The Law of Evidence

Fifth Edition

The Law of Evidence

Fifth Edition

I.H. Dennis, M.A., PH.D.
of Gray's Inn, Barrister-at-Law
Professor of English Law, University College London

SWEET & MAXWELL

 THOMSON REUTERS

First Edition	1999, Reprinted 2000	by Ian Dennis
Second Edition	2002	by Ian Dennis
Third Edition	2007	by Ian Dennis
Fourth Edition	2010	by Ian Dennis
Fifth Edition	2013	by Ian Dennis

Published in 2013 by Sweet & Maxwell, 100 Avenue Road, London NW3 3PF part of Thomson Reuters (Professional) UK Limited (Registered in England & Wales, Company No 1679046.

Registered Office and address for service: Aldgate House, 33 Aldgate High Street, London EC3N 1DL)

For further information on our products and services, visit *www.sweetandmaxwell.co.uk*

Typeset by Letterpart Ltd, Reigate, Surrey

Printed in Great Britain by TJ International Ltd, Padstow, Cornwall.

No natural forests were destroyed to make this product; only farmed timber was used and re-planted.

A CIP catalogue record of this book is available for the British Library.

ISBN Mainwork: 978-0-41402-562-2

Preface to the Fifth Edition

The law of evidence continues to be a fast-moving subject. It is only three years since the last edition of this book, but numerous case law developments since 2010 amply justify the appearance of the fifth edition. I have revised the text at many points to take account of important new decisions. The extent of change is most marked in Chapter 17, where the law of hearsay in criminal cases has required considerable updating. The headline development here is the long-awaited judgment of the Grand Chamber of the European Court of Human Rights in *Al-Khawaja and Tahery v United Kingdom*, and the follow-up decisions of the Court of Appeal in *Ibrahim* and *Riat*. In consequence I have completely rewritten the section on hearsay evidence and art.6 of the European Convention on Human Rights. Another key case considered in this chapter is *Twist*, in which an illuminating judgment from Hughes L.J. has done much to resolve the confusion created by a string of inconsistent decisions on the admissibility of mobile phone text messages. I have added a final section in this chapter on the claim that anonymous hearsay is never admissible in English law. In so far as this claim does not distinguish between cases where the identity of the maker of a hearsay statement is known, and cases where it is not, the claim is too widely stated.

Several other important new cases deserve highlighting. *Brewster and Cromwell* is now the leading authority on the admission of evidence of the bad character of a non-defendant under s.100 of the Criminal Justice Act 2003. Disclosure continues to be problematic, particularly as regards defence statements, and Chapter 9 notes the significant checks on disadvantages to the defence established in *Newell* and in *Rochford*. In relation to the standard of proof *Majid* confirms the current preference for directing juries to be sure of guilt before convicting; the classic formula of "beyond reasonable doubt" is now to be avoided. Chapter 20 notes a number of recent decisions in which the Court of Appeal is finally beginning to take a stronger line on the form and admissibility of different types of forensic science evidence. The Law Commission's recommendation for a *Daubert*-style gatekeeping role for judges in relation to expert evidence seems unlikely to be enacted in the near future, but there are signs that the common law may be moving slowly in that direction. The Scottish cases of *Cadder v HM Advocate* and *HM Advocate v P* have significant implications for English law on confessions obtained where defendants have had not the opportunity to take legal advice before interview, and on the admissibility of evidence obtained in consequence of such a confession. These implications are considered in Chapters 6 and 8, which also note the ruling of the European Court of Human Rights in *Gafgen v Germany* on evidence obtained in violation of art.3 of the ECHR.

In order to keep the book within reasonable limits I have cut out some material which is now largely of historical interest. This is most noticeable in Chapters 9 and 18, where I have pruned the discussion of the common law on disclosure and the "similar facts" rule respectively, to the minimum necessary to appreciate the background to the modern statutory provisions. Comment on these exclusions and on possible other changes to my coverage of evidential topics would be welcome.

Finally, I would like once again to record my thanks to Dr Abenaa Owusu-Bempah for her valuable research assistance. As ever my biggest debt is to Sue for her encouragement, and her sympathetic tolerance of my bad working habits.

I hope the book is up to date as at 31 December, 2012.

Ian Dennis

February 12, 2013

TABLE OF CONTENTS

PART II
OBTAINING EVIDENCE: PRE-TRIAL PROCEDURES AND THE REGULATION OF ACCESS

5. THE PRIVILEGE AGAINST SELF-INCRIMINATION AND THE RIGHT TO SILENCE

**PART III
ADDUCING EVIDENCE: TRIAL PROCEDURES AND THE
PRINCIPLES OF PROOF**

11. BURDEN AND STANDARD OF PROOF

12. FORMS OF PROOF AND ALTERNATIVES TO PROOF

PART IV
USING EVIDENCE: THE SCOPE AND LIMITS OF
EXCLUSIONARY RULES

16. HEARSAY AT COMMON LAW AND IN CIVIL PROCEEDINGS

17. THE MODERN LAW OF HEARSAY IN CRIMINAL CASES

18. CHARACTER AND CREDIBILITY: AN OVERVIEW

19. EVIDENCE OF BAD CHARACTER IN CRIMINAL CASES

20. OPINION AND EXPERT EVIDENCE

TABLE OF CASES

TABLE OF STATUTES

TABLE OF STATUTORY INSTRUMENTS

TABLE OF EUROPEAN, INTERNATIONAL AND FOREIGN LEGISLATION

Abbreviations

The following abbreviations appear throughout the book. They are listed here for ease of reference.

Archbold — *Criminal Pleading Evidence and Practice* 61st edn (London: Sweet & Maxwell, 2012).

Auld Review — Lord Justice Auld, *Review of the Criminal Courts of England and Wales* (London, 2001).

CLRC Eleventh Report — Criminal Law Revision Committee, *Eleventh Report Evidence (General)*, London (Cmnd. 4991, 1972).

Cross and Tapper — Sir R. Cross and C. Tapper, *Cross and Tapper on Evidence* 12th edn (Oxford: Oxford University Press, 2010).

Emmerson, Ashworth and Macdonald — Ben Emmerson Q.C., Andrew Ashworth Q.C. and Alison Macdonald, *Human Rights and Criminal Justice* 2nd edn (London: Sweet & Maxwell, 2007).

Law Com. No. 245 — *Evidence in Criminal Proceedings: Hearsay and Related Topics* (Law Com. No. 245, Cm. 3670, The Stationery Office, London, 1997).

Law Com. No. 273 — *Evidence of Bad Character in Criminal Proceedings* (Law Com. No. 273, Cm. 5257, The Stationery Office, London, 2001).

RCCJ Report — Report of the Royal Commission on Criminal Justice (Cm. 2263, 1993).

RCCP Report — Report of the Royal Commission on Criminal Procedure (Cmnd. 8092, London, 1981).

Redmayne — M. Redmayne, *Expert Evidence and Criminal Justice* (Oxford: Oxford University Press, 2001).

Roberts and Zuckerman — *Criminal Evidence* 2nd edn (Oxford: Oxford University Press, 2010).

Wigmore — J.H. Wigmore, *Evidence in Trials at Common Law*, 10 vols (as revised at various dates).

Zuckerman, *Principles* — A.A.S. Zuckerman, *The Principles of Criminal Evidence* (Oxford: Oxford University Press, 1989).

PART I

UNDERSTANDING EVIDENCE: THE FOUNDATIONS OF THE LAW

CHAPTER 1

AN INTRODUCTION TO THE LAW OF EVIDENCE

A. EVIDENCE, INFERENCE AND PROOF

Evidence is information. It is information that provides grounds for belief that a   **1–001**
particular fact or set of facts is true. As such there is nothing particularly "legal"
about the concept of evidence and its function.[1] Many different people use
evidence to inquire into the existence or non-existence of an infinite number of
facts for a wide variety of different purposes. Historians, scientists, doctors,
journalists and detectives are just some of the groups whose daily work involves
them in the collection and evaluation of evidence. Sometimes different types of
inquirer may inquire successively into the same fact or set of facts: the identity of
a murderer, for example, might be investigated in turn by a police officer, a
forensic scientist, a court of law, an investigative journalist and a historian. Each
inquirer may use different procedures for collecting and evaluating the
information needed for the inquiry. The procedures used will depend on the type

---

[1] Since "evidence" is not a technical term in the law (unlike "judicial evidence"—discussed in Ch.12)
this book does not propose to offer a technical definition. The functional statement made here is
derived from W. M. Best, *A Treatise on the Principles of the Law of Evidence*, 4th edn (London,
1866), p.10: "[Evidence is] . . . any matter of fact, the effect, tendency or design of which is to produce
in the mind a persuasion, affirmative or disaffirmative, of the existence of some other matter of fact".
For a longer statement to the same effect see Wigmore (Tillers rev., 1983), Vol.1 s.1.

of person making the inquiry, the purposes of the inquiry and the resources available for it. Some procedures, such as forensic science investigations, require specialist qualifications and experience.

Despite their differences in aims and methods, different types of inquirer are essentially engaged in the same intellectual process. The process is founded on the assumption that knowledge of the world, of past events and present states of affairs, may be gained by anyone through observation and reason. Cohen has described this assumption as the principle of "universal cognitive competence".[2] The principle permits the belief that the truth of facts, whose existence is in question, may be established by drawing conclusions (inferences) from information that the inquirer has collected for that purpose. Because of the limitations of human knowledge "truth" for this purpose has to be regarded as a question of probability. We can never be confident to the point of absolute certainty that our evidence is always accurate and complete, and that we have always drawn the correct inferences from it. Perfect knowledge is unattainable in an imperfect world. The law, like other fields of human inquiry, has to be satisfied with degrees of probability of accurate truth-finding.[3]

When the existence or non-existence of a fact has been established to the degree of satisfaction required by the inquirer's procedures we can say that, as far as that inquirer is concerned, the matter has been proved. For example, a court of law determining whether a person is guilty of an offence has to be satisfied of guilt beyond reasonable doubt; this is known as the criminal standard of proof. Proof is a term with a variable meaning. In legal discourse it may refer to the outcome of the process of evaluating evidence and drawing inferences from it, or it may be used more widely to refer to the process itself and/or to the evidence which is being evaluated. It is usually clear from the context which meaning is intended.

1–002   For the purposes of the law it is frequently necessary to determine the truth of disputed or uncertain questions of fact. Substantive legal rights, duties and liabilities generally depend on such questions. When such questions arise a variety of actors in the relevant legal process may be concerned with the collection and evaluation of evidence. In the criminal process crucial decisions about the guilt of a suspect have to be made at an early stage by police officers and prosecutors on the basis of the evidence available to them. The ultimate inquirer is the court or tribunal charged with the determination of the particular legal dispute or other proceeding. If the proceeding reaches the stage of a trial or hearing before the court or tribunal it is the law of evidence which regulates the process of proof in the trial or hearing.

This is not to say that the law of evidence is exclusively trial-centred, although the trial tends to be the focus of attention for reasons to be discussed later. Much of the law of evidence is concerned with the presentation and use of evidence at trial but an important part deals with pre-trial processes involving the collection of evidence. For example, the Police and Criminal Evidence Act 1984 ("PACE")

---

[2] See L. J. Cohen, "Freedom of Proof" in W.L. Twining (ed), *Facts in Law* (1983), pp.1, 10. For a historical treatment of this assumption see J. D. Jackson, "Theories of Truth Finding in Criminal Procedure: An Evolutionary Approach" (1988) 10 Cardozo L.R. 475.

[3] This point is explored further in Ch.4.

and its associated Codes of Practice contain a detailed set of rules of conduct for police officers engaged in obtaining evidence relating to the commission of an offence. The reception of evidence at trial may be significantly affected by non-compliance with these rules.

This chapter provides a short introduction to the law of evidence. Section B explains the main concepts and terminology. Section C deals with some key characteristics of evidence law. Section D concludes with some general comments about the development of the law. At this stage the aim is not to explore any of these matters in detail, but to give an overview of the subject and a guide to the further analysis and discussion which is undertaken in later chapters.

B. CONCEPTS AND TERMINOLOGY

The law of evidence uses a number of concepts which are fundamental to an understanding of the subject. This section introduces these concepts by stating a number of general propositions about them and about their relationships. The propositions are stated in summary form, with more detailed explanation given later.

1–003

1. Evidence must be *relevant* in order for a court to receive it. This means that it must relate to some fact which is a proper object of proof in the proceedings.[4] The evidence must relate to the fact to be proved in the sense that it tends to make the existence (or non-existence) of the fact more probable, or less probable, than it would be without the evidence. A simple example is a case where a fact to be proved is the identity of the accused as the person who stole certain goods. Evidence that the goods were found in the accused's house is relevant because it makes the existence of the fact that he is the thief more probable.

2. Evidence must also be *admissible*, meaning that it can properly be received by a court as a matter of law. The most important rule of admissibility is that the evidence must be relevant; irrelevant evidence is always inadmissible. Generally speaking evidence that is relevant is also admissible, but certain rules of law prohibit the reception of certain types of evidence, even though the evidence is relevant. An example is the rule against hearsay evidence, which, broadly speaking, forbids the reception of evidence of a statement made by a person on another occasion when the purpose of adducing[5] the evidence is to ask the court to accept that the statement was true. These rules are often called the *exclusionary rules*, to indicate their function of excluding certain evidence from the court's consideration. The rules are complex because they are often accompanied by exceptions, some of which may be narrow and precisely defined, others may be in broad and flexible terms. Questions of admissibility of evidence are questions of law and are decided by the judge.

3. In addition to exclusionary rules, there is also *exclusionary discretion*. In criminal cases a trial judge may exclude prosecution evidence that is relevant and

---

[4] The facts which are proper objects of proof are sometimes called material facts, but materiality is a slippery term which can be used with more than one meaning. See the discussion in the text below.

[5] "Adducing" evidence is a term often used to denote the process of presenting evidence to a court in one of the approved forms, most commonly in the form of the testimony of a witness.

admissible (in the sense that it is not excluded by an exclusionary rule) in the exercise of a discretion conferred on the judge by the common law or by s.78 of PACE. The statutory discretion is to prevent the admission of the evidence from adversely affecting the fairness of the proceedings. The main application of the common law discretion is to exclude evidence the prejudicial effect of which outweighs its probative value. Probative value refers to the potential weight of the evidence (see next paragraph), whereas prejudicial effect refers to the tendency of evidence to prejudice the court against the accused, so as to lead the court to make findings of fact against him for reasons not related to the true probative value of the evidence. The relationship between exclusionary rules and exclusionary discretion, and the differences between them, are discussed in Ch.3. Broadly speaking, exclusionary rules derive from the dangers thought to be presented by certain types of evidence and apply to all cases. The discretion to exclude evidence is exercised according to the circumstances of particular cases.

4. At the end of a contested trial the court will have to evaluate the relevant and admissible evidence that it received. The *weight* of the evidence is the strength of the tendency of the evidence to prove the fact or facts that it was adduced to prove. This is a matter for the tribunal of fact to decide. In civil cases the judge who tries the case is generally the judge of issues of both law and fact. In criminal cases the tribunal of fact is different according to whether the case is tried on indictment or summarily. The jury is the tribunal of fact for cases tried on indictment. In summary trial the magistrates (justices) deal with issues of both law and fact; lay magistrates have the guidance of their clerk on questions of law. This book uses the term "factfinder" to refer generally to a tribunal of fact, unless the context requires a specific reference to a judge, jury or magistrate. When a factfinder has to determine the weight of evidence it will examine carefully, amongst other things, the credibility and reliability of the evidence. These terms are not always used with a consistent meaning. Credibility is most commonly used in connection with the testimony of a witness and refers to the extent to which the witness can be accepted as giving truthful evidence in the sense of honest or sincere testimony. Reliability refers most commonly to the truthfulness of testimony in the sense of its accuracy. Honest witnesses may sometimes give evidence that is inaccurate; mistaken evidence of identification by eyewitnesses is a classic example.

1. Materiality and the objects of proof

1–004 The objects of proof are the facts in a given set of legal proceedings in respect of which evidence can properly be adduced. For the purposes of exposition it is convenient to classify them under a number of headings.

(A) Facts in issue

1–005 The most important category of objects of proof consists of the facts in issue. These are sometimes called the *material facts*, and may also be referred to by the Latin term *facta probanda*. These are all the facts that it is necessary for a party to prove in order to succeed in the litigation. They comprise the facts constituting a cause of action in a civil proceeding, or the facts that make up the offence charged in a criminal case, together in either case with any facts that must be proved by the defendant to establish a defence. In any given case the facts in issue are determined by reference to the substantive law and the statements of case, which include for this purpose the indictment, information or written charge[6] in criminal proceedings.

In a typical civil action the claimant might claim damages for injuries caused by the defendant's negligence. The question whether the defendant owed the claimant a duty of care is a question of law (the law of tort) about which the parties may present argument but not evidence. Whether the defendant was in breach of a duty of care is a question of fact. The claimant is required by the rules of court to specify in the particulars of claim the precise respects in which the defendant is alleged to have been negligent. If the defendant, in the defence, formally denies negligence the claimant will have to adduce evidence to prove at least one of the alleged particulars of negligence. Again, depending on what is admitted or denied in the defence, the claimant will have to prove as a fact that the defendant's negligence caused the claimant's injuries. The nature and extent of the injuries and the amount of any special damages would also have to be proved as facts if not admitted. If the defendant alleged contributory negligence and the claimant denied it the defendant would have to adduce evidence to prove the issue. It follows that in a civil action the substantive law determines the elements of the cause of action and the classification of the elements into issues of law and fact. The statements of case determine which questions of fact are actually in dispute in the action.

In a criminal case the substantive law specifies the elements of the offence charged. The indictment or information or written charge provides brief particulars of the allegations of fact which constitute that offence. It used to be the case that the defendant had no obligation at any stage to state which, if any, of the prosecution's allegations he admitted and which he denied. Now, however, the defendant has a statutory obligation under s.5 of the Criminal Procedure and Investigations Act 1996 to provide a defence statement in certain circumstances, setting out the nature of his defence, indicating the matters of fact on which he takes issue with the prosecution and the reasons why.[7] At trial the defendant simply pleads "guilty" or "not guilty" to the charges. Accordingly:

> "... whenever there is a plea of not guilty, everything is in issue, and the prosecution has to prove the whole of their case, including the identity of the accused, the nature of the act and the existence of any necessary knowledge or intent."[8]

To this should be added the point that the prosecution may also have to prove the absence of certain defences if there is evidence sufficient to raise the issue of

1–006

---

[6] An indictment is the formal statement of the charge in proceedings on indictment in the Crown Court. Informations and written charges are formal statements of charges in summary proceedings in magistrates' courts. For the introduction of written charges see the Criminal Justice Act 2003 s.29.

[7] See Ch.9 for further discussion.

[8] per Lord Goddard C.J. in Sims [1946] K.B. 531 at 539 CCA. If at trial the defendant puts forward a defence which is different from any defence set out in his pre-trial defence statement the court may draw adverse inferences against the defendant in determining his guilt: see Criminal Procedure and Investigations Act 1996 s.11.

their existence. For example, in a murder case, following a not guilty plea, the prosecution must prove that it was the accused who unlawfully killed the deceased, that he or she did so with the necessary state of mind (i.e. malice aforethought, judicially defined as the intention to kill or cause serious injury) and, if the issue is disclosed by the evidence, that he or she did so not, say, while acting in lawful self-defence.

(B) Evidentiary facts (facts relevant to the facts in issue)

1–007   The terms "facts in issue" and "material facts" are sometimes used more widely to include both the facts in issue in the sense just described and also other disputed facts that, analytically, fall within a second category of objects of proof. This category consists of facts introduced into the proceedings as a means of proof of the facts in issue. The party introducing them seeks to argue that the facts in issue may be proved indirectly by logical inference from such facts. They are known therefore as evidentiary facts, or facts relevant to the facts in issue. It is suggested that to avoid confusion it is better to use one of these terms in preference to the wide use of "facts in issue". Occasionally references are seen to the Latin term *factum probans*, denoting a fact offered to prove another fact (*factum probandum*). An example from a criminal case of an evidentiary fact is the presence or absence of a motive on the part of a defendant to commit the offence charged. Motive, in the sense of a reason or explanation for a criminal act, is not an element of the offence which must be proved by the prosecution. It is not therefore a fact in issue in the narrower sense. However, the existence of a motive may increase the probability of the fact that the defendant did commit the offence charged.

If evidentiary facts are not formally admitted or judicially noticed they must themselves, like facts in issue, be proved by evidence in an approved form. The approved forms of evidence (the forms of judicial evidence) are the testimony of witnesses, documentary and real evidence. These are considered, along with alternatives to proof, in more detail in Ch.12.

Accordingly, if the existence of the defendant's alleged motive for the offence were disputed, evidence suggestive of that motive would need to be given in an appropriate form. In this way an evidentiary fact may, as its name implies, be both an object of proof and, if proved, a means of proof (evidence) of the facts in issue.

1–008   At this stage a word may be said about the terms *direct* and *circumstantial* evidence. Direct evidence is testimony given by a witness of the witness's perception by her own senses (sight, hearing etc) of one or more of the facts in issue. It can also include the presentation of documents or things in issue to the tribunal of fact,[9] when the tribunal may be asked to act on its own perception of the nature or quality of the document or thing. Direct evidence of facts in issue may give rise to questions concerning the credibility and reliability of the testifying witness, but does not normally present problems of relevance. Circumstantial evidence is often used as a compendious term to describe any

---

[9] Such as clear CCTV images; see, e.g. *Goring* [2011] EWCA Crim 2 at [51].

evidence of facts relevant to the issue.[10] There are a great many types of circumstantial evidence. It would be a largely pointless exercise to attempt to compile a complete list. Several of the more important types will be mentioned in the course of Ch.3, which deals in detail with the subject of relevance. It is in relation to circumstantial evidence that problems of relevance may occur.

There is no distinction in principle between direct and circumstantial evidence as a means of proof of facts in issue. Neither form of evidence is considered superior to the other although it is recognised that circumstantial evidence may present more difficulties of evaluation. These difficulties have led the courts to require trial judges to direct juries about the approach they should adopt in evaluating certain types of circumstantial evidence. The lies of the accused, the failure of the accused to mention to the police in interview facts later relied on in defence, and the failure of the accused to testify at his trial, are the most prominent examples.[11] Provided appropriate directions are given when required, it is possible for even the most serious cases to be proved entirely by circumstantial evidence. For example, in *McGreevy v DPP*[12] the defendant was convicted of murder, despite the absence of a witness to the killing, on a mass of evidence relating to such matters as the time and circumstances of the death, the defendant's opportunity to commit the murder, blood stains found on the clothing of the deceased and of the defendant and footprints found at the scene of the murder. In this case, the House of Lords rejected an attempt to draw a formal distinction between direct and circumstantial evidence of facts in issue. It was held, dismissing the defendant's appeal, that the trial judge, when directing the jury in a case depending entirely on circumstantial evidence, need give only the standard direction regarding the burden and standard of proof. He would, therefore, have to tell the jury that the prosecution had to satisfy them of the accused's guilt beyond reasonable doubt before they could convict, but there was no rule requiring him to add that the evidence not only had to be consistent with guilt but also inconsistent with any other rational conclusion. While acknowledging the point that competing hypotheses or inferences may sometimes be drawn from circumstantial evidence, Lord Morris of Borthy-Gest took the view that it would be unnecessary and undesirable to lay down a special form of direction for such a case. A trial judge might sometimes offer guidance to the jury in the terms suggested but should not be bound by a stereotyped form of words to do so.[13]

Facts relevant to the issue must not be understood as being restricted to items of circumstantial evidence having a demonstrable bearing on the facts in issue. As McCormick puts it:

1–009

---

[10] For a useful concise account see A. Samuels, "Circumstantial Evidence" (2001) 165 J.P. 682.

[11] Guidance as to these and many other jury directions is given in the *Crown Court Bench Book—Directing the Jury*, published online at *http://www.judiciary.gov.uk* [Accessed January 23, 2013].

[12] *McGreevy v DPP* [1973] 1 All E.R. 503 HL.

[13] See also *R. v P* [2007] EWCA Crim 3216; [2008] 2 Cr.App.R. 6 at [68], applying the approach in *McGreevy* to the decision of the judge whether there is a case to answer.

> "In addition to evidence that bears directly on the issues, leeway is allowed even on direct examination for proof of facts that merely fill in the background of the narrative and give it interest, color and lifelikeness."[14]

Such facts might be described as part of the context or setting of the facts in issue. This category also includes information which may enable other evidence to be better understood and evaluated. McCormick gives the examples of maps, diagrams and charts as aids to understanding. Photographs of the scene of a crime are another example. Eggleston has pointed out that the addition of detail and circumstance to a narrative is "not only essential to its proper appreciation by those who hear it, but provides the material by which the inherent consistency or probability of the narrative can be tested".[15] This may be particularly important in assessing the credibility of a witness or the reliability of a disputed confession.

The common law recognised the admissibility of what was often called "background" evidence. In *Sawoniuk*,[16] discussed below, Lord Bingham C.J. commented:

> "Criminal charges cannot fairly be judged in a factual vacuum. In order to make a rational assessment of evidence directly relating to a charge it may often be necessary for a jury to receive evidence describing, perhaps in some detail, the context and circumstances in which the offences are said to have been committed."[17]

1–010 It was said not to be a bar to admissibility that such background evidence showed the defendant in a bad light or even that he had committed other offences not charged. In *Sawoniuk* the defendant was convicted on two counts of murder of Jews in Belarus in 1942. The Court of Appeal upheld the trial judge's decision to admit evidence showing the defendant's participation in a "search and kill" operation against Jewish survivors of an earlier massacre. This was relevant to the accuracy of the eyewitness identification evidence relating to the murders charged, because the killer belonged to the group involved in the operation. This decision as to the specific relevance of the evidence would have been enough to decide the case.[18] However, the court held that the admission of the evidence was also justified as background evidence that was essential to help the jury to understand the significance of the eyewitness evidence in the exceptional context of the case. Immediately after stating the principle set out above, Lord Bingham C.J. cited a passage from the judgment of the Court of Appeal in the unreported case of *Pettman*[19]:

> "Where it is necessary to place before the jury evidence of part of a continual background of history relevant to the offence charged in the indictment and without the totality of which the account placed before the jury would be incomplete or incomprehensible, then the fact that the

---

[14] *McCormick on Evidence*, 6th edn (St Paul: Thomson West, 2006), p.306.

[15] R. Eggleston, "Relevance and Admissibility" in H. Glass (ed)*Seminars on Evidence* (Melbourne, 1970), p.76. See further the discussion in Ch.4 of the "story-telling" theory of factfinding.

[16] *Sawoniuk* [2000] 2 Cr.App.R. 220 CA.

[17] *Sawoniuk* [2002] 2 Cr.App.R. 220 CA at [234].

[18] Although it is not easy to reconcile this decision with *Blastland* [1986] A.C. 41 HL, discussed in Ch.3.

[19] *Pettman* May 2, 1985.

whole account involves including evidence establishing the commission of an offence with which the accused is not charged is not of itself a ground for excluding the evidence."[20]

Similarly in *TM*,[21] the Court of Appeal relied on this passage to uphold the admission in a case of sexual abuse by TM of his sister of evidence that TM had been forced at an earlier time to watch and then take part in other acts of sexual abuse committed by older members of the family. The value of this background evidence was that it put the evidence of the victim in an essential context which explained why she did not feel able to seek protection against her brother from the rest of the family.

Cases such as *TM* and *Sawoniuk*[22] were not easy to distinguish from those in which evidence of the accused's bad character and other misconduct was held inadmissible under the general exclusionary rule at common law discussed in Ch.18. "Similar fact" evidence, as it was often called, required a high degree of probative value on an issue in the case before it could overcome the exclusionary rule. On the face of it this was a more demanding test than the explanatory value required for background evidence, yet the risk of prejudice that might be caused by evidence demonstrating the accused's other discreditable behaviour was equally real. However, the gap between the two rules was narrowed by the existence of the judge's exclusionary discretion, referred to above. In *Sawoniuk*, the trial judge had expressly concluded that the probative value of the evidence of the search and kill operation outweighed its likely prejudicial effect. In *TM*, the Court of Appeal thought that there was no reason to exclude the evidence of the other sexual abuse under s.78 of PACE, given the trial judge's direction to the jury as to the limited use that could be made of it.

The concept of background evidence has received statutory recognition as "explanatory evidence". As we shall see, the Criminal Justice Act 2003 replaced the common law rules relating to the admission of evidence showing the accused's bad character and other misconduct with a scheme intended to clarify and enlarge the admissibility of such evidence. Broadly speaking, under this scheme, such evidence continues to be inadmissible unless it can be admitted through one of the seven statutory "gateways". One of the gateways permits the admission of evidence of bad character where it is "important explanatory evidence". The statutory definition[23] states that evidence is important explanatory evidence if:

1–011

(a)   without it, the court or jury would find it impossible or difficult properly to understand other evidence in the case; and
(b)   its value for understanding the case as a whole is substantial.

In summary, therefore, relevant background or explanatory evidence which does not show the bad character of a person within the meaning of the Criminal

---

[20] *Sawoniuk* [2000] 2 Cr.App.R. 220 at [234].
[21] *TM* [2000] 2 Cr.App.R. 266.
[22] For other cases on the relevance of past incidents and relationships involving the defendant, see *Williams* (1987) 84 Cr.App.R. 298; *Sidhu* (1994) 98 Cr.App.R. 59; *Fulcher* [1995] 2 Cr.App.R. 251. See also *Dolan* [2003] EWCA Crim 1859; [2003] 1 Cr.App.R. 18 at [281].
[23] Criminal Justice Act 2003 s.102.

Justice Act 2003[24] continues to be admissible at common law. Where background or explanatory evidence does show bad character it will have to satisfy the test of admissibility under the Act.

(C)   Facts relating to the credibility of witnesses

1–012   As indicated above, questions may arise concerning the credibility[25] of a witness who testifies about the facts in issue or facts relevant to the issue. The maker of a statement out of court which is admitted in evidence might also have his credibility called into question. A witness's credibility can be attacked on various grounds: common examples are defective vision or hearing, bias towards a party, bad character, mental disability, and so on. Such matters are contingently related (collateral) to the proceedings in that they affect the weight to be placed on the witness's testimony. Facts relating to the credibility of witnesses become objects of proof when, exceptionally, evidence is permitted to be given concerning their existence or extent. For example, in the old case of *Thomas v David*[26] a witness who denied in cross-examination that she was the mistress of the party for whom she was testifying was contradicted by evidence allowed to be called in rebuttal of the denial. The general principle, discussed more fully in Ch.14, is that answers to questions in cross- examination concerning credibility must be taken as final. In certain exceptional cases evidence may be adduced concerning these collateral facts when their effect may be to colour the whole of the witness's testimony in the eyes of the jury. The existence of a relationship suggesting bias is one obvious example. Where the evidence relating to credibility is evidence of the witness's bad character, such as the previous convictions of the witness, the conditions of admissibility imposed by s.100 of the Criminal Justice Act 2003 must be complied with.

The distinction between facts relevant to the issue and collateral facts relevant to credit is fundamental in the law of evidence. But it can be a difficult distinction to apply, notably in cases involving the evidence of complainants of sexual offences.[27] A further difficulty can arise where evidence of an accused's previous convictions or bad character is admitted under the provisions of the Criminal Justice Act 2003. The evidence may be admitted as relevant to the issue of the accused's guilt and/or as relevant to his credibility, and the judge may have to direct the jury about the difference between permitted uses of the evidence.[28] Much scepticism has been expressed in the past about the intelligibility of such a direction.

(D)   Facts relating to the admissibility of evidence

1–013   The final category of objects of proof is facts relating to the admissibility of evidence. These are facts brought into issue as the result of the operation of the

---

[24] As defined by Criminal Justice Act 2003 ss.98 and 112. See further Chs 14 and 19.
[25] In this context credibility includes reliability.
[26] *Thomas v David* (1836) 7 C. & P. 350.
[27] See Chs 14 and 15.
[28] See Ch.19.

law of evidence itself. A number of rules prescribe factual conditions for the admissibility of certain evidence. An illustration is the rule that a confession by an accused person must not have been obtained by oppression of that person or by anything said or done likely to render any confession by that person unreliable.[29] If an accused disputes the existence of the factual condition and claims, for example, to have been tortured into confessing, the trial judge may hear evidence of the circumstances of the interrogation before ruling on the admissibility of the confession. In the Crown Court such evidence is heard by the judge in the absence of the jury, using the procedure known as the *voir dire*, or the trial within the trial. This procedure follows the normal rules for taking evidence, so that witnesses as to the facts relating to the admissibility of the evidence in question are called, examined and cross-examined as in the main trial.[30]

2. Relevance and admissibility

The root principles of the relationship of relevance and admissibility were stated with great clarity by Thayer: **1–014**

> "(1) ... without any exception, nothing which is not, or is not supposed to be, logically relevant is admissible; and (2) ... subject to many exceptions and qualifications, whatever is logically relevant is admissible ..."[31]

This elegant antithesis has formed the basis of many subsequent statements of principle in Anglo-American law. In *Hollington v F Hewthorn & Co Ltd,*[32] Goddard L.J. explained that:

> "nowadays it is relevance ... that is the main consideration, and, generally speaking, all evidence that is relevant to an issue is admissible, while all that is irrelevant is excluded."

Rule 402 of the American Federal Rules of Evidence is to the same effect:

> "All relevant evidence is admissible, except as otherwise provided by the Constitution of the United States, by Act of Congress, by these rules, or by other rules prescribed by the Supreme Court pursuant to statutory authority. Evidence which is not relevant is not admissible."

Questions of admissibility of evidence are questions of law for the judge. Because relevance is the most important condition of admissibility it follows that the judge also decides issues of relevance. Relevance and admissibility are discussed further in Ch.3. As noted above, the weight of evidence is generally classified as a question of fact for the factfinder in the proceedings; in jury trials this is of course the jury. In other trials the judge or magistrates will be the judge of both law and fact. Even in jury trials the judge's decisions on admissibility may sometimes require consideration of the probative value of the evidence and

---

[29] PACE s.76(2), discussed in Ch.6.

[30] See Ch.6.

[31] J.B. Thayer, *A Preliminary Treatise on Evidence at the Common Law* (Boston: Little Brown, 1898), p.226.

[32] *Hollington v F Hewthorn & Co Ltd* [1943] K.B. 587 at 594 CA.

thus involve estimates of its potential weight. This is particularly the case in relation to decisions about the exercise of exclusionary discretion. The respective roles of judge and jury are considered more fully in Ch.4.

C.   THE CHARACTER OF THE LAW OF EVIDENCE

1–015   Four fundamental points are worth making at an early stage about the character of the modern law of evidence. The first is that the law has a broad scope, with rather uncertain limits. Thus the law of evidence deals with issues of obtaining evidence before trial, adducing evidence at trial, and using and evaluating evidence. However, the boundary between the law of evidence and the other body of adjectival law, the law of procedure, is not fixed. The classification of certain issues as evidential or procedural may consequently be largely a matter of taste. This book does not cover, for example, the law on estoppel and double jeopardy, whereas some other evidence texts do. More fundamentally, there has been some tendency in civil proceedings for these two bodies of adjectival law to merge; for example, the Civil Evidence Act 1995 abolished the rule of inadmissibility of hearsay evidence in civil proceedings and substituted a provision requiring a party to give notice of intention to adduce hearsay evidence.[33]

Secondly, the origins of the modern law of evidence lie, broadly speaking, in the common law rulings of the judges from the 17th century onwards. Statutory intervention began to take place from the nineteenth century and has markedly accelerated in recent decades. Both these sources of law show the profound influence of two key features associated with the adversarial procedure traditionally used to conduct litigation in English law.[34] These are the features of party autonomy and orality of evidence. According to the principle of party autonomy litigation is initiated and conducted by the parties to a legal dispute.[35] The parties define the issues on which they wish the court or tribunal to adjudicate. They carry out the pre-trial investigations into the facts of the dispute and present the evidence to support their claims. The role of the court as adjudicator is essentially passive, limited to hearing the evidence and argument presented by the parties and ruling on the issues of fact and law arising. Litigation in this form takes on the character of a contest or fight between two or more opponents, both aiming to present their own cases in the best possible light and to

---

[33] See further Ch.16.
[34] For general discussion see, in relation to civil cases, I. H. Jacob, *The Fabric of English Civil Justice* (London, 1987), Ch.1. For criminal cases, see M. Damaska, "Evidentiary Barriers to Conviction and Two Models of Criminal Procedure: A Comparative Study" (1973) 121 U.Pa.L.R. 506. See also M. Damaska, *The Faces of Justice and State Authority* (New Haven, 1986); Australian Law Reform Commission, *Report on Evidence* (Canberra, 1987); M. Damaska, *Evidence Law Adrift* (New Haven, 1997). The last of these contains numerous thought-provoking reflections on the implications of 20th-century changes to what he describes as the traditional pillars of evidence law.
[35] This description includes the prosecutor in criminal proceedings, irrespective of whether the prosecution is brought by a private individual or by the state. Even in the latter case the form of the dispute is the same; competing claims are presented to and determined by independent adjudicative tribunals. Adversarial criminal process is sometimes referred to as accusatorial procedure, but the latter is a concept incorporating distinctive moral and political values; see A. Goldstein, "Reflections on Two Models: Inquisitorial Themes in American Criminal Procedure" (1974) 26 Stanford L.R. 1009, 1016.

cause maximum damage to the case of the opponent.[36] The court sits in the middle acting as umpire. There is also the possibility that the parties may choose not to fight but to compromise the dispute. In practice civil litigation is usually settled by agreement.[37] In criminal cases many defendants plead guilty,[38] often as the result of a bargain with the prosecution. It follows that adversary litigation does not purport to be, and is unlikely in practice to amount to, a free-ranging official enquiry into the truth of disputed or uncertain facts. It is more of a process in which, if the matter ever gets to trial, two or more parties present competing versions of a past or present reality and invite the adjudicator to choose between them.

The principle of orality is the principle that evidence on disputed questions of fact should be given by witnesses called before the court to give oral testimony of matters within their own knowledge. Historically the principle is intimately connected with the importance attached by the common law to the oath, to the demeanour of the witness, and to cross-examination as guarantees of reliability. Oral testimony from witnesses physically present before the court also helps to legitimise the adjudication in other ways. It reinforces the drama and solemnity of the occasion, and it allows for maximum participation in decision-making in the sense that parties can confront their accusers and challenge the evidence against them in the most direct way possible by cross-examination. In the United States parties have constitutional rights, guaranteed by the Sixth Amendment, to confrontation and cross-examination of witnesses.

Thirdly, the law of evidence is not a tidy system of clearly defined rules with each rule having its own distinct scope and limits. It is doubtful how far the law has ever had such a character, but at the present time the law of evidence is indisputably untidy and extremely complex. It contains a mixture of specific rules,[39] open-textured rules with a good deal of flexibility in their application,[40] and discretions which may be "weak" or "strong" in nature, depending on how much freedom they confer on the persons who exercise them to formulate the criteria for their exercise.[41] The discretions sometimes overlap, and their relationship with rules of evidence is sometimes obscure. Moreover, this mixture is in a continual state of flux. In recent years the law has undergone profound changes as a result of extensive statutory reform. A further important influence is human rights law. Many parts of the law of evidence have come under scrutiny

1–016

---

[36] For the classic exposition of the "fight" theory of adversary litigation see J. Frank, *Courts on Trial* (1949), Ch.VI. See further L. Bennett and M. Feldman, *Reconstructing Reality in the Courtroom* (1981), and the discussion in Ch.4.

[37] See the brief but informative account of settlement in P. F. Smith and S. H. Bailey, *The Modern English Legal System*, 5th edn (London, 2007), paras 11–025–11–030.

[38] In 2010, the guilty plea rate in the Crown Court was 70%: *Judicial and Court Statistics* (Ministry of Justice, 2011). See further M. Zander, "What the Annual Statistics Tell Us About Pleas and Acquittals" [1991] Crim. L.R. 252.

[39] e.g. the rule that in criminal proceedings the evidence of a child under 14 must be given unsworn: Youth Justice and Criminal Evidence Act 1999 s.55(2)(a).

[40] e.g. the rules relating to the admissibility of evidence of bad character of defendants under the provisions of the Criminal Justice Act 2003: see Ch.19.

[41] See Ch.3.

for their compatibility with the right to a fair trial under art.6 of the European Convention on Human Rights ("ECHR"), following the incorporation of the Convention into English law.[42]

Fourthly, the rules of evidence developed at common law, as overlaid by statutory intervention, are sometimes referred to as "the strict rules of evidence"[43] in the context of defining the nature of civil and criminal proceedings. However, it soon becomes apparent to any investigator of evidence law that there is not one unitary law of evidence applicable to all legal proceedings. Rather there are several different laws of evidence. The content of the law varies with the particular legal process under consideration.

1. Civil and criminal proceedings distinguished

1–017

In surveying the different laws of evidence the most important distinction to be made is between criminal and civil proceedings. As will be seen in later chapters there are major differences in the law on certain key topics: these include the standard of proof, the admissibility of hearsay evidence, and judicial discretion to exclude evidence. Several evidential issues arising in connection with the investigation of offences, which have generated a substantial amount of law, do not arise in the civil context. Hence the law of criminal evidence is much more extensive than the law of civil evidence.

The civil process itself is not a unitary whole. Many statutes contain provisions regulating specific questions of evidence in different types of civil proceeding.[44] More fundamentally there is a distinction between proceedings in the ordinary civil courts and proceedings before administrative tribunals.[45] There are numerous different types of administrative tribunal. Most are established by a statute conferring a specific jurisdiction over matters relating to such disparate subjects as employment, social security benefits, immigration, VAT and so on. It is impossible to generalise about the rules of evidence applicable in proceedings conducted before such bodies. The relevant statute sometimes prescribes the application of the rules in the civil courts[46]; sometimes it excludes them,[47] and sometimes it gives the tribunal power to determine its own procedure.[48] Consequently there are great variations of style and detail. Where Parliament has

---

[42] Human Rights Act 1998, discussed in Ch.2.

[43] See Civil Evidence Act 1995 s.11; Criminal Justice Act 2003 s.134. In *Re T* [2004] 2 F.L.R. 838 Butler-Sloss P. stated that "the strict rules of evidence applicable in a criminal trial, which is adversarial in nature, are to be contrasted with the partly inquisitorial approach of the court dealing with children cases in which the rules of evidence are considerably relaxed."

[44] Important examples would include the Partnership Act 1890 s.15 (admission by a partner concerning partnership affairs is evidence against the firm); Family Law Reform Act 1969 s.20 (evidence of scientific tests on the issue of parentage of any person); Senior Courts Act 1981 s.72 (removal of privilege against self-incrimination in proceedings for infringement of rights relating to intellectual property).

[45] See E. Campbell, "Principles of Evidence and Administrative Tribunals" in *Well and Truly Tried* L. Waller and E. Campbell (eds), (Sydney: Law Book Company, 1982), p.36.

[46] See, e.g. Equality Act 2006 ss.16, 20, 31 Sch.2 para.10(3)(b) (power of the Commission for Equality and Human Rights to require the production of information and documents does not extend to information and documents which a person could not be compelled to disclose in civil proceedings in the High Court).

not stipulated a particular procedure the courts have required a broad general principle of natural justice to be followed in the holding of a hearing or inquiry.[49]

However, it is clear that the content of natural justice in this context is flexible; the procedure adopted should depend on the nature of the proceeding in question and its purposes.[50] It would seem, broadly speaking, that the more "judicial" in character the proceeding, and the closer it approaches the model of a criminal prosecution, the more likely there is to be a fuller range of rules of evidence.[51]

2. Criminal proceedings

The fullest range of evidence law is to be found in criminal proceedings. Traditional common law rules, refined by the courts over three centuries, have been combined with a substantial amount of statute-based law to create an extensive and complex legal regime. This regime has been the subject of a fierce and continuing debate for many years.

1–018

In criminal proceedings there may be differences in the rules of evidence at different stages of the same process.[52] In magistrates' courts, for example, magistrates conducting committal proceedings have no discretion to exclude evidence,[53] but in summary trials they have the general discretion conferred by s.78(1) of PACE.[54] In the Crown Court, where an issue arises concerning the factual basis for sentencing a convicted offender, the law governing the

---

[47] e.g. r.15(2)(a)(i) of the Tribunal Procedure (First-tier Tribunal) (Health, Education and Social Care Chamber) Rules 2008 (SI 2008/2699) permits the relevant tribunal to admit evidence whether or not it would be inadmissible in a civil trial in England and Wales.

[48] e.g. reg.3 of the Employment Tribunals (Constitution and Rules of Procedure) Regulations 2004 (SI 2004/1861) provides that the chairman of an employment tribunal must deal justly with the case. Schedule 1 r.14(2) goes on to state that the chairman or tribunal shall seek to avoid formality in his or its proceedings and shall not be bound by any enactment or rule of law relating to the admissibility of evidence in proceedings before the courts.

[49] *R. v Deputy Industrial Injuries Commissioner Ex p. Moore* [1965] 1 Q.B. 456; *Bushell v Secretary of State for the Environment* [1981] A.C. 75; *Mahon v Air New Zealand* [1984] A.C. 808. More recent cases talk in terms of fairness rather than natural justice: see, e.g. *R. (on the application of Smith) v Parole Board* [2005] UKHL 1; [2005] 1 All E.R. 755 HL.

[50] *R. v Commission for Racial Equality Ex p. Cottrell & Rothon (a firm)* [1980] 3 All E.R. 265. For an interesting discussion of evidence in social security cases see J. G. Logie and P. Q. Watchman, "Social Security Appeal Tribunals: An Excursus on Evidential Issues" (1989) 8 C.J.Q. 109.

[51] Thus the Judicial Committee of the Privy Council has held that the onus and standard of proof in disciplinary proceedings before the Professional Conduct Committee of the General Medical Council and the relevant legal principles are those applicable to a criminal trial: *Lanford v General Medical Council* [1990] A.C. 13.

[52] Thus the ordinary rules of criminal evidence do not apply in applications for extension of custody time limits: *Wildman v DPP* [2001] Crim. L.R. 565. Similarly the Divisional Court has held that art.6 of the European Convention on Human Rights does not apply in hearings for breach of bail conditions: *R. (on the application of the DPP) v Havering Magistrates' Court* [2001] 2 Cr.App.R. 12.

[53] PACE s.78(3). This provision will be repealed if and when the provisions of the Criminal Justice Act 2003 replacing committal proceedings are brought into effect (ss.41 and 332 Schs 3 and 37 Pt 4).

[54] See *Vel v Owen* (1987) 151 J.P. 510 holding that magistrates may deal with an application to exclude when it arises or leave the decision until the end of the hearing. See also *Halawa v Federation Against Copyright Theft* [1995] 1 Cr.App.R. 21. In *Sang* [1980] A.C. 402, Lord Scarman had stated (obiter, at 456) that at common law magistrates had the same discretion as the judge in a jury trial to exclude legally admissible evidence in the interests of ensuring a fair trial for the accused.

applicable rules of evidence was said some years ago to be still in the process of development.[55] Although some of the rules applicable to the trial on liability apply to *Newton* hearings on sentencing,[56] it is clear that there are some differences.[57] These differences have to be accounted for by reference to the different purposes and circumstances of the post-conviction hearing. Similarly, it has been held that confiscation proceedings following conviction are an extension of the sentencing hearing and therefore criminal in nature, but by virtue of the Criminal Justice Act 1993 the applicable rules of evidence are different from those in criminal trials and include, for example, the civil standard of proof and the use of hearsay that would be inadmissible in a criminal trial.[58]

There are also some differences in the rules of evidence applicable to the two forms of criminal trial. Dock identifications are permissible and customary in some circumstances in summary trials,[59] but are disapproved in trials on indictment.[60] Magistrates may act on their personal knowledge of facts in issue, but this is not the case for factfinders in trials on indictment.[61] It has been convincingly argued that in practice the common law rule against evidence of the accused's bad character and other misconduct was not and could not be systematically applied in magistrates' courts in view of the regularity with which known offenders reappeared before the same justices.[62]

---

[55] M. Wasik, "Rules of Evidence in the Sentencing Process" [1985] C.L.P. 187.

[56] Named after the leading case of *Newton* (1983) 77 Cr.App.R. 13 which established the procedure for determining disputed questions of fact for the purpose of sentencing.

[57] In *Smith* (1988) 10 Cr.App.R.(S.) 271 the Court of Appeal held that in deciding what the factual situation of an offence was a sentencer was not bound by the rules of admissibility applicable in the trial of the issue of guilt or innocence. He could therefore take account of witness statements, depositions and evidence heard in the trial of co-defendants, all of which would be hearsay as against the defendant. The defendant must however be given every opportunity to put his own version of events. cf. *Gandy* (1989) 11 Cr.App.R.(S.) 564: a sentencer should direct himself as if he were a jury and should therefore, in a case of disputed identification, follow the guidelines in *Turnbull* [1977] Q.B. 224 CA; *Underwood* [2005] 1 Cr.App.R. 13: "the judge must, of course, direct himself in accordance with ordinary principles, such as, for example, the burden and standard of proof".

[58] *Silcock and Levin* [2004] EWCA Crim 408; [2004] 2 Cr.App.R. (S) 61 at [323]. cf. *Chal* [2007] EWCA Crim 2647; [2008] 1 Cr.App.R. 18 at [247]: the rules of evidence applicable in criminal trials apply equally to determinations by juries under s.4A of the Criminal Procedure (Insanity) Act 1964 of whether a person unfit to plead had committed the acts with which he is charged.

[59] *Barnes v Chief Constable of Durham* [1997] 2 Cr.App.R. 505 DC; *Karia v DPP* [2002] EWHC 2175.

[60] See Ch.7.

[61] See the discussion of judicial notice and personal knowledge in Ch.12.

[62] P. Darbyshire, "Previous Misconduct and Magistrates' Courts—Some Tales from the Real World" [1997] Crim. L.R. 105. The validity of Darbyshire's argument is unlikely to be affected by the changes to the admissibility of evidence of bad character made by the Criminal Justice Act 2003.

3. The multiplicity of styles of legal proceedings

Collectively the variations outlined above suggest that the law of evidence is a **1–019** flexible instrument of legal process. Some of the rules apply in one type of proceeding and not in another[63]; others apply differently in different proceedings,[64] and a third group may be enforced less rigorously in some contexts than others.[65]

A final addition to an already complex picture is the existence of a number of "inquisitorial" procedures. These are inquiries initiated and conducted by officials into facts of legal significance in which the avowed aim is to establish an independent truth.[66] Inquests in coroners courts[67] and statutory regimes for the investigation of insolvency and fraud[68] are prominent examples. The latter have become particularly controversial in view of their rejection of the privilege against self-incrimination,[69] traditionally one of the great cornerstones of the common law of evidence. Inquisitorial process is commonly contrasted with adversarial process in debates about the nature and reform of the law of evidence. We shall return to this topic in Ch.4.

The existence of so many varieties of legal process, and of significant variations in the evidential rules applicable to each, might suggest that it is difficult to make statements about the aims of the law of evidence which are accurate but yet not so general as to be vacuous. It does not take us very far to say that in any particular legal process the applicable law of evidence regulates the process of proof. This is an accurate description of the law's function, but it does not address the issue of the ends to which the regulation should be directed. The question about the aims and objectives of evidence law is a question with both descriptive and normative dimensions. An adequate answer to it requires a coherent theoretical context. This issue will be explored in Ch.2.

---

[63] Thus the rules of admissibility which apply in courts of law may be expressly disapplied in proceedings before certain tribunals; see fnn.47 and 48 above.

[64] The different regimes in civil and criminal cases for the admission of documentary hearsay afford a clear example; see Ch.17.

[65] e.g. the rule against the admission of evidence of other similar conduct by the defendant is applied less strictly in civil than in criminal cases: *Mood Music Publishing Co Ltd v De Wolfe Ltd* (1976) 1 All E.R. 763 CA; *O'Brien v Chief Constable of South Wales Police* [2005] UKHL 26; [2005] 2 All E.R. 931 HL; and see Ch.18.

[66] It is beyond the scope of this book to compare adversarial and inquisitorial procedures in detail, much less to offer an evaluation of their respective merits. There is an extensive literature, much of which is referred to in the volume of essays, *Adversarial versus Inquisitorial Justice: Psychological Perspectives on Criminal Justice Systems* edited by Koppen and Penrod, (New York: Springer, 2003). See also J. McEwan, "Ritual, Fairness and Truth: The Adversarial and Inquisitorial Models of Criminal Trial" in *The Trial on Trial* edited by Duff, Farmer, Marshall, and Tadros, (Portland: Hart Publishing, 2004) vol.1, p.51.

[67] Matthews, Paul *Jervis on Coroners*, 12th edn (Sweet & Maxwell: London, 2002), paras 1–07 onwards.

[68] Companies Act 1985 ss.432–434; Insolvency Act 1986 ss.235–236; Criminal Justice Act 1987 s.2.

[69] *Re London United Investments Plc* [1992] 2 All E.R. 842 CA; *Bishopsgate Investment Management Ltd v Maxwell* (1992) 2 All E.R. 856 CA; *R. v Director of Serious Fraud Office Ex p. Smith* [1993] A.C. 1 HL.

D.   THE DEVELOPMENT OF THE LAW OF EVIDENCE

1.   Legislative reform

1–020   The point has already been made that much change has taken place in the law of criminal evidence in recent years. Much of this change has been introduced by legislation: PACE, the Criminal Justice Act 1988, the Criminal Justice and Public Order Act 1994, the Youth Justice and Criminal Evidence Act 1999 and the Criminal Justice Act 2003. Yet there has been no systematic overall design to these reforms, no clearly articulated statement of the objectives of a modern law of evidence. The reforms have proceeded from a variety of sources with different concerns and priorities.

These sources are mostly a series of reports by a variety of different organisations or individuals charged with making an inquiry into aspects of the criminal justice system in general or rules of evidence in particular. The sequence of reports began in 1972 with the publication of the Eleventh Report of the Criminal Law Revision Committee ("CLRC") on Evidence (General).[70] This reviewed virtually the whole of the law of criminal evidence, and made numerous proposals for reform based on the Committee's general philosophy that the law should be simplified, with fewer exclusionary and restrictive rules. In particular, the CLRC proposed the curtailment of some traditional protective rules for the accused, such as the right to silence, on the basis that they were no longer needed in modern times and might operate in practice as an unjustified hindrance to the efficient prosecution and conviction of the guilty. This stance proved extremely controversial. It was founded squarely on what Packer has famously described as "crime control" values,[71] and was unsympathetic to some received notions of "due process" for defendants.[72] More than a decade was to pass before any of the CLRC's proposals were enacted.

In the meantime the Royal Commission on Criminal Procedure reported in 1981.[73] That Commission was explicitly concerned to strike a balance between the rights of suspects and the public interest in obtaining reliable evidence of guilt. The balance included, amongst other things, maintenance of the right to silence. A key proposal of the Commission was for a statutory clarification and reform of police powers, including various powers to obtain evidence from suspects in investigations. The proposal was taken up in PACE, the first of the modern reforming statutes. PACE incorporated many of the Commission's recommendations and added to them some of the CLRC's less controversial proposals.

---

[70] Cmnd.4991 (1972).

[71] H. L. Packer, *The Limits of the Criminal Sanction* (Stanford: Stanford University Press, 1968), pp.153 onwards.

[72] H. L. Packer, *The Limits of the Criminal Sanction* (1968). Packer's models of criminal justice systems provide a useful starting-point for understanding aspects of the development of the law of criminal procedure and evidence in England, but the models are not discussed in detail here. Chapter 2 offers a different framework for considering the aims of the law of evidence.

[73] Cmnd.8092 (1981).

In 1986, the report of the Roskill Committee on fraud trials[74] made important **1–021** recommendations in relation to the use of documents in evidence, including much greater admissibility of hearsay documents.[75] These proposals, like those of the CLRC, were inspired by the desire to modernise and simplify the law in the interests of efficiency and the prevention of what the Committee saw as unmeritorious technical objections to admissibility. Concern also began to develop in the 1980s about the treatment by the law of evidence of victims and vulnerable witnesses; in 1989 the Pigot Committee produced an influential report,[76] recommending measures aimed at reducing the stress associated with the traditional method of giving oral testimony in open court.

At the end of the 1980s and the beginning of the 1990s the criminal justice system was badly damaged by the publicity attached to a series of spectacular cases of miscarriage of justice. The Guildford Four, the Maguire family, the Birmingham Six, Judith Ward, Stefan Kiszko, the Tottenham Three, and others,[77] all involved defendants convicted of major crimes. Many of them had served long sentences of imprisonment before their convictions were quashed. In nearly all these cases evidential problems provided the main reasons for quashing the convictions; the problems included the fabrication or extortion by the police of confessions by the accused, unreliable expert evidence, and non-disclosure to the defence of material evidence tending to undermine the prosecution case. The public concern about the Guildford and Birmingham cases led to the appointment of the Royal Commission on Criminal Justice, the second Royal Commission to report[78] on the criminal justice system within a dozen years.

The report of this second Commission turned out to be a disappointment. It is true, as the Commission said,[79] that it was not appointed to look into individual cases. Nevertheless, commentators were surprised to find the Commission making little effort to analyse the causes of miscarriage in any of the notorious cases which led to its appointment or which came to light afterwards. The Commission acknowledged that public confidence in the criminal justice system had been shaken by these cases and it was clear that restoration of confidence was one of its aims. It would seem an elementary necessity therefore to have offered some diagnosis of the problems before the prescription for their cure. Instead the Commission concentrated firmly on its terms of reference which were to examine:

"the effectiveness of the criminal justice system in England and Wales in securing the conviction of those guilty of criminal offences and the acquittal of those who are innocent."

This wording placed the focus of the inquiry squarely on the importance of accurate outcomes of criminal process and on the efficacy of the "system" in

---

[74] Fraud Trials Committee Report (London: Stationery Office Books, 1986).

[75] Ch.5.

[76] Report of the Advisory Group on Video Evidence (Home Office: London, 1989).

[77] For discussion, see JUSTICE, "Miscarriages of Justice" (London: 1989); I. Dennis, "Miscarriages of Justice and the Law of Confessions: Evidentiary Issues and Solutions" [1993] P.L. 291; C. Walker, "Introduction" in C. Walker and K. Starmer (eds), *Justice in Error* (London: Blackstone Press Ltd, 1993), p.1.

[78] Report of the Royal Commission on Criminal Justice (RRCJ Report) Cm.2263 (1993).

[79] RCCJ Report, Ch.1 para.3.

promoting accuracy. The Benthamite goal of "rectitude of decision" was thus impliedly adopted. The key institutions and officials were then impliedly assigned a managerial role in efficiently achieving effective (accurate) outcomes. Some of the Commission's recommendations to carry forward this agenda were taken up; in particular a new regime governing disclosure by both prosecution and defence was introduced in the Criminal Procedure and Investigations Act 1996.

1–022   In 2001 came Lord Justice Auld's report entitled *Review of the Criminal Courts of England and Wales*.[80] This mammoth report of some 700 pages covered a very large number of topics concerned with the delivery of criminal justice by the courts. Auld L.J.'s remit was very broad. He was asked to inquire into:

> "the practices and procedures of, and the rules of evidence applied by, the criminal courts at every level, with a view to ensuring that they deliver justice fairly, by streamlining all their processes, increasing their efficiency and strengthening the effectiveness of their relationships with others across the whole of the criminal justice system, and having regard to the interests of all parties including victims and witnesses, thereby promoting public confidence in the rule of law."

It was a major achievement to produce a report of such breadth and detail in a relatively short time. The strengths of the report were its impartiality and its concern with the quality of justice. Auld had no overt crime control agenda of the type that marked the Eleventh Report of the CLRC. Moreover, there is no managerialist emphasis in the report of the type that was latent in the Runciman Commission Report and which became overt in the White Paper *Criminal Justice: The Way Ahead*.[81] Auld's objective was to balance the various interests mentioned in his terms of reference, taking account of the human rights implications of the incorporation of the ECHR into English law.[82] The result was a report that was closer in tone to the 1981 Report of the Royal Commission on Criminal Procedure than to any of the other official inquiries of recent years into criminal justice. Auld's proposals were presented for the most part in a measured even-handed style, well supported by reference to relevant literature.

However, the Auld Review had certain weaknesses. First, it was much concerned with efficiency, again reflecting its remit, but the projected efficiency gains from proposed reforms were mostly speculative since the proposals were not costed. Secondly, the Review as a whole lacked empirical foundations since Auld commissioned little in the way of research, apart from an extensive study of the literature on juries. Thirdly, the long list of 328 recommendations formed a disparate set of proposals which varied greatly in their generality and importance. They represented one man's judgment of the correct balance across a wide sweep of criminal justice issues. They were not parts of an integrated overall plan. Consequently the Government was able to cherry-pick the proposals; many of Auld's recommendations found their way into the Criminal Justice Act 2003, but

---

[80] London, The Stationery Office, 2001 ("Auld Review").

[81] Cm.5074 (2001); for comment see [2001] Crim. L.R. 261.

[82] The Human Rights Act 1998, which effected the incorporation, is discussed in more detail in Ch.2. For comment on Auld's balancing technique see A. Duff, L. Farmer, S. Marshall and V. Tadros, "Introduction: Towards a Normative Theory of the Criminal Trial" in Duff, *The Trial on Trial* (Oxford: Hart Publishing, 2004), Vol. I pp.6–7.

others were simply discarded including, regrettably, the recommendation for a comprehensive review of the law with a view to its reform and codification.[83]

Alongside this series of one-off reports should be placed the work of the Law Commission, the statutory body established in 1965 to review and reform the law of England and Wales as a whole. From the 1980s onwards the Commission has been active in promoting reform both of civil and criminal evidence, based on its established tradition of producing well-researched, high-quality consultation papers, followed by final reports containing proposals for legislation and draft Bills. Much use of this material is made throughout this book. Particularly important are the Law Commission reports in the 1990s on hearsay in civil and criminal cases respectively, the recommendations of which were enacted largely unaltered.[84] The Commission's most recent project in the evidence field is an important report on expert evidence, discussed in Ch.20.

1–023

2. Recent developments

The Criminal Justice Act 2003 was a massive piece of legislation which made extensive changes to the law of criminal procedure and evidence, and also to the law of sentencing. The inspiration for its procedural and evidential reforms came from a number of sources, including the Auld Review, the White Paper *Justice For All*,[85] and the Law Commission's work on hearsay evidence, noted above. As well as making substantial reforms to the law on hearsay the Act completely recast the law on evidence of bad character, formally discarding a great deal of old learning in the process. This revision was a key element in the Government's professed aim of "rebalancing" the criminal justice system away from defendants to more favourable treatment for victims and witnesses. The objective was to reduce the extent to which witnesses could have their credibility attacked through evidence of their bad character, while allowing greater admissibility of evidence of a defendant's previous convictions and other misconduct where this was relevant to an issue in the case. The new law relating to the bad character of defendants is set out in a group of complex and detailed provisions, discussed in Ch.19.

1–024

In summary, therefore, the process of reform of the law of evidence has been piecemeal, as successive governments have adopted particular recommendations in particular reports and blended them into the legislation with their own policy initiatives. Although there has been no overall grand design, many of the reforms have adopted a strategy which involves a greatly increased reliance on discretion on the part of trial judges in admitting evidence and directing juries about it. Much of the reform effort has been directed at eliminating or relaxing technical rules of the common law which constrain the behaviour of trial judges, and substituting much more open-textured standards of fairness. The move away from restrictive rules is linked in turn to a wish to give factfinders more opportunity for

---

[83] Auld Review, p.546 para.77.
[84] See Civil Evidence Act 1995, giving effect to proposals in Law Com.No.216, *The Hearsay Rule in Civil Proceedings* (London, 1993); Criminal Justice Act 2003, giving effect to proposals in Law Com.No.245, *Evidence in Criminal Proceedings: Hearsay and Related Topics* Cm.3670 (1997).
[85] Cm.5563 (2002).

hearing evidence and more scope for exercising common sense in evaluating it. Thus factors which previously affected the admissibility of evidence, such as potential unreliability or the risk of manufacture, have been shifted to considerations of weight. However, extending the powers of trial judges and factfinders in this way has its costs. Not the least of these is indeterminacy. Looser criteria for the admission and evaluation of evidence inevitably mean more uncertainty in the preparation and conduct of trials.[86] As noted above, another strong policy theme in much of the reforming legislation has been greater protection of the interests of witnesses, particularly witnesses who are victims of crime. The impact of this policy is discussed in the chapters on witnesses.

1–025 Finally, we should note the Criminal Procedure Rules 2012.[87] These are a unified set of rules of criminal procedure which were first introduced in 2005.[88] They apply, in general, to all criminal cases in magistrates' courts and the Crown Court and in all cases in the Criminal Division of the Court of Appeal. The Rules have a number of aims. One is to bring together in an accessible form a mass of rules previously scattered across a large number of statutory instruments. This consolidation is seen as an essential first step in the creation of a criminal procedural code. Secondly, the Rules are intended to promote a culture change in criminal case management. In the words of the Lord Chief Justice, introducing the Rules in 2005:

> "they introduce new rules, written in plain English, that give courts explicit powers and responsibilities to manage cases actively, with the object of reducing the numbers of ineffective hearings that cause avoidable distress to witnesses and inconvenience and expense to everyone."

The emphasis on active case management marks a significant inroad into the adversarial tradition, with its commitment to principles of party autonomy and judicial passivity. This development has received strong criticism from McEwan, who deplores the transfer of power from the parties to the court and suggests that it carries dangers of diminishing due process protections for defendants.[89] This is perhaps debatable, given the importance of art.6 of the ECHR in maintaining a number of fair trial rights and the duty of the court under s.6 of the Human Rights Act 1998 to act compatibly with Convention rights. However, one consequence of the development has certainly been a strong judicial insistence that criminal trials are no longer to be regarded as a game in which the defence refuse to reveal their hand until the last possible moment. In *Malcolm v DPP*,[90] for example, the Divisional Court emphasised that the defence have a duty under the Rules to assist the court to achieve the "overriding objective" of dealing with cases justly,

---

[86] For further criticism of these developments see C. Tapper, "The law of evidence and the rule of law" [2009] C.L.J 67.

[87] Criminal Procedure Rules 2012 (SI 2010/1726). The Rules were drafted by the Criminal Procedure Rules Committee, chaired by the Lord Chief Justice. The Committee was established by the Courts Act 2003.

[88] The Rules have been regularly updated since their introduction. The current version is the Criminal Procedure Rules 2012 (SI 2010/1726), in force from October 1, 2012.

[89] J. McEwan, "From adversarialism to managerialism: criminal justice in transition" (2011) 31 L.S. 519.

[90] *Malcolm v DPP* [2007] Crim. L.R. 894.

and that this includes making the defence to the charge clear to the prosecution and the court at an early stage. The statement of the overriding objective and what it means is one of the most interesting aspects of the Rules. It is central to the aims of the law of evidence, the topic to which we now turn in Ch.2.

CHAPTER 2

THE AIMS OF THE LAW OF EVIDENCE

A. Introduction: Evidence, Legal Process and Adjudication

Chapter 1 identified the law of evidence as a form of adjectival law. This means **2–001** the law which sets out the legal mechanisms for implementing and enforcing substantive legal rights duties and liabilities. The particular function of the law of evidence is to regulate the process of proof of facts for the purposes of legal proceedings. This is a straightforward description of the law's instrumental function, but it does not without more reveal anything about the purposes of the regulation of proof. What, in other words, are the aims of the law of evidence, given its character as adjectival law? This is the issue taken up in this chapter.

A useful starting-point for approaching the question of aims is to recall that most of the legal proceedings in question are concerned with adjudication. Adjudication is usually thought of as a form of dispute-resolution, but it may sometimes be concerned with the implementation of law, where any "dispute" is a matter of form rather than substance. Adjudication by public officials of questions of rights, duties, liabilities and status is one of the defining characteristics of virtually all legal systems.[1]

---

[1] See H. L. A. Hart, *The Concept of Law* (Oxford: Clarendon Press, 1961), esp. pp.94–95; J. Finnis, *Natural Law and Natural Rights* (Oxford: Clarendon Press, 1980). esp. pp.266 ff.

The principal attributes of adjudication, as described by Fuller,[2] are that the parties involved participate in the decision by presenting proofs and reasoned arguments. By "proofs" Fuller means evidence designed to persuade the adjudicator to uphold a particular party's factual contentions by drawing the appropriate favourable inferences. The term "reasoned arguments" embodies the idea that the dispute is to be resolved within an institutional framework governed by rationality. In other words, the adjudicator is expected to decide the dispute by the exercise of reason in determining the relevant issues of fact and law. Personal prejudice and irrelevant reasons would not be acceptable grounds for decision. This analysis fits best the adjudicator who is a professional judge; the judge makes a public announcement of the decision and presents a reasoned justification for it. Juries, on the other hand, also make public announcements of their decisions, but do not give their reasons. To that extent the rationality of juries has to be taken on trust.[3] For a variety of reasons it is thought that the stability of jury verdicts should not be open to disturbance by parties subjecting the reasoning of lay factfinders to detailed scrutiny.

2–002　From this perspective the question about the aims of the law of evidence needs to be placed in the context of a wider question about the aims of adjudication. The issue can be reformulated accordingly: what are the goals of adjudication and in what ways does the law of evidence promote them? After discussion of this issue, the chapter goes on to deal with the place of rights in the analysis of the aims of the law of evidence. This involves consideration of the Human Rights Act 1998 and the effects of incorporation of the European Convention on Human Rights into English law. The chapter concludes with an exposition of the theory that the aims of the law of evidence are best accounted for in terms of promoting the legitimacy of verdicts and judgments in adjudication. In summary, the theory argues that legitimacy is an essential attribute of verdicts and judgments, and that it is derived from a combination of their factual accuracy, their moral authority, and their expressive value as official applications of the relevant law.

B.　THE RATIONALIST MODEL OF ADJUDICATION

2–003　Consideration of the goals of adjudication, and the role of the law of evidence in their realisation, can usefully begin with the theoretical model developed by Twining, which he describes as the "rationalist model of adjudication".[4] This presents an ideal or prescriptive theory of adjudication ultimately based on utilitarian principles but constructed in such a way as to allow for possible points

---

[2] L. Fuller, "The Forms and Limits of Adjudication" (1978) 92 Harv. L.R. 353. See also the penetrating discussion by D. J. Galligan, *Due Process and Fair Procedures* (Oxford: Clarendon Press, 1996), pp.241 onwards, who correctly describes Fuller's account of adjudication as tied closely to the adversarial traditions of common law systems.

[3] Although it should be noted that English adjectival law seeks to promote rationality of decision-making by juries through requirements for judicial directions on the issues the jury has to decide and on the reasoning process jurors should use in evaluating certain types of evidence. These requirements, and associated warnings, are discussed in later chapters.

[4] W. L. Twining, *Rethinking Evidence*, 2nd edn (Cambridge: Cambridge University Press, 2006), pp.75 onwards.

of departure or disagreement.[5] Twining claims that the principal features of the theory have by and large been accepted by the leading scholars in the Anglo-American tradition of specialist writings on evidence.[6] The theory can be concisely summarised by saying that it asserts that the fundamental aim of adjudication is rectitude of decision-making. Rectitude is achieved by the correct application of substantive law to the true facts of the dispute. The facts are determined through the accurate evaluation of relevant and reliable evidence by a competent and impartial adjudicator applying the specified burden and standard of proof. There must be adequate safeguards against corruption and mistake and adequate provision for review and appeal.

As Twining indicates, this is an instrumentalist model.[7] It presupposes that rectitude of decision is a necessary condition of the administration of justice under the law. The model then embodies the idea that the pursuit of truth through reason is a necessary means of achieving rectitude. In the light of the model some of the instrumental aims of the law of evidence become clearer. At a straightforward level the law should aim to assist in the achievement of rectitude by ensuring that as far as possible the evidence before the adjudicator is relevant and reliable, that it is presented in a form which is designed to bring out truth and discover untruth and that the appropriate burdens and standards of proof are clearly specified.

For Bentham, from whose work Twining's model is ultimately derived, the aim of rectitude was best achieved by adoption of what he called the Natural System of Procedure.[8] This was a system characterised by the absence of technical rules, particularly rules that excluded certain types of relevant evidence or attempted to specify the relevance or weight of different pieces of evidence. It was better, in Bentham's view, to adopt a general principle of admitting all evidence probative of the factual issues in the case and to give the factfinder a free hand in its assessment. Any "rules" of evidence should take the form of guidelines addressed to the decision-maker's understanding rather than to the will. In other words, the law should not attempt to control factfinding by having rules dictating what evidence can be received and how it should be evaluated. Instead the law should aim to improve the quality and accuracy of factfinding by educating the factfinder about the factors affecting the relevance and weight of evidence, and by giving guidance as to appropriate reasoning in the evaluation of evidence. Under this system, therefore, the reliability of evidence would invariably be an issue for the factfinder to determine. It would not be correct to employ a risk of unreliability as a justification for "technical" rules of exclusion or use of evidence.[9]

---

[5] W. L. Twining, *Rethinking Evidence*, (2006), p.76.
[6] W. L. Twining, *Rethinking Evidence*, (2006), p.76.
[7] W. L. Twining, *Rethinking Evidence*, (2006), p.83.
[8] J. Bentham, *Rationale of Judicial Evidence*, J. S. Mill (ed) (London: Hunter and Clarke, 1827), Vol.2 pp.425–434; Vol.4 pp.5–12, 428 onwards. Bentham's work on adjudication and evidence is illuminatingly discussed by W. L. Twining, *Theories of Evidence: Bentham and Wigmore* (London: Stanford University Press, 1985), Ch.2, and by G. Postema, *Bentham and the Common Law Tradition* (Oxford: Clarendon Press, 1986), Chs 10 onwards.
[9] For a modern version of this argument see L. Laudan, *Truth, Error and Criminal Law* (Cambridge: Cambridge University Press, 2006).

2–004 However, consistently with principles of utility, Bentham allowed for the modification of his Natural System by reference to its costs. If the benefits of receiving certain evidence in aid of rectitude were to be exceeded by the costs, in terms, as he put it, of the "preponderant" vexation, expense or delay its reception would cause, then it would be right to exclude the evidence from consideration. This is a matter of fundamental importance. Bentham's concession to the claims of these costs was a recognition of the necessity for constraints on a theory which would argue for the free admission and evaluation of all probative evidence; a theory, in other words, of "free proof".[10] In a world of unlimited time and resources, and with an absence of the intrusion of values competing with rectitude, free proof might be an attainable ideal.[11] But, as Bentham himself implicitly acknowledged, in a context of practical decision-making where these conditions do not obtain, limits have to be set. Part of the aims of the law of evidence is therefore to articulate and justify the constraints on the principle of free proof which the rationalist model of adjudication might otherwise logically adopt.

At this point it is helpful to note that rules of evidence may have different kinds of significance. Rules with "epistemic" significance relate to the truthfinding objective of adjudicative proceedings; they are intended to promote truthfinding and hence rectitude of decision. There are numerous examples of such rules to be found throughout this book. Important examples include rules dealing with evidence thought to present risks of unreliability, such as identification evidence,[12] and rules designed to ensure that expert evidence is given only by persons appropriately qualified.[13] Rules with 'non-epistemic' significance are designed to give effect to values other than truthfinding which may bear on evidential issues in the proceedings. Again this book contains several examples. Important examples of such values include police probity in the investigation of offences,[14] and the protection of confidentiality in the public interest.[15] Giving effect to these values may generate rules allowing for the exclusion of relevant evidence, or restrictions on questioning, which might otherwise promote the truthfinding obejctive. Many rules of evidence have both epistemic and non-epistemic significance. A notable example is the right to confront witnesses[16]; this serves the truthfinding objective by providing a means of evaluating the credibility and reliability of a witness's testimony, and, as

---

[10] See further, on freedom of proof and its assumptions, L. J. Cohen, "Freedom of Proof" in W.L. Twining (ed), *Facts in Law* (1983), pp.1, 10; W. L. Twining, *Rethinking Evidence*, (2006), pp.208–210; J. D. Jackson, "Theories of Truth Finding in Criminal Procedure: An Evolutionary Approach" (1988) 10 Cardozo L.R. 475; A. Stein, "The Refoundation of Evidence Law" (1996) IX *Canadian Journal of Law and Jurisprudence* 279. A fuller account of Stein's views is set out in his *Foundations of Evidence Law* (Oxford: Oxford University Press, 2005).

[11] But see Stein, *Foundations of Evidence Law* (2005) arguing that freedom of proof fails to deal fairly with the risk of error in adjudicative factfinding, and advocating a "refoundation" of evidence law according to principles of risk-allocation.

[12] Discussed in Ch.7.

[13] Discussed in Ch.20.

[14] Discussed in Chs 6 and 8.

[15] Discussed in Ch.9.

[16] Discussed in Chs 15 and 16.

explained below, it also gives effect to an important 'process value' of enabling a party to participate fully in the adjudication.

The following discussion argues that accounting for the constraints on free proof may involve both epistemic and non-epistemic considerations. The discussion shows that the law of evidence frequently has competing objectives, particularly where epistemic and non-epistemic considerations pull in different directions.[17] A major issue then arises of how competitions between different objectives should be resolved.

1. Constraints on freedom of proof

(A)   Expense and delay

The aim of minimising expense and delay in adjudication is widely, if not universally, accepted. Hearing any evidence involves the expenditure of time and money. If the evidence is of no use, the expenditure is unjustified. It follows that no one could reasonably object to a rule that evidence which is not relevant to the litigation should be inadmissible. Irrelevant evidence is no use, and is therefore wasteful of resources.[18] Indeed a rule excluding irrelevant evidence is clearly called for by the logic of the rationalist model itself. It follows that the non-epistemic value of efficiency of legal process and the epistemic value of truthfinding both support the exclusion of irrelevant evidence. The criteria of relevance and the problems of evidence with marginal or an insufficient degree of relevance will be considered in Ch.3.

The aim of cost-reduction may also be part of the rationale for other more controversial rules of the common law. An example is the rule that, in general, the statements of a witness made out of court that are consistent with present testimony are not admissible. Consistency in a witness may be a virtue, but traditionally such statements were regarded as having doubtful probative value because of the risk that they might amount only to superfluous repetition or, in the case of a party, be deliberately manufactured.[19] On this view such benefits as they might have would therefore be generally outweighed by the expense and delay incurred in admitting them. There were always exceptions to this general rule, and these were enlarged by the Criminal Justice Act 2003, so that not only are more previous statements by witnesses admissible but they are also capable of being evidence of the facts stated rather than going only to bolster the witness's credibility.[20] However, s.126 of the Act gives the court a discretion to exclude

2–005

---

[17] For illuminating discussion see L. Laudan, *Truth, Error and Criminal Law* (2006).

[18] This is quite apart from any other "costs" it may have, such as distracting the factfinder and confusing the issues; see Ch.3.

[19] See, e.g. the much-quoted dictum of C. B. Eyre in *Hardy* (1794) 12 St. Tr. 199 at 1093: "[T]he presumption . . . is, that no man would declare anything against himself unless it were true; but that every man, if he was in a difficulty, or in the view to any difficulty, would make declarations for himself". The topic of previous consistent statements is discussed in Ch.14.

[20] See Ch.14.

these, and any other, hearsay statements on the ground that their admission, taking account of the value of the evidence, would result in undue waste of time.[21]

(B) Procedural fairness

2–006   Secondly, there is broad agreement that adjectival law, including the law of evidence, should aim to promote minimum standards of procedural fairness. This is a concept whose contours are somewhat blurred because it appears that it may have different applications in different contexts. Nevertheless its central elements can be stated with reasonable confidence. They derive from the principles of natural justice[22] and comprise the ideas that parties to adjudication should have adequate notice of the allegations of their opponents,[23] a reasonable opportunity to present their own cases (which implies reasonable opportunities to gain access to evidence), a reasonable opportunity to challenge the evidence against them by cross-examination of witnesses or otherwise, and finally that the adjudication should be conducted within a reasonable time in public in an orderly and impartial manner.[24]

Put in these terms, procedural fairness has both epistemic and non-epistemic significance. First, it can be argued that procedural fairness is instrumentally important for adjudication. It arguably promotes rectitude of decision by enabling all parties to locate, produce and test all the relevant and worthwhile evidence on the facts in dispute.[25] However, there are two countervailing considerations which suggest that in some respects procedural fairness can operate as a constraint on free proof. The first is that the procedure involved is the adversary process. As noted in Ch.1, this allows parties to screen out from the adjudication certain issues and evidence if they wish. From the standpoint of the adjudicator, this freedom of the parties to circumscribe the scope of the enquiry may well reduce accuracy of decision-making. Judges in civil cases are well aware of this,

---

[21] See Ch.17.

[22] The basic principles are spelt out in art.6 of the European Convention on Human Rights, discussed in more detail below. See further D. J. Galligan, *Due Process and Fair Procedures* (Oxford: Clarendon Press, 1996); M. Bayles, *Procedural Justice* (London: Kluwer Academic, 1990); P. Jackson, *Natural Justice*, 2nd edn (London: Sweet & Maxwell, 1979); P. Stein and J. Shand, *Legal Values in Western Society* (Edinburgh: Edinburgh University Press, 1974), pp.77 onwards.

[23] See, e.g. *A v United Kingdom* (2009) 49 E.H.R.R. 29; *Secretary of State for the Home Department v AF (No.3)* [2009] UKHL 28; [2009] 3 All E.R. 643.

[24] A further principle might be that the parties have a right to know the reasons for the decision (see Bayles, *Procedural Justice* (1990), Ch.4), but the principle is applied patchily in English law. Parties to cases in the superior courts are entitled to a reasoned judgment but juries, lay magistrates and many administrative tribunals do not give reasons. For discussion of the giving of reasons for administrative decisions, see D. J. Galligan, *Due Process and Fair Procedures* (1996), pp.429–437.

[25] Zuckerman has described the principle of access to evidence as "particularly important in an adversary system of adjudication where litigants have to rely on their own efforts to find and present evidence": A. A. S. Zuckerman, "Privilege and Public Interest" in C. Tapper (ed), *Crime Proof and Punishment* (London: Butterworths, 1981), p.248.

and occasionally comment on it.[26] The second point is that procedural fairness embodies a principle of equality of opportunity for parties to litigation.[27] But parties are plainly not equal in their ability or their resources to conduct legal disputes. Hence it is generally considered essential to allow them to be legally represented; in turn, effective legal representation is generally considered to require that parties should be able to have confidential access to legal aid and advice. The doctrine of legal professional privilege permits parties to refuse to disclose confidential communications with their lawyers.[28] Such communications may contain information that a thoroughgoing inquiry into the truth of the matter would think was important. Nevertheless the doctrine of legal professional privilege enables this information to be withheld from the adjudication.

Secondly, procedural fairness is important for non-epistemic reasons as a component in the acceptability of decisions. Parties who have had a full opportunity to participate in the decision-making process are more likely to accept the outcome as a legitimate resolution of the dispute.[29] Respect for full participation as a "process value" may also help to make decisions more acceptable to the public at large.[30] This is an aspect of the maxim that "justice must not only be done but be seen to be done".

(C) Avoidance of error

Thirdly, any adjudicative decision carries a risk of error. The rationalist model **2–007** makes a fundamental epistemological assumption that, in principle, the truth about past events and present states of affairs is capable of being accurately inferred from evidence.[31] However, it must be recognised that the evidence presented by the parties may be incomplete or unreliable, or may be evaluated incorrectly. Mistakes can then occur. If the mistake is of such a kind that it results in a wrong decision (whether wrongful conviction, acquittal or judgment) a miscarriage of justice takes place. Rectitude of decision is not achieved. Therefore an important aim of the law of evidence is to allocate the risks of error in the adjudicative process so as to minimise the chance of a miscarriage of

---

[26] See, e.g. *Air Canada v Secretary of State for Trade* [1983] 2 A.C. 394 at 438 per Lord Wilberforce: "It often happens, from the imperfection of evidence, or the withholding of it, sometimes by the party in whose favour it would tell if presented, that an adjudication has to be made which is not, and is known not to be, the whole truth of the matter".
[27] "Equality of arms" is an essential element of the right to a fair trial under art.6 of the European Convention on Human Rights ("ECHR"): *X v Federal Republic of Germany* (1151/61) (1962) 7 *Collection of Decisions of the European Commission of Human Rights* 118. See further below.
[28] See Ch.10.
[29] Bayles, *Procedural Justice* (1990), pp.127–135; T. Tyler, *Why People Obey the Law* (1990). This point is discussed more fully below.
[30] See R. S. Summers, "Evaluating and Improving Legal Processes: A Plea for Process Values" (1974) 60 Cornell L.R. 1.
[31] For discussion of various forms of scepticism about the law's epistemology see W. L. Twining, *Rethinking Evidence*, 2nd edn (2006), Ch.4. See also Z. Bankowski, "The value of truth: fact scepticism revisited" (1981) 3 L.S. 257, and the discussion in Ch.4 below.

justice.[32] The most obvious mechanisms employed for this purpose are the burden of proof and the standard of proof. These are devices which, as explained above, are an integral part of the rationalist model. They can be varied according to the importance attached to avoiding particular types of erroneous outcome. The high standard of proof required in criminal cases is intended to reduce the risk of a wrongful conviction.

Constraints on free proof arise if it is decided that rules of admissibility and use of evidence are necessary to avoid particular types of erroneous outcome. Hence the need to reduce the risk of wrongful conviction is part of the explanation of some of the more restrictive rules of criminal evidence. For example, most people would consider a person's criminal record a relevant item of evidence in deciding whether the person had committed a particular offence. However, at common law it was generally excluded from evidence on the ground that the risk of it being misused by the factfinder to the prejudice of the accused outweighed the probative value it might have.[33] The reforms made by the Criminal Justice Act 2003 were intended to result in greater admissibility of defendants' criminal records, but the Court of Appeal has made it clear that where the record is admitted a specific direction to the factfinder is required in order to prevent misuse of this evidence.[34] The detailed rules governing the obtaining of statements from a suspect by the police are designed at least in part to ensure that confessions are reliable, and to lessen the chance of a wrongful conviction.[35] Many of these restrictive rules continue to attract controversy, either on the ground that they are insufficiently protective of innocent accused, or that they are over-protective of defendants at the expense of victims and the community in general.

(D) Pursuit of other values

2–008   Fourthly, it must be emphasised that accuracy of factfinding (via the pursuit of truth) is not the only value at stake in the adjudicative process. As noted above, non-epistemic values may make significant claims to protection, and these claims may compete for priority with the value attached to truth-finding. An interest in the protection of any of these values might call in a particular case for the exclusion of certain evidence, or restrictions on questioning, to the detriment of accuracy in factfinding. An illustration would be evidence of the contents of a secret diplomatic despatch alleged to be defamatory of the claimant. If the interests of the state protect this letter from disclosure to, and use by, the claimant

---

[32] Australian Law Reform Commission, *Report on Evidence* (ALRC 39, Canberra, 1987), paras 35 onwards. See also A. Stein, *Foundations of Evidence Law*, 2005 arguing that allocation of the risk of error is *the* foundation principle of the law of evidence; L. Laudan, *Truth, Error and Criminal Law,* (2006).

[33] See Ch.18.

[34] *Hanson* [2005] EWCA Crim 824; [2005] 2 Cr.App.R. 299.

[35] See Ch.6.

in litigation, the action will fail for want of proof of the libel. It follows that the law of evidence has an important objective of allocating priorities among competing interests in adjudication.[36]

This may well be a complex and controversial task. It is not an easy matter to determine how high a value to place on truth-finding as an aid to rectitude of decision. Unless criteria can be established to enable judgments about competing interests to be made coherently and systematically there is a danger that the law may develop in an unprincipled and inconsistent fashion. A further complication is the constraints already referred to. How should the various claims of free proof, avoidance of error, human rights, procedural fairness and competing interests be determined? To take some concrete examples, how should the law of evidence approach the question of a confession obtained by torture, or a claim by, say, a rape victim, that it is wrong in principle that the accused need not give evidence at trial to answer a prima facie case? Adjusting competing claims can also be a problem in civil contexts. For example, in what civil proceedings, if any, should a person suspected of fraud have a privilege against self-incrimination?

A model of adjudication which is concerned only with rectitude of decision supplies no answer to such questions, unless it is the robust response that the implicit principle of free proof is overriding in all cases. But this stance is not convincing. A law of evidence which, for example, abolished legal professional privilege and which contained no special protections at all for the accused in criminal cases would be unlikely to command much support. This is because it would fail to give effect to values of individual autonomy that, in a liberal democratic society, are strongly felt to be fundamental to the administration of justice. As noted above, even Bentham allowed for modifications to his natural system of procedure on the grounds of the avoidance of vexation, expense and delay. However, as pointed out by Twining[37] and echoed by Galligan,[38] Bentham's failure to define "vexation" left a large question about the extent of the modification and the criteria for determining it. We turn therefore to the techniques for resolving competing priorities.

2. Settling competing objectives

We can consider three possible approaches to this central issue of how to settle competing objectives. The first is some reasonably comprehensive version of Benthamite utilitarianism. This would begin by conceding a high value to rectitude of decision, essentially for the reasons given by Bentham; that because the law raises expectations and enables people to regulate their conduct, it is necessary to satisfy such expectations and maintain security and stability by correct application of the law[39] It would then be necessary to consider the precise

2–009

---

[36] The importance of this task has increased with the incorporation of the ECHR. Many of the Convention's rights now figure in litigation, and many conflicts of rights can emerge; a witness's right to privacy under art.8 versus a defendant's right to examine witnesses against him under art.6(3)(d) is a key example.

[37] W. L. Twining, *Theories of Evidence: Bentham and Wigmore* (1985), pp.91–94.

[38] D. J. Galligan, "More Scepticism About Scepticism" (1988) 8 O.J.L.S. 249, 253.

[39] J. Bentham, *Treatise on Judicial Evidence,* E. Dumont (ed) (London: 1825), p.2.

mix of rules and discretion required to maximise accuracy of factfinding[40] Finally this approach would acknowledge the existence of other social goals such as the security of the state, or police propriety, and the need to establish how those goals might be furthered or hindered by particular rules of evidence. A complex calculation of overall gains and losses to utility would be required where such goals conflicted with rectitude.

There are some difficult problems to be overcome with this approach. The most fundamental is whether the whole enterprise is misconceived: how can one meaningfully undertake a cost-benefit analysis of values which may be incommensurable? It is hard to see, for example, how state security, or the sensitivities of witnesses, can be weighed in the same currency as accuracy of adjudicative decisions. This point underlies much of the criticism directed at law reform and other official bodies which have purported to "balance" conflicting interests in the criminal justice process. As Ashworth and Redmayne have argued, the metaphor of "balancing" sometimes turns out to be no more than a rhetorical device for a conclusion, a value preference, put forward without proper argument.[41] If the term "balancing" is to be used at all, it is better understood as the description of a complex process of identifying relevant rights and interests, explaining the criteria for inclusion and exclusion, and providing justifying argument for different weights and priorities; all of this should be, in Ashworth and Redmayne's terms, "a properly researched, reasoned and principled course of argument". Even then, the problems for a utilitarian of carrying out this prescription on a systematic basis should not be underestimated.[42] Relatively few objective data exist about the efficacy of different rules, or no rules, in achieving accuracy of decision. It is even harder to determine the effect of evidential rules on more generalised non-epistemic aspects of the public welfare. The application of the rules is likely to be mediated by the occupational culture of the social groups that administer the laws; the police are an obvious case in point, as far as criminal justice is concerned. The result of these factors is that even the most uncompromising utilitarian is likely to have to resort to subjective judgments about what particular rules might achieve.[43] In relation to the epistemic objective, a further problem is whether to give different weight to different interests in formulating the law and, if so, how this is to be done. If a wrongful conviction is considered to be a worse evil than a mistaken acquittal, does it follow that special precautions should be taken to prevent it? What sort of precautions should they be? Is there an acceptable level of risk of wrongful conviction? If all possible steps were taken to eliminate the risk, would the price in terms of unjustified acquittals be too high? There is plainly much scope for disagreement on these questions where a consequentialist analysis is employed that takes no account of individual rights.

---

[40] D. J. Galligan, "More Scepticism About Scepticism" (1988) 8 O.J.L.S. 249, 256–257.
[41] A. Ashworth and M. Redmayne, *The Criminal Process*, 4th edn (Oxford: Oxford University Press, 2010), pp.41–45.
[42] D. J. Galligan, "More Scepticism About Scepticism" (1988) 8 O.J.L.S. 249, 258.
[43] The Auld Review, noted in Ch.1, offers many examples of such judgments on a whole range of criminal justice issues.

C. INDIVIDUAL RIGHTS AND THE LAW OF EVIDENCE

1. The foundation values for individual rights

An alternative to utility as a method for settling objectives and ordering priorities **2–010** may be based on the notion of rights in legal process. This approach switches the primary focus of the law from generalised public welfare to the protection of individual interests. Rights theorists argue that rights are possessed by individuals and they derive from decisions to attach high values to certain individual interests. The essence of a right, as elaborated by Dworkin,[44] is that it enjoys a high level of legal protection and is not to be freely traded against generalised social goals.

The justification for particular rights will be found in the moral and political values of the society in question. It will frequently be necessary to explore these to determine the nature and importance of the interest to be protected by the right, and to decide on the appropriate form and extent of the legal protection constituting the right. It is not the purpose of this chapter to offer a general jurisprudential analysis of rights in legal process; but it is helpful to consider the values which provide the foundation for two rights which are central to debates about the aims of the law of evidence, particularly criminal evidence. These rights are, first, the right of an accused person not to be wrongly convicted of an offence, and, secondly, the right of any person to a fair hearing in the determination of that person's civil rights and obligations and of criminal charges against him. Both of these rights are clearly recognised in English law. They have been strengthened, and possibly enlarged, by the formal incorporation into English law of the ECHR. Article 6 of the Convention sets out expressly the right to a fair trial. The right against wrongful conviction does not appear in express terms in the Convention, but it is implicit in arts 5 and 7 relating to the right to liberty, and to no punishment without law, respectively.

The issues raised by incorporation of the Convention, and about the scope of art.6 in particular, are considered later. It is helpful in understanding these issues to have some appreciation of the foundation values which underlie human rights instruments in their application to adjectival law. Accordingly, a brief summary of these is given, and we will then consider further the right against wrongful conviction. The next section of the chapter will return to the ECHR.

Ideas drawn from dominant streams of Western political and legal philosophy lie **2–011** at the heart of international human rights law. International human rights instruments are founded on the doctrine of the rule of law, and on a conception of the individual as an autonomous moral agent who is accorded an entitlement to certain fundamental rights. The principles involved are familiar ones in Anglo-American jurisprudence. A lucid statement is provided by Maher,[45] summarising Lon Fuller's conception of law:

---

[44] R. M. Dworkin, *Taking Rights Seriously* (London: Gerald Duckworth & Co Ltd, 1977).
[45] G. Maher, "Natural Justice as Fairness" in D. N. McCormick and P. B. H. Birks (eds), *The Legal Mind: Essays for Tony Honore* (1986), pp.103, 114.

"law as a special means of subjecting human conduct to the governance of rules necessarily adopts a specific conception of moral personality, one which respects the autonomy of those subject to the legal order."

Equally familiar to many lawyers and philosophers is the link between natural justice and the rule of law, as restated most notably in the work of John Rawls.[46] According to the liberal theory of dispositive justice, adjudicative decisions affecting the rights of individuals must be made in accordance with procedures that respect the autonomy of individuals. Maher again provides a useful summary:

"just as the rule of law insists upon respecting the moral status of people generally, the rules of natural justice receive their justification in the way in which they particularise this general principle in the application of general rules to concrete cases ...
    The idea ... is that the best justification of natural justice lies in the moral requirement of respect for the autonomy of the party affected by a decision; this leads to using a procedure which gives him a role in it and can thus explain to him the basis on which the application of the rule or policy to him is justified."[47]

Maher has argued that the principle of fairness provides the best justifying account of the rules of natural justice. Fairness in adjudicative contexts consists partly of equality of treatment for the parties concerned,[48] which presupposes an independent and impartial tribunal, and partly of informed participation in the process of adjudicative decision.[49] These broad principles of equality and informed participation are important not just instrumentally (because they tend to promote factually correct outcomes of decisions), but normatively, because requirements of due process demonstrate respect for the dignity and rights of individuals.[50]

2.   The right against wrongful conviction

2–012   Concern for individual autonomy is given further expression in the right against wrongful conviction. This right is generally agreed to be a fundamental safeguard of the liberty of the individual. English law recognises this right in the following way. If it is established on the accused's appeal against conviction that the conviction is unsafe, the Court of Appeal must quash the conviction.[51] This duty used to be subject to the express proviso "that the Court may, notwithstanding that they are of opinion that the point raised in the appeal might be decided in favour of the appellant, dismiss the appeal if they consider that *no miscarriage of justice has actually occurred*" (emphasis supplied). The proviso was dropped

---

[46] J. Rawls, *A Theory of Justice* (rev. ed. 1999), pp.209–210.

[47] G. Maher, "Natural Justice as Fairness" in D. N. McCormick and P. B. H. Birks (eds), *The Legal Mind: Essays for Tony Honore* (1986), pp.115, 116.

[48] M. Bayles, *Procedural Justice* (1990), p.131.

[49] See generally L. Fuller, "The Forms and Limits of Adjudication" (1978) 92 Harv. L.R. 353; R. S. Summers, "Evaluating and Improving Legal Processes: A Plea for Process Values" (1974) 60 Cornell Law Review 1; D. J. Galligan, *Discretionary Powers* (1986), pp.242, 332–337.

[50] R. M. Dworkin, "Principle, Policy, Procedure" in C. Tapper (ed.), *Crime Proof and Punishment* (London: Butterworths, 1981), p.193.

[51] Criminal Appeal Act 1968 s.2(1) and (2), as substituted by the Criminal Appeal Act 1995.

when the Criminal Appeal Act 1995 substituted a new provision in accordance with a recommendation by the Royal Commission on Criminal Justice to clarify the basis on which the Court of Appeal should quash a conviction, but it was not intended that any change of substance should be made.[52] The strength of the right against wrongful conviction is shown by the fact that the correctness of the conviction can be reopened many years later, long after the original appeal process has been exhausted.[53] This is not normally the case with acquittals, where the general rule is that there can be no second prosecution for the same offence,[54] or with judgments in civil cases unless there is evidence that the judgment was procured by fraud,[55] or there are exceptional circumstances.[56]

What is the basis of this right? Wrongful conviction is plainly something to be avoided on a standard utilitarian calculus because of its considerable costs, the distress caused to the accused, his family and friends, and the alarm and insecurity that knowledge of such convictions creates in society at large. But, in an undifferentiated approach to maximising rectitude of decision, this set of costs would then be weighed against other sets, particularly those resulting from failure to convict the guilty. A "pure" utilitarian might argue that in deciding on the optimal arrangement of rules of evidence, the legislator might simply trade off one set of costs against the other, without attaching any special weighting to either set. Some might say that the Criminal Law Revision Committee came close to this approach in formulating its recommendations in the Eleventh Report.

On the other hand, a rights-based approach would argue that the value attached to individual autonomy and liberty is such that wrongful conviction and punishment of the innocent is an end particularly to be avoided; the moral harm involved means that it is a significantly worse event than non-punishment of the guilty.[57] On this view, avoidance of this outcome is a moral and political imperative, and talk of weighing costs of outcomes, and indeed the use of utilitarian calculations generally, is out of place. Furthermore, the argument continues that if the legal system does recognise a right against an outcome of wrongful conviction, then it ought to recognise in addition ancillary rights to

---

[52] RCCJ Report, Ch.10 paras 27–34.

[53] The procedure requires a reference of the case back to the Court of Appeal by the Criminal Cases Review Commission: Criminal Appeal Act 1995 s.9.

[54] On the plea of autrefois acquit see Archbold, *Criminal Pleading Evidence and Practice* (2012 edn) para.4–116; M. Friedland, *Double Jeopardy* (Oxford: Clarendon Press, 1969). There are two exceptions: one for an acquittal tainted by interference with or intimidation of a juror or witness (Criminal Procedure and Investigations Act 1996 s.54), the other for an acquittal of a qualifying offence where there is new and compelling evidence of guilt and it is in the interests of justice for the defendant to be retried (Criminal Justice Act 2003 ss.75–97).

[55] Spencer Bower and Turner, *Res Judicata*, 2nd edn (London: Butterworths, 1969), pp.322–330, and the authorities there cited.

[56] Civil PR r.52.17; confirming *Taylor v Lawrence* [2002] 2 All E.R. 353, where the Court of Appeal held that it had jurisdiction to reopen a perfected appeal if it was clearly established that a significant injustice had probably occurred and that there was no alternative effective remedy. This case concerned an allegation of the appearance of bias on the part of a county court judge, which would amount to a breach of natural justice if bias were established. For examples of later cases, one on each side of the line, see *Couwenbergh v Valkova* [2004] EWCA Civ 676; *Re U (A Child) (Serious Injury: Standard of Proof) (Permission to Reopen Appeal)* [2005] EWCA Civ 52.

[57] See R. M. Dworkin, "Principle, Policy, Procedure" in C. Tapper (ed), *Crime Proof and Punishment* (1981), p.193; D. J. Galligan, "More Scepticism About Scepticism" (1988) 8 O.J.L.S. 249, 260.

special rules that are designed to protect individuals against that outcome. In this way a rights-based approach might justify particular rules of evidence on the ground that they give effect to a special concern not to convict the innocent. The burden of proof on the prosecution, the high standard of proof in criminal cases, exclusionary rules, exclusionary discretion, judicial warnings and a number of other rules and procedures might all be accounted for in this way.

2–013 However, this approach does not necessarily dispose of all disputes about the degree of legal protection to be afforded to the right against wrongful conviction. Given that mathematical certainty of guilt is unattainable, the logical extreme of this approach is that no one could ever be convicted of anything, in view of the inescapable possibility of a mistake. Such an uncompromising stance would destroy the criminal justice system. In setting the level of accuracy required for conviction, and hence the number and scope of protections aimed at promoting accuracy, the costs of the trial and the costs of acquitting the guilty cannot be ignored. The more difficult it is made to convict any accused of an offence, the greater the risk of acquitting a person who is in fact guilty. This point leads Galligan to suggest that a principle of proportionality is required:

"the level of accuracy sought should represent a sense of proportion between the importance of the substantive right [i.e. that a person should not be wrongly punished] and the resources that society can be expected to make available in maintaining it."[58]

Such decisions of proportionality, he says, are difficult but in principle possible.

This is an important constraint on the rights-based approach. It envisages a necessary limitation on pursuit of the goal of inhibiting conviction of the innocent by means of rules of evidence; the limitation is derived from the social costs of the rules, particularly the non-conviction of the guilty. Judgments about the significance of these costs are not fixed, and they may shift from time to time with changes in moral and political sentiment. This may in turn lead to pressure to restrict or abrogate rules protective of the accused.

A further source of limits on the scope of protective rules is the idea of victims' rights. The needs and entitlements of victims of crime were much neglected by the criminal justice system generally until recent years.[59] Increasing consciousness of the extent to which some victims have been treated unfairly by certain rules of evidence has produced significant reform, including the abandonment of some traditional protections for the accused. A good example of the influence of these factors is the abolition of corroboration requirements for the evidence of young children, and of complainants of sex offences.[60] Until relatively recently corroboration was required for the evidence of young children, on the ground of the presumed unreliability of children as witnesses.[61] Those rules were abolished[62] partly as a result of research showing that children's

---

[58] D. J. Galligan, "More Scepticism About Scepticism" (1988) O.J.L.S. 249, 261.
[59] See Ashworth and Redmayne, *The Criminal Process* (2010), p.13 and generally.
[60] See Ch.15.
[61] See I. Dennis, "Corroboration Requirements Reconsidered" [1984] Crim. L.R. 316, 330.
[62] By the Criminal Justice Act 1988 s.34.

evidence was more reliable than had been thought previously,[63] and partly because of a growing sense that the rules unduly inhibited conviction of persons guilty of serious offences against children.[64] In the case of adult complainants of sex offences, powerful arguments were developed that the common law's requirement for corroboration warnings about the evidence of complainants— warnings designed to protect the accused against wrongful conviction—resulted in unjustified acquittals of dangerous offenders, under-reporting of rape offences and a general failure of the law to protect women. These consequentialist arguments were reinforced by the objection that the requirement was unfair in principle, demeaning to women and stigmatised them as inferior types of witness.[65] The warning requirement for complainants was abolished in 1994.[66]

It seems, therefore, that the evidential procedures secured by the right against wrongful conviction are not absolute. They may be qualified by reference both to their necessity and to their negative effects on rectitude of decision. In some cases they may also yield to other social goals.[67] This reinforces the general point that, although a rights-based approach starts from clearly defined priorities in the task of settling the objectives of evidential rules, it cannot escape the need to acknowledge the limiting influence of factors founded on general utility or on competing rights. We need to bear this well in mind as we return to consider the effects of incorporation into English law of the ECHR.

2–014

D.   THE HUMAN RIGHTS ACT 1998

The Human Rights Act 1998[68] incorporated into English law the provisions of the ECHR. The Act has had, and will continue to have, a profound impact on the creation, interpretation and application of legislation and case law throughout the whole of English law, and the law of evidence is no exception. Indeed, the law of criminal procedure and evidence has proved to be one of the most significant areas of contention as the implications of the Convention, and of art.6 in particular, have been considered.

2–015

Before the Act came into force the Convention had the same formal status in English law that it had had ever since the United Kingdom ratified the

---

[63] See J. R. Spencer and R. Flin, *The Evidence of Children*, 2nd edn (London: Blackstone Press, 1993), Ch.11.

[64] Spencer and Flin, *Evidence of Children* (1993).

[65] See Dennis, "Corroboration" [1984] Crim. L.R. 316; J. Temkin, *Rape and the Legal Process*, 2nd ed (Oxford: Oxford University Press 2002), pp.255 onwards.

[66] Criminal Justice and Public Order Act 1994 s.32.

[67] e.g. the protection of police sources of information may result in an accused being unable to call witnesses or develop a particular line of cross-examination: see Ch.9. Similarly the accused is restricted in the extent to which he can cross-examine a complainant of a rape offence on her previous sexual history; the justification is founded on considerations of the right to privacy and the undesirable consequences of this type of questioning in terms of the distress caused to complainants and the discouragement of other complainants: see Ch.15.

[68] The Act received the Royal Assent on November 9, 1998. A substantial period of preparation was allowed before the Act came fully into force on October 2, 2000. For comment on the constitutional implications of the legislation, see S. Fredman, "Bringing Rights Home" (1998) 114 L.Q.R. 538; A. T. H. Smith, "The Human Rights Act and the Criminal Lawyer: The Constitutional Context" [1999] Crim. L.R. 251.

international treaty containing the Convention.[69] The Convention was like any other international treaty ratified by the United Kingdom but not formally incorporated into English law by Act of Parliament. It was not part of English law,[70] and it could not therefore override any unambiguous domestic law, statutory or case law, with which it was inconsistent. However, where English law was not clearly established, the Convention could be used as an aid to the interpretation of a statute. This was on the basis that the courts would presume, in the absence of clear words, that Parliament did not intend to legislate in conflict with the Convention.[71] If the statutory language was reasonably capable of bearing a meaning consistent with the Convention, the courts would adopt that meaning on the assumption that the legislature intended to give effect to the international obligations of the United Kingdom.[72] The position was similar with regard to case law. Where the law was not clearly settled, the courts could resolve the ambiguity in accordance with the Convention. Finally, in *Khan (Sultan)*[73] the House of Lords held that the apparent breach of a Convention right was a factor which a judge might take into account in the exercise of the exclusionary discretion under s.78 of PACE, but it was left unclear whether the judge had a duty to do so.

Under the procedure that used to apply, individuals who complained of breaches of their rights under the Convention could not obtain a remedy directly. Instead they had to make an application to the European Court of Human Rights[74] for an adjudication whether they had suffered a breach of their rights under the Convention at the hands of the Member State in question. A ruling against the Member State did not change any domestic law or give an individual any directly enforceable right in domestic law. However, the Member State would usually make any necessary changes to domestic law to bring it into line with the Convention, as interpreted in the rulings of the European Court of Human Rights. The United Kingdom had an embarrassing record as a respondent to cases in Strasbourg, having been found to be in breach of the Convention in many cases in the 1980s and 1990s.[75] This was one of the main reasons, although by no means the only reason, that persuaded the Labour Government that took office in 1997 to take the step of incorporation of the Convention into English law.[76]

2–016   Since the Human Rights Act 1998 came into force it is no longer necessary for aggrieved individuals to seek redress in Strasbourg. This is because of the duties imposed by the Act, and the remedies provided by the Act for alleged breaches of Convention rights. First, courts, tribunals and other public authorities are under a

---

[69] The UK ratified the treaty in 1951. The Convention came into force in 1953. The UK has allowed the right of individual petition to Strasbourg since 1966.
[70] *R. v Chief Immigration Officer Ex p. Bibi* [1976] 1 W.L.R. 979 at 984, 988.
[71] *R. v Home Secretary Ex p. Brind* [1991] 1 A.C. 696 HL.
[72] See, generally, *Garland v British Rail Engineering Ltd* (1983) 2 A.C. 751 HL; and in relation to the Convention, *Att-Gen v Guardian Newspapers Ltd (No.2)* [1990] 1 A.C. 109 at 283 per Lord Goff.
[73] *Khan (Sultan)* [1996] 3 All E.R. 289 HL.
[74] The procedure was more complex and time-consuming until recently, requiring an application to the European Commission of Human Rights (now abolished) for a ruling whether the complaint was admissible; the European Court of Human Rights used to hear only those complaints ruled admissible.
[75] Ashworth and Redmayne, *The Criminal Process* (2010), p.30.
[76] See further A. T. H. Smith, "Human Rights Act" [1999] Crim. L.R. 251, 251–252.

duty not to act in a way which is incompatible with a Convention right.[77] Such action is declared by the Act to be unlawful.[78] It follows that when courts apply rules of criminal procedure and evidence they must do so in a way which complies with the right to a fair trial under art.6 of the Convention. The duty is reinforced by a second duty under the Act requiring courts and tribunals to take account of what we may call Convention jurisprudence, when determining a question arising in connection with a Convention right. The jurisprudence consists of relevant judgments, decisions, declarations and advisory opinions of the European Court of Human Rights, opinions and decisions of the European Commission of Human Rights, and decisions of the Committee of Ministers of the Council of Europe.[79]

However, the reference to "taking account of" this jurisprudence means that, while decisions of the European Court of Human Rights must be considered, they are not binding on the English courts.[80] Two important consequences follow. First, the English courts are not limited in enlarging human rights under the ECHR by the current boundaries of the Strasbourg case law. In particular there is nothing in the Human Rights Act to prevent an English court from developing art.6 protections to a greater extent than Strasbourg has so far done.[81] Secondly, where the Strasbourg jurisprudence is inconsistent with established English case law, then the domestic doctrine of precedent prevails. In *Lambeth LBC v Kay*[82] Lord Bingham, with whom all the other six members of the court agreed, stated that where a court would ordinarily be bound by the rules of precedent to follow the decision of another court higher in the domestic hierarchy, but that decision appeared to be inconsistent with a subsequent ruling of the European Court of Human Rights, the court should follow the binding precedent. In his view the degree of certainty required for justice was best achieved, even in the ECHR context, by adhering to the rules of precedent.

This ruling clarified the position of courts below the level of the House of Lords, now the Supreme Court, in the domestic hierarchy. It left open the position of the highest court in the hierarchy. What then is the position of the Supreme Court? Must it follow a Strasbourg decision, even where the Supreme Court believes the decision to be wrong? Two views have been taken about this question. In *Secretary of State for the Home Department v AF (No.3)*[83] the House of Lords allowed an appeal against a refusal of judicial review in view of the earlier judgment of the European Court of Human Rights on a similar issue in *A v United Kingdom*.[84] The House appeared to regard itself as bound to follow the Strasbourg decision; in the words of Lord Rodger, "We have no choice …

---

[77] HRA 1998 s.6(1).

[78] HRA 1998 s.6(1).

[79] HRA 1998 s.2.

[80] A. T. H. Smith, "Human Rights Act" [1999] Crim. L.R. 251, 256.

[81] It is clear that the courts have done this in the context of reverse onuses; see the discussion in Ch.11.

[82] *Lambeth LBC v Kay* [2006] UKHL 10; [2006] 4 All E.R. 128.

[83] *Secretary of State for the Home Department v AF (No.3)* [2009] UKHL 28; [2010] 2 A.C. 269.

[84] *A v United Kingdom* (2009) 49 E.H.R.R. 29. The issue concerned the extent of the obligation on the Home Secretary to disclose to the applicant the grounds for reasonably suspecting him of involvement in terrorism-related activity.

Strasbourg has spoken, the case is closed".[85] This was on the basis that, as Lord Hoffmann put it, "The UK is bound by the Convention, as a matter of international law, to accept the decisions of the European Court of Human Rights on its interpretation".[86] However, some months later in *Horncastle*[87] Lord Phillips robustly asserted the Supreme Court's independence from the Strasbourg court and made it clear that the Supreme Court will if necessary reject a Strasbourg ruling that it regards as wrong:

> "The requirement to 'take into account' the Strasbourg jurisprudence will normally result in this Court applying the principles that are clearly established by the Strasbourg Court. There will, however, be rare occasions where this court has concerns as to whether a decision of the Strasbourg Court sufficiently appreciates or accommodates particular aspects of our domestic process. In such circumstances it is open to this court to decline to follow the Strasbourg decision, giving reasons for adopting this course. This is likely to give the Strasbourg Court the opportunity to reconsider the particular aspect of the decision that is in issue, so that there takes place what may prove to be a valuable dialogue between this court and the Strasbourg Court. This is such a case."[88]

The issue in *Horncastle* concerned a Strasbourg limitation on the use of hearsay evidence to the effect that untested hearsay could not form the 'sole or decisive' evidence for conviction without violating art 6. The Supreme Court rejected the supposed rule, as confirmed by the Fourth Section of the European Court of Human Rights in *Al-Khawaja and Tahery v United Kingdom,*[89] and invited the Grand Chamber of the Court to reconsider it. The Grand Chamber's response,[90] and its implications, is considered in detail in Ch.17. For now we may note that the Grand Chamber backed away from confrontation with the Supreme Court, holding that the supposed "sole or decisive" rule was not to be applied inflexibly in all circumstances. In a concurring judgment, Judge Bratza, the British judge on the Court, endorsed Lord Phillips' call for dialogue between the Supreme Court and the European Court of Human Rights.[91] The result of this episode appears to be that for now at least these courts are in a position of near, if not complete, equality in the interpretation of the ECHR. The UK Supreme Court is not alone in Europe in adopting this stance. Krisch has shown that the German Constitutional Court has taken a similar line, and that the French and Spanish courts both retain flexibility in the weight they accord to Strasbourg judgments.[92]

---

[85] *Secretary of State for the Home Department v AF (No.3)* [2009] UKHL 28; [2010] 2 A.C. 269 at [98].

[86] *Secretary of State for the Home Department v AF (No.3)* [2009] UKHL 28; [2010] 2 A.C. 269 at [70]. Lord Hoffmann had earlier expressed the view that the Strasbourg decision was wrong but stated that the House of Lords had no choice but to submit to it.

[87] *Horncastle* [2009] UKSC 14; [2010] 2 A.C. 373, refusing to follow the decision of the Fourth Section of the European Court of Human Rights in *Al-Khawaja and Tahery v UK* (2009) 49 E.H.R.R. 1 that the defendant's right to a fair trial is violated where hearsay evidence forms the sole or decisive evidence for conviction. See Ch.17

[88] *Horncastle* [2009] UKSC 14; [2010] 2 A.C. 373 at [11].

[89] *Al-Khawaja and Tahery v United Kingdom* (2009) 49 E.H.R.R. 1.

[90] *Al-Khawaja and Tahery v United Kingdom* (2012) 54 E.H.R.R. 23.

[91] *Al-Khawaja and Tahery v United Kingdom* (2012) 54 E.H.R.R. 23 at [2].

[92] N. Krisch, "The Open Architecture of European Human Rights Law" (2008) 71 M.L.R. 183.

Turning to legislation, the English courts have no power to disapply a provision in UK primary legislation on the ground that it is incompatible with the ECHR. Under s.3(1):

> "So far as it is possible to do so, primary legislation and subordinate legislation must be read and given effect in a way which is compatible with the Convention rights."

If this is not possible, the court must still apply the legislation. There is no power in the court to repeal primary legislation or to declare it void.[93] Where the court is satisfied that the relevant provision of primary legislation is incompatible with a Convention right, it may make a declaration of that incompatibility.[94] This does not invalidate the legislation or anything done under it,[95] but the expectation is that the legislation will then be amended to bring it into line with the Convention. A "fast-track" procedure for doing this is provided in s.10.

Section 3 has been described as giving the courts a powerful canon of interpretation,[96] and as an emphatic adjuration by the legislature which applies even if there is no ambiguity in the statutory language.[97] Leading cases under the Human Rights Act show that the courts are willing to use s.3 to depart from the natural meaning of a statutory text in favour of a secondary meaning that is compatible with art.6, but which is unexpected or contrived.[98] A clear reluctance to make declarations of incompatibility has emerged.[99]

2–017

The duties under the Human Rights Act are of fundamental constitutional importance. They have had a significant impact in some areas of the law of evidence, such as reverse onuses and sexual history evidence, and the jurisprudence associated with art.6 is still developing. However, there are undoubtedly some areas where the courts are likely to say that the relevant English law encapsulates Convention law. This is particularly so in relation to instances where the exclusionary discretion under s.78 of PACE is used to safeguard the fairness of the proceedings. It will be surprising if previous judicial implementations of notions of fairness, whether as part of the common law's right to a fair trial or pursuant to the statutory discretion, are held not to coincide in most cases with the requirements of art.6 of the Convention.

---

[93] On the other hand, the Act envisages that subordinate legislation can be declared void for incompatibility: see HRA 1998 ss.4(3) and (4), 10(4).

[94] HRA 1998 s.4(1) and (2).

[95] HRA 1998 s.4(6).

[96] *R. v DPP Ex p. Kebilene* [2000] 2 A.C. 326 at [373] per Lord Cooke of Thorndon.

[97] *R. v A (No.2)* [2001] UKHL 25; [2001] 2 Cr.App.R. 351 at [369] per Lord Steyn). See also Lord Hoffmann in *R. v Secretary of State for the Home Department Ex p. Simms* [1999] 3 All E.R. 400 at 412–413, emphasising that s.3 reinforces the "principle of legality" that fundamental rights cannot be overridden by general or ambiguous words in a statute.

[98] Prominent examples are *Lambert* [2001] UKHL 37; [2001] 2 Cr.App.R. 511; *R. v A (No.2)* [2001] UKHL 25; [2001] 2 Cr.App.R. 351; *Sheldrake v DPP* [2004] UKHL 43; [2005] 1 A.C. 264. But cf. Lord Hoffmann in *R. (on the application of Wilkinson) v IRC* [2005] UKHL 30; [2006] 1 All E.R. 529 at [17], emphasising that s.3 was not intended to have the effect of requiring courts to give the language of statutes "acontextual meanings".

[99] See in particular *R. v A (No.2)* [2001] UKHL 25; [2001] 2 Cr.App.R. 351 HL; *Sheldrake v DPP* [2004] UKHL 43; [2005] 1 A.C. 264. See also *Ghaidan v Godin-Mandoza* [2004] 3 W.L.R. 113 HL, confirming that a Convention-compliant interpretation under s.3 is the primary remedial measure for incompatibility and a declaration of incompatibility under s.4 an exceptional course.

Remedies are provided for in s.7 of the Act. A person who claims that a public authority has acted (or proposes to act) unlawfully under s.6 may bring proceedings against the authority under the Act in the appropriate court or tribunal, or rely on the Convention right(s) concerned in any legal proceedings, but in either case only if he is or would be a victim of the unlawful act.[100] Accordingly, in criminal proceedings Convention rights may be relied on by possessors of those rights at all stages of the proceedings, including pre-trial procedures, trial and appeal.

2–018   It is now appropriate to consider art.6 and to make some general points about its scope and limits. Article 6 provides:

> "1.   In the determination of his civil rights and obligations or of any criminal charge against him, everyone is entitled to a fair and public hearing within a reasonable time by an independent and impartial tribunal established by law. Judgment shall be pronounced publicly but the press and public may be excluded from all or part of the trial in the interest of morals, public order or national security in a democratic society, where the interests of juveniles or the protection of the private life of the parties so require, or to the extent strictly necessary in the opinion of the court in special circumstances where publicity would prejudice the interests of justice.
>
> 2.   Everyone charged with a criminal offence shall be presumed innocent until proved guilty according to law.
>
> 3.   Everyone charged with a criminal offence has the following minimum rights:
>
> (a)   to be informed promptly, in a language which he understands and in detail, of the nature and cause of the accusation against him;
>
> (b)   to have adequate time and facilities for the preparation of his defence;
>
> (c)   to defend himself in person or through legal assistance of his own choosing or, if he has not sufficient means to pay for legal assistance, to be given it free when the interests of justice so require;
>
> (d)   to examine or have examined witnesses against him and to obtain the attendance and examination of witnesses on his behalf under the same conditions as witnesses against him;
>
> (e)   to have the free assistance of an interpreter if he cannot understand or speak the language used in court."

This is a concise and basic provision.[101] Essentially it sets out fundamental principles of fair trial, couched in open-ended language that positively demands interpretation. In this sense it is clear that art.6 represents a starting-point. The expectation is that interpretation will be necessary and that it should be expansive. Paragraph 3 states that the rights it lists are "minimum rights". In *Delcourt v Belgium*[102] the European Court of Human Rights said:

> "In a democratic society within the meaning of the Convention, the right to a fair administration of justice holds such a prominent place that a restrictive interpretation of Article 6(1) would not correspond to the aim and the purpose of that provision."

---

[100] HRA 1988 s.7(1). A person is a victim of an unlawful act only if he would be a victim for the purposes of art.34 of the Convention if proceedings were brought in the European Court of Human Rights in respect of that Act: s.7(7).

[101] For discussion, see Emmerson, Ashworth and Macdonald, especially Chs 2, 4, 9, 14 and 15; F. G. Jacobs and R. C. A. White, *The European Convention on Human Rights*, 4th edn (Oxford: Oxford University Press, 2006), Ch.8; A. Ashworth, "Article 6 and the Fairness of Trials" [1999] Crim. L.R. 261.

[102] *Delcourt v Belgium* (1979–80) 1 E.H.R.R. 355 at 25.

In *Jespers v Belgium*,[103] the European Commission of Human Rights developed the point further:

> "Article 6 does not define the notion of a fair trial in criminal cases. Paragraph 3 of that Article lists certain specific rights which constitute essential elements of that general notion. The term 'minimum' [in srt.6(3)] clearly shows that the list of rights in paragraph 3 is not exhaustive and that a trial could well not fulfil the general conditions of a fair trial even if the minimum rights guaranteed by paragraph 3 were respected."

Accordingly the Strasbourg jurisprudence associated with art.6 has considerably **2–019** expanded the scope of the article. The content of the right to a fair trial under the Convention is not now adequately captured by the terms of art.6. It should also be noted that art.6 does not explain the application of any limits on the express rights set out in paras 2 and 3.[104] These rights can be qualified in certain circumstances, as can any further rights implied into art.6. For these reasons the text of art.6 is better treated as a restatement of basic principles of natural justice than as a legislative code of the conditions of fair trial. As a code it is incomplete and the apparently absolute terms used to describe the rights can be misleading.

The scope and content of art.6 has expanded in a number of ways. First, the European Court and Commission of Human Rights has implied into art.6 several rights additional to the rights expressly stated. These include a right against compelled self-incrimination,[105] a right of access to undisclosed material in the possession of the prosecution,[106] and a right to private and confidential communication with a legal adviser.[107] This list is not closed and may be added to as the interpretation of art.6 evolves.[108] Secondly, the application of art.6 is not restricted to the criminal "trial" as that term is understood in English law. The object of the article is to protect a person throughout the criminal process from the moment he is charged with an offence up to and including final appeal or review.[109] Being "charged" with an offence is an autonomous concept under the Convention. Its meaning is not controlled by the domestic law of the Member State in question, and the European Court of Human Rights has said that it will give the term a "substantive" rather than a "formal" interpretation.[110] Thus "charge" has been held to mean:

> "[the] official notification given to an individual by the competent authority of an allegation that he has committed a criminal offence, a definition that also corresponds to the test whether the situation of the [suspect] has been substantially affected."[111]

---

[103] *Jespers v Belgium* (1981) 27 D.R. 61 at 54.
[104] Compare para.1 of art.6, where permissible limits on the right to a public hearing are set out in detail.
[105] *Funke v France* (1993) 16 E.H.R.R. 297; *Saunders v United Kingdom* (1997) 23 E.H.R.R. 313 and see Ch.5.
[106] *Jespers v Belgium* (1981) 27 D.R. 61; *Edwards v United Kingdom* (1993) 15 E.H.R.R. 417; and see Ch.9.
[107] *S v Switzerland* (1992) 14 E.H.R.R. 670; and see Ch.10.
[108] See, e.g. *T and V v United Kingdom* (2000) 30 E.H.R.R. 121, finding a violation of art.6 in the failure of the UK Government to adapt Crown Court trial procedures so as to ensure a fair trial for juveniles charged with murder.
[109] Jacobs and White, *Human Rights* (2006) pp.159–163.
[110] *Adolf v Austria* (1982) 4 E.H.R.R. 313.
[111] *Deweer v Belgium* (1979–80) 2 E.H.R.R. 439; *Eckle v FRG* (1983) 5 E.H.R.R. 1.

The relevant official notification may be the date of a formal charge, but earlier official acts may imply the allegation that the person in question has committed an offence, and such acts may indicate that his position has been substantially affected. Depending on the circumstances this might include the date of arrest,[112] and it is clear that custodial interrogation by the police with a view to obtaining evidence for use in a possible prosecution engages art.6.[113] Similarly, an interview at which the police propose to issue a caution to the defendant instead of charging him also engages art.6, thus triggering an implied right to disclosure to the defendant's legal adviser of statements the defendant made at an earlier interview.[114]

2–020 However, art.6 does not attempt to set out detailed rules of evidence for Member States to incorporate in their national laws. The European Court of Human Rights has said that:

> "while art.6 of the Convention guarantees the right to a fair trial, it does not lay down any rules on the admissibility of evidence as such, which is therefore primarily a matter for regulation under national law."[115]

The ECHR does not therefore either require or prohibit particular rules of evidence. These are for each state to decide. What the rules must do is ensure that the right to a fair trial is respected. It follows that there is no rule, either of Strasbourg jurisprudence or of English law, that evidence obtained in violation of a Convention right and used to prove guilt makes a trial unfair under art.6.[116] The ECHR requires effective remedies to secure Convention rights but does not stipulate what the remedies should be. However, in this respect the Strasbourg jurisprudence is not always consistent. Where the European Court of Human Rights has indicated limits to the qualifications that may be made to art.6 rights, the expression of those limits has sometimes taken on the appearance of a rule of evidence. Thus, for example, the court repeatedly said that untested hearsay evidence may not form the sole or decisive evidence for conviction,[117] and a similar limitation has been said to apply to adverse inferences from the accused's failure to mention facts when questioned by the police that are later relied on in defence.[118]

On the other hand the court has also emphasised that its task is not to review the national law as such, but to review the applicant's trial as a whole in order to

---

[112] *Foti v Italy* (1983) 5 E.H.R.R. 313.

[113] *Murray v United Kingdom* (1996) 22 E.H.R.R. 29; *Cadder v HM Advocate* [2010] UKSC 43, and see Ch 6 para.6.31.

[114] *DPP v Ara* [2001] 4 All E.R. 559, DC; discussed in Ch.9. cf. *R. (on the appplication of R) v Durham Constabulary* [2005] UKHL 21; [2005] 2 All E.R. 369 (final warning to young offender).

[115] *Schenk v Switzerland* (1998) 13 E.H.R.R. 242 at [46]. See also *Heglas v Czech Republic* (2009) 48 E.H.R.R. 44 at [84].

[116] *Khan v United Kingdom* (2001) 31 E.H.R.R. 1016; *Heglas v Czech Republic* (2009) 48 E.H.R.R. 44.

[117] See *Al-Khawaja and Tahery v United Kingdom* (2009) 49 E.H.R.R. 1, reviewing a line of earlier decisions stating this proposition. However, the subsequent judgment of the Grand Chamber in this case ((2012) 54 E.H.R.R. 23) modified this stance and held that the "rule" is not to be applied inflexibly. See further Ch.17.

[118] *Condron v United Kingdom* (2001) 31 E.H.R.R. 1, and see Ch.5.

determine whether the proceedings were fair.[119] In some cases the court has concluded that the impact of a particular rule or practice resulted in the defendant not receiving a fair trial. When this happens the court makes a declaration that there was a violation of art.6, but does not pronounce on the compatibility of the rule or practice as such. This may be contrasted with the power of English courts to make declarations of incompatibility of legislative provisions with Convention rights under s.4 of the Human Rights Act 1998.

In reviewing the trial as a whole the European Court of Human Rights will require a fair balance between the parties which gives effect to the principle of "equality of arms". The principle applies to both civil and criminal proceedings: "Each party must be afforded a reasonable opportunity to present his case–including his evidence–under conditions that do not place him at a substantial disadvantage vis-à-vis his opponent".[120] The essential counterpart to the right of presentation, which seems necessarily to imply a right of access to evidence, is what Jacobs and White[121] describe as the right to an adversarial trial. This refers to an opportunity for the parties to have knowledge of and comment on the observations filed or evidence adduced by the other party.[122] The fair balance required by art.6 must respect the rights of the defence. This means that any measure restricting the rights of the defence, such as restrictions on the right to question certain witnesses, must be strictly necessary[123] and must not be such as to impair the essence of the right.[124] The rights of the defence obviously include the rights expressly set out in art.6 and the rights implied into art.6 by the Strasbourg jurisprudence. But they go further than this. In *Heglas v Czech Republic* the European Court of Human Rights set out the following statement of principle[125]:

> "To determine whether the proceedings as a whole were fair, one must also consider whether the rights of the defence were respected. One must in particular check whether the applicant was offered the possibility to question the authenticity of the evidence and to object to its use. One must also take into account the quality of the evidence, including the question of knowing whether the circumstances in which it was gathered put into doubt its reliability or accuracy. Where a problem of fairness does not necessarily arise where the evidence obtained is not corroborated by other proofs, it must be noted that where it is very solid and gives rise to no doubt, the need for other supporting evidence becomes less."

Reflecting the Convention's concern with substance rather than form, the European Court of Human Rights has insisted on several occasions that the Convention is "intended to guarantee not rights that are theoretical and illusory

2–021

---

[119] *Kostovski v The Netherlands* (1989) 12 E.H.R.R. 434 at [39]; *Ludi v Switzerland* (1993) 15 E.H.R.R. 173 at [43]; *Saidi v France* (1993) 17 E.H.R.R. 251 at [251]; *Doorson v The Netherlands* (1996) 22 E.H.R.R. 330 at 67; *Van Mechelen v The Netherlands* (1997) 25 E.H.R.R. 547 at 49.

[120] *Dombo Beheer NV v The Netherlands* (1994) 18 E.H.R.R. 213 at 33. This was a civil case. For an application of the principle of equality of arms in a criminal case, see *Borgers v Belgium* (1993) 15 E.H.R.R. 92.

[121] Jacobs and White, *Human Rights* (2006) p.176.

[122] *Ruiz-Mateos v Spain* (1993) 16 E.H.R.R. 505.

[123] *Van Mechelen v The Netherlands* (1997) 25 E.H.R.R. 547.

[124] *Heaney and McGuinness v Ireland* (2001) 33 E.H.R.R. 12, a case concerned with the privilege against self-incrimination.

[125] *Heglas v Czech Republic* (2009) 48 E.H.R.R. 44 at [86].

but rights that are practical and effective".[126] This principle can have significant implications. It might, for example, lead a court to find a violation of art.6 where the defence lawyer, appointed to represent the defendant on legal aid, was incompetent and gave bad advice which prejudiced the defendant's position.[127]

The general right under art.6 to a fair trial is absolute; unlike the rights in arts 8–11 for example, it does not admit of any qualifications.[128] It is therefore a strong right which cannot be overridden by interests of public welfare, for example in the control of crime. However, this is not to say that the particular rights conferred by art.6, whether listed expressly in the paragraphs of the article, or implied into it, are also absolute. Both Strasbourg jurisprudence and recent English case law have made it clear that the particular rights can be qualified or restricted. For English courts the criteria for a valid qualification or restriction are to be found in the concepts of legitimate aim and proportionality. A restriction on an art.6 right is valid if it is imposed pursuant to a legitimate aim, which may be an important goal of public policy, such as the reduction of death and injury caused by the misuse of motor vehicles,[129] or the protection of complainants of sexual offences from intrusive and distressing questioning.[130] The restriction must be proportionate to the aim in the sense that it represents a fair balance between the importance of the community interest in the goal to be achieved and the importance of the interest in the protection of the defendant's fundamental rights. Furthermore it must not go beyond what is necessary to achieve the aim. The Strasbourg jurisprudence also recognises these criteria, which have been said to be inherent in the whole of the Convention.[131]

It remains to note that the procedural context of disputes about the application of art.6 may well differ as between Strasbourg and the English courts. This may in turn affect the approach to interpretation. A case can reach Strasbourg only after all the national proceedings have been concluded, so the whole course of the trial is known. The European Court of Human Rights thus always examines a case retrospectively, but it is able to examine the whole of the proceedings. Now that the Convention forms part of English law, issues about violations of it may arise at any stage during the proceedings. Issues about the scope of cross-examination, for example, could surface during a trial or at a pre-trial plea and case management hearing. The English courts have to decide these issues as and when they arise. To some extent this requires a sharper focus on the scope

---

[126] See, e.g. *Artico v Italy* (1981) 3 E.H.R.R. 1 at [33]; *Soering v United Kingdom* (1989) 11 E.H.R.R. 439 at [87].

[127] cf. *Artico v Italy* (1981) 3 E.H.R.R. 1.

[128] However, it is probably not the case that a violation of art.6 automatically renders a conviction "unsafe" for the purposes of s.2 of the Criminal Appeal Act 1968. Some dicta in the House of Lords suggest that it does (*Forbes* [2001] 1 All E.R. 686 at [697] per Lord Bingham; *R. v A (No.2)* [2001] UKHL 25; [2001] 2 Cr.App.R. 351 at [366] per Lord Steyn), but the Court of Appeal is more equivocal (*Davis Johnson and Rowe* [2001] 1 Cr.App.R. 115; *Togher Doran and Parsons* [2001] 3 All E.R. 463). See further Emmerson, Ashworth and Macdonald, pp.525–531; Dennis, "Fair Trials and Safe Convictions" [2003] C.L.P. 211; Taylor and Ormerod, "Mind the Gaps: Safety, Fairness and Moral Legitimacy" [2004] Crim. L.R. 266.

[129] *Brown v Stott* [2001] 2 All E.R. 97 HL.

[130] *R. v A (No.2)* [2001] UKHL 25; [2001] 2 Cr.App.R. 351 HL.

[131] *Sporrong and Lonroth v Sweden* (1983) 5 E.H.R.R. 35 at 69; *Soering v United Kingdom* (1989) 11 E.H.R.R. 439 at 89.

and limits of the art.6 guarantees as procedural imperatives. It is possible that an English court will find a violation caused by the operation of a particular rule of procedure or evidence at a stage before the proceedings are complete, in circumstances where the European Court might hold, with the benefit of hindsight, that the proceedings were not unfair taken as a whole.

E.   LEGITIMACY OF ADJUDICATION

A third approach to the problem of settling competing objectives does not begin **2–022** from concern with public welfare or with protection of individual rights. It begins with the adjudicative process itself and with recognition of the point already made that adjudication is a form of official decision-making concerned with the resolution of disputes and the implementation of law. This remains true whether the forum of the dispute is a criminal court, a civil court or an administrative tribunal. If official adjudications are to succeed in gaining acceptance and respect as authoritative decisions,[132] it is essential that they are, and are seen to be, legitimate. Legitimacy of decision is not the same concept as (factual) rectitude of decision, although the two are closely related. This relationship will now be explored. The argument will be developed that the aims of the law of evidence are ultimately referable to an overall objective of promoting legitimacy of decision in adjudication, and that priorities as between competing rights and interests should be settled according to how best legitimacy of decision will be promoted.

Rectitude of decision was defined earlier as the correct application of substantive law to the true facts of the dispute. The "true facts", as distinct from those that may be asserted by one party or the other, are determined by accurate evaluation of the relevant and reliable evidence. Legitimacy of decision, on the other hand, refers to a larger concept, of which factual accuracy is a major part, but which includes additional notions of moral authority and expressive value. In essence, legitimacy signifies an aspiration that an adjudicative decision should as far as possible be factually accurate and also consistent with other fundamental moral and political values embedded in the legal system. The objective is that the decision should claim not only to be factually accurate, thus fulfilling the truthfinding aim of the legal process, but also to be morally authoritative, and to express the value of the rule of law. A decision with these qualities provides the state with the standing to call for the acceptance of the decision by the person or persons to whom it is addressed and by the public at large.

These claims will be further developed in the rest of this section. It may be noted at this point that if they are accepted they offer a promising solution to the problem of settling the aims of the law of evidence. The aims will be to promote legitimacy of decision-making in adjudication through law designed to ensure that verdicts and judgments are factually accurate, morally authoritative, and expressive of the rule of law. It is important to note at this point that the moral and political values with which adjudicative decisions should be consistent may differ according to the nature of the dispute. Accordingly the legitimacy of a

---

[132] H. Hart and J. McNaughton, "Evidence and Inference in the Law" in D. Lerner (ed), *Evidence and Inference* (1958), p.52.

particular resolution of a particular dispute depends on the kind of dispute it is. It follows that competing claims in the law of evidence may need to be settled in different ways for different types of adjudication.

2–023 Further exploration begins with the proceedings in which rules of evidence operate to the fullest extent. Criminal proceedings are concerned with the application of the criminal law. The foundation moral and political principles of the criminal law are well established. The primary aim of the criminal law is to influence behaviour. Hart sums up the point concisely: "The aim of making an act criminal is to announce to society that these acts are not to be done and to secure that fewer of them are done".[133] In constructing liability for a criminal offence, the law reflects a moral and political concern to accord to all citizens equal respect and dignity.[134] As part of this concern the law accords persons the status of autonomous moral agents with an entitlement to freedom of action and the ability to exercise self-determination in their choice of actions.[135] The fundamental doctrine that there is in general no criminal liability without mens rea is a clear expression of this moral principle. A person's freedom of action is not to be interfered with until it appears to have been knowingly abused. Punishment—the chief distinguishing characteristic of the criminal law— involves the imposition of both a legal sanction, such as imprisonment or a fine, and a moral sanction in the form of the stigma of conviction.[136] The basic principle of the distribution of punishment is that in general it should only be applied to a person who chose to break the law and who deserves to be punished.[137]

It is helpful to bear in mind these fundamental precepts when considering the criminal process, particularly criminal trials. A criminal trial is a formal process of application of the criminal law to a citizen, and it is essentially a public process.[138] The process should be open to public inspection and in general be freely reportable by the media. This concern for publicity is an important clue to the purposes of criminal trials and to the law of evidence that regulates them. It underlines the point that the criminal trial has traditionally been regarded by the

---

[133] H. L. A. Hart, *Punishment and Responsibility* (Oxford: Oxford University Press, 1968), p.6.

[134] R. M. Dworkin, *Law's Empire* (London: 1986), Chs 6 and 7; H. Gross, *A Theory of Criminal Justice* (Oxford: Oxford University Press, 1979), pp.32–33; A. Duff, *Trials and Punishments* (Cambridge: Cambridge University Press, 1986), pp.89–90, 97–98, 144–145.

[135] H. Packer, *The Limits of the Criminal Sanction* (Stanford: Stanford University Press, 1968), pp.74 onwards; *Lynch v DPP for Northern Ireland* [1975] A.C. 653 at 689 HL per Lord Simon of Glaisdale; A. Ashworth, *Principles of Criminal Law*, 5th edn (Oxford: Oxford University Press, 2006), pp.158–159.

[136] N. Walker, *Punishment Danger and Stigma* (Oxford: Blackwell, 1980), Ch.7.

[137] Hart, *Punishment and Responsibility* (1968), Chs I and VIII, esp.pp.8–13, 207–209; Glanville Williams, *Textbook of Criminal Law*, 2nd edn (London: Steven & Sons, 1983), pp.36 onwards.

[138] Bentham regarded the publicity of legal proceedings as the key instrument for ensuring accuracy of decision-making: see W. L. Twining, *Theories of Evidence: Bentham and Wigmore* (London: 1985), Ch.2, synthesising Bentham's numerous remarks on the subject in the *Rationale of Judicial Evidence*. See also A. Duff, *Trials and Punishments* (1986), p.148; R. Pattenden, *Judicial Discretion and Criminal Litigation* (Oxford: Clarendon Press, 1990), Ch.5; A. Duff, L. Farmer, S. Marshall and V. Tadros, "Introduction: Towards a Normative Theory of the Criminal Trial" in Duff (eds), *The Trial on Trial* (2004), Vol.1 p.1. See also the essay in the same volume by M. M. Dubber, "The Criminal Trial and the Legitimation of Punishment", p.85.

state as a medium of communication with the public at large.[139] Within the trial the value attached to freedom and dignity requires that the state should justify its claim that formal condemnation and punishment of the defendant should take place. The importance of this value is expressed in the presumption of innocence, a principle that is found in all international instruments of human rights and the constitutions of many states. The presumption of innocence generates the rule that the burden of proof is on the prosecution to prove the defendant's guilt.

Satisfying this burden and making out the claim for condemnation and punishment has more than one dimension. This is seen plainly when the functions of the verdict in a criminal trial are considered. A verdict of guilty or not guilty is more than a purely factual statement. It is no more like a pathologist's report than the criminal trial is like a diagnostic procedure.[140] The criminal trial in common law jurisdictions is a procedure which aims to be both demonstrative and justificatory. A defendant who pleads not guilty puts the prosecution to proof of their allegations. He requires them to demonstrate his guilt to the satisfaction of both himself and the public. At one level the verdict represents a conclusion that the factual demonstration has or has not been made out.

But this is not the only message that the verdict carries. "Guilt" is a moral concept. A verdict of "guilty" also conveys moral condemnation of the defendant. It is an expression of moral blame. As Duff puts it:

> "to indict someone for a criminal offence is to offer a particular criticism of his conduct; to try him is to seek to determine the justice of that criticism; to convict him is to blame him publicly for that offence."[141]

In addition to these functions of communicating factual decisions and moral blameworthiness, the criminal verdict has a third function. A guilty verdict is additionally an expression of the norms of the criminal law and of the consequences of breach of such norms.[142] Thus the verdict does not just communicate the result of one particular trial. Its further function is expressive. It confirms the importance of the rule of law and the consequences of not abiding by it. It emphasises the behavioural constraints imposed by the criminal law and points to the example of the defendant to increase the effectiveness of the message. This wider function of the verdict is well understood by the policy-oriented organs of the state. They frequently emphasise the importance of convictions in furthering a policy of crime control. Acquittals do little to reinforce behavioural constraints.

Understanding these three dimensions of the verdict in a criminal trial is crucial to an understanding of the aims of the law of evidence. The factual judgment, that the defendant did or did not commit the offence, is a judgment on the probative value of the evidence. The moral judgment, that the defendant

2–024

---

[139] See, e.g. D. Hay, "Property, Authority and the Criminal Law" in Hay (eds), *Albion's Fatal Tree* (London: Pantheon Books 1975), p.28, showing vividly the use of criminal courts in the 18th century as ideological platforms.

[140] A. Duff, *Trials and Punishments* (1986), Ch.4.

[141] A. Duff, *Trials and Punishments* (1986), p.39.

[142] For discussion see C. Nesson, "The Evidence or the Event: On Judicial Proof and the Acceptability of Verdicts" (1985) 98 Harv. L.R. 1357.

should or should not be convicted (publicly blamed) and punished, is more complex. Clearly it is not independent of the factual judgment. A factual judgment that the defendant did not commit the offence should always result in an acquittal. A conclusion that the defendant deserved to be convicted despite not having committed the offence would be unacceptable. It would be inconsistent with the fundamental principles of responsibility and punishment outlined above.

A judgment that the defendant did commit the offence should, presumptively, result in a conviction. It would tend to undermine the aims of the criminal law if those adjudged to have broken its terms were not convicted.[143] However, neither the moral authority of the verdict, nor its expressive value, is necessarily to be equated with the factual judgment. We need only consider the example of a confession obtained by torture to see this point. The confession might be reliable in proving that the defendant in fact committed the offence; its truth might be confirmed by independent evidence insufficient in itself to prove guilt. But a verdict of guilty would not be acceptable as a morally justified statement of the defendant's blameworthiness and fitness for punishment, or as an expression of the values of the criminal law. The use of torture by the state is a serious illegality[144] that also amounts to a gross violation of the ethical principle of political morality which accords all citizens respect and dignity. Such a violation destroys the moral and expressive authority of the verdict. This is because a verdict which is derived from a disregard for the core values of the criminal law is self-contradictory. It cannot fulfil its integral functions, that is, of making morally justified criticism of the defendant and of conveying an expressive message that the criminal law incorporates values that it is necessary to uphold by punishment, while appearing to be based itself on a deliberate flouting of those values.[145] As well as being flawed by their internal contradictions such verdicts carry significant risks of generating a loss of public confidence in the criminal process and in the criminal law itself.[146]

---

[143] The point is well made by A. A. S. Zuckerman, "Illegally Obtained Evidence: Discretion as a Guardian of Legitimacy" [1987] C.L.P. 55, 56.

[144] It is a crime under national and international law: see *A v Secretary of State for the Home Department (No.2)* [2005] UKHL 71; [2006] 1 All E.R. 575.

[145] In *A v Secretary of State for the Home Department (No.2)* [2005] UKHL 71; [2006] 1 All E.R. 575 the House of Lords held that evidence obtained by torture is inadmissible as a matter of law. According to Lord Bingham, torture evidence is excluded as unreliable, unfair, offensive to ordinary standards of humanity and decency and incompatible with the principles which should animate a tribunal seeking to administer justice. See also *Jalloh v Germany* (2007) 44 E.H.R.R. 32, the Grand Chamber of the European Court of Human Rights, holding that evidence, whether in the form of a confession or real evidence, obtained by torture in violation of art.3 of the ECHR, should never be admitted as proof of guilt. Its admission would automatically violate the defendant's right to a fair trial under art.6.

[146] A verdict is a judgment arrived at on the basis of evidence. But, as Zuckerman ("Illegally Obtained Evidence" [1987] C.L.P. 55) has commented in relation to illegally obtained evidence, "today the investigative process is seen as part of the administration of justice". Therefore a verdict assessing the defendant's guilt and fitness for punishment is very likely to contain an element of judgment upon the conduct of the proceedings of which the evidence is an integral part. For this reason it is difficult to accept Nesson's insistence that acceptable verdicts must aim to project legal rules rather than proof rules: (1985) 98 Harv. L.R. 1357, 1357–1358, 1390–1392. Acceptable verdicts will surely project both. See also A. Duff, L. Farmer, S. Marshall and V. Tadros, "Introduction: Towards a Normative Theory of the Criminal Trial" in Duff (eds), *The Trial on Trial* (2004), p.25, who say "serious breaches of due process, serious failures to address the defendant as a responsible

This analysis suggests that the law of evidence in criminal cases has aims which **2–025** are not fully accounted for by references only to the promotion of truth finding, accuracy of decision-making and/or the protection of individual rights. Recognising that the verdict serves a number of important public functions, the law is constructed so as to ensure that the verdict will be able to discharge those functions. This means that it will be concerned not just with factual accuracy, and hence with reliability of evidence, but also with ensuring the moral authority and expressive value of the verdict. The law's initial premise is rightly that in principle all relevant evidence should be admitted, because this will tend to promote factually accurate judgments. In other words, epistemic considerations, those which go to the truthfinding objective of criminal proceedings, should be the starting-point. Factually accurate judgments should, and usually will, carry both moral authority and expressive value. This is on the basis that the state has good reason to enforce its criminal law and has the standing to call for acceptance of the verdict given its commitment to standards of probity and legality in its legal system. However, restrictive rules may be needed for either or both of two reasons. First, if relevant evidence carries significant risks of unreliability it may not be safe to give the factfinder a free hand in its evaluation. The avoidance of error, particularly of wrongful conviction, may require the adoption of precautionary measures. These may take a variety of forms: exclusionary rules, exclusionary discretion, corroboration requirements, judicial warnings and so on. The precise form required in any particular case will depend on the nature and degree of the perceived risk.

Secondly, apparently reliable evidence may need to be excluded altogether if it carries significant risks of impairing the moral authority and/or the expressive value of the verdict. As explained above, such authority and value are functions of the factual accuracy of the verdict and of its consistency with other fundamental values embedded in the criminal justice system. These may be of a substantive or procedural nature, and are to be discovered by analysis of legal materials and relevant moral and political discourse. Substantive values, reflected in the core principles of responsibility and punishment set out above and amplified in the ECHR, include respect for human autonomy and dignity, security of person and property from unjustified interference, privacy and freedom from discrimination. Examples of procedural values include the presumption of innocence, fair trial according to principles of natural justice, and probity on the part of state agencies entrusted with coercive powers. Verdicts must be consistent with such values, because it is not in the public interest that verdicts should be returned which lack moral authority and/or expressive value. They are not satisfactory either for justifying individual punishment or for affirming the values of the criminal law. Accordingly, if we exclude relevant evidence because of our concerns about factual accuracy and/or moral authority or expressive value, we will be giving effect to values which are an essential part of the process of proof in criminal cases.

---

citizen, undermine the legitimacy of the trial as a process that calls citizens to account to answer charges of wrongdoing, and thus also undermine the legitimacy of the verdict as a judgment that is to emerge from such a process".

Some important conclusions follow from this approach. The factual accuracy of the decision ceases to be the primary goal of the adjudicative process. Truth-finding becomes a means, in fact the major means, by which a legitimate verdict is secured, but it is the legitimacy of the verdict which is the ultimate goal.[147] As has been shown, this is a larger notion than rectitude of decision. A factually inaccurate or doubtful conviction can never be legitimate; it is inconsistent with the fundamental moral basis of the criminal law. But a decision may be factually correct and yet lack the elements of moral authority and expressive value necessary for the further functions of the verdict. So, in the case where X has confessed under torture to robbery, it might well be factually correct to say that "X committed robbery", but a conviction for robbery would lack moral authority and expressive value because of the use of torture to obtain the evidence on which X is convicted.

2–026   Establishing this larger notion of the ultimate aim of adjudication enables competing claims in the law of evidence to be settled in a more coherent way. Where competition arises, a calculation will be necessary about the arrangement that best promotes legitimacy of decision. This will require account to be taken both of the need for accuracy of factfinding and of the values affecting the moral authority and expressive value of the decision. In some cases, as we shall see, such calculations have been made by Parliament or the courts in adopting a particular set of rules or principles. In other cases a good deal is left to the discretion of officials in the criminal process. We shall note numerous examples of different calculations in the succeeding chapters of this book.

At this point we should make one important distinction between the three functions of the verdict. The defendant is the subject of the criminal proceedings, the central figure. He is the person charged and therefore the person at risk of conviction and punishment. The evidence in the case is focused on his alleged guilt of the offence. Clearly society in general and the victim of the offence in particular have important interests in the probative value of the evidence and the factual accuracy of the verdict founded on the evidence.[148] But the defendant has a unique interest in the sense that if a verdict of guilty is incorrect he is the person who will suffer unjust blame and punishment. As we have seen, Dworkin has argued powerfully that in liberal democratic states individuals have a special moral right against the moral harm involved in wrongful conviction.[149] This moral right supports both a legal right against that outcome, and also a further right to procedures which aim to safeguard against that outcome.

However, the defendant does not have similar unique interests in the other functions of the verdict. This is clearly so in relation to its expressive value. Whether the state should be able to uphold a verdict founded on its agents' deliberate violation of the rule of law—a clear example would be a confession obtained by torture—is a matter that concerns all its citizens. As Australian law

---

[147] cf. J. D. Jackson, "Managing Uncertainty and Finality: The Function of the Criminal Trial in Legal Inquiry" in Duff (eds), *The Trial on Trial* (2004), Vol.I, p.121, stressing the importance of finality of decision in accounting for the relationship between truth-finding and the rules of procedure and evidence.

[148] See *Horncastle* [2009] UKSC 14 at [18].

[149] "Principle, Policy, Procedure" in Tapper (ed) *Crime Proof and Punishment* (Butterworths, 1981), 193; D. J. Galligan, "More Scepticism About Scepticism" (1988) 8 O.J.L.S. 249.

recognises, the question whether illegally obtained evidence should be excluded from a criminal trial is principally a question of public policy, not individual right.[150] The answer to the question makes an important statement about the kind of state it is and the values it respects and upholds.[151] The values in question, namely the probity of state agents and the commitment of the state to legality, are plainly non-epistemic.

In relation to moral authority, a fundamental principle of political morality underpinning the criminal process is that the defendant, as a citizen of the state, should be treated with concern and respect for his liberty and dignity.[152] The principle might be described as the principle of fair treatment, and it forms part of the justification for the defendant's right to a fair trial. But this principle does not apply uniquely to the defendant. It applies to all citizens of the state. In particular other citizens involved in the proceedings against the defendant, namely victims and witnesses, also have justifiable claims to fair treatment.[153] They have interests which may be put at risk by the operation of the criminal process, as the European Court of Human Rights recognised in its landmark ruling in *Doorson v The Netherlands*.[154] These interests, and the conflicts they generate with defendants' rights, have been an increasing preoccupation in modern law.[155]

It follows that this fundamental principle of political morality is not solely defendant-focused. Arguably, therefore, for a guilty verdict to have moral authority it is not necessary that the process should have sole regard to the defendant's claim to fair treatment. Indeed many jurisdictions would now regard it as unacceptable that the process should always accord priority to this interest of the defendant. Thus, for example, in *HM Advocate v Murtagh*[156] the Privy Council held that although "an accused's right to fair disclosure is an inseparable part of his right to a fair trial",[157] it does not require automatic disclosure of convictions of a prosecution witness that are not material to her credibility and which would be embarrassing or damaging to her if disclosed. In this way a defence claim to an entitlement that is not founded on its instrumental value for safeguarding the factual accuracy of the verdict may yield to the claims of other participants in the process.

---

[150] *Bunning v Cross* (1978) 141 C.L.R. 54; *Ridgeway v R.* (1995) 184 C.L.R. 19, esp. at 38 ("Ordinarily … any unfairness to the particular accused will be of no more than peripheral importance"); Evidence Act 1995 (NSW and Cth) s.138.

[151] It is notable that the exclusionary rule developed by the Supreme Court of the US for breaches of a defendant's constitutional right against unlawful search and seizure is founded on rationales of deterrence of police impropriety and the maintenance of judicial integrity: *Mapp v Ohio*(1961) 367 U.S. 643; *Herring v US* (2009) 129 S. Ct. 695.

[152] See A. Ashworth and M. Redmayne, *The Criminal Process,*4th edn (Oxford: Oxford University Press, 2010), Ch.2, identifying this principle as supporting defendants' rights in criminal process.

[153] See, e.g. L. Ellison, *The Adversarial Process and the Vulnerable Witness* (Oxford: Oxford University Press, 2001), 65ff; J. McEwan, "Ritual, Fairness and Truth: The Adversarial and Inquisitorial Models of Criminal Trial" in Duff (eds), *The Trial on Trial* (2004), Vol.I, p.51, p.60. In a different context the European Court of Human Rights remarked in *Pretty v UK*(2002) 35 E.H.R.R. 1 at [65]: "The very essence of the Convention is respect for human dignity and human freedom".

[154] *Doorson v The Netherlands* (1996) 22 E.H.R.R. 330.

[155] As recently demonstrated in *HM Advocate v Murtagh*[2009] UKPC 36, see below.

[156] *HM Advocate v Murtagh* [2009] UKPC 36.

[157] per Steyn L.J. in *Brown (Winston)* [1994] 1 W.L.R. 1599 at 1606.

All this is not to say that the theory of legitimacy is simply a description of whatever decisions about rules of evidence are arrived at in particular contexts. It can and should be used as a critical principle—notably to test decisions to exclude evidence as a matter of rule or discretion. Its starting-point in every case is a presumption in favour of rules which will promote the factual accuracy of decision-making, since factual accuracy is the major component of legitimacy. Accordingly it is worth emphasising again that the main rule of evidence should be the one advocated by Bentham. *In general*, all relevant evidence should be admitted because this will maximise the opportunities for factfinders to reach factually accurate decisions. Exclusion of relevant evidence as a matter of *rule* should always require justification by appeal to significant systemic risks of unreliability of evidence of that type and/or to significant risks that use of evidence of that type will undermine the moral authority or expressive value of verdicts. Exclusion of items of relevant evidence as a matter of *discretion* always requires justification by appeal to a significant risk of unreliability in the circumstances of the particular case and/or to a significant risk that use of the evidence will undermine the moral authority or expressive value of the verdict in the particular case. These principles are developed systematically in the succeeding chapters of this book as particular rules of evidence are analysed.

This approach tries to relate the aims of the law of criminal evidence internally to the purposes and values of the criminal law. It rejects any idea of the independence of the law of evidence from the substantive law of crime. Rather it offers a normative conception of the criminal process as an integrated whole. Accordingly it is essential to analyse any particular aspect in context and with reference to the concerns and characteristics of the process as a whole. A major theme of this book is that the law of evidence cannot be properly understood without reference to its various contexts, and this is particularly true of the criminal context.

2–027   Before turning to civil contexts, it is appropriate at this point to return to the question of why the law of evidence is so concerned with trial processes when, as we have seen in Ch.1, most civil and criminal litigation is not actually tried out. The answer begins with the observation that the possibility of a trial casts a long shadow over the investigative and preparatory stages. Parties know that if they cannot settle their disputes they will eventually have to submit them to public adjudication. That process has its own internal imperative of legitimacy that places constraints on the principles of unfettered investigation that the parties might otherwise wish to adopt in their dealings.

The remainder of the answer concerns the nature of the administration of justice in England. This has tended to adopt what Damaska has called a "co-ordinate" style of judicial organisation.[158] The co-ordinate style is characterised by party control of litigation, by a substantial lay element in decision-making, by considerable reliance on community standards for decision and

---

[158] M. Damaska, *The Faces of Justice and State Authority* (Yale University Press, 1986). Damaska's analysis of legal processes and their relationship to structures of authority is illuminating. His contrasts are between ideal types; it is not his contention that particular legal systems fall squarely

common sense in the evaluation of evidence, and by limited systems of appeal and review.[159] Damaska contrasts this with what he calls the hierarchical style, which is characterised by bureaucratic control of litigation, "professional" decision-making, reliance on precisely defined standards for decision and comprehensive systems of appeal and review.[160] In the system of co-ordinate authority, the trial assumes particular importance because it is the original and presumptively the final adjudicator of the dispute. It is where community standards may be applied by lay decision-makers in resolving a dispute that the parties have failed to settle for themselves. Rights of appeal are limited and there is considerable reluctance to interfere with the decisions on fact reached at the trial. There is a peculiar urgency therefore attached to trial decisions being both accurate and legitimate. The law of evidence has a major role to play in securing these outcomes.

If we move now to the civil context, certain differences from the criminal process are immediately apparent. Because the civil process does not generally employ the practice of blaming and punishing,[161] civil judgments do not have the justificatory function, in terms of making moral criticism of persons found liable, that criminal verdicts have. Secondly, unlike the criminal law, the civil law does not generally have a primary behaviour-guiding function.[162] Its principal concerns are with redress of grievances, conferral of benefits, regulation of lawful activity and the effecting of private arrangements.[163] These concerns may involve the enforcement of rights and liabilities relating to distribution of losses, the management of a business, questions of status and so on, but overall the aim of adjudication is to settle disputes within a framework of economic, social and political relations that attaches considerable value to self-determination.[164] Adjudicative decisions may play some part in guiding future behaviour, but that is not their main purpose. It follows that civil judgments do not generally share the expressive functions of criminal verdicts. Thirdly, as we have seen, there is not the same strong right against wrongful decision. A factually inaccurate

---

within one type or the other. As he points out, most modern legal systems are hybrids containing a variety of forms, but his co-ordinate model does offer valuable insights into key features of English criminal process.

[159] Damaska, *The Faces of Justice and State Authority* (1986), pp.23–28, 38–46, 57–70.

[160] Damaska, *The Faces of Justice and State Authority* (1986), pp.16–23, 29–38, 47–56. Broadly speaking the co-ordinate style is associated with adversarial procedure and the hierarchical style with inquisitorial procedure, but there are many variations in different jurisdictions, as seen in Ch.1 in relation to England and Wales. For recent comparative discussion see Koppen and Penrod (eds), *Adversarial versus Inquisitorial Justice: Psychological Perspectives on Criminal Justice Systems*, (New York: Springer, 2003).

[161] An exception is the award of exemplary damages as a mark of disapproval of the defendant's conduct. Such awards are controversial at least partly because they are made in the absence of the restrictions and safeguards of the criminal process.

[162] Although, from a law and economics perspective, the possibility of damages for the commission of civil wrongs may function as an incentive to risk-averse individuals to maximise wealth by avoidance of the commission of wrongs.

[163] R. Summers and C. Howard, *Law, its Nature, Function and Limits*, 2nd edn (1972), pp.21 onwards.

[164] R. M. Dworkin, *Law's Empire* (1986), Ch.8. See also Stein and Shand, *Legal Values* (1974), Chs 5 and 6. On the aims of civil justice more generally see H. Genn, *Judging Civil Justice* (Cambridge: Cambridge University Press, 2010) esp.Ch.1.

judgment in a civil case will generally stand after the appeal process has been exhausted, unless there is evidence that the judgment was procured by fraud or there are exceptional circumstances which enable the court to reopen the decision. The importance of finality in the settlement of civil disputes generally takes priority.

2–028 These points suggest that the aims of the civil process have at least as much to do with the restoration of equilibrium and harmony (via the peaceful and acceptable settlement of disputes) between warring parties as with the implementation of state policy on matters of civil law.[165] The restoration of equilibrium and harmony enables the parties to resume their chosen means of self-determination within the legal framework provided by the state. From this perspective, truth-finding may become a less urgent imperative for the adjudicator. Procedural fairness and equality of treatment for parties in the litigation process may assume greater importance.[166] This is not to say that a court will not strive to achieve rectitude of decision within the confines of the issues and the evidence which the parties choose to present. This is still a major component of legitimacy, and inaccuracy, if detected in time, should be grounds for reversal. Nevertheless the fairness and impartiality of the adjudication will be crucial factors in its acceptability. This has been clearly indicated by the courts themselves. In *Air Canada v Secretary of State for Trade*,[167] a case concerned with a disputed claim for public interest immunity for certain documents, Lord Wilberforce commented:

> "In a contest purely between one litigant and another, such as the present, the task of the court is to do, and be seen to be doing, justice between the parties, a duty reflected by the word 'fairly' in the rule. There is no higher or additional duty to ascertain some independent truth. It often happens, from the imperfection of evidence, or the withholding of it, sometimes by the party in whose favour it would tell if presented, that an adjudication has to be made which is not, and is known not to be, the whole truth of the matter; yet, if the decision has been in accordance with the available evidence and with the law, justice will have been fairly done."[168]

The topic of public interest immunity will be considered in detail in Ch.9. For the moment it is worth stressing Lord Wilberforce's express modification of the rationalist model of adjudication. The duty of the court is to decide on the basis of the evidence provided by the parties; there is no duty to assume an activist role by seeking out additional evidence, even where the means to do so is at hand. The public interest will be satisfied by fairness in the settlement of the dispute. Rectitude of decision thus becomes a relative concept. It is the fairness of the adjudication that is the key to its legitimacy.

---

[165] J. Weinstein, "Some Difficulties in Devising Rules for Determining Truth in Judicial Trials" (1966) 66 Col. L.R. 223, 241 onwards.
[166] Australian Law Reform Commission, Report on Evidence (ALRC 39, Canberra, 1987), paras 31 onwards.
[167] *Air Canada v Secretary of State for Trade* [1983] 2 A.C. 394.
[168] *Air Canada* [1983] 2 A.C. 394 at 438.

The subordinate role of truth-finding in civil litigation is strikingly demonstrated in the Civil Procedure Rules. Rule 1.1 sets out the "overriding objective", to which the court must seek to give effect when it exercises any power given to it by the Rules:

> "1.1—(1) These Rules are a new procedural code with the overriding objective of enabling the court to deal with cases justly.
>
> (2) Dealing with a case justly includes, so far as is practicable—
>> (a) ensuring that the parties are on an equal footing;
>> (b) saving expense;
>> (c) dealing with the case in ways which are proportionate—
>>> (i) to the amount of money involved;
>>> (ii) to the importance of the case;
>>> (iii) to the complexity of the issues; and
>>> (iv) to the financial position of each party;
>> (d) ensuring that it is dealt with expeditiously and fairly; and
>> (e) allotting to it an appropriate share of the court's resources, while taking into account the need to allot resources to other cases."

There is not a word here, or in r.1.4, that sets out the court's duty of active case management, about the court having a duty to determine the true facts of the dispute. The interests of efficient case management must, however, take account of the interests of justice. The latter might, for example, require the amendment of procedural directions to allow the admission of video evidence that would substantially undermine the claimant's case in a personal injury action.[169] In this way an outcome might be avoided where a person acquires a judicial award to which he or she was demonstrably not entitled.

It is instructive to contrast this statement of the "overriding objective" of civil proceedings with the equivalent statement for criminal cases. The Criminal Procedure Rules 2012 state:

2–029

> "(1) The overriding objective of this new code is that criminal cases be dealt with justly.
>
> (2) Dealing with a criminal case justly includes—
>> (a) acquitting the innocent and convicting the guilty;
>> (b) dealing with the prosecution and the defence fairly;
>> (c) recognising the rights of a defendant, particularly those under art.6 of the European Convention on Human Rights;
>> (d) respecting the interests of witnesses, victims and jurors and keeping them informed of the progress of the case;
>> (e) dealing with the case efficiently and expeditiously;
>> (f) ensuring that appropriate information is available to the court when bail and sentence are considered; and
>> (g) dealing with the case in ways that take into account–
>>> (i) the gravity of the offence alleged,
>>> (ii) the complexity of what is in issue.
>>> (iii) the severity of the consequences for the defendant and others affected, and
>>> (iv) the needs of other cases."

The Criminal Procedure Rules begin with the same proposition as the Civil Procedure Rules, namely that their objective is to enable courts to deal with cases justly. However, the difference in their conceptions of justice is striking. The

---

[169] See *Rall v Hume* [2001] 3 All E.R. 248 CA.

Criminal Procedure Rules state the importance of accurate outcomes as their first priority whereas, as we have seen, the Civil Procedure Rules do not refer to outcomes at all. There is no reference to procedural rights in the Civil Procedure Rules whereas the importance of the rights of the defendant is emphasised at an early stage in the Criminal Procedure Rules. Efficiency of process is mentioned in both sets of Rules, but is a lower priority for criminal cases. These differences confirm the need for a theoretical account of the aims of the law of evidence that locates the adjectival law in the context of the relevant substantive law.

CHAPTER 3

RELEVANCE AND ADMISSIBILITY

A. INTRODUCTION

3–001 Relevance is the fundamental condition of admissibility of evidence. We have seen in Ch.1 that evidence that is irrelevant is inadmissible.[1] Relevant evidence is prima facie admissible, on the basis that its admission will tend to promote the aims of the law of evidence.[2] It may, however, be made inadmissible by virtue of an exclusionary rule. Exclusionary rules now operate mainly in criminal cases. In modern law there are fewer exclusionary rules in civil cases; and those that still exist, such as the rule against evidence of character and other misconduct,[3] tend to be less strict.

A judge may also exclude evidence in the exercise of a discretion. In criminal cases this may be either the discretion at common law, to exclude prosecution evidence, which is founded on the judge's duty to secure a fair trial for the accused, or the discretion under s.78 of PACE to exclude prosecution evidence the admission of which would so adversely affect the fairness of the proceedings that it ought not to be admitted. Other statutory provisions provide for a discretion in criminal cases to admit or exclude specific types of evidence.[4] In civil cases the court has a discretion under the Civil Procedure Rules to exclude evidence that would otherwise be admissible[5]; exclusion must be aimed at furthering the overriding objective under r.1.1.

Section B of this chapter discusses the concept of relevance in English law. Section C deals generally with admissibility, making some brief comments about exclusionary rules, and section D discusses in more detail the nature and scope of exclusionary discretion.

B. RELEVANCE

1. Stephen's definition

3–002 In contrast to all modern codes of evidence, English law has no authoritative statutory or common law definition of the core concept of relevance. The absence of the limits that might be imposed by such a definition permits flexibility in the application of the concept. However, as is so often the case in English law, flexibility is purchased at the cost of some obscurity and inconsistency.

---

[1] Although it is inadmissible, where irrelevant evidence has been admitted for the prosecution, the Court of Appeal will not find a conviction to be unsafe unless the evidence is unfairly prejudicial to the accused. See, e.g. *Sammon* [2011] EWCA Crim 1199, where Pitchford L.J. said at [55], "The ultimate question which this Court will consider is whether there is a real risk that the jury was improperly influenced by the inadmissible material ... The answer to this question will depend not just on the nature and objectively prejudicial effect of the inadmissible material but also upon the terms, if any, of any warning to the jury and the other evidence in the case. The assessment of the influence of prejudice is intensely fact and case sensitive".

[2] See Ch.2.

[3] See Ch.18.

[4] Examples are s.114(1)(d) of the Criminal Justice Act 2003 (discretion to admit otherwise inadmissible hearsay evidence in the interests of justice) and s.126 of the same Act (discretion to exclude admissible hearsay where there is a danger that its admission would result in undue waste of time).

[5] CPR r.32.1(2).

Many modern accounts of relevance begin with Stephen's influential definition in the Digest:

> "The word 'relevant' means that any two facts to which it is applied are so related to each other that according to the common course of events, one either taken by itself or in connection with other facts proves or renders probable the past, present or future existence or non-existence of the other."[6]

This definition needs to be qualified and supplemented in certain respects, but it does have distinct merits which are worth highlighting. First, the opening words emphasise that relevance is concerned with the *relationship between facts:* the relationship between the fact sought to be proved and the fact offered in evidence. The question whether a given item of evidence is relevant in a given case cannot be answered in the abstract. The evidence must be relevant to something—the something being a proper object of proof in the case. Thus the answer requires a precise analysis of the factual issue to which the evidence is claimed to be connected. Secondly, Stephen's definition requires relevance to be assessed *according to the common course of events.* In deciding whether something may be inferred about the existence of fact A from proof of fact B, reliance is to be placed on the common stock of knowledge about the world; in other words, on logic, common sense and general experience. This is what Thayer meant when he said that "the law furnishes no test of relevancy".[7] In evaluating factual relationships of cause, effect and association, there is in general no stipulated criterion in law. The only "laws" which identify the existence of a relationship between facts are the laws of nature and human behaviour. Occasionally courts prescribe certain matters to be "relevant"[8] or "irrelevant",[9] but these rulings essentially concern the scope of particular substantive rules of law. Deemed relevance or irrelevance does not necessarily correspond to logical relevance.

It follows that some background generalisation about the world is always present when we judge one fact relevant to the existence of another. In most cases there is no necessity to articulate the generalisation because it is uncontroversial. For example, if identity is in issue on a charge of murder, it is usually considered relevant to prove that the defendant had a motive for killing the victim. If asked to justify the claim of relevance, most people would offer an explanation to the effect that an intentional act such as murder is generally done for a reason and

---

[6] J. F. Stephen, *Digest of the Law of Evidence,* 12th edn (London: Macmillan, 1948), art.1. Note the difference between this and the definition in the first edition (London: 1876). Article 9 of the first edition stated: "Facts, whether in issue or not, are relevant to each other when one is, or probably may be, or probably may have been—the cause of the other; the effect of the other; an effect of the same cause; a cause of the same effect: or when the one shows that the other must or cannot have occurred, or probably does or did exist, or not, which in the common course of events would either have caused or have been caused by the other".

[7] J. B. Thayer, *A Preliminary Treatise on Evidence at the Common Law* (Boston: Little, Brown, 1898), p.265.

[8] e.g. under the former law of provocation, that the age and sex of the defendant are always relevant in considering whether a reasonable man would have done as the defendant did when provoked to lose his self-control: *DPP v Camplin* [1978] A.C. 705 HL, interpreting the Homicide Act 1957 s.3.

[9] e.g. that evidence of the defendant's voluntary intoxication is irrelevant and inadmissible in considering the defendant's criminal liability for an offence of "basic intent": *DPP v Majewski* [1977] A.C. 443 HL.

that motiveless killings are rare. Therefore, showing that D had a reason to kill P increases the probability of D's guilt; it does this by placing him in a limited class of persons more likely than others to have committed the murder. The form of reasoning involved is inductive. Given that the law provides no test which could ground logical deductions about the relevance of evidence, it is clear that the "logic" relied on is the logic of everyday experience, supplemented by expert knowledge where necessary. What we have called background generalisations are formulated on the basis of such experience and knowledge, and they are authoritative only to the extent that their truth is generally accepted.[10]

3–003   In cases where the relevance of evidence is in doubt, it may be useful to test the point by constructing a syllogism. A syllogism is a logical construct consisting of a major premise, a minor premise, and a conclusion. The major premise is an empirical proposition of a general nature whose truth is likely to be accepted by the factfinder. The classical example is the proposition "All men are mortal". The minor premise is a specific proposition of fact, the truth of which is admitted or which can be proved by evidence. In the classical example, the minor premise is the statement "Socrates is a man". The conclusion is obtained by dividing the minor premise into the major premise: "Therefore Socrates is mortal". In the context of the law of evidence the item of evidence of doubtful relevance is the minor premise. The task will then be to decide whether an acceptable background generalisation can be formulated as the major premise so as to permit a reasonable factfinder to draw the suggested conclusion. Although this technique appears to cast the problem as one of deductive analysis the validity of the conclusion still rests ultimately on the persuasiveness of the major premise. That in turn depends on the degree to which the hypothesis involved conforms with common knowledge, or with expert knowledge in a case where that is required. The technique is useful, however, in demonstrating the need for careful articulation of a background generalisation where the relevance of evidence is disputed.

In the old case of *Hollingham v Head*,[11] the plaintiff sued the defendant for the price of a quantity of guano sold and delivered to the defendant. The defence was no liability to pay because of breach of a condition as to quality. In order to prove the existence of the alleged condition the defendant wished to adduce evidence of other contracts containing the condition made by the plaintiff with other persons. The Court of Common Pleas upheld the trial judge's rejection of the evidence. Willes J., after stating that evidence offered for the purpose of establishing probability must at least afford a reasonable inference as to the matter in dispute, continued:

---

[10] For an instructive case where a generalisation was not accepted, see *Bracewell* (1978) 68 Cr.App.R. 44 CA. The defendant argued that it was relevant to show that his co-accused had used violence on his mistress in support of his case that it was the co-accused who had mounted a violent and fatal assault on the victim of a joint burglary. The Court of Appeal doubted the validity of a generalisation that "a man who, when he uses violence to his mistress, does not know when to stop, is more likely to have been guilty of a violent assault on a man in the course of a burglary than a man who has not used violence to his wife or mistress".

[11] *Hollingham v Head* (1858) 27 L.J.C.P. 241.

"It appears to me that the evidence, which was proposed to be given in this case, would not have shewn that it was probable that the plaintiff had made the contract, which the defendant contended he had made; for I do not see how the fact, that a man has once or more in his life acted in a particular way, makes it probable that he so acted on a given occasion."[12]

Willes J. was thus expressly refusing to accept a background generalisation based on the tendency of human behaviour to repeat itself. But his rejection of this premise is problematic. It is contradicted by a good deal of common experience; it is well-known that human behaviour generally is often repetitive. More particularly, many businessmen and traders use standard-form contracts to deal with their customers. Even in the mid-nineteenth century, a trader such as the plaintiff, who was in the habit of attending agricultural markets to promote his new product, might well have offered the same inducement to purchase to all his prospective customers. It is not convincing to say that the evidence relating to the plaintiff's other contracts had no logical relevance. The decision in the case is better based on the ground of insufficient relevance of the evidence, given the delay, expense and inconvenience of enquiring into transactions unrelated to the one in issue. As we shall see, courts are often reluctant to broaden the issues in a case by investigating other matters or engaging in "satellite" litigation. The question of sufficiency of relevance is considered further below.

A third valuable feature of Stephen's definition is the reminder that the relevance of a fact can be assessed taking the fact *either by itself or in connection with other facts*. The relevance of an item of evidence need not be considered in isolation from the other evidence in the case. Indeed, the state of the other evidence may critically affect the formulation of a background generalisation. It may therefore be crucial in determining both the existence and the degree of relevance. Suppose that the defendant is charged with the murder of her husband and pleads that she killed him in a rage, having lost her self-control as a result of his grossly offensive behaviour.[13] Evidence that she loathes and despises her neighbour does not seem by itself to have any logical relevance to the issue of whether she lost her self-control. But further evidence that her husband's offensive behaviour included repeated taunts, comparing her unflatteringly with her neighbour, alters the judgement of relevance, because it makes it more likely that she did lose her self-control as a result of these insults.

3–004

The extent to which other evidence may affect a judgement about the *degree* of logical relevance of a given item of evidence is illustrated by the instructive case of *Ball*.[14] The defendants were brother and sister, both adults, charged with incest. Police officers gave evidence that when they visited the house which the defendants shared, they found one bedroom in use containing a double bed. The trial judge admitted evidence that before the Punishment of Incest Act 1908 the defendants had lived together openly and that they had conceived a child. The House of Lords upheld the admission of the evidence as showing a "guilty passion" on the part of the defendants, leading to the inference that sexual relations had continued between them after incest had become a crime. Suppose, however, that the other evidence had been that when the police visited the house

---

[12] *Hollingham v Head* (1858) 27 L.J.C.P. 241 at 242.
[13] Coroners and Justice Act 2009 ss.54, 55(4).
[14] *Ball* [1911] A.C. 47 HL.

they found two bedrooms in use and nothing else to suggest that the defendants were sharing a bed. The relevance of their past association is now significantly different. Instead of being highly relevant to resolve a doubt arising from other incriminating evidence (the purpose for which they were sharing a bed), its relevance now rests in the general claim that their previous conduct showed a disposition that they were likely to continue to indulge despite the criminalisation of such conduct. At this point the degree of relevance is much less, and the evidence begins to look more prejudicial than probative. Hoffmann was surely right to suggest that it would almost certainly have been excluded at common law in the hypothetical case.[15]

3–005   One difficulty with the Stephen test arises from the proposition that the evidentiary fact must *prove or render probable* the existence of the fact in issue. If this test is applied literally it seems to set the standard too high. It would tend to rule out much circumstantial evidence that most people would intuitively consider relevant. To revert to the example of motive in a murder case, we would not accept a bare assertion that because D had a motive to kill P, therefore D probably killed P. The background generalisation involved—that people who have reasons to kill probably do kill—is overstated. To require the evidence to prove probability in this sense is to require it to prove too much; the existence of a motive increases suspicion against D, but it cannot normally prove the crime or suggest the high degree of likelihood that seems to be contemplated by a test of "probability". It may be that the test of probability represents a confusion between the relevance and the sufficiency of evidence. The sufficiency of evidence to prove a case is a function of all the evidence in the case, not of individual items. A common tendency of students new to evidence is to argue that a particular item of circumstantial evidence "can't be relevant because it doesn't prove the issue". This is clearly misconceived. Items of circumstantial evidence are frequently compared to bricks in a wall or strands in a rope.[16] It is not necessary that any particular item has to be substantial enough to function as a wall or strong enough to bear the weight of the case on its own.

It might be thought that the difficulty could be overcome by using Stephen's reference to "other facts" to argue that probability is always to be assessed having regard to the other evidence in the case. In this way evidence of motive, for example, would become relevant if, when considered together with the other evidence, it raised a probability of D's guilt. However, given that evidence emerges in stages during the course of a trial, such an approach would entail saying that much circumstantial evidence having some bearing on the facts in issue must be admitted conditionally, with the court waiting to see whether other evidence helps it to create a "probability" of the facts in issue. But this is not the way in which the concept of conditional admissibility is applied in practice.[17] Courts do not admit evidence plainly having some degree of logical relevance on

---

[15] L. H. Hoffmann, "Similar Facts After *Boardman*" (1975) 91 L.Q.R. 193, 202. Whether it would be excluded under the statutory regime created by the Criminal Justice Act 2003 for bad character evidence (see Ch.19) is more debatable, but it is submitted that the answer should be the same.

[16] See, e.g. Pollock C.B. in *Exall* (1866) 4 F. & .F 922 at 929.

[17] Cross and Tapper, pp.71–72.

the basis that it can only be considered if its potential weight is increased by other evidence. It seems therefore that Stephen's reference to probability must not be taken literally.

2. Logical relevance

An alternative conception of relevance modifies the reference to probability while impliedly accepting the rest of Stephen's definition. In the words of r.401 of the Federal Rules of Evidence:

> "'Relevant evidence' means evidence having any tendency to make the existence of any fact that is of consequence to the determination of the action more probable or less probable than it would be without the evidence."

In *DPP v Kilbourne,* Lord Simon of Glaisdale expressed the view that:

> "Evidence is relevant if it is logically probative or disprobative of some matter which requires proof. I do not pause to analyse what is involved in 'logical probativeness' except to note that the term does not of itself express the element of experience which is so significant of its operation in law, and possibly elsewhere. It is sufficient to say, even at the risk of etymological tautology, that relevant (i.e. logically probative or disprobative) evidence is evidence which makes the matter which requires proof more or less probable."[18]

This conception, which might be called the theory of bare or minimum logical relevance, does not require that the evidence of fact B should make the existence of fact A (the object of proof) probable or improbable; it requires only that fact B should increase or decrease the probability of the existence of fact A. In other words, if in doubt, we could ask what is the probability of the fact to be proved (its prior probability) in the absence of the evidence in question? Having established this figure, whether by inference from other evidence or by the adoption of some normative figure,[19] we can then ask whether the evidence in question tends to alter that probability? If so, the evidence is relevant. On this view relevance is a threshold criterion; provided that the evidence tends to increase or decrease the probability of a fact to be proved, it can be said to have potential probative value. It is not necessary on this approach that the evidence should have any particular degree of probative value.

However, in *Randall* Lord Steyn restated Lord Simon's proposition and then added a reference to degrees of relevance:

> "A judge ruling on a point of admissibility involving an issue of relevance has to decide whether the evidence is capable of increasing or diminishing the probability of the existence of a fact in issue. The question of relevance is typically a matter of degree to be determined, for the most part, by common sense and experience."[20]

3–006

3–007

---

[18] *DPP v Kilbourne* [1973] A.C. 729 at 756 HL.
[19] For further discussion of the difficulty of assessing prior probabilities, see Ch.4.
[20] *Randall* [2003] UKHL 69; [2004] 1 Cr.App.R. 26 at [20]; citing Keane, *The Modern Law of Evidence*, 5th edn (2000), p.20.

We will return to the question of degrees of relevance below. It is worth noting at this point that common sense and experience will indicate whether a given item of evidence has any logical relevance, and, if it does, what degree of relevance it has. But if relevance is a question of degree we still need another criterion to tell us whether that particular degree of relevance is sufficient for the evidence to be admitted. This is a question of law to which common sense and experience cannot supply an answer.

3. Logical relevance and exclusionary discretion: the "costs" of admission

3–008   Evidence that is logically relevant might be objected to on one or more of various grounds. These are independent of the rules of admissibility which relate to such matters as hearsay, opinion or character evidence. They include claims that evidence is too remote, or prejudicial, or likely to multiply the issues, or may mislead or confuse the jury, or lead to unnecessary delay and expense. Arguments of efficiency and fairness may support the exclusion of evidence on one or more of these grounds. The admission of evidence of little probative value may marginally promote accuracy of decision, but any gains in this direction may have to be offset against the costs, both literal and metaphorical, of its admission. If the evidence is likely to confuse or distract the factfinder, it may reduce the chances of accuracy of decision. The evidence may unfairly prejudice the party against whom it is admitted because the factfinder is likely to over-value it, or because it will influence the factfinder to find against a party for reasons unrelated to the probative value of the evidence.

The theory of bare or minimum logical relevance deals with these claims by the creation of an exclusionary discretion.[21] Thus, r.403 of the Federal Rules of Evidence provides:

"Although relevant, evidence may be excluded if its probative value is substantially outweighed by the danger of unfair prejudice, confusion of the issues, or misleading the jury, or by considerations of undue delay, waste of time, or needless presentation of cumulative evidence."

This method of structuring the decision whether to admit the evidence requires a trial judge first to determine the logical relevance of the evidence. The judge must then weigh its potential probative value against the possible costs of admission mentioned in the rule. If the judge concludes that the costs substantially outweigh the probative value of the evidence, then it ought to be excluded. Characterising such an exclusionary decision as one of "discretion" is important, because it has the effect of restricting the powers of an appeal court. Under the prevalent approach in Anglo-American law to the exercise of discretionary power, an appeal court will only interfere with a trial judge's exercise of discretion if the decision was so unreasonable as to be perverse, or if the judge erred in principle in reaching the decision, for example by taking into account irrelevant

---

[21] In common law jurisdictions exclusionary rules are often used in criminal cases to deal with the problem of prejudice arising from evidence of the accused's other misconduct.

considerations or failing to consider relevant ones. It will not be sufficient that the appeal court would simply have exercised the discretion differently.

In English law a trial judge has a discretion at common law and under statute to exclude evidence in *criminal* proceedings. It is controversial how far these discretions extend, a matter which is discussed below. In *civil* proceedings, it seems reasonably clear that there was no equivalent in English common law to r.403. In a civil case a judge formerly had no discretion to exclude evidence which was otherwise relevant and admissible, either on the ground that it was obtained unlawfully,[22] or on any of the grounds mentioned in r.403.[23] However, it also seems to be clear that matters such as prejudice, multiplication of the issues, waste of time, and so on, were not simply ignored by judges in civil proceedings in deciding whether the evidence in question should be received. It appears that these matters could be taken into account in the initial decision as to whether the evidence was relevant at all. In *Vernon v Bosley*, Hoffmann L.J. stated as a general principle that:

> "the degree of relevance needed for admissibility is not some fixed point on a scale, but will vary according to the nature of the evidence and in particular the inconvenience, expense, delay or oppression which would attend its reception."[24]

The Civil Procedure Rules, which came into force in 1999, introduced a general **3–009** exclusionary discretion into civil proceedings. Rule 32.1(2) of the Civil Procedure Rules authorises a court to use its power under r.32.1 to control evidence to exclude evidence that would otherwise be admissible. Exclusion will have to be aimed at furthering the overriding objective under r.1.1. A cautious approach to this new discretion was taken in *Great Future International Ltd v Sealand Housing Corp*,[25] where the Court of Appeal indicated that the exclusionary power should be exercised with great circumspection for the purpose of achieving the overriding objective of dealing with cases justly.[26]

What this means has been considered in dicta in a number of subsequent cases; these dicta suggest a growing awareness of the possibilities for use of the exclusionary discretion. Thus in *O'Brien v Chief Constable of South Wales Police*[27] Lord Phillips commented that dealing with a case justly includes dealing with the case in a way which is proportionate to what is involved in the case, and in a manner which is expeditious and fair. In this case the House of Lords suggested that the case management decision whether to exclude otherwise admissible evidence would take into account the burdens entailed by admission in

---

[22] *Helliwell v Piggott-Sims* [1980] F.S.R. 582 CA.
[23] *Bradford City Metropolitan Council v K* [1990] Fam. 140; *Re C (Minors)* [1993] 4 All E.R. 690; *Vernon v Bosley* [1994] P.I.Q.R. 337; Cross and Tapper, pp.212–215; R. Pattenden, "The discretionary exclusion of relevant evidence in English civil proceedings" (1997) 1 E. & P. 361.
[24] *Vernon v Bosley* [1994] P.I.Q.R. 337. In this case the Court of Appeal rather blurred the distinction by saying that appellate review of such balancing decisions by trial judges would be limited to the principles used for review of exercises of discretion. In criminal proceedings it seems clear that this is not so for many cases, and that decisions on relevance are treated for the most part as judgments on questions of law. See the discussion in the text below.
[25] *Great Future International Ltd v Sealand Housing Corp* [2002] EWCA Civ 1183.
[26] Citing *Grobbelaar v Sun Newspapers Ltd*, The Times, August 12, 1999.
[27] *O'Brien v Chief Constable of South Wales Police* [2005] UKHL 26; [2005] 2 All E.R. 931 at [54].

terms of time, cost and the resources necessary to deal with the evidence, together with any likelihood that admission of the evidence would distort the trial and distract the attention of the decision-maker by focusing on collateral issues, or would cause unfair prejudice.[28] In *Post Office Counters Ltd v Mahida,*[29] the Court of Appeal referred to the exclusionary power as designed to allow the court to stop cases getting out of hand, and gave the example of excluding admissible hearsay evidence to prevent hearings becoming interminable. In *Jones v University of Warwick,*[30] Lord Woolf C.J. said that proactive management of civil proceedings was concerned not only with the individual piece of litigation before the court but with litigation as a whole. In exercising its exclusionary power the court could take account of unlawful means used by a party to obtain evidence, such as a breach of the claimant's human rights, and the effect on litigation generally of the court not censuring the conduct in question. This marks a departure from the common law and introduces an element of public policy into the exercise of exclusionary discretion in civil cases. In the light of these dicta it now seems clear that the discretion provided for by the Civil Procedure Rules has incorporated the factors mentioned in r.403 of the Federal Rules. However, it remains to be seen whether this will make a significant difference in practice to the former judicial habit of treating the "costs" of admission as a factor in the calculation of whether the evidence has sufficient relevance to justify its admission in the first place.

The emphasis on relevance as a matter of degree represents a third, distinctive, conception of relevance, and it is to this conception that we will now turn.

4.   Sufficient relevance

3–010   This third conception[31] regards relevance as a variable quality of evidence. To qualify for admissibility, evidence must not only have logical relevance in the sense of increasing or decreasing the probability of the fact to be proved, but must have a sufficient degree of relevance to outweigh the "costs" of its admission.[32] This overlaps with Wigmore's idea that all evidence must have a

---

[28] *O'Brien v Chief Constable of South Wales Police* [2005] UKHL 26. See Lord Bingham at [6], Lord Phillips at [55] and [56], Lord Carswell at [77].

[29] *Post Office Counters Ltd v Mahida* [2003] EWCA Civ 1583.

[30] *Jones v University of Warwick* [2003] 3 All E.R. 760.

[31] There is a 4th conception, namely "legal" relevance, which characterises exclusionary rules as cases where the law deems evidence to be irrelevant. On this view evidence is legally relevant and hence admissible if it is logically relevant and not deemed by the law to be irrelevant. See J. F. Stephen, *Digest of the Law of Evidence* (1876), art.9. This approach has never commanded general acceptance, not least because it looks artificial and misleading. Some evidence ruled out by a rule of exclusion such as hearsay may have a high degree of logical relevance. For further discussion of theories of relevance see G.F. James, "Relevancy, probability and the law" (1941) 29 Cal. L.R. 689; H. L. Trautman, "Logical or legal relevancy–a conflict in theory" (1952) 5 Vand. L.R. 385; Wigmore, Vol.1A (Tillers rev. Boston, 1983), para.37; A. Stein, "The Refoundation of Evidence Law" (1996) IX *Canadian Journal of Law and Jurisprudence* 279; Roberts and Zuckerman, *Criminal Evidence,* 2nd edn (Oxford: Oxford University Press, 2010), pp.99–108.

[32] We can recall Lord Steyn's statement in *Randall* [2003] UKHL 69; [2004] 1 Cr.App.R. 26 (p.375), cited above: "the question of relevance is typically a matter of degree to be determined, for the most part, by common sense and experience". As noted above, if relevance is a question of degree, common

"plus value" in order to be relevant enough to be submitted to a jury for consideration.[33] Wigmore's idea is implicit in Cowen and Carter's claim that "the law prescribes a minimum quantum of probative value for evidence before it will regard it as relevant".[34] However, the notion that relevance is a matter of degree in all cases is not precisely the same as saying that a "plus value" is always required; the "plus value" is not necessarily related to the "costs" of admission, although in practice it might often be convenient to make the link. The principle adopted in English law is necessarily imprecise because the degree of relevance and the costs of particular items of evidence will vary greatly with the circumstances of each case.

Treating the "costs" of admission as part of the initial decision on relevance logically entails treating the balancing decision involved as a matter of *judgment* on a question of law. If a decision is one of judgment on law rather than the exercise of a discretion, an appeal court may substitute its own view for that of the trial judge, if persuaded that the judge came to the wrong conclusion. Both this approach, based on sufficient relevance, and the approach based on logical relevance plus exclusionary discretion, are agreed on the factors to be taken into account in the decision on admissibility. The difference is that the second regards all of these factors as the subject of an exclusionary discretion, to be exercised after the judgment of logical relevance, whereas the first regards most of them as part of the judgment of relevance itself. In practice it will not matter which approach the trial judge adopts, since the result is likely to be the same. But, as indicated above, the difference may be important on appeal if the court is scrupulous about the extent to which it is willing to interfere with an exercise of discretion as opposed to a judgment on a question of law.

In criminal cases it is clear that the courts generally regard as exercises of discretion decisions as to whether the probative value of evidence is outweighed by its prejudicial effect. This was a well-established head of discretion at common law[35]; it is unclear after PACE whether this head of discretion has been absorbed by the general discretion under s.78,[36] or whether it has been preserved as a separate head of discretion by s.82(3). Whichever is the case, it is still the general view that the judge's decision is an exercise of *discretion*. However, decisions about the other grounds for exclusion mentioned in r.403 are not so clearly classified in English law. It is proposed to discuss the matter under a number of headings corresponding to different kinds of "costs" of admission. It should be emphasised that this classification is not pure because some of the categories overlap; in addition it is not always possible to assign particular cases to particular categories. Frequently, more than one of the cost factors will combine to produce a conclusion that the disadvantages of admitting the evidence outweigh any probative value it may have. Nevertheless, with these caveats in

---

sense and experience may indicate what degree of relevance the evidence has, but another criterion is needed before a court can say that that degree of relevance is sufficient for the evidence to be admitted. The most obvious and appropriate criterion is the "costs" of admission; the degree of relevance should be enough to exceed the costs.

[33] Wigmore, Vol.1A (Tillers rev., Boston, 1983), para.28.

[34] Z. Cowen and P. B. Carter, *Essays on the Law of Evidence* (Oxford: Clarendon Press, 1956), p.125.

[35] *Sang* [1980] A.C. 402 HL.

[36] As assumed in *R. v King's Lynn Magistrates' Court Ex p. Holland* [1993] 2 All E.R. 377 DC.

mind, the classification still offers a useful means of analysing a number of cases. Taken as a whole the analysis suggests that English law tends to regard these cost factors as being subject either to particular rules of admissibility or to exercises of judgment on law by trial judges.

(A)   Superfluity, delay and expense

3–011   The admission of evidence which is superfluous or of little probative value is a waste of litigants' time and money. It also uses up scarce resources of the legal system without adequate justification and contributes to inefficiency. In Ch.2 it was suggested that these points formed one of the main rationales for the common law rule that the previous consistent statements of witnesses are generally inadmissible. In other contexts it would seem, though reported examples are hard to find, that a trial judge may say that evidence is insufficiently relevant, simply on the basis of its superfluity, or because of the unjustifiable delay and expense that its reception would cause.[37] The Royal Commission on Criminal Justice thought that if such a power existed, it was not exercised frequently enough by trial judges. The Commission recommended the express enactment of a provision in similar terms to r.403 of the Federal Rules of Evidence.[38]

By itself, the admission of superfluous evidence would hardly be a ground for interference with the verdict or judgment of a trial court. However, if the evidence might have had the effect of causing prejudice to the defendant in a criminal case, then intervention may be justified, given that the probative value of the evidence is slight. As mentioned above, such a calculation of probative value and prejudicial effect is usually regarded as a matter of the trial judge's discretion, but the courts are not always consistent. In *Berry*,[39] the Court of Appeal held that the trial judge in a murder case should not have admitted evidence of a previous relationship between the defendant and his deceased mistress to establish a motive of jealousy on his part and, by inference, an intention to kill. The evidence was said, first, to be remote from the killing, because the relationship had finished a few weeks before the death and, secondly, to be prejudicial to the defendant. The claim of remoteness is not particularly convincing in view of the relatively short lapse of time involved, and in view of the link with the other evidence of the defendant's continuing jealousy after the relationship had finished. This other evidence was cogent and undisputed. It consisted of the defendant's admissions to the police of his jealousy and of statements in letters he had written to the deceased after their relationship ended.

---

[37] *Tooke* (1990) 90 Cr.App.R. 417 is a reasonably clear example: see Lord Lane C.J. at 421. For civil cases see *Vernon v Bosley* [1994] P.I.Q.R. 337 (Hoffmann L.J.); and *Hollingham v Head* (1858) 27 L.J.C.P. 241, both cited in Pattenden, "Discretionary exclusion" (1997) 1 E. & P. 361, 375–379. The latter case shows how in practice these efficiency concerns will frequently be allied to concerns about multiplication of the issues and confusion of the factfinder. Note that a trial judge now has a statutory discretion in criminal proceedings to exclude (admissible) hearsay evidence if admitting it would result in undue waste of time, taking account of the value of the evidence: Criminal Justice Act 2003 s.126.

[38] RCCJ Report para.8.13. A similar call was made, in the context of a civil case, by Butler-Sloss L.J. in *Re M and R (Minors)* [1996] 4 All E.R. 239 at 255.

[39] *Berry* (1986) 83 Cr.App.R. 7 CA. See also *Byrne* [2002] EWCA Crim 632; [2002] 2 Cr.App.R. 21.

Evidence of the history of the relationship would have added little to what was already available. It is suggested therefore that it would have been better regarded as superfluous rather than too remote. Although the Court of Appeal clearly regarded the probative value of the evidence as outweighed by the risk of prejudice, the judgment interestingly makes no reference to any "discretion" on the part of the trial judge in respect of the admission of this evidence. It was assumed that a question of judgment of relevance was involved on which the judge could and should be reversed.[40]

In *Phillips (Alun)*,[41] the Court of Appeal emphasised that a decision to admit evidence of the history of a relationship as "background" evidence:

> "may well involve a careful exercise of judgment on the part of the judge. This is not, strictly speaking, an exercise of discretion . . . In a case such as the present, where it is not in issue that some background material of a certain category is relevant, it is a question of fact and degree how much material of that category should be admitted".[42]

Later in the judgment the court stated that the judge could limit the scope of background evidence if contentious material was likely to lead to prolonged examination and cross-examination; it seems clear that this "cost" of admission was regarded as something to be taken into account in the decision on relevance.

(B)   Multiplicity of issues

Several cases illustrate the reluctance of courts to allow the parties to multiply the issues by introducing evidence of other incidents and transactions where these are not related to the one in question. In *Whitehead*,[43] an unlicensed surgeon was charged with manslaughter. Maule J. ruled that the defence could not call evidence from other patients to prove that the defendant had treated them successfully: "Neither on the one hand or the other can other cases treated by the prisoner be gone into".[44] In *Agassiz v London Tramway Co*,[45] a passenger on a tram claimed damages for personal injuries sustained in a collision which she alleged was caused by the negligence of the defendants' driver. Kelly C.B. is reported as having rejected evidence of a statement by the conductor to a fellow passenger that the driver was new and had been reported because he had been off the line five or six times that day. The statement would have been hearsay but was apparently rejected because of the many side issues to which it would have given

3–012

---

[40] The court nonetheless applied the proviso to uphold the conviction in view of the other evidence. On the relevance of past incidents and relationships involving the defendant, see further *Williams* (1987) 84 Cr.App.R. 298; *Sidhu* (1994) 98 Cr.App.R. 59; *Fulcher* [1995] 2 Cr.App.R. 251. In *Phillips (Alun)* [2003] EWCA Crim 1379; [2003] 2 Cr.App.R. 35 the Court of Appeal said that *Berry* should be disregarded insofar as it cast doubt on the proposition stated by Lord Atkinson in *Ball* [1911] A.C. 47 that in a murder case evidence of the accused's previous acts and words towards the deceased is admissible to prove not only motive but the fact of the killing by the accused.
[41] *Phillips (Alun)* [2003] EWCA Crim 1379; [2003] 2 Cr.App.R. 35.
[42] *Phillips (Alun)* [2003] EWCA Crim 1379; [2003] 2 Cr.App.R. 35 at [35].
[43] *Whitehead* (1843) 3 Car. & Kir. 202.
[44] *Whitehead* (1843) 3 Car. & Kir. 202 at 203.
[45] *Agassiz v London Tramway Co* (1872) 21 W.R. 199.

rise. In *Hollingham v Head*,[46] as mentioned above, the Court of Common Pleas upheld the refusal of the trial judge to admit evidence of other contracts made by the plaintiff in that case.

The objections to multiplication of the issues rest on a combination of familiar concerns about delay and expense, and anxiety that the factfinder may be distracted from concentrating on the case in hand. In *Hollingham v Head*, Willes J. justified the rejection of the evidence of other contracts by the need "to obviate the prejudice, the injustice, and the waste of time to which the admission of such evidence would lead", and continued, "bearing in mind the extent to which it might it be carried, and that litigants are mortal, it is necessary not only to adhere to the rule, but to lay it down strictly".[47] In *Whitehead*, Maule J. stated the rule cited above and added: "The attention of the jury must be confined to the present case".[48]

(C) Confusion and misleading of the jury

3–013 An important influence in the historical development of the law of evidence in Anglo-American jurisdictions has been a felt need to protect a jury from being misled or confused by certain types of evidence.[49] This concern appears at several points in the rules of admissibility, and it may well affect decisions as to whether evidence has sufficient relevance to be admitted. It may, for example, be the best explanation for the decision of the Court of Criminal Appeal in *Quinn and Bloom*.[50] The defendants, who were charged with keeping a disorderly house, sought to use in evidence a filmed reconstruction of striptease performances made three months after the performances that had led to the charges. Upholding the trial judge's refusal to admit the evidence, Ashworth J. highlighted the potential unreliability of such evidence:

> "It is obvious that to allow such a reconstruction would be introducing a method of proof which would be most unsatisfactory for the reason that it would be almost impossible to analyse motion by motion those slight differences which may in the totality result in a scene of quite a different character from that performed on the night in question."[51]

Although the judgment does not bring out the point, it seems clear that a jury might well have been misled by this piece of self-serving evidence. Indeed the defendants impliedly admitted as much by conceding that some of the movements in the film, such as ones of a snake, could not be said with any certainty to be the same as those made at the material time. Thus, although the film had some relevance in illustrating the testimony of the police officers who had witnessed the performances in question, it was insufficient to outweigh the risk of leading the jury astray. The Court of Criminal Appeal in fact explained the

---

[46] *Hollingham v Head* (1858) 27 L.J.C.P. 241.

[47] *Hollingham v Head* (1858) 27 L.J.C.P. 241 at 242.

[48] *Whitehead* (1843) 3 Car. & Kir. 202 at 203.

[49] On the other hand, the interests of avoiding confusion and bewilderment of the jury may sometimes justify the admission of evidence of background and context that will enable the evidence going to the facts in issue to be better understood: see, e.g. *Sawoniuk* [2000] 2 Cr.App.R. 220 CA.

[50] *Quinn and Bloom* [1962] 2 Q.B. 245 CCA.

[51] *Quinn and Bloom* [1962] 2 Q.B. 245 at 257 CCA.

exclusion of the evidence with a terse claim that it was "not the best evidence".[52] This evidentiary ghost puts in a fleeting appearance from time to time in modern cases, but the "best evidence" rule long ago lost any claims it had to universality.[53] It is now best regarded as a general principle of good practice which may be invoked to lend support to decisions reached on other grounds. The potential unreliability of evidence is commonly said to be a matter of weight for the factfinder to assess, but the Court of Criminal Appeal clearly took the view that in some cases, of which this was one, a judgment could be made that the problem was so great as to make the evidence inadmissible in law. There is no reference in the judgment of the court to exclusion in this case being a matter of discretion.

(D) Remoteness

Remoteness is a term which figures prominently in many discussions of relevance. It is sometimes used in a rather general way so that evidence may be described as too remote if it has one or more of the characteristics discussed above under the headings of superfluity, multiplicity of issues and confusion of the jury.

3–014

A narrower usage is concerned with the separate argument that evidence may be insufficiently relevant (too remote) if it invites the jury to draw speculative inferences for which there is no independent foundation. The leading authority is the difficult and controversial case of *Blastland*.[54] The defendant was charged with the buggery and murder of a 12-year-old boy. In evidence the defendant admitted meeting the boy on the evening in question and engaging in an act of attempted buggery with him, but claimed that he panicked and ran off when he saw another man nearby who might have observed what he had been doing. He had given a description of the other man, who had been fully investigated by the police. It was the defendant's case that it was this man, identified in the appeal as Mark, who must have carried out the buggery and murder. At trial the prosecution had made certain formal admissions relating to the police investigation of Mark, to Mark's movements on the evening of the murder and to his known past homosexual acts with adults but not with children. The issue of Mark's identity as the murderer was therefore squarely before the jury, but what the jury had not known was that Mark had made and retracted a series of confessions to the offences with which the defendant was charged. Those confessions were inadmissible hearsay at common law if testified to by a person other than Mark, and the trial judge had refused leave to the defence to call Mark as a witness and treat him as hostile so as to be able to cross-examine him on what he had said at the police interviews.[55] The defence had then sought to call witnesses to testify

---

[52] *Quinn and Bloom* [1962] 2 Q.B. 245 CCA.

[53] The history of the rule is summarised in *Cross on Evidence*, 5th edn (1979), pp.15–17. In *Masquerade Music Ltd v Springsteen* [2001] EWCA Civ 563; [2001] E.M.L.R. 654 at [85] Parker L.J. declared that the rule, long on its deathbed, had finally expired.

[54] *Blastland* [1986] A.C. 41 HL.

[55] Mark would have been entitled to invoke the privilege against self-incrimination in refusing to answer any such questions.

that Mark had told them, before the body had been discovered, that a boy had been murdered. The trial judge ruled this evidence inadmissible.

The House of Lords upheld the ruling and dismissed the defendant's appeal. The evidence of Mark's knowledge of the murder was agreed to be inadmissible. This was not, as the judge had thought, because it was excluded by the hearsay rule, but because it was insufficiently relevant. According to Lord Bridge, evidence of a third party's state of mind is only admissible when the state of mind "is either itself directly in issue at the trial or is of direct and immediate relevance to an issue which arises at the trial".[56] Lord Bridge's analysis of this point deserves careful consideration. It was clear, as he said, that Mark's knowledge of the boy's murder was not a fact in issue at the trial. Was it a fact relevant to the issue of the defendant's guilt? The answer, equally clearly, was that it might be, depending on how that knowledge had been acquired. But, as Lord Bridge indicated, there was no admissible evidence as to the source of Mark's knowledge. Therefore any inference that it was acquired because it was he rather than the defendant who had committed the murder was necessarily speculative. The inference might or might not be correct.

3–015   The difficulty with accepting this as a valid argument for exclusion is that competing inferences may be drawn from a great deal of circumstantial evidence that no one doubts is rightly admitted.[57] Suppose, further, that the prosecution had been seeking to adduce the evidence of Mark's knowledge in support of a charge that *he* was the murderer. There can be no question but that it would have been admitted in proof of his guilt. It would not by itself make his guilt certain, or even probable, but it would increase the apparent probability of his guilt. The murderer had to be a member, possibly the only member, of a class of persons with knowledge of the murder before the body was discovered, and the evidence placed Mark as a member of that class. If the evidence of Mark's knowledge increased the probability of his guilt, it must tend therefore to decrease the probability of Blastland's guilt, given that there was nothing to suggest that he and Mark had been acting in concert.

At this point it is clear that a major collision between logic and policy is taking place. The prosecution may use circumstantial evidence of special knowledge to prove the identity of the defendant as the murderer, but the defendant may not, apparently, use such evidence to weaken the prosecution case by throwing suspicion on to another. Why should this be so? Part of the answer may derive from the values of the criminal process. Viewed from the perspective of crime control values, it would be contrary to efficiency and to the aim of convicting the guilty to allow defendants to engage in endless speculation about other persons who, as a result of inference from evidence such as their special knowledge, might be thought to have committed the offence in question. In this way trials would be unacceptably prolonged, issues multiplied and, most crucially, the attention of factfinders diverted from the strength of the case against the defendant. The main part of the answer, as far as the House of Lords was concerned, was the internal consistency of the rules of admissibility. Lord Bridge

---

[56] *Blastland* [1986] A.C. 41 at 54.
[57] e.g. evidence of the accused's lies to the police, discussed below. See also *Sanders* [1997] Crim. L.R. 751 CA.

pointed to "the very odd result" of holding that a defendant may not give evidence of an oral confession by a third party,[58] but may try to achieve the same effect indirectly by evidence of a third party's statements showing special knowledge of the crime. From this perspective the decision in *Blastland* simply represents a refusal to permit the ban on third-party confessions to be outflanked by the hearsay exception for evidence of states of mind.

However, the decision also demonstrates an uneasy compromise with the parallel objective of not convicting the innocent. Lord Bridge commented that the formal admissions and evidence relating to Mark's movements on the evening of the murder were all:

> "properly put before the jury as relevant and admissible material which they could be invited to weigh in the scales against the powerful case adduced for the Crown in deciding whether it might have been Mark, not the appellant, who murdered [the boy]."[59]

This amounts to saying in effect that, in the interests of due process and the avoidance of wrongful conviction, the defendant may use some types of circumstantial evidence against a third party but not others. On the facts of the case the difference cannot be justified on the basis of different degrees of relevance. As well as being reliable, the evidence of Mark's special knowledge was on the face of it more incriminating than the general evidence of his opportunity and character. There is therefore a contradiction in *Blastland* which makes the reasoning of the decision even more unconvincing.

Unease about this case is increased by the earlier decision of the Court of Appeal in *Steel*.[60] A trial judge had refused to permit the defendant to cross-examine a police officer about lies told by a third party, who had been suspected of the offence, concerning his whereabouts and movements at the material time. In upholding the judge's refusal Lord Lane C.J. stated: "what Mr R may or may not have been doing... at this particular time was an irrelevance".[61] Although relevance is a question to be determined according to the facts of each case, this decision looks inconsistent in principle with the approval given in *Blastland* to the admission of certain items of circumstantial evidence tending to incriminate Mark.

It is plain that the law in this area is confused and hard to justify. There cannot be any doubt that a defendant may adduce direct evidence that a third party committed the offence.[62] A witness in *Blastland* who had seen Mark kill the boy would have been able to testify to that fact. Equally, if Mark had been called as a witness, the defence could have asked him whether he had committed the

3–016

---

[58] *Blastland* [1986] A.C. 41 at 53. Such evidence was inadmissible hearsay at common law, and a third-party confession remains hearsay under the definition in ss.114 and 115 of the Criminal Justice Act 2003. However, an oral or written confession by a third party who is not available as a witness may now be admissible under s.116 of the Criminal Justice Act 2003. A third-party confession might also be admissible under the inclusionary discretion conferred by s.114(1)(d). See Ch.17.
[59] *Blastland* [1986] A.C. 41 at 51.
[60] *Steel* (1981) 73 Cr.App.R. 173 CA.
[61] *Steel* (1981) 73 Cr.App.R. 173 at 186 CA.
[62] Confirmed by the Court of Appeal in *Greenwood* [2004] EWCA Crim 1388; [2005] 1 Cr.App.R. 7 at [41](i).

murder.[63] However, it is equally clear that the common law rule in *Turner*,[64] confirmed in *Blastland*, prevented the admission of a third party confession made out of court, and in principle the confession remains inadmissible hearsay under the statutory scheme for hearsay evidence enacted by the Criminal Justice Act 2003.[65] The decision in *Blastland* excludes evidence of a third party's state of mind when it is sought to use that evidence as the equivalent of an implied confession. With other types of circumstantial evidence the position is unclear. It may be excluded as irrelevant or speculative, but much will depend on the particular facts of each case and what, if anything, the prosecution are prepared to admit.[66]

This last point is well illustrated by *Greenwood*,[67] where the Court of Appeal emphasised the use of formal admissions by the prosecution as a pragmatic means of doing justice in this type of case. The defendant, who had volunteered a confession to a murder three years earlier, wished to cast doubt on his confession and guilt by reference to facts pointing to the possible commission of the murder by one or other of two other men, neither of whom had been charged. The prosecution was prepared to make admissions as to these facts, which included a tape-recorded interview with the victim in which she had given an account of violence she had previously suffered at the hands of one of the men, Parkinson, a former boyfriend. On a retrial, the first trial having resulted in a hung jury, the judge excluded the admissions relating to Parkinson as irrelevant, saying that there was no evidence to suggest his involvement in the murder and implying that the evidence of his motive (via the tape-recording) would simply be an invitation to the jury to speculate. The Court of Appeal quashed the defendant's conviction for manslaughter on the ground that the admissions had been wrongly excluded. According to Waller L.J.:

> "The practice of the Crown being prepared to make admissions in relation to facts which 'might' point to a third party having committed the crime, which the defendant denies having committed, is long-standing. Such evidence is relevant and admissible to be weighed in the scales against the evidence adduced by the Crown that it was the defendant they have charged. Of course the Crown cannot be forced to make admissions if it does not accept that the admission points to the possibility of a third party being the perpetrator. Furthermore, if it is prepared to make an admission it can seek other admissions from the defence or put in evidence of its own in order that the admission can go fairly in its context before the jury".[68]

3–017 How far courts will take this endorsement of prosecution admissions remains to be seen. Many prosecutors may have reservations about the Court of Appeal's further suggestion that they may have some obligation to make admissions, on

---

[63] Although, as noted above, he could invoke the privilege against self-incrimination and refuse to answer.

[64] *Turner* (1975) 61 Cr.App.R. 67 at 88 CA.

[65] It might be admitted as an exception under s.116 or s.114(1)(d); see above.

[66] See further A. Choo, "The Notion of Relevance and Defence Evidence" [1993] Crim. L.R. 114.

[67] *Greenwood* [2004] EWCA Crim 1388; [2005] 1 Cr.App.R. 7.

[68] *Greenwood* [2004] EWCA Crim 1388; [2005] 1 Cr.App.R. 7 at [40]. At [38] per Waller L.J. commended the use of admissions to circumvent the hearsay rule where a "strict application of the rule could lead to the possibility of injustice". The rule's application to the tape-recording was not analysed in detail: the recording clearly was hearsay evidence, but would have been admissible under s.23 of the Criminal Justice Act 1988 since the maker of the hearsay statement was dead and therefore unavailable as a witness.

the basis of a proposition that a defendant must be entitled to produce any evidence that points to another person having a motive to commit the murder, or any other evidence that would point to the possibility that another person might have done it.[69] This proposition is extremely wide. Unqualified, it is inconsistent in principle with *Blastland*, since it seems to open the door to numerous speculative inferences. Trial judges are likely to be concerned about proliferation of issues and distraction of the jury if admissions were to be made extensively on this basis.

In summary, all the cases discussed under this and the previous three headings seem to treat the relevance of evidence as involving not just a question of the existence of its logical relevance, but also a question of its degree. The cases suggest that decisions about relevance require a judgment[70] that the degree of relevance is sufficient to outweigh the costs of admission so as to make the evidence admissible in law. Such judgments can be reversed on appeal if the appeal court regards the trial judge's decision as wrong.

5. Case study of relevance I: "lifestyle" evidence in drugs cases

A series of cases has involved offences related to controlled drugs, where the prosecution have adduced evidence of the accused's possession of large amounts of cash, or evidence of the accused's lavish lifestyle, or evidence of the accused's possession of drugs paraphernalia. The issue may be whether the accused was knowingly in possession of drugs found on his premises, or, in a smuggling case, in his luggage. His defence may be that the drugs were planted on him by the police or a third party. More commonly, the issue is whether the accused's admitted possession of a quantity of drugs was with intent to supply, or whether the drugs were intended only for his own use.

3–018

Two questions have been said to arise in these cases.[71] The first is the relevance of the evidence to the issues in the case. Does evidence of cash or lifestyle increase the probability that the defendant was knowingly in possession of drugs found on him, or that he intended to supply drugs found on him?[72] If it does not, the evidence is irrelevant and should be excluded as a matter of law. The second question concerns prejudice. If the judge thinks that the evidence has probative value, the admission of the evidence may nonetheless be prejudicial. The jury may infer that the cash and the lifestyle represent the fruits of previous offences, and that the defendant is likely to be guilty because he has committed similar offences in the past. This is the "forbidden chain of reasoning" that the common law rule against evidence of bad character and other misconduct generally prohibited. However, the Criminal Justice Act 2003 abolished the common law rule and introduced a new scheme of admissibility for evidence of

---

[69] *Greenwood* [2004] EWCA Crim 1388; [2005] 1 Cr.App.R. 7 at [41](i).
[70] Note, however, the statutory *discretion* to exclude (admissible) hearsay evidence as an undue waste of time (Criminal Justice Act 2003 s.126), and the *discretion* at common law and under PACE s.78 to exclude evidence where its prejudicial effect would outweigh its probative value. See further below.
[71] *Morris* [1995] 2 Cr.App.R. 69 CA.
[72] Evidence of possession of large amounts of cash and of lavish lifestyle may also be relevant to charges of conspiracy to supply drugs: see, e.g. *Malik* [2000] 2 Cr.App.R. 8.

bad character, which includes making admissible evidence of the defendant's propensity to commit offences of the kind with which he is charged.[73] In view of this change it is now unlikely, although not impossible, that a judge, having found such evidence to be relevant, will then exclude it on the basis that its prejudicial tendency exceeds its probative value.

Returning to the question of relevance, in *Batt*,[74] one of the earliest cases in the series, the defendant was charged with possession of 500 grammes of cannabis with intent to supply. The drugs had been found in a rabbit hutch in the garden of the defendant's house; the defendant denied any knowledge of the drugs. The trial judge admitted evidence that £150 in cash had been found in a kettle in the defendant's house. Allowing the appeal, the Court of Appeal held that possession of the money was not probative of the offence charged, since the money could not have anything to do with an intention to supply in the future the cannabis that had been found. Given the small amount of money found, an inference from it that the defendant was a drug-dealer was little more than speculative. Many people might keep that amount of cash about the house for payment of bills. The decision is probably right on the facts.

3–019　　However, in some cases the prosecution may be able to show that the defendant is in possession of much larger amounts of cash as well as a quantity of drugs. In these cases it can be argued that the jury can draw a strong inference that the defendant is engaged in a continuing course of drug-dealing. In *Wright*,[75] the defendant was found in possession of a quantity of cocaine, £16,000 in cash and a gold necklace worth about £9,000. The Court of Appeal held that evidence of the defendant's possession of the cash and the necklace had been rightly admitted. It was relevant, according to the court, on the issue of the intention with which the defendant was in possession of the cocaine. Beldam L.J. spelt out the background generalisations involved:

> "Substantial capital in hard cash is essential for someone who is minded to deal in these drugs, and so it comes about that those who carry on the trade are frequently found to have in their possession large amounts of cash, either because they have received it for sales already made or because they need it to take advantage of any opportunity which may arise for the purchase of fresh supplies of the drug."[76]

The tendency of the courts subsequently has been to follow the approach in *Wright*, on the issue of intent to supply, in any case where a sizeable amount of cash has been found on the accused personally or at his home.[77] *Batt* has been explained as a decision on the particular facts of the case, and as not laying down a strict rule that evidence of possession of money is never admissible on a charge of possession of drugs with intent to supply. In *Grant*, where the defendant was found in possession of a quantity of crack cocaine and £912 in cash, Lord Taylor C.J. confirmed that the finding of money is capable of being relevant to the issue

---

[73] See Ch.19.

[74] *Batt* [1994] Crim. L.R. 592 CA.

[75] *Wright* [1994] Crim. L.R. 55 CA.

[76] This passage from Beldam L.J.'s judgment is set out in *Morris* [1995] 2 Cr.App.R. 69 at 75.

[77] *Gordon* [1995] 2 Cr.App.R. 61 CA; *Morris* [1995] 2 Cr.App.R. 69 CA; *Brown* [1995] Crim. L.R. 716 CA; *Grant* [1996] 1 Cr.App.R. 73 CA; *Edwards* [1998] Crim. L.R. 207 CA.

of intent to supply, on the basis that it may indicate the defendant's ongoing trade in drugs. Lord Taylor C.J. went on to say that the judge had to give a direction concerning the jury's evaluation of this evidence. The jury had to be told that they must consider any explanation which the accused put forward for possession of the money. They could treat the evidence of the money as probative only if they rejected any such innocent explanation and rejected any possibility of the money being in the defendant's possession for reasons other than drug-dealing.[78] If they concluded that the money showed not merely past dealing, but an *ongoing* dealing in drugs, then they could take this into account in deciding whether the necessary intention had been proved.[79]

What about charges of possession of drugs, or of smuggling, where the accused denies knowledge of drugs found on him or in his luggage or premises? Does evidence of the finding of cash, or of the defendant's lavish lifestyle, yield an inference that he is "knowingly" in possession of drugs? The initial reaction of the courts was to say "No". In *Halpin*,[80] Rougier J. said that it was:

3–020

> "unarguable that such evidence cannot afford any probative value when the issue is possession ... it is not and cannot be relevant to the issue of whether or not the defendant was in possession of the drug."[81]

Later cases have been more cautious, and the dictum in *Halpin* has had a mixed reception. It has been cited without disapproval on more than one occasion,[82] but in *Guney*[83] the Court of Appeal doubted it and refused to follow it. In *Guney*, a large quantity of heroin was found in a wardrobe in the defendant's house along with a box containing nearly £25,000 in cash and a handgun. The defendant did not dispute possession of the money, which he explained as savings he had made whilst a bankrupt to pay off debts. He claimed that the drugs and the gun had been planted on him. However, these items were physically close to the box of cash which the defendant had placed in the wardrobe the evening before his arrest. In addition the defendant, when interviewed, had either lied or given inconsistent explanations about the source of the cash. The Court of Appeal held that in these circumstances evidence of the finding of the money was relevant and rightly admitted:

> "The question whether evidence is relevant depends not on abstract legal theory but on the individual circumstances of each particular case ... Accordingly although evidence of cash

---

[78] In *Malik* [2000] 2 Cr.App.R. 8 the Court of Appeal explained that this did not require the judge to direct the jury in terms that if they rejected the defendant's explanation for the wealth and lifestyle they then had to rule out all other possible explanations other than the prosecution's before treating this as evidence of a conspiracy to supply. The court was rightly concerned not to prompt juries into engaging in "fact-free speculation".

[79] *Grant* was followed in *Graham* [2007] EWCA Crim 1499, but Toulson L.J. commented (at [25]) that in view of the admissibility of propensity evidence under the Criminal Justice Act 2003 a distinction between treating possession of cash as evidence that D is an [ongoing] drug dealer and evidence that he has dealt in drugs in the past and has a propensity to do so is a distinction without a practical difference.

[80] *Halpin* [1996] Crim. L.R. 112 CA.

[81] This dictum is set out in *Guney* [1998] 2 Cr.App.R. 242 at 264.

[82] *Scott* [1996] Crim. L.R. 652 CA; *Richards* Unreported February 24, 1997 CA.

[83] *Guney* [1998] 2 Cr.App.R. 242 CA. See also *Edwards* [1998] Crim. L.R. 207 at 208.

and lifestyle may only rarely be relevant where the charge is simple possession, we are unable to accept that as a matter of law such evidence must, automatically, be excluded as irrelevant...

...where possession with intent is charged, there are numerous sets of circumstances in which cash and lifestyle evidence may be relevant and admissible to the issue of possession itself, not least to the issue of knowledge as an ingredient of possession...

...The coincidence that his cash was physically close to firearms and drugs which belonged to someone else, and that the appellant either lied or gave inconsistent explanations about the source of the cash when interviewed, were... all matters for consideration by the jury when considering the defence that he was ignorant of the presence of the drugs and firearms and therefore not knowingly in possession of them."[84]

In *Yalman*,[85] the issue was whether the defendant was "knowingly" involved in the illegal importation of heroin by his elderly father whom the defendant had met at the airport off a flight from Cyprus. The Court of Appeal again commented that the relevance of evidence depends on the nature of the charge and the particular facts of the case. The court went on to hold that evidence of the defendant's drug dependency and of his possession of drugs paraphernalia was relevant on the issue of the defendant's knowledge, once it was established that there was a prima facie case that the defendant was involved in the illegal importation of the drugs. Evidence of involvement included the curious fact that, although the defendant met his father at the airport, he did not greet his father at the first opportunity, but waited until his father had reached the entrance to the airport. It would have been even more curious if, by coincidence, the drugs had been planted on the father of a drug user without the knowledge of either of them.

In the great majority of these drugs cases the Court of Appeal has upheld the admission of evidence of cash or lifestyle, while emphasising that the issue is to be determined by a close examination of the circumstances of the case and the precise issue to which the evidence is claimed to be relevant. If that is so, there is really no need for the plethora of reported cases on the subject. Now that it has been established that there are no absolute rules prohibiting the use of such evidence, the general principles of relevance and exclusionary discretion are capable of dealing with the questions of admissibility.[86]

6.   Case study of relevance II: the lies of the accused

3–021   If the accused has told lies in connection with the offence charged, most people would intuitively consider that fact to be relevant to the issue of his guilt of the offence. They would ask the obvious question: why did the defendant lie about the matter? Many would then answer this question with what looks like an equally obvious response: he knew he was guilty and therefore lied to get out of trouble. In this way the lies of the accused would be treated as having probative value on the issue of guilt. They would be evidence of guilt and would tend to support other evidence of guilt.

---

[84] *Guney* [1998] 2 Cr.App.R. 242 at 265–267.
[85] *Yalman* [1998] 2 Cr.App.R. 269 CA.
[86] See also the case-note on *Yalman* and *Guney* by M. Redmayne, "Drugs, money and relevance" (1999) 3 E. & P. 128.

This superficially attractive common sense reasoning has a potential flaw. Defendants do not always lie because they know they are guilty. They may lie for a number of possible reasons other than guilt. This point was well made by the trial judge in *Burge and Pegg*[87] in directing the jury:

"Defendants in criminal cases may have lied for many reasons, for example to bolster a true defence. They may feel that they are wrongly implicated and although innocent that nobody will believe them and so they lie just to conceal matters which look bad but which in truth are not bad. They may lie to protect someone else. They may lie because they are embarrassed or ashamed about other conduct of theirs which is not the offence charged. They may lie out of panic or confusion. All sorts of reasons."

Consequently a factfinder should not be too quick to jump to conclusions from evidence that the accused has lied. Alternative explanations for the lie, other than the accused's consciousness of his guilt, ought to be considered and rejected before any adverse inference is drawn. In the leading case of *Lucas*,[88] the Court of Appeal held that juries should be given a specific warning direction from the judge about the use that they could make of evidence of lies by the accused. The direction has to include a reminder about the possible innocent reasons for lying. *Lucas* was, however, a case under the old law of corroboration, and the warning set out the conditions which had to be satisfied before the jury could treat the defendant's lies as corroboration of evidence given against him by an accomplice. With the abolition of corroboration requirements, not all these conditions are now in point, although lies may still have probative value on the issue of guilt. Subsequently, in *Burge and Pegg*,[89] the Court of Appeal said that a *Lucas* direction should if possible be tailored to the circumstances of the case, but it will normally be sufficient if it makes two basic points.

The jury should be told that before they can treat the lie as evidence of the accused's guilt two conditions must be satisfied.   **3–022**

"1.   that the lie must be admitted or proved beyond reasonable doubt, and
2.   that the mere fact that the defendant has lied is not in itself evidence of guilt since defendants may lie for innocent reasons, so only if the jury is sure that the defendant did not lie for an innocent reason can a lie support the prosecution case."[90]

When must such a direction be given? One situation where it is not required is what the Court of Appeal in *Burge and Pegg* called "the normal case where there is a straight conflict of evidence".[91] Suppose, for example, that V testifies that D raped her. In his evidence D admits the intercourse but maintains that it was with V's consent. The jury will have to decide which of V and D is telling the truth. If the jury concludes that it is V, so that the intercourse was without her consent, the case is proved against D. He is guilty of rape.[92] It then follows that he has lied in

---

[87] *Burge and Pegg* [1996] 1 Cr.App.R. 163 at 171 CA.
[88] *Lucas* [1981] Q.B. 720 CA.
[89] *Burge and Pegg* [1996] 1 Cr.App.R. 163 at 174 CA.
[90] An "innocent" reason need not be wholly innocent and may include a fear of acknowledging a lesser guilt: *Bullen* [2008] EWCA Crim 4 at [42].
[91] *Burge and Pegg* [1996] 1 Cr.App.R. 163 at 173. See also *Harron* [1996] 2 Cr.App.R. 457 CA, where the authorities are reviewed.
[92] That is, assuming that he does not raise a separate issue of reasonable belief in consent.

the witness box, but this is not a lie which the prosecution are seeking to use as an item of evidence in itself to prove guilt. Where the question is whether the jury believe the prosecution witnesses, who say that the defendant committed the offence, or the defendant, who says that he did not, the issue of whether the defendant is lying is co-extensive with the central issue of guilt. A *Lucas* direction in such a case does not just add complexity to the jury's task in deciding the credibility conflict. It is confusing because it is a kind of "bootstraps" argument. It is incoherent for a jury to say that they believe the prosecution witnesses in preference to the defendant, and then to use the conclusion that the defendant must have lied as a further reason for believing the prosecution witnesses.

A second situation where a *Lucas* direction may not be required arises where an accused tells a lie in a police interview and also fails to mention a fact which he later relies on in his defence. If he subsequently produces the *same* explanation for the lie and for the failure to mention the fact relied on in defence, it is usually wrong, because confusing, for a judge to give both a *Lucas* direction and a direction under s.34 of the Criminal Justice and Public Order Act 1994 about the possibility of an adverse inference from the failure to mention the fact in question. The judge should select and adapt the direction more appropriate to the facts and issues in the case. This will usually be the s.34 direction, which can incorporate if appropriate the point of the *Lucas* direction that a lie may have an innocent explanation. If the jury accept an accused's later explanation for a lie as true, it would be inconsistent for them then to draw an adverse inference under s.34 on the basis that the same explanation, when offered to account for the non-disclosure of the fact in question, was a late invention.[93]

A *Lucas* direction *is* required where the prosecution are seeking to use a lie by the accused as equivalent to an implied admission of guilt. This will be where the lie relates to a material issue, but one which is essentially about some subsidiary or collateral matter, so that the lie provides additional support for other evidence pointing to guilt. In *Burge and Pegg* the Court of Appeal summarised the circumstances where the direction is usually required. The first is where the defence relies on an alibi. If the alibi is then admitted by the defendant to be false, or is independently shown to be false, its falsity may provide support for an identification which the defendant alleges to be mistaken. However, the jury must be directed that before they can treat as probative the defendant's lie about his opportunity to commit the offence, they must be satisfied that the lie was a deliberate attempt to deceive, and not the result of an innocent motive.[94] Secondly, the direction must be given:

"where the judge considers it desirable or necessary to suggest that the jury should look for support or corroboration of one piece of evidence from other evidence in the case, and amongst that other evidence draws attention to lies told, or allegedly told, by the defendant."[95]

---

[93] See *Hackett* [2011] EWCA Crim 380, summarising the effect of earlier authorities.

[94] *Turnbull* [1977] Q.B. 224 CA; *Goodway* [1993] 4 All E.R. 894 CA. See also *Peacock* [1998] Crim. L.R. 681 CA, and commentary by Professor D. J. Birch.

[95] *Burge and Pegg* [1996] 1 Cr.App.R. 163 at 173. This was the situation in *Lucas* [1981] Q.B. 720.

To these well-established categories of case the Court of Appeal in *Burge and Pegg* added two more. In effect these generalise the specific cases just referred to and overlap with them:

> "3.   Where the prosecution seek to show that something said, either in or out of the court, in relation to a separate and distinct issue was a lie, and to rely on that lie as evidence of guilt in relation to the charge which is sought to be proved.
> 4.   Where although the prosecution have not adopted the approach to which we have just referred, the judge reasonably envisages that there is a real danger that the jury may do so."[96]

To illustrate these principles, suppose D is charged with unlawfully wounding P, a man whom D knows, by hitting him with a beer glass in a pub. D denies the attack, saying that P inflicted the injury himself and is trying to frame D in revenge for D taking up with P's girlfriend. If the jury reject this story and believe P, they necessarily have no choice but to convict D as a matter of logic.[97] A *Lucas* direction is not required. D's untruthful story relates to the central issue of his guilt of unlawful wounding; it is not a case where a lie about a subsidiary matter forms a link in a chain of reasoning intended to demonstrate guilt. Compare this with the situation where D says that he was drinking wine in the pub and did not have a beer glass in his hand at any time. The prosecution call the barman who testifies that he served D with a pint of beer shortly before the attack on P. If the jury accept the barman's evidence, it seems to follow that D has lied about his possession of a weapon of the type used in the attack. The prosecution might argue that the jury could infer from the lie about having the weapon that D had in fact used it to attack P. Even if the prosecution did not make this an express part of their case, there is a danger that the jury might do so anyway. A *Lucas* direction would therefore be required.

C.   EXCLUSIONARY RULES

One of the most striking characteristics of the common law of evidence is the existence of a significant number of rules which forbid the reception of logically relevant evidence. The common law rule against hearsay prohibited the admission of statements made other than by a testifying witness as evidence of the facts stated.[98] The opinion rule stipulates that ordinary witnesses must speak only as to fact and not as to the inferences that they draw from the facts. Expert witnesses can give their opinion on matters requiring expertise, but should not express a view on the ultimate issue in the case. The common law rule against evidence of bad character and other misconduct generally prohibited the giving of

3–023

3–024

---

[96] *Burge and Pegg* [1996] 1 Cr.App.R. 163 confirming the dictum to this effect in *Goodway* [1993] 4 All E.R. 894 at 900–902 CA. A direction is not required where the lie is relevant only to the accused's credibility as a witness: *Smith* [1995] Crim. L.R. 305.

[97] See the judgment of North P. in *Dehar* [1969] N.Z.L.R. 763 at 765.

[98] The common law rule against hearsay was abolished by the Criminal Justice Act 2003 (s.118(2)), but the new statutory regime for the admissibility of hearsay evidence is still founded on a principle that hearsay evidence is excluded unless and until certain conditions additional to relevance have been satisfied—see Criminal Justice Act 2003 s.114(1), discussed in Ch.17.

evidence of other crimes committed by a defendant.[99] The rule of legal privilege protects confidential communications between lawyer and client. The doctrine of public interest immunity asserts that certain types of evidence must be withheld from the adjudication if their disclosure would be injurious to the public interest. Evidence may not in general be given of a witness's previous consistent statements.

The rationale of each rule will be considered when the topic is dealt with in detail. It is worth making the point at this stage that the rationale will often include some of the constraints already discussed in connection with relevance and will represent a judgment that the "costs" of the type of evidence in question are sufficiently great to justify a general rule of restriction, rather than an ad hoc decision on the facts of each case. Other parts of the rationale of particular rules may be referable to the need to protect certain rights of parties to litigation or the need to ensure legitimacy of decision in the adjudication.

However, it is important not to overestimate the impact of the formal rules of admissibility in practice. There are three reasons for this. First, some of the rules are concerned with the purpose for which certain evidence may be adduced. They may prohibit use for one purpose but not for another. This means that the evidence will go before the factfinder with, in the case of the jury, an appropriate limiting instruction from the judge. There is considerable scepticism about the efficacy of such instructions in some cases and whether juries are capable of understanding and applying some of the more refined distinctions. Secondly, the formal rules are generally accompanied by formal exceptions that may cut down the ambit of the restriction very severely. For example, even at common law there were numerous exceptions to the hearsay rule. While they did not always achieve the objectives of admitting reliable hearsay when it was the best evidence available, they did ameliorate some of the worst effects of the original rule. Modern statutory reforms, particularly in civil cases, may reduce the importance of some of the common law's exclusionary rules virtually to vanishing point. Thirdly, there is a persistent tension between the strict application of the formal rules and the desire of the judges to admit evidence that appears to be both relevant and reliable. In some cases this may lead to exceptions being expanded or the general rules being reformulated or reinterpreted or, in the last resort, simply ignored.

3–025   This last point led Zuckerman to argue some years ago that in many contexts it would be more accurate to speak of guiding principles, rather than binding definitions of legal rules.[100] He suggested that courts should move, and in practice have tended to move, towards the position where the law of criminal evidence is regarded as laying down principles that guide courts in the exercise of a discretion to see that justice is done. There is much force in this argument, which might be regarded as applying to the system of criminal litigation a process which has already happened to a large extent in civil litigation. However, the process of change is erratic and its speed should not be exaggerated. There are certainly cases in which "the courts refuse to observe strict definitions when they

---

[99] The common law rules governing the admissibility of evidence of bad character were abolished by the Criminal Justice Act 2003 (s.99(1)). For discussion of the new statutory regime see Ch.19.
[100] Zuckerman, *Principles*, pp.6–13.

consider the result of observance unsatisfactory".[101] But equally, as Zuckerman acknowledged, "many judges are unaware of the extent of the discretion they possess and they are consequently discouraged from paying close attention to the general principles according to which it should be exercised".[102] In this passage Zuckerman used the term "discretion" in a weak sense to denote a judicial power of choice in making decisions about the application of the exclusionary rules. We now turn to consider the nature and scope of the more general exclusionary discretions vested in the trial judge and the principles for their exercise.

D.   EXCLUSIONARY DISCRETION IN CRIMINAL CASES

It is important to make two general points at the beginning of this section. **3–026** Questions about the existence and the exercise of a discretion to exclude evidence in a criminal case arise most often in the context of evidence which has been obtained by means that are alleged to be unlawful or unfair. Consequently many of the principles governing the discretion have been worked out in the cases on this topic, and these cases will be considered in detail in Ch.8. However, the exclusionary discretion has never been limited to cases of improperly obtained evidence, either at common law or under s.78 of PACE. The discretion to exclude evidence that is otherwise admissible goes beyond improperly obtained evidence, which is why it is appropriate to consider it at this stage.

Secondly, the term "discretion" needs clarification. As noted above, it is a term that is used with more than one meaning in the law of evidence, as in the law generally.[103] In its first, weaker, sense "discretion" refers to a legal standard, cast in broad and flexible terms, which gives the judge a good deal of latitude in its application to a given set of facts. However, once the judge concludes that the standard is satisfied on the facts before him, it is his duty to apply the standard. He is not then free to disregard it. "Discretion" in the second, stronger, sense refers to a power of the judge to act in any way that he thinks fit on the facts before him. An example of this second sense is to be found in s.8(1) of the Civil Evidence Act 1995. This section deals with proof of statements contained in documents, where such statements are admissible as evidence in civil proceedings. Before being admitted, the document must be authenticated, but the statute provides that it may be authenticated "in such manner as the court may approve". Thus once the court finds the statement in the document to be admissible it may choose any criteria for authentication of the document that it considers appropriate.

On the other hand, the statutory power to exclude evidence in criminal proceedings is an example of discretion in the first sense. Section 78(1) of PACE provides, in summary, that a court "may" refuse to allow prosecution evidence to be given if its admission would have such an adverse effect on the fairness of the

---

[101] Zuckerman, *Principles*, p.11.
[102] Zuckerman, *Principles*, pp.12–13.
[103] See generally R. M. Dworkin, *Taking Rights Seriously* (1977), esp. pp.31–33; D. J. Galligan, *Discretionary Powers* (Oxford: 1986); R. Pattenden, *Judicial Discretion and Criminal Litigation* (Oxford: Clarendon Press, 1990).

proceedings that the court ought not to admit it.[104] In *Chalkley* the Court of Appeal held that, despite the permissive word "may", a judge who concluded that admission of the evidence would have the effect referred to in the section could not then logically "exercise a discretion" to admit the evidence.[105] At this stage the judge would have no discretion; there would be a duty to exclude the evidence once the judge decided that the broad test in the section was satisfied.

1. Discretionary exclusion at common law

3–027   Since at least the case of *Christie*[106] the common law has recognised the existence of some discretion to exclude otherwise admissible evidence in criminal cases. The precise scope and limits of this discretion have never been completely settled, but it is generally agreed that the relevant principles include at least the following.

(A)   Evidence whose prejudicial effect exceeds its probative value

3–028   This was the first type of case to be recognised. The principle that the judge has a discretion to exclude evidence the prejudicial effect of which exceeds its probative value has been confirmed on numerous occasions,[107] and was put beyond doubt by the authoritative statement of the House of Lords in *Sang*.[108] In this case the certified question for the House was whether a trial judge has any discretion "to refuse to allow evidence, being evidence other than evidence of admission, to be given in any circumstances in which such evidence is relevant and of more than minimal probative value". All the members of the Appellate Committee were agreed that, whatever the exact limits of the discretion, it certainly included cases where the probative value of the evidence was exceeded by its prejudicial effect.[109] This was said to be founded on the judge's duty to secure a fair trial for the accused by preventing unfair use of evidence at trial.[110]

In *Sang*, Lord Diplock referred to three examples of cases subject to this type of discretion. They were cases of "similar fact" evidence,[111] cases of cross-examination of the accused on his previous convictions and bad character

---

[104]   The full text of s.78(1) is set out below.

[105]   *Chalkley* [1998] 2 Cr.App.R. 79 at 105, confirming *Middlebrook and Caygill* unreported February 18, 1992 CA.

[106]   *Christie* [1914] A.C. 545 HL.

[107]   Including *Noor Mohammed v R.* [1949] A.C. 182 PC; *Harris v DPP* [1952] A.C. 694 HL; *Selvey v DPP* [1970] A.C. 304 HL.

[108]   *Sang* [1980] A.C. 402.

[109]   This formulation resolved the earlier doubt whether the discretion was available only where the evidence in question was of minimal or trifling probative value. It was quite clear after *Sang* that it was not.

[110]   *Sang* [1980] A.C. 402 at 436–437 per Lord Diplock; 445 per Lord Salmon); 450 per Lord Fraser of Tullybelton); 454 per Lord Scarman.

[111]   That is, cases involving use by the prosecution of evidence of the accused's bad character and misconduct on other occasions. See Ch.18.

under s.1(f) of the Criminal Evidence Act 1898,[112] and cases involving repeated accusations of the offence made in the presence of the accused, where the issue is whether the accused's response can be inferred to be an implied admission of the truth of the accusation.[113] It seems clear that the principle is not restricted to these three types of case. Even before *Sang* this discretion had been applied in at least one case to exclude a voluntary but unreliable confession,[114] and in *Sang* Lord Diplock stated the principle in general terms when giving his answer to the certified question. There is no doubt that it would extend, for example, to the exclusion of gruesome pictures likely to inflame the jury unfairly against the accused.[115]

Evidence is unfairly prejudicial to the accused if its use at trial would tend to lead the factfinder to convict the accused for reasons other than the proper probative value of the evidence. This idea is discussed in more depth in Ch.18, where a distinction is developed between "reasoning prejudice" and "moral prejudice". Broadly speaking, reasoning prejudice may occur where the nature of the evidence may cause the factfinder significantly to overestimate the probative value of the evidence, whereas moral prejudice may occur where the nature of the evidence may cause the factfinder to convict the defendant regardless of the probative value of the evidence.

(B) Fairness to the accused

This head of discretion at common law was almost exclusively concerned with   3–029
evidence obtained by illegal or unfair means. For this reason its history, and the detailed analysis it received in *Sang*, is discussed in Ch.8. The terms of the certified question in *Sang* also covered this head of discretion. The majority of the House of Lords agreed with Lord Diplock's answer, which set out a very restrictive view of the discretion:

> "Save with regard to admissions and confessions and generally with regard to evidence obtained from the accused after the commission of the offence, [the judge] has no discretion to refuse to admit relevant admissible evidence on the ground that it was obtained by improper or unfair means. The court is not concerned with how it was obtained."[116]

This proposition expresses very clearly the traditional concern of the common law with the criminal trial. From this standpoint, the quality of the evidence adduced at the trial is the major preoccupation. The law of evidence aims to ensure the reliability of the evidence presented to the factfinder, and the avoidance of prejudice, by a whole battery of legal devices: exclusionary rules, exclusionary discretion, judicial warnings and directions about permitted uses of evidence. The orientation to events at the trial meant that the common law was not much concerned with what happened in the pre-trial stages of the case. How

---

[112] This provision was later renumbered s.1(3) of the Criminal Evidence Act 1898. It was repealed by the Criminal Justice Act 2003, which made new provision regarding the admissibility of evidence of the accused's bad character. See Ch.19.

[113] *Christie* [1914] A.C. 545 HL; see Ch.5.

[114] *Stewart* (1972) 56 Cr.App.R. 272.

[115] *Murphy* (1987) 37 A.C.R. 118 at 127; *Baker* [1989] 3 N.Z.L.R. 635.

[116] *Sang* [1980] A.C. 402 at 437.

the police, for example, obtained the evidence was immaterial in the general run of cases. This was a coherent position to take as far as *non-confessional* evidence was concerned; as we shall see in Ch.8, the reliability of such evidence is rarely a problem. Evidence, for example, of the accused's possession of drugs or stolen goods, found during an illegal search, is cogent proof of guilt in the absence of an allegation that the evidence was planted.

The great exception to this indifference of the common law to pre-trial events was evidence of incriminating statements by the accused. These were regarded with suspicion by the courts for many years and treated as potentially unreliable, on the ground that the accused might have been improperly induced to make a confession that was in fact false.[117] Curiously, in *Sang*, Lord Diplock fractured the coherence of the common law by reinterpreting the rationale of the rule against involuntary confessions in terms of the privilege against self-incrimination. This enabled him to explain that the discretion to exclude non-confessional evidence was limited, by analogy to the confessions rule, to evidence obtained from the accused by means which violated the privilege against self-incrimination, such as evidence obtained from the accused by deception. This evidence might be reliable, but might still be excluded on the basis that the accused had been unfairly induced to incriminate himself. Given, then, that the privilege against self-incrimination was being contrasted with reliability as the rationale of the confessions rule, Lord Diplock's concern seems to have been not so much with the quality of the evidence as with the unfair treatment of the accused that produced it.

3–030   This exception recognised by Lord Diplock was narrow, probably unduly narrow, and *Sang* is an unsatisfactory case in many respects.[118] Nevertheless, it was the first clear acknowledgment at the highest judicial level in England that the common law ought to have concerns that go further than the quality of the evidence adduced at the trial, and how the evidence might be used or misused by the factfinder. Although the general stance was maintained that the courts were not concerned with the means of obtaining evidence, the exception allowed that this could not be absolute. This limited recognition that the pre-trial process could not be wholly insulated from the trial was then carried a good deal further in PACE.

It was subsequently made clear that fairness to the accused was not exclusively concerned with protection of the accused from the consequences of pre-trial impropriety. In *Scott and Barnes v R*,[119] the question arose whether a trial judge had discretion to exclude the depositions of witnesses who were unavailable to testify at the trial. The Privy Council held that *Sang* had not exhaustively defined the categories of case where a judge had discretion to exclude evidence in the interests of securing a fair trial for the accused. Lord Griffiths said that the House of Lords in *Sang* had not considered the problem of depositions of absent witnesses. He went on to hold that there was a discretion to exclude the sworn deposition of a deceased witness, although a discretion to be exercised with great restraint.

---

[117] *Warickshall* (1783) 1 Leach 263; *Baldry* (1852) 16 J.P. 276; *Ibrahim v R.* [1914] A.C. 599.
[118] See the critique of the case in Ch.8.
[119] *Scott and Barnes v R.* [1989] A.C. 1242 PC. See also *Grant v R.* [2006] UKPC 2 at [21(3)].

2.   PACE section 82(3): the preservation of the common law

PACE has two provisions dealing with judicial discretion to exclude evidence in   **3–031**
criminal trials. These are ss.78(1) and 82(3). The more straightforward provision
is s.82(3). This provides:

> "Nothing in this Part of this Act shall prejudice any power of a court to exclude evidence
> (whether by preventing questions from being put or otherwise) at its discretion."

It is generally accepted that this section is intended to preserve any existing
exclusionary discretion at common law, whatever the ambit of that discretion
might be. It follows that the law discussed above remains good law as far as it
recognises categories of case in which an exclusionary discretion exists. The
status of decisions, such as the decision in *Sang* itself, that there is no such
discretion in certain cases of improperly obtained evidence, is considered in Ch.8.
The common law can therefore still be invoked by the defendant in a suitable
case, such as where the police have tricked him into providing incriminating
evidence against himself. An example occurred in the trial of Colin Stagg for the
murder of Rachel Nickell on Wimbledon Common. A female police officer,
working undercover, had engaged, in the words of Ognall J., in "a skilful and
sustained enterprise to manipulate the accused. Sometimes subtle, sometimes
blatant in its technique, it was designed by deception to manoeuvre and seduce
him to reveal fantasies of a suggested incriminating character".[120] Ognall J. ruled
that the evidence so obtained should be excluded in the light of the principles
stated in *Sang* relating to self-incrimination at common law. The court's powers
in this respect, he said, were preserved by s.82(3).[121]

In practice, however, the common law has been very largely superseded by
s.78(1). There is little reference to s.82(3) amongst the numerous cases on
exclusionary discretion under PACE. Only one clear case has been identified, in
relation to illegally or unfairly obtained evidence, where the preserved common
law applies in a situation where s.78 cannot. Where a trial judge admits
prosecution evidence, but decides at a later stage in the trial that it should be
excluded, the judge cannot utilise s.78 for this purpose because that refers to a
court refusing to allow prosecution evidence "to be given". In *Sat-Bhambra*,[122]
the Court of Appeal said, obiter, that once evidence has been admitted, s.78, like
s.76, ceases to operate.[123] In that case it was suggested that a judge who wished to

---

[120] This quotation is from a transcript of the judge's ruling dated September 15, 1994.

[121] He added that the evidence could equally well be excluded under the fairness discretion conferred
by s.78. The story of the police operation against Stagg is told by Paul Britton, the criminal
psychologist who acted as consultant to the operation, in *The Jigsaw Man* (London: Corgi Books,
1997). When the judge excluded the evidence the case against Stagg collapsed, thus averting a
potential miscarriage of justice. Some years later Robert Napper admitted to the murder of Rachel
Nickell.

[122] *Sat-Bhambra* (1988) 88 Cr.App.R. 55.

[123] cf. *Barker* [2010] EWCA Crim 4, where the Court of Appeal said that s.78 could be used to
exclude the evidence of a video-recorded interview that had been admitted as the complainant's
evidence in chief but which the trial judge subsequently wished to exclude having reconsidered the
complainant's competency as a witness. *Sat-Bhambra* (1988) 88 Cr.App.R. 55 was not cited in
Barker.

reconsider a decision to admit the accused's confession, in the light of subsequent evidence about the circumstances in which it was obtained, could act under s.82(3). Accordingly the judge could direct the jury to ignore the confession, or if necessary in a case where a direction would be an inadequate remedy, discharge the jury from giving a verdict.

3.   PACE section 78: protection of the fairness of the proceedings

3–032

"(1)   In any proceedings the court may refuse to allow evidence on which the prosecution proposes to rely to be given if it appears to the court that, having regard to all the circumstances, including the circumstances in which the evidence was obtained, the admission of the evidence would have such an adverse effect on the fairness of the proceedings that the court ought not to admit it.

(2)   Nothing in this section shall prejudice any rule of law requiring a court to exclude evidence."

The precise scope of s.78, and the extent to which it enlarges the exclusionary discretion at common law, is still not settled. There are powerful arguments that it was intended to widen significantly the limited approach taken in *Sang*. Some decisions, and numerous judicial opinions, suggest that it has had this effect. On the other hand, there is a line of judicial thinking that s.78 does no more than put into statutory form the substance of Lord Diplock's answers in *Sang* to the question certified for the House of Lords. In *Chalkley*,[124] the Court of Appeal appeared to adopt an even more restrictive interpretation of the section. We will look first at the arguments for a wide view of the section before turning to analyse the reasoning adopted in *Chalkley*.

(A)   The legislative history of section 78

3–033

The legislative history of s.78[125] is important because it explains why PACE contains two provisions which, on the face of it, appear to overlap, if not actually to do much the same job. The Police and Criminal Evidence Bill originally contained only the clause which became s.82(3) of the Act. This reflected the recommendations of the Royal Commission on Criminal Procedure[126] to retain the exclusionary discretion at common law, but to reject any rule of inadmissibility for illegally obtained evidence. Such a stance was controversial,[127] and led to continuing concern over the adequacy of the Bill in dealing with improper police conduct. During the Committee stage of the Bill in the House of Lords, Lord Scarman successfully moved an amendment to insert a "reverse onus" provision requiring the prosecution to justify the admission of any evidence[128] obtained improperly. Impropriety was not defined, but was clearly capable of extending to all forms of unlawful conduct in the obtaining of

---

[124] *Chalkley* [1998] 2 Cr.App.R. 79.

[125] For a helpful summary see M. Zander, *The Police and Criminal Evidence Act 1984*, 5th edn (London: Sweet & Maxwell, 2005), pp.362–363.

[126] RCCP, Cmnd.8092, London, 1981, paras 4.131–4.134.

[127] See Zander, *The Police and Criminal Evidence Act 1984* (2005), p.362 fn.49.

[128] That is, any evidence other than a confession. Confessions were dealt with separately in the clause which became s.76.

evidence. It would probably also include cases where the police had taken unfair advantage of the accused to obtain evidence by, for example, violating the privilege against self-incrimination. The prosecution would have to justify admission in all cases of impropriety either by satisfying the court that the impropriety was of no material significance and could be disregarded, or that the public interest in the fair administration of justice required the evidence to be given. The provision would have drastically altered the common law and would have brought English law much more into line with the rule in Scots law.[129]

The Government refused to accept the Scarman amendment. When the Bill returned to the House of Commons the Home Secretary set out a number of objections: it was not appropriate for evidence to be excluded as a disciplinary measure for police misconduct, the onus on the prosecution was too heavy and would lead to the acquittal of too many guilty people for reasons unrelated to the fairness of the trial, and there would be unacceptably numerous and complex trials within trials on issues of admissibility. He therefore brought forward a new amendment in the form of a clause which he described as "simple and clear in form, yet suitably flexible".[130] This was the clause which in due course became s.78. The section was thus added to the Bill at a late stage to respond to strongly felt political opposition to the perceived limitations of the common law in dealing with improperly obtained evidence. It seems reasonably clear therefore that the section was intended to have the effect of widening the common law.

(B)   The ordinary meaning of section 78 read in the context of PACE

If the words of the section are given their ordinary meaning, there are several indications that the section has a wide scope. First, the "fairness" discretion is not restricted to evidence obtained from the accused; s.78 refers simply to "evidence on which the prosecution proposes to rely".[131] There is no restriction on the source of the evidence. Secondly, there is an express reference in s.78 to "the circumstances in which the evidence was obtained" as a factor to be considered in assessing the fairness of admitting it. This contrasts with the rejection in *Sang* of the idea that the court should be concerned with how evidence is obtained. Thirdly, s.78 contains no limitation to evidence obtained by means which violate the accused's privilege against self-incrimination. The reference to the circumstances in which the evidence is obtained is unqualified. Fourthly, the section requires the court to estimate the effect of admitting the evidence on the fairness of the *"proceedings"*, rather than the fairness of the trial. If Parliament had

3–034

---

[129] *Lawrie v Muir* [1950] J.C. 19. In *Sang* [1980] A.C. 402, Lord Scarman had cited the Scottish approach with approval: [1980] A.C. 402 at 457.

[130] *Hansard*, HC Vol.60, col.1014 (October 29, 1984).

[131] This point is strengthened by the fact that in the debate in the House of Lords over the Scarman amendment, Lord Hailsham, the Lord Chancellor, put forward his own amendment which would have given the courts a general discretion to exclude evidence, but only where it was obtained from the accused. Section 78 was modelled on the Hailsham draft but with the limitation to evidence obtained from the accused removed.

intended to restrict the discretion to preventing the unfair use of evidence at *trial*, in accordance with *Sang*, it would have been easy to say so.[132]

This reading of the section strongly supports the view, suggested by the legislative history, that s.78 was intended to be a general provision, giving trial judges a wide and flexible standard to apply in ensuring the fairness of the proceedings. By expressly referring in unqualified terms to the circumstances in which the evidence was obtained as a relevant factor to be considered, the section seems to envisage trial judges finding that fairness could be adversely affected by both unfair use of evidence *and* unfair treatment of the accused. In this way the section recognises that the criminal trial should no longer be insulated from the pre-trial proceedings. It apparently charges the judge with the task of superintending the fairness of the proceedings as a whole, on the basis that the investigative phase and the trial phase are seen as two intimately related parts of an integrated process.[133]

Is there any reason why s.78 should not be interpreted according to its ordinary meaning? Would any principle of interpretation support reading back into the section the limits imposed by *Sang* on exclusionary discretion? In *Fulling*,[134] Lord Lane C.J. said that PACE was a codifying Act. This important dictum[135] means that the principles stated by Lord Herschell in the leading case of *Bank of England v Vagliano Brothers*[136] are applicable to the interpretation of s.78:

> "I think the proper course is in the first instance to examine the language of the statute and to ask what is its natural meaning, uninfluenced by any considerations derived from the previous state of the law, and not to start with inquiring how the law previously stood, and then, assuming that it was probably intended to leave it unaltered, to see if the words of the enactment will bear an interpretation in conformity with this view."

3–035   Following these principles, there would seem to be no warrant for reintroducing into s.78 the limits imposed by *Sang*. There is nothing in the language of the section which requires them; indeed, incorporating them would entail a complete rewriting of the provision.

---

[132] PACE ss.77 and 79 refer respectively to a duty and a discretion of the court at a *trial*. The choice of the different word proceedings looks therefore like a deliberate contrast. In *R. v King's Lynn Magistrates' Court Ex p. Holland* [1993] 2 All E.R. 377 Beldam L.J. described as unsustainable the argument that "proceedings" in s.78 is intended to refer only to the proceedings of a trial.

[133] J. R. Spencer in [1998] C.L.J. 633, reviewing P. Mirfield, *Silence, Confessions and Improperly Obtained Evidence* (Oxford: Clarendon Press, 1997). In *Teixeira de Castro v Portugal* (1999) 28 E.H.R.R. 101 the European Court of Human Rights held that the applicant, who had been incited by undercover police officers to procure drugs on their behalf, had been deprived by this entrapment of a fair trial from the outset.

[134] *Fulling* [1987] Q.B. 426 at 431 CA.

[135] See also the dictum of Lord Steyn in *Hasan* [2005] UKHL 22; [2005] 2 Cr.App.R. 22 at [52]: "Subject to the discretion of a trial judge under the common law to exclude evidence where its likely prejudicial effect outweighs its probative value (see s.82(3); *R. v Sang* . . .) the provisions of s.76, read with s.82(1) [of PACE] and s.78, constitute a part-codification of the law governing criminal evidence".

[136] *Bank of England v Vagliano Brothers* [1891] A.C. 107 at 144–145 HL.

(C)   Judicial opinion supporting a wide application of section 78

There is a good deal of authority to support a wide view of s.78. We can consider **3–036** first the central problem of evidence obtained improperly. In *R. v Horseferry Road Magistrates' Court Ex p. Bennett*,[137] Lord Griffiths stated, obiter, that s.78 enlarges a judge's discretion to exclude evidence obtained by unfair means.[138] This dictum was cited by the Court of Appeal in *Khan, Sakkaravej and Pamarapa*,[139] in holding that s.78 gives a judge power to exclude evidence obtained by means of an illegal search of the accused. In this case the Court of Appeal refused to interfere with a judge's decision to admit evidence of drug-smuggling by a diplomat who was abusing his privilege. There was no unfairness in admitting overwhelmingly cogent evidence that had been discovered by a search that was technically illegal only because the diplomat was not present when his bag was searched. It may well be that exclusion of the fruits of unlawful searches will be rare, but this does not detract from the significance of recognising that s.78 confers a discretion to exclude such evidence. This case would not be covered by Lord Diplock's statement in *Sang* of the discretion.

One part of the decision of the House of Lords in *Sang* was that there is no discretion at common law to exclude evidence obtained by entrapment of the accused. However, in *Smurthwaite*,[140] the Court of Appeal held that s.78 does permit a judge to exclude evidence obtained by entrapment if its admission would have such an adverse effect on the fairness of the proceedings that it ought not to be admitted. This necessarily implies that the section has reversed the effect of the decision of the House of Lords in *Sang* on this point.[141] In *Latif and Shahzad*,[142] the House of Lords appears to have accepted that s.78 could in principle be used to exclude evidence obtained by entrapment, although the argument for exclusion failed on the facts.[143] Finally, in *Looseley*,[144] the House of Lords confirmed that s.78 may be used to exclude evidence obtained by entrapment, although it was made clear that the normal remedy in a case of unacceptable entrapment should be a stay of the proceedings for abuse of process.[145]

In *Khan (Sultan)*,[146] the House of Lords assumed that s.78 could extend to the exclusion of evidence of incriminating conversations obtained by the use of a listening device unlawfully attached to the wall of a house. Lord Nolan, who gave the leading speech, said that he agreed with Lord Taylor C.J. in *Smurthwaite* "that the power conferred by s.78 to exclude evidence in the interests of a fair trial is at

---

[137] *R. v Horseferry Road Magistrates' Court Ex p. Bennett* [1994] 1 A.C. 42 at 61 HL.
[138] See also *Cooke* [1995] 1 Cr.App.R. 318 at 328 (per Glidewell L.J.: "it is now clear that s.78 has given the courts a substantially wider discretion to refuse to admit evidence improperly obtained").
[139] *Khan, Sakkaravej and Pamarapa* [1997] Crim. L.R. 508.
[140] *Smurthwaite* [1994] 1 All E.R. 898.
[141] Although Lord Taylor C.J. was careful to say that s.78 has not altered the substantive rule of law that entrapment is no defence as such to a criminal charge.
[142] *Latif and Shahzad* [1996] 2 Cr.App.R. 92.
[143] *Latif and Shahzad* [1996] 2 Cr.App.R. 92 at 101–102.
[144] *Looseley* [2001] 4 All E.R. 897.
[145] For further discussion see Ch.8.
[146] *Khan (Sultan)* [1996] 3 All E.R. 289.

least as wide as that conferred by the common law".[147] In fact, it is very doubtful whether the principles stated in *Sang* would cover this case, since there was no violation of the privilege against self-incrimination. An extension of the common law seems to have been involved. It is notable that when Khan's case reached the European Court of Human Rights the court accepted that s.78 enables an English court to safeguard the fairness of the proceedings, for the purposes of art.6 of the ECHR, by exclusion of evidence.[148] This proposition was expressed generally, without qualification. In *R. v P*,[149] which concerned the admissibility of foreign intercepts of mobile telephone conversations, the House of Lords cited the relevant passage from *Khan v United Kingdom* as confirmation that s.78 is an appropriate safeguard of the fairness of the trial. Lord Hobhouse referred to:

> "the vital role of s.78 as the means by which questions of the use of evidence obtained in breach of article 8 are to be resolved at a criminal trial. The criterion to be applied is the criterion of fairness in article 6 which is likewise the criterion to be applied by the judge under s.78."[150]

In *R. v P* the intercepted conversations were those of a prosecution witness, not one of the defendants. It is therefore a necessary implication of the reasoning in this case that the s.78 discretion is not restricted to evidence obtained from the accused but extends to any prosecution evidence that may have been obtained in breach of Convention rights. In *Hasan,* Lord Steyn referred to "the unrestricted capability of s.78 to avoid injustice by excluding any evidence obtained by unfairness".[151]

3–037   We can turn now to consider other types of evidence. Section 78 has not been restricted to evidence obtained improperly. There are numerous cases upholding its application to evidence of the convictions of third parties, where these would otherwise be admissible against the accused under s.74 of PACE.[152] No question of impropriety, or pre-trial unfair treatment of the accused, is involved. Nevertheless, it may be unfair to use such evidence at the trial, not least because it may result in the effective reversal of the burden of proof and/or the admission against the accused of what is in effect untested hearsay evidence.[153] In *O'Loughlin,*[154] it was held that s.78 could be used to exclude the depositions of certain witnesses absent from the trial. Identification evidence was involved, and in the absence of cross-examination of the witnesses the jury would have little guidance on how much weight to give the evidence. Similarly, it appears to be generally agreed that s.78 can be used to exclude other admissible hearsay

---

[147] *Khan (Sultan)* [1996] 3 All E.R. 289 at 298, citing [1994] 4 All E.R. 426 at 435.
[148] *Khan v United Kingdom* (2000) 8 B.H.R.C. 310. See also *PG and JH v UK* [2002] Crim. L.R. 308.
[149] *R. v P* [2001] 2 All E.R. 58.
[150] *R. v P* [2001] 2 All E.R. 58 at 70.
[151] *Hasan* [2005] UKHL 22; [2005] 2 Cr.App.R. 22 at [62].
[152] See Ch.20.
[153] The point being that the effect of allowing the prosecution to prove the conviction may be to put before the jury a statement by a co-accused incriminating the defendant, made at an earlier trial when the defendant had no opportunity to cross-examine the co-accused. See *O'Connor* (1987) 85 Cr.App.R. 298 CA.
[154] *O'Loughlin* [1988] 3 All E.R. 431.

statements. In *Horncastle*, Lord Phillips, giving the judgment of the Supreme Court in a case concerned with the admission of the hearsay statements of unavailable witnesses, referred to "the very important general safeguard in section 78(1)".[155] In *Flynn*, the Court of Appeal held that a trial judge was wrong not to have excluded under s.78 certain voice recognition evidence of police officers, because of the officers' failure to make appropriate notes.[156] It seems to have been assumed that s.78 could be used in a suitable case to exclude an alibi notice adduced as part of the prosecution case,[157] and expert evidence where a scientific examination altered vital evidence before a defence expert could examine it.[158]

Finally, in *Quinn*,[159] Lord Lane C.J. summarised the discretion under s.78 in general terms. These terms strongly suggest that Lord Lane considered s.78 to apply to any relevant prosecution evidence:

> "The function of the judge is . . . to *protect the fairness of the proceedings*, and normally proceedings are fair if a jury hears *all* relevant evidence which either side wishes to place before it, but proceedings may become unfair if, for example, one side is allowed to adduce relevant evidence which, for one reason or another, the other side cannot properly challenge or meet, or where there has been an abuse of process, e.g. because evidence has been obtained in deliberate breach of procedures laid down in an official code of practice. One important factor in the exercise of its discretion will be for the court to weigh the probative effect of the disputed evidence against its prejudicial effect."[160]

(D) Judicial opinion rejecting a wide application of section 78

Dicta in a number of cases before *Chalkley* gave a narrow interpretation to s.78. In *Mason*,[161] Watkins L.J. said that the section did no more than restate the power which judges had at common law before PACE. On this view s.78 is simply a legislative restatement of the common law, setting out in statutory form the discretion stated in *Sang* and other cases. The section would thus add nothing to s.82(3) which, as we have seen, expressly preserves any discretion at common law to exclude evidence. In *Christou*,[162] Lord Taylor C.J. said that the criteria of fairness are the same whether the judge is exercising his discretion at common law or under the statute. The context suggests that Lord Taylor C.J. was distinguishing the issue of the test of "fairness" from the separate issue of the

3–038

---

[155] *Horncastle* [2009] UKSC 14 at [28].
[156] *Flynn* [2008] EWCA Crim 970. The court held that the evidence should also have been excluded on the ground that its prejudicial effect far outweighed its probative value.
[157] *Fields and Adams* [1991] Crim. L.R. 38 CA (the point appears in the commentary by Sir John Smith at 40). On the facts, the Court of Appeal rejected the argument that the judge was wrong to allow the prosecution to put in the notice of alibi.
[158] *DPP v British Telecommunications Plc* [1991] Crim. L.R. 532 DC. The Divisional Court held in this case that the justices had been wrong to exclude the evidence on the facts, but appear to have accepted that s.78 was capable of applying in this situation. Similarly in *Robb* (1991) 93 Cr.App.R. 161 the Court of Appeal seems to have assumed that in a suitable case s.78 could be used to exclude expert evidence where the evidence was potentially unreliable.
[159] *Quinn* [1990] Crim. L.R. 581 CA.
[160] This passage from the transcript of *Quinn* is conveniently set out in the judgment of Beldam L.J. in *R. v King's Lynn Magistrates' Court Ex p. Holland* [1993] 2 All E.R. 377 at 379 DC.
[161] *Mason* [1987] 3 All E.R. 481 CA.
[162] *Christou* (1992) 95 Cr.App.R. 264 at 269.

types of case in which the fairness discretion can be exercised, but this is made unclear by the fact that he then discussed fairness solely in terms of the common law concerns with tricks and self-incrimination. Certainly it is possible to read the section as giving statutory authority to the common law[163]; the critical issue is whether this exhausts the effect of the section.

In *Chalkley*,[164] the Court of Appeal was in no doubt that s.78 did not enlarge the common law. The defendant had been convicted of conspiracy to commit robbery, the main evidence against him being tape-recordings of highly incriminating conversations between the defendant and his co-accused. The police had covertly installed a listening device in the defendant's house to make the recordings, having been able to gain entry to the house as a result of arresting the defendant and his partner in connection with an unrelated matter concerning the fraudulent use of a credit card. The trial judge had admitted the evidence after conducting a careful balancing exercise for the purpose of applying s.78. He took into account the fact that the police had breached provisions of PACE, had infringed the civil law of trespass and violated the defendant's right to privacy under art.8 of the ECHR. He then weighed these considerations against the facts that the police had not acted in bad faith,[165] the recordings constituted reliable evidence of the commission of a serious crime, and they showed that there was a risk of the defendant committing serious offences in the future involving danger to the public. He concluded that it would not be an affront to the conscience of a right-thinking person to admit the evidence of the recordings, despite the circumstances in which they were obtained. Dismissing the appeal, the Court of Appeal held that the judge had been wrong to embark on the balancing exercise. According to Auld L.J. the judge had confused the issue of the fairness of admitting evidence under s.78 with the discretion to stay criminal proceedings as an abuse of process:

> "Depending on the circumstances, the latter may require consideration, not just of the potential fairness of a trial, but also of a balance of the possibly countervailing interests of prosecuting a criminal to conviction and discouraging abuses of power. However laudable the end, it may not justify any means to achieve it."[166]

Auld L.J. went on to say that the exercise of the discretion under s.78 did not require an analogous balancing exercise. In the view of the Court of Appeal the inclusion in s.78 of the words "the circumstances in which the evidence was obtained" did not mean that the court could exclude the evidence as a mark of

---

[163] Thus in a number of cases courts have referred to s.78 as continuing the discretion to exclude evidence whose prejudicial effect exceeds its probative value: *Quinn* [1990] Crim. L.R. 581; *R. v King's Lynn Magistrates' Court Ex p. Holland* [1993] 2 All E.R. 377; *Hasson and Davey* [1997] Crim. L.R. 579. Note, however, the alternative view that the rule requiring probative value to be weighed against prejudicial effect is a rule which falls outside s.78: *O'Leary* (1988) 87 Cr.App.R. 387 at 391–392 CA.

[164] *Chalkley* [1998] 2 Cr.App.R. 79 CA.

[165] There were reasonable grounds to suspect the defendant and his partner of having committed the fraud offence, hence the arrest was arguably lawful despite the police's ulterior motive of getting the defendant out of the house so that the listening device could be installed. The investigating officer had obtained authorisation from his Chief Constable for the installation of the device.

[166] *Chalkley* [1998] 2 Cr.App.R. 79 at 105 CA.

disapproval of the way in which it had been obtained. Nor were they intended to widen the common law rule, as stated by Lord Diplock in *Sang*. Auld L.J. then stated this rule in terms that:

> "save in the case of admissions and confessions and generally as to evidence obtained from the accused after the commission of the offence there is no discretion to exclude evidence unless its quality was or might have been affected by the way in which it was obtained."[167]

Since the judge had adopted the wrong approach, the Court of Appeal exercised the discretion afresh. The court held that the recordings were relevant, highly probative of guilt and otherwise admissible; and none of the unlawful conduct of the police had affected the quality of the evidence.

Curiously, however, Auld L.J. also noted that the evidence "had not resulted from incitement, entrapment or inducement or any other conduct of that sort".[168] If s.78 really does no more than restate the effect of *Sang*, then the presence of incitement or entrapment is irrelevant. *Sang* decided that there is no discretion to exclude evidence obtained by entrapment. It should not therefore be a factor in the application of s.78, if *Chalkley* is right.[169]

3–039

It is suggested, with respect, that it is not right. The judgment on the s.78 point[170] is extremely unsatisfactory for several reasons. First, it interprets "proceedings" in s.78 to mean "trial", without referring to the significance of the section in its context in PACE. Parliament used "trial" in s.77 and 79; Parliament could easily have used "trial" in s.78 if that is what was intended. Secondly, *Chalkley* makes no reference to the legislative history of the section, or to the fact that PACE has been held to be a codifying Act. *Fulling* (above) was not cited to the court. Thirdly, it fails to account for s.82(3), which is simply not mentioned. Fourthly, there is no discussion of, or even any reference to, the authorities supporting a wide view of s.78. *Chalkley* was inconsistent in its approach to the section with *Smurthwaite*,[171] *Khan*,[172] *Quinn*,[173] and *R. v King's Lynn*

---

[167] *Chalkley* [1998] 2 Cr.App.R. 79 at 105–106. With respect to Auld L.J. this was not quite what Lord Diplock said in *Sang*. Lord Diplock did not refer to impropriety affecting the *quality* of the evidence; he referred to the discretion being available to exclude evidence "which the accused has been induced to produce voluntarily if the method of inducement was unfair": [1980] A.C. 402 at 436. By introducing the idea that the impropriety has to affect the quality of the evidence, Auld L.J. narrowed even further what was already a narrow discretion.

[168] *Chalkley* [1998] 2 Cr.App.R. 79 at 107.

[169] And, as noted above, it has now been confirmed that s.78 has had the effect of reversing *Sang* on the existence of a discretion to exclude evidence obtained by entrapment.

[170] The case is also of major importance on other points, most notably the interpretation of the amended form of s.2(1) of the Criminal Appeal Act 1995. The case appears to hold that the Court of Appeal is concerned only with the "safety" of a conviction in the sense of whether the conviction is factually reliable, and is not concerned with whether the conviction might be "unsatisfactory" for other reasons: see [1998] 2 Cr.App.R. 79 at 98. It is beyond the scope of this book to investigate this issue in more detail, but it should be noted that this interpretation is extremely controversial. It is hard to see how it can be reconciled with the duty of the courts under s.6 of the Human Rights Act 1998 to ensure that a defendant received a fair trial compliant with art.6 of the ECHR. For discussion of the later authorities, most of which do not follow *Chalkley* on this point, see Dennis, "Fair Trials and Safe Convictions" [2003] C.L.P. 211.

[171] *Smurthwaite* [1994] 1 All E.R. 898 CA.

[172] *Khan* [1997] Crim. L.R. 508 CA.

[173] *Quinn* [1990] Crim. L.R. 581 CA.

Magistrates' Court Ex p. Holland,[174] none of which were cited to the court. Fifthly, the decision takes a very restrictive view of the decision of the House of Lords in *Khan (Sultan)*.[175] The Court of Appeal cites the decision as support for its stance on s.78, but fails to acknowledge that the House of Lords did not rule out the possibility that the fairness of the proceedings might be compromised by impropriety in obtaining the evidence even where the evidence itself is reliable. Sixthly, the Court of Appeal concludes its analysis of s.78 by misstating the test: it says that the exercise for the trial judge under the section is an examination of the question whether it would be unfair to the *defendant* to admit the evidence in question (emphasis supplied). This is not what the section says. It directs attention to the effect of admission of the evidence on the fairness of the *proceedings*, and there is authority that an overall judgment of fairness to both sides is required.[176]

Collectively, these objections constitute a compelling argument for saying that the decision, that s.78 merely restates the common law, is simply wrong.[177] In the first edition of this book it was suggested that the failure to take account of *Fulling* and *Smurthwaite*, in particular, which were binding on the Court of Appeal, might mean that the decision in *Chalkley* as to the effect of s.78 was actually *per incuriam*. *Smurthwaite*, but not *Fulling*, was cited to the Court of Appeal in the subsequent case of *Shannon*[178] where the court referred to *Chalkley* with approval. *Shannon* was a case of alleged entrapment. In reaching the conclusion that s.78 might allow for the exclusion of evidence obtained by entrapment the Court of Appeal appeared to say that s.78 had had the effect of restoring the ambit of exclusionary discretion to what it was at common law *before Sang*.[179] With respect it has to be said that this is a bizarre reading of s.78. There is absolutely nothing in the words of the section or its legislative history to support the view that Parliament intended s.78 to reverse *Sang* on the entrapment point while leaving the ambit of exclusionary discretion as otherwise restated in that case. If the Court of Appeal meant that s.78 overturned *Sang* altogether, this is inconsistent with the court's approval of *Chalkley*, which held the opposite. It is submitted that *Shannon* also is wrong on the scope of s.78 and cannot stand against the mass of other authority supporting the view that it applies to any prosecution evidence.

3–040   On the assumption that this is the correct view, the question remains whether *Chalkley* was right in suggesting that s.78 permits exclusion only where the *quality* of the evidence was or might have been affected by the way in which it was obtained. In many cases an impropriety in obtaining the evidence may well have a potentially significant effect on its quality: breaches of the requirements in PACE for the recording of interviews with suspects[180] or for the conduct of

---

[174] *R. v King's Lynn Magistrates' Court Ex p. Holland* [1993] 2 All E.R. 377 DC.

[175] *Khan (Sultan)* [1996] 3 All E.R. 289.

[176] *R. v King's Lynn Magistrates' Court Ex p. Holland* [1993] 2 All E.R. 377.

[177] Auld L.J. himself has subsequently described the above as a "powerful critical analysis of this case": the Auld Review, at p.562, fn.122.

[178] *Shannon* [2001] 1 Cr.App.R. 12.

[179] *Shannon* [2001] 1 Cr.App.R. 12 at [30]–[32], citing three first instance decisions allowing for exclusion of evidence obtained by entrapment. These decisions were overruled in *Sang*.

[180] See Ch.6.

identification procedures[181] are clear examples. However, evidence obtained by unacceptable entrapment or by unlawful searches or by unlawful surveillance may be of excellent quality. On the authorities cited earlier such evidence may still be subject to the exclusionary discretion under s.78. The importance attached to the presence of bad faith[182] on the part of the police or other law enforcement agents is a further indication that fairness for the purposes of s.78 is not just a quality control issue. There is no necessary connection between a deliberate breach of investigative powers and the quality of the evidence obtained thereby. Breaches of fundamental rights of the accused, whether or not in bad faith, which prejudice the accused but which do not necessarily affect the quality of the evidence obtained in consequence, may also give rise to exclusion under s.78.[183] Section 78 applies in extradition proceedings, where it should (only) be used to exclude evidence obtained in a way that "outraged civilised values".[184] The relevant authorities do not suggest that exclusion in such cases depends on the quality of the evidence being affected by the impropriety. It would seem therefore that *Chalkley* is not correct on this point either.

(E)   General principles relating to the application of section 78

Whatever its precise scope, certain general principles have been established regarding the application of s.78. These can be summarised as follows:

3–041

(1)   The section applies only to prosecution evidence. It does not apply to evidence tendered by an accused or a co-accused. A trial judge has no equivalent discretion to exclude defence evidence.[185]

(2)   It will normally be the defence that raise the issue of exclusion of prosecution evidence under s.78. The court may take the point itself if the defence do not, since the section is concerned with interests wider than those of the defence. The Divisional Court has said that the concept of burden of proof has no part to play under s.78. The section does not require any fact to be proved, hence it is more accurate to speak of a burden of persuasion under the section. If the defence raise the issue, it might be thought that they should bear the burden of persuasion, but the better view is that the section is neutral as between the prosecutor and the defence.[186]

(3)   The exercise of the trial judge's discretion can be reviewed only on *Wednesbury* principles.[187] The Court of Appeal will not substitute its own

---

[181]   See Ch.7.

[182]   See the discussion of the cases on bad faith in Chs 6 and 7, and for some theoretical considerations see the next section of this chapter.

[183]   See, e.g. *Kirk* [1999] 4 All E.R. 698 CA.

[184]   *R. v Governor of Brixton Prison Ex p. Levin* [1997] A.C. 741 at 748 HL (Lord Hoffmann); *Re Proulx* [2001] 1 All E.R. 57 DC.

[185]   *Lobban v R.* [1995] 2 All E.R. 602 PC. Note, however, that a judge can refuse, under s.132(5) of the Criminal Justice Act 2003, to admit hearsay evidence tendered by a defendant where the defendant failed to give the required notice under the Criminal Procedure Rules and the admission of the evidence would be unfair to a co-accused: *Musone* [2007] EWCA Crim 1237; [2007] 2 Cr.App.R. 29.

[186]   *R. (on the application of Saifi) v Governor of Brixton Prison* [2000] 1 W.L.R. 1134.

[187]   *Associated Provincial Picture Houses Ltd v Wednesbury Corp* [1948] 1 K.B. 223.

judgment for that of the trial judge simply because it takes a different view of the case. The trial judge must be shown to have erred in principle before the court will interfere.[188]

(4)   The state of the other incriminating evidence is important in estimating the adverse effect of admitting the evidence in question on the fairness of the proceedings.[189] Section 78 requires a decision to be made on a matter of degree. It may be unfair to admit certain evidence, but by itself this is not enough. The admission of the evidence has to have such an adverse effect on fairness that the court ought not to admit it. Where the other evidence is strongly incriminating, fairness is unlikely to be seriously affected. If the disputed evidence is the sole or main prosecution evidence against the accused, fairness is likely to be significantly affected by its admission.

4.   The rationale of discretionary exclusion

3–042   In order to discuss the rationale of exclusion of evidence in the judge's discretion it is necessary to anticipate some points that will be made in more detail in Ch.8. Many of the cases on exclusionary discretion have concerned evidence obtained by means alleged to be unlawful or unfair. These cases of improperly obtained evidence present a confusing picture as far as the rationale of exclusion is concerned.[190] Traditionally, three competing principles are canvassed as possible accounts of exclusionary decisions. Each of these is problematic as a self-contained account, as we shall see; yet it is clear that all three present relevant considerations on the issue of the fairness of admitting the evidence in question. This is true whether we are considering the discretion at common law or under s.78 of PACE. This in turn suggests the need for some kind of over-arching theory that can help to explain how these principles relate to the overall aims of the law of evidence.

The first principle is concerned with the *reliability* of the evidence. A theoretical position might be that a particular item of evidence is excluded, as a matter of discretion, because of the significant risk that in the circumstances of the particular case the evidence is unreliable. Its weight is thought to be so uncertain that it is not safe to allow the factfinder to evaluate the evidence, in view of the significant risk of error. In these circumstances the use of such evidence by the prosecution is unfair to the defendant. Some cases under the well-established head of discretion that allows for the exclusion of evidence whose prejudicial effect exceeds its probative value can be founded on this principle; an example is the exclusion of a confession by a person suffering from mental disability where the risk of its probative value being over-estimated is significant. It is also possible to point to some cases of improperly obtained evidence where this consideration is decisive. As noted above, breaches of the

---

[188] *O'Leary* (1988) 87 Cr.App.R. 387 CA; *Christou* (1992) 95 Cr.App.R. 264 CA; *Thompson v R.* [1998] A.C. 811 at 838–839 PC.
[189] *Keenan* [1990] 2 Q.B. 54 CA; *Weekes* (1993) 97 Cr.App.R. 222 CA; cf. *Walsh* (1990) 91 Cr.App.R. 161 CA.
[190] For a helpful discussion, see P. Mirfield, *Silence, Confessions and Improperly Obtained Evidence* (1997), Chs 2, 6 and 12.

requirements of PACE for recording statements by the accused may mean that police evidence of the defendant's alleged oral confession is significantly suspect. It may be unfair to use this evidence at trial if the defendant was never afforded the opportunity to challenge the accuracy of the police account at the time it was made. On the other hand, much improperly obtained evidence has a high degree of reliability. An illegal search may yield evidence of the defendant's possession of drugs or stolen goods. A bodily sample illegally taken from the defendant may yield a match with a DNA profile from the victim. If such evidence is to be excluded, this cannot be on the ground that it is unfair to use unreliable evidence.

The second principle is concerned with *deterrence*. A theoretical position might **3–043** be that exclusion of evidence obtained improperly is a deterrent to investigating authorities against the use of improper methods. The argument is that if the police and other investigating agencies know they cannot use the results of impropriety in evidence, they will not be tempted to resort to it as a way of proving the case. An element of education may also be involved; the police, for example, may learn through the experience of exclusion of evidence both the correct application of the rules and the importance of following them. In this way the police might internalise the value of rule-following as good practice. Courts have regularly denied that disciplining the police and deterring them from misbehaviour is part of the judicial function.[191] However, some decisions concerned with breaches of PACE and the Codes of Practice show strong disapproval of police malpractice and contain clear messages to the police about the importance of respecting the rules laid down by PACE. *Keenan*[192] and *Canale*[193] are leading cases illustrating the concern of the Court of Appeal to communicate to the police that the Codes are to be taken seriously and must be properly applied. On the other hand evidence may still be excluded under s.78 where the police have acted in good faith and made a mistake about the extent of their powers. Deterrence of the police from misbehaviour cannot account for decisions such as *Samuel*[194] and *Walsh*,[195] where the police unlawfully denied the accused access to legal advice but acted in good faith.

There are other difficulties with this principle. The Royal Commission on Criminal Procedure commented that the exclusionary sanction can only be effective in a minority of cases, because most of the persons subject to police action are either not arrested, or not charged, or not prosecuted, or plead guilty or do not contest the legality of police action.[196] Zuckerman argued that the efficiency of the deterrent sanction is further put in doubt by the existence of countervailing influences on police behaviour, such as peer expectations and public pressure.[197] In very high-profile cases the pressure on the police to deliver

---

[191] See *Sang* [1980] A.C. 402 at 436 per Lord Diplock; *Mason* [1987] 3 All E.R. 481 at 484 per Watkins L.J.; *Hughes* [1994] 1 W.L.R. 876 at 879 per Lord Taylor C.J.

[192] *Keenan* [1990] 2 Q.B. 54 CA.

[193] *Canale* [1990] 2 All E.R. 187 CA.

[194] *Samuel* [1988] Q.B. 615 CA.

[195] *Walsh* (1990) 91 Cr.App.R. 161 CA.

[196] RCCP, Cmnd.8092, London, 1981, para.4.125. The accused might not contest the legality of police action for fear of having his previous convictions admitted under gateway (g) of s.101 of the Criminal Justice Act 2007. See Ch.19.

[197] *Principles*, pp.349–350. See also Roberts and Zuckerman, pp.185–188.

a culprit may be almost overwhelming. There is also the problem of the remoteness of the sanction from the time of the improper behaviour.

3–044   The third principle is *remedial,* concerned with protection of the rights of the accused. The common law concept of the right to fair trial has embraced the principles that the accused may be tried and convicted only for an offence properly charged and according to the evidence relating to that charge.[198] If the evidence is likely to be misused by the factfinder, because its prejudicial effect exceeds its probative value, its exclusion is necessary to uphold this right. Its exclusion might also be grounded in the right of the accused against wrongful (factually inaccurate) conviction, discussed in Ch.2.

Accused persons have many other rights, both substantive and procedural. A theoretical position might be that exclusion of evidence obtained in breach of the accused's rights is necessary to vindicate those rights. Exclusion would restore the accused to the position as regards evidence of the offence that he would have enjoyed but for the breach. This principle has undeniable attractions. The accused's right of unfettered access to a lawyer, for example, is one of the essential elements of the right to a fair trial under art.6 of the ECHR. Denial of access,[199] or police deception of the lawyer,[200] may result in the accused being placed at a significant evidential disadvantage. Exclusion of the evidence obtained in consequence of the police action may therefore be necessary to remedy the unfairness. Other remedies, such as a civil action for damages or a police disciplinary proceeding, are inadequate to prevent the disadvantage being converted into the permanent form of conviction. In *Mohammed v The State,*[201] the Privy Council stated that if the right breached was a constitutional right of the accused, such as in that case the right of access to a lawyer, that would be a cogent factor militating in favour of exclusion of the accused's subsequent confession. According to Lord Steyn: "the stamp of constitutionality on a citizen's rights is not meaningless: it is clear testimony that an added value is attached to the protection of the right".[202] A presumption of exclusion would indicate respect for the constitutional character of the infringed right and accord it a high value.

However, like the reliability and deterrent principles, the remedial rights-protective principle faces some significant difficulties. If the evidence in question is relevant and reliable, the price of its exclusion may be the acquittal of a guilty and possibly dangerous offender. The social costs of this may be considerable. There may be a failure to protect the public, as well as a failure to provide satisfaction to a victim of the offence. This conflict between the claims of social defence and the protection of individual rights is sharpened by a further definitional problem. What are to count as rights for this purpose? Is the exclusionary remedy limited to what might be called "process" rights, that is rights relating to the procedures for obtaining evidence against suspects? What about breach of rights that protect substantive interests, such as freedom of the

---

[198]   Roberts and Zuckerman, pp.22–23, make the same point in slightly different language.
[199]   *Samuel* [1988] Q.B. 615 CA; *Murray v United Kingdom* (1996) 22 E.H.R.R. 29.
[200]   *Mason* [1987] 3 All E.R. 481 CA.
[201]   *Mohammed v The State* [1999] 2 A.C. 111.
[202]   *Mohammed v The State* [1999] 2 A.C. 111 at 123.

person, or privacy? In Ch.5 it will be argued that the law of evidence is not an appropriate mechanism for protecting substantive rights: the latter are the concern of the law of tort (and the criminal law, in some cases), and they need to be vindicated by a remedy that is available in all cases and is available as a matter of right, not as a matter of exclusionary discretion.[203] As regards "process" rights, the PACE Codes, for example, contain numerous detailed provisions regulating the treatment and questioning of persons in custody. Are we to regard all of them as generating rights whose violation will lead to exclusion of evidence obtained subsequently? If not, what distinctions are to be made and on what basis?[204]

These three principles—reliability, deterrence and protection—sometimes combine to produce an overwhelming case for exclusion of evidence. The deliberate introduction at a late stage of unverified police notes of an alleged oral confession would justify a court invoking all three principles to exclude the evidence. On the other hand, they can produce very different results in certain cases. Suppose that the police extort a confession from an accused which leads to the discovery of incriminating real evidence. The latter is reliable, but it is arguable that it should be excluded on deterrent and protective principles. Compare an unlawful search of a house belonging to the accused's neighbour, E.[205] If this turns up evidence incriminating the accused it might be excluded on a deterrent principle but not on a reliability principle, nor on a protective principle because it is not the accused's rights which have been infringed.

The existence of such cases, coupled with the difficulties identified above, suggests the need for an alternative justifying account of the exclusion of improperly obtained evidence. Australian courts have for some time invoked a principle of judicial integrity,[206] whereby it is argued that the courts should not be seen to be taking advantage of the impropriety of government agents by acting on evidence unlawfully or unfairly obtained.[207] A similar idea underlies the Canadian principle that evidence may be excluded under the Charter of Rights and Freedoms if its admission would tend to bring the administration of justice into disrepute.[208] Both the Australian and Canadian approaches regard the exclusion of improperly obtained evidence as a broad question of public policy. Trial judges have to weigh against each other:

> "two competing requirements of public policy, thereby seeking to resolve the apparent conflict between the desirable goal of bringing to conviction the wrongdoer and the undesirable effect of curial approval, or even encouragement, being given to the unlawful conduct of those

---

[203] See *Khan v United Kingdom* (2000) 8 B.H.R.C. 310.

[204] cf. A. Ashworth and M. Redmayne, *The Criminal Process*, 4th edn (2010), pp.344–362, for a defence of a remedial rights-based approach, particularly in cases involving breach of a defendant's rights under PACE.

[205] cf. *Khan (Sultan)* [1996] 3 All E.R. 289 HL.

[206] See A. Ashworth, "Exploring the Integrity Principle in Evidence and Procedure" in P. Mirfield and R. Smith (eds), *Essays for Colin Tapper*, (London: LexisNexis, 2003).

[207] *Bunning v Cross* (1978) 141 C.L.R. 54; *Ridgeway v R.* (1995) 129 A.L.R. 41. See also the Evidence Act (Commonwealth) 1995 s.138, and the discussion in Mirfield, *Silence, Confessions* (1997), pp.358–365.

[208] Charter of Rights and Freedoms s.24(2). This provision has generated an extensive case law. For a useful introduction, see Mirfield, *Silence, Confessions* (1997), pp.365–370.

whose task it is to enforce the law. This being the aim of the discretionary process ... it follows that it by no means takes as its central point the question of unfairness to the accused."[209]

Factors relevant to this calculation include whether the impropriety was deliberate or reckless, the probative value of the evidence, any necessity for its immediate preservation by unlawful action, the importance of the evidence, the nature of the offence and the seriousness of the impropriety.

3–045 It seems that the judge should weigh these various factors according to the overall effect on what Mirfield has described[210] as "public attitude integrity"—meaning that the judge should exclude the evidence if its admission would be contrary to the "public interest in ensuring that public confidence in the justice system is not undermined by the perception that the courts of law condone or encourage unlawful or improper conduct on the part of those who have the duty to enforce the law".[211] It is almost certainly the case that public confidence and public attitudes are not empirically determined for this purpose. Much public opinion is overtly punitive, heavily swayed by short-term passions and media publicity. It is a fair bet that many people might say, in answer to an opinion poll, that the police ought to be able to override any individual rights in order to bring criminals to justice. For this reason it has been said in Canada that the test is whether the admission of the evidence would bring the administration of justice into disrepute according to the views of the hypothetical, reasonable, well-informed and dispassionate person in the community.[212] This person's views are of course a construction of the judiciary themselves, although the test does require the judges at least to address the issue of community values on the assumption that the hypothetical reasonable person will wish to see them upheld by the courts.

The theory of legitimacy developed in this book likewise locates the issues presented by improperly obtained evidence in a wider context. This context is the functions of the criminal process itself and the verdict that constitutes the culmination of the process. The moral authority and expressive value of the verdict may be significantly imperilled by improperly obtained evidence. The danger can be present in various forms: unreliable evidence that detracts from the factual accuracy of the verdict, evidence obtained in breach of the accused's fundamental right to a fair trial that detracts from the moral authority of the verdict, and evidence obtained by deliberate police abuse of power that detracts from both the moral authority and the expressive value of the verdict. On this approach it is always relevant to consider the traditional principles discussed above, but they must be considered both individually and cumulatively, and the final question is always one of the impact of the impropriety on the legitimacy of the verdict.

3–046 In Ch.2 it was argued that exclusion of items of relevant evidence as a matter of *discretion* always requires justification by appeal to a significant risk of

---

[209] per Stephen and Aickin JJ. in *Bunning v Cross* (1978) 141 C.L.R. 54 at 74–75.

[210] Mirfield, *Silence, Confessions* (1997), pp.24, 360.

[211] per McHugh J. in *Ridgeway v R.* (1995) 129 A.L.R. 41 at 89.

[212] See Sopinka J. in *Burlingham* (1995) 2 S.C.R. 206 at 210, commenting on the earlier judgment of Lamer J. in *Collins* (1987) 1 S.C.R. 265.

unreliability in the circumstances of the particular case, and/or to a significant risk that use of the evidence will undermine the moral authority and/or expressive value of the verdict in the particular case. This is the key to understanding the proper scope and limits of s.78. The section makes most sense when interpreted as capable of applying to *all* prosecution evidence, irrespective of the nature or the source of the evidence, and irrespective of how it was obtained. The "proceedings" should be understood as referring to the whole of the proceedings against the accused. The fairness of the proceedings as a whole may be adversely affected if admission of the prosecution evidence in question means that the prosecution have an advantage that is inconsistent with the fundamental moral and political values of the criminal justice system. This advantage may be the use of evidence that is unreliable and prejudicial, or it may be the use of evidence obtained in violation of the accused's human rights, or it may be evidence obtained by deliberate abuse of process, and so on. Section 78 enables the trial judge to calculate whether the extent of the unfair advantage is such as to require the exclusion of the evidence. In this way the judge is able to safeguard the legitimacy of the verdict in the exceptional case where there is a significant risk that this will be undermined by the admission of the evidence.

CHAPTER 4

FACTS AND FACTFINDING

A.   INTRODUCTION

The third of the fundamental concepts of the law of evidence, after relevance and   **4–001**
admissibility, is that of weight. Weight is a concept employed in the evaluation of
evidence. Assume that the judge has admitted the evidence in question, having
decided that it is relevant to the facts in issue, that it is admissible in law in the
sense that it does not fall foul of any exclusionary rule, and that it should not be
excluded in the exercise of judicial discretion. It is then the task of the factfinder
to assess the extent to which the evidence as a whole proves the facts in issue in
the case. The weight of any particular item of evidence is the strength of its
tendency to prove one or more of the facts in issue, when considered in
conjunction with the other evidence in the case.[1]

Weight differs from relevance in this way. When a judge decides that evidence
is relevant, the judge is deciding that it is *capable* of affecting the probability of a
fact in issue in the estimation of a rational factfinder, on the assumption that the
factfinder could find the evidence to be credible and reliable. In this sense the
relevance of evidence is its *potential* weight as tending to prove one or more facts
in issue. When a factfinder decides on the weight of the evidence, the factfinder is

---

[1] It will of course have to be considered by itself if it is the only evidence in the case (sometimes the
only prosecution evidence of guilt is the accused's confession), or if it is the only evidence relating to
one of the facts in issue.

[111]

estimating the degree to which the evidence *does* affect the probability of a fact in issue, on the assumption that the factfinder has found the evidence to have a degree of credibility and reliability. Evidence that the factfinder rejects as incredible or wholly unreliable has no weight. A risk of unreliability reduces the weight of the evidence.

The term "probative value" ought also to be mentioned at this point. According to the Law Commission, evidence has probative value where it is both true and relevant to a fact in issue.[2] The use of the word "true" here is too strong and potentially misleading; the "truth" of a particular item of evidence, in any absolute sense, is not a condition of its having probative value. Evidence of identification from a credible eyewitness has probative value, even though there may be a question mark over its accuracy. A judge would not have to be satisfied that it was a true (i.e. accurate) identification before admitting the evidence. It would be more accurate simply to say that the probative value of evidence is the extent to which it tends to increase or decrease the probability of a fact in issue. Thus in one usage "probative value" means the same as weight when we are talking about the decisions of a factfinder. In another usage the term can refer to the degree of relevance that certain evidence has.[3] The degree of relevance is the judge's estimate of the extent to which the evidence could affect the probability of a fact in issue, in the judgment of a rational factfinder. The judge may have to make this estimate of probative value whenever a question arises of whether the evidence is likely to have a prejudicial effect on the factfinder. For example, suppose that in an assault case the prosecution adduce evidence from a doctor about the nature and extent of the injuries. The prosecution then seek to supplement the testimony with grisly police photographs of the injuries. They have little probative value in the circumstances (assuming the doctor's testimony to be credible and reliable), but as a visual medium they may have a significant emotional impact on a jury. That may in turn increase the jury's sympathy for the victim and arouse hostility towards the accused. If this tendency is clearly disproportionate to the rational strength of the evidence as a means of proof, the exclusionary discretion is available to prevent an accused suffering prejudice.[4]

4–002   The evaluation of evidence raises a number of issues which will be considered in this chapter. The first section deals with the identity of factfinders in criminal and civil proceedings. It discusses the fundamental distinction between issues of law and fact and the associated division of function in jury trials between judge and jury, a division that has had a profound influence on the structure and content of the law of evidence. The second section examines the formal controls on the factfinding process, such as withdrawal of issues, judicial warnings and instructions, judicial powers to comment to juries on evidence, and possibilities of reversing decisions of fact on appeal.

---

[2] Law Com. Consultation Paper No.141, *Evidence in Criminal Proceedings: Previous Misconduct of a Defendant* (London: 1996), para.6.2.

[3] Sometimes statute requires evidence to have "substantial probative value" to be admissible: see, e.g. Criminal Justice Act 2003 ss.100(1)(b) and 101(1)(e). In *Braithwaite* [2010] EWCA Crim 1082; [2010] 2 Cr.App.R. 18 at [15] the Court of Appeal distinguished this standard from "simple relevance".

[4] See *Murphy* (1987) 37 A.C.R. 118 at 127; *Baker* [1989] 3 N.Z.L.R. 635; R. Pattenden, *Judicial Discretion and Criminal Litigation* (1990), p.244.

It will be seen that in the construction of its rules the law makes certain assumptions concerning the nature of "facts" and the process of reasoning about disputed questions of fact. These assumptions raise major theoretical issues that have been much debated in the literature on evidence and related disciplines in recent years. The interest and importance of these issues is such that no modern study of evidence can afford to neglect them. An extended treatment is not possible in a work of this nature, but the third and fourth sections of the chapter aim to provide some introductory discussion of some of the main themes of the debates. The third section deals with "fact-scepticism" and associated theories about the way in which "knowledge" is or may be socially constructed. The fourth section looks at theories concerned with the process of factfinding. This discussion will include some consideration of probability theory and of the uses and limits of mathematical models of reasoning about disputed questions of fact.

B.   QUESTIONS OF FACT AND QUESTIONS OF LAW

1.   *The basic distinction and the allocation of decision-making*

The division of issues in legal proceedings into questions of fact and questions of law is fundamental. It represents the distinction, in Zuckerman's words, between "the question of what happened and the legal consequences of that which happened".[5] Official adjudication of disputes is founded on the assumption that facts of cases exist independently of the law. Accordingly, it is conceived to be part of the function of legal process to "find" the facts, either in the form of what the parties agree are the facts, or by means of authoritative rulings after the hearing of evidence. This must be done before the law, which states normative rules for certain fact-situations can be applied to the particular facts of the dispute. Certain ancillary principles are founded on the distinction between law and fact; the most important is that decisions on questions of law may constitute binding precedents for other cases, whereas decisions on questions of fact do not.[6]

4–003

In jury trials the distinction also signifies the allocation of function between jury and judge. The general principle is that the judge decides questions of law, and generally does so on the basis of the arguments about legal texts which are advanced by the lawyers in the case. Questions of fact are for decision by the jury on the basis of the evidence adduced in the case and the inferences to be drawn from the evidence. In civil trials without a jury the judge decides all questions of law and fact, but the distinction between law and fact has some importance at the appeal stage. Appeal courts will not hesitate to reverse a judge on a point of law, if persuaded that the ruling was wrong, but their attitude to reversing decisions on fact is more complex. Generally appeal courts will rarely interfere with a judge's findings of primary facts.[7] This is because they take the view that the judge was

---

[5] Zuckerman, *Principles*, p.22.

[6] Note also the procedural principle that in civil cases the parties must plead facts and not law.

[7] "Primary facts are facts which are observed by witnesses and proved by oral testimony or facts proved by the production of a thing itself, such as original documents": per Denning L.J. in *British Launderers Assoc v Hendon Rating Authority* [1949] 1 K.B. 462.

the person best placed to make such findings, given that he saw and heard all the witnesses and had the general feel of the case. However, where the issue is the inferences to be drawn from the evidence given by the witnesses, rather than assessments of the witnesses' credibility and demeanour, an appeal court may regard itself as well placed as the judge to draw the necessary inferences. It might therefore be more prepared to reassess the judge's conclusions.[8] In all proceedings before magistrates the bench is responsible for decisions on both law and fact. On questions of law, lay magistrates are expected to take the advice of their clerk.

In general, questions of law include questions relating to the substantive law that governs the rights, duties and liabilities of the parties. Questions such as: What are the elements of murder? Did the defendant owe a duty of care to the claimant? Is a testator's unsigned will valid? are clear examples of questions of law. The duties and powers of the tribunal hearing the proceedings are also questions of law. This heading takes in such matters as the court's power to admit or exclude evidence, a judge's power to withdraw an issue from the jury, the judge's duty to direct the jury on the burden and standard of proof, and so on. Questions of fact include such questions as the credibility and reliability of the witnesses, the weight of the evidence given in the proceedings, and whether the burden of proof has been satisfied. In jury trials these questions of fact are decided by the jury.

These are elementary principles. They need a certain amount of expansion and qualification because the distinction between law and fact is not as sharp and straightforward as first appears, nor does it provide a wholly accurate account of the division of functions in jury trial.

2. *Qualifying the distinction and blurring the division of function in jury trials*

4–004   First, the general principles are subject to the point that some issues may be regarded as mixed questions of law and fact, with judge and jury having separate functions in relation to the issue. An illustration is provided by the law of criminal attempts: statute provides that where there is evidence sufficient in law to support a finding that a person had done an act more than merely preparatory to the commission of an offence, the question whether the act was more than merely preparatory is a question of fact.[9] In jury trials the former issue is a question of law for the judge, whereas the latter question is for the jury to decide.

Secondly, particular issues may be stipulated to be ones of law or fact, and the classification may not correspond to Zuckerman's distinction between "what happened" and "the legal consequences of what happened". The classification may be made for reasons of expediency, and these reasons may dictate that the

---

[8] *Whitehouse v Jordan* [1981] 1 All E.R. 267 HL. In *Grant* [2005] EWCA Crim 1089; [2005] 2 Cr.App.R. 28 at [43] the Court of Appeal said that it would take a very exceptional case for it to accede to an argument that it should overturn a decision by an experienced judge on a voir dire when the judge had heard much live evidence, but went on to hold that the judge's conclusions from the evidence he had heard in the case were unpersuasive.

[9] Criminal Attempts Act 1981 s.4(3).

general principles on the allocation of functions should not be followed. A good example is questions of foreign law, that is questions relating to the law of any jurisdiction outside England and Wales. These questions involve the interpretation of legal texts in the same way as questions of English law. Nevertheless, they are treated as questions of fact to be decided by the judge.[10] In order to make the decision the judge will hear evidence as to the relevant foreign law. The evidence will usually come from expert witnesses; in the event of a contest the judge will have to decide the same kinds of issues of credibility and weight that may confront juries in dealing with other kinds of expert evidence. Evidence of foreign law may also take the form of a previous decision on the point by an English court of superior status. In this context, unusually, previous decisions on questions of "fact" may constitute precedents in future cases involving the same point.

This is not the only situation in which judges in jury trials make decisions on questions of fact, and more is said about this below. Equally, some jury decisions are arguably decisions of law. To explore this point further it is helpful to note that there are different types of question of "fact" involved in legal proceedings. Glanville Williams, in an important article,[11] suggested a fourfold classification of "facts".

First, there are what may be called "primary" or "brute" facts. These are events **4–005** and circumstances existing in the world and experienced by persons with their own senses. In legal proceedings their existence is reported by witnesses either as things they did or said themselves, or as things they directly observed with their own senses: physical acts, the colour of a vehicle, a person's oral statement, and so on. The weight of the evidence of such facts depends on the credibility and reliability of the witnesses involved.

Secondly, there are "inferential" facts. These are events and circumstances whose existence in the world is inferred from other facts, which may themselves be primary or inferential. Fingerprints found at the scene of a crime are primary facts. The prints may be inferred to be those of the accused if they match the prints he was observed to have given at the police station. If the prints are on a knife found in a victim's back, and the accused was observed entering the victim's room with an upraised knife, it may be inferred first that the knives are the same and secondly that the accused stabbed the victim with the requisite intent for murder. The weight of the evidence of inferential facts depends, first, on the credibility and reliability of the witnesses to the facts from which inferences are being drawn and, secondly, on the strength of the inferences which can be drawn from those facts.

---

[10] Administration of Justice Act 1920 s.15, applied in criminal proceedings by *Hammer* [1923] 2 K.B. 786; Senior Courts Act 1981 s.69(5); County Courts Act 1984 s.68. Note that the law of the European Community is not foreign law for this purpose: s.3 of the European Communities Act 1972 provides for the taking of judicial notice of European law. The Supreme Court of the United Kingdom takes judicial notice of the law of Scotland and Northern Ireland by virtue of being the final court of appeal for those jurisdictions, but in other courts in England and Wales Scots and Northern Irish law must be proved by evidence.

[11] G. Williams, "Law and Fact" [1976] Crim. L.R. 472, 532.

The third of Williams' categories is "evaluative" facts.[12] These are judgments of value made by comparing primary and inferential facts to a legal standard: whether an accused's use of force was "reasonable" force in self-defence is an example. Legal standards of this type require factfinders to make the necessary value judgments of degree by using social standards that they supply themselves.

4–006 Fourthly, there are what Williams called "denotative" facts.[13] These are decisions of classification in the sense that they require a judgment whether primary and inferential facts fall within a particular legal description. Examples include the questions whether a victim's injuries amounted to "grievous bodily harm" for the purposes of s.18 of the Offences Against the Person Act 1861, and whether a person's conduct was "dishonest" for the purposes of the crime of theft. This category of "fact" is controversial because many of the questions of classification involved could be regarded as questions of law in the sense that they are capable of stipulative legal definition. The description "grievous bodily harm", for example, could be expanded to include a catalogue of types of injury. It is sometimes argued that leaving such classificatory issues at large is an improper delegation to factfinders of questions that ought to be dealt with as issues of law. Dishonesty, which is arguably the main inculpatory element of theft,[14] is particularly controversial left to a jury as a largely indeterminate question of "fact".[15]

In jury trials, therefore, it can be seen that the factfinder's function extends to deciding some issues that could well be dealt with as questions of law. By contrast, some decisions reserved for the judge are decisions on issues of fact.[16] The most obvious are facts forming conditions of admissibility of evidence. Because admissibility is itself a question of law, the determination of factual issues on which admissibility depends has been treated as part of the legal question and hence as part of the judicial function. Accordingly a judge may have to decide whether the tape of an interview reveals that the police made promises of favour to a suspect in return for a confession (primary fact) and, if so, whether this amounted to something said likely to render unreliable any confession by the suspect[17] (an inferential fact).

If the facts on which admissibility depends are disputed, the judge will have to hear evidence about the facts. The procedure for doing so is known as the voir dire and is in effect a trial within a trial. It involves evidence as to the relevant

---

[12] Also called "normative" facts: D. A. Binder and P. Bergman, *Fact Investigation* (Minn.: St Paul, 1984), pp.6–7.

[13] They are similar to Hohfeld's "operative facts": W. N. Hohfeld, *Fundamental Legal Conceptions as Applied in Judicial Reasoning* (New Haven: Yale University Press, 1923), pp.32–35. For further discussion of the law/fact distinction, deploying Hohfeldian terminology, see Roberts and Zuckerman, pp.129–137.

[14] As a result of *Gomez* [1993] A.C. 442; and *Hinks* [2001] 2 A.C. 241.

[15] I. Dennis, "The Critical Condition of Criminal Law" [1997] C.L.P. 213. The first part of the well-known test devised by the Court of Appeal in *Feely* [1973] 1 Q.B. 530; and *Ghosh* [1982] Q.B. 1053 asks whether the accused's conduct was dishonest according to the current standards of ordinary decent people. This is about as indeterminate as it is possible to get, and of course it assumes a social consensus about dealings with other people's property that may not exist.

[16] For an illuminating analysis see R. Pattenden, "Pre-verdict judicial fact-finding in criminal trials with juries" (2009) 29 O.J.L.S. 1.

[17] PACE s.76(2), discussed in Ch.6.

facts being given on oath in the normal way, with the witnesses being examined and cross-examined by the parties. Counsel address the judge on the issues arising and the judge then rules on the admissibility of the disputed evidence. Such evidence will be heard in the absence of the jury if there is any risk of the jury hearing disputed evidence that could be prejudicial to the accused, such as a confession or previous convictions.

3. Submissions of no case to answer

A judge may also have to make preliminary determinations of the weight of evidence. A submission of no case to answer at the close of the prosecution evidence[18] will entail a decision whether the prosecution have produced sufficient evidence on which a reasonable jury[19] could convict. In *Galbraith*,[20] the Court of Appeal held that this test required only an assessment of the potential weight of the evidence; assuming that a reasonable jury accepted the evidence and the inferences sought to be drawn from it, was it capable of proving the case beyond reasonable doubt? It was not part of the judge's function to form a view of the actual weight of the evidence in the sense of how creditworthy he found the witnesses or of how persuasive he found the inferences from their testimony. The judge could only stop the case if there was no evidence that the crime alleged was committed by the defendant or the evidence was so tenuous that no jury could properly convict on it.[21] It should be noted that the judge has a continuing responsibility throughout the case not to allow a jury to consider evidence on which they could not properly convict. This responsibility continues to the close of all the evidence.[22] If at that stage the judge thinks that no reasonable jury could properly convict he should raise the issue with counsel even if the defence have not made a submission of no case to answer.

4–007

The *Galbraith* rule has sometimes been criticised[23] for allowing too many weak prosecution cases to reach the jury, with consequent dangers of a miscarriage of justice. The Royal Commission on Criminal Justice recommended reversal of *Galbraith* and its replacement by a power in the judge to withdraw an issue (or even the whole case) from the jury if the judge considers the evidence to be too weak or to be demonstrably unsafe or unsatisfactory.[24] This would modify

---

[18] On applications for dismissal of charges under s.6 of the Criminal Justice Act 1987 see *R. v Crown Court at Kingston* [2001] 4 All E.R. 721 DC.

[19] Or bench of magistrates: *CPS v S* [2007] EWHC Admin 3313.

[20] *Galbraith* [1981] 1 W.L.R. 1039.

[21] For an example of a case where a judge found the prosecution evidence "tenuous" see *Shippey* [1988] Crim. L.R. 767 (Turner J. ruled that "frankly incredible" parts of a complainant's testimony and "really significant inherent inconsistencies" in the testimony meant that a jury could not properly convict on her evidence). cf. *CPS v S* [2007] EWHC Admin 3313 (Divisional Court held that a magistrates' ruling of no case to answer on the basis of inconsistencies between prosecution witnesses was perverse).

[22] In *Brown (Davina)* [2002] 1 Cr.App.R. 46 the Court of Appeal confirmed that a judge has a power and a duty to withdraw a case from the jury at any time after the close of the prosecution case if he is satisfied that no jury properly directed could convict.

[23] See R. Pattenden, "The Submission of No Case—Some Recent Developments" [1982] Crim. L.R. 558; A. Ashworth and M. Redmayne, *The Criminal Process*, 4th edn (2010), pp.340–342.

[24] RCCJ Report, Ch.4, para.42.

significantly the traditional principle that the assessment of the credibility and reliability of witnesses is a jury matter, but this principle has already been modified for weak, unsupported identification evidence[25] and for unsupported confessions made by persons suffering from serious mental defects.[26] Section 125 of the Criminal Justice Act 2003 has created a third exception, giving a judge power to stop a prosecution case based wholly or partly on unconvincing hearsay evidence. It seems highly desirable to generalise these exceptions in the interests of preventing possible wrongful convictions. Given that the Court of Appeal has a duty to quash a conviction it regards as unsafe,[27] it would be logical and efficient, as well as right in principle, for the trial judge to refuse to give the jury the opportunity to bring in a verdict of guilty that in his view would be unsafe. However, in *CPS v F*,[28] the Court of Appeal recently confirmed and restated the *Galbraith* test in the context of a historic sex abuse case where the complaint was much delayed. The court held that the adequacy of the complainant's explanation for the delay was a matter for the jury not the judge. Even if the judge thought that the explanation was unsatisfactory, the question was not whether in the judge's view a conviction would be safe but whether on the evidence a jury, properly directed, could properly convict.[29]

C.   LEGAL CONTROLS ON FACTFINDING

4–008   One of the principal functions of the law of evidence is to control and direct the process of factfinding. The rules of admissibility are one of the most obvious manifestations of this function, and it was noted in Ch.1 that these rules are numerous and complex. It is commonly said by contrast that English law has no rules of weight. The meaning of this claim is that the law does not prescribe the weight of particular types or forms of evidence, such as eyewitness identification evidence or documents under seal. Instead, evaluation of witnesses and of the cogency of the evidence are left as questions at large for the factfinder. However, while it is true that there is no system of formal proofs in English law, there are several mechanisms which place significant constraints on the unregulated power of factfinders to determine issues of weight of evidence. Some of these mechanisms, such as the specimen directions issued by the Judicial Studies Board (see below), are intended only for use in jury trial. Others have more general application to other forms of criminal and civil trial as well as juries.

---

[25] *Turnbull* [1977] 1 Q.B. 224; *Fergus* (1994) 98 Cr.App.R. 313. See also *Daley v R.* [1993] 4 All E.R. 86 PC, where Lord Mustill offered an alternative explanation of the relationship between *Galbraith* (a rule about leaving decisions on credibility to juries) and *Turnbull* (a rule about not leaving unreliable identification evidence to juries); see further Ch.7.

[26] *Mackenzie* (1993) 96 Cr.App.R. 98. The Court of Appeal purported to apply *Galbraith*, but it seems clear that it created an exception to the general rule that the assessment of the reliability of a witness is a matter for the jury. See further Ch.6.

[27] Criminal Appeal Act 1968 s.2(1).

[28] *CPS v F* [2011] EWCA Crim 1844.

[29] The court also emphasised that the *Galbraith* test for withdrawing the case from the jury should not be confused with the test for stopping the prosecution as an abuse of process. The latter test is whether the defendant can receive a fair trial. In the context of delay this requires consideration of how far the defendant has been prejudiced by the delay.

As stated above, judges must withdraw issues from juries if they consider that the prosecution has adduced insufficient evidence to satisfy the standard of proof. There is a duty to direct an acquittal in such a case. On the other hand, according to the House of Lords in *Wang*,[30] there are no circumstances in which a trial judge in a criminal case is entitled to direct a jury to convict.[31] It makes no difference that the defendant does not contest the prosecution evidence; even where uncontested evidence is sufficient to prove all the elements of the offence charged, the defendant still has a right to the jury's verdict. This right to what may be in effect a perverse verdict is controversial, but it is consistent with the theory that the jury is a constitutional guarantor of legitimacy in serious cases. As discussed later in this chapter, a residual power to exercise jury equity to acquit in rare cases where conviction could not be morally justified is arguably a functional necessity of the criminal justice system.

As regards defences, the right to the jury's verdict does not entitle a defendant to ask the jury to consider factual defences to the charge if there is no foundation for them. The judge must leave to the jury any defence for which there is evidential support, however thin,[32] and whether or not it is expressly raised by the defendant.[33] A judge has no duty to leave a defence to the jury if it is speculative and has no evidence to support it.[34] In non-jury trials successful submissions of no case to answer will result in dismissal of the charge in question or a verdict for the party against whom the evidence was given.

Where rules of evidence stipulate that certain evidence may only be used in certain ways, judges must direct juries to this effect and must apply the rules themselves in non-jury trials. There is much scepticism that some of these rules of use of evidence are too complex or unacceptably technical to be understood or correctly applied by juries,[35] but it is a formal requirement that the appropriate directions be given. In other contexts, judges are required in effect to educate juries by means of discourses on the risks attached to particular types of evidence

4–009

---

[30] *Wang* [2005] UKHL 9; [2005] 2 Cr.App.R. 8, approving the majority opinions of the House of Lords in *DPP v Stonehouse* [1978] A.C. 55.

[31] cf. however, *Hill and Hall* (1989) 89 Cr.App.R. 74 CA, where the Court of Appeal upheld a conviction after the trial judge ruled that the defendants' defence to admitted facts was not a defence in law, and directed the jury to convict. In *Wang* [2005] UKHL 9; [2005] 2 Cr.App. R. 8 Lord Bingham commented that *Hill and Hall* is not easy to reconcile with the majority opinions in *Stonehouse*.

[32] Including the exculpatory part of a pre-trial mixed statement: *Silverman* (1987) 86 Cr.App.R. 213 CA; *Bass* [1992] Crim. L.R. 647 CA.

[33] *Mancini v DPP* [1942] A.C. 1 HL (provocation); *Kachikwu* (1965) 52 Cr.App.R. 538 CCA (self-defence); *Bashir* (1982) 77 Cr.App.R. 60 CA (belief in consent). See further S. Doran, "Alternative Defences: the 'invisible burden' on the trial judge" [1991] Crim. L.R. 878.

[34] *Briley* [1991] Crim. L.R. 444 CA; *Acott* [1997] 2 Cr.App.R. 94 HL.

[35] Scepticism may be reinforced by the research finding in Cheryl Thomas's report for the Ministry of Justice, *Are Juries Fair?* (MOJ, 2010), p.37) that "while over half the jurors at Winchester (68 per cent) perceived the judge's directions [on self-defence] as easy to understand, only a minority fully understood the directions in terms used by the judge". See also L. Ellison and V. E. Munro, "Getting to (not) guilty: examining jurors' deliberative processes in, and beyond, the context of a mock rape trial" (2010) 30 L.S. 74, esp. pp.95–96. To improve juror comprehension many trial judges now supply juries with written summaries of the directions and documents such as a suggested "Route to Verdict"; for strong support for this development see H.H. Judge Madge, "Summing-Up—A Judge's Perspective" [2006] Crim. L.R. 817.

and on the techniques to be employed in its evaluation. The instructions which have to be given about eyewitness identification evidence which is alleged to be mistaken are an important illustration of how the law seeks both to inform and to structure factfinders' decision-making about the assessment of problematic evidence. Other instances of "caution" warnings are less elaborate, but in general the warnings must still be given.[36]

For some years the Judicial Studies Board issued a series of specimen directions for trial judges to use in directing juries as to the issues the jury had to decide. These were widely followed, not least because their use was thought to make the summing-up more appeal-proof. However, the specimen directions were sometimes given rather mechanistically without sufficient regard to the needs of the individual case, a tendency reinforced by the practice of some defence counsel of arguing that departures from the specimen directions rendered convictions unsafe. Concern about these developments led in March 2010 to the specimen directions being overtaken by a new edition of the Crown Court Bench Book, also published by the Judicial Studies Board.[37] The new form of the Bench Book is intended to help and encourage trial judges to craft directions that are appropriately tailored to the individual case, and aims to discourage the culture of criticising any deviations from the general forms of words suggested in the specimen directions.

Finally, it is an accepted part of the judicial function in English law to give juries guidance on evaluating evidence. A judge's summing-up may include comment on assessing the credibility of witnesses, comment on the inferences that may be drawn from the evidence and comment on the weight of the evidence. There is a large element of discretion in the content and style of such comment, and the Court of Appeal will be reluctant to interfere provided that the judge has complied with the duty to present the defence case fairly. Within that constraint the judge has considerable latitude in deciding the emphasis and the language of the summing-up.[38]

D.   FACT-SCEPTICISM AND THE CONSTRUCTION OF KNOWLEDGE

1.   *Reconstructing a "true" reality*

4–010   In Ch.2 it was noted how the rationalist model of adjudication seems to adopt a "correspondence" theory of truth. According to this theory, facts have an objective existence in the physical world. They are capable of being experienced by human beings using their senses, in ways that correspond to their reality, and their existence is therefore capable of being reported to an inquirer such as a court. A court inquiring into past facts will not have experienced the facts itself, but may nonetheless reconstruct the facts through a process of inference. The

---

[36] See Ch.15.

[37] The *Crown Court Bench Book—Directing the Jury* is published online at www.judiciary.gov.uk [Accessed January 24, 2013]. The Judicial Studies Board is now the Judicial College.

[38] No one interested in this important topic should overlook the unique insight provided by Devlin J. into his summing-up in the notorious murder case involving Dr Bodkin Adams. See P. Devlin, *Easing the Passing* (London: The Bodley Head, 1985), Ch.20.

inferences may be founded on the estimated reliability of reports of persons with direct experience of the facts in issue. Alternatively, or in addition, inferences may be founded on circumstantial evidence, that is, evidence of facts relevant to the facts in issue. By this process of inference the theory argues that an accurate reconstruction can be made that corresponds to the reality of past events.

However, the possibility of accurate reconstruction is contingent on the existence of certain conditions. The fulfilment of these conditions is in practice so problematic that the goal of recreating the events in question to a standard of mathematical certainty[39] is unattainable. We will first look at why this is so, before considering the response to the problem, then we will go on to consider some important strands of sceptical thinking about the enterprise of factfinding in legal contexts.

To ensure a wholly accurate reconstruction of past events we would first have to be certain that we were in possession of all the relevant evidence. The information from which inferences were to be drawn would have to be complete, with no possibility of any relevant material being overlooked or unavailable. Two obvious difficulties arise. How do we know when information is complete? Only a literally omniscient being could make a confident claim that there was nothing further to be known about a past reality. For ordinary mortals, such an epistemological claim is inherently conjectural. Moreover, the very notion of relevance depends, as we have seen, on the acceptance of background generalisations that may be contestable or open to differing interpretation. Secondly, we would have to be certain that witnesses who gave direct evidence of the facts in issue had made complete and correct observations, had recalled the events from their memory fully and accurately and had reported their observations to the factfinder fully, honestly and without ambiguity. These are demanding standards. In relation to the identification of persons we shall note in Ch.7 extensive psychological research suggesting that eyewitness identification is so inherently fallible that one could never confidently assert in a given case that it is reliable to the point of mathematical certainty. Thirdly, as far as circumstantial evidence is concerned, in addition to the problems of completeness and reliability we would have to be certain that the inferences being drawn as to the facts in issue were also complete and accurate, in the sense that no other inferences were possible that might cast any degree of doubt on our conclusions.

It is for these reasons that the correspondence theory, which aspires to a faithful present replication of a past reality, promises a goal that remains permanently elusive. At all stages of the legal process the necessary conditions provide scope for errors in factfinding. In consequence, for the purposes of use in a practical but imperfect world, the correspondence theory has had to settle for the truth of past events to be treated as a matter of probability rather than certainty. Inquirers in legal contexts, such as police officers and courts, may strive to eliminate errors as far as possible but they must ultimately acknowledge that decisions cannot be made to depend on a standard of perfect correspondence between present

4–011

---

[39] Standard mathematical notation expresses probabilities on a scale from nought to one. Nought signifies the certain negative of proposition x, one signifies the certain affirmative of x. For an introduction to mathematical reasoning about probabilities see R. Eggleston, *Evidence, Proof and Probability*, 2nd edn (London: 1983).

knowledge and past history. Even in criminal cases, where the stakes are frequently highest, the standard of proof cannot be made more stringent than beyond reasonable doubt if the system of conviction and punishment is to work at all.

Acceptance of these points suggests that all that factfinders can do, and all that we can reasonably expect them to do, is to reach the best decision that they can in conditions of uncertainty.[40] The best decision for this purpose is the one that gets closest to "what happened" in the world "out there", but accuracy cannot be guaranteed. It is because "truth" can only ever be a matter of probability that the rationalist model of adjudication pays so much attention to procedures that are intended to reduce the possibility of error.

There is in any event scope for scepticism about how far legal processes are suited to serving the epistemological aspirations of the rationalist model. The model presupposes that truth-finding is the principal aim of adjudication, but we have already noted the view that the common law adversarial procedure does not function as an open-minded and open-ended inquiry into the "truth" of a past reality. The American realist Jerome Frank[41] was one of the first and most influential exponents of a common view amongst legal practitioners that adversarial procedure resembles a contest or "fight" in which the aim is to persuade the factfinder to accept one of the two or more competing versions of reality that the parties construct and then present to the court. The version chosen then constitutes the official "truth" for the purposes of the adjudication. Clearly, a factfinder may decide not to accept any of the partisan versions in its entirety but to construct a further version modified according to the factfinder's preferences for particular features of the partisan models. This does not affect the essential validity of the "fight" theory, since the factfinder's freedom of inquiry is still largely curtailed by the parties' autonomy in choosing the issues on which to fight and the evidence adduced on those issues. Frank's criticism was that the "truth" arrived at by this procedure was essentially contingent and haphazard. It might correspond to historical reality, depending on how thoroughly the parties prepared their cases and how conscientiously the factfinder evaluated them, but the system was not structurally designed to maximise the chance of achieving this result.

4–012   It was an implicit assumption of Frank's critique, as Twining has noted,[42] that the concept of a historical truth was meaningful. Frank was not a "fact-sceptic" in any strong sense; for him, historical facts had an objective existence that was capable of being discovered by rational inquiry. He wanted to improve accuracy of factfinding and to avoid miscarriages of justice. His concern was with the means adopted to discover the truth in adjudicative proceedings, his point being that the parties did not present the court with all the available means of discovery, complete and unedited.

---

[40] See, for further discussion, A. Stein, "The Refoundation of Evidence Law" (1996) IX *Canadian Journal of Law and Jurisprudence* 279; and Ch.2 of his *Foundations of Evidence Law* (Oxford: Oxford University Press, 2005).

[41] See in particular J. Frank, *Courts on Trial* (Princeton: Princeton University Press, 1949).

[42] W. Twining, "Some Scepticism about Some Scepticisms" in *Rethinking Evidence*, 2nd edn (2006), p.118.

Many defence lawyers would deny that this is their job. A common view amongst practitioners is that in an adversarial system of criminal justice the purpose of the trial is to test the prosecution case. On this view the responsibility of the defence lawyer is not to help the court discover some independent historical truth. It is rather to test the truth of the accusation made by the prosecution that the defendant committed the offence charged. Certainly one way of doing this is by setting up an alternative version of past events and inviting the jury to accept that version in preference to the one constructed by the prosecution. Alternatively the defence might simply adopt the strategy of challenging the credibility and reliability of the prosecution evidence—"putting the prosecution to proof"—and arguing that it fails to prove the charge, either beyond reasonable doubt or at all. Those who take this view are particularly resistant to any idea that the duty to give a defence statement under s.5 of the Criminal Procedure and Investigations Act 1996 should require the defence to set out a positive case in response to the prosecution case.

2. *The social contingency of facts*

Later theorists of legal process and of the sociology of knowledge have taken matters considerably further. Broadly speaking, two major critiques have developed. One body of work has been concerned with the extent to which the "facts" of a case are actively constructed, or reconstructed, by the parties in legal processes before the factfinder comes to attempt the reconstruction required for the purpose of deciding the case. From this standpoint facts do not have, or do not necessarily have, an independent static quality that can be discovered by an impartial enquirer. Rather they are, or may be, socially contingent; a product of the social process used to determine them and hence possessing a dynamic and dependent quality.

4–013

Socio-legal research into pre-trial criminal investigations has emphasised the ways in which the "facts" can be manipulated by the participants in the process. McConville, Sanders and Leng comment:

> "at each point of the criminal justice process 'what happened' is the subject of interpretation, addition, subtraction, selection and reformulation. This process is a continuous process... [Case construction] involves not simply the selection and interpretation of evidence but its creation."[43]

One of the clearest examples of this process may occur in the interrogation of suspects. McConville, Sanders and Leng suggest that interrogation is used not only to unlock factual information that the suspect already has, but also in a creative way to bring facts into existence in the form of admissions produced and structured by the form and manner of questioning.[44] Obtaining evidence of mens rea in this way is common. A suspect might be led to admit that he must have been conscious of taking a risk of causing injury to someone when doing a

---

[43] M. McConville, A. Sanders and R. Leng, *The Case for the Prosecution* (London: Routledge 1991), p.12.
[44] M. McConville, A. Sanders and R. Leng, *The Case for the Prosecution* (1991) pp.65–67.

particular act, and therefore that he acted recklessly,[45] whereas the reality may have been different. The risk might have been obvious, but the suspect may not in fact have thought about it at the time. A further important feature of interrogation is how it may be used to repress or marginalise exculpatory information from the suspect. This is a particular danger where a police officer approaches an interview on the assumption that the suspect is guilty and that the only purpose of the interview is to produce a confession. Explanations not amounting to admissions are not likely to be of interest to such an officer and hence may not be pursued. It should be noted, however, that para.3.5 of the Code of Practice under Pt II of the Criminal Procedure and Investigations Act 1996 states that the investigator should pursue all reasonable lines of inquiry, whether these point towards or away from the suspect. What is reasonable in each case will depend on the particular circumstances. Despite this duty, there remains a danger that the record of the interview may represent a filtering of the information from the suspect about the "facts" of the case and a misleading picture of the reality.

4–014   A similar process of control may be exerted by the lawyers at the trial.[46] When lawyers question witnesses they prefer not to ask open questions that permit the witness to make a free report of what the witness knows.[47] This is because they do not want to give the witness an opportunity of qualifying favourable evidence or of saying something positively damaging to the case of the party conducting the questioning.[48] Consequently questions are often phrased so as to require short definite answers that fit the version of the facts being put forward by the questioner. Witnesses will be discouraged from volunteering additional material and will be required to tailor their answers to the framework imposed by the lawyers' questions. In this way again a filtered and possibly misleading account of the facts may be presented to the factfinder.

Such perceptions have led some commentators to raise epistemological questions about the concept of truth itself and about the extent to which there is ever an objective reality that can be discovered by means of inference from the "facts" as presented by witnesses.[49] The other development which has reached radical sceptical conclusions is the philosophical critiques of some postmodernist and feminist writers.[50] Such work often makes forceful denials of the law's claim

---

[45] For the purposes of an offence, say, of maliciously inflicting grievous bodily harm under s.20 of the Offences Against the Person Act 1861.

[46] D. McBarnet, *Conviction* (Oxford: Macmillian, 1981), pp.16 onwards; J. McEwan, *Evidence and the Adversarial Process*, 2nd edn (Oxford: Hart Publishing, 1998), p.13; P. Rock, *The Social World of an English Crown Court* (Oxford: Clarendon Press, 1993), pp.59–60, 177.

[47] See, e.g. P. Murphy and D. Barnard, *Evidence and Advocacy* (London: 1984), Ch.8, esp. p.123.

[48] This is particularly important in cross-examination, where control may be exercised by the device of not asking certain questions. See Murphy and Barnard, *Evidence and Advocacy* (1984), pp.164–165.

[49] See D. Nicolson, "Truth, Reason and Justice: Epistemology and Politics in Evidence Discourse" (1994) 57 M.L.R. 726. Nicolson's later essay, "Gender, Epistemology and Ethics: Feminist Perspectives on Evidence Theory" in M. Childs and L. Ellison (eds), *Feminist Perspectives on Evidence* (London: Cavendish Publishing, 2000), p.13 seems less unreceptive to some notion of objective truth, referring at one point to ways in which feminist approaches might lead to "more accurate [sic] forms of factfinding" (p.14).

[50] A typical conclusion is expressed by P. Smith in *Feminist Jurisprudence* (Oxford: Oxford University Press, 1993), p.212. Writing of adjudication, she comments:

to objectivity and rationality.[51] However, it is not always clear how far such denials are being taken.[52] Strong versions of these forms of epistemological scepticism run into major difficulties with concepts of mistakes and miscarriages of justice. For example, one extreme stance is unqualified relativism. On this view "truth" does not have an objective existence; it is constituted by the legal process of interpreting the past and represents no more than the outcome of the process officially used to determine the existence of the facts in issue.[53] It then seems to follow that each adjudicative decision on a question of fact must be as good, or as bad, as the next. We have no scope and no criteria for evaluating the correctness of the decision. The concept of a miscarriage of justice is grossly attenuated if even the possibility of objective truth is rejected. The only type of miscarriage that can exist on this view is procedural failure to observe the stipulated rules of proof.

This conclusion is so unpalatable that it must be rejected by anyone seriously concerned with the legitimacy of adjudication. It may be, as Bankowski argues, that our procedures for certifying the truth are flawed.[54] As noted earlier, the power of selection of evidence inherent in the principle of party autonomy is not necessarily conducive to truth-finding. It can also be admitted that certain kinds of "facts" are to a greater or lesser extent artefacts of the legal process.[55] This is undoubtedly true of evaluative facts that always involve the application of normative standards. Judgments in legal contexts of, for example, the reasonableness of a person's conduct, inevitably reflect, indeed are intended to reflect, the value preferences of a particular culture at a particular moment in time. The utility of the "reasonableness" standard is that it can accommodate the shifts in values that may occur over time. A good example is social perceptions of what amounts to "reasonable" chastisement of children by parents exercising the common law right to use force for the purpose of discipline. Society will not now tolerate the degree of force thought acceptable in Victorian times,[56] and there is a strong body of opinion that physical force should not be used on children at all.

Some primary and inferential "facts" may also represent social constructions, as was suggested above. These may be deliberate, as in the case of the engineered   **4–015**

"It is not clear ... whether objective truth is a realistic goal in law. Although there is no single unified feminist position on the nature of truth and knowledge in law, the feminist intellectual movement, like many postmodern movements, regards the truth of all propositions relating to society and certainly to law as depending on context, perspective and situation. Every perspective is just that, a perspective".

[51] For a particularly striking example, see A. Orenstein, " 'MY GOD!' A Feminist Critique of the Excited Utterance Exception to the Hearsay Rule" (1997) 85 Cal. L.R. 159, 189–191.

[52] Note the ambiguity in the notions of "realistic" goals, and "perspectives" on truth, in the passage quoted from P. Smith in *Feminist Jurisprudence* (1993).

[53] This seems to be the view taken by M. Freeman, "The Jury on Trial" [1981] C.L.P. 65, 95 and fn.76. Referring to another paper by Freeman, in which the same view is expressed, Twining has called this strong form of scepticism a "descent into irrationalism": *Scepticism* (2006), p.124.

[54] Z. Bankowski, "The value of truth: fact scepticism revisited" (1981) 1 L.S. 257.

[55] See further D. McBarnet, *Conviction* (Oxford: 1981), who propounds (at p.25) the argument that "Both in its concepts and its form the legal system copes with the problems of proof and truth by redefining them".

[56] Children Act 2004 s.58 restricts the common law defence by making it unavailable to offences under ss.18, 20 and 47 of the Offences Against the Person Act 1861 and s.1 of the Children and Young Persons Act 1933.

confession or the controlled testimony of a witness. Alternatively they may unwittingly reflect social values, beliefs and prejudices; consider, for example, a person's report that as a child she was sexually abused by her father. This might be a reliable report of a real incident of assault that the person has never forgotten. It might, however, be the product of a later reinterpretation of certain events treated by both parties at the time as "innocent"—a reinterpretation possibly suggested in interviews with therapists or social agencies. A further possibility is that it might be a "memory" of a forgotten incident that the person has been encouraged by a therapist to "recover" during counselling. There is fierce controversy over the extent to which such a memory is ever "true".[57]

On the other hand, certain facts seem to be resistant to characterisation as social constructions. Suppose a security camera records an incident in which a masked person walks into a bank, demands money at gunpoint, and when the cashier refuses to hand over any money, shoots the cashier who falls dead with a bullet in her brain. It seems impossible to deny the historical primary fact that a killing has taken place. Equally, if X is convicted of the murder of the cashier, perhaps on the basis of an engineered confession, but is subsequently shown to have been recorded on camera shopping in a town 100 miles away at the time of the killing, it seems undeniable that he was not the killer and that a miscarriage of justice has taken place.

It follows that admitting the defects of truth-finding procedures and the contingent value-laden nature of many "facts" in litigation need not commit us to the extreme view that all objective truth is a myth.[58] Such admissions compel us to look critically at factfinding procedures; they do not compel rejection of the whole enterprise of seeking truth as an illusion. Unqualified scepticism about the concept of "truth" overstates the case, not least because it fails to distinguish sufficiently carefully between the different types of fact that can be the subject of adjudication.[59]

E.   THEORIES OF FACTFINDING

4–016   Traditionally, evidence textbooks tended to deal only with the rules of evidence and had little to say about the analysis of evidence. In this respect writers followed the judges who created the common law of evidence. The question of how factfinders evaluate evidence and reach decisions on disputed issues of fact was largely ignored by judges and textwriters. Certainly writers generally made the point that English law has no formal rules or approved methods for analysing

---

[57] See S. Brandon, J. Boakes, D. Glaser and R. Green, "Recovered memories of childhood sexual abuse" (1998) British Journal of Psychiatry 172 at 296. The issue of recovered memory is discussed further in Ch.15.

[58] Stephen Guest has pointed out to me that there is a sense in which all knowledge of facts is socially constructed, because it depends on the use of social conventions to organise the facts by categories and to frame them linguistically; a description of the incident mentioned in the previous paragraph as a "killing" makes the point. We accept these facts as true because we accept the conventions as durable and workable.

[59] See further M. L. Seigel, "A Pragmatic Critique of Modern Evidence Scholarship" (1994) 88 Northwestern L.R. 995, esp. pp.1015–1017; Hock Lai Ho, *A Philosophy of Evidence Law* (Oxford: Oxford University Press, 2008) Ch 2.

and weighing evidence. This was often coupled with statements to the effect that the law relies instead on factfinders using their common sense and experience in the evaluation of evidence. However, the discussion generally stopped at this point, and there was no further theorising about the processes of analysis and decision-making.

This neglect of theory is surprising. The issue of how jurors and other factfinders evaluate evidence is vitally important. Many of the formal rules of admissibility and presentation of evidence have been based on untested assumptions about how jurors in particular behave when evaluating evidence. No doubt the legal barrier to empirical research on real juries is part of the explanation.[60] A more significant factor may be a further assumption that the use of common sense and experience to evaluate evidence is an essentially unproblematic notion on which there was nothing useful to say. Alternatively there may have been a feeling that further exploration of the evaluative process involved extra-legal concepts and methodologies and was thus not relevant to the enterprise.

This attitude gradually changed in the light of the so-called "new evidence scholarship", which developed from the 1960s onwards. This term, coined by a leading American scholar,[61] described an international awakening of interest in the process of proof and the development of a number of theories regarding the ways in which factfinders in adjudicative contexts approach their task and reach decisions. The resulting literature is rich and complex and has given rise to much controversy and debate. Some of the complexity of the debate results from the fact that a substantial part of the literature has a sophisticated mathematical focus. Moreover it is sometimes unclear whether the theorising is at the descriptive level, or at the normative level, or oscillating between the two. The aim of this section is to introduce the principal approaches to the task of theorising the process of adjudicative factfinding. At the risk of some oversimplification, an attempt will be made to clarify their nature and analyse some of their implications.

The first approach is descriptive and consists of what Hastie has called an "intuitions" response.[62] This approach utilises the assumptions and intuitions of commentators about how factfinders generally, and juries in particular, behave in practice. Sometimes the claims made are buttressed by anecdotal evidence, sometimes relevant expert research is discussed, but often appeal is made simply to the supposed shared values and experience of "common sense". Such assumptions and intuitions generally characterise jurors as essentially amateur logicians. The argument is usually that they evaluate evidence by inductive reasoning founded in common sense and general experience. The reasoning may

4–017

---

[60] Contempt of Court Act 1981 s.8. The RCCJ recommended amendment of this provision to permit properly conducted academic research on juries (RCCJ Report, Ch.1 para.8). No governmental action was taken on this recommendation, and the possibility of action was further reduced by Auld L.J.'s recommendation against amendment to enable research into individual juries' deliberations: Auld Review, p.168 para.87.

[61] R. Lempert, "The New Evidence Scholarship: Analyzing the Process of Proof" (1986) 66 Boston U.L.R. 439.

[62] R. Hastie, "Introduction" in R. Hastie (ed), *Inside the Juror* (Cambridge: Cambridge University Press, 1993), p.4.

be undisciplined but it is generally competent. As Hastie has noted, this approach has been one of the predominant influences on the formation and application of policy on evidential issues. It has informed numerous legislative and judicial developments of evidence law, but has always lacked an adequate theoretical base. The lack of discipline in the method of evaluation was a primary target of Wigmore. His attempt to devise a much more rigorous and systematic analytical method is discussed below.

A second approach has centred on the thesis that analysis of evidence might proceed according to mathematical models of probability and inference. This thesis is founded on the principle that reasoning about disputed questions of fact is essentially "atomistic", meaning that it proceeds by analysing individual items of evidence in terms of their effect on a given hypothesis—for example, that it was the defendant who committed the offence charged. An extensive interdisciplinary debate has developed around the claim that such atomistic reasoning follows mathematical principles. The debate has been sharpened by the increasing use of statistical evidence in many different types of legal proceedings. This has produced legal issues of how far courts should be instructed in the relevant mathematical techniques of analysis. This approach has a strongly normative emphasis. The advocates of the virtues of mathematical techniques of factfinding usually do not claim that this is how factfinders generally behave in practice. They may, however, claim that the technique known as Bayes' Theorem could be used in practice as an appropriate method of combining statistical and non-statistical evidence. An alternative claim is that Bayesian analysis offers a standard that can be used to test the reasoning of factfinders who employ other methods to reach their conclusions.

By contrast, a third important branch of the new evidence scholarship is rooted in empirical research and tends to be descriptive rather than prescriptive. This approach is centred on the thesis that reasoning about disputed questions of fact, particularly reasoning by juries, is not "atomistic" and does not proceed by either logical analysis or according to mathematical principles. Instead, the claim is that such reasoning should be characterised as "holistic". This term is used to describe a process whereby factfinders assess evidence as a whole. The assessment takes the form of a narrative or story, constructed by the factfinder, that aims to account as coherently and plausibly as possible for the evidence in the case. The factfinder will then use the story to decide the case according to the verdict options available.

4–018   It is beyond the scope of this book to discuss these three approaches, and the debates they have generated, in any substantial detail. However, it is important to have some understanding of the nature and implications of the main theories. It is clear that the analysis of evidence raises issues of interest and importance to all lawyers. Major policy issues turn on how we think certain evidence is or should be handled by factfinders. Statistical evidence in particular is capable of being seriously mishandled, as the well-known "Prosecutor's Fallacy" (discussed below) clearly shows. The admissibility of expert evidence of mathematical models of reasoning has presented an issue for the courts, with the Court of Appeal ruling out such evidence for jury trials, but the question remains open in other proceedings.

1. *Wigmorean analysis*

The main precursor of the modern debates on probability and inference was **4–019**
Wigmore, whose classic work *The Science of Judicial Proof*[63] advocated the use
of an elaborate system for charting the analysis of individual items of evidence
and their inferential relationships to the facts in issue. Wigmore argued that there
is a logical relationship between evidence and conclusions of fact that can be
dissected, rationalised and presented in diagrammatic form. Accordingly, his
chart method requires each inferential step in the reasoning process to be
articulated in the form of a proposition which is logically related to the ultimate
probandum in the case—the proposition of fact on which the legal rights, duties
and liabilities of the parties are contingent. It must therefore be determined by
analysis of the controlling law to identify the factual elements requiring proof.

In a murder case, for example, the ultimate probandum might be the
proposition that "D unlawfully killed V with the intention to kill V or to cause V
serious injury and without lawful justification or excuse". Typically an ultimate
probandum is a compound and complex proposition; once formulated it can then
helpfully be divided into a number of simpler penultimate or intermediate
probanda, such as "A wound caused V's death", "It was D who wounded V", "D
intended to kill V", and so on. The chart can then be constructed according to the
relevance of items of evidence to one or more of the probanda, remembering that
relevance may be direct or indirect. Evidence may be indirectly relevant, for
example, if it bears on a collateral factual proposition in issue, such as whether a
particular witness is biased in favour of the party calling the witness. By setting
out the process of inferential reasoning using Wigmore's symbolic notation it can
be shown how particular conclusions of fact are reached on the basis of the
evidence. If the analysis is carried out fully, a complete map of the argument in
the case—the argument that the evidence proves a given hypothesis such as "D
unlawfully killed V with the intention to kill V or to cause V serious injury"—can
be constructed. Such a map must necessarily reflect the volume and complexity
of the evidence in the case. This is because the relationship of each piece of
evidence to the ultimate probandum, or to intermediate probanda, must be
charted, and if certain items of evidence support more than one inference, each
inferential chain must be included.

It follows that Wigmorean analysis is rigorous and comprehensive when
properly carried out. It also follows, as Anderson and Twining have pointed out,[64]
that it is laborious and time-consuming. Consequently it may not be a practicable
tool for regular use in forensic contexts. However, it has considerable value as a
form of intellectual training for the analysis of evidence. Amongst other benefits,
it enables the analyst to depict in graphic form the evidence supporting (or
negating) each element of a complex probandum, and the extent to which items
of evidence converge or diverge in the conclusions they support. It also has the

---

[63] Wigmore, *The Science of Judicial Proof*, 3rd edn (Boston, 1937). For a modern approach to
Wigmorean analysis see T. Anderson, D. Schum and W. Twining, *Analysis of Evidence*, 2nd edn
(Cambridge, 2005), esp. Ch.5. See also D. A. Schum, *The Evidential Foundations of Probabilistic
Reasoning* (New York, 1994), pp.160–169. The whole of this important text is worth study.
[64] T. Anderson, D. Schum and W. Twining, *Analysis of Evidence*, 2nd edn (Cambridge: Cambridge
University Press, 2005), p.118.

merit of heightening awareness of the concealed assumptions and background generalisations that underpin all inductive "common sense" reasoning.

4–020   Space does not permit a full explanation of Wigmore's complex symbolic notation or a fully worked illustration.[65] However, to introduce the method and to highlight its value as an analytical tool we can undertake a microanalysis of two items of evidence in a simple hypothetical.

Suppose that D is charged with robbery from a post office in Brighton on May 1.[66] This charge generates the ultimate probandum in the case: "D used force in order to steal property belonging to another, at a post office in Brighton on May 1". This is the proposition of fact of which the prosecution must satisfy the factfinder in order to establish D's guilt of robbery under the controlling criminal law. Its elements are derived from the definition of robbery in s.8 of the Theft Act 1968 and the particulars of the offence as they would be stated in the indictment. One item of evidence in the case is the authenticated tape of an interview in which D stated to the investigating police officer that he was at home in London at the time of the robbery. A second item is the testimony of an eyewitness, W, that she saw D in Brighton on May 1 half an hour before the robbery. From W's testimony, two possible inferential arguments can be constructed to support the ultimate probandum. These arguments can be set out in the form of a sequence of propositions that would be part of a much larger "Key list" of propositions expounding the whole of the argument in the case:

A:

    (1)   —W's testimony that she saw D in Brighton on May 1 half an hour before the relevant time > (supports the inference that)

    (2)   —D was in Brighton on May 1, half an hour before the relevant time >

    (3)   —D remained in Brighton until the relevant time >

    (4)   —D had the opportunity to commit the offence >

    (5)   —D committed the offence.

B:

    (1)   —W's testimony that she saw D in Brighton on May 1, half an hour before the relevant time >

    (2)   —D was in Brighton on May 1, half an hour before the relevant time >

    (3)   —D was not in London on May 1, at the relevant time >

    (4)   —D lied about his whereabouts at the relevant time (note that the chart would need to include at this point D's statement that he was in London as proved by the tape) >

    (5)   —D committed the offence.

---

[65] For a helpful, simplified, Wigmorean scheme see T. Anderson, D. Schum and W. Twining, *Analysis of Evidence*, 2nd edn (2005), Ch.3, and for a modern illustration of the technique see B. Robertson, "John Henry Wigmore and Arthur Allan Thomas: an example of Wigmorean analysis" (1990) 20 Victoria U. of Wellington L.R. 181.

[66] The time and place of the robbery are particulars of the offence necessary to identify it, although they are not of course elements of the offence itself.

It is apparent that each step in each of the two arguments rests on certain assumptions and generalisations. These may often be contestable and give rise to doubts about the strength of the inference. In order to evaluate the weight of the evidence it is highly instructive to articulate all such assumptions and generalisations. This might be done as follows for the two chains of reasoning:

A: (1) > (2) "Eyewitnesses make correct identifications and remember accurately dates and times". These statements are very problematic as unqualified empirical generalisations. Experience and psychological research have demonstrated that eyewitnesses make a high percentage of errors in identification of persons.[67] Questions might also be raised about the possibility of W being mistaken about the date and time of her observation of D. In some circumstances there might be further doubt about W's credibility as a witness if she had a reason to lie about her identification of D. These factors might lead to considerable uncertainty over the weight that could safely be attached to W's testimony.

(2) > (3) "Persons in one place at a particular time stay in that place for indeterminate periods of time". This is sometimes called the factual presumption of continuance; it would be generally agreed that the strength of the inference it supports depends on such issues as the place in question, the time in question, what the person is doing at the time, the opportunities for leaving, the reasons for staying or leaving, and so on.

(3) > (4) "Persons physically present in a place have an opportunity to commit an offence in the place". This seems self-evident, if not tautologous, if "place" means either Brighton, or the post office in Brighton, on both occasions when the word is used. But proposition (4) makes an unspoken assumption either that W saw D at the post office, or that D moved from wherever it was in Brighton that W saw him to the post office, an assumption concealed by the ambiguity of the word "place".

(4) > (5) "Persons who have an opportunity to commit an offence take advantage of the opportunity". Plainly this is overstated. The existence of an opportunity merely brings D within a class of persons who could possibly have committed the offence. We cannot conclude that he is the robber, or even that he is probably the robber, without more.

B: (1) > (2) The same analysis as for A: (1) > (2).

(2) > (3) "Persons cannot get from Brighton to London in half an hour". This is an empirical claim. Most people would accept the physical impossibility of making such a journey in half an hour by train or car, and would dismiss the speculative possibility that D flew by helicopter in the absence of any evidence of this.

(3) > (4) "Persons who wrongly state their whereabouts on a particular day at a particular time do so deliberately". Like A: this is

---

[67] See Ch.7.

an overstated generalisation about human behaviour. A lie is one explanation for the false statement, but mistake is an alternative. To estimate the strength of the inference that D lied, we would need to know more. Did he have any reason for remembering his whereabouts on that day? Is there any corroboration of his statement? (4) > (5) "Persons who construct false alibis do so in order to conceal their guilt". This assertion about the motivation for lies about opportunities to commit offences has an intuitive appeal, but we cannot safely draw the conclusion without ruling out other possible reasons for lying. Was D's statement produced by panic or by fear of the police? If he was trying to hide something, was it necessarily the offence, or some other discreditable conduct?

4–021 This short discussion shows the existence of numerous points of doubt and possible alternative inferences at various stages of the two chains of reasoning. As already indicated all such alternatives would themselves have to be charted and located in the overall analysis of the case.

2. *Mathematical models of reasoning*

4–022 The Wigmorean method assumes that analysis of evidence is atomistic, proceeding on the basis of inferences from individual items of evidence as to the probability of the facts in issue. It also assumes that the process of inferential reasoning is inductive, but it does not attempt to theorise the relationship between inference and probability, or to analyse the kind of probability involved in legal decision-making.[68] A major strand of the new evidence scholarship has been concerned to fill this gap. An extensive body of literature has developed, with the principal theoretical debates centred on the question how far the reasoning of legal factfinders about the probability of disputed facts does or should follow mathematical principles. Speaking very broadly, and with a degree of oversimplification, there has been a major contest[69] between those, who argue in favour of mathematical models based on the use of Bayes' Theorem, or some other theory of probability, as a device for estimating the impact of items of evidence on a given hypothesis, and those who maintain that the reasoning involved is in principle non-mathematical and that probability judgments are founded rather on a vast mass of inductive generalisations about human behaviour and about cause and effect in the world. Wigmore's approach was essentially the latter, although this is not to say that he would necessarily have rejected mathematical theories as either inaccurate or undesirable.

It is important to make this point to avoid the misconception that these approaches are necessarily rivals and mutually exclusive. Advocates of mathematical reasoning do not generally claim that it is appropriate for all

---

[68] An excellent summary of the issues surrounding probability theory is in A. Ligertwood and G. Edmond, *Australian Evidence,* 5th edn (London: LexisNexis Butterworths, 2010), 14-41.
[69] The seminal work setting up the contest was L.J. Cohen, *The Probable and the Provable* (Oxford: Oxford University Press, 1977).

disputed questions of fact in legal process.[70] Such reasoning has often tended to focus on issues apparently invoking a probability judgment, such as the standard of proof in civil cases, or on issues which are objectively verifiable, such as the identity of a person alleged to have done a criminal act. Evaluative issues and some inferential issues, such as a person's intent, which may incorporate elements of moral judgment, do not lend themselves to mathematical proof.[71] Equally, those who are sceptical about the use of mathematical methods for deciding about the occurrence of unique events would not challenge their use in some other legal contexts, such as a case involving an issue of a statistical nature: percentage of market share, discrimination in the workplace, and so on.[72]

The starting-point for the modern debates is the notorious Californian case of *People v Collins*,[73] which remains an object-lesson in the misuse of statistics. The two defendants were charged with robbery in the Los Angeles area, mainly on the basis that they matched eyewitness descriptions of the robbers. The prosecution relied on a number of features of the descriptions: that the robbers were an inter-racial couple, they drove a yellow car, the girl had blonde hair and a ponytail, the man had a moustache, he was black and also had a beard. They assigned a probability to each of these features occurring in the Los Angeles area, for example the estimated number of yellow cars on the road. The prosecution then applied the multiplication rule,[74] according to which the probability of any random couple having all the relevant features of the robbers was taken to be the product of each of the individual probabilities multiplied together. This gave a figure of 1/12,000,000, which was represented to be the odds against the defendants being innocent, and which seems to have so impressed the jury that they convicted. The Supreme Court of California, recognising the flaws in the prosecution argument, overturned the convictions. The first problem was that there was no objective basis for the assigned probabilities; they seem to have been mostly guesswork. Secondly, the features chosen were plainly not independent of each other. It was absurd to assign separate probabilities for men with moustaches and black men with beards, since many of the latter might be expected to have moustaches. This meant that the multiplication rule was inapplicable because it presupposes independent variables.[75] Thirdly, even if the final figure was correct, it does not follow that there was only a 1/12,000,000 probability that the defendants were innocent. This is the classic "Prosecutor's Fallacy": the probability of a random match is not necessarily the same as the probability of innocence of a person who provides a particular match. This point is explored further below.

---

[70] See, e.g. the articles by R. D. Friedman (a leading Bayesian enthusiast), "Answering the Bayesioskeptical challenge" (1997) 1 E. & P. 276 and "Towards a (Bayesian) convergence?" (1997) 1 E. & P. 348.

[71] See further A. A. S. Zuckerman, "Law, Fact or Justice?" (1986) 66 Boston U.L.R. 487.

[72] R. J. Allen (a leading Bayesian sceptic) concedes that Bayes' Theorem would be a useful analytical tool in situations involving "virtually purely statistical evidential bases": see his "Rationality, algorithms and juridical proof: a preliminary inquiry" (1997) 1 E. & P. 254, 258.

[73] *People v Collins* (1968) 438 P. 2d 33.

[74] For an explanation of the multiplication rule see R. Eggleston, *Evidence, Proof and Probability*, 2nd edn (London: 1983), p.13.

[75] For a different, and more charitable, interpretation of the prosecutor's approach, see W. B. Fairley and F. Mosteller, "A Conversation About *Collins*" (1974) 41 U. Chic. L.R. 242, 244–247.

4–023   The *Collins* case was the catalyst for the development of an extensive literature discussing the nature and appropriateness of mathematical analyses of evidence.[76] It is beyond the scope of this book to review all aspects of this discussion, some of which became somewhat abstruse and remote from practical reality. Instead, the focus is on one of the central issues, namely the use and limits of Bayesian theory as a method of determining probabilities in legal contexts. Bayes' Theorem, named after the eighteenth-century English clergyman who devised it, offers a way of updating probabilities in the light of further evidence. The Theorem is generally accepted as an accurate statement of mathematical logic, although there is acute controversy over the feasibility and desirability of its application to factual determinations in legal contexts.

The Bayesian method works as follows.[77] We assume we wish to know the weight of a particular item of evidence. The method is most suited to evidence of a scientific nature, and much of the debate in recent years about Bayesian approaches has concerned the assessment of DNA profiling carried out by forensic scientists. In order to determine the extent to which such evidence affects the assessment of guilt or innocence, we need to know the *prior probability* of guilt. This figure will generally be arrived at on the basis of the other evidence in the case. There are problems with the subjectivity of such assessments that can be put aside for the moment. We will need to return to them later. For the purposes of exposition it is helpful to consider a hypothetical example. Suppose that in a rape case the victim states that her attacker was a man whose face she did not see, but during the rape he told her that he lived in a certain town. Enquiries establish that approximately 10,000 adult males live in the town. A jury that knew nothing about the defendant other than that he lived in the town might reasonably conclude that the empirical prior probability of his guilt of the rape was represented by odds of one in 10,000.[78] Expert scientific evidence is then given that a DNA sample taken from the defendant matched the DNA profile obtained from a sample of semen found on the victim. The expert witness states that the chance of a match between the crime sample and a sample from an innocent individual chosen randomly from an appropriate population is one in 100,000. The question arising is the significance of this figure and its effect on the prior probability of guilt.

---

[76] A starting-point for further reading is M. O. Finkelstein and W. B. Fairley, "A Bayesian Approach to Identification Evidence" (1970) 83 Harv. L.R. 489, and the powerful reply by L. H. Tribe, "Trial by Mathematics: Precision and Ritual in the Legal Process" (1971) 84 Harv. L.R. 1329. The subsequent progress of the debate can be traced in Wigmore, *Evidence* (Tillers rev. 1983), Vol.1A para.37 and the collections of papers published in (1986) 66 Boston U.L.R., (1991) 13 Cardozo L.R. and (1997) 1 E. & P. 253.

[77] There are numerous discussions of Bayesian approaches to factfinding that vary greatly in their complexity and accessibility. Excellent starting-points are R. Eggleston, *Evidence, Proof and Probability*, 2nd edn (1983); P. Dawid: "Appendix on Probability and Proof" in Anderson, Schum and Twining, *Analysis of Evidence* (2005), p.385; D. J. Balding and P. Donnelly, "The Prosecutor's Fallacy and DNA Evidence" [1994] Crim. L.R. 711; M. Redmayne, "Science, Evidence and Logic" (1996) 59 M.L.R. 747. What follows here is a highly simplified account.

[78] Bayes' Theorem can be expressed in more than one form, but the odds form is probably the easiest to understand and the most useful for illustrative purposes when examining the significance of a single item of evidence. The odds given here ought to be adjusted to take account of the possibility that the rapist was lying about where he lived, but in the interests of simplicity this refinement is omitted.

In the example, the expert has testified in terms of the *likelihood ratio* of this evidence. As Balding and Donnelly explain it, this is:

> "the ratio of the probability of a match given that the defendant is guilty to the probability of a match given that the defendant is innocent. This is usually calculated as one divided by the probability of a match given that the defendant is innocent, that is one divided by the match probability."[79]

It is essential to distinguish at this point two separate questions arising from the scientific evidence. One is the probability that the defendant's DNA profile matches the DNA profile from the crime sample, on the assumption that he is innocent. This is the proper subject of expert testimony since it involves knowledge and skill in interpreting the traces obtained by DNA sampling methods and selecting appropriate populations for purposes of comparison. The other is the probability that the defendant is innocent, given that his DNA profile matches the DNA profile from the crime sample. This is the crucial issue in the case, and is a question for the factfinder charged with the task of determining guilt or innocence. The questions should not be confused because the answer to the second depends on the presuppositions that we start with about the defendant's innocence, and these are determined in large measure by the state of the other evidence before the scientific evidence is considered. The "Prosecutor's Fallacy" is to treat the answer to the first question as the answer to the second, when the figures involved may be quite different.

4–024

This is clearly revealed if symbolic notation is used to develop the analysis of the hypothetical. In the following notation, P stands for probability, E for evidence, G for guilt, I for innocence and "/" means "given" or "on the assumption that".

The prior probability of guilt on the other evidence, compared with the prior probability of innocence, can be stated as:

$$\frac{P(G|(other)E)}{P(I|(other)E)} = \frac{1}{10,000}$$

The expert's testimony about the likelihood ratio, that is the odds of finding the evidence according to whether the defendant is assumed to be guilty or innocent, can be stated as[80]:

4–025

$$\frac{P(E|G)}{P(E|I)} = \frac{100,000}{1}$$

The figure now required is P(G/(all)E). The latter figure is known as the *posterior probability* of guilt. Bayes' Theorem states that it can be derived by multiplying the prior probability by the likelihood ratio. It can be set out in the following equation:

---

[79] Balding and Donnelly, "The Prosecutor's Fallacy" [1994] Crim. L.R. 711, 713.
[80] The odds stated must of course correspond to the match probability. In this case it is assumed that the probability of finding a match if the defendant is guilty is 1 (certain), whereas the probability of finding a match if the defendant is innocent is 1/100,000, or 0.00001. This translates into odds of 100,000 to 1 for the purposes of the Theorem.

$$\frac{P(G|(all)E)}{P(I|(all)E)} = \frac{P(G|(other)E)}{P(I|(other)E)} \times \frac{P(E|G)}{P(E|I)} = \frac{1}{10,000} \times \frac{100,000}{1} = \frac{10}{1}$$

The posterior probability of guilt is thus represented by odds of ten to one on, meaning that there are ten chances out of 11 that the defendant is guilty; in percentage terms, approximately a 91 per cent probability of guilt. This figure would alter significantly if the prior probability of guilt were greater. If the defendant had said that he lived in a small village containing 100 men, giving a prior probability of one in 100, the posterior probability using the same likelihood ratio would be 100 to one on; in percentage terms, a 99 per cent probability of guilt.

4–026   The use of Bayes' Theorem in criminal trials was considered by the Court of Appeal in *Adams (Denis)*.[81] This was a rape case in which the prosecution case rested entirely on DNA evidence based on a sample of semen found in the complainant's vagina. The prosecution expert testified as to a match between the DNA profiles of the defendant and the semen sample. He gave it as his opinion that the chances of a match between the sample and a randomly chosen unrelated man were one in 200,000,000. That figure was doubted by the defence expert, who spoke of the right figure being more like one in 2,000,000. To assist the jury in evaluating the significance of that statistic the defence introduced evidence of Bayes' Theorem. The aim was to enable the jury to compare the limited non-statistical evidence in the case with the evidence relating to the DNA samples. The other evidence was favourable to the defence in the sense that it consisted of an absence of any eyewitness testimony (the complainant had failed to pick out the defendant on an identification parade), and the defendant testified as to an alibi that was supported by his girlfriend. The defence evidence proceeded on the illustrative speculation that the initial probability of the defendant's guilt was one in 200,000 (a figure arrived at by taking a number of possible local suspects as 150,000 and multiplying it by the 25 per cent probability that the rapist was not a local man: both these figures were admittedly arbitrary). That probability, the defence argued, was lowered by the probability of guilt given the favourable evidence, but was then increased by the probability of guilt given the DNA evidence. On this basis the defence were able to suggest that after making the appropriate calculations, the posterior probability of the defendant's guilt on the defence expert's figure for the DNA evidence was only 0.5, which translates to odds of one to two. In other words, on these calculations the defendant was twice as likely to be innocent as guilty. On the other hand, if the prosecution were right in putting the chance of a random match at 1 in 200,000,000 the odds on guilt turned into 55 to 1 in favour of guilt. The difference between these results may help to explain why both the prosecution and defence were willing for the jury to hear the statistical evidence and decide which figure they preferred. In the event the jury convicted.

The Court of Appeal allowed the defendant's appeal and ordered a retrial. The court held that the trial judge, having admitted the evidence of Bayes' Theorem, had failed to direct the jury adequately as to the substance of the evidence and how it could be used. The details of the misdirection are not material; what is

---

[81] *Adams (Denis)* [1996] 2 Cr.App.R. 467.

important for present purposes is the clear dictum that evidence of Bayes' Theorem or any similar statistical method of analysis is not appropriate for jury trial and should not be admitted. Such evidence was said to distract the jury with unnecessary theory and complexity and to trespass on what was uniquely their province to evaluate the relationship between one piece of evidence and another. The dictum undoubtedly sent a strong signal to judges in jury trials to have no truck with statistical methods of assessing the probability of guilt.[82]

The judgment in *Adams (Denis)* pointed out a number of problems with the use of Bayes' Theorem in jury trials. The first issue concerns the fixing of prior probabilities of guilt. How is this to be done? Are there any criteria available for undertaking this crucial task? It is generally agreed that the Theorem itself does not supply an answer. It only offers a method of updating probabilities in the light of further evidence; it cannot supply the starting-point for the calculations. Most theorists take the view that establishing the prior probability of guilt is ultimately a matter of subjective judgment—each jury will have to decide this for themselves. At this point serious difficulties begin to emerge. The Court of Appeal notes the obvious point that 12 jurors may well disagree on the appropriate figure. This is a particular danger if they are given no guidance on possible starting-points; the process is then almost certain to be speculative and impressionistic. In the absence of agreement on the prior probability of guilt, Bayes' Theorem cannot be used at all. Disagreement might be overcome by taking an average of the individual views, but this is an artificial solution and it is also potentially misleading, in the sense that the average view might not represent the view of any individual juror.

Possible guidance could be derived from either normative or empirical considerations. Stein, for example, has suggested that a normative figure for the prior probability of guilt could be derived from the standard of proof; it would represent the permissible percentage of wrong convictions where proof is required beyond reasonable doubt—say 1 in 100.[83] This is attractive to the extent that it is a coherent way of giving effect to the presumption of innocence in criminal cases. However, it is one thing to admit that mistakes may occasionally occur in criminal adjudication. It is quite another to quantify acceptable degrees of risk of error as a social value preference. Tribe argued some years ago, in relation to the standard of proof, that it is wrong in principle to quantify degrees

4–027

---

[82] The Court of Appeal repeated the message on two further occasions: *Doheny and Adams* [1997] 1 Cr.App.R. 369 at 374 (the second defendant was a different Adams); *Denis Adams (No.2)* [1998] 1 Cr.App.R. 377 at 384–385. The second of these two cases concerned the retrial of Denis Adams. The retrial seems to have been virtually a carbon copy of the first trial, including the admission again of evidence of Bayes' Theorem at the instance of the defence. The operation of the Theorem was very fully explained by the defence expert who supplied the jury with a detailed questionnaire to use. The trial judge's direction on this aspect of the case made it clear that it was for the jury themselves to decide whether to use the "statistical approach" or the "common sense approach" in reaching their verdict. Dismissing the appeal against conviction, the Court of Appeal held that the direction was not open to criticism. Lord Bingham C.J. went on to say that, in the absence of special features, "expert evidence should not be admitted to induce juries to attach mathematical values to probabilities arising from non-scientific evidence adduced at the trial" (p.385).

[83] A. Stein, "Judicial Fact-Finding and the Bayesian Method: The Case for Deeper Scepticism about their Combination" (1996) 1 E. & P. 25, 37.

of doubt in criminal cases.[84] His point seems equally applicable at this stage of the analysis of evidence. A further query relates to whether a normative criterion should have universal application. Should the same figure apply in all cases irrespective of the charge? On a formal basis the answer is presumably "Yes", but some might argue that the acceptability of the figure is contingent on the type of case involved: a wrongful conviction for murder is much worse for the person convicted than a wrongful conviction for a minor offence of, say, theft or assault. Thus even normative figures might not be constant, and might even vary for different offences charged in the same proceedings. Moreover, for particularly stigmatic offences, such as assaults on children, there would be a serious risk of juries deviating from the norm in the interests of social defence or because of sheer prejudice. We might also ask whether it is appropriate to use a low prior probability in a case where the evidence suggests it should be fairly high; an example would be where a child has been killed, and it seems clear that the killer must have been either or both of its parents.[85]

Empirical assessments are even more problematic, as *Adams (Denis)* suggests. A sceptical juror might query why in that case the geographical area defining a "local" man was set at 10 miles radius from the scene of the incident, thereby excluding large centres of population a little further away. Enlarging the population base would make the prior probability even lower. On the other hand, another equally sceptical juror might well think that the police did not happen upon the defendant at random, but were led to him in a way that had not been revealed. Such a juror might then view the prior probability of guilt as dependent on a calculation of the probability that the police had acted maliciously or on mistaken information. Clearly this would tend to produce a very much higher figure than the population base approach. Another juror might argue that since a high percentage of defendants who plead not guilty are found guilty (say, for the sake of argument, about half) the prior probability of guilt of any one defendant should reflect the overall distribution. On this basis the prior probability would be a figure of 0.5. This is of course inconsistent with the presumption of innocence, as generally understood, but the point is that there is nothing in the Bayesian method to rule out such a choice of starting-point.

A second problem noted by the Court of Appeal in *Adams (Denis)* is that the weight of particular pieces of evidence depends on their relationship with all the other pieces of evidence in the case. It is artificial and potentially seriously misleading to evaluate the effect of each piece independently and sequentially on prior probabilities. The probability that a confession is true or false, for example, is greatly affected by the extent to which its detail is confirmed or contradicted by other evidence: medical, ballistic, eyewitness, circumstantial, and so on. This objection can be met by a sufficiently all-encompassing conditionalisation of probabilities, so that, to take another example, the probability of W's eyewitness identification of D existing if D is not guilty can be estimated conditionally according to such other evidence as W's acquaintance with D, the state of W's eyesight, the lighting conditions at the time, W's previous conviction for perjury, and so on. Each of these items affects and is affected by each of the others. The

---

[84] Tribe, "Trial by Mathmatics" (1971) 84 Harv. L.R. 1329.
[85] I am indebted to Mike Redmayne for this point.

problem then is that the mathematical calculations quickly become impossibly large and complex. One writer has commented:

> "for the consistent use of Bayesian theory for the updating of probabilities by conditionalization, where thirty items of evidence are introduced relevant to an inference, one must record a billion probabilities."[86]

In the practical context of decision-making by lay juries it is inconceivable that a case of any degree of complexity could be handled in this way.

A third problem is concerned not with the viability of Bayesian method but with its essential validity as a means of accurate assessment of evidence in adjudicative contexts. Bayesian calculations proceed on the basis of probability judgments that are assumed to be of equal validity in the sense that they all have a rational foundation. However, this overlooks the point that in adjudicative contexts the informational base for each judgment may vary widely in its adequacy; in other words the judgments of probability may have different degrees of weight according to how solidly they are grounded. Some may have a foundation which is empirically verifiable—for example that the murderer of a person on an island must have been one of the 100 people proved to have been on the island at the time. Where all the relevant probabilities are objectively grounded, the application of Bayes' Theorem is not open to objection on this score.

4–028

However, some probabilities may rest on nothing more than subjective generalisations about human experience—for example that people who have a motive to kill are more likely to kill than people who do not have a motive—but how securely can such a generalisation fix the figure we assign for the probability of finding evidence of a motive if a particular person is guilty, compared to finding evidence of a motive if he is innocent? In such situations there is no unified standard for measuring the adequacy of the informational base for making probability judgments in adjudicative contexts. Furthermore, because these are all unique "one-off" situations, one cannot run parallel controlled trials to standardise the data. If different subjective probability judgments have different weights they may be incommensurable and the multiplication rule makes little sense.

In *Adams (Denis)* the Court of Appeal robustly rejected the theory that jury evaluation of evidence is in principle mathematical. Juries evaluate evidence "by the joint application of their individual common sense and knowledge of the world to the evidence before them".[87] If this is so, the argument runs, then not only do they not need expert help but it may confuse them and distract them from their proper task. The Court of Appeal emphasised this point in *Denis (Adams) (No.2)*[88] by describing evidence of Bayes' Theorem as "a recipe for confusion, misunderstanding and misjudgment". Underlying the approach of the Court of

4–029

---

[86] C. Callen, "Second Order Considerations, Weight, Sufficiency and Schema Theory: A Comment on Professor Brilmayer's Theory" (1986) 66 Boston U.L.R. 715, 726 fn.72. See also Callen's earlier article in (1982) 57 Indiana L.J. 1.

[87] *Adams (Denis)* [1996] 2 Cr.App.R. 467 at 481.

[88] *Denis (Adams) (No.2)* [1998] 1 Cr.App.R. 377 at 384.

Appeal is a traditional reluctance to allow jury evaluation of evidence to be replaced by trial by expert, whether psychiatrist, psychologist, statistician or any other specialist. This resistance to the wider use of expert opinion is discussed further in Ch.20.

However, it is worth emphasising that statistical evidence needs skilled interpretation if it is not to be mishandled, as *People v Collins* graphically demonstrates.[89] This reflects the more general point that common sense and world knowledge will only take a jury so far. On technical matters, expert help is not only advisable, it is essential if the evidence is not to be misunderstood. This is why the Court of Appeal has rightly laid down detailed guidelines for the use of prosecution evidence of DNA profiling[90]; a primary aim is to enable the defence to have the necessary information regarding the methods employed to compile the evidence so as to be in a position to test or challenge it effectively.

3. *Narrative and story-telling*

4–030   We turn now to the third approach to factfinding. This acknowledges the key role played by common sense and experience, but locates it in a very different model of decision-making. Both Wigmorean analysis and mathematical models of reasoning are challenged by "holistic" theories of jury decision-making. Such theories reject the idea that factfinders do in practice evaluate evidence by a meticulous sequential analysis of individual items. It makes no difference, according to this view, whether the "atomistic" analysis is structured in terms of the effect of each item on the probability of a given hypothesis (e.g. guilt of the defendant), or whether it takes the form of a chart of the logical inferences relevant to the ultimate probanda in the case. Holistic theories draw on research in cognitive psychology to argue that juries evaluate evidence as a whole in terms of a narrative or story that aims to account coherently for the evidence. The method is strongly inductive, in the sense that the narrative is grounded in the jury's collective knowledge and experience of the world. That knowledge and experience is used not only as the basis for inferences from the evidence that actually exists but also to supply elements in the narrative where evidence is missing.

As a descriptive theory of how factfinders, particularly lay factfinders, actually reason about disputed questions of fact, the holistic approach is intuitively appealing. It is well recognised that narrative structures play a pervasive role in our understanding of human action in society. In the context of legal practice Twining has commented:

> "It is widely acknowledged that stories play a significant role in factfinding in adjudication and that the 'logic of proof' is founded in common-sense reasoning in which background generalisations ('general experience') play an important part."[91]

---

[89] The English case of *Clark* [2003] EWCA Crim 1020 is an even more troubling example of flawed statistical evidence; see Ch.20.

[90] *Doheny and Adams* [1997] 1 Cr.App.R. 369, updated in the light of developments in DNA profiling technology in *Reed and Reed* [2009] EWCA Crim 2698; [2010] 1 Cr.App.R.23.

[91] W. Twining, "Anchored Narratives—A Comment" (1995) 1 *European Journal of Crime, Criminal Law and Criminal Justice* 106, 108.

McCormick has taken the point further by arguing that "the *only* type of test which we have available to us for verifying contested assertions about the past is this test of 'coherence'; taking all that has been presented to us in the way of real or testimonial evidence we work out a story that hangs together, which makes sense as a coherent whole" (emphasis supplied).[92]

The leading advocates of a "narrative" theory of factfinding, based on research, are Pennington and Hastie. In a series of papers[93] they have developed a sophisticated story model founded on their empirical research in cognitive psychology. It is helpful to describe the main features of the model before considering aspects of it in more detail. The model divides the decision-making process into three stages. The first stage is concerned with the evaluation of the evidence presented to the factfinder in the case. The model states that during evidence evaluation a juror constructs "a selective summary of the evidence that tends to represent an intuitively coherent version of what happened in the events referred to in testimony".[94] In other words, the juror tends to organise the mixed mass of evidence with which he has been presented into the form of a story that aims to account for the existence of the evidence. A story is coherent for this purpose if it respects the principles that determine whether narrative structures (stories) are well-formed and plausible. These principles are discussed further below.

4–031

The model's second stage of decision-making occurs towards the end of the trial when the judge explains to the jury the verdict options. This may be a matter of considerable complexity. In a criminal case, depending on the charges, the judge may have to explain not only the different elements of different offences but also the elements of various defences, possible alternative verdicts, and the burden of proof in relation to all these matters. A murder case, for example, that raised issues of causation, mens rea and both general and special defences, would result in an extensive direction on the law canvassing four possible verdicts: guilty of murder, guilty of manslaughter, guilty of attempted murder, not guilty of any offence. It has been suggested that learning verdict options is a difficult "one-off" task for jurors.[95] They may retain only an incomplete and jumbled memory of verdicts as lists of features or elements of crimes, particularly if the directions are oral and only heard once. This reinforces the point made earlier in this chapter that it is desirable for judges to give juries written instructions on verdict options, certainly in a case of any degree of complexity.

The third stage comes when the juror compares the story that he or she has constructed to represent the evidence with the verdict categories. The aim at this stage is to find the best match:

"If a subjectively satisfactory match is found, the juror will conclude with the corresponding verdict and a degree of confidence proportional to the perceived goodness of match, subjective completeness and coherence of the story."[96]

---

[92] N. McCormick, *Legal Reasoning and Legal Theory* (Oxford: Oxford Uinversity Press, 1978), p.90.
[93] Referred to and summarised in N. Pennington and R. Hastie, "The story model for juror decision making" in R. Hastie (ed), *Inside the Juror* (1993), p.192.
[94] R. Hastie (ed), *Inside the Juror* (1993), p.26.
[95] Pennington and Hastie, "The story model for juror decision making" (1993), p.200.
[96] R. Hastie (ed), *Inside the Juror* (1993), p.26.

4–032   Before discussing features of the story model in more detail it should be noted that the empirical research used to develop and test this model has taken place in mock-jury and laboratory settings. The researchers acknowledge that it has not been possible for them to carry out research with real juries in real trials. To that extent they counsel caution before assuming that the theories will generalise from the experimental situation to the context of actual courtrooms. Nevertheless, Hastie has argued that:

> "there are so many converging results concerning juror behavior from laboratory studies and from surveys of actual jurors that most of the conclusions from the studies reported are surely accurate descriptions of juror behavior in real trials."[97]

This view seems to be widely shared, as the comment by Twining, quoted above, acknowledges.

A second note of caution is that the story model does not attempt to theorise the role of "jury equity". Hastie has commented that "the juror's sense of justice" is given relatively short shrift in his summary of the model, but he adds that there is little evidence from his work that jurors depart from the factfinding task to follow the dictates of conscience or to apply their sense of fair play when deciding criminal trial verdicts.[98] He does suggest, however, that conflicts may occasionally arise between jurors' notions of equity and justice and "official" legal definitions of the jury's task. This is surely right. The existence of such conflicts and the way in which juries respond to them is illustrated by some celebrated cases in England where juries have acquitted defendants in the teeth of evidence pointing to their legal guilt.[99]

Opinions differ on how far this practice can be justified,[100] but from the normative perspective adopted in this book the use of jury equity is defensible in isolated cases. Given that factual accuracy is the major component of legitimate verdicts, juries should as a general rule apply themselves solely to the factfinding task. A decision which is factually accurate will be morally authoritative in the overwhelming majority of cases. However, as argued in Ch.2, the ultimate aim of procedural law is to promote legitimacy of verdicts. The jury secure legitimacy of conviction, not only by deciding that the defendant is in fact guilty of the offence charged, but also by certifying, as the constitutional representative of the community, that he is properly to be blamed and punished for breach of a criminal prohibition that ought to be observed. In rare and exceptional cases it should be acceptable for the jury, through their general verdict of not guilty, to refuse this certification. There may be a tiny number of cases where a jury may be persuaded that a defendant, although factually "guilty", should nevertheless not be convicted. This might be because the defendant is perceived as being morally blameless, and hence not a fit object for the stigma of conviction and punishment. Alternatively a jury might be unwilling to enforce the particular

---

[97] R. Hastie (ed), *Inside the Juror* (1993), p.28.
[98] R. Hastie (ed), *Inside the Juror* (1993), pp.28–29.
[99] The acquittal of Clive Ponting of a charge under s.2 of the Official Secrets Act 1911, arising out of the leaking of documents relating to an incident during the Falklands War, is the best-known example in recent years.
[100] See further M. Matravers, " 'More Than Just Illogical': Truth and Jury Nullification" in Duff, Farmer, Marshall and Tadros (eds), *The Trial on Trial* (2004), Vol.I, p.71.

criminal law in question because of its serious disharmony with community values or because of the jury's disapproval of the particular prosecution. It is clear that the power should only be used in rare and exceptional cases. Any wider use would tend to undermine both the authority of the legislature and the aim of the criminal justice system to enforce the criminal law. But as a dispensing power of last resort jury equity is a coherent device.

A more detailed account of the story model begins with the point that it is of course possible to construct more than one narrative to account for any given mass of evidence. Individual jurors will generally be presented with at least two stories in a contested case—the versions of events constructed by the prosecution and defence lawyers respectively. Jurors may then construct variations of their own according to how far they accept particular features of the stories presented by the parties and how far they wish to add elements of their own creation. Pennington and Hastie suggest that two "certainty" principles govern which of a number of possible stories will be accepted.[101] The two certainty principles are coverage and coherence. Because the theory states that the story that the juror constructs determines the juror's decision, it follows that these certainty principles will also help to determine the selection of verdict and the confidence level with which a particular decision will be made. Coverage is concerned with how far the story accounts for the evidence presented to the jury. The greater the coverage, the more acceptable the story is likely to be and the greater the juror's confidence in a decision based on it. Conversely, a story that leaves evidence unaccounted for will generate lower levels of juror acceptability and confidence.

    The coherence of a story relates to certain qualities it has as a narrative. To be coherent a story should be internally consistent; it should not contain contradictions within itself and should not contradict evidence believed to be true. The story should also be plausible in the sense that it is consistent with the decision-maker's knowledge and general experience of the world. It should be complete in its structure and have no missing elements of any significance. The more coherent the story is according to these criteria the more acceptable it is likely to be and the greater the confidence level the juror will have in it. At this point reference should also be made to the criterion of uniqueness. Uniqueness refers to the desirability of there being only one coherent story. More than one coherent story obviously reduces the confidence which can be placed in any one of them as the basis of a verdict decision.

    According to the theory jurors construct stories which are divided into a number of episodes.[102] An episode has a typical structure that begins with an initiating event, often a human action. This causes characters in the story to have psychological responses and to conceive goals. The goals or objectives motivate their subsequent actions, which lead to the occurrence of certain consequences and states of affairs. One episode in a typical murder story might consist of an incident in which the deceased provoked the defendant by an assault, or by insults and abuse, leading to the defendant suffering feelings of anger and humiliation and planning a revenge attack. Episodes are similarly linked together by

4–033

---

[101] Pennington and Hastie, "The story model for juror decision making" (1993), pp.198–199.
[102] Pennington and Hastie, "The story model for juror decision making" (1993), p.197.

relationships of causality and intention in such a way as to demonstrate the coherence and completeness of the story.

4–034   This structure of stories and episodes is the key to understanding the creative role that may be played by jurors' common sense and general experience. The evidence in the case may directly establish a number of the events and causal relationships that form part of the story. Often the evidence will not be complete, and jurors will be invited to infer the existence of other events and causal relationships to fill out the episodic structure of the story. Such inferences will be founded on jurors' expectations about what is necessary to constitute a coherent and complete story and their own knowledge and beliefs about causation and intentionality in the world. The empirical research suggests that the inferential components of the story may be extensive. Pennington and Hastie conducted interviews with a sample of adult volunteers who were shown a realistic filmed re-enactment of a murder trial and who were then questioned about the evidence in the case. The "verbal protocols" (summaries of the responses) obtained from the interviews showed that only 55 per cent of the references to the events out of which the case arose were to events actually included in testimony. "The remaining 45 per cent were references to inferred events–actions, mental states, and goals that 'filled in' the stories in episode configurations."[103] It would be unwise to generalise too far from this small-scale study, but its conclusions tend to confirm both that factfinders may use inferential reasoning extensively to supplement the actual evidence in the case and that when they do so they tend to structure its use in narrative form. It is also important to note that if it is the case that factfinders can create almost half the evidence by inference, it is not surprising that different factfinders may construct very different stories about what happened and therefore reach different verdicts.

Pennington and Hastie's work has focused on lay jurors. A group of Dutch scholars has put forward a broadly similar theory about the reasoning of judicial factfinders.[104] These authors suggest that judges also evaluate evidence in story form. The judicial task, it is argued, consists of determining the plausibility of the stories put forward by the prosecution and the defence, the underlying theory being that evidence only derives its meaning from a story context: "Without a context, any evidence is meaningless . . . Detached from a story facts do not prove anything".[105] A plausible story must be consistent and coherent. It must be supported by evidence, and the evidence itself must be anchored in a general rule. These general anchoring rules are ones that cannot be sensibly contested; they are generally acknowledged to be true because they constitute common sense facts of life. It follows that the degree of confidence the judge has in the evidential support for the story will reflect the terms of the anchoring rule. The authors cite the example of eyewitness testimony.[106] Such testimony will only prove something if we accept that eyewitnesses are reliable—that is, that they do not lie or make mistakes. Clearly this is not true as a general rule. Experience and

---

[103] Pennington and Hastie, "The story model for juror decision making" (1993), p.206.
[104] W. A. Wagenaar, P. J. van Koppen and H. F. M. Crombag, *Anchored Narratives* (Hemel Hempstead: Prentice-Hall, 1993).
[105] W. A. Wagenaar, P. J. van Koppen and H. F. M. Crombag, *Anchored Narratives* (1993), p.33.
[106] W. A. Wagenaar, P. J. van Koppen and H. F. M. Crombag, *Anchored Narratives* (1993), p.15.

research suggest that lies and mistakes are common. The rule must therefore be qualified, and it follows that the judge will have to be satisfied before placing reliance on the eyewitness that this is not one of the exceptional cases; the possibility of a lie or mistake must be ruled out, perhaps by supporting evidence that is itself safely anchored.

It seems likely that lay factfinders and professional judges do adopt similar strategies for evaluating evidence. The story model is underpinned by a cognitivist psychology that assigns a key role to common sense and general experience in the forming of mental representations of information. Judges have no greater access to the stock of common knowledge than lay persons, and must ultimately base their reasoning on the same foundations.[107] If it is right that the development of narratives is a pervasive method of comprehending events in the world, then judges will not reason very differently in form from lay tribunals. What we might fairly expect, however, is that judges, by virtue of their training and experience, will have a greater awareness of gaps in evidence and of the need for careful analysis of the inferences they make to fill the gaps.

All this is not to say that the story model should be accepted uncritically. There are problems with it at both a descriptive and a normative level, and this section concludes with an examination of some of the criticisms that can be made of it as a theory of factfinding in adjudicative contexts.

First, it appears that the model may blur an important distinction between a story and an argument. As Twining puts it,[108] a story is a narrative of particular events arranged in a time sequence and forming a meaningful totality. An argument is a number of propositions related to each other within an inferential structure; time and particularity are not defining elements of arguments, unlike stories. The significance of evidence may often be understood by locating it in the context of a story, but there are many evidential facts that do not need a story context to be meaningful. An item of scientific evidence such as a match between DNA profiles is not a story, and does not need to be made part of a story before it can be used as a step in an argument that a particular person is the perpetrator of an offence.[109] Reasoning about disputed questions of fact in legal contexts is a discourse of argument because it is directed to the establishment or the negativing of specific propositions. The whole or part of an argument may be presented in narrative form because of its psychological appeal as a way of connecting and explaining different pieces of evidence, but a story is not a necessary or defining element of an argument.

4–035

Secondly, it is important to note Twining's further point[110] that stories can be dangerous. The danger resides precisely in the creative scope they allow for invention and gap-filling. It is not difficult to list the practical risks: the

---

[107] W. A. Wagenaar, P. J. van Koppen and H. F. M. Crombag, *Anchored Narratives* (1993), p.16.

[108] W.L. Twining, "Anchored Narratives—A Comment" (1995) 1 *European Journal of Crime, Criminal Law, and Criminal Justice* 106, 110.

[109] Such evidence needs to be connected with the events charged in the indictment, but this can be done by a hypothesis, e.g. "It was the defendant who attacked the victim and raped her". This is not a story, except in a most impoverished sense.

[110] W.L. Twining, "Anchored Narratives—A Comment" (1995) 1 *European Journal of Crime, Criminal Law, and Criminal Justice* 106, 112. See also Ch.11 of Twining's *Rethinking Evidence*, 2nd edn (2006).

incorporation of unproved or irrelevant facts, the use of innuendo, the distortions produced by deliberate or unconscious bias or stereotyping. A more fundamental problem is defining the "story" itself. Stories are not self-defining; they do not present themselves with predetermined and unalterable limits. The addition of further episodes may produce radical changes to the story.

This point has interesting implications for the law of evidence. The admission of "background" evidence adds further episodes to the story of the case. As noted in Ch.1, part of the justification for this is to enable the evidence concerning the facts in issue to be better understood and evaluated. The meaning of the central episodes becomes clearer when they are placed in an expanded context that provides more information about the history and motivations of the main characters in the story. A further justification that is now apparent is the value of background evidence in displacing speculation and possible prejudice on the part of the factfinder. There is less risk of missing parts of the story being supplied inaccurately.

4–036 However, where the background evidence is discreditable, problems arise. Evidence of bad character and other misconduct may have only indirect (and limited) relevance to the facts in issue, but the party seeking to adduce the evidence may feel strongly that it gives a context to the party's story of which the factfinder should be be aware. Both the prosecution and the defence in a criminal case may argue that the interests of fairness call for an enlargement of the story by the addition of further episodes revealing the character of the accused or a prosecution witness respectively. The problems then are distraction and prejudice; the effect may be to shift the focus of the factfinder from the facts in issue to an evaluation of the extra episodes. The dangers presented by the introduction of the accused's criminal record have been recognised for many years. A clear example the other way is provided by the unregulated use of sexual history evidence in rape cases. Extensive questioning of a rape complainant about her sexual experiences with men other than the defendant may well have the effect of diverting a jury's attention from the defendant's actions to the complainant's character. Such questioning is a deliberate addition to the "story" of the rape.

PART II

OBTAINING EVIDENCE: PRE-TRIAL PROCEDURES AND THE REGULATION OF ACCESS

CHAPTER 5

THE PRIVILEGE AGAINST SELF-INCRIMINATION AND THE RIGHT TO SILENCE

A. INTRODUCTION

5–001　Part II of this book deals with a number of evidential issues arising in connection with the pre-trial stages of criminal and civil proceedings. In recent years questions of rights of access to evidence, and countervailing rights to refuse to make disclosure, have become much more prominent. In criminal cases the traditional focus of the law of evidence on the regulation of contested trials has broadened as the course of trials has increasingly had to take account of pre-trial events. A court may exclude evidence in a criminal case on the basis that the fairness of a trial may be compromised by unfairness earlier in the proceedings, including impropriety in the way the evidence was obtained. This is one aspect of a more general perception that pre-trial process is no longer to be regarded as something separate from the formal trial. In *R. v Horseferry Road Magistrates' Court Ex p. Bennett*[1] the House of Lords stayed a prosecution for abuse of process where the police procured the presence of the defendant in the United Kingdom by means that violated international law and deliberately disregarded extradition procedures. The Lords considered that, however fair the conduct of the actual trial might be, the legitimacy of the judicial process was in question. Lord Lowry said that to try the defendant at all would offend "the court's sense of justice and propriety".[2]

In this way legal process is now seen more as a continuum rather than as a succession of discrete episodes, with the trial as the central episode. Reflecting this development, much of the growth of the law of evidence in recent years has concerned the regulation of the investigation of offences, and the rules and procedures governing the disclosure of evidence. The Human Rights Act 1998 consolidated this wider remit of the law of evidence by incorporating the right to a fair trial under art.6 of the ECHR. As noted in Ch.2, the Strasbourg jurisprudence shows that the "determination... of [a] criminal charge" for the purposes of art.6 is interpreted widely. It is not restricted to the events occurring at a formal trial, but can include much of the pre-trial proceedings. This is because a "charge" is an autonomous concept under the Convention. It has been defined broadly to include the first official notification to a person "of an allegation that he has committed an offence, a definition that also corresponds to the test whether the situation of the [person] has been substantially affected".[3] This may be as early as the date of arrest.[4] As a result of this expansive view of the criminal process the European Court of Human Rights consistently takes account of pre-trial events in evaluating the fairness of a trial.[5]

---

[1] *R. v Horseferry Road Magistrates' Court Ex p. Bennett* [1994] 1 A.C. 42 HL; [1993] 3 All ER 138.

[2] *R. v Horseferry Road Magistrates' Court Ex p. Bennett* [1993] 3 All ER 138 at 161.

[3] *Deweer v Belgium* (1979–80) 2 E.H.R.R. 439 at 46; *Eckle v FRG* (1983) 5 E.H.R.R. 1 at 73.

[4] *Foti v Italy* (1983) 5 E.H.R.R. 313 at 52.

[5] See, e.g. *Edwards v United Kingdom* (1993) 15 E.H.R.R. 417 (non-disclosure of material evidence to the defence); *Saunders v United Kingdom* (1997) 23 E.H.R.R. 313 (questioning of the accused under compulsion); *Teixeira de Castro v Portugal* (1999) 28 E.H.R.R. 101 (entrapment). See also *Forbes* [2001] 1 All E.R. 686 at 697 per Lord Bingham: "... it is always necessary to consider all the facts and the whole history of the proceedings in a particular case to judge whether a defendant's right to a fair trial has been infringed or not."

This first chapter in Pt II considers the closely related topics of the privilege against self-incrimination and the right to silence. Both topics deal with the issue of compulsion of a person to provide evidence that may incriminate him. Broadly speaking, the difference between them is that the privilege against self-incrimination deals with questions of direct compulsion of an accused person to provide evidence against himself, whereas the right to silence covers certain situations of indirect compulsion. The common law privilege against self-incrimination entitles a person in any legal proceedings to refuse to answer questions or produce documents that may incriminate him. Questions of direct compulsion arise where statute intervenes to empower various officials to require the answering of questions or delivery of documents, with the sanction of criminal penalties for refusal. The use of these penalties, and the use of information or documents obtained by direct compulsion, may raise problems of fair trial under art.6. The right to silence deals with the evidential consequences in a criminal case of an accused's failure to answer police questions in pre-trial investigations or to give evidence at his trial. There is no directly enforceable duty to speak in these situations. But if adverse inferences may be drawn from a decision by a person to remain silent, then there is a form of indirect compulsion upon him to answer questions that may incriminate him. Again issues may arise of compatibility with art.6.

Section B explores in more detail the relationship between the privilege and the right to silence in criminal cases. Section C discusses the scope and limits of the privilege against self-incrimination at common law, the statutory restrictions upon the privilege, and the consequential problems that have arisen under art.6. This is followed in section D by a corresponding analysis of the right to silence at common law, its restriction by the Criminal Justice and Public Order Act 1994, and the art.6 issues. Finally, section E discusses the underlying theory of these doctrines. The discussion seeks to relate the purposes and values involved to the overall aims of the law of evidence. The focus in this last section is on the right to silence in particular, for the following reason.

5–002

The right to silence has been controversial ever since Bentham's famous attack on it,[6] and for more than 20 years from 1972 it provided one of the major battlegrounds of the modern law of evidence. The battle exemplified Packer's classic distinction between the "crime control" and "due process" models of criminal justice.[7] Reformers claimed that the so-called "right" was an unjustified obstruction to the efficient prosecution and conviction of guilty persons, whereas their opponents argued that it provided an essential protection for suspects in the criminal justice process and that it was an essential component of a fair trial. The battle seemed to have ended in victory for the reformers with the passing of the Criminal Justice and Public Order Act 1994, which significantly curtailed the right to silence as it had developed at common law. However, this victory has turned out not to be comprehensive. A combination of Strasbourg jurisprudence and somewhat restrictive interpretation by the Court of Appeal has meant that the reform to the right to silence in the police station is less radical in certain respects than it might have been. At the same time s.34 of the 1994 Act, which gave effect

---

[6] J. Bentham, *Treatise on Evidence*, E. Dumont (ed) (London: 1823).
[7] H. L. Packer, *The Limits of the Criminal Sanction* (Stanford: Stanford University Press, 1968).

to this reform, has led to considerable difficulties for trial judges in directing juries correctly about the drawing of adverse inferences from silence. There has been debate whether s.34 is more trouble than it is worth, and suggestions for a return to the common law.[8] A theoretical perspective on this debate offers considerations of principle to go with those of policy and expediency. In section E an approach to the right to silence is suggested that aims to move beyond the entrenched positions of the traditional debate. A principle derived from the theory of the legitimacy of the verdict is offered as the most coherent way forward. This principle cuts across the "crime control versus due process" opposition; it argues for the reinstatement of the accused's right to silence in the police station, but concedes that vital differences in the procedural context mean that the justification for a right to silence at trial is weak.[9]

B. THE RELATIONSHIP OF THE PRIVILEGE AGAINST SELF-INCRIMINATION AND THE RIGHT TO SILENCE

5–003   One of the problems in clarifying the relationship between the privilege against self-incrimination and the right to silence is that the latter term has a variable meaning. It is sometimes used as a synonym for the privilege against self-incrimination, but sometimes it refers to a legal rule of wider or narrower scope.[10] In *R. v Director of Serious Fraud Office Ex p. Smith*,[11] Lord Mustill suggested that the right to silence is a term used somewhat loosely to refer to any one or more of a "disparate group" of six immunities which "differ in nature, origin, incidence and importance". He continued:

> "Amongst these may be identified: (1) a general immunity, possessed by all persons and bodies, from being compelled on pain of punishment to answer questions posed by other persons and bodies; (2) a general immunity, possessed by all persons and bodies, from being compelled on pain of punishment to answer questions the answers to which may incriminate them; (3) a specific immunity, possessed by all persons under suspicion of criminal responsibility whilst being interviewed by police officers or others in similar positions of authority, from being compelled on pain of punishment to answer questions of any kind; (4) a specific immunity, possessed by accused persons undergoing trial, from being compelled to give evidence, and from being compelled to answer questions put to them in the dock; (5) a specific immunity, possessed by persons who have been charged with a criminal offence, from having questions material to the offence addressed to them by police officers or persons in a similar position of authority; (6) a a specific immunity (at least in certain circumstances, which it is unnecessary to explore), possessed by accused persons undergoing trial, from having adverse comment made on any failure (a) to answer questions before the trial, or (b) to give evidence at the trial."

Despite these differences the unifying feature of the immunities described by Lord Mustill is that they are all concerned with the legal significance of silence in the face of *questioning*. The privilege against self-incrimination is a term that

---

[8] D. J. Birch, "Suffering in Silence: A Cost-Benefit Analysis of Section 34 of the Criminal Justice and Public Order Act 1994" [1999] Crim. L.R. 769.
[9] This chapter does not otherwise deal with the accused's right to silence at trial. The evidential consequences of an accused's failure to testify are discussed in Ch.13.
[10] See further P. Mirfield, *Silence, Confessions and Improperly Obtained Evidence* (1997), pp.13–16.
[11] *R. v Director of Serious Fraud Office Ex p. Smith* [1993] A.C. 1 at 30–32 HL.

may also be employed in this context,[12] but neither in theory nor in current doctrine is its application restricted to the issue of whether persons can be compelled to answer questions. The issues for the privilege are much broader. In essence they are the justification and limits of the principle that no one should be obliged to produce *evidence* against themselves,[13] an enquiry which extends well beyond compulsory questioning.

In beginning this wider enquiry we note a conceptual distinction between what may be called primary and derivative applications of the privilege against self-incrimination. In its primary form the privilege against self-incrimination defines the scope of legal duties to co-operate in certain legal procedures. The investigation of offences may involve a variety of pre-trial procedures for the collection of evidence from a suspect. These procedures take different forms but they all involve obtaining evidence from the suspect, and they depend in the first instance for their efficacy on the suspect's co-operation. Thus they might require suspects to answer questions, to give information, to hand over documents or material objects, to take part in forensic investigations such as fingerprinting or the taking of samples, to permit searches of the suspect's person or property, to consent to the conduct of identification procedures. A privilege against self-incrimination might, in principle, exempt a person under investigation from complying with any or all of such procedures if compliance might tend to incriminate him.[14] As Mirfield puts it, the principle *nemo debet prodere se ipsum*, a term that he prefers to what has been described here as the privilege against self-incrimination, would entail that the police may not *engage the will* of the suspect so as to compel him to provide evidence against himself.[15] The mechanism for such protection would be a rule that no legal sanction could be imposed for a refusal to co-operate. A refusal would not be punishable as an offence or as a contempt. However, current English law is narrower than any such abstract principle. The rule of primary application, as noted above, is that "a man is not bound to provide evidence against himself by being forced to answer

---

[12] The term is often used interchangeably with the right to silence when Lord Mustill's 2nd and 6th immunities are under discussion.

[13] This is the Latin maxim, referred to by Lord Diplock in *Sang* [1980] A.C. 402, *nemo debet prodere se ipsum*. On the origins and development of the privilege against self-incrimination, see Wigmore, Vol. VIII (McNaughton rev. 1961), para.2250; L. W. Levy, *Origins of the Fifth Amendment* (New York: 1968); J. H. Langbein, "The Historical Origins of the Privilege Against Self-Incrimination at Common Law" (1994) 92 Mich. L.R. 1047; R. Helmholz, *The Privilege Against Self-Incrimination: Its Origins and Development* (Chicago: University Of Chicago Press, 1997); M. R. T. Macnair, "The Early Development of the Privilege Against Self-Incrimination" (1990) 10 O.J.L.S. 66.

[14] Where a procedure, such as a search or the taking of a sample, involves a violation of a suspect's interest in the security of person or property, consideration of the privilege might seem to be unnecessary in view of the general protection afforded to such interests by the substantive law of crime and tort. Nevertheless the privilege could supply an independent reason for not permitting exceptions to the substantive law for investigative procedures: see *Tate Access Floors v Boswell* [1991] Ch. 512, where Sir Nicolas Browne-Wilkinson V.C. held that the privilege could be relied on to defeat parts of an *Anton Piller* order requiring a defendant to permit the plaintiff to search the defendant's premises and seize documents related to alleged infringements of copyright.

[15] P. Mirfield, *Silence, Confessions and Improperly Obtained Evidence* (1997), p.16.

questions or produce documents".[16] Other evidence-collecting procedures fall outside the scope of the common law privilege.

5–004   Again as a matter of principle, the notion that persons should not be obliged to incriminate themselves is capable of considerable expansion. The privilege, if suitably interpreted, could become the basis for one or more of a group of ancillary or derivative applications. These might be designed to give more comprehensive effect to a broad principle that, in the words of the Fifth Amendment to the United States Constitution, "no one can be compelled to be a witness against himself". Such derivative applications of the privilege might include, first, the right to silence. In this context the term has a more precise usage. As indicated above, it describes an evidential immunity from comment on, and adverse inferences from, silence. The jury may not be invited by the prosecution or the judge to draw adverse inferences from an accused's failure to mention facts to the police when questioned or from his election not to testify at trial.[17] Without such an immunity, there would be an element of indirect compulsion to answer questions that may be incriminating. Secondly, these applications might include various exclusionary principles. Under this heading might be found a rule that an involuntary confession is inadmissible, or a rule that evidence obtained as a result of police deception and entrapment of the accused is liable to exclusion. If evidence is excluded on the basis of the privilege a further possibility arises of excluding other evidence discovered as a result of the unlawful or unfair action by the investigating authorities ("the fruit of the poisoned tree"). Thirdly, the privilege might be regarded as supporting warnings of the type set out in *Miranda v Arizona*[18] designed to make the privilege more available and effective for suspects generally. These warnings would include informing the suspect of the privilege, of the right of access to legal advice and of the right to refuse to be questioned.[19]

It does not follow that the privilege is the only possible rationale of these measures. It is possible to give a number of different accounts of, for example, a rule that coerced confessions are inadmissible.[20] The rationale of this rule will be

---

[16] per Sir Nicholas Browne-Wilkinson V.C. in *Tate Access Floors v Boswell* [1991] Ch. 512 at 529; citing *Rank Film Distributors Ltd v Video Information Centre* [1982] A.C. 380 HL. See also *R. v Director of Serious Fraud Office Ex p. Smith* [1993] A.C. 1 at 30–32 per Lord Mustill.

[17] This is the 6th of the "disparate group of immunities" described by Lord Mustill in *R. v Director of Serious Fraud Office Ex p. Smith* [1993] A.C. 1 at 30–32.

[18] *Miranda v Arizona* (1966) 384 U.S. 436.

[19] For English law see PACE Code of Practice C, paras 3.1, 3.15, 6, 10 and 11.2. These matters are discussed fully in Ch.6.

[20] English law was thought for a long time to base the rule that an involuntary confession was inadmissible on unreliability (see *Warickshall* (1783) 1 Leach 263; *R. v Ibrahim* [1914] A.C. 599 PC); but in *Sang* [1980] A.C. 402 at 436 HL, Lord Diplock expressed the view that the underlying rationale of the common law rule was the principle *nemo debet prodere se ipsum*. In saying this Lord Diplock went further than Lord Reid in *Commissioners of Customs and Excise v Harz and Power* [1967] 1 A.C. 761 at 820 HL who had opined that this principle and reliability were joint rationales for the voluntariness rule. Under PACE the notion of involuntariness was dropped. Confessions are now inadmissible if procured by oppression or by anything said or done likely to render unreliable any confession by the suspect (s.76(2)). See Ch.6. The architects of the reform based their proposals on a combination of reliability, disciplinary and protective principles: see the Eleventh Report of the Criminal Law Revision Committee, para.64; Report of the Royal Commission on Criminal Procedure, Cmnd.8092 (1981), paras 4.131–4.132.

discussed further in Ch.6. For the moment it is worth emphasising that despite the rhetoric sometimes used in support of the privilege against self-incrimination[21] the extensive range of applications that it might have in theory is significantly limited in practice. The limitation may take the form of a denial that the privilege is applicable at all, or a statutory abolition or restriction of the privilege. Such limitations have increased in recent years. How and why this has happened will be explored in the succeeding sections of this chapter.

C. THE PRIVILEGE AGAINST SELF-INCRIMINATION

1. *The privilege against self-incrimination at common law*

(A) *Civil proceedings*

The Civil Evidence Act 1968 s.14 refers to the privilege against self-incrimination as:

5–005

> "(1)   The right of a person in any legal proceedings other than criminal proceedings to refuse to answer any question or produce any document or thing if to do so would tend to expose that person to proceedings for an offence or for the recovery of a penalty."

This has been said[22] to restate the common law, and subsequent references to the privilege in the case law are consistent with the statutory formulation.[23] At common law the privilege has a general application to all persons in all civil proceedings. Thus it is available equally to witnesses, and to the parties to civil litigation,[24] both at trial and in pre-trial proceedings, such as discovery of documents,[25] the grant of search orders[26] and the issue of freezing injunctions.[27]

---

[21] See, e.g. the remarks of Murphy J. in *Pyneboard Pty Ltd v Restrictive Trade Practices Commission* (1983) 152 C.L.R. 328 at 346.

[22] By Lord Diplock in *Rio Tinto Zinc Corp v Westinghouse Electric Corp* [1978] A.C. 547 at 636 HL. See generally *Phipson on Evidence*, 16th edn (London: Sweet & Maxwell, 2005), paras 24–40 and 24–65.

[23] See *Rank Film Distributors Ltd v Video Information Centre* [1982] A.C. 380 HL; *Tate Access Floors v Boswell* [1991] Ch. 512.

[24] See, e.g. *Blunt v Park Lane Hotel Ltd* [1942] 2 K.B. 253, where the question was whether a plaintiff in a slander action could rely on the privilege to refuse to answer interrogatories about whether she had committed adultery. The Court of Appeal held that since the jurisdiction of the old ecclesiastical courts over adultery was obsolete, the privilege no longer had this extension.

[25] *AT & T Istel Ltd v Tully* [1993] A.C. 45 HL.

[26] For search orders see Civil Procedure Act 1997 s.7; CPR r.25.1(h). On the availability of the privilege against self-incrimination against *Anton Piller* orders (the predecessors of search orders) see *Rank Film Distributors Ltd v Video Information Centre* [1982] A.C. 380 HL; *Tate Access Floors v Boswell* [1991] Ch. 512. The decision in the former case was quickly reversed by the Senior Courts Act 1981 s.72, withdrawing the privilege in cases concerned with infringement of intellectual property rights and passing off.

[27] For freezing injunctions see CPR r.25.1(f). On the availability of the privilege against self-incrimination against *Mareva* injunctions (the predecessors of freezing injunctions) see *Sociedad Nacional de Combustivies de Angola UEE v Lundqvist* [1991] 2 Q.B. 310.

In the absence of the privilege, the person claiming it would have a legal duty to answer questions or produce documents or things, and would be liable in contempt for failing to comply.

The privilege includes a right to refuse to incriminate one's spouse,[28] but its extent is limited in all cases to "criminal offences under the law of any part of the United Kingdom and penalties provided for by such law".[29] "Penalties" referred historically to the statutory penalties recoverable by common informers who brought proceedings against certain types of wrongdoer. In modern law such proceedings are obsolete, and the main penalties in respect of which privilege is now available are administrative penalties imposed by the EC Commission for breach of European Union law,[30] certain statutory penalties, such as those recoverable under fiscal legislation, and penalties for civil contempt.[31]

The privilege includes both answers that would incriminate the person directly and those which might incriminate indirectly, by forming part of a line of inquiry leading to the obtaining of evidence against the person.[32] However, in *C Plc v P*[33] the Court of Appeal held that the privilege did not extend to "independent" evidence in the form of indecent images of children found on a computer which the appellant had delivered up pursuant to a search order in intellectual property proceedings. The court drew a distinction between things which a person is compelled to produce and things which are discovered in the course of executing a court order. It appears that the common law privilege would apply to the former; a stolen computer might be an example of an incriminating "thing" which the defendant could not be compelled to produce. But the privilege would not apply to things discovered independently; the court made an analogy with the finding of controlled drugs in counterfeit bags seized pursuant to a search order, and a solicitor executing a search order observing an illegal weapon in the defendant's house. This distinction is consistent with the rule for evidence discovered in consequence of an inadmissible confession,[34] which the Court of Appeal cited, but in the context of the case it requires us to distinguish between an order for the delivery of a thing incriminating in itself, and the delivery of a thing not incriminating in itself but which has incriminating contents. This is hardly satisfactory, and is difficult to square with the rule stated at the beginning of this paragraph. The better approach would be to say that the privilege should apply only to the compelled production of incriminating communications from the defendant, and not to documents or things which exist independently of the defendant's will.[35]

---

[28] Civil Evidence Act 1968 s.14(1)(b), changing the common law which restricted the privilege to the claimant: *Rio Tinto Zinc Corp v Westinghouse Electric Corp* [1978] A.C. 547 at 637 HL per Lord Diplock.

[29] Civil Evidence Act 1968 s.14(1)(a).

[30] *Rio Tinto Zinc Corp v Westinghouse Electric Corp* [1978] A.C. 547 HL.

[31] *Bhimji v Chatwani (No.2)* [1992] 4 All E.R. 912; *Memory Corp Plc v Sidhu* [2000] 1 All E.R. 434.

[32] *Slaney* (1832) 5 C. & P. 213. See further *Lamb v Munster* (1882) 10 Q.B.D. 110.

[33] *C Plc v P* [2007] EWCA Civ 493; [2007] 3 All ER 1034.

[34] See Ch.6.

[35] This is the rule enunciated by the European Court of Human Rights in *Saunders v United Kingdom* (1997) 23 E.H.R.R. 313, discussed below. In *C Plc v P* [2007] EWCA Civ 493 at [46] Lawrence Collins L.J. accepted that there is "a powerful case in policy terms for there being no privilege with respect to disclosure of free-standing documents or other material not brought into existence under

Indeed, strong views have been expressed about the continued availability of the privilege at all in civil cases. In *AT & T Istel Ltd v Tully*,[36] Lord Templeman was particularly critical:

> "It is difficult to see any reason why in civil proceedings the privilege against self-incrimination should be exercisable so as to enable a litigant to refuse relevant and even vital documents which are in his possession or power and which speak for themselves : . . . I regard the privilege against self-incrimination exercisable in civil proceedings as an archaic and unjustifiable survival from the past when the court directs the production of relevant documents and requires the defendant to specify his dealings with the plaintiff's property or money."

5–006

Such criticism reflects a belief that the underlying rationale for the privilege is restricted to the protection of suspects and defendants in the criminal process.[37] Those who are sceptical whether it should have any wider application generally argue that any unfairness in requiring parties and witnesses in civil proceedings to disclose incriminating evidential material can be dealt with by "use immunity" measures. These are statutory provisions[38] which prohibit the use in a subsequent prosecution of material disclosed under compulsion. It is thought that by this means the aims of civil proceedings will not be hampered by claims of privilege, whilst the person seeking the protection of privilege will not be significantly disadvantaged by the compelled disclosure. These considerations will need to be borne in mind when we turn to consider the human rights aspects of the privilege.

(B)   Criminal proceedings

The common law privilege applies in criminal proceedings. Witnesses in criminal trials may rely on it as a justification for refusing to answer questions tending to incriminate them, and this includes the accused who testifies in defence, as far as incrimination of offences other than those currently charged is concerned.[39] As regards pre-trial criminal investigations, it is clear, as Lord Mustill acknowledged in *R. v Director of Serious Fraud Office Ex p. Smith*,[40] that all persons, including suspects, have a liberty at common law not to answer any questions from the police, whether or not the questions are incriminating. In this sense any privilege against self-incrimination is swallowed up in the wider citizen's privilege not to co-operate with law enforcement authorities. However, the narrower privilege undoubtedly still exists at this stage as an independent rule. This is apparent from the decision in *R. v Director of Serious Fraud Office* that, when Parliament gave the Director of the Serious Fraud Office powers of compulsory questioning of

5–007

---

compulsion", citing A. Zuckerman, *Civil Procedure*, 2nd edn (London: Sweet & Maxwell, 2006), Ch.17. In *Malik v Manchester Crown Court* [2008] EWCA 1362 (Admin); [2008] 4 All E.R. 403 the Divisional Court expressed the view that the ratio of *C Plc v P* was that no privilege exists in relation to pre-existing documents, *sed qu.*

[36] *AT & T Istel Ltd v Tully* [1993] A.C. 45 at 53 HL.

[37] See *AT & T Istel Ltd v Tully* [1993] A.C. 45 at 53 per Lord Templeman, 57 per Lord Griffiths.

[38] e.g. Theft Act 1968 s.31; Senior Courts Act 1981 s.72(3) and (4); Fraud Act 2006 s.13.

[39] The Criminal Evidence Act 1898 s.1(2) removes the privilege against self-incrimination in respect of questions in cross-examination that would tend to criminate him as to the offence charged.

[40] *R. v Director of Serious Fraud Office Ex p. Smith* [1993] A.C. 1 HL.

persons suspected of serious fraud,[41] it not only expressly removed the liberty of non-co-operation but also impliedly removed the privilege against self-incrimination.

2. *Statutory restrictions on the privilege*

5–008   Parliament has made numerous inroads into the privilege against self-incrimination. Many statutes require individuals to answer questions, provide information and produce documents in a variety of procedural contexts, with a threat of criminal sanctions for non-compliance. Some statutes expressly remove the privilege in such cases; an example is s.31 of the Theft Act 1968, which provides that the privilege does not excuse a person from answering any question in proceedings for the recovery or administration of any property, for the execution of any trust or for an account of any property or dealings with property.[42] In other cases the statute may be silent about the availability of the privilege; it then becomes a question of construction for the courts as to whether the statute has impliedly removed the privilege. In certain statutory investigations where fraud is suspected, the courts have invariably found that the privilege has been impliedly removed; more is said about these cases below.

Statutes imposing positive duties to answer questions, provide information and produce documents may or may not contain provisions about the use that can be made of statements and documents produced under such legislative compulsion. Section 31 of the Theft Act 1968, for example, provides that no statement or admission made in answering a question covered by the section is admissible in criminal proceedings for an offence under the Theft Act.[43] Where the statute does not expressly provide for immunity from use of compelled statements, the courts generally hold the legislative intention to be that no immunity is available and therefore that the statements can be used in evidence against their maker.[44]

Some of the most important exceptions to the privilege against self-incrimination are concerned with investigations into fraud. Various agencies and office-holders, such as the Serious Fraud Office, the Department for Business, Enterprise and Regulatory Reform,[45] and liquidators of insolvent companies, have statutory powers to investigate individuals and companies, where the business in question may involve possibly serious fraud. These powers include powers to require any person (including a person under suspicion) to answer questions, to supply information and to disclose documents. The existence of such powers is generally argued to be essential for establishing how relevant enterprises were managed and for tracing the whereabouts of missing assets. The

---

[41] Criminal Justice Act 1987 s.2.

[42] See also Fraud Act 2006 s.13.

[43] There are similar provisions in the Criminal Damage Act 1971 s.9, Senior Courts Act 1981 s.72, and Children Act 1989 s.98. The Fraud Act 2006 s.13 provides for use immunity for an offence "under this Act or a related offence"; for discussion of "related offence" see *Kensington International Ltd v Republic of Congo* [2007] EWCA Civ 1128.

[44] *Scott* (1856) Dears. & B. 47 is the leading case establishing this principle of interpretation. For modern examples see *Kansal* [1993] Q.B. 244; *Bishopsgate Investment Management Ltd v Maxwell* [1993] Ch.1. All three cases concern statutory investigations into personal or corporate insolvency.

[45] Formerly the Department of Trade and Industry ("DTI").

courts have consistently held that these are powers of an inquisitorial nature that impliedly remove the privilege against self-incrimination.[46] A person under investigation may thus be faced with the choice either (a) of voluntary incrimination through compliance with requests or orders for disclosure; or (b) of criminal penalties for a refusal to comply or for the giving of false information.

The extent to which use can be made of information or documents disclosed under these powers varies according to the particular legislation. The general position used to be that civil investigators such as liquidators or DTI inspectors had a power to hand over incriminating statements or documents to the prosecuting authorities for possible use as part of an affirmative prosecution case.[47] There was no "use immunity" for material disclosed under compulsion in this type of investigation. However, statements obtained from a suspect by the Serious Fraud Office, which is a criminal investigation agency, could be used only to prove perjury in the making of the statement or to contradict inconsistent testimony at trial.[48] This latter rule, which might be viewed as a residual concession to the privilege against self-incrimination, did not prevent the use in evidence of facts discovered in consequence of compulsorily disclosed material, such as the location of a foreign bank account.

    5–009

In justification of those decisions, the English courts referred to the public interest element in the relevant proceedings.[49] They argued that it was not just a question of protecting the interests of shareholders or creditors. Parliament had chosen to regard the public interest in being protected from fraud as being sufficiently important to override the privilege. Such recognition of the claims of collective interests in crime control failed to explain how fraud could be distinguished from major crimes such as murder, armed robbery or rape. The privilege may be relied on in these cases to resist questioning by the police, yet the public interest in being protected from murderers, robbers and rapists would seem arguably stronger. Certainly the argument for the special position of fraud offences did not impress the European Court of Human Rights. In *Saunders v United Kingdom*,[50] the court held that the use at the first Guinness trial[51] of statements obtained from Saunders by DTI inspectors under their compulsory powers had deprived him of his right to a fair hearing within the meaning of art.6(1). In reaching this conclusion the court confirmed the emphatic rejection by the European Commission of Human Rights of the UK Government's public interest justification.[52]

---

[46] *Re London United Investments Plc* [1992] Ch. 578 CA (powers of DTI inspectors under ss.432 and 434 of the Companies Act 1985); *Bishopsgate Investment Management Ltd v Maxwell* [1993] Ch. 1 CA (powers of liquidators of an insolvent company under ss.235 and 236 of the Insolvency Act 1986); *R. v Director of Serious Fraud Office Ex p. Smith* [1993] A.C. 1 HL (powers of the Director of the Serious Fraud Office under s.2 of the Criminal Justice Act 1987).

[47] See generally D. N. Kirk and A. J. J. Woodcock, *Serious Fraud: Investigation and Trial*, 2nd edn (London: Butterworths, 1998).

[48] Criminal Justice Act 1987 s.2(8).

[49] See in particular *Re London United Investments Plc* [1992] Ch. 578, 594; *R. v Director of Serious Fraud Office Ex p. Smith* [1993] A.C. 1 at 44.

[50] *Saunders v United Kingdom* (1997) 23 E.H.R.R. 313.

[51] That is, the first of a series of trials involving a number of prominent businessmen on charges of theft and related offences arising out of a bitterly contested takeover battle in the 1980s.

[52] *Saunders v United Kingdom* (1997) 23 E.H.R.R. 313 at [74].

As a direct result of the *Saunders* case, the Youth Justice and Criminal Evidence Act 1999 s.59 and Sch.3 inserted "use immunity" provisions into a large number of the statutory powers concerned with fraud-related investigations. These are discussed further below; for the moment it should be noted that they provide immunity for *answers* and *statements* made in response to compulsory questioning under the relevant powers. They do not protect pre-existing *documents* disclosed under compulsion. It should also be noted that these provisions apply only to the statutory powers set out in Sch.3 to the Youth Justice and Criminal Evidence Act 1999. They do not extend to many other statutory powers to require persons to answer questions and give information.

5–010 Before leaving the subject of fraud, it is worth noting one point of distinction between fraud and other serious offences. This is that the procedural context may be different. As Jackson has pointed out, a person required to attend for interview at the Serious Fraud Office is given advance notice in writing of what is required from him and he is positively advised to have a legal advisor present during the interview.[53] A police interview of a person in custody at a police station may take a quite different form. Insofar as the privilege against self-incrimination protects persons in vulnerable positions in police custody it is arguably less necessary in the changed conditions of a fraud investigation.

Furthermore all these inquisitorial powers in fraud cases are vested in persons other than police officers—namely accountants, lawyers and civil servants. Such groups may have different occupational cultures from the police, and the relevant procedures have different systems of accountability. A company liquidator is a senior accountant and a court-appointed officeholder; Departmental inspectors appointed under the Companies Act are either senior barristers or accountants who report directly to the Department; the Director of the Serious Fraud Office is a senior civil servant who discharges his functions under the supervision of the Attorney-General. While these matters of status and report do not guarantee that investigations will be conducted with an absence of pressure and in accord with principles of natural justice[54] they do suggest that the risks of abuse of power sometimes associated with police investigations may be much less.

It might also be argued that the overruling of the privilege in commercial fraud cases can be justified by analogy with fiduciary principles. A person voluntarily accepting an office, such as that of company director or auditor, with public and/or private duties, e.g. to shareholders and creditors, could fairly be said to accept a responsibility to answer questions about the discharge of his duties and the management of assets. The argument is attractive as far as it applies to office-holders who are the principal targets of the relevant legislation. But the argument is under-inclusive, in that the legislation does not limit the duty to speak to office-holders.[55]

---

[53] J. D. Jackson, "The Right of Silence: Judicial Responses to Parliamentary Encroachment" (1994) 57 M.L.R. 270, 274.

[54] In *Re Pergamon Press Ltd* [1971] Ch. 388 the Court of Appeal held that the subject of questioning by DTI inspectors need not be told of what he is suspected.

[55] Thus under the Companies Act 1985 s.434(2) and (3) a Departmental investigator may require an officer or agent of the company being investigated *or any other person* to produce documents and answer questions on oath.

3.   *The privilege against self-incrimination and ECHR article 6*

(A)   *Incorporation of the privilege into article 6*

Article 6 of the ECHR does not expressly state either the privilege against **5–011** self-incrimination or the right to silence as elements of the right to a fair trial. However, the European Court of Human Rights has consistently declared that art.6 states only minimum rights and that it should receive an expansive application.[56] As part of the expansion the court has implied into art.6 both the privilege against self-incrimination and the right to silence. It has described them as "generally recognised international standards lying at the heart of the notion of a fair procedure".[57]

In the landmark case of *Funke v France*,[58] the European Court of Human Rights held that art.6(1) includes the right of anyone charged with a criminal offence to remain silent and not to contribute to incriminating himself. Accordingly the court resolved that the conviction of the applicant for failing to produce bank statements to the French customs authorities on request was a violation of art.6(1). The applicant had argued that the Customs had brought criminal proceedings for non-production that were calculated to compel him to co-operate in a prosecution to be mounted against him for offences against regulations governing financial dealings with foreign countries. The court agreed, holding that the special features of French customs law could not justify such an infringement of art.6(1).

This was a bold and far-reaching decision. It incorporated into the Convention a principle of the common law that, on the face of it, is at odds with the inquisitorial traditions of much of continental Europe. Secondly, in doing so, the court appeared[59] to give the privilege the same scope that it has in English common law, as opposed to the more restricted American rule.[60] Thirdly, and crucially, the court held that the statutory right of inspection of documents under art.65–1 of the French Customs Code was ineffective to override the privilege. Despite its unqualified terms the Code provision was held to be incapable of justifying the infringement of the right not to contribute to self-incrimination.

---

[56] *Delcourt v Belgium* (1979–80) 1 E.H.R.R. 355 at [25]; *Moreida de Azvedo v Portugal* (1992) 13 E.H.R.R. 731 at [66].

[57] *Murray v United Kingdom* (1996) 22 E.H.R.R. 29 at [45]; *Saunders v United Kingdom* (1997) 23 E.H.R.R. 313 at [68]; *Heaney and McGuinness v Ireland* (2001) 33 E.H.R.R. 264.

[58] *Funke v France* (1993) 16 E.H.R.R. 297.

[59] Appearances may be deceptive. The extension of the privilege to include pre-existing documents is doubtful, as discussed below.

[60] That is, by allowing the privilege to protect a person from having to produce pre-existing documents as well as from having to make testimonial disclosures. In *Fisher v United States* (1976) 425 U.S. 391 the Supreme Court introduced the "act of production" doctrine whereby the privilege may not bar the state from compelling the production of incriminating material from the accused as long as the process involved does not compel the accused to create an incriminating testimonial response by complying with the state's order. The production of bank statements, where the existence of the relevant accounts is not in issue, would seem not to be covered by the privilege according to this doctrine. cf. *United States v Doe* (1984) 465 U.S. 605, and see the discussion in *McCormick on Evidence*, 6th edn (West, St Paul, 2006), para.138; Berger, "American perspectives on self-incrimination and the compelled production of evidence" (2002) 6 E. & P. 218 at 230 onwards.

Following this decision it was uncertain whether the right against self-incrimination which the court had implied into art.6 was absolute and allowed for no restrictions.

5–012   However, since the court's later decision in *Murray v United Kingdom*,[61] it has become clear that both the privilege against self-incrimination and the right to silence can be qualified or restricted.[62] The key question is when this can happen without a violation of art.6. There is now a significant body of case law dealing with the human rights issues presented by statutory powers to acquire information and documents by direct compulsion. From the point of view of human rights there are two problems to be considered. One problem arises where a person refuses to comply with a demand under one of these powers for information or documents. Does prosecution and conviction of him for failure to comply violate art.6? The other problem arises where the person does comply and discloses information or documents. If that information or those documents are used in a subsequent prosecution is there a violation of art.6?

The case law on these problems is complex and in some respects inconsistent. Two distinctions have emerged as significant for the law in this area, but both present difficulty. The first difficulty emerged in *Saunders v United Kingdom*.[63] The European Court of Human Rights commented at one point in the judgment:

> "The right not to incriminate oneself, in particular, presupposes that the prosecution in a criminal case seek to prove their case against the accused without resort to evidence obtained through methods of coercion or oppression in defiance of the will of the accused. In this sense the right in question is closely linked to the presumption of innocence contained in Art.6(2) of the Convention."[64]

This statement does two important things. It explains the rationale of the privilege in terms of freedom from abuse of state power; this is the point of the reference to obtaining evidence by methods of coercion or oppression. It links this freedom from abuse of power to the principle of the presumption of innocence, a fundamental principle in the liberal democratic tradition of criminal justice. The other thing the statement does is to introduce an important limitation on the notion of abuse. The objection is to the use of coercion or oppression to obtain evidence in defiance of the will of the accused.

5–013   This is where the difficulty arises. If this idea of obtaining evidence against the will is taken literally it would mean, for example, that compelling a reluctant suspect to take a breath test or allow his fingerprints to be taken, would violate the privilege. But the court was at pains to explain in *Saunders* that the privilege did not go this far (neither did the common law, as noted earlier). It said later in the judgment that there was a distinction between *statements* made under compulsion, to which the privilege applied, and evidence having an existence

---

[61] *Murray v United Kingdom* (1996) 22 E.H.R.R. 29.
[62] The European Court of Human Rights has confirmed the non-absolute nature of these rights on a number of occasions. See, on the right to silence, *Condron v United Kingdom* (2001) 31 E.H.R.R. 1 at [56]; *Averill v United Kingdom* (2001) 31 E.H.R.R. 839 at [42]–[43]; and, on the privilege against self-incrimination, *Heaney and McGuinness v Ireland* (2001) 33 E.H.R.R. 264 at [47].
[63] *Saunders v United Kingdom* (1997) 23 E.H.R.R. 313.
[64] *Saunders v United Kingdom* (1997) 23 E.H.R.R. 313 at [68].

independent of the will of the suspect, such as alcohol in breath, to which the privilege did not apply. This second category of evidence would obviously include pre-existing documents—these exist independently of the suspect's will and are not brought into existence under compulsion. But in *Funke v France* the court had decided that the privilege did attach to the pre-existing bank statements that the French customs authorities wanted M. Funke to produce under compulsion. *Saunders* was inconsistent with *Funke* on this point, and the inconsistency has produced difficulty ever since, as appears below.

Moreover, the distinction made in *Saunders* is not always either straightforward or satisfactory. In *R. v S and A*,[65] the Court of Appeal had to decide whether the privilege applied to a requirement to disclose the encryption key to certain computer files. The court noted that although the key itself existed independently of the defendant's will (like the key to a locked drawer), the defendant's disclosure in a statement of his *knowledge* of it might be incriminating in itself. On that basis the privilege was held to apply, although it would not apply to the data held in the computer files. In *Jalloh v Germany*,[66] an issue arose of the use of evidence in the form of drugs swallowed by the defendant, where the evidence had been obtained by forcibly administering an emetic to the defendant. The European Court of Human Rights held that the privilege was applicable and had been violated by the procedure used to retrieve the evidence. The court reasoned that although the drugs hidden in the defendant's body were real evidence and had an existence independent of his will, force was used to obtain them *in defiance of* his will, and the degree of force used differed significantly in gravity from the degree of compulsion normally required to obtain the types of material referred to in *Saunders* as existing independently of the defendant's will. This argument blurs the distinction made in *Saunders* to the point where it is almost meaningless.

Before discussing the second key distinction it is useful to note an important check on attempts to restrict the privilege. The European Court of Human Rights has said on more than one occasion that any degree of compulsion must not be such as to destroy the "very essence" of the privilege against self-incrimination.[67] In *Heaney and McGuinness v Ireland*,[68] the court found a violation of art.6 where the applicants were given sentences of six months' imprisonment under Irish anti-terrorist legislation for refusing to give evidence about their movements on the night of a murder. In the court's view, the essence of the privilege was destroyed where they were compelled to choose between the threat of imprisonment for failing to provide information and the risk presented by providing information relevant to very serious charges that might be brought against them. But the case did not clarify the crucial question of the criteria for when compulsion will or will not have this effect; this is a matter to which we shall return shortly.

---

[65] *R. v S and A* [2008] EWCA Crim 2177.
[66] *Jalloh v Germany* (2007) 44 E.H.R.R. 32.
[67] The court first alluded to this principle in *Murray v United Kingdom* (1996) 22 E.H.R.R. 29 at [49].
[68] *Heaney and McGuinness v Ireland* (2001) 33 E.H.R.R. 264.

(B)   Scope of the privilege

5–014   The second key distinction is between administrative inquiries and criminal investigations. In *IJL, GMR and AKP v United Kingdom*,[69] three of the other defendants in the first Guinness trial claimed that the compulsory questioning of them by DTI inspectors under s.434 of the Companies Act 1985 violated their privilege against self-incrimination under art.6. The European Court of Human Rights rejected this argument. The court held that a legal requirement for an individual to give information demanded by an administrative body does not infringe art.6. It seems that where the body in question is essentially a regulatory body, such as the DTI inspectors, whose job is to discover and record facts, then art.6 is not applicable because the body is not engaged in the determination of a criminal charge. Such an inquiry is not part of the process of investigation and prosecution. Accordingly sanctions for failure to comply with a demand for information or documents will not result in a violation of art.6. This is not to say that a so-called administrative investigation can never involve the determination of a criminal charge, as the court had recognised earlier in *Saunders v United Kingdom*.[70] It is likely to depend on whether the body in question has the power to adjudicate on the person's liability.

A similar distinction for types of investigation was made by the House of Lords in *R. v Herts CC Ex p. Green Environmental Industries*.[71] In this case a local authority had requested a company to supply factual information about clinical waste found on unlicensed sites. Failure to provide the information was an offence under s.71(3) of the Environmental Protection Act 1990. The House of Lords held that the company and its managing director could not invoke the privilege against self-incrimination to justify their non-compliance. According to Lord Hoffmann art.6 is anchored to the fairness of the criminal trial and is not concerned with "extra-judicial inquiries".[72] He stated that although the local authority had power to bring criminal proceedings under the Act for illegal waste disposal, its request for information under s.71 could not be described as an adjudication either in form or substance. Nor did the request for information invite any admission of wrongdoing. This decision is consistent with the rulings in the Guinness cases in Strasbourg. However, it does not offer much further help on the problem of distinguishing administrative "extra-judicial" inquiries from criminal investigations.[73]

---

[69] *IJL, GMR and AKP v United Kingdom* (2001) 33 E.H.R.R. 11.
[70] *Saunders v United Kingdom* (1997) 23 E.H.R.R. 313.
[71] *R. v Herts CC Ex p. Green Environmental Industries* [2000] 1 All E.R. 773 HL.
[72] *R. v Herts CC Ex p. Green Environmental Industries* [2000] 1 All E.R. 773 at [781].
[73] The distinction is reasonably clear where investigators have only a factfinding role and have no powers to adjudicate on a person's liabilities or take decisions on prosecution. Thus in *Kearns* [2002] EWCA Crim 748; [2003] 1 Cr.App.R. 7 the Court of Appeal upheld the defendant's conviction of an offence under s.354(3)(a) of the Insolvency Act 1986 where he failed to give information on request to the Official Receiver in bankruptcy about certain receipts and payments of money. The Receiver was carrying out his statutory duty to investigate and report on the estate of the bankrupt. His demand was not made in order to provide evidence to prove a case against the defendant. Where investigating officials do have adjudicative powers the courts will have to examine the substance of the investigation to decide whether it involves the "determination of a criminal charge". Inland Revenue

It is clear, however, that although a person may be validly compelled on pain of punishment to give information in an administrative inquiry, the use of answers and statements in a subsequent prosecution may result in a violation of art.6.[74] This is so even if the statements are not overtly incriminating. They were not in *Saunders*, and yet the European Court of Human Rights held that their use in his subsequent prosecution hampered him in the conduct of his defence and thereby violated his right to a fair trial. As we have seen, the United Kingdom's response to this decision was the "use immunity" provisions in Sch.3 to the Youth Justice and Criminal Evidence Act 1999. These apply to a large number of compulsory powers in administrative inquiries. They provide that no evidence relating to answers and statements made in compliance with the powers may be adduced by the prosecution in criminal proceedings. Where no such use immunity provision exists, there will be an issue for the judge at the criminal trial whether to exclude evidence of the statements under s.78 of PACE. The same issue can of course arise where a person makes statements under compulsion in a criminal investigation. According to the Court of Appeal in *R. v K*,[75] the same approach applies in both types of case. This approach is discussed below; for the moment it can be noted that in *R. v K* the defendant made admissions, which incriminated him in possible tax evasion, in the course of compulsory disclosure of his assets for the purposes of an application for ancillary relief in divorce proceedings. The Court of Appeal held that evidence of the admissions should be excluded under s.78 in a prosecution for tax evasion, on the ground that the nature of the sanction to be applied to enforce the compulsory disclosure (imprisonment for contempt) would be a disproportionate response to the social purpose of suppressing tax evasion.

The provisions in the 1999 Act do not include *documents* produced under compulsion. What then is the position where a person delivers up pre-existing documents under compulsion in an administrative inquiry? If the documents do not contain statements made under compulsion, does their use in a subsequent prosecution violate art.6? This issue arose in *Attorney-General's Reference (No.7 of 2000)*,[76] where the Court of Appeal answered the question with a firm "No". The reference arose out of a case where a bankrupt delivered up to the Official Receiver various documents relating to his affairs leading up to the bankruptcy. These included documents showing his gambling activities. Failure to comply with the obligation to make such delivery would have been punishable as a contempt under s.291(6) of the Insolvency Act 1986. He was subsequently prosecuted for an offence under s.362(1)(a) of the Insolvency Act of materially contributing to his insolvency by gambling. The trial judge had ruled the documents inadmissible on the ground that their admission would result in a violation of art.6. Disagreeing, the Court of Appeal followed the distinction made by the European Court of Human Rights in *Saunders v United Kingdom* between

5–015

---

[74] and Customs investigations may present difficulty: see further *Funke v France* (1993) 16 E.H.R.R. 297; *JB v Switzerland* [2001] Crim. L.R. 748; *Allen (No.2)* [2001] 4 All E.R. 768.

[74] See *Saunders v United Kingdom* (1997) 23 E.H.R.R. 313; followed in *IJL, GMR and AKP v United Kingdom* (2001) 33 E.H.R.R. 11.

[75] *R. v K* [2009] EWCA Crim 1640.

[76] *Attorney-General's Reference (No.7 of 2000)* [2001] EWCA Crim 888; [2001] 2 Cr.App.R. 19.

statements made under compulsion and evidence having an existence independent of the will of the accused. These documents were held to fall into the latter category. They were outwith the scope of the privilege against self-incrimination and therefore their use would not violate art.6. The court noted that the trial judge would still have the discretion under s.78 of PACE to exclude documents if their admission would adversely affect the fairness of the particular proceedings. The court said that in so far as *Saunders* conflicted with *Funke v France*[77] it preferred the approach in *Saunders* as a matter of principle.[78]

5–016   We may now turn to compulsory questioning in investigations forming part of criminal proceedings. Assuming that the person being questioned has been notified, or is aware, that he is being seriously investigated with a view to prosecution, there is a "determination of a criminal charge" and art.6 is clearly engaged. So the first issue is whether the imposition of a penalty for failing to give information that may be incriminating is a violation.

This is a major issue, on which the case law from Strasbourg and London appeared for a time to be in conflict. The initial response in Strasbourg was to say that there is a violation if the accused is subject to direct compulsion to disclose potentially incriminating information in criminal proceedings. Thus in *Heaney and McGuinness v Ireland*,[79] as noted above, the applicants were held to have been denied a fair trial when they were convicted and imprisoned for six months for failing to comply with a compulsory request to account for their movements. The degree of compulsion imposed by the relevant legislation was said to have destroyed the "very essence" of their privilege against self-incrimination. A different answer was given by the Privy Council in *Brown v Stott (Procurator Fiscal, Dunfermline)*.[80] Mrs Brown was suspected of driving with excess alcohol to a store where she stole a bottle of gin. After she had been arrested for theft the police made an oral request under s.172(2)(a) of the Road Traffic Act 1988 that she identify the person who had driven her car to the store. Refusal to give the name is an offence punishable with a maximum £1,000 fine and endorsement of licence. When Mrs Brown admitted that she had driven the car she was breathalysed. The result was positive. The procurator fiscal intended to rely on her admission of being the driver at her forthcoming prosecution for theft and driving with excess alcohol. She alleged that the use of her admission would violate art.6. The Privy Council reversed the decision of the High Court of Justiciary in Scotland and held that there would be no violation of art.6. Lord Bingham argued that the privilege against self-incrimination in art.6 is not absolute. It could be restricted, he said, in pursuance of a legitimate aim, provided that the restriction is proportionate to the aim to be achieved. The legitimate aim in this case was the enforcement of road traffic legislation designed to reduce the high incidence of death and injury on the roads caused by the misuse of motor vehicles. This was a very serious problem that needed to be addressed in an effective way for the benefit of the public. The restriction was proportionate

---

[77] *Funke v France* (1993) 16 E.H.R.R. 297.
[78] *Saunders v United Kingdom* [2001] 2 Cr.App.R. 286 at 299 per Rose L.J., citing also *L v United Kingdom* (2000) 2 F.L.R. 322.
[79] *Heaney and McGuinness v Ireland* (2001) 33 E.H.R.R. 264.
[80] *Brown v Stott* [2001] 2 All E.R. 97.

because it required only an answer to a simple question; there was no element of improper coercion or oppression that might give rise to unreliable admissions. The penalty for refusal to answer was non-custodial and moderate.

This judgment was problematic because it appeared to be inconsistent in principle with *Heaney and McGuinness v Ireland*. Mrs Brown's admission was essential to prove that she had been driving at a time when she had excess alcohol in her blood. From her standpoint this use of her compelled statement destroyed the "very essence" of her privilege by facilitating her conviction. On the other hand, one intelligible distinction might be that in *Heaney* the penalty for refusal to give information could be custodial, and of course any incriminating statement might expose the defendant to life imprisonment for murder. The defendants were likely to be imprisoned whatever they did. In *Brown v Stott* the penalty for refusal to give information was non-custodial, so the dilemma for the defendant was less severe. However, this distinction seemed to be ruled out by the court's approval in *Heaney* of the decision in *Funke v France*, where the penalty for refusing to hand over the bank statements was a continuing fine.

The conflict now seems to have been resolved, at least as far as the use of compulsion in road traffic legislation is concerned, by the decision of the Grand Chamber of the European Court of Human Rights in *O'Halloran and Francis v United Kingdom*.[81] Both applicants' vehicles had been caught on camera speeding. The first applicant responded to a s.172 notice by admitting that he was the driver at the relevant time. At his trial for the speeding offence he tried unsuccessfully to have his admission excluded and was convicted. The second applicant refused to disclose the identity of the driver, relying on the privilege against self-incrimination and the right to silence. He was subsequently convicted of failing to provide the information required by the s.172 notice. The European Court of Human Rights considered that the cases, although concerned with different offences, raised the same central issue of whether coercion of a person charged with a speeding offence to make statements which incriminated him or which could lead to his incrimination was compatible with art.6. To this question the court, by a substantial majority of 14–2, returned the answer Yes. In reaching this conclusion the court cited and adopted the justifying arguments used by Lord Bingham in *Brown v Stott*, although, curiously, it did not refer to his description of the test as being one of proportionality. The crucial factors in the justification of the restriction were said to be the nature and degree of compulsion used to obtain the evidence, the existence of any relevant safeguards in the procedure, and the use to which any material so obtained was put. In the court's view, the special nature of the regulatory regime for road traffic, involving the acceptance of obligations by citizens who own or drive cars, the limited nature of the information sought, the absence of any element of prolonged questioning and of any risk of unreliable admissions, the moderate and non-custodial penalties involved, and the fact that the identity of the driver was only one element in the offence of speeding, amounted to a combination of circumstances which did not destroy the essence of the privilege. This approach seems to be one of proportionality in all but name, being based on a weighting of various factors in the particular context. This impression is strengthened by the citation of the

---

[81] *O'Halloran and Francis v United Kingdom* (2008) 46 E.H.R.R. 21.

court's earlier decision in *Jalloh v Germany*,[82] where a further justifying factor was mentioned of the weight of the public interest in the investigation and punishment of the offence at issue.

As far as the English courts are concerned it is clear that this approach now governs all cases involving compulsory disclosure of information which engage the privilege.[83] It remains to be seen whether the more permissive stance of the Strasbourg court will extend to legislative compulsion in relation to other offences, or whether the court will regard road traffic legislation as in effect a special case. But it certainly follows from *O'Halloran and Francis v United Kingdom* that the use in a prosecution of a statement made by a person under compulsory questioning in a criminal investigation is not necessarily a violation of art.6. The contrary view was arguably a necessary implication of *Heaney*, and of course it is a conclusion that seemed to follow from *Saunders*. In that case, the court had held that the use in a prosecution of a compelled statement made in an *administrative* inquiry was a violation of art.6. However, the English courts had refused to find a violation where the use of compulsion to obtain a statement was justified by reference to the criteria of legitimate aim and proportionality,[84] and this conclusion has effectively now been endorsed by the European Court of Human Rights.

Finally under this heading we can consider whether the imposition of a penalty for failing to produce in a criminal investigation a *pre-existing document* that may be incriminating is a violation of art.6. In two cases the European Court of Human Rights has said "Yes". One case is *Funke v France*, noted above. The other is *JB v Switzerland*.[85] This was a complicated tax case in which a Swiss taxation authority imposed "disciplinary fines" on the applicant for a refusal to submit documents relating to investments in certain companies that the applicant had not declared for tax purposes. The judgment is very poorly reasoned. It does little more than set out the facts, rehearse the contentions of the parties and then state that the court considers there to have been a violation. The little more is a citation from *Saunders* of the distinction between material having an existence independent of the person concerned and material obtained by means of coercion in defiance of the will of the person concerned. In making this citation the court failed to notice that the documents in issue in the case fell into the first category (where the privilege does not apply) rather than the second (where it does). This is yet another example of the failure of Strasbourg to resolve the problems created by the inconsistency between *Funke* and *Saunders*.

---

[82] *Jalloh v Germany* (2007) 44 E.H.R.R. 32.
[83] See *R. v S and A* [2008] EWCA Crim 2177 (compelled disclosure of encryption key to computer files relevant to charges relating to terrorism held to be proportionate). cf. *R. v K* [2009] EWCA Crim 1640 (compelled disclosure in ancillary divorce proceedings of information relevant to charges of tax evasion held to be disproportionate).
[84] *DPP v Wilson* [2001] EWHC Admin 198; following *Brown v Stott* [2001] 2 All E.R. 97.
[85] *JB v Switzerland* [2001] Crim. L.R. 748.

D. THE RIGHT TO SILENCE

1. *The relevance of silence*

What is the probative value of silence? In what way or ways can it help the prosecution to show that the accused failed to answer certain questions, or failed to take advantage of an opportunity to disclose certain information? In principle there seem to be four possibilities for the relevance of silence in the context of pre-trial investigation:

5–017

(1) a person's failure to answer questions or to disclose information yields a direct inference that the person is guilty or, which amounts to the same thing, that the person remains silent because he or she is conscious of his or her guilt;

(2) a person's failure to deny an accusation, in circumstances where it would be reasonable to expect a denial if the accusation is untrue, yields an inference that the person is accepting the truth of the accusation;

(3) a person's failure, at the first reasonable opportunity, to disclose facts subsequently relied on in his or her defence weakens the defence because of the inference that the person concerned either fabricated the defence at a later stage or deliberately chose not to mention it for fear that the police would investigate it and expose its falsity;

(4) a person's failure to explain away incriminating prosecution evidence strengthens the prosecution case where the means of explanation are within the person's special knowledge, because of the inference that the person is unable to provide any explanation, or at least an explanation that will stand up to scrutiny.

Prior to the statutory reforms, all four possibilities had been considered by the courts in relation to the official investigation of offences. Before examining the authorities is important to note that principle (2), the principle that silence may be an implied admission of the truth of an accusation, was established as a general principle in the law of evidence well before the practice of questioning of suspects by the police became established. For example, in the 19th century case of *Cramp*,[86] the defendant was confronted by P, an irate father, who accused the defendant of supplying P's daughter with instruments to procure abortion. The defendant did not deny the supply, but said that he would give P money to go away. The trial judge directed the jury that they could treat the defendant's reaction as evidence that he had accepted the truth of P's accusation.

In the leading case of *Christie*,[87] the House of Lords considered and restated the principle. The facts of this case, which is relevant to several topics in the law of evidence, were that a young boy aged five alleged that the defendant had indecently assaulted him. The boy had gone to play in fields in the morning. He returned in a distressed condition 30 minutes later. His mother and a police officer then accompanied him back to the fields, where he identified the

---

[86] *Cramp* (1880) 14 Cox C.C. 390.
[87] *Christie* [1914] A.C. 545.

defendant by saying "That is the man" and putting his hand on the defendant's sleeve. He then described what the defendant had done to him. The defendant's response was to say "I am innocent. I have been asleep in the fields since 8 o'clock last night". At the defendant's trial the boy gave unsworn testimony as to the assault and made a dock identification of the defendant as the man responsible. The boy was not asked about any previous act of identification. His mother and the police officer both testified as to the act of identification in the fields and the boy's statement in the defendant's presence. The defendant was convicted but the Court of Criminal Appeal quashed the conviction, holding that the evidence of the boy's statement was inadmissible because the defendant had denied the accusation. On an appeal by the Crown the House of Lords reversed the ruling of the Court of Criminal Appeal but dismissed the appeal on the separate ground that the trial judge had misdirected the jury that the evidence of the mother and the police officer could corroborate the boy's testimony. The Lords held that there is no rule that informal accusations must be excluded if denied by the person accused. The question was whether the accused by his demeanour had wholly or partly accepted the statement of accusation; a defendant "may deny the statement in such a manner and under such circumstances as may lead a jury to disbelieve him, and constitutes evidence from which an acknowledgment may be inferred by them".[88] A rule of practice was suggested that statements accusing the defendant in his presence should not be admitted until a foundation was laid for admission by proof of facts from which a reasonable inference might be drawn that the defendant had accepted the statement in whole or part.

5–018   It is clear that the Lords intended this principle, of the possible acceptance of accusing statements by demeanour, to apply equally to whatever form a defendant's reaction took. Denials, physical conduct and silence all seem to have been thought capable of interpretation as an informal admission of the truth of the statement. In relation to silence, in the form of a failure to deny the accusation, it became clear that an inference of acceptance could be drawn where a denial could reasonably be expected if the accusation were untrue. A critical factor in deciding this issue is whether the parties were on equal terms[89]; if they were, it would prima facie be reasonable to expect the accused to deny a false accusation.[90] Parties are generally on even terms in informal settings where one is not in a position of authority over the other.

---

[88] *Christie* [1914] A.C. 545 at 554 per Lord Atkinson.

[89] *Mitchell* (1892) 17 Cox C.C. 508; *Parkes v R.* [1976] 1 W.L.R. 1251 PC.

[90] Although not, apparently, if an accusation of some offence or impropriety is contained in a letter: *Wiedemann v Walpole* [1891] 2 Q.B. 534. According to Lord Esher M.R. "it is the ordinary and wise practice of mankind not to answer such letters". cf. *Bessela v Stern* (1877) 2 C.P.D. 265 (silence in the face of an oral accusation of breach of promise to marry).

2. The common law right to silence in the police station

We can now turn to consider the common law on silence in the context of pre-trial criminal process. Silence following the old form of police caution,[91] or following a formal charge, e.g. at committal proceedings, could not be treated as an item of evidence in itself against the accused. In *Leckey*,[92] the defendant's response when the police charged and cautioned him was "I have nothing to say until I have seen someone, a solicitor". The trial judge commented to the jury on this silence, saying that an innocent man might have been expected to deny the charge. The Court of Criminal Appeal quashed the defendant's conviction for murder on the ground that the comment was improper and prejudicial. The court observed that were the position otherwise, the caution would become a trap for the accused—it would be inconsistent to tell the defendant he was not obliged to say anything and then to use his silence against him. This was a case where the effect of the judge's comment was to suggest that guilt could be inferred directly from silence.

5–019

The same result occurred where it was sought to use silence as an implied admission of the truth of an accusation. In *Hall v R.*,[93] a police officer investigating a drug offence told the defendant that a co-accused had said that the drug in question belonged to the defendant, who had not been cautioned at this stage. He made no reply to the officer's statement. The trial judge and the Court of Appeal in Jamaica treated the statement as containing an implied accusation and held that the jury were entitled to infer from the defendant's silence his tacit acceptance of the accusation. The Privy Council allowed the defendant's appeal and quashed his conviction for possession of the drug. It was held that silence alone on the part of a person who has been informed by a police officer that someone has made an accusation against him cannot give rise to an inference that the person is accepting the truth of the accusation. The court made no distinction between the position before the defendant has been cautioned and his silence after caution. Lord Diplock relied on a general principle that an accused person has no duty to answer police questions or to comment on police statements. The fact of a caution was immaterial:

> "The caution merely serves to remind the accused of a right which he already possesses at common law. The fact that in a particular case he has not been reminded of it is no ground for inferring that his silence was not in exercise of that right, but was an acknowledgment of the truth of the accusation."[94]

---

[91] "You do not have to say anything unless you wish to do so but what you say may be given in evidence." This was the wording required by PACE Code C para.10.4 until the caution was changed in 1995 when ss.34–39 of the Criminal Justice and Public Order Act 1994 came into force.

[92] *Leckey* [1944] 1 K.B. 80. See also *Naylor* [1933] 1 K.B. 685; *Sullivan* (1966) 51 Cr.App.R. 102 CCA.

[93] *Hall v R.* [1971] 1 W.L.R. 298.

[94] *Hall v R.* [1971] 1 W.L.R. 298 at 301, disapproving *Feigenbaum* [1919] 1 K.B. 431. In *Collins and Keep* [2004] EWCA Crim 83; [2004] 2 Cr.App.R. 11 the Court of Appeal applied this reasoning when holding that mere silence by a defendant when a lie was told to the police in his presence by a co-defendant about what they were doing did not without more provide a sufficient evidential basis for leaving to the jury whether by his reaction the defendant had adopted the lie. The defendants had

Subsequently, in *Chandler*,[95] the Court of Appeal doubted the width of Lord Diplock's dicta in *Hall* insofar as they appeared to suggest that the principle stated by the House of Lords in *Christie* could never apply in the context of a police officer questioning a suspect. In *Chandler* the defendant had been questioned by a police officer in the presence of his solicitor both before and after he had been cautioned. The defendant answered some questions, but he refused to answer other questions about whether he knew certain persons whom the police suspected of being involved with him in a conspiracy to defraud. The trial judge directed the jury to consider whether the defendant had remained silent, before caution, in the exercise of his common law right or because he feared to incriminate himself. The Court of Appeal quashed the defendant's conviction for misdirection, holding that the judge had improperly telescoped the reasoning that the jury should have applied in considering the probative value of the defendant's silence. He should have directed the jury to consider two questions (not one):

(a)   Did the defendant's silence amount to an acceptance of what was said? (In other words, was he impliedly admitting that he did know the persons referred to?)

(b)   If so, could his guilt of the offence charged be reasonably inferred from what he had accepted?

5–020   The logic of this analysis is impeccable, although cynics may be forgiven for wondering whether the average juror would have the patience or the ability to distinguish so precisely the evidential limits of silence, particularly since the judge's question could hardly be ignored in any consideration of the significance of the defendant's silence. Be that as it may, the main importance of the case lies in the Court of Appeal's denial of the generality of the dicta in *Hall* and in the recognition that the *Christie* principle might operate even in the context of police questioning. The court seems to have been in no doubt that the principle could not operate *after* caution, but thought that it could apply where the accused and the police were speaking on even terms before the police had administered the caution. In this case the court noted that the defendant had his solicitor with him, available to give advice and to act as a witness to what was said at the interview. Lawton L.J. then stated:

> "The law has long accepted that an accused person is not bound to incriminate himself; but it does not follow that a failure to answer an accusation or question when an answer could reasonably be expected may not provide some evidence in support of an accusation ... [On the facts of this case] some comment on the defendant's lack of frankness before he was cautioned was justified."[96]

In further dicta Lawton L.J. expanded on the assumption that the question of "even terms" is not determined exclusively by the status of the police officer as

---

been stopped by the police in the street. Neither had been cautioned, but the court appears to have assumed that they were not on equal terms with the police for the purposes of a possible application of the *Christie* principle.

[95]   *Chandler* [1976] 1 W.L.R. 585.
[96]   *Chandler* [1976] 1 W.L.R. 585 at 589.

an authority figure. He suggested that the court should consider the realities of the power relationship and the character of the personalities involved:

> "We do not accept that a police officer always has an advantage over someone he is questioning . . . A young detective questioning a local dignitary in the course of an enquiry into alleged local government corruption may be very much at a disadvantage. This kind of situation has to be contrasted with that of a tearful housewife accused of shoplifting or of a parent being questioned about the suspected wrongdoing of his son."[97]

On the face of it, *Chandler* appeared to make a substantial inroad into the right of silence in the police station, but its practical impact depended on the time when the suspect is first cautioned. It was clearly accepted in *Chandler* that the *Christie* principle could not apply after caution. Under PACE the police are required to caution a person when they have grounds to suspect that the person has committed an offence. The grounds do not have to consist of admissible evidence; an anonymous tip-off could be sufficient. It follows that in a great many cases the caution will have to be administered at the beginning of an interview and that there will be no scope for the application of the *Christie* principle.

The use of pre-trial silence to weaken a defence raised for the first time at trial was considered by a strong Court of Appeal in *Gilbert*.[98] In this case the defendant was charged with murder. At trial he raised the issue of self-defence, not having mentioned this to the police when first questioned about the death of the victim. The trial judge's comment to the jury invited them, in the words of the Court of Appeal, "to reject self-defence as D had not mentioned it in his statement". This comment was held to be improper. The Court of Appeal rejected the purported distinction between silence as evidence of guilt and silence as affecting the weight of a subsequent defence. The latter was thought to be no more than an indirect or oblique way of inferring the former.[99] This was an important decision in terms of basic principle because it consolidated the suspect's right to silence in the police station and provided a significant contrast to the limits expressed in *Chandler*.

5–021

There are, however, further limits to the right to silence at common law. In *Smith (RW)*,[100] the Court of Appeal held that the defendant's refusal to give the police a sample of his hair for purposes of matching hair found at the scene of a robbery was corroborative of his identity as one of the robbers. The court rejected an argument that the defendant was protected by the privilege against self-incrimination. It was held that the context and terms of the refusal meant that the case was in a "wholly different category from evidence of a failure to answer when a caution has been administered or a failure to answer in sufficient detail".[101] The context was that the defendant had his solicitor with him during the interview and was therefore regarded as being on equal terms with the police.

---

[97] *Chandler* [1976] 1 W.L.R. 585 at 590.
[98] *Gilbert* (1977) 66 Cr.App.R. 237.
[99] Note, however, that the defendant's conviction was upheld by application of the proviso; rectitude of decision (no significant risk of an erroneous outcome) triumphed over process values.
[100] *Smith (RW)* (1985) 81 Cr.App.R. 286.
[101] *Smith (RW)* (1985) 81 Cr.App.R. 286 at 292.

After receiving the request for a sample the solicitor had asked where the hairs in question had been found. The reply was that they were found at the scene of the robbery, whereupon the defendant had said "In that case, no". The common law was strengthened by PACE which gave the police statutory powers to take fingerprints and non-intimate samples from a suspect under certain conditions without consent. If consent is withheld the police may use reasonable force to override the unwillingness to co-operate. Intimate samples may only be taken with consent, but a refusal without good cause to give consent can be used to draw adverse inferences in determining the issue of guilt.[102]

Similarly the privilege against self-incrimination does not extend to a failure to provide an explanation of prima facie circumstantial evidence such as the defendant's possession of recently stolen goods. In this sense the accused's silence pre-trial may lend weight to incriminating prosecution evidence. In *Raviraj*,[103] the Court of Appeal confirmed that guilty knowledge that goods were stolen could be inferred from the defendant's failure to provide an innocent explanation for the stolen goods found on premises occupied by him. The court distinguished the cases on the right to silence, referring to a general proposition that "where suspicious circumstances appear to demand an explanation, and no explanation or an entirely incredible explanation is given, the lack of explanation may warrant an inference of guilty knowledge in the defendant".[104] Where stolen goods are found in a defendant's possession there is anyway a clear inference of guilty knowledge, on the basis that people in possession of articles usually know where they have come from. What *Raviraj* is really indicating is that this inference becomes overwhelming in the absence of explanation; in this way silence has evidential value in strengthening the existing prosecution evidence. It seems that this is a general principle relating to failure to answer a prima facie case, particularly where the defendant has special means of knowledge of an innocent explanation, if there is one.[105] The point is not restricted to a failure to account for recently stolen goods, although this situation provides one of the main examples.

3. *Statutory reform of the right to silence*

5–022   The Criminal Justice and Public Order Act 1994 ("CJPOA") made controversial reforms to the right to silence. Sections 34–39 provide for the drawing of adverse inferences from silence in a number of situations. The provisions are modelled on the provisions of the Criminal Evidence (Northern Ireland) Order 1988.[106] The

---

[102] PACE s.62(10). For discussion of the exclusion of bodily samples from the scope of the privilege against self-incrimination, and of some difficulties associated with it, see S. Easton, "Bodily Samples and the Privilege Against Self-Incrimination" [1991] Crim. L.R. 18.

[103] *Raviraj* (1987) 85 Cr.App.R. 93.

[104] *Raviraj* (1987) 85 Cr.App.R. 93 at 103.

[105] The European Court of Human Rights has accepted that silence may have such an effect as a matter of common sense, and the use of it to strengthen the prosecution case does not make a trial unfair: *Murray v United Kingdom* (1996) 22 E.H.R.R. 29.

[106] Criminal Evidence (Northern Ireland) Order 1988 (SI 1988/1987).

Act made some modifications,[107] but in general terms the scheme of the Act was to extend to England and Wales the reforms that had been in effect in Northern Ireland since the end of 1988.

In relation to pre-trial investigations, s.34 indicates that a court or jury may draw such inferences as appear proper from evidence that the accused, on being questioned under caution about the offence for which he is being tried, failed to mention any fact relied on in his defence, being a fact which in the circumstances existing at the time he could reasonably have been expected to mention.[108] The inferences may be drawn both in determining whether there is a case to answer and in determining whether the accused is guilty of the offence charged. The provision applies in relation to questioning by constables and also to questioning by other persons charged with the duty of investigating offences or charging offenders.

The Court of Appeal has said on a number of occasions that the mischief at which this provision is primarily directed is the case where the accused relies at trial on a positive defence following a "no comment" interview and/or a defence that was not disclosed to the police during interview, the so-called "ambush defence".[109] When the provision operates it clearly allows the prosecution to invite the court or jury to infer from its late appearance that the defence is a sham.[110] Section 35 deals with the accused's silence at trial and is discussed in Ch.13. The provisions of ss.36 and 37 relate to the accused's failure to account for objects, substances or marks (s.36), or his presence at a particular place (s.37), in circumstances where such matters are reasonably believed by an investigating constable to be incriminating. Such failures, like failure to mention facts relied on subsequently, may ground adverse inferences both in determining whether there is a case to answer and in determining the guilt of the accused.[111]

The overall effect of these sections is to place pressure on suspects to co-operate with police investigations, to disclose defences at the earliest opportunity and, at trial, to respond to a prima facie case and submit themselves to cross-examination by the prosecution. It is not an offence or a contempt to fail to do any of these things,[112] and in this sense the Act has not abolished primary applications of the privilege against self-incrimination. There is still no directly enforceable duty to make incriminating disclosure.[113] However, there is an equivalent indirect

5–023

---

[107] The most significant of these was the introduction of the requirement that the accused must have been cautioned before inferences can be drawn from his failure to mention facts when questioned about the offence.

[108] This is the effect of s.34(1)(a). Inferences can also be drawn where the accused fails to mention any such fact "on being charged with the offence or officially informed that he might be prosecuted for it": s.34(1)(b).

[109] *Brizzalari* [2004] EWCA Crim. 310; *Beckles* [2004] EWCA Crim. 2766; [2005] 1 Cr.App.R. 23; *Troy Smith* [2011] EWCA Crim. 1098.

[110] Thus reversing *Gilbert* (1977) 66 Cr.App.R. 237 CA.

[111] In *Compton* [2002] EWCA Crim. 2835 the CA stressed that s.36 requires D to account for a "specific state of fact". It is not enough that D has referred in an earlier interview to other facts, from which it could be inferred what his account might be.

[112] CJPOA s.35(4) states in terms that the section does not render the accused compellable to give evidence on his own behalf. He will not therefore be guilty of contempt by failing to do so.

[113] See, however, Ch.9, for discussion of the duty to make a defence statement under the provisions of the Criminal Procedure and Investigations Act 1996.

obligation through the threat that, to put it crudely, silence will make conviction more likely. These provisions represent a radical departure from one of the traditional foundations of Anglo-American criminal proceedings. The reforms made by the Act were extremely controversial. Many commentators were profoundly unconvinced by the arguments put forward by the Government.[114] The reforms were carried through despite support for the right to silence expressed by two successive Royal Commissions.[115] Both Commissions had undertaken important empirical research on the exercise of the right by suspects, but their findings were largely brushed aside. It is clear that the restrictions imposed by the Act were essentially a political move based on strongly held perceptions by the police in particular about the operation of the right in practice.[116] Those perceptions were largely unsupported by the available evidence. In particular, the "common sense" belief that silence in the police station provides reliable evidence of guilt was demonstrated to be systemically flawed.[117]

The reforms have been in place for some years. During this time they have faced considerable obstacles. On one side there is the European Convention on Human Rights and the issue of how far ss.34–38 of the 1994 Act are compatible with the right to a fair trial under art.6. On the other side there has been some significant judicial dislike of s.34 in particular. At one time this manifested itself in a reluctance to give s.34 any kind of generous interpretation. In *Bowden,*[118] Lord Bingham C.J. was explicit about the need for a conservative approach:

> "Proper effect must of course be given to these provisions [of the CJPOA]. But since they restrict rights recognised at common law as appropriate to protect defendants against the risk of injustice, they should not be construed more widely than the statutory language requires."[119]

In consequence of these obstacles numerous issues of interpretation have arisen on s.34, and to a lesser extent on the other provisions. These issues have generated an extensive and complex case law.[120] The general effect of the case law can perhaps be summarised in the following way. Section 34 has survived challenge in Strasbourg and is now most unlikely to be declared incompatible

---

[114] For analysis and criticism see, e.g. I. Dennis, "The Criminal Justice and Public Order Act 1994: the Evidence Provisions" [1995] Crim. L.R. 4; S. Easton, *The Case for the Right to Silence*, 2nd edn (Aldershot: Ashgate Publishing, 1998), Ch.5.

[115] Royal Commission on Criminal Procedure Report, Cmnd.8092 (1981) Report, para.4.53; RCCJ Report, Ch.4, paras 22–25.

[116] Police criticism of the right to silence began with the Dimbleby Lecture in 1973 by Sir Robert Mark, then Metropolitan Police Commissioner, and continued for 20 years: F. McElree and K. Starmer, "The Right to Silence" in C. Walker and K. Starmer (eds), *Justice in Error* (London, 1993), pp.72–73, summarising the submission from the Police Service to the RCCJ.

[117] See the valuable study by M. McConville and J. Hodgson, *Custodial Legal Advice and the Right to Silence* (RCCJ Research Study No.16, London, 1993).

[118] *Bowden* [1999] 2 Cr.App.R. 176.

[119] *Bowden* [1999] 2 Cr.App.R. 176 at 181. In *Webber* [2004] UKHL 1; [2004] 1 Cr.App.R. 40, Lord Bingham commented that his statement in *Bowden* was made with particular reference to the statutory provisions not modifying the law on legal professional privilege. He emphasised, however, that if the statutory provisions were not to be an instrument of unfairness or abuse the statutory safeguards should be strictly observed and jury directions carefully framed.

[120] So complex that Birch has argued for repeal of the section on the ground that any evidential gains from it are outweighed by its costs in terms of the traps and difficulty it presents for trial judges: D.

with art.6. The English courts have given "proper effect" to the section in a number of respects. On the other hand, a combination of the Strasbourg jurisprudence and a process of restrictive interpretation in some of the English cases has resulted in adverse inferences under s.34 playing a more limited role in criminal trials than might have been the case with a more sympathetic treatment.[121]

4. *Section 34 and the ECHR*

Like the privilege against self-incrimination the right to silence is not expressly set out in art.6 but has been implied into it by the European Court of Human Rights.[122] Again like the privilege the implied right to silence is not absolute. It can be qualified or restricted under certain conditions. However, unlike the privilege, the Strasbourg jurisprudence on restrictions of the right to silence is reasonably clear and consistent.

5–024

First, the European Court of Human Rights has made clear that the drawing of inferences from a person's silence in the police station is not necessarily incompatible with art.6. This is true whether we are dealing with a non-jury trial or a jury trial. In *Murray v United Kingdom*,[123] the court held that the drawing of inferences from an accused's silence in interview, under the Northern Ireland version of s.34, did not vitiate the fairness of the trial. But *Murray* was a trial before a Diplock court, where the judge gave a reasoned judgment on fact. It was speculated that the court might take a different view of inferences in jury trials, where juries do not give reasoned decisions that can be scrutinised for fairness. This point was raised by the applicants in *Condron v United Kingdom*,[124] but the court rejected it. The court said that particular caution was required in drawing any inferences from silence (as *Murray* had indicated), and that there should be appropriate safeguards for the defence. This meant that in a jury trial the judge should give a particularly careful direction about the conditions under which an inference could be drawn. On the facts of *Condron* the court held that the direction was inadequate (see further below), but it is necessarily implicit in the

---

Birch, "Suffering in Silence: A Cost-Benefit Analysis of Section 34 of the Criminal Justice and Public Order Act 1994" [1999] Crim. L.R. 769. For a thoughtful review of the key issues see M Redmayne, "English Warnings" (2008) Cardozo L.R. 1047.

[121] See further I. Dennis, "Silence in the Police Station: The Marginalisation of Section 34" [2002] Crim. L.R. 25. Several of the research findings in the study by T. Bucke, R. Street and D. Brown, *The right of silence: the impact of the Criminal Justice and Public Order Act 1994* (Home Office Research Study 199, London, 2000) suggest that judicial coolness towards the section is matched by a tendency for its value in practice to be limited. Thus CPS respondents considered that in the general run of cases silence in the police station would play only a marginal role (if any) in the decision to prosecute (p.43). Prosecutors take the view that other evidence is necessary to mount a successful prosecution, and this view is shared by prosecuting barristers. Some barristers are reluctant to use the provisions of the 1994 Act because they feel that they are unfair on defendants or may be perceived by juries as unfair (p.49). The Act appears to have had no demonstrable impact on conviction rates (p.67).

[122] The first case was *Murray v United Kingdom* (1996) 22 E.H.R.R. 29.

[123] *Murray v United Kingdom* (1996) 22 E.H.R.R. 29.

[124] *Condron v United Kingdom* (2001) 31 E.H.R.R. 1.

court's judgment that if the judge had got it right, then the fact that the jury's reasoning could not be known and therefore could not be reviewed was not a fatal objection.

It appears also from *Condron* that a *balance* has to be struck between the exercise of the right to silence and the drawing of an adverse inference. The notion of balance between the defendant's rights and the public interest is a pervasive theme in Convention jurisprudence, although it is not always clear how the balance is to be arrived at. The drawing of adverse inferences from silence may infringe art.6, depending on the circumstances of the case. The court has said that it will pay "particular regard to the situations where inferences may be drawn, the weight attached to them by the national courts in their assessment of the evidence and the degree of compulsion in the situation".[125] It seems that in this context the "balance" requires a number of conditions to be satisfied. It is suggested that an inference may fairly be drawn for the purposes of art.6 from a person's silence in pre-trial interview if four conditions are satisfied.[126] These conditions are currently the minimum necessary to satisfy human rights law:

(1)   The defendant must have been afforded access to legal advice before being interviewed. This requirement formed the basis of the decision in *Murray* that the applicant had been denied a fair trial. The European Court of Human Rights held that since adverse inferences might be drawn from a failure to answer questions, it was of "paramount importance" that the accused should be given access to legal advice; delay might result in his position being irretrievably prejudiced.[127] The court applied similar reasoning in *Averill v United Kingdom*.[128] The accused had been refused access to his lawyer for the first 24 hours of detention, during which time he was interviewed about his involvement in a double murder. As in *Murray,* the court found no violation in the drawing of inferences from the accused's failure to explain to the police strongly incriminating evidence against him,[129] but held that the possibility of adverse inferences (about which the accused was warned by the words of the caution) created a "fundamental dilemma" for the accused making access to legal advice essential for a fair trial. The requirement was incorporated into s.34 (as subs.(2A)) by s.58 of the Youth Justice and Criminal Evidence Act 1999.

(2)   The jury must have been properly directed to consider the accused's reason for silence. They must be told that they can draw an adverse inference only if they are satisfied that the reason for silence was that the defendant had no story to give at the time of the interview or no story that he was prepared to have questioned or investigated. As indicated above, the judge had failed to give such a direction in *Condron v United Kingdom*. The European Court of

---

[125] *Murray v United Kingdom* (1996) 22 E.H.R.R. 29 at 61.

[126] The first condition is now a statutory requirement. The remaining three are all supported by the English case law and appear as part of the guidance on s.34 given to trial judges in the *Crown Court Bench Book—Directing the Jury.*

[127] There was therefore a violation of art.6(3)(c).

[128] *Averill v United Kingdom* (2001) 31 E.H.R.R. 839.

[129] Fibres found on his hair and clothing matched those found on balaclavas and gloves discovered in a burnt-out car used by the gunmen.

Human Rights thought that such a direction was more than merely "desirable"[130]; it was essential because the failure to give it meant that the jury were left at liberty to draw an adverse inference "notwithstanding that it may have been satisfied as to the plausibility of the explanation" (that the applicant's silence was the result of legal advice not to answer questions when they were not fit to be interviewed). However, in *Adetoro v United Kingdom*,[131] the European Court of Human Rights declined to find a violation of art.6 when the trial judge omitted to give this direction, on the ground that in this case D's explanation for the failure to mention the facts relied on in defence was inextricably linked to his substantive defence to the charges. His defence to charges of armed robbery was that he was engaged in dealing in stolen cars, and he claimed that he did not mention this to the police because he did not want to incriminate his accomplices. The court took the view that since the jury had rejected the defence to the charges they must necessarily have rejected the explanation as well. The judge's omission could not therefore have caused any unfairness.

(3)   An adverse inference from silence must not be the sole or main evidence for conviction. This is a further point confirmed by *Condron* about the balance that has to be struck in these cases on silence. The reference to an inference from silence not being the *main* evidence for conviction is a qualification of the 1994 Act. This states in s.38(3) only that a person may not be convicted *solely* on an inference drawn under any of ss.34–37. This is a significant modification of the legislative scheme.[132] In conjunction with the next point it confirms that, as far as Strasbourg is concerned, a s.34 inference can play no more than a supporting role.

(4)   The facts—as established by the other evidence—must clearly call for an explanation from the accused, an explanation to be taken into account in assessing the persuasiveness of the evidence adduced by the prosecution. The European Court of Human Rights has not said in terms that this is a necessary condition for compatibility of adverse inferences from silence with art.6. Nevertheless, it was expressly referred to in *Murray v United Kingdom*[133] and in *Condron v United Kingdom* as one of the factors making it not unfair to draw inferences from a failure to mention exculpatory facts to the police. It is also consistent with the requirement that silence should not constitute the sole or main evidence for conviction. Jennings, Ashworth and Emmerson have suggested that ss.36 and 37 of the CJPOA provide

---

[130] Thereby rejecting the approach of the Court of Appeal in *Condron and Condron* [1997] 1 Cr.App.R. 185.

[131] *Adetoro v United Kingdom* [2010] ECHR 609.

[132] In *Petkar and Farquhar* [2003] EWCA Crim 2668; [2004] 1 Cr.App.R. 22 the Court of Appeal restated the requirements of a "well-crafted" direction as including a direction that if the jury do draw an adverse inference they should not convict wholly or mainly on the strength of it.

[133] In *Murray v United Kingdom* (1996) 22 E.H.R.R. 29, the applicant had been found guilty of aiding and abetting unlawful imprisonment following his arrest on premises where the IRA had detained a suspected police informer. The court held that in the circumstances of the case there was a very strong prosecution case which called for an answer from the applicant and that it was not unfair to draw "common sense" inferences from his failure to provide an explanation.

examples of the kind of facts that call for an explanation[134]—where there are objects, substances or marks on the accused or his clothing reasonably believed to be attributable to his participation in a specified offence, or where he is found at the place where and about the time when the offence was committed and his presence is reasonably believed to be attributable to his participation. In these situations if no satisfactory explanation is forthcoming a common sense inference may be permissible that there is no explanation other than an incriminating one. It would seem to be implicit in this requirement that the other evidence should amount to at least a prima facie case against the accused.[135] An adverse inference can then provide support for such a case, but it can play no more than a supporting role.

5.   The interpretation of section 34

(A)   The statutory conditions and the nature of the test

5–025   A number of conditions have to be complied with before adverse inferences can be drawn under s.34. In *Argent*,[136] the Court of Appeal summarised the statutory requirements in the form of a list of six conditions.[137] To this list we must now add a seventh condition. The accused must have been allowed an opportunity to consult a solicitor before being questioned or charged.[138] The list of conditions in *Argent* is as follows:

(1)   there must be proceedings against the accused for an offence;
(2)   the failure to mention facts must occur before the accused is charged;
(3)   the failure must occur during questioning of the accused under caution by a constable;
(4)   the questioning must be directed to trying to discover whether or by whom the alleged offence had been committed;
(5)   the failure must be to mention some fact on which the accused relies in defence in the proceedings[139];

---

[134] *Condron v United Kingdom* [2000] Crim. L.R. 879at [887]. citing *Averill v United Kingdom* (2001) 31 E.H.R.R. 839.
[135] Supported by *Gill* [2001] 1 Cr.App R. 11; *Chenia* [2002] EWCA Crim 2345; [2003] 2 Cr.App.R. 6, and see further below.
[136] *Argent* [1997] 2 Cr.App.R. 27.
[137] These conditions apply where the prosecution relies upon subs.(1)(a); this is the usual case.
[138] See s.34(2A), inserted by s.58 of the Youth Justice and Criminal Evidence Act 1999. Section 58 inserted similar provisions also into ss.35–37 of the CJPOA. Where a suspect is not given the opportunity to take legal advice, the protection given by s.34(2A) involves the disapplication of the adverse inference provisions in s.34; it does not render inadmissible any answers given by him during questioning: *Ibrahim* [2008] EWCA Crim 880; [2008] 2 Cr. App. R. 23 at [77].
[139] CPJOA s.34 can still apply where the defendant does not give evidence at trial (*Bowers* [1998] Crim. L.R. 817 CA), since he can rely for his defence on a fact adduced in evidence by defence witnesses or through cross-examination of prosecution witnesses. Where the defendant gives no evidence himself and adduces no evidence, and simply puts the prosecution to proof, the section cannot apply: *Moshaid* [1998] Crim. L.R. 420 CA.

(6)   the fact which the accused fails to mention must be one that, in the circumstances existing at the time, he or she could reasonably have been expected to mention when questioned.

In *Argent* the Court of Appeal clarified two important general points about the application of the last condition. The phrase "in the circumstances" is not to be construed restrictively. It includes all the relevant circumstances relating to the accused as well as to the circumstances of the interview itself. Thus account should be taken of such matters as the accused's age, experience, mental capacity, physical state, sobriety and personality, in addition to factors such as the availability of legal advice. Secondly, the test is partly subjective in the sense that the fact in question must be one that *the accused* could reasonably be expected to mention. This may necessitate an inquiry into the accused's capacities, his knowledge and understanding of the offence under investigation and the legal advice he has received about it. The Court of Appeal emphasised that the test does not refer to some hypothetical reasonable accused of ordinary fortitude.[140]

(B)   Facts which it would be reasonable to expect the accused to mention

Inferences can only be drawn under s.34 from a failure to mention a "fact" relied on in defence. When directing the jury on the possibility of adverse inferences under s.34 the judge must identify the specific facts that it is claimed the defendant failed to mention in interview and on which he now relies in defence.[141] The judge should also identify the inferences (conclusions) that it is suggested might be drawn from the failure to mention such facts, to the extent that they may go beyond the standard inference of late fabrication.[142]

5–026

The notion of a "fact" for the purposes of s.34 has received a good deal of judicial consideration. In the leading case of *Webber*,[143] Lord Bingham, giving the opinion of the House of Lords, said:

> "Since the object of s.34 is to bring the law back into line with common sense, we think it clear that 'fact' should be given a broad and not a narrow or pedantic meaning. The word covers any alleged fact which is in issue and is put forward as part of the defence case: if the defendant advances at trial any pure fact or exculpatory explanation or account which, if it were true, he could reasonably have been expected to advance earlier, s.34 is potentially applicable."

As noted above, it is not necessary for the purposes of s.34 that the defendant should give evidence himself of the facts on which he now relies and which he failed to mention in interview. Evidence of such facts can be adduced by defence witnesses or in cross-examination of prosecution witnesses.[144] In *Webber*,[145] the House of Lords went further and held that a defendant relied on a fact or matter in his defence not only when he gave or adduced evidence of it, but also when a

---

[140]   *Argent* [1997] 2 Cr.App.R. 27 at 33.
[141]   *Webber* [2004] UKHL 1; [2004] 1 Cr.App.R. 40.
[142]   *Petkar and Farquhar* [2003] EWCA Crim 2668; [2004] 1 Cr.App.R. 22.
[143]   *Webber* [2004] UKHL 1; [2004] 1 Cr.App.R. 40.
[144]   *Bowers* [1998] Crim. L.R. 817.
[145]   *Webber* [2004] UKHL 1; [2004] 1 Cr.App.R. 40 at 513.

specific or positive case was put on his behalf to prosecution witnesses, whether or not the witnesses accepted the suggestions made, or when the defendant adopted the evidence of a co-defendant. However, questions simply intended to probe or test the prosecution case ("Are you really sure you saw your assailant for half a minute?") are not facts relied on for the purposes of s.34.[146] Counsel should not put a specific or positive case to witnesses without instructions. If a judge is in doubt whether counsel is testing the prosecution evidence or advancing a positive case the judge should ask counsel to make his position clear.[147]

5–027   A further distinction needs to be drawn in relation to explanations for facts asserted by the prosecution. It is clear that a "fact" relied on is not restricted to a new factual issue asserted by the defence, such as a claim that the accused was acting under duress. It includes a factual explanation for a fact asserted by the prosecution. This was confirmed in *Milford*[148]—a drug-smuggling case where the defendant produced at trial a previously unmentioned explanation for his association with his co-conspirators that he was an entrepreneur selling boat cradles. This is the sort of specific or positive factual assertion that could have been investigated had it been mentioned in interview. On the other hand, in *Nickolson*,[149] the Court of Appeal suggested that a fact relied on does not include a theory or speculative explanation for facts asserted by the prosecution. This seems right in principle. If the defendant produces at trial a hypothetical reason for some incriminating fact (for example, a possible motive of jealousy for a complaint), and the reason does not have a foundation of fact known to the defendant at the time of the interview, then a s.34 inference is inappropriate. It is not a situation of a positive assertion about which the defendant could have been interviewed at the time.[150]

A fact relied on does not include a bare admission of a fact asserted by the prosecution. In *Betts and Hall*,[151] Hall had refused to answer questions in interview after receiving legal advice not to do so because the police had made inadequate disclosure of the facts of the offence. At trial he admitted knowing that the victim of the offence had had an affair with the wife of Hall's friend. The Court of Appeal held that the judge had erred in identifying this as a "fact" relied on by the defendant at trial. A bare admission of a fact asserted as part of the prosecution case—that is, that Hall knew about the affair, which was the reason for the attack—could not be said to be the assertion of a fact. The failure to make this admission in interview could not therefore ground a s.34 inference. The judgment in this case shows the strong influence of the judgment of the European Court of Human Rights in *Condron v United Kingdom*.[152] The Court of Appeal argued that the balance required by *Condron* is found by restricting inferences

---

[146] *Webber* [2004] UKHL 1; [2004] 1 Cr.App.R. 40 at [34].
[147] *Webber* [2004] UKHL 1; [2004] 1 Cr.App.R. 40 at [36].
[148] *Milford* [2001] Crim. L.R. 330.
[149] *Nickolson* [1999] Crim. L.R. 61; *B(MT)* [2000] Crim. L.R. 181.
[150] cf. *Webber* [2004] UKHL 1; [2004] 1 Cr.App.R. 40 at [22], where the House of Lords cited with apparent approval a comment by Professor Birch in [1999] Crim. L.R. 61 that it might go too far to say that any speculation by the defendant seeking to explain away the prosecution case does not amount to reliance in his defence on the facts forming the basis of the speculation.
[151] *Betts and Hall* [2001] 2 Cr.App.R. 257.
[152] *Condron v UK* [2001] 31 E.H.R.R. 1.

from silence to cases where the accused makes positive assertions at trial.[153] The point of s.34 is to allow such positive assertions to be investigated and tested beforehand so that the jury can have the benefit of the prosecution's informed response to the assertion. The same consideration does not apply to a bare admission.[154]

Hall had "relied on" this admission in the sense that it seems to have formed part of a claim that, although he knew of the victim, he did not know him by sight and could not therefore have picked him out for attack. The victim had testified that he did know Hall and had recognised him as one of the assailants. The Court of Appeal rejected a defence argument that Hall's denial of this fact relied on by the prosecution was not a "fact" for the purposes of s.34: "The appellant was asserting that he and Mr Caris did not know one another. That, if true, is a fact".[155] Thus admissions and denials are treated differently, despite the point that both the admission and denial were of facts put in issue by the victim's evidence. At first sight this looks difficult to justify, and Birch has commented that in neither case does a new fact come into play.[156] On the other hand a denial, if known in time, would enable the police to make further investigations that are simply unnecessary in the case of an admission.[157] Finally, there is no exclusion from the application of s.34 of cases where the fact relied on by the defence is the central issue in the case.[158]

Assuming that the defendant is relying on a fact that he failed to mention in interview, the question then is whether it is a fact that he could reasonably have been expected to mention when interviewed. The application of the reasonable expectation test has caused considerable difficulty where the defendant claims that he relied on legal advice as the reason for not mentioning the fact. The authorities are in some disarray, but the most recent pronouncements of the Court of Appeal indicate that a normative standard is still to be applied even if the jury consider that there was genuine reliance on legal advice to remain silent in interview. This issue is discussed more fully below. More generally, the natural meaning of s.34 would suggest that the reasonable expectation test ought to take account of the nature of the fact in question. The jury ought to ask themselves what ordinary people sharing the accused's characteristics would be likely to do in relation to this fact and what he or she could therefore fairly be expected to do. On this basis there are some facts that most people would know or believe to be relevant to the offence being investigated and that they would be likely to mention. It would be reasonable to expect the accused to mention these, with or

5–028

---

[153] *Betts and Hall* [2001] 2 Cr.App.R. 257 at [264]–[265].

[154] In *Webber* [2004] UKHL 1; [2004] 1 Cr.App.R. 40 the HL confirmed that failure to mention something which is agreed to be true cannot as a general proposition give rise to an adverse inference. See also *Troy Smith* [2011] EWCA Crim 1098.

[155] *Betts and Hall* [2001] 2 Cr.App.R. 257 at [264] per Kay L.J.

[156] Commentary on *Betts and Hall* [2001] 2 Cr.App.R. 257 in [2001] Crim. L.R. 757.

[157] However, recent cases suggest that where D declines to answer questions in interview and gives evidence, "putting forward no more than a bare denial of an essential part of the prosecution's case" (*Troy Smith* [2011] EWCA Crim 1098), or evidence which is "little if anything more than a denial of the offence" (*R. v M(I)* [2011] EWCA Crim 868; [2012] 1 Cr.App.R. 3, a s.34 direction is not appropriate.

[158] See *Webber* [2004] UKHL 1; [2004] 1 Cr.App.R. 40, effectively overruling the earlier CA decisions in *Mountford* [1999] Crim. L.R. 575 and *Gill* [2001] 1 Cr.App.R. 160.

without the benefit of legal advice. Examples would be that a blow was struck in self-defence, or that the person complaining of rape consented to intercourse. In other cases an accused, like most people, might not be aware that he can rely on certain facts until he has received legal advice. An example might be where property is taken temporarily, but the accused does not know that unauthorised borrowing is not usually theft.[159]

(C)   Failure to "mention"

5–029   The fact must be one that the defendant failed to "mention" in interview. An important point here is the status of a prepared statement by the defendant that he or his solicitor hands to the police. This is a common device.[160] The written statement is usually accompanied by an oral declaration that the defendant will not answer questions about the written statement. In *Ali*[161] two defendants gave the police prepared statements. One omitted to mention two facts relied on in evidence. The other set out an alibi in similar terms to the defendant's subsequent evidence. The Court of Appeal held that a s.34 direction was appropriate in the first case but not the second. This is an important ruling. Clearly an inference cannot be drawn that the defendant's explanation at trial is a late invention if it was there in the prepared statement. The Crown argued in *Ali* that it was still possible to infer that the defendant was unwilling to have his story questioned or investigated and therefore that s.34 could operate. This argument was rightly rejected. If the argument had succeeded it would mean that s.34 had effectively created a duty to answer police questions, even where the defendant had disclosed his defence. This is not what the section says, and the court refused to do more than give it its literal meaning. The defendant had not failed to mention the fact relied on in evidence. Moreover, although it might be inferred that he was unwilling to be questioned about it, an inference could not safely be drawn that he was unwilling for the police to investigate it independently.

In *Knight*,[162] the Court of Appeal confirmed that while the aim of s.34 is to require early disclosure of a suspect's account, it is not, separately and distinctly, to require the subjection of that account to police cross-examination. Where the account in the prepared statement was wholly consistent with the defendant's evidence at trial, a direction that adverse inferences could be drawn from the defendant's failure to answer police questions on the account should not have been given. The court allowed the defendant's appeal.

These decisions[163] give the green light to the use of prepared statements in all cases where the defendant has a story that he will stick to at trial, although the Court of Appeal emphasised in *Knight* that the prepared statement would provide no automatic immunity from adverse inferences if it was either incomplete in comparison with the defendant's account at trial or in any way inconsistent with

---

[159] Leaving aside the complications of s.6 of the Theft Act 1968, as to which a person would undoubtedly need legal advice.

[160] Its use is noted by Bucke, Street and Brown, *The right of silence* (2000), p.26 fn.9.

[161] *Ali* [2001] 6 Archbold News 2.

[162] *Knight* [2003] EWCA Crim 1977; [2004] 1 Cr.App.R. 9.

[163] See also *Turner* [2004] 1 All E.R. 1025, to the same effect as *Knight* [2003] EWCA Crim 1977.

it.[164] The defendant will normally need to give evidence at trial of the facts relied on, or adduce evidence from other witnesses, since the statement to the police is not generally admissible in evidence for the defence as evidence of the facts stated. Nor can the prosecution be required to adduce as part of their evidence a pre-prepared wholly self-serving statement by the defendant.[165] Nevertheless the prepared statement is certainly admissible as relevant circumstantial evidence to show as a fact that the defence was disclosed at interview and to rebut any claim that the defendant failed to mention the facts on which he is relying at trial.

(D)   Reasons for silence and legal advice to remain silent

Two main points arise under this heading. The first is the judge's direction that a jury may draw an adverse inference only if they are satisfied that the reason for silence was that the defendant had no story to give at the time of the interview or no story that he was prepared to have questioned or investigated. In the early cases on s.34 only the first alternative was referred to (see, for example, *Condron and Condron*[166]). But later cases accepted that recent invention is not the only incriminating reason for silence[167]; another reason may be that the accused has a story but is reluctant to have it scrutinised by the police.[168] In *Condron v United Kingdom*,[169] the European Court of Human Rights adopted the two alternatives, and in *Gill*,[170] the Court of Appeal followed the *Condron v United Kingdom* formulation.[171] These later cases are surely correct as a matter of construction. As noted above, the primary purpose of s.34 was to deal with the supposed problem

5–030

---

[164] In *Turner* [2004] 1 All E.R. 1025 the CA suggested that where there are differences between what D says in a prepared statement and the evidence he gives at trial the jury might be better directed to consider a difference as constituting a previous lie rather than as the foundation for a s 34 inference. See also *Maguire* [2008] EWCA Crim 1028, where the Court of Appeal suggested that a s.34 direction was unnecessary in a case where a defendant advanced inconsistent defences in a police interview and in evidence at trial, and the Crown's case was that his evidence was untruthful because of the change of story. According to the court, the use of formalised directions under s.34 should be discouraged where their effect was to over-formalise common sense. cf.*Hackett* [2011] EWCA Crim 380; [2011] 2 Cr.App.R. 3, suggesting that a s.34 direction is more appropriate than a *Lucas* direction where D puts forward the same explanation for a statement in interview alleged to be a lie and for his failure to mention at the time the fact relied on at trial.

[165] *Knight* [2003] EWCA Crim 1977; [2004] 1 Cr.App.R. 9 at [14]; following *Pearce* (1979) 69 Cr.App.R. 365. See further Ch.14.

[166] *Condron and Condron* [1997] 1 Cr.App.R. 185.

[167] *Daniel* [1998] 2 Cr.App.R. 373; *Beckles and Montague* [1999] Crim. L.R. 148; *Milford* [2001] Crim. L.R. 330.

[168] The recognition of this alternative means that an accused cannot avoid the possibility of a s.34 inference by the device of mentioning to his solicitor at an early stage the facts he will rely on. This device is effective to counter a claim of recent fabrication (*Wilmot* (1989) 89 Cr.App.R. 341; *Seaton* [2010] EWCA Crim 1980; [2011] 1 Cr.App.R. 2), but will not meet the claim that he was unwilling to have his story questioned or investigated by the police. See Birch, "Suffering in Silence" [1999] Crim L.R. 769, 776.

[169] *Condron v UK* (2001) 31 E.H.R.R. 1.

[170] *Gill* [2001] 1 Cr.App.R. 11 at [29] and [30].

[171] As did the Court of Appeal in *Betts and Hall* [2001] EWCA Crim 224; [2001] 2 Cr.App.R. 16, where the court replaced the reference in *Condron v United Kingdom* to the accused having no answer that would stand up to "cross-examination" with the phrase "questioning and investigation". As Kay L.J. noted (at p.269), the former reference is taken from *Cowan* [1996] 1 Cr.App.R. 1, but is more appropriate to a case under s.35 of the CJPOA.

of late and/or ambush defences. An ambush defence may well be a recent fabrication, but it does not have to be. An accused might decide at interview what line he is going to take at trial, but be unwilling to open it up to the police for questioning and investigation.

The second point is related to the first. It is the issue of the effect of legal advice to the defendant to remain silent and not to answer questions. If the defendant gives a no comment interview following legal advice can s.34 still operate to permit adverse inferences? This crucial question has caused the courts much difficulty. In *Condron and Condron*,[172] Stuart-Smith L.J. said in the Court of Appeal that the fact of such advice having been given could not by itself prevent a s.34 inference, because otherwise the section would be rendered "wholly nugatory".[173] This must be correct, because the fact of legal advice by itself is not necessarily related to the accused's reason for not answering questions. The real problem, which *Condron and Condron* left unclear, is presented by the answer to a question of causation. What is the position of the accused who claims that his failure to mention facts was the result of his *reliance* on legal advice to say nothing? Does the fact of reliance on legal advice defeat s.34 without more, or does the jury still have to make an evaluative judgment whether the defendant could reasonably have been expected to mention the facts on which he relies later?[174] The authorities on this issue are in some disarray, although in its later decisions the Court of Appeal denied any inconsistency and tried to reach an accommodation. As we shall see, this accommodation does require the jury to make a normative assessment of the defendant's silence in interview, but does not require an assessment of the quality in legal terms of the advice the defendant received.

The problem derives from another collision in the law of evidence between logic and policy. Logically it should follow that if the defendant kept silent on legal advice, and not because he had no story to give or none that would stand up to scrutiny, then it should not matter whether the advice was well-grounded, or whether the jury thinks he should have revealed his defence at that stage anyway. The point is that the failure to mention the facts is not an incriminating one, given the causal test that the courts have built into s.34 and which Strasbourg has approved. The Court of Appeal recognised the force of this point in *Betts and Hall*[175] where an additional reason for allowing the appeal was that the judge had told the jury they could draw adverse inferences if they thought that the defendants had no good or valid reasons for refusing to answer questions. It should be remembered that they had been legally advised not to do so. The Court of Appeal held that the reference to the quality of the decision to keep silent was a misdirection. It was the genuineness of the decision that mattered. Kay L.J. stated:

---

[172] *Condron and Condron* [1997] 1 Cr.App.R. 185.

[173] *Condron and Condron* [1997] 1 Cr.App.R. 185 at 191.

[174] In which case, as Rose L.J. recognised in *Roble* [1997] Crim. L.R. 449, the reasons for the advice might have to be disclosed in order to determine whether they were good reasons.

[175] *Betts and Hall* [2001] EWCA Crim 224; [2001] 2 Cr.App.R. 16.

> "If it is a plausible explanation that the reason for not mentioning facts is that the [defendant] acted on the advice of his solicitor and not because he had no, or no satisfactory, answer to give then no inference can be drawn."[176]

The court went on to give a model direction[177] which emphasised that the jury's task was to make a decision of fact and causation. The model direction indicated that the jury might conclude that the defendant was simply hiding behind the legal advice, and the real reason for silence was that he had no story to give. In this situation inferences would be possible. But if the jury concluded that legal advice might be the true explanation for his failure to mention facts, "then you may not hold his failure against him nor draw any adverse inference from the failure".

This case appeared to establish an important point of principle. It is strongly arguable that a defendant who genuinely relies on legal advice given in good faith (and not to cover the lack of a story) should not be penalised for doing so. A typical scenario would be where a defendant is advised to "keep his powder dry" until the police case becomes clearer or there is greater disclosure of the evidence against the defendant. In such a case what is the point of insisting that a person should have access to legal advice before being interviewed if the jury are to be given the opportunity to say that although he relied on the advice to remain silent he should not have done?

5–031

Acknowledgment of this logic would not entail a conclusion that s.34 is effectively dead, on the basis that legal advisors will always advise suspects not to answer questions. There is first the obvious point that silence may not always be in the suspect's best interests. In some circumstances co-operation with the police may be the best course, as where the evidence of guilt is overwhelming. Secondly, reliance on the advice is a question of fact, and the defendant will always have to take the risk that the jury may not believe that his alleged reliance was genuine. Two matters need to be borne in mind at this stage. The Court of Appeal noted in *Betts and Hall* that:

> "the adequacy of the explanation advanced may well be relevant as to whether or not the advice was truly the reason for not mentioning the facts. A person, who is anxious not to answer questions because he has no or no adequate explanation to offer, gains no protection from his lawyer's advice because that advice is no more than a convenient way of disguising his true motivation for not mentioning facts."[178]

A feeble story, in other words, is likely to damage the defendant's credibility on this issue. A further relevant consideration is the reasons for the legal advice. These may be important *evidentially* as a guide to the genuineness of the defendant's claim to have relied on the advice. The stronger the reasons for the advice the more likely a jury will be to accept that the defendant's reliance was genuine. A bare statement that the defendant was advised to say nothing may not carry much conviction, especially if the facts relied on are ones that it would

---

[176] *Betts and Hall* [2001] EWCA Crim 224; [2001] 2 Cr.App.R. 16 at [53].
[177] *Betts and Hall* [2001] EWCA Crim 224; [2001] 2 Cr.App.R. 16 at [57].
[178] *Betts and Hall* [2001] EWCA Crim 224; [2001] 2 Cr.App.R. 16 at [54].

obviously be reasonable to mention in interview. So, if the defendant is going to give a no comment interview on advice, then disclosure of the reasons for the advice is likely to be desirable.

5–032   Despite these arguments, in other decisions the Court of Appeal has considered that the policy of s.34 would be thwarted if actual reliance on legal advice would be an adequate justification for silence in all cases. This policy has been expressed in different ways. In *Beckles*,[179] Lord Woolf C.J. made the historically accurate statement, noted above, that "the mischief at which the provision was primarily directed was the positive defence following a 'no comment' interview and/or the ambush defence". He did not suggest further purposes for s.34. Other judges, however, have taken the view that the purpose of s.34 is not restricted to the procedural aim of ensuring early disclosure of the accused's defence. In *Hoare and Pierce*,[180] Auld L.J. emphasised its instrumental relationship with the substantive issue of the defendant's guilt:

> "The whole basis of s.34, in its qualification of the otherwise general right of an accused to remain silent and to require the prosecution to prove its case, is an assumption that an innocent defendant—as distinct from one who is entitled to require the prosecution to prove its case—would give an early explanation to demonstrate his innocence . . . the s.34 inference is concerned with flushing out innocence at an early stage or supporting other evidence of guilt at a later stage . . ."

In *Howell*,[181] Laws L.J. placed s.34 in the context of what he saw as a general move towards a more participatory style of procedure which imposes normative expectations on the accused:

> "It seems to us that this provision is one of several enacted in recent years which has served to counteract a culture, or belief, which had long been established in the practice of criminal cases, namely that in principle a defendant may without criticism withhold any disclosure of his defence until the trial. Now, the police interview and the trial are to be seen as part of a continuous process in which the suspect is engaged from the beginning . . . This benign continuum from interview to trial, the public interest that inheres in reasonable disclosure by a suspected person of what he has to say when faced with a set of facts which accuse him, is thwarted if currency is given to the belief that if a suspect remains silent on legal advice he may systematically avoid adverse comment at his trial. And it may encourage solicitors to advise silence for other than good objective reasons."

In accordance with this view Laws L.J. went on to hold in *Howell* that the fact of reliance on legal advice was not sufficient by itself to avoid adverse inferences. There had to be:

> "soundly based objective reasons for silence, sufficiently cogent and telling to weigh in the balance against the clear public interest in an account being given by the suspect to the police."

In the circumstances of the case he held that it was not a good reason for advising silence that there was no written statement to the police by the victim of an alleged attack by the defendant. The court made it clear in *Howell* that it was

---

[179] *Beckles* [2004] EWCA Crim 2766; [2005] 1 Cr.App.R. 23 at [6].
[180] *Hoare and Pierce* [2004] EWCA Crim 784; [2005] 1 Cr.App.R. 22 at [53] and [54].
[181] *Howell* [2003] EWCA Crim 1; [2005] 1 Cr.App.R. 1 at [23] and [24].

not following *Betts and Hall* on the construction of s.34. Instead the court cited the language of Strasbourg in support of its evaluative approach. In *Condron v United Kingdom* the European Court of Human Rights had referred to the need for the fact of legal advice to be given "appropriate weight" by the domestic court, because there may be "good reason why such advice may be given". This loose language had seemed to leave open the possibility of the jury finding that the accused relied on legal advice but that in the circumstances the advice lacked sufficient grounds to justify the accused's silence. *Howell* was approved by the Court of Appeal in *Knight*,[182] in another judgment given by Laws L.J. However, there remained a widespread view that the decision was in conflict with *Betts and Hall* in so far as *Howell* required an assessment of the legal quality of the advice as well as the factual issue of whether it was relied on.

The Court of Appeal subsequently sought to resolve the conflict by adopting an intermediate position. In *Hoare and Pierce*[183] the trial judge directed the jury that:

5–033

> "when you are considering whether it was reasonable for the defendant to rely on the advice and whether he actually did so, or whether he simply latched on to it as a convenient excuse, you are entitled to look at the explanation for the advice and whether that was a reasonable ground for advising the client not to answer."

This seems to retain a requirement that reliance must be reasonable but does not impose a condition that the reasons for the advice must be objectively good. In upholding the direction Auld L.J. commented that an accused cannot reasonably be expected to assess the quality of his legal advice—to second-guess it.[184] Nor, we might add, can a jury reasonably be expected to say whether the legal advice was good or bad. Auld L.J. stated that the question for the jury in the end is whether regardless of advice, genuinely given and genuinely accepted, an accused has remained silent not because of that advice but because he had no or no satisfactory explanation to give. This might imply that an accused who does have a story that he could give in interview but who is advised to delay giving it is immune from adverse inferences if he relies on the advice. But this is difficult to fit with the claim in the judgment that the purpose of s.34 is to flush out innocent explanations at the earliest opportunity. It seems that the Court of Appeal thought that a jury should be able to decide that, despite the advice, it was unreasonable for an accused not to give his story when interviewed.

This interpretation gets support from *Beckles*,[185] which approved the reasoning and decision in *Hoare and Pierce*. Lord Woolf C.J. emphasised that the ultimate question is whether the facts relied on at the trial were facts that the defendant could reasonably have been expected to mention at interview. He continued:

> "If they were not, that is the end of the matter. If the jury consider that the defendant genuinely relied on the advice, that is not necessarily the end of the matter. It *may still not have been*

---

[182] *Knight* [2003] EWCA Crim 1977; [2004] 1 Cr.App.R. 9.
[183] *Hoare and Pierce* [2004] EWCA Crim 784; [2005] 1 Cr.App.R. 22.
[184] *Hoare and Pierce* [2004] EWCA Crim 784; [2005] 1 Cr.App.R. 22 at [58].
[185] *Beckles* [2004] EWCA Crim 2766; [2005] 1 Cr.App.R. 23.

reasonable for him to rely on the advice, or the advice may not have been the true explanation for his silence . . . If it is possible to say that the defendant genuinely acted upon the advice, the fact that he did so because it suited his purpose may mean he was not acting reasonably in not mentioning the facts. His reasonableness in not mentioning the facts remains to be determined by the jury. If they conclude he was acting unreasonably they can draw an adverse inference from the failure to mention the facts."[186] (emphasis addeded)

5–034   *Beckles* seems to have settled the matter for the time being. It is unlikely that the Court of Appeal will wish to revert in a future case to either the *Betts and Hall* or the *Howell* approach. It seems therefore the jury now have to operate a two-stage process of decision. Stage one is the decision whether the defendant had no story to give at the time or no story that he was prepared to have investigated, and that this was the case even if he did genuinely rely on legal advice to remain silent. If the jury decide against the defendant on this point then adverse inferences can be drawn from the failure to mention the facts relied on at trial. If the jury decide the point in his favour then stage two requires them to consider whether such genuine reliance was reasonable in the circumstances, on the necessary assumption that the defendant did have a story to give, and there is a question why he did not give it at the time. If it was reasonable not to mention the facts at the time then no adverse inferences are possible. The circumstances will invariably include the reasons for the advice, which will need to be disclosed to the court. In *Howell* Laws L.J. suggested that the kind of circumstances that would most likely justify silence would be such matters, for example, as:

"the suspect's condition (ill-health, in particular mental disability; confusion, intoxication, shock, and so forth . . .), or his inability genuinely to recollect events without reference to documents which are not to hand, or communication with other persons who may be able to assist his recollection."[187]

If the reason for the advice is inadequate disclosure by the police[188] then it would seem to be important to say this at the time of the interview. It should be remembered that disclosure of the reasons for legal advice not to answer questions will constitute a waiver of legal professional privilege in the

---

[186] *Beckles* [2004] EWCA Crim 2766; [2005] 1 Cr.App.R. 23 at [46].

[187] *Howell* [2003] EWCA Crim 1; [2005] 1 Cr.App.R. 1 at [24]. See also *Essa* [2009] EWCA Crim 43 at [15].

[188] The law on disclosure obligations prior to committal is still in the process of development: see *R. v DPP Ex p. Lee* [1999] 2 Cr.App.R. 304; *DPP v Ara* [2001] 4 All E.R. 559; although it has been held that s.34 does not require the police to reveal the whole of their case before interview: *Imran and Hussain* [1997] Crim. L.R. 754. But it is necessarily the case that what facts the defendant can reasonably be expected to mention depends on his knowledge of the case against him. Other reasons for legal advice not to answer questions might include a lack of evidence against the client, or a belief that the client is vulnerable due to a mental condition (see Bucke, Street and Brown, *The right of silence* (2000), p.25 fn.9). A lawyer may believe that the police already have enough evidence to charge the client, but it is doubtful whether this would justify advice not to answer questions (on the basis that an interview would then be in breach of Code C). A balance of authority holds that even where the police believe they have a prima facie case, an informed decision on whether there is "sufficient evidence to prosecute" necessarily involves consideration of any explanation or information from the accused, in which case an interview would not be in breach of the Code. See *Van Bokkum* [2000] 6 Archbold News 2; preferring *McGuinness* [1999] Crim. L.R. 318; and *Ioannou* [1999] Crim. L.R. 586; to *Gayle* [1999] Crim. L.R. 502.

communications between lawyer and client.[189] If the defendant testifies at trial—and he will normally have to in order to get in evidence of the facts that he did not mention in interview—he can be cross- examined on his discussions with his solicitor since these will be relevant to the question of the genuineness of his reliance. Similarly, if the defence call the solicitor to give evidence of the reasons for the advice the solicitor can also be cross-examined. According to Lord Bingham C.J. in *Bowden*,[190] if the solicitor has made a statement before trial disclosing the reasons for the advice, that statement can be put in by the prosecution as admissible evidence against the defendant (it is a statement made by his authorised agent). Lastly, on the issue of waiver, any indirect compulsion to waive privilege by disclosing the reasons for legal advice does not violate art.6 of the ECHR. The argument that it might was raised in *Condron v United Kingdom*[191] but was rejected by the European Court of Human Rights. According to the court:

> "The fact that the applicants were subjected to cross-examination on the content of their solicitor's advice cannot be said to raise an issue of fairness under Art.6 . . . They were under no compulsion to disclose the advice given, other than the indirect compulsion to avoid the reason for their silence remaining at the level of a bare explanation. The applicants chose to make the content of their solicitor's advice a live issue as part of their defence. For that reason they cannot complain that the scheme of s.34 is such as to override the confidentiality of their discussions with their solicitors."[192]

(E) Prima facie case

It now seems to be clear that the jury have to be satisfied that there is a prima facie case against the defendant before they can draw any adverse inference from his failure to mention facts relied on in defence. This was denied by the Court of Appeal in *Doldur*,[193] but the requirement is implicit in the approach of the European Court of Human Rights in *Condron v United Kingdom*, and it was applied by the Court of Appeal in *Gill*.[194] In *Gill* the failure of the trial judge to direct the jury to find a prima facie case before considering an inference from silence formed one of the grounds for allowing the appeal.[195]

5–035

This is a requirement which the courts have now imported into both s.34 and s.35. In *Cowan*[196] Lord Taylor C.J. restricted the scope of s.35 by including this requirement in the directions the judge has to give in relation to a s.35 inference.

---

[189] *Bowden* [1999] 2 Cr.App.R. 176, where the Court of Appeal indicated that disclosure of the fact that the accused received legal advice not to answer questions will not waive privilege, but that opening up the reasons for the advice will be an implied waiver.

[190] *Bowden* [1999] 2 Cr.App.R. 176 at 183.

[191] *Condron v United Kingdom* [2001] 31 E.H.R.R. 1.

[192] *Condron v United Kingdom* [2001] 31 E.H.R.R. 1 at [60].

[193] *Doldur* [2000] Crim. L.R. 178. Similarly in *Daniel* [1998] 2 Cr.App.R. 373 Otton L.J. said that it was not necessary to direct the jury to be satisfied that the prosecution had established a case to answer before they could draw any adverse inference from the defendant's failure to answer questions at interview.

[194] *Gill* [2001] 1 Cr.App.R. 11.

[195] As it did in *Milford* [2001] Crim. L.R. 33. See also *Chenia* [2002] EWCA Crim 2345; [2003] 2 Cr.App.R. 6.

[196] *Cowan* [1996] 1 Cr.App.R. 1.

The requirement does not form part of the statutory wording, although it is necessarily implicit in s.35 that the *judge* has to be satisfied that there is a case to answer, otherwise the question of the defendant giving evidence does not arise. Lord Taylor's judgment in *Cowan* has been influential in the s.34 cases, particularly after the circumscribed approach to inferences from silence in the police station adopted by the European Court of Human Rights in *Condron v United Kingdom*.[197] The incorporation of the prima facie case requirement in s.34 does, however, produce something of an anomaly. Under s.34(2)(c) the court may draw adverse inferences from failure to mention facts in determining whether there is a case to answer in the first place. This allows for the possibility of silence playing a more significant role than merely providing support for an already established prima facie case. It is then somewhat inconsistent to insist that a jury may not consider silence unless satisfied that the other evidence discloses a prima facie case. However, the requirement is probably now essential to comply with the ECHR restriction that silence may not provide the sole or main evidence for conviction.

It is possible that the requirement goes further than an insistence on a bare prima facie case. In *Murray v United Kingdom*,[198] the European Court of Human Rights referred to the strength of the prosecution case which "called for an answer" from the applicant. In *Murray v DPP*,[199] a case concerned with the Northern Ireland equivalent of s.35, the House of Lords held that failure to testify may yield a general inference of guilt, but that the inference may only be properly drawn if the prosecution have made out a clear or strong prima facie case calling for an answer. Similarly in *Birchall*,[200] the Court of Appeal said that the jury must be directed that they should not draw adverse inferences from the defendant's failure to testify until they have concluded that the prosecution have made out a sufficiently compelling case to answer as to call for an answer by the defendant. Leading authorities have taken the same line in relation to inferences under s.34.[201]

(F)   Proper inferences

5–036   There is some tendency to confuse the accused's reason for silence with the inference that may be drawn from that silence regarding the facts relied on. In *Condron and Condron*,[202] Stuart-Smith L.J. conflated the two issues by saying that s.34 only operated where the jury were satisfied that the accused did not mention the facts relied on because he invented them subsequently. But the difference between motive for silence and the truth of the facts relied on is

---

[197]   *Condron v United Kingdom* (2001) 31 E.H.R.R. 1.
[198]   *Murray v United Kingdom* (1996) 22 E.H.R.R. 29.
[199]   *Murray v DPP* (1993) 97 Cr.App.R. 151.
[200]   *Birchall* [1999] Crim. L.R. 311.
[201]   *Petkar and Farquhar* [2003] EWCA Crim 2668; [2004] 1 Cr.App.R. 22 at [51] (vi), restating as an essential element of a model direction that an inference should only be drawn if, apart from the defendant's failure to mention facts later relied on in his defence, the prosecution case is so strong that it clearly calls for an answer by him. See also *Beckles* [2004] EWCA Crim 2766; [2005] 1 Cr.App.R. 23 at [35].
[202]   *Condron and Condron* [1997] 1 Cr.App.R. 185.

apparent when the other incriminating reason for silence is considered. For example, D might not mention his alibi in interview because he could not supply details of where he was and who he was with without further inquiry, and was therefore unwilling to be questioned at that stage. Even if he might reasonably have been expected to mention the fact that he had an alibi, so that an adverse inference might be drawn, it does not necessarily follow that the alibi is false.

If the conditions of use are satisfied, so that s.34(2) applies, the court or jury may draw such inferences as appear proper from the failure to mention facts relied on subsequently. However, the Act gives no further guidance on what inferences might be proper. The courts have now said, as they have done in relation to legislation restricting the right to silence at trial,[203] that what inferences are proper depends upon the circumstances of the particular case, being a question to be decided by applying fairness and common sense.[204] The most obvious inference is that the previously undisclosed fact is untrue.[205] The jury might conclude that it is simply a late invention, or a story tailored to fit the prosecution case or to tie in with the case of a co-accused. Whether such an inference can form part of a chain of reasoning leading to a conclusion that the accused is guilty ought to depend on the issue in the case, the nature of the fact in question and the state of the other evidence. If the "fact" is in the nature of a "confession and avoidance" defence, whereby the accused admits the actus reus and mens rea of the offence but sets up some independent ground of justification or excuse such as self-defence, then the rejection of that defence is almost certain to lead to the conclusion that the accused has no defence at all and is guilty. On the other hand, if the issue is identity, and the other evidence against the accused is circumstantial, the rejection of a fact offered as an innocent explanation of one piece of circumstantial evidence may not necessarily yield a further inference of guilt. This suggests that it would be wrong for a court to conclude simply that because an accused fails to mention a fact relied on subsequently he is therefore guilty. Accordingly trial judges will have to direct juries carefully on the inferences that may fairly be drawn from such failures. In *Petkar and Farquhar,* the Court of Appeal confirmed that the inferences that it is suggested might be drawn from failure to mention facts should be identified by the judge in his direction, to the extent "that they may go beyond the standard inference of late fabrication".[206]

---

[203] *Haw Tua Tau v Public Prosecutor* [1981] 3 All E.R. 14 at 21; *Murray v DPP* (1993) 97 Cr.App.R. 151 at 160.

[204] *Cowan* [1996] Q.B. 373 CA; *Condron* [1997] 1 Cr.App.R. 185 CA.

[205] It seems clear that the section cannot be restricted only to such inferences—meaning that the effect of the section is simply to reverse *Gilbert* (1977) 66 Cr.App.R. 237 CA. This is what Mirfield describes as the "limited force" view of the section (*Silence, Confessions* (1997), p.258), but such a reading would be artificial because it would ignore the logical implications of concluding that the fact in question was untrue. At the same time, an "extensive force" view that the section permits a direct inference of guilt from a failure to mention a fact seems to invite unfair logical jumps—in effect telescoping what may be quite complex chains of inference.

[206] *Petkar and Farquhar* [2003] EWCA Crim 2668; [2004] 1 Cr.App.R. 22 at [51](ii).

(G)   Exclusionary discretion

5–037   Section 34 refers to *evidence* being given of the accused's failure to mention facts. Since this is evidence on which the prosecution propose to rely, it is subject to the judge's exclusionary discretion under s.78 of PACE. Are there any circumstances that might justify a judge in concluding that admission of the evidence of silence would have such an adverse effect on the fairness of the proceedings that it ought not to be admitted? Silence is in one sense the converse of a confession, but since the prosecution will be seeking to use it to the same incriminating effect, it can be argued that the principles that the courts have developed in relation to confessions should apply by analogy. From this perspective there are a number of possible exclusionary scenarios.

The first is what might be called the "silent verbal". The accused relies at trial on facts that he says he mentioned[207] to the police in an untaped interview. The officer's notebook records that questions were asked under caution to which the accused replied "No comment". The record was not shown to the accused or signed by him. Unless there is good reason for the failure to ask the accused to verify the record, this should be regarded as a "significant and substantial" breach of PACE Code C for the purposes of s.78.[208] Secondly, any deception by the police about the meaning of the caution or the state of the evidence against the accused should be regarded as tainting the evidence of silence in a subsequent interview.[209] Thirdly, it may be quite unsafe to attach any probative significance to the failure of a suspect suffering from severe mental illness or mental handicap to mention facts later relied on in his defence. In such a case the evidence should not be permitted to go before the jury at all.[210]

Section 34(4) extends the section to cover questioning by persons other than constables who are charged with the duty of investigating offences or charging offenders. This is the same wording as used in PACE for the application of the Codes of Practice. It will be very surprising if it is interpreted differently in the CJPOA. Under PACE it is a question of fact who falls within this wording.[211] Persons who have been held to do so include Customs officials, Inland Revenue officers conducting "*Hansard*" interviews, commercial investigators employed by companies to investigate possible crimes, and store detectives, depending on the terms of their employment.[212] The absence of a caution by such a person could be grounds for excluding the evidence of silence in any event under s.78 of PACE.[213]

---

[207] The notion of a fact relied on being "mentioned" is not without difficulty. How specific does the reference have to be? Does the accused have to indicate an intention to rely upon the fact?

[208] *Keenan* [1990] 2 Q.B. 54 CA; *Canale* [1990] 2 All E.R. 187 CA.

[209] *Mason* [1987] 3 All E.R. 481 CA.

[210] See *Mackenzie* (1993) 96 Cr.App.R. 98 CA.

[211] *Seelig and Spens* [1992] 1 W.L.R. 148 at 158; *Bayliss* (1993) 98 Cr.App.R. 235 CA.

[212] See Ch.6, fnn.38–41 for the relevant authorities.

[213] cf. *Twaites and Brown* (1991) 92 Cr.App.R. 106 CA.

(H)   Continued application of common law

What is the status of evidence of silence (in the sense of failure to mention facts) that does not satisfy the conditions of s.34(1)? Suppose, for example, that the accused has not been cautioned before being questioned. Subsection (2) does not then apply, but is the evidence of silence still admissible, and if so, for what purpose?   **5–038**

The answer is that the common law, supplemented by s.78 of PACE, still applies. Section 34(5) provides that the section does not:

> "(a)   prejudice the admissibility in evidence of the silence or other reaction of the accused in the face of anything said in his presence relating to the conduct in respect of which he is charged, in so far as evidence thereof would be admissible apart from this section; or
>
> (b)   preclude the drawing of any inference from any such silence or other reaction of the accused which could properly be drawn apart from this section."

This has the effect of preserving the *Christie*[214] principle and means that the decision in *Chandler*[215] thus remains good law insofar as it relates to silence pre-caution.[216] For the principle to operate in the police-suspect context, however, there must not only be a failure to caution, but the police and the suspect must be on "even terms", as when the accused has his solicitor with him at the time. Under PACE the conjunction of these events is inherently unlikely.[217]

Where the possibility of drawing inferences under s.34 does not arise, other common law limitations on the use of silence remain. Indeed the Court of Appeal has gone one stage further. In *McGarry*,[218] D was interviewed twice about a suspected assault in which V suffered grievous bodily harm. On legal advice D refused to answer questions at the first interview. At the beginning of the second interview five weeks later he handed the police a prepared written statement in which he said that V had lunged at him and that he had punched V in self-defence. He then answered "no comment" to questions about the incident. At trial D testified to having acted in self-defence. The Crown took the view that no adverse inferences could properly be drawn from D's silence in the two interviews and did not cross-examine D about it. The trial judge, however, directed the jury that they might wish to take into account D's failure at the second interview to mention details about the defence that D did not reveal until he gave evidence. The Court of Appeal held that this was a misdirection and quashed D's conviction. Once the judge had concluded that the requirements of s.34 were not satisfied, so that it was not open to him to leave to the jury the possibility of drawing adverse inferences, he had a *duty* to direct the jury positively that they should not draw any adverse inferences from D's silence. The   **5–039**

---

[214] *Christie* [1914] A.C. 545 HL.

[215] *Chandler* [1976] 3 All E.R. 105 CA.

[216] This is still the case even where the conditions of s.34 are satisfied, as a result of subs.(5).

[217] This of course assumes that the *Christie* principle applies unaltered, notwithstanding the effects of the Act and the revised caution. For an argument against this assumption see Mirfield, *Silence, Confessions* (1997), pp.270–271.

[218] *McGarry* [1998] 3 All E.R. 805.

court was strongly influenced in reaching this decision by its perception that "by s.34 Parliament was making a limited modification to a firmly established rule of the common law".[219]

E.   THEORIES OF UNDERLYING PURPOSES AND VALUES

5–040   Having considered the law relating to the privilege against self-incrimination and to its derivative application of the right to silence, we now return to issues of theory. In this section we examine four leading accounts of the privilege against self-incrimination. Other purposes and values have been ascribed to the privilege from time to time,[220] but only one of them will be considered further here.

The first two theories are concerned with what Arenella has called "accusatorial process norms".[221] One is the theory concerned with outcomes of the criminal process, which argues that the privilege protects the innocent against the danger of wrongful conviction. The other is the theory concerned with methods of discharging the criminal burden of proof, which argues that the privilege is an application of the presumption of innocence. The remaining two theories are concerned with upholding substantive values derived from a core principle of respect for human autonomy. The values in question are those of privacy from state intrusion and freedom from the imposition by the state of cruel choices.

These theoretical accounts are defective because they all fail, for different reasons, to provide us with a coherent theory of the proper scope and justification of the privilege. A more convincing account is needed, and the section concludes by arguing that the best justification is to be found in the idea that the privilege is necessary to prevent the abuse of state power. Prevention of abuse of state power is in turn referable to the overall aim of the law of evidence to safeguard the legitimacy of criminal proceedings and of the verdict that is their outcome.

---

[219] *McGarry* [1998] 3 All E.R. 805 at 809, Hutchison L.J. *Gilbert* was cited as authority for this rule.
[220] For critical reviews of such accounts, see Wigmore, para.2251; J. T. McNaughton, "The Privilege Against Self-Incrimination: Its Constitutional Affectation, Raison d'etre and Miscellaneous Implications" (1960) 51 J. Crim. Law, Criminology & Police Science 138. More recent sceptical writing has tended to focus on the four theories discussed here; see in particular D. Dolinko, "Is There a Rationale for the Privilege Against Self-Incrimination?" (1986) 33 U.C.L.A. L.R. 1063; D. Dripps, "Self-incrimination and self-preservation: a skeptical view" [1991] U.Illinois L.R. 329. For a more sympathetic treatment of both rights-based and consequentialist arguments see S. Easton, *The Case for the Right to Silence*, 2nd edn (Aldershot, 1998), Ch.6; S. Schulhofer, "Some kind words for the privilege against self-incrimination" (1991) 26 Valparaiso L.R. 311. For a different approach see M. Redmayne, "Rethinking the Privilege Against Self-Incrimination" (2007) 27 O.J.L.S. 209, arguing for a rationale of the privilege as a distancing mechanism, enabling defendants to "disassociate" themselves from prosecutions.
[221] P. Arenella, "*Schmerber* and the Privilege Against Self-Incrimination: A Reappraisal" (1982) 20 Am.Crim. L.R. 31 at 37.

1. *Protection of the innocent against wrongful conviction*

This fundamental concern underlies many of the restrictions that the law of criminal evidence places on freedom of proof. The theory argues that the privilege has an essential instrumental function. It is seen as a device intended, like a number of other adjectival rules, to minimise the risk of a particular erroneous outcome of the criminal justice process.[222] The wrongful conviction of the innocent is considered a species of moral harm so severe as to warrant special measures to prevent its occurrence.[223] If the measures make it more difficult to convict the truly guilty, this is a price the system must pay.

5–041

As far as pre-trial processes are concerned, this account of the privilege is incomplete. It is largely restricted to the particular context of interrogation of suspects in police custody because it links the privilege closely to the reliability rationale for the rule against involuntary confessions. On this theory the perceived risk is that coercive or manipulative questioning may lead the suspect to make incriminating statements that are false. Thus this theory aims to account for restrictions on *questioning*, including the right to silence, the derivative application of the privilege described above. If coercion or manipulation leads the suspect to produce other non-confessional evidence clearly probative of guilt, the issue of protection of the innocent does not generally arise.[224] Such other evidence might consist of pre-existing incriminating documents, which are currently covered by the privilege. Thus the justifying argument of protection of the innocent is plainly under-inclusive. It does not account for this aspect of the privilege, and it therefore becomes necessary to appeal to other interests that the privilege may protect if the present scope of the privilege is to be satisfactorily accounted for.

Moreover, even when limited to the context of custodial interrogation, the theory is weak. In relation to interrogation the theory is that the privilege grants the power to suspects to refuse to answer questions; this right of silence (in its broader sense) then reduces the likelihood that the police will engage in oppressive questioning and enables the suspect to resist it better if it occurs.[225] But there are problems with this argument, as a contextual analysis of questioning demonstrates. Research on the conduct of police investigations has emphasised that the interview with the suspect is the central investigative strategy of the police,[226] and for good reason. It uses limited resources efficiently and more often than not produces what from the police point of view is a clear and satisfactory result. Many studies have shown that the great majority of suspects do make

---

[222] Notable advocates of this view were the majority of the members of the Royal Commission on Criminal Justice. RCCJ Report, Ch.4, para.22.

[223] For further discussion see Ch.2, paras 2–12 to 2–13.

[224] If a suspect is bullied or tricked into producing his knife that is stained with the victim's blood, there may be reasons for excluding this evidence, but unreliability is not one of them.

[225] For a restatement of this view see S. Greer, "The Right to Silence: A Review of the Current Debate" (1990) 53 M.L.R. 709.

[226] M. McConville, A. Sanders and R. Leng, *The Case for the Prosecution* (London and New York: Routledge, 1991), Ch.4, esp. pp.56–57.

statements to the police[227] and that the majority of these are incriminating.[228] The great majority of those who confess then plead guilty at trial.[229] Thus, as Dixon observed when discussing the right of silence:

> "criminal justice . . . is organised around interrogation, confession and the guilty plea: the right of silence disrupts this normal process, and this is why, even if it is exercised rarely, it 'so often angers the police'."[230]

5–042 It follows that the occupational culture of the police is inimical to the privilege; it is in police interests to exert pressure on suspects to waive the privilege rather than to provide any support or encouragement for its exercise. The psychological pressure on suspects that this generates is well-recognised.[231] The environment of the police station, the isolation of the suspect and the clearly expressed expectation of the police that the suspect will talk combine to create an atmosphere in which it may take an abnormal effort of will to assert the privilege effectively.[232] In these circumstances it becomes doubtful whether the privilege is capable of functioning as an adequate protection against false incrimination. This must be particularly true for the weak or vulnerable suspect who is frequently claimed to be the person most at risk from abandonment of the privilege.[233] The notorious miscarriage of justice cases[234] and the psychological research carried out by Gudjonsson[235] and others indicate that it is precisely the frightened and the suggestible who are most likely to confess under the existing pressure of custodial interrogation. PACE introduced a scheme of having "appropriate adults" present at interviews with certain types of vulnerable suspect (juveniles,

---

[227] The research evidence presented in the RCCJ Report gave varying figures. At their lowest, at least 72% of suspects answered all or some significant police questions (see p.53), and in some studies the percentage was much higher; see in particular R. Leng, *The Right to Silence in Police Interrogation: A Study of Some of the Issues Underlying the Debate* (RCCJ Research Study No.10, London, 1993) who found that the right to silence was relied on in less than 5% of cases. The more recent study, by Bucke, Street and Brown, *The right of silence* (2000), p.31, found that 6% of suspects refused to answer all questions and another 10% refused to answer some questions.

[228] Bucke, Street and Brown, *The right of silence* (2000), p.34 give a figure for confession rates of 55% of interviewees. This is consistent with M. McConville, *Corroboration and Confessions* (RCCJ Research Study No.13, London, 1993), who found that the incidence of confessions by suspects varied between 53% and 61% (see p.61). Earlier studies are discussed by G. Gudjonsson, *The Psychology of Interrogations and Confessions: A Handbook* (Chichester: 2003), Ch.4. Bucke, Street and Brown suggest that the effect of s.34 of the Criminal Justice and Public Order Act 1994 is that fewer suspects are exercising the right to silence, but the confession rate is unchanged because more are telling lies.

[229] In McConville's study (cited in the previous note), of those who confessed during custodial interrogation where the outcome of the case is known, 93.6% pleaded guilty: p.32.

[230] D. Dixon, "Politics, Research and Symbolism in Criminal Justice: The Right of Silence and the Police and Criminal Evidence Act 1984" (1991) 20 Anglo-American L.R. 27, 38.

[231] For an excellent review see Gudjonsson, *Psychology of Interrogations* (2003).

[232] B. Irving, *Police Interrogation: A Case Study of Current Practice* (Royal Commission on Criminal Procedure Research Study No.2, London, 1980), p.153.

[233] See most recently the RCCJ Report at p.54, discussing possible restriction of the right to silence.

[234] Discussed by I. H. Dennis, "Miscarriages of Justice and the Law of Confessions: Evidentiary Issues and Solutions" [1993] P.L. 291; C. Walker, "Introduction" in C. Walker and K. Starmer (eds), *Justice in Error* (London, 1993), p.1.

[235] Gudjonsson, *Psychology of Interrogations* (2003).

mentally disordered and mentally handicapped persons) to provide support and protection, but the evidence for the effectiveness of appropriate adults is not encouraging.[236]

If this is so, it follows that the most likely beneficiaries of the privilege, on the theory we are considering, are hardened, but innocent, suspects who would use a right to silence and who would be at risk from increased pressure if it were unavailable. It seems unlikely that this is a large group, given the relatively small numbers of suspects, both guilty and innocent, who do remain silent in the police station. We may also be sceptical as to whether removal of the right to silence will make much difference to the hardened suspect who, ex hypothesi, has reasons for not explaining his innocence to the police in interview.

In examining this instrumentalist account of the privilege we should consider the efficacy of other safeguards against the perceived danger of coercive and manipulative questioning. This topic is dealt with in detail in the next chapter, but it is worth noting here one or two important points. The most severe forms of police oppression have always been subject to direct legal sanction in the shape of the criminal law. There is no special dispensation for law enforcement officers to subject suspects to torture and violence. Similarly police officers are civilly liable for torts of assault and false imprisonment committed in the course of their employment, and their employers will incur vicarious liability for such torts. Since 1986 the general criminal and civil law has been supplemented by the provisions of PACE and the Codes of Practice. These represent what the Court of Appeal has described as "a rigorously controlled legislative regime"[237] that governs the detention, treatment and questioning of persons by police officers and others charged with the duty of investigating offences. In addition to the statutory rule under s.76 of PACE against the use of oppression or other techniques likely to produce unreliable confessions the provisions of Codes C and E stipulate in much detail how powers of questioning are to be exercised. The requirement for taping of formal interviews is particularly important in this context.

As the next chapter makes clear, the Codes have been reinforced by the willingness of the courts in some cases to apply the statutory discretion under s.78 of PACE so as to exclude evidence obtained by the police following breaches of the rules. This tendency has been particularly noticeable in relation to incriminating statements made after an unjustified denial of the right of access to legal advice, a right described in the leading case as a "fundamental right" of the accused.[238] The courts have also been willing to exclude evidence of confessions where the requirements for the recording of interviews have not been observed.[239] Interestingly, the judges have not sought to justify their use of the exclusionary discretion under PACE by reference to the privilege against

5–043

---

[236] See A. Sanders, R. Young and M Burton, *Criminal Justice*, 4th edn (Oxford, 2010), pp.201-205.
[237] *Bailey and Smith* (1993) 97 Cr.App.R. 365 at 375 CA.
[238] *Samuel* [1988] Q.B. 615 CA. See also *Parris* (1989) 89 Cr.App.R. 68 CA; *Walsh* (1990) 91 Cr.App.R. 161 CA; *Chung* (1991) 92 Cr.App.R. 314 CA.
[239] *Keenan* [1990] 2 Q.B. 54 CA; *Canale* [1990] 2 All E.R. 187 CA; *Bryce* (1992) 95 Cr.App.R. 320 CA.

self-incrimination.[240] They have preferred to look instead to other traditional justifications for the exclusion of illegally or unfairly obtained evidence. These include the need for evidence to be reliable,[241] particularly as regards both the making and the content of incriminating statements, the need for statutory rights to be respected[242] and the need for police propriety in the obtaining of evidence.[243]

It seems therefore that the privilege against self-incrimination is probably ineffective to prevent compelled false incrimination of innocent suspects.[244] Moreover, such limited protection as it may offer is unnecessary where the custodial regime is closely regulated by legislation, provided that the legislative controls are backed by the willingness of courts to apply exclusionary principles where appropriate. The circumstances where exclusion of incriminating statements is appropriate are discussed in the next chapter.

2. *Presumption of innocence*

5–044   The privilege against self-incrimination can be defended on a broader ground than the protection of the innocent against the outcome of wrongful conviction. In reality the truly "innocent" are merely a subset of a larger group of all suspects in the criminal process. However, it may be claimed that the interest of all suspects, whether factually guilty or innocent, in not being obliged to incriminate themselves is sufficiently important to justify its protection by some or all of the primary and derivative applications described above. This interest derives from the values attached to the freedom and dignity of the individual. It is embodied in the fundamental procedural principle that it is for the prosecution to prove the accused's guilt, and not for the accused to prove innocence.

According to this theory the fundamental rule concerning the burden and standard of proof in criminal cases expresses more than a bare rule of decision for the court in situations of uncertainty, and more than a rule about the allocation of the risks of misdecision.[245] In addition it makes a political statement about the relationship between the state and the citizen. This statement is to the effect that the state, which has greater resources for the purpose, must prove its case without help from the suspect. If he or she is presumed innocent, it is wrong in principle

---

[240] In *Keenan* [1990] 2 Q.B. 54 at 61 CA, Hodgson J. referred to protection against self-incrimination being provided primarily by PACE s.76. Even this is debatable; see fn.20 at para.5–004 above and the discussion in the text below.

[241] See, e.g. *Parris* (1989) 89 Cr.App.R. 68 CA; *Keenan* [1990] 2 Q.B. 54 CA; *Canale* [1990] 2 All E.R. 187 CA; *Chung* (1991) 92 Cr.App.R. 314 CA.

[242] See, e.g. *Parris* (1989) 89 Cr.App.R. 68 CA; *Samuel* [1988] Q.B. 615 CA; *Walsh* (1990) 91 Cr.App.R. 161 CA.

[243] See, e.g. *Walsh* (1990) 91 Cr.App.R. 161 CA; *Canale* [1990] 2 All E.R. 187 CA.

[244] For a sophisticated argument that the privilege protects innocent persons indirectly see Daniel J. Seidmann and Alex Stein, "The Right to Silence Helps the Innocent: A Game Theoretic Analysis of the Fifth Amendment Privilege" (2000) 114 Harv. L.R. 431, but see also the cogent critique by Roberts and Zuckerman, *Criminal Evidence,* 2nd edn (2010), 560–563.

[245] The leading advocate of conceptualising the function of the law of evidence as the allocation of the risks of misdecision is A. Stein, "The Refoundation of Evidence Law" (1996) IX *Canadian Journal of Law & Jurisprudence* 279. His argument is developed further in *Foundations of Evidence Law* (2005).

to compel the suspect to be a source of incriminating evidence.[246] The burden of proof must be discharged by the prosecution without recourse to such methods. Accordingly the suspect must be given the privilege of declining to co-operate in procedures designed to establish guilt.[247] Derivative applications, particularly the right to silence, can be justified by an appeal to the same principle.[248]

Normatively this argument presents difficulties. If it is accepted without qualification it follows that the state may be denied access to a good deal of relevant and reliable evidence. It is pretty much self-evident that the accused may be a potent source of incriminating evidence. For example, cogent evidence of identity (much more cogent than the notoriously fallible testimony of eyewitnesses)[249] may be provided by fingerprints and bodily samples. Highly incriminating real evidence, say, of the possession of drugs, explosives or stolen property, may result from searches of person or property. The results of intoximeter tests or blood/urine samples provide essential proof of guilt in drink-driving cases. Reliable confessions produced by legitimate questioning may be essential to prove one or more elements of particular offences. This is especially true in relation to offences that occur in private and that may leave little or no tangible trace of their occurrence, such as child sexual abuse. Confessions also have an important role in offences for which forms of subjective mens rea are prescribed.[250] Questioning of suspects may also be the only way of acquiring reliable information about aspects of the management of business enterprises and the whereabouts of missing assets.

Denial of access to these types of evidence may have great costs. There is a considerable risk that the adjudication will be less accurate as a result; rectitude of decision may well be significantly diminished. Given that the factual accuracy of the verdict is the major component of its legitimacy, it is plain that public confidence in the criminal process may be compromised by the failure to gain access to such evidence. Perceptions may arise that guilty persons are not prosecuted for lack of evidence, or are wrongly acquitted at trial. In turn this may lead to a loss of confidence in "just deserts" principles, where these form the basis of penal policy, or a belief that the deterrent function of the criminal law is being undermined. The law may additionally be seen as failing to deliver satisfaction to victims, giving rise to consequential risks of private revenge and vigilanteism.

5–045

In practice, these considerations have significantly restricted the scope of the privilege against self-incrimination. We have already seen that the protection of

---

[246] For arguments along these lines see, e.g. *Murphy v Waterfront Commission* (1964) 378 U.S. 52 at 55 per Goldberg J.; Wigmore, Vol.VIII (McNaughton rev., 1961), para.2251; Report of the Royal Commission on Criminal Procedure, Cmnd.8092 (1981), para.4.51.

[247] cf. Redmayne's argument for a "disassociation" rationale ("Rethinking the Privilege Against Self-Incrimination" (2007) 27 O.J.L.S. 209). Redmayne does not ground his argument on the presumption of innocence, although his focus is similarly the value of a defendant's liberty not to co-operate with a prosecution. As he acknowledges, his argument faces a similar problem of potential over-inclusiveness.

[248] See, e.g. *Justice on Trial* (London: 1993), para.9.19. This report by the Independent Civil Liberty Panel on Criminal Justice relied also on the argument that the right to silence helps to protect the innocent from wrongful conviction.

[249] See Ch.7.

[250] M. McConville, A. Sanders and R. Leng, *The Case for the Prosecution* (1991), pp.67 onwards.

the innocent theory fails at the descriptive level; it is under-inclusive in accounting for the current scope of the privilege. Conversely, the theory based on the presumption of innocence is descriptively over-inclusive. It does not explain why, for example, the privilege does not extend to investigative processes concerned with the collection of real evidence by means of searches and the taking of fingerprints and samples. English law has taken the view that such evidence has great probative value, sufficient to justify the use of compulsory powers to obtain it. In this way public interests in truth-finding and the conviction of the guilty prevail over interests in maintaining the integrity of the principle that the suspect should not be used as a source of incriminating evidence.

One response might be that this presentation of the theory is overstated. Supporters of the theory might argue that it is concerned only with incrimination by compulsion of the suspect to disclose evidence that would otherwise be unobtainable. The theory, in other words, would be that the state may not compel the suspect to bring into existence incriminating communications (such as a confession) and may not therefore use a failure to communicate as incriminating evidence. On this basis the right to silence is justified, but evidence existing independently of the suspect's communications, such as fingerprints, would be obtainable by the state, which would be entitled to use compulsory powers to obtain it. However, it is not clear why the theory should be restricted in this way; there seems to be nothing in the premise of the presumption of innocence to justify it. Moreover the modification runs into difficulties over the protection for pre-existing documents. These exist independently of the suspect and constitute evidence obtainable by the state. If the privilege nonetheless enables the suspect to refuse to assist the investigation by producing them, it is not at all easy to see why the privilege should not permit the suspect to refuse to assist the investigation in other ways.[251]

5–046   The final point addresses a further argument that is focused exclusively on the right to silence. This is the claim that allowing positive inferences of guilt from silence is inconsistent with the burden of proof and the presumption of innocence. The claim can be considered at two levels. At the doctrinal level the argument clearly fails.[252] The legal burden of proof is not reversed by the restriction of the right to silence; if the tribunal of fact is left with a reasonable doubt after consideration of all the evidence, the accused must be given the benefit of it. It is not for the accused to "prove" innocence. The provisions of the Criminal Justice and Public Order Act 1994 do not affect this fundamental rule.[253] At the level of principle the objection to allowing inferences of guilt from silence in pre-trial investigations is right, but for the wrong reasons. The objection is developed more fully later; for the moment we can say that it rests on a combination of the potential unreliability of silence as evidence in this context and on the failure of police interviews to conform with principles of natural justice. Founding the objection on the presumption of innocence proves too much. It seems to imply a claim that it is necessarily improper to draw any inferences from a person's

---

[251] As Lord Bingham noted in *Brown v Stott* [2001] 2 All E.R. 97 at 116.
[252] C. R. Williams, "Silence in Australia: Probative Force and Rights in the Law of Evidence" (1994) 110 L.Q.R. 629, 637, 648.
[253] Confirmed by the Court of Appeal in *Cowan* [1996] Q.B. 373.

failure to explain away incriminating evidence. This is contrary both to common sense and to existing law. Common sense argues that if other evidence yields a prima facie inference of guilt a failure to provide an innocent explanation suggests that one does not exist.[254]

3. *Protection of privacy*

The idea that the privilege against self-incrimination protects substantive interests in privacy has received much support in the literature.[255] The underlying purpose and value is well summed up by Galligan:

5–047

> "privacy is important because it protects personal identity and autonomy. Without a zone of privacy, identity, autonomy, personality cannot exist. This is easily shown: suppose that your every action could be monitored, that every thought, urge and desire could be known and recorded, to be used for any purposes by a stranger. Identity and autonomy, let us use the general term personality, under such conditions would be seriously distorted if not destroyed. It follows that a zone of privacy is essential to personality … The right of silence serves privacy, which in turn serves this basic sense of personality."[256]

According to this view, privacy is sufficiently important to justify duties on others to respect it. Hence it may provide the ground for a privilege against self-incrimination; given that the police have no special relationship with the suspect, they have no claim on the information about the suspect's actions, thoughts and motives other than the general claim based on the collective interest in crime control. Galligan argues that this interest is not generally sufficient to justify serious incursions into privacy, particularly where the incursion takes the form of intrusion into consciousness through "prolonged and discursive" questioning. He suggests that there is no difference in principle between requiring the suspect to reveal disadvantageous information through speech, and plugging the suspect into a painless mind-reading machine. Both, he maintains, are procedures to which objection may be taken.[257]

However, this account of the privilege faces difficulties similar to those discussed in relation to the theory based on the presumption of innocence. We can begin with the question of scope. If the purpose is to protect privacy, it is hard to see why the privilege does not protect the suspect from having his person and property searched, or from having his fingerprints taken, or from having to provide samples of breath or other bodily substances. All these procedures involve invasions of interests in privacy, and this is true whether we conceive of privacy as meaning seclusion (the right to be let alone), or secrecy (the right not

---

[254] See, e.g. *Raviraj* (1987) 85 Cr.App.R. 93 (failure to explain possession of recently stolen goods yields prima facie inference of guilty knowledge; but, on the presumption of innocence theory, why does the privilege not apply in such a case?).

[255] R. S. Gerstein, "Privacy and Self-Incrimination" (1970) 80 *Ethics* 87; P. Arenella, "*Schmerber* and the Privilege Against Self-Incrimination" (1982) 20 Am.Crim. L.R. 31; D.J. Galligan, "The Right to Silence Reconsidered" [1988] C.L.P. 69.

[256] Galligan, "The Right to Silence Reconsidered" [1988] C.L.P. 69 at 88. For critical comment, see B. Robertson, "The Right to Silence Ill considered" (1991) 21 *Victoria University of Wellington* L.R. 139.

[257] Galligan, "The Right to Silence Reconsidered" [1988] C.L.P. 69, 89.

to give personal information), or some combination of both. Yet the privilege is not available in such cases. Therefore an unqualified claim that the privilege protects privacy is plainly over-inclusive.

5–048   A common response to this point is to say that privacy must be understood in a narrower sense of an interest in mental privacy. In other words the individual's right is one of freedom from intrusion into consciousness. Arenella, discussing the landmark case of *Schmerber v California*,[258] says that the decision distinguishes between "the individual's right to limit accessibility to his mind and his right to limit accessibility to his body".[259] He adds that the "focus on invasions of mental privacy accurately reflects the core value underlying the privilege's historical development".[260]

Whether or not the historical claim is accurate, this more limited theory is still problematic. Is it really true that personal privacy is more deeply or significantly infringed by questions, say, about a person's movements on a particular day, than by a strip search or the taking of a urine sample? As Stuntz has commented, this argument seems counter-intuitive.[261] Secondly, it is not easy to see how an interest in mental privacy justifies privilege for pre-existing documents. Can the argument for freedom from intrusion into consciousness coherently extend to a decision to hand over something that exists independently of the suspect's consciousness? Thirdly, as a rule of the law of evidence, the privilege protects against the use of compelled disclosures. If immunity from evidential use is granted, the privilege can be overridden.[262] But this limitation on the scope of the privilege does not make sense in the context of the protection of privacy. Because privacy is a substantive value, it should be the nature of the disclosure that is important, rather than its consequences.[263] Privacy is still infringed by a compelled communication, even if no evidential use is made of it. It follows that the protection of the privilege is significantly incomplete if the privacy theory is correct.

These problems may lead us to be justifiably suspicious of a theory that seeks to use an evidential principle as if it were a tortious remedy. Inevitably the principle will protect substantive rights in a partial and somewhat arbitrary fashion, because its application will depend on a host of factors that may influence the course and outcome of individual cases in unpredictable ways. Moreover, since English common law did not recognise a generic legal right to privacy,[264] a claim that the protection of privacy was the primary rationale of the common law evidential privilege against self-incrimination lacks conviction. To say this is not to say that privacy is unimportant, or to say that the law of evidence

---

[258] *Schmerber v California* (1966) 384 U.S. 757.
[259] Arenella, "*Schmerber* and the Privilege Against Self-Incrimination" (1982) 20 Am.Crim. L.R. 31, 41.
[260] Arenella, "*Schmerber* and the Privilege Against Self-Incrimination" (1982) 20 Am.Crim. L.R. 31, 41.
[261] W. Stuntz, "Self-Incrimination and Excuse" (1988) 88 Col. L.R. 1227, 1277.
[262] See, e.g. Theft Act 1968 s.31; *AT & T Istel v Tully* [1993] A.C. 45 HL.
[263] The point is clearly made by Stuntz, "Self-Incrimination and Excuse" (1988) 88 Col. L.R. 1227, 234.
[264] The lack of a general right to privacy at common law was confirmed in *Malone v Metropolitan Police Commissioner (No.2)* [1979] 2 W.L.R. 700.

has no role in its protection. Privacy of communication with a lawyer, for example, is a key element of a practical and effective right to legal advice.[265] Breach of privacy is a factor that might need to be taken into account in decisions whether to exclude evidence.[266]

4. *Protection from cruel choices*

A fourth theory is that the privilege prevents suspects from being subjected by the state to cruel choices.[267] In the context of police interrogation the choices would be, in the absence of the privilege, to lie in answer to questions, to refuse to answer and so prolong the interview, as well as run the risk of silence being interpreted as an admission of guilt, or to answer truthfully and incriminate oneself. The privilege enables the suspect to refuse to answer without the risk that adverse inferences may be drawn. A variation of this theory argues that the instinct for self-preservation is likely to cause suspects to lie, and that it is preferable to allow suspects to remain silent rather than positively to mislead the police.[268]

5–049

This theory transposes to the pre-trial context a familiar argument for the privilege being available to accused persons at trial. The avoidance of a "cruel trilemma" for defendants testifying on oath has received considerable support as a justifying argument from adherents of the privilege.[269] It does have the advantage of focusing clearly on the issue of communication. On this view the privilege should be available in the pre- trial context to ensure that decisions to make disclosures to the police, whether of admissions or of pre-existing documents, are truly voluntary. Procedures for the collection of other evidence, which do not depend on the choice of a suspect to disclose information, are outside the scope of the privilege. In this way the theory accounts for the scope of the privilege more coherently than any of the other theories we have examined.

However, the weakness of the theory is that, unlike the other theories, its underlying premise assumes that the suspect is guilty. An innocent suspect would, at least in theory, have nothing to lose by answering questions truthfully. There is therefore no cruelty involved in requiring the innocent suspect to speak. Once the

---

[265] In *Brennan v United Kingdom* (2001) 34 E.H.R.R. 507 the European Court of Human Rights found a violation of art.6 where a terrorist suspect's first consultation with his solicitor took place within the sight and earshot of a police officer who was in close proximity. The court stated at [58]: "an accused's right to communicate with his advocate out of hearing of a third person is part of the basic requirements of a fair trial".

[266] In *Khan (Sultan)* [1996] 3 All E.R. 289 the House of Lords held that evidence obtained by a breach of privacy in the form of taped conversations recorded by surveillance devices attached to a person's house was not inadmissible as a matter of law, but was subject to discretionary exclusion in a suitable case.

[267] K. Greenawalt, "Silence as a Moral and Constitutional Right" (1981) 23 *William and Mary Law Review* 15.

[268] cf. P. Westen and S. Mandell, "To Talk, to Balk, or to Lie: The Emerging Fifth Amendment Doctrine of the 'Preferred Response'" (1982) 19 Am. Crim. L.R. 521.

[269] *Murphy v Waterfront Commission* (1964) 378 U.S. 52 at 55; *Pennsylvania v Muniz* (1990) 110 S.Ct. 2638 at 2648; Westen and Mandell, "To Talk, to Balk, or to Lie" (1982) 19 Am. Crim. L.R. 521. The trilemma is the choice between punishment for perjury (lies on oath), punishment for contempt (silence on oath) or punishment for the offence (truthful incrimination).

true nature of the premise is recognised, the argument loses much of its claim to moral force. It becomes difficult to accept that the interest of a guilty person in escaping conviction by not disclosing evidence of the crime is worthy of official legal protection. Almost two centuries ago Bentham ridiculed arguments of this type, as founded on what he called "the old woman's reason"[270] or "the foxhunter's reason",[271] and suggested that neither had a serious claim to our attention.[272] This is still a persuasive critique, and it can be reinforced by the point that it is extremely hard to see how the state can justify giving priority to the interests of guilty suspects over those of their victims. From the perspective of the victim there is a double wrong perpetrated if the state refuses to vindicate the victim by placing evidential pressure on the offender to admit the offence.

5 *Legitimacy and abuse of power*

5–050 Despite the deficiencies of the justifications for the privilege discussed above it still exerts a powerful appeal. Many people would still regard it as expressing a fundamental principle about the relationship between a state and its citizens. In a number of jurisdictions the privilege has the status of a constitutional right. It appears in terms in the International Covenant on Civil and Political Rights cl.14(3)(g) of which states that a person has the right "not to be compelled to testify against himself or to confess guilt". As explained above, the European Court of Human Rights has introduced the privilege into the European Convention as part of the right to a fair hearing. However, none of these instruments does more than state a relatively bare general principle; it remains a matter of interpretation how far the primary and derivative applications of the privilege extend, and when, if ever, the privilege may be overruled.

Perhaps the way forward towards a critical principle should begin by noting a recurrent theme of the discussion so far. This is that there is an important distinction between custodial interrogation by the police involving direct demands for evidence (usually in the form of incriminating statements) and other procedures for the collection of incriminating evidence. We may then reflect further on the two arguments for the privilege as an element of due process. It was suggested above that an appeal to the value of the presumption of innocence was over-broad, and also failed to furnish an adequate explanation for distinctions between procedures for the collection of different types of evidence. By contrast an appeal to the importance of the protection of the innocent against wrongful conviction was under-inclusive, and also failed to acknowledge the likely ineffectiveness of the protection in most cases. However, an important sense of unease does seem to be reflected in the arguments founded on these values. It reflects a sentiment, ultimately founded on the political and moral values of liberal ideology, about power and propriety in criminal process where agencies of the state both investigate and adjudicate on the behaviour of citizens. The unease

---

[270] Namely, that it is a hardship on the defendant to require him to confess, truthfully, his guilt. Bentham was referring here to the accused's testimony at trial, but the point is transferable to the context of pre-trial questioning.

[271] Namely, that the defendant must be given a sporting chance to escape rightful conviction.

[272] Bowring (ed), *Rationale of Judicial Evidence* (1843), Vol.VII B.IX pp.452–454.

can perhaps be expressed in terms that, in an adversary system of criminal adjudication based on formal equality of parties, there is an inherent danger of unfairness in the state exploiting its enforcement power to place an individual in a vulnerable position. The vulnerability consists of a risk either that investigative powers may be used to obtain evidence that is factually unreliable or that they may be misused to compel the production of incriminating evidence by means inconsistent with the fundamental values of the criminal law. If either of the risks materialises, the legitimacy of the criminal verdict may be compromised.

If this danger is taken seriously it offers a possible contribution to the development of a critical principle. Before formulating the principle with more precision it is necessary to return for a moment to the two arguments for the privilege that are based on substantive values of privacy and freedom from cruel choices. Like the systemic rationales these both suffer from deficiencies as self-contained justifying accounts of the privilege against self-incrimination. However, there is an important common feature of the arguments that requires further emphasis. As we have seen the principal concern of the privilege is with the compulsion of suspects to co-operate in investigative procedures. The fundamental objection to the use of compulsion, reflected in the privacy and cruel choices arguments, is that it amounts to treating a suspect as an object for the extraction of evidence. On Kantian principles this is prima facie an infringement of the core value attached to the claims of all human beings to respect and dignity.

Recognising the validity of this claim does not commit us to saying that infringements can never be justified. As explained above, it would tend to defeat most of the aims of criminal justice if the accused could never be used as a source of incriminating evidence. As a practical reality it is very doubtful whether any society could afford to give effect to all possible primary and derivative applications of the privilege. It is therefore possible to say that the public interest in the enforcement of the criminal law by means of legitimate verdicts at criminal trials may provide the necessary justification for overriding the core value. On this basis the critical principles can be stated as follows. There should be no compulsion of persons to comply with procedures for the collection of evidence except where such procedures can be justified by reference to other values internal to the process of criminal adjudication. The relevant values would be the need to secure reliable evidence that is probative of guilt and the collection of such evidence by procedures based on natural justice to individuals or with other safeguards aimed at ensuring that state power is exercised in accordance with fundamental principles. It is submitted that these ideas constitute the heart of the concept of fairness in investigative processes.

5–051

Such critical principles have clear implications for the privilege against self-incrimination. They do not seek to argue that compulsion is never permissible. They concede the importance of the factual accuracy of criminal adjudications by allowing for procedures for the compulsory collection of reliable evidence probative of guilt. In this way procedures can be specified, for example, for fingerprinting, the taking of samples and the carrying-out of searches, all of which override a suspect's unwillingness to co-operate. The precise conditions under which such procedures can be carried out must depend on the weighting to be given to a number of variables. These will include the nature and degree of the risk of abuse of power, the extent to which important interests of the suspect, such as privacy, are infringed by the procedure, the ways in which those who exercise the procedure can be held accountable, the importance of the evidence and any circumstances of necessity for its collection or preservation.

It is in relation to custodial interrogation by the police that the potential for systemic abuse of law enforcement powers is greatest. As indicated earlier, there is a risk of considerable physical and psychological pressure being applied to suspects to co-operate by making incriminating statements or by handing over evidence such as documents. It is well-recognised that such pressure, if carried to extremes, may be inconsistent with the fundamental values of the criminal law and may in addition produce confessions that are unreliable. Moreover, even where no confession is forthcoming, it may be quite unsafe to draw adverse inferences from silence. This is therefore the context in which claims for primary and derivative applications of the privilege have the greatest cogency. But this is not to say that all questioning with an element of compulsion is necessarily unacceptable so as to require the application of the privilege. Judicial questioning of a suspect under conditions of natural justice, for example, does not in modern times present the same kind of risk of abuse of power or of unreliability. In this or a related context the claim that compulsory incrimination is unfair should therefore be given less weight when considering the extent to which the pursuit of factual accuracy of criminal adjudication should be compromised.

5–052 An important conclusion follows from this approach to the nature and operation of the privilege against self-incrimination. The privilege is characterised not as a "human right", a notion that in an unqualified form begs some difficult questions, but as a functional device required in some contexts by the need of the criminal justice system to retain its internal coherence. Adoption of this view entails some rethinking of the primary and derivative applications of the privilege. In some cases the boundaries will be drawn differently from those currently determined by a view of the privilege as a human right.[273] An example would be a notice from the police requiring the owner of a vehicle caught speeding on camera to identify its driver at the time. This is not a situation in which there is any significant risk of abuse of power. To say that there is a "human right" not to make such a disclosure seems to stretch the concept well beyond its proper limits and at the same time to trivialise it. Equally, however, the functional view of the privilege does not entail agreement with a "crime control" very restrictive approach. The curtailment of the right to silence in the police station is objectionable because of the risk of abuse of state power associated with custodial interrogation. Section 34 of the Criminal Justice and Public Order Act 1994 ought to be repealed as a matter of principle. The same objection does not

---

[273] In this connection it is interesting to note the claim by the European Court of Human Rights, stated rather than argued, that the rationale of the right to silence and the privilege against self-incrimination "lies, inter alia, in the protection of the accused against improper compulsion by the authorities thereby contributing to the avoidance of miscarriages of justice and to the fulfilment of the aims of Article 6": *Saunders v United Kingdom* (1997) 23 E.H.R.R. 313 at 68.

hold for inferences from failure to testify at trial where the procedural context of the accused's silence is wholly different. Section 35 of the Act is therefore supportable.[274]

---

[274] See Ch.13 for further discussion.

CHAPTER 6

CONFESSIONS[1]

---

[1] See P. Mirfield, *Silence, Confessions and Improperly Obtained Evidence* (Oxford, 1997) for valuable although partly dated discussion.

A. INTRODUCTION

1. *Confessions and criminal justice*

6–001   Confessions have a crucial function in the criminal justice process. The previous chapter showed that questioning of suspects is a central investigative strategy of the police, not least because it is frequently successful in eliciting statements that can be used in evidence against the suspect. The majority of suspects questioned by the police make full or partial admissions, and the great majority of those confessing go on to plead guilty at trial.[2] Guilty pleas are officially encouraged by the system of sentencing discounts because they contribute to the efficient processing of cases and relieve victims and witnesses from the stress of testifying at a contested trial. Where trials are contested, it was estimated some years ago that confession evidence is significant or crucial in 20–30 per cent of cases.[3] In some cases, including ones of great gravity, it may constitute virtually the whole of the prosecution case.[4] Even where there is independent evidence of the commission of an alleged criminal act, statements by the defendant in interview may be essential to establish mens rea.[5]

Confessions are therefore potent instruments for securing two fundamental goals of the criminal justice system, namely the conviction of the guilty and the protection of victims and potential victims of crime. They may also have other positive values. They may, for example, have psychological benefits for the suspects who make them. A study by Gudjonsson and Petursson of convicted prisoners in Iceland revealed that in more than a third of cases confessions were made in order to relieve feelings of guilt and of a need to talk about the offence to a person in authority.[6] Particularly significant in this context was the finding that "sex offenders confessed more frequently than other offenders because of a strong internal need to confess".[7] It may be dangerous to generalise from such a limited study, although Gudjonsson reported that he had replicated it in Northern Ireland with very similar results.[8] Certainly such findings suggest that the therapeutic possibilities of confession should not be overlooked, even if we might not wish to go as far as Wigmore, who asserted:

---

[2] See Ch.5 para.5–041 fnn.227–229 and accompanying text.

[3] M. McConville and J. Baldwin, *Courts, Prosecution and Conviction* (Oxford: Oxford University Press, 1981), pp.136–137. The figures for cases *dependent* on confession evidence may well be much lower: see M. McConville, *Corroboration and Confessions*, RCCJ Research Study No.13 (London, 1993), esp. p.87.

[4] As it did in the case of the Guildford Four: *Richardson, The Times*, October 20, 1989. For a recent example see *Wilding* [2010] EWCA Crim 2799.

[5] M. McConville, A. Sanders and R. Leng, *The Case for the Prosecution* (London), pp.67 onwards. See also C. Walker and D. Wall, "Imprisoning the Poor: Television Licence Evaders and the Criminal Justice System" [1997] Crim. L.R. 173, 178, on the importance of confessions in providing evidence of the offence of using a television without a licence.

[6] G. Gudjonsson, *The Psychology of Interrogations, Confessions and Testimony: A Handbook* (Chichester: John Wiley & Sons, 2003), pp.152–154.

[7] G. Gudjonsson, *The Psychology of Interrogations, Confessions and Testimony: A Handbook* (2003), p.153.

[8] G. Gudjonsson, *The Psychology of Interrogations, Confessions and Testimony: A Handbook* (2003), p.153.

> "[E]very guilty person is almost always ready and desirous to confess, as soon as he is detected and arrested . . . The nervous pressure of guilt is enormous . . . and when detection comes the pressure is relieved; and the deep sense of relief makes confession a satisfaction."[9]

Further support for this psychological point comes from professionals working in the area of child sexual abuse. Many would regard a voluntary admission of responsibility by an alleged abuser as a key factor in both the rehabilitation of the offender and the recovery of the victim.[10] Given that these are also important goals of criminal justice, the point strengthens the case for taking a positive view of the role of confessions.

However, despite the importance of their role, or perhaps because of it, **6–002** confessions are among the most significant causes of miscarriage of justice. In several of the notorious cases that came to light some years ago the Court of Appeal quashed convictions for murder and other serious offences in response to substantial doubts about the reliability of the confession evidence on which the defendants were convicted.[11] Cases such as the Guildford Four, the Birmingham Six, Judith Ward, the Tottenham Three and others raised a variety of issues about the dangers of confession evidence and about the adequacy of the legal regime regulating the obtaining and use of such evidence. These issues are set out and discussed later in the chapter.

2. *The meaning of "confession"*

The term "confession" has an extended meaning in the law of evidence. In **6–003** ordinary speech a confession is a frank admission of guilt, and in practice many confessions by suspects do consist of full acknowledgments of the commission of an offence. But the term is not restricted to this meaning. Section 82(1) of PACE defines "confession" to include "any statement wholly or partly adverse to the person who made it". Thus any incriminating statement falling short of a full acknowledgment of the commission of an offence is still treated as a confession for the purposes of the regulatory scheme established by PACE.[12] It follows that a mixed statement, consisting of partly incriminating and partly exculpatory elements, is also a "confession" for the purposes of PACE.[13] However, to qualify as a confession a statement must be adverse to its maker at the time it is made. A statement that is wholly exculpatory when made is not within the definition of a

---

[9] Vol.III (Chadbourn rev., 1970), para.851. Wigmore overstated his point, but it is undeniable that voluntary confessions prompted by guilt do occur and are occasionally reported as news items. One example is the case of Andrew Aiken who walked into a police station and confessed to the murder of a friend seven years earlier: *The Times*, September 9, 1997.

[10] D. Glaser and J. R. Spencer, "Sentencing, Children's Evidence and Children's Trauma" [1990] Crim. L.R. 371, 374.

[11] See I. Dennis, "Miscarriages of Justice and the Law of Confessions: Evidentiary Issues and Solutions" [1993] P.L. 291.

[12] Authoritative dicta stated that the same principle applied at common law: *Commissioners of Customs and Excise v Harz and Power* [1967] 1 A.C. 760 at 817–818 HL per Lord Reid; *Sharp* [1988] 1 All E.R. 65 at 68 HL per Lord Havers.

[13] *Sharp* [1988] 1 All E.R. 65 HL; *Aziz* [1996] 1 A.C. 41 at 50 HL per Lord Steyn.

confession.[14] It makes no difference if the statement can be shown subsequently to be a lie[15] or to be inconsistent with the accused's testimony at trial.[16] In *Hasan*,[17] Lord Steyn, with whom the other members of the House of Lords agreed, held that it would be a strained interpretation of s.82(1) to read "confession" to include a wholly exculpatory statement, which was not compelled by anything in the statutory context. He emphasised what he called the "unrestricted capability of s.78 to avoid injustice by excluding any evidence obtained by unfairness"[18]; this power could extend to excluding wholly exculpatory or neutral statements obtained by oppression.

Section 82(1) expressly states that a confession may be "made in words or otherwise". A nod of the head in response to a question such as "Did you take the purse?" will be just as much a confession as a spoken or written "Yes".[19] Similarly, the accused's silence, demeanour or conduct may amount to an implied admission of the truth of an accusation made in his presence,[20] and will thus have to satisfy the conditions of admissibility for a confession. One form of admission by conduct that has become increasingly prominent is a re-enactment by the accused of the offence. A voluntary demonstration by the accused, recorded on video, of how he committed the offence may provide compelling evidence of guilt. In *Li Shu-Ling v R.*,[21] the Privy Council confirmed that such a video-recording is admissible as a confession,[22] provided it is made clear to the accused beforehand that his participation is not compulsory and provided that he has an opportunity to view the recording after completion and have recorded any comments he wishes to make about the film.[23]

3. *The issues raised by confession evidence*

6–004   The miscarriage of justice cases show that confessions may present a variety of problems. These problems can be categorised under three broad headings: authenticity, legitimacy and reliability. The categories are analytically distinct in the sense that authenticity is concerned with the question whether an alleged confession was made at all and, if so, in what terms; legitimacy is concerned with the question whether the means used to procure the confession were lawful and fair; reliability is concerned with the question whether a legitimate confession is

---

[14] *Hasan* [2005] UKHL 22; [2005] 2 Cr.App.R. 22, rejecting the contrary view of the Court of Appeal in the court below, reported sub nom. *R. v Z* [2003] 2 Cr.App.R. 12; and approving *Sat-Bhambra* (1989) 88 Cr.App.R. 55 CA; and *Park* (1994) 99 Cr.App.R. 270 CA.

[15] *Sat-Bhambra* (1989) 88 Cr.App.R. 55; *Doncaster* [2008] EWCA Crim 5 at [35].

[16] *Park* (1994) 99 Cr.App.R. 270 CA.

[17] *Hasan* [2005] UKHL 22; [2005] 2 Cr.App.R. 22.

[18] *Hasan* [2005] UKHL 22; [2005] 2 Cr.App.R. 22 at [62].

[19] The type of example given by the CLRC to illustrate the application of the definition (Eleventh Report, p.214, Annex 2).

[20] See Ch.5.

[21] *Li Shu-Ling v R.*[1989] 1 A.C. 270.

[22] Provided the conditions of admissibility of confessions are satisfied; if illegal or unfair means have been used to secure a prior oral confession, they may have the effect of "tainting" the subsequent re-enactment: see *Lam Chi-Ming v R.* [1991] 2 A.C. 212 PC.

[23] If the re-enactment is preceded by an oral confession, as it usually will be, the video-recording should be made reasonably soon afterwards.

true or false. In practice, cases may well give rise to more than one of these issues, as when a defendant alleges that he was induced by unlawful means into making a confession that was in fact untrue. There are also several ancillary issues concerning confessions, mostly concerning the scope and consequences of a ruling that confession evidence is inadmissible. These issues are dealt with towards the end of this chapter.

The authenticity of a confession is called into question when a defendant alleges that it was fabricated. Fabrication may take a number of forms and it may relate to the whole or part only of the confession. One form is the invention of an alleged oral admission, the practice often referred to as "verballing". This is a long-standing problem in England. Its existence was noted by both the Criminal Law Revision Committee[24] and the Royal Commission on Criminal Procedure,[25] and it was one of the main abuses that PACE aimed to eradicate by the introduction of the regulatory regime that now includes the taping of all interviews in police stations. This measure is discussed further below. An example of the problem comes from the Birmingham Six case, in which two of the defendants claimed that they were the victims of police "verbals".[26] A second form of fabrication consists of tampering with a written statement after it has been signed by the defendant. In the Birmingham Six and Tottenham Three cases evidence was presented to the Court of Appeal that pages containing incriminating remarks appeared to have been added to the defendants' statements after they had been signed.[27] A third form, which shades into the legitimacy issue, may occur where a police officer writes out a confession that the defendant claims to have been coerced or tricked into signing.

Despite Wigmore's claims about the willingness of suspects to confess, it is apparent that some pressure or encouragement is inevitable in police interviewing, and is likely to be necessary in some cases if suspects are to make admissions.[28] The issue then arises of the proper limits of that pressure and of the legitimacy of admitting in evidence a confession obtained in breach of them. Again the miscarriage of justice cases demonstrate the range of problems involved. The defendants in the Guildford Four and Birmingham Six cases alleged that their written confessions were extracted from them by the use of one or more of various improper inducements. This term is used here to refer to unacceptable manipulative techniques of interrogation. These include directly coercive practices such as overt torture and violence, intimidation, degrading treatment, sleep deprivation, sustained lengthy periods of interrogation and other forms of oppression. They may also include threats and promises about such matters as the grant or refusal of bail, the number and gravity of charges, the involvement of members of the suspect's family, and so on. Manipulative techniques may in some cases, although not necessarily, be combined with denials of the suspect's rights of due process. There may be a failure by the police

---

[24] At Eleventh Report para.52(ii).
[25] RCCP Report, p.70. For judicial acknowledgment of the existence of the problem, see *Turner* (1975) 61 Cr.App.R. 67 at 76–77 per Lawton L.J.
[26] See Dennis, "Miscarriages of Justice" [1993] P.L. 291, 295–296.
[27] "Miscarriages of Justice" [1993] P.L. 291, 296–297, 300.
[28] G. Gudjonsson, *The Psychology of Interrogations, Confessions and Testimony: A Handbook* (2003), p.627.

to caution the suspect, a failure to advise of the right to legal advice, an unjustified refusal of access to a lawyer, and so on. The use of inducements and denials of due process in the interviewing of suspects presents difficult problems for the law of evidence and has led to the development of a complex legal regime.

6–005 The third main issue is the reliability of the confession. Is it true or false? Every police officer of any experience knows that some voluntary confessions are completely false. The story is often told of how more than 200 people falsely confessed to the kidnapping of the Lindbergh baby.[29] Such anecdotal experience is backed by a substantial body of research showing a number of possible reasons why people may make false confessions.[30] First, confessions may be volunteered to well-publicised crimes; in such cases they tend to be made by persons seeking notoriety or suffering from generalised guilt feelings or indulging in criminal fantasies. Judith Ward's voluntary incriminating statements are a clear example of this type of unreliable confession.[31] Other unreliable confessions may come from persons subjected to stress and fatigue, particularly vulnerable suspects such as juveniles, and persons suffering from mental disability or mental disorder. Stress appears to be a key factor in many false confessions. Gudjonsson, a distinguished forensic psychologist with much experience in miscarriage of justice cases, has developed the theory of interrogative suggestibility.[32] Certain people, he argues, have a psychological make-up which makes it difficult for them to resist the pressure of interrogation. This pressure is present to some degree in all formal interviews but may be increased by the police deliberately for suspects whom they believe to be guilty of serious crimes. Some suspects are by nature more willing to accept suggestions made by their interrogators. The risk is that they will then make a false confession, which may be one of two types.

A "coerced-compliant" confession may result from aggressive questioning of a compliant and suggestible suspect. Such a person may tell the police what he thinks they want to hear in order to please those in authority or to gain some short-term advantage: release, bail or simply the ending of a situation the suspect finds intolerable. No thought may be given to the consequences of confessing or there may be a belief that the record can be put right later. Gudjonsson suggested that Carole Richardson (of the Guildford Four) and Hugh Callaghan (of the Birmingham Six) were both false confessors of this type.[33] Characteristically, the confession is retracted once the stress induced by the interrogation has dissipated. The other type is the "coerced-internalised" confession. The suspects in these cases believe, at least temporarily, that they are guilty of the offences to which they have confessed. Such confessions may be the product of one or more of a number of factors, e.g. mental confusion, intoxication, bad memory, suggestibility, immaturity, generalised guilt feelings. A compliant suspect who confesses may come later to believe the confession; Carole Richardson is again a case in

---

[29] S. M. Kassin and L. S. Wrightsman, "Confession Evidence" in S.M. Kassin and L.S. Wrightsman (eds), *The Psychology of Evidence and Trial Procedure* (Sage Publications, 1985), pp.67, 76.

[30] RCCJ Report, p.57.

[31] *Ward* [1993] 1 W.L.R. 619 CA.

[32] G. Gudjonsson, *The Psychology of Interrogations, Confessions and Testimony: A Handbook* (2003), Ch.14.

[33] Dennis, "Miscarriages of Justice" [1993] P.L. 291, 303.

point.[34] The suggestibility scale developed by Gudjonsson does give some indication of how an individual is likely to react to a given situation when asked leading questions and subjected to interrogative pressure. When he administered the relevant tests to all the members of the Birmingham Six, the two who obtained significantly low scores were the same two who did not sign written confessions but who were alleged to have made oral admissions.

It follows that the characteristics and personality of the defendant and the circumstances and style of the interview may be relevant in determining both whether a confession was improperly induced and whether the confession is reliable. This point has implications for the admissibility and use of expert psychological and psychiatric evidence on behalf of the defence. In *Blackburn*,[35] the Court of Appeal stated that the phenomenon of coerced-compliant confessions fell outside the experience of a jury and was therefore a topic on which expert evidence was admissible. In this case the court accepted the evidence of a forensic psychologist that coerced-compliant confessions might be made by normal persons not suffering from any personality disorder or abnormal suggestibility, but rendered compliant, in the face of aggressive questioning, by fatigue and vulnerability due to age or other factors.

We now turn to the law that regulates the obtaining, admissibility and use of evidence of confessions. This law was substantially recast by the Police and Criminal Evidence Act 1984 ("PACE"). PACE replaced the voluntariness rule at common law[36] with a new rule of admissibility and provided for the issue of detailed Codes of Practice to replace the inadequate Judges Rules relating to the exercise of police powers of detention, treatment and questioning of suspects. It should be noted that PACE applies the Codes also to persons other than police officers who are charged with the duty of investigating offences or charging offenders. It is a question of fact who falls within this wording[37]; the list includes Customs officials,[38] Inland Revenue officers conducting "*Hansard*" interviews,[39] commercial investigators employed by companies to investigate possible crimes,[40] and store detectives, depending on the terms of their employment.[41] The new regime generated much case law in the first few years of its operation. Many of the cases have been concerned to clarify the scope and application of the rule of admissibility in s.76(2), but the majority of appeals have sought to take advantage of the general exclusionary discretion introduced by s.78. That section was discussed in Ch.3 where the point was made that a substantial amount of the

6–006

---

[34] Dennis, "Miscarriages of Justice" [1993] P.L. 291, 303.

[35] *Blackburn* [2005] 2 Cr.App.R. 30.

[36] This rule stated that the prosecution could not give in evidence a confession by the accused unless the prosecution could prove that it was a voluntary statement in the sense that it had not been obtained from the accused by fear of prejudice or a hope of advantage excited or held out by a person in authority or by oppression. The leading cases establishing the modern rule were *Ibrahim v R.* [1914] A.C. 599 PC; *DPP v Ping Lin* [1976] A.C. 574 HL; *Callis v Gunn* [1964] 1 Q.B. 495 CCA. For criticism and reform proposals, substantially enacted in PACE, see CLRC, Eleventh Report paras 53–66; RCCP Report paras 4.68–4.73, 4.131–4.135.

[37] *Seelig and Spens* [1992] 1 W.L.R. 148 at 158; *Bayliss* (1994) 98 Cr.App.R. 235 CA.

[38] *Sanusi* [1992] Crim. L.R. 43.

[39] *Gill* [2004] 1 Cr.App.R. 20.

[40] *Twaites and Brown* (1991) 92 Cr.App.R. 106.

[41] *Bayliss* (1994) 98 Cr.App.R. 235.

jurisprudence of exclusionary discretion is concerned with evidence of incriminating statements made by defendants to police and other law enforcement officials.

B.   SECTION 76: THE RULES OF ADMISSIBILITY

1.   *Confessions admissible as exceptions to the hearsay rule*

6–007   Exposition of the law begins with s.76(1) of PACE:

> "In any proceedings a confession made by an accused person may be given in evidence against
> him in so far as it is relevant to any matter in issue in the proceedings and is not excluded by
> the court in pursuance of this section."

The effect of the subsection is to enact the common law rule that a confession is admissible against its maker as an exception to the hearsay rule. The traditional rationale for admitting hearsay of this type is the same as for any admission by a party to litigation, namely that a person would not generally admit something against his interest unless it were true.[42] The fact that some confessions may be false does not seriously detract from the essential common sense underlying this claim. It does, however, put us on notice that certain safeguards may be needed if there is reason to think that a confession may be untrue.

PACE did not maintain one aspect of the common law relating to confessions. Section 82(1), which provides the definition of a confession, states that it is immaterial whether or not the confession is made to a person in authority. This provision gave effect to a recommendation of the Criminal Law Revision Committee to reverse the old common law rule that inducements to confess only rendered a confession involuntary, and therefore inadmissible, if they emanated from a person in authority such as a police officer.[43] It does not now matter to whom a confession was made. If the prosecution wish to rely upon it they must satisfy the rule of admissibility in s.76(2).

6–008   Subsection (1) states that a confession made by an accused is admissible "against him". These words give effect to the common law rule that a confession is admissible only against its maker and not against anyone else such as a co-accused who may be named in it.[44] A judge who admits under this provision a confession made by D1 must give the jury a formal direction that the confession

---

[42] CLRC Eleventh Report para.53. This argument goes to the reliability of such hearsay statements. For a second reason going to the fairness of admitting such statements see J. C. Smith, "Exculpatory Statements and Confessions" [1995] Crim. L.R. 280, 282, arguing that under the adversary theory of litigation a party cannot complain about the use against himself of his own hearsay statements.

[43] A "person in authority" was, broadly, anyone with authority over the accused or over the investigation of the offence or over the prosecution for the offence (*Deokinanan v R.* [1969] 1 A.C. 20). This definition led to much technicality which the CLRC considered to serve no useful purpose (Eleventh Report para.58); note, however, that echoes of the concept linger on in the notions of torture, and inhuman or degrading treatment, impliedly by officials, under s.76(2)(a) of PACE.

[44] *Gunewardene* (1951) 35 Cr.App.R. 80 CCA; *Spinks* [1982] 1 All E.R. 587.

may only be used in considering the guilt of D1, and may not be used in considering the case against D2, even if the jury know that D2 has been named in it.[45]

The rationale of this rule is based partly on fairness to the co-accused, who had no opportunity to challenge a confession by another made out of court in his absence, and partly on reliability. The parts of D1's confession that incriminate D2 are not against D1's interest, and therefore the assumption of their likely truth does not apply. Moreover, there is a real risk that D1 will have had a motive for casting blame on D2.[46] However, the rule is qualified, and is subject to other hearsay exceptions. First, if the confession is made in the co-accused's presence, his reaction to it may amount to an admission of the truth of the parts that accuse him of complicity, under the principle discussed in Ch.5. Secondly, in cases of conspiracy or joint venture, statements by one conspirator or joint venturer in furtherance of the common purpose are admissible against other conspirators or joint venturers to prove the the nature and scope of the common purpose, although not their participation in the conspiracy or joint venture, under the doctrine of implied agency. This is considered further in Ch.17. The third qualification derives from the majority decision of the House of Lords in *Hayter*.[47]

In this case Hayter (D2) was charged with murder, on the basis that he was the middleman between Ryan (D1), the alleged killer of the partner (P) of Bristow (D3), who had taken out a contract for P's death. The prosecution's evidence against D1 consisted entirely of admissions alleged to have been made to his girlfriend, which incriminated D2 and D3. It was accepted that the evidence against D2 was circumstantial, and that the case against him depended on the prosecution being able to prove that D1 was the killer and D3 the procurer. The trial judge directed the jury that D1's confession was not evidence against D2, but he also said that if the jury concluded that D1 was the killer, on the basis of his admissions, they could use the fact of D1's guilt in considering the guilt of D2. On appeal a bare 3–2 majority of the House of Lords held that the direction was correct and dismissed D2's appeal. For the majority there was a difference between using the contents of D1's confession in evidence against D2 to "confront" his defence (a use prohibited by the common law rule), and using it to establish D1's own guilt and then using the fact of his guilt as a building block in the case against D2, which should be permitted. The decision of the majority was much influenced by the existence of s.74 of PACE.[48] This allows the prosecution to prove the *conviction* of another person for an offence where it is relevant to any issue in the proceedings against the accused to show that the other committed the offence in question. Accordingly Lords Steyn and Brown (with whom Lord Bingham agreed) argued that since the prosecution would have been able to use D1's conviction for murder of P at D2's trial, had D1 been tried separately before D2 and convicted, policy suggested they should be able to achieve the same effect in a joint trial. In support of this conclusion is the point that in a joint trial

---

[45] *Jefferson* [1994] 1 All E.R. 270 CA.
[46] See Lord Brown in *Hayter* [2005] UKHL 6; [2005] 2 Cr.App.R. 3 at [85].
[47] *Hayter* [2005] UKHL 6; [2005] 2 Cr.App.R. 3.
[48] Discussed in Ch.20.

D2 is in a better position to challenge the evidence pointing to D1's guilt and does not incur the burden of proof he would have where s.74 applies.[49] Lords Steyn and Brown also argued that if in the joint trial D1's guilt were established by evidence other than his confession (an eyewitness, fingerprint, etc.) the judge would be entitled to direct the jury that they could take account of their finding of D1's guilt in considering the case against D2. It would be illogical if the jury could not do this where D1's guilt was proved by his confession.

6–009   For the minority in *Hayter*, Lords Rodger and Carswell, this reasoning simply amounted to turning inadmissible evidence into admissible evidence, thereby obliterating the hearsay rule as it applies to statements of co-defendants in a joint trial. Lord Rodger thought that it was not for the House of Lords in its judicial capacity to effect such a destruction of the rule, particularly given the very recent reforms to the hearsay rule made by Parliament in the Criminal Justice Act 2003, which had not included what was now being done.[50] This, with respect, is a formal approach to the issue. Its merit is called into question by Lord Carswell's concession that "adherence to the accepted principles of the common law governing the admission and exclusion of evidence in criminal trials may well result in the acquittal of a defendant against whom the evidence, if admitted, would make a strong case for his guilt".[51] We should be sceptical of any evidential rule that excludes strongly probative evidence of guilt (or innocence). In line with the theory of legitimacy set out in Ch.2 we should consider excluding such evidence only where there is a substantial risk that the evidence will be unreliable or its admission will imperil the moral or expressive authority of the verdict. It is suggested that there is no such risk in a case like *Hayter*, and for that reason the decision of the majority should be regarded as correct in principle.[52] However, the principle in *Hayter* may be restricted to cases of alleged joint offences. Alternatively, or in addition, the principle may not be applicable to a mixed statement by a co-accused, where it is the exculpatory part of the confession that tends to implicate the defendant. *Hayter* was distinguished on both these grounds by the Privy Council in *Persad v Trinidad and Tobago*,[53] where the issue was which of three defendants was guilty of an offence of buggery carried out by one of them during a joint robbery. Persad was implicated as to the buggery by confessional statements from his co-accused, notably Kelly. The Privy Council held that the trial judge should have ruled that Kelly's statement could not be used in the case against Persad since the buggery was not alleged to be a joint offence, and the exculpatory part of Kelly's confession was not a declaration against his interest and was therefore "materially less likely to be true".[54]

     Fourthly, the scheme for admissibility of hearsay evidence in the Criminal Justice Act 2003 now enables a hearsay statement to be admitted under

---

[49] A point made by Birch, commenting on the decision of the Court of Appeal in *Hayter* [2003] Crim. L.R. 887, cited with approval by Lords Steyn and Brown.

[50] See *Hayter* [2005] 2 Cr.App.R. 3 at [54]–[57].

[51] *Hayter* [2005] 2 Cr.App.R. 3 at [77].

[52] For other approval of the majority decision see McGourlay, "Is criminal practice impervious to logic?: *R. v Hayter*" (2006) 10 E. & P. 128.

[53] *Persad v Trinidad and Tobago* [2007] UKPC 51; [2008] 1 Cr.App.R. 9.

[54] *Persad v Trinidad and Tobago* [2007] UKPC 51; [2008] 1 Cr.App.R. 9 at [18].

s.114(1)(d) "in the interests of justice". In *R. v Y*,[55] the Court of Appeal confirmed that this is a general provision capable of applying to a confession by a co-accused. However, the court emphasised that this does not mean that police interviews of one defendant can routinely be admitted against another defendant. In applying the "interests of justice" test the judge must have regard to the factors listed in s.114(2). These include the reliability of the maker of the statement, the circumstances in which the statement was made, and the difficulty for a co-accused in challenging the statement. The court thought that "in the great majority of cases" such factors would point away from admission of a confession against any person other than its maker.[56] Accordingly, if the prosecution fails to persuade the court to admit the confession under this provision, it remains admissible under s.76(1) of PACE only against its maker, and a jury must be directed that it is not evidence against anyone else named in it.[57]

So far we have referred to the prosecution leading evidence of the confession as part of their affirmative case against the accused. Subsection (1) does not, however, expressly restrict the use of the confession in this way. The subsection says nothing about the position of a co-accused. Can one accused (D1) make use of a confession by another accused (D2) if the confession is relevant to D1's defence? This apparently simple question is in fact analytically complex. Further discussion is postponed to the end of the chapter until the use of confession evidence by the prosecution has been considered in full.

2. *Prohibited methods of obtaining confessions—procedural issues*

Section 76(2) replaced the voluntariness rule at common law. It deals with the methods used to obtain confessions and requires the prosecution to prove that the actual confession in question was not obtained by the methods prohibited by the section: **6–010**

> "If, in any proceedings where the prosecution proposes to give in evidence a confession made by an accused person, it is represented to the court that the confession was or may have been obtained—
> (a) by oppression of the person who made it; or
> (b) in consequence of anything said or done which was likely, in the circumstances existing at the time, to render unreliable any confession which might be made by him in consequence thereof, the court shall not allow the confession to be given in evidence against him except in so far as the prosecution proves to the court beyond reasonable doubt that the confession (notwithstanding that it may be true) was not obtained as aforesaid."[58]

The words "represented to the court" envisage the defence specifically raising the issue, either by directly alerting the prosecution before the trial, or by formal

[55] *R. v Y* [2008] EWCA Crim 10; [2008] 2 All ER 484, explaining *McLean* [2007] EWCA Crim 219; [2008] 1 Cr.App.R. 11.
[56] *R. v Y* [2008] EWCA Crim 10 at [57].
[57] To avoid the risk of prejudice to a co-accused named in a confession it may be edited at the judge's discretion: see *Silcott* [1987] Crim. L.R. 765; *Jefferson* [1994] 1 All E.R. 270.
[58] PACE s.76(2) applies equally to trial on indictment and summary trial. It does not apply in committal proceedings: s.76(9), inserted by Criminal Procedure and Investigations Act 1996 Sch.1 Pt II para.25.

submission at the trial. Cross-examination of prosecution witnesses with a view to showing that the confession was obtained by one of the prohibited methods does not amount by itself to a representation.[59] Once the defence has raised the issue the burden is on the prosecution to prove the factual conditions of admissibility laid down in the section. These conditions must be proved to the normal criminal standard of proof beyond reasonable doubt. Under s.76(3) the court is given power to raise the issue of its own motion and to require the prosecution to prove the admissibility of the confession under s.76(2). A court might do this, for example, in a case where the defendant in a magistrates' court is not legally represented.

The defendant may want to challenge evidence of his confession on grounds both of legitimacy and authenticity. He may claim that he did not make the confession and that it was not voluntary because of police ill-treatment of him at the time. The Privy Council has made it clear that these claims are not necessarily contradictory:

> "In all cases where the accused denies authorship of the contents of a written statement but complains that the signature or signatures on the document which he admits to be his own were improperly obtained from him by threat or inducement, he is challenging the prosecution's evidence on both grounds and there is nothing in the least illogical or inconsistent in his doing so."[60]

6–011   In *Thongjai v R.*,[61] the Privy Council extended this analysis to the case of oral admissions.[62] If the defendant claims that he did not make the alleged oral admission, and that he was ill-treated by the police before or at the time of the alleged admission, he is regarded as raising two issues that are not mutually exclusive. Given the division of functions in a jury trial between judge and jury, the legitimacy issue has to be taken first. As the court explained, the judge first has to decide whether, on the assumption that the alleged admission was made, it is inadmissible as a matter of law.[63] "The second issue, which is for the jury to decide if the judge rules that the alleged admission is admissible in evidence, is whether the admission was in fact made."[64]

Since an issue of fact is involved under s.76(2) the court will almost certainly have to hear evidence of the making of the confession. This will be done under the procedure known as the voir dire, or the trial within the trial.[65] A defendant

---

[59] See *R. v Liverpool Juvenile Court Ex p. R* [1988] Q.B. 1.

[60] *Ajodha v The State* [1982] A.C. 204 at 220 per Lord Bridge.

[61] *Thongjai v R.* [1997] 3 W.L.R. 667.

[62] As the High Court of Australia had already done in *MacPherson v R.* (1981) 147 C.L.R. 512.

[63] Or, presumably, excluded in the exercise of the statutory or common law discretion.

[64] *Thongjai v R.* [1997] 3 W.L.R. 667 at 673.

[65] See para.4–006 above. Note that the issue of fact whether a confession is true or false is a question for the jury and does not by itself normally present a problem of admissibility; nor does a challenge by the accused only to the authenticity of an alleged confession; if the prosecution say that the defendant made an oral admission and the defendant says that he did not, the issue is again a question of fact for the jury (*Ajodha v The State* [1982] A.C. 204 at 222). This is subject to a possible application by the defendant under s.78 of PACE for exclusion of the evidence of the alleged confession. Such an application will be determined by the judge in the absence of the jury and may necessitate a voir dire if the facts relevant to the issue of exclusion are in dispute. For a case where the judge did not hold a voir dire but should have done see *Dhorajiwala* [2010] EWCA Crim 1237. It seems clear that in the

who challenges the legitimacy of the methods used to obtain the confession will invariably have to testify on the voir dire. It is only by giving his side of the story that a defendant will stand a realistic chance of persuading the judge that there is at least a reasonable doubt on the issue.

This in turn raises questions about the scope of the voir dire and its relationship with the main trial before the jury. The first of these questions is whether the prosecution may cross-examine the accused on the voir dire as to the *truth* of the confession, in addition to questioning him about the making of the confession. The common law authorities conflicted, with a majority of the Privy Council in *Wong Kam-Ming v R.*,[66] saying "No" and rejecting the decision to the contrary of the Court of Criminal Appeal in *Hammond*.[67] PACE does not deal directly with this issue, but s.76(2) of PACE does provide that the truth of the confession is immaterial to its admissibility. This supports the Privy Council's view in principle, and there are dicta of the Court of Appeal after PACE to the effect that *Wong Kam-Ming* is strong persuasive authority that the accused should not be cross-examined on the voir dire as to the truth of his confession.[68]

The second question is then whether, in the main trial, the prosecution can lead evidence of statements by the accused on the voir dire, or cross-examine the accused on his statements on the voir dire. This question raises tricky problems where the accused makes any kind of incriminating statement on the voir dire. Such a statement will constitute a (further) confession under the wide definition in s.76(1), which results in that confession being admissible for the prosecution if the conditions of admissibility in s.76(2) are satisfied. Invariably they will be, because questioning of the accused on the voir dire is highly unlikely to amount to oppression or things said or done likely to render any confession by the accused unreliable. Thus it seems that the express wording of s.76 has displaced the second part of the decision in *Wong Kam-Ming*. This was that the prosecution could not lead evidence of statements by the accused on the voir dire, and could cross-examine on such statements only in the situation where the out-of-court confession is admitted in the main trial and the accused then testifies inconsistently with his statements on the voir dire.[69] On the argument just put, this part of the decision continues only in respect of statements that are not in any way adverse to the accused.

However, ss.78 and/or 82(3) of PACE may come to the rescue of an accused who claims that he was unfairly placed in the position of not being able to challenge the admissibility of the out-of-court confession without running the risk of statements made in the course of the challenge being used against him in the main trial. In this way it could be argued that the virtual necessity to give

---

Crown Court the judge must decide the admissibility question before the jury hear evidence of the confession: *Manji* [1990] Crim. L.R. 512. In magistrates' courts the decision may be postponed whether the defence is relying on s.76 or s.78 as grounds for exclusion: *R. v Liverpool Juvenile Court Ex p. R* [1988] Q.B. 1 (s.76); *Vel v Owen* (1987) 151 J.P. 510 (s.78); P. Mirfield, *Silence, Confessions and Improperly Obtained Evidence* (Oxford, 1997), pp.40–43.
[66] *Wong Kam-Ming v R.* [1980] A.C. 247.
[67] *Hammond* [1941] 3 All E.R. 318.
[68] *Davis* [1990] Crim. L.R. 860; *Cox* [1991] Crim. L.R. 276.
[69] In *Brophy* [1982] A.C. 476, the House of Lords confirmed that *Wong Kam-Ming v R.* correctly stated English law on the point.

evidence on the voir dire results in the accused effectively being deprived of the right not to testify before the jury. Even after the restriction on the right to silence at trial made by s.35 of the Criminal Justice and Public Order Act 1994, this argument has considerable force and could be reinforced by the recognition given by the European Court of Human Rights to the privilege against self-incrimination as an essential component of the right to a fair trial. An exclusionary discretion may be the best way of dealing with the problem,[70] short of a legislative amendment to s.76 restating the second part of the decision in *Wong Kam-Ming*.[71]

6–012   The final point in this section is that if the judge rejects a defence claim that a confession should be excluded by reason of impropriety in the way that it was obtained, the defence may revive the question of impropriety before the jury. Until the decision of the House of Lords in *Mushtaq*,[72] it was thought that this did not enable the defence to invite the jury to disregard the confession on the ground only that it was obtained improperly. Rather, the law was that the defence could argue that the confession was factually unreliable because of the way that it was obtained. The judge would then direct the jury to consider the evidence of the circumstances in which the confession was made in deciding upon the weight to be given to the confession.[73] In *Mushtaq*, the trial judge had admitted D's confession after ruling on a voir dire that the prosecution had proved that the confession had not been obtained by oppression as D alleged. In the trial D cross-examined the police officers concerned putting to them the same allegations of oppression, which they strenuously denied. D did not give evidence. The judge directed the jury in accordance with the law just stated and followed the then Judicial Studies Board model direction by saying that if the jury were sure that the confession was true, they could rely upon it even if it was or might have been made as a result of oppression or other improper circumstances. On appeal a majority of the House of Lords held that this was a misdirection.[74] Disapproving the earlier authorities, Lord Rodger, with whom Lord Steyn and Lord Phillips agreed, considered that the judge is now required to tell the jury that if they think that the confession was, or may have been, obtained by oppression or other improper means as described by the defendant in evidence, then they must disregard it.[75] It is necessarily implicit in the view of the majority that the jury must do this even if they think that the confession is in fact true.

---

[70] cf. P. Mirfield, *Silence, Confessions and Improperly Obtained Evidence* (1997), pp.71–75.

[71] In *Brophy* [1982] A.C. 476, a decision at common law, Lord Fraser emphatically rejected an argument that the availability of exclusionary discretion would ameliorate any prejudice to the accused arising from a decision to permit the use in the main trial of statements made by him on the voir dire (at 483). He preferred to regard as absolute the accused's right to give evidence at the voir dire without affecting his right to remain silent at the substantive trial.

[72] *Mushtaq* [2005] UKHL 25; [2005] 2 Cr.App.R. 32.

[73] The leading cases were *Chan Wai-Keung v R.* [1967] 2 A.C. 160 PC; *Burgess* [1968] 2 Q.B. 112 CA; *Prasad v R.* [1981] 1 W.L.R. 469 PC.

[74] Although all the Lords agreed that since there was no evidence of oppression or any other improper means (D had given no evidence and the police witnesses had denied the claims put to them) the misdirection could not have affected the fairness of the trial or the safety of D's conviction. His appeal was therefore dismissed.

[75] *Mushtaq* [2005] UKHL 25; [2005] 2 Cr.App.R. 32 at [55]. See also Lord Carswell at [75].

This is a troubling decision because it appears to duplicate the function of judge and jury, and to allow the jury to second-guess the judge on the issue of how the confession was obtained. We need therefore to examine the reasoning of the majority. Lord Rodger employed two arguments in support of his conclusion. The first was what he regarded as the logic of PACE. In his view the object of s.76(2) is to prevent a confession obtained by improper means from playing any part in the jury's verdict. Accordingly, "it flies in the face of that policy to say that a jury are entitled to rely on a confession even though, as the ultimate arbiters of all matters of fact, they properly consider that it was, or may have been, obtained by oppression or any other improper means".[76] However, as Lord Hutton pointed out, this interpretation is not what was intended by the Criminal Law Revision Committee, which provided the draft clause on which s.76(2) is based.[77] Under its scheme the test set out in s.76(2) is a test for the admissibility of evidence, which is a matter for the judge. The reference in the provision to "the court" confirms the point[78]; this is apt to refer to the judge in a trial on indictment or the magistrates in a summary trial. When Parliament intends a statutory provision dealing with decisions about evidence to extend to a jury the legislation generally refers to "a court or jury".[79] Secondly, to describe the jury as "the ultimate arbiters of fact" simply begs the question; the history of s.76(2) and the meaning of "court" suggest strongly that Parliament intended to allocate two distinct questions of fact to two different decision-makers.

Lord Rodger's second argument, also adopted by Lord Carswell, was based on **6–013** art.6 of the ECHR. Their Lordships reasoned that if the jury could rely on a confession, which they thought was or might have been obtained by oppression or other improper means, they would be acting unlawfully under s.6 of the Human Rights Act 1998 because they would be acting in a way that was incompatible with a defendant's right against self-incrimination as implied in art.6. Now it is certainly possible to found the rule against coerced confessions on the privilege against self-incrimination,[80] although other rationales for the rule are equally possible. But this concession does not mean that the argument must succeed. The argument turns on two assumptions: that where a court is composed of judge and jury they have separate and distinct identities as a "public authority" for the purposes of s.6(3) of the Human Rights Act, and that art.6 of the ECHR requires both decision-makers to protect the right against self-incrimination. These assumptions are challenged by Lord Hutton, who describes the first one as artificial, and the second as not mandated by the Strasbourg jurisprudence. His analysis of these assumptions[81] is convincing. Strasbourg has made it clear that it is for national law to lay down rules of evidence. Under the common law system of procedure:

---

[76] *Mushtaq* [2005] UKHL 25; [2005] 2 Cr.App.R. 32 at [46].
[77] See CLRC Report, paras 2 and 12.
[78] As Lord Carswell pointed out *Mushtaq* [2005] UKHL 25; [2005] 2 Cr.App.R. 32 at [69].
[79] For recent examples see Criminal Justice Act 2003 ss.100(2)(a), 102, 105(1)(a), etc.
[80] There is common law (*Lam Chi-Ming v R.* [1991] 2 A.C. 212 PC) and Strasbourg (*Saunders v United Kingdom* (1997) 23 E.H.R.R. 313) authority in support. See further below.
[81] See *Mushtaq* [2005] UKHL 25; [2005] 2 Cr.App.R. 32 at [18]–[23].

> "it is the judge who protects the defendant's right not to incriminate himself by being compelled to make a confession (even if it is true) against his will, and the judge also protects the accused against the danger that a confession may go before the jury which may well be untrue because it was obtained by oppression or improper conduct. In addition the jury provide further protection to the defendant because they will be entitled to reject the confession as unreliable on the ground that there is a reasonable possibility that it is untruthful if (contrary to the view which the judge will have formed on the voir dire) they are not satisfied that it was not obtained by oppression or improper conduct."

Judge and jury act collectively to ensure a fair trial for the defendant. But, as the Court of Appeal said in the court below, this does not mean that the jury should take on the function that the system entrusts to the judge. "Provided each fulfils its role the accused will receive a fair trial." It is submitted therefore that the reasoning of the majority in *Mushtaq* is flawed and that the minority view is preferable. However, the decision stands,[82] and accordingly the accused is able to have two goes at the legitimacy issue; if he fails before the judge he can ask the jury in effect to reverse the judge's decision.

3. *The rule against oppression*

6–014   The partial definition of oppression in s.76(8) of PACE states that "in this section 'oppression' includes torture, inhuman or degrading treatment, and the use or threat of violence (whether or not amounting to torture)". This is based on art.3 of the ECHR, which provides that no one shall be subjected to torture or inhuman or degrading treatment. The Royal Commission on Criminal Procedure had expressed a clear view that confessions obtained by such methods were unacceptable as a means of proof.[83] Several arguments of principle and policy support this view. First, the exclusion of the confession is a vindication of the accused's right not to be subjected to the unlawful use of force or threat of force by the police.[84] The means referred to in s.76(8) will invariably amount to at least a common assault. Exclusion of the confession demonstrates that there is no exception to the right for police interrogation, however reasonable the suspicions of the accused's guilt may be. Secondly, where the privilege against self-incrimination is regarded as an independent procedural right of the accused, exclusion of a confession coerced by force would seem to be essential to uphold the right. Thirdly, exclusion is necessary as a deterrent to the police to engage in such practices. Inadmissibility of a confession obtained by force may not, as Zuckerman has suggested,[85] necessarily be sufficient to counteract all other pressures on the police. Interests of securing a suspect's co-operation in other ways might be unaffected by such a rule. However, without such a rule, the temptation of some police officers to resort to the use of force might prove irresistible. In this sense, exclusion helps to minimise the risk. Finally, the rule of exclusion is a clear public statement that the use of the prohibited means is not a

---

[82]   It has been cited and applied twice by the Privy Council: *Wizzard v R.* [2007] UKPC 21; *Benjamin v Trinidad and Tobago* [2012] UKPC 8. See also *Pham* [2008] EWCA Crim 3182.

[83]   RCCP Report, para.4.132.

[84]   A. J. Ashworth, "Excluding Evidence as Protecting Rights" [1977] Crim. L.R. 723.

[85]   A. A. S. Zuckerman, "Illegally Obtained Evidence: Discretion as a Guardian of Legitimacy" [1987] C.L.P. 55, 59.

legitimate method of investigation. It was argued in Ch.2 that a conviction based on a confession obtained by torture lacks moral authority and fails to fulfil the moral and expressive functions of the criminal verdict.[86]

It makes no difference to any of these arguments whether the confession is true. Section 76(2) states in a parenthesis that the confession is inadmissible, "notwithstanding that it may be true".[87] Thus, even if the accused admits in a later interview that an earlier coerced confession was true, the first confession remains inadmissible. What then is the status of the second confession in such a case? Is this admissible even though the first confession is not, or is the second "tainted" because it was made in consequence of a first confession procured by illegal means?[88] The answer begins with the proposition that the same rules apply to both confessions. Therefore, under s.76(2), the prosecution must prove that the making of the second confession was not obtained by oppression of the person who made it. If the police conduct relied on by the accused is the same conduct that rendered the first confession inadmissible, then the court will have to be satisfied that its influence had ceased to operate by the time of the second confession. This may often necessitate an inquiry into events occurring between the first and second confessions. In *Glaves*,[89] the defendant made further admissions of involvement in burglary and manslaughter eight days after his first admissions. The trial judge excluded the first admissions under s.76 of PACE because of police misconduct in insisting that the defendant answer questions and in refusing to accept his repeated denials of involvement. However, the judge admitted the later admissions on the assumption that the defendant had received legal advice in the intervening period. This assumption was in fact incorrect. The Court of Appeal held that the later admissions should have been excluded also because the defendant might have been subject to the continuing influence that had caused him to confess earlier. At the same time the court indicated that the judge's view could have been supported if the defendant had received legal advice before the second round of interviews. The point seems to be that such advice would have informed the defendant of his right to silence and would have counteracted the effect of the police misconduct. This authority suggests that it will therefore be a question of fact in each case whether earlier oppression continues to operate on the defendant's mind.[90] In many cases there is likely to be

---

[86] The use of torture renders inadmissible at common law any evidence obtained thereby: *A v Secretary of State for the Home Department (No.2)* [2005] UKHL 71; [2006] 1 All E.R. 575. In *Jalloh v Germany* (2007) 44 E.H.R.R. 32 the Grand Chamber of the European Court of Human Rights stated that evidence, whether in the form of a confession or real evidence, obtained by torture in violation of art.3 of the ECHR should never be admitted as proof of guilt irrespective of its probative value (at [105]). It appears that in the court's view this would automatically violate the defendant's right to a fair trial under art.6.

[87] This suggests that presumed unreliability of the actual confession is *not* the rationale for exclusion, although it can be argued that part of the utility of the rule against the admission of confessions obtained by oppression is to reduce the total number of unreliable confessions.

[88] See, generally, P. Mirfield, "Successive Confessions and the Poisonous Tree" [1996] Crim. L.R. 554.

[89] *Glaves* [1993] Crim. L.R. 685.

[90] The Court of Appeal said that it did not take the view that in circumstances like this there must inevitably be a continuing blight on any subsequent confession: [1993] Crim. L.R. 686. See also *Ismail* [1990] Crim. L.R. 109 (second confession excluded under s.78). For further discussion see Mirfield, "Successive Confessions" [1996] Crim. L.R. 554 at 563–565.

an inference that its effect is continuing unless something positive has intervened to curtail its effect. The inference of continuance may be particularly strong where there has been physical ill-treatment at an earlier stage. Even if a solicitor is present at the later interview the defendant may feel obliged to repeat a confession for fear of subsequent retribution if it is not confirmed.

(A)   "Torture, inhuman or degrading treatment"

6–015   PACE does not define further any of the three concepts of "torture", "inhuman treatment" or "degrading treatment", and to date no English court has had to consider them.

However, "torture" is defined elsewhere in English law, namely for the purposes of the offence of torture, set out in s.134 of the Criminal Justice Act 1988. That definition refers to the "intentional infliction ... of severe physical or mental pain and suffering by a public official, or by a person acting in an official capacity, in the performance ... of his official duties". A court is likely to find this test helpful if confronted with an allegation that a police officer tortured a suspect under interrogation into making a confession.

Further help on interpretation comes from the Strasbourg jurisprudence on art.3 of the Convention. In the *Greek Case*,[91] the European Commission of Human Rights defined "inhuman treatment" as such treatment "as deliberately causes severe suffering, mental or physical", and "degrading treatment" as treatment that "grossly humiliates the individual before others or drives him to act against his will or conscience". The European Court of Human Rights expanded these notions in *Republic of Ireland v United Kingdom*.[92] In this case, the court was concerned with five techniques of interrogation practised for a short period in 1971 on a group of terrorist suspects in Northern Ireland. The techniques were aimed at disorientation or sensory deprivation of the suspects and involved wall-standing, hooding, subjection to continuous noise, deprivation of sleep and deprivation of food and drink. The court held that the techniques amounted to inhuman treatment because they caused intense physical and mental suffering and also led to acute psychiatric disturbances during interrogation. They were also degrading because they were such as to arouse in their victims feelings of fear, anguish and inferiority capable of humiliating and debasing them and possibly breaking their physical or moral resistance. These explanations clearly contemplate major abuses of power. They underline the point that serious and deliberate breaches of international standards of human rights are never acceptable as methods of obtaining incriminating statements from suspects.

---

[91] Greek Case (1969) 12 Yearbook of the European Convention on Human Rights 186.
[92] *Republic of Ireland v United Kingdom* (1978) 2 E.H.R.R. 25.

(B)   The use or threat of violence (whether or not amounting to torture)"

This is not as self-explanatory as first appears. In the context of the law of assault, "violence" can refer to any application of unlawful force to a person.[93] If this applies without modification to s.76 of PACE, it means that, say, giving a person a single push, or holding a person by the lapels of a coat, is enough to render a subsequent confession by that person inadmissible. Cross and Tapper suggest[94] that "violence" in this context must indicate more than a mere battery and should be construed as connoting a substantial application of force. There is something to be said for this view if the use of force is confined to a single minor incident, but repeated assaults, or assaults likely to cause bodily harm, should clearly be regarded as "violent" conduct. Different forms of aggressive or hostile behaviour (shouting, insults, invasions of personal space, etc.) may amount to a threat of violence as well as falling within the residual meaning of oppression now to be considered.

6–016

(C)   Other forms of "oppression"

Section 76(8) states that oppression "includes" the means listed in the subsection. The question arises of what other cases fall within the prohibition on the use of oppression. What, in other words, is the meaning of this term in cases outside the partial definition? At common law, oppression had a wide meaning. It denoted something which "sapped the accused's free will" so that "he spoke when otherwise he would have remained silent".[95] In his address to the Bentham Club in 1968, Lord MacDermott expanded upon this notion[96]:

6–017

> "[Oppressive questioning is] questioning which by its nature, duration or other attendant circumstances (including the fact of custody) excites hopes (such as the hope of release) or fears, or so affects the mind of the suspect that his will crumbles and he speaks when otherwise he would have remained silent."

Taken literally, this principle made questioning of suspects in police custody virtually impossible. A prime object of questioning is to persuade the reluctant suspect to talk. As noted above, few confessions will be forthcoming without some element of persuasion and pressure. Numerous statements and actions by the police might have the effect of lowering a suspect's resistance to making a statement. It is well recognised that in one sense the whole situation of detention and questioning in police custody is oppressive.

In practice the courts resolved this apparent contradiction by generally requiring extreme conduct on the part of the police before the threshold of oppression was reached. Oppression was regarded as a matter of degree which

---

[93] See Blackstone's *Commentaries on the Laws of England*, 17th edn (Edward Christian, 1830), Vol.3 p.120; *Collins v Wilcock* [1984] 3 All E.R. 374 at 378 per Goff L.J.
[94] Cross and Tapper, p.672.
[95] *Priestley* (1965) 51 Cr.App.R. 1 per Sachs J.
[96] Lord MacDermott, "The Interrogation of Suspects in Custody" (1968) 21 C.L.P. 1, 10.

depended to a considerable extent on the circumstances of the interrogation[97] and the character of the suspect. In *Prager*,[98] questioning of a naval officer suspected of espionage occurred over fourteen-and-a-quarter hours. Questioning occupied nine-and-a-quarter hours, the last six hours being consecutive. The Court of Appeal held that this did not amount to oppression. On the other hand, in *Hudson*,[99] a civil servant suspected of corruption was taken from his home in the early hours of the morning to a police station many miles away where he was held in custody for five days and questioned on and off throughout. The Court of Appeal accepted the defence argument that his confession had been obtained by oppression. When PACE was enacted it made express provision for the possibility of extended detention of suspects for the purpose of questioning. This made the emphasis given in *Hudson* to the period that the defendant spent in custody look distinctly problematic.

6–018   It is therefore an important question whether the common law meaning of oppression survived the enactment of PACE. In *Fulling*,[100] the Court of Appeal answered the question with a firm "No". The defendant was suspected of having acted in concert with her lover to obtain property by deception. After her arrest she at first remained silent, despite persistent questioning. She eventually confessed to the offence after allegedly being told by the interviewing officer that her lover had been having an affair with a woman occupying the cell next to the defendant. On appeal against conviction she argued that the confession should have been excluded on the ground that it had been obtained by oppression. She claimed to have been so distressed by the information that she had confessed in the hope that she could thereby escape from an intolerable situation.

The Court of Appeal's rejection of the common law approach to oppression begins with the proposition that PACE was a codifying Act and was therefore to be interpreted according to its natural meaning, without any presumption as to the continuance or otherwise of the previous law.[101] This is debatable. PACE contained a handful of provisions on criminal evidence. It was plainly not a codification of the law of criminal evidence. It was not even a codification of the law of confessions, since there were several aspects of that law with which it did not deal at all.[102] On the other hand, PACE was undoubtedly a codification of the law of police powers. It dealt comprehensively with the powers of the police to investigate offences. Furthermore, the legislative history of the Act showed that it embodied reforms in s.76 which were intended to replace the voluntariness rule at common law.[103] Oppression was an essential component of that rule. Thus it is

---

[97] In *Mohammed Ali Bin Burut v Public Prosecutor* [1995] 2 A.C. 579 the Privy Council was in no doubt that "For the police to interview an arrested person while he is manacled and hooded is plainly oppressive conduct calculated to sap the will of the person being interviewed".

[98] *Prager* [1972] 1 W.L.R. 260.

[99] *Hudson* (1980) 72 Cr.App.R. 163. See also *Westlake* [1979] Crim. L.R. 652.

[100] *Fulling* [1987] 2 All E.R. 65.

[101] Applying the principle laid down in *Bank of England v Vagliano Bros* [1891] A.C. 107 at 144–145.

[102] e.g. the status of mixed inculpatory and exculpatory statements, and questioning the accused on the voir dire about the truth of the confession.

[103] The architects of the reforms in s.76 were the Criminal Law Revision Committee, in its Eleventh Report (1972), and the Royal Commission on Criminal Procedure, in its Report (1981). Their

plausible, particularly given the relationship of paras (a) and (b) of s.76(2) (discussed further below), that the common law meaning of oppression was not intended to survive the Act.

In any event, having reached the conclusion that the "artificially wide" definition approved in *Prager* no longer applied, the Court of Appeal ruled that oppression should have its ordinary meaning. Surprisingly, the court did not refer to the partial definition in subs.(8) but instead consulted the dictionary for guidance.[104] Accordingly the court declared the ordinary meaning to be "the exercise of authority or power in a burdensome, harsh or wrongful manner; unjust or cruel treatment of subjects, inferiors etc; the imposition of unreasonable or unjust burdens". The court went on to add:

> "There is not a word in our language which expresses more detestable wickedness than oppression . . . We find it hard to envisage any circumstances in which such oppression would not entail some impropriety on the part of the interrogator."[105]

Applying this principle, the court held that even if the police statement was made as the defendant alleged it was not so improper as to amount to oppression. Both the principle and its application in this case have been criticised.[106]

6–019

However, it can be argued that the partial definition in subs.(8) shows that oppression is essentially concerned with police misconduct; the definition sets out the central cases of misconduct amounting to a violation of the suspect's human rights. Cases not falling within the list should be construed *ejusdem generis*, as the Court of Appeal assumed with its reference to impropriety.[107] It follows from this fairly narrow interpretation that any broader inquiries into the circumstances of the interrogation and their effect on the particular suspect will be undertaken under para.(b) of s.76(2). Under this provision the court will ask whether anything said or done was likely to render unreliable any confession by the defendant. Lord Lane C.J. commented in *Fulling* that para.(b) now covers some of the ground that was formerly covered by oppression at common law.[108]

What *Fulling* has emphasised is that the court will no longer inquire, if indeed it ever seriously did, into the question of whether the confession was truly voluntary. In *Miller*,[109] a case decided on the common law, the Court of Appeal held that there was no rule at common law that the prosecution had to prove that the defendant had a free choice whether to confess. The decision rejected

---

proposals for replacing the voluntariness rule were based on a combination of principles aimed at ensuring the reliability of confessions generally, the propriety of police conduct and the protection of suspects' rights.

[104] Astonishingly Lord Carswell stated in *Mushtaq* [2005] UKHL 25; [2005] 2 Cr.App.R. 32 at [64] that "oppression is not defined in PACE", and made no reference to s.76(8). He then adopted Lord MacDermott's definition in his address to the Bentham Club, noted above, citing *Prager* [1972] 1 W.L.R. 260 but not *Fulling* [1987] 2 All E.R. 65. Since the meaning of "oppression" was not in issue in *Mushtaq* it is submitted that these remarks should be regarded as aberrant dicta.

[105] *Fulling* [1987] 2 All E.R. 65 at 69, citing the *Oxford English Dictionary*.

[106] Zuckerman, "Illegally Obtained Evidence" [1987] C.L.P. 55, 333.

[107] For a different view, see P. Mirfield, *Silence, Confessions and Improperly Obtained Evidence* (1997), pp.77 onwards.

[108] *Fulling* [1987] 2 All E.R. 65 at 69. Arguably the defendant's confession would have been ruled involuntary at common law, according to the wide test of oppression discussed above.

[109] *Miller* [1986] 3 All E.R. 119 CA.

Australian[110] and New Zealand[111] authority to the contrary, perhaps recognising the philosophical and psychological difficulties that would be generated by a forensic inquiry into the state of a person's free will in a police station. However, *Miller* was inconsistent in principle with *Prager*, which seemed to envisage just such an inquiry. *Fulling* resolved the inconsistency in favour of a more pragmatic and focused inquiry into the degree of police misconduct.

This is not to say that the test is an easy one to apply. It calls for a judgment of the moral quality of police conduct, since it is only when the conduct can be characterised as "harsh" or "unjust" or "detestably wicked" that the threshold of oppression is reached. These are essentially contestable concepts and much will depend on the particular facts of each case. However, certain points about the application of the principle are reasonably clear and will now be considered.

6–020   First, the reference in the *Fulling* definition to "wrongful" conduct must be treated with care. This is certainly capable of extending to conduct that amounts to a breach of PACE or the Codes of Practice, such as where the suspect is deprived of sleep and questioned for long periods without a break.[112] However, the fact that police conduct is independently unlawful is neither a necessary nor a sufficient condition for it to be characterised as oppressive. It is not necessary, in the sense that there may be oppression by conduct not explicitly prohibited by the legislation, such as bullying, shouting and the extensive repetition of accusations of guilt. It is not sufficient, in the sense that the concept of impropriety, coupled with descriptions of conduct as cruel and wicked, suggests that at least a deliberate and serious breach will be required. A breach of PACE or the Codes made in good faith is unlikely to be oppressive. In *Miller*,[113] the admissibility of a confession made by a suspect suffering from paranoid schizophrenia was in issue. The trial judge had found that the interviewing officer had not deliberately set out to exploit the defendant's disordered state of mind. The Court of Appeal expressed the view, obiter, that had the finding been otherwise, the confession would have had to be excluded as obtained by oppression. This is an important dictum since on the facts the case did not involve a breach of any legislative prohibition. When the courts have considered discretionary exclusion of evidence for breaches of PACE or the Codes they have similarly attached much weight to the question whether the breach was in bad faith.[114]

In *Paris, Abdullahi, Miller*,[115] ("the Cardiff Three") the third defendant had confessed to murdering his girlfriend. His admissions were made during interviews totalling 13 hours spread over five days. The Court of Appeal allowed his appeal and quashed his conviction for murder on the ground that the admissions were obtained by oppression. The interviews were oppressive, taken as a whole, because of their length and tenor. The Court of Appeal, which listened to the tapes of the interviews, pointed to the officer's "bullying and hectoring" manner, his shouting at the defendant and his continual repetition of what he

---

[110] *Sinclair v R.* (1946) 73 C.L.R. 316; *Starecki* [1960] V.R. 141.
[111] *Williams* [1959] N.Z.L.R. 502.
[112] Contrary to Code C, paras 12.2 and 12.8 respectively.
[113] *Miller* [1986] 3 All E.R. 119 CA.
[114] *Alladice* (1988) 87 Cr.App.R. 380 at 385; *Walsh* (1990) 91 Cr.App.R. 161, and see the text below.
[115] *Paris, Abdullahi, Miller* (1992) 97 Cr.App.R. 99 CA.

wanted the defendant to say, despite the fact that the defendant denied involvement in the murder more than 300 times. The convictions of the co-accused were also quashed on the ground that they were possibly tainted by the inadmissible confession. The court thought that the jury might have used the confession prejudicially against them despite the judge's instruction not to do so.

A particularly disturbing feature of this case is the fact that the defendant's solicitor was present throughout the interviews but did not intervene at any stage. The Court of Appeal expressed surprise at his passivity. The fact that he was unable or unwilling to prevent the oppression offers a salutary reminder that the presence of a legal advisor is not necessarily a safeguard against police impropriety in all cases.[116]

This case can usefully be compared with *Heaton*[117] to underline the point that oppression is a matter of degree. In *Heaton* the defendant had confessed to manslaughter in the course of a 75-minute interview in the presence of his solicitor. Amongst other things he complained that the interviewing officers raised their voices and repeated questions. Having listened to the tape of the interview the Court of Appeal held that there was no shouting and no oppressive hostility shown to the defendant. Some repetition of questions was appropriate. The court distinguished *Paris* on the facts, having referred with approval to the dictum in the earlier case, that it is:

6–021

> "perfectly legitimate for officers to pursue the interrogation of a suspect with a view to eliciting his account or gaining admissions. They are not required to give up after the first denial or even after a number of denials."[118]

The use of deliberate deception on a suspect may contribute to a finding of oppression. In the trial of George Heron[119] for the murder of a young girl at the block of flats where he was a caretaker, the judge excluded Heron's confession on the grounds both of the bullying manner of the interview and the lies told to Heron that two witnesses had identified him as being at the spot where the girl was last seen alive. In the earlier case of *Mason*,[120] the Court of Appeal held that a lie that the defendant's fingerprints had been found on an article used in the offence should have resulted in exclusion of his confession under s.78. This seems not to have been regarded as oppressive for the purposes of s.76(2)(a), but the point was not fully argued, possibly because no other impropriety was alleged against the police.

6–022

Emotional cruelty, as possibly exemplified in *Fulling*, is more difficult to assess because of its infinite variations of degree and because the personal characteristics of the accused will be an important factor in deciding on its severity. What may be harsh or cruel in relation to a vulnerable individual may

---

[116] For an illuminating study of the nature and quality of legal advice to suspects, see the research study for the RCCJ carried out by M. McConville and J. Hodgson, *Custodial Legal Advice and the Right to Silence* (London: Stationary Office Books, 1993). As a postscript to the Cardiff Three case it is worth noting that 15 years after the murder another man, Jeffrey Gafoor, was convicted of it on the strength of a matching DNA profile and his subsequent confession: *The Times*, July 5, 2003.

[117] *Heaton* [1993] Crim. L.R. 593 CA. See also *Emmerson* (1990) 92 Cr.App.R. 284 CA.

[118] *Paris* (1992) 97 Cr.App.R. 99 at 104.

[119] *R. v Heron, The Times*, November 22, 1993.

[120] *Mason* [1987] 3 All E.R. 481 CA.

not be so to a phlegmatic or hardened suspect.[121] The officer's statement in *Fulling*, which if it was made appears to have been true, may fairly be described as callous and unfeeling. Whether that is enough to qualify it as oppressive under the test set out in the case is a matter on which opinions will almost inevitably differ. Had it been a deliberate lie calculated to distress the suspect, or had it been coupled with other forms of objectionable behaviour, the case for the exclusion of the defendant's confession would have been much stronger.

4. *The scope and application of the "reliability" rule*

(A) *A hypothetical test*

6–023   Under para.(b) of s.76(2) the prosecution must prove that the confession was not obtained in consequence of anything said or done likely in the circumstances to render unreliable any confession by the accused. The provision is based on a proposal of the CLRC in the Eleventh Report.[122] The Committee envisaged that the trial judge would have to reconstruct in his mind the course of dealing between the police and the suspect. In other words the judge would have to imagine being in the role of the "fly on the wall", observing the progress of the interview and keeping in mind the other circumstances of the interview and of the suspect's detention in the police station. At the point when the actual confession was made the judge should ask whether at that stage any confession that the accused might have made was likely to be unreliable as a result of something said or done.

It should be stressed at the outset that this test is concerned with a hypothetical issue. The question is the likely reliability of any[123] confession the accused might have made at the point of time that the actual confession was made. The court is not concerned therefore with the reliability of the actual confession itself.[124] The prosecution must prove an absence of causation between what was said and done and the actual confession, but otherwise the importance of the actual confession is simply to fix the moment of time at which the hypothetical question must be answered. The Court of Appeal has had to remind trial judges of this point more than once.[125] It follows that because the court is dealing only with the hypothetical issue at the particular moment in the interview, the prosecution cannot overcome problems about the reliability of a confession by using extrinsic

---

[121] The common law allowed individual characteristics and susceptibilities to be taken into account in applying the voluntariness test (see *Priestley* (1966) 51 Cr.App.R. 1), and in this respect the position has not changed. See, e.g. *Seelig and Spens* [1992] 1 W.L.R. 148 CA.

[122] Eleventh Report para.64.

[123] "Any" confession means any such confession as the accused actually made: *Re Proulx* [2001] 1 All E.R. 57 DC.

[124] Although, of course, if the court concludes that the actual confession is likely to be unreliable, *as a result of something said or done*, then it must exclude the confession because the prosecution have failed to prove that it was not obtained in consequence of anything said or done likely to "render unreliable any confession which might be made by him in consequence thereof". The risk of the actual confession being unreliable for other reasons is a matter of weight for the factfinder, subject to the court's discretion to exclude the confession where no reasonable factfinder could safely rely upon it: see below.

[125] *Cox* [1991] Crim. L.R. 276; *Kenny* [1994] Crim. L.R. 284; *Blackburn* [2005] 2 Cr.App.R. 30.

evidence that it is likely to be true.[126] Similarly, it is immaterial whether the actual confession subsequently turns out to be true. In *McGovern*,[127] the accused's first confession to murder was subsequently admitted to be true. Quashing the conviction, the Court of Appeal held that the confession should not have been admitted because the prosecution had failed to discharge the burden of proof under s.76(2)(b). The defendant's later admission of the truth of the confession was not a relevant factor in this decision. As the subsection itself indicates, the judge must exclude a confession where the prosecution fail to satisfy para.(b), "notwithstanding that the confession may be true".

On the face of it, the result in *McGovern* is a remarkable one. It suggests the need for further discussion of the rationale of this part of s.76(2). The key to understanding the provision is the point that, like para.(a), it is concerned with the issue of the methods used to obtain the confession (the "legitimacy" issue) and not with the issue of whether the actual confession itself is true or false (the "reliability" issue). This point appears clearly in the judgment of Stuart-Smith L.J. in *Crampton*[128]:

> "the words of the subsection seem to postulate some words spoken by the police or acts done by them which were likely to induce unreliable confessions. The word 'unreliable', in our judgment, means 'cannot be relied upon as being the truth'. What the provision of subs.2(b) is concerned with is the nature and quality of the words spoken or the things done by the police which are likely to, in the circumstances existing at the time, render the confession unreliable in the sense that it is not true. It is quite plain that if those acts and words are of such a quality, whether or not the confession is in fact true, it is inadmissible."

Under the PACE scheme the reliability issue is essentially a question of weight for the factfinder.[129] The issue under s.76(2) is essentially the legitimacy of the methods used by the police to obtain confessions. In summary, the message the provision conveys is that the police should not abuse their power to oppress a suspect into making a confession and they should not adopt other techniques of interrogation likely to lead to an unreliable confession. The two paragraphs of s.76 thus reflect the two dimensions of legitimate verdicts. The oppression rule is intended to safeguard the moral authority and expressive value of the verdict, whereas the "reliability" rule in para.(b) is a rule intended to promote the factual accuracy of verdicts generally that are based on confession evidence. However, it is fair to say that if this is the correct analysis of the rationale of para.(b), the provision is extremely uninformative about the interviewing methods to be avoided. Code C gives some help,[130] but any further legislative detail is necessarily limited by the point that s.76(2)(b) is concerned with the reliability of any confession that might be made *by the accused*. As Mirfield rightly says:

6–024

---

[126] *Blackburn* [2005] EWCA Crim 1349; [2005] 2 Cr.App.R. 30.

[127] *McGovern* (1991) 92 Cr.App.R. 228.

[128] *Crampton* (1991) 92 Cr.App.R. 369 at 372.

[129] This is why s.76(2)(b) is careful to refer to the likely reliability of *any* confession the accused might have made; by not deciding on the reliability of the actual confession the judge does not usurp the function of the jury.

[130] As in para.11–5, relating to the giving of information to the suspect about future police action.

"it is unclear what *generalizable* lesson the police will learn from exclusion of a confession because this accused, with his own individual characteristics, quirks even, and specific circumstances, might have confessed unreliably."[131]

It follows from this characterisation that whereas deliberate impropriety by the police is a key element of oppression it is not a necessary condition of invalidating a confession under para.(b). Confessions may still be rendered unreliable as a result of police conduct performed in good faith and even with the interests of the suspect in mind. In *Fulling*, Lord Lane C.J. commented that a confession may fall to be excluded under para.(b) where there is no suspicion of impropriety,[132] and this dictum has been approved subsequently.[133]

(B)   "Anything said or done"

6–025   It also follows from correct identification of the rationale of s.76(2)(b) that there must be something said or done that is external to the accused and is likely to influence the accused to make a confession. This point was clarified by the Court of Appeal in *Goldenberg*.[134] The defendant was a heroin addict who had been in police custody for five days after his arrest and who had been charged with conspiracy to supply diamorphine. He asked for an interview, in the course of which he made a confession. On appeal against conviction he argued that the confession should have been excluded at trial as being unreliable because it might have been made in the hope that he would be granted bail. The Court of Appeal held that the words "anything said or done" did not include things said or done by the person making the confession. They were limited to something external to that person and to something likely to have some influence on him. The fact that the defendant might have had a motive for confessing to secure his release on bail was not therefore something that affected the admissibility of the confession. Implicit in this decision is a finding not only that the police had not held out any inducement to the defendant to confess but also that the mere holding of the interview in response to his request was not itself something said or done likely to produce an unreliable confession.[135] Given that the concern of s.76(2)(b) is with behaviour-influencing methods of dealing with suspects, this decision looks right on the facts. A defendant's possible anxiety to confess to secure some advantage, when not induced by the police themselves, is something that, under the PACE scheme, goes to the weight to be attached to the confession. It is regarded as an issue for the jury, not one of admissibility for the judge.[136] Similarly, s.76 does

---

[131]   At p.100. See also *R. v M* (2000) 8 Archbold News 2 (hostile interventions by D's solicitor).

[132]   *Fulling* [1987] 2 All E.R. 65 at 70.

[133]   *Walker* [1998] Crim. L.R. 211 CA. cf. *Brine* [1992] Crim. L.R. 122 CA.

[134]   *Goldenberg* (1988) 88 Cr.App.R. 285.

[135]   In *Crampton* (1991) 92 Cr.App.R. 369 the Court of Appeal doubted whether interviewing a heroin addict undergoing withdrawal symptoms was, without more, "something done" for the purposes of s.76(2)(b). See also *R. v W* [1994] Crim. L.R. 130.

[136]   *Crampton* (1991) 92 Cr.App.R. 369; *Wahab* [2002] EWCA Crim 1570; [2003] 1 Cr.App.R. 15. The same principle applied at common law: *Rennie* [1982] 1 All E.R. 385, cited with approval in *Crampton* and in *Wahab*. In *Wahab* the Court of Appeal upheld the judge's admission of D's confession to drug dealing which he made after his solicitor reported back to him a conversation that the solicitor had had with the police on D's instructions. The police had made no promises, and the

not rule out a possibly unreliable confession by a person of very low IQ if there was nothing "said or done" likely to influence the person into making a confession.[137] Individual vulnerabilities on their own go to the issue of weight, unless the judge takes the view that the confession is so unconvincing that no reasonable jury could convict on it, when he should withdraw the case from the jury if there is no other evidence.[138]

Admittedly there may sometimes be a difficult line to draw between this principle and the principle that a suspect's individual vulnerabilities are relevant in determining the application of the test under para.(b). In *Delaney*,[139] the defendant was convicted of indecent assault on a girl aged three. The only evidence against him was his admissions, which he began to make after some 90 minutes' questioning. The defendant was aged 17, educationally subnormal with an IQ of 80, and there was psychological evidence that he was subject to quick emotional arousal, which might lead him to wish to rid himself of an interview as quickly as possible. The interviewing officers admitted that they had taken pains to minimise the gravity of the offence to the defendant and had suggested to him that such an offender needed psychiatric help rather than punishment. These suggestions might well have been enough on their own to justify exclusion of the confessions under para.(b). Even if well-intentioned, they were things said which were likely to produce from this vulnerable defendant a false confession in order to escape the pressure of the interview. In allowing the appeal the Court of Appeal also took into account breaches of the recording requirements for interviews.[140] It was held that these deprived the court of the best evidence of what was said and done during the interviews. The court could not be sure therefore that the prosecution had discharged their burden of proof under s.76(2)(b), particularly given the suggestions made by the police.

McGovern[141] is a case to similar effect. The defendant was aged 19, with a greater degree of mental subnormality (IQ of 73 and a mental age of ten). She was also six months pregnant, was physically ill before the interview and emotionally distressed during it. The things "said and done" by the police in this case consisted of an unlawful refusal of access to a solicitor and breaches of the recording requirements. As in *Delaney* the Court of Appeal held that the confession (to murder) should have been excluded on the ground that the prosecution had failed to discharge the burden of proof under s.76(2)(b). It was said that the denial of access to a solicitor was likely to render any confession by this defendant unreliable in the circumstances. The assumption appears to have been that a solicitor would have prevented the interview taking place at all on the basis that the defendant was not then fit to be interviewed and might say

---

court thought that D's belief that a confession might lead to the release of members of his family from police custody did not affect the reliability of his confession. In relation to the solicitor's advice about the conversation the court held that advice properly given to a defendant by his solicitor does not normally provide a basis for excluding a subsequent confession under s.76(2)(b).

[137] See *Lewis (Martin)* [1996] Crim. L.R. 260 CA.

[138] *Mackenzie* (1992) 96 Cr.App.R. 98 CA; *Wood* [1994] Crim. L.R. 222 CA.

[139] *Delaney* (1988) 88 Cr.App.R. 338 CA.

[140] The court found that the officers were in breach of paras 11.3 and 11.4 of Code C by failing to make a contemporaneous record of the interview.

[141] *McGovern* (1991) 92 Cr.App.R. 228 CA.

anything. *McGovern* is a strong case. It illustrates the impact of s.76(2)(b) in a murder case, and, in addition, exemplifies the operation of the "tainting" principle. In a second interview a day later, with a solicitor present, the defendant had made a longer, more detailed and more coherent confession. The Court of Appeal held that this also should have been excluded. It was tainted by the first confession in the sense that the second interview was a direct consequence of the first interview, but the solicitor had not been informed of the breach of s.58 of PACE. Had she been she might have prevented the second interview taking place.

6–026   It is apparent also from *McGovern*, and a number of other cases, that "anything said or done" is much wider than the notion of an inducement at common law. The phrase certainly includes inducements[142] such as holding out the possibility of release on bail,[143] or suggesting that offences could be taken into consideration rather than specifically charged,[144] or offering a hope of treatment rather than punishment.[145] It also includes such matters as the length of detention and the number of interviews. In *Moss*,[146] the Court of Appeal quashed convictions for indecent assault on young children where the defendant's main admissions came in his eighth interview after he had been in custody for six days. The defendant was mentally handicapped, or nearly so, and no solicitor was present. Inducements from persons other than police officers may result in a confession being held inadmissible.[147]

Police failures to comply with what may be called the due process requirements of PACE are a common feature of the cases under s.76(2)(b). Thus breach of the statutory right of access to legal advice may well lead the court to conclude that the prosecution cannot discharge the burden of proof. This is on the basis that a solicitor might have prevented a vulnerable suspect from being interviewed at all, or have advised the suspect not to answer further questions after repeated denials of the offence. Similar thinking underlies the decision in *Everett*[148] where the Court of Appeal quashed the conviction of the defendant for indecent assault. The court held that the trial judge had failed to take into account medical evidence of the defendant's mental condition when considering the admissibility of his admissions. The defendant was aged 42 but had a mental age of eight. In the view of the Court of Appeal, under Code C he should have been interviewed in the presence of an independent mature person. Such a person could presumably have been expected to exercise a protective role for the defendant.[149] Other failures of due process, such as a failure to caution, or breach

---

[142] For an interesting discussion of the use of inducements in Inland Revenue investigations into suspected tax evasion see D. Ormerod, "Hansard invitations and confessions in the criminal trial" (2000) 4 E. & P. 147.

[143] *Barry* (1992) 95 Cr.App.R. 384.

[144] *Phillips* (1988) 86 Cr.App.R. 18.

[145] *Delaney* (1989) 88 Cr.App.R. 338.

[146] *Moss* (1990) 91 Cr.App.R. 371.

[147] See, e.g. *Roberts (Neil)* [2011] EWCA Crim 2974: statement by D's manager that the police would not be involved if D confessed to a suspected theft was likely to render a confession unreliable.

[148] *Everett* [1988] Crim. L.R. 826.

[149] See also *Wilding* [2010] EWCA Crim 2799 (absence of an appropriate adult at the interview of a vulnerable suspect).

of the recording requirements, where they do not logically affect the reliability of the confession, are more appropriately considered as a matter of exclusionary discretion under s.78 of PACE.[150]

C. DISCRETIONARY EXCLUSION OF CONFESSION EVIDENCE

1. *The general principles of discretionary exclusion under PACE section 78*

A confession which passes the test of admissibility in s.76(2) may nonetheless be excluded under s.78. This section deals with prosecution evidence the admission of which may adversely affect the fairness of the proceedings.

6–027

Subsection (1) of s.78 provides:

> "In any proceedings the court may refuse to allow evidence on which the prosecution proposes to rely to be given if it appears to the court that, having regard to all the circumstances, including the circumstances in which the evidence was obtained, the admission of the evidence would have such an adverse effect on the fairness of the proceedings that the court ought not to admit it."

The general principles relating to exclusionary discretion, and to s.78 in particular, are discussed in Ch.3. Most of the authorities on s.78 agree that it gives a trial judge a discretion to exclude any evidence on which the prosecution propose to rely, including evidence admissible under other statutory provisions. In this sense it is an overriding power, founded on the obligation placed on trial judges to safeguard the overall fairness of criminal proceedings. The wide terms of the section have very largely swallowed up the discretion at common law to exclude prosecution evidence in order to ensure a fair trial for the accused.[151] In relation to confessions, the only situation where it is necessary to rely on the common law rather than s.78 is where a confession has already been given in evidence. In *Sat-Bhambra*,[152] the Court of Appeal stated, obiter, that ss.76 and 78 of PACE are directed solely to the situation before the confession goes before the jury. Once the judge rules that the confession should be admitted, the sections cease to have effect. If the judge decides later to exclude confession evidence that has already been heard by the jury, the judge will have to invoke the common law to do so, directing the jury to disregard the evidence. This is almost certainly only a formal difference in the source of the judge's power. In this context the criteria of unfairness seem to be the same at common law and under s.78.[153]

The subject of confession evidence has proved fertile ground for argument about the use of s.78. Following the important decision in *Mason*,[154] in some cases defence counsel can have at least two bites at the exclusionary cherry. If the legitimacy of the confession is in issue it may first be argued that the confession

6–028

---

[150] Although the courts sometimes confuse the reasoning, as in *Doolan* [1988] Crim. L.R. 747. cf. *Menard* [1995] 1 Cr.App.R. 306 CA.

[151] This discretion is preserved by PACE s.82(3).

[152] *Sat-Bhambra* (1988) 88 Cr.App.R. 55.

[153] See *Mason* [1987] 3 All E.R. 481 CA; *Christou* [1992] Q.B. 979 CA.

[154] *Mason* [1987] 3 All E.R. 481 CA.

was obtained by oppression or by means likely to produce an unreliable confession and is therefore inadmissible as a matter of law under s.76– Alternatively or in addition, it may be argued that, having regard to the way it was obtained, admission of the confession would have such an adverse effect on the fairness of the proceedings that it ought not to be admitted.[155] An example of a case where a two-stage argument of this type is likely is where a vulnerable suspect has been unlawfully denied access to legal advice. In some cases where counsel has relied on both ss.76 and 78 the courts have not always indicated precisely on which section they are relying, in holding that the confession in question ought to have been excluded,[156] or whether they are relying on both.[157]

Section 78 may be relevant to all three of the main issues that can arise with confession evidence. As just indicated it can be relied upon where the defendant claims that a confession was unlawfully or unfairly obtained. It has also been invoked in numerous cases in relation to the authenticity issue. Here the defendant mounts a direct challenge to the evidence of the making of the confession, usually arguing that the evidence should be excluded because breaches by the police of Code C have placed him at an unfair disadvantage. A further possible use for the section is in relation to the reliability issue. Although the truth or falsity of a confession is normally a question of fact for the jury, a defendant might argue that in the circumstances no weight could safely be attached to his confession and that it would therefore be unfair to admit it. The courts undoubtedly acknowledge the existence of a discretion to exclude confessions where there is a serious risk of unreliability. In such a case the prejudicial effect of admitting the confession outweighs its probative value.[158] It remains somewhat obscure after PACE whether the source of the discretion is s.78 or the common law discretion preserved by s.82(3) of PACE, but there seems to be no difference in substance on this point.[159]

Most of the jurisprudence of s.78 in relation to confessions is concerned with the effect of breaches by the police of provisions of PACE or the Codes of Practice. The general principle established by the leading cases of *Absolam*,[160] *Keenan*[161] and *Walsh*[162] is that only breaches that are "significant and substantial" are likely to affect the fairness of the proceedings so adversely that the evidence of the confession ought not to be admitted. Not every breach will have this quality, and it must not be assumed that s.78 is an available remedy for all instances of unlawful behaviour by the police. A breach of PACE or of Code C

---

[155] See, e.g. *Elleray* [2003] EWCA Crim 553; [2003] 2 Cr.App.R. 11, where the defendant unsuccessfully argued that his confession to rape, made in an interview with a probation officer for a pre-sentence report, should have been excluded under s.78.

[156] See, e.g. *Re Walters* [1987] Crim. L.R. 577 DC.

[157] See, e.g. *Moss* (1990) 91 Cr.App.R. 371 CA.

[158] *Stewart* (1972) 56 Cr.App.R. 272; *Miller* [1986] 3 All E.R. 119 CA.

[159] In *DPP v R.* [2007] EWHC 1842 (Admin) the Divisional Court was in no doubt that evidence of a police interview with a severely mentally handicapped boy of 13, apparently containing admissions to sexual assault, should be excluded under s.78 since it had no value in view of his disability and high level of suggestibility.

[160] *Absolam* (1988) 88 Cr.App.R. 332 CA.

[161] *Keenan* [1990] 2 Q.B. 54 CA.

[162] *Walsh* (1990) 91 Cr.App.R. 161 CA.

does not result in automatic, or even presumptive, exclusion under s.78. It all depends on the nature of the breach and its consequences.

As far as the application of this principle is concerned there does not appear to be any difference between the words "significant" and "substantial". They appear to be used in conjunction to emphasise that an important question of degree is involved. In one case, *Park*,[163] the Court of Appeal characterised a particular breach of the recording requirements as not being a "significant *breach* causing substantial prejudice". It seems clear, however, that substantial prejudice is not a requirement in all cases. For example, where the police have acted in bad faith it does not appear that the defendant has to show that he has suffered serious adverse consequences. To repeat, therefore, the principle requires the court to form a judgment about the quality of the breach, and it is only when the breach is of the appropriate degree of seriousness that exclusion may be possible. Various factors are relevant in determining whether a breach is significant and substantial. These have been worked out mostly in the context of the due process requirements of PACE and the Codes. The breaches in question often involve an unjustified denial of the right of access to legal advice and/or a failure to comply with the requirements for the recording of interviews. These will now be considered in more detail and we will then look at other types of case under s.78.

6–029

2. *Breach of the right to legal advice*

The right of a suspect to have access to legal advice was described by the Court of Appeal in *Samuel*[164] as a "fundamental right".[165] Its importance is underlined by art.6(3)(c) of the ECHR which sets out a right to legal assistance as part of the right to a fair hearing in the determination of a criminal charge. Section 58 of PACE imposes a duty on the police to grant a suspect access to legal advice on request. There is a further obligation on the custody officer to inform the defendant of the right to consult privately with a solicitor and of the fact that independent legal advice is available free of charge.[166] Access may be delayed in certain circumstances, but these are narrowly defined.[167] Under s.58(8) the suspect must have been detained in connection with an indictable offence but not yet charged, and an officer of the rank of superintendent or above must have reasonable grounds for believing that the exercise of the right:

6–030

(i) will lead to interference with or harm to evidence connected with an indictable offence or interference with or physical injury to other persons; or

(ii) will lead to the alerting of other persons suspected of having committed such an offence but not yet arrested for it; or

---

[163] *Park* (1993) 99 Cr.App.R. 270.
[164] *Samuel* [1988] Q.B. 615 CA.
[165] For re-affirmation of the importance of the right, and for the consequences of breach for the safety of a conviction see *James* [2008] EWCA Crim 1869.
[166] Code C para.6.1.
[167] PACE s.58(8) and (8A); Code C paras 6.5 and 6.6, and Annex B.

(iii)   will hinder the recovery of any property obtained as a result of such an offence.[168]

In *Samuel,*[169] the Court of Appeal gave real substance to the test of reasonable grounds. The court held that the officer in question must have a genuine belief that one of the stipulated consequences will occur, and that this belief must be founded on something that is known or reasonably suspected about the particular solicitor or the particular suspect. It will not be sufficient that the officer has a generalised fear that, for example, the solicitor may unwittingly carry a message from the suspect alerting his accomplices. It is not a good reason for refusing or delaying access that the officer fears that the solicitor will advise the suspect to remain silent and not answer police questions.[170]

Where access is refused or delayed for a reason bad in law, a distinction has been suggested between cases of bad faith, where access is deliberately denied for a reason known to be bad, and good faith, where the police are merely mistaken about the extent of their powers. In *Alladice,*[171] Lord Lane C.J. commented that if the police had acted in bad faith in refusing access, the court would have little difficulty in ruling any confession inadmissible. In *Walsh,*[172] Saville J., giving the judgment of the Court of Appeal, expanded on this notion:

> "although bad faith may make substantial or significant that which might not otherwise be so, the contrary does not follow. Breaches which are in themselves significant and substantial are not rendered otherwise by the good faith of the officers concerned."

Walsh was important also because it made clear that even significant and substantial breaches do not result in automatic exclusion of evidence under s.78. Prima facie they will always adversely affect the fairness of the proceedings, but the section still requires the judge to make a judgment of degree. The judge must decide in every case whether the adverse effect is such that "justice requires the evidence to be excluded".[173] This will often be the case where bad faith is involved, because deliberate flouting of the rules will invariably undermine the moral authority and expressive value of the verdict. It is difficult to see how an intentional unlawful denial of access to legal advice could be justified by reference to other considerations once the right of access is characterised as fundamental. Certainly it would be dangerous to allow the gravity of the offence to be relied on. That would suggest that the worse the offence suspected the more the rules of due process can be ignored.[174] This is not to say that the court will not

---

[168] Delay may also be authorised under s.58(8A) where the officer has reasonable grounds for believing that the person detained for the indictable offence has benefited from his criminal conduct and the recovery of the value of the property constituting the benefit will be hindered by the exercise of the right conferred by s.58.

[169] *Samuel* [1988] Q.B. 615.

[170] Code C Annex B para.4; *Samuel* [1988] Q.B. 615 at 626 CA.

[171] *Alladice* (1988) 87 Cr.App.R. 380 at 386.

[172] *Walsh* (1990) 91 Cr.App.R. 161 at 163.

[173] *Walsh* (1990) 91 Cr.App.R. 161. Note that denial of access to legal advice may well contravene art.6 of the ECHR: see below.

[174] For a full discussion of the complex issues involved in the relationship between offence seriousness and due process see Andrew Ashworth's Hamlyn lectures, *Human Rights, Serious Crime and Criminal Procedure* (London: Sweet & Maxwell, 2002).

inquire into how far the defendant was prejudiced by a breach in bad faith. An element of prejudice will provide further support for exclusion.

Where access to legal advice has been refused in good faith the judge will inquire into the extent to which the defendant was prejudiced by the refusal. In *Samuel*,[175] the Court of Appeal held that a confession to robbery ought to have been excluded when made following the police's second refusal to allow the defendant to see his solicitor. The defendant had admitted burglary after being interviewed four times but had consistently denied robbery. The court accepted that the defendant's experienced solicitor would have advised him to answer no further questions and that the defendant would have accepted that advice. On the other hand, in *Alladice*,[176] the Court of Appeal took the view that the defendant was well aware of his right to silence and was capable of using it if he wished. The court reasoned therefore that the denial of access had not placed the defendant at any material disadvantage.[177] This, with respect, was too narrow a view of a solicitor's value to a suspect in the police station. As well as providing legal advice, a solicitor can be a witness to an interview, thereby discouraging any possibility of "verballing".[178] In *Parris*,[179] a case turning on disputed oral admissions, the Court of Appeal acknowledged the importance of the solicitor's presence by holding that the police evidence of the admissions ought to have been excluded where access had been unlawfully refused. More generally, a solicitor can provide psychological support to a suspect, as well as a check on the conditions of the suspect's detention and treatment.[180]

6–031

The English authorities must now be read in the light of recent developments in human rights law. As noted above, art.6(3)(c) of the ECHR provides for a person charged with a criminal offence to have the right to legal assistance. In *Salduz v Turkey*,[181] the European Court of Human Rights held that in order for the right to a fair trial under art.6(1) to be practical and effective:

> "as a rule, access to a lawyer should be provided as from the first interrogation of a suspect by the police, unless it is demonstrated that there are compelling reasons to restrict this right. Even where compelling reasons may exceptionally justify denial of access to a lawyer, such restriction—whatever its justification—must not unduly prejudice the rights of the accused under Article 6. The rights of the defence will in principle be irretrievably prejudiced when incriminating statements made during police interrogation without access to a lawyer are used for a conviction."[182]

---

[175] *Samuel* [1988] Q.B. 615.

[176] *Alladice* (1988) 87 Cr.App.R. 380.

[177] See also *Dunford* (1990) 91 Cr.App.R. 150 CA.

[178] *Dunn* (1990) 91 Cr.App.R. 237 CA.

[179] *Parris* (1989) 89 Cr.App.R. 68.

[180] Given the value of a solicitor to a suspect in the police station it is interesting to note that still only an overall minority of suspects request and receive legal advice. See P. Pleasence, V. Kemp and N. J. Balmer, "The Justice Lottery: Police Station Advice 25 Years on from PACE" [2011] Crim. L.R. 3, giving a figure of around 45% of suspects requesting advice. See also L. Skinns, "The Right to Legal Advice in the Police Station: Past, Present and Future" [2011] Crim. L.R. 19 for a study of the reasons why so many suspects choose not to request legal advice despite being told that it is free.

[181] *Salduz v Turkey* (2009) 49 E.H.R.R. 19.

[182] *Salduz v Turkey* (2009) 49 E.H.R.R. 19 at [55].

This insistence on the overriding importance of access to legal advice for a suspect detained by the police had originated some years earlier in the Strasbourg cases on the right to silence, [183]and is founded on the European Court's concern to protect suspects from being unfairly compelled to incriminate themselves during interrogation. *Salduz* signalled an apparent hardening of the Court's view of the right of access by its statement that access should be denied only for compelling reasons, as distinct from "good cause",[184] and the further statement that admitting a suspect's incriminating statement made without access to legal advice will "irretrievably prejudice the rights of the defence". In *Cadder v HM Advocate*,[185] the Supreme Court considered the implications of the *Salduz* ruling for the Scottish procedure of detention for questioning,[186] whereby a suspect could notify a lawyer of the fact of detention but was not entitled to obtain legal advice before questioning. In a landmark decision[187] it was held that art.6 was breached where the Crown relied on admissions made by the accused without legal advice when in detention under this provision. The ratio of this case is restricted to the Scottish procedure since English law has no comparable provision. However, the Supreme Court's analysis of the art.6 point has inescapable significance for the English law of confessions. In the court's view the *Salduz* ruling has given rise to a 'clear and constant' Strasbourg jurisprudence, the effect of which is that:

> "contracting states are under a duty to organise their systems in such a way as to ensure that, unless in the particular circumstances of the case there are compelling reasons for restricting the right, a person who is detained has access to advice from a lawyer before he is subjected to police questioning."[188]

Lord Hope expressed the view that it followed that evidence of any incriminating answers obtained by the police from a detainee who is subjected to police questioning without access to legal advice is inadmissible.[189] The point is yet to be tested in England, but it seems unlikely that the courts will take a different view. Assuming that Lord Hope's dictum is followed, the result is that where a court is satisfied that there was a breach of s.58, and that access was denied unlawfully, a subsequent confession in a police interview should either be held inadmissible as a matter of law, or excluded under s.78 of PACE. This conclusion should now follow irrespective of whether the breach was in bad or good faith. The effect of the *Salduz* ruling would seem to be that prejudice is to be presumed. How far the exceptional cases set out in s.58(8) can provide "compelling reasons" for lawfully denying access remains to be seen. It may well be that, as applied in the light of *Samuel,* they will be held to be compatible with art.6.

---

[183] In particular *Murray v UK* (1996) 22 E.H.R.R. 29; see further the discussion in Ch 5.

[184] A phrase used in *Murray v UK* (1996) 22 E.H.R.R. 29 at [63].

[185] *Cadder v HM Advocate* [2010] UKSC 43; [2010] 1 W.L.R. 2601.

[186] Under s.14 of the Criminal Procedure (Scotland) Act 1995.

[187] For discussion of this case and its aftermath see P. R. Ferguson, "Repercussions of the Cadder Case: the ECHR's fair trial provision and Scottish criminal procedure" [2011] Crim. L.R. 743, and R. M. White and P. R. Ferguson, "Sins of the Father? The 'Sons of Cadder'" [2012] Crim. L.R. 357.

[188] *Cadder v HM Advocate* [2010] UKSC 43; [2010] 1 W.L.R. 2601 at [48].

[189] *Cadder v HM Advocate* [2010] UKSC 43; [2010] 1 W.L.R. 2601 at [55]

3. Breach of the requirements for recording of interviews

The requirements in PACE for the tape-recording of interviews, and for the **6–032** recording in writing of any statements not made in formal interview, were expressly designed for two related purposes. One was to prevent the continuation of the practice of some police officers of "verballing" suspected offenders, the other was to protect police officers from unfounded allegations of verballing.[190] In the latter respect at least, the introduction of tape-recording seems to have been a considerable success.[191] However, there have been numerous cases since PACE came into force of police officers giving evidence of alleged oral admissions by defendants where the officer concerned has not complied with the recording provisions of Code C.[192] Commonly the alleged statement was not recorded contemporaneously, no reason or an inadequate reason is given for this, and the record was not shown to the accused for verification.[193] In the leading case of *Keenan*[194] the defendant had been committed for trial on a charge of possessing an offensive weapon. A home-made spear was said to have been found in a car he had been driving when arrested. After committal, the prosecution served two statements as additional evidence from the arresting officers recording admissions about the spear made by the defendant in an interview at the police station. The interview had not been contemporaneously recorded, no reason for this was stated in the police notebooks, and the defendant had not been shown the record. Having stated that these were significant and substantial breaches, the Court of Appeal quashed the conviction. It was unfair to admit the police statements because they placed the defendant at a substantial disadvantage. If his case was that the admissions were fabricated, he would effectively be forced to give evidence to this effect. He would thereby lose his right of silence and also put his character in issue by attacking the police. If the case was that the interview was inaccurately recorded he was handicapped by having been given no contemporaneous opportunity to correct any inaccuracies and he had no contemporaneous note of his own.

Keenan was followed in *Canale*[195] where the Court of Appeal found that breaches of the recording requirements were "flagrant, deliberate and cynical". The police officers involved had given as a reason for not making a contemporaneous recording that it was the "best way", which the court dismissed as "not a reason at all".[196] The officers had also failed to 'show the record to the defendant for verification. Quashing the defendant's convictions for robbery and transferring a firearm, the Court of Appeal held that he had been prejudiced by the breaches. They had deprived the judge of the best evidence to enable him to

---

[190] See *Keenan* [1990] 2 Q.B. 54 at 63 (Hodgson J.); *DPP v Lawrence* [2007] EWHC 2154 (Admin); [2008] 1 Cr.App. R. 10.
[191] J. Baldwin, "The Police and Tape Recorders" [1985] Crim. L.R. 695; RCCJ Report, Ch.3, para.65.
[192] Part 11 of Code C contains the relevant requirements for interview records.
[193] Such failures would amount to breaches of paras 11.7, 11.10 and 11.11 of Code C respectively.
[194] *Keenan* [1990] 2 Q.B. 54.
[195] *Canale* [1990] 2 All E.R. 187.
[196] *Canale* [1990] 2 All E.R. 187 at 190.

decide on the defendant's submissions that the confessions he made in later, properly recorded, interviews had been induced by tricks by the police in the earlier, improperly recorded, interviews.

This case is a good example of the court attaching considerable weight to the policy of police propriety in the investigation of offences. Clearly disturbed by the bad faith shown by the officers concerned, and by the claim that they were largely ignorant of PACE procedures, the court sent out a blunt message: "If, which we find it hard to believe, police officers still do not appreciate the importance of [PACE] and the accompanying Code, then it is time that they did".[197] This is not to say that the purpose of exclusion is overtly punitive. The orthodox view, restated by Lord Lane C.J. in *Delaney*[198] and approved in subsequent decisions,[199] is that "it is no part of the duty of the court to rule a statement inadmissible simply in order to punish the police for failure to observe the Code of Practice".[200] The statement in *Canale* should rather be understood as expressing a concern that wilful disregard of the statutory procedures will have such an impact on the fairness of the proceedings that exclusion of any confession will be very likely.

6–033   However, the degree of unfairness will be lessened if on the facts the risk of verballing is not strong. In *Matthews, Dennison and Voss,*[201] the Court of Appeal upheld a trial judge's decision to admit evidence of an oral confession by the first defendant, despite breaches of the recording requirements. The confession admitted to kidnapping and assaulting the victim who had been stripped of his clothes in the attack. The clothes were found subsequently in the place indicated in the statement. The judgment does not spell out the reason for the decision, but it is not difficult to distinguish this case from *Keenan*. The finding of the clothes meant that a defence of fabrication would be implausible, given the unlikelihood of a coincidental discovery by the police. Similarly, the finding was highly incriminating and meant that the defendant would probably need to testify in any event to stand any chance of acquittal. Therefore the failure to show the note of the statement to the defendant did not place her at any significant disadvantage.[202]

This case was one of a number of decisions concerned with the meaning of the term "interview". The question of when a police-suspect interaction amounts to an interview for the purposes of the recording requirements has proved problematic, and different versions of Code C have provided different definitions of the term. The current definition is in Code C para.11.1A, which provides:

---

[197]   *Canale* [1990] 2 All E.R. 187.
[198]   *Delaney* (1988) 88 Cr.App.R. 338.
[199]   *Oliphant* [1992] Crim. L.R. 40 CA; *Christou* [1992] Q.B. 979 CA; *Hughes* [1994] 1 W.L.R. 876 CA.
[200]   *Delaney* [1998] 88 Cr.App.R. 338 at 341.
[201]   *Matthews, Dennison and Voss* (1990) 91 Cr.App.R. 43.
[202]   See also *Dunn* (1990) 91 Cr.App.R. 237 (evidence of defendant's confession rightly admitted, despite serious breaches of the recording requirements, because defendant's solicitor's clerk was present during the disputed conversation).

"An interview is the questioning of a person regarding their involvement or suspected involvement in a criminal offence or offences which, under para.10.1, must be carried out under caution."[203]

Paragraph 10.1 then sets out in more detail the test of the purpose of the questioning. This determines whether a caution has to be given, and hence whether it amounts to an interview:

"A person whom there are grounds to suspect of an offence, see Note 10A,[204] must be cautioned before any questions about an offence, or further questions if the answers provide the grounds for suspicion, are put to them if either the suspect's answers or silence (i.e. failure or refusal to answer or answer satisfactorily) may be given in evidence to a court in a prosecution. A person need not be cautioned if questions are for other necessary purposes, e.g.:
(a)   solely to establish their identity or ownership of any vehicle;
(b)   to obtain information in accordance with any relevant statutory requirement, see para.10.9;
(c)   in furtherance of the proper and effective conduct of a search, e.g. to determine the need to search in the exercise of powers of stop and search or to seek co-operation while carrying out a search;
(d)   to seek verification of a written record as in para.11.13."

Code C contains a further important provision against verballing. This requires **6–034** the police to give the defendant an opportunity to verify an alleged oral confession on tape. Paragraph 11.4 is based on a proposal of the Royal Commission on Criminal Justice.[205] It stipulates that at the beginning of an interview (which must be recorded on tape in accordance with Code E) the interviewing officer must, after cautioning the suspect, put to him any significant statement or silence which occurred in the presence and hearing of a police officer or other police staff before the start of the interview and which have not been put to the suspect in the course of a previous interview. The interviewer must ask the suspect whether they confirm or deny that earlier statement or silence and if they want to add anything. A significant statement is defined as one which appears capable of being used in evidence against the suspect, in particular a direct admission of guilt. A significant silence is defined as a failure or refusal to answer a question or answer satisfactorily when under caution, which might give rise to an adverse inference under the relevant provisions of the Criminal Justice and Public Order Act 1994.[206] It is likely that any unexplained failure to comply with this requirement will be regarded as a significant and substantial breach for the purposes of the exclusionary discretion under s.78.

The requirements of Pt 11 of Code C relating to "interviews" do not apply to what a person is alleged to have said as part of the offence itself, for example, where a person is charged with the use of threatening, abusive or insulting words or behaviour under s.5 of the Public Order Act 1986. In *DPP v Lawrence,*[207] the

---

[203] The test of whether there are grounds to suspect a person of an offence is objective: *Nelson and Rose* [1998] 2 Cr.App.R. 399; *Williams* [2012] EWCA Crim 264.
[204] Paragraph 10A explains that there must be some reasonable objective grounds for the suspicion, based on known facts or information that are relevant to the likelihood that the offence has been committed and the person to be questioned committed it.
[205] RCCJ Report Ch.4 para.50.
[206] These definitions are in para.11.4A of Code C.
[207] *DPP v Lawrence* [2007] EWHC 2154 (Admin); [2008] 1 Cr.App.R. 10.

Divisional Court held that Pt 11, and in particular para.11.13,[208] is directed at what a suspect is alleged to have said of a self-incriminating nature on or after arrest for the conduct in question. This follows from its rationale of preventing verballing in the investigation of offences.

4. *Other breaches of PACE or the Codes of Practice*

6-035   Other breaches of due process may form the basis for excluding a confession under s.78. As with unlawful denials of access to legal advice and failures to observe the recording requirements, the courts are unwilling to constrain the discretion by laying down detailed guidelines. Everything depends on the circumstances of each case and the degree to which the defendant was disadvantaged by the breach.[209] In *Twaites and Brown*,[210] the first defendant made a written confession to theft from the betting shop where she was the manageress. She made the confession to commercial investigators hired by her employers. The investigators did not caution her before the interview. After holding that s.67(9) of PACE applies the Codes of Practice to such investigators, if they are charged with the duty of investigating offences, the Court of Appeal went on to say that the trial judge's consideration of the fairness discretion might have been affected if he had been referred to this provision. This, with respect, is clearly right. The defendant was not in police custody when questioned and might well have felt able to exercise a right of silence if she had been told she had one. Other cases confirm that a failure to caution may justify exclusion of a confession under s.78,[211] although exclusion may be unlikely in the absence of other breaches as well, or of evidence that the accused was prejudiced by the failure to caution.[212]

Similarly, if the police interview a vulnerable suspect, meaning a juvenile, or a person suffering from mental disorder or mental handicap, without an "appropriate adult" being present,[213] this failure grounds a strong argument for exclusion.[214] Exclusion may well be under s.76(2)(b), on the basis that this is something done which is likely to render any confession by such a suspect unreliable.[215] Alternatively, the imbalance of power between police and suspect

---

[208] Paragraph 11.13 provides that a written record shall be made of any comments made by a suspect outside the context of an interview but which might be relevant to the offence.

[209] See, e.g. *King* [2012] EWCA Crim 805 (breach of s.30 of PACE).

[210] *Twaites and Brown* (1990) 92 Cr.App.R. 106.

[211] *Keenan* [1990] 2 Q.B. 54 CA; *Nelson and Rose* [1998] 2 Cr.App.R. 399 CA.

[212] See *Oni* [1992] Crim. L.R. 183 CA; *Pall* (1992) 156 J.P.R. 424 CA; *Gill* [2003] EWCA Crim 2256; [2004] 1 Cr.App.R. 20 (where the statements relied on by the prosecution were lies by the defendants rather than confessions, but the Court of Appeal applied the same principles in holding that evidence was fairly admitted of what they said in an interview that should have been conducted after caution). See also *Devani* (2007) EWCA Crim 1926; [2008] 1 Cr.App.R. 4.

[213] In breach of Code C para.11.15. See also Code C paras 11.1 and 11.18 for limited exceptions to this requirement. For the meaning of "appropriate adult" see Code C para.1.7, and for discussion see B. Littlechild, "Reassessing the Role of the 'Appropriate Adult' " [1995] Crim. L.R. 540; J. Hodgson, "Vulnerable Suspects and the Appropriate Adult" [1997] Crim. L.R. 785.

[214] See P. Mirfield, *Silence, Confessions and Improperly Obtained Evidence* (1997), pp.284 onwards.

[215] As in *Everett* [1988] Crim. L.R. 826 CA; *Moss* (1990) 91 Cr.App.R. 371 CA; *Cox* [1991] Crim. L.R. 276 CA.

in this situation, and the scope for manipulation of the suspect, suggest that it would be prima facie unfair under s.78 to admit an incriminating statement by the suspect.

A balance of authority supports the view that the state of the other evidence is important in considering the exclusionary discretion. In *Keenan*,[216] it was pointed out that weak or non-existent other evidence increases the risks attached to possible verballing, and this was echoed by the Court of Appeal in *Weekes*.[217] The contrary remark in *Walsh*[218] that the presence or absence of other evidence against the defendant "makes little or no difference" should perhaps be read in the context of the finding in that case that the accused had been substantially prejudiced in any event by the denial of access to a solicitor.

The state of the other evidence was always relevant in considering the possible application of the proviso in a case where the Court of Appeal held that evidence should have been excluded. Under the Criminal Appeal Act 1995 the question in all cases is whether the conviction is safe. It is thought that the state of the other evidence will continue to be an essential factor in estimating the safety of a conviction where evidence is held to have been wrongly admitted.

6–036

D.   OTHER ISSUES RELATING TO CONFESSIONS

1.   *Relevance of confessions for reasons other than their truth*

A statement by the accused may be relevant for a reason other than the truth of the statement. It may be relevant, for example, to show that the accused writes or speaks in a particular way. Peculiarities of spelling or expression may help to identify the accused as the perpetrator of the offence. In *Voisin*,[219] the body of a murder victim was found with a piece of paper beside it on which were written the words "Bladie Belgiam". Suspicion fell on the defendant. After his arrest the police asked him whether he would write out the words "bloody Belgian". He agreed and proceeded to write out "Bladie Belgiam". The Court of Criminal Appeal held that this writing was clearly admissible at common law, despite the fact that the defendant had not been cautioned before doing the writing. The CLRC thought the principle of the case was sound and recommended that it should apply even where the evidence in question is contained in an otherwise inadmissible confession.[220]

Accordingly, s.76(4) of PACE provides:

6–037

> "The fact that a confession is wholly or partly excluded in pursuance of this section shall not affect the admissibility in evidence—
> (a)   . . .
> (b)   where the confession is relevant as showing that the accused speaks, writes or expresses himself in a particular way, of so much of the confession as is necessary to show that he does so."

---

[216] *Keenan* [1990] 2 Q.B. 54 CA.
[217] *Weekes* (1993) 97 Cr.App.R. 222.
[218] *Walsh* (1990) 91 Cr.App.R. 161 at 164.
[219] *Voisin* [1918] 1 K.B. 531.
[220] Eleventh Report para.69.

2. *Evidence of subsequently discovered facts*

6–038   Paragraph (a) of s.76(4) and subs.(5) and (6) deal with two problems that caused considerable difficulty at common law. Suppose the accused's confession leads the police to the discovery of relevant facts such as the location of a murder weapon or the ownership of a foreign bank account. If the confession is inadmissible because of the way in which it was obtained, two questions arise about the evidence of the subsequently discovered facts. Can any evidence be given of the facts discovered as a result of the inadmissible confession? If so, can evidence be given that they were discovered as a result of a statement by the accused?

A further question relates to the confession. Can all or any part of the confession be admitted on the basis that its truth is confirmed by the facts discovered as a result of it? The answer to this has already been provided in the discussion of s.76(2). That provision states expressly that a confession obtained by oppression or by anything said or done likely to render any confession unreliable is inadmissible "notwithstanding that it may be true". It is therefore immaterial whether facts found in consequence of the confession confirm the reliability of the whole or any part of it. It remains inadmissible as to the whole; no severance is made of any part specifically shown to be reliable by subsequently discovered facts.[221]

The questions about the subsequently discovered facts are answered as follows. Under s.76(4):

> "The fact that a confession is wholly or partly excluded in pursuance of this section shall not affect the admissibility in evidence—
> (a)   of any facts discovered as a result of the confession."

The section continues:

> "(5)   Evidence that a fact to which this subsection applies was discovered as a result of a statement made by an accused person shall not be admissible unless evidence of how it was discovered is given by him or on his behalf.
> (6)   Subsection (5) above applies—
>   (a)   -to any fact discovered as a result of a confession which is wholly excluded in pursuance of this section; and
>   (b)   -to any fact discovered as a result of a confession which is partly so excluded, if the fact is discovered as a result of the excluded part of the confession."

6–039   Section 76(4)(a) thus makes clear that the admissibility of the subsequently discovered facts is not tainted by the exclusion of the confession. There is no "fruit of the poisoned tree" doctrine in English law.[222] However, the facts in question must satisfy the normal rules of admissibility, including of course the requirement of relevance. In order to be relevant to the issue of the accused's guilt, the facts must tend to incriminate the accused. If they cannot do this without reference to the inadmissible confession, they cannot affect the issue one way or the other and will be inadmissible as part of the prosecution case. This

---

[221] See *Lam Chi-Ming v R.* [1991] 2 A.C. 212 PC.
[222] For the position under the ECHR see below.

was the principle established in the old case of *Warickshall*[223] where evidence of the finding of stolen goods in the defendant's bed was held admissible, although the confession in which she disclosed their whereabouts was not. A modern application is seen in the Privy Council decision in *Lam Chi-Ming v R*.[224] The defendant made a confession to murder that was ruled inadmissible as having been obtained by oppression. Part of the confession disclosed that the knife used in the murder had been thrown into a particular spot in Hong Kong harbour. The defendant agreed to re-enact on video the disposal of the knife, which was duly recovered from the spot he indicated. The Judicial Committee of the Privy Council held that the video should have been excluded as merely a repetition of an unlawfully obtained confession. It then followed that there was nothing to link the finding of the knife with the accused, and the conviction was quashed.

This point has an important implication for the rationale of the rule in s.76(2) concerning the admissibility of confessions. If the rationale of that rule is the privilege against self-incrimination, as some authorities suggest,[225] it would be logical to extend the exclusion of a confession to other evidence obtained as a result of the confession. If such evidence is admitted despite its causal link with the unlawfully induced confession the protection of the privilege turns out to be partial at best, illusory at worst. Despite this, the rule now embodied in s.76(4) of PACE has always preferred to acknowledge that subsequently discovered real evidence is likely to be reliable and will contribute to the factual accuracy of the verdict. This suggests again that the rules in s.76 represent the outcome of a weighting of principles for the achievement of legitimate verdicts, rather than a derivative application of the privilege against self-incrimination.

Interests of legitimacy are further recognised by the limitation in s.76(5) that the prosecution may not reveal that the source of the discovery of the later evidence was an (excluded) statement of the accused.[226] Only the accused may make this link. This is consistent with the view that state reliance on tainted evidence weakens the moral authority and expressive value of the verdict. It follows that the later evidence must incriminate the accused independently so that reference to the earlier confession is unnecessary. However, even where the later evidence can stand on its own, exclusion is still possible under s.78. A judge might take the view, for example, that a deliberate use of violence in order to coerce the accused into revealing the location of a weapon or of prohibited goods had such an adverse effect on the fairness of the proceedings that the evidence of the finding of the weapon or goods should not be admitted.

Such a view would be reinforced in certain cases by consideration of art.6 of the ECHR. Where a confession has been procured by torture, in breach of a suspect's rights under art.3, Strasbourg case law holds that art.6 will be violated

---

[223] *Warickshall* (1783) 1 Leach 263.

[224] *Lam Chi-Ming v R.* [1991] 2 A.C. 212.

[225] *Keenan* [1990] 2 Q.B. 54 at 61 CA per Hodgson J.; *Lam Chi-Ming v R.* [1991] 2 A.C. 212 at 220 PC per Lord Griffiths, who added the rationales of possible unreliability and the importance of police propriety.

[226] This clarifies a point on which the common law authorities were in conflict. The provision gives effect to a minority view of the CLRC (Eleventh Report para.69). Clearly it may cause problems for the prosecution where there is no evidence, apart from the confession, to link the accused with the facts discovered in consequence of it.

not only by the admission of the confession, but also by the admission of other evidence obtained as a result of torture, irrespective of its probative value.[227] In *Gafgen v Germany,* D confessed to murdering a boy he had kidnapped, after he was threatened with torture if he did not reveal the boy's whereabouts.[228] The European Court of Human Rights found that such a threat was not itself an act of torture but did amount to inhuman and degrading treatment in breach of art.3. The court confirmed that the admission of a confession obtained in this way would have rendered the proceedings as a whole unfair.[229] It then went on to consider the admission by the German court of items of real evidence discovered as a result of the confession. These had been admitted not to prove D's guilt as such, but to confirm (in accordance with German law) the truth of a second confession he had made voluntarily at his trial. In these circumstances the European court held that the breach of art.3 had not had an impact on his conviction sufficient to render the trial unfair. Nevertheless, the judgment strongly suggests that if a member state were to seek to use as part of a prosecution case real evidence obtained by inhuman or degrading treatment art. 6 would require the evidence to be excluded. It is almost certain that an English court would follow this guidance and would use s. 78 of PACE for this purpose.[230]

However, the Supreme Court made it clear in the Scottish case of *HM Advocate v P*[231] that it does not regard the European Court of Human Rights as laying down any *general* principle that the fruit of the poisoned tree must always be excluded. The case concerned proposed evidence from a friend of D that in a phone call to the friend D had made a partly incriminating statement that he had had sex with a woman he was accused of raping. D had given the police the name of the friend in an interview without access to legal advice. Any statement D made in the interview was therefore inadmissible, following *Cadder v HM Advocate.*[232] The Supreme Court held that leading the friend's evidence at D's trial would not be incompatible with D's rights under art. 6. In the leading speech Lord Hope stressed the importance of distinguishing between evidence of incriminating statements *created* by the defendant in response to impermissible questioning, and evidence which exists independently of those statements. The friend's evidence of the phone call existed independently of D's statement in the interview and could be adduced without reference to the interview. The police could have found it by some other means, however unlikely such discovery might have been. In such a case it seems that the trial judge may still exclude the evidence in the interest of securing a fair trial but is not obliged to do so.

---

[227] *Jalloh v Germany* (2007) 44 E.H.R.R. 32; *Gafgen v Germany* (2011) 52 E.H.R.R. 1 at [167].

[228] *Gafgen v Germany* (2011) 52 E.H.R.R. 1. The German police had believed, wrongly, that the boy was still alive and were desperate to find him.

[229] *Gafgen v Germany* (2011) 52 E.H.R.R. 1 at [166].

[230] See the judgments of Lords Hope and Brown in *HM Advocate v P* [2011] UKSC 44.

[231] *HM Advocate v P* [2011] UKSC 44.

[232] *Cadder v HM Advocate* [2010] UKSC 43. There was no question in *HM Advocate v P* [2011] UKSC 44 of a breach by the police of art.3.

3.   *Mixed statements*

An aspect of the law of confessions that has caused some difficulty is the problem **6–040** of the "mixed" statement. This is a statement which is partly an admission and partly an exculpatory or self-serving statement. An example would be an acknowledgment by D that he hit P, coupled with a claim that he did so in self-defence.[233] When an out-of-court self-serving statement stands on its own, it is not generally admissible. The hearsay rule prevents it being admitted as evidence of the facts stated, and the common law rule against narrative prevents it being admitted as a previous statement consistent with the accused's testimony as a witness. There is a somewhat ill-defined exception at common law that permits the admission in evidence of the accused's statements to the police in interview. These are used as part of the "general picture" to show the accused's reaction when questioned about the offence.[234] This is a cloudy notion since it appears that the jury may take such statements into account, but they are not evidence of the truth of any denial or explanation they contain.

When such self-serving statements accompany incriminating statements, the courts have balked at requiring trial judges to direct juries that the incriminating parts are evidence of their truth, but that the exculpatory parts are not and are something less. After some divergence of view in the Court of Appeal the law was settled by the House of Lords in *Sharp*.[235] This followed the line of authority in the Court of Appeal represented by *Duncan*.[236] In the case of a mixed statement the judge should direct the jury to consider the whole of the statement, in deciding where the truth lies. In this sense the jury are exceptionally permitted to treat the favourable parts as evidence of their truth. However, the judge may also tell the jury that the favourable parts may deserve less weight because of the ease with which they can be manufactured. If the accused does not testify, the judge can make an adverse comment on the quality of the exculpatory parts, reminding the jury that the accused has not been cross-examined on them.[237] These principles apply not just to mixed statements made to the police but to any mixed statement tendered by the prosecution.

4.   *Safeguards against unreliability*

A word needs to be said about the judge's power to withdraw a case from the jury. **6–041** As a general rule, the jury is entrusted with the responsibility of deciding whether a confession is reliable in the sense of being true and hence whether it is proper to convict upon it. However, the rule is subject to the residual power of the judge to withdraw the case from the jury where certain conditions apply to render a conviction unsafe. In *Mackenzie*[238] Lord Taylor C.J. spelt out the conditions:

---

[233] The test of a "mixed" statement is one of the contents of the statement, not whether the prosecution is relying on any admissions in it: *Western v DPP* [1997] 1 Cr.App.R. 474 DC.
[234] See Ch.14.
[235] *Sharp* [1988] 1 All E.R. 65; *Aziz* [1996] 1 A.C. 41 HL.
[236] *Duncan* (1981) 73 Cr.App.R. 359.
[237] *Aziz* [1996] 1 A.C. 41 HL.
[238] *Mackenzie* (1993) 96 Cr.App.R. 98 at 108. See also *Wood* [1994] Crim. L.R. 222.

"applying the guidance given by this court in *Galbraith* [1981] 1 W.L.R. 1039, we consider that where (1) the prosecution case depends wholly upon confessions; (2) the defendant suffers from a significant degree of mental handicap; and (3) the confessions are unconvincing to a point where a jury properly directed could not properly convict upon them, then the judge, assuming he has not excluded the confessions earlier, should withdraw the case from the jury. The confessions may be unconvincing, for example, because they lack the incriminating details to be expected of a guilty and willing confessor, or because they are inconsistent with other evidence, or because they are otherwise inherently improbable. Cases depending solely or mainly on confessions, like cases depending upon identification evidence, have given rise to miscarriages of justice. We are therefore of opinion that when the three conditions tabulated above apply at any stage of the case, the judge should, in the interests of justice, take the initiative and withdraw the case from the jury."

The formulation of these conditions reflects the facts of the case, which involved a series of confessions by a mentally handicapped suspect to a series of murders, some of which the police did not believe he could have committed. There seems no reason in principle why the power to withdraw wholly unconvincing confessions from the jury should be restricted to confessions by this one class of suspects. Confessions by other vulnerable suspects are candidates for inclusion in an expanded list: suspects suffering from mental illness or personality disorder and juveniles are the most obvious groups. Choo has gone further and posed the question whether the power should not be exercisable whenever the prosecution case depends wholly on confessions that are so unconvincing that no properly directed jury could properly convict on them, regardless of whether the unreliability of the confessions is attributable to mental handicap or to some other factor.[239] There is much to be said for this position, particularly if we are to continue to have no corroboration requirement for confessions.

5.   *Use by an accused of a confession by a co-accused*[240]

6–042   Finally, we return to the question posed earlier of whether one accused (D1) may make use of a confession by a co-accused (D2) where D2's confession is relevant to D1's defence. Suppose that in a police interview D2 has admitted sole responsibility for the offence, in a case where D1 says that he, D1, had nothing to do with it.[241] If the prosecution adduce D2's confession in evidence against D2, then D1 has no problem. Once the evidence is admitted he will be able to take advantage of it for the purposes of his own defence. However, difficulties emerge where the prosecution do not adduce D2's confession in evidence. There may be several possible reasons for this. The trial judge may rule the confession inadmissible under s.76(2) of PACE, or may exclude it in the exercise of his discretion under s.78. The prosecution may decide not to use the confession because it does not fit the case they are presenting at trial. A further possibility is that the prosecution is simply unaware of its existence, as may be the case where D2 makes the confession to someone other than a police officer.[242] The question then is whether D1 can adduce evidence of D2's confession in any or all of these situations.

---

[239] A. Choo, *Evidence Text and Materials* (London, 1998), p.407.
[240] See M. Hirst, "Confessions as Proof of Innocence" [1998] C.L.J. 146.
[241] cf. *Beckford and Daley* [1991] Crim. L.R. 833 CA.
[242] cf. *Campbell and Williams* [1993] Crim. L.R. 448 CA.

One obvious problem is the hearsay rule. The rule prevents a party adducing evidence of a statement made by a person otherwise than while giving oral evidence in the proceedings as evidence of the facts stated. In this context, the effect of the rule is that D1 cannot prove the fact that D2 committed the offence charged by evidence that D2 made a statement of that fact out of court, unless an exception to the rule applies. The common law did not recognise an exception for a confession by a third party, where the third party was not a co-accused.[243] There was, however, a hearsay exception at common law for admissions by parties to litigation. This exception was of course confirmed by s.76(1) of PACE as far as use of confessions by the prosecution is concerned. The use of a confession by a co-accused caused some difficulty until the decision of the House of Lords in *Myers*,[244] which clarified most of the issues, but left one problem unresolved.[245] The Criminal Justice Act 2003 dealt with this problem and placed the law on a statutory footing by inserting a new s.76A into PACE as part of its extensive reforms to the hearsay rule.

Section 76A is based on a recommendation of the Law Commission that the rules relating to the admissibility of confessions should be the same whether evidence of the confession is adduced by the prosecution or by a co-accused. Accordingly s.76A is closely modelled on s.76. Section 76A(1) provides:

> "In any proceedings a confession made by an accused person may be given in evidence for another person charged in the same proceedings (a co-accused) in so far as it is relevant to any matter in issue in the proceedings and is not excluded by the court in pursuance of this section."

The conditions of admissibility of the confession[246] for the co-accused[247] set out in subs.(2) are the same as for the prosecution. A co-accused, like the prosecution, will not be able to adduce evidence of an accused's confession if the confession was obtained by oppression or anything likely to render such a confession unreliable.[248] Subsection (2) of s.76A also sets out the court's duty to exclude the confession if the conditions of admissibility are not met, but makes one change from the equivalent wording of s.76(2):

6–043

---

[243] *Turner* (1975) 61 Cr.App.R. 67 CA; *Blastland* [1986] A.C. 41 HL; *Callan* (1994) 94 Cr.App.R. 467 CA. A confession by a third party may now be admissible under the provisions for admissible hearsay in the Criminal Justice Act 2003 ss.114(1)(d), 116, 117. See Ch.17.

[244] *Myers* [1998] A.C. 124.

[245] For an account of the law before the Criminal Justice Act 2003 see the second edition of this book at pp.210–213.

[246] The definition of "confession" in s.82(1) of PACE is applicable, so a mixed statement will be included; see *Nazir* [2009] EWCA Crim 213, explaining the doubt expressed in *Finch* [2007] EWCA Crim 36; [2007] 1 Cr.App.R. 33. The written basis of an earlier guilty plea by the accused is still a "confession" even though the accused was subsequently permitted to vacate the plea: *Johnson* [2007] EWCA Crim 1651.

[247] Where the accused (the maker of the confession) has pleaded guilty and is no longer charged in the same proceedings as the co-accused s.76A is not applicable: *Finch* [2007] EWCA Crim 36; [2007] 1 Cr.App.R. 33. As the Court of Appeal noted in *Finch*, the accused is then a compellable witness for the co-accused.

[248] This was the point left unresolved by *Myers* [1998] A.C. 124.

"If, in any proceedings where a co-accused proposes to give in evidence a confession made by an accused person, it is represented to the court that the confession was or may have been obtained—

(a)   by oppression of the person who made it; or

(b)   in consequence of anything said or done which was likely, in the circumstances existing at the time, to render unreliable any confession which might be made by him in consequence thereof,

   the court shall not allow the confession to be given in evidence for the co-accused except in so far as it is proved to the court on the balance of probabilities that the confession (notwithstanding that it may be true) was not so obtained."

The difference is that the co-accused has to prove the conditions only to the civil standard of balance of probabilities,[249] whereas the prosecution must establish them beyond reasonable doubt. This is in accordance with the normal principles regarding proof of facts in criminal proceedings. A second important point of difference between the co-accused and the prosecution as regards adducing evidence of an accused's confession is that no exclusionary discretion is available in relation to the co-accused. Section 78 provides for exclusionary discretion for evidence on which the *prosecution* propose to rely, and a judge has no discretion at common law to exclude relevant and admissible defence evidence.[250] Once the co-accused satisfies the court as to the conditions specified in s.76A(2) the court must admit the evidence of the confession.

One situation that needs further explanation occurs where the accused (D2) gives evidence at trial incriminating the co-accused (D1), but the testimony is inconsistent with D2's earlier confession. Can D1 cross-examine D2 on D2's confession as a previous inconsistent statement under ss.4 and 5 of the Criminal Procedure Act 1865? If D2 can prove the conditions of admissibility of the confession under s.76A then the cross-examination is on relevant and admissible evidence and can proceed. But if the judge decides that D2's confession was obtained by oppression, it is inadmissible both for the prosecution and a co-accused. This would suggest that D1 cannot use it in cross-examination as a means of discrediting D1.[251] However, before the enactment of s.76A, it was settled at common law that D1 could cross-examine D2 on D2's previous inconsistent statements on the ground that these were relevant to D1's defence. Such statements included self-incriminating statements by D2 that the prosecution were unable to adduce, either because the statements were liable to be excluded in the judge's discretion,[252] or because they were not made voluntarily and hence were inadmissible for the prosecution in law.[253] As regards admissibility, the problem of the hearsay rule did not arise in this situation at common law. Under ss.4 and 5 of the Criminal Procedure Act 1865,[254] which provide the authority for the proof of previous inconsistent statements by

---

[249] The judge must make a finding that the confession is admissible under s.76A if the issue of admissibility is raised: *L & R v R.* [2011] EWCA Crim 649.

[250] *Lobban v R.* [1995] 1 W.L.R. 877 PC.

[251] See *Treacy* [1944] 2 All E.R. 228, where the Court of Criminal Appeal refused to allow the prosecution to do this.

[252] *Rowson* [1986] Q.B. 174 CA, where the Crown chose not to lead a statement by D2 made in breach of the Judges Rules.

[253] *Lui Mei Lin v R.* [1989] A.C. 288 PC; *Corelli* [2001] Crim. L.R. 913.

[254] Discussed in Ch.14.

witnesses, such statements were held to be relevant only to the credibility of the witness and could not be used as evidence of the facts stated.[255] If this were still the position it is arguable that it would fall outside s.76A, and the previous law would continue to apply. But the rule about the use of previous inconsistent statements has changed. Section 119 of the Criminal Justice Act 2003 provides that a previous inconsistent statement that is admitted by a witness, or that is proved against him under ss.4 or 5 of the Criminal Procedure Act 1865, is admissible as evidence of any matter stated of which the witness could have given oral evidence. If D2's confession can thus be used as a hearsay statement it would seem to be a logical necessity that it must be proved to be admissible under s.76A. On the other hand, it is unfair, and could lead to a miscarriage of justice, if D1 is not permitted to demonstrate to the jury that D2's incriminating testimony against D1 is inconsistent with D2's earlier confession.

---

[255] See *Myers* [1998] A.C. 124 at 139–140 per Lord Hope; citing *Rowson* [1986] Q.B. 174; and *Lui Mei Lin v R.* [1989] A.C. 288.

CHAPTER 7

IDENTIFICATION EVIDENCE

A. INTRODUCTION

7–001   Identity is an issue in many criminal cases.[1] Unless the defendant admits that he committed the relevant criminal act, the prosecution will have to prove it at trial. This means that evidence identifying the defendant as the offender will be necessary.

Evidence of identity can take various forms. One form is expert scientific evidence. This generally consists of expert opinion that a comparison of material obtained from the accused matches material from the scene of the crime or the victim of the offence. Such material can itself take many different forms: they include fingerprints, bodily samples used to construct DNA profiles, fibres from clothing, substances on clothing and shoes, samples of handwriting and so on. Some of these types of evidence may provide cogent proof of identity,[2] although the expert's methods and conclusions may well be contested by the defence. A second form is circumstantial evidence. This might include evidence, for example, that the defendant was found in the vicinity of the crime and failed to account satisfactorily for his presence,[3] or that the defendant was found in possession of materials used in connection with the offence or goods stolen during the offence. Motive may also be relevant to prove identity. The use and weaknesses of circumstantial evidence were considered in Ch.3. A third possibility is real evidence in the form of photographs taken at the scene of the crime, e.g. by a security camera, or tape recordings of the offender's voice. The factfinder may be invited to make the identification itself by comparing the image on the photograph with the appearance of the defendant, or by comparing the voice on the tape with the defendant's voice.

By far the most problematic form of identification evidence is the testimony of eyewitnesses. Eyewitnesses may have seen the actual commission of the offence, or they may have seen something else which tends to connect the accused with the offence. Eyewitness testimony that purports to identify the defendant as the person seen at the material time is notorious for its high risk of unreliability. Mistaken eyewitness evidence of identity has been responsible for some major miscarriages of justice. Yet its use may be essential in many cases where other forms of identification evidence are lacking, or it is desired to use different forms to support each other.

---

[1] It may of course arise as an issue in civil matters, such as paternity or succession to an estate. This chapter is concerned exclusively with identification in criminal cases.

[2] At one time fingerprints were considered to provide almost certain evidence of identity. It was "conservatively" estimated that the chance of two finger impressions from different people being identical were 1 in 64,000,000,000: see D. Campbell, "Fingerprints: A Review" [1985] Crim. L.R. 195. In *Buckley* (1999) 163 J.P. 561 the Court of Appeal said "it has long been known that fingerprint patterns vary from person to person and that such patterns are unique and unchanging throughout life". Recent developments have subjected fingerprint evidence to more critical scrutiny: see the report of the US National Academy of Sciences, *Strengthening Forensic Sciences in the United States: A Path Forward* (2009); the report by Sir Anthony Campbell, *The Fingerprint Inquiry: Scotland* (2011); *Smith (Peter)* [2011] EWCA Crim 1296; [2011] 2 Cr.App.R. 174; S. Cole and A. Roberts, "Certainty, Individualisation and the Subjective Nature of Expert Fingerprint Evidence" [2012] Crim. L.R. 824.

[3] See Criminal Justice and Public Order Act 1994 s.37.

Identification evidence has some parallels with confession evidence. Because **7–002** identity is frequently in issue, evidence of identity is as central in many cases to the proof of guilt as a confession. The Crown Court Study for the Royal Commission on Criminal Justice found that there was "very important" or "fairly important" identification evidence in almost 25 per cent of contested cases.[4] Of these, probably about half involved eyewitness testimony. Yet, like confession evidence, identification evidence may be unreliable on occasion. It can also raise similar problems of legitimacy in the way it is obtained. Examples might be the commission of an assault on the defendant to procure a bodily sample,[5] or a deliberate decision by the police to substitute for an identification parade an inferior and unfair identification procedure.[6] It is not surprising, therefore, that as with confessions, a complex legal regime has evolved to regulate the obtaining and use of identification evidence. This chapter examines this regime and asks whether the legal response to the problems of identification evidence is adequate, or whether more needs to be done to prevent miscarriages of justice and unfair convictions.

The structure of the chapter is that section B discusses the risks associated with eyewitness evidence of identity. Section C analyses how the law regulates the obtaining by the police of eyewitness evidence of identity. Section D deals with some issues concerning the way in which identification evidence is adduced at trial. Section E considers the evaluation of eyewitness identification evidence, including the instructions which a judge must give in a jury trial. Finally, section F makes some general points regarding expert evidence of identity.

B.   THE PROBLEMS OF EYEWITNESS EVIDENCE OF IDENTITY

1.   Miscarriages of justice

It is trite to say that eyewitness evidence of identity carries a significant risk of **7–003** being mistaken. It took a long time for the problem to be officially acknowledged, but there has been general agreement for many years that this form of evidence has the potential to cause serious miscarriages of justice. In 1972 the Criminal Law Revision Committee commented in the Eleventh Report[7]: "We regard mistaken identification as by far the greatest cause of actual or possible wrong convictions". The Devlin Report[8] in 1976 quoted[9] Scarman L.J. in the Court of Appeal as referring to "the vexed question of how the court should deal with identification evidence" and saying later, "we all know there is no branch of human perception more fallible than identifying a person". The report went on to say:

---

[4] M. Zander and P. Henderson, RCCJ Research Study No.19 (London, 1993), pp.92–93. On eyewitness identification evidence in magistrates' courts cases see A. Roberts, "Does Code D Impose an Unrealistic Burden on the System of Summary Justice?" (2001) 165 J.P. 756.
[5] See *Cooke* [1995] 1 Cr.App.R. 318 CA.
[6] See *Nagah* (1991) 92 Cr.App.R. 344 CA, discussed below.
[7] Eleventh Report para.196.
[8] *Report to the Secretary of State for the Home Department of the Departmental Committee on Evidence of Identification in Criminal Cases* (HMSO, 1976).
[9] *Evidence of Identification in Criminal Cases* (1976) para.4.21, citing *Dunne*, October 4, 1974 CA.

"We are satisfied that in cases which depend wholly or mainly on eyewitness evidence of identification there is a special risk of wrong conviction. It arises because the value of such evidence is exceptionally difficult to assess; the witness who has sincerely convinced himself and whose sincerity carries conviction is not infrequently mistaken."[10]

Well-known cases of miscarriage of justice resulting from mistaken evidence of identity start with Adolf Beck, who early in the last century was twice convicted of fraud on the mistaken identification evidence of 15 women (11 on the first occasion and four on the second). He spent several years in prison as a result of the first conviction.[11] The concern aroused by his case led to the establishment of the Court of Criminal Appeal in 1907, the first court constituted for the specific purpose of hearing criminal appeals. Oscar Slater was wrongly convicted of murder in 1909 after two witnesses had identified him leaving the house where the murder took place and another 12 had identified him as the man who had earlier been seen watching the house. He served 19 years before his conviction was quashed.[12] In the 1970s, Luke Dougherty was wrongly convicted of theft after two employees identified him from police photographs as the man they had seen shoplifting in the store where they worked. At the time of the theft he was on a bus trip with some 50 other people. He served several months in prison before the Court of Appeal quashed his conviction in March 1974 as unsafe and unsatisfactory. One month later the Home Secretary recommended the grant of a free pardon to Laszlo Virag and ordered his immediate release from prison. Virag had been convicted of offences of theft of parking meter coin boxes, using a firearm to resist arrest, and wounding a police officer with intent to cause grievous bodily harm or resist arrest. He had been identified as the man concerned in the various incidents that were the subject of the charges by a total of eight witnesses, including five police officers. He served nearly five years before further investigation revealed that the offences in question had almost certainly been committed by another man.

The concern aroused by the cases of Dougherty and Virag led to the establishment of a Home Office Committee of inquiry chaired by Lord Devlin. The Committee's report, published in 1976,[13] reviewed the whole subject of identification evidence in criminal cases and made a series of recommendations relating both to the way in which such evidence was obtained pre-trial and to the way in which it was handled at trial. The latter recommendations included a drastic general rule that it should not be possible to convict upon eyewitness identification evidence alone unless the circumstances of the identification were exceptional or the eyewitness evidence was supported by substantial evidence of another sort. In the event this recommendation was never enacted. It was overtaken shortly afterwards by some belated judicial legislation. Spurred on by the Devlin Report, the Court of Appeal took decisive action. In *Turnbull*,[14] the court laid down detailed guidelines for trial judges to follow in dealing with cases

---

[10] *Evidence of Identification in Criminal Cases* (1976) para.8.1.

[11] See the Report of the Committee of Inquiry into the case of Mr Adolf Beck, Cd.2315 (1904); E.R. Watson (ed) *The Trial of Adolf Beck* (London: William Hodge & Co, 1924).

[12] See W. Roughead (ed) *The Trial of Oscar Slater*, 4th edn (London: 1950).

[13] *Report to the Secretary of State for the Home Department of the Departmental Committee on Evidence of Identification in Criminal Cases* (HMSO, 1976).

[14] *Turnbull* [1977] Q.B. 224.

of disputed identification. In formulating the guidelines the court said that it had tried to give effect to the Devlin recommendations, but in fact introduced a significant modification based on the quality of the identification evidence.[15] The guidelines are fully discussed in Section E below.

These cases are among the best-known examples of a problem that existed on a much bigger scale.[16] Figures quoted in the Devlin Report[17] indicated that in the 30 years from 1945 to 1974 there were up to 125 cases in which the defendant's conviction was declared to be wrong or unsafe in circumstances where the correctness of eyewitness identification was the principal issue. A Home Office study of 38 cases showed 30 positive but wrong identifications from 62 witnesses at identity parades—an error rate of nearly 50 per cent.

7–004

A notable feature of the miscarriage of justice cases was the number of witnesses who mistakenly identified the same man. Normally, other independent witnesses giving evidence to the same effect as witness A would provide strong support for the correctness of A's testimony, but this common sense assumption was consistently falsified in identification cases. This conclusion has two profoundly important implications for criminal justice. It suggests first that eyewitness identification evidence has systemic flaws, dangers of inaccuracy that are not peculiar to particular witnesses or types of witness, and hence that a plurality of witnesses is not necessarily a safeguard against mistakes. Secondly, it suggests that factfinders may not be aware of these dangers and may overestimate the accuracy of eyewitness identifications. If so, questions arise about the efficiency of the techniques available to factfinders in the evaluation of such evidence. These issues of the systemic flaws of identification evidence, and the difficulty of evaluating identification evidence, have greatly interested cognitive and social psychologists who have been conducting research on eyewitness identification for many years. It is to their work that we can now turn as we examine in more detail the reasons why this type of evidence carries such significant risks of unreliability and such potential for causing miscarriages of justice.

2.   The psychological research

Valuable surveys of the psychological research are contained in the studies by Cutler and Penrod,[18] and Wilcock, Bull and Milne.[19] This section draws on their analyses and conclusions. The research has investigated many possible factors

7–005

---

[15] This modification did not commend itself to Lord Devlin, who roundly criticised the Court of Appeal: see his book, *The Judge* (Oxford: Oxford University Press, 1981), pp.188 onwards.

[16] The discussion here concentrates on wrongful conviction as a result of mistaken identity. We should not lose sight of Twining's point that misidentification may have serious consequences for innocent people at all stages of the criminal justice process, involving potential liability to arrest, detention for questioning, search of premises and so on. See W. Twining, *Rethinking Evidence* (1990), Ch.5.

[17] *Evidence of Identification in Criminal Cases* (1976) Apps G and H.

[18] B. L. Cutler and S. D. Penrod, *Mistaken Identification—The Eyewitness, Psychology and the Law* (Cambridge: Cambridge University Press, 1995).

[19] R. Wilcock, R. Bull and R. Milne, *Witness Identification in Criminal Cases: Psychology and Practice* (Oxford: Oxford University Press, 2008). Much useful material is also to be found in S. M.

relating to the accuracy of eyewitness identifications and to their evaluation. There are various ways of classifying these factors; Cutler and Penrod divide sources of identification error into witness factors, perpetrator, event and post-event factors, and they include a separate discussion of the effects of suggestive identification procedures on identification accuracy. For the purposes of the discussion here it is more useful to draw distinctions between factors relating to the original observation by the witness, factors relating to the storage and retrieval of the witness's memory of the observation, and factors affecting the evaluation of the witness's testimony.

(A)   Observation

7–006   It does not of course need a psychologist to point out the obvious problems in relying on an identification by a witness with defective vision, or with some other perceptual disorder. Bad eyesight, colour blindness and so on may clearly affect the witness's reliability, however confident the witness may claim to be about the accuracy of the observation. Similarly, an identification by a witness who had a poor opportunity for observing the offender has an obvious question mark over its accuracy. Common sense tells us that it is easy to make a mistake, for example, at night, or when the view is obstructed, particularly if the witness only sees the person identified for a few seconds.

The distinctive contribution of psychology is in clarifying the effect that certain other factors may have on the likely accuracy of the observations on which later identifications are based. Some factors have relatively little effect. For example, a factor only weakly related to accuracy is the gender of the witness, although there is some evidence that both men and women may be more accurate in recognising faces of people of their own gender.[20] Factors of intelligence and personality seem not to be reliable predictors of identification performance.[21] On the other hand, the age of the witness may be an important predictor of accuracy: in the studies reviewed by Cutler and Penrod the young and the elderly subjects performed significantly less well than other adults.[22] As regards malleable characteristics of the observer the only one that seems to have

---

A. Lloyd-Bostock and B. R. Clifford (eds), *Evaluating Witness Evidence* (1983); I. McKenzie and P. Dunk, "Identification parades: psychological and practical realities" in A. Heaton-Armstrong, E. Shepherd and D. Wolchover (eds), *Analysing Witness Testimony* (London; Oxford University Press, 1999), p.178, and several of the contributions in A. Heaton-Armstrong, E. Shepherd, G. Gudjonsson and D. Wolchover (eds), *Witness Testimony* (Oxford: Oxford Uinversity Press, 2006), esp. Chs 1 and 16.

[20] R. Wilcock, R. Bull and R. Milne, *Witness Identification in Criminal Cases: Psychology and Practice* (Oxford: Oxford University Press, 2008), pp.39, 79.

[21] B. L. Cutler and S. D. Penrod, *Mistaken Identification—The Eyewitness, Psychology and the Law* (1995), pp.84–85; R. Wilcock, R. Bull and R. Milne, *Witness Identification in Criminal Cases: Psychology and Practice* (2008), pp.63, 65-67.

[22] B. L. Cutler and S. D. Penrod, *Mistaken Identification—The Eyewitness, Psychology and the Law* (1995), pp.82–83. See also R. Wilcock, R. Bull and R. Milne, *Witness Identification in Criminal Cases: Psychology and Practice* (2008), p.39 for similar conclusions. On child witnesses generally, see Ch.13 below.

a significant effect is intoxication, which unsurprisingly decreases accuracy.[23] However, one interesting finding of some research studies concerns the accuracy of police officers. Wilcock reports that police officers may be significantly better than civilians at remembering details of a crime they have witnessed (such as the type of knife used), but seem to be no better at making accurate identifications of perpetrators.[24] This is potentially important because it is counter-intuitive: a lay factfinder might well reason that a police officer is likely, by virtue of training and experience, to be more reliable, but the empirical data do not bear this out.[25] Finally in relation to observer factors, we should note the possible distorting effects of bias. Bias may take the crude form of stereotyping, as where a witness expects the perpetrator of an offence to be a member of a particular racial group and makes an identification accordingly.[26] Alternatively, the bias may be in the more subtle form of an expectation aroused by past experience, as where a person is wrongly identified as a member of a gang committing an offence by virtue of the fact that the witness has seen him or her before in the company of other members of the gang.[27]

Turning to factors related to the offender rather than to the observer, it seems that the gender and race of the person identified do not by themselves affect the accuracy of the identification. However, there is substantial research evidence of an "own-race" bias in accuracy.[28] Members of particular racial groups are generally better at identifying members of the same group than members of other racial groups, and this seems to be true for all groups. One factor which increases accuracy is the distinctiveness of the "target". People who have a highly distinctive facial appearance are more likely to be accurately identified than those of a more neutral appearance.[29] On the other hand, changes in facial appearance and the use of disguises significantly decrease accuracy. Cutler and Penrod give a striking illustration of how the use of a hat to obscure the hair and the hairline can make different faces look very similar.[30] The use of a weapon in the commission

---

[23] B. L. Cutler and S. D. Penrod, *Mistaken Identification—The Eyewitness, Psychology and the Law* (1995), p.90; R. Wilcock, R. Bull and R. Milne, *Witness Identification in Criminal Cases: Psychology and Practice* (2008), pp.77–78.

[24] R. Wilcock, R. Bull and R. Milne, *Witness Identification in Criminal Cases: Psychology and Practice* (2008), p.67.

[25] Judges agree: in *Reid v R.* [1990] 1 A.C 363 Lord Ackner stated that experience had shown that police identification could be just as unreliable as identification by ordinary members of the public (p.392).

[26] See E. Loftus, *Eyewitness Testimony* (Cambridge MA: Harvard University Press, 1979), p.39. For further discussion see R. Wilcock, R. Bull and R. Milne, *Witness Identification in Criminal Cases: Psychology and Practice* (2008), Ch.6.

[27] E. Loftus, *Eyewitness Testimony* (1979) .

[28] B. L. Cutler and S. D. Penrod, *Mistaken Identification—The Eyewitness, Psychology and the Law* (1995), p.104; R. Wilcock, R. Bull and R. Milne, *Witness Identification in Criminal Cases: Psychology and Practice* (2008), pp.78–79.

[29] B. L. Cutler and S. D. Penrod, *Mistaken Identification—The Eyewitness, Psychology and the Law* (1995), p.98.

[30] B. L. Cutler and S. D. Penrod, *Mistaken Identification—The Eyewitness, Psychology and the Law* (1995), p.100.

of the offence may have the effect of focusing the witness's attention on the weapon rather than the person wielding it; this again may adversely affect accuracy of identification.[31]

(B)   Storage and retrieval of memory[32]

7–007   A number of post-event factors can significantly affect the accuracy of a subsequent identification. It is a commonplace of experience that memory fades over time, and the psychological research confirms that the accuracy of identification declines with the period of delay between the original observation and the act of identification.[33] The longer the memory is stored, the fewer correct identifications are made. The research experiments do not give sufficiently consistent results to support reliable predictions about the effect of particular delays, although one extensive group of studies some years ago suggested that there is a significant decline in accuracy after four months.[34]

The research also suggests that retrieval of memory can be strongly influenced by the conduct of identification procedures. For example, a witness may pick out a person on a parade, having previously identified the person from a police photograph. In such a case the parade identification "is probably not an independent recollection of the crime perpetrator but is based in part on familiarity rooted in having identified the person from a mugshot".[35] In other words, the witness may be retrieving a memory of the photograph rather than the original observation. Secondly, Cutler and Penrod suggest, on the basis of an extensive review, that there is convincing evidence that suggestive identification instructions influence eyewitness performance.[36] "Biased" instructions that suggest to witnesses that a perpetrator is present in a parade when this is not the case significantly increase the rate of false identifications. Interestingly, however, the rate of false identifications from "perpetrator-absent" procedures is substantially reduced when the choice of persons is presented to the witness in sequence rather than simultaneously. The value of this alternative style of presentation may be particularly important in relation to the showing of photographs to witnesses as a means of identifying a suspect. It might help to reduce the risk of the witness picking out from a group of photographs all seen at

---

[31] B. L. Cutler and S. D. Penrod, *Mistaken Identification—The Eyewitness, Psychology and the Law* (1995), pp.101–102; R. Wilcock, R. Bull and R. Milne, *Witness Identification in Criminal Cases: Psychology and Practice* (2008), pp.76–77.

[32] On the characteristics and weaknesses of memory generally see *Guidelines on Memory and the Law*, a Report of the Research Board of the British Psychological Society (2008), discussed by A. Keane, "The Use at Trial of Scientific Findings relating to Human Memory" [2010] Crim. L.R. 19.

[33] B. L. Cutler and S. D. Penrod, Mistaken *Identification—The Eyewitness, Psychology and the Law* (1995), pp.105–106, R. Wilcock, R. Bull and R. Milne, *Witness Identification in Criminal Cases: Psychology and Practice* (2008), p.40.

[34] J. W. Shepherd, "Identification after long delays" in S. M. A. Lloyd-Bostock and B. R. Clifford (eds), *Evaluating Witness Evidence* (Chichester: Wiley-Blackwell, 1983), p.173.

[35] B. L. Cutler and S. D. Penrod, *Mistaken Identification—The Eyewitness, Psychology and the Law* (1995), p.110.

[36] B. L. Cutler and S. D. Penrod, *Mistaken Identification—The Eyewitness, Psychology and the Law* (1995), p.122.

the same time the one that most resembles the person seen, rather than one of a person whom the witness actually recognises as the person seen. Resemblance is not the same as recognition.

Further possible sources of contamination of memory include discussion with other witnesses and information about the offence or the suspect communicated to the witness by the police. These inputs could cause the witness to modify the memory to make it correspond with the additional information.[37] The risk of contamination of memory is increased if police interviewers ask the witness only closed or leading questions. The courts have shown themselves sensitive to the risks of inaccuracy and unfairness resulting from eyewitnesses being together before an identification procedure takes place.[38]

(C) Evaluation of eyewitness accuracy

A factfinder relying on common sense in deciding whether to accept a witness's testimony as reliable might well be tempted to attach importance to two factors. One is the witness's consistency: to what extent does the prior description that the witness gave to the police match the appearance of the person whom the witness has identified? The greater the congruence and completeness of the description, the more the factfinder might accept the accuracy of the identification. The other factor is the witness's confidence. The more confident the witness is in his or her accuracy, the more inclined the factfinder might be to accept the identification. The psychological research offers some interesting perspectives on these tendencies. The review by Cutler and Penrod concludes that consistency of testimony (of crime details and person descriptions) is unrelated to identification accuracy.[39] Consistent witnesses do not have higher rates of accuracy than inconsistent ones. The necessary implication is that inconsistencies between the description and the identification may not detract significantly from the reliability of the latter. This is undoubtedly counter-intuitive. It contradicts the received wisdom of the courts and the established practice at the criminal Bar; defence barristers habitually make a great deal of these discrepancies, and some judgments have highlighted them as grounds for doubting the correctness of a conviction.[40] Clearly this is a matter on which further research is needed. As regards the factor of confidence, early studies suggested that placing a lot of weight on a witness's confidence in the correctness of an identification might be a mistake. It seemed that there was no significant positive correlation between confidence and accuracy.[41] However, Wilcock et al report that more recent research has found that confidence may be related to accuracy in certain

7–008

---

[37] R. Wilcock, R. Bull and R. Milne, *Witness Identification in Criminal Cases: Psychology and Practice* (2008), pp.41–43.

[38] See, e.g. *Finley* [1993] Crim. L.R. 50; *Martin and Nicholls* [1994] Crim. L.R. 218.

[39] B. L. Cutler and S. D. Penrod, *Mistaken Identification—The Eyewitness, Psychology and the Law* (1995), p.95.

[40] See, e.g. *Fergus* (1994) 98 Cr.App.R. 313.

[41] R. Wilcock, R. Bull and R. Milne, *Witness Identification in Criminal Cases: Psychology and Practice* (2008), p.68.

experimental situations.[42] How far such findings provide solid empirical support for a 'common sense' belief in the relationship between confidence and accuracy is unclear; again further research is called for. Meanwhile the *Turnbull* guidelines will continue to require trial judges to warn juries that even honest and confident witnesses can make mistakes in identification.

C. OBTAINING EYEWITNESS EVIDENCE OF IDENTITY: THE LEGAL RESPONSE

7–009 Given the problems associated with eyewitness identification evidence, the adequacy of the legal response is a critical issue. Broadly speaking, this response takes two forms. One form consists of the statutory regulation of procedures for obtaining eyewitness identification evidence in the investigatory stage. The aims of the regulation are to ensure that, as far as possible, the procedures are fair to the suspect and the evidence obtained from them is reliable. The other form consists of the judicial guidelines that a trial judge must follow in dealing with disputed eyewitness identification evidence at trial. The object of the guidelines is the avoidance of miscarriages of justice by wrongful conviction, hence a major concern is the direction to be given to juries to educate them as to the dangers of this type of evidence on the assumption that these are dangers of which they may be unaware. Both techniques—the statutory regulation of police procedures and the judicial control of the evaluation of identification evidence—have developed in recent decades. They have now reached a level of considerable detail and sophistication. It would, however, be dangerous to assume that they have resolved all the problems. Cases of wrongful identification still occur from time to time,[43] although it is also fair to say that the level of public anxiety about the subject is much less than it was in the 1970s. The Royal Commission on Criminal Justice received little evidence on the treatment of identification evidence, and its recommendations on the subject were restricted to minor modifications of Code D of PACE.[44]

In this section we examine the pre-trial procedures for the obtaining of identification evidence from eyewitnesses. Following a recommendation by the Royal Commission on Criminal Procedure,[45] Parliament decided in 1984 to make the procedures subject to statutory control; accordingly the Codes of Practice issued pursuant to s.66 of PACE include in Code D a code of practice for the identification of persons by police officers.[46] This title is misleading, since the Code is largely concerned with the procedures by which the police obtain evidence of identification by witnesses who are ordinary members of the public. Code D also regulates a number of other procedures by which the police may

---

[42] R. Wilcock, R. Bull and R. Milne, *Witness Identification in Criminal Cases: Psychology and Practice* (2008), pp.68–71.

[43] For example see *McGranaghan* [1995] 1 Cr.App.R. 559.

[44] RCCJ Report Ch.2 paras 9–2.

[45] RCCP Report para.3.138.

[46] Code D incorporates, inter alia, recommendations of the Devlin Committee on pre-trial procedures: see the Devlin Report, *Evidence of Identification in Criminal Cases* (1976), paras 8.9–8.20. For comment on the legal regime, see A. Roberts, "The problem of mistaken identification: some observations on process" (2004) 8 E. & P. 100.

obtain evidence of identification, including fingerprints and bodily samples. However, Code D is not comprehensive. It covers in detail formal procedures for obtaining identification by witnesses, and cases in which the police produce a suspect to the eyewitness,[47] but there are a number of informal and other procedures that it does not cover. We will look first at the general issue of the purpose and scope of Code D; we will then consider the problematic issue of how far Code D applies to "on the spot" investigations by police and eyewitnesses; lastly we will consider the detailed application of Code D and the consequences of breach of the Code.

1. The purpose and scope of Code D generally

Like the other PACE codes, Code D applies to police officers and other persons charged with the duty of investigating offences or charging offenders. The importance of the Codes in guiding and directing police investigations has been stressed by the courts on many occasions. In *Popat*,[48] Hobhouse L.J. reiterated this point and continued:

7–010

> "But there is a more fundamental purpose which is to provide standards which can be applied to police conduct and to ensure, as far as it is practicable to do so, the quality and reliability of the evidence collected by police officers and used in criminal proceedings. The areas of interviewing and obtaining admissions from suspects are one example of this; another is identification evidence. Thus the Codes have a direct bearing upon questions arising under ss.76–78 of the Act. At a trial, the trial judge has to consider any question of compliance with the Code in deciding the question of fairness under s.78."[49]

The purpose and scope of Code D has been conveniently summarised by Birch[50]:

> "Formal identification is governed by Code D, which seeks, by laying down strict procedural guidelines, to ensure fairness in identifications conducted under the supervision of the police. Code D does not of itself prevent the prosecution relying on, say, an informal identification by the eyewitness of the suspect; nor could it do so, as the code is not in any sense a rule of admissibility. Rather, it provides guidance on the sort of identification which will keep the police on the right side of s.78 of PACE, which provides the mechanism for the exclusion of 'unfair' identifications.
>
>   It follows that informal identifications may be given in evidence provided they give rise to no unfairness, and that the risk run by the police if they resort to informal procedures where Code D provides a formal alternative is that they may be suspected of seeking to frustrate the possibility of a fairer and more suitable procedure taking place at a later stage."

It is worth stressing Birch's point that Code D does not state rules of admissibility. Like the other PACE Codes, it sets out procedures to be followed by the police in the investigation of offences. Breach of the procedures does not make any evidence obtained in consequence inadmissible in law; rather such breach is taken into account by the court in deciding whether to exercise its

---

[47] *Popat* [1998] 2 Cr.App.R. 208 CA.
[48] *Popat* [1998] 2 Cr.App.R. 208 CA. The actual decision in this case was overruled by the House of Lords in *Forbes* [2001] 1 All E.R. 686, but this does not affect the accuracy of Hobhouse L.J.'s dictum.
[49] *Popat* [1998] 2 Cr.App.R. 208 at 212.
[50] In her Commentary to *Oscar* [1991] Crim. L.R. 778 CA.

powers of discretionary exclusion of evidence, notably the power under s.78 of PACE. As we have seen, this is a general power to exclude any evidence on which the prosecution proposes to rely. Accordingly it will apply equally to any identification evidence obtained by procedures falling either within or outwith the scope of Code D. Similarly the Court of Appeal's power of review of the safety of a conviction embraces the whole of the evidence admitted in the case.

7–011   The importance of these general powers is clearly seen in one situation where Code D has no application, namely where members of the public adopt their own informal methods of identification. In *O'Leary*,[51] a young girl told her parents she had been assaulted a few minutes earlier. She described the clothes her attacker was wearing, whereupon her father went to see if he could find the man. He saw a man, the defendant, wearing clothes that matched the description. He took the defendant back to his house after a struggle and asked his daughter whether this was the man. She said it was. The defendant denied the incident, and although he told some lies to the police, they did not amount to corroboration of the girl's story. The Court of Appeal, with some hesitation, refused to interfere with the trial judge's decision to admit the evidence of this informal confrontation,[52] but allowed the defendant's appeal on the basis of a "lurking doubt"[53] about the safety of the conviction. The doubt arose from the circumstances of the confrontation, involving a distressed little girl brought face to face with a man in the clutches of her father, and the lack of any other evidence supporting the accuracy of her identification. One might reinforce the doubt by pointing out that the clothes in question—black leather jacket and jeans—are not uncommon and might well have been worn by more than one man in the area at the time.

O'Leary can be compared in this respect with *Oscar*,[54] where a witness saw a man wearing distinctive clothing trying to burgle nearby premises. She called the police, describing the man's clothing. The police arrested the defendant close by, and apparently hiding, a few minutes later. On arrest he was wearing the distinctive clothing mentioned by the witness who immediately identified him as the man she had seen. In the circumstances of this case the court was positive that it was not unfair to admit the evidence of identification and that there was nothing unsafe about the conviction.

Other cases to which Code D does not apply include accidental meetings between a witness and a person whom the witness then identifies,[55] recognition of the defendant's voice as opposed to his face,[56] and identifications carried out abroad under arrangements made by foreign police forces.[57] The last of these is

---

[51] *O'Leary* (1988) 87 Cr.App.R. 387 CA. See also *R. v I* [2007] EWCA Crim 923; [2007] 2 Cr. App. R. 24 (informal identification from photographs shown to the witness by the school attended by the defendant).

[52] Taking the view that the decision to admit the evidence was not *Wednesbury* unreasonable: (1988) 87 Cr.App.R. 387 at 392.

[53] Applying the test laid down by Widgery L.J. in *Cooper (Sean)* [1969] 1 Q.B. 267.

[54] *Oscar* [1991] Crim. L.R. 778 CA.

[55] *Long* [1991] Crim. L.R. 453 CA.

[56] *Deenik* [1992] Crim. L.R. 578 CA. Ormerod has argued strongly that there should be an analogous code for obtaining evidence of voice identification: "Sounds familiar?—Voice Identification Evidence" [2001] Crim. L.R. 595, and see the discussion in Section F below.

[57] See *Quinn* [1990] Crim. L.R. 581 CA.

probably only a formal exclusion in the sense that an English court, when applying the fairness test in s.78 of PACE, is very likely to compare the fairness of the actual procedure used against the standards prescribed by Code D. It has also been held that Code D did not apply in circumstances where witnesses were asked whether they recognised the defendant from a contemporary photograph as someone they had worked with 18 years earlier, and the defendant's appearance had changed substantially in the intervening period.[58] Finally, the Court of Appeal has expressed the view that Code D does not apply to police officers viewing CCTV footage to see whether they recognise anyone shown in the photographs.[59]

2. The purpose and scope of Code D: on-the-spot investigations

A point raised by *Oscar* and several other cases is how far Code D applies when the police are engaged in investigations at the scene of the crime shortly after its commission. Typically such investigations begin when a victim and/or a witness reports an offence and usually gives a description of the person who committed it. Such reports and descriptions can be followed up in more than one way. The witness may identify the offender to the police when the police arrive on the scene. The police may try to find the offender by taking the witness on a tour of the area to see if the witness can point out the person in question on the street. The police may conduct a search of the area themselves, find a person matching the description and then ask the witness whether this is the person in question. The police and the witness may maintain observation over a period of time in the hope that the offender will reappear.

7–012

There are two provisions of the Code that need to be considered in this context. The first is para 3.2. This applies where the identity of the suspect is not known. Paragraph 3.4 states that references to a suspect being "known" mean that there is sufficient information known to the police to justify the arrest of a particular person for suspected involvement in the offence. According to Lord Bingham in *Forbes*[60] there will not be "sufficient information" for this purpose unless the police have some apparently reliable evidence implicating that person. Paragraph 3.2 begins:

> "In cases when the suspect's identity is not known, a witness may be taken to a particular neighbourhood or place to see whether they can identify the person they saw. Although the number, age, sex, race, general description and style of clothing of other people present at the location and the way in which any identification is made cannot be controlled, the principles applicable to the formal procedures under paragraphs 3.5 to 3.10 shall be followed as far as practicable. For example ... "

The paragraph goes on to list five examples of principles for the police to follow where witnesses are making "on-the-spot" identifications. In summary these are: where practicable a record should first be made of the witness's description of the suspect; care should be taken not to direct the witness's attention to any particular

---

[58] *Folan* [2003] EWCA Crim 908.
[59] *Chaney* [2009] EWCA Crim 21 at [30].
[60] *Forbes* [2001] 1 All E.R. 686 at [692].

individual unless this cannot be avoided; multiple witnesses should be kept separate; once a witness makes a positive identification so as to give the police sufficient information to justify an arrest the formal identification procedures set out from para.3.4 onwards take over; a detailed record should be made of all the circumstances of the on-the-spot identification.

7–013   According to May L.J. in *El-Hannachi*,[61] interpreting the predecessor of this paragraph, it:

> "applies most readily to circumstances, of which the facts of *Popat* are a clear example, where, after due consideration and without any specific need for urgency, the police take a witness to what they regard as a likely place to observe whether the witness can identify a person who may pass by."

In *Popat*,[62] the witness, a victim of two separate incidents of assault and attempted rape by the same man, kept watch on several occasions from the window of her flat, accompanied by a police officer. On the fifth occasion she observed a man in the street whom she told the officer she recognised as her assailant. This was a case where the witness had reported the incidents to the police and had already given a description of the assailant. In *El-Hannachi* a witness to an affray in a car park was taken in a police car almost immediately afterwards along a road where participants in the affray had dispersed. She was asked by a police officer to say whether she recognised anyone, and she pointed out the defendants as having been involved in the affray. May L.J. was clearly doubtful whether the case came within the paragraph at all, but held that if it did, there was no breach of it by the police since it was not practicable for a record to be made of the witness's descriptions of the suspects before she was driven up the road.

Where the suspect is "known" and "available",[63] the formal identification procedures set out from para.3.4 onwards apply. The crucial provision is para.3.12, which deals with the circumstances in which one of these identification procedures must be held. This provides that whenever:

> "(i)   a witness has identified a suspect or purported to have identified them prior to any identification procedure set out in paragraphs 3.5 to 3.10 having been held; or
>
> (ii)   there is a witness available, who expresses an ability to identify the suspect, or where there is a reasonable chance of the witness being able to do so, and they have not been given an opportunity to identify the suspect in any of the procedures set out in paragraphs 3.5 to 3.10,
>
> and the suspect disputes being the person whom the witness claims to have seen, an identification procedure shall be held unless it is not practicable or it would serve no useful purpose in proving or disproving whether the suspect was involved in committing the offence. For example, when it is not disputed that the suspect is already well known to the witness who claims to have seen them commit the crime."

---

[61] *El-Hannachi* [1998] 2 Cr.App.R. 226 at 236 CA.

[62] *Popat* [1998] 2 Cr.App.R. 208 CA.

[63] A suspect is "available" if he is immediately available or will be within a reasonably short time and willing to take an effective part in at least one of the procedures that it is practicable to arrange: para.3–4.

The relationship between the duty to conduct a formal identification procedure **7–014** and the power to enable a witness to make an on-the-spot identification was settled by the House of Lords in *Forbes*.[64] Resolving a conflict of authority in the Court of Appeal on the interpretation of the predecessors to paras 3.2 and 3.12, the House held that the paragraph in Code D creating the duty was to be read literally. Therefore, where an eyewitness informally identified a suspect to the police, for example, by picking him out on the street in accordance with the procedure permitted for on-the-spot investigations, and the suspect disputed the identification, an identification parade[65] would still be required. In this way the two paragraphs were held to have a sequential and cumulative effect. Although the wording of the two paragraphs has changed to some extent in the latest version of Code D, it seems clear that the relationship remains as stated in *Forbes*.[66] It follows that as a general rule a suspect who disputes an identification has a right under para.3.12 to a formal identification procedure. Even where the witness has previously made a positive street identification in good conditions, the suspect is entitled to put that to the test, in the interests of reliability and fairness. Lord Bingham, who delivered the unanimous opinion of the House in *Forbes*, stated that Code D is an "intensely practical" document. It sets out clear rules for the police to follow, and in his view there was no warrant for qualifying the plain language of the paragraph. Lord Bingham added that the right to a parade was intended to protect suspects from the risk of a miscarriage of justice. It was not to be subject to a police officer's judgment on whether a satisfactory identification had already taken place.

The right to an identification procedure is not, however, absolute. There is an exception for cases where a procedure would not be practicable; these are discussed in the next section. There is also an exception for cases where a procedure would serve no useful purpose. The example given in para.3.12 is where it is not disputed[67] that the suspect is already well known to the witness. This echoes a dictum of Lord Bingham in *Forbes* that suggested that the mandatory obligation would not apply where the case was one of "pure recognition" of someone well known to the witness. Whether a person is "well known" to the recognising witness is of course a question of degree; this may sometimes present the police with difficult decisions on when a formal procedure can safely be dispensed with.[68] Lord Bingham referred also to cases where

---

[64] *Forbes* [2001] 1 All E.R. 686.

[65] Now a video identification: see below.

[66] See para.3.2(d) which states that it is not necessary for a witness who has made a positive identification under para.3.2 to take part in a further procedure, *subject to paragraph 3.12* .. (emphasis added).

[67] Where this is disputed in a case of alleged "recognition", a failure to hold an identification procedure is likely to be a breach of Code D: see *Harris* [2003] EWCA Crim 174.

[68] In *Fergus* [1992] Crim. L.R. 363 the Court of Appeal held that a parade should have been held where the witness had seen the suspect only once before and knew his name only by hearsay. cf. *Reid* [1994] Crim. L.R. 442, where the witness had met the defendant on a number of occasions and had been threatened by him earlier on the night in question. No parade took place. The Court of Appeal held that it was acceptable for the trial judge to admit evidence of a dock identification instead. Lapse of time may make a difference: in *McKenna v DPP* [2005] EWHC 677 (Admin), Newman J. held that it was a breach of para.3.12 not to hold a parade where the witness recognised the defendant in the street as someone she had known 14 years earlier and seen maybe twice since.

holding a parade would be futile because the witness makes it plain that he cannot identify the culprit or can only identify clothing. But again there may be problematic cases. Suppose a witness says that he or she caught only a glimpse of the suspect's face but would recognise the suspect's distinctive clothing. Should the suspect be entitled to demonstrate that the witness cannot pick him out on a formal procedure?[69] Does this serve a useful purpose? In cases of uncertainty, given the mandatory nature of para.3.12, the principle should be that if there is any reasonable doubt that a useful purpose might be served, and the identification is disputed, a formal procedure should be conducted.

It should be noted at this point that a breach of the obligation to hold a formal procedure will not automatically render evidence of the informal identification inadmissible. Lord Bingham confirmed in *Forbes* that exclusion will continue to be a matter for the trial judge's discretion under s.78 of PACE, taking account of all the circumstances of the case. He did not comment further on the criteria for exercising the discretion but held that the informal identification evidence in *Forbes* was rightly admitted, despite the breach of the duty to hold a parade:

> "The evidence was compelling and untainted, and was supported by the evidence (which it was open to the jury to accept) of what the appellant said at the scene, it did not suffer from such problems or weaknesses as sometimes attend evidence of this kind, as, for example, where the suspect is already visibly in the hands of the police at the moment he is identified to them by the complainant."[70]

7–015   In the light of this approach, exclusion may be unlikely where there is no allegation of bad faith against the police in the failure to hold a formal procedure, the informal identification was a positive one made fairly in good conditions, and it is supported by other evidence.[71] Lord Bingham indicated in *Forbes* that if the judge does admit the evidence, despite the breach of Code D, then he should give an appropriate direction to the jury inviting them to consider the possible effect of the breach on the reliability of the informal identification. Such a direction is intended to counter any prejudice arising to the defendant from the breach. The trial judge had not given such a direction in *Forbes*, but the House of Lords considered that the conviction was nonetheless safe in view of the strength of the identification evidence.[72]

The ultimate question in such cases remains one of whether the evidence that the prosecution proposes to give of an on-the-spot identification would so adversely affect the fairness of the proceedings that it ought not to be admitted. The principles mentioned above will be important considerations on the issue of fairness. Among the matters that the judge will need to take into account are

---

[69] Should it be relevant that identification procedures may be expensive in terms of police time and resources? In relation to identification parades Roberts, "Does Code D Impose an Unrealistic Burden" (2001) 165 J.P. 756, 757, cited police estimates of £605 per parade (West Midlands Police) and £1,200 (Metropolitan Police).

[70] *Forbes* [1999] 2 Cr.App.R. 501 at 517 (a citation from the Court of Appeal in *Forbes*).

[71] Thus in *McKenna v DPP* [2005] EWHC 677 (Admin) Newman J. held it was not unfair to admit the evidence of the street identification despite the breach; the witness was an honest off-duty special constable, it was a case of recognition rather than identification, the recognition was made under good conditions, and there was supporting circumstantial evidence which D admitted.

[72] cf. *Harris* [2003] EWCA Crim 174, where an appeal was allowed for failure to give such a direction.

whether witnesses were allowed to be together before making their identifications, whether the police failed to obtain descriptions from the witnesses before the identifications occurred (assuming that this was practicable) and whether a record was kept of what the witnesses said when viewing suspects arrested. Any defects in the procedures revealed by the answers to these questions would adversely affect the fairness of the trial because they would make it that much harder for the defendant to challenge the reliability of the identifications. In this connection it is likely to be particularly important, where there are multiple witnesses, for the police to keep back at least one eyewitness for use in a formal procedure later.

3.   The application of Code D and the consequences of breach

(A)   An overview of Code D

Before discussing the consequences of breach of Code D in more detail, it is necessary to consider the formal regulatory regime that it establishes. The duty created by para.3.12, to conduct identification procedures where the case involves disputed eyewitness identification evidence and the identity of the suspect is known to the police, has been noted. Paragraph 3.13 provides that such a procedure may also be held if the officer in charge of the investigation considers that it would be useful. Code D sets out a number of methods of formal identification. In order of preference they are:

7–016

(i)   video identification;
(ii)   identification parade;
(iii)   group identification;
(iv)   confrontation.

The first safeguard against the risk of unreliable identifications is the requirement that the responsibility for arranging and conducting these procedures shall rest with an officer who is independent of the investigation (the "identification officer") and who is not below the rank of inspector.[73] The Code aims to prevent possible contamination of the identification witnesses by prohibiting any officer involved with the investigation of the case from taking any part in the procedures.[74]

A video identification is the first method of choice. When the duty under para.3.12 to hold an identification procedure applies, the suspect is initially to be offered a video identification, unless this is not practicable, or an identification parade is more practicable and more suitable than a video identification, or a group identification is more suitable than either and the identification officer considers it practicable to arrange. The identification officer and the officer in charge of the investigation should consult each other to decide which option is to

---

[73] Code D para.3.11. The identification officer can delegate the procedures, but only if he can supervise effectively and either intervene or be contacted for advice.
[74] Code D para.3.11.

be offered.[75] A suspect is not required to consent to take part in any of these three procedures,[76] but if he refuses the procedure first offered he will be asked to state his reason and he will be allowed to make representations as to why another procedure should be used.[77] It should be explained to the suspect that if he does not consent to any of the three procedures his refusal may be given in evidence in any subsequent trial and, perhaps more importantly, that the police may proceed covertly without his consent to test whether a witness can identify him.[78] In these circumstances most suspects are well advised to co-operate in one of the procedures, since they and their legal advisers will then be able to satisfy themselves that the procedure is fairly conducted.

7–017   A video identification must be carried out in accordance with Annex A of Code D. The procedure is that the witness views a set of video images that must include the suspect and at least eight other people who, so far as possible, resemble the suspect in age, general appearance and position in life.[79] Moving images must be used,[80] and they must, as far as possible, show the suspect and other people in the same positions or carrying out the same sequence of movements. Unusual physical features of the suspect, such as scars, tattoos or hair colour, may either be concealed or replicated on the images of the other people.[81] The suspect's solicitor, but not the suspect, may attend the showing of the images to the witness.[82] If no representative attends, the viewing must be recorded on video. Annex A also contains detailed instructions for the conduct of the video identification; these include telling the witness to view the whole set of images at least twice before making any decision whether they can pick someone out as the person they saw on the earlier occasion.

Identification parades are carried out in accordance with Annex B to Code D. The procedure tests whether the witness can pick out the person previously observed from a line of people of similar appearance to the suspect. A parade can take place in a normal room or one equipped with a one-way viewing screen, so that the witness cannot be seen by the suspect.[83] The suspect has a right to have a solicitor or friend present. Where the witness views the parade from behind a screen, and there is no representative of the suspect, the viewing shall be recorded on video.[84] Composition of the parade is similar to the requirements for video identifications: at least eight people in addition to the suspect who, so far as possible, resemble him in age, height, general appearance and position in life.[85] If the suspect has an unusual physical feature steps may be taken with his

---

[75] Code D para.3.14.
[76] Code D para.3.17(iv).
[77] Code D para.3.15.
[78] Code D para.3.17(v).
[79] Code D Annex A para.2. There is no requirement that the other persons should resemble the suspect in *height*, unlike the rule for identification parades (Annex B para.9).
[80] Subject to 2 exceptions (see para.3.5 of Code D), when still images may be used.
[81] Code D Annex A para.2A.
[82] Code D Annex A para.9.
[83] Code D Annex B para.2.
[84] Code D Annex B para.2.
[85] Code D Annex B para.9.

agreement to conceal the location of that feature on him and the other members of the parade.[86] There are detailed instructions in Annex B for the conduct of the parade.

An alternative to both video identifications and parades is a group identification. The only situation expressly envisaged by Code D for a group identification is where the suspect is known but not available, in which case the group identification may take place covertly.[87] A second possibility implicitly envisaged is where, because of the unusual appearance of the suspect, it would not be practicable to assemble sufficient people who resemble him to make a video identification or a parade fair.[88] Group identifications are carried out in accordance with Annex C to Code D. In such a case the suspect is viewed by a witness amongst an informal group of people.[89] Such a procedure typically takes place in the street, a shopping centre, an Underground station—any location where other people are passing by, or waiting around informally, in groups such that the suspect is able to join them and be capable of being seen by the witness at the same time as others in the group.[90] If the procedure takes place with the suspect's consent he is entitled to have a solicitor or friend present.[91]

If none of these three procedures is practicable the identification officer may arrange for the suspect to be directly confronted by the witness.[92] A confrontation does not require the suspect's consent, but force may not be used to make the suspect's face visible to the witness.[93] Like identification parades, confrontations may be carried out either in a normal room, when witness and suspect will be face-to-face, or in a room equipped with a one-way viewing screen.[94] Any confrontation should take place in the presence of the suspect's solicitor, interpreter or friend unless this would cause unreasonable delay.[95] Annex D to Code D sets out further requirements for the conduct of confrontations.

7–018

In all cases where a suspect is asked for his consent to an identification procedure, he must be given certain information as specified by Code D.[96] This includes an explanation of the procedure and of his right to have a solicitor or friend present, the consequences of refusal to take part, whether the witnesses have been shown any photographs by the police during the investigation before the identity of the suspect became known, and so on. This extensive right to information is not, however, accompanied by an equally extensive right of control over the procedure. For example, when a parade was the preferred method of formal identification, it was held that the suspect has a right to a

---

[86] Code D Annex B para.10.
[87] Code D para.3.21. An alternative in this situation is a video identification using either moving or still images, if necessary obtained covertly.
[88] See Code D Annex C para.7.
[89] Code D Annex C para.4.
[90] Code D Annex C para.4.
[91] Code D Annex C para.13.
[92] Code D para.3.23.
[93] Code D Annex D para.3.
[94] Code D Annex D para.7.
[95] Code D Annex D para.4.
[96] Code D para.3.17.

parade,[97] but not if it was impracticable to hold one. He could object to the makeup of the parade and ask for reasonable time to find persons of similar appearance to stand on the parade if the police were unable to assemble the required number.[98] He could not, however, insist on persons of his own choice if the police had found enough people of similar appearance.[99] As we have seen, although the suspect can object to a parade and refuse to take part, the other procedures can all be conducted without his consent.

The showing of photographs to witnesses is also covered by Code D. Where the identity of the suspect is not known, witnesses may be shown photographs, or computerised or other images, by the police to see if they can identify a suspect.[100] This must be done in accordance with Annex E to Code D. The basic principles are that the witness should be asked whether he or she can pick out, unprompted, a photograph of the person observed from a group (not less than 12) of photographs of a similar type, and witnesses should not be given an opportunity to influence each other. Once a suspect has been identified in this way the normal procedures for obtaining identification evidence under Code D should be followed. Photographs must not be shown to witnesses if the identity of the suspect is known and the suspect is available to take part in a video identification, an identification parade, or a group identification.[101]

7–019   The question then arises of the evidential status of identification from photographs. Such evidence is relevant, but should there be restrictions on its admissibility? From the point of view of the defence, admissibility is a double-edged sword. Proof that the witness had picked out the suspect from photographs before identifying him in a parade could be used to cast doubt on the reliability of the parade identification, through the suggestion that the witness was remembering the photograph rather than the person originally seen. On the other hand, the fact that the police had photographs of the defendant is potentially prejudicial because it tends to suggest that he has a criminal record. From the point of view of the prosecution, evidence of identification from photographs demonstrates the witness's consistency if the witness has subsequently identified the same person, and has independent probative value[102] if there was no subsequent identification or the normal procedures were not followed. The courts have accommodated these competing interests by saying that as a general principle the prosecution should not lead evidence that a witness identified the defendant from a police photograph.[103] The reason for this is that the prejudice that would be caused to the defendant by the revelation that he had a criminal

---

[97] *Conway* (1990) 91 Cr.App.R. 143 CA; *Rutherford and Palmer* (1994) 98 Cr.App.R. 191 CA.

[98] *Britton and Richards* [1989] Crim. L.R. 144 CA.

[99] *Thorne* [1981] Crim. L.R. 702 CA.

[100] Code D para.3.3.

[101] cf. *Folan* [2003] EWCA Crim 908, where a single photograph was shown for recognition purposes of a suspect whose identity was known. Code D was held not to apply in view of the passage of time between the offence and the recognition 18 years later, but the Court of Appeal held that it would have been wise to follow procedures in Annex E in the interests of fairness.

[102] Assuming of course that the procedure for making an identification from photographs was itself fair. For cases where it was not see *Hope, Limburn and Bleasdale* [1994] Crim. L.R. 118; *Campbell* [1994] Crim. L.R. 357. For an excellent discussion of the whole subject of identification from photographs see *Alexander v R.* (1981) 145 C.L.R. 395 High Ct of Australia.

[103] *Lamb* (1980) 71 Cr.App.R. 198 CA. cf. *Campbell* [1994] Crim. L.R. 357 CA.

record would generally outweigh the probative value of the identification.[104] However, evidence of identification from photographs can be admitted if on the facts no prejudice arises,[105] or if the purpose of admission is to rebut a defence suggestion that a witness's identification on a parade was a recent mistake.[106]

(B)   Breach of Code D

Where there is a breach of Code D, the question of excluding the evidence of identification under s.78 of PACE is likely to arise. In determining this question the courts have followed the same general approach that they take to the exclusion of confession evidence in cases of breach of Code C. Thus, although the identification cases do not always refer in terms to the test of a "significant and substantial" breach,[107] they do inquire into the extent to which the defendant was prejudiced by the breach and the effect of such prejudice on the fairness of the proceedings.

7–020

If the breach was or may have been in bad faith, the court has been likely to exclude the evidence, particularly if the breach consisted of the failure to hold a parade.[108] In such a case it is easy to find that the defendant was unfairly deprived of the best opportunity to test the witness's reliability. In *Nagah*,[109] the Court of Appeal quashed a conviction for attempted rape where the police had engaged in a "complete flouting" of Code D. They had substituted an unsatisfactory street identification for the parade that the defendant had agreed to go on and that it was practicable to hold. The unfairness of this tactic was compounded by the large discrepancies between the victim's description of her attacker and the defendant's appearance. Similarly, in *Graham*,[110] the Court of Appeal characterised a failure to hold a parade, to which the defendant had agreed, as a plain breach for which no legitimate explanation was given. This led to the defendant being deprived of an advantage to which he was entitled, namely a parade that might prove favourable to him if no positive identification were made.[111] Other intentional breaches of Code D are also likely to result in exclusion of evidence. In *Marcus*,[112] the defendant was of unusual appearance. The police first conducted a video identification with appropriately masked images of the other persons in the procedure. When this failed to yield a result the police, amazingly with the agreement of the CPS, conducted a second procedure with unmasked footage of the suspect and the other persons. The inspector in charge admitted in evidence that the defendant stood out and that the procedure was blatantly unfair. It was a plain breach of the requirement that the other persons should resemble the

---

[104] See *Bleakley* [1993] Crim. L.R. 203 CA.

[105] As in *Allen* [1996] Crim. L.R. 426 CA, where the defence put in the defendant's record for tactical reasons; therefore no prejudice was caused by revealing that the police had photographs of him.

[106] *Bleakley* [1993] Crim. L.R. 203.

[107] For a case where the court did, see *R. v B* [2008] EWCA Crim 1524.

[108] That is, when a parade was the first-choice procedure under earlier versions of Code D.

[109] *Nagah* (1991) 92 Cr.App.R. 344 CA.

[110] *Graham* [1994] Crim. L.R. 212 CA.

[111] See also *Conway* (1990) 91 Cr.App.R. 143 CA; *Allen* [1995] Crim. L.R. 643 CA.

[112] *Marcus* [2004] EWCA Crim 3387; [2005] Crim. L.R. 384.

suspect as far as possible. The Court of Appeal held that this was a deliberate device to evade the Code and therefore that the identification evidence should have been excluded.

It may be that in cases of suspected bad faith, even the appearance of unfairness in the procedure is enough to trigger the exclusionary discretion. In *Gall*,[113] where an investigating officer took part in the conduct of a parade,[114] the Court of Appeal held that the judge should have excluded the witness's evidence of identification, and agreed that: "a prisoner could well feel considerable suspicion of what might be going on if an investigating officer comes into the parade room, has a look at the parade, has the opportunity to talk to the witness, and then the witness is introduced into the parade". In *Finley*,[115] multiple breaches of Code D had taken place: eyewitnesses had been invited to pick out a suspect from a set of photographs only one of which looked at all like the defendant[116]; the four eyewitnesses all worked together and were left together before the parade[117]; the parade was unfair because the defendant's appearance did not match that of the other persons.[118] The Court of Appeal held that the judge should not have let the case go to the jury because the case was inherently weak and because the defendant would have a justifiable lack of confidence in the fairness of the identification procedure.

7–021 In cases such as *Gall* and *Finley* the police have complied with the duty to hold a parade, but they have done it in such a way as to raise the suspicion that the parade has been robbed of most of its value. The abuse of process this suggests generates a powerful case for exclusion on the ground of unfairness when allied to the potential prejudice caused to the defendant. When the breach is in good faith, so that the element of deliberate abuse of process drops out of the picture, the issue of prejudice becomes central to the argument for exclusion. As with breaches of Code C, relating to questioning of suspects, the defence will have to show that on the facts of the case substantial prejudice was caused by the breach. This is a claim which the courts will investigate carefully by reference to all the circumstances of the case. Everything turns on the particular combinations of facts in individual cases. In *Preddie*,[119] the Court of Appeal held that evidence of a street identification should have been excluded where there was no necessity to hold one because the police were already in the process of arresting the defendant, and in addition the police failed to record both the first description of the offender and the fact that a street identification had been made. As the court said, since the witness had identified the defendant as he was being arrested the video identification procedure which took place later the same day could not be of any value. It could not be a fair test of the witness's ability to pick out the defendant from a group of people of similar appearance. The defendant had

---

[113] *Gall* (1990) 90 Cr.App.R. 64 at 69 CA.
[114] Contrary to Code D para.2.2.
[115] *Finley* [1993] Crim. L.R. 50 CA.
[116] See now Code D Annex E para.4.
[117] See now Code D Annex B para.14.
[118] Code D Annex B para.9.
[119] *Preddie* [2011] EWCA Crim 312. *Nethercott* [2011] EWCA Crim 2987 is another case where cumulative breaches of Code D were held to have required exclusion of the identification evidence.

therefore been substantially prejudiced by the breaches. In *Ryan*,[120] an identification by confrontation took place at the police station in the presence of the defendant's solicitor. The witness was taken to the police station by an investigating officer and moved from one place to another in the station by other investigating officers. The Court of Appeal agreed with the trial judge that this amounted to a breach of Code D, but held that the judge had been right not to exclude the evidence because no unjust prejudice had been caused to the defendant.[121] This seems to be a reasonable conclusion, given that a confrontation between witness and suspect was involved. The result would probably have been different if the procedure had been a parade,[122] because of the suspicion that the officer was priming the witness as to the person to pick out.[123]

The authorities state little in the way of general principles for decision, but some further case comparisons offer useful insights into the relative weight that may be attached to particular features of the procedure adopted in a given case. For example, in relation to the failure to hold a parade, the Court of Appeal has sometimes found that no unfairness was caused to the defendant by the adoption of an alternative procedure. In *Tiplady*,[124] trading standards officers organised a group identification of the defendant in the foyer of the magistrates' court. A parade could and should have been held, but the Court of Appeal accepted that the officers had acted in good faith. The procedure adopted was not unfair because there was a fair mix of people similar in age to the defendant, and the defendant's solicitor had not objected to it at the time. This can be compared with *Martin and Nicholls*,[125] where schoolboy eyewitnesses identified the defendants in the crowd outside the court on the day of the hearing. The Court of Appeal took the view that it was unfair to have admitted this evidence having regard to the unsatisfactory conditions of the witnesses being together beforehand and there being no fair mix of people.

In *Hope, Limburn and Bleasdale*,[126] the Court of Appeal held that the showing of photographs of the defendants to the victim of an assault was not an acceptable alternative to the holding of a parade where the identity of the suspects was known. Clearly such a procedure does not supply any test of the witness's ability to pick out the persons seen from a group of others of similar appearance. On the other hand, if the procedure adopted is fair in substance, a failure to comply with formal statutory requirements is unlikely to amount to significant prejudice. The Court of Appeal has upheld convictions where the police decided that it was impracticable to hold a parade but then failed to inform the defendant that they

---

[120] *Ryan* [1992] Crim. L.R. 187 CA.

[121] See also *H v DPP* [2007] EWHC 2192 (Admin), where the police failed to make the record required by Code D para.3.2(e) in a case of an "on the spot" identification. The Divisional Court upheld the conviction on the basis that the district judge had found no bad faith on the part of the police, and there was no unfairness to the defendant given that he had admitted being at the scene of the offence.

[122] Compare *Gall* (1990) 90 Cr.App.R. 64.

[123] The Court of Appeal has though indicated that in deciding whether to exclude evidence for breach of Code D the judge should consider all the trial safeguards against possible unfairness in admitting the evidence: *R. v B* [2008] EWCA Crim 1524.

[124] *Tiplady* [1995] Crim. L.R. 651 CA. *Penny* (1992) 94 Cr.App.R. 345 CA is similar.

[125] *Martin and Nicholls* [1994] Crim. L.R. 218 CA.

[126] *Hope, Limburn and Bleasdale* [1994] Crim. L.R. 118 CA.

were holding a group identification instead,[127] and where the defendant was detained in custody beyond the permitted time before an identification by confrontation took place.[128]

7–022 Where the breach has resulted in significant prejudice to the defendant, but the trial judge admitted the evidence of identification, the Court of Appeal is likely to quash a conviction. This is generally on the ground that the evidence should have been excluded under s.78 of PACE,[129] although it should be remembered that in such a case the court is reviewing an exercise of discretion and will not interfere with the judge's decision unless persuaded that the judge erred in principle in admitting the evidence. As noted above, there is also the general power in the Court of Appeal to quash a conviction as unsafe. This has occasionally been used where the court has had a doubt about the conviction but has not been prepared to say that the trial judge was wrong to admit the evidence in question.[130] A conviction may be upheld, despite an element of significant prejudice, if the judge has given a proper direction on the possible effects of the breach on the reliability of the evidence[131] and/or there is strong other evidence of guilt.[132]

Finally, it should be noted that compliance with Code D does not guarantee that the Court of Appeal will uphold a conviction. In *Knowles*,[133] the victim of an attack picked out his assailant from photographs. The police took the view that it was not practicable to hold a parade in view of the suspect's unusual appearance. They therefore held a confrontation after the defendant refused to take part in a group identification. The Court of Appeal held that no breaches of Code D had occurred, but said that the identification evidence was nonetheless unsafe and unsatisfactory. The victim's description of his attacker contained serious omissions about the defendant's appearance that should have been mentioned if the victim, as he claimed, did get a good look at the attacker in good light. The conviction was quashed.[134]

D. PROBLEMS OF ADDUCING IDENTIFICATION EVIDENCE AT TRIAL

1. Dock identifications

7–023 The term "dock identification" refers to the procedure whereby a witness is asked whether he or she can see in the courtroom the person who committed the offence, and the witness then identifies the defendant in the dock. It has been recognised for many years that such identifications may be very unsatisfactory

---

[127] *Grannell* (1990) 90 Cr.App.R. 149.
[128] *Taylor (Leroy)* [1991] Crim. L.R. 541.
[129] As in *Gall* (1990) 90 Cr.App.R. 64; *Nagah* (1991) 92 Cr.App.R. 344; *Graham* [1994] Crim. L.R. 212; *Martin and Nicholls* [1994] Crim. L.R. 218; *Allen* [1995] Crim. L.R. 643.
[130] See, e.g. *Quinn* [1995] 1 Cr.App.R. 480.
[131] *Khan* [1997] Crim. L.R. 584 CA.
[132] See, e.g. *Joseph* [1994] Crim. L.R. 48 CA; *Rutherford and Palmer* (1994) 98 Cr.App.R. 191 CA; *McEvoy* [1997] Crim. L.R. 887 CA.
[133] *Knowles* [1994] Crim. L.R. 217.
[134] See also *O'Leary* (1988) 87 Cr.App.R. 387 (informal confrontation).

where identity is in dispute.[135] If the witness has not previously identified the defendant, substantial doubts may arise over the reliability of the dock identification partly because of the inevitable lapse of time between the original observation and the court hearing, and partly because the isolation of the defendant in the dock means that there is no fair test of the witness's ability to pick out the person observed from a group of persons of similar appearance. If the witness has identified the defendant previously, a dock identification adds very little in the way of independent probative value because of the strong likelihood that the witness is remembering the previous identification rather than the person originally observed. In all cases there is a risk that a jury would be over-impressed by a dramatic scene of recognition in the courtroom, hence dock identifications have considerable potential for prejudicing a defendant.

Evidence of a dock identification is not, however, inadmissible at common law. The Privy Council has confirmed this point on a number of occasions,[136] and in *Tido v R.*,[137] rejected a suggestion[138] that it should be admissible only in the most exceptional circumstances. However, the Privy Council went on to insist that a trial judge must always consider whether the admission of evidence of a dock identification, especially if it was the first occasion when the accused was identified, might imperil the fairness of the trial. The reason why a prior identification parade was not held is a crucial factor; if there was no good reason that would militate against the admission of the evidence. If dock identification evidence is admitted it is always necessary to give the jury careful directions as to the dangers of relying on it. In particular the judge should warn the jury of the disadvantages to the accused of having been denied the opportunity to take part in an identification parade if he had been deprived of the opportunity.

As far as the Crown Court in England is concerned, there is long-standing authority that dock identifications are undesirable[139] and should be excluded wherever possible. If the witness has made a previous identification the prosecution should lead evidence from the witness about that before asking the witness to confirm as a purely formal step that the person identified is the person in the dock. However, one situation where it is appropriate to exercise the discretion to admit evidence of a dock identification is where the defendant has refused to attend a parade or to take part in any other procedure.[140] Another is where the witness claims to recognise the defendant as someone he or she knows

---

[135] Formal proof that the offender is the person in the dock is of course essential in any criminal case. Where identity is not in dispute there is no objection to dock identification. For an authoritative discussion and some (unenacted) recommendations, see the Devlin Report, *Evidence of Identification in Criminal Cases* (1976) paras 4.89–4.109.

[136] *Pop (Aurelio) v R.* [2003] UKPC 40; *Pipersburgh and Robateau v R.* [2008] UKPC 11; *Tido v R.* [2011] UKPC 16; [2011] 2 Cr.App.R. 23.

[137] *Tido v R.* [2011] UKPC 16; [2011] 2 Cr.App.R. 23.

[138] In the judgment of the Privy Council in *Edwards v R.* [2006] UKPC 23.

[139] *Cartwright* (1914) 10 Cr.App.R. 219. cf. *Robinson* [2006] Crim. L.R. 427, where evidence was admitted at a murder trial of a witness who claimed that she recognised the defendant's voice when he began to give evidence. The commentary by Professor Ormerod notes that this was the equivalent of a dock identification.

[140] *John* [1973] Crim. L.R. 113.

well from previous acquaintance.[141] Holding a formal identification procedure in such a case will not serve any useful purpose, as discussed above.

In *Barnes v Chief Constable of Durham*,[142] the Divisional Court held that the position in magistrates' courts was different from that in the Crown Court. Popplewell J. stated that dock identifications were customary in magistrates' courts to provide proof of identity in driving cases. Otherwise a situation could arise where a person charged with a driving offence, who had made no statement to the police, could sit back and submit that the prosecution had not proved that he was the driver. The whole process of justice in the magistrates' courts, it was said, would be severely impaired if an identification parade had to be held in every case where a person did not positively admit to being the driver. The practical force of this argument from necessity can be appreciated, and it is notable that the defendant in the case did not raise the issue of identity until his trial, on a charge of failing to provide a specimen, several months after being charged. On the facts, therefore, it was probably not unfair to allow a dock identification to deal with what seems to have been essentially a formal objection to the prosecution case.[143] At the same time, the identification by the police officer who had been present when the driver in question was interviewed was of doubtful weight. The interview had taken place almost three years earlier, and it does not appear that the officer ever gave a description of the driver before making his identification. The officer said he remembered the defendant because of his manner in interview, but it must be a very frequent experience for police officers to be given "hassle" by persons they interview. It is not obvious why this particular defendant should have stood out in this way.

7–024   As Popplewell J. said, there is no logic in distinguishing between the acceptability of dock identifications in Crown Courts and magistrates' courts.[144] It is unclear whether the decision in this case acknowledges a special rule for driving cases,[145] or whether the argument from necessity represents a more open-ended principle for use in magistrates' courts. If the latter, there are clear dangers in allowing the safeguards of the formal PACE procedures to be bypassed on grounds of expediency.[146]

---

[141] The emphasis should be on the witness knowing the suspect *well*.

[142] *Barnes v Chief Constable of Durham* [1997] 2 Cr.App.R. 505 DC.

[143] The driver in question had originally given a different name and date of birth to that of the defendant. If the defendant was not that driver, it is inexplicable that he did not raise this when arrested more than 2 years after the incident.

[144] *Barnes v Chief Constable of Durham* [1997] 2 Cr.App.R. 505 at 512.

[145] *Barnes* was followed by Burnton J. in *Karia v DPP* [2002] EWHC 2175, who held in another driving case that it was fair to permit the prosecution to rely on a dock identification, to prevent an unmeritorious formal objection that the prosecution had failed to identify the defendant as the driver, when he had given no prior notice that he wished to raise the issue of identity. In *Holland v HM Advocate* [2005] UKPC D1 Lord Rodger commented, in the context of discussing the compatibility of dock identifications in Scotland with art.6 of the ECHR, that the practice of permitting dock identifications in magistrates' courts in England applied to driving offences.

[146] See T. Watkin in [2003] Crim. L.R. 463.

2. Evidence of previous identifications by witnesses

The above discussion of dock identifications has proceeded on the assumption   **7–025**
that it will normally be the witness who testifies about a previous act of
identification if he or she has made one. The practice of permitting witnesses to
do this has existed for many years. The authority for it is usually said to be the
decision of the House of Lords in *Christie*.[147] The defendant was charged with
indecent assault on a young boy. The boy gave unsworn evidence at the trial in
which he described the assault and made a dock identification of the defendant as
the man responsible. He was not asked about any previous act of identification.
His mother and a police officer then testified that shortly after the incident and in
their presence the boy had touched the sleeve of the defendant's coat, saying
"That is the man". The boy had then gone on to describe what the man had done
to him. This evidence raised a number of evidential issues; those relating to
evidence of statements made in the presence of the accused and to the use of the
testimony of the mother and the police officer as corroboration of the boy's
testimony are considered elsewhere in this book. The actual decision of the
House of Lords was that the trial judge had misdirected the jury on corroboration.
In relation to the admissibility of the testimony as evidence of a previous act of
identification the Lords were divided or unclear. Lord Atkinson was in no doubt
that the testimony of the mother and the police officer was admissible as evidence
of the boy's previous identification.[148] Lord Haldane L.C. thought that its
relevancy was to show "that the boy was able to identify at the time and to
exclude the idea that the identification of the prisoner in the dock was an
afterthought or a mistake".[149] However, he also shared Lord Moulton's doubt[150]
that this testimony ought not to have been given unless the boy himself had first
given primary evidence of his earlier identification. Lord Reading simply noted
that the defendant's counsel had not in fact objected to the admissibility of
evidence of the boy's previous identification, and went on to conclude that the
additional statement describing the assault could not be admitted as part of the act
of identification unless the boy had given evidence of it first.[151]

Despite this dubious foundation, *Christie* was treated as authority for the
proposition that at common law evidence is admissible of an act of prior
identification by a witness, not only from the witness personally, but also from
another person who observed it. According to this rule, if the eyewitness has
identified the defendant at trial, the previous identification shows the witness's
consistency and so diminishes any element of doubt surrounding the reliability of
the identification at trial. In this way the law avoided the potential problem of the
hearsay rule, because the evidence of the previous act of identification was not
admitted to prove its truth. However, the hearsay problem does arise if evidence
is given of an out-of-court identification by the witness, say by a police officer

---

[147] *Christie* [1914] A.C. 545 HL.
[148] *Christie* [1914] A.C. 545 at 553. Lord Parker agreed with Lord Atkinson.
[149] *Christie* [1914] A.C. 545 at 551.
[150] *Christie* [1914] A.C. 545 at 558. Lord Moulton's view was cited with approval by Lord Normand in *Teper v R.* [1952] A.C. 480 at 488 PC, and by Lord Morris of Borth-y-Gest in *Sparks v R.* [1964] A.C. 964 at 981 PC.
[151] *Christie* [1914] A.C. 545 at 563.

who attended the procedure where the witness made the identification, but the witness cannot identify the defendant at trial, whether because of amnesia, fear or some other reason. In this case the purpose of admitting the evidence of the previous identification can only be to prove its truth. A hearsay purpose is necessarily involved.

The hearsay point was overlooked in *Osborne and Virtue*,[152] where the Court of Appeal held that a police officer, who had attended an identification parade, could give evidence of the identifications made at the parade by two eyewitnesses of a robbery. The witnesses had been called to testify at the trial but had failed to identify either defendant in court. In the later case of *McCay*,[153] an eyewitness testified that he had picked out a person at a parade, but could not now remember who it was. The police officer who conducted the parade was called to testify that the witness said "It is number 8", thereby indicating the defendant. In response to the argument that the officer's evidence was hearsay, the Court of Appeal offered two reasons for holding the evidence admissible. One was that the words spoken by the witness at the parade were part of a relevant act of identification that the words accompanied and explained, and were thus admissible under the res gestae principle.[154] The other was that s.67(11) of PACE provided by implication for the admission of evidence of identification carried out in accordance with the provisions of Code D. This was a distinctly creative interpretation since the subsection refers to the provisions of the codes of practice themselves being admissible in evidence and makes no mention of evidence obtained via the procedures of the codes. This ground for the decision seems clearly to be wrong.[155] Of course, it would be highly inconvenient, and contrary to the interests of justice, if a technical objection based on the hearsay rule prevented the court hearing details of a previous identification where this is important evidence.[156]

7–026   The common law on previous identifications has been affected by the reforms to the hearsay rule made by the Criminal Justice Act 2003. First, the effect of s.120(4) and (5) is that a previous statement by a witness is admissible as evidence of any matter stated if the statement identifies or describes a person, object or place, and while giving evidence the witness indicates that to the best of his belief he made the statement and that it is true. Accordingly, a previous identification by an eyewitness, who can confirm at trial making the statement of identification and confirm its truth, is now admissible as evidence of the facts

---

[152] *Osborne and Virtue* [1973] Q.B. 678 CA.

[153] *McCay* (1990) 91 Cr.App.R. 84 CA.

[154] This point is considered further in Ch.17.

[155] In *Lynch* [2007] EWCA Crim 3035; [2008] 1 Cr. App. R. 24 the Court of Appeal doubted the validity of this ground for the decision in *McCay* (1990) 91 Cr.App.R. 84 CA. *Lynch* concerned a statement by an identifying witness, after she had picked out the defendant at a parade, stating what she had seen him do. Distinguishing *McCay*, the Court of Appeal held that this hearsay statement made after the act of identification was not admissible as part of the res gestae, but was rightly admitted in the interests of justice under s.114(1)(d) of the Criminal Justice Act 2003. See Ch.17.

[156] Another route to admission is the suggestion in *McCay* (1990) 91 Cr.App.R. 84 CA of showing the witness his contemporaneous statement for the purpose of refreshing his memory before he testified at trial as to whom he had identified at the parade. This procedure could also be used for the kind of statement in issue in *Lynch* [2007] EWCA Crim 3035.

stated. It is a statutory exception to the rule against hearsay. In *Chinn*,[157] the Court of Appeal made an important clarification of the scope of s.120(5), saying that it was necessary to have regard to the purpose for which a statement identifying or describing a person, object or place was adduced in the criminal proceedings. The statement had to be placed in the context of the proceedings; it was of no use in a vacuum. Accordingly, under this provision the statement of a witness was admissible that she had seen the defendant, who was charged with an offence of unlawful wounding in a nightclub, present in the club at the time and throw a glass bottle that hit the victim.[158] At the trial the witness claimed to have no memory of the incident but confirmed that she had made the statement to the police when the matter was fresh in her memory and that it stated the truth.

This provision will not help in cases such as *Osborne and Virtue* and *McCay*, where the witness cannot remember making the earlier identification or cannot confirm its truth. Secondly, however, s.118 preserves certain common law categories of admissible hearsay. These include the rule of res gestae, whereby a statement is admissible as evidence of any matter stated if it accompanied an act that can be properly evaluated as evidence only if considered in conjunction with the statement.[159] This is the rule which provided the first reason for upholding the admission of the identification evidence in *McCay*. Despite the somewhat artificial reasoning that involves the court distinguishing between an act of identification and the statement expressing it, it seems safe to assume that the courts will wish to use this rule to ensure the admission of previous identifications where the witness is forgetful or fearful at trial.[160]

A converse type of situation arises where the witness has failed to make a positive identification at a formal pre-trial procedure; does this rule out any evidence of identification from the witness? In *George*,[161] the Court of Appeal confirmed that such a failure is no bar to the witness giving relevant evidence describing the event or the person he or she saw at the time. Clearly the failure to pick out the defendant at the formal procedure as the person seen affects the weight to be given to such a description. It is a weakness that the judge would be expected to highlight in the *Turnbull* warning. Witnesses may of course have degrees of certainty about their identifications, and in *George* the court commented that in at least two situations a qualified formal identification might be relevant and probative. One is where the qualified identification supports or is at least consistent with other evidence indicating that the defendant committed the offence. The other is where the witness can give an explanation for their lack of certainty that helps to place the qualified identification in its proper context and may show that other evidence given by the witness is likely to be correct. This might be particularly significant where, as happened in this case, the defendant substantially changed his appearance between the crime and the identification procedure that took place a considerable time later.

---

[157] *Chinn* [2012] EWCA Crim 501; [2012] 2 Cr.App.R. 4.
[158] Other parts of her statement, which went beyond identifying or describing the defendant and the fact that he threw the bottle, were held to be inadmissible under s.120(4) and (5).
[159] CJA 2003 s.118 subs.(1) para.4(b).
[160] A further alternative is the general inclusionary discretion for hearsay evidence to be admitted in the interests of justice under s.114(1)(d) of the Criminal Justice Act 2003.
[161] *George* [2002] EWCA Crim 1923; [2003] Crim. L.R. 282.

Finally, the situation may arise where a witness makes an identification which the witness later attempts to retract. In *Parvez*,[162] the witness W had made a statement to the police which included a statement saying that he had recognised the defendant D as one of the offenders responsible for an attempted murder. At D's trial W was called for the prosecution but claimed not to be able to identify him as one of the offenders. The prosecution obtained leave to treat W as hostile and so was able to cross-examine him on his witness statement.[163] The Court of Appeal held that the trial judge was correct not to withdraw the case from the jury. Under s.119 of the Criminal Justice Act 2003 once the witness statement was admitted the jury was entitled to treat it as being true. They could thus prefer W's earlier identification of the defendant to his denial at the trial if they thought W had retracted the identification through fear.

3. Identification by the court: evidence of recordings, photographs and photofits

7–027 Recordings made, and photographs taken, at the time and place of the offence are clearly relevant to show the nature and circumstances of the offence and the identity of the person or persons who committed it. When the images are of good quality, an automatic recording such as CCTV footage is one of the best forms of identification evidence because it does not depend on fallible human powers of observation and memory. The courts have been quick to recognise the benefits to factfinding of the impact of new technologies, for both making and interpreting such recordings. They have refused to be deflected from the pursuit of accuracy in decision-making by what are seen as essentially technical and contrived arguments for exclusion. Steyn L.J. summed up the approach concisely:

> "It is essential that our criminal justice system should take into account modern methods of crime detection. It is no surprise, therefore, that tape recordings, photographs and films are regularly placed before juries. Sometimes that is done without expert evidence, but, of course, if that real evidence is not sufficiently intelligible to the jury without expert evidence, it has always been accepted that it is possible to place before the jury the opinion of an expert in order to assist them in their interpretation of the real evidence... There are no closed categories where such evidence may be placed before a jury. It would be entirely wrong to deny to the law of evidence the advantages to be gained from new techniques and new advances in science."[164]

This is not to say, of course, that new technologies are infallible, or that expert opinion about the interpretation of recordings may not be challenged. The reliability of expert evidence generally is considered in Ch.20. The point for present purposes is that objections to the use of new technologies in proving identity have generally been regarded as going to weight rather than to admissibility. There are no systemic reasons for excluding the evidence provided by automatic recordings, and powerful reasons of relevance and best evidence for admitting it.

---

[162] *Parvez* [2010] EWCA Crim 3229.
[163] Under the provisions of the Criminal Procedure Act 1865 s.3; see Ch.14.
[164] *Clarke* [1995] 2 Cr.App.R. 425 at 429–430.

Recordings and photographs may be admitted as real evidence,[165] provided they are duly authenticated.[166] According to the Court of Appeal in the leading case of *Attorney-General's Reference (No.2 of 2002)*,[167] where identity is disputed, there are four ways in which evidence of a photographic image from the scene of the crime can be admitted with a view to persuading the court to conclude that it was the defendant who committed the offence:

(1) if the image is sufficiently clear, the jury may make the identification itself by comparing the image on the photograph or the recording with the appearance of the defendant sitting in the dock[168];

(2) if a witness knows the defendant sufficiently well to recognise him as the offender depicted in the photographic image he or she can give evidence of this[169];

(3) where a witness who does not know the defendant has spent time viewing and analysing the photographic images from the scene, thereby acquiring special knowledge the jury does not have, the witness can give (expert) evidence of identification based on a comparison between those images and a reasonably contemporary photograph of the defendant, provided that the images and the contemporary photograph are available for the jury[170];

(4) where a witness is suitably qualified in facial mapping, he or she can give expert opinion evidence of identification based on a comparison between images from the scene (whether expertly enhanced or not) and a reasonably contemporary photograph of the defendant, provided both are available for the jury.[171]

A word needs to be said about photofit and identikit pictures. These are graphic images of suspects, drawn by police artists or compiled as composite pictures by police investigators, from descriptions by eyewitnesses of persons they saw committing offences. Such pictures have been in use for some time as investigative tools and their composition has become more sophisticated with the advent of computer technology. At common law they were held to be admissible in evidence on the basis that they were a species of evidence sui generis

7–028

---

[165] See *Kajala v Noble* (1982) 75 Cr.App.R. 149 CA; *Dodson and Williams* (1984) 79 Cr.App.R. 220 CA; *Taylor v Chief Constable of Cheshire* [1987] 1 All E.R. 225 DC; *Clarke* [1995] 2 Cr.App.R. 425 CA.

[166] On authentication, see Ch.12.

[167] *Attorney-General's Reference (No.2 of 2002)* [2002] EWCA Crim 2373; [2003] 1 Cr.App.R. 21.

[168] *Dodson and Williams* (1984) 79 Cr.App.R. 220 CA. cf. *Jaber* [2010] EWCA Crim 130.

[169] *Fowden and White* [1982] Crim. L.R. 588 CA; *Kajala v Noble* (1982) 75 Cr.App.R. 149. This may be so even if the original photographic image is no longer available for the jury: *Taylor v Chief Constable of Cheshire* [1987] 1 All E.R. 225. Where the recognising witness is a police officer viewing CCTV footage, the officer should follow the guidance as regards making an appropriate record of the circumstances of the viewing and recognition issued in response to the call made by the Court of Appeal in *Dean Smith* [2008] EWCA Crim 1342. See also *Jaber* [2010] EWCA Crim 130; *Moss* [2011] EWCA Crim 252.

[170] *Clare and Peach* [1995] 2 Cr.App.R. 333 CA. See the discussion by R. Munday in (1995) 159 J.P. 547.

[171] *Stockwell* (1993) 97 Cr.App.R. 260 CA (facial mapping); *Clarke* [1995] 2 Cr.App.R. 425 CA (facial mapping by video superimposition).

analogous to a photograph.[172] They were admissible as real evidence in the same way as photographs, and their admission did not therefore infringe either the hearsay rule or the rule against previous consistent statements. This reasoning was flawed because any such picture, no matter who compiles it, necessarily incorporates the witness's statement as to the person's appearance. If that picture is adduced in evidence as an accurate representation of the appearance of the person the witness observed, the court is being asked to rely on the witness's out-of-court assertion of what the person looked like as a true representation of the person's appearance. The photofit does not speak for itself in the way that a photograph does. It is the product of a human mind (the witness) making an intentional communication. It is therefore hearsay evidence when adduced for the purpose of showing that it is a true likeness of the offender. The point was recognised in the Criminal Justice Act 2003. A "statement" for the purposes of the rule against hearsay is defined in s.115(2) to include a representation made "in a sketch, photofit or other pictorial form". This reverses the common law position. It means that photofits will be treated as regards admissibility in the same way as other previous verbal identifications by the witness. They will continue to be admissible, but as exceptions to the hearsay rule in accordance with the rules discussed above.

E.   THE EVALUATION OF EYEWITNESS EVIDENCE OF IDENTIFICATION

1.   The Turnbull guidelines

7–029   In the leading case of *Turnbull*,[173] the Court of Appeal responded to the contemporary concern about eyewitness identification evidence by setting out a detailed set of guidelines for trial judges to follow in the handling of such evidence. The guidelines are not of course a statute, and the courts have said that they should not be treated as if they were.[174] Nevertheless, in some respects they do function as the judicial equivalent of a statutory code of practice. A good deal of case law has developed on their interpretation, and a failure to comply with them will provide grounds for appeal. Appeal courts are likely to find that a failure to follow the guidelines makes a conviction unsafe.[175] In *Reid v R.*,[176] Lord Ackner put the matter very strongly by saying that a significant failure to follow the guidelines will cause a conviction to be quashed because it will have resulted in a substantial miscarriage of justice. However, it is clear that this is not a blanket rule. Exceptionally a conviction may be upheld, despite a failure to follow the guidelines, if the court is convinced that the result would have been the same had the guidelines been followed.[177] This may be the case, for example, if

---

[172] *Cook* [1987] 1 All E.R. 1049 CA.
[173] *Turnbull* [1977] Q.B. 224.
[174] *Keane* (1977) 65 Cr.App.R. 247 at 248, where Scarman L.J. points out that *Turnbull* does not establish a rigid pattern or a catechism; *Mills v R.* [1995] Crim. L.R. 884 (see Commentary by D.J.B.).
[175] *Keane* (1977) 65 Cr.App.R. 247.
[176] *Reid v R.* [1990] 1 A.C. 363 at 384 PC.
[177] *Hunjan* (1978) 68 Cr.App.R. 99.

uncorroborated identification evidence is of exceptionally good quality,[178] or where other prosecution evidence makes the case exceptionally strong.[179]

The guidelines are set out here in detail. We will then look at how they have been interpreted.

Lord Widgery C.J., giving the judgment of the Court of Appeal in *Turnbull*, said[180]:

> "In our judgment the danger of miscarriages of justice occurring can be much reduced if trial judges sum up to juries in the way indicated in this judgment.
>
> First, whenever the case against an accused depends wholly or substantially on the correctness of one or more identifications of the accused which the defence alleges to be mistaken, the judge should warn the jury of the special need for caution before convicting the accused in reliance on the correctness of the identification or identifications. In addition he should instruct them as to the reason for the need for such a warning and should make some reference to the possibility that a mistaken witness can be a convincing one and that a number of such witnesses can all be mistaken. Provided this is done in clear terms the judge need not use any particular form of words.
>
> Secondly, the judge should direct the jury to examine closely the circumstances in which the identification by each witness came to be made. How long did the witness have the accused under observation? At what distance? In what light? Was the observation impeded in any way, as for example by passing traffic or a press of people? Had the witness ever seen the accused before? How often? If only occasionally, had he any special reason for remembering the accused? How long elapsed between the original observation and the subsequent identification to the police? Was there any material discrepancy between the description of the accused given to the police by the witness when first seen by them and his actual appearance? If in any case, whether it is being dealt with summarily or on indictment, the prosecution have reason to believe that there is such a material discrepancy they should supply the accused or his legal advisers with particulars of the description the police were first given. In all cases if the accused asks to be given particulars of such descriptions, the prosecution should supply them. Finally, he should remind the jury of any specific weaknesses which had appeared in the identification evidence. Recognition may be more reliable than identification of a stranger; but, even when the witness is purporting to recognise someone whom he knows, the jury should be reminded that mistakes in recognition of close relatives and friends are sometimes made.
>
> All these matters go to the quality of the identification evidence. If the quality is good and remains good at the close of the accused's case, the danger of a mistaken identification is lessened; but the poorer the quality, the greater the danger. In our judgment, when the quality is good, as for example when the identification is made after a long period of observation, or in satisfactory conditions by a relative, a neighbour, a close friend, a workmate and the like, the jury can safely be left to assess the value of the identifying evidence even though there is no other evidence to support it; provided always, however, that an adequate warning has been given about the special need for caution."

Lord Widgery C.J. then gave examples of good quality identification evidence that could be left to a jury without supporting evidence. These included the recognition by a kidnap victim of his captor who had been with him for many days during the kidnap, and the identification by a police officer of a suspected drug supplier whom he had previously had under repeated observation. Lord Widgery continued:

---

[178] See, e.g. *Freemantle v R.* [1994] 3 All E.R. 225 PC, where the identification took the form of a recognition of the accused in good conditions by two witnesses, one of whom said to the accused that he recognised him. The accused had responded by appearing to acknowledge the recognition.
[179] See, e.g. *Clifton* [1986] Crim. L.R. 399.
[180] *Turnbull* [1997] Q.B. 224 at 228–231.

"When, in the judgment of the trial judge, the quality of the identifying evidence is poor, as for example when it depends solely on a fleeting glance or on a longer observation made in difficult conditions, the situation is very different. The judge should then withdraw the case from the jury and direct an acquittal unless there is other evidence which goes to support the correctness of the identification. This may be corroboration in the sense lawyers use that word; but it need not be so if its effect is to make the jury sure that there has been no mistaken identification . . .

The trial judge should identify to the jury the evidence which he adjudges is capable of supporting the evidence of identification. If there is any evidence or circumstance which the jury might think was supporting when it did not have this quality, the judge should say so. A jury, for example, might think that support for identification evidence could be found in the fact that the accused had not given evidence before them. An accused's absence from the witness box cannot provide evidence of anything and the judge should tell the jury so.[181] But he would be entitled to tell them that when assessing the quality of the identification evidence they could take into consideration the fact that it was uncontradicted by any evidence coming from the accused himself.

Care should be taken by the judge when directing the jury about the support for an identification which may be derived from the fact that they have rejected an alibi. False alibis may be put forward for many reasons: an accused, for example, who has only his own truthful evidence to rely on may stupidly fabricate an alibi and get lying witnesses to support it out of fear that his own evidence will not be enough. Further, alibi witnesses can make genuine mistakes about dates and occasions like any other witness can. It is only when the jury are satisfied that the sole reason for the fabrication was to deceive them and there is no other explanation for its being put forward, that fabrication can provide any support for identification evidence. The jury should be reminded that proving the accused has told lies about where he was at the material time does not by itself prove that he was where the identifying witness says he was.

In setting out these guidelines for trial judges, which involve only changes of practice, not law, we have tried to follow the recommendations set out in the report which Lord Devlin's committee made to the Secretary of State for the Home Department in April 1976. We have not followed that report in using the phrase 'exceptional circumstances' to describe situations in which the risk of mistaken identification is reduced. In our judgment, the use of such a phrase is likely to result in the build-up of case law as to what circumstances can properly be described as exceptional and what cannot. Case law of this kind is likely to be a fetter on the administration of justice when so much depends on the quality of the evidence in each case. Quality is what matters in the end. In many cases the exceptional circumstances to which the report refers will provide evidence of good quality, but they may not; the converse is also true.

A failure to follow these guidelines is likely to result in a conviction being quashed and will do so if in the judgment of this court on all the evidence the verdict is either unsatisfactory or unsafe."

2.   When do the guidelines apply?

7–030 Lord Widgery C.J. himself said that the *Turnbull* guidelines applied primarily to the "fleeting glimpse" type of case.[182] However, other authorities have made it clear that they apply generally whenever eyewitness identification evidence is alleged to be mistaken,[183] subject only to certain exceptional cases.[184] Thus the judge should still give a warning where the identification evidence is of good quality, as where the witness had good opportunities for observation and is

---

[181] See now Criminal Justice and Public Order Act 1994 s.35; discussed in Ch.13.

[182] *Oakwell* (1978) 66 Cr.App.R. 174 at 178.

[183] *Keane* (1977) 65 Cr.App.R. 247 CA; *Scott and Barnes v R.* [1989] A.C. 1242 PC; *Bowden* [1993] Crim. L.R. 379 CA; *Bentley* (1994) 99 Cr.App.R. 342 CA; *Bradley* [2004] EWCA Crim 1481 CA.

[184] See below.

convinced that the identification is correct.[185] It makes no difference to the requirement for the warning that the witness has picked out the accused on a parade.[186]

The warning must also be given where the identifying witness claims to have recognised the accused from previous acquaintance.[187] In *Bentley*,[188] the Court of Appeal quashed a conviction for wounding with intent to do grievous bodily harm where the trial judge had failed to give a *Turnbull* warning in respect of the victim's identification of the defendant as his attacker. The victim knew the defendant and claimed to have recognised him as the person who collided with him in a club and then attacked him with a glass. The victim was very drunk at the time. Lord Taylor C.J. explained the justification for treating recognition cases as subject to the *Turnbull* guidelines:

> "The recognition type of identification... [cannot] be treated as straightforward or trouble-free... Each of us, and no doubt everyone sitting in this Court, has had the experience of seeing someone in the street whom we know, only to discover later that it was not that person at all. The expression 'I could have sworn it was you' indicates the sort of warning which the judge should give, because that is exactly what the witness does. He swears that it was the person he thinks it was. He may nevertheless have been mistaken even where it is a case of recognition rather than one of identification."[189]

The exceptional cases where a *Turnbull* warning is not necessary include, first, the identification of a car or, presumably, any other vehicle. In *Browning*,[190] the Court of Appeal held that a car does not change its shape or appearance in the way that a human facial expression does, hence a *Turnbull* direction is not required. Even in this type of case, however, the judge should draw the jury's attention to the witness's opportunity to view the car at the material time, the witness's ability to distinguish makes of cars and their characteristics, and to the danger of the witness not having a genuine recollection but of repeating information about the car absorbed from elsewhere, or of inventing a memory.

Secondly, a warning is unnecessary where the defendant admits his presence at the scene of the crime, there is no possibility of him being mistaken for another and the issue is one of what he was doing at the time. Thus, in *Slater*,[191] the defendant denied assaulting P in a pub, although he admitted that he was in the pub when the assault occurred. The defendant was six feet six inches tall, and there was no suggestion that anyone else present was remotely near that height. Since there was no possibility that the defendant had been mistaken for someone else, the only question was what, if anything, he had done. Accordingly the Court of Appeal upheld the trial judge's decision not to give the warning about the risk

7–031

---

[185] *Tyson* [1985] Crim. L.R. 48.

[186] *Scott and Barnes v R.* [1989] A.C. 1242.

[187] In *Turnbull* itself Lord Widgery C.J. expressly referred to recognition cases as falling within the guidelines, and a line of authority has confirmed that they do. See *Beckford v R.* (1993) 97 Cr.App.R. 409 PC; *Bowden* [1993] Crim. L.R. 379 CA; *Thomas* [1994] Crim. L.R. 128 CA; *Bentley* (1994) 99 Cr.App.R. 342 CA; *Wait* [1998] Crim. L.R. 68 CA.

[188] *Bentley* (1994) 99 Cr.App.R. 342.

[189] *Bentley* (1994) 99 Cr.App.R. 342 at 344.

[190] *Browning* (1992) 94 Cr.App.R. 109 CA.

[191] *Slater* [1995] 1 Cr.App.R. 584.

of mistaken identification. On the other hand, in *Thornton*,[192] the defendant denied assault at a wedding reception, although he admitted being present at the reception when the attack took place. Here there was a possibility of a mistaken identification, since four people were involved in the attack and there were other guests at the reception dressed similarly to the defendant. The Court of Appeal held that the full *Turnbull* warning should have been given.

Thirdly, a warning may not be necessary where the issue is not whether the witness has made a mistake but is only whether the witness is telling the truth. Logically a claim that the witness has deliberately made a false identification does not, without more, raise an issue of honest mistake. Consequently, there is some Court of Appeal authority that in recognition cases, where the defence is that the identifying witness is lying, a *Turnbull* warning would be unnecessary and confusing.[193] However, the Privy Council took a more cautious view in *Shand v R.*,[194] saying that even where credibility was the sole line of defence, the judge should normally direct the jury that they had to be satisfied that the identifying witnesses were not only honest, but also not mistaken. It would only be in a "wholly exceptional" case, according to the Privy Council, that the warning could be dispensed with entirely.[195] Despite the strength of these words, it seems that the issue depends essentially on the facts of the case and the nature of the identification. If mistake remains a possibility on the facts of the case the warning should be given.[196] If a *Turnbull* direction would add nothing of substance to the judge's other directions it is not necessary.[197] So where the quality of the identification evidence was exceptionally good and the challenge was only to the witness's credibility, the absence of a *Turnbull* direction was not fatal to a conviction.[198]

Fourthly, a *Turnbull* direction is inappropriate where a jury are invited to make their own identification from photographs or video recordings taken at the scene of the crime. In *Blenkinsop,*[199] video film and still photographs were taken at the scene of a violent demonstration. These were shown to the jury along with a police photograph of the accused taken after his arrest the following day. The jury were invited to say whether the film and the photographs at the scene showed the accused taking part in the violence. Dismissing his appeal against a conviction for violent disorder the Court of Appeal held that the *Turnbull* direction for a case of identification by a *witness* is not required where the jury are making the identification. It is necessary, and sufficient, if the judge warns the jury of the risk

---

[192] *Thornton* [1995] 1 Cr.App.R. 578.
[193] *Courtnell* [1990] Crim. L.R. 115; *Cape* [1996] 1 Cr.App.R. 191. cf. *Ryder* [1994] 2 All E.R. 859, where it was held that a *Turnbull* warning was required in a case of recognition, but since the fundamental issue was the credibility of the witness, no miscarriage of justice had resulted from the omission to give the warning.
[194] *Shand v R.* [1996] 2 Cr.App.R. 204.
[195] *Shand v R.* [1996] 2 Cr.App.R. 204 at 209. See, e.g. the illustration given by Lord Lowry in *Beckford v R.* (1993) 97 Cr.App.R. 409 at 415.
[196] See, e.g. *Grieves v R.* [2011] UKPC 39; [2012] Crim. L.R. 212.
[197] See *Capron v R.* [2006] UKPC 34; *Giga* [2007] Crim. L.R. 571.
[198] See *Freemantle v R.* [1995] 1 Cr.App.R. 1; *Shand v R.* [1996] 2 Cr.App.R. 204. In both cases the Privy Council applied the proviso to uphold convictions despite the absence of a warning. See also *Giga* [2007] Crim. L.R. 571.
[199] *Blenkinsop* [1995] 1 Cr.App.R. 7.

of a mistake and of the need to exercise particular care in any identification the jury make for themselves. In giving this warning the judge should direct the jury on the importance of such factors as the quality of the photographs, the extent of the exposure of the facial features of the person photographed, any evidence of a change in the defendant's appearance and the opportunity the jury have had to observe the defendant in court.[200]

Where a witness does not purport to identify the defendant but has given a general description of a person seen that matches the appearance of the defendant, it has been suggested that a *Turnbull* direction would be prudent.[201] This is surely correct, unless the prosecution's case depends very largely on circumstantial evidence of identity, and a resemblance between the defendant and the witness's description is effectively a minor piece of supporting evidence. Such a case would not be one resting wholly or mainly on the correctness of a disputed eyewitness identification.[202]

7–032

3.   The terms of the warning

It is worth repeating that *Turnbull* is not a statute, and the guidelines should not be applied as if they were legislative provisions. This means that there is no set formula of words that must be recited to the jury.[203] The purpose of the guidelines is to ensure that the judge educates the jury about dangers of which they might not otherwise be aware. This means that the judge must, as Lord Taylor C.J. put it in *Bentley*[204]:

7–033

> "alert the jury to the dangers which are inherent in cases where identification is in issue; . . . alert them to the potential fallibility of the identifying process, and to the many cases where convinced and convincing witnesses have been shown later to have been hopelessly and dangerously mistaken about their so-called recognition of the defendant."

The court will look carefully at the judge's direction to ensure that the fundamental requirements laid down in *Turnbull* are met and that the message has been made clear to the jury. Provided this has been done, the direction does not

---

[200] *Dodson and Williams* (1984) 79 Cr.App.R. 220. In *Downey* [1995] 1 Cr.App.R. 547 Evans L.J. stated that a direction on the perils of jury identification from photographs was not mandatory. This can be accepted insofar as it indicates that there is no imperative requirement to mention particular factors that might affect the reliability of such an identification unless an issue arises on them on the facts of the case. If the statement indicates that a jury need not be warned about the risk of mistaken identification generally it goes too far and should not be followed. In *Downey* a *Turnbull* direction had been given in respect of an identification witness, so that the risks of mistake were present to the jury's mind in any event and an additional warning was superfluous. See also *Ali* [2008] EWCA Crim 1522.
[201] *Andrews* [1993] Crim. L.R. 590, but see now *Thomas* [2010] EWCA Crim 148, where the Court of Appeal distinguished between identification evidence and descriptive evidence, for which a *Turnbull* warning was not required. See also *Nyanteh* [2005] EWCA Crim 686, where the precise basis of the identification was unclear, and the trial judge gave a *Turnbull* direction, the terms of which the Court of Appeal upheld.
[202] Compare *Spencer* [1995] Crim. L.R. 235, where a small child's visual identification was an essential element of the prosecution's case and a full *Turnbull* warning was required.
[203] *Pattinson and Exley* [1996] 1 Cr.App.R. 51 at 53 per Henry L.J.
[204] *Bentley* (1994) 99 Cr.App.R. 342 at 344.

have to follow a rigid pattern or contain particular key words.[205] The courts have generally resisted attempts to confine the guidelines within verbal straitjackets. These features of appellate review—the concentration on the substance of the direction and the refusal to be imprisoned by form—are seen clearly in the leading cases on key elements of the direction.

For example, it is essential that the judge brings out the point that mistakes can be made by honest witnesses, even apparently convincing ones.[206] In *Reid v R.*,[207] Lord Ackner suggested that this is a risk greater than the ordinary risk of mistake in human recollection,[208] and a jury may not be aware of the extent of the risk. Hence the need to draw their attention specifically to the point. It is not, however, necessary to use the word "convincing" in explaining that an honest witness can be mistaken.[209] It is sufficient to stress the danger of mistake so that the jury know that they must consider the identifying witness's reliability as well as their credibility.

7–034   In an appropriate case the judge should warn that even a number of honest witnesses may be mistaken. Such a warning is always required where a number of identifications, none of which is independently established, are said to support each other.[210] Similarly, the judge should normally refer to the experience of miscarriages of justice through mistaken identification. Again this is something that a jury may not be aware of unless specifically warned. However, such a warning is unnecessary and unhelpful in a jurisdiction in which there is no such history of miscarriages of justice.[211]

A *Turnbull* direction must point out to the jury any specific weaknesses in the identification evidence. In *Fergus*,[212] the Court of Appeal quashed a conviction for assault with intent to rob where the sole evidence against the accused was an eyewitness identification by the victim that contained nine specific weaknesses, including major discrepancies between the victim's description of the assailant and the defendant's appearance. The trial judge had not reviewed these weaknesses in the direction to the jury. The court held that:

> "in a case dependent on visual identification, and particularly where that is the only evidence, *Turnbull* makes it clear that it is incumbent on a trial judge to place before the jury any specific weaknesses which can arguably be said to have been exposed in the evidence. And it is not sufficient for the judge to invite the jury to take into account what counsel for the defence said

---

[205] Although the Court of Appeal has stressed the value of the model Judicial Studies Board direction derived from *Turnbull* and warned trial judges of the danger of diluting or glossing it: *Shervington* [2008] EWCA Crim 658.

[206] *Amore v R.* (1994) 99 Cr.App.R. 279 PC; *Bentley* (1994) 99 Cr.App.R. 342 CA; *Phillips* [2007] EWCA Crim 1042.

[207] *Reid v R.* [1990] 1 A.C. 363 PC.

[208] *Reid v R.* [1990] 1 A.C. 363 at 381. The duty on a judge to emphasise the special need for caution in acting on the correctness of an eyewitness identification was stressed by the Privy Council in *Farquharson v R.* (1994) 98 Cr.App.R. 398.

[209] *Rose v R.* [1995] Crim. L.R. 939; *Mills v R.* [1995] Crim. L.R. 884.

[210] *Weeder* (1980) 71 Cr.App.R. 228; *Breslin* (1984) 80 Cr.App.R. 226; *Grant* [1996] 2 Cr.App.R. 272 at 281 CA.

[211] *Amore v R.* (1994) 99 Cr.App.R. 279 PC, on appeal from Jamaica.

[212] *Fergus* (1994) 98 Cr.App.R. 313.

about the specific weaknesses. Needless to say, the judge must deal with the specific weaknesses in a coherent manner so that the cumulative impact of those specific weaknesses is fairly placed before the jury."[213]

At another point in the judgment in *Fergus* it was suggested that the judge should "summarise" for the jury any specific weaknesses.[214] Subsequently the Court of Appeal was quick to reject defence arguments that such a summary was a mandatory requirement.[215] A summary may be appropriate in some cases, when it must be a summary of the whole case, both for the prosecution and the defence. In other cases it may be more convenient to give specific reminders in relation to specific parts of the evidence as they come to be dealt with in the course of the summing-up.[216] Given that a summing-up should be tailored to the evidence in each case, this refusal to tie the hands of the trial judge too closely is welcome. Having said that, in a case of any complexity it may often be desirable to focus on an identification issue as a whole, reviewing the evidence of identity systematically. This is likely to be more helpful to a jury than if the judge gives a general warning about the dangers of mistaken identity and then comes back to the issue intermittently in the course of a lengthy summing-up.

4. Good and poor quality identifications

According to *Turnbull*, a case resting wholly or mainly on a disputed identification that is of poor quality and unsupported by other evidence should be withdrawn from the jury. Such a case was *Daley v R.*,[217] where the sole evidence on a murder charge was an eyewitness identification by the victim's husband who hid after intruders broke into his house to carry out a robbery and shot his wife. He had had a very limited opportunity to observe the intruders, but identified the defendant on a parade four months later. There was no corroboration of his identification. Quashing the defendant's conviction the Privy Council held that the judge should have withdrawn the case from the jury in view of the poor quality of the identification evidence and the weaknesses that gave it such a slender basis as to make it unreliable. Similarly, in *Fergus*[218] the Court of Appeal, having held that the trial judge had failed to give an adequate *Turnbull* direction, went further and held that the judge should have withdrawn the case from the jury in view of the poor quality and specific weaknesses of the unsupported identification by the victim of a mugging.

In both these cases the initial observation was for a short period under difficult circumstances. However, not all "fleeting glimpse" cases will necessarily be

7–035

---

[213] *Fergus* (1994) 98 Cr.App.R. 313 at 318. See also *R. v I* [2007] EWCA Crim 923; [2007] 2 Cr. App. R. 24, where the Court of Appeal held that a judge must not only identify the weaknesses in the evidence but must also explain why they are weaknesses.

[214] *Fergus* (1994) 98 Cr.App.R. 313 at 321 per Steyn L.J.

[215] See *Mussell and Dalton* [1995] Crim. L.R. 887; *Pattinson and Exley* [1996] 1 Cr.App.R. 51; *Qadir* [1998] Crim. L.R. 829 CA.

[216] *Mussell and Dalton* [1995] Crim. L.R. 887; *Pattinson and Exley* [1996] 1 Cr.App.R. 51.

[217] *Daley v R.* (1994) 98 Cr.App.R. 447 PC. See also *Hutton* [1999] Crim. L.R. 74: a witness's limited opportunity of seeing a robber, plus defects in the conduct of the identification parade, meant that the case should not have been allowed to go to the jury.

[218] *Fergus* (1994) 98 Cr.App.R. 313.

classified as poor quality identifications. In *Reid*,[219] the victim of an attempted murder had claimed to recognise the defendant as the man who had shot him through a car window. Upholding the judge's decision to let the case go to the jury the Court of Appeal held that this was not a case of a fleeting glimpse of a stranger. It was "a view of somebody that the complainant did know in a car very close by, with a streetlight five yards away, for a matter of some seconds".[220] Such cases underline the point that the difference between good and poor quality identifications is a matter of degree. Relatively small increases in the length of time for observation and in the strength of the light, or the fact that the witness had seen the person in question before, may result in the case reaching the jury rather than being thrown out at half time.[221]

5. Supporting evidence

7–036   The judge decides whether there is evidence capable of supporting the correctness of an eyewitness identification. He should explain to the jury what this evidence is while making it clear that it is for the jury to decide whether the evidence does in fact support the identification. The judge should also explain any evidence that is not capable of providing support where there is a danger that the jury might think that it does.

Lord Widgery C.J. stated in *Turnbull* that supporting evidence does not have to amount to corroboration in its legal meaning.[222] In many cases supporting evidence will be independent evidence that itself implicates the accused in the commission of the offence (e.g. a confession, or the accused's possession of cash stolen in a robbery[223]), but it need not necessarily have this quality if it nonetheless tends to suggest that the witness's identification is correct. The accused's false alibi may have this effect if the jury are satisfied that the reason for its falsity is that it was a deliberate fabrication intended to deceive the jury. Another example is the accused's possession of a car matching the description of the getaway vehicle.[224]

F.   SCIENTIFIC AND OTHER EXPERT EVIDENCE

7–037   Some forms of scientific evidence of identification depend on access to a sample from the defendant, such as a fingerprint, or a specimen of blood or hair. PACE sets out the statutory procedures that provide the police with the powers to obtain the relevant material from a suspect.[225] Fingerprints and non-intimate samples can be taken without consent. An intimate sample can be taken only with a suspect's consent, but a refusal to consent without good cause may be the subject

---

[219] *Reid* [1994] Crim. L.R. 442 CA.

[220] *Reid* [1994] Crim. L.R. 442 at 443. *Rose v R.* [1995] Crim. L.R. 939 is similar.

[221] cf. *Samson* [2004] EWCA Crim 2171. See also *Shervington* [2008] EWCA Crim 658.

[222] See Ch.15.

[223] See, e.g. *Rutherford and Palmer* (1994) 98 Cr.App.R. 191 CA.

[224] See, e.g. *Penny* (1992) 94 Cr.App.R. 345 CA.

[225] PACE s.61 (fingerprinting); s.62 (intimate samples); s.63 (non-intimate samples). See also ss.64 and 65.

of adverse inferences.[226] If the police obtain or retain a fingerprint or a sample unlawfully, the evidence remains admissible in law, but the judge may exclude it as a matter of discretion in accordance with the principles discussed in Ch.8.

There are other instances in which expert evidence is admissible on issues of identification. Such cases include facial mapping, earprints,[227] voice recognition[228] and evidence of handwriting.[229] However, it is submitted that expert evidence is not admissible in English law on the general issue of the weaknesses of eyewitness identification evidence.[230] Educating the jury in this regard will remain the prerogative of the judge. At first sight this is curious. The *Turnbull* guidelines are premised on the assumption that juries are unaware of the risks attached to this kind of evidence, and expert evidence is admissible in many cases to furnish the jury with relevant information outside their usual experience. However, its exclusion in identification cases may be accounted for on two grounds. First, it probably does not pass the 'necessity' test for the admission of expert evidence[231] given that it is general in nature and the judges themselves are required to warn juries about the risks associated with mistaken eyewitness identification. Secondly, its weight is likely to be quite unclear. This is because its conclusions are derived from laboratory studies and it is therefore speculative on how far the findings of those studies can be generalised to real trials with real juries, much less to the specific circumstances of one particular trial.[232] Accordingly concerns about side issues and the risk of confusing rather than helping the jury would be likely to arise. For the time being therefore England is unlikely to follow those American jurisdictions that have permitted psychologists to testify generally on the reliability of identification evidence.

However, this point is subject to an important qualification. Although the *Turnbull* guidelines are widely regarded as having been successful in alerting factfinders to the dangers of unreliable eyewitness identification evidence, they should still be treated as laying down minimum requirements. The Court of Appeal and trial judges should be prepared to expand them if necessary, as and when experience and research demonstrate the existence of factors influencing eyewitness accuracy that the guidelines do not currently include.

---

[226] PACE s.62(10).

[227] *Dallagher* [2002] EWCA Crim 1903; [2003] 1 Cr.App.R. 12; *Kempster (No.2)* [2008] EWCA Crim 975; [2008] 2 Cr.App.R. 19.

[228] *Robb* (1991) 93 Cr.App.R. 161; *Flynn and St John* [2008] EWCA Crim 970; [2008] 2 Cr.App.R. 20.

[229] See, e.g. *Montgomery* [1996] Crim. L.R. 507 CA, where the prosecution led the evidence of a handwriting expert in a fraud case in preference to possible testimony from a defrauded purchaser who had given a description of the fraudsman that did not fit the defendant. The Court of Appeal held that the decision not to hold a parade was not a breach of Code D because there was no reasonable possibility that the purchaser could make an identification and therefore there was no disputed identification evidence.

[230] There is no appellate English authority directly on point, but such evidence has been ruled inadmissible in Scotland: *Gage v HM Advocate* [2011] H.C.A.J.C. 40, discussed by A. Roberts in (2012) 16 E. & P. 93.

[231] *Turner* [1975] Q.B. 834, discussed in Ch.20.

[232] As researchers themselves have acknowledged: see S. M. A. Lloyd-Bostock and B. R. Clifford, *Evaluating Witness Evidence* (1983), Introduction.

7–038   Finally, there is increasing recognition that the danger of mistaken identification is not restricted to eyewitness identification, but applies equally to other forms of identification evidence. This is particularly the case in relation to voice identification.[233] Ormerod, in a thorough review of the subject,[234] argued that there is a need to develop safeguards against error analogous to those in Code D, but taking account of the significant differences between eyewitness and earwitness evidence and the lessons from the scientific research. Since the Court of Appeal had held that Code D applies only to visual and not to voice identification,[235] Ormerod's proposal was the right way forward. In 2003 the government published a circular giving guidance to police forces on the use of voice identification parades, modelled on the provisions for eyewitness parades in Code D. Subsequently the Court of Appeal noted in *Flynn and St John*,[236] that the ability of a lay listener correctly to identify voices is subject to a number of variables, including the quality of the recording of the disputed voice, the nature and duration of the speech which is sought to be identified, and the degree of familiarity of the listener with the known voice. The court went on to say that where police officers purport to identify a voice on tape they should take great care to make a proper record of the procedures they have adopted to avoid the risks of unfairness and inaccuracy in making the identification. Given the difficulties the defence may have in challenging police evidence of voice recognition, such records are essential if the prejudicial effect of the evidence is not to outweigh its probative value. The court expressed the view that where the prosecution seek to rely on such evidence they should instruct an expert to give an independent opinion on its validity.

Where voice recognition evidence is properly admitted, it is permissible for the jury to compare the voice heard on the relevant recording with the voice of the defendant whom they have heard give evidence in the trial.[237] The judge should direct the jury to listen to the tapes guided by the evidence of the voice recognition witness, whether an expert or a lay witness. In addition a suitably adapted version of the *Turnbull* warning is required for all voice identification cases.[238] The trial judge should take particular care to highlight the danger of mistaking one voice for another.

---

[233] See R. Bull and B. Clifford, "Earwitness Testimony" in A. Heaton-Armstrong, E. Shepherd and D. Wolchover (eds), *Analysing Witness Testimony* (1999), p.194, for a summary of relevant research. See also R. Wilcock, R. Bull and R. Milne, *Witness Identification in Criminal Cases: Psychology and Practice* (2008), pp.89–97.

[234] D. Ormerod, "Sounds Familiar?—Voice Identification Evidence" [2001] Crim. L.R. 595. See also his subsequent article, "Sounding Out Expert Voice Identification" [2002] Crim. L.R. 771.

[235] *Gummerson and Steadman* [1999] Crim. L.R. 680.

[236] *Flynn and St John* [2008] EWCA Crim 970; [2008] 2 Cr.App.R. 20.

[237] *Flynn and St John* [2008] EWCA Crim 970; [2008] 2 Cr.App.R. 20 at [56], doubting *Chenia* [2002] EWCA Crim 2345; [2003] 2 Cr.App.R. 6.

[238] *Hersey* [1998] Crim. L.R. 281; *Gummerson and Steadman* [1999] Crim. L.R. 680; *Roberts* [2000] Crim. L.R. 183.

CHAPTER 8

EVIDENCE OBTAINED BY ILLEGAL OR UNFAIR MEANS

A. INTRODUCTION

This chapter deals with evidence that has been obtained by illegal or unfair   **8–001**
means. A convenient term to describe such evidence is improperly obtained
evidence. Some aspects of this topic have already been discussed in the previous
two chapters dealing with confessions and eyewitness identification evidence
respectively. Both these types of evidence are governed by a detailed regulatory
regime devised in large part as a response to their potential for causing
miscarriages of justice. We have seen how confession and identification evidence
obtained in breach of the PACE Codes of Practice may be excluded in the
exercise of the trial judge's discretion under s.78 of PACE.

We now consider the problem of impropriety more generally, taking account
of other forms of evidence that may be obtained by the use of illegal or unfair

[301]

means on the part of investigating authorities. Potentially there are many such forms. They include real evidence discovered as the result of illegal searches of person or property, the results of breathalyser and blood or urine tests in drink-driving cases, expert evidence derived from samples unlawfully obtained from the accused, evidence of a person's conduct and statements obtained by techniques involving deception, entrapment, eavesdropping and covert surveillance, evidence that has been stolen or obtained in breach of confidence, and so on.

The great majority of the investigative techniques concerned are now regulated by statute. PACE deals with search and seizure, and the obtaining of fingerprints and bodily samples. The Road Traffic Act 1988 deals with the administration of breath and blood/urine tests in driving cases. The Regulation of Investigatory Powers Act 2000 provides comprehensive regulation[1] of the interception of communications, including telephone-tapping and mail-opening.[2] This Act also covers various forms of covert surveillance, such as the use of concealed microphones on property or in vehicles,[3] and establishes authorisation procedures for the use of covert human intelligence sources (undercover officers and police agents).[4] Statutory authority is necessary to legitimate police actions that would otherwise amount to trespass against the person or property. Statutory authority is also necessary where investigative techniques might violate the right to privacy in art.8 of the ECHR. Interference with privacy can be justified under the Convention, but it has to be in accordance with the law.[5] Other forms of proactive policing, such as the use of certain kinds of traps, that do not involve invasions of legally protected interests, do not need statutory authority. They may however be subject to administrative guidelines.

8–002   A question may arise concerning the admissibility of evidence if the relevant statutory procedures have not been complied with, or if the means used to obtain the evidence are challenged as otherwise unlawful or unfair. Improperly obtained evidence raises a number of problems concerning admissibility. The first two concern fairness to the accused, but they relate to different aspects of fairness. First, there is the possible impact of improperly obtained evidence on rectitude of decision. If the evidence carries a significant risk of unreliability or is more prejudicial than probative, its use at trial may be unfair because of the danger that it will lead to a verdict of guilty that is factually inaccurate. Secondly, if unfair means have been used to obtain the evidence this may impact on the moral authority of the verdict. Improperly obtained evidence involving unfair treatment

---

[1] It is beyond the scope of this book to deal with this major statute in detail, but aspects of it are referred to in this chapter. For further discussion of the Regulation of Investigatory Powers Act 2000 ("RIPA") see the articles by Y. Akdeniz, N. Taylor and C. Walker, "www.Bigbrother.gov.uk: State surveillance in the age of information and rights" [2001] Crim. L.R. 73; P. Mirfield, "Regulation of Investigatory Powers Act 2000: Evidential Aspects" [2001] Crim. L.R. 91. On telephone-tapping see D. Ormerod and S. McKay, "Telephone Intercepts and their Admissibility" [2004] Crim. L.R. 15.

[2] RIPA Pt I, replacing the Interception of Communications Act 1985.

[3] RIPA ss.26–28– See also Police Act 1997 Pt III.

[4] RIPA s.29.

[5] And be necessary in a democratic society in the interests of one of a number of specified purposes: see below. The need to provide appropriate legal authority for interferences with the right to privacy by interception of communications and covert surveillance was one of the main objectives of the RIPA.

of the accused before the trial may compromise the legitimacy of the verdict by significantly undermining its moral foundation. Thirdly, if the means used to obtain the evidence involve illegality on the part of the state this may demonstrate the state's disregard for the rule of law and thereby threaten both the moral authority and the expressive value of the verdict.

However, where the evidence improperly obtained is not confession evidence or eyewitness identification evidence, the scale of the first problem is much reduced. A great deal of evidence outside these two categories is highly reliable and highly probative. Some of it, such as fingerprint or DNA profile evidence, may in some cases be virtually conclusive on the factual issue of the defendant's guilt. Since factual accuracy is the major component of legitimate adjudication, it follows that the natural and correct tendency is to admit it at trial. In addition, some of the investigative techniques concerned are less open to oppression and abuse of power than the questioning of persons in custody. These points help to explain why exclusion of non-confessional improperly obtained evidence has tended to be regarded as exceptional in English law and as something to be undertaken only in limited circumstances.

The law in this area is complex and still developing. Statute occasionally provides rules governing the admissibility of evidence obtained by particular methods.[6] Where the statute is silent, or there is no relevant legislation, the general rule at common law applies. This rule states that the admissibility of evidence is not affected by the means used to obtain it. The use of illegal or unfair techniques to obtain evidence does not generally make otherwise relevant and admissible evidence inadmissible. There is a small number of exceptions to this rule; these are discussed below. In addition, the general rule is subject to judicial discretion, existing both at common law and under statute, to exclude admissible prosecution evidence.[7] The scope and limits of exclusionary discretion were discussed generally in Ch.3, where the point was made that the discretion to exclude prosecution evidence is not limited to evidence obtained by illegal or unfair means. However, it is in relation to this kind of evidence that the exercise of the discretion is most controversial. It now seems to be established that the discretion under s.78(1) of PACE is wider than the discretion at common law,[8] but the limits of the statutory discretion remain obscure, and there is considerable doubt about the underlying rationale of the exclusionary decisions. As explained in Ch.3, there is an important theoretical debate about whether the purpose of exclusion is to ensure reliability of evidence, or to vindicate certain rights of the accused,[9] or to maintain police propriety (by, for example, controlling certain policing methods), or to maintain the integrity of judicial proceedings or, more generally, to promote legitimacy of adjudicative decision-making. A further element of complexity is added to the subject of improperly obtained evidence by

---

[6] See, e.g. RIPA ss.17–18 (interception of communications).
[7] See Ormerod and Birch, "The Evolution of the Discretionary Exclusion of Evidence" [2004] Crim. L.R. 767.
[8] Subject to *Chalkley* [1998] 2 Cr.App.R. 79 CA, discussed and criticised in Ch.3.
[9] The ECHR dimension is discussed by A. Ashworth, "The Exclusion of Evidence Obtained by Violating a Fundamental Right: Pragmatism Before Principle in the Strasbourg Jurisprudence" in P. Roberts and J. Hunter (eds), *Criminal Evidence and Human Rights* (Oxford: Hart Publishing, 2012), Ch.6.

the expansion in recent years of the abuse of process doctrine. When successfully invoked this has the effect of stopping a prosecution in its tracks. The relationship of this procedure to exclusionary discretion is still being worked out.

The structure of this chapter is as follows. Section B deals with improperly obtained evidence at common law. Section C discusses s.78 of PACE and restates the general principles of its application. Section D then deals in some detail with the use of s.78 in relation to various types of illegally or unfairly obtained evidence. Section E concludes the chapter with a short discussion of abuse of process and its relationship to the exclusion of evidence.

B. THE COMMON LAW RELATING TO ILLEGALLY OR UNFAIRLY OBTAINED EVIDENCE

1. *The general rule*

8–003   The general rule at common law was and remains clear and unambiguous. The means by which evidence is obtained does not affect its admissibility as a matter of law. Provided the evidence is relevant it is admissible in law, and it is not rendered inadmissible because illegality or unfairness is used to obtain it. A classic statement of the attitude of 19th century judges was the terse observation of Crompton J. in *Leatham*[10]: "It matters not how you get it; if you steal it even, it would be admissible in evidence".

The inspiration for this common law position came largely from civil cases,[11] where the court has traditionally conceived its function as that of doing justice between the parties according to the evidence the parties choose to present. From this standpoint it is immaterial how the parties come by their evidence. Any unlawfulness in obtaining the evidence can be left to the injured party as an independent grievance for which the party can pursue whatever legal remedies are available. The application of this rule to the prosecutor in criminal cases made sense in a procedural context where historically the prosecutor was usually a private individual. This was the situation prior to the emergence of regular police forces in the middle decades of the nineteenth century.[12] However, the development of the police was not considered to call for a change in the basic rule. The orthodox theory was that a police officer, although holding the office of

---

[10] *Leatham* (1861) 8 Cox C.C. 498 at 501.

[11] The issue in *Leatham* (1861) 8 Cox C.C. 498 concerned the use in a prosecution of a document referred to by the accused in a statement that by statute could not be used against him. The document had come into the hands of the prosecutor independently. The court of Queen's Bench held that the defendant could not object to its production and use by the person who had it. Crompton J.'s observation, made in the course of argument, was stressing the point that in the absence of a formal prohibition on admissibility the means by which the evidence was obtained were immaterial. Hill J. supported the decision with a reference to the rule that secondary evidence of a privileged document is admissible, a rule that had already been said to apply even where the secondary evidence had been unlawfully obtained: *Lloyd v Mostyn* (1842) 10 M. & W. 478. For other early authorities see J. D. Heydon, "Illegally Obtained Evidence" [1973] Crim. L.R. 603.

[12] See J. M. Beattie, *Crime and the Courts in England 1660–1800* (Oxford: Oxford University Press, 1986), Ch.2.

constable under the Crown,[13] was an independent agent who derived his authority and powers from the common law.[14] At this stage in their development it was not clear that the police had powers that were greater than those of the ordinary citizen. Stephen, for example, writing in the 1880s, noted that the police had no greater powers of questioning or evidence-gathering than were available to private persons.[15] Well into the 20th century the Royal Commission on Police Powers and Procedure maintained:

"The Police... have never been recognised, either in law or in tradition, as a force distinct from the general body of citizens... [the] principle remains that a Policeman... is only a person paid to perform, as a matter of duty, acts which if he were so minded he might have done voluntarily. Indeed, a policeman possesses few powers not enjoyed by the ordinary citizen, and public opinion, expressed in Parliament and elsewhere, has shown great jealousy of any attempts to give increased authority to the Police."[16]

This representation of the police as "citizens in uniform" meant that the common law rule about the means used to obtain evidence could still be coherently applied to evidence obtained by the police. If the police, even when investigating and prosecuting crime, were doing so in the same way as private citizens, they need not be identified with the state as the administrator of criminal justice. The courts could therefore distance themselves from the methods employed by the police in the gathering of evidence. Thus in *Jones v Owen*,[17] which concerned a charge of unlawful fishing, the court admitted evidence that the accused was found with young salmon after a constable had unlawfully searched him. It was said that to exclude evidence obtained by illegal means would be a dangerous obstacle to the administration of justice.

The rule that relevant evidence is admissible, even if improperly obtained, was firmly established in the nineteenth century; the only major exception recognised at that time was the rule relating to the inadmissibility of an involuntary confession by the accused.[18] The rule has remained in place despite the most profound changes in the role and powers of the police in more recent times. Although the constitutional form of the independent constable has been retained, in substance the police have become official state investigators of crime. Their organisation has become increasingly centralised,[19] many of their operations have

---

[13] *Fisher v Oldham Corp* [1930] 2 K.B. 364.

[14] See L. Lustgarten, *The Governance of Police* (London, 1986), Ch.2.

[15] *History of the Criminal Law* (1883), Vol.1 pp.493–494. In *Wright v Court* (1825) 4 B. & C. 596, a case decided shortly before the establishment of the first police force in 1829, it was held that a constable who arrested a man on suspicion of felony had no power to detain him while the private prosecutor collected the necessary evidence. The constable's duty was to take the man before a magistrate as soon as he reasonably could.

[16] *Report of the Royal Commission on Police Powers and Procedure* Cmd.3297, (London, 1929), p.6. This was still the orthodox view as late as 1962: the Royal Commission on the Police (Final Report, London, 1962) restated the "principle that police powers are mostly grounded in the common law and differ little from those of ordinary citizens" (p.11).

[17] *Jones v Owen* (1870) 34 J.P. 759.

[18] See Ch.6.

[19] Recent developments include the introduction of the Serious Organised Crime Agency ("SOCA"), pursuant to the Serious Organised Crime and Police Act 2005. SOCA is an investigative, intelligence and enforcement agency. It replaced the National Crime Squad and the National Crime Intelligence Service, and has also taken on aspects of Customs enforcement, so that it combines the legal powers

been subject to Home Office guidelines for many years,[20] and, most importantly, they have been equipped for their functions of investigating and preventing crime with statutory powers far exceeding any available to private citizens. By codifying and extending the law of police powers PACE administered the last rites to the concept of the "citizen in uniform", but the concept had become increasingly untenable as an accurate representation of the police for many years previously.[21]

8–004 Moreover, since 1985 we have had a Crown Prosecution Service ("CPS") responsible for the great majority of criminal prosecutions in England and Wales. The CPS has worked closely with the police since its inception. It has now taken over from the police responsibility for charging persons against whom there is sufficient evidence[22]; such decisions are made according to whether the published criteria for prosecution are satisfied.[23] The criminal process is thus not only more organised and more integrated than it was in the nineteenth century, but it is also effectively in the hands of different state agencies from start to finish. Police, the CPS and the courts are, quite rightly, operationally independent of central government, but collectively they represent the enforcement and administration of criminal justice by the state. This has the important consequence that the old common law analogy between the parties to civil actions and police investigator/prosecutors in criminal cases has broken down completely. Modern trial courts cannot distance themselves from the pre-trial stages of criminal process in the way that their nineteenth-century predecessors could.

Nevertheless, throughout this period of significant change in the role and powers of the police, the courts have continued to apply the rule that illegality or unfairness in obtaining evidence does not affect its admissibility as a matter of law. Several of the leading cases have concerned evidence found during unlawful searches of person or property,[24] but the rule has also been applied in other

---

of police, customs and immigration services. SOCA is subject to the central supervision and direction of the Home Secretary, who may, among other things, determine its strategic priorities (s.9), issue codes of practice for the exercise of any of its functions (s.10) and allocate its funding (s.18). See also the Policing and Crime Act 2009, Pt 1 of which gives the Home Secretary powers to direct the making or termination of collaboration agreements between police forces.

[20] The use of these pre-dated PACE by some considerable time. In 1930, for example, a Home Office circular was issued to the police explaining the Judges Rules: see I. Brownlie, "Police Questioning, Custody and Caution" [1960] Crim. L.R. 298, 299. R. Plehwe, "Police and Government: The Commissioner of Police for the Metropolis" [1974] P.L. 316, 329, notes that in 1881 Sir William Harcourt, the Home Secretary, announced in Parliament that he had issued a directive to police authorities that they were not to use methods of entrapment without direct authorisation by the Home Office.

[21] It is difficult to be precise about when the change occurred, because it was a gradual process rather than a single event or series of events. Notable milestones were the Judges Rules (first issued in 1912 and revised in 1964); Magistrates' Courts Act 1952 s.38(2) (grant of police bail); *Dallison v Caffery* [1965] 1 Q.B. 348 CA; Report of the Royal Commission on Criminal Procedure (London, 1981); *Holgate-Mohammed v Duke* [1984] 2 W.L.R. 660 HL. On the development of police detention for questioning see D. Dixon, *Law in Policing* (Oxford: Oxford University Press, 1997), Ch.4.

[22] Criminal Justice Act 2003 s.28 Sch.2.

[23] See the *Code for Crown Prosecutors,* 2013 edn, issued pursuant to the Prosecution of Offences Act 1985.

[24] *Kuruma v R.* [1955] A.C. 197 (search of person); *King* [1969] 1 A.C. 304 (search of property); *Jeffrey v Black* [1978] Q.B. 490 (search of property).

contexts. Its continuing force was assumed by the House of Lords in the leading case of *Sang*,[25] in which the House gave extensive consideration to the question of how far there was a judicial discretion at common law to exclude evidence because of the means by which it had been obtained. The case concerned evidence of an offence procured by an alleged *agent provocateur* acting in collusion with the police. The decision, discussed below, that there was no discretion to exclude evidence obtained by these means, as well as the whole of their Lordships' dicta relating to other aspects of the exclusionary discretion, proceeded on the basis that the admissibility of evidence is not affected as a matter of law by the means used to obtain it. In *Khan (Sultan)*,[26] a case involving covert recordings of private conversations, the House of Lords confirmed that the rule of admissibility for illegally or unfairly obtained evidence is a well-established rule of law of general application. It seems clear that the rule has not been affected by the European Convention on Human Rights, or by PACE or any other statutory regulation of investigative powers, such as covert surveillance, unless the statute expressly provides for inadmissibility of evidence obtained in prohibited ways. In *Khan (Sultan)*, the police obtained recordings of incriminating conversations by means of a listening device surreptitiously attached to the outside wall of a house. The attachment of the device to the wall constituted a civil trespass against the occupier, a probable offence of criminal damage, and a breach of art.8 of the European Convention on Human Rights, guaranteeing the right to privacy. The House was in no doubt that the recordings were admissible in law,[27] and then proceeded to consider defence arguments for their exclusion under the discretion given by s.78 of PACE.

There are certain exceptions to the general common law rule. The longest-established of these exceptions concerns confessions. As noted in Ch.6, at common law the prosecution had to prove that a confession made to a person in authority had been made voluntarily and not in response to inducements or oppression. Under s.76 of PACE the common law rule was replaced by a duty on the prosecution to prove that a confession was not made in consequence of oppression or of anything said or done likely to render unreliable any confession by the accused.[28] The confession is inadmissible unless the prosecution can discharge this burden of proving beyond reasonable doubt that the confession was not obtained in either of the prohibited ways.

The second exception to the general rule is related to the first but was identified **8–005** much more recently. This exception concerns evidence obtained by torture. In *A v Secretary of State for the Home Department (No.2)*,[29] the question for the House of Lords was whether the Special Immigration Appeals Commission ("SIAC"), when hearing an appeal under s.25 of the Anti-terrorism, Crime and Security Act 2001 by a person certified and detained under the Act, could receive evidence that had or might have been obtained by torture, inflicted in order to obtain evidence,

---

[25] *Sang* [1980] A.C. 402.

[26] *Khan (Sultan)* [1996] 3 All E.R. 289.

[27] Following the decision in *Sang*: see [1996] 3 All E.R. 289 at 298 per Lord Nolan.

[28] The duty is triggered where it is represented to the court that a confession was or may have been obtained by such means, or the court may take the issue of its own motion. See further Ch.6.

[29] *A v Secretary of State for the Home Department (No.2)* [2005] UKHL 71; [2006] 1 All E.R. 575.

by officials of a foreign state without the complicity of British authorities. The House answered the question with an emphatic "No", holding that evidence obtained by torture is inadmissible in judicial proceedings. In a landmark judgment Lord Bingham founded his decision firmly on the common law:

> "The principles of the common law, standing alone, in my opinion compel the exclusion of third party torture evidence as unreliable, unfair, offensive to ordinary standards of humanity and decency and incompatible with the principles which should animate a tribunal seeking to administer justice."[30]

Lord Bingham discussed the rule at common law against involuntary confessions, noting that it provided a partial analogy with a rule against evidence obtained by torture. Clearly the rules will overlap where torture is used to obtain an incriminating statement from the defendant. But, as Lord Bingham pointed out, the analogy is inexact. The confessions rule applies only to statements by defendants, whereas the rule against torture will extend to evidence obtained from third parties. On the other hand the confessions rule provides for exclusion of statements on grounds much wider than torture, including inducements and other things said or done likely to produce an unreliable confession. Two other points about this case merit comment. The first is Lord Bingham's emphasis on the rule against torture as an issue of constitutional principle; he said that it trivialised the issue to treat it as an argument about the law of evidence.[31] Certainly the issue is far too important to be regarded as a matter for "technical" rule-making, but nonetheless the constitutional principle invoked by him finds its expression in a rule of admissibility of evidence. To that extent the decision is a striking affirmation of the argument made earlier in this book that the law of evidence has concerns that go much wider than the reliability of the evidence, and hence the factual accuracy of verdicts, against individual defendants.

The second point relates to evidence other than statements obtained by torture. Suppose a defendant, or a third party, is tortured by the police into revealing the location of real evidence that incriminates the defendant, for example explosives concealed in a garage rented by him. Lord Bingham commented in relation to *Warickshall*[32] that there is an obvious anomaly in treating an involuntary statement as inadmissible while treating as admissible evidence that would never have come to light but for the involuntary statement.[33] He went on to describe the anomaly as a pragmatic compromise accepted by the common law based on the desirability of admitting probative (real) evidence where this can be done without

---

[30] *A v Secretary of State for the Home Department (No.2)* [2005] UKHL 71; [2006] 1 All E.R. 575 at [52]. Lord Bingham also held that the common law principles were supported by the ECHR, interpreted in the context of the prohibition in international law of the use of torture and of the use in evidence of statements procured by torture. In *Jalloh v Germany* (2007) 44 E.H.R.R. 32 the European Court of Human Rights said that evidence obtained by torture in violation of art.3 of the ECHR should never be used in a trial. In *Gafgen v Germany* (2012) 52 E.H.R.R. 1 the court repeated the proposition and confirmed that art.6 would also be violated by the use of a confession obtained in breach of art.3 by means amounting to inhuman or degrading treatment (in that case a threat of torture).

[31] *A v Secretary of State for the Home Department (No.2)* [2005] UKHL 71; [2006] 1 All E.R. 575 at [51].

[32] *Warickshall* (1783) 1 Leach 263; discussed in Ch.6.

[33] *A v Secretary of State for the Home Department (No. 2)* [2005] UKHL 71; [2006] 1 All E.R. 575 at [16].

relying on the involuntary statement; he might have added that the compromise was endorsed by Parliament in s.76(4) of PACE. But *Warickshall* was not a case involving torture. Does English law's refusal to adopt a "fruit of the poisoned tree" doctrine for real evidence obtained in consequence of involuntary confessions still apply where the discovery of the real evidence results from a statement made under torture? This was left unclear in *A v Secretary of State for the Home Department (No.2)*. However, there is recent Strasbourg authority that the use of real evidence obtained as a direct result of acts of torture would make the proceedings as a whole automatically unfair, in breach of art. 6.[34] In Ch.6 above it was suggested that an English court could be expected to follow this ruling and could invoke the s.78 exclusionary discretion in such a case. This would require the court to read down s.76(4) of PACE to the effect that it states only that there is no *general* rule of inadmissibility for real evidence discovered in consequence of an inadmissible confession. There would then be room for discretionary exclusion of evidence where this was necessary to satisfy fair trial requirements.

A third exception to the common law rule, applying in both civil and criminal cases, concerns a party's privileged documents that the party brings into court. If an opposing party then uses trickery to obtain the documents he or she will not be permitted to adduce the documents or copies of them in evidence. In *ITC Film Distributors v Video Exchange Ltd*,[35] Warner J. stated two reasons for this decision. One was that the use of deception to obtain documents in these circumstances is probably a contempt of court; the court should not condone such an abuse of its process by admitting the evidence. The second was that the public interest in truth-finding in litigation is outweighed by the public interest in ensuring that parties who bring documents into court should not be at risk of having them filched and used by their opponents. At first sight this seems to be an example of how the value attached to rectitude of decision, which argues for the admission of any relevant evidence however obtained, may sometimes be defeated by the value attached to unhindered participation in the adjudicative process. However, it is likely that the court's protection of its own integrity was the critical factor in the decision; had the documents been filched in the same way outside the court, say from the solicitor's office, they, and copies of them, would have been admissible.[36]

---

[34] *Gafgen v Germany* (2012) 52 EHRR 1 at [173].

[35] *ITC Film Distributors v Video Exchange Ltd* [1982] Ch. 431.

[36] Under the secondary evidence rule at common law: *Lloyd v Mostyn* (1842) 10 M.& W. 478; *Calcraft v Guest* [1898] 1 Q.B. 759. The common law rule is subject to the equitable jurisdiction to restrain a breach of confidence where the documents have not yet been used in evidence: see *Ashburton v Pape* [1913] 2 Ch. 469; *Goddard v Nationwide Building Society* [1986] 3 All E.R. 264, and the discussion in Ch.10.

2. Exclusionary discretion at common law

(A) The development of the "fairness" discretion

8–006 Given the clear basic rule, most of the law in this area concerns the ambit of the judicial discretion to exclude evidence otherwise admissible in law. As explained in Ch.3, a discretion has been recognised at common law since at least the case of *Christie*[37] to exclude evidence the prejudicial effect of which outweighs its probative value. However, this head of discretion has relatively little application to the issue of illegally or unfairly obtained evidence. This is because, as already noted, outside the problematic areas of confessions and eyewitness identification evidence, such evidence often has a high degree of probative value. Evidence produced by an unlawful search, for example, may be highly incriminating. Its value is unlikely to be outweighed by prejudicial effect, whether prejudice is defined in terms of a tendency to cause the factfinder significantly to overestimate the probative value of the evidence, or a tendency to cause the factfinder to convict the accused for reasons unrelated to the probative value of the evidence.

A more appropriate head of discretion to consider is based on conceptions of fairness, but at common law the "fairness" discretion was limited both in theory and practice. The existence of some discretion to exclude evidence for reasons of fairness to the accused was first recognised in *Kuruma v R*. Lord Goddard C.J., giving the opinion of the Privy Council in a case where the defendant was found to be in possession of ammunition after an unlawful search, said[38]:

> "No doubt in a criminal case the judge always has a discretion to disallow evidence if the strict rules of admissibility would operate unfairly against the accused. This was emphasised in the case before this Board of *Noor Mohammed v R.*,[39] and in the recent case in the House of Lords of *Harris v Director of Public Prosecutions*.[40] If, for example, some admission of some piece of evidence, e.g., a document, had been obtained from a defendant by a trick, no doubt the judge might properly rule it out."

Lord Goddard's last sentence appeared to introduce a novelty into the law, although it is not clear that he intended it as such.[41] It was at best only a dictum since he held on the facts that there was no unfairness involved in admitting the evidence. Nonetheless, Lord Parker, Lord Goddard's successor as Lord Chief Justice, repeated the substance of the dictum in *Callis v Gunn*[42] and expanded it to take in other forms of police conduct:

---

[37] *Christie* [1914] A.C. 545 HL.

[38] *Kuruma v R.* [1955] A.C. 197 at 204.

[39] *Noor Mohammed v R.* [1949] A.C. 182.

[40] *Harris v DPP* [1952] A.C. 694. Both these cases cited by Lord Goddard C.J. concerned "similar fact" evidence and the discretion to exclude evidence whose probative value is outweighed by its prejudicial effect.

[41] See the restrictive interpretation placed on his words by Lord Diplock in *Sang* [1980] A.C. 402 at 436, suggesting that Lord Goddard C.J. was referring only to confessions obtained in breach of the Judges Rules and evidence analogous to a confession, such as an incriminating document, which the defendant was unfairly induced to produce by means violating the privilege against self-incrimination.

[42] *Callis v Gunn* [1964] 1 Q.B. 495 at 502 DC. The case concerned fingerprints which the police had obtained from the accused without informing him that he could refuse to supply them or that they

"[the] discretion, as I understand it, would certainly be exercised by excluding the evidence if there was any suggestion of it having been obtained oppressively, by false representations, by a trick, by threats, by bribes, anything of that sort."

There is a third, and even wider, dictum in *Jeffrey v Black*,[43] an unlawful search case where the police arrested the defendant for theft of a sandwich from a public house, charged him, and then went on to search his home for drugs. After holding that the search was unlawful in the absence of the defendant's consent or a warrant, Lord Widgery C.J. went on to consider the justices' decision to exclude the evidence of the finding of drugs in the defendant's home. He emphasised that the discretion was exceptional in nature, and continued:

"But if the case is exceptional, if the case is such that not only have the police officers entered without authority, but they have been guilty of trickery or they have misled someone, or they have been oppressive or they have been unfair, or in other respects they have behaved in a manner which is morally reprehensible, then it is open to the justices to apply their discretion and decline to allow the particular evidence to be let in as part of the trial."[44]

Lord Widgery C.J. then held that on the facts, the justices had been wrong to exclude the evidence since the police officers had done no more than enter without the appropriate authority. Assuming that the dicta of three successive Lord Chief Justices represented the law, it seems clear that in practice it was extremely difficult to persuade the courts to find a sufficient degree of police misconduct to justify excluding this kind of evidence, given that the non-confessional evidence obtained in these cases is highly probative of guilt. In no reported case between 1955 and 1979 was evidence produced by an unlawful search excluded. In fact during this period the only reported instances of non-confessional evidence being excluded by an appellate court for reasons of unfairness concerned two motorists arrested on suspicion of drink-driving offences.[45] They had consented to medical examinations after being told that the purpose of the examination was to determine if they were suffering from any illness or disease. The Court of Criminal Appeal held that the examining doctors should not have been permitted to testify that in their opinion the accused were unfit to drive through drink. The accused had in effect been tricked into incriminating themselves; had they known the true purpose of the examination they could have refused consent to it.

8–007

(B) R. v Sang

In *Sang,* Lord Diplock explained these cases as examples of the court giving effect to the privilege against self-incrimination.[46] This was consistent with the view that he took about the rationale of the law relating to involuntary confessions. If a confession were excluded because it was induced from the

8–008

---

might be used in evidence against him. There was no legal requirement to give this information. Allowing the prosecutor's appeal, the Divisional Court held that the magistrates had not been justified in excluding the fingerprint evidence.

[43] *Jeffrey v Black* [1978] Q.B. 490.
[44] *Jeffrey v Black* [1978] Q.B. 490 at 498.
[45] *Payne* [1963] 1 All E.R. 848. See also *Court* [1962] Crim. L.R. 697.
[46] *Sang* [1980] A.C. 402 at 435.

suspect by means violating the privilege against self-incrimination, then it would be logical for courts to exclude non-confessional evidence on the same grounds. This analogy overlooked the point that the voluntariness rule for confessions was a rule relating to admissibility as a matter of *law*, whereas exclusion of non-confessional evidence was a matter of *discretion*, yet the accused's interest in the vindication of the privilege would be the same in both cases.

Nevertheless, Lord Diplock used this theory to ground his view of the scope of exclusionary discretion at common law. Before considering this view in more detail it is important to note the actual decision in the case. In *Sang* the accused was charged with conspiracy to utter forged banknotes. The prosecution case was that the defendant and his associates went to a prearranged rendezvous with a large quantity of forged US banknotes and walked straight into a police ambush. The defendant's counsel tried to persuade the trial judge to hold a voir dire on whether the defendant's acts had been procured by an *agent provocateur*, acting in collusion with the police, who had posed as a buyer of banknotes and set up the rendezvous. Counsel's object was to argue that in these circumstances the judge should exercise discretion to exclude the prosecution evidence. The judge ruled that even if the facts were as the defendant alleged he had no discretion to exclude evidence on the ground that it had been unfairly obtained. The defendant thereupon changed his plea to guilty and challenged the ruling on appeal. Because the argument raised a general issue as to the scope of exclusionary discretion at common law, the Court of Appeal certified a point of law of general public importance that went a good deal further than was involved in the use of entrapment by *agents provocateurs*:

> "Does a trial judge have a discretion to refuse to allow evidence, being evidence other than evidence of admission, to be given in any circumstances in which such evidence is relevant and of more than minimal probative value?"

The Law Lords did not give a unanimous answer to this general question. They were, however, unanimous on the specific issue in the case. All agreed that the judge had no discretion to exclude evidence of the commission of the offence on the ground that the offence had been instigated by an *agent provocateur*. This followed, they thought, from the rule of substantive criminal law that entrapment is no defence to criminal liability.[47] To allow evidence to be excluded as a matter of discretion on the ground of entrapment would be inconsistent; it would have the effect of admitting the defence indirectly and thus give the judge the power to disregard at his or her discretion the rule that the defence is not directly available.

8–009   The wider review of the exclusionary discretion produced different opinions, although none of the Lords was willing to concede that a general discretion existed to exclude any prosecution evidence obtained by any improper means. It was accepted in all the speeches that there was a discretion to exclude evidence whose prejudicial effect outweighed its probative value. This was said to be founded on the judge's duty to secure a fair trial for the accused by preventing

---

[47] *Sang* [1980] A.C. 402 at 432–433 per Lord Diplock, 441 per Viscount Dilhorne, 443 per Lord Salmon, 446 per Lord Fraser, 455 per Lord Scarman. The Lords confirmed as correct the decisions of the Court of Appeal in *McEvilly and Lee* (1973) 60 Cr.App.R. 150; and *Mealey and Sheridan* (1974) 60 Cr.App.R. 59 that the defence of entrapment is unknown to English law.

unfair use of evidence at trial. Lord Diplock, with whom Viscount Dilhorne generally agreed, then gave this answer to the certified question:

> "Save with regard to admissions and confessions and generally with regard to evidence obtained from the accused after the commission of the offence, [the judge] has no discretion to refuse to admit relevant admissible evidence on the ground that it was obtained by improper or unfair means. The court is not concerned with how it was obtained."[48]

Lord Diplock rationalised this saving on the basis that it aimed to protect the accused's privilege against self-incrimination:

> "there is no discretion to exclude evidence discovered as the result of an illegal search but there is discretion to exclude evidence which the accused has been induced to produce voluntarily if the method of inducement was unfair."[49]

This approach had a degree of plausibility, derived from the coherence of using the privilege against self-incrimination both to explain the exclusion of involuntary confessions and as the test of unfairness in determining whether to exclude non-confessional evidence obtained from the accused.[50] However, the logical application of this criterion would produce some uncomfortable results. Was Lord Diplock really accepting that if the police deceived the defendant into handing over incriminating evidence, say by pretending that they had a search warrant, the judge had a discretion to exclude the evidence, but that if the police simply forced their way into the defendant's house without a warrant and against his will, there was no discretion to exclude the fruits of the search?

Possibly it was consciousness of this result that led the other Lords to take a less circumscribed view of the discretion. Lord Salmon, in a short speech, declared that the categories of cases in which the judge could exclude prosecution evidence, on the ground that it would make the trial unfair, were not closed and could not be closed except by statute.[51] He added mysteriously that he understood Lord Diplock to accept this proposition. His open-ended view of the discretion was confirmed by his refusal to comment on the correctness of the dicta in the earlier cases of *Callis v Gunn* and *Jeffrey v Black*, dicta which Viscount Dilhorne had rejected as wrong.[52] Lord Salmon said simply, but unhelpfully, that "the decision whether evidence may be excluded depends entirely on the particular facts of each case and the circumstances surrounding it, which are infinitely variable".[53]

Lord Fraser of Tullybelton accepted the correctness of the dicta in the earlier cases, but doubted whether they were intended to apply to evidence obtained from "sources other than the accused himself *or from premises occupied by him*" (emphasis added).[54] He then expressed agreement with Lord Diplock's answer to

8–010

---

[48] *Sang* [1980] A.C. 402 at 437.
[49] *Sang* [1980] A.C. 402 at 436.
[50] Note though that Lord Diplock's approach marked a switch from the earlier theory that the rationale of the rule against involuntary confessions was the risk of unreliability; see Ch.6.
[51] *Sang* [1980] A.C. 402 at 445.
[52] *Sang* [1980] A.C. 402 at 441.
[53] *Sang* [1980] A.C. 402 at 444.
[54] *Sang* [1980] A.C. 402 at 450.

the certified question. However, it is not at all clear that the rest of Lord Fraser's speech was consistent with Lord Diplock's answer. Lord Fraser accepted that the criteria for discretionary exclusion were the judges' subjective views of what was "unfair or oppressive or morally reprehensible",[55] whereas Lord Diplock seemed to restrict the possibility of exclusion to cases where the evidence was obtained by means violating the privilege against self-incrimination. Secondly, Lord Fraser's express reference to the possibility of excluding evidence obtained from the accused's premises is contradicted by Lord Diplock's statement, referred to above, that there is no discretion to exclude evidence discovered as the result of an illegal search.

Lord Scarman's speech was equivocal and somewhat confused. He emphasised that the function of the judge is to ensure a fair trial for the accused, and that the judge's exclusionary discretion is directed to the *use* that is made of evidence at trial.[56] He continued this theme by saying that the principle of fairness was exclusively concerned with the use of evidence at trial, but added that the principle "is not susceptible to categorisation or classification, and is wide enough in some circumstances to embrace the way in which, after the crime, evidence has been obtained from the accused".[57] The second part of this proposition partly conflicts with the first because the context seems to make it clear that it is only when the evidence is obtained from the accused, and only when the means used to obtain the evidence infringe the privilege against self-incrimination, that any discretion can arise. Moreover, this qualification is itself rendered doubtful by Lord Scarman's apparent approval of certain Scottish cases dealing with the admissibility of evidence found in consequence of illegal searches of the accused's premises,[58] where the issue does not necessarily depend on violations of the privilege against self-incrimination.

Sang is an unsatisfactory authority from many points of view.[59] The speeches are inconsistent, they give confusing and unclear guidance on the scope of the fairness discretion at common law, and they misleadingly treat as comparable categories of fairness at trial the separate principles that the accused should not be convicted on prejudicial evidence and the principle that the accused should receive fair treatment in the evidence-gathering process. Most fundamentally of all, *Sang* completely failed to address the changing role and powers of the police in the investigation of offences and the implications this might have for the courts as the guardians of the legitimacy of criminal trials. Lord Diplock simply repeated the mantra that it was not the judges' function to discipline the police over their methods of obtaining evidence.[60] This position may be defensible but it rather misses the point of the extent to which the legitimacy of guilty verdicts may be compromised if they are founded on evidence obtained improperly. The importance attached to the privilege against self-incrimination was a recognition that more was at stake than issues of reliability and factual accuracy of decision.

---

[55] *Sang* [1980] A.C. 402.
[56] *Sang* [1980] A.C. 402 at 452.
[57] *Sang* [1980] A.C. 402 at 456–457.
[58] *Lawrie v Muir* [1950] J.C. 19; *HM Advocate v Turnbull* [1951] S.C.(J.) 96.
[59] See P. G. Polyviou, "Illegally Obtained Evidence and *R. v Sang*" in *Crime Proof and Punishment* (C. Tapper (ed.), London, 1981), p.226.
[60] *Sang* [1980] A.C. 402 at 436.

However, this emphasis was both misplaced, in the undiscriminating priority it gave to the privilege, and inadequately theorised, in its failure to locate this type of unfairness in a wider consideration of the aims of the law of evidence.

Subsequent cases, decided before the advent of PACE, applied *Sang*,[61] but did little to clarify the relevant principles. In *Trump*,[62] a police constable had obtained a specimen of blood from a motorist after giving the motorist a statutory warning under the wrong section of the Road Traffic Act 1972. The Court of Appeal held that the error did not make the evidence inadmissible in law, but did raise the issue of whether the case came within the principles set out in *Sang*. This was on the basis that giving the blood sample, which showed an excessive blood alcohol level, was very close to making an admission that the accused had consumed too much alcohol. Upholding the trial judge's decision not to exclude the evidence, the court held that the constable had acted in good faith. There was therefore no need to exclude the evidence as a disciplinary measure, nor would the admission of the evidence undermine the fairness of the trial. The explicit reference to exclusion as a sanction for police misconduct ran directly counter to Lord Diplock's rejection of this idea in *Sang*, while the distinction between action in good faith and deliberate misconduct should be immaterial in the context of protecting an accused's privilege against self-incrimination.

8–011

In *Fox*,[63] another breathalyser case, a motorist gave a sample of breath in the police station after having been arrested unlawfully. The House of Lords held that this illegality did not affect the admissibility of the evidence of the sample and held, further, that there was no ground for excluding the evidence as a matter of discretion since the defence conceded that the police officers concerned had acted in good faith. Lord Fraser of Tullybelton, with whom all the other Lords expressed agreement, commented that "if the appellant had been lured to the police station by some trick or deception, or if the police officers had behaved oppressively towards the appellant, the justices' jurisdiction to exclude otherwise admissible evidence recognised in *Sang* might have come into play".[64] This statement, like Lord Fraser's speech in *Sang* itself, leaves it unclear whether he was accepting that a violation of the privilege against self-incrimination was a prerequisite for discretionary exclusion where evidence was illegally or unfairly obtained. On the other hand, in *Apicella*,[65] the Court of Appeal clearly did accept this condition when deciding that there was no ground for excluding evidence derived from a sample of the accused's body fluid taken without his consent. The court said that no trick had been practised on the accused, although he had in fact

---

[61] cf. *Scott and Barnes v R.* [1989] A.C. 1242, where the Privy Council held that *Sang* had not exhaustively defined the categories of case where a judge had discretion to exclude evidence in the interests of securing a fair trial for the accused. In particular, said Lord Griffiths, there was a discretion to exclude the sworn deposition of a deceased witness, albeit a discretion to be exercised with great restraint. See also *Grant v R.* [2006] UKPC 2, where Lord Bingham said that in the opinion of the Privy Council it is clear that the judge has an overriding discretion to exclude evidence which is judged to be unfair to the defendant in the sense that it will put him at an unfair advantage or deprive him unfairly of the ability to defend himself (para.21(3)).

[62] *Trump* (1980) 70 Cr.App.R. 300.

[63] *Fox* (1986) 82 Cr.App.R. 105.

[64] *Fox* (1986) 82 Cr.App.R. 105 at 111.

[65] *Apicella* (1986) 82 Cr.App.R. 295 CA.

submitted to the sample being taken only because a prison officer had told him that he had no choice. This was apparently not thought to amount to a violation of the privilege, despite the element of compulsion.

C.   THE STATUTORY DISCRETIONS TO EXCLUDE EVIDENCE

1.   *PACE section 82(3)*

8–012   The effect of s.82(3) of PACE is to preserve any discretion at common law to exclude evidence. Accordingly the law discussed in the previous section remains good law after PACE. The point was made in Ch.3 that since PACE came into force, there has been very little reference to s.82(3), and no attempt at all to clarify more precisely the scope and limits of the discretion at common law to exclude evidence. It seems to have been generally assumed that the discretion discussed in *Sang*, founded on fairness to the accused, has been absorbed into the discretion under s.78 to safeguard the fairness of the proceedings. The major preoccupation, as exemplified in *Chalkley*,[66] has been whether s.78 is a restatement or an enlargement of the limits of the common law discretion as set out in *Sang*. The courts have very largely ignored s.82(3) in these discussions.

It seems clear from the legislative history of s.78[67] that Parliament itself did not think through the implications of having two provisions in PACE both dealing with exclusionary discretion. On any reading of PACE the provisions overlap to a considerable extent, and it is a somewhat artificial exercise to try to interpret them as having distinct areas of operation. One tempting possibility is to regard s.82(3) as mainly preserving the discretion at common law to exclude evidence the prejudicial effect of which exceeds its probative value. This gains some plausibility from its express reference to the power of the court to prevent "questions being put", a form of words apt to describe the judge's former power to control cross-examination of the accused under s.1(3) of the Criminal Evidence Act 1898 where the accused lost the shield against questions about his criminal record and bad character.[68] This was one of the examples given by Lord Diplock in *Sang* to illustrate the operation of the discretion to weigh prejudicial effect against probative value. On this view all other aspects of fairness, including issues about evidence obtained as a result of unlawful or unfair treatment of the accused before trial, would be dealt with by s.78. This approach would make for a reasonably tidy state of the law, but it is not the way the courts have approached the two sections up to now. Moreover, this approach would run into a problem where a judge decides to exclude evidence on fairness grounds *after* the evidence has been given. It seems that the source of the power to exclude has to be s.82(3) in such a case.[69]

---

[66] *Chalkley* [1998] 2 Cr.App.R. 79 CA.
[67] See Ch.3.
[68] This provision was repealed by the Criminal Justice Act 2003 as part of the recasting of the law relating to evidence of bad character. See Chs 18 and 19.
[69] *Sat-Bhambra* (1988) 88 Cr.App.R. 55 CA, and see Ch.3.

2.   PACE section 78

"(1)   In any proceedings the court may refuse to allow evidence on which the prosecution proposes to rely to be given if it appears to the court that, having regard to all the circumstances, including the circumstances in which the evidence was obtained, the admission of the evidence would have such an adverse effect on the fairness of the proceedings that the court ought not to admit it.

(2)   Nothing in this section shall prejudice any rule of law requiring a court to exclude evidence."

The legislative history of s.78, and its relationship to the common law, has been discussed in detail in Ch.3. The discussion concluded that the authorities are in conflict on the extent to which s.78 has restated or enlarged the discretion to exclude evidence as it had developed at common law, but that there is a compelling case for saying that the statutory discretion is wider than the common law. How much wider is still uncertain. However, if it is accepted that the narrow scope of the discretion expounded by Lord Diplock in *Sang* has been abandoned, then it would be appropriate to hold that s.78 applies to *any* evidence on which the prosecution propose to rely. The discretion would not be limited either by the source of the evidence or by the means used to obtain it. This interpretation corresponds with the natural meaning of the words used in s.78. There is a further powerful argument for regarding s.78 as conferring a general discretion to safeguard the fairness of the proceedings. In *Khan v United Kingdom*,[70] the applicant claimed that the use in evidence against him of a covert recording obtained in violation of art.8 was a breach of art.6. Rejecting this claim the European Court of Human Rights held that the opportunity to argue for the exclusion of the evidence under s.78 was an adequate safeguard of the fairness of the trial. As we have seen this was a case where the quality of the evidence was not affected by the means used to obtain it. It seems therefore that the Court treated s.78 as a provision of general application which the English courts could use to ensure that art.6 was respected. In *R. v P*,[71] the House of Lords accepted this role for s.78, and in *Rosenberg*,[72] the Court of Appeal confirmed that the admissibility of evidence obtained in breach of art.8 is to be determined by the right to a fair trial under art.6 and s.78.

---

[70] *Khan v United Kingdom* (2001) 31 E.H.R.R. 1016. See also *PG and JH v United Kingdom* [2002] Crim. L.R. 308. In *Heglas v Czech Republic* (2009) 48 E.H.R.R. 44 the European Court of Human Rights repeated that it is not the job of the Court to rule on the admissibility of evidence obtained unlawfully, but to examine whether the rights of the defence were respected in determining whether he received a fair trial. For this purpose the rights of the defence were said to include the possibility of objecting to the use of the evidence ([84]–[86]). This case concerned a covert recording obtained in violation of art.8; for the position in relation to evidence obtained in violation of the absolute right under art.3 against torture and inhuman or degrading treatment see *Jalloh v Germany* (2007) 44 E.H.R.R. 32; *Gafgen v Germany* (2012) 52 E.H.R.R. 1.

[71] *R. v P* [2001] 2 All E.R. 58.

[72] *Rosenberg* [2006] Crim. L.R. 540. See also *Hardy* [2002] EWCA Crim 3012; [2003] 1 Cr.App.R. 30.

D.   THE APPLICATION OF SECTION 78

1.   *General principles*

8–014   Before reviewing the main types of case in which the courts have considered illegally or unfairly obtained evidence, it is useful to recall the general principles relating to the exclusionary discretion under s.78. These are presented in summary form, having been discussed above or in Ch.3:

- On the argument just put, s.78 applies to *any* evidence on which the prosecution propose to rely. It does not apply to evidence tendered by an accused or a co-accused.[73]
- It is not restricted to evidence obtained from the accused.
- It is not restricted to evidence not regulated by any other provision. It extends, for example, to confessions, whose admissibility in law is determined by s.76 of PACE,[74] and to the convictions of third parties, the admissibility of which in law is regulated by s.74 of PACE.[75]
- The Divisional Court has said that the concept of burden of proof has no part to play under s.78.[76] The section does not require any fact to be proved, and in any event the section confers a power wide enough for its exercise on the court's own motion.[77] There is some authority that it is for the defence to persuade the court that prosecution evidence should not be admitted by virtue of s.78,[78] but the better view is that the section is neutral as between the prosecution and the defence.[79]
- Impropriety is not a necessary condition of exclusion under s.78.[80]
- The exercise of the trial judge's discretion under s.78 can only be reviewed on *Wednesbury* principles.[81] The Court of Appeal will not substitute its own judgment for that of the trial judge simply because it takes a different view of the case. The trial judge must be shown to have erred in principle before the Court of Appeal will interfere. A breach of the European Convention on Human Rights is always a relevant factor for trial judges to take into account in deciding whether or not to exclude evidence.[82]
- The element of "fairness of the proceedings" refers to fairness to the prosecution as well as fairness to the defence. Fairness of the proceedings is normally satisfied if all the relevant evidence on both sides is admitted. Fairness may be upset by, for example, abuse of process, breach of natural

---

[73] See *Lobban v R.* [1995] 2 All E.R. 602 at 612 per Lord Steyn.

[74] *Mason* [1987] 3 All E.R. 481 CA, and see further Ch.6.

[75] See Ch.20.

[76] *R. (on the application of Saifi) v Governor of Brixton Prison* [2000] 1 W.L.R. 1134 at [1153].

[77] *R. (on the application of Saifi) v Governor of Brixton Prison* [2000] 1 W.L.R. 1134 at [1153].

[78] *Cooke* [1995] 1 Cr.App.R. 318 at 328 per Glidewell L.J. It is more accurate to speak of the burden of persuasion under s.78 than the burden of proof, as noted in the text above. Arguably, in a case of real doubt, the burden should be on the prosecution to persuade the court not to exclude the evidence.

[79] *R. (on the application of Saifi) v Governor of Brixton Prison* [2000] 1 W.L.R. 1134 at [1153].

[80] See Ch.3 para.3.37.

[81] *Christou* (1992) 95 Cr.App.R. 264 CA.

[82] In *Khan (Sultan)* [1996] 3 All E.R. 289 the House of Lords accepted that a breach of the Convention was a matter relevant to the exercise of the discretion under s.78.

justice, the admission of evidence whose prejudicial effect exceeds its probative value, and the reversal of the presumption of innocence.[83]
- The state of the other incriminating evidence is likely to be important in estimating the adverse effect of admitting the evidence in question on the fairness of the proceedings.[84]

The concept of "fairness" has not been analysed in any depth in any of the cases.[85] It seems, however, that it is wide enough to account for exclusionary decisions intended to achieve one or more of the following goals:

- Reliability of evidence: the discretion may be used to exclude evidence that, in the circumstances, carries significant risks of unreliability such that it would be unsafe to act upon it. This is linked to the next point.
- Elimination of prejudice: the discretion may be used to exclude evidence whose prejudicial effect outweighs its probative value.[86]
- Vindication of the accused's rights: the discretion may be used to exclude evidence as a remedy for breach of the accused's rights designed to put the accused in the same position as if the rights in question had been respected.[87]
- Promotion of police propriety: the discretion may be used as a means of expressing the court's disapproval of police conduct and of affirming the importance of respect for the value of the rule of law. This is not the same as using exclusion as a punitive sanction against individual police officers. A number of authorities reject this as a proper function of the courts.[88]
- Protection of the integrity of the criminal process: this is linked to the previous goal in so far as the discretion may be used to protect the administration of justice from being tainted by an association with improperly obtained evidence.[89] This idea is also connected with the more general theory, discussed in Chs 2 and 3, that the fundamental aim of the law of criminal evidence is to safeguard the legitimacy of the verdict.

2. *Illegally obtained evidence*

(A) *Breaches of PACE and the Codes Of Practice*

PACE has established detailed schemes to regulate the questioning of suspects by police officers and the obtaining of identification evidence from eyewitnesses.

8–015

---

[83] See Ch.3 para.3–037.
[84] *Keenan* [1990] 2 Q.B. 54 CA; *Weekes* (1993) 97 Cr.App.R. 222 CA.
[85] The vagueness of the fairness test in s.78 is criticised by Ormerod and Birch, "The Evolution of the Discretionary Exclusion of Evidence" [2004] Crim. L.R. 767.
[86] Exclusion on this ground may also be authorised by s.82(3).
[87] e.g. where the police have in good faith unlawfully denied a suspect access to legal advice: see Ch.6 para.6–031.
[88] See Ch.6 para.6–032.
[89] In *Looseley* [2001] 4 All E.R. 897 the House of Lords confirmed that s.78 could be used to exclude evidence obtained by entrapment, although a stay of prosecution for abuse of process would normally be the appropriate remedy. See further below.

The consequences of breach of the regulatory schemes for the admission of evidence of confessions and identification have been discussed in detail in Chs 6 and 7 respectively. In summary the courts have taken the view that not every breach of PACE or a Code of Practice will result in exclusion under s.78. Exclusion is not automatic: it is only if the breach is "significant and substantial" that the admission of the evidence is likely to have such an adverse effect on the fairness of the proceedings that it ought not to be admitted.[90] The first criterion to be applied in deciding whether a breach is significant and substantial is whether it was made in bad or good faith. A deliberate breach in bad faith will prima facie adversely affect the fairness of the proceedings: the court will find it easy to exclude evidence obtained by such means.[91] The objectives of exclusion in such cases include the maintenance of police propriety and the protection of the integrity of the criminal process from being tainted by deliberate malpractice. The courts do not seem to be concerned here so much with vindicating rights of the accused, since they may not inquire in cases of bad faith into the actual effect of the breach on the accused's position.[92] This inquiry is made, however, when the breach is in good faith. Then the courts will examine how far the accused was prejudiced by the breach. Prejudice in this sense refers to the extent to which the accused was disadvantaged by the breach.[93] Disadvantage can take a number of different forms. It can include, for example, both the case where the effect of the breach is to cause the accused to produce incriminating evidence such as a confession or a lie, and the case where the effect of the breach is to make it more difficult for the accused to challenge incriminating evidence.[94] Significant disadvantage from a proven breach is a key element in the judgment of whether the breach is "significant and substantial" for the purposes of the exclusionary decision. If the evidence is then excluded so as to cancel the disadvantage it is clear that protection of the accused's rights is one of the main objectives in these cases.

It should be noted, however, that there must be a causal link between the breach and the disadvantage suffered by the accused. In *Gill*,[95] for example, Inland Revenue officials conducting a *"Hansard"* interview with the defendants failed to caution them in breach of Code C. The Court of Appeal, after holding that the breach was not caused by any bad faith on the part of the Revenue or any "flagrant disregard" of the provisions of Code C, concluded that even if a caution had been administered the defendants would not have done anything different from what they did in making statements subsequently relied on by the prosecution as lies. They had been fully informed as to the purpose of the

---

[90] *Absolam* (1988) 88 Cr.App.R. 332; *Keenan* [1990] 2 Q.B. 54; *Walsh* (1990) 91 Cr.App.R. 161.

[91] *Alladice* (1988) 87 Cr.App.R. 380; *Walsh* (1990) 91 Cr.App.R. 161; *Gill* [2004] 1 Cr.App.R. 20.

[92] As in some of the cases concerned with breach of Code D: see Ch.7 para.7.20. See also *King* [2012] EWCA Crim 805, which concerned the covert recording of a conversation in a police car between two arrested suspects, in alleged breach of s.30 of PACE. The Court of Appeal commented ([26]): "In our judgment, the deliberate flouting of a statutory duty" [in this case, to take an arrested person to a police station as soon as practicable] "for the purpose only of creating an opportunity for a covert recording may, depending on the circumstances, result in the exclusion of evidence".

[93] *Wright* [1994] Crim. L.R. 55.

[94] Multiple breaches of Code C may have both effects, as in *Williams* [2012] EWCA Crim 264 (failure to caution plus several breaches of the recording requirements for interviews).

[95] *Gill* [2003] EWCA Crim 2256; [2004] 1 Cr.App.R. 20.

interview, they had been advised to have professional representation at the interview but had chosen not to, and they had been warned that even if they made a full confession to tax fraud they might still be prosecuted. The court thought that the defendants must have known that they were not obliged to answer the questions in the interview.

So far this approach is reasonably clear. Problems begin when we turn to consider such factors as the gravity of the offence, the probative value of the evidence and circumstances of necessity for its collection or preservation. In some situations these factors are relevant to the question whether or not there has been a breach of PACE or the Codes at all. Section 58(8) of PACE, for example, permits the police to deny a suspect access to a solicitor on various grounds, including reasonable belief that giving access immediately will lead to the destruction of evidence of the offence. In other cases these factors might in theory offer grounds of justification or excuse for prima facie breaches of PACE.[96] The prosecution might want to argue in a suitable case that the unfairness of admitting evidence obtained in consequence of a significant and substantial breach of PACE was sufficiently mitigated by the necessity to obtain the evidence, or by the public interest in bringing to justice a very serious offender, that the evidence should not be excluded. A further, related, problem is whether anything turns on the importance of the obligation breached; the duties imposed on the police by PACE and the Codes vary greatly in their importance, and it would be a rigid and far-reaching approach to insist on them all being treated equally for the purposes of exclusionary discretion. The denial of access to a solicitor, for example, is much more significant in the ordinary case than the refusal to have a break after the first two hours of questioning. A third issue is whether the "significant and substantial" test applies in respect of breaches of other provisions of PACE outside the areas of confessions and identification evidence.

8–016

The courts have yet to provide clear answers to these questions. In particular, as we have seen, the question of what factors the trial judge must or may take into account in exercising the exclusionary discretion under s.78, where these factors do not affect the quality of the evidence, remains controversial. However, some guidance emerges from cases dealing with the use of evidence derived from samples from the defendant that the police have unlawfully obtained or retained. In *Nathaniel*,[97] the defendant was convicted of rape on prosecution evidence that included evidence of a match between the defendant's DNA profile and the DNA profile of a semen sample taken from the victim. The defendant's DNA profile was obtained from a blood sample that the defendant had provided in connection with a previous charge of rape, of which he had been acquitted at trial. He was told before giving the sample that if he were acquitted, the sample and the DNA

---

[96] In a series of breathalyser cases it has been held that the right to legal advice under s.58 of PACE can be balanced against the legitimate aim of the suppression of drink-driving and the importance of not significantly delaying the obtaining of breath specimens. Accordingly, some delay in affording the defendant access to legal advice does not amount to a significant and substantial breach for the purposes of s.78: *DPP v Billington* [1988] 1 W.L.R. 535; *Kennedy v DPP* [2002] EWHC 2297 (Admin); *Gearing v DPP* [2008] EWHC 1695 (Admin).

[97] *Nathaniel* [1995] 2 Cr.App.R. 565.

profile would be destroyed in accordance with the statutory duty then[98] imposed on the police by PACE s.64.[99] The police did not destroy the profile after the acquittal but entered it on a computer database; the computer subsequently revealed a match with the profile from the later victim. The Court of Appeal held that the judge should have excluded the DNA evidence in view of the failure of the police to destroy the profile as they had promised and as they had a duty to do. The judgment assumed that s.64 was a further example of a provision in PACE which created a procedural right in the defendant that can be vindicated by the law of evidence. The judgment did not refer to the "significant and substantial" test when discussing the breach of s.64, but clearly the breach in this case was significant and substantial, and it had prejudiced the defendant, who had been disadvantaged in the sense that the breach resulted in evidence being available that led to his conviction.

Should the evidence have been excluded in consequence of the breach? In mitigation of the police action it might be argued that the case involved a very serious charge, the evidence was highly probative of guilt, and there was no allegation of bad faith on the part of the police. The defence were in a position to challenge the evidence by calling their own expert witness. It is unclear whether these matters would have been sufficient to excuse the breach of statutory duty if that had stood alone.[100] The judgment refers to both the breach of duty *and* the breach of the promise to the defendant that the sample would be destroyed. The interest violated by the latter breach was the defendant's interest in not being obliged to incriminate himself. By excluding the evidence resulting from the violation the Court of Appeal gave the privilege against self-incrimination a derivative application. It was argued in Ch.5 that the privilege against self-incrimination should not be treated as a fundamental right, partly because of the weakness of its justification, and partly because of the drastic effects it may have in excluding reliable and important evidence if it is given wide derivative applications. *Nathaniel* is a good example of this danger. It is suggested that, in the absence of any finding that the police had deliberately set out to manipulate the defendant and abuse their powers under PACE, the trial judge was right to admit the evidence and the Court of Appeal wrong to allow the appeal.[101] It will be argued later in this chapter that where the police have not acted in bad faith,

---

[98] Subsequently the law changed. Section 82 of the Criminal Justice and Police Act 2001 amended s.64 of PACE so that fingerprints and samples from persons who were not prosecuted or who were cleared were no longer required to be destroyed. They could be retained for purposes of criminal investigation and the conduct of future prosecutions. Retrospective authorisation was given for the retention and use of the large number of samples that ought to have been destroyed previously under s.64 but that were not. A comprehensively revised scheme for the destruction, retention and use of such evidential material is now contained in Pt 1 of the Protection of Freedoms Act 2012.

[99] He was also told, truthfully, that if he refused without good cause to give the sample the jury could draw adverse inferences from his refusal in considering his guilt on a charge of rape: see PACE s.62(10).

[100] In *Cooke* [1995] 1 Cr.App.R. 318, which also concerned a charge of rape, the Court of Appeal upheld the trial judge's refusal to exclude evidence of a DNA profile from a sample of the defendant's hair obtained (assumedly) unlawfully without the defendant's consent. Importance was attached to the reliability of the evidence, which was not affected by the means (assault) of obtaining it.

[101] It is worth noting that a second DNA profile based on a hair sample from the defendant was held to have been rightly admitted. This had been obtained following a lawful arrest. The fact that the arrest was founded on evidence of a previous DNA profile that was held to have been wrongly

evidence should be excluded only if the defendant has been significantly disadvantaged by the breach and the breach violated a fundamental norm of the criminal justice process. Only some breaches will have this quality. The right to legal advice is correctly regarded as a fundamental norm, but the privilege against self-incrimination should not be so regarded.

In *Attorney-General's Reference (No.3 of 1999)*,[102] a similar problem had arisen in another rape case, but with two points of difference. No express promise was made to the defendant about destruction of the sample taken from him in the event of his acquittal on the first charge, and in this case the prosecution had relied on a second sample taken from the defendant after the computer database had revealed a match between the sample from the victim and the unlawfully retained sample from the defendant. The decision of the House of Lords was that, contrary to the view of the trial judge and the Court of Appeal in the case, the then s.64(3)(B) of PACE did not make the evidence derived from the second sample inadmissible. The House was not asked to consider the correct approach of a trial judge under s.78 where the prosecution tender DNA evidence in these circumstances.[103] However, Lord Steyn said pointedly[104] that he was not to be taken as endorsing the reasoning of the trial judge who had stated that he would have excluded the evidence under s.78 had he not concluded that it was in any event inadmissible. Lord Hutton went further, commenting that in exercising the discretion under s.78 it was necessary to consider the interests of the victim and the public as well as of the defendant.[105] Immediately before this statement he referred to the "very grave crimes" committed against the victim in this case. There was no issue in this case as to the quality of the evidence. The approach taken by Lord Hutton strongly suggests that he thought that the admitted breach of PACE could ground exclusion under s.78, despite the breach not affecting the quality of the evidence, but that it would not be unfair to admit the evidence where the breach was in effect excused by the seriousness of the offence and the need to protect victims.[106]

8–017

(B) Breaches of the Road Traffic Act in drink-driving cases

After some initial uncertainty about the effect of s.78 on the common law, the Divisional Court took the view that the principles applicable to breaches of PACE apply also to breaches of the breathalyser law in the Road Traffic Act. In *Matto v Wolverhampton Crown Court*,[107] a Crown Court had found that the police had acted in bad faith and in excess of their statutory powers in arresting the

8–018

---

admitted was not thought to affect the fairness of admitting the second profile. However, this second profile was insufficiently probative of the defendant's guilt.

[102] *Attorney-General's Reference (No.3 of 1999)* [2001] 1 All E.R. 577.

[103] *Attorney General's Reference (No.3 of 1999)* [2001] 1 All E.R. 577 at 583 per Lord Steyn.

[104] *Attorney General's Reference (No.3 of 1999)* [2001] 1 All E.R. 577 at 583 per Lord Steyn.

[105] *Attorney General's Reference (No.3 of 1999)* [2001] 1 All E.R. 577 at 590.

[106] In *Warren v Attorney-General of Jersey* [2011] UKPC 10; [2011] 2 Cr.App.R. 29 Lord Brown commented (at [77]) that in *Attorney-General's Reference (No.3 of 1999)* "... the House clearly contemplated that the judge could properly have exercised his s.78 discretion in favour of admitting the relevant evidence".

[107] *Matto v Wolverhampton Crown Court* [1987] R.T.R. 337.

defendant at a time when they knew that he had withdrawn their implied licence to be on his premises. The Divisional Court held that in these circumstances the Crown Court had failed to consider whether the evidence of a positive breath specimen was so tainted by the oppressive conduct of the police that it should have been excluded under s.78. The defendant's appeal was allowed. It seems that the court thought that the same result could have been achieved at common law. Subsequently, in *Thomas v DPP*,[108] the Divisional Court treated *Matto* as authority for the proposition that a finding of bad faith was a *necessary* condition for the exclusion of evidence of the defendant's failure to provide a specimen following an unlawful arrest. This restriction could only be justified on a view that s.78 did not enlarge the exclusionary discretion at common law. The use of oppression or a trick sufficient to invoke the principle in *Sang* presupposes deliberate impropriety on the part of the police.

However, in two further cases the Divisional Court rejected such a limitation of s.78 and doubted the authority of *Thomas v DPP*. In *DPP v McGladrigan*,[109] it was pointed out that *Samuel*[110] had not been cited in *Thomas*. Hodgson J., giving the judgment of the Divisional Court, went on to say that *Samuel* established that bad faith was not necessary for the exclusion of evidence under s.78. This application of the principle in the context of the Road Traffic Act was obiter since on the facts the court held that D had not been unlawfully arrested. There was therefore no basis for exclusion of evidence of a positive breath specimen in any event. Nonetheless, in *DPP v Godwin*,[111] the Divisional Court repeated that bad faith or oppression were not necessary conditions for exclusion under s.78. The court refused to interfere with the decision of the justices to exclude evidence of a positive specimen supplied by D after his unlawful arrest, despite the absence of a finding of bad faith:

> "The justices were entitled to conclude that the substantial breach by the constable of the protection afforded to members of the public by s.6 [of the Road Traffic Act 1988] was denied to the defendant, that as a result the prosecutor obtained evidence which he would not otherwise have obtained, and that as a result the defendant was prejudiced in a significant manner."[112]

This is an important recognition of the generality of the principles established by the cases concerned with breaches of PACE. A second feature of the decision is the recognition of the scope for variations in judgments of fairness. Bingham L.J. commented that other justices might have made the opposite decision on the facts without acting unreasonably. It seems to be clear that the Divisional Court applies the normal *Wednesbury* principles of review to exclusionary decisions by justices, and will only interfere where the justices have gone wrong in principle, as where there is no basis in fact for the exclusionary decision.

---

[108] *Thomas v DPP* [1991] R.T.R. 292.
[109] *DPP v McGladrigan* [1991] R.T.R. 297.
[110] *Samuel* [1988] Q.B. 615 CA.
[111] *DPP v Godwin* [1991] R.T.R. 303.
[112] *DPP v Godwin* [1991] R.T.R. 303 at 305.

(C)   Other forms of unlawful conduct

The admissibility of evidence obtained or retained in breach of other statutory requirements is sometimes dealt with expressly by the relevant legislation. A useful illustration is provided by s.17 of the Regulation of Investigatory Powers Act 2000 ("RIPA"), which deals with evidence of intercepted communications.[113] Section 17 replaced the rule of admissibility formerly contained in s.9 of the Interception of Communications Act 1985 ("IOCA"). Section 1 of RIPA, like s.1 of IOCA before it, creates an offence of intentional interception of a communication in the course of transmission by post or by means of a telecommunications system (telephone tapping). An offence is not committed if the interceptor has lawful authority: the main cases are interception under a warrant issued by the Secretary of State, or where the interceptor reasonably believes that the person by whom, or to whom, the communication is sent had consented to the interception and the interception took place in the course of authorised surveillance.[114] Section 17 of RIPA, like s.9 of IOCA, provides that no evidence shall be adduced that tends to suggest that an offence has been committed under s.1, or that a warrant has been issued for an interception.

8–019

After some uncertainty the courts interpreted s.9 of IOCA as rendering inadmissible any evidence obtained by interception carried out in England.[115] This was a purposive interpetation to give effect to the policy of the legislation to maintain the secrecy of surveillance operations within the jurisdiction, involving interception of communications. According to Lord Hobhouse in *R. v P* the protection of sources of information is a key reason for preferring secrecy to disclosure of covertly obtained material.[116] However, s.9 did not prevent the admission of evidence obtained by foreign telephone tapping; there was no breach of the 1985 Act in such a case.[117] In the latter case, though, there may be a question of discretionary exclusion under s.78 of PACE if the interception was carried out abroad without the consent of the person whose telephone was tapped, because a breach of art.8 of the European Convention on Human Rights may be involved.[118] Article 8 provides:

> "1.   Everyone has the right to respect for his private and family life, his home and his correspondence.
>
> 2.   There shall be no interference by a public authority with the exercise of this right except such as is in accordance with the law and is necessary in a democratic society in

---

[113] See Mirfield, "Regulation of Investigatory Powers Act 2000" [2001] Crim. L.R. 91.

[114] See RIPA ss.3 and 5, replacing IOCA s.1(2). The defence of belief in consent will cover cases, for example, where the telephone of a person being blackmailed is tapped with his agreement.

[115] See *R. v P* [2001] 2 All E.R. 58 HL, where the authorities are reviewed.

[116] *R. v P* [2001] 2 All E.R. 58 at [71]. It is beyond the scope of this book to deal with the law on intercepts in detail. The law is complex and controversial, and in the view of many there is a strong argument for repealing the relevant provisions of RIPA and allowing intercept evidence to be generally admissible as it is in virtually all other jurisdictions. The case is succinctly put by J. R. Spencer, "Intercept Evidence: The Case for Change" (2008) 172 J.P. 651, 671. Successive governments have kept the law under review but to date no legislation for change has been forthcoming.

[117] *Aujla* [1998] 2 Cr.App.R. 16 CA, approved by the House of Lords in *R. v P* [2001] 2 All E.R. 58.

[118] See generally D. Ormerod, "ECHR and the Exclusion of Evidence: Trial Remedies for Article 8 Breaches?" [2003] Crim. L.R. 61.

the interests of national security, public safety or the economic well-being of the country, for the prevention of disorder or crime, for the protection of health or morals, or for the protection of the rights and freedoms of others."

In *Aujla*,[119] the defendants were charged with conspiracy to smuggle illegal immigrants into the United Kingdom by means of light aircraft flown from the Netherlands. Two other parties to the conspiracy were resident in the Netherlands. They were convicted by the Dutch courts of being involved in facilitating the illegal entry of immigrants into the United Kingdom. Part of the evidence against them was tapes of telephone conversations between them and the defendants; the intercept had been placed on the telephone of the Dutch offenders in the Netherlands. The Court of Appeal held that the tapes were admissible in evidence at the trial of the defendants in England, and that the trial judge was correct in refusing to exclude them under s.78. This was because there was no breach of art.8: the intercept in the Netherlands had been authorised by the Dutch authorities, so that the interference with privacy had been in accordance with the law, and the interference had been necessary in a democratic society for the prevention of crime. Moreover, the evidence was relevant and there was no issue as to the accuracy of the tapes.

8–020 Similar issues arise in connection with evidence obtained by means of hidden listening devices, where unlawful conduct by the police in placing the devices may have been involved; again it is necessary to consider art.8 of the ECHR and s.78 of PACE. The leading case is *Khan (Sultan)*[120] but the speeches in the House of Lords do not engage fully with the issues of unlawfully obtained evidence and the use of s.78. This is partly a result of the way the case was argued. The police had installed an electronic listening device on the outside of a house without the knowledge or consent of the occupier. By means of the device the police were able to record an incriminating conversation involving the defendant, a visitor to the house. During the conversation, the defendant indicated that he had been involved in an importation of heroin some months earlier. Heroin had been found in the possession of the defendant's cousin when the defendant and his cousin were both searched on arrival at Heathrow from Pakistan. No drugs had been found on the defendant, who had been released without charge. At the defendant's trial the prosecution admitted that the installation of the device constituted a civil trespass against the occupier of the house and may have amounted to a (minor) offence of criminal damage.[121] Counsel for the defendant did not, however, make these forms of unlawful conduct central to his argument that the evidence from the device ought to have been excluded under s.78.[122] Instead he contended that

---

[119] *Aujla* [1998] 2 Cr.App.R. 16.

[120] *Khan (Sultan)* [1996] 3 All E.R. 289 HL. For discussion, see C. Tapper, "Overhearing and oversight" (1997) 1 E. & P. 162.

[121] It should be noted that the police had complied with the 1984 Home Office "Guidelines on the use of Equipment in Police Surveillance Operations", but these did not of course provide statutory or any other authority for breach of the law. The use of such devices was subsequently regulated by Police Act 1997 Pt III, summarised in P. B. Carter, "Evidence Obtained by Use of a Covert Listening Device" (1997) 113 L.Q.R. 468, 474–476.

[122] This may have been because they were not unlawful as against the accused, hence any "unfairness" in using the evidence against him could not be founded on a breach of his rights under English law.

the secret recording of the conversation constituted a breach of the defendant's right to privacy under art.8 of the ECHR.[123] Lord Nolan, giving the main speech in the House of Lords, noted that under English law there is in general nothing unlawful about a breach of privacy. He expressly rejected an argument that evidence obtained in breach of art.8 was inadmissible in law and impliedly rejected an alternative position that a violation of the Convention was per se a ground for excluding otherwise admissible evidence. He went on to accept that an apparent breach of the Convention was a matter that the trial judge could take into account as relevant to the exercise of the s.78 discretion, but held that on the facts:

> "the judge was fully entitled to hold that the circumstances in which the relevant evidence was obtained, even if they constituted a breach of art.8, were not such as to require the exclusion of the evidence."[124]

It is disappointing, although not surprising, given the specific focus of the case, that the House of Lords did not think it necessary to review the application of s.78 generally to unlawful police action. It is disappointing in particular that there is no discussion in *Khan (Sultan)* of the s.78 cases dealing with breach of PACE and other statutory provisions. More generally it is regrettable that we have no further guidance from the House of Lords on the relative importance of the various factors relevant to the exercise of the exclusionary discretion. On the substantive issue of fairness the result of the case is in line with other authorities upholding the admission of covert recordings of incriminating acts and statements.[125] It seems that the House of Lords attached importance to the probative value of the evidence[126] and to the fact that its use did not make the trial unfair in the sense of prejudicing the rights of the defence.[127] When this case reached the European Court of Human Rights as *Khan v United Kingdom*[128] the court reiterated its stance that rules of admissibility of evidence are a matter for the national law.[129] It was held that since the applicant had had the opportunity to argue for the exclusion of the evidence as unfair under s.78 there had been no violation of his right to a fair trial under art.6.[130]

---

[123] He also argued unsuccessfully that the recording was inadmissible by analogy with the prohibition on evidence obtained from telephone tapping (Interception of Communications Act 1985 s.9) and that it amounted to an inadmissible confession which the defendant had been induced to make. Lord Nolan had no difficulty in disposing of both these optimistic arguments.

[124] *Khan (Sultan)* [1996] 3 All E.R. 289 at 302. It seems clear that there was a breach of art.8 in this case because the interference with privacy was not "in accordance with the law": see above.

[125] *Bailey and Smith* (1993) 97 Cr.App.R. 365 CA; *Smurthwaite* (1994) 98 Cr.App.R. 437 CA. Both cases are discussed below.

[126] See Lord Nolan's comment at 302: "It would be a strange reflection on our law if a man *who has admitted his participation* in the illegal importation of heroin should have his conviction set aside on the grounds that his privacy has been invaded" (emphasis added).

[127] See the citation of the decision of the European Court of Human Rights in *Schenk v Switzerland* (1988) 13 E.H.R.R. 242 by Lord Slynn of Hadley and by Lord Nolan: [1996] 3 All E.R. 289 at 292 and 300 respectively.

[128] *Khan v United Kingdom* (2000) 8 B.H.R.C. 310.

[129] *Schenk v Switzerland* (1988) 13 E.H.R.R. 242.

[130] The court reached the same conclusion in another covert taping case, *PG and JH v United Kingdom* [2002] Crim. L.R. 308; and in a case of covert filming, *Perry v United Kingdom* [2003]

Future operations of the type involved in this case will be authorised under the provisions of Pt III of the Police Act 1997 or Pt II of RIPA. The interferences with privacy that they entail will therefore be in accordance with the law, and consequently should not involve a breach of art.8. This does not mean that the evidence they produce will necessarily be immune from exclusion under s.78, although exclusion seems very unlikely given that evidence of incriminating conversations recorded by the devices will presumably be both reliable and highly probative of guilt.[131]

3. *Unfairly obtained evidence*

(A) *Deception in questioning and abuse of the police role*

8–021   The concept of "abuse of the police role" appears in the judgment of Lord Taylor C.J. in *Smurthwaite*.[132] In that case he used it with reference to the adoption by a police officer of an undercover pose in order to question a suspect so as to circumvent the requirements of Code C. It can be conveniently widened to refer generally to cases in which the police use deception in order to interrogate the accused and to elicit incriminating statements. One kind of direct deception is lies about the evidence against the accused. In *Mason*,[133] the police falsely informed the defendant and his solicitor that the defendant's fingerprints had been found on a fragment of a glass bottle containing petrol used in an arson attack on a car. The solicitor advised co-operation with the police, whereupon the defendant made a full confession of his part in the offence. The truth of the confession does not seem to have been disputed. However, the Court of Appeal held that the trial judge had failed to take into account the deception practised on the solicitor. Had he done so he could not have failed to exercise his discretion to exclude the confession.

This was a case where the defendant was induced to waive the privilege against self-incrimination by a deliberate deception of his legal advisor. The Court of Appeal did not spell out why it regarded such deception as peculiarly significant. The judgment simply refers tersely to the solicitor's duty to advise his client "unfettered by false information from the police".[134] This claim may suggest that particular importance was attached to the accuracy and objectivity of

---

Crim. L.R. 281. See also *R. v P* [2001] 2 All E.R. 58 where the House of Lords accepted that s.78 is an appropriate safeguard of the fairness of the trial under art.6 in cases of intercepted communications and covert surveillance.

[131] cf. *Chalkley* [1998] 2 Cr.App.R. 79 CA, which concerned evidence of incriminating conversations recorded by a device secretly planted in the defendant's home. As in *Khan (Sultan)* [1996] 3 All E.R. 289 there was only executive authority for the operation, and the Court of Appeal seems to have assumed that there was a breach of art.8. Nevertheless the court was in no doubt that it was fair to admit the evidence:

"there was no dispute as to its authenticity, content or effect; it was relevant, highly probative of the appellants' involvement in the conspiracy and otherwise admissible; it did not result from incitement, entrapment or inducement or any other conduct of that sort; and none of the unlawful conduct of the police ... affects the quality of the evidence" (at 107).

[132] *Smurthwaite* (1994) 98 Cr.App.R. 437 CA.

[133] *Mason* [1987] 3 All E.R. 481.

[134] *Mason* [1987] 3 All E.R. 481 at 485.

legal advice. If so, such a concern might in turn be referable to a desire to protect the innocent from wrongful conviction or, more generally, to promote rational and informed participation by all suspects in the process of decision-making as to their guilt or innocence. As we have seen, respect for participation as a process value may be a significant component in the acceptability of decisions.[135]

It is unclear what the position would have been in this case if only the defendant himself had been deceived. There is no prohibition as such in PACE or the Codes of Practice on the use of deception to obtain admissions. But the use of such a tactic might affect admissibility in one of several ways. If the deceit were regarded as sufficiently serious to amount to oppression, or as a tactic likely in the circumstances to induce an unreliable confession, a resulting confession would be inadmissible under s.76(2) of PACE. It does not appear to have been argued in *Mason* that the lie about the state of the evidence against the suspect rendered his confession inadmissible as a matter of law.[136] Ironically, however, this may be because the defendant had his solicitor advising him at the relevant interview. In a case where the suspect is being interviewed on his own in custody important lies, for example, that he has been positively identified at the scene of the crime, or that a co-accused has incriminated him, might persuade the court that the prosecution could not discharge the burden of proof under s.76(2).[137] Alternatively, such lies might be regarded, as they were in *Mason*, as adversely affecting the fairness of the proceedings for the purposes of discretionary exclusion under s.78. It may be significant that in *Mason* the defendant was interviewed in police custody. The vulnerable position in which this places a suspect has been treated in one or two of the later cases as a reason for distinguishing the decision.[138]

A suspect in custody who is induced into incriminating himself may be able to claim that it is unfair to admit the evidence against him if he was not warned adequately about the possible consequences of his actions. This is a kind of deception by omission. In *De Silva*,[139] the defendant, who had been arrested at Gatwick airport in possession of cocaine concealed in his suitcase, was persuaded to take part in telephone calls to other persons involved in the importation by promises from Customs officers that any help he gave them would result in a reduction in his sentence. Since the calls required him to behave as if he were guilty of the importation, they were incriminating. The prosecution adduced evidence of them to prove his guilty knowledge of the cocaine (which he denied), but the Court of Appeal held that the evidence of the calls should have been excluded under s.78. The court said that it was fundamentally unfair to use the calls against him when he had not been warned in terms that the evidence might

8–022

---

[135] R. Summers, "Evaluating and Improving Legal Processes: A Plea for Process Values" (1974) 60 *Cornell Law Review* 1. See the discussion of legitimacy in Ch.2.

[136] The trial judge was referred to s.76 of PACE but is said by the Court of Appeal to have decided to admit the confession in his discretion after discussing the provisions of s.78: *Mason* [1987] 3 All E.R. 481 at 483.

[137] In *Heron, The Times*, November 22, 1993 the trial judge excluded Heron's confession to murder on the ground of oppression. The police questioning included the making of false claims to Heron that two witnesses had identified him at the place where the victim (a little girl) was last seen alive.

[138] *Christou* (1992) 95 Cr.App.R. 264 CA. See also *Maclean and Kosten* [1993] Crim. L.R. 687 CA.

[139] *De Silva* [2002] EWCA Crim 2673; [2003] 2 Cr.App.R. 5.

be used not only against others but also against himself. A conventional caution was not sufficient for this purpose. Although it was accepted that the officers had acted in good faith the court clearly took the view that the defendant had effectively been misled into incriminating himself. The same result might well have been reached at common law in this case.

The Court of Appeal has also rejected the form of deceit that consists of the adoption of an undercover pose in order to question a suspect without the constraints of the Codes of Practice. In *Bryce*,[140] a police officer posing as a buyer for a stolen car gave evidence of the defendant's incriminating answers to questions about the car when the two of them met at a rendezvous arranged by telephone. The defendant was charged with theft and handling stolen goods, and the questions were central to the issue of dishonesty since they concerned the defendant's knowledge of how long the car had been stolen. Quashing the conviction for handling the Court of Appeal held that Code C applied to the questions asked by the undercover officer. They amounted to a series of questions about the defendant's suspected commission of an offence. As the court said, "[it was] ... an interrogation with the effect, if not the design, of using an undercover pose to circumvent the Code".[141] Consequently there were clear breaches of the Code. The defendant had not been cautioned or notified of his right to legal advice. No contemporaneous record had been made of the interview. Breaches of the Code do not result in automatic exclusion of statements under s.78, but in this case they were held to affect adversely the fairness of the proceedings. The defendant challenged the alleged conversation as a fabrication, and there was no neutral, reliable record of what was said.

The position is likely to be different where the police deceive a defendant as to the reason for a stop and search. If the search yields reliable evidence of a serious offence, the court may well take the view that this outweighs any unfairness. In *McCarthy*,[142] the police pretended to the defendant that they had stopped her car for a routine stop and search instead of indicating to her that they suspected her to be engaged in drug trafficking. The search of the car produced a package containing a very large amount of cash. Upholding the trial judge's refusal to exclude this evidence, the Court of Appeal held that any breach of Code A of PACE was not significant and substantial and that it would not be unfair to admit the evidence. Clearly the police would have discovered the package whether or not they had complied with their duty to give the correct reason for the stop. In that sense the defendant had not been prejudiced, and since the court refused to say that the police had acted in bad faith, it is difficult to see a convincing reason for exclusion.

(B)　　Tricks and traps[143]

8–023 A second group of cases deals with the use of various police stratagems to obtain evidence of the commission of offences. The common feature of these cases is

---

[140] *Bryce* (1992) 95 Cr.App.R. 320. See also *Okafor* (1994) 99 Cr.App.R. 97 CA.

[141] *Bryce* (1992) 95 Cr.App.R. 320 at 325.

[142] *McCarthy* [1996] Crim. L.R. 818.

[143] A.J. Ashworth, "Should the police be allowed to use deceptive practices?" (1998) 114 L.Q.R. 108.

that they all involve the use of deception in situations where the police are not engaged in questioning the accused with a view to obtaining a confession. In these cases the police strategy is to facilitate the doing of an incriminating act or the making of an incriminating statement by the accused who will thus provide evidence against himself of his earlier commission of the offence. The police techniques involved are all covert, in the sense that the accused will of course be unaware that the police are observing his behaviour.

When direct interrogation fails because suspects exercise the right to silence, the secret bugging of conversations of suspects in police stations has sometimes been resorted to. The Court of Appeal considered the fairness of this tactic in *Bailey and Smith*.[144] The defendants had been remanded into police custody after being charged with robbery. During earlier interviews both had exercised the right of silence. They were placed in a cell together after some play-acting by the investigating officers who had indicated that they did not wish the custody officer to do this. The object was to trick the defendants into believing that the cell was not bugged. The trick worked and the police were able to record incriminating conversations. The Court of Appeal upheld the trial judge's admission of the tapes. The court argued that this method of obtaining evidence was not prohibited by the legislative regime for detention and questioning, nor should it be regarded as unfair. The police, it was said, were investigating very serious crimes, committed by men who had engaged in trickery and worse, and there was no suggestion of oppression or that the confessions were unreliable.

Defence counsel argued in this case that the police trick was aimed expressly at undermining the defendants' right to silence and at misleading them into incriminating themselves. He relied on *Mason* to support the argument. The Court of Appeal, however, preferred to regard *Mason* as a case concerned with overt questioning of a person in police custody and as distinguishable from cases involving covert investigation and surveillance. There was previous authority that evidence obtained by eavesdropping and secret recording was admissible.[145] The court added[146]:

> "We recognise finally that some may well think it odd and perhaps even unsatisfactory that alongside a rigorously controlled legislative regime governing the detention, treatment and questioning of those in police custody, parallel covert investigations of this nature can legitimately continue. But all that said, we not merely believe ourselves bound by the principles enunciated in *Ali (Shaukat)* but see no reason to decry the police's conduct in the present case nor to doubt the essential fairness of this evidence having been held admissible."

This decision represents a notable refusal to extend the right of silence, which is **8–024** a derivative application of the privilege, beyond the situation of overt questioning

---

[144] *Bailey and Smith* (1993) 97 Cr.App.R. 365. Note that covert surveillance on a person held in police custody is now governed by RIPA ss.26(3) and 48(1). Lawful authority for such surveillance is required if it is not to violate art.8 of the ECHR: see *PG and JH v United Kingdom* [2002] Crim. L.R. 308 European Court of Human Rights.

[145] *Maqsud Ali* [1966] 1 Q.B. 688 CCA; *Jelen and Katz* (1990) 90 Cr.App.R. 456 CA; *Ali (Shaukat), The Times*, February 19, 1991; *Roberts* [1997] 1 Cr.App.R. 217 CA.

[146] *Bailey and Smith* (1993) 97 Cr.App.R. 365 at 375.

and demands on the accused to supply incriminating evidence.[147] This limitation is reinforced by the leading case dealing with undercover operations. In *Christou*,[148] the police mounted an elaborate trap aimed at thieves and burglars. Two undercover officers opened a shop masquerading as shady jewellers who were prepared to buy stolen goods. Sales to them were recorded on camera and tape without the knowledge of the sellers. They asked questions of the sellers, who included the defendants, of the type which shady jewellers "might be expected to ask". The Court of Appeal held that the trial judge's exercise of discretion to admit the evidence could not be impugned. The court reasoned that although the evidence had been obtained by a trick the defendants, unlike in *Mason*, had not been in police custody and there was no unfairness in that they were not persuaded to do anything that they would not have done otherwise. "Putting it in different words, the trick was not applied to the appellants; they voluntarily applied themselves to the trick."[149]

A similar approach is seen in *Williams v DPP*.[150] As part of a crime prevention initiative the police placed temptation in the form of an insecure and unattended van parked on a public road. The van contained dummy cartons of cigarettes. The defendants were seen to reconnoitre the van and then to remove some of the cartons. Upholding the convictions (for interference with the contents of a motor vehicle with intent to commit theft)[151] the Divisional Court held that even if the defendants had been tricked, the trick did not have an adverse effect on the fairness of the proceedings. Citing the decision in *Christou*, Farquharson L.J. commented:

> "in my judgment, it [the police conduct] is an entirely legitimate enterprise on the part of the police and of a permissible character for the detection of crime."[152]

The court rejected an argument that the police had acted as *agents provocateurs*. They had done nothing to persuade the defendants to commit the offence and had not participated in it.[153] The defendants, it was said, had done the acts voluntarily with no pressure and with full understanding of their own dishonesty. It is significant that in this case, as in *Bailey and Smith*, the judgment uses the word "legitimate" in connection with police procedure for the obtaining of evidence. This provides some indirect support for the theory advanced in Ch.3 as to the rationale of exclusionary decisions under s.78.

---

[147] *Bailey and Smith* was approved by the Court of Appeal in *Mason* [2002] EWCA Crim 385; [2002] 2 Cr.App.R. 38, another case of covert recording of suspects' conversations in police stations. In *Mason* and also in *Button* [2005] EWCA Crim 516 (covert video recordings) the court held that the recordings had been made in breach of the defendants' rights to privacy under art.8 of the ECHR, but the trial judges' decisions not to exclude them under s.78 did not result in an unfair trial in breach of art.6. For critical comment see the Commentary to *Button* in [2005] Crim. L.R. 571.

[148] *Christou* (1992) 95 Cr.App.R. 264 CA.

[149] *Christou* (1992) 95 Cr.App.R. 264 at 269.

[150] *Williams v DPP* (1994) 98 Cr.App.R. 209 DC.

[151] Criminal Attempts Act 1981 s.9(1).

[152] *Williams v DPP* (1994) 98 Cr.App.R. 209 at 215.

[153] This is not a straightforward point. The police had not incited the defendants but they had aided the commission of the offence in the same way as an employee who is bribed to leave goods in a place where they can be stolen. Presumably the police would not be guilty either because they lacked mens rea or because a law enforcement defence would be open to them.

One point of distinction with *Christou* might have been that in that case the undercover officers were seeking to obtain evidence of offences already committed. In *Williams v DPP,* the police were in effect seeking to catch habitual offenders through the attempted commission of fresh offences. It might be argued that traps in the first situation were acceptable, but that devices to tempt crime were not. The use of such devices could be regarded as an example of "entrapment" analogous to the situation of incitement or instigation of crime discussed in the next section of this chapter. The Divisional Court rejected this analogical argument,[154] pointing out that it sets up a distinction that is unworkable, quite apart from whether it is desirable in principle. A police officer, for example, may have to act as a decoy or bait to lure a suspected attacker. In such a case both objectives are necessarily involved. On the point of principle one may surmise that public opinion would not tolerate the exclusion of evidence, say, of the identity of a dangerous sex offender caught by such means.

This group of cases shows that the courts are unwilling to exclude evidence obtained by deception that does not infringe any statutory rights of the accused. In such cases they will not give the privilege against self-incrimination derivative applications in the absence of manipulation of the accused to do something that he would not otherwise have done. This is a desirable approach. It is not unfair to admit relevant and reliable evidence of guilt where the accused has voluntarily chosen to incriminate himself. **8–025**

(C)   Entrapment and agents provocateurs[155]

The Law Commission noted that "entrapment" is not a term of art and has no precise definition.[156] It can be used with varying shades of meaning.[157] In its widest sense it refers to any involvement of police officers in any form of trick or trap to obtain evidence of the commission of an offence. The police involvement might take place before or after the commission of the offence. This usage would embrace all the cases discussed in the two preceding sections of this chapter. For example, "manna from heaven" operations that facilitate the commission of offences, such as the operation carried out in *Williams v DPP*, are sometimes described as examples of entrapment.[158] **8–026**

A narrower, more precise, usage describes the activity of an *agent provocateur*. The classic definition of an *agent provocateur* was given by the Royal Commission on the Police in 1929:

---

[154] *Williams v DPP* (1994) 98 Cr.App.R. 209 at 214.

[155] See generally S. Bronitt and D. Roche, "Between rhetoric and reality: sociolegal and republican perspectives on entrapment" (2000) 4 E. & P. 77; D. Ormerod and A. Roberts, "The trouble with Teixeira: Developing a principled approach to entrapment" (2002) 6 E. & P. 38; A. Ashworth, "Re-drawing the boundaries of entrapment" [2002] Crim. L.R. 159; Hock Lai Ho, "State Entrapment" (2011) 31 L.S. 71.

[156] Law Com No.83, *Report on Defences of General Application* (London, 1977), para.5.1.

[157] See D. Birch, "Excluding Evidence from Entrapment: What is a 'Fair Cop'?" [1994] C.L.P. 73.

[158] As in G. Robertson, "Entrapment Evidence: Manna from Heaven, or Fruit of the Poisoned Tree?" [1994] Crim. L.R. 805.

> "a person who entices another to commit an express breach of the law which he would not otherwise have committed and then proceeds or informs against him in respect of such offences."[159]

In this context the claim of "entrapment" is a claim by the accused that he was induced to commit the offence by pressure or persuasion from a police officer or a person acting as a police agent. "Entrapment" is not an ideal term for this purpose since it fails to capture the element of positive instigation of the offence that is the distinguishing feature of the *agent provocateur*, but it is a well-recognised usage.[160] A third form of entrapment, lying somewhere between the narrow and wide meanings just described, is the "test purchase" case, where an undercover police officer or his agent makes a purchase from a person suspected of trading illegally, in circumstances where the sale is unlawful.

There is a long history of fear of the use of entrapment by the police. It dates back to a time before the establishment of regular police forces when law enforcement was largely a matter of private initiative. Then it was not uncommon for "thief-takers" to set up crimes by encouraging vulnerable individuals to steal; arrest and prosecution would follow, in the hope that the informer would recover any financial penalty imposed.[161] The fear that this practice could become institutionalised was one of the factors in the opposition to the setting-up of the police,[162] and concern continued to be expressed about police entrapment well into the modern era.[163] In recent years the concern has been tempered by a realisation of the force of police claims that proactive methods are essential for investigating some forms of ongoing or organised crime where there are no victims to report the offences. Drug-smuggling and illegal trading are two of the main types of crime where the police may need to become involved with the commission of fresh offences in order to obtain direct evidence of the activity. This has led to a compromise position in the evidential rules.

8–027   The substantive criminal law rule, confirmed by the House of Lords in *Sang*,[164] is that there is no defence of entrapment in English law.[165] It is not a ground of exculpation for the voluntary commission of an offence that the defendant was trapped into committing it. The Lords held further in *Sang* that there was no discretion at common law to exclude evidence obtained by entrapment. As explained above, it was argued that to hold otherwise would be to undermine the

---

[159] *Report of the Royal Commission on Police Powers and Procedure* Cmd.3297 (1929).

[160] The Law Commission used it in this restricted sense in Law Com No.83, *Report of Defences of General Application* (1977).

[161] See L. Radzinowicz, *A History of English Criminal Law and its Administration from 1750* (London: 1956), Vol.2 pp.326–337; D. Hay and F. Snyder (eds), *Policing and Prosecution in Britain 1750–1850* (Oxford: 1989), Ch.7.

[162] T. A. Critchley, *A History of Police in England and Wales* (London: 1967), p.160.

[163] See, e.g. the reaction in Parliament and in the press to the police operation in *Titley* (1880) 14 Cox C.C. 502. This case involved an undercover policeman persuading a chemist, suspected of being concerned in the illegal procuring of abortions, to supply chemicals intended to procure a miscarriage of the policeman's wife. The public reaction is noted in J. Morton, *Supergrasses and Informers: An Informal History of Undercover Police Work* (London: Little, Brown & Company, 1995), p.203. For judicial hostility see the remarks of Lord Goddard C.J. in *Brannan v Peek* [1947] 2 All E.R. 572.

[164] *Sang* [1980] A.C. 402.

[165] This rule is unaffected by s.78 of PACE, and the first part of the decision in *Sang* [1980] A.C. 402 remains good law: *Looseley* [2001] 4 All E.R. 897 HL.

rule of substantive law. After some uncertainty[166] it is now settled that s.78 of PACE reversed the second part of the decision in *Sang*. The discretion under s.78 to exclude prosecution evidence to safeguard the fairness of the proceedings extends to evidence obtained by entrapment.[167] However, courts also have a power at common law to stay a prosecution on the ground that it is an abuse of process. It is established law that an abuse of process may be constituted by pre-trial police impropriety which makes it unfair to try the defendant at all.[168] Accordingly the abuse of process doctrine is capable of extending to a case of entrapment.

Given this double jurisdiction to prevent the prosecution from taking advantage of the fruits of entrapment, two questions arise. In what circumstances is it appropriate in a case of entrapment to exercise the preventive jurisdiction? If such a case arises, which is the appropriate remedy: should the relevant evidence be excluded or should the prosecution be stopped altogether? The first question entails consideration of the ECHR. In *Teixeira de Castro v Portugal*,[169] the European Court of Human Rights held that a person was deprived of the right to a fair trial under art.6 of the Convention from the outset, in a case where police officers incited him to supply drugs to them in circumstances where he was not known to be already engaged in drug-dealing. This was distinguished from the situation where police officers posed as potential purchasers in a drug deal that was already underway.[170]

Both questions were fully considered by the House of Lords in the leading case of *Looseley*.[171] This case reports two conjoined hearings before the House that raised the same issues. In *Looseley* the defendant appealed against his convictions on three counts of supplying a Class A controlled drug. He supplied heroin to an undercover police officer "Rob" at Rob's request on three separate occasions. The requests were part of an undercover operation set up following police concern about trade in Class A drugs from a pub. Rob had been given the defendant's name by someone at the pub as a potential source of supply. The trial judge had refused to stay the prosecution as an abuse of process or to exclude the evidence of Rob under s.78 of PACE. In *Attorney-General's Reference (No.3 of 2000)* the defendant had been charged on one count of supplying a Class A controlled drug (heroin) and on a second count of being concerned in supplying heroin. The trial judge stayed the prosecution as an abuse of process after hearing evidence that the undercover police officers to whom the heroin had been supplied had offered the defendant cheap contraband cigarettes as an inducement. The officers had sought to persuade the defendant on a number of occasions to

---

[166] Compare dicta in *Harwood* [1989] Crim. L.R. 285 with *Gill and Ranuana* [1989] Crim. L.R. 358.

[167] *Looseley* [2001] 4 All E.R. 897 HL; confirming *Smurthwaite* (1994) 98 Cr.App.R. 437 CA.

[168] *R. v Horseferry Road Magistrates' Court Ex p. Bennett* [1994] 1 A.C. 42 HL, and see the discussion in Section E.

[169] *Teixeira de Castro v Portugal* (1999) 28 E.H.R.R. 101. See also *Ramanauskas v Lithuania* [2008] Crim. L.R. 639, where the European Court of Human Rights found a violation of art.6 in a case where a prosecutor was repeatedly pressed to accept a bribe. He had not committed any previous offences, all the contacts had been initiated by the police officer concerned, and there was no evidence that he would have committed the offence in the absence of the repeated offers.

[170] *Ludi v Switzerland* (1993) 15 E.H.R.R. 173.

[171] *Looseley* [2001] 4 All E.R. 897. For a recent review see the discussion in *Moore* [2013] EWCA Crim 85, citing Ormerod, "Recent Development in Entrapment" [2006] *Covert Policing Review* 65.

supply heroin. There was evidence that the defendant was "not really into" heroin and only supplied it as a return favour for the cigarettes. In reaching his decision the judge applied the ruling of the European Court of Human Rights in *Teixeira de Castro v Portugal*. On a reference by the Attorney-General the Court of Appeal had taken the view that the judge had been wrong to stop the prosecution. The court then referred to the House of Lords a point of law in the following terms:

> "In a case involving the commission of offences by an accused at the instigation of undercover police officers, to what extent, if any, have: (i) the judicial discretion conferred by s.78 of [PACE]; and (ii) the power to stay the proceedings as an abuse of the court; been modified by art.6 of the [ECHR] and the jurisprudence of the European Court of Human Rights?"

8–028   The House of Lords dismissed the appeal in *Looseley* and upheld the defendant's convictions. The Lords held that the trial judge was entitled to find that Rob presented himself only as a customer for drugs, and did not incite the defendant to commit an offence that he would not have committed otherwise. In the *Attorney-General's Reference (No.3 of 2000)* the Lords disagreed with the Court of Appeal and held that the trial judge had been right to stay the proceedings. This was because the officers did more than give the defendant the opportunity to commit the offence of supplying heroin. They instigated the offence because they offered him inducements that would not ordinarily be associated with the commission of such an offence.

The speeches in *Looseley* range widely over the issues presented by entrapment cases. Several key principles emerge. As noted above the House confirmed its earlier decision in *Sang* that there is no substantive defence of entrapment in English law. The House also confirmed a trial judge's discretion to stay proceedings as an abuse of process. The test that the judge should apply is whether continuance of the prosecution would be "an affront to the public conscience" or "deeply offensive to ordinary notions of fairness". It was held that the judge may also exclude under s.78 of PACE evidence obtained by entrapment. Section 78 had reversed the effect of the decision in *Sang* that no such discretion existed at common law.

It was generally agreed that if a procedure is needed in a particular case to prevent the prosecution from making use of evidence obtained by unacceptable entrapment then the appropriate remedy is the abuse of process doctrine. According to Lord Nicholls this is because entrapment goes to the propriety of there being a prosecution at all for the relevant offence, having regard to the state's involvement in the circumstances in which it was committed.[172] He thought that it was simply not acceptable that the state through its agents should lure its citizens into committing acts forbidden by the law and then seek to prosecute them for doing so: "That would be a misuse of state power and an

---

[172] *Looseley* [2001] 4 All E.R. 897 at [17]. On so-called "private" entrapment by journalists and other non-state agents, where the issue is whether the state should be able to take advantage of evidence of a crime instigated by others, see *Shannon v United Kingdom* [2005] Crim L.R. 133; *Re Saluja* [2006] EWHC 2784 (Admin); K. Hofmeyr, "The Problem of Private Entrapment" [2006] Crim. L.R. 319, arguing that the appropriate remedy for entrapment by a non-state agent is exclusion of evidence under s.78.

abuse of the process of the courts".[173] Lord Hoffmann, agreeing, thought that exclusion of evidence is not an appropriate response to entrapment.[174] But he noted that proceedings are not always conducted logically and that issues about the participation of state agents in the commission of the crime might emerge once a trial was underway. They would be relevant to the exercise of the discretion under s.78. In such circumstances "an application to exclude evidence under s.78 may be in substance a belated application for a stay. If so, it should be treated as such and decided according to the principles appropriate to the grant of a stay".[175] This is an important recognition of the possible scope and purposes of s.78 since Lord Hoffmann had previously said that a stay of prosecution is a procedure designed to protect the integrity of the criminal justice system.[176]

Turning from the appropriate remedy to the substance of the matter, the question is the acceptable limits of proactive investigative conduct in which the police initiate the commission of the offence. According to the Lords in *Looseley* it is acceptable if the police did no more than present the defendant with an unexceptional opportunity to commit a crime. The word "unexceptional" signifies an ordinary temptation. The question is whether the police conduct was no more than might have been expected from other "ordinary" customers in the circumstances.[177] The fact that the police instigated the offence in the sense of initiating the transaction that amounts to or involves the offence is not enough by itself to constitute unacceptable entrapment.[178] The straightforward deception that the officer is a member of the public is therefore not unfair.

8–029

It follows from this principle that a test purchase from a suspected illegal trader by a police officer or his agent is on the right side of the line, provided that the officer or agent behaves like an ordinary member of the public.[179] Similarly, plain clothes officers who flag down an unlicensed taxi and request a particular destination do not unfairly trap the driver into an offence,[180] provided that they do "not wave £50 notes or pretend to be in distress".[181] These examples exemplify the operation of the causal test expressed by Lord Bingham C.J. in *Nottingham City Council v Amin*.[182] Lord Bingham distinguished between cases where a person committed an offence only because he had been "incited, instigated,

---

[173] *Looseley* [2001] 4 All E.R. 897 at [1].
[174] *Looseley* [2001] 4 All E.R. 897 at [36].
[175] *Looseley* [2001] 4 All E.R. 897 at [44].
[176] *Looseley* [2001] 4 All E.R. 897 at [39]. Lord Hutton agreed at [104].
[177] *Looseley* [2001] 4 All E.R. 897 per Lord Nicholls at [23]; Lord Hoffmann at [54]–[55]; Lord Hutton at [112]–[114].
[178] *Looseley* [2001] 4 All E.R. 897 per Lord Nicholls at [3]. See also Lord Hoffmann at [69]–[70], doubting the distinction between "active" and "passive" conduct on the part of the undercover policeman or informer, suggested by Lord Taylor C.J. in *Smurthwaite* (1994) 98 Cr.App.R. 437. So a police officer pretending to be a girl aged 12 replying to an invitation written on a train toilet door, for the purpose of obtaining evidence of the defendant's incitement of a child under 13 to engage in penetrative sexual activity, was held not to have instigated this offence: *Jones* [2007] EWCA Crim 1118; [2007] 2 Cr. App. R. 21.
[179] *DPP v Marshall* [1988] 3 All E.R. 683 DC; *Ealing LBC v Woolworths Plc* [1998] Crim. L.R. 58 DC; *Looseley* [2001] 4 All E.R. 897 per Lord Nicholls at [3]; Lord Hoffmann at [55].
[180] *Nottingham City Council v Amin* [2000] 1 W.L.R. 1071 DC.
[181] *Looseley* [2001] 4 All E.R. 897 at [54] per Lord Hoffmann.
[182] *Nottingham City Council v Amin* [2000] 1 W.L.R. 1071 DC.

persuaded, pressurised or wheedled into committing it by a law enforcement officer", from cases where the officer had merely presented the defendant with an opportunity to break the law. If the defendant freely took advantage of the opportunity in circumstances where it appeared that he would have behaved in the same way if the opportunity had been offered by anyone else, then the police conduct would not be objectionable. While the causal test works well in many cases, particularly those involving the commission of regulatory offences, it may need modification in certain circumstances. As Lord Hoffmann commented, ordinary members of the public do not become involved in major crime such as contract murder or large-scale drug dealing.[183] In this type of case appropriate standards of police behaviour are more problematic and require a sharper focus on the nature of the police conduct.

It also follows from the "unexceptional opportunity" principle that repeated requests and some degree of importunity may equally be acceptable if that is what might be expected from an ordinary customer. This point is particularly relevant in the context of purchasing drugs from a suspected dealer. A customer who is not already known to the dealer may have to make a number of requests before the dealer is prepared to trust him.[184] This is to be distinguished from:

"a case where an undercover policeman repeatedly badgers a vulnerable drug addict for a supply of drugs in return for excessive and ever increasing amounts of money. Eventually the addict yields to the importunity and pressure, and supplies drugs. He is then prosecuted for doing so. Plainly this result would be objectionable ... as artificial or state created crime."[185]

8–030   The Lords make it clear that in assessing the propriety of police conduct it is important to have regard to a number of other factors in addition to those already mentioned. The first such factor is necessity. Depending on the nature of the offence:

"the use of proactive techniques is more needed and hence, more appropriate, in some circumstances than others. The secrecy and difficulty of detection, and the manner in which the particular criminal activity is carried on, are relevant considerations."[186]

Lord Hoffmann, agreeing, suggested that:

"consensual offences such as dealing in unlawful substances or offences with no immediate victim like bribery or offences which victims are reluctant to report are obvious candidates for such methods. So is the infiltration of conspiracies."[187]

---

[183] *Looseley* [2001] 4 All E.R. 897 at [55].
[184] *Looseley* [2001] 4 All E.R. 897 per Lord Hoffmann at [69]; Lord Hutton at [102].
[185] *Looseley* [2001] 4 All E.R. 897 per Lord Nicholls at [4]. For a case where a conviction was quashed on this ground see *Moon* [2004] EWCA Crim 2872.
[186] *Looseley* [2001] 4 All E.R. 897 at [4] per Lord Nicholls.
[187] *Looseley* [2001] 4 All E.R. 897 at [66]. In *Jones* [2007] EWCA Crim 1118; [2007] 2 Cr. App. R. 21 the Court of Appeal noted that offences of inciting children to engage in sexual activity, carried out by text messages, might necessitate covert activity by police to identify the user of the mobile phone in question. See also *Brett* [2005] EWCA Crim 983, where the Court of Appeal made it clear that covert policing of this type need not be the last resort, nor is it a reason for staying proceedings that other methods might have worked.

A second additional factor is the reason for the police operation.[188] The police must act in good faith. There must be no vendettas against particular individuals or groups. According to Lord Nicholls:

> "having reasonable grounds for suspicion is one way good faith may be established, but having grounds for suspicion of a particular individual is not always essential. Sometimes suspicion may be centred on a particular place, such as a particular public house or a bus station.[189] Sometimes random testing may be the only practicable way of policing a particular trading activity."

Lord Nicholls added the important limitation that the defendant's criminal record is unlikely to be relevant, unless it can be linked to other factors grounding reasonable suspicion that the defendant is *currently* engaged in criminal activity (emphasis supplied).[190] This rejection of a record as a sufficient reason by itself for targeting a particular individual is consistent with the rejection in *Looseley* of the "predisposition" justification of entrapment. This justification focuses on the defendant's criminal intent: it argues that if the defendant already had the intent (was predisposed) to commit the crime, then it was not objectionable for the police merely to provide the opportunity. It would be different, the argument goes, if the police were responsible for implanting the necessary intent. That would be state-created crime. Lord Nicholls did not regard this as an adequate principle for establishing the limits of acceptable police conduct. Leaving aside the point that predisposition is inherently speculative, he thought that it was going too far to say that a person who was ready and willing to commit a certain kind of crime could never be entrapped into committing it. Citing Lamer J. in the Supreme Court of Canada,[191] Lord Nicholls commented that it is always possible that it was the conduct of the police that led the defendant into committing the crime in the particular case, notwithstanding the defendant's disposition. As he put it, "predisposition does not make acceptable what would otherwise be unacceptable conduct on the part of the police or other law enforcement agencies. Predisposition does not negative misuse of state power".[192]

Thirdly, the nature and extent of the police participation in the offence must be taken into account.[193] This is not just a question of the degree of pressure exerted by the police on the defendant. That is certainly relevant: "the more forceful or persistent the police overtures, the more readily may a court conclude that the police overstepped the boundary".[194] But it is also relevant to consider such matters as reasonable suspicion and proper supervision of the police operation. Reasonable suspicion is a valuable threshold requirement for an undercover operation involving entrapment, not least because it may check any tendency to

8–031

---

[188] *Looseley* [2001] 4 All E.R. 897 at [27] per Lord Nicholls.
[189] *Moon* [2004] EWCA Crim 2872.
[190] *Looseley* [2001] 4 All E.R. 897 at [29].
[191] *R. v Mack* (1988) 44 C.C.C. (3d) 513 at 551.
[192] *Looseley* [2001] 4 All E.R. 897 at [22].
[193] *Looseley* [2001] 4 All E.R. 897 at [28] per Lord Nicholls; at [56]–[65], per Lord Hoffmann.
[194] *Looseley* [2001] 4 All E.R. 897, Lord Nicholls at [28].

discriminatory policing and will help to restrict infringements of privacy.[195] Lord Hoffmann attached importance to official authorisation of investigations involving the possible use of entrapment. Such authorisation would help to prevent dangers of doctored evidence, oppression, extortion and corruption. He also thought that it would help to ensure respect for the requirement of reasonable suspicion. Authority for the use of undercover agents is now required by s.29 of the Regulation of Investigatory Powers Act 2000, which sets out the procedures to be followed.

Finally, the Lords in *Looseley* considered that the principles they had set out ensured that English law would be consistent with the requirements of art.6 of the ECHR.[196] The decision of the European Court of Human Rights in *Teixeira de Castro v Portugal* was thought to be right on the facts. Lord Hoffmann pointed to the lack of any judicial supervision of the investigation, and to the fact that the competent authorities had no good reason to suspect the defendant of being a drug trafficker. Lord Hutton emphasised the instigation of the offence by the officers concerned, and the lack of anything to suggest that without their intervention it would have been committed.[197] The Lords rejected, however, any idea that the case supports a general principle that the police must always act passively if they are to stay on the right side of art.6.

The "unexceptional opportunity" principle adopted in *Looseley* can be securely grounded in the theory that the law of evidence aims to promote the legitimacy of verdicts. The evidence secured through the instigation of an offence may be wholly reliable in proving that the defendant in fact committed the offence. It is difficult to argue with, say, film from a hidden camera that shows the defendant handing a quantity of heroin to undercover police officers in exchange for money. However, the promotion of a crime that would not otherwise take place at all strikes at the core reason for the existence of criminal law. A guilty verdict in such a case cannot function as an expressive message that the values of the criminal law are to be respected if the sole reason for the occurrence of the offence is that it was procured by state officials whose duty is to uphold the law. In this way the state forfeits its moral authority to call for the imposition of blame and punishment of the defendant. It is right therefore that the prosecution should be prevented from taking advantage of evidence obtained in this way.

---

[195] D. Ormerod and A. Roberts, "The trouble with *Teixeira*: Developing a principled approach to entrapment" (2002) 6 E. & P. 38, 47–48, and for the significance of the reasonable suspicion requirement in the context of the ECHR see *Fox, Campbell and Hartley v United Kingdom* (1990) 13 E.H.R.R. 157.

[196] *Looseley* [2001] 4 All E.R. 897 at [30] per Lord Nicholls; at [72]–[75], per Lord Hoffmann; at [109]–[112], per Lord Hutton; at [123]–[124], per Lord Scott of Foscote.

[197] For a more sceptical view see D. Ormerod and A. Roberts, "The trouble with *Teixeira*" (2002) 6 E. & P. 38, esp. 43–46.

E.   ABUSE OF PROCESS AND EXCLUSIONARY DISCRETION

Judges have a discretion at common law to stay a prosecution altogether on the   **8–032**
ground that it constitutes an abuse of process.[198] It is beyond the scope of this
book to consider the doctrine of abuse of process in detail, because much of it
deals with matters outside the reach of the law of evidence. For example, the
question whether a prosecution should be stopped because it is oppressive,[199] or
because of the prejudice caused to the defendant by unjustifiable delay in
bringing the prosecution,[200] belongs more to the realm of criminal procedure
rather than criminal evidence. The question does not raise issues about the proper
admissibility and use of evidence at trial. In *R. v Horseferry Road Magistrates'
Court Ex p. Bennett*,[201] the power to stay was exercised where it was alleged that
the defendant had been forcibly abducted and brought to England to face trial in
disregard of extradition laws.[202] The question whether it is an abuse of process to
try a defendant in these circumstances is not a question which raises evidential
issues.

However, it is clear that there is some overlap between the functions of the
abuse of process doctrine and the exclusion of evidence under s.78 of PACE. This
was confirmed by the House of Lords in the context of entrapment in *Looseley,*[203]
and by the Supreme Court in the context of prosecutorial misconduct in
Maxwell.[204] It was implicit in the way the Court of Appeal in *Beckford*[205] referred
to the two main types of case which they identified as covered by the jurisdiction
to stay proceedings:

> "(a)   cases where the court concludes that the defendant cannot receive a fair trial;
> (b)   cases where the court concludes that it would be unfair for the defendant to be
> tried."[206]

The reference in both these types of case to the concept of fairness invites
comparison with the reference in s.78 to the fairness of the proceedings. In
particular, some situations of pre-trial impropriety by investigating or prosecuting
authorities raise the kinds of problems discussed in the earlier part of this chapter.
The use of entrapment provides an example. In *Latif and Shahzad*,[207] the House
of Lords was invited to say that it was an abuse of process for customs officers to

---

[198] *Connelly v DPP* [1964] A.C. 1254 HL; *DPP v Humphrys* [1977] A.C. 1 HL. See generally A.
Choo, *Abuse of Process and Stays of Judicial Proceedings*, 2nd edn (Oxford, 2008); D. Corker and D.
Young, *Abuse of Process in Criminal Proceedings*, 2nd edn (London, 2003).
[199] *Riebold* [1967] 1 W.L.R. 674; *R. v Horsham JJ Ex p. Reeves* (1980) 75 Cr.App.R. 236.
[200] See *Attorney-General's Reference (No.1 of 1990)* (1992) 95 Cr.App.R. 296 CA.
[201] *R. v Horseferry Road Magistrates' Court Ex p. Bennett* [1994] 1 A.C. 42 HL.
[202] The case was decided on these assumed facts. For a fuller and rather different account of events
see the judgment of Lord Hope in *Warren v Attorney-General of Jersey* [2011] UKPC 10; [2011] 2
Cr.App.R. 29.
[203] *Looseley* [2001] 4 All E.R. 897.
[204] *Maxwell* [2010] UKSC 48; [2011] 2 Cr.App.R. 31 at [11] per Lord Dyson. See also the remarks of
Lord Brown in *Warren v Attorney-General of Jersey* [2011] UKPC 10; [2011] 2 Cr.App.R. 29 at
[77]–[78].
[205] *Beckford* [1996] 1 Cr.App.R. 94.
[206] *Beckford* [1996] 1 Cr.App.R. 94 at 101.
[207] *Latif and Shahzad* [1996] 2 Cr.App.R. 92 HL.

lure an organiser in the heroin trade into the jurisdiction so that he could be arrested and tried for being concerned in an illegal importation of heroin. Lord Steyn noted that, even if there was an element of entrapment, a fair trial had been possible in this case and had in fact taken place. He went on to set out the principle on abuse of process:

> "the issue is whether, despite the fact that a fair trial was possible, the judge ought to have stayed the criminal proceedings on broader considerations of the integrity of the criminal justice system. The law is settled. Weighing countervailing considerations of policy and justice, it is for the judge in the exercise of his discretion to decide whether there has been an abuse of process, which amounts to an affront to the public conscience and requires the criminal proceedings to be stayed . . . in a case such as the present the judge must weigh in the balance the public interest in ensuring that those who are charged with grave crimes should be tried and the competing public interest in not conveying the impression that the court will adopt the approach that the end justified any means."[208]

8–033   Rejecting the argument for a stay, Lord Steyn held that the judge had been entitled to take the view that Shahzad was an organiser in the heroin trade who took the initiative in proposing the importation. Even if the undercover customs officer who brought the drugs to England had committed an offence, his conduct:

> "was not so unworthy or shameful that it was an affront to the public conscience to allow the prosecution to proceed. Realistically, any criminal behaviour of the customs officer was venial compared to that of Shahzad."[209]

Finally, Lord Steyn held that the defence's alternative argument that the evidence against Shahzad should have been excluded under s.78 failed also. Given the judge's finding that Shahzad had not been prejudiced in the presentation of his defence, there were no further factors that had not been considered already on the abuse of process argument. Subsequently, in *Looseley*[210] the House of Lords held that where unacceptable entrapment is made out the appropriate remedy is usually a stay for abuse of process and not exclusion of the evidence, although s.78 may need to be invoked where the issue of entrapment does not emerge until the trial is underway.

In contexts other than entrapment the relationship between the power to exclude evidence and the power to stay the proceedings is somewhat obscure. In *Aujla*,[211] the prosecution sought to adduce evidence obtained by telephone tapping carried out abroad. The Court of Appeal rejected a defence submission that the evidence should be excluded under s.78, and then went on to consider an alternative submission that the use of the evidence would be an abuse of process. It seems that defence counsel was trying to use the abuse of process doctrine as an exclusionary principle rather than as a plea barring the court's jurisdiction, and the Court of Appeal was plainly not convinced that the doctrine could be used in this way: "We have not had our attention drawn to any case where the principles of abuse of process have been used successfully to exclude evidence that would

---

[208] *Latif and Shahzad* [1996] 2 Cr.App.R. 92 at 101.
[209] *Latif and Shahzad* [1996] 2 Cr.App.R. 92 at 101.
[210] *Looseley* [2001] 4 All E.R. 58.
[211] *Aujla* [1998] 2 Cr.App.R. 16 CA.

otherwise be relevant and admissible".[212] The court rejected the alternative submission, saying that the circumstances of the case fell well short of establishing that the evidence had been obtained unlawfully or that its use would offend against any fundamental principle of justice.

This still leaves open the possibility of staying the proceedings on the ground that the admission of the evidence would make the trial unfair. This is a drastic remedy, and its use would necessarily have to be founded on a view that the exclusionary discretion under s.78 was inadequate or inappropriate for the purpose. Such a narrow view of s.78 is implicit in the judgment of the Court of Appeal in *Chalkley*.[213] The court's general approach in that case to the interpretation of s.78 is set out and criticised in Ch.3. It should be noted here that the Court of Appeal held that the determination of the fairness of admitting evidence under s.78 was distinct from the determination of whether to stay proceedings as an abuse of process. In the view of the Court of Appeal the trial judge had erred in adopting a balancing test under s.78, whereby he weighed factors favouring the effective prosecution of crime against factors relating to the nature of the police conduct, the protection of human rights and the public interest in discouraging abuse of power. These factors, the court said, were appropriately considered as part of the decision on whether to stay the proceedings; under s.78 the judge should be concerned only with whether the methods used to obtain the evidence affected the quality of the evidence (which seems to refer to its reliability). However, in *Attorney-General's Reference (No.1 of 1990)*,[214] which was not cited in *Chalkley*, Lord Lane C.J. said that the trial process itself was equipped to deal with the bulk of complaints used to found an argument for a stay of proceedings. He went on to refer to police impropriety in relation to evidence, and approved an earlier statement of principle by Watkins L.J. in *Heston-Francois*[215]:

> "However reprehensible conduct of this kind may be it is not, at least in circumstances such as the present, an abuse, or, in another word, a misuse of the court's process. It is conduct which in these circumstances falls to be dealt with in the trial itself by *judicial control upon admissibility of evidence*, the judicial power to direct a verdict of not guilty, usually at the close of the prosecution's case, or by the jury taking account of it in evaluating the evidence before them." (emphasis added)

In the light of this, and in the light of the other criticisms made in Ch.3, it is suggested again that *Chalkley* is wrong in its construction of s.78. Properly interpreted, the section provides the appropriate principle for ensuring the fairness of the proceedings, as far as the admission of evidence is concerned. Fairness in this context should be understood as covering both unfair use of evidence at trial, and unfair treatment of the accused in the obtaining of evidence before trial, where the unfair treatment presents a significant risk of impairing the moral authority and expressive value of the verdict. On this basis the trial judge was right in *Chalkley* to take into account the more general factors mentioned that did not bear solely on the issue of the reliability of the evidence. Questions of

8–034

---

[212] *Aujla* [1998] 2 Cr.App.R. 16 at 22 per Roch L.J.
[213] *Chalkley* [1998] 2 Cr.App.R. 79.
[214] *Attorney-General's Reference (No.1 of 1990)* (1992) 95 Cr.App.R. 296 CA.
[215] *Heston-Francois* [1984] Q.B. 278 at 290.

police conduct in bad faith, breach of human rights and entrapment are all matters which the cases discussed in this chapter show to be relevant to the exercise of the discretion under s.78. These matters do not necessarily affect the quality of the evidence obtained, but they may certainly affect those aspects of fairness not directly concerned with reliability of evidence and the factual accuracy of the verdict.

That said, it should be noted that the use of s.78 to exclude evidence improperly obtained would leave open the possibility that a trial could continue if there were other, properly obtained, evidence of guilt. Should a defendant still be able to be convicted on untainted evidence where there has been serious pre-trial impropriety by the police in relation to the gathering of (excluded) evidence against the defendant? An application of the abuse of process doctrine would of course prevent this possibility.

On this crucial point there are conflicting signals in the case law. The decision of the Court of Appeal in *Grant*[216] is a strong indication that the abuse of process jurisdiction is appropriate in this situation. The police had placed covert recording devices in a police exercise yard in order to tape privileged conversations between the defendant and his solicitor. In fact the tapes yielded no evidence that the Crown relied on at the trial or that they might have deployed to undermine the defence case. Despite the lack of prejudice to the defendant from the police conduct the Court of Appeal quashed the defendant's conviction for conspiracy to murder, saying that they were in no doubt that the judge should have stopped the prosecution. Laws L.J.:

> "...unlawful acts of the kind done in this case, amounting to a deliberate violation of a suspected person's right to legal professional privilege, are so great an affront to the integrity of the justice system, and therefore the rule of law, that the associated prosecution is rendered abusive and ought not to be countenanced by the court."[217]

8–035 In his Note of Dissent to the Runciman Report,[218] Zander posed the question whether the Court of Appeal should uphold a conviction, "despite the most serious misconduct by the prosecution", if there is other reliable and sufficient evidence that the defendant committed the offence. His concerns related to cases where evidence had been fabricated or suppressed or where the defendant had been subjected to serious violence to produce a confession. The problem of impropriety is of course wider than this, as Zander himself recognised. Zander's response to his question was that "the moral foundation of the criminal justice system requires that if the prosecution has employed foul means the defendant must go free even though he is plainly guilty".[219] To support this uncompromising conclusion he prayed in aid the argument from legitimacy[220] referred to above in connection with s.78. *Grant* is powerful support for this position.

---

[216] *Grant* [205] EWCA Crim 1089; [2005] 2 Cr.App.R. 28.

[217] *Grant* [2005] EWCA Crim 1089; [2005] 2 Cr.App.R. 28 at [54]. The RIPA Pt II provides for such covert recording of private and privileged consultations to be lawful, but only as authorised intrusive surveillance: see *In re McE* [2009] UKHL 15.

[218] RCCJ Report (London, 1993).

[219] RCCJ Report, Note of Dissent, para.68.

[220] RCCJ Report para.72.

However, there is a danger of over-extending the legitimacy argument in this context. The theory claims that s.78 may be rightly used to exclude evidence in the interests of ensuring the moral authority and expressive value of a guilty verdict. In an appropriate case this could include all evidence obtained, directly or indirectly, by impropriety. But if there is other, genuinely independent, evidence of guilt it is not so clear that a guilty verdict would necessarily be illegitimate. To prevent a conviction at all in such circumstances may pay inadequate regard to the important goals of punishing the guilty and of vindicating the interests of victims. If the untainted evidence is causally unrelated to the police malpractice, is sufficient for conviction, and the defendant has not been prejudiced by the malpractice so that a fair trial is possible, then it would seem desirable for the court to balance the competing considerations of public policy. In *Grant* Laws L.J. explained that "it is the court's duty to protect the public from crime, especially serious crime; that consideration may militate in favour of refusal of a stay".[221] But he went on to make it clear that the balancing exercise will entail an inquiry into the gravity of the illegal conduct by police or state prosecutors. If the conduct "is so grave as to threaten or undermine the rule of law itself, the court may readily conclude that it will not tolerate, far less endorse, such a state of affairs and so hold that its duty is to stop the case".[222]

Recently the Supreme Court and the Privy Council have gone out of their way to disapprove the decision in *Grant. Maxwell*[223] concerned an appeal to the Supreme Court against an order for a retrial after the Court of Appeal had quashed convictions for murder and robbery in view of gross misconduct by the investigating police, involving non-disclosure of significant benefits provided to the chief prosecution witness, forgery of a custody record and perjury at the defendant's trial. However, after his convictions the defendant had made a number of voluntary confessions to the offences. These confessions could be proved independently in a retrial, although it was accepted that they would not have come into existence but for the earlier misconduct leading to the convictions. Lord Brown, who dissented on the issue in the case, commented in a dictum that he had "the gravest doubts as to the correctness of the court's decision in *Grant.*"[224] Lord Dyson, for the majority dismissing the appeal, agreed, saying that he had "considerable reservations as to whether that case was correctly decided".[225] Lord Dyson returned to the point in his judgment in the Privy Council in *Warren v Attorney-General of Jersey,*[226] where the issue was whether a prosecution for drug smuggling should have been stayed on the ground that key incriminating evidence had been procured by unlawful conduct of the part of the police, including lying to authorities in France and misleading the Attorney General and Chief Officer of Police in Jersey. In the course of dismissing the appeal against a refusal of a stay Lord Dyson stated in terms that the decision in

---

[221] *Grant* [2005] 2 Cr.App.R. 28 at [55].
[222] *Grant* [2005] 2 Cr.App.R. 28 at [56].
[223] *Maxwell* [2010] UKSC 48; [2011] 2 Cr.App.R. 31.
[224] *Maxwell* [2010] UKSC 48; [2011] 2 Cr.App.R. 31 at [96].
[225] *Maxwell* [2010] UKSC 48; [2011] 2 Cr.App.R. 31 at [28].
[226] *Warren v Attorney-General of Jersey* [2011] UKPC 10; [2011] 2 Cr.App.R. 29. For criticism of both this case and *Maxwell* see P. O'Connor QC, "Abuse of Process After *Warren* and *Maxwell*" [2012] Crim. L.R. 672.

Grant was wrong.[227] He argued that the seriousness of the crime involved, and the fact that no prejudice resulted to the accused from the police misconduct, meant that the Court of Appeal should not have interfered with the trial judge's decision to refuse a stay in that case. Neither *Maxwell* nor *Warren* lay down any new principle on abuse of process. They agree that a balancing exercise is involved in the second type of case set out in *Beckford,* although they emphasise that the focus should be on protecting the integrity of the criminal justice system rather than fairness to the individual defendant. Neither case discusses the exclusion of evidence under s.78, although it is implicit in the decision in *Warren* that the Privy Council would not have interfered with the decision to admit the unlawfully obtained evidence. Given the scale of the police misconduct in the case, and its deliberate nature, this is a surprising conclusion which contrasts markedly with the cases on breach of PACE discussed earlier in this chapter.

---

[227] *Warren v Attorney-General of Jersey* [2011] UKPC 10; [2011] 2 Cr.App.R. 29 at [36].

CHAPTER 9

DISCLOSURE AND IMMUNITY

A. INTRODUCTION

9–001 The subject of disclosure of evidence brings into collision two fundamental interests, and the law in this area is best understood as a shifting and uneasy attempt to settle the competing priorities.

On one side is the interest that all parties to legal proceedings have in gaining access to all the evidence that is relevant to the determination of the subject-matter of the proceedings. This includes evidence in the hands of third parties as well as evidence in the possession of opposing parties to the proceedings. The interest in access to evidence has both a private and a public dimension. Zuckerman has argued that access to evidence is so important for the parties to litigation that it should be recognised as their constitutional right:

> "It is a fundamental principle in the administration of justice that parties to litigation have a right to bring before the court all evidence relevant to their case and to call on others to produce such evidence as they may have. This right is derivative from the right to equal and just trial. Without it the efficacy of substantive rights would be much reduced and rendered uncertain. This principle—which may for convenience be termed the principle of unimpeded access to evidence—is therefore of cardinal constitutional significance and bears close relation to the constitutional right of unimpeded access to the the courts generally."[1]

This argument gains considerable support from art.6 of the ECHR. The European Court of Human Rights has held that the right to a fair trial under art.6 has as one of its elements the right of access to evidence. In *Edwards v United Kingdom*,[2] the court held that art.6 entitles the defendant to disclosure of all material evidence for or against him. The prosecution in this case had failed to disclose before the trial evidence bearing on the credibility of the police witnesses, but on the facts that failure was held to have been remedied by the procedure adopted in the Court of Appeal. The evidence had been disclosed by that stage, but the defendant had not sought an order for a fresh cross-examination of the police witnesses. There was therefore no violation of art 6. Nevertheless, the principle that in criminal proceedings the prosecution may not hold back relevant material was clearly established.

9–002 From the standpoint of the parties to civil litigation, obtaining access to evidence is instrumentally important in enabling them to settle their disputes before trial, because it enables better estimates to be made of the strengths and weaknesses of their respective cases. Access to evidence is essential in all cases for determining what evidence can be adduced if a dispute proceeds to trial; a denial of access may diminish the accuracy of the adjudication through the inability of the party denied access to present its case properly. As well as its importance to the outcome of litigation, access is also a key participation value. Parties may well feel aggrieved and complain that they have not had a fair hearing if they have not been able to adduce relevant evidence because access to it has been denied.

---

[1] A. A. S. Zuckerman, "Privilege and public interest" in C. Tapper (ed), *Crime Proof and Punishment* (London: Butterworths, 1981), p.248.
[2] *Edwards v United Kingdom* (1993) 15 E.H.R.R. 417. See also *Attorney-General's Guidelines on Disclosure* (2005), para.1: "Fair disclosure to an accused is an inseparable part of a fair trial".

As noted in Ch.2, there is an important and self-evident public interest in the protection of individual rights. It matters to all citizens of a state what rights citizens have in litigation and how effectively those rights are protected. In addition there are other important public interests in the securing of access to evidence. These derive from the need to provide effective mechanisms for the enforcement of adjectival rights. The objective of securing access to evidence can be argued to be a functional necessity of the adversarial system for adjudication of disputes. If courts rely on the parties to present the relevant evidence for the adjudication, they should afford the parties the means to obtain the evidence. If they do not, the danger of making decisions on incomplete evidence is increased and hence there is an increased risk of miscarriage of justice. Miscarriages of justice damage the legitimacy of the system of official adjudication of disputes. Arguments of efficiency are also relevant; there is an undoubted public interest in the most efficient use of expensive legal machinery, and this includes an interest in the facilitation of settlement of disputes, and informed preparation for trial.

In this way private and public interests combine to support the case for unrestricted access to evidence, even evidence in the possession of an opponent. The case for disclosure then argues for two forms of compulsory process. One is a procedure for ensuring that evidence (that a party knows to exist) is available at trial if it is needed. This procedure takes the form of a summons directed to a witness to attend court to give evidence, or to produce documents to the court.[3] The other is a procedure for pre-trial discovery and inspection of material in the possession of opponents and third parties, so that the party seeking disclosure can find out what is relevant and available.

Opposed to such interests in disclosure are interests in secrecy. Such interests **9–003** may arise out of a desire to maintain privacy in one's affairs generally, or out of the need to protect confidentiality of certain communications, or because a wider public interest argues for non-disclosure. The value attached to these interests in particular contexts has led to the development of a number of legally recognised claims to privilege or immunity from disclosure of evidence. Some of these claims, such as legal professional privilege, may have an absolute quality to them that marks them out as strong procedural rights. Others, such as public interest immunity, depend upon a balancing of interests and may operate differently in civil and criminal proceedings. The conflict between interests in access to evidence and interests in secrecy is sharpened by the fact that both types of interest have human rights dimensions. Access to evidence is one of the elements of the right to a fair trial, as noted above, but it may run counter to the right to privacy in art.8 of the Convention[4] or the right to freedom of expression in art.10. The latter includes the "freedom . . . to receive and impart information . . . without interference by public authority", and is a crucial measure for the protection of the freedom of the press. It follows that where a party to litigation seeks disclosure of a journalist's sources of information the rights in question are

---

[3] CPR r.34.2.

[4] Which may result in some restriction of the right to disclosure of, for example, a prosecution witness's previous convictions: *HM Advocate v Murtagh* [2009] UKPC 36.

directly opposed. The battleground in English law for this particular conflict is s.10 of the Contempt of Court Act 1981, to which we shall return later in this chapter.

The next two sections of this chapter consider the general rules of disclosure in civil and criminal proceedings respectively. Sections D and E then examine the law relating to claims that resist disclosure on the ground of public interest immunity. Section F deals briefly with the privilege against disclosure that attaches to communications made for the purposes of conciliation and settlement of disputes. Since interests of public policy directly support confidentiality for these types of communications, it is appropriate to mention them in this chapter. Other forms of privilege are dealt with elsewhere in this book. The privilege against self-incrimination is discussed in Ch.5 along with its derivative application, the "right to silence" in pre-trial criminal investigations.[5] The topic of legal professional privilege is treated separately in Ch.10.

B.   DISCLOSURE IN CIVIL CASES[6]

9–004   Pre-trial disclosure of documents takes place in civil litigation after the exchange of the parties' statements of case (formerly known as pleadings). These are the formal documents in which the parties set out the nature of their claims: the claimant (formerly plaintiff) initiates the exchange with service of his claim form and particulars of claim, the defendant responds with a defence (and counterclaim, if any), and the claimant may then file a reply to the defence. Generally speaking, allegations of fact in a statement of case are taken to be admitted unless the opponent's statement of case states that they are denied or not admitted. In this way the statements of case clarify the facts that are in issue between the parties and that will have to be proved at trial.

The process of disclosure of documents was formerly known as discovery. In accordance with Pt 31 of the Civil Procedure Rules 1998 the parties exchange lists of the documents, which are or have been in their possession, and on which they rely, or which support another party's case, or which adversely affect their own or another party's case. They must make available for inspection all such documents currently in their possession unless they can claim privilege or immunity from disclosure, or they state that they will not permit inspection on the ground that to do so would be disproportionate to the issues in the case. Any such claim must be specified in the list and must sufficiently identify the documents or class of documents to which it refers. Any dispute about the validity of the claim can be the subject of an interlocutory application by the party seeking disclosure. If the claim is upheld disclosure will be refused, but even if the claim is not upheld, inspection will not automatically be ordered. A court may exercise its general powers of management under r.3.1 to refuse an order for inspection in the interests of furthering the overriding objective (r.1.1). This objective requires the

---

[5] The accused's right to silence at trial is discussed in Ch.13.
[6] This topic is dealt with only in outline. For further detail readers are advised to consult specialist works on civil procedure.

court to deal with the case justly, which includes saving expense and ensuring fairness and equality for the parties. According to Lord Clarke in *Al-Rawi v Security Service*:

> "As to disclosure, the general principle is that if the court is satisfied that it is necessary to order certain documents to be disclosed and inspected in order fairly to dispose of the proceedings then ... the law requires that such an order should be made."[7]

The implications of such a necessity requirement are discussed below in connection with claims of public interest immunity.

This right of mutual disclosure applies only as between the parties[8] to civil litigation. Litigants have no equivalent right to compel witnesses and third parties to make any disclosure before trial of relevant documents in their possession. Interests of privacy and confidence are considered to take precedence over the interests of parties to litigation in searching for relevant evidence from non-parties. However, this is subject to two substantial qualifications.[9] First, s.34 of the Senior Courts Act 1981 gives the High Court power to order disclosure of documents by a person who is not a party to the proceedings and who is likely to have in his possession, custody or power any documents relevant to an issue arising out of the claim. Any party to the proceedings may apply for such an order, which may be granted in such circumstances as are specified in the Civil Procedure Rules.[10] These orders are not limited to particular types of proceeding, and consequently have numerous important applications. For example they enable a claimant in a personal injuries action to obtain discovery before trial of hospital records relating to his medical treatment. The claimant would be able to obtain the production of the records at trial by means of a witness summons, but clearly previous sight of them will greatly facilitate preparation for trial.

Secondly, in *Norwich Pharmacal Co v Commissioners of Customs and Excise*,[11] the House of Lords held that in certain circumstances third parties could be compelled to disclose the identity of wrongdoers so as to enable proceedings to be brought against them. The principle is that where a person through no fault of his own, and voluntarily or as a matter of duty:

9–005

---

[7] *Al-Rawi v Security Service* [2011] UKSC 34; [2012] 1 All E.R. 1 at [140], citing *Science Research Council v Nasse* [1980] A.C. 1028.

[8] Note that s.33(2) of the Senior Courts Act 1981 confers a power on the High Court to order disclosure of documents before the commencement of the action by a person likely to be a party to the proceedings and who is likely to have or have had in his possession, custody or power any documents relevant to an issue arising or likely to arise out of the claim.

[9] Note also that certain statutory procedures may include a power to call on any person thought capable of providing relevant information to produce documents and, in some cases, to attend for oral examination. See, e.g. Insolvency Act 1986 s.236 (liquidation of an insolvent company); Companies Act 1985 ss.431–432 (inspection of company by inspectors appointed by the Secretary of State). Important public interests in the obtaining of information are said to justify these compulsory powers, which frequently include a provision overriding the privilege against self-incrimination (see Ch.5).

[10] CPR r.31.17, which includes a requirement that the documents sought are likely to support the case of the applicant or adversely affect the case of one of the other parties to the proceedings. "Likely" means "may well" rather than the higher test of "more probable than not": *Three Rivers DC v Bank of England (No.4)* [2002] 4 All E.R. 881 CA.

[11] *Norwich Pharmacal Co v Commissioners of Customs and Excise* [1974] A.C. 133 HL.

"gets mixed up in the tortious acts of others so as to facilitate their wrongdoing he may incur no personal liability but he comes under a duty to assist the person who has been wronged by giving him full information and disclosing the identity of the wrongdoers . . . justice requires that he should co-operate in righting the wrong if he unwittingly facilitates its perpetration."[12]

Applying this principle, the House of Lords ordered the disclosure of documents identifying the importers of goods that the plaintiffs claimed were being imported in breach of patent rights. As well as identifying the wrongdoers, the documents would of course provide evidence of the illegal importation.[13] This remedy is not available as of right. The claimant must show a real interest in pursuing a remedy against the wrongdoer, and must also show that this interest in the pursuit of justice outweighs any countervailing public interest, for example in the protection of sources of information.[14] However, the remedy is also a flexible one, and it has been held to extend to disclosure of information and documents necessary for a person's defence to serious criminal charges brought against him in a foreign jurisdiction, where there was evidence of facilitation by agents of the UK Government of wrongdoing by the foreign government.[15]

In addition to their pre-trial obligations to make mutual disclosure of documents, parties to civil proceedings must also exchange witness statements.[16] This duty is part of the radical shift in recent years towards the avoidance of surprise and greater openness in civil litigation, a shift that reflects a developing policy of more proactive management of civil cases and official encouragement of parties to settle disputes before trial.[17] A witness statement is a "written statement signed by a person which contains the evidence which the person would be allowed to give orally".[18] Such statements will stand at trial as the evidence in chief of the witness, unless the court orders otherwise, and the party calling the witness is not allowed without good reason to adduce any evidence from the witness that was not included in the statement.[19] Moreover, a party who has not provided a witness statement in compliance with the direction for

---

[12] *Norwich Pharmacal* [1974] A.C. 133 at 175.

[13] See also *Mackinnon v Donaldson Lufkin and Jenrette Securities Corp* [1986] Ch. 482; *Khanna v Lovell White Durrant (a firm)* [1995] 1 W.L.R. 121.

[14] *British Steel Corp v Granada Television Ltd* [1981] A.C. 1096 HL. See also *Ashworth Hospital Authority v MGN Ltd* [2002] UKHL 29; [2002] 4 All E.R. 193 HL.

[15] *R. (on the application of Mohammed) v Foreign Secretary* [2008] EWHC 2048 (Admin). This case also confirms that proof of causation of another's wrongdoing is not required; it is enough if the person from whom disclosure is sought has facilitated the wrongdoing, albeit innocently. The judgment of the Divisional Court on the scope of the *Norwich Pharmacal* principle was not challenged in the appeal brought on a different point in *R. (on the application of Mohammed) v Foreign Secretary* [2010] EWCA Civ 65, but was approved, obiter, by Lord Judge C.J.

[16] CPR r.32.4.

[17] See, e.g. the remarks of Lord Donaldson M.R. in *Mercer v Chief Constable of Lancashire* [1991] 1 W.L.R. 367 at 373. Further development of this policy was a major recommendation of the report on civil litigation by Lord Woolf, *Access to Justice* (London, 1996). Woolf's proposal that the courts should effectively take over the management of civil litigation from the parties represented a further stage in the diminution of the traditional adversarial principle of party autonomy. The force of this can be seen in CPR r.32.1 whereby the court may control the evidence by giving directions as to the issues on which it requires evidence, the nature of the evidence which it requires to decide those issues, and the way in which the evidence is to be placed before the court.

[18] CPR r.32.4(1).

[19] CPR r.32.5(3) and (4).

exchange of witness statements will not be allowed to adduce evidence covered by the direction without the leave of the court.[20] A party cannot refuse to disclose the contents of a witness statement on the ground of litigation privilege.[21] This is necessary to promote the avoidance of surprise, and is not unfair, because if the party providing the statement does call the witness the party thereby waives privilege. Note, however, that if the party who has served a witness statement does not call the witness to give evidence at trial, or put the witness statement in as hearsay evidence, any other party may put the witness statement in as hearsay evidence.[22]

C.   DISCLOSURE IN CRIMINAL CASES[23]

1.   *The disclosure issue in context*

The Criminal Procedure and Investigations Act 1996 ("CPIA") instituted a new regime of pre-trial disclosure of material in criminal cases. This made significant changes to the common law which had previously applied.[24] The duties of disclosure imposed by the CPIA are aimed at ensuring fair disclosure of material that may be relevant to an investigation and that does not form part of the prosecution case. Disclosure under the CPIA takes place primarily as part of the preparations for *trial*.[25] Thus, where the accused is to be tried on indictment, the prosecution's duty of disclosure under s.3 of the CPIA arises only after committal.[26] However, issues of disclosure may arise much earlier in the proceedings, including the stages that take place in the police station, in connection with decisions to be made before trial. Such disclosure issues continue to be regulated by common law, which is still in the process of development (see below). Not only is the law on disclosure in criminal proceedings somewhat complex as a result, but there is considerable concern that the CPIA does not work satisfactorily in practice.[27]

9–006

It is important to note the institutional context of the disclosure issue, because the traditional arrangements for the investigation of offences, and the imbalance of resources between state and defendant,[28] produce an inherent conflict. The state bears the primary responsibility for investigating suspected offences through the official agencies it funds, most notably the police, but also including customs

---

[20] CPR r.32.10.

[21] Litigation privilege is discussed in Ch.10.

[22] CPR r.32.5(5).

[23] This section now deals only with the general principles of disclosure under the Criminal Procedure and Investigations Act 1996. For the historical background to the present law see the fourth edition of this book, and for further detail readers are advised to consult specialist works on criminal procedure.

[24] See *Ward* (1993) 96 Cr.App.R. 1; *Keane* (1994) 99 Cr.App.R. 1.

[25] See the *Attorney-General's Guidelines on Disclosure* (2005), para.3

[26] CPIA s.1(2)(a).

[27] See the Auld Review of the Criminal Courts of England and Wales (2001), pp.444–476; the review by Gross L.J., *Review of Disclosure in Criminal Proceedings* (2011), and the review by Gross and Treacy LJ.J., *Further review of disclosure in criminal proceedings: sanctions for disclosure failure* (2012), the latter reviews available at www.judiciary.gov.uk [Accessed January 2013].

[28] A point recognised by Lloyd L.J. in *McIlkenny* (1991) 93 Cr.App.R. 287 at 312 CA (the "Birmingham Six" case).

and excise officers, tax inspectors, trading standards officers, and so on. The defence very rarely have the money, the time or the expertise to carry out a full investigation, quite apart from the fact that they lack the statutory investigative powers available to official agencies. The defence may interview potential defence witnesses, and may commission scientific investigations, but generally and inevitably they have to rely on the police doing the investigation as thoroughly as possible.

Consequently the defence have a strong interest in gaining access to all the fruits of the police investigation. This is the only way in which the principle of "equality of arms", one of the foundations of the adversarial system of adjudication, can be roughly upheld. However, any obligation placed on the prosecution to disclose unused material inevitably involves the police in considering whether they have acquired material that could help the defence, and in making such material available. This sets up a potential conflict in that it requires the police to act in a way that is inconsistent with their occupational interest in building a case against the accused. Research has suggested that this interest may sometimes lead the police to marginalise or repress any information that does not fit the police case.[29] There is no doubt that non-disclosure by the police of important evidence for the defence has contributed to some serious miscarriages of justice.[30] A further problem can arise where other official investigators, such as forensic scientists or pathologists, identify with the prosecution and fail to disclose information that would significantly assist the defence.[31]

9–007   These systemic problems still exist,[32] although important efforts have been made to address them First, under the Code of Practice issued under Pt II of the CPIA, investigating officers have a duty to record all information received and to make disclosure of it to the prosecutor.[33] Secondly, the Code of Practice requires an investigator to pursue all reasonable lines of inquiry, whether these point towards or away from the suspect.[34] If the police are aware of a possible defence there is a duty to investigate it. Thirdly, the Court of Appeal has repeatedly stressed that expert witnesses like forensic scientists and pathologists have, in addition to the duty which they owe to the party retaining their services, an overriding duty to

---

[29] M. McConville, A. Sanders and R. Leng, *The Case for the Prosecution* (1991), Ch.4 esp. pp.65–75. For further discussion of police interviewing strategies see A. Sanders, R. Young and M. Burton, *Criminal Justice*, 4th edn (Oxford: Oxford University Press, 2010), Ch.5.

[30] For some well-known examples see *Stefan Kiszko, The Times* February 19, 1992; *Judith Ward* (1993) 96 Cr.App.R. 1; *Taylor and Taylor* (1994) 98 Cr.App.R. 361.

[31] See, e.g. *Maguire* [1992] Q.B. 396; *Judith Ward* (1993) 96 Cr.App.R. 1; *Sally Clark* [2003] EWCA Crim 1020.

[32] Other problems identified in the reviews mentioned above include inadequate training of police disclosure officers, late and/or incomplete disclosure by the CPS and an over-abundance of guidance on the operation of the CPIA. The guidance includes the Code of Practice, the Attorney-General's Guidelines of 2005, the Protocol of 2006, the Attorney-General's *Supplementary Guidelines on Disclosure: Digitally Stored Material* of 2011, and the Criminal Procedure Rules 2012.

[33] Code of Practice paras 4.1, 4.4, 7.1 onwards.

[34] Code of Practice para.3.5. See also PACE Code C para.11B, and the *Attorney-General's Guidelines on Disclosure* (2005), paras 36 and 37, setting out the duty of prosecutors to advise investigators to pursue reasonable lines of inquiry pointed to by the defence statement.

the court; these duties include an obligation to disclose all their relevant data.[35] Fourthly, the Code for Crown Prosecutors, made under statutory authority, states that prosecutors must be "fair, independent and objective".[36] It is their duty to make sure that the right person is prosecuted for the right offence. In doing this "they must always act in the interests of justice and not solely for the purpose of obtaining a conviction". They also have a specific obligation to make sure that all relevant evidence is put before the court.[37] In *R. v H and C*,[38] Lord Bingham referred to the duty of prosecuting counsel as not to obtain a conviction at all costs but to act as a minister of justice. This imposes "a duty to see that all available legal proof of the facts is presented: it should be done firmly and pressed to its legitimate strength but it must also be done fairly".[39]

The prosecution have for many years had a duty to disclose to the defence the evidence on which they propose to rely at committal proceedings for an indictable offence.[40] Since 1985 a similar duty has existed in respect of either way offences.[41] These duties require the prosecution to serve the defence with copies of written statements by the persons whom the prosecution propose to call as witnesses at the trial. The critical question then is how much of the *other* material gathered in the investigation the prosecution must disclose, even if they do not propose to use that material in evidence at trial. In any large investigation the volume of unused material[42] will be very considerable. Some of the material may simply be irrelevant. Some of it may tend to undermine the prosecution case, for example inconsistent statements by prosecution witnesses or negative results of scientific tests. There may be statements supporting the defence by witnesses whom the prosecution do not regard as credible. There may be information about the character of witnesses, such as their criminal records, and so on.

2.   *Disclosure from arrest to committal*

As noted above, the period from arrest to committal is not covered by the duties set out in the CPIA. It is clear that the common law as stated in *Keane,*[43] the leading case before the CPIA, does not apply. This would require more disclosure

9–008

---

[35] See above, and *Harris* [2005] EWCA Crim 1980; [2006] 1 Cr.App.R. 5; *R. v B(T)* [2006] EWCA Crim 417; [2006] 2 Cr.App.R. 3.

[36] Code for Crown Prosecutors (2013), para.2.4.

[37] Code for Crown Prosecutors (2013), para.2.2.

[38] *R. v H and C* [2004] UKHL 3; [2004] 2 Cr.App.R. 10.

[39] *Boucher v R.* [1955] S.C.R. 16 at 24–25 Sup. Ct. of Canada per Rand J.

[40] The requirements for service of the written statements, depositions etc admissible in evidence in the modern form of committal proceedings are contained in the Magistrates' Court Act 1980 ss.5A–5F.

[41] Magistrates' Courts (Advance Information) Rules 1985 (SI 1985/601), made pursuant to Criminal Law Act 1977 s.48. Paragraph 57 of the *Attorney-General's Guidelines on Disclosure* (2005) extends disclosure requirements by stating that the prosecutor should provide to the defence all evidence upon which the Crown proposes to rely in a summary trial. Such provision should allow the accused or their legal advisers sufficient time properly to consider the evidence before it is called.

[42] In *Saunders* unreported September 29, 1989 Henry J. ruled that "it is clear the term 'unused material' may apply to virtually all material collected during the investigation of a case". See R. Card and R. Ward, *The Criminal Procedure and Investigations Act 1996* (Bristol: 1996), para.2.23.

[43] *Keane* [1994] 1 W.L.R. 746 CA.

than the Act and would make the Act redundant.[44] However, it is also clear that some duty of disclosure rests on both the police and the prosecution during this period.[45] In relation to the police there is authority that they may have to make such disclosure as is necessary to enable the defendant's solicitor to give his client informed legal advice. In *DPP v Ara*,[46] a solicitor was advising a client whether to accept the offer of a police caution. He requested disclosure of a copy of an earlier taped interview in which the client made an admission that rendered him suitable for caution. The police refused disclosure whereupon the solicitor advised against acceptance of the caution. The Divisional Court upheld the justices' decision to stay the subsequent prosecution as an abuse of process. The question of whether a defendant should accept a caution was inextricably linked to his entitlement to legal advice. A necessary condition of informed legal advice was that the solicitor knew accurately the terms of the interview on the basis of which the police were prepared to issue a caution. Rose L.J. made it clear that there is no general duty on the police to disclose material before charge; this would often be impracticable and in some cases highly undesirable, as where there was an ongoing investigation.

Nevertheless, *Ara* is a welcome recognition of the need for sufficient disclosure in the earlier stages of criminal process to enable informed legal advice to be given about crucial decisions that a defendant may have to make. Another example of such a decision is whether to answer police questions in interview. A solicitor cannot give informed advice without knowing the nature of the case against the defendant, and this will require the police to make adequate disclosure for this purpose.[47]

Disclosure by the prosecution before committal was considered by the Divisional Court in *R. v DPP Ex p. Lee*.[48] On an application for judicial review of a prosecutor's refusal to make disclosure before committal to the extent requested by the defence, the court held that the defence had asked for too much too soon and the prosecution had offered too little too late. After reviewing the common law authorities and the scheme of the CPIA Kennedy L.J. stated that some disclosure might be required before committal but that it could not normally exceed the duty under the Act of primary disclosure after committal. The test is what justice and fairness requires of the responsible prosecutor in the circumstances of each case.[49] The application of this very general test again appears to involve consideration of what is necessary to enable the defendant to participate effectively in the proceedings against him. Kennedy L.J. gave a number of examples of the kind of material that ought to be disclosed under the test[50]:

---

[44] *R. v DPP Ex p. Lee* [1999] 2 Cr.App.R. 304 at 317–318 CA.
[45] As anticipated by CPIA s.3(1)(a).
[46] *DPP v Ara* [2001] 4 All E.R. 559 DC.
[47] See the discussion of s.34 of the Criminal Justice and Public Order Act 1994 in Ch.5.
[48] *R. v DPP Ex p. Lee* [1999] 2 Cr.App.R. 304.
[49] *R. v DPP Ex p. Lee* [1999] 2 Cr.App.R. 304 at 317–318. See also the *Attorney-General's Guidelines on Disclosure* (2005), para.55.
[50] *R. v DPP Ex p. Lee* [1999] 2 Cr.App.R. 304 at 318.

"(a)   Previous convictions of a complainant or deceased if that information could reasonably be expected to assist the defence when applying for bail.

(b)   Material which might enable a defendant to make a pre-committal application to stay the proceedings as an abuse of process.

(c)   Material which might enable a defendant to submit that he should only be committed for trial on a lesser charge, or perhaps that he should not be committed for trial at all.

(d)   Material which will enable the defendant and his legal advisors to make preparations for trial which may be significantly less effective if disclosure is delayed (e.g. names of eyewitnesses who the prosecution do not intend to use)."

These are all what might be called "purpose-specific" situations. In most cases **9–009** the duty of disclosure is likely to be triggered by a request from the defence for particular material, although a prosecutor might become aware of a need to make disclosure of material from his own consideration of the papers.[51] However, the prosecutor does not at this stage have to review the whole file, as the duty of disclosure under the CPIA requires him to do after committal. Still less does he have to make what Kennedy L.J. described as "full blown common law discovery" at the pre-committal stage.[52]

3.   The Criminal Procedure and Investigations Act 1996

(A)   The scheme of the Act

The original scheme of the CPIA[53] was amended by the Criminal Justice Act **9–010** 2003. The amended scheme applies in respect of investigations that began on or after April 4, 2005. The amended disclosure provisions of the CPIA need to be read together with the revised edition of the Code of Practice issued under the Act, and the revised Attorney-General's Guidelines on Disclosure applicable to the amended scheme. There is also a Protocol for the control and management of unused material in the Crown Court, the origins and status of which are somewhat obscure,[54] but it has received the blessing of the Court of Appeal, which has said that it should be applied by trial judges.[55]

The CPIA provides for a staged scheme of disclosure. In summary the prosecutor has an initial duty of disclosure of any unused material that might reasonably be considered capable of undermining the case for the prosecution or of assisting the case for the accused. Following initial disclosure the defence has a duty to provide a defence statement setting out the nature of the accused's defence and a number of accompanying details. The prosecutor has a continuing duty of disclosure of any further material which satisfies the test for initial disclosure. We will now look at the scheme in more detail.

---

[51] "Where the need for such disclosure is not apparent to the prosecutor, any disclosure will depend on what the defendant chooses to reveal about the defence": *Attorney-General's Guidelines on Disclosure* (2005), para.56.

[52] *R. v DPP Ex p. Lee* [1999] 2 Cr.App.R. 304 at 318.

[53] For the history and details of the original scheme see previous editions of this book.

[54] The Protocol was issued on February 20, 2006. The text is set out in *Archbold* (2013 edn), Appendix N-52. Its origins and status are critically examined in *Criminal Law Week* 2006/08/51.

[55] *R. v K (Note)* [2006] EWCA Crim 724; [2006] 2 All E.R. 552.

(B)   The prosecutor's duties of disclosure

9–011   A "criminal investigation" is defined as:

> "an investigation which police officers or other persons have a duty to conduct with a view to its being ascertained—
> (a)   whether a person should be charged with an offence, or
> (b)   whether a person charged with an offence is guilty of it."[56]

The Code of Practice explains that this definition includes investigations into crimes that have been committed, investigations whose purpose is to ascertain whether a crime has been committed, with a view to the possible institution of criminal proceedings, and investigations that begin in the belief that a crime may be committed, for example, when the police keep premises or individuals under observation for a period of time, with a view to the possible institution of criminal proceedings.[57] Accordingly, the beginning of an investigation is not restricted to cases where the police respond to a report that an offence has been committed or investigate a suspected offence. An investigation can begin before any offence is committed, as may well happen in cases of intelligence-led policing involving surveillance or covert operations.

Under the amended s.3 of the CPIA the prosecutor has an initial duty of disclosure. Subsection (1) provides that the prosecutor must:

> "(a)   disclose to the accused any prosecution material which has not previously been disclosed to the accused and which might reasonably be considered capable of undermining the case for the prosecution or of assisting the case for the accused, or
> (b)   give to the accused a written statement that there is no material of a description mentioned in paragraph (a)."

9–012   "Material" has a very wide definition that takes in material of all kinds, including information and objects of all descriptions.[58] It will thus include all documents, all items of real evidence, information stored on computer and so on. Where information is given orally during an investigation it should be recorded[59]; the record of it will be disclosable. "Prosecution material" is defined as material:

> "(a)   which is in the prosecutor's possession, and came into his possession in connection with the case for the prosecution against the accused; or
> (b)   which, in pursuance of a code operative under Part II, he has inspected in connection with the case for the prosecution against the accused."[60]

Paragraph (b) covers material in the hands of the police or of third parties that the prosecutor has seen, but is not (yet) in his possession. Under the Code of Practice the investigating police officer is required to make a record of all relevant

---

[56]   CPIA s.1(4). "Other persons" will include customs and excise officers, trading standards officers and numerous other officials employed by investigatory agencies. By s.26(1) of the Act other persons having a duty to conduct a criminal investigation must have regard to any relevant provision of the Code of Practice which would apply if they were police officers.

[57]   Code of Practice, para.2.1.

[58]   CPIA s.2(4).

[59]   See ss.3(4), 23(3) and the Code of Practice, para.4.1.

[60]   CPIA s.3(2).

information obtained in the investigation.[61] This will include information that comes to the knowledge of investigators as a result of liaison with third parties, such as doctors, accountants, local authorities and so on.[62] The police "disclosure officer", who may or may not be the same person as the investigating officer, is responsible for examining the material retained during the investigation and revealing material to the prosecutor during the investigation.[63] This task involves the preparation of schedules of unused material, divided into sensitive and non-sensitive material.[64] The prosecutor is entitled to inspect any material not already copied to him by the police. As noted above, experts such as forensic scientists who are retained for the purposes of the investigation, have a duty at common law to disclose to the prosecutor material of which they know and that may have a bearing on the offence charged and the surrounding circumstances of the case.[65]

The test set out in s.3 is an objective test of material that might *reasonably* be considered capable of undermining the prosecution case or of assisting the case for the accused. The use of the single objective test at the initial stage is a considerable improvement on the previous law which provided for different tests at different stages of disclosure, leading to much confusion and disparity of application. Two situations in particular are now clarified. Where the prosecution know what the defence is likely to be (for example, from interview or a prepared statement) any unused material tending to support the defence is now disclosable in advance of the defence statement, even if it does not undermine the prosecution case. Any material that could reasonably be considered capable of undermining the prosecution case must be disclosed, even if the prosecutor himself thinks it does not. It will not matter at this stage that the defence may be unknown or not apparent from the prosecution papers. There is an exception from the duty of disclosure for material that it is not in the public interest to disclose,[66] and the prosecutor must not disclose material the disclosure of which is prohibited by s.17 of the Regulation of Investigatory Powers Act 2000 (relating to the product of intercepted communications).[67]

Section 7A of the CPIA creates a continuing duty of disclosure on the prosecution. The duty arises after compliance with the duty of initial disclosure under s.3, and runs until the accused is convicted or acquitted or the prosecutor decides not to continue with the case.[68] The duty imposes the same test for continuing disclosure as for initial disclosure and is subject to the same savings. Since the duty is one of continuing review of prosecution material, disclosure under s.7A is not dependent on the giving of a defence statement, although if the accused does give a defence statement any disclosure required under the section must be made within specified time limits.

9–013

---

[61] Code of Practice para.4.4.

[62] See *Attorney-General's Guidelines on Disclosure* (2005), para.53.

[63] Code of Practice para.2.1.

[64] Code of Practice paras 6.2–6.4. The treatment of "sensitive" material is dealt with in paras 6.12–6.14.

[65] *Maguire* [1992] 2 All E.R. 433 at 447 CA.

[66] CPIA s.3(6). On public interest immunity see further below.

[67] CPIA s.3(7).

[68] CPIA s.7A(1).

The Attorney-General's Guidelines on Disclosure list examples of material that might be considered capable of undermining the prosecution case or of assisting the case for the accused.[69] The list is clearly not intended to be exhaustive, and some of the categories of material overlap, but it is useful to indicate the scope of the duty of disclosure by giving some illustrations based on the list:

- "Any material casting doubt upon the accuracy of any prosecution evidence." The prosecution rely on a forensic scientist's report that swabs taken from D's hands after his arrest show that he had recently handled explosives. A second report indicates that the test employed by the forensic scientist is not specific for explosives, and that handling other substances could give a positive result. The second report must be disclosed.
- "Any material which may point to another person, whether charged or not (including a co-accused) having involvement in the commission of the offence." The prosecution rely on a statement by an eyewitness W identifying D as the offender. A statement by another eyewitness X identifies as the offender someone else or a person of a different description from D. X's statement must be disclosed.
- "Any material which may cast doubt upon the reliability of a confession." The prosecution rely on a taped interview in which D admitted murder. The tape of a second interview a day later reveals that D repeated the admission but added some details that the police know are untrue. The tape of the second interview must be disclosed.
- "Any material that might go to the credibility of a prosecution witness." The prosecution rely on an identification of D as the offender by an eyewitness W who picked out D on a parade. The prosecutor is in possession of a statement by W to the police in which W gave a description of the offender that does not match D's appearance. W's statement must be disclosed. If W has a previous conviction that fact must be disclosed.
- "Any material that might support a defence that is either raised by the defence or apparent from the prosecution papers." D is interviewed without the benefit of legal advice and admits 'stealing' a policeman's helmet during a drunken spree, not knowing that the crime of theft requires an intention permanently to deprive the owner of the property appropriated. The prosecutor is in possession of a statement by an eyewitness who states that he heard the defendant tell the officer that he was only borrowing the helmet. The statement must be disclosed.
- "Any material which may have a bearing on the admissibility of any prosecution evidence." D admits in a taped interview to robbery. He later retracts the admission and alleges that he made it as the result of threats by the interviewing officer to charge his wife with the offence. A prisoner E, who was in the cell next to D in the police station, has stated to the police that he heard the officer making this threat to D. E's statement must be disclosed. It is immaterial that the police and prosecutor believe that E is lying.

---

[69] Guidelines on Disclosure para.12.

The Guidelines also provide important guidance to investigators and prosecutors who know or believe that third parties, including government departments, are in possession of material that might be relevant to an issue in the case. Reasonable steps should be taken to try to procure the material for consideration and possible disclosure.[70]

Non-disclosure of material that satisfies the statutory test for disclosure will provide a ground of appeal against conviction. If the material might have significantly assisted the defence the Court of Appeal is likely to quash the conviction as unsafe.[71]

9–014

(C) Defence disclosure

Section 5(5) of the CPIA imposes a duty on the accused, where he is charged with an indictable offence and the prosecution have complied with the duty of initial disclosure under s.3, to give a defence statement to the court and the prosecutor. Section 5A, which was inserted by the Criminal Justice Act 2003 and which is not in force at the time of writing, empowers the court to order an accused to give a defence statement to any other accused in the proceedings. However, it should be noted in this connection that if an accused gives to the prosecutor a defence statement that might reasonably be considered to assist the case of a co-accused the prosecutor should disclose that statement to the co-accused under the prosecutor's duty of continuing disclosure.[72] Under s.6, where the accused is charged with a summary offence or an either way offence that is to be tried summarily, and the prosecution have given initial disclosure, the accused may voluntarily give a defence statement.

9–015

The contents of the defence statement are prescribed by s.6A. Subsection (1) provides that a defence statement is a written statement:

(a) setting out the nature of the accused's defence, including any particular defences on which he intends to rely;

(b) indicating the matters of fact on which he takes issue with the prosecution;

(c) setting out, in the case of each such matter, why he takes issue with the prosecution;

---

[70] See paras 47–52. See also *Brushett* [2001] Crim. L.R. 471; *Protocol for the Control and Management of Unused Material in the Crown Court* (2006), paras 52–62. On the duties of the prosecutor when material is in the hands of third parties abroad in countries outside the European Union see *R. v RF* [2009] EWCA Crim 678. Where material in the hands of third parties, such as records relating to children in the social security files of local authorities, is ordered to be disclosed, the judge may limit the use of the material and order that the relevant documents may not be put before the jury without his agreement: *R. v J (DC)* [2010] EWCA Crim 385; [2010] 2 Cr.App.R. 2.

[71] For recent examples see *Barkshire* [2011] EWCA Crim 1885; [2012] Crim. L.R. 453; *Joof* [2012] EWCA Crim 1475.

[72] See *Cairns* [2003] EWCA Crim 2838; [2003] 1 Cr.App.R. 38 at [78], referring to the prosecutor's obligation under the original scheme of the CPIA to give secondary disclosure, but the reasoning is equally applicable to the duty of continuing disclosure under the amended scheme, and is reinforced, as the Court of Appeal said, by the right of the co-accused under art.6(3)(b) of the ECHR to have adequate time and facilities for the preparation of his defence.

(ca)   setting out particulars of the matters of fact on which he intends to rely for the purposes of his defence[73]; and

(d)   indicating any point of law (including any point as to the admissibility of evidence or an abuse of process) that he wishes to take, and any authority on which he intends to rely for that purpose.

Subsection (2) provides that a defence statement that discloses an alibi must give particulars of it, including the name, address and date of birth of any witness the accused believes is able to give evidence in support of the alibi, or as many of those details as are known to the accused when the statement is given.

9–016   Under s.6E a defence statement given by the accused's solicitor on his behalf is deemed to be given with his authority unless the contrary is proved. The effect of this is that even if the accused has not signed the statement it will still be regarded as his statement made by his authorised agent. That means that the statement will be admissible as part of the prosecution case if it contains admissions, or inconsistencies with the accused's testimony at trial.[74] The judge may direct that a defence statement is to be given to the jury if the judge thinks that seeing a copy of the statement would help the jury to understand the case or resolve any issue in the case.[75] The judge can make this direction of his own motion. But since this provision envisages the jury being able to use the statement as evidence in the case it would seem necessary that the statement should first be admitted in evidence in the normal way.

As regards the content of a defence statement, the accused is now required to specify his defence with particularity. Under the original CPIA scheme the requirement was simply to set out the accused's defence "in general terms". Particular defences for the purposes of s.6A will clearly include any general defence in criminal law, such as self-defence or duress. Special statutory defences, such as due diligence or reasonable excuse, will also be included, and presumably the nature of any such excuse should be spelt out. Also included will be "defences" that deny elements of the offence, such as absence of causation, lack of intention or knowledge, mistake, intoxication. The defence are also required to indicate the matters of *fact* on which they take issue, as against the original requirement to indicate the *matters* on which they took issue. The significance of this change is unclear. During proceedings in Parliament on the Criminal Justice Bill the Government denied that it would mean civil-style pleading to all allegations of fact in the prosecution's witness statements. It was suggested that the requirement related to the "main facts" alleged by the

---

[73] Subsection (1)(ca) was added by the Criminal Justice and Immigration Act 2008 s.60(1). It does not apply in relation to offences into which a criminal investigation began before April 4, 2005, or in relation to cases to which Pt I of the CPIA applied by virtue of s.1(1) or (2) before November 3, 2008.

[74] However, where the statement is inconsistent with an earlier statement by D's counsel on a PCMH form, the Court of Appeal has said that the court should use its discretion under s.78 of PACE to exclude the earlier statement where it is satisfied that the defence were conducting the case in accordance with the letter and spirit of the Criminal Procedure Rules: *Newell* [2012] EWCA Crim 650; [2012] 2 Cr.App.R. 10, not following the decision of the Divisional Court in *R. (on the application of Firth) v Epping Magistrates' Court* [2011] EWHC 388 (Admin); [2011] 1 Cr.App.R. 32.

[75] CPIA s.6E(4) and (5).

prosecution,[76] but this construction of the provision is not obvious and would seem to need judicial authority or delegated legislation.[77] The duty to indicate points of law to be taken and the authorities to be relied on seems unobjectionable.

The Criminal Justice Act 2003 inserted three further defence duties into the CPIA. Section 6B creates a duty of updated defence disclosure. An accused who gives a compulsory or voluntary defence statement will have a duty to update it if changes are needed. This is the counterpart to the prosecution's duty of continuing disclosure under s.7A and does not raise any issues of principle. The section has not yet been brought into force.

9–017

Section 6C requires the accused to give to the court and the prosecutor a notice indicating whether he intends to call any persons as witnesses (other than himself) at his trial. If so, he has to give their names, addresses and dates of birth, or information to assist in identifying or finding any such witness. The duty does not extend to indicating the evidence that the witnesses will give, or even the issues to which their evidence will relate. This requirement was and remains controversial. Concerns were expressed, particularly by defence lawyers, about police wishing to interview defence witnesses and, whether or not consciously, frightening them off giving testimony in support of the accused. Section 40 of the Criminal Justice Act 2003 attempted to address this concern by providing for the Home Secretary to prepare a Code of Practice for police interviews of witnesses notified by the defence.[78] Accordingly the Code includes guidance in relation to information to be given to the interviewee and the accused about such an interview, notification to the accused's solicitor of the interview, attendance of the interviewee's solicitor and the accused's solicitor, and the attendance of an appropriate person taking account of the age or disability of the interviewee. It is unclear as yet whether the fears about possible intimidation of defence witnesses were well-founded.

Section 6D, which has not yet been brought into force, requires the accused to notify the court and the prosecutor of the names and addresses of any experts he instructs with a view to the expert providing an expert opinion for possible use at the accused's trial. The duty is only to disclose the expert's name and address. The section does not override litigation privilege so as to require disclosure of any unused experts' reports.[79] In these circumstances the question arises as to what is the point of this disclosure. There is no property in a witness,[80] so the prosecution can if they wish interview the expert with the aim of soliciting his opinion. But the expert may not reveal any of the instructions from the accused since these are privileged, and if his opinion cannot readily be severed from the instructions the opinion is privileged as well.[81] In most cases it seems likely that

---

[76] See *Hansard*, Standing Committee B, col.234, January 9, 2003.

[77] CPIA s.6A(4) empowers the Home Secretary to make regulations as to the details of the matters to be included in defence statements.

[78] For critical discussion see P. Hungerford-Welch, "Prosecution Interviews of Defence Witnesses" [2010] Crim. L.R. 690.

[79] If the accused intends to call the expert as a witness he will have to disclose the expert's evidence in advance: Criminal Procedure Rules 2012 Pt 33.

[80] See the discussion of litigation privilege in Ch.10.

[81] See *R. v R* [1994] 4 All E.R. 260.

the prosecution will not be able to get anything useful out of knowing about the defence's unused experts, apart from the fact that the accused may have shopped around for a supportive expert opinion. It is not clear what use the prosecution could or would want to make of this fact. It is submitted that this duty of notification is therefore largely a waste of time.

9–018   Where the accused is at fault in the disclosure procedure, for example the accused fails to give a defence statement under s.5, or gives it late, or departs at trial from the defence put forward in a defence statement, then under the amended CPIA s.11(5):

> "(a)   the court or any other party may make such comment as appears appropriate;
> (b)   the court or jury may draw such inferences as appear proper in deciding whether the accused is guilty of the offence concerned."

There is an obvious parallel here with the provisions of the Criminal Justice and Public Order Act 1994 relating to the accused's failure to mention facts in interview[82] and failure to testify in defence at trial.[83] Those who take a strong view of the accused's right to silence as founded on the presumption of innocence oppose s.5 in principle; Zander's forthright Note of Dissent to the report of the Royal Commission on Criminal Justice[84] is a good example. Zander argued that because the burden of proof lies on the prosecution throughout, the defendant's only task is to defend himself. "[It] is wrong to require the defendant to be helpful by giving advance notice of his defence and to penalise him by adverse comment if he fails to do so".[85] The Royal Commission had proposed the introduction of defence disclosure for essentially pragmatic reasons: it would prevent ambush defences, facilitate better trial preparation, encourage guilty pleas or discontinuances by the prosecution, and improve efficiency by enabling better estimates of length and cost of trial. Some of these reasons have been challenged—in particular, there is much dispute about the frequency of ambush defences and the alleged difficulty prosecutors have in meeting them.[86] Zander's objection raised a fundamental question of principle, but this in turn was challenged. Uglow argued that defence disclosure would promote the goal of truth-finding by defining the issues to be decided and how the parties intend to answer the other's evidence. He suggested that "concealment of evidence until a late stage by either side necessarily leads to the jury being unable to assess the weight or probative quality of such evidence".[87]

---

[82]   CJPOA s.34, discussed in Ch.5.

[83]   CJPOA s.35, discussed in Ch.13.

[84]   RCCJ Report p.221.

[85]   RCCJ Report, Note of Dissent para.2.

[86]   Zander's study for the RCCJ (M. Zander and P. Henderson, *Crown Court Study*, RCCJ Research Study No.19, (London, 1993)) found considerable differences in perception of the frequency of ambush defences. Prosecution counsel saw them in 7% of cases, the CPS 10% and the police 23%. Counsel saw them as a serious problem in 3% of cases.

[87]   S. Uglow, *Evidence Text and Materials* (London: Sweet & Maxwell, 1997), p.319. See also the support for the principle of defence statements in the Auld Review pp.454–462. For further discussion see the thoughtful article by Redmayne, "Criminal Justice Act 2003 (1) Disclosure and its Discontents" [2004] Crim. L.R. 441, esp. 449–454.

It is now clear that the requirement of defence disclosure is not incompatible with art.6 of the ECHR. It does not violate the presumption of innocence in art.6(2) because s.5, like s.34 of the Criminal Justice and Public Order Act 1994, does nothing to alter the burden of proof in criminal cases. The prosecution will still have to prove the defendant's guilt beyond reasonable doubt at the trial. A second line of attack might be founded on the privilege against self-incrimination. It might be argued that requiring the defendant to state how much of the prosecution's case he disputes is indirectly requiring him to incriminate himself. He is in effect being compelled to make admissions by the threat of adverse inferences at the trial if he fails to make a defence statement or if he departs from the statement made. However, any adverse inferences are only permissive and not mandatory, and a person cannot be convicted solely on an inference drawn under s.11(5).[88] In *Essa*,[89] the Court of Appeal was in no doubt that s.11(5) of the CPIA is compatible with art.6. Making an analogy with s.34 of the Criminal Justice and Public Order Act 1994, the court referred to the power of judicial control over the Crown's right to comment on the absence of a defence statement. The judge can intervene to prevent unfair cross-examination of the defendant on the issue, and direct the jury to ignore such cross-examination if necessary. Similarly in *Rochford*,[90] the Court of Appeal insisted that both the privilege against self-incrimination and legal professional privilege survive the duty to give a defence statement:

> "What the defendant is required to disclose by s 6A is what is going to happen at the trial. He is not required to disclose his confidential discussions with his advocate, although of course they may bear on what is going to happen at the trial. Nor is he obliged to incriminate himself if he does not want to. Those are fundamental rights and they have certainly not been taken away by s 6A ..."[91]

It follows, as the Court of Appeal said, that the defendant can, if he wishes, still sit back and put the prosecution to proof of their case. But if the defendant wishes to put forward any form of positive case, as opposed to making a simple denial of guilt, then this must be set out in the defence statement. The judge is entitled to ask "insistently and trenchantly" about the nature of the defence to be put, but the judge is not entitled to require counsel to reveal the defendant's instructions. Equally the judge has no power to find the defendant to be in contempt of court if the defendant refuses to comply with a direction to amplify a defective defence statement. In *Rochford* the Court of Appeal quashed a finding of contempt in these circumstances on the ground that the sanction for non-compliance with the statutory obligation to give a defence statement is in s.11 of the CPIA. It was not

---

[88] CPIA s.11(10). The European Court of Human Rights would probably say that art.6 requires convictions not to be based "solely or mainly" on adverse inferences under s.11, by parity of reasoning with adverse inferences from failure to mention facts in interview under s.34 of the Criminal Justice and Public Order Act 1994. See Ch.5.

[89] *Essa* [2009] EWCA Crim 43. It was claimed that no defence statement had been served on legal advice, to which the Court of Appeal responded by saying that it did not understand how any lawyer could give such advice in view of the duty created by s.5 of the CPIA. The *Protocol for the Control and Management of Unused Material in the Crown Court* (2006) contains stern warnings to defence lawyers to comply with the statutory duty and give full and detailed defence statements: paras 34–42.

[90] *Rochford* [2010] EWCA Crim 1928; [2011] 1 Cr.App.R. 11.

[91] *Rochford* [2010] EWCA Crim 1928; [2011] 1 Cr.App.R. 11 at [21].

open to the court to add an extra-statutory sanction of punishment for contempt. The recent review by Gross and Treacy LJ.J. of sanctions for non-disclosure[92] does not recommend any additional sanctions for failures by the defence.

D.   PUBLIC INTEREST IMMUNITY IN CIVIL PROCEEDINGS

1.   *General principles*

(A)   *The nature of the claim for public interest immunity*

9–019   In civil proceedings documents may be withheld from production if their disclosure would be contrary to the public interest. This is known as the rule of public interest immunity. The rule applies at all stages of civil proceedings, including the trial where it may be invoked to prevent witnesses adducing in evidence documents that ought not in the public interest to be revealed.[93] In practice, the question of the immunity is most likely to arise at the stage of disclosure, where it can give rise to lengthy interlocutory proceedings.

Until 1973 the rule was often referred to as the rule of "Crown privilege",[94] reflecting the fact that most claims to the immunity were made on behalf of central government by ministers of the Crown. In *Rogers v Home Secretary*,[95] Lord Reid said that this term was wrong and misleading. An evidential privilege, such as legal professional privilege, can only be claimed by the person who has the privilege, and can be freely waived by that person. Lord Reid pointed out that it is open to any person to assert that the public interest requires non-disclosure,[96] although a minister of the Crown will often be the most appropriate person to do so.

There are two other reasons for rejecting the concept of "Crown privilege". The first concerns the difference between an immunity and a privilege. The doctrine of public interest immunity operates as an exclusionary rule of the law of evidence. If it is not in the public interest to disclose certain documents, then no evidence of them will be admissible at trial. It will make no difference that the party seeking disclosure is in a position to give secondary evidence of the document in question.[97] The situation may be different, however, if the party is in

---

[92] See above.

[93] In addition the immunity would logically justify a witness's refusal to give oral evidence of some particular fact that ought not to be disclosed in the public interest, such as a national defence secret.

[94] Although Lord Simon had criticised the use of this expression as early as 1942: *Duncan v Cammell Laird* [1942] A.C. 624 at 641 HL.

[95] *Rogers v Home Secretary* [1973] A.C. 388 HL. The case was on appeal from *R. v Lewes Justices Ex p. Secretary of State for the Home Department*, and is frequently referred to by that name. In this book it is cited as *Rogers v Home Secretary*.

[96] And the judge may have a duty to raise the issue if no one else does so: *Rogers v Home Secretary* [1973] A.C. 388 at 400.

[97] Authority for this logical proposition is not extensive, but see *Cooke v Maxwell* (1817) 2 Stark 183; *Chatterton v Secretary of State for India* [1895] 2 Q.B. 189 at 193 and 195; Lord Simon, "Evidence Excluded by Considerations of State Interest" [1955] C.L.J. 62, 68–72. In *Rogers v Home Secretary* [1973] A.C. 388 the plaintiff had possession of a copy of the document held to be immune from disclosure; it does not appear to have been suggested that the copy was admissible as secondary evidence.

a position to give independent evidence of the matters dealt with by the documents. For example, a court will not generally order disclosure of a document containing the name of an informer who has given information to the police or to a prosecutor,[98] but if the defendant knows the identity of the informer he may give evidence of it if it is relevant to his defence. A privilege, on the other hand, protects only against compelled disclosure; secondary evidence of a privileged document or conversation is admissible at common law.[99]

Secondly, in modern law the immunity is not restricted to the Crown in the sense of the executive or central government. The public interest to be protected may be an interest in the work of local authorities or non-governmental organisations ("NGOs"). An example of the latter is *D v NSPCC*,[100] where the House of Lords held that the defendants, a national charity with certain statutory functions relating to child protection, could invoke the immunity to justify refusing to disclose the name of an informant who had reported a suspected case of child abuse. The court took the view that if anonymity could not be guaranteed to informants, the supply of information to the NSPCC might well dry up and make it more difficult for the Society to carry out its functions. Other examples of the reach of the immunity beyond the executive include confidential information supplied to the Gaming Board,[101] the child protection records of local authorities,[102] and reports by investigating officers into police misconduct made under the statutory procedure for dealing with complaints against the police.[103]

9–020

(B)   Establishing the grounds of a claim

The grounds for a claim of public interest immunity traditionally distinguished between "contents" claims and "class" claims. The distinction went back to the decision of the House of Lords in *Duncan v Cammell Laird*.[104] The plaintiffs were the dependants of a number of the defendants' employees who died when a submarine built by the defendants sank during trials in 1939. The plaintiffs brought an action under the Fatal Accidents Acts, alleging negligence in the construction of the submarine. The defendants had built the submarine under contract with the Admiralty; at the stage of discovery of documents the defendants, acting under instructions from the Admiralty, objected to producing contractual documents relating to the construction of the submarine and the salvage reports. The ground of objection was that production of the documents would endanger national security. Bearing in mind that this was wartime and that the submarine carried secret equipment, the objection was undoubtedly a strong

9–021

---

[98]   *Marks v Beyfus* (1890) 25 Q.B.D. 494, and see the text below.
[99]   See Ch.10.
[100]   *D v NSPCC* [1978] A.C. 171 HL.
[101]   *Rogers v Home Secretary* [1973] A.C. 388 HL.
[102]   *Gaskin v Liverpool City Council* [1980] 1 W.L.R. 1549 CA. cf. *Campbell v Tameside MBC* [1982] Q.B. 1065 CA.
[103]   *Taylor v Anderton* [1995] 2 All E.R. 420 CA.
[104]   *Duncan v Cammell Laird* [1942] A.C. 624.

one.[105] It probably outweighed the importance of the plaintiffs having access to documents that might be crucial to their case. The House of Lords did not, however, engage in any exercise of balancing the importance of the plaintiffs' access to relevant evidence against the need for military secrecy. It was held that the certificate furnished by the minister, the First Lord of the Admiralty, was conclusive on the question whether disclosure would be contrary to the public interest. A certificate in proper form could not be questioned by the court. This was enough to decide the case, but Viscount Simon L.C. went on to deal generally with the grounds for making a claim to withhold documents in the public interest. He stated that the claim could be put on either of two bases:

(1)   a *contents* claim: that disclosure of the contents of particular documents would damage the public interest by, for example, endangering national security or compromising diplomatic relations.
(2)   a *class* claim: that the particular documents belonged to a class of documents which ought not to be disclosed in the interests of "the proper functioning of the public service".

The second basis was much wider than the first. Class claims could extend potentially to vast swathes of official documents, depending on how harm to the proper functioning of the public service was conceived. Such documents might vary greatly in their importance: from minutes of Cabinet meetings, to high-level policy communications between ministers and civil servants, to policy documents of lesser significance, to reports of a routine nature, and so on. For some years following *Duncan v Cammell Laird* there was a tendency for the executive to take full advantage of the apparently wide reach of the law. Class claims were made for all manner of government records, including cases where the need for secrecy was dubious, if not non-existent.[106] This tendency was encouraged by the courts' self-imposed rule that ministerial certificates asserting that disclosure would result in harm to the public interest were conclusive.

Criticism of the law mounted, until in 1968 the House of Lords took the opportunity to abandon the rule that the certificate could not be questioned. In *Conway v Rimmer*,[107] the Home Secretary claimed immunity for five confidential reports on a probationary police constable. The litigation concerned an action for malicious prosecution brought by the constable against his former police superintendent, arising from a prosecution of the constable on a charge of theft of which he had been acquitted. All the reports had been made by the defendant, and both he and the plaintiff believed them to be relevant to the issue of malice and wished them to be disclosed. The House of Lords unanimously reversed the rule derived from *Duncan v Cammell Laird* and held that the court was the final arbiter of whether the public interest required non-disclosure of relevant

---

[105] Although some of the documents in question had already been produced before an earlier tribunal of inquiry into the loss of the submarine, presided over by Bucknill J., and had been referred to in his Report, Cmd.6190 (1940).
[106] Examples include *Ellis v Home Office* [1953] 2 Q.B. 135 CA (Home Office medical and other reports on prisoners); *Broome v Broome* [1955] P. 190 (War Office conciliation records relating to servicemen and their spouses).
[107] *Conway v Rimmer* [1968] A.C. 910.

evidence. The Lords made it clear that the court should balance one public interest against another: the public interest in litigants having access to relevant evidence for the purposes of the adjudication should be set against the public interest, such as the proper functioning of the public service, said to be put in danger of harm by disclosure of documents. After inspecting the reports in question the House of Lords ordered their production. It was very doubtful whether any harm to the public interest would result from disclosure, whereas the reports might prove to be vitally important to the litigation.

Conway v Rimmer was a landmark case. It established that the courts, and not the executive, were the final arbiters of what the public interest requires in the context of adjudication. It also marked the beginning of a trend to question the validity of class claims, a trend that has become more marked in recent years. This point will be developed in more detail below, but first it is necessary to place decisions about the validity of claims to public interest immunity in their procedural context. Just because a claim to immunity is made in pre-trial proceedings does not mean that the court will automatically have to engage in the exercise of balancing different aspects of the public interest.

9–022

(C) Pre-trial procedure and the rules of disclosure

Pre-trial disclosure of documents is complicated by the interaction of the evidential rules with the procedural rules of disclosure. A party to a private law claim is entitled as a general principle to inspect all relevant documents in the possession of the opponent that are not protected by law from disclosure. Therefore the initial burden is on the party resisting disclosure to make out a prima facie case that documents are protected by public interest immunity. This is usually done by means of a certificate from a minister, or other appropriate official, setting out the grounds of the claim. Although the certificate is not conclusive, it will normally be sufficient to satisfy the burden of showing a valid claim unless the grounds stated are plainly inadequate. According to the House of Lords in *Air Canada v Secretary of State for Trade (No.2)*[108] the applicant who seeks an order for discovery of documents that are prima facie protected must first persuade the court to inspect the documents. This requires the party to show that there is a reasonable likelihood that the documents in question will positively assist the party's case,[109] as opposed to having some general relevance to the litigation, and that there is a doubt whether the public interest does require non-disclosure. The first of these requirements is founded on the courts' reluctance to let litigants embark on "fishing expeditions", but it has been justly criticised for its difficulty. How can a party show that the documents are likely to help his case if he has not yet seen them?[110] If strictly applied, this requirement

9–023

---

[108] *Air Canada v Secretary of State for Trade (No.2)* [1983] 2 A.C. 394.
[109] In *Al-Rawi v Security Service* [2011] UKSC 34; [2012] 1 All E.R. 1 at [102], Lord Mance referred to the obligation on the party inviting the court to inspect the material to show that the material "is likely to give substantial support" to the party's case.
[110] Arguably the onus should be on the party resisting disclosure to show that the documents need not be disclosed. One way of demonstrating this would be by showing that they are not likely to assist the applicant's case.

would result in much of the ground gained by *Conway v Rimmer* being lost. The second requirement again brings into play the contents/class distinction. The courts are unlikely to question a ministerial certificate that disclosure of the *contents* of a particular document would be harmful to the public interest,[111] hence they are unlikely to exercise the power to inspect in such a case.[112]

Assuming that the applicant can get over these hurdles, the court may be persuaded to inspect the documents itself to see whether production of them to the applicant is necessary for disposing fairly of the case. This was the procedural rule set out expressly in the former Rules of the Supreme Court.[113] If after inspection the court decides that disclosure is not necessary for disposing fairly of the case, the application can be dismissed on the rules of discovery. This was the outcome in *Burmah Oil Co Ltd v Bank of England*.[114] The plaintiff company (Burmah) had been rescued by the defendant (the Bank) when it ran into acute financial difficulty. The rescue plan included a sale of Burmah shares to the Bank at a price that Burmah subsequently alleged to be unconscionable. In proceedings to have the sale set aside, Burmah sought discovery of documents relating to negotiations that took place between the Bank and the government about the rescue plan. These documents were high-level government policy papers consisting of communications between ministers and/or senior civil servants. The House of Lords held after looking at the documents that they would not materially assist Burmah and refused to order disclosure.

If, on the other hand, the court decides that the documents would assist the applicant, and therefore that disclosure would be necessary for fairly disposing of the case, then the court must apply the evidential rule. This requires the court to balance the public interest in the proper administration of justice, which argues in favour of disclosure, against the public interest in non-disclosure as presented in the certificate setting out the claim. As far as the burden of proof is concerned, there is a heavy burden of proof on any authority that makes a class claim to justify the claim.[115] If the claim is well-founded, so that the court has to balance

---

[111] *Conway v Rimmer* [1968] A.C. 910 at 943 per Lord Reid; *Burmah Oil Co Ltd v Bank of England* [1980] A.C. 1090 at 1143 per Lord Scarman. But in *R. (on the application of Al-Sweady) v Secretary of State for Defence* [2009] EWHC 1687 (Admin), where a Ministerial PII certificate was subsequently admitted to contain false assertions, the Divisional Court stated in a strongly worded judgment that the court would approach the content of future PII certificates from the Ministry of Defence "with very considerable caution" ([25]).

[112] In *Balfour v Foreign Office* [1994] 1 W.L.R. 681 at 688 the Court of Appeal said that the court should not inspect once an actual or potential risk to national security had been demonstrated by an appropriate certificate. This goes too far; where the applicant can show convincingly that the document would materially assist his case the court should be prepared to consider inspection, since it might be possible to order partial disclosure, or restricted disclosure to the applicant's legal advisers.

[113] RSC Ord.24 r.13. It does not appear in terms in the Civil Procedure Rules but may well be an implicit element of the court's duty to give effect to the overriding objective (r.1.2).

[114] *Burmah Oil Co Ltd v Bank of England* [1980] A.C. 1090.

[115] per Lord Reid in *Rogers v Home Secretary* [1973] A.C. 388 at 400 HL; cited by Ackner L.J. in *Campbell v Tameside MBC* [1982] 2 All E.R. 791 at 796 CA; and by Lord Woolf in *R. v Chief Constable of the West Midlands Police Ex p. Wiley* [1995] 1 A.C. 274 at 290.

the public interests in disclosure and non-disclosure, the scales must come down decisively in favour of the party seeking discovery before the court orders disclosure.[116]

(D)   The weakness of class claims

At this point we return to the justification for class claims. Class claims have always been controversial because the objection to disclosure rests not on the sensitivity of the particular documents in question, but on the cogency of the argument for withholding all documents of that type. Such arguments are necessarily general and formalistic, and some of the rationales offered for class claims have attracted much scepticism. In *Duncan v Cammell Laird*, Viscount Simon L.C. referred to protecting a class of communications within a public department because of the danger of prejudicing "the candour and complete-ness"[117] of such communications by the possibility of disclosure.[118] As Le Sueur and Sunkin put it:

9–024

> "[the] concern was the familiar one that if policymakers and their advisors feared that their internal papers could later become public this would discourage free discussion and be detrimental to the quality of governmental decision-making."[119]

However, in *Conway v Rimmer*,[120] Lord Reid gave little weight to the idea that public servants might be inhibited in their communications with one another by the thought of possible disclosure of those communications in civil litigation; as he pointed out, the argument has not prevented disclosure of "class" documents in criminal cases.[121] In *Burmah Oil Co Ltd v Bank of England*,[122] Lord Keith went further, describing the candour argument as "grotesque" and "utterly insubstantial"[123] as a reason for denying a litigant access to relevant evidence. This denunciation should be treated with care. While it may have force when applied to communications between civil servants on matters of general policy, it is less convincing as far as the making of confidential reports on the conduct of individuals is concerned. Frankness of judgment might depend on how far the reporter was assured of confidentiality.

---

[116]   per Lord Edmund-Davies in *Burmah Oil Co Ltd v Bank of England* [1980] A.C. 1090 at 1127 HL, citing Lord Cross in *Alfred Crompton Amusement Machines Ltd v Customs and Excise Commissioners* [1974] A.C. 405 at 434 HL.

[117]   *Duncan v Cammell Laird* [1942] A.C. 624 at 635.

[118]   See also the Parliamentary statement by Viscount Kilmuir L.C. in 1956, concerning future government practice as to claims of Crown privilege, which asserted the need for candour of communication as the justification for class claims: *Hansard*, HL cols 741–748 (June 6, 1956).

[119]   *Public Law* (London: 1997), p.504.

[120]   *Conway v Rimmer* [1968] A.C. 910 HL.

[121]   *Conway v Rimmer* [1968] A.C. 910 at 942. See section D below for further discussion of public interest immunity in criminal proceedings.

[122]   *Burmah Oil Co Ltd v Bank of England* [1980] A.C. 1090 HL.

[123]   *Burmah Oil Co Ltd v Bank of England* [1980] A.C. 1090 at 1133. cf. however, the comments of Lord Wilberforce in *Burmah Oil*, viewing the argument more favourably and saying that it had "received an excessive dose of cold water": [1980] A.C. 1090 at 1112. His comments were cited with apparent approval by Lord Fraser in *Air Canada v Secretary of State for Trade (No.2)* [1983] 2 A.C. 394 at 433 HL.

An alternative argument for class claims, preferred by Lord Reid in *Conway v Rimmer*, is founded on the protection of the public service from unfair criticism, and the difficulty of conducting public administration in the glare of publicity:

> "To my mind the most important reason [sc. for non-disclosure] is that such disclosure would create or fan ill-informed or captious public or political criticism. The business of government is difficult enough as it is, and no government could contemplate with equanimity the inner workings of the government machine being exposed to the gaze of those ready to criticise without adequate knowledge of the background and perhaps with some axe to grind."[124]

The difficulty with this is, first, that in some cases at least criticism might be well-merited, and beneficial if it led to improvements in the "inner workings of the government machine".[125] In such cases the public interest would in the long-term be enhanced by disclosure. Secondly, it should not be the concern of the courts to protect the government from mere criticism,[126] however ill informed and captious. Criticism may be annoying and embarrassing, but it is too tenuous an interference with the work of government to justify broad undifferentiated protection for official documents. Thirdly, the moves in recent years towards more open government and freedom of information[127] make general arguments for official secrecy increasingly less attractive.

9–025   As noted above, the weakness of these general rationales for class claims has led the courts in recent years to be more demanding in their attitude to such claims. In *R. v Chief Constable of West Midlands Police Ex p. Wiley*,[128] Lord Woolf said that the recognition of a new class-based public interest immunity requires clear and compelling evidence that it is necessary. Claims for the protection of broadly defined classes of documents are likely to receive particularly careful examination. Questions will arise whether the class can be narrowed or refined, or whether it is possible to reveal part of the documents in question.[129] This suggests some merging of contents and class claims, but the distinction has not collapsed altogether. In *Taylor v Anderton*,[130] Sir Thomas Bingham M.R., after citing Lord Woolf's statement in *Ex p. Wiley* and noting the "existence of a current of opinion strongly flowing in favour of openness and disclosure", held that reports and working papers prepared by officers investigating police conduct[131] formed a class of documents entitled to public interest immunity. His Lordship accepted a justification based on a modified version of the candour of communication argument:

---

[124] *Conway v Rimmer* [1968] A.C. 910 at 952.
[125] See the comments of Lord Keith in *Burmah Oil Co Ltd v Bank of England* [1980] A.C. 1090 at 1134 HL, relating the point to the trend towards more open government.
[126] As Viscount Simon L.C. recognised in *Duncan v Cammell Laird* [1942] A.C. 624 at 642 HL.
[127] See, e.g. A. Tomkins, "Public Interest Immunity: Freedom of Information and Judicial Discretion" in P. Leyland and T. Woods (eds), *Administrative Law Facing the Future: Old Constraints and New Horizons* (London, 1997), pp.321, 342–346.
[128] *R. v Chief Constable of West Midlands Police Ex p. Wiley* [1995] 1 A.C. 274 HL.
[129] See Sir Simon Brown, "Public Interest Immunity" [1994] P.L. 579, 581.
[130] *Taylor v Anderton* [1995] 2 All E.R. 420 at 437 CA.
[131] Pursuant to the procedure for the investigation of complaints against the police established by Pt IX of PACE.

"I have no difficulty in accepting the need for investigating officers to feel free to report on professional colleagues or members of the public without the apprehension that their opinions may become known to such persons. I can readily accept that the prospect of disclosure in other than unusual circumstances would have an undesirably inhibiting effect on investigating officers' reports."[132]

An important development came in the wake of the Scott Report,[133] which was highly critical of the use of class claims to public interest immunity, and recommended that they should no longer be made in criminal cases. The government accepted this recommendation, and in fact went further. Ministerial statements in Parliament announced a new approach. This applies equally to criminal and civil cases. The approach effectively abandons the contents/class distinction and focuses instead directly on any damage to the public interest that would be caused by the disclosure of sensitive documents. Ministers will claim immunity only when they believe that disclosure will cause serious harm to the public interest. Such harm or damage might result from, for example, an immediate threat to the safety of an individual, or to the national economic interest or the country's relations with a foreign state; harm might also be more indirect, in the form of damage to a "regulatory process". This approach therefore abolishes class claims as far as central government is concerned, although we should not forget that the guidelines containing this approach do not have the force of law, and no government minister is legally bound to follow them. Assuming, however, that the new approach is followed, any documents that contain genuinely sensitive material will be dealt with by contents claims. Consequently, class claims cannot be made in future for internal policy advice by civil servants, nor for documents that relate generally to matters of national security.

This approach[134] does not apply to non-governmental organisations, but it has unmistakeable implications for them. If contents claims are now thought to be adequate to protect the functioning of central government, it is hard to see why they should not suffice for NGOs. Thus this new approach severely undermines the basis for class claims by other bodies, such as local authorities, and it should encourage the courts to increase their reluctance to uphold such claims.

9–026

(E) Duty or discretion to make a claim

The Scott Report dealt with one further important issue. In the failed prosecution which led to the Scott Report Ministers who had signed public interest immunity certificates stated that they had been advised by government lawyers that they had a duty to make the claim. The Attorney-General's view had been that ministers had no power to waive the immunity where the documents in question

9–027

---

[132] *Taylor v Anderton* [1995] 2 All E.R. 420 at 437.
[133] Sir Richard Scott, *Reports of the Inquiry into the Export of Defence Equipment and Dual-Use Goods to Iraq and Related Prosecutions*, HC 115 (1996). *Hansard*, HL Vol.576, cols 1507–1517 (December 18, 1996) Lord Chancellor; *Hansard*, HC Vol.287, cols 949–958, (December 18, 1996), Attorney-General.
[134] This approach is set out in *Hansard* HL Vol. 576, cols 1507–1517, and discussed by C. Forsyth, "Public Interest Immunity: Recent and Future Developments" [1997] C.L.J. 51.

fell within a recognised class of documents for which immunity was available. This view was founded on certain dicta of Bingham L.J. in *Makanjuola v Commissioner of Metropolitan Police*,[135] to the effect that public interest immunity is an exclusionary rule of the law of evidence, and that it is for the court, not the parties, to decide the balance of public interest in the proceedings. Accordingly, where there is a public interest in non-disclosure, litigants should assert it: "[P]ublic interest immunity cannot in any ordinary sense be waived, since, although one can waive rights, one cannot waive duties".[136]

However, despite the supposed existence of a duty to make a claim, there were several examples of cases where a claim could have been made but was not. The Scott Report cited the prosecution of Clive Ponting in 1984 for leaking government information to an MP about the sinking of the Argentine battleship General Belgrano during the Falklands War. The Government voluntarily disclosed a document known as the "Crown Jewels", a detailed Ministry of Defence review of the events leading up to the sinking. No claim for public interest immunity was made.[137] In Scott's view, Bingham L.J.'s dicta in *Makanjuola* had been misunderstood:

> "[T]he . . . passage . . . nowhere states or implies that a Minister is under a duty to claim PII for documents that he does not think the public interest requires to be withheld . . . The duty to claim PII arises if the Minister is of the opinion that the disclosure of the documents to the defendant would be damaging to the public interest. Ministers are well able to decide whether Government documents of a confidential or secret nature should be disclosed for the purposes of some greater interest."[138]

Moreover, in *Ex p. Wiley* Lord Woolf envisaged that a minister might decide on reviewing the documents not to make a claim because, in the minister's view, any public interest in non-disclosure would be outweighed by the public interest in access to the document for the purposes of the litigation. As Lord Woolf said, it is then difficult to conceive that a court would feel it appropriate to disagree.[139] The courts should not be more executive-minded than the executive, particularly where access to evidence, one of the ingredients of the right to a fair trial, is concerned.

9–028   In the light of these developments, and the government's reaction to the Scott Report, it is clear that any duty to make a claim only arises *after* the minister has considered the public interests involved. By announcing that certain types of class claim would no longer be made the government abandoned the position that there is a duty to claim public interest immunity in all possible cases. Under the parliamentary announcement the minister's duty is first to consider whether any serious harm to the public interest is likely to follow from disclosure. This may well involve the minister in a consideration of whether the degree of harm involved in disclosure is outweighed by the desirability of disclosure in the

---

[135] *Makanjuola v Commissioner of Metropolitan Police* [1992] 3 All E.R. 617 CA.
[136] *Makanjuola* [1992] 3 All E.R. 617 at 623.
[137] Scott Report paras G18.61–18.64. A further example is *M v Home Office* [1992] Q.B. 270 (minutes of meeting between Home Secretary and senior civil servants). See also Forsyth, "Public Interest Immunity" [1997] C.L.J. 51, 55–56.
[138] Scott Report para.G18.60.
[139] *Ex p. Wiley* [1995] 1 A.C. 274 at 296.

interests of justice. If the minister takes the view that there is a risk of serious harm from disclosure, then there should be a duty to bring this to the court's attention. The court as an impartial tribunal can then decide on which side the balance of public interest comes down.

The balancing exercise should be conducted in accordance with the principles set out in *R. v Chief Constable of the West Midlands Ex p. Wiley*.[140] A number of factors are relevant in estimating the strength of the public interest in the administration of justice. One is the importance of the documents to the litigation; if the evidence provided by the documents is obtainable from another source, disclosure will not generally be necessary and injustice will not be done to the applicant by refusing an order for production. If the evidence is not available elsewhere and is crucial to the case of the party seeking disclosure, the court will need to consider the factors of the nature of the litigation, the importance of the party's claim, the nature and degree of risk to a public interest, and how far that interest can be protected by limited disclosure in the form of summaries or redactions or other methods.[141] We can now examine how the balance between access and secrecy works out in a number of different types of claim for immunity.

2. *Balancing public interests in different contexts*

(A) *National security and defence*

As noted above, the courts are likely to accept a certificate that disclosure of the contents of a particular document would be injurious to the interests of national security or defence. Arguments for maintaining the secrecy in wartime of military campaign plans,[142] and of the details of the construction of military equipment,[143] are self-evidently powerful. The House of Lords expressed a clear view in *Conway v Rimmer* that the decision on the facts in *Duncan v Cammell Laird* was justifiable. However, acceptance of the risk of damage to these interests does not mean that they will necessarily take priority in a balancing exercise. The Divisional Court in *R. (on the application of Mohammed) v Foreign Secretary*,[144] held that the risk to national security from terrorism favoured non-disclosure, in a claim under the *Norwich Pharmacal* jurisdiction, of certain redacted material where its release might result in the United States government withdrawing intelligence-sharing arrangements with the UK government. But the court reached this conclusion only after conducting a detailed and careful weighing of the public interests involved and then deciding to accord priority to the claim in the certificate for secrecy of the material. It seems therefore that even contents claims relating to these centrally important interests may be subject to rigorous scrutiny where there is a case for saying that need for secrecy is outweighed by

9–029

---

[140] *Ex p. Wiley* [1995] 1 A.C. 274.
[141] See, e.g. *R. (on the application of Mohammed) v Foreign Secretary* [2009] EWHC 152 (Admin).
[142] *Asiatic Petroleum Co Ltd v Anglo-Persian Oil Co Ltd* [1916] 1 K.B. 822.
[143] *Duncan v Cammell Laird* [1942] A.C. 624 HL.
[144] *R. (on the application of Mohammed) v Foreign Secretary* [2009] EWHC 152 (Admin).

other interests. Accordingly it is worth emphasising the government's position that it will no longer make *class* claims for documents relating to national security.

(B)   International relations

9–030   Other obvious interests of state are interests in the maintenance of good diplomatic relations and international comity. Here again the courts are unlikely in civil proceedings to question a ministerial certificate that these interests would be harmed by the disclosure of certain documents. What was in effect a class claim for such documents was recognised in *Hennessey v Wright*.[145] The refusal of the Secretary of State for the Colonies to permit disclosure of the reports of a colonial governor was upheld on the ground that these were state documents. Field J. referred in somewhat alarmist terms to the "danger to the nation" and the possibility of war arising from the publication of a document of this type. In more modern times Brightman L.J. has suggested that protection would be given to "the contents of confidential documents addressed to, or emanating from sovereign states, or concerning the interests of sovereign states, arising in connection with an international territorial dispute between sovereign states … such an immunity is a public interest of the United Kingdom".[146] In *R. v Governor of Brixton Prison Ex p. Osman (No.1)*[147] the Divisional Court upheld a refusal to disclose documents in the interests of not prejudicing the diplomatic relations between the United Kingdom and Malaysia.[148]

(C)   State papers: matters of high-level government policy

9–031   In *Conway v Rimmer*,[149] the House of Lords was in no doubt that documents relating to the formation and discussion of high-level government policy formed a class for which public interest immunity could be claimed. This class includes minutes of Cabinet meetings, and departmental communications at the level of ministers and senior civil servants on matters of national policy.[150] Lord Reid expressed the view that documents such as Cabinet minutes ought not to be disclosed as a general rule, whatever their contents.[151] In support of this view he explained and contrasted the "candour" and "criticism" justifications of class claims discussed in the previous section. Dicta in later cases have softened Lord Reid's presumptive protection, making it clear that the immunity is not automatic and that the court will, if necessary, inspect the documents and order disclosure if the balance of public interest requires it.[152]

---

[145] *Hennessey v Wright* (1888) 21 Q.B.D. 509.
[146] *Buttes Gas & Oil Co v Hammer (No.3)* [1981] Q.B. 223 at 265 CA (the case was reversed on other grounds: [1982] A.C. 888 HL).
[147] *R. v Governor of Brixton Prison Ex p. Osman (No.1)* [1992] 1 All E.R. 108 DC.
[148] See also *R. (on the application of Mohammed) v Foreign Secretary* [2009] EWHC 152 (Admin).
[149] *Conway v Rimmer* [1968] A.C. 910.
[150] See, e.g. *Burmah Oil Co Ltd v Bank of England* [1980] A.C. 1090 at 1133–1134 per Lord Keith of Kinkel; *Air Canada v Secretary of State for Trade (No.2)* [1983] 2 A.C. 394 at 445 per Lord Scarman.
[151] *Conway v Rimmer* [1968] A.C. 910 at 952.
[152] See above.

Where the documents are relevant to a party's claim, factors favouring disclosure would include the lapse of time since the relevant discussion took place,[153] the seriousness of the party's claim, and the extent to which the government itself is alleged to be a party to wrongdoing. All three of these were taken into account in the Australian case of *Sankey v Whitlam*,[154] where the High Court of Australia ordered production of Cabinet minutes and other documents to the applicant, a private prosecutor who had instituted proceedings for conspiracy against a former prime minister and members of his Cabinet. Gibbs A.C.J. noted that the documents related to matters that had occurred more than three years earlier, and that were no longer of any significance to the national interest. He added:

> "Moreover, if the documents can be withheld, the informant will be unable to present to the court his case that the defendants committed criminal offences while carrying out their duties as Ministers. If the defendants did engage in criminal conduct, and the documents are excluded, a rule of evidence designed to serve the public interest will instead have become a shield to protect wrongdoing by Ministers in the execution of their office . . . For these reasons I conclude that the public interest in the administration of justice outweighs any public interest in withholding documents of this class."[155]

The government announcement indicating that class claims would no longer be made seems clearly to rule out any blanket protection for internal Whitehall policy communications. It remains to be seen whether this will extend to all types of state papers concerned with government policy.

(D)   Low-level policy communications and routine reports

Where an applicant can satisfy the court that documents in these classes are likely to assist the applicant's case the court will almost certainly inspect the documents. There will invariably be a doubt whether the public interest requires them to be protected. If disclosure is necessary for disposing fairly of the case, it seems safe to say that the balance of public interest will usually favour disclosure. Arguments for protection based on the need for candour of communication, or the need to avoid unfair criticism, are unlikely to be given much weight. In *Conway v Rimmer*, the House of Lords inspected the reports on the plaintiff, a probationary police officer, of which disclosure was sought and ordered their

9–032

---

[153] See *Att-Gen v Jonathan Cape Ltd* [1976] Q.B. 752.

[154] *Sankey v Whitlam* (1978) 142 C.L.R. 1. See also the judgment of the Supreme Court of the United States ordering disclosure of the Watergate tapes: *Nixon v US* (1974) 418 U.S. 683.

[155] *Sankey v Whitlam* (1978) 142 C.L.R. 1 at 46–47. See also T. R. S. Allan, "Abuse of Power and Public Interest Immunity: Justice Rights and Truth" (1985) 101 L.Q.R. 200, arguing cogently that where the actions of government ministers are alleged to be unlawful there is a direct public interest in the vindication of public law. This factor was largely ignored by the House of Lords when it refused to inspect the documents at issue in *Air Canada v Secretary of State for Trade (No.2)* [1983] 2 A.C. 394, a case which concerned allegations that the Trade Secretary had acted unlawfully in forcing the British Airports Authority to increase landing charges at Heathrow. In *R. (on the application of Mohammed) v Foreign Secretary* [2009] EWHC 152 (Admin) the Divisional Court rejected an argument that there is an absolute rule that PII cannot be claimed to prevent disclosure of evidence of serious misconduct by officials of the UK. The balancing exercise was held to apply in all cases.

production. In *Campbell v Tameside MBC*,[156] the plaintiff, a middle-aged female schoolteacher, had been assaulted by an 11-year-old pupil. Her action for damages for personal injuries against the local education authority alleged negligence in allowing the pupil to attend an ordinary school. She sought discovery of certain reports on the pupil by teachers and psychologists. Ordering production after inspecting the reports, the Court of Appeal held that allowing immunity would result in a denial of justice to the plaintiff. The court gave short shrift to the defendants' argument that protection was necessary to ensure the candour of such reports. Ackner L.J. commented crisply that some people "might regard the occasional and rare exposure of these reports to the public gaze as a spur to greater efficiency in their production and intelligibility in their expression".[157] Certainly arguments about the danger of inhibiting the writers of such reports look insignificant when set against the facts that the plaintiff had suffered substantial personal injury and probably had no other means of redress. There was also the point that it would be unfair in effect to require her to bear the costs of an educational experiment that went wrong.

Where reports are not of a routine nature, such as the conclusions of an investigation into specific allegations of police misconduct, the courts may be more sympathetic to claims for public interest immunity. In *Taylor v Anderton*,[158] as noted above, the Court of Appeal upheld a claim for immunity for the report of such an investigation on the basis of ensuring candour in the making of such reports. The decision stands in contrast to *Ex p. Wiley* where the House of Lords refused a class immunity for documents created in the course of the investigation such as witness statements.[159] The reasoning in *Taylor v Anderton* is also somewhat undermined by the concession that the officer making the report would know that his report might have to be disclosed in criminal proceedings if it was necessary to help establish the innocence of the accused. The psychological assumption underpinning the candour argument really only makes sense if disclosure is not permitted under any circumstances.

(E) Confidentiality and the protection of sources of information

9–033   This is now one of the most important types of claim for public interest immunity. The confidentiality of communications, whether within organisations or with third parties, is not by itself sufficient for a claim. This was made clear by Lord Cross in *Alfred Crompton Amusement Machines Ltd v Customs and Excise Commissioners*[160] who confirmed that confidentiality "is not a separate head of privilege, but it may be a very material consideration to bear in mind when privilege is claimed on the ground of public interest". This means that the court will consider to what extent the proper functioning of the public service depends on the protection of confidence. The question will be how far the public functioning of the organisation concerned would be harmed by the disclosure of

---

[156] *Campbell v Tameside MBC* [1982] Q.B. 1065 CA.
[157] *Campbell v Tameside MBC* [1982] Q.B. 1065 at 1077.
[158] *Taylor v Anderton* [1995] 2 All E.R. 420 CA.
[159] See *Ex p. Wiley* [1995] 1 A.C. 274. The House of Lords overruled a line of authority in the Court of Appeal to the contrary.
[160] *Alfred Crompton* [1974] A.C. 405 at 433 HL.

its confidential communications, particularly with third parties. There is an essential distinction here between public functions and private interests, a distinction that is not necessarily related to the form or constitution of the organisation. In *Science Research Council v Nasse*,[161] which concerned a complaint of discrimination in employment, the House of Lords refused to grant the Council immunity for confidential reports on its employees made in accordance with its procedure for promotions.[162] Even though the employers were a public body, the efficiency of their promotion scheme was regarded as a matter of private interest in the same way as it would be for a limited company.

In reaching this conclusion the House of Lords put a brake on the expansionist tendencies of the law on public interest immunity suggested by its earlier decision in *D v NSPCC*.[163] In the latter case, as noted above, the House of Lords refused to order disclosure of documents revealing the identity of an informant who had reported suspected child abuse to the NSPCC. The Society is constitutionally a voluntary society incorporated by royal charter, but it discharges certain statutory functions related to the protection of children.[164] The House of Lords accepted that there was a public interest in the free flow of information from members of the public to the Society about possible cases of child abuse, and that without an effective promise of confidentiality that information was less likely to be forthcoming. This interest overrode the interest in enabling the plaintiff to obtain the information necessary to institute proceedings against a possibly malicious informant. Certain dicta in two of the speeches in the House of Lords[165] suggested considerable potential for the expansion of public interest immunity. Lord Hailsham expressed the view that the categories of public interest were not closed and might alter by restriction or extension as social conditions and social legislation developed. In relation specifically to confidential matters Lord Edmund-Davies suggested that where a confidential relationship exists, and disclosure would be in breach of some ethical or social value involving the public interest, the court might uphold a refusal to disclose if the balance of public interest was in favour of exclusion. In *Science Research Council v Nasse* Lord Scarman expressly dissented from both dicta. Saying that the area of public interest immunity was very restricted, he insisted that it existed "to protect from disclosure only information the secrecy of which is essential to the proper working of the Government of the State".[166] He went on to say that *D v NSPCC* was a "very special" case that should not be seen as a departure from established principle. The history of public interest immunity in

---

[161] *Science Research Council v Nasse* [1980] A.C. 1028 HL.

[162] Note, however, that in deciding whether to exercise its discretion to grant an application for discovery, the court may take account of any need to preserve confidentiality, and will therefore consider carefully whether discovery is necessary for disposing fairly of the case and whether, for example, the necessary information can be obtained from other sources not involving a breach of confidence: *Science Research Council v Nasse* [1980] A.C. 1028 at 1065–1066 HL per Lord Wilberforce.

[163] *D v NSPCC* [1978] A.C. 171.

[164] These functions were prescribed by the Children and Young Persons Act 1969 s.1.

[165] *D v NSPCC* [1978] A.C. 171 at 230 per Lord Hailsham and 245 per Lord Edmund-Davies.

[166] *Science Research Council v Nasse* [1980] A.C. 1028 at 1087.

the 30 years since Lord Scarman's judgment is a bumpy one, as the Scott Report attests, but at the present time his restrictive approach looks to have been vindicated.

Certainly it is possible to take a narrow view of the basis of the decision in *D v NSPCC*, as indeed Lord Diplock did in his judgment in the case. This view grounds the decision in an express analogy with the protection traditionally given to police and prosecution sources of information. Lord Diplock regarded information about neglect or ill-treatment of children as serving a public interest of similar importance and therefore justifying the same rule of anonymity.[167] In this area, as in others, the "police informer" rule has been highly influential, and it is this rule that will now be considered in more detail.

9–034   The protection of informers is based on the public interest in the enforcement of the criminal law by the police and prosecutors. In the leading case of *Marks v Beyfus*[168] the plaintiff in an action for malicious prosecution had called the Director of Public Prosecutions as a witness in order to ascertain the information on which the Director had acted in directing a prosecution of the plaintiff. The Court of Appeal held that the trial judge had been right to allow the Director to refuse to disclose the names of his informants and the nature of their information. The rationale is that a good deal of the work of prevention and detection of crime is facilitated by the use of informers, and that this work would be adversely affected if the identity of informers was liable to be revealed because the sources of information would soon dry up. A further reason is the protection of the informers themselves from reprisals if their identity became known.

Although the topic of informer anonymity is often discussed in the context of public interest immunity, the courts have sometimes said that the protection of informants is a matter of rule. On this view the availability of the protection is not a matter of discretion in the sense that it is a decision that requires in each case a balancing of aspects of the public interest. Lord Esher M.R. emphasised in *Marks v Beyfus* that a rule of law was involved, and this was confirmed, obiter, by Lord Diplock in *D v NSPCC* who described the uniform practice of the judges as having hardened into a rule whereby the balance always comes down in favour of non-disclosure.[169] The principal exception to this rule is in criminal proceedings where disclosure of the identity of the informer is necessary for the defence of the accused. In such a case the interests of ensuring a fair trial for the accused and avoiding a possible wrongful conviction prevail. However, in recent civil cases the strictness of Lord Diplock's approach has been softened. The Court of Appeal has upheld exercises of balancing the public interest in the protection of informers against that of securing a fair trial, citing in support of this approach the need for case-specific analysis emphasised in the jurisprudence of human rights law.[170]

The informer "rule" has influenced a number of decisions to grant public interest immunity where the court has been persuaded that the proper functioning

---

[167] *D v NSPCC* [1978] A.C. 171 at 219.
[168] *Marks v Beyfus* (1890) 25 Q.B.D. 494 CA.
[169] *D v NSPCC* [1978] A.C. 171 at 218.
[170] See *Chief Constable of Greater Manchester Police v McNally* [2002] EWCA Civ 14; [2002] 2 Cr.App.R. 37, and the cases there cited.

of a body exercising public functions depends on information received from third parties in confidence. *D v NSPCC* has already been mentioned. In *Rogers v Home Secretary*,[171] the House of Lords held that a letter from a Chief Constable to the Gaming Board concerning the character of an applicant for a gaming licence was protected from production in evidence. The Gaming Board had a statutory duty to make inquiries about the character of applicants for licences. The court was clear that the Board's sources of information should be protected, particularly given the connections between the control of gambling and organised crime. Where the communication was from an identified police officer, as was the case, protection was still necessary since the communication might give clues as to the sources of the police information.[172]

A more debatable decision on the facts was *Alfred Crompton Amusement Machines Ltd v Customs and Excise Commissioners*.[173] In pursuance of their statutory duty to levy purchase tax (a forerunner of VAT), the Commissioners obtained confidential information from third parties relating to the value for tax of the plaintiffs' amusement machines. The House of Lords upheld the Commissioners' refusal to produce the relevant documents on the ground that they were covered by public interest immunity.[174] It was successfully argued that disclosure would be resented by those who had supplied the information; they would be less co-operative in future, thus making the statutory duties of the Commissioners more difficult to carry out. Even assuming this to be true, it was hardly a strong argument because the Commissioners had a statutory power to *compel* relevant information to be given, unlike the situation of the police, the Gaming Board and the NSPCC, all of whom depend on the voluntary supply of information.

9–035

The *Alfred Crompton* case can be compared with the contemporary decision of the House of Lords in *Norwich Pharmacal Co v Customs and Excise Commissioners*.[175] In the latter case the House of Lords ordered the Commissioners to disclose to the plaintiffs documents revealing the identity of persons who had been importing a certain pharmaceutical product into the United Kingdom in breach of the plaintiffs' patent. The Commissioners had acquired this information by virtue of their statutory duty to obtain information relating to the importation of goods. They argued that it would be contrary to the public interest to disclose such information given in confidence, but the House of Lords held that wrongdoers did not deserve the protection that the claim of public interest immunity would give them. Since honest importers would not be deterred from giving information by knowledge that the identity of wrongdoers would be disclosed, it followed that the Commissioners' functioning would not be significantly impaired.

---

[171] *Rogers v Home Secretary* [1973] A.C. 388, HL.
[172] A further factor in the balance of public interest in *Rogers* was the nature of the applicant's claim. He had originally sought a privilege (the grant of a gaming licence) in which he voluntarily put his character and reputation in issue, and had then brought proceedings for criminal libel on the basis of an unfavourable reference. It seems clear that the public interest in the administration of justice is not greatly damaged if such a claim cannot be pursued because the reference is excluded from evidence.
[173] *Alfred Crompton* [1974] A.C. 405 HL.
[174] A separate claim for legal professional privilege failed: see Ch.10.
[175] *Norwich Pharmacal* [1974] A.C. 133.

In *British Steel Corp v Granada Televison Ltd,*[176] the House of Lords took matters a significant stage further by recognising a public interest in the free flow of information to the media. The Lords confirmed that at common law journalists do not have a privilege as such in their sources of information; there is nothing analogous to legal professional privilege for such communications.[177] However, it was held that in exercising a discretion whether to order discovery,[178] the court could have regard to the duty of confidence between journalist and source in view of the public interest in the transmission of information to the media. The strength of this interest is variable, and it can be overridden where the interests of justice require that the plaintiff should be able to pursue a legal remedy against a wrongdoer. Although the decision on the facts went against the defendants, it was something of a landmark because it represented an acknowledgment that a public interest could attach to the proper functioning of a body that was not part of government and was not discharging any statutory functions that depended on the receipt of information from third parties.

9–036   Shortly after the decision in this case, the government decided to provide statutory protection for the media's sources of information.[179] Section 10 of the Contempt of Court Act 1981 provides:

> "No court may require a person to disclose, nor is any person guilty of contempt of court for refusing to disclose, the source of information contained in a publication for which he is responsible, unless it be established to the satisfaction of the court that disclosure is necessary in the interests of justice or national security or for the prevention of disorder or crime."

The courts have stated that they will give this provision a wide construction to promote its purpose of safeguarding the effective functioning of the press. In *Secretary of State for Defence v Guardian Newspapers Ltd,*[180] Griffiths L.J. said in the Court of Appeal:

> "The press have always attached the greatest importance to their ability to protect their sources of information. If they are not able to do so, they believe that many of their sources would dry up and this would seriously interfere with their effectiveness. It is in the interests of us all that we should have a truly effective press, and it seems to me that Parliament by enacting s.10 has clearly recognised the importance that attaches to the ability of the press to protect their sources . . . I can see no harm in giving a wide construction to the opening words of the section

---

[176] *British Steel Corp v Granada Television Ltd* [1981] A.C. 1096 HL.

[177] This decision is in line with other cases refusing privilege for confidential communications with members of other professional groups: priests (*Normanshaw v Normanshaw and Measham* (1893) 69 L.T. 468); doctors (*Hunter v Mann* [1974] Q.B. 767); bankers (*Robertson v Canadian Imperial Bank of Commerce* [1995] 1 All E.R. 824). Despite the lack of a formal privilege, a court is most unlikely to compel disclosure of such a confidence unless persuaded that disclosure is essential in the interests of the administration of justice.

[178] Of the identity of a wrongdoer; this was a case brought under the *Norwich Pharmacal* jurisdiction by the plaintiff corporation which was seeking to identify a "mole" who had leaked confidential documents to the defendant television company.

[179] For discussion see R. Costigan, "Protection of journalists' sources" [2007] P.L. 464.

[180] *Secretary of State for Defence v Guardian Newspapers Ltd* [1985] A.C. 339 HL.

because by the latter part of the section the court is given ample powers to order the source to be revealed where in the circumstances of a particular case the wider public interest makes it necessary to do so."[181]

In accordance with this approach the provision has been held to cover information that is communicated and received for the *purpose* of publication, even if that information has not in fact been published.[182] Despite the express reference in s.10 to "information contained in a publication", the House of Lords was in no doubt that the policy of the statute should apply as much to intended publication as to actual publication. Secondly, s.10 applies both where the applicant is seeking discovery of the identity of a wrongdoer,[183] and where the applicant is asserting a proprietary right to a document or thing in the hands of the defendant.[184] In this way the section may operate to defeat vested proprietary rights. Thirdly, it is enough that disclosure might, but not necessarily would, cause the identity of the source to be revealed.[185] Fourthly, once the statutory protection is available, it applies unless and until the party seeking disclosure can discharge the burden of satisfying the court by evidence that, on the balance of probabilities, disclosure is necessary in the interests of one of the four matters of public concern listed at the end of the section.[186]

There is therefore no discretion in the judge to decide whether the statutory protection is prima facie available. No "balancing" needs to be done at the stage of seeing whether the statutory condition exists of "information contained in a publication for which the person is responsible". If the condition exists the statutory protection follows as of right. But this does not mean that notions of discretion and balancing of public interests have disappeared altogether. According to Lord Bridge in *X Ltd v Morgan-Grampian Ltd*, the judge does have a "discretion" in relation to the application of the exceptions in the section. At this second stage of decision, the concept of the "balancing exercise" re-emerges in the guise of whether it is necessary to order disclosure for one of the four stated purposes. Lord Bridge stated that the judge will start with the assumption that the protection of sources is a matter of "high public importance", and will then have to consider whether there is a sufficient necessity to override it in the interests of "another matter of high public importance".[187] Thus a judgment about the relative importance of different public interests will be required, and it follows that the necessity referred to in s.10 does not have a fixed meaning that applies indifferently across all four exceptions; it is a flexible concept that takes its "colour from its context".[188]

9–037

---

[181] *Guardian Newspapers* [1984] Ch. 156 at 166–167 CA; a passage cited with approval by Lord Bridge in *X Ltd v Morgan-Grampian Ltd* [1991] 1 A.C. 1 HL.

[182] *X Ltd v Morgan-Grampian Ltd* [1991] 1 A.C. 1 at 40 per Lord Bridge and 54–55 per Lord Lowry.

[183] Pursuant to *Norwich Pharmacal* [1974] A.C. 133.

[184] *Secretary of State for Defence v Guardian Newspapers Ltd* [1985] A.C. 339 at 349 per Lord Diplock.

[185] *Guardian Newspapers* [1985] A.C. 339.

[186] *X Ltd v Morgan-Grampian Ltd* [1991] 1 A.C. 1 at 41 per Lord Bridge.

[187] *X Ltd v Morgan-Grampian Ltd* [1991] 1 A.C. 1 at 41 per Lord Bridge.

[188] *Re An Inquiry under the Company Securities (Insider Dealing) Act 1985* [1988] A.C. 660 at 704 per Lord Griffiths.

Factors that are relevant in estimating the importance of protecting the source of the information include the nature of the information itself. The greater the legitimate public interest in it, the greater will be the importance of protection.[189] It would seem therefore that "whistleblowers" who report to the press malpractice or negligence in any matter affecting the public at large should expect to receive a high degree of protection. Where the source is not exposing iniquity, an important factor will be the manner in which the source obtained the information. If the information was obtained lawfully, this will enhance the importance of protection. The use of illegal means, such as theft or computer misuse, will diminish the importance of protection.[190] This last point shows that the importance of protecting the functioning of the press is qualified by an implied message from the courts that the press should not encourage illegality.[191]

E. PUBLIC INTEREST IMMUNITY IN CRIMINAL PROCEEDINGS

1. *The extent of the application of PII in criminal proceedings*

9–038   Public interest immunity applies in criminal proceedings. This point was in some doubt at common law, but a series of cases in the Court of Appeal in the early 1990s that were concerned with the prosecution's duty of disclosure assumed as settled law the application of public interest immunity to criminal cases.[192] Since 1997 the matter has been settled on a statutory basis. The Criminal Procedure and Investigations Act 1996 provides that the prosecutor must not make disclosure of material that the court, on an application by the prosecutor, concludes it is not in the public interest to disclose.[193]

The Act does not define the grounds on which public interest immunity can be claimed. However, the Code of Practice issued under the Act describes sensitive material as material, the disclosure of which, the disclosure officer believes, would give rise to a real risk of serious prejudice to an important public interest.[194] The Code goes on to set out an extensive list of examples of sensitive material that a disclosure officer may believe it is not in the public interest to disclose.[195] These examples cover a wide range. At one end of the range are broad categories of material relating to national security, material received from the intelligence and security agencies, and material relating to intelligence from foreign sources that reveals sensitive intelligence-gathering methods. At the other end are more narrowly focused categories such as material containing details of persons taking part in identification parades and material relating to the private life of a witness. In the leading case of *R. v H and C*,[196] Lord Bingham noted:

---

[189] *X Ltd v Morgan-Grampian Ltd* [1991] 1 A.C. 1 at 44 HL per Lord Bridge.

[190] *X Ltd v Morgan-Grampian Ltd* [1991] 1 A.C. 1 at 44 HL.

[191] For further discussion of s.10 and the interpretation of the exceptions readers are advised to consult specialist works on media law.

[192] *Ward* (1993) 96 Cr.App.R. 1 CA; *Davis, Johnson and Rowe* [1993] 1 W.L.R. 613 CA; *Keane* [1994] 1 W.L.R. 746 CA.

[193] CPIA ss.3(6).

[194] Code of Practice para.2.1.

[195] Code of Practice para.6.12.

[196] *R. v H and C* [2004] UKHL 3; [2004] 2 Cr.App.R.10 at [18].

"The public interest most regularly engaged is that in the effective investigation and prosecution of serious crime, which may involve resort to informers and undercover agents, or the use of scientific or operational techniques (such as surveillance) which cannot be disclosed without exposing individuals to the risk of personal injury or jeopardizing the success of future operations."

In *R. v H and C* the House of Lords reviewed the subject of public interest immunity in criminal cases in the light of the Strasbourg jurisprudence on art.6. The considered opinion of the House, delivered by Lord Bingham, restated the principles for decision-making that prosecutors and courts should follow when dealing with questions of non-disclosure in the public interest. The *Attorney-General's Guidelines on Disclosure* endorse the principles and advise that they should be rigorously applied.[197] Scrupulous attention to the principles is particularly necessary where material has to be examined in the absence of the accused, so as to ensure that the procedure is compliant with art.6.

2. Process of decision-making in PII cases

Lord Bingham emphasised that the "golden rule" is that full disclosure should be made to the defence of any material held by the prosecution that weakens its case or strengthens that of the defendant. As he rightly said, bitter experience has shown that miscarriages of justice may occur where such material is withheld from disclosure.[198] For this purpose the parties' respective cases should be carefully (although not restrictively) analysed to ascertain the specific facts the prosecution seek to establish and the specific grounds on which the charges are resisted. The defence should not be permitted to make general and unspecified allegations and then seek far-reaching disclosure in the hope that material may turn up to make them good. Neutral material or material damaging to the defendant need not be disclosed and should not be brought to the attention of the court.[199]

9–039

Lord Bingham's approach clearly requires prosecutors to review the unused material and apply the CPIA test of prosecution disclosure conscientiously. His implied message is that prosecutors should not "give the defence the keys to the warehouse",[200] and let the defence trawl through all of the non-sensitive material for something useful. How far this exhortation is effective, given the resource constraints on the police and the CPS, is unclear. He also suggested that only in truly borderline cases should the prosecution seek a judicial ruling on the disclosability of material in their hands. Read in context this must mean that in general the prosecution should follow the golden rule and make full disclosure; only in cases of real difficulty should prosecutors make PII applications to the

---

[197] *Attorney-General's Guidelines on Disclosure* (2005), 22.
[198] *R. v H and C* [2004] UKHL 3; [2004] 2 Cr.App.R. 10 at [14].
[199] *R. v H and C* [2004] UKHL 3; [2004] 2 Cr.App.R. 10 at [35].
[200] A phrase used in the *Protocol for the Control and Management of Unused Material in the Crown Court* (2006), para.31, which emphasises that this should not be done.

court.[201] Lord Bingham went on to say that when any issue of derogation from the golden rule of full disclosure comes before it the court must address a series of questions[202]:

(1)   What is the material that the prosecution seek to withhold? This must be considered by the court in detail.

(2)   Is the material such as may weaken the prosecution case or strengthen that of the defence? If "No", disclosure should not be ordered. If "Yes", full disclosure should (subject to (3), (4) and (5) below) be ordered.

(3)   Is there a real risk of serious prejudice to an important public interest (and, if so, what) if full disclosure of the material is ordered? If "No", full disclosure should be ordered.

(4)   If the answer to (2) and (3) is "Yes", can the defendant's interest be protected without disclosure or disclosure be ordered to an extent or in a way that will give adequate protection to the public interest in question and also afford adequate protection to the interests of the defence? This question requires the court to consider, with specific reference to the material that the prosecution seek to withhold and the facts of the case and the defence as disclosed, whether the prosecution should formally admit what the defence seek to establish or whether disclosure short of full disclosure may be ordered. This may be done in appropriate cases by the preparation of summaries or extracts of evidence, or the provision of documents in an edited or anonymised form, provided the documents supplied are in each instance approved by the judge. In appropriate cases the appointment of special counsel may be a necessary step to ensure that the contentions of the prosecution are tested and the interests of the defendant protected. In cases of exceptional difficulty the court may require the appointment of special counsel to ensure a correct answer to questions (2) and (3), as well as (4).

(5)   Do the measures proposed in answer to (4) represent the minimum derogation necessary to protect the public interest in question? If "No", the court should order such greater disclosure as will represent the minimum derogation from the golden rule of full disclosure.

(6)   If limited disclosure is ordered pursuant to (4) or (5) may the effect be to render the trial process, viewed as a whole, unfair to the defendant? If "Yes", then fuller disclosure should be ordered even if this leads or may lead the prosecution to discontinue the proceedings so as to avoid having to make disclosure.

(7)   If the answer to (6) when first given is "No", does that remain the correct answer as the trial unfolds, evidence is adduced and the defence advanced?

---

[201] If the prosecution decide to withhold material relevant to the defence on PII grounds without notifying the court at all (i.e. neither the judge nor the Court of Appeal) there will be a violation of art.6: see *Dowsett v United Kingdom* (2004) 38 E.H.R.R. 41.

[202] *R. v H and C* [2004] UKHL 3; [2004] 2 Cr.App.R. 10 at [36]. The prosecutor must provide the court with full and accurate information: *Attorney-General's Guidelines on Disclosure* (2005), para.21. For a case where the Court of Appeal quashed a conviction, despite D's plea of guilty, because of inadequate disclosure plus dishonest prosecution evidence on a voir dire PII hearing, see *Early* [2002] EWCA Crim 1904; [2003] 1 Cr.App.R. 19.

It is important that the answer to (6) should not be treated as a final, once-and-for-all, answer but as a provisional answer that the court must keep under review.

Question (4), and Lord Bingham's answer to it, should be placed in the context of the procedure for dealing with a PII claim. The procedure is set out in rules of court made pursuant to s.19 of the Criminal Procedure and Investigations Act 1996.[203] The rules replace, but broadly follow, the common law principles stated by the Court of Appeal in *Davis, Johnson and Rowe*.[204] There are three types of application. The first procedure, which is the one generally to be followed, is that the prosecutor must apply to the court, with notice to the accused, and the hearing of the application shall be inter partes with both sides being entitled to make representations. The application will normally be heard by the trial judge. The accused will have been given notice of the nature of the material to which the application relates. The European Court of Human Rights has held that the entitlement of the accused under art.6 of the ECHR to disclosure of relevant evidence is not an absolute right, and may be balanced against competing interests such as national security or the need to protect witnesses at risk of reprisals or keep secret police methods of investigation of crime.[205] However, only such measures restricting the rights of the defence that are strictly necessary are permissible under art.6, and the decision-making procedure in such cases must comply as far as possible with the requirements of adversarial proceedings and equality of arms. The inter partes procedure respects the rights of the defence to make the case before the judge for disclosure of the relevant material and therefore is normally compliant with art.6.[206]

Secondly, the prosecutor may decline to include in the notice of the application a specification of the nature of the material where he has reason to believe that to reveal to the accused the nature of the material to which the application relates would have the effect of disclosing that which he contends should not in the public interest be disclosed.[207] In this situation the defence is under a significantly greater handicap. Not only does the defence not know the nature of the material in question; the hearing may be ex parte when only the prosecutor is entitled to make representations to the court.[208] However, it seems that the involvement of the trial judge, who has a duty to ensure the fairness of the trial, together with the notice to the defence of the application, and the opportunity for the defence to make written submissions to the judge, are sufficient to satisfy art.6.[209] In *Jasper v United Kingdom*,[210] and in *Fitt v United Kingdom*,[211] the

9–040

---

[203] CPR Pt 22.

[204] *Davis, Johnson and Rowe* [1993] 1 W.L.R. 613.

[205] *Rowe and Davis v United Kingdom* (2000) 30 E.H.R.R. 1.

[206] By implication from *Rowe and Davis v United Kingdom* (2000) 30 E.H.R.R. 1.

[207] CPR r.22. 3(3)(b).

[208] CPR r.22 3(6).

[209] Where the prosecution does not disclose the material to the trial judge, but does disclose it to the Court of Appeal with a PII application, there may or may not be a violation of art.6 depending on the facts and circumstances of the case. Compare *Botmeh and Alami v United Kingdom* (2007) 46 E.H.R.R. 659 (no violation); with *Rowe and Davis v United Kingdom* (2000) 30 E.H.R.R. 1; and *Atlan v United Kingdom* (2001) 34 E.H.R.R. 833 (violation). Crucial factors include the procedure

European Court of Human Rights by a bare majority found no violation in such circumstances and rejected any necessity for the appointment of security-cleared "special counsel" to make submissions on behalf of the defence. As Lord Bingham explained in *R. v H and C*,[212] such counsel can be appointed under statutory authority in certain types of proceeding, and it appears that judges in ordinary criminal trials can ask the Attorney-General to sanction their appointment to deal with PII applications. However, there are ethical and practical problems with special counsel. They are not able to take full instructions from their clients, are not responsible to them, and do not report to them. When these difficulties are added to the predictable problems of expense and delay, it seems clear that such appointments should always be exceptional rather than the norm. According to Lord Bingham, a trial judge should not order appointment of special counsel unless and until satisfied that no other course will adequately meet the overriding requirement of fairness to the defendant.[213]

Thirdly, in rare cases the prosecutor may make an application ex parte, without any notice to the accused, if he has reason to believe that to reveal to the accused the fact that an application is being made would have the effect of disclosing that which the prosecutor contends should not in the public interest be disclosed.[214] The handicaps for the defence in this situation are clearly greater than in the second type of case since the defence is not in a position to present adversarial argument on the issue. Compliance with art.6 is therefore more difficult. In *Edwards and Lewis v United Kingdom*,[215] the European Court of Human Rights found a violation of art.6 in circumstances where the accused were hampered in arguing that they had been entrapped into committing the offences charged because the trial judge, who had to decide the issue of improper entrapment as a question of fact, had decided at an earlier *ex parte* PII hearing that certain relevant information should not be disclosed to the defence. Moreover, the judge had seen certain discreditable information relating to Edwards at the PII hearing that the judge might have regarded as relevant to the entrapment issue and that the accused had had no opportunity of challenging. The court did not say in terms that the appointment of special counsel was the only way in which the fairness of the trial would be safeguarded, but that is a strong implication of the decision. This case was strongly relied on by the defendants in *R. v H and C*, who argued for the appointment of special counsel to safeguard their interests at any ex parte PII hearing that might be held in their absence concerning disclosure of material that might support their applications for a stay of proceedings for abuse of process or exclusion of evidence under s.78 of PACE. Applying the principles set out above, the House of Lords held that the trial judge's appointment of special counsel, which the Court of Appeal had reversed, was premature. This decision

---

followed by the Court of Appeal, the significance of the undisclosed material for the defence, and how far the Court of Appeal is in a position to ensure the overall fairness of the proceedings.

[210] *Jasper v United Kingdom* (2000) 30 E.H.R.R. 441.
[211] *Fitt v United Kingdom* (2000) 30 E.H.R.R. 480.
[212] *R. v H and C* [2004] UKHL 3; [2004] 2 Cr.App.R. 10.
[213] *R. v H and C* [2004] UKHL 3; [2004] 2 Cr.App.R. 10 at [22].
[214] CPR r.22. 3(2).
[215] *Edwards and Lewis v United Kingdom* (2005) 40 E.H.R.R. 24, judgment of the Grand Chamber, confirming the judgment of the Fourth Section, reported in [2003] Crim L.R. 891.

rather leaves matters in the air. The House of Lords clearly hoped that issues of disclosure can be resolved by conscientious application of the CPIA test. But if this does not prove possible it may well be that the appointment of special counsel is the only way of keeping on the right side of art.6, at least for applications that the judge has to determine as a question of fact and which may be determinative of the case.[216]

3. *Fairness and the public interest*

An issue left unclear in *R. v H and C* is exactly when the interests of fairness to the accused will require disclosure of sensitive material. In what circumstances do these interests override the public interest in secrecy of the relevant information? If the material is simply irrelevant then clearly the statutory test for disclosure is not satisfied. If the material is relevant, but does not undermine the prosecution's case or assist the accused's case then again the statutory test is not satisfied and there is no need for disclosure. The problem arises where the sensitive material is relevant and might undermine the prosecution case or assist the accused's case.

9–041

One view is that the right to a fair trial means that if the material passes these tests of relevance and potential value to the defence then it should be disclosed, or the prosecution should be discontinued.[217] If this were the law then the right to disclosure would undoubtedly be a strong defence right since it would not permit any kind of "balancing" or offsetting of the value of the material to the defence against the public interest. However, this view has relatively little support in either the English or the Strasbourg case law. Taking the Strasbourg jurisprudence first, the European Court of Human Rights has used the language of balancing of interests. In *Edwards and Lewis v United Kingdom* the court repeated what it said earlier in *Rowe and Davis v United Kingdom*,[218] namely that:

> "... the entitlement to disclosure of relevant evidence is not an absolute right. In any criminal proceedings there may be competing interests, such as national security or the need to protect witnesses at risk of reprisals or keep secret police methods of investigation of crime, which must be *weighed* against the rights of the accused. In some cases it may be necessary to withhold certain evidence from the defence so as to preserve the fundamental rights of another individual or to safeguard an important public interest."[219] (emphasis added)

This might suggest an unstructured and flexible balancing test, not requiring any particular level of probative value for the sensitive material. Nevertheless, the court was careful to qualify its approach by incorporating a saving that any measures restricting the rights of the defence must be "strictly necessary"—by implication, to protect the interest that is competing with the defence interest in disclosure. And any difficulties caused to the defence by a limitation on its rights must be sufficiently counterbalanced by the procedures followed by the judicial

---

[216] cf. *May* [2005] EWCA Crim 97; [2005] 1 W.L.R. 2092. On ex parte applications to "disclosure judges" in Northern Ireland see *McKeown v United Kingdom* (2012) 54 E.H.R.R. 7.
[217] For discussion of such wider principles of disclosure see D. Ormerod, "Improving the Disclosure Regime" (2003) 7 E. & P. 102.
[218] *Rowe and Davis v United Kingdom* (2000) 30 E.H.R.R. 1.
[219] *Rowe and Davis v United Kingdom* (2000) 30 E.H.R.R. 1 at [61].

authorities.[220] In *Botmeh*,[221] the Court of Appeal followed this approach, holding that there is no absolute right to disclosure of relevant defence evidence. In *R. v H and C,* Lord Bingham, after citing the the passage above and other extracts from the Strasbourg jurisprudence, expressed the view that there is no dissonance between the principles of domestic law and those recognised in the Convention jurisprudence.[222] However, Lord Bingham seemed to envisage a threshold test for probative value of sensitive material to the defence. He said that where sensitive material is withheld from the defence, and the material is of *significant help* (emphasis supplied) to the defendant, there must be a very serious question whether the prosecution can succeed.[223] This notion of significant help is not discussed further in the case, which is mainly focused on the procedure for decision of PII claims. It would seem that something more than mere relevance is required for this threshold,[224] but how much help is significant, and for what purposes, remains unclear. In these circumstances it may be helpful to look at a group of earlier English authorities dealing with police sources of information. These cases have tended to employ a necessity test; the question has been constructed as one of whether disclosure is "necessary" for the defence (as opposed to the question from the Strasbourg cases, which is whether non-disclosure is necessary to protect the competing interest).

9–042   It was noted earlier in this chapter that public interest immunity has for many years protected police sources of information. Courts have refused to order disclosure of material that could lead to the identification of informers. The justification for protection is partly the interests of the efficient functioning of the police, who depend on a regular flow of confidential information to facilitate their prevention and detection of crime, and partly the safety of the informers themselves.[225]

The exception to the informer rule is where disclosure of the identity of an informant is necessary to enable the accused in a criminal case to establish his innocence.[226] In *Keane*,[227] the Court of Appeal talked in terms of a balancing exercise between competing interests, but added that if the disputed material may prove the defendant's innocence or avoid a miscarriage of justice, "then the balance comes down resoundingly in favour of disclosing it".[228] Thus in *Agar*,[229] the Court of Appeal held that the identity of an informer should have been disclosed where the defendant, who was charged with possession of drugs, claimed that the informer had acted in concert with the police to frame him for the offence. Disclosure was necessary for the proper presentation of the defence

---

[220] *Rowe and Davis v United Kingdom* (2000) 30 E.H.R.R. 1.
[221] *Botmeh* [2001] EWCA Crim 2226; [2002] 1 W.L.R. 531.
[222] *R. v H and C* [2004] UKHL 3; [2004] 2 Cr.App.R. 10 at [33].
[223] *R. v H and C* [2004] UKHL 3; [2004] 2 Cr.App.R. 10 at [37].
[224] For an example of a case where the relevance of the material was insufficient see *Morrow, Geach and Thomas* [1994] Crim. L.R. 58.
[225] Hence if the informer wishes to waive anonymity he will not be automatically prevented from doing so by the doctrine of public interest immunity, since the primary justification for the doctrine will have disappeared: *Savage v Chief Constable of Hampshire* [1997] 2 All E.R. 631 CA.
[226] *Marks v Beyfus* (1890) 25 Q.B.D. 494 CA.
[227] *Keane* [1994] 1 W.L.R. 746.
[228] *Keane* [1994] 1 W.L.R. 746 at 751.
[229] *Agar* [1990] 2 All E.R. 442 CA.

because identifying the informer added weight to the defendant's testimony. The Court of Appeal reached a similar conclusion in *Turner*,[230] while adding a cautionary note that judges should scrutinise applications for disclosure of details about informants with great care, and be astute to see that such details really are essential to the running of the defence.[231] If the informant is *only* an informant, disclosure of his identity is unlikely to be necessary. Where the informant has, or may have, participated in the offence, careful analysis of his role in relation to the issues of interest to the defence will be required. In *Menga and Marshalleck*,[232] the defence to charges of attempted robbery and a firearms offence was that the accused wrongly believed that the intended victim of the "robbery" was a knowing accomplice, whereas he was allegedly a police informer. The trial judge refused to order disclosure of the police "informer contact sheets" that would have revealed whether this was so. After inspecting the documents, the Court of Appeal upheld this ruling on the basis that there was nothing in the documents materially to support the defence of wrongful belief. This is problematic: if the point of the defence is that the accused were set up by the "victim", the fact that he is an informer lends some weight to the claim that the accused were trapped into taking part in what they believed to be a sham robbery.[233]

The rule protecting the identity of informants has been extended to cover the location of police surveillance points, but only insofar as this is necessary to safeguard the identity of members of the public who have co-operated with the police in permitting use of their premises for observation.[234] The location of such surveillance points may be important for cross-examination on the weight of police evidence of their observations. The defence may want to know, for example, the distance of the point from the incidents observed, the officers' angle of vision and the presence of any obstructions to their view. In *Johnson*,[235] the defendant had been convicted of offences of possession and supply of controlled drugs on the basis of police observations from private premises. The defendant argued on appeal that he had not received a fair trial because his defence had been hampered by the trial judge's refusal to order disclosure of the location of the premises. Dismissing the appeal, the Court of Appeal held that the judge had acted rightly in refusing disclosure while safeguarding the defendant's position by careful directions to the jury about any disadvantages incurred by the defendant as a result of the restraints placed on cross-examination by the judge's ruling. The court went on to say that a judge should only order non-disclosure once a proper evidential foundation had been provided by the prosecution:

---

[230] *Turner* [1995] 3 All E.R. 432.
[231] For cases where on analysis they were not, see *Slowcombe* [1991] Crim. L.R. 198 CA; *Menga and Marshalleck* [1998] Crim. L.R. 58.
[232] *Menga and Marshalleck* [1998] Crim. L.R. 58 CA.
[233] See the commentary by D. C. Ormerod, "Improving the Disclosure Regime" (2003) 7 E. & P. 102.
[234] *Rankine* [1986] Q.B. 861 CA. cf. *Brown and Daley* (1988) 87 Cr.App.R. 52, where the Court of Appeal refused to extend the rule to cover the identification of unmarked police cars used for surveillance work. There is no analogy with informers for police investigative methods that do not presuppose co-operation with third parties. Therefore, if the defence need to cross-examine on the details of the surveillance, information sufficient to identify the vehicles should be supplied.
[235] *Johnson* [1989] 1 All E.R. 121 CA.

"The minimum evidential requirements seem to us to be the following. (a) The police officer in charge of the observations to be conducted, and no one of lower rank than a sergeant should usually be acceptable for this purpose, must be able to testify that beforehand he visited all observation places to be used and ascertained the attitude of occupiers of premises, not only to the use to be made of them but also to the possible disclosure thereafter and of the occupiers. He may, of course, in addition inform the court of difficulties, if any, usually encountered in the particular locality of obtaining assistance from the public. (b) A police officer of no lower rank than a chief inspector must be able to testify that immediately prior to the trial he visited the places used for observation, the results of which it is proposed to give in evidence, and ascertained whether the occupiers are the same as when the observations took place and, whether they are or not, what the attitude of those occupiers is to the possible disclosure of the use previously made of the premises and of facts which could lead at the trial to identification of premises and occupiers."[236]

9–043 The measures taken in this case offer useful examples of the kind of measures that can be taken, in the language of Strasbourg, to counterbalance any difficulties caused to the defence by the limitation on its right to disclosure.

F. PRIVILEGE: NEGOTIATIONS FOR SETTLEMENT AND CONCILIATION

9–044 It is public policy to encourage the parties to civil litigation to settle their disputes by negotiation if possible, instead of fighting them out to a lengthy, expensive, and often acrimonious, finish. Such negotiations will often involve the making of concessions and offers which, if they were later revealed in court, could be interpreted as admissions by the client. In this way the client's case could be significantly damaged by the efforts made to avoid a trial. Accordingly the law affords protection to all communications, written or oral, made for the purpose of effecting a settlement of the dispute. Since the privilege is a joint one, partly founded on the implied agreement of the parties as well as public policy, such communications may not be disclosed subsequently without the consent of both parties.[237] The purpose of communications for settlement is frequently signalled by the use of the term "without prejudice", meaning that any statements made are without prejudice to the right of the party to pursue his case fully if the negotiation fails. It is not, however, necessary to use this term to attract the privilege. The question is one of the intention of the parties,[238] and if the circumstances show an attempt to compromise the dispute,[239] the absence of words like "without prejudice" is not fatal. Evidence of the content of the negotiations will still be inadmissible as a general rule.[240]

There are several exceptions to the rule.[241] One exception applies where there is an issue subsequently whether the negotiations did in fact reach a settlement. Where one party sues on an alleged agreement to settle, evidence of the

---

[236] *Johnson* [1989] 1 All E.R. 121 CA at 128.

[237] *Walker v Wilsher* (1889) 23 Q.B.D. 335 CA.

[238] The test of intention is objective: *Pearson Education Ltd v Prentice Hall India Private Ltd* [2005] EWHC 636. cf. *Schering Corp v Cipla Ltd* [2004] EWHC 2587.

[239] The privilege is not restricted to cases where litigation has formally begun. It can apply to negotiations between the parties where they contemplated or might reasonably have contemplated litigation if they could not agree on a settlement of their dispute: *Barnetson v Framlington Group Ltd* [2007] 3 All E.R. 1054 CA.

[240] *Rush and Tompkins Ltd v GLC* [1989] A.C. 1280 HL.

[241] See the judgment of Walker L.J. in *Unilever Plc v Procter & Gamble* [2000] 1 W.L.R. 2436.

negotiations is admissible to show that agreement was reached and the terms of the agreement.[242] Similarly, evidence of facts communicated during settlement negotiations is admissible as an aid to the interpretation of the settlement agreement. It makes no difference that the communications were without prejudice since the parties would expect the agreement to mean the same in both cases.[243] The privilege is not available at all where a letter headed "without prejudice" is not an attempt to settle, but is itself a substantive act of bankruptcy, as where a debtor tells his creditors that he cannot pay.[244] Similarly, a letter acknowledging the existence of a debt as an undisputed liability and dealing only with whether, and to what extent, the debtor can meet that liability, is not privileged because there is no dispute to be compromised.[245] No privilege attaches to a communication containing an illegal threat[246] or a libel.

In the leading case of *Rush and Tompkins Ltd v GLC*,[247] the House of Lords made it clear that the privilege can protect against use by third parties of settlement negotiations. In building construction disputes, for example, there would otherwise be a risk that concessions made by a main contractor in an attempt to settle a dispute with subcontractor A might be held against him in a separate dispute with subcontractor B. It was held that evidence of settlement negotiations is inadmissible in any subsequent litigation connected with the same subject-matter.[248] It would follow that the third party would not only be unable to obtain discovery of the negotiations but would also be unable to use any secondary evidence of them that was available. However, where a "without prejudice" communication containing an admission comes into the hands of the prosecuting authorities, there is no rule that the evidence of the admission is inadmissible in subsequent criminal proceedings. The Court of Appeal so held in *R. v K*,[249] following the rule that evidence of the defendant's legally privileged communications is admissible where it is has fallen into the hands of the prosecution.[250] The court thought that the public interest in prosecuting crime outweighed the public interest in facilitating the settlement of civil disputes, although it also noted the possible use of the exclusionary discretion under s.78 of PACE where the admission of the evidence would adversely affect the fairness of the criminal proceedings.

Finally, an analogous privilege protects communications with a conciliator in matrimonial disputes.[251] This again is founded on public policy considerations; the law is concerned to encourage spouses to settle their differences and achieve

---

[242] *Tomlin v Standard Telephones and Cables Ltd* [1969] 1 W.L.R. 1378 CA.

[243] *Oceanbulk Shipping and Trading SA v TMT Asia Ltd* [2010] UKSC 44; [2010] 4 All E.R. 1011.

[244] *Re Daintrey Ex p. Holt* [1893] 2 Q.B. 116.

[245] *Bradford and Bingley Plc v Rashid* [2006] UKHL 37; [2006] 4 All E.R. 705.

[246] *Kitcat v Sharp* (1882) 48 L.T. 64.

[247] *Rush and Tompkins Ltd v GLC* [1989] A.C. 1280.

[248] See also *Ofulue v Bossert* [2009] UKHL 16, where the House of Lords held that an acknowledgment of the claimant's title to property, made during without prejudice negotiations to settle an action for possession of the property, could not be relied on by the claimant in a separate later action for possession of the same property. It was immaterial that the claimant's title was not disputed in the earlier action.

[249] *R. v K* [2009] EWCA Crim 1640.

[250] See Ch.10 paras 10–19, 10–21.

[251] See *Pais v Pais* [1971] P. 119; *Re D (Minors)* [1993] Fam. 231.

reconciliation if possible, and additionally there is an important concern with the welfare of any children involved. The law here is still in the process of development and may not have exactly the same scope and limits as the usual "without prejudice" privilege.

CHAPTER 10

LEGAL PROFESSIONAL PRIVILEGE[1]

A. INTRODUCTION

One of the most important grounds on which access to evidence can be refused is   **10–001**
that the evidence in question is protected by legal professional privilege. This
doctrine gives legal recognition to a person's interest in maintaining the secrecy
of confidential communications in connection with his legal affairs. The doctrine
originated at common law, and for most purposes its scope and limits are still
determined by the common law. However, Parliament has given the privilege

---

[1] A useful monograph is J. Auburn, *Legal Professional Privilege: Law and Theory* (Oxford: Hart
Publishing, 2000).

statutory expression for certain purposes.[2] The best-known formulation is in s.10(1) of PACE, which Lord Goff has stated reproduces the common law[3]:

"(1) Subject to subs.(2) below, in this Act 'items subject to legal privilege' means—
(a) communications between a professional legal adviser and his client or any person representing his client made in connection with the giving of legal advice to the client;
(b) communications between a professional legal adviser and his client or any person representing his client or between such an adviser or his client or any such representative and any other person made in connection with or in contemplation of legal proceedings and for the purposes of such proceedings; and
(c) items enclosed with or referred to in such communications and made—
(i) in connection with the giving of legal advice; or
(ii) in connection with or in contemplation of legal proceedings and for the purposes of such proceedings,
when they are in the possession of a person who is entitled to possession of them."

This section gives effect to the two forms of the privilege at common law. One form protects communications between a client and a lawyer made in connection with a purpose of the client obtaining or receiving legal advice from the lawyer. This is sometimes referred to as lawyer-client privilege, or legal advice privilege to distinguish it from the other form of legal professional privilege known as litigation privilege. Litigation privilege protects communications between a client, or the client's lawyer, and a third party[4] made for the dominant purpose of the client obtaining or receiving advice or information in connection with litigation that is in existence or is contemplated as a definite prospect. Under both forms the privilege is that of the client, not the lawyer or the third party. The privilege gives the client a right to refuse to disclose a privileged communication,[5] a right to refuse to give evidence about it[6] and a right that the lawyer (or the third party) shall not be compelled to disclose or give evidence about it without the client's consent.[7] The lawyer owes a corresponding duty to the client not to disclose a privileged communication without the client's consent.[8] Such consent can be freely given or withheld. If the client does disclose or give evidence about a privileged communication, or consents to the lawyer (or a third party) doing so, the privilege is said to be waived.

It is convenient to deal with the two forms of the privilege separately because the litigation privilege differs from the legal advice privilege in a number of important ways, although in other respects the law is the same. The differences

---

[2] The terminology is not always consistent. Alternatives are "legal privilege" and "professional privilege".

[3] See *R. v Central Criminal Court Ex p. Francis and Francis* [1989] A.C. 346 at 392 HL. The formulation in s.10 is expressed to be for the purposes of PACE; principally the scope of powers of search and seizure.

[4] Litigation privilege is available to an unrepresented litigant, as Laws L.J. confirmed in *R. (on the application of Kelly) v Warley Magistrates' Court* [2007] EWHC 1836 (Admin); [2008] 1 Cr.App.R. 14 at [18]; to that extent the reference to "professional" privilege is a misnomer.

[5] *Minet v Morgan* (1873) 8 Ch. App. 361, confirming earlier authorities.

[6] *Minter v Priest* [1930] A.C. 558 at 579 per Lord Atkin.

[7] *Greenough v Gaskell* (1833) 1 Myl. & K. 98 (lawyer); *Harmony Shipping Co v Davis* [1979] 3 All E.R. 177 at 181 (third party witnesses).

[8] *Greenough v Gaskell* (1833) 1 Myl. & K. 98 at 101–102.

reflect the facts that the two types of privilege have different rationales, and that for certain purposes the legal advice form has an absolute quality to it that does not apply to litigation privilege.[9]

B. THE LAWYER-CLIENT (LEGAL ADVICE) PRIVILEGE

1. *Statement and rationale*

The law has recognised a type of legal advice privilege for centuries. According to Wigmore,[10] the earliest references appear in the late sixteenth century when cases were reported holding that solicitors and counsel were exempt from examination touching the matter on which they were acting for the client.[11] In this early period the courts regarded the privilege as that of the lawyer rather than the client. It was thought that a lawyer, when giving evidence, ought not in honour to be required to disclose what he had been told in confidence.[12]

10–002

The modern form of the privilege was settled in the 19th century as courts of equity refined their process of pre-trial discovery. A series of leading cases[13] established two propositions that are crucial for an accurate identification of the modern rationales for the privilege. The first is that the privilege is that of the client rather than the lawyer.[14] The second is that the privilege attaches to confidential communications in connection with a purpose of legal advice irrespective of whether litigation is in existence or contemplated. In *Greenough v Gaskell*,[15] Lord Brougham L.C. held that a solicitor was bound to withhold communications sent or received and documents made in the course of professional employment on the client's behalf. This protection, he said, was not qualified by any reference to proceedings pending or in contemplation. Such a restriction would exclude a very important class of communications, namely those made with a view to the avoidance of litigation in the future or the successful conduct of any litigation which did arise. This wider rule for legal advice privilege found favour with the judges of the period so that by the time of

---

[9] *Re L (A Minor) (Police Investigation: Privilege)* [1997] A.C. 16 HL.

[10] (McNaughton rev., 1961) Vol.VIII, para.2290.

[11] *Berd v Lovelace* (1577) Cary 62 (solicitor); *Dennis v Codrington* (1579) Cary 100 (counsel).

[12] Wigmore, (McNaughton rev., 1961) para.2290.

[13] *Greenough v Gaskell* (1833) 1 Myl. & K. 98; *Lawrence v Campbell* (1859) 4 Drew 485; *Minet v Morgan* (1873) 8 Ch. App. 361; *Anderson v Bank of British Columbia* (1876) 2 Ch.D. 644, confirming that the rules of equity governed the procedure of discovery after the fusion of law and equity by the Judicature Acts.

[14] This had already been stated by Buller J. in *Wilson v Rastall* (1792) 4 Term Rep. 753, following the rejection by the House of Lords in *The Duchess of Kingston's Case* (1776) 20 How. St. Tr. 586 of "point of honour" as a valid ground for refusal to testify; see Wigmore, (McNaughton rev., 1961), para.2286. The theory of the privilege as that of the client in fact first appeared some time earlier: Wigmore, para.2290, citing Gilbert, *The Law of Evidence* (London edn, 1756), p.138. Since the lawyer cannot waive his client's privilege the lawyer may sometimes find himself in difficulty, e.g. where a wasted costs order is made against him; see *Medcalf v Mardell* [2002] 3 All E.R. 721 HL.

[15] *Greenough v Gaskell* (1833) 1 Myl. & K. 98.

Minet v Morgan,[16] 40 years later, Lord Selborne L.C. was able to describe the rule as "well settled and established in this Court".[17]

This form of legal professional privilege has more than one rationale. The first is the need for full and frank disclosure by the client to the lawyer. In the leading case of *R. v Derby Magistrates' Court Ex p. B*,[18] Lord Taylor of Gosforth C.J., after reviewing earlier authorities, summarised this rationale as follows:

> "The principle which runs through all these cases . . . is that a man must be able to consult his lawyer in confidence, since otherwise he might hold back half the truth. The client must be sure that what he tells his lawyer in confidence will never be revealed without his consent. Legal professional privilege is thus much more than an ordinary rule of evidence, limited in its application to the facts of a particular case. It is a fundamental condition on which the administration of justice as a whole rests."[19]

10–003 This reference to the administration of justice merits further discussion. The argument is that the privilege of keeping communications with a lawyer secret facilitates the representation of clients by legal advisers. It encourages lay clients to consult professional legal advisers and not to hold anything back that might be relevant. This is important because the law is complex and difficult for the lay person to understand, hence a client needs skilled and informed advice if he is to be able to arrange his affairs with confidence and security. The importance of this interest clearly increases with the gravity of the matter in question. For example, a client who consults a solicitor after being charged with a serious crime has a strong interest in not permitting the police or the prosecution to have access to discussions about the defence to the charge.

In addition to such individual interests in confidentiality is an important public interest. This is based in part on considerations of efficiency. Lawyers need full information from their clients if they are to do their jobs effectively with minimum cost and delay. The state provides machinery for the resolution of legal disputes, which include accusations that a person has committed an offence, but the machinery is expensive and time-consuming to run. Since it is ultimately provided at public expense there is a public interest in the establishment of rules, such as legal privilege, that enable it to function as cost-effectively as possible. Lawyers who are fully briefed will be in a better position to give their clients reliable advice on the avoidance of litigation, or on settlement of civil disputes or on guilty pleas in a criminal case. One judge has commented, in relation to the privilege, that the public interest requires "that hopeless and exaggerated claims and unsound and spurious defences be so far as possible discouraged, and civil actions so far as possible settled without resort to judicial decision".[20] A lawyer can only give full and candid advice about the client's legal position if the client has disclosed all the material facts.

---

[16] *Minet v Morgan* (1873) 8 Ch. App. 361.

[17] *Minet v Morgan* (1873) 8 Ch. App. 361 at 368.

[18] *R. v Derby Magistrates' Court Ex p. B* [1996] 1 A.C. 487 HL.

[19] *R. v Derby Magistrates' Court Ex p. B* [1996] 1 A.C. 487 at 540. Lord Taylor's proposition was approved by the Privy Council in *B v Auckland District Law Society* [2003] UKPC 38; [2003] 2 A.C. 736.

[20] *Ventouris v Mountain* [1991] 3 All E.R. 472 at 475 per Bingham L.J.

Secondly, and following the theme of the public interest, there is a rationale for legal privilege based on the interest in maintaining the fundamental moral and political values on which the legal system is founded. A major value, discussed in Ch.2, is that all citizens are entitled to equal concern and respect. Legal representation is itself an acknowledgment of the elementary truth that not all citizens are equal in their power and resources to organise their affairs. Allowing confidentiality to communications with lawyers maximises the potential of legal representation to iron out such inequalities of wealth and ability. This point connects with the status of the right to legal representation as a human right, discussed below.

Thirdly, in *Three Rivers DC v Governor and Company of the Bank of England (No.6)*,[21] Lord Scott set out what he called the "rule of law rationale", which emphasises the importance of the privilege in protecting the interests of citizens in privacy and security:

> "... it is necessary in our society, a society in which the restraining and controlling framework is built upon a belief in the rule of law, that communications between clients and lawyers, whereby the clients are hoping for the assistance of the lawyers' legal skills in the management of their (the clients) affairs, should be secure against the possibility of any scrutiny from others, whether the police, the executive, business competitors, inquisitive busybodies or anyone else ... this idea ... justifies, in my opinion, the retention of legal advice privilege in our law, notwithstanding that as a result cases may sometimes have to be decided in ignorance of relevant probative material."[22]

In the *Derby Magistrates* case the House of Lords took a strong view of the privilege. Lord Taylor, with whose speech the majority of the Lords agreed, described it as "absolute", meaning that it was not subject to new exceptions devised by the courts on the basis of balancing the interest recognised by the privilege against other public interests.[23] The precise issue in the case is discussed later in this chapter; for present purposes the point is that the privilege is itself based on a judgment that in general the public interest in protecting the confidentiality of legal advice outweighs the public interest in ensuring unimpeded access to evidence. The fact that the privilege does not yield to contrary calculations of the public interest shows that it is a strong right, with a status significantly greater than an "ordinary rule of evidence". In *R. (on the application of Morgan Grenfell & Co Ltd) v Special Commissioner of Income Tax*,[24] Lord Hoffmann described legal professional privilege as "a fundamental human right long established in the common law". In this case the House of Lords held that the privilege could be overridden by Parliament only by express words or necessary implication.[25] Even then, as will shortly be seen, there might be an issue whether a statutory abrogation of the privilege is compatible with the ECHR.

10–004

---

[21] *Three Rivers DC* [2004] UKHL 48; [2005] 1 A.C. 610.

[22] *Three Rivers DC* [2004] UKHL 48; [2005] 1 A.C. 610 at [34].

[23] *Derby Magistrates* [1996] 1 A.C. 487 at 508.

[24] *R. (on the application of Morgan Grenfell & Co Ltd) v Special Commissioner of Income Tax* [2003] 1 A.C. 563.

[25] "A necessary implication is not the same as a reasonable implication ... [it] necessarily follows from the express provisions of the statute construed in their context ... A necessary implication is a matter of express language and logic not interpretation": *R. (on the application of Morgan Grenfell &*

The right to legal representation is recognised internationally as a fundamental human right. Article 6.3(c) of the ECHR states that:

> "Everyone charged with a criminal offence has the following minimum rights ... to defend himself in person or through legal assistance of his own choosing or, if he has not sufficient means to pay for legal assistance, to be given it free when the interests of justice so require."[26]

There is no express reference to legal professional privilege in art.6,[27] but the European Court of Human Rights has made clear its view that confidentiality of communication between lawyer and client is necessary to guarantee the effectiveness of the right to legal representation.[28] By emphasising the importance of confidentiality of the lawyer-client relationship the court has implied the substance of legal advice privilege into art.6.[29] This means in particular that discussions between the accused and his lawyer should be conducted out of the hearing of third parties. Surveillance of the discussion may result in a finding of a violation of art.6, on the basis that the accused was directly affected by this restriction on the exercise of the rights of the defence. In *Brennan v United Kingdom,* the court found a breach of art.6(3)(c) and 6(1) where a police officer was present within sight and hearing of the defendant's first consultation with his solicitor after being arrested on suspicion of murder:

> "... the Court cannot but conclude that the presence of the police officer would have inevitably prevented the applicant from speaking frankly to his solicitor and given him reason to hesitate before broaching questions of potential significance to the case against him. Both the applicant and the solicitor had been warned that no names should be mentioned and that the interview would be stopped if anything was said which was perceived as hindering the investigation. It is immaterial that it is not shown that there were particular matters which the applicant and his solicitor were thereby stopped from discussing. The ability of an accused to communicate freely with his defence lawyer ... was subject to express limitation. The applicant had already made admissions before the consultation, and made admissions afterwards. It is indisputable that he was in need at that time of legal advice, and that his responses in subsequent interviews, which were to be carried out in the absence of his solicitor, would continue to be of potential relevance to his trial and could irretrievably prejudice his defence."[30]

Co Ltd) v Special Commissioner of Income Tax* [2003] 1 A.C. 563 at [45] per Lord Hobhouse; applied by the Privy Council in *B v Auckland District Law Society* [2003] UKPC 38; [2003] 2 A.C. 736. This principle was applied by the Divisional Court in *R. (on the application of Kelly) v Warley Magistrates' Court* [2007] EWHC (Admin) 1836; [2008] 1 Cr.App.R. 14 in holding that a district judge had no power under the Criminal Procedure Rules to override legal professional privilege by requiring the applicant to disclose pre-trial the identity and other details of his defence witnesses.

[26] See also art.21 of the Statute of the International Tribunal for Yugoslavia, providing in virtually identical terms for an accused's right of legal representation in the determination of any charge pursuant to the statute.

[27] Compare r.97 of the Rules of Procedure and Evidence of the International Tribunal for Yugoslavia, which creates a lawyer-client privilege for all communications between lawyer and client, subject only to the client's consent to disclosure, or voluntary disclosure by the client to a third party. A form of litigation privilege appears in r.70, which protects from disclosure "reports, memoranda, or other internal documents prepared by a party, its assistants or representatives in connection with the investigation or preparation of the case".

[28] *S v Switzerland* (1992) 14 E.H.R.R. 670 at [48]; *Brennan v United Kingdom* (2002) 34 E.H.R.R. 18 at [58]; *Modarca v Moldova* (2009) 48 E.H.R.R. 39, at [87]–[89].

[29] In *R. v Derby Magistrates' Court Ex p. B* [1996] 1 A.C. 487, Lord Taylor stated explicitly that legal professional privilege was a fundamental human right protected by the European Convention.

[30] *Brennan v United Kingdom* (2002) 34 E.H.R.R. at [62].

In this case the accused and his solicitor were aware of the officer's presence. The finding of a violation of art.6 is premised on the inhibiting effect of his presence. What happens if the officer engages in covert surveillance of the consultation, or intercepts the client's correspondence with the solicitor, and the prosecution then seek to use evidence of the privileged communications against the accused at his trial? The evidence has been obtained in breach of confidence and possibly illegally.[31] In these circumstances the accused may apply for a stay of the proceedings as an abuse of process.[32] In *Grant*,[33] where the police had secretly recorded privileged conversations between the defendant and his solicitor in a police exercise yard, the Court of Appeal was in no doubt that such a deliberate violation of the right to legal privilege was so great an affront to the integrity of the justice system and therefore the rule of law that the prosecution was abusive and should be stopped. This was a strong decision because the court held that it made no difference that the defendant had not in fact suffered any prejudice from the breach. As discussed in Ch.8, the decision in *Grant* was subsequently disapproved by the Supreme Court in *Maxwell*[34] and by the Privy Council in *Warren v Attorney-General of Jersey*.[35] Both courts seem to have taken the view that it was not enough by itself that there had been a deliberate interference with a fundamental right, where the defendant was charged with a very serious crime and had suffered no disadvantage from the police misconduct. This view of the appropriate balance in such a case is debatable, although if the prosecution have sufficient independent and untainted evidence to support a conviction it is not apparent that a guilty verdict would be illegitimate. However, it is submitted that if in a case like *Grant* the eavesdropping does yield incriminating evidence on which the prosecution proposes to rely, then, whatever the fate of an abuse of process application, there is a compelling case for the exclusion of the evidence under s.78 of PACE.

Finally, eavesdropping on confidential discussions, or interfering with confidential correspondence, is prima facie a breach of the right to privacy under art.8 of the ECHR.[36] Article 8 provides additional protection for privileged communications, protection that is not dependent on there being a trial, as required for art.6. In *Foxley v United Kingdom*,[37] the court found a violation of art.8 where a receiver and trustee in bankruptcy had opened and copied the defendant's correspondence with his lawyers after obtaining a court order[38] authorising the re-direction of the defendant's mail. The court held that there was no justification for the actions of the receiver, which had contravened the principles of

10–005

---

[31] The Regulation of Investigatory Powers Act 2000 Pt II provides for covert recording of private and privileged consultations to be lawful, but only as authorised intrusive surveillance: see *In Re McE* [2009] UKHL 15.

[32] Applying the test of whether the police conduct was such a serious abuse of power that the prosecution amounts to an affront to the public conscience: *Looseley* [2001] 4 All E.R. 897.

[33] *Grant* [2005] EWCA Crim 1089; [2005] 2 Cr.App.R. 28.

[34] *Maxwell* [2010] UKSC 48; [2011] 2 Cr.App.R. 31.

[35] *Warren v Attorney-General of Jersey* [2011] UKPC 10; [2011] 2 Cr.App.R. 29.

[36] *Campbell v United Kingdom* (1992) 15 E.H.R.R. 137. Authorisation of such activity as intrusive surveillance under Pt II of the Regulation of Investigatory Powers Act 2000 may provide a sufficient justification under art.8(2): see *In Re McE* [2009] UKHL 15.

[37] *Foxley v United Kingdom* (2001) 31 E.H.R.R. 637.

[38] Under the Insolvency Act 1986 s.371.

confidentiality and professional privilege attaching to relations between a lawyer and his client. The court noted the close relationship in this context between art.8 and art.6:

> "The Court recalls that, where a lawyer is involved, an encroachment on professional secrecy may have repercussions on the proper administration of justice and hence on the rights guaranteed by art.6."[39]

However, it was held that it was unnecessary to consider further the applicant's complaint under art.6, given the finding of a violation of art.8. It was noted also that the applicant had not provided the court with any information about the conduct and outcome of the receivership proceedings. It was not clear, therefore, how the applicant's exercise of the rights of the defence had been affected by the interference.

2. *Extent of the privilege*

(A) *The meaning of "lawyer"*

10–006   The most obvious example of a lawyer for the purposes of the privilege is a solicitor in private practice, but the scope of the privilege is not restricted to communications with such lawyers. It extends to communications with counsel, who is regarded either as the client's legal adviser or as the solicitor's alter ego,[40] salaried legal advisers employed by corporations, government departments and other organisations ("in-house lawyers")[41] and foreign lawyers.[42] The privilege also protects communications made by or through the lawyer's clerk or other employee or agent.[43]

There is a related privilege attached to communications with certain persons who are not lawyers in any of the senses just mentioned but who provide legal advice to the client in specific contexts. Statute has given protection to communications with patent agents[44] and licensed conveyancers.[45] Section 190 of the Legal Services Act 2007 extends legal professional privilege to communications with individuals, not being barristers or solicitors, who as "authorised persons" under the Act provide advocacy services in relation to the exercise of rights of audience, or litigation services in relation to the conduct of litigation, or conveyancing services in relation to reserved instrument activities, or probate

---

[39] *Foxley* (2001) 31 E.H.R.R. 637 at [50]. See also *Niemietz v Germany* (1993) 16 E.H.R.R. 97, and generally Emmerson, Ashworth and Macdonald, paras 14–14 to 14–24.

[40] *Bristol Corp v Cox* (1884) 26 Ch.D. 678.

[41] *Alfred Crompton Amusement Machines Ltd v Customs and Excise Commissioners (No.2)* [1974] A.C. 405 (the decision of the Court of Appeal on this point was not challenged in the further appeal to the House of Lords); *AM & S Europe Ltd v Commission of the European Communities* [1983] 1 All E.R. 705 at 733 CJEC per Advocate-General Slynn.

[42] *Re Duncan* [1968] P. 306; *IBM Corp v Phoenix International (Computers) Ltd* [1995] 1 All E.R. 413 Ch. D.

[43] *Parkins v Harkshaw* (1817) 2 Stark. N.P. 239; *Taylor v Forster* (1825) 2 C.& P. 195.

[44] Copyright, Designs and Patents Act 1988 s.280. Similarly the Trade Marks Act 1994 s.87 attaches privilege to communications with trade mark agents.

[45] Administration of Justice Act 1985 s.33.

services in relation to probate activities. There is some authority for privilege attaching to communications with legally unqualified representatives of parties to proceedings before industrial tribunals with a view to the conduct of the proceedings.[46] This might have paved the way for the development of a general principle that privilege ought to be available whenever a client is being advised or represented by another person in connection with litigation, whether or not the adviser is legally qualified. However, later authorities have refused to extend privilege to communications with legally unqualified persons.[47] In *R. (on the application of Prudential plc) v Special Commissioner of Income Tax*,[48] a majority of the Supreme Court held that legal professional privilege does not apply at common law to any professional adviser other than a qualified lawyer. It does not therefore extend to accountants giving legal advice on tax matters, despite the fact that many clients might consult their accountants on fiscal liabilities rather than their solicitors. The court was emphatic that such an extension of privilege would raise serious questions of its scope and application that only Parliament could properly answer. Privilege was held not to arise either where a client of a firm of claims and project-handling consultants received advice from a legally qualified person but the retainer was not to provide legal advice as such.[49]

(B)   Clients and their employees and agents

Because the privilege is that of the client it follows that the benefit of the privilege cannot be claimed by any other party to the privileged communication. In *Schneider v Leigh*,[50] the defendant, a doctor, wrote a libellous medical report on the plaintiff. The defendant wrote the report for the solicitors of a company that the plaintiff had sued in other proceedings. The company therefore had the benefit of litigation privilege for the report, but the Court of Appeal held that legal privilege was not available to the defendant as author of the report. He was therefore liable to disclose the report to the plaintiff. At the same time it should be noted that a defendant in such circumstances might have a defence of qualified privilege to an action for libel, but this is a substantive rule of the law of tort and is not the same as the rule of the law of evidence that we are now considering.

10–007

However, it is possible for privilege to be held jointly by more than one person. A lawyer may be asked to advise, for example, both a company as to its corporate legal position and its directors as to their individual responsibilities. For joint privilege to arise it is necessary that there should be a joint retainer by the clients concerned, or that the parties have a joint interest in the subject matter of the relevant communication at the time that it comes into existence and that the facts demonstrate that all those sharing the privilege and the lawyers concerned

---

[46] *M & W Grazebrook Ltd v Wallens* [1973] 2 All E.R. 868 NIRC.
[47] *Umoh* (1987) 84 Cr.App.R. 138 CA (no privilege for conversation of prisoner with prison legal aid officer, but public interest immunity may apply); *New Victoria Hospital v Ryan* [1993] I.C.R. 201 EAT (no privilege for communications by employers with personnel consultants in relation to the dismissal of an employee).
[48] *R. (on the application of Prudential plc) v Special Commissioner of Income Tax* [2013] UKSC 1.
[49] *Walter Lilly & Co Ltd v Mackay* [2012] EWHC 649 (TCC); (2012) 141 Con. LR 102.
[50] *Schneider v Leigh* [1955] 2 Q.B. 195. cf. *Lee v South West Thames RHA* [1985] 2 All E.R. 385 CA.

knew, or from the objective evidence ought to have known, that they enjoyed legal professional privilege with the others.[51] In the case of a corporate representative this will require evidence that he communicated with the lawyer to seek advice in an individual capacity, that the lawyer knew or ought to have appreciated that he was communicating with the individual in that individual capacity and that others with whom the joint privilege is claimed knew or ought to have appreciated the legal position. The holders of a joint privilege do not retain any privilege as against one another, but can assert the privilege against the rest of the world. Because the privilege is joint it can only be waived jointly and not by one party alone.[52]

Privilege may also be claimed by a client's successor in title. The rule is that the client's privilege attaches to the relevant communications so that they acquire a privileged status that does not come to an end when the particular transaction or litigation is concluded. The privilege remains in existence and can be invoked by the client and his successors in title in subsequent proceedings, whether or not the subject-matter or the parties are the same. This can produce remarkable results. In *Calcraft v Guest*,[53] the Court of Appeal upheld a claim of privilege for the original proofs of witnesses and notes on evidence in an action over fishing rights involving the plaintiff's predecessor in title no less than a century earlier. In giving judgment Lindley M.R. uttered the famous aphorism, "once privileged, always privileged", raising the possibility of privilege claims subsisting into eternity. It is doubtful how far the rationale of the need for full and frank disclosure by the original clients is a convincing justification for the blanket protection given to the interests of future generations. However, the rule is well-established,[54] and it was recently affirmed, obiter, by the House of Lords in *R. v Derby Magistrates' Court Ex p. B.*[55]

A client may use an employee or agent to communicate with a legal adviser,[56] but lawyer-client privilege will be available only as long as the employee or agent is no more than a channel of communication.[57] If, however, the employee or agent is instructed to prepare a report for the legal adviser, on the basis of material supplied or collected by the employee or agent, then the report is regarded as coming from a third party. This means that it can only attract privilege under the litigation form of legal privilege. Litigation must be in existence or contemplated as a definite prospect. In *Re Highgrade Traders*,[58] Oliver L.J. rejected an argument that reports commissioned by an insurance company from firms of loss adjusters, fire investigation specialists and

---

[51] See *R. (on the application of Ford) v FSA* [2011] EWHC 2583 (Admin); [2012] 1 All E.R. 1238.
[52] *Hellenic Mutual War Risks Association (Bermuda) Ltd v Harrison, The Sagheera* [1997] 1 Lloyds Rep. 160.
[53] *Calcraft v Guest* [1898] 1 Q.B. 759.
[54] See *The Aegis Blaze* [1986] 1 Lloyd's Rep. 203 CA. It is immaterial that the parties to the subsequent litigation are not the same, or that the subject-matter is different.
[55] *R. v Derby Magistrates' Court Ex p. B* [1996] 1 A.C. 487 at 506 per Lord Taylor C.J., with whom Lord Keith of Kinkel and Lord Mustill agreed and at 509 per Lord Lloyd of Berwick.
[56] *Reid v Langlois* (1849) 1 Mac. & G. 627.
[57] *Wheeler v Le Marchant* (1881) 17 Ch.D. 675 at 684 CA. See also *Jones v Great Central Rail Co* [1910] A.C. 4 HL (no privilege for information given by dismissed employee to a trade union official, since the latter had to make a decision whether to refer the employee's claim to the union's lawyers).
[58] *Re Highgrade Traders* [1984] B.C.L.C. 151 CA.

accountants were communications by agents of the insurers for the purposes of lawyer-client privilege. He recognised that a client may communicate with a lawyer through an employee or agent, but emphasised that the legal advice privilege applies only where the employee or agent is no more than the medium of communication. The latter point, he said, is not directed to the case "where, there being no litigation in progress or contemplation, the client or solicitor procures a third-party to provide information collected by the third-party to the solicitor". This rule was reviewed and confirmed by the Court of Appeal in *Three Rivers DC v Governor and Company of the Bank of England (No.5)*,[59] where privilege was refused for documents prepared by employees of the Bank of England for submission to the Bank's solicitors. The solicitors had been retained to give advice to the Bank on the presentation of its case to a statutory inquiry into the collapse of a bank under the supervision of the Bank. It was accepted that litigation privilege did not apply since the statutory inquiry was not an adversarial proceeding. In holding that legal advice privilege was not available the Court of Appeal relied, inter alia, on *Waugh v British Railways Board*.[60] In this leading case on legal privilege the House of Lords had discussed the possibly privileged status of an accident report, compiled by the defendants' own officers on instructions from the defendants, exclusively in terms of the litigation privilege.

This is an important point in practice for many different types of report. **10–008** Background reports, briefing papers, accident investigations, financial and other investigations for insurance companies, reviews of safety equipment and procedures and risk assessments of all kinds may well raise issues of the extent of legal privilege. Characterising all such documents as third party reports, and giving them protection only on the basis of litigation privilege, seems to be at odds with the recent trend in English law to expand the scope of protection for lawyer-client privilege.[61] However, it is consistent to some degree with one of the rationales for legal advice privilege. We have seen that one rationale is the need for full and frank disclosure by the client to the lawyer. It is not clear how far this justification can apply where a third party makes factual investigations and presents conclusions in a report written independently of the client. By hypothesis the client's information will be incomplete and there will be less reason to hold back information to the third party. An independent third party will generally have no reason not to state the facts and conclusions fully and frankly. Hence secrecy for such reports would not seem to be warranted, except where they are part of the preparations for the client's brief for litigation. However, the inclusion of employees within the rule applicable to third parties is problematic. First, employees may feel a greater identity of interest with the employer and have more incentive to edit what they say. Secondly, where the employer is a corporate body it is nominally the client for the purposes of legal privilege, but it can act only through its officers and employees. A question then arises as to which of these represent the corporation for the purposes of attracting privilege,

---

[59] *Three Rivers DC (No.5)* [2003] EWCA Civ 474; [2003] Q.B. 1556.
[60] *Waugh v British Railways Board* [1980] A.C. 521 HL.
[61] A trend demonstrated by the increasing protection available in cases of inadvertent disclosure (see paras 10–021 to 10–022, below) and the refusal of the courts to "balance" the privilege against other public interests (see paras 10–024 to 10–026, below).

and which are third parties for the purposes of the rule. How is the distinction to be made? Since a corporation can only make disclosure to its legal advisers on the basis of information held by its officers and employees it is arguable that it is artificial to distinguish between its employees in relation to the information they hold. It would seem that for the privilege to be effective the information of the corporate client should be treated as the sum of the information held collectively by all its employees. The decision of the Court of Appeal in *Three Rivers DC v Governor and Company of the Bank of England (No.5)*, mentioned above, is controversial. In *Three Rivers DC v Governor and Company of the Bank of England (No.6)*,[62] which concerned a different point in the same litigation (discussed below), the House of Lords declined an invitation to review that decision, but clearly thought that there was room for debate as to its correctness.[63] It seems likely that the courts will revisit this issue in due course.[64]

(C)   The protected communications

10–009   The communication between lawyer and client must be confidential. Confidentiality is implied by law as one of the defining characteristics of the fiduciary relationship between lawyer and client.[65] Confidentiality, and therefore privilege, may also exist where the communication is made with a view to establishing the relationship.[66] It should be emphasised that the privilege protects communications and not facts. A lawyer can be required to disclose his client's identity,[67] and to testify about facts that he has directly perceived in the course of the relationship with the client, such as the client's handwriting.[68] The court also has jurisdiction to order a solicitor to reveal the client's confidential contact details, although the court must be alert not to make any order which might inhibit the fundamental right of the client to seek and obtain legal advice.[69]

In general the privilege will protect confidential communications if they are made in connection with a purpose of giving or receiving legal advice.[70] Clear examples of documents privileged under this principle are a client's instructions to a solicitor, a solicitor's instructions to counsel, counsel's opinion and the

---

[62] *Three Rivers DC (No.6)* [2004] UKHL 48; [2005] 1 A.C. 610.
[63] See *Three Rivers DC (No.6)* [2004] UKHL 48 at [46]–[48] per Lord Scott and [118] per Lord Carswell.
[64] For comment see R. Preston-Jones and J. Paterson, (2004) 154 N.L.J. 1709; C. Passmore, (2006) 156 N.L.J. 668.
[65] See *Bristol and West Building Society v Mothew* [1996] 4 All E.R. 698 at 711–712 per Millett L.J., and see generally *Cordery on Solicitors*, 9th edn (London: Butterworths, 1998), Vol.1, J [59] onwards.
[66] *Minter v Priest* [1930] A.C. 558 HL.
[67] *Bursill v Tanner* (1885) 16 Q.B.D. 1.
[68] *Dwyer v Collins* (1852) 7 Exch. 639.
[69] *JSC BTA Bank v Solodchenko* [2011] EWHC 2163 (Ch); [2012] 1 All E.R. 735, where Henderson J. held that the order should be made where its primary purpose was to aid enforcement of an order for the committal of the client to prison for contempt of a previous court order.
[70] *Minter v Priest* [1930] A.C. 558 at 581 HL per Lord Atkin; *Balabel v Air-India* [1988] 2 All E.R. 246 at 254 CA per Taylor L.J. A relationship of client and legal adviser may exist between the police and the Director of Public Prosecutions where the police seek the Director's advice on matters with which they are concerned: *Goodridge v Chief Constable of Hampshire Constabulary* [1999] 1 All E.R. 896.

solicitor's advice to the client. A number of points now need to be made by way of expansion and qualification of the general principle.

According to Taylor L.J. in *Balabel v Air-India*,[71] the purpose of legal advice has to be interpreted broadly. It is not restricted to communications making a specific request for legal advice or that convey such advice. It includes communications that provide information as part of a continuous course of dealing between solicitor and client. Many transactions pass through a number of stages when information will be exchanged between solicitor and client as part of an overall purpose of providing legal advice as and when needed. Communications fairly referable to this purpose will be covered by privilege. Furthermore, legal privilege is not restricted to the giving of advice on matters of law or the drafting or construction of documents. It can extend to non-legal advice, such as advice on the commercial wisdom of entering a particular transaction, provided this is directly related to the performance by the lawyer of his professional duty as legal adviser of the client.[72] However, this is not to say that all communications to or from clients that take place in the ordinary course of a solicitor's business are protected, even if they are confidential.[73] A record of a transaction such as a conveyance has been held not to be privileged since its purpose is not the provision of legal advice.[74] Similarly, a free-standing instruction by a client to a solicitor, for example to offer terms of settlement[75] or to collect rents from tenants,[76] will not attract privilege unless it contains an implied request for advice.

In *Three Rivers DC v Governor and Company of the Bank of England (No.6)*,[77] the House of Lords reconsidered the scope of legal advice privilege and confirmed an important application of it to "presentational" advice. This decision was part of extensive litigation arising from the collapse of the Bank of Credit and Commerce International in 1991. It concerned the issue of whether communications between the Bank of England and their solicitors and counsel relating to the statement submitted by the Bank to the Bingham Inquiry into the collapse of BCCI were privileged from disclosure. The claim for discovery of these documents succeeded in the Court of Appeal, which held that the legal advice form of legal professional privilege covered only advice as to the Bank's legal rights and liabilities and did not extend to advice as to presentation of the Bank's case to the Inquiry. The judgment of Lord Phillips M.R. had expressed some scepticism as to the justification for any legal advice privilege outside the context of litigation. The decision, and these further remarks, caused considerable disquiet in government and the profession and led to interventions by the Attorney-General, the Law Society and the Bar Council in the appeal to the

---

[71] *Balabel v Air-India* [1988] 2 All E.R. 246 CA.

[72] *Nederlandse Reassurantie Groep Holding NV v Bacon & Woodrow (a firm)* [1995] 1 All E.R. 976 QBD.

[73] Dicta to the contrary in such cases as *Carpmael v Powis* (1846) 1 Ph. 687; and *Great Atlantic Insurance Co v Home Insurance Co* [1981] 2 All E.R. 485 were not followed by the Court of Appeal in *Balabel v Air-India* [1988] 2 All E.R. 246.

[74] See *R. v Crown Court at Inner London Sessions Ex p. Baines & Baines* [1987] 3 All E.R. 1025 DC, applying s.10 of PACE.

[75] See *Conlon v Conlons Ltd* [1952] 2 All E.R. 462.

[76] *Balabel v Air-India* [1988] 2 All E.R. 246 at 255 per Taylor L.J.

[77] *Three Rivers DC (No.6)* [2004] UKHL 48; [2005] 1 A.C. 610.

Lords. The House of Lords reversed the Court of Appeal and allowed the Bank's appeal. All their Lordships endorsed the approach to legal advice privilege of the Court of Appeal in *Balabel v Air-India*, in particular the statement by Taylor L.J. that "legal advice is not confined to telling the client the law; it must include advice as to what should prudently and sensibly be done in the relevant legal context". Lord Scott, with whom Lord Rodger, Baroness Hale and Lord Brown expressed agreement, held that "relevant legal contexts" clearly include rights, liabilities and obligations in public law as well as private law. In this case the context was the Bingham Inquiry and the question whether the Bank had properly discharged its public law duties under the Banking Acts. Presentational advice or assistance given by lawyers to clients whose conduct might be the subject of criticism by the Inquiry was advice or assistance that might serve to avoid the need to invoke public law remedies against the clients. Lord Carswell pointed out that presentational advice required the skills of a lawyer in assembling the facts and handling the evidence as much in a statutory inquiry as in a court of law, and added that the availability of competent legal advice would materially assist the inquiry by reducing irrelevance and encouraging the making of proper admissions. Accordingly the House agreed that presentational advice in the context of an inquiry was properly to be regarded as legal advice, and that communications between lawyer and client relating to the advice should attract privilege because they fell within the policy underlying the justification for legal advice privilege. Lord Scott's analysis of this policy is discussed above.

10–010   This is a strong endorsement of the traditional common law approach to legal advice privilege. It rejects any suggestion that privilege should be restricted either to the litigation context or to communications directly concerning rights and liabilities. Provided that a relevant legal context can be identified, and that the advice in question involves the exercise of the skills of a lawyer, clients and lawyers can be reassured that legal advice about the clients' affairs will remain privileged. Lord Brown put it in these terms:

> "I would go so far as to state as a general principle that the process by which a client seeks and obtains his lawyer's assistance in the presentation of his case for the purposes of any formal inquiry—whether concerned with public law or private law issues, whether adversarial or inquisitorial in form, whether held in public or in private, whether or not directly affecting his rights or liabilities—attracts legal advice privilege. Such assistance to my mind clearly has the character of legal business. It is precisely the sort of professional service for which lawyers are ordinarily employed by virtue of their expertise and experience."[78]

However, it is important to emphasise that the "purpose" test for legal privilege relates to the purpose for which the document is brought into existence. Privilege is available only where the purpose of legal advice or of use in litigation accounts for the existence of the document. A document that comes into existence for other reasons before any issue of its use for legal advice or in litigation arises cannot subsequently acquire privilege because it is used for those purposes. It acquires no greater protection in the hands of the solicitor than it had in the hands of the

---

[78] *Three Rivers DC (No.6)* [2004] UKHL 48; [2005] 1 A.C. 610 at [120].

client.[79] This is a logical consequence of the basic rules of privilege. So in *Ventouris v Mountain* the Court of Appeal rejected the defendant's claim of privilege for documents that came into existence before the litigation arose but which were acquired by his solicitors for use in the litigation. Bingham L.J. stated, after an extensive review of authority:

> "I think the effect of the authority overall is to reinforce the plaintiff's argument in principle. I can see no reason in principle why a pre-existing document obtained by a solicitor for purposes of litigation should be privileged from production and inspection . . . [save in one type of case] . . . I find nothing in anything [sic] of the cases which suggests, let alone justifies, such a result. Such a rule would in my view pose a threat to the administration of justice."[80]

The last sentence of this quotation has particular significance for criminal cases. It would be highly undesirable if an accused could throw a cloak of legal privilege over incriminating documents, and other evidence of the offence, simply by submitting it all to a solicitor with a request for legal advice. In the earlier case of *King*,[81] the Court of Appeal had refused a claim of privilege for a pre-existing document (a purported invoice) sent by the defence to a handwriting expert for an opinion. The communications with the expert, in the form of the letters requesting and delivering his opinion, were agreed to be privileged but the court held that protection did not extend to the chattels or documents on which the opinion was based. There was no difference between criminal and civil cases in this respect. As Dunn L.J. commented:

> "it would be strange if a forger could hide behind a claim of legal professional privilege by the simple device of sending all the incriminating documents in his possession to his solicitors to be examined by an expert."[82]

This rule for pre-existing original documents is subject to one clear exception, noted by Bingham L.J. in the quotation above from *Ventouris v Mountain*. Where a solicitor makes a collection of, or selects from, pre-existing unprivileged documents the collection or selection is privileged if disclosure would tend to reveal the nature of the legal advice to the client. In *Lyell v Kennedy (No.3)*,[83] the Court of Appeal upheld a claim of privilege for a solicitor's copies of entries in registers and public records and photographs of tombstones and houses. Cotton L.J. stated that to order production would be giving the other parties "a clue to the advice which had been given by the solicitor, and giving them the benefit of the professional opinion which had been formed by the solicitor". As the decision in this case shows the exception applies equally to original documents and to copies of originals.

10–011

A related issue, on which there is conflicting authority, is whether a copy of an unprivileged original can ever attract privilege on the ground only that the copy

---

[79] *R. v Peterborough Justices Ex p. Hicks* [1977] 1 W.L.R. 1371 DC (search of solicitor's premises for forged document submitted to solicitor by client and seizure of same—privilege not applicable).
[80] *Ventouris v Mountain* [1991] 3 All E.R. 472 at 484.
[81] *King* [1983] 1 W.L.R. 411 CA. See also, to similar effect, *R. v Peterborough Justices Ex p. Hicks* [1977] 1 W.L.R. 1371 DC. Dicta to the contrary by Swanwick J. in *Frank Truman Export Ltd v Metropolitan Police Commissioner* [1977] Q.B. 952 were doubted by the Court of Appeal in *King*.
[82] *King* [1983] 1 W.L.R. 411 at 414.
[83] *Lyell v Kennedy (No.3)* (1884) 27 Ch.D. 1 at 26.

has been taken for the purpose of legal advice or for use in litigation. It is hard to see why in principle there should be any difference in the status of originals and copies. Certainly it has not been doubted that a copy of a privileged original is also privileged.[84] It would follow logically that a copy of an unprivileged original is also unprivileged,[85] and it would be odd if the holder of an unprivileged original could claim privilege for a copy made for the purpose of legal advice while remaining liable to produce the original in evidence under a witness summons. Dicta in modern cases show a marked aversion to any idea that the rules of privilege might apply differently as between copies and originals. In *Dubai Bank Ltd v Galadari*,[86] Dillon L.J. expressed incredulity that the availability of privilege could depend on such a fine distinction, and in *Lubrizol Corp v Esso Petroleum Co Ltd*,[87] Aldous J. commented, "I also find it incredible that in these days of the photocopier, the computer and the fax, that any distinction concerning privilege can be drawn between a copy and the original".[88] In the former case the Court of Appeal held that privilege could not attach in law to a copy of an affidavit where the affidavit had not been brought into existence for the purpose of legal advice or for the conduct of an action. In reaching this conclusion the Court of Appeal distinguished two earlier decisions and doubted a third. The cases it felt able to distinguish were *The Palermo*[89] and *Watson v Cammell Laird & Co (Shipbuilders and Engineers) Ltd*.[90] In both, privilege had been held to attach to copies taken by solicitors of documents not originally privileged, but in *Dubai Bank Ltd v Galadari* the Court of Appeal explained that in those cases the originals of the documents in question had never been in the hands of the solicitors. Hence in taking copies the solicitors were collecting the evidence for the trial and their clients were held able to claim privilege. This is not a satisfactory distinction if only because it may be a matter of chance whether a client or his solicitor has the original document, and in any event the original remains producible in the hands of a third party. These cases are "ripe for authoritative reconsideration",[91] and it seems fair to expect that on a suitable occasion they will be formally overruled.

The decision doubted in *Dubai Bank Ltd v Galadari* was *R. v Board of Inland Revenue Ex p. Goldberg*[92] where a Divisional Court allowed a claim of privilege for a large number of copy documents relating to a client's tax affairs that had been supplied by the client's solicitor to a QC for advice. The Court of Appeal in *Dubai Bank* held that this went too far if the ground of decision was that copies made for the sole purpose of obtaining legal advice were privileged. However, it may be that *Goldberg* can be justified on the basis that the solicitor had exercised professional skill and judgment in reviewing and selecting the relevant

---

[84] See Lord Denning M.R. in *Buttes Gas and Oil Co v Hammer (No.3)* [1981] Q.B. 223 at 244 CA.
[85] A Divisional Court so ruled in *Chadwick v Bowman* (1886) 16 Q.B.D. 561.
[86] *Dubai Bank Ltd v Galadari* [1990] Ch. 98 at 104 CA.
[87] *Lubrizol Corp v Esso Petroleum Co Ltd* [1992] 1 W.L.R. 957.
[88] *Lubrizol Corp v Esso Petroleum Co Ltd* [1992] 1 W.L.R. 957 at 961.
[89] *The Palermo* (1883) 9 P.D. 6.
[90] *Cammell Laird* [1959] 1 W.L.R. 702.
[91] *Ventouris v Mountain* [1991] 3 All E.R. 472 at 481 per Bingham L.J.
[92] *Goldberg* [1989] Q.B. 267.

documents for copying to counsel, so as to bring the case within the principle of *Lyell v Kennedy (No.3)* mentioned above.

3. Loss of privilege

This is a convenient heading to describe a number of situations in which a claim of lawyer-client privilege will or may fail, despite the fact that the claim relates to a communication between a lawyer and a client. The first situation is where the communication is in furtherance of a crime or fraud on the part of the client. In this case it is more accurate to say not that privilege is lost, but that it never arises in the first place. In the second situation privilege does arise but the client subsequently waives the privilege. In the third situation the client has not waived privilege but a third party has nonetheless acquired possession of the original or of a copy of a privileged document, or is otherwise in a position to give evidence of a privileged communication. Finally we will consider to what extent, if at all, a court may order disclosure of privileged communications in order to protect an interest that the court regards as having a higher priority.

10–012

(A)   Communications in furtherance of crime or fraud

In the leading case of *Cox and Railton*,[93] the defendants consulted a solicitor about the drawing-up of a bill of sale that the prosecution alleged was fraudulent. The Court for Crown Cases Reserved held that the solicitor had been rightly compelled to testify at the defendants' trial on a charge of obtaining money by false pretences about the defendants' communications with him. The privilege attaching to communications with legal advisers did not extend to cases where the advice was sought by the client in furtherance of a crime or fraud the client intended to perpetrate. It should be noted that the solicitor in this case was unaware of the purpose for which his advice was wanted. If he had not been ignorant and had given the advice requested he would have become a party to the offence and would have ceased to act as a lawyer.[94]

10–013

Although *Cox and Railton* concerned a fraud that amounted to a criminal offence the doctrine is not limited to such frauds. It has been said to extend to the tort of deceit and to include "all forms of fraud and dishonesty such as fraudulent breach of contract, fraudulent conspiracy, trickery and sham contrivances".[95] In *Barclays Bank Plc v Eustice*,[96] the defendants entered into transactions for an undervalue involving the creation or transfer of interests in property that represented the plaintiff's security for a substantial loan to the defendants. The Court of Appeal upheld the judge's order for disclosure of documents passing between the defendants and their legal advisers relating to the transactions. Privilege was held not to apply because of the strong prima facie case that the purpose of the transactions was to prejudice the interests of the plaintiff as the

---

[93] *Cox and Railton* (1884) 14 Q.B.D. 153.
[94] *Russell v Jackson* (1851) 9 Hare 387 at 392–393; *Cox and Railton* (1884) 14 Q.B.D. 153 at 168.
[95] *Crescent Farm (Sidcup) Sports Ltd v Sterling Offices Ltd* [1972] Ch. 553 at 565 per Goff J.
[96] *Barclays Bank Plc v Eustice* [1995] 4 All E.R. 511.

defendants' creditor. According to Schiemann L.J. this purpose was sufficiently iniquitous for public policy to require disclosure.[97]

The reference to iniquity does not seem to have been intended as a statement of a new test, since Schiemann L.J. referred to the traditional phrase "crime or fraud" without disapproval and noted that "fraud" was used in a relatively wide sense in this context.[98] Certainly the transactions in the case might well be thought to be examples of "sham contrivances". The use of the concept of iniquity to indicate the limits of privilege is appropriate in the sense that it reflects the established principle of equity that there is no confidence in iniquity.[99] On the other hand it is a more indeterminate test even than fraud in "a wide sense" and thus makes the limits of this exception to privilege more uncertain.

10–014   The difficulty of establishing the limits is shown by the unwillingness of the courts to extend the exception to communications relating to any intended legal wrong. In *Crescent Farm (Sidcup) Sports Ltd v Sterling Offices Ltd*,[100] the plaintiff claimed damages for breach of contract, interference with contract and conspiracy in respect of the first defendant's sale of land to the second defendant contrary to the plaintiff's right of pre-emption. In according privilege to counsel's opinion concerning the conveyance Goff J. held that the plaintiff's causes of action did not come within the ambit of the exception to privilege for communications in furtherance of crime or fraud. In his view:

> "It is clear that parties must be at liberty to take advice as to the ambit of their contractual obligations and liabilities in tort and what liability they will incur whether in contract or tort by a proposed course of action without thereby in every case losing professional privilege."[101]

One of the relevant factors in deciding the limits of the exception is likely to be the stage at which legal advice is sought or given. A court may be more willing to refuse privilege where a client seeks advice on how to structure a transaction yet to be carried out than if he seeks advice on the effect of what has already been done.[102] A purpose to defraud may be easier to infer in the former case. Clearly a court may be reluctant to force a lawyer to disclose what a client said when seeking advice on how to respond to a criminal charge already made. However, where there is evidence, for example, of a specific agreement to pervert the course of justice, which is free-standing and independent in the sense that it does not require any judgment to be reached in relation to the issues to be tried in the case in question, the court will be in a position to evaluate the claim to privilege and is likely to refuse it.[103] But in "the ordinary run of cases" privilege is not

---

[97] *Barclays Bank Plc v Eustice* [1995] 4 All E.R. 511 at 524. The decision in this case was doubted, obiter, by Lord Neuberger in *In Re McE* [2009] UKHL 15 at [109].

[98] *Barclays Bank Plc v Eustice* [1995] 4 All E.R. 511 at 521. It includes deliberate misrepresentation made by a borrower to a building society for the purpose of procuring an advance: *Nationwide Building Society v Various Solicitors, The Times*, February 5, 1998. Mortgage frauds will generally constitute criminal offences under ss.1 and 2 of the Fraud Act 2006.

[99] *Gartside v Outram* (1856) 26 L.J. Ch. 113; *Initial Services Ltd v Putterill* [1968] 1 Q.B. 396.

[100] *Crescent Farm (Sidcup) Sports Ltd v Sterling Offices Ltd* [1972] Ch. 553.

[101] *Crescent Farm* at 565.

[102] *Barclays Bank Plc v Eustice* [1995] 4 All E.R. 511 at 522 per Schiemann L.J.

[103] See *R. (on the application of Hallinan Blackburn Gittings & Nott (a firm) v Middlesex Guildhall Crown Court* [2004] 1 W.L.R. 766.

excluded for communications by a client to a lawyer regarding the conduct of his case in criminal or civil proceedings merely because the communication is untrue and would, if acted upon, lead to the commission of perjury in the proceedings.[104]

For the exception to apply it is clear that the communication must be in furtherance of a crime or fraud. It is not enough that the communication between lawyer and client is relevant to a charge of crime or fraud against the client. In *Butler v Board of Trade*,[105] the defendants had commenced a prosecution against the plaintiff for offences of fraudulent trading. In separate proceedings the plaintiff sought a declaration that a letter written to him by his solicitor was privileged. The letter was written on the solicitor's own initiative and warned the plaintiff of the potential criminal consequences involved in pursuing a certain course of conduct. Goff J. held that the exception would apply only if, looking at the matter on a prima facie basis, there was a necessary inference that the letter was not just relevant to the alleged criminal or fraudulent design but was actually preparation for or in furtherance of the design. On the facts there was no evidence[106] to justify an inference that the letter was in furtherance of any fraudulent trading by the plaintiff. It was simply a factual warning to the plaintiff of the legal risks he was running. Therefore the original letter did attract legal privilege. The separate issue of whether the defendants could use a copy of the letter in the prosecution is dealt with below.

Section 10(2) of PACE excludes from privilege under the Act "items held with the intention of furthering a criminal purpose". In *R. v Central Criminal Court Ex p. Francis & Francis*,[107] a majority of the House of Lords interpreted these words to refer either to the intention of the actual holder of the item or to the intention of any other person. Accordingly a firm of solicitors was ordered to hand over to the police conveyancing files relating to the purchase of a property.[108] The police suspected on reasonable grounds that a third party had laundered the proceeds of drug-trafficking by financing the purchase of property by members of his family. Although the family members (the clients) and the lawyers were innocent of this purpose they were not able to claim privilege for the documents in view of the third party's criminal intention. The majority adopted a purposive interpretation of the provision partly to further the policy of Pt II of PACE to give the police powers to enable them to detect the perpetrators of crime.[109] The decision allows the police to trace the proceeds of crime by overriding privilege even for documents in the hands of innocent holders; any other interpretation would mean that the evidential trail would stop as soon as an offender succeeded in constituting an unaware client or lawyer as holder of a relevant document. A further reason for a purposive interpretation was what the majority saw as the

10–015

---

[104] *R. v Central Criminal Court Ex p. Francis & Francis* [1989] A.C. 346 at 397 per Lord Goff. See also *Kuwait Airways Corp v Iraqi Airways Co* [2005] EWCA Civ 286; [2005] 1 W.L.R. 2734.

[105] *Butler v Board of Trade* [1971] Ch. 680.

[106] In deciding whether the communications came into existence in furtherance of a criminal purpose of the client the court may if necessary inspect the communications themselves: *R. v Governor of Pentonville Prison Ex p. Osman* [1989] 3 All E.R. 701 at 729–730 DC.

[107] *R. v Central Criminal Court Ex p. Francis & Francis* [1989] A.C. 346.

[108] Pursuant to an order by a circuit judge under s.27 of the Drug Trafficking Offences Act 1986.

[109] See *Francis & Francis* [1989] A.C. 346 at 380–381 per Lord Brandon of Oakbrook, 383 per Lord Griffiths and 392–393 per Lord Goff of Chieveley.

absurdity of a literal construction of s.10(2). The majority argued that if this construction was right the exception to legal privilege applied only where the actual holder of the document was holding it with an intention to further a criminal purpose. It could not therefore apply where the relevant purpose had already been fulfilled. The exception would only be of use in the investigation of future offences, "whereas in the nature of things, the police are almost always investigating past crimes".[110] Moreover, as Lord Griffiths pointed out, on the literal view, where an innocent solicitor was acting for a client who was a drug dealer:

> "copies of letters written by the solicitor to his client, but retained in his office, which contained advice that facilitated laundering drug money would be subject to legal privilege, but the originals of that advice, in the hands of the client, would not be subject to legal privilege."[111]

It would make no sense to protect the copy but not the original.

These cogent arguments failed to persuade the minority. In a robust dissenting speech Lord Bridge of Harwich declined to depart from what he saw as the plain grammatical meaning of the subsection. In his view, before an order could be given for access to material in the possession of a solicitor that would otherwise be subject to legal privilege under s.10(1), the judge would have to be satisfied both that the material was intended to further a criminal purpose and that the solicitor was a party to that intention.[112] Lord Oliver of Aylmerton, also dissenting, thought that this interpretation was consistent with a legislative intention to protect innocent solicitors who would be under a duty to their clients to claim privilege. If the law were otherwise such solicitors would be put in a position where their duty to take a stand on legal privilege depended on an intention of which they knew nothing and where they might be liable for contempt of court if they got it wrong.[113] The majority probably have the better of the debate,[114] but it has to be recognised that their decision does some violence to the statutory language. The case represents a striking example of judicial willingness to rewrite an unsatisfactorily worded provision where the court feels sure of its ground in public policy.[115]

10–016   Although the case turned on the interpretation of the statutory provision, Lord Goff expressed the view that s.10(2) encapsulated the common law. Therefore, he said, at common law the criminal purpose exception to legal privilege applied equally whether the purpose was that of the client or of a third party using the

---

[110] *Francis & Francis* [1989] A.C. 346 at 384 per Lord Griffiths.

[111] *Francis & Francis* [1989] A.C. 346.

[112] *Francis & Francis* [1989] A.C. 346 at 379.

[113] *Francis & Francis* [1989] A.C. 346 at 389.

[114] For a contrary view see A. L. E. Newbold, "The Crime/Fraud Exception to Legal Professional Privilege" (1990) 53 M.L.R. 472, who argues that the majority misinterpreted the common law authorities and misunderstood the relationship between the common law and s.10 of PACE.

[115] Note that correspondence between solicitor and client, and enclosures, even if not privileged will still be "special procedure material" for the purposes of the search and seizure provisions of PACE. See *R. v Guildhall Magistrates' Court Ex p. Primlaks Holdings Co* (1989) 89 Cr.App.R. 215 DC. It is beyond the scope of this book to deal with these and related procedures.

client as an innocent tool. In either case the protection of such communications could not be otherwise than injurious to the public interest.

(B) Waiver

A client may waive privilege in a communication by knowingly disclosing it, or by giving evidence about it or by authorising the lawyer to do so.[116] Waiver can also be implied by law. A client who brings a civil action against his lawyer is held to waive by implication legal privilege in all communications with the lawyer relevant to the action.[117] The doctrine of implied waiver in such cases is designed to prevent the unfairness of a client opening up the confidential relationship with the solicitor while simultaneously seeking to enforce the obligation of confidence by asserting privilege.[118] Once a client has waived privilege in a particular communication he cannot claim it subsequently in the same proceedings. However, it is possible to waive privilege for a limited purpose only.[119] Thus a client who makes privileged documents available to the police for use in a criminal prosecution against a defendant does not thereby either expressly or impliedly waive privilege in the documents for the purposes of his subsequent civil action against the same defendant.[120]

10–017

When waiver of privilege does take place tricky problems can arise over its extent. In relation to single documents the rule is that waiver of privilege in part of a document amounts to a waiver of privilege in the whole document.[121] This is certainly the case where the document is used in evidence at trial. There is an exception where the undisclosed part of the document deals with a separate subject-matter so that the document can be severed without becoming misleading.[122] This may be a question of degree, and ultimately the judge has to apply a test of fairness after reading the whole of the document. In *Great Atlantic*

---

[116] Inadvertent disclosure, or deliberate disclosure without authorisation, is discussed below in connection with secondary evidence. It should be noted, however, that legal advisers who represent a client in litigation have ostensible authority to conduct the case as they think best in the interests of the client. Therefore when counsel introduces a document into the trial record, without the client's agreement, he effectively waives any privilege in that document. See *Great Atlantic Insurance Co v Home Insurance Co* [1981] 2 All E.R. 485 CA.

[117] *Lillicrap v Nalder & Son (a firm)* [1993] 1 All E.R. 724 CA. This case shows that where it is relevant to refer to transactions between the parties other than the one that is the subject-matter of the action the implied waiver of privilege will be held to extend to the documents in the other transactions.

[118] *Paragon Finance Plc v Freshfields* [1999] 1 W.L.R. 1183; approving *Nederlandse Reassurantie Groep Holding NV v Bacon & Woodrow (a firm)* [1995] 1 All E.R. 976 QBD; and doubting *Kershaw v Whelan* [1996] 2 All E.R. 404 QBD.

[119] *B v Auckland District Law Society* [2003] UKPC 38; [2003] 2 A.C. 736.

[120] *British Coal Corp v Dennis Rye Ltd (No.2)* [1988] 3 All E.R. 816 CA, where Neill L.J. held that it would be contrary to public policy to regard such action as amounting to a waiver of privilege. However, where privileged material is made available for the purposes of criminal proceedings the client cannot limit the use of it in those proceedings: *Ungvari* [2003] EWCA Crim 2346. In civil litigation the privilege is not waived, as regards a plaintiff, where one defendant discloses his privileged communications to another defendant under an express or implied obligation of confidentiality: *Gotha City v Sothebys* [1998] 1 W.L.R. 114 CA.

[121] *Great Atlantic Insurance Co v Home Insurance Co* [1981] 2 All E.R. 485 CA.

[122] *Great Atlantic Insurance Co v Home Insurance Co* [1981] 2 All E.R. 485 at 490.

Insurance Co v Home Insurance Co,[123] Templeman L.J. assumed that the same rules extended to pre-trial discovery of privileged documents, and it would seem right in principle to apply the same rules at different stages of the same litigation.[124] However, the dicta in question were doubted subsequently by Hoffmann L.J. in *GE Capital Corporate Finance Group Ltd v Bankers Trust Co,*[125] who pointed to the long-standing practice of permitting parties giving discovery to seal or cover up parts of documents that were irrelevant to the issues in the case. He suggested that this practice should apply where a party wished to maintain privilege for part of a document while giving discovery of a part that was not privileged; there should be no additional requirement of showing that a separate subject-matter was involved.[126] This proposition does not directly address the case of part-waiver of a document privileged as a whole, and it is submitted that Templeman L.J.'s view is to be preferred.

A further issue then arises concerning communications that are mentioned in, or are related to, communications in which privilege has been waived. Does waiver of privilege in document A also amount to a waiver of privilege in document B either where A refers to B or where A and B are dealing with the same subject-matter? According to Geoffrey Lane J. in *George Doland Ltd v Blackburn Robson Coates & Co,*[127] a waiver by the plaintiffs of legal advice privilege in an oral conversation prior to litigation did not result in waiver of the litigation privilege protecting documents brought into existence subsequently for the purposes of the litigation, even if the documents related to the subject-matter of the conversation. However, up until the point in time when litigation privilege arose, the defendants were entitled to disclosure of any documents relating to the subject-matter of the conversation. This approach to the problem was doubted by Hobhouse J. in *General Accident Fire and Life Assurance Corp Ltd v Tanter*[128] who pointed out that the decision could produce an "almost infinite regress"[129] of disclosure if privilege was waived, as it was in the *Tanter* case, in a memorandum protected by both legal advice and litigation privilege. His Lordship went on to hold that there could be no waiver of privilege in other related documents until the principal document in question had been "deployed in evidence", and that in any event waiver was confined to documents relevant to the transaction with which the principal document was concerned (e.g. the terms of an alleged oral conversation reported in the document) and did not extend to all documents relevant to the subject-matter of the transaction (e.g. what was said at other dates about the matters discussed in the conversation). This way of dealing with the

---

[123] *Great Atlantic Insurance Co v Home Insurance Co* [1981] 2 All E.R. 485.

[124] In *Dunlop Slazenger International Ltd v Joe Bloggs Sports Ltd* [2003] EWCA Civ 901 the Court of Appeal held that the principle against "cherry-picking" (a party cannot waive privilege in selected parts of documents while maintaining privilege for other relevant parts) applied where the document was deployed in pre-trial proceedings.

[125] *GE Capital Corporate Finance Group Ltd v Bankers Trust Co* [1995] 2 All E.R. 993 CA.

[126] *GE Capital Corporate Finance Group Ltd v Bankers Trust Co* [1995] 2 All E.R. 993 at 997.

[127] *George Doland Ltd v Blackburn Robson Coates & Co* [1972] 3 All E.R. 959 QBD.

[128] *General Accident Fire and Life Assurance Corp Ltd v Tanter* [1984] 1 All E.R. 35 QBD.

[129] *Tanter* [1984] 1 All E.R. 35 at 42.

extent of "waiver by association" seems to be commanding general support,[130] but there may be a need for further consideration at an appellate level.

In criminal proceedings a defendant may waive privilege in communications with his lawyer by giving evidence about them or by calling the lawyer to do so. A defendant might wish to do this, for example, to rebut a suggestion that his own evidence is a recent fabrication or has been tailored to meet the prosecution case.[131] Proof that he told his solicitor the same story at an earlier time would be an effective counter to such suggestions. A second example would be where the defendant wants to adduce evidence of the reasons his solicitor gave for advising him not to answer questions in a police interview.[132] Where privilege is waived the defendant can be cross-examined on exactly what passed between him and his solicitor on the topic, but the waiver is not necessarily entire and general. By waiving privilege in some communications the defendant does not automatically make available to all other parties all the communications with the solicitor on every occasion: the test of the extent of the waiver is fairness and the avoidance of a misleading impression.[133]

(C)   Secondary evidence[134]

Several interesting and difficult questions arise if a third party acquires possession of a privileged document or overhears a privileged conversation.[135] Suppose, for example, that the defendant in a civil case obtains a copy of the instructions to counsel prepared by the solicitor for the claimant. Can he give evidence of the privileged communication? If the evidence is admissible in the hands of the third party, does it matter how he gained access to the evidence (e.g. unlawfully)? Assuming the evidence is admissible, does the person who would have been entitled to claim privilege have any legal remedy to prevent the evidence being used and, if so, what is the nature and scope of the jurisdiction involved? There is a considerable body of case-law dealing with these questions. Although the law on most of the issues is now reasonably clear the last question in particular has produced much controversy and the cases are to some extent in conflict.

The topic is discussed under the heading of secondary evidence of privileged communications, although this term is not quite accurate for the case where the

10–018

---

[130] See the discussion in *Phipson on Evidence*, 16th edn (London: Sweet & Maxwell, 2005), paras 26–23 to 26–29.

[131] See *Seaton* [2010] EWCA Crim 1980; [2011] 1 Cr.App.R. 2, explaining *Wilmot* (1989) 89 Cr.App.R. 341.

[132] Where the defendant is seeking to avoid an adverse inference under s.34 of the Criminal Justice and Public Order Act 1994: see *Condron* [1997] 1 Cr.App.R. 185; *Bowden* [1999] 2 Cr.App.R. 176, and the discussion in Ch.5.

[133] *Loizou* [2006] EWCA Crim 1719; *Seaton* [2010] EWCA Crim 1980; [2011] 1 Cr.App.R. 2.

[134] See generally C. Tapper, "Privilege and Confidence" (1972) 35 M.L.R. 83; J. D. Heydon, "Legal Professional Privilege and Third Parties" (1974) 37 M.L.R. 601; P. B. Matthews, "Breach of confidence and legal privilege" (1981) 1 L.S. 77; N. Andrews, "The Influence of Equity upon the Doctrine of Legal Professional Privilege" (1989) 105 L.Q.R. 608; A. L. E. Newbold, "Inadvertent Disclosure in Civil Proceedings" (1991) 107 L.Q.R. 99.

[135] Unauthorised surveillance or interception of a client's privileged communications will violate the client's rights under art.8 of the ECHR: see above.

third party seeks to use in evidence the original of a privileged document. The issue of admissibility of secondary evidence was clarified in two important civil cases in the nineteenth century. In *Lloyd v Mostyn*,[136] the question arose whether the plaintiff's attorney was entitled to adduce in evidence a copy of a bond. The original of the bond was held by the defendant's lawyer, who objected to produce it on the ground of privilege. The assize judge had allowed the objection to production of the original but had admitted the copy in evidence. The Court of Exchequer was in no doubt that the ruling on admissibility was correct. Parke B. commented:

> "Where an attorney intrusted confidentially with a document communicates the contents, or suffers another to take a copy, surely the secondary evidence so obtained may be produced. Suppose the instrument were even stolen, and a correct copy taken, would it not be reasonable to admit it?"[137]

On its own this case is not a strong authority. Despite the trial judge's decision to uphold the claim of privilege it is not clear that the bond was in fact privileged, as opposed simply to being held by the lawyer in confidence. This may help to explain Parke B's reference to an attorney being "intrusted confidentially with a document". Moreover, Parke B.'s statement was made during the course of argument and not as part of the judgment, which was devoted to a different point. Nevertheless, *Lloyd v Mostyn* was followed by the Court of Appeal in *Calcraft v Guest*[138] where the documents in question were expressly held to be privileged. They were proofs of witnesses and notes on evidence prepared for the plaintiff's predecessor in title in an action over a right of fishery a century earlier. The documents had been found and handed to the defendants in a subsequent action over the same fishing rights. The defendants had taken copies of these documents before returning the originals to the plaintiffs. The Court of Appeal cited and applied Parke B.'s statement of principle as clear authority that the copies were admissible as secondary evidence in the current action. The short judgment of Lindley M.R. did not elaborate further on the reasoning that might support this conclusion, or on any limits there might be to use by a third party of privileged documents. Despite its somewhat slender foundations, this decision has been regarded for more than 100 years as having settled the law on whether secondary evidence of privileged documents is admissible as a matter of law. Logically the principle must extend to the case where the third party is in possession of the original of a privileged communication.[139] It would be absurd if someone in a position to adduce the original in evidence could only rely upon a copy.

10–019   The rule in *Calcraft v Guest* applies in criminal cases also. This was so stated by Goff J. in *Butler v Board of Trade*,[140] discussed below, and confirmed by the

---

[136] *Lloyd v Mostyn* (1842) 10 M. & W. 478.
[137] *Lloyd v Mostyn* (1842) 10 M. & W. 478 at 481–482.
[138] *Calcraft v Guest* [1898] 1 Q.B. 759.
[139] A conclusion supported by Swinfen-Eady L.J. in *Ashburton (Lord) v Pape* [1913] 2 Ch. 469 at 476–477; Cooke J. in *Uljee* [1982] 1 N.Z.L.R. 561 at 563; Andrews, "Legal Professional Privilege" (1989) 105 L.Q.R. 608 611–612.
[140] *Butler v Board of Trade* [1971] Ch. 680.

Court of Appeal in the unusual case of *Tompkins*.[141] During the course of a criminal trial the defendant wrote an incriminating note to his counsel. This note was found on the floor of the court at the end of the day and handed to prosecution counsel. The following day prosecution counsel put questions to the defendant in cross-examination based on the contents of the note, although the trial judge excluded the note itself from evidence in the exercise of his discretion. In the course of rejecting the defendant's argument that the cross-examination amounted to a breach of natural justice, Ormrod L.J.[142] made a general statement about criminal cases that, it is submitted, accurately represents current English[143] law:

> "Privilege, in this context, relates only to production of a document; it does not determine its admissibility in evidence. The note, though clearly privileged from production, was admissible in evidence once it was in the possession of the prosecution."

Presumably, therefore, the note could have been adduced as part of the prosecution evidence provided the prosecution could have proved that it was written by the defendant.

This line of authority based on *Calcraft v Guest* treats privilege as a rule against disclosure and production of evidence rather than a rule of admissibility. On this approach, A cannot compel B to give evidence of B's privileged communications, but if A is able to adduce primary or secondary evidence of the communications the fact that they are privileged in the hands of B is not an objection to the admissibility of A's evidence. Furthermore, the view at common law was that it did not matter how admissible evidence was obtained. Provided the evidence of the communications was relevant it was immaterial whether the party adducing it had obtained it by lawful or unlawful means. This appears clearly from the statement of Parke B. in *Lloyd v Mostyn*. In the criminal case of *Leatham*,[144] Crompton J. repeated the point that evidence is still admissible at common law even if it has been stolen.

However, three important qualifications must now be made. First, in criminal cases a trial judge has a discretion to exclude prosecution evidence that is otherwise relevant and admissible.[145] The common law discretion was founded on the judge's duty to secure a fair trial for the accused. The precise scope of the common law discretion was controversial, but in *Tompkins* the Court of Appeal seems to have been in no doubt that it could be used to limit prosecution use of

---

[141] *Tompkins* (1977) 67 Cr.App.R. 181.

[142] *Tompkins* (1977) 67 Cr.App.R. 181 at 184. Ormrod L.J. cited *Rice* [1963] 1 Q.B. 857 for the proposition that counsel is entitled to put questions based on the contents of a document even if he is barred, as he was in the case, from referring directly to the document itself.

[143] *Tompkins* (1977) 67 Cr.App.R. 181 was followed by the Court of Appeal in *Cottrill* [1997] Crim. L.R. 56, but was disapproved and not followed by the New Zealand Court of Appeal in *Uljee* [1982] N.Z.L.R. 581, where it was held that a constable's evidence of a conversation he had overheard between the defendant and his solicitor was inadmissible. In *Goddard v Nationwide Building Society* [1986] 3 All E.R. 264 CA Nourse L.J., obiter, expressed a preference for the rule in *Uljee*, but suggested that only the House of Lords could now reverse the English rule. See further T. R. S. Allan, "Legal Privilege and the Principle of Fairness in the Criminal Trial" [1987] Crim. L.R. 449.

[144] *Leatham* (1861) 8 Cox C.C. 498 at 501. See also *Kuruma v R.* [1955] A.C. 197 PC; *Khan (Sultan)* [1996] 3 All E.R. 289 HL; and for civil cases *Helliwell v Pigott-Sims* [1980] F.S.R. 582 CA.

[145] See generally Ch.3.

the defendant's privileged communication. In modern law the common law discretion is supplemented, and in practice largely replaced, by the statutory discretion under s.78 of PACE. In *Cottrill*,[146] the defendant's solicitors had voluntarily disclosed[147] to the prosecution a statement by the defendant that was inconsistent with the evidence the defendant gave at trial. The Court of Appeal held that the judge had acted entirely within his discretion under s.78 in refusing to exclude the statement, which the prosecution had used to cross-examine the defendant. However, as argued earlier in this chapter, deliberate malpractice by the police to obtain evidence of the defendant's privileged communications with his solicitor would ground a compelling argument for exclusion under s.78 if the prosecution sought to use them in evidence against him.[148] Where police have been able to record, covertly but lawfully,[149] a privileged consultation, it is unclear whether the prosecution would be permitted to use evidence of the client's statements against the client.[150]

10–020   Secondly, a limited exception to the rule in *Calcraft v Guest* exists to protect privileged documents brought into court. In *ITC Film Distributors v Video Exchange Ltd*,[151] the defendant had obtained some of the plaintiff's privileged documents by a trick practised on the plaintiff's representative at an earlier hearing in the action. Warner J. held that the rule in *Calcraft v Guest* did not apply where a party to litigation filched or obtained by stealth documents that the other party had brought into court. He ordered the defendant to return the documents and any copies made, and granted an injunction restraining the defendant from making any use of the documents.[152] The decision is grounded in considerations of public policy,[153] and can also be regarded as an exercise of the court's inherent jurisdiction to deal with conduct of a party amounting to a contempt.

10–021   Thirdly, in civil cases the courts have made the common law rule of admissibility of secondary evidence of privileged communications effectively subject to the equitable jurisdiction to protect confidential information. This well-established jurisdiction enables courts to grant remedies against breach of confidence by restraining persons from disclosing or making use of confidential information that has come into their hands and ordering them to deliver up confidential documents not belonging to them and any copies they have made. Given that

---

[146] *Cottrill* [1997] Crim. L.R. 56.
[147] Apparently in an effort to persuade the prosecution to drop the case. The disclosure was without the defendant's knowledge.
[148] See para.10–004 above.
[149] See *In Re McE* [2009] UKHL 15.
[150] In *In Re McE* [2009] UKHL 15 Lord Hope thought that "basic rules of fairness strongly indicate the contrary" ([66]). Since the privilege is that of the client there would seem to be no comparable argument of unfairness against use of statements by the *solicitor* if the solicitor were charged, for example, with doing acts intended to pervert the course of justice.
[151] *ITC Film Distributors v Video Exchange Ltd* [1982] 2 All E.R. 241 Ch. D.
[152] Except in relation to copies exhibited to an affidavit, which the judge had already looked at for the purposes of the application in question.
[153] *Goddard v Nationwide Building Society* [1986] 3 All E.R. 264 at 272 per Nourse L.J.; this dictum gains support from Warner J.'s inclusion of a reference to a passage in the speech of Lord Simon in *D v NSPCC* [1978] A.C. 171 at 233, giving examples of exclusion of evidence as a matter of public policy. See also Ch.8 at para.8–5.

communications between lawyer and client have to be made in confidence in order to be privileged, a question was certain to arise sooner or later about the scope of the equitable remedies in relation to the use of secondary evidence of the communications. This issue was not raised in *Calcraft v Guest*, which was decided solely on the basis of the common law rule. However, some years later in *Ashburton (Lord) v Pape*,[154] the Court of Appeal had to confront the potential conflict between the rule of admissibility and the jurisdiction to restrain disclosures in breach of confidence. Pape, the defendant in these proceedings, was a bankrupt who was applying in separate bankruptcy proceedings for his discharge. Ashburton was one of Pape's creditors and was opposing his discharge. By collusion with a solicitor's clerk Pape had obtained certain correspondence between Ashburton and his solicitor, which he had copied before returning it. He was now proposing to use the copies in evidence at the bankruptcy hearing against Ashburton. Ashburton sought and obtained an injunction in the Chancery Division restraining Pape from publishing or making use of the copy letters or any of the information contained in them. The Court of Appeal subsequently upheld the injunction granted at first instance by Neville J. and also removed an exception that Neville J. had made "for the purpose of the pending proceedings in the defendant's bankruptcy and subject to the direction of the Bankruptcy Court".

The reason for the exception and the precise significance of the decision to remove it have been disputed.[155] The natural interpretation of the Court of Appeal's decision, however, is that the court was preventing Pape from carrying out his intention to use the copy letters in evidence. To that extent the court was using the equitable jurisdiction to override the rule in *Calcraft v Guest*. Subsequent Court of Appeal cases have taken the decision as authority for the proposition that a court may restrain a person in possession of another's privileged documents from using them in evidence. The facts that they are admissible and that the person intends to use them in evidence are no answer to a claim by the person entitled to privilege for their return and for an injunction forbidding their use.[156] In *Goddard v Nationwide Building Society*,[157] a solicitor had acted for both the plaintiff and the defendant building society in a mortgage transaction for house purchase. When the plaintiff subsequently brought an action alleging negligence on the part of the defendant's surveyor the solicitor passed to the defendant a copy of an attendance note that recorded earlier conversations between himself and the plaintiff. The defendant pleaded the substance of the note in its defence and clearly intended to rely on the copy as secondary evidence in the trial of the action. The Court of Appeal held that since the solicitor had written the note in his capacity as the plaintiff's solicitor the plaintiff could claim

---

[154] *Ashburton (Lord) v Pape* [1913] 2 Ch. 469.

[155] Principally by Matthews, "Breach of confidence" (1981) 1 L.S. 77, who argues on the basis of earlier authorities and certain ambiguities in the judgments of Cozens-Hardy M.R. and Kennedy L.J. that the Court of Appeal did not intend to deal with questions of admissibility of evidence at all. This is not, however, how the decision has been interpreted by the majority of later cases and commentators. See further Andrews, "The Influence of Equity" (1989) 105 L.Q.R. 608, 614–618.

[156] *Goddard v Nationwide Building Society* [1986] 3 All E.R. 264 at 270 per May L.J. Nourse L.J., the other member of the Court of Appeal, agreed (at 271).

[157] *Goddard v Nationwide Building Society* [1986] 3 All E.R. 264 CA.

privilege for it, and, following *Ashburton (Lord) v Pape*, was entitled to an order striking out the passages in the defence referring to the note and an injunction restraining the defendant from using or relying on the note. Similarly, in *Guinness Peat Properties Ltd v Fitzroy Robinson Partnership*,[158] the defendants succeeded in obtaining an injunction restraining the plaintiff company from making use of or relying on a privileged letter inadvertently disclosed by the defendants during discovery in an action by the plaintiff for professional negligence.

However, there is some authority that the civil courts will not employ this jurisdiction to control the use of evidence in a criminal case, at least as far as a public prosecution is concerned. In *Butler v Board of Trade*,[159] the defendants were in possession of a copy of a letter written to the plaintiff by his solicitor. The defendants wished to use the letter in their prosecution of the plaintiff for offences of fraudulent trading. Goff J. refused to grant a declaration having the effect of restraining the Crown from doing so, saying that this would not be a permissible exercise of the equitable jurisdiction in confidence. In his view the Crown's interest in the prosecution of offenders had to prevail over the plaintiff's limited proprietary right in equity to prevent a breach of confidence. He expressly left open the position with regard to a private prosecution. The distinction between public prosecutions and other legal proceedings is dubious, and in *Goddard v Nationwide Building Society* Nourse L.J. expressed the view that there was much to be said for having the spirit of *Ashburton (Lord) v Pape* supreme in both civil and criminal proceedings.[160] The emphasis in *R. v Derby Magistrates' Court Ex p. B*,[161] on the "absolute" nature of the privilege, and the refusal of the House of Lords to balance privilege against competing public interests, provide further reasons for regarding *Butler v Board of Trade* as a doubtful authority.[162] On the other hand, if a prosecutor is in possession of relevant evidence of guilt it is not obvious that the interest in maintaining confidentiality of privileged communications necessarily outweighs the public interest in the enforcement of the criminal law. It seems preferable to allow the criminal courts to regulate their own process, particularly now that they have the wide-ranging discretion under s.78 of PACE to exclude prosecution evidence in the interests of preserving the fairness of the proceedings.[163]

10–022 A further point of controversy is whether the jurisdiction to prevent the admission of secondary evidence of privileged communications is founded solely on their confidential nature, or on the fact that they are both confidential and privileged.

---

[158] *Guinness Peat Properties Ltd v Fitzroy Robinson Partnership* [1987] 2 All E.R. 716 CA.

[159] *Butler v Board of Trade* [1971] Ch. 680.

[160] *Goddard v Nationwide Building Society* [1986] 3 All E.R. 264 at 272.

[161] *R. v Derby Magistrates' Court Ex p. B* [1996] 1 A.C. 487 HL.

[162] *Butler v Board of Trade* [1971] Ch. 680 was not cited in *R. v Derby Magistrates' Court Ex p. B* [1996] 1 A.C. 487 HL.

[163] It should be noted that the Court of Appeal has held that in criminal proceedings the Crown Court has jurisdiction similar to that of the civil courts to restrain use of material inadvertently disclosed, according to what justice requires: *R. v G and B* [2004] EWCA Crim 1368; [2004] 2 Cr.App.R. 37 (the material in that case was subject to public interest immunity). It remains to be seen how this jurisdiction will develop; the court declined to define the circumstances in which the Crown Court might exercise its powers.

One view is that the rules of privilege and confidence are completely separate.[164] On this view, privilege protects a client only from compelled disclosure pursuant to legitimate authority, and it is the law of confidence alone that determines the use a third party can make of privileged documents. The significance of this approach is that the equitable remedies for breach of confidence simpliciter are fully discretionary, meaning that in each case the court has to balance the competing interests of the parties, taking into account such considerations as the conduct of the third party, the importance of the documents to the litigation in question and whether the documents would have to be disclosed in any event. There is support for this view in the first instance judgment of Scott J. in *Webster v James Chapman & Co.*[165] In this case, which concerned a plaintiff's expert report mistakenly disclosed to the defendant firm of solicitors, Scott J. described *Calcraft v Guest* and *Ashburton v Pape* as "examples of two independent and free-standing principles of jurisprudence".[166] He went on to say that once a privileged document passed into the hands of some other party prima facie the benefit of the privilege was lost. Therefore evidence of it could be used at trial. However, the privileged document would almost invariably also be a confidential document and would therefore be eligible for protection against unauthorised disclosure and use under the law relating to confidential information:

> "The law regarding confidential information is, I think, now relatively well settled. The court must, in each case where protection of confidential information is sought, balance on the one hand the legitimate interests of the plaintiff in seeking to keep the confidential information suppressed and on the other hand the legitimate interests of the defendant in seeking to make use of the information. There is never any question of an absolute right to have confidential information protected. The protection is the consequence of the balance to which I have referred coming down in favour of the plaintiff."[167]

A different view was expressed by Nourse L.J. in *Goddard v Nationwide Building Society*.[168] Taking the point that not all confidential communications are privileged (e.g. those between doctor and patient), he doubted whether equity would restrain a litigant in possession of such a communication from using it for the purposes of litigation:

> "It cannot be the function of equity to accord a *de facto* privilege to communications in respect of which no privilege can be claimed. Equity follows the law."[169]

Therefore, he argued, the equitable jurisdiction can prevail over the rule of evidence only where the communication is both confidential and privileged. There is force in this point, although it is not impossible to imagine cases where a court might feel that a third party who had obtained confidential, but unprivileged, documents by unlawful means should not be permitted to take advantage of his wrongdoing by using the documents in evidence. It may be unwise to assume that an injunction is never available in such a case. Having

---

[164] See A. L. E. Newbold, "Inadvertent Disclosure in Civil Proceedings" (1991) 107 L.Q.R. 99.
[165] *Webster v James Chapman & Co* [1989] 3 All E.R. 939 Ch D.
[166] *Webster v James Chapman & Co* [1989] 3 All E.R. 939 at 943.
[167] *Webster v James Chapman & Co* [1989] 3 All E.R. 939 at 945.
[168] *Goddard v Nationwide Building Society* [1986] 3 All E.R. 264 CA.
[169] *Goddard v Nationwide Building Society* [1986] 3 All E.R. 264 at 271.

insisted that privilege is a necessary condition of the equitable protection, Nourse L.J. then indicated that no balancing exercise is required in order to grant protection. The jurisdiction did not, he said, depend on the conduct of the third party, nor was there discretion in the court to refuse to exercise the jurisdiction according to its view of the materiality of the communication or the justice of admitting or excluding it: "The injunction is granted in aid of the privilege which, unless and until it is waived, is absolute".[170]

Later authorities are in disarray. In *Webster v James Chapman & Co* Scott J. doubted these statements of Nourse L.J., describing them as dicta, but in the later case of *Derby & Co Ltd v Weldon (No.8)*,[171] Vinelott J. disagreed and adopted them as a correct analysis of the law after *Ashburton v Pape*. The judgment of Dillon L.J. in the Court of Appeal in *Derby & Co Ltd v Weldon (No.8)*,[172] did not deal at length with the issue, but was nonetheless emphatic that no balancing exercise is required when a party seeks to vindicate privilege in documents mistakenly disclosed. In *Istil Group Inc v Zahoor*,[173] Lawrence Collins J. reviewed the authorities and, in a careful judgment, attempted to restate the principles. In his view protective injunctions and orders for the return of privileged documents involve the equitable jurisdiction to prevent breach of confidence. Therefore the normal rules for the grant of equitable remedies apply, such as the absence of delay and "clean hands" of the party seeking the injunction. However, the court will not be concerned with the materiality of the document and the justice of admitting it, and ordinarily the court should intervene to protect confidence. In this sense there is no balance to be struck between privilege and truth. But other public interest factors may apply, particularly the principle that the court should not restrain publication of material in relation to misconduct that ought in the public interest to be disclosed. He cited the well-known proposition that "there is no confidence in the disclosure of iniquity". It remains to be seen how far this judgment might provide a basis for further clarification of the law.

In relation to the conduct of the party in possession of the other party's privileged documents, it should be noted that innocent recipients of documents disclosed by mistake may be restrained from using them in the same way as a party who acquired them by fraud. Mistakes in pre-trial disclosure have been a growing problem in large-scale commercial litigation. In *Guinness Peat Properties v Fitzroy Robinson Partnership*,[174] the defendants' solicitors inadvertently failed to claim privilege for a certain letter that they left in the files of correspondence disclosed to the plaintiffs on discovery. The plaintiffs inspected and took a copy of the letter. The Court of Appeal held that, although it was generally too late to claim privilege after documents had been inspected,[175] the

---

[170] *Goddard v Nationwide Building Society* [1986] 3 All E.R. 264 at 272. He made clear, however, that an injunction can be refused on general principles affecting discretionary remedies, such as inordinate delay.

[171] *Derby & Co Ltd v Weldon (No.8)* [1990] 3 All E.R. 762.

[172] *Derby & Co Ltd v Weldon (No.8)* [1990] 3 All E.R. 762 at 779.

[173] *Istil Group Inc v Zahoor* [2003] EWHC 165 (Ch); [2003] 2 All E.R. 252.

[174] *Guinness Peat Properties v Fitzroy Robinson Partnership* [1987] 2 All E.R. 716 CA.

[175] Following Hoffmann J. in *Re Briamore Manufacturing Ltd* [1986] 3 All E.R. 132. Note that *Ashburton v Pape* was not cited to Hoffmann J. in that case.

Court had power under the equitable jurisdiction to restrain use of the documents where the inspecting party had procured the inspection by fraud or must have realised that an obvious mistake had been made. Since, on the facts of the case, the mistake was obvious, Slade L.J. dismissed the plaintiffs' appeal against the injunction granted to the defendants.[176]

The difficult case is where the mistake is not obvious. This was the situation in *Webster v James Chapman & Co*[177] where the plaintiff's solicitors notified the defendants that they intended to rely on an expert report at the trial and mistakenly included a copy of the report with the letter. Scott J. refused to grant the plaintiff an order for the return of the report and an injunction restraining the defendants from making use of it. Given that the plaintiff proposed to rely on a later report from the same experts, which was inconsistent with the report disclosed to the defendants, Scott J. considered that it would be unfair to the defendants if they could not make use of their knowledge of the original report, knowledge that they had acquired without fault on their part. He reached this conclusion adopting the balancing exercise discussed above. On the alternative approach of Nourse L.J. it is difficult to see how an injunction could be refused in aid of privilege, even in the case of a non-obvious mistake, provided the documents have not yet been used in evidence. It may be, however, that in such a case a court would be more willing to find that privilege had been waived.[178]

An important procedural point is that an injunction is obtainable in the same proceedings. It is not now necessary to make a separate application in fresh proceedings.[179] However, the party desiring protection must still seek it before the other party has used the confidential information in evidence or otherwise relied on it at trial. After that it is too late. Finally, it must be noted that, under r.31.20 of the Civil Procedure Rules, where a party inadvertently allows a privileged document to be inspected, the party who has inspected the document may use it or its contents only with the permission of the court.[180]

10–023

(D) Court-ordered disclosure: proof of innocence and other public interests

Until the decision of the House of Lords in *R. v Derby Magistrates' Court Ex p. B*[181] it was thought that a further category of case existed in which privilege could be lost. This was where an accused person in a criminal case sought disclosure of

10–024

---

[176] For other applications of this principle see *English and American Insurance Co v Herbert Smith & Co* (1987) 137 N.L.J. 148; *Derby & Co Ltd v Weldon (No.)* [1990] 3 All E.R. 762 CA. The test is whether the mistake would be obvious to a hypothetical reasonable solicitor who would realise, inter alia, that where complex and substantial discovery is carried out under a tight timetable there is a risk of mistakes being made: see *IBM Corp v Phoenix International (Computers) Ltd* [1995] 1 All E.R. 413 Ch. D.

[177] *Webster v James Chapman & Co* [1989] 3 All E.R. 939.

[178] cf. *Al Fayed v Commissioner of Police for the Metropolis* [2002] EWCA Civ 780 (non-obvious mistake; on the facts it was not unreasonable for the claimants to conclude that privilege had been waived; it was not just and equitable to grant an injunction and order the return of the documents).

[179] *Goddard v Nationwide Building Society* [1986] 3 All E.R. 264 at 271 per Nourse L.J.

[180] The same principles apply to the exercise of the court's discretion under this rule as to the grant of an injunction: *Al Fayed v Commissioner of Police for the Metropolis* [2002] EWCA Civ 780.

[181] *R. v Derby Magistrates' Court Ex p. B* [1996] 1 A.C. 487.

a third party's privileged documents on the ground that they were necessary for the conduct of his defence. There was authority that privilege could be lost or overridden where disclosure was necessary for this purpose, although the cases on the point, *Barton,*[182] and *Ataou,*[183] stated different principles for decision.[184] However, the ultimate question in both cases was one of priorities of fundamental rights. Both held that in certain circumstances the right against wrongful conviction, with its ancillary right of access to evidence to establish innocence, prevailed over the right to legal privilege.

10–025   In *R. v Derby Magistrates' Court Ex p. B* the House of Lords reversed these priorities and overruled both *Barton* and *Ataou*. The appellant applied for judicial review of witness summonses directed to the appellant and his solicitor requiring them to produce certain attendance notes and proofs of evidence. These documents disclosed the factual instructions that the appellant had given after he had been charged with murder as a result of his confession that he alone was responsible for it. Before his trial, but after giving the instructions, he had changed his story and alleged that his stepfather had committed the murder. The appellant was acquitted of murder. Some years later the stepfather was charged with the murder. At the committal proceedings the appellant gave evidence against him, whereupon counsel for the stepfather sought to cross-examine the appellant on the clearly inconsistent statements he had made to his solicitor. The appellant declined to waive privilege in the instructions, at which point the witness summonses were issued. The House of Lords unanimously allowed the appeal, holding that lawyer-client privilege was absolute and permanent in its nature and that no exception should be allowed to it. It followed therefore, according to Lord Taylor C.J., that *Barton* and *Ataou* were wrongly decided and should be overruled.

The assertion that no exception should be allowed to privilege must be read in the context of the argument that the court had power to engage in a balancing of interests. It is this proposition that the Lords were at pains to deny, founding on the argument that the balance of public interest was settled "once and for all in the sixteenth century",[185] when the law in effect recognised legal privilege as one of the fundamental conditions of the administration of justice. There is nothing, however, to suggest that their Lordships were intending to cast doubt on any of the other cases in which privilege may be lost.

The only note of hesitation in what is otherwise a strong and unequivocal decision was sounded by Lord Nicholls. His Lordship reserved his "final view" on the case where the client no longer has any interest to protect by claiming privilege. He thought that this situation did not arise on the facts because the appellant had a legitimate interest in not disclosing material that would point to his guilt of a horrific murder of which he had been publicly acquitted. But his Lordship was clearly doubtful about upholding privilege where the privilege has become spent:

---

[182] *Barton* [1972] 2 All E.R. 1192.
[183] *Ataou* [1988] Q.B. 798.
[184] For discussion of the different principles see previous editions of this book.
[185] *R. v Derby Magistrates' Court Ex p. B* [1996] 1 A.C. 487 at 508.

"I would not expect a law, based explicitly on considerations of the public interest, to protect the right of a client when he has no interest in asserting the right and the enforcement of the right would be seriously prejudicial to another in defending a criminal charge or in some other way."[186]

None of the other Lords addressed this point directly. It is unclear therefore whether they would recognise an exception in the limited form envisaged by Lord Nicholls, although it has to be said that the categorical nature of the speeches by Lord Taylor C.J. and Lord Lloyd of Berwick does not suggest that this is likely. The upshot of the case is that process values take precedence over rectitude of decision. The interests of persons in the confidentiality of legal advice are given a higher priority than the interests of defendants in avoiding the risk of a miscarriage of justice in the form of wrongful conviction.

This ordering of priorities can be strongly criticised as contrary to fundamental **10–026** principle.[187] It is undoubtedly problematic from the perspective of human rights law. The stepfather would have a right under art.6 of the ECHR of access to evidence necessary for his defence.[188] The appellant has a right to protection for his privileged communication, but it is a right under art.8. The appellant's rights under art.6 are not engaged because he has already been tried, and the rule against double jeopardy prevents reopening of the acquittal.[189] The art.8 right is a qualified one. One ground for interference with it is "the protection of rights and freedoms of others". The argument is strong that it is necessary to interfere with the appellant's right to privacy to protect the stepfather's art.6 right of access to evidence. The court could couple an order for disclosure with measures to protect the appellant from any adverse publicity that might result from his privileged communications being used in cross-examination. If this analysis is correct, the inescapable conclusion is that human rights considerations will require the court to engage in precisely the kind of balancing exercise that the House of Lords was at such pains to reject.

Finally, it is extraordinary that an exception to privilege that appeared to Caulfield J. in *Barton* to be a matter of natural justice should be abolished on the ground that the highest court in the land is bound by conceptions of the public interest prevailing four centuries ago. The Australian Evidence Act 1995 reversed a similar decision by the High Court of Australia,[190] and it is submitted that Parliament should do the same in England. There seems to be little chance of the courts reconsidering their stance on this issue after *B v Auckland District Law Society*,[191] where the Privy Council, following the *Derby Magistrates* case, held that the "full and frank disclosure" rationale of legal privilege compelled the conclusion that the public interest in upholding legal privilege could not be the subject of a balancing exercise against other public interests.

---

[186] *R. v Derby Magistrates' Court Ex p. B* [1996] 1 A.C. 487 at 513.

[187] See also the forceful critique of the decision by C. Tapper, "Prosecution and Privilege" (1996) 1 E. & P. 5.

[188] *Jespers v Belgium* (1981) 27 D.R. 61; *Edwards v United Kingdom* (1993) 15 E.H.R.R. 417.

[189] Subject to the possibility of new and compelling evidence becoming available against him: see Criminal Justice Act 2003 Pt 10.

[190] See s.123 of the Act, overturning *Carter v Managing Partner, Northmore, Hale, Davey & Leake* (1995) 129 A.L.R. 593.

[191] *B v Auckland District Law Society* [2003] UKPC 38; [2003] 2 A.C. 736.

C.   LITIGATION PRIVILEGE

1.   *Statement and rationale*

10–027   Litigation privilege protects material coming into existence for the purpose of litigation to which the client is a party. This includes the identity and other details of witnesses to be called in adversarial litigation, whether civil or criminal.[192] Obviously it may include material that would in any event be covered by legal advice privilege, such as the client's correspondence with his solicitor about the conduct of the litigation. Litigation privilege, like legal advice privilege, also covers confidential work done by the client's legal advisors on behalf of the client, such as legal research, counsel's notes, draft opinions and so on. However, litigation privilege is wider than legal advice privilege in one major respect. It extends privilege to confidential communications by the client or the lawyer with third parties for the dominant purpose of acquiring advice or information in connection with the litigation. Such communications typically include witness statements, proofs of evidence, expert reports and so on. At common law the rule is that the client may refuse to disclose these documents, and the lawyer or third party may not disclose them without the client's consent. This basic rule is now qualified by the rules of court that require advance disclosure in civil cases of witness statements and experts' reports.[193] Generally speaking, in civil cases litigation privilege is now an issue only when a party does not intend to adduce evidence of the statement in question, made to him or his solicitor by a third party. In criminal cases the prosecution must disclose statements and reports constituting unused material in accordance with the rules laid down in Pt I of the Criminal Procedure and Investigations Act 1996.

The rationale of this form of privilege is generally agreed to be the adversary system of procedure in criminal and most civil proceedings.[194] This system is founded on the principle of party autonomy whereby the parties to legal proceedings decide on the presentation of their case and the evidence they will use to support it. Just as they can decide not to rely on evidence adverse to their case so they cannot build their case by calling upon their opponents to reveal their own preparations and evidence.[195] Litigation privilege thus derives from the logic of the adversary process, and it is reinforced by the argument that legal representation is essential to ensure equality of arms in adversarial litigation. Since the object of legal representation is to enable the client's case to be put as effectively as possible, this would be undermined if all preparations for the litigation had to be disclosed.

---

[192] *R. (on the application of Kelly) v Warley Magistrates' Court* [2007] EWHC 1836 (Admin); [2008] 1 Cr.App.R. 14.

[193] CPR r.32.4(2) (witness statements) and r.35.13 (experts' reports).

[194] *Waugh v British Railways Board* [1980] A.C. 521 at 536 per Lord Simon of Glaisdale; *Re L (A Minor) (Police Investigation: Privilege)* [1997] A.C. 16 at 25 per Lord Jauncey of Tullichettle, with whom Lord Lloyd of Berwick and Lord Steyn agreed.

[195] Where the preparations for litigation are covered by both litigation privilege and legal advice privilege they share a common, or at least an overlapping, rationale, namely the need to protect the confidentiality of the materials in question: *R. (on the application of Kelly) v Warley Magistrates' Court* [2007] EWHC 1836 (Admin); [2008] 1 Cr. App. R. 14 at [22] per Laws L.J.

However, in *Re Barings Plc*,[196] Sir Richard Scott V.C. rejected a conception of litigation privilege as a free-standing doctrine of the law of evidence. In his view it was essentially ancillary to legal advice privilege. After referring to a number of authorities,[197] he continued:

> "These citations make clear, in my opinion, that documents brought into being by solicitors for the purposes of litigation were afforded privilege because of the light they might cast on the client's instructions to the solicitor or the solicitor's advice to the client regarding the conduct of the case or on the client's prospects. There was no general privilege that attached to documents brought into existence for the purposes of litigation independent of the need to keep inviolate communications between client and legal adviser. If documents for which privilege was sought did not relate in some fashion to communications between client and legal adviser, there was no element of public interest that could override the ordinary rights of discovery and no privilege."[198]

This restrictive view of litigation privilege is difficult to square with the rule that the privilege is available to a litigant in person who has no legal adviser acting for him.[199] It is also inconsistent with a number of the modern cases that do not make this explicit link with legal advice privilege. In particular, statements in the Court of Appeal decisions of *Re Highgrade Traders Ltd*[200] and *Guinness Peat Properties Ltd v Fitzroy Robinson Partnership*[201] indicate that where litigation is reasonably in prospect, documents brought into being for the purpose of enabling a solicitor to advise whether a claim should be made or resisted are privileged provided only that that is the dominant purpose for which they were made.[202] In *Re Barings Plc* Sir Richard Scott V.C. doubted the correctness of these statements, but acknowledged that he was bound by the decisions, which he then distinguished on the facts. It remains to be seen whether in the current climate of increasing openness in civil litigation his view will command support in future.[203]

10–028

2. *Extent of the privilege*

(A)   The meaning of "lawyer"

This has been dealt with in the section on lawyer-client privilege.

10–029

---

[196] *Re Barings Plc* [1998] 1 All E.R. 673 Ch. D.
[197] *Lyell v Kennedy* (1884) 27 Ch.D. 1 CA; *Anderson v Bank of British Columbia* (1876) 2 Ch.D. 644 CA; *Wheeler v Le Marchant* (1881) 17 Ch.D. 675 CA.
[198] *Re Barings Plc* [1998] 1 All E.R. 673 at 681–682.
[199] A rule confirmed obiter by Laws L.J. in *R. (on the application of Kelly) v Warley Magistrates' Court* [2007] EWHC 1836 (Admin); [2008] 1 Cr.App.R. 14.
[200] *Re Highgrade Traders Ltd* [1984] B.C.L.C. 151.
[201] *Guinness Peat Properties Ltd v Fitzroy Robinson Partnership* [1987] 2 All E.R. 716.
[202] See Oliver L.J. in *Re Highgrade Traders Ltd* [1984] B.C.L.C. 151 at 172; Slade L.J. in *Guinness Peat Properties Ltd v Fitzroy Robinson Partnership* [1987] 2 All E.R. 716 at 723.
[203] But not from Rosemary Pattenden who defends the adversary process rationale in "Litigation privilege and expert opinion evidence" (2000) 4 E. & P. 213. It did appeal, however, to Lawrence Collins J. in *Istil Group Inc v Zahoor* [2003] 2 All E.R. 252, who described the traditional rationale as ripe for reconsideration.

(B)   Clients and third parties

10–030   The section on lawyer-client privilege has already discussed issues arising about the identity of the "client" in the case of corporations, and whether employees and agents who supply information and advice to other employees identified as the "client" are regarded as third parties for the purposes of lawyer-client privilege.

It should be remembered at this point that a third party who provides advice or information to a client or a client's lawyer for purposes of litigation is a potential witness in the litigation. An eyewitness who makes a statement, or an employee or agent who compiles an expert's report, may well find themselves required to give evidence if the matter goes to trial. However, the law does not recognise any property in a witness.[204] A client who chooses not to call a particular witness with whom he has had confidential communications cannot prevent an opposing party calling the witness. Nor can he prevent the witness giving evidence of expert opinion based on documents and facts that the witness has observed in circumstances that were not privileged. However, a client can claim privilege for communications with the witness,[205] and for the witness's knowledge or expert opinion about the relevant facts where that knowledge or opinion is based on privileged material and cannot be divorced from it.[206]

(C)   The protected communications

10–031   Two major issues require discussion. The first is the requirement that for privilege to attach to communications with third parties, litigation must either be in existence or at least contemplated by the client. The second is that the dominant purpose of the communication must be the supply of advice or information in connection with the litigation. These will be dealt with in turn.

The leading case that establishes that communications with third parties are privileged only if made in connection with litigation is *Wheeler v Le Marchant*.[207] This was an action for specific performance of a building contract to lease building land from the defendants. The defendants claimed privilege for correspondence by their solicitors with a firm of surveyors about the land in question. The solicitors apparently sought information about the state of the property in order to enable them to advise the clients, but at the time no litigation had yet arisen. The Court of Appeal refused the defendants' claim, holding that privilege could only be claimed for communications with third parties that came into existence after a dispute arose and that were prepared with a view to obtaining advice or information for the purpose of the actual or contemplated

---

[204] *Harmony Shipping Co SA v Davis* [1979] 3 All E.R. 177 CA; *Re L (A Minor)* [1997] A.C. 16 HL.
[205] And also for items, such as a blood sample, brought into existence for the purposes of the proceedings; these are "subject to legal privilege" under s.10(1)(c) of PACE: *R. v R* [1994] 4 All E.R. 260 CA.
[206] *Davies* [2002] EWCA Crim 85; (2002) 166 J.P. 243.
[207] *Wheeler v Le Marchant* (1881) 17 Ch.D. 675 CA.

litigation. Jessel M.R. explicitly rejected the defendants' attempt to extend legal advice privilege to a case involving a communication with a third party[208]:

> "it has never hitherto been decided that documents are protected merely because they are produced by a third person in answer to an inquiry made by the solicitor. It does not appear to me to be necessary, either as a result of the principle that regulates this privilege or for the convenience of mankind, so to extend the rule."[209]

The question then is what degree of contemplation is necessary to attract litigation privilege? Is it enough, for example, that the client anticipates litigation as a possibility? It is clear from the authorities that it is not necessary that litigation should actually be in existence or that there should have been formal notice of intention to commence proceedings. It is equally clear that contemplating litigation as a mere possibility, or having a general apprehension of future litigation, is not enough. The appropriate test appears to be whether litigation must have been reasonably in prospect. This can be expressed by saying that the client must have contemplated litigation as a "real likelihood" as opposed to a mere possibility, provided this is not understood to mean a greater than 50 per cent chance of litigation.[210] It seems therefore that if something has happened that is likely in the client's view to result in litigation, privilege can attach to communications with third parties for the purposes of such litigation. In *Alfred Crompton Amusement Machines Ltd v Commissioners of Customs and Excise (No.2)*,[211] the plaintiff company gave formal notice to the defendants that it was dissatisfied with the agreed formula on which it had been paying purchase tax on the amusement machines with which it dealt. The notification was given in 1967 and was followed by an agreed procedure whereby the defendants stated their opinion about the basis on which purchase tax was payable. If the opinion was not accepted the procedure provided for the dispute to go to arbitration. The opinion was given in 1968 and was followed in due course by arbitration. In the course of the High Court litigation that succeeded the arbitration the defendants claimed privilege for confidential correspondence with third parties about the value of the company's machines. The House of Lords held that the defendants had reasonably contemplated litigation in the form of arbitration since 1967 when they received the notice of dissatisfaction. At this stage it was clear that a dispute had arisen that was likely to result in litigation. The court held that the claim failed on the facts, however, because the communications with the third parties were made for the purpose of enabling the defendants to decide on the basis on which purchase tax was payable; they were not made for the purpose of enabling the defendants' lawyers to advise on the case to be put in arbitration.[212]

The "purpose" test functions as an important limitation on the scope of litigation privilege. Depending on how widely or narrowly it is interpreted it can have the effect of refusing or permitting access to evidence of great probative value. A

10–032

---

[208] That is, a third party who was not a mere channel of communication between client and lawyer; see paras 10–007 to 10–008 above.

[209] *Wheeler v Le Marchant* (1881) 17 Ch.D. 675 at 681.

[210] See *United States v Philip Morris Inc* [2004] EWCA Civ 330; (2004) 1 C.L.C. 811.

[211] *Alfred Crompton* [1974] A.C. 405 HL.

[212] An alternative claim for non-disclosure based on public interest immunity succeeded; see Ch.9.

report of an accident investigation, for example, that is conducted very soon after the accident, is likely to contain statements of witnesses made when events were fresh in their memory as well as findings of fact by expert investigators. Such a report may well be the best evidence of the nature and cause of the accident. Access to the report is obviously vital to an injured claimant seeking compensation and to a court charged with the task of determining liability for the accident. The nature of the test for privilege was authoritatively settled by the House of Lords in *Waugh v British Railways Board*[213] in favour of a narrow test of the "dominant purpose" for which the communication in question was made. The plaintiff was the widow of an employee of the defendants who had been killed in a railway accident. Two days after the accident two of the defendants' officers prepared a "joint inquiry report" in accordance with the defendants' usual practice. In support of their refusal to give discovery of the report the defendants swore an affidavit stating that the report had been prepared for two purposes: to establish the cause of the accident with a view to taking appropriate safety measures and to provide material to be placed before the defendants' solicitors for advice in respect of the anticipated litigation. These purposes were said to be of equal rank or weight. This would have been more than sufficient to ground the claim of privilege according to the bulk of previous Court of Appeal authority, which tended to prefer a test of whether submission to the legal adviser was one of the purposes, albeit subsidiary, of the document in question.[214] The House of Lords rejected this line of authority as stating a test that was wider than necessary to serve the interests of parties in preparing for litigation. Lord Wilberforce argued that the public interest in the due administration of justice strongly required disclosure of such reports that were contemporaneous, contained statements by eyewitnesses and were almost certainly the best evidence of the cause of the accident. To override this public interest, preparation for litigation ought to be at least the dominant purpose for which the report was prepared. Lord Edmund-Davies, agreeing, commented that "justice is better served by candour than by suppression" and added that in his view:

> "the test of dominance will ... be difficult to satisfy when inquiries are instituted and reports produced automatically whenever any mishap occurs, whatever its nature, its gravity or even its triviality."[215]

Applying the "dominant purpose" test, the defendants' claim in *Waugh* failed because on their own admission the two purposes for which the report was prepared were of equal importance. A subsequent decision made it clear that the courts will scrutinise carefully claims about the dominant purpose for which communications with third parties are made. In *Neilson v Laugharne*,[216] the Court of Appeal refused privilege for statements taken during an investigation under s.49 of the Police Act 1964 pursuant to a complaint by the plaintiff against

---

[213] *Waugh v British Railways Board* [1980] A.C. 521.
[214] *Birmingham and Midland Motor Omnibus Co Ltd v London and North Western Railway Co* [1913] 3 K.B. 850; *Ankin v London and North Eastern Railway Co* [1930] 1 K.B. 527; *Ogden v London Electric Railway Co* (1933) 49 T.L.R. 542.
[215] *Waugh v British Railways Board* [1980] A.C. 521 at 543–544.
[216] *Neilson v Laugharne* [1981] Q.B. 736.

the police. It was held that the dominant purpose of the statements was use in the police inquiry and not, as the defendant chief constable claimed, use in the later civil proceedings. However, the fact that a report was made for two or more independent purposes will not necessarily be fatal to a claim for privilege. Privilege will still apply if the party claiming it can show that other purposes were subsidiary to the main purpose of using the report to enable legal advice on the prospects of an anticipated claim.[217]

In *Guinness Peat Properties v Fitzroy Robinson Partnership*,[218] the Court of Appeal held that the dominant purpose is to be discovered by an objective assessment of all the evidence. This includes the intentions not only of the creator of the document but also the intentions of the person or body under whose direction the document is brought into existence. In that case the document was a notification by a firm of architects to their insurers of an intended claim against the architects for professional negligence. The defendants had made the notification as required by the terms of their indemnity policy. The Court of Appeal considered that the fact that their purpose was compliance with the policy did not mean that the document was not privileged. The relevant persons to be considered were the insurers who had the real interest in defending the claim. The insurers' evidence, which the court accepted, was that they required the clients to make such notifications (which included comments on the merits of the claim) for submission to the insurers' solicitors for legal advice on the claim.[219]

The nature of the claim in this case may have been an important factor in the decision. It is more plausible to argue a dominant purpose for third-party reports of legal advice in a case of professional negligence,[220] which is quite likely to raise complex issues of law and fact, than in a routine insurance claim for theft or accident. The initial decision on whether to admit or resist the latter type of claim is generally made by an insurer's claims manager or claims department. Reports from third parties, whether the insured or assessors or investigators, that form part of the materials for the initial decision will not be privileged in such a case. Even if the report is intended to go subsequently to the legal adviser in the event of a denial of liability this is likely to be regarded as a contingent purpose, and therefore secondary to the dominant purpose of enabling the initial decision to be made.[221]

10–033

---

[217] See, e.g. *McAvan v London Transport Executive* (1983) 133 N.L.J. 1101 CA.

[218] *Guinness Peat Properties v Fitzroy Robinson Partnership* [1987] 2 All E.R. 716.

[219] This case is a useful illustration of the principle of common interest whereby the position of the firm is equated with that of their insurers. Thus the insurers' solicitors became the clients' solicitors for the purposes of the litigation to which the client was a party. See further *Buttes Gas and Oil Co v Hammer (No.3)* [1981] Q.B. 223 CA.

[220] The claims manager of the defendants' insurers gave evidence on affidavit that virtually all claims against architects were submitted to legal advisers for advice.

[221] See, e.g. *Melik v Norwich Union* [1980] 1 Lloyd's Rep. 523, where Woolf J. refused privilege on this basis for an assessor's report on an insurance claim for loss caused by theft. Much, though, depends on the circumstances of the case and the insurers' evidence: compare the result in the fire insurance case of *Re Highgrade Traders Ltd* [1984] B.C.L.C. 151 CA (assessors' reports held to be privileged). Compare further *Guardian Royal Exchange v Stuart* [1985] 1 N.Z.L.R. 596 (fire insurance claim–assessors' reports not privileged), and see generally A. Borrowdale, "Insurers and Legal Professional Privilege in New Zealand" (1989) 8 C.J.Q. 249.

A very different approach to the availability of litigation privilege is apparent in the decision of Sir Richard Scott V.C. in *Re Barings Plc*.[222] After the collapse in 1995 of Barings Bank, solicitors acting for the administrators of the bank prepared a report on the conduct of the directors of the bank. The administrators commissioned the report in compliance with their statutory duty to report to the Department of Trade and Industry under s.7(3) of the Company Directors Disqualification Act 1986. The statutory purpose of the report was to provide material to the Secretary of State for the purpose of assisting in the Secretary's decision whether to begin disqualification proceedings against the directors. Distinguishing the cases of *Re Highgrade Traders Ltd* and *Guinness Peat Properties Ltd v Fitzroy Robinson Partnership*, Sir Richard Scott V.C. held that the question of whether such a statutory report was privileged depended on a balancing of public interests. In his judgment disclosure of the report was necessary on the facts for disposing fairly of the case and for saving costs; he went on to say that there was no public interest that required privilege to be given to the report sufficient to override the public interest in the administration of justice reflected in the right to discovery. This decision was strongly influenced by his view that litigation privilege is ancillary to legal advice privilege, and that it should protect communications with third parties only when disclosure of such communications would "impinge on the inviolability of lawyer-client communications".[223] While there is something to be said for this view, making the availability of privilege depend on a balancing of public interests seems to confuse privilege and public interest immunity. It is also hard to reconcile in principle with the approach adopted to legal advice privilege by the House of Lords in *R. v Derby Magistrates' Court Ex p. B*.[224] A more satisfactory solution would be for the legislation requiring the making of such reports to state expressly whether they are to be privileged.

3.   *Loss of privilege*

10–034   The rules relating to communications in furtherance of crime or fraud, waiver and secondary evidence are the same as for legal advice privilege and have been discussed above. There is a need to consider further the issue of court-ordered disclosure, because the House of Lords has held that in one respect at least there is a substantial difference between the two forms of privilege.

(A)   *Court-ordered disclosure: litigation privilege and non-adversarial proceedings*

10–035   In *Re L (A Minor) (Police Investigation: Privilege)*,[225] an issue arose whether a judge had jurisdiction to order disclosure to the police of a pathologist's report on a child who was the subject of care proceedings brought by a local authority.[226]

---

[222] *Re Barings Plc* [1998] 1 All E.R. 673 Ch. D.
[223] See the discussion in the text above.
[224] *R. v Derby Magistrates' Court Ex p. B* [1996] 1 A.C. 487.
[225] *Re L (A Minor) (Police Investigation: Privilege)* [1997] A.C. 16 HL.
[226] Under Pt IV of the Children Act 1989.

The child's parents were both drug addicts. The child had been admitted to hospital after ingesting a quantity of methadone. The mother's explanation was that the child had swallowed it by accident whereas the police suspected that it had been administered deliberately. In the course of the care proceedings the mother obtained leave to commission a report from a consultant pathologist on the frequency of the child's consumption of methadone. The effect of the report was to cast serious doubt on the mother's story, hence the police interest in securing access to it. In resisting the police application for disclosure the mother argued, inter alia, that the report was protected by legal privilege. By a majority of three to two the House of Lords rejected the argument, holding that no privilege attached to the report because litigation privilege was excluded by necessary implication from the terms and overall purpose of the Children Act 1989. Lord Jauncey of Tullichettle, who gave the main speech for the majority, reasoned that litigation privilege is an essential component of a fair trial under the adversarial system, but that it did not have a role to play in care proceedings under the Act, which, like wardship proceedings, were concerned with the welfare of the child and were essentially non-adversarial. This conclusion, he said, did not affect the lawyer-client form of legal privilege, which continued to be available in non-adversarial proceedings.

There is much to be said in favour of the majority view, given a procedural context in which the parties not only have no property in the opinion of the expert witness but in addition cannot withhold from the court evidence obtained with leave of the court that is relevant to the future of the child.[227] If the mother had been able to maintain litigation privilege for the pathologist's report this might have indirectly subordinated the interests of the child to those of the mother, contrary to the object of the Act. However, such reasoning did not appeal to Lord Nicholls of Birkenhead. In his dissenting speech,[228] he rejected any sharp distinction between adversarial litigation and inquisitorial family proceedings, pointing out that the latter may be just as confrontational as other civil litigation, and saying that the distinction distracted attention from the real issue of the requirements of fairness in all forms of proceedings. This can be readily conceded, as can his point that legal advice privilege is an essential element of a fair hearing in family proceedings as much as any other. What is less convincing, with respect, is the argument that the purpose of legal advice privilege would be frustrated if the legal adviser could not approach potential witnesses in confidence before advising the client.[229] This argument makes two assumptions. One is that the legal adviser would be inhibited from disclosing to the third party anything adverse to the client that would otherwise remain secret. This problem did not arise in the case itself because the expert's report was prepared on the basis of the child's hospital case notes, which had already been filed as part of the court papers available to all parties. There is no suggestion in the report of the case that the mother's lawyers had been unable to advise her properly. At best therefore this is a hypothetical difficulty that might be met in a suitable case by an

---

[227] *Oxfordshire CC v M* [1994] 2 All E.R. 269 at 278 per Sir Stephen Brown P.; approved by Lord Jauncey in *Re L (A Minor)* [1997] A.C. 16 at 28.

[228] With which Lord Mustill agreed.

[229] *Re L (A Minor)* [1997] A.C. 16 at 33.

exercise of the judge's admitted discretion not to order disclosure. The other assumption is that a legal adviser might not approach a witness in any event for fear of eliciting an adverse response that would then be disclosable. Many would say that it would not be unfair to require a client to take this risk, given the existence of countervailing public interests in accessing material relevant to both the welfare of the child and the enforcement of the criminal law.[230]

Re L (A Minor) is an important case for litigation privilege generally.[231] It confirms the trend established by *Waugh v British Railways Board*[232] to confine this form of privilege within relatively narrow limits, and it recognises that the different rationales of the two forms of legal professional privilege[233] may generate important differences in the scope and limits of the two forms. The majority were careful to distinguish the earlier decision of the House in *R. v Derby Magistrates' Court Ex p. B*[234] as being concerned only with lawyer-client privilege. Inevitably this raises the question whether, if litigation privilege is not "absolute", it can be waived by the court in other contexts by reference to a balancing of the interests concerned. For example, could a court order disclosure of a communication protected only by litigation privilege where it is necessary to do so for the defence of an accused in criminal proceedings? Suppose that S, a solicitor acting for D1 who has been charged jointly with D2 with robbery, contacts a potential defence witness for a statement. The witness makes a written statement to S that only one person was involved in the robbery and that it was D1. Assuming that the witness is unavailable to testify at the trial, can D2 issue a witness summons to S to produce the written statement?[235]

The statement is covered by litigation privilege, but D2 can argue forcefully that he requires it to help prove his innocence. On the other hand D1 has an equally strong interest in maintaining confidentiality. The approach in *R. v Derby Magistrates' Court Ex p. B* suggests that privilege would not be waived, but it does not seem to be in the interests of justice that D1 can suppress the statement of a third party adverse to himself where this may have the effect of preventing the acquittal of an innocent person.

---

[230] In *L v United Kingdom* [2000] F.L.R. 322 the European Court of Human Rights held that the application by the mother in *Re L (A Minor)* [1997] A.C. 16, alleging violations of arts 6 and 8 in respect of the order for disclosure to the police of the expert's report, was inadmissible.

[231] It was applied in the context of adversarial civil litigation in *Vernon v Bosley (No.2)* [1999] Q.B. 18 CA.

[232] *Waugh v British Railways Board* [1980] A.C. 521 HL.

[233] cf. *Re Barings Plc* [1998] 1 All E.R. 673 Ch. D, discussed above.

[234] *R. v Derby Magistrates' Court Ex p. B* [1996] 1 A.C. 487 HL.

[235] This hypothetical situation makes the further assumption that the statement would be admitted as an exception to the hearsay rule under s.117 of the Criminal Justice Act 2003.

PART III

ADDUCING EVIDENCE: TRIAL PROCEDURES AND THE PRINCIPLES OF PROOF

CHAPTER 11

BURDEN AND STANDARD OF PROOF

A. Introduction

Part III of this book moves the focus from the problems associated with obtaining **11–001**
evidence before trial, which were discussed in Pt II, to the trial itself. The aim in
this group of five chapters is to deal with the principles of proof applicable to the
common law adversarial trial. These principles embrace questions of the
allocation of the burden and standard of proof, the forms of proof and alternatives

to proof, and the competence and examination of witnesses. We begin in this chapter with the burden and standard of proof in adversarial trials.

The organisation of the chapter is that section B contains a preliminary discussion of the concepts of burden and standard of proof, and explains the different burdens that arise in relation to proof of facts. The chapter then gives separate consideration to criminal and civil cases because the rules differ substantially. Section C discusses the allocation of burdens in criminal cases. Section D deals with the allocation of burdens in civil cases. Sections E and F deal with the standard of proof in criminal and civil cases respectively. The final section of the chapter, section G, deals with the burden and standard of proof of facts which are conditions of the admissibility of evidence.

B.   THE CONCEPTS OF BURDEN AND STANDARD OF PROOF

1.   *General definitions*

11–002   The term "burden of proof", also known as the "onus of proof", refers to the legal obligation on a party to satisfy the factfinder, to a specified standard of proof, that certain facts are true. The facts for this purpose are the facts in issue—the facts on which the legal rights and liabilities of the parties to the case depend. As noted in Ch.1, the facts in issue in any particular case are determined by reference to the substantive law and the statements of case or pleadings in the case (for this purpose, "pleadings" include the indictment or information in a criminal case). There may be several facts in issue in a given case, and the burden of proof of different issues may be differently allocated amongst the parties. For example, in a civil action for damages for personal injuries caused by negligent driving, the claimant will bear the burden of proof of the defendant's negligence and of the causation of the claimant's injuries by the negligent driving. If the defendant alleges contributory negligence by the claimant, the defendant will bear the burden of proving it.

A burden of proof also rests on a party to establish the existence of any facts on which the admissibility of evidence to be adduced by the party depends—for example, that the defendant's confession to an offence was not obtained by oppression.[1]

11–003   The term "standard of proof", also known as the "quantum of proof", refers to the degree of probability to which facts must be proved to be true. In adjudicative proceedings truth is generally conceived to be a matter of probability; since there can be degrees of probability a question arises of what is the appropriate degree for the proceedings in question. Because of the inherent limitations of human knowledge,[2] no party is ever required to prove facts to a standard of absolute, mathematical, certainty.

11–004   It is essential to know which party has the burden of proof in a given case for the following reasons. First, the procedural question of which party has the right to begin calling evidence at the trial is answered by determining the allocation of the

---

[1] This is discussed in more detail in section G below.
[2] See Ch.4.

burden of proof of the facts in issue. Generally speaking, the party who bears the burden of proof on the first issue will have the right to begin. In this sense the allocation of the burden of proof is a crucial question for the lawyers in the case.

The second reason relates to a crucial question for the judge in the case. Where there is a submission of no case to answer, the judge will need to know the allocation of the burden of proof in order to rule on the submission. If the party bearing the burden of proof has not adduced sufficient evidence capable of satisfying a reasonable factfinder to the requisite degree, the submission will succeed and the case will end at that point.

Thirdly, the allocation of the burden of proof is important for the factfinder. When the factfinder comes to decide the issues after all the evidence has been heard, the burden and standard of proof is crucial in determining by whom and how far the factfinder has to be persuaded that facts are true. The function of the rules on burden and standard of proof at this stage of a trial is to provide authoritative guidance for the resolution of uncertainty. If the factfinder is left in some doubt, perhaps because the witnesses contradict each other and the factfinder is unsure whom to believe, the rules determine what decision the factfinder should reach. A further function of the rules, particularly the rules on standard of proof, is to distribute the risk of error in the process of adjudication. Given that truth is a matter of probability, there is always a possibility that a particular determination of fact will be mistaken. The question of which party ought to bear the risk of a mistake by the factfinder is one of vital importance. It raises fundamental issues about the values at stake in different types of legal proceedings. We will return to this question when we consider the allocation of the burden and standard of proof in criminal cases and the presumption of innocence.

Fourthly, the rules on burden and standard of proof are important on appeal when an appeal court has to decide whether they were correctly applied at the trial. In a criminal case tried by jury, for example, the judge has a duty to direct the jury as to the burden and standard of proof. An incorrect direction, or a failure to give a direction at all,[3] will be grounds for quashing a conviction.[4]

2.   *The different types of burden*

There is more than one type of burden known to the law. The fundamental distinction is between the burden of proof and the burden of adducing evidence. The burden of proof, as described above, is often called the "legal burden".[5] Different terminology is sometimes used that emphasises different characteristics of the burden; the most common alternatives are the "persuasive burden",[6] the

11–005

---

[3] In *Edwards* (1983) 77 Cr.App.R. 5, the trial judge, having correctly directed on the burden of proof, omitted to direct the jury as to the standard of proof. The Court of Appeal held that the omission was a serious defect, but that in view of the overwhelming evidence against the accused the proviso should be applied to uphold the conviction.

[4] For an emphatic reaffirmation of this point see *Bentley* [2001] 1 Cr.App.R. 307 CA.

[5] A usage coined by A. T. Denning (later Lord Denning M.R.), "Presumptions and Burdens" (1945) 61 L.Q.R. 379.

[6] Glanville Williams, *Criminal Law The General Part*, 2nd edn (London: Stevens & Sons, 1961), Ch.23; *Lambert* [2001] UKHL 37; [2002] 2 A.C. 545 at [47] per Lord Hope of Craighead.

"probative" burden[7] and the "fixed burden of proof".[8] The classic example of a legal burden is the rule that in a criminal case the prosecution bear the burden of proving the elements of the offence charged, to the standard of beyond reasonable doubt. If the prosecution fail to persuade the factfinder to this standard of one or more of the elements of the offence charged, then the prosecution will not have discharged their legal burden and the factfinder must acquit on that charge. For this reason Wigmore called the burden of proof the "the risk of non-persuasion".[9] Legal burdens are allocated by rules of law and are fixed at the beginning of the case. They do not shift during the course of a trial.

The burden of adducing evidence is often called the "evidential burden", to contrast it with the "legal burden". It is the obligation to adduce sufficient evidence to raise an issue for the court to consider. Its nature, and its relationship with the legal burden, is best explained by the example of a criminal case. As a general rule, the prosecution have the legal burden of proving the elements of the offence charged.[10] The prosecution cannot discharge this burden unless they produce sufficient evidence capable of satisfying a reasonable jury that the elements of the offence are proved to the required standard; in other words, the prosecution have an evidential burden of making out a case for the defendant to answer—a prima facie case, as it is sometimes known.

The question of who has an evidential burden on a particular issue is determined, like the legal burden, by substantive rules. Generally speaking, a party who bears a legal burden of proving a particular issue will also bear an evidential burden on that issue; this means that the party must adduce sufficient evidence on the issue in one or more of the accepted forms of judicial evidence.[11] Sometimes, however, the operation of a legal presumption may have the effect of relieving a party of the obligation to adduce evidence on a point, other than evidence of the fact forming the foundation of the presumption. There are also cases where a party can ask the court to take judicial notice of the existence of a fact, in which case the court will not require evidence of the fact to be adduced. The forms of judicial evidence, and the use of presumptions and judicial notice as alternatives to "proof", are considered in the next chapter.

11–006 It is important to note that a party may have an evidential burden in relation to a particular issue without necessarily having a legal burden. To revert to the example of a criminal case, an accused who wants to rely on a special or a general defence to the charge, such as loss of control (in a murder case) or self-defence, must produce some evidence, or point to some evidence already adduced by the prosecution, that raises a reasonable doubt whether he killed as a result of loss of control, or committed the offence in self-defence. Even if the defendant does not expressly raise the issue of a defence, the judge must still direct the jury on it if there is sufficient evidence to raise a reasonable doubt about its existence.[12] Once this evidential burden has been discharged, the

---

[7] *DPP v Morgan* [1976] A.C. 182 HL.

[8] N. Bridge (later Lord Bridge), "Presumptions and Burdens" (1949) 12 M.L.R. 273, 274.

[9] Vol.IX (Chadbourn rev., 1981), para.2485.

[10] For the exceptions to the rule, see section C below.

[11] Namely, testimony documents and real evidence. See Ch.12.

[12] *Mancini v DPP* [1942] A.C. 1 HL. See generally S. Doran [1991] Crim. L.R. 878.

prosecution's legal burden comes into play. As part of their task of proving the defendant's guilt the prosecution will not only have to prove the elements of the offence (unless the defendant admits them), but also that the offence was not committed after loss of control or in self-defence. By successfully raising the issue of such a defence, the defendant increases the scope of the legal burden on the prosecution.

In the case of these defences the accused is raising a new issue. An important recent development in criminal cases is that the accused may also bear a burden of adducing evidence if he wishes to prevent adverse inferences being drawn from other evidence, where that other evidence is relevant to an issue on which the prosecution already bear the legal and evidential burdens. An example is the reason for an accused's failure to testify in his own defence. Suppose that the prosecution adduce a prima facie case that the defendant committed the elements of the offence charged. The defendant does not give evidence in his own defence. If the defendant then seeks to invite the factfinder not to draw an adverse inference under s.35 of the Criminal Justice and Public Order Act 1994, on the basis that there is an "innocent" explanation for the failure to testify, he must adduce evidence of the explanation for the factfinder to consider.[13] The development is criticised by Pattenden,[14] who argues that it is inconsistent with the fundamental principle that an accused can contest the prosecution case without calling evidence.[15] Pattenden's criticism is cogently put, and it is of course true that before the Criminal Evidence Act 1898 the accused could not have been required to give evidence himself in support of his innocent explanations of prosecution evidence. He was an incompetent witness in his own defence at a trial on indictment. Nevertheless, the law has moved on substantially since 1898, and in recent years criminal proceedings have increasingly been taking on the flavour of a "dialogue" between the prosecution and the defence,[16] a dialogue in which the defendant is being obliged to participate. This development is a further example of this tendency. In this connection it is worth remembering the point discussed above that the accused has for many years had the burden of adducing evidence of defences of the "confession and avoidance" type,[17] the rationale being that it would be unreasonable to expect the prosecution to negative all possible defences when they could not know in what form any such defence might be raised. There is an analogy with the prosecution negativing all possible innocent explanations for the accused's lies, or his failure to testify, before treating these matters as incriminating. How, realistically, can this be done when the prosecution do not know what reasons are in issue and in what form?

---

[13] *Cowan* [1996] Q.B. 373 CA. See also *Argent* [1997] 2 Cr.App.R. 27 CA (reason for the accused's failure to disclose to the police a fact subsequently relied on at trial); *Bateson, The Times*, April 10, 1991 CA (reason for the accused's lies).

[14] R. Pattenden, "Silence: Lord Taylor's Legacy" (1998) 2 E. & P. 141 at 152–154, 156–158.

[15] At common law the accused has always had the right to put the prosecution to proof, requiring them to demonstrate his guilt by evidence that he can test and challenge. This right does not impose on the accused any obligation to put forward a positive case in his defence.

[16] Witness the introduction of the obligation to make pre-trial disclosure of the defence case (see Ch.9), the effective obligation on the accused to mention facts to the police to be relied on in defence (see Ch.5), and the effective obligation on the accused to testify at trial (see Ch.13).

[17] On which see Glanville Williams, "Evidential Burdens on the Defence" (1977) 127 N.L.J. 182.

Two points encapsulate the difference between the legal and the evidential burden. When a judge is deciding whether an evidential burden has been discharged, he looks only at the evidence favouring the party who bears the evidential burden. The question for decision is whether the favourable evidence is sufficient by itself to raise an issue for the court to consider; the fact that there may be substantial other evidence contradicting the favourable evidence is immaterial at this stage. When a factfinder (judge, jury or bench of magistrates) is deciding whether a legal burden has been discharged, the factfinder looks at *all* the evidence adduced in the case. Thus the factfinder will take into account the evidence that first served to discharge the evidential burden plus any other evidence that tends to confirm or rebut it. The second point is that the discharge of an evidential burden does not involve a decision that any fact has been proved.[18] All it signifies is that a question has been validly raised about the possible existence of a material fact; the decision is only that enough evidence has been adduced to justify a possible finding in favour of the party bearing the burden. It is therefore technically incorrect to refer to this burden as an "evidential burden of proof".[19] The discharge of the legal burden occurs at a later stage in the trial, when the factfinder is required to decide on the existence or non-existence of facts whose possible existence is in issue. In jury trials the two burdens are adjudicated upon by different participants in the trial. The judge decides whether an evidential burden has been discharged when deciding what issues are to be left to the jury. The jury decide whether the legal, or persuasive, burden has been discharged when they consider their verdict.[20]

11–007 The distinction between these two burdens is well-established and has been judicially recognised on a number of occasions.[21] At the same time, it has to be said that the judges have not always used terminology clearly or consistently. In particular there has been a confusing tendency to conflate the evidential burden with a third concept, namely the "tactical" or "provisional" burden.[22] This should not be regarded as a term of art in the same way as the legal and evidential burdens. It is merely a useful explanatory term to describe a straightforward idea. When a party has discharged an evidential burden and raised an issue for the court to consider, there arises a tactical onus on the other party to respond with

---

[18] *Jayasena v R.* [1970] A.C. 618 at 624 PC per Lord Devlin; *Hunt* [1987] A.C. 352 at 385 HL per Lord Ackner.

[19] As Lord Bingham confirmed in *Sheldrake v DPP* [2004] UKHL 43; [2005] 1 All E.R. 237 at [1].

[20] See further Glanville Williams, "The Evidential Burden: Some Common Misapprehensions" (1977) 127 N.L.J. 156. In *R. v M* [2007] EWCA Crim 3228 the Court of Appeal appears to have contemplated the possibility that a judge might leave to the jury the question whether the defendant had discharged the evidential burden of raising the defence under s.28 of the Misuse of Drugs Act 1971 to a charge of possession of a controlled drug. It is submitted, with respect, that this is quite plainly misconceived. It is for the judge to rule whether the issue has been raised by the evidence in the case, and then to direct the jury on the burden and standard of proof or disproof of the issue. It is a recipe for immense confusion if the judge has to direct the jury about the discharge of two different burdens in relation to the same issue. The court then made matters worse by referring to whether the "evidential burden can be discharged on a balance of probabilities" (at [11]), which confuses the evidential and legal burdens. This case should be quietly forgotten.

[21] See, e.g. *Jayasena v R.* [1970] A.C. 618 PC; *Edwards* [1975] Q.B. 27 CA; *Hunt* [1987] A.C. 352 HL; *Lambert* [2001] UKHL 37; [2002] 2 A.C. 545 HL.

[22] See, e.g. Lord Simon in *DPP v Morgan* [1976] A.C. 182 at 217 HL.

some rebutting evidence. There is no legal obligation to adduce (further) evidence on the issue, but the party against whom the evidence has been adduced increases the risk of losing on the issue if nothing is done to challenge the evidence. Suppose D is charged with maliciously wounding P with intent to do him grievous bodily harm. P testifies that in an argument in a pub D suddenly produced a knife and stabbed him. This testimony is sufficient to discharge the prosecution's evidential burden, because it provides prima facie evidence of all the elements of the offence under s.18 of the Offences Against the Person Act 1861. If D does not try to counter P's testimony, D runs the risk that the jury are very likely to decide that P's testimony is true. The jury are then very likely to infer that D had the requisite intention to cause P grievous bodily harm. If it is D's case that the stabbing was accidental, then as a practical matter D will have to give evidence to that effect. There is no legal obligation on him to do so, in the sense that he will necessarily lose on the issue if he does not, but tactical considerations dictate the need to meet the presumption that the jury may well otherwise make about his intention.[23] However, in some situations courts have recently held that juries need not consider possible innocent explanations of certain matters unless there is evidence to support those explanations.[24] These are undoubtedly new evidential burdens.

C. ALLOCATION OF BURDENS IN CRIMINAL CASES

1. *The presumption of innocence and the general rule on the burden of proof*

The presumption of innocence states that a person is presumed to be innocent until proven guilty. In one sense this simply restates in different language the rule that the burden of proof in a criminal case is on the prosecution to prove the defendant's guilt. As explained above, the burden of proof rule has a number of functions, one of which is to provide a rule of decision for the factfinder in a situation of uncertainty. Another function is to allocate the risk of misdecision in criminal trials. Because the outcome of wrongful conviction is regarded as a significantly worse harm than wrongful acquittal the rule is constructed so as to minimise the risk of the former. The burden of overcoming a presumption that the defendant is innocent therefore requires the state to prove the defendant's guilt.

11–008

In another more profound sense the presumption of innocence reflects moral and political values that are regarded as sufficiently important in liberal states to elevate the rule about the burden of proof to the status of a fundamental human right.[25] The values involved are those of the liberty, dignity, privacy and

---

[23] Juries may infer that persons intend the natural and probable results of their actions, but are not bound to do so: Criminal Justice Act 1967 s.8.

[24] See above.

[25] ECHR art.6(2). For further discussion of the scope and significance of the presumption see A. J. Ashworth, "Four Threats to the Presumption of Innocence" (2006) 10 E. & P. 241; A Stumer, *The Presumption of Innocence* (Oxford: Hart Publishing, 2010); Hock Lai Ho, "The Presumption of Innocence as a Human Right" in P. Roberts and J. Hunter (eds), *Criminal Evidence and Human Rights* (2012), p.259.

reputation of the individual. An individual's interest in the maintenance of these values is invaded by a criminal prosecution, with its associated risks of the adverse publicity and degradation of a trial, the stigma of conviction and the various forms of punishment. From this standpoint it is essential that the state should justify fully its invasion of the individual's interests by proof that the individual has committed an offence, thereby abusing the freedom of action accorded to him or her by the liberal state.

This imperative is at the heart of the presumption of innocence. The significance of the presumption is not and should not be affected by the seriousness of the offence in question. Sachs J. put the point well in *State v Coetzee*[26]:

> "There is a paradox at the heart of all criminal procedure in that the more serious the crime and the greater the public interest in securing convictions of the guilty, the more important do constitutional protections of the accused become. The starting-point of any balancing enquiry where constitutional rights are concerned must be that the public interest in ensuring that innocent people are not convicted and subjected to ignominy and heavy sentences massively outweighs the public interest in ensuring that a particular criminal is brought to book ... Hence the presumption of innocence, which serves not only to protect a particular individual on trial, but to maintain public confidence in the enduring integrity and security of the legal system. Reference to the prevalence and severity of a certain crime therefore does not add anything new or special to the balancing exercise. The perniciousness of the offence is one of the givens, against which the presumption of innocence is pitted from the beginning, not a new element to be put into the scales as part of a justificatory balancing exercise. If this were not so, the ubiquity and ugliness argument could be used in relation to murder, rape, car-jacking, housebreaking, drug-smuggling, corruption ... the list is unfortunately almost endless, and nothing would be left of the presumption of innocence, save, perhaps, for its relic status as a doughty defender of rights in the most trivial of cases."

11–009   Roberts has suggested three further practical arguments in favour of the presumption.[27] Each reflects in a different way aspects of a general principle of fairness in the treatment of citizens by the state. One is that a contest between state and individual is not a contest of equals; because the state has much greater resources for investigation and conduct of a case than the individual[28] it is right that the state should have the burden of obtaining and presenting convincing evidence of guilt. Secondly, if the burden were generally on the defendant to prove innocence, the factfinder would have to convict in any case in which the factfinder remained undecided about the facts determining guilt or innocence. This is thought not to be acceptable in a criminal justice system that attaches a high value to not convicting the innocent.[29] Thirdly:

---

[26] *State v Coetzee* [1997] 2 L.R.C. 593 South African Constitutional Court. This passage was cited with approval by Lord Steyn in *Lambert* [2001] UKHL 37; [2002] 2 A.C. 545 at [34].

[27] P. Roberts, "Taking the Burden of Proof Seriously" [1995] Crim. L.R. 783.

[28] Sometimes the state has exclusive access to evidence, as in the case of a sample from a victim that is destroyed in the process of testing. It is hard to see how an accused could ever have a fair trial where the state not only requires him to prove his innocence but has also made it impossible for him to obtain the evidence that might do so.

[29] This was one of the arguments used by Lord Clyde in *Lambert* [2001] UKHL 37; [2002] 2 A.C. 545 at [156], in rejecting a legal burden on the accused to prove lack of knowledge of possession of a controlled drug under s.28(2) and (3)(b) of the Misuse of Drugs Act 1971. See further below.

"for as long as criminal proceedings are initiated and structured by the prosecutor's presentation of a prima facie case to answer on specified charges—as opposed, say, to requiring each of us to undergo monthly confessionals before an inquisitor—placing the burden of proof on a defendant will often deprive him of a fair opportunity to answer the allegations against him."[30]

In other words, the defendant may be required to do too much to defend himself at too late a stage, when witnesses' memories have faded, documents have gone missing and so on.

There is more than one dimension involved in identifying the moral and political values underpinning the rule about the burden of proof. It enables us to highlight the importance of the rule as a human right, and consequently to criticise unwarranted deviations from it; this is a principal target of the article by Roberts cited above.[31] A further point is that the rule about the burden of proof is a corollary of the human right to be presumed innocent, but it is not necessarily the only one. Some would argue that the right to be presumed innocent can generate, or at least support, other rules of the law of evidence. One of the standard justifications of the privilege against self-incrimination appeals to the presumption of innocence.[32] Another possibility is the rule that a legal presumption cannot operate to prove particular facts against the accused in a criminal trial.[33]

The extent of the prosecution's burden of proof in a criminal trial was considered by the House of Lords in the landmark case of *Woolmington v DPP*.[34] The defendant had been convicted of the murder of his wife by shooting her in the kitchen of her mother's house. The defendant testified at trial that the shooting was an accident. His story was that his wife had left him and returned to live with her mother; he had gone to the house to persuade her to come back to him, with the plan of producing the gun and threatening to shoot himself if she refused. On her refusal he duly produced the gun, but somehow it went off accidentally and shot her. Swift J., an experienced judge, had directed the jury that once the prosecution had proved that the deceased had died at the hands of the accused, then that was presumed to be murder unless the defendant could satisfy the jury that it was an accident. In this way the judge clearly placed on the defendant the burden of proof of lack of mens rea. His direction looks thoroughly heretical to modern eyes, but there was considerable authority for it as an accurate statement of the law.[35] Nonetheless, the House of Lords held decisively that it was wrong, and allowed the defendant's appeal. In a classic judgment Lord Sankey L.C. declared that the prosecution had the burden of proving not only that the defendant had killed the deceased, but that the killing was not an accident—that the defendant had done it with the malice required for the offence of murder. He went on in resonant language to generalise the rule about the burden of proof in criminal cases:

---

[30] Roberts, "Taking the Burden of Proof Seriously" [1995] Crim. L.R. 783, 786.
[31] See also Roberts and Zuckerman, Ch.8, esp. pp.344–360.
[32] This argument is discussed in Ch.5.
[33] See Ch.12.
[34] *Woolmington* [1935] A.C. 462.
[35] Sir M. Foster, *Crown Law* (1762), p.255; *Greenacre* (1837) 8 C. & P. 35; J. F. Stephen, *Digest of the Criminal Law*, 7th edn (1926), p.235; *Archbold*, 29th edn (1934), p.873.

"Throughout the web of the English Criminal Law one golden thread is always to be seen, that it is the duty of the prosecution to prove the prisoner's guilt subject to ... the defence of insanity and subject also to any statutory exception. If, at the end of and on the whole of the case, there is a reasonable doubt, created by the evidence given by either the prosecution or the prisoner, the prosecution has not made out the case and the prisoner is entitled to an acquittal. No matter what the charge or where the trial, the principle that the prosecution must prove the guilt of the prisoner is part of the common law of England and no attempt to whittle it down can be entertained."[36]

11–010   The significance of *Woolmington* was profound in two ways.[37] First, it changed the previous law by rejecting Foster's doctrine of the presumption of malice, and by insisting that the burden of proof of mens rea was on the prosecution in all criminal cases, not just murder. Secondly, its reference to the duty of the prosecution to prove the accused's guilt paved the way for a series of cases holding that the prosecution also had the burden of disproving any common law defences that the accused had specifically raised.[38] Thus, depending on the issues raised, the prosecution may have to prove that the accused did not act in self-defence,[39] or under duress,[40] or in a state of sane automatism,[41] or under provocation (in a murder case).[42] It ought to have had two further effects. *Woolmington's* insistence on the fundamental nature of the burden of proof ought to have affected important issues concerning the enactment and interpretation of statutory offences. It ought to have acted as a brake on any tendency of the legislature to reverse the onus of proof by express provision, and it ought to have been a weighty factor in judicial decisions on whether Parliament had impliedly reversed the onus of proof in a statutory offence. It is doubtful how far it has had either effect, even after the Human Rights Act 1998.

2.   The common law exception to the general rule: the defence of insanity

11–011   In *Woolmington v DPP*, Lord Sankey L.C. expressly excluded the defence of insanity from the scope of the rule that the burden is on the prosecution to prove guilt. He gave no reason for this exclusion, other than that it rested on the authority of *M'Naughton's Case*,[43] which he described as "quite exceptional". The rules on insanity stated by the judges in 1843 clearly placed the burden of

---

[36] *Woolmington* [1935] A.C. 462 at 481.

[37] See J. C. Smith, "The Presumption of Innocence" (1987) 38 N.I.L.Q. 223.

[38] By the discharge of an evidential burden on him. "It is generally accepted that *Woolmington* changed the law as to the burden of proof in the case of common law defences such as self-defence and non-insane automatism": per Lord Hope of Craighead in *Lambert* [2001] UKHL 37; [2002] 2 A.C. 545 at [82].

[39] *Lobell* [1957] 1 Q.B. 547 CCA.

[40] *Gill* [1963] 1 W.L.R. 841 CCA.

[41] *Bratty v Attorney-General for Northern Ireland* [1963] A.C. 386 HL. A plea of insane automatism is the same as insanity, the burden of proof of which is, exceptionally, on the accused.

[42] *Mancini v DPP* [1942] A.C. 1 HL. Provocation at common law has now been replaced by the statutory defence of loss of control (Coroners and Justice Act 2009 s.54). Once the defence is raised the burden of disproof is on the prosecution: s.54(5).

[43] Lord Sankey L.C. cited the report in (1843) 4 St.Tr.(N.S.) 847. It is more commonly cited as *M'Naghten* (1843) 10 Cl. & Fin. 200.

proof of insanity on the accused, but that was not surprising at the time, since the accused seems to have borne the burden of proof in respect of all common law defences.[44] Nevertheless, given the unique quasi-legislative status of the M'Naghten Rules, Lord Sankey L.C. was plainly not prepared to overrule them on this point. The fact remains that there is really no good reason in principle or policy why the accused should bear a legal burden of proving insanity as opposed to a burden of adducing evidence to raise the issue.[45] In 1972 the Criminal Law Revision Committee described the rule for insanity as anomalous and recommended that it be changed in line with the Committee's general proposal that all burdens on the accused should be evidential only.[46] No action has been taken on this proposal and insanity remains an exception to the general rule.

The accused also bears the burden of proof of the related statutory defence of diminished responsibility.[47] The standard of proof where the accused bears the burden of proving either insanity or diminished responsibility is the lower standard of the balance of probabilities.[48] Under s.6 of the Criminal Procedure (Insanity) Act 1964, where the accused on a trial for murder raises the issue either of insanity or of diminished responsibility, the prosecution may respond with evidence tending to prove the other issue. So if the defendant pleads diminished responsibility the prosecution may try to show that he was insane at the time of the act in question. In such a case the prosecution have the legal burden of proving the issue they raise, and the standard of proof is the usual prosecution standard of beyond reasonable doubt.[49] Similarly, under s.4 of the Criminal Procedure (Insanity) Act 1964, the issue of the accused's fitness to plead may be raised either by the defence or by the prosecution; if raised by the prosecution, they will bear the legal burden of proving beyond reasonable doubt the accused's unfitness to plead.[50]

---

[44] W. M. Best, *A Treatise on the Principles of the Law of Evidence* (London: S. Sweet, 1849), para.306; *Jayasena v R.* [1970] A.C. 618 at 623 PC per Lord Devlin.

[45] The arguments are discussed and criticised by T. H. Jones, "Insanity, Automatism, and the Burden of Proof on the Accused" (1995) 111 L.Q.R. 475. The only argument with any real substance is that a burden of proving the accused's sanity would be too difficult for the prosecution to discharge. This is not because insanity is allegedly easily faked; Jones is rightly critical (at 492–493) of the majority of the Supreme Court of Canada who accepted this claim in *Chaulk* [1990] 3 S.C.R. 1303. It is because psychiatry is not an exact science and there may be acute disagreements amongst the expert witnesses about the nature and effects of mental illness, as vividly demonstrated in the *Hinckley* case in the United States. On this view reasonable doubts are not difficult to create, but very difficult to rebut. This point should not be persuasive. It is doubtful whether many defendants in England would want the uncertainties associated with a special verdict, even if the rule on burden of proof were different, and in any event it is surely right in principle that a case of genuine doubt on the issue ought to be resolved in favour of the accused.

[46] *Eleventh Report* para.140.

[47] Homicide Act 1957 s.2(2), as substituted by the Coroners and Justice Act 2009 s 52. The Court of Appeal has held that the placing of the legal burden of proving diminished responsibility on the accused does not infringe art.6 of the ECHR: *Lambert Ali and Jordan* [2001] 1 Cr.App.R. 205. See further below.

[48] *Oliver Smith* (1911) 6 Cr.App.R. 19 at 20 CCA; *Carr-Briant* [1943] K.B. 607 CCA (insanity); *Dunbar* [1958] 1 Q.B. 1 (diminished responsibility).

[49] *Grant* [1960] Crim. L.R. 424 CCA.

[50] *Robertson* [1968] 1 W.L.R. 1767 CA.

3. *Express statutory exceptions to the general rule*

11–012   In *Woolmington,* Lord Sankey L.C. also excluded from the scope of the general rule on the burden of proof in criminal cases "any statutory exception". Statutory exceptions are commonly said to be of two types: express and implied. There were examples of both types in existence when *Woolmington* was decided, and by making reference to them Lord Sankey L.C. was merely acknowledging the constitutional truism that Parliament was able to legislate for exceptions to even the most fundamental of rules.[51] As a result of the Human Rights Act 1998, this traditional theory is qualified to the extent that the court has power under s.4 of the Act to make a declaration that provisions of legislation are incompatible with a right under the European Convention of Human Rights ("ECHR"). This could include a provision expressly placing a legal burden on the accused, in possible violation of the presumption of innocence in art.6(2) of the ECHR. However, where incompatibility is found, it has become clear that the courts will exercise the interpretative power under s.3 of the Act, if it is possible to do so, to "read down" the provision so that the burden on the accused is only an evidential burden.[52]

Many statutes expressly impose a burden of proof on the accused in respect of some matter relating to his guilt of the offence charged. It would be pointless to attempt a catalogue or a classification of these provisions. They include not only special defences, such as the defence to murder of diminished responsibility, and numerous defences of "due diligence" to various offences of a regulatory type, but also provisions concerned with the elements of an offence. An example of the latter is the Criminal Justice and Public Order Act 1994 s.51(7), dealing with the offence of witness intimidation, which provides that the requisite intention to obstruct justice is to be presumed from proof of an act of intimidation, done in the knowledge or belief that the victim is a witness in proceedings for an offence, "unless the contrary is proved". Provisions referring to the accused "proving" or "showing" some matter are invariably interpreted as imposing a legal burden on the accused, although it is also the case that the standard of proof to be reached by the accused is always the lower standard of the balance of probabilities.[53] All such reverse onuses will raise an issue of compatibility with the presumption of innocence under the ECHR.

Ashworth and Blake have demonstrated the extent to which Parliament derogates from the *Woolmington* principle in relation to indictable offences.[54] Their research found that no fewer than 40 per cent of offences triable in the Crown Court violate the presumption of innocence by requiring the defendant to prove a statutory defence or (dis)prove at least one element of the offence. Some of these cases involve offences that the courts have interpreted as imposing a

---

[51] See the observations of Lord Ackner in *Hunt* [1987] A.C. 352 at 380 HL.
[52] See the discussion in the text below.
[53] *Carr-Briant* [1943] K.B. 607 CCA.
[54] A. Ashworth and M. Blake, "The Presumption of Innocence in English Criminal Law" [1996] Crim. L.R. 306.

legal burden on the accused,[55] but there are clearly a good many where it is the legislation itself that has expressly reversed the onus of proof. The authors comment:

"It is a fair conclusion from the evidence presented here that many of those who prepare, draft and enact criminal legislation for England and Wales either fail to recognise these violations of the presumption of innocence or its application in this sphere, or fail to appreciate what can be achieved by placing only an evidential burden (rather than the legal burden) on defendants in respect of defences."[56]

4. *Implied statutory exceptions to the general rule*

In the leading case of *Hunt*,[57] Lord Ackner stated that Parliament may impose a burden of proof on the accused "either expressly or by necessary implication". He rejected, as did the other Law Lords, an argument that the reference by Lord Sankey L.C. in *Woolmington* to "any statutory exception" was limited to express statutory exceptions. He was in no doubt that interpretation of legislative provisions might show a necessary implication, from the words used in the statute, that Parliament intended to place a burden of proof on the accused, even though Parliament had chosen not to give effect to its intention expressly. He was of course right to say that the courts cannot ignore a clear parliamentary intention to reverse the onus of proof, but the emphasis placed on the courts' constitutional position rather obscures the creative judicial task that may be involved in the interpretation of statutes.

11–013

A clear case of necessary implication is where the express words of the legislation require a particular logical deduction. An example comes from the Terrorism Act 2000. Section 118 lists a number of provisions in the Act that create statutory defences to various offences under the Act and indicates that these impose only an evidential burden.[58] Once the issue of such a defence is raised the legal burden is on the prosecution to prove beyond reasonable doubt that the defence is not available on the facts of the case. In *Attorney-General's Reference (No.4 of 2002)*,[59] the House of Lords had no hesitation in deciding that the defence under s.11(2) of the Act was intended to impose a legal burden since it was not one of those listed in s.118.

A second type of necessary implication arises from the rule of interpretation embodied in s.101 of the Magistrates' Courts Act 1980. This applies to all *summary* trials, and a provision of this type has formed part of the law since well before *Woolmington*. The original provision was contained in the Summary

---

[55] See the next section of this chapter, on implied exceptions.
[56] Ashworth and Blake, "The Presumption of Innocence" [1996] Crim. L.R. 306, 315.
[57] *Hunt* [1987] A.C. 352 HL.
[58] This provision was the legislative response to the doubts expressed by the House of Lords in *R. v DPP Ex p. Kebilene* [2000] 2 A.C. 326 about the compatibility with the ECHR of a reverse onus in s.16A of the Prevention of Terrorism (Temporary Provisions) Act 1989. It can be seen as an example of what has been called the "democratic dialogue" between the judiciary and government: see Richard Clayton QC, "Judicial deference and 'democratic dialogue': the legitimacy of judicial intervention under the Human Rights Act 1998" [2004] P.L. 33.
[59] *Attorney General's Reference (No.4 of 2002)* [2004] UKHL 43; [2005] 1 All E.R. 237.

Jurisdiction Act 1848,[60] which reformed magistrates' courts and established a new system of summary jurisdiction. Section 101, the modern descendant of that provision, provides:

> "Where the defendant to an information or complaint relies for his defence on any exception, exemption, proviso, excuse or qualification, whether or not it accompanies the description of the offence or matter of complaint in the enactment creating the offence or on which the complaint is founded, the burden of proving the exception, exemption, proviso, excuse or qualification shall be on him; and this notwithstanding that the information or complaint contains an allegation negativing the exception, exemption, proviso, excuse or qualification."

11–014   The effect of the section is that where, in a summary trial, the defendant relies for a defence on any exception, exemption, proviso, excuse or qualification to the statutory offence charged, the burden of proving that exception, etc is on the defendant. The court will therefore have to interpret the statute in order to decide whether the particular provision on which the defendant is relying is an "exception, etc." to the offence in question. The section makes clear that for this purpose it does not matter whether the provision relied on forms part of the clause containing the description of the offence,[61] or whether it appears elsewhere in the statute. It is also immaterial whether the statement of the charge contains an allegation that no exception, etc. is applicable; as far as s.101 is concerned, there is no necessary correlation between the form of the pleading and the rules of proof. Where the section applies and the defendant is held to have a burden of proving an exception, etc. the burden is a legal burden, and the defendant will have to prove the exception, etc. on the balance of probabilities.[62]

There is no corresponding statutory rule for trials on indictment. However, in *Edwards*,[63] the Court of Appeal held that s.101 restated an earlier rule of common law that applied to all criminal trials, including those on indictment. In *Hunt*,[64] the House of Lords confirmed this conclusion. Lord Griffiths[65] stated in terms that *Edwards* was rightly decided on this point,[66] and Lord Ackner impliedly accepted its correctness, while emphasising, as did all the Lords in *Hunt*, that the essential question is one of the interpretation of the particular statutory provisions in question. In accepting the ruling in *Edwards*, Lord Griffiths attached importance to consistency between the two modes of trial. He thought it unlikely that Parliament would have knowingly created confusion in 1848 by providing for different rules on burden of proof in summary trials and trials on indictment. The value of consistency is strengthened, as he noted, by the growth in the

---

[60] Summary Jurisdiction Act 1848 s.14. This was amended and replaced by s.39(2) of the Summary Jurisdiction Act 1879, which became in turn s.81 of the Magistrates' Courts Act 1952, then s.101 of the Magistrates' Courts Act 1980.

[61] Although, if it does, a "particularly difficult" problem of construction can arise: per Lord Griffiths in *Hunt* [1987] A.C. 352 at 374.

[62] *Gatland v Metropolitan Police Commissioner* [1968] 2 Q.B. 279 DC. It is clear that a legal burden on the accused held to arise under s.101 must now pass the test of compatibility with art.6(2) of the ECHR: *R. (on the application of Grundy & Co Excavations Ltd) v Halton Division Magistrates' Court* [2003] EWHC 272; (2003) 167 J.P. 387. See further below.

[63] *Edwards* [1975] Q.B. 27 CA.

[64] *Hunt* [1987] A.C. 352.

[65] With whom Lord Keith of Kinkel and Lord Mackay of Clashfern expressed agreement.

[66] *Hunt* [1987] A.C. 352 at 375–376.

twentieth century of offences triable either way: "The law would have developed on absurd lines if in respect of the same offence the burden of proof today differed according to whether the case was heard by the magistrates or on indictment".[67] He referred also to the position in Scotland, where a similar rule to s.101 is expressly applied to both trials on indictment and summary trials.[68]

The rule embodied in s.101 envisages a court distinguishing between those statutory elements of criminal liability that the prosecution must prove—which are "the description of the offence"—and those statutory elements amounting to an exception, exemption, proviso, excuse or qualification, which the defendant must prove. In *Hunt,* the latter are referred to as statutory "defences".[69] This is a convenient shorthand term, but it has the potential to mislead. It might suggest that s.101 exceptions are analogous to the general defences at common law that the defendant has an evidential burden to raise. These are usually defences of the "confession and avoidance" type, such as self-defence or duress, whereby the defendant admits committing an actus reus with mens rea, but claims to have had a justification or excuse for doing so. Some of the special statutory "defences" are of the confession and avoidance type, but others require the defendant to prove matters that, on the face of it, seem to be part of the "description of the offence". An example is the offence of driving without a licence. The courts have held that the burden is on the prosecution to prove the driving, but on the defendant to prove possession of a licence to drive.[70] This can be brought within s.101 on the basis that a licence is a "qualification", but on another view the absence of a licence is an essential element of the actus reus of the offence. As Smith has pointed out, a "description" of this offence as simply "driving" would be plainly wrong[71]; the act of driving is only prohibited if it is done in the specified circumstance that the driver does not have a licence. There is a grammatical analogy with the offence of rape that has a similar form for the expression of the actus reus: penetration without consent. It has never been doubted that the prosecution must prove both penetration and the absence of consent. It seems clear therefore that the interpretative task does not depend on any generally recognised distinction between "offences" and "defences".[72] It is also clear that

---

[67] *Hunt* [1987] A.C. 352 at 373.

[68] Criminal Procedure (Scotland) Act 1975 ss.66 and 312(v).

[69] *Hunt* [1987] A.C. 352 at 374 per Lord Griffiths, 379–380 per Lord Ackner.

[70] *John v Humphreys* [1955] 1 W.L.R. 325 DC. See, to similar effect, *Oliver* [1944] K.B. 68 (a wartime offence of dealing in sugar without a licence); *Ewens* [1967] 1 Q.B. 322 CCA (possession of drugs without a prescription). All these cases were decided according to a purported general rule, repudiated by the Court of Appeal in *Edwards* [1975] Q.B. 27 CA, that "if a negative averment be made by one party which is peculiarly within the knowledge of the other, the party within whose knowledge it lies, and who asserts the affirmative, is to prove it and not he who asserts the negative": *Turner* (1816) 5 M. & S. 206 at 211 per Bayley J.

[71] Smith, "The Presumption of Innocence" (1987) 38 N.I.L.Q. 223, 230.

[72] Such a distinction is much debated in the literature on the substantive criminal law. The finer details of the debate are beyond the scope of this book, but see K. Campbell, "Offence and Defence" in I. Dennis (ed), *Criminal Law and Justice* (London: 1987), p.73, for one cogently argued view of the distinction. A Stein, "After *Hunt*: The Burden of Proof, Risk of Non-Persuasion and Judicial Pragmatism" (1991) 54 M.L.R. 570 has argued that s.101 should apply to defences of excuse but not defences of justification, which go to the lawfulness of the defendant's act and which the prosecution should disprove. This is an interesting thesis, but it depends on a formal distinction between excuses and justifications that English law does not currently employ and which is problematic in itself.

s.101 itself gives no clue as to how the distinction it sets up is to be operated. The job of classification is left entirely to the courts as a question of the interpretation of the particular statute,[73] which is the point stressed by the House of Lords in *Hunt*.

11–015   Nonetheless, the courts have attempted to give some general guidance for interpretation. In *Edwards*, Lawton L.J., giving the judgment of the Court of Appeal, said that this exception to the general rule on the burden of proof was limited to:

> "offences arising under enactments which prohibit the doing of an act save in specified circumstances or by persons of specified classes or with specified qualifications or with the licence or permission of specified authorities."[74]

This formulation suited the issue in that case, which concerned the burden of proof in relation to the possession of a justices' licence to sell intoxicating liquor.[75] The prosecution had proved the sale of liquor by the defendant, but had called no evidence that the defendant did not have a licence. The Court of Appeal, interpreting the offence according to the principle cited, held that the prohibited act was the sale of liquor, and that the burden was on the defendant to prove that he had a licence. Since he had not done so the Court of Appeal held that he was rightly convicted.

The difficulty with the principle stated by Lawton L.J. is partly that it is unhelpful where the offence-creating provisions make no reference to specific licences or qualifications to do certain acts.[76] According to the Divisional Court in *DPP v Wright*,[77] it is also narrow, being limited to matters which are

---

[73] This is abundantly clear from the inconsistent way in which the courts apply, or fail to apply, s.101. Smith, "The Presumption of Innocence" (1987) 38 N.I.L.Q. 223, 232, contrasts s.161 of the Highways Act 1980 (an offence to deposit any thing on a highway without lawful authority or excuse—burden on the defendant to prove lawful authority or excuse: *Gatland v Metropolitan Police Commissioner* [1968] 2 Q.B. 279) with s.137(1) of the same Act (an offence wilfully to obstruct the highway without lawful authority or excuse—burden on the prosecution to prove absence of lawful authority or excuse: *Nagy v Weston* [1965] 1 All E.R. 78). Identical grammatical constructions produce opposite results. This example shows also that there is no generally accepted drafting convention that would enable courts to distinguish between offences and defences, a point confirmed by F. Bennion, "Statutory Exceptions: A Third Knot in the Golden Thread" [1988] Crim. L.R. 31.
[74] *Edwards*, [1975] Q.B. 27 at 40.
[75] Licensing Act 1964 s.160(1)(a).
[76] A good illustration is provided by *Nimmo v Alexander Cowan & Sons Ltd* [1968] A.C. 107 HL, which concerned a civil action by an employee against his employers for damages for breach of statutory duty under s.29(1) of the Factories Act 1961. The duty, breach of which is also a criminal offence, is to make safe any place of work "so far as is reasonably practicable". Assuming that the plaintiff could prove that his place of work was unsafe, the question was whether the burden was on him (and similarly on the prosecution in criminal proceedings) to prove that it was reasonably practicable for the employers to make the place safe, or for the defendants to prove that it was not reasonably practicable so to do. The principle stated in *Edwards* cannot settle this question. The House of Lords held that, in interpreting this provision, they were not confined to looking only at the arrangement of the sections of the Act and the forms of expression used in them. They could also consider matters of policy, including the practical consequences of holding that the burden rested on the one party or the other. In the event the majority of the court held that the burden lay on the defendants.
[77] *DPP v Wright* [2009] EWHC 105 (Admin) at [54].

straightforward for the defendant to prove. More fundamentally, the problem is that the principle is essentially a restatement—albeit a sophisticated one—of the question of classification rather than a resolution of it.[78] It does not explain how or why a court should decide to classify a particular matter as part of the prohibited act to be proved by the prosecution or as a specified circumstance, etc. to be proved by the defendant. These are questions of policy and principle as well as of grammatical construction. The House of Lords had already recognised the wider ramifications of interpretation once before in *Nimmo v Alexander Cowan & Sons Ltd*.[79] In *Hunt* the House of Lords took the opportunity to restate and develop the methodology of interpretation.

The defendant was charged with possession of a controlled drug, contrary to s.5(2) of the Misuse of Drugs Act 1971. During a search of his home the police had found a paper fold containing a white powder. An analyst's report stated that the powder consisted of morphine, which is a Class A controlled drug, mixed with caffeine and atropine, neither of which is a controlled drug. A compounded preparation of morphine falls within the definition of a controlled drug. However, the report did not state the percentage of morphine in the powder. Under Pt II of the Misuse of Drugs Regulations 1973,[80] which is headed "Exemptions from Certain Provisions of the Misuse of Drugs Act 1971", a preparation containing not more than 0.2 per cent of morphine is excepted from the prohibition on possession set out in s.5 of the Act. At trial the defendant submitted unsuccessfully that he had no case to answer because the prosecution had adduced no evidence to show that the powder contained more than 0.2 per cent morphine and therefore that the exception did not apply. The issue for the House of Lords was where the burden of proof lay. If the provision in the Misuse of Drugs Regulations was an "exception" within the meaning of s.101 of the Magistrates' Courts Act 1980, then the defendant's conviction was correct. The burden of proof would have been on him, but he had adduced no evidence to show that there was less than 0.2 per cent morphine in the compound. If the provision was not an "exception", but was an element of the offence that the prosecution had to prove, then the defendant's conviction was wrong since the prosecution had produced no evidence of the amount of the morphine. The House of Lords held unanimously that the second interpretation was the correct one and quashed the defendant's conviction.

In reaching the conclusion that it was an essential ingredient of the offence that the defendant should be in possession of more than 0.2 per cent of morphine, the House of Lords said that the classification of the relevant regulation for the purposes of s.101 was not necessarily determined by its location in the legislation, which in this case was quite separate from the provision creating the offence of possession. Nor was the question of classification necessarily settled by the form of words used in the legislation to describe the regulation. This is important. It shows that the courts' insistence that interpretation of statutory offences entails trying to discover Parliament's intentions is something of a myth.

11–016

---

[78] See the excellent article by A. A. S. Zuckerman, "The Third Exception to the Woolmington Rule" (1976) 92 L.Q.R. 402.

[79] *Nimmo v Alexander Cowan & Sons Ltd* [1968] A.C. 107; see above.

[80] Misuse of Drugs Regulations 1973 (SI 1973/798) reg.4(1) and Sch.1 para.3.

On the face of it, there was a formidable formal argument[81] that Parliament must be taken to have known of s.101 when it was enacting the legislation on misuse of drugs, and therefore it must have used the descriptions "exemptions" and "exceptions" intentionally, knowing that they would result in the imposition of the burden of proof on the accused. Nevertheless, the House of Lords implicitly rejected the argument, preferring to adopt a more sophisticated approach to the question of interpretation. Similarly, in *DPP v Wright*,[82] the Divisional Court was doubtful whether the reference in s.1 of the Hunting Act 2004 to "exempt" hunting brought the case within s.101, given the variety of exemptions provided for in the Act and the fact that the offence of hunting under s.1 was plainly not intended to be absolute.

The approach adopted in *Hunt* takes account of a number of factors. The location of the provision in the legislation and the form of the provision are clearly important, not to say potentially decisive, and therefore courts will generally look at these factors first. If they do not conclusively settle the issue, then, according to Lord Griffiths,[83] the court should also take account of:

- the mischief at which the Act was aimed;
- practical considerations affecting the burden of proof, such as the ease or difficulty that the respective parties would encounter in discharging the burden of proof;
- the seriousness of the offence.

The first factor is an echo of the argument often used to justify strict liability: that an examination of the Act may show that its purpose was to regulate an area of activity in the public interest by prohibiting certain acts absolutely. In this context a court may hold that Parliament's intention was to make an apparently absolute prohibition subject to the defendant proving that his act falls within a defined exception, etc. The second factor incorporates a principle that a court is more likely to classify a provision as a statutory defence if it would not be difficult for the defendant to discharge the burden of proving it. The licence cases can be justified on this principle: if the defendant has a licence to drive, or to sell intoxicating liquor, it is not a great hardship to ask him to produce it. On the other hand, according to Lord Griffiths, "Parliament can never lightly be taken to have intended to impose an *onerous* duty on a defendant to prove his innocence in a criminal case, and a court should be very slow to draw any such inference from the language of a statute".[84] The third factor is mentioned by Lord Griffiths as one that helps to resolve any ambiguity in favour of the defendant in a case where the question of construction is one of real difficulty. The prosecution should have the burden of proving the commission of serious statutory offences, such as the misuse of hard drugs, where consideration of the other factors does not clearly disclose Parliament's intention. Both he and Lord Ackner regarded Lawton L.J.'s

---

[81] It does not appear from the report that counsel for the prosecution put any part of his case precisely in these terms, but they are largely assumed in the argument that he did make. See *Hunt* [1987] A.C. 352 at 360–363.

[82] *DPP v Wright* [2009] EWHC 105 (Admin).

[83] *Hunt* [1987] A.C. 352 at 374, 378.

[84] *Hunt* [1987] A.C. 352 at 374 (emphasis added).

statement of principle in *Edwards* as a useful guide to the interpretation and application of s.101, rather than a complete statement of this exception to the *Woolmington* rule.[85]

Applying this approach to the issue in the case, Lord Griffiths held that although **11–017** Pt II of the Misuse of Drugs Regulations 1973 was concerned generally with exceptions to what would otherwise be unlawful acts, reg.4(1) relating to the percentage of morphine in a compound was concerned with the definition of the essential ingredients of the offence of possession. His reasoning began with the point that reg.4(2) disapplied the offence altogether in relation to poppy-straw. This leaves no room for a burden of proof on the accused; it is simply not an offence to be in possession of poppy-straw. Applying a similar construction to the other part of reg.4 suggested that Parliament had created an offence of having morphine in one form, but not in another; it was therefore necessary for the prosecution to prove that the defendant possessed morphine in the prohibited form. Lord Griffiths then reinforced this conclusion by saying that it would not be difficult for the prosecution to prove the percentage of morphine in the compound since they had to obtain an analyst's report in any event. On the other hand, it might be very difficult for the defendant to discharge a burden of proof on the issue. He would no longer have the substance because the police would have seized it, and he has no statutory right to a proportion of it for testing purposes. In any event the substance might be destroyed in the prosecution's testing process. Finally, Lord Griffiths referred to the seriousness of the offence, saying that it was right to resolve the interpretative ambiguity in favour of the defendant.

The actual decision in *Hunt* is undoubtedly correct. The alternative interpretation would in effect have required the defendant to do the impossible. With respect, the House of Lords was also right to reject the formalism that would have determined the burden of proof solely on the basis of the location and syntax of the regulation.

Nevertheless, the interpretative approach adopted in the case has not escaped criticism.[86] Critics have argued in particular that ease of proof should not be a criterion for the allocation of burdens in criminal cases. Although the criterion worked to the accused's advantage in this case, the fear is that it might be used in other cases to impose burdens on the accused that would be equally easy (or difficult) for the prosecution to discharge, or that would violate the spirit of the *Woolmington* rule. After all, the defendant has better access than the prosecution to his state of mind at the time of his act, but mens rea is an essential element of guilt and ought to be proved affirmatively by the prosecution. This leads to a more fundamental point. The principle that it is for the prosecution to prove guilt is not one of the interpretative factors expressly mentioned in *Hunt*. Indeed Lord Templeman said that the decision in *Woolmington* was not relevant to the issue to

---

[85] *Hunt* [1987] A.C. 352 at 375 and 386 respectively.
[86] Smith, "The Presumption of Innocence" (1987) 38 N.I.L.Q. 223; P. Healy, "Proof and Policy: No. Golden Threads" [1987] Crim. L.R. 355; P. Mirfield, "The Legacy of *Hunt*" [1988] Crim. L.R. 19; Glanville Williams, "The Logic of 'Exceptions' " [1988] C.L.J. 261. For a more sympathetic appraisal of the decision see D. J. Birch, "Hunting the Snark: The Elusive Statutory Exception" [1988] Crim. L.R. 221; but see also Mirfield, "An Ungrateful Reply" [1988] Crim. L.R. 233.

be decided.[87] This is a surprising and somewhat alarming statement. When the courts are interpreting statutes to decide whether it was Parliament's intention to make an offence one of strict liability, the courts begin with a presumption of mens rea, and then analyse the statute to see whether the presumption is rebutted.[88] An analogous approach to burden of proof, for which *Woolmington* could have provided direct inspiration, would be to say that the courts should begin with a presumption that Parliament's intention is to impose the burden on the prosecution to prove all elements of guilt, including the absence of a defence. Section 101 indicates that such a presumption is rebuttable, and no doubt the courts would take into account the factors mentioned in *Hunt* in deciding whether it was rebutted in a particular case. This approach might not in practice yield many different results, but it would place the emphasis in the right place and might discourage too ready a reliance on ease of proof as a reason for reversing the onus.

One encouraging development in this direction is the decision of the Court of Appeal in *Charles*.[89] The defendant was charged with breaching the conditions of an ASBO (anti-social behaviour order) without reasonable excuse. The issue was whether the defendant had the burden of proving a reasonable excuse for doing the acts in question, or whether the prosecution had to prove the absence of such excuse. The court was emphatic that Parliament could not have intended to place the burden on the defendant, since the terms of an ASBO are set by the court, often imprecisely, and they may criminalise "conduct that Parliament itself has not criminalised and has not provided the terms in which that can be done". It therefore upheld the guidance provided by the Judicial Studies Board that the burden on the defendant is only evidential. If the issue of reasonable excuse is raised it is for the prosecution to disprove it.

5. Reverse onuses and compatibility with the presumption of innocence[90]

11–018   All consideration of reverse onuses, whether imposed expressly or by implication, must take account of the presumption of innocence in art.6(2) of the ECHR. Article 6(2) states quite simply: "Everyone charged with a criminal offence shall be presumed innocent until proved guilty according to law".

As discussed above, the presumption is the foundation of the fundamental rule that the onus lies on the prosecution to prove the defendant's guilt of the offence charged beyond reasonable doubt. The problem is that on the face of it a reverse onus is inconsistent with the presumption.[91] Unless the presumption can be

---

[87] *Hunt* [1987] A.C. 352 at 364.
[88] For forceful reaffirmations of this approach see *B (A Minor) v DPP* [2000] 2 A.C. 428 HL; *R. v K* [2001] 3 All E.R. 897 HL.
[89] *Charles* [2009] EWCA Crim 1570.
[90] This section draws heavily on Dennis, "Reverse Onuses and the Presumption of Innocence: In Search of Principle" [2005] Crim. L.R. 901. See also Ashworth, "Four Threats to the Presumption of Innocence" (2006) 10 E. & P. 241; Stumer, *The Presumption of Innocence* (2010), Chs 4 and 5.
[91] *Johnstone* [2003] UKHL 28; [2003] 2 Cr.App.R. 493 at [47] per Lord Nicholls; *Sheldrake v DPP* [2004] UKHL 43; [2005] 1 All E.R. 237 at [41] per Lord Bingham; *Makuwa* [2006] EWCA Crim 175; [2006] 2 Cr.App.R. 11 at [28]. cf. the approach of the Court of Appeal in *Attorney-General's*

qualified the terms of art.6(2) seem to require the prosecution to prove any and all matters comprising the guilt of the defendant.[92] This in turn presents a difficulty for a court in implementing a reverse onus because under s.6 of the Human Rights Act 1998 it is unlawful for it to act in a way that is incompatible with a Convention right.

The first response to this difficulty requires a return to the distinction between the legal and the evidential burden. The significance of the distinction in this context is that evidential burdens are regarded as compatible with the presumption of innocence.[93] This may be because, unlike legal burdens, they do not require the accused to assume the risk of being convicted because he fails to prove some matter relating to his innocence.[94] The important consequence follows that a court can avoid the problem of incompatibility if it can interpret the legislation so as to impose only an evidential and not a legal burden on the defendant. Where a legal burden is not expressly imposed, the court might be able to do this at the initial stage of construing the legislation according to the ordinary principles of interpretation, which would include for this purpose the rule embodied in s.101 of the Magistrates' Courts Act 1980. Alternatively, if the legislation is held to impose, whether expressly or impliedly, a legal burden on the defendant, and if that legal burden is then held to be incompatible with the presumption of innocence, it may be possible for the court to use the power under s.3 of the Human Rights Act 1998 to "read down" the legal burden to an evidential burden.

The second response is that a legal burden is not necessarily incompatible with art.6(2). The Strasbourg jurisprudence and the English authorities agree that art.6(2) does not state an absolute rule.[95] The presumption of innocence can be qualified, provided certain conditions are fulfilled. We will deal first with the Strasbourg jurisprudence on art.6(2), which is not extensive. The leading case is *Salabiaku v France*,[96] one of the less illuminating judgments of the European Court of Human Rights. The applicant had been convicted of a customs offence of smuggling prohibited goods (cannabis). The French courts had taken account of a provision in the French Customs Code that provided that "the person in

11–019

Reference (No.4 of 2002) [2003] EWCA Crim 762; [2003] 2 Cr.App.R. 22, convincingly criticised by V. Tadros and S. Tierney, "The Presumption of Innocence and the Human Rights Act" (2004) 67 M.L.R. 402, 420–422.

[92] Compare the apparently absolute terms of art.6(2) with the express savings built into art.6(1) and arts 8–11.

[93] *R. v DPP Ex p. Kebeline* [2000] 1 Cr.App.R. 275 at 324 per Lord Hope; *Lambert* [2001] UKHL 37; [2002] 2 A.C. 545; *Sheldrake v DPP* [2004] UKHL 43; [2005] 1 All E.R. 237.

[94] None of the cases has explored the arguments supporting the claim that an evidential burden does not infringe art.6(2). The most obvious point is that art.6(2) is not engaged by evidential burdens because it is concerned with *proof*, and an evidential burden does not require the defendant to prove anything. But even if art.6(2) is engaged, it can be argued that it is not incompatible with the presumption of innocence to require the defendant to raise the issue of a matter going to his innocence, *provided* the matter is one of which he has personal knowledge. In a hypothetical extreme case of a statute requiring a court to presume the existence of *all* the elements of an offence, unless the defendant raised a reasonable doubt about one or more of them, art.6(2) could well be engaged and the evidential burden would be likely to be regarded as disproportionate. I am indebted to David Prendergast for this example.

[95] *Salabiaku v France* (1988) 13 E.H.R.R. 379.

[96] *Salabiaku v France* (1988) 13 E.H.R.R. 379.

possession of contraband goods is deemed liable for the offence", on the basis that he is presumed to have known that the drugs he physically imported were in his possession. The majority of the European Court of Human Rights found that there had been no violation of art.6(1) or (2), since the legislation allowed for the possibility that the defendant could escape liability by proving *force majeure*, and that in any event the courts did not resort automatically to the presumption but considered all the evidence in making their assessment. The offence in question was a relatively minor offence, carrying a maximum penalty of three months' imprisonment.

The court's approach began with the proposition that there was no objection in principle to strict liability in criminal law:

> "Contracting States may, under certain conditions, penalise a simple or objective fact as such, irrespective of whether it results from criminal intent or from negligence."[97]

The court went on to say that presumptions of fact or law operate in every legal system, and that the Convention did not prohibit such presumptions in principle. However, the court added that art.6(2) did not necessarily regard presumptions of fact or law in criminal cases with indifference:

> "It requires States to confine them within reasonable limits which take into account the importance of what is at stake and maintain the rights of the defence."[98]

11–020   Although this qualification is vague and offers very little in the way of guidance, the judgment as a whole is significant for its explicit recognition that the presumption of innocence in art.6(2) is not an absolute right. Like the other detailed rights contained in art.6, it can be restricted. What then are the criteria for a valid restriction? In *Janosevic v Sweden*,[99] the European Court of Human Rights, following *Salabiaku*, said:

> "in employing presumptions in criminal law, the Contracting States are required to strike a balance between the importance of what is at stake and the rights of the defence; in other words, the means employed have to be reasonably proportionate to the legitimate aim to be achieved."

In *Lambert* two members of the House of Lords referred explicitly to these criteria[100] (that had already been adopted by the Privy Council in *Brown v Stott*,[101] to test the validity of restrictions on the privilege against self-incrimination), and the decision of the House proceeded on the basis that the legal burden in that case was disproportionate to the legitimate aim of assisting the prosecution of drug offences. Similarly, the approach of the House of Lords in *Sheldrake v DPP* was to identify the aim of the legislation and then to consider the proportionality of the reverse onus in relation to the aim.[102]

---

[97] *Salabiaku v France* (1988) 13 E.H.R.R. 379 at [27].
[98] *Salabiaku v France* (1988) 13 E.H.R.R. 397 at [28].
[99] *Janosevic v Sweden* (2004) 38 E.H.R.R. 473 at [101].
[100] *Lambert* [2002] 2 A.C. 545 at [88] per Lord Hope and [198] per Lord Hutton.
[101] *Brown v Stott* [2003] 1 A.C. 681.
[102] *Sheldrake v DPP* [2004] UKHL 43; [2005] 1 All E.R. 237 at [50] per Lord Bingham.

The question then is how are these criteria of legitimate aim and proportionality to be applied? What are the factors to be considered? The English courts have had considerable difficulty in settling how these criteria are to be applied. They have rejected any general rule on reverse onuses[103] and said that each case has to be decided according to its particular circumstances.[104] But the law cannot stop at this point: courts and lawyers need to know the relevant factors to be taken into account in decisions on the allocation of the burden of proof. They also need to know how these factors are to be weighed and how far there are general principles to structure decision-making. Clear guidance is all the more essential given the importance of what is at stake. The presumption of innocence is one of the most fundamental principles of criminal justice, with constitutional status in many jurisdictions.

In the five years after the Human Rights Act came into force there were four leading cases in the House of Lords on the compatibility issue, plus several more in the Court of Appeal and the Divisional Court. The flow of case-law has continued since then, albeit at a slower rate. The cases have canvassed a variety of factors, but there is considerable judicial disagreement or uncertainty about their significance, and the results of the cases show some inconsistency in the weight accorded to the various factors. Rather than embark on a lengthy recitation of all the cases we will take as case-studies the four early decisions of the House of Lords, and then consider an analysis of six relevant factors in decision-making on the compatibility question.

11–021

In *Lambert*,[105] the defendant was convicted of possession of cocaine (a Class A controlled drug) with intent to supply. He had been arrested after taking possession of a duffle bag that was found to contain two kilograms of cocaine. He claimed that he had been paid to collect the bag and thought it contained scrap jewellery. His trial took place before the Human Rights Act 1998 came into force. The trial judge directed the jury according to the law as it was then thought to be, namely that once the prosecution had proved that the defendant was knowingly in possession of the bag, that the defendant knew that there was something in the bag, and that the bag in fact contained a controlled drug, the burden was then on the defendant under s.28(2) and (3)(b) of the Misuse of Drugs Act 1971 to prove on the balance of probabilities that he did not know that the bag contained a controlled drug. His appeal to the House of Lords was heard after the Human Rights Act came into force. By a majority the House of Lords held that the Act did not have retrospective application, but went on to consider whether in any event the imposition of a legal burden on the defendant to prove absence of knowledge violated the presumption of innocence in art.6(2) of the ECHR.

It was held by the majority (Lord Hutton dissenting) that the imposition of a legal burden on the defendant was a disproportionate means of achieving the justified aim of easing the difficult task of the prosecution in proving the

---

[103] e.g. the proposal of the Criminal Law Revision Committee that any onus on the defendant should be evidential only: *Eleventh Report* para.140. Almost 20 years ago, in *Hunt* [1987] A.C. 352, Lord Griffiths commented that such a fundamental change could only be effected by Parliament and not by the House of Lords. In *Sheldrake v DPP* [2004] UKHL 43; [2005] 1 All E.R. 237 at [42] Lord Bingham confirmed this view.

[104] *Lambert* [2002] 2 A.C. 545 at [34], [152]; *Sheldrake v DPP* [2004] UKHL 43 at [21].

[105] *Lambert* [2001] UKHL 37; [2002] 2 A.C. 545.

defendant's knowledge in this type of case where the drugs are in a container. One reason for this decision seems to have been a felt sense of where the fair balance lay in reconciling the interests of the defendant against the wider public interest in controlling the abuse of drugs. Lord Steyn, whose analysis of the proportionality issue was the most developed, noted that s.28 requires the defendant to prove lack of knowledge of his possession of the drug. Knowledge is a form of mens rea, and goes to the defendant's moral blameworthiness. As such it ought to be proved by the prosecution, despite appearing in the statute in the form of a defence.[106] He reinforced this conclusion by pointing to the importance of the seriousness of the offence, which is punishable with life imprisonment, and to the unfairness that would result if the jury were obliged to convict where they thought that the accused's version of events was as likely to be true as not.[107]

11–022   Having concluded that a legal burden would be disproportionate, the Lords then held that compatibility with art.6(2) would be preserved if s.3 of the Human Rights Act 1998 were used to "read down" the words of s.28 of the Misuse of Drugs Act 1971 to impose only an evidential burden on the defendant.[108] In the words of Lord Hope:

> "I would therefore read the words 'to prove' in section 28(2) as if the words used in the subsection were 'to give sufficient evidence', and would give the same meaning to the words 'if he proves' in section 28(3). The effect which is to be given to this meaning is that the burden of proof remains on the prosecution throughout. If sufficient evidence is adduced to raise the issue, it will be for the prosecution to show beyond reasonable doubt that the defence is not made out by the evidence."[109]

Lambert is an instructive example of the power of the interpretative tool given to the courts by s.3 of the Human Rights Act 1998.[110] In this context it enables the courts to give the words "to prove" in a reverse onus provision their natural meaning of a legal burden, *provided* this can be justified as a proportionate restriction on the presumption of innocence. Where a legal burden cannot be so justified, the words can be given an alternative, less natural, meaning of a burden of adducing sufficient evidence.

In *Johnstone*,[111] the defendant was convicted of an offence under s.92 of the Trade Marks Act 1994 of being in possession of goods that infringed a registered

---

[106] The Court of Appeal took a similar line in *Keogh* [2007] EWCA Crim 528; [2007] 3 All E.R. 789 in reading down express legal burdens on the defendant under ss.2(3) and 3(4) of the Official Secrets Act 1989 to prove that he did not know or have reasonable cause to believe that disclosures he had made of official documents related to defence or international relations, or would be damaging. In the court's view a reverse burden was not necessary because the prosecution should be able to establish mens rea from such matters as the nature of the material disclosed and extrinsic facts about the defendant which did not depend on his subjective knowledge.

[107] *Lambert* [2001] UKHL 37; [2002] 2 A.C. 545 at [38] per Lord Steyn and [156] per Lord Clyde.

[108] The final step in the reasoning in *Lambert* [2001] UKHL 37 was to say that if the judge had directed the jury on the basis that the burden on the defendant was evidential only, the jury would have reached the same result and therefore the conviction was not unsafe. Contrast *Choudhury* [2008] EWCA Crim 3179, where the Court of Appeal followed *Lambert* in holding that the trial judge had misdirected the jury by telling them the defendant bore the burden of proof under s.28, and went on to quash the convictions.

[109] *Lambert* [2001] UKHL 37; [2002] 2 A.C. 545 at [94].

[110] For an even more striking example see *R. v A* [2001] 2 Cr.App.R. 351 HL, discussed in Ch.15.

[111] *Johnstone* [2003] UKHL 28; [2003] 2 Cr.App.R. 493.

trade mark. This offence, which is targeted at those who deal in counterfeit goods, carries a maximum penalty on conviction on indictment of 10 years' imprisonment. Section 92(5) provides a defence if the defendant can prove (a legal burden) that he had a reasonable belief that the goods in question were not infringing goods. The House of Lords upheld the reverse onus as proportionate, on the basis that the facts were within the defendant's own knowledge, he had engaged in trade in branded products knowing of the risk of counterfeit goods, and that it is Parliament, not the courts, that has primary responsibility for policy decisions as to the constituent elements of a criminal offence.

In *Sheldrake v DPP*,[112] the defendant was convicted of an offence under s.5(1)(b)   **11–023**
of the Road Traffic Act 1988 of being in a charge of a motor vehicle while being over the prescribed alcohol limit. Under s.5(2) it is a defence for the defendant to prove (a legal burden) that there was no likelihood of him driving the vehicle while over the limit. The offence is punishable with six months' imprisonment and/or a fine. The House of Lords first held that it was not objectionable to criminalise such conduct without requiring the prosecution to prove criminal intent. As noted above, art.6(2) does not prohibit offences requiring proof only of simple objective facts. The Lords then upheld the reverse onus as proportionate, on the basis that since the likelihood of the defendant driving was a matter closely conditioned by his own knowledge and state of mind at the time, it was not unfair for Parliament to impose the burden on him to show that he was outside the risk with which the offence was dealing.

In *Attorney-General's Reference (No.4 of 2002)*, a conjoined appeal reported together with *Sheldrake v DPP*, a point of law was referred arising out of the acquittal of a defendant of charges under s.11(1) of the Terrorism Act 2000 of being a member, and professing to be a member, of a proscribed organisation. The maximum penalty on conviction is 10 years' imprisonment. Section 11(2) provides that it is a defence to prove that the organisation was not proscribed when the defendant became a member, or began to profess to be a member, and that he had not taken part in any of its activities while it was proscribed. At the trial, s.11(2) was treated as imposing only an evidential burden on the defendant. The trial judge ruled that there was no case to answer on the charges under s.11(1). The question referred was whether the defence in s.11(2) imposed a legal, rather than an evidential burden, and, if so, whether that was compatible with the ECHR. By a 3–2 majority the House of Lords held that s.11(2) imposed a legal burden, but that this was disproportionate to the legitimate aim of the provision and should be read down to an evidential burden. For the majority Lord Bingham focused on the width of the offences in s.11(1), saying that they could catch persons who were innocent of any blameworthy or properly criminal conduct. There was a real risk of unfair conviction if such persons could exonerate themselves only by establishing the defence in s.11(2) on the balance of probabilities. He referred also to the high maximum penalty for the offences, and to the difficulty of proof. While a defendant might reasonably be expected to

---

[112] *Sheldrake v DPP* [2004] UKHL 43; [2005] 1 All E.R. 237.

show that the organisation was not proscribed when he became a member, it might be all but impossible for him to show that he had not taken part in its activities when it was proscribed.[113]

It is clear from these cases, and others in the Court of Appeal and Divisional Court, that six factors have figured prominently in discussions about the justifiability of particular reverse onuses. We can now consider these factors, and the principal points of judicial uncertainty and inconsistency.[114]

(A) Judicial deference

11–024 One key question concerns the relationship between the courts, on the one hand, and the legislature and executive, on the other. How much weight should the courts give to the decisions of democratically accountable bodies as to the placing of the burden of proof? How far should they defer to the judgment of Parliament? The starting-point for exploring this factor is a statement of Lord Hope in *R. v DPP Ex p. Kebilene*. Referring to what he called the "discretionary area of judgment" Lord Hope said[115]:

> "In some circumstances it will be appropriate for the courts to recognize that there is an area of judgment within which the judiciary will defer, on democratic grounds, to the considered opinion of the elected body or person whose act or decision is said to be incompatible with the Convention ... It will be easier for such an area of judgment to be recognized where the Convention itself requires a balance to be struck, much less so where the right is stated in terms which are unqualified. It will be easier for it to be recognized where the issues involve questions of social or economic policy, much less so where the rights are of high constitutional importance or are of a kind where the courts are especially well placed to assess the need for protection."

In identifying the parameters of judicial deference Lord Hope did not expressly distinguish between the criteria of legitimate aim and proportionality. Nor did Lord Nicholls in *Johnstone*, where he stated the principle of deference in stronger terms. Describing the court's role as one of review, he commented:

> "Parliament, not the court, is charged with the primary responsibility for deciding, as a matter of policy, what should be the constituent elements of a criminal offence ... the court will reach a different conclusion from the legislature only when it is apparent the legislature has attached insufficient importance to the fundamental right of an individual to be presumed innocent until proved guilty."[116]

The Court of Appeal took a similarly strong line in *Attorney-General's Reference (No.1 of 2004)*,[117] where Lord Woolf C.J. ruled that the assumption should be that Parliament would not have made an exception to the presumption of innocence without good reason. However, in *Sheldrake v DPP*, Lord Bingham was at pains to indicate that courts should not duck the issue in this way. He cast doubt on Lord Woolf's proposition, saying that such an approach may lead the court to

---

[113] *Sheldrake v DPP* [2004] UKHL 43; [2005] 1 All E.R. 237 at [51].
[114] For a fuller treatment see Dennis, "Reverse Onuses and the Presumption of Innocence" [2005] Crim L.R. 901.
[115] *R. v DPP Ex p. Kebilene* [2000] 2 A.C. 326 at [381].
[116] *Johnstone* [2003] UKHL 28; [2003] 2 Cr.App.R. 493 at [51].
[117] *Attorney-General's Reference (No.1 of 2004)* [2004] EWCA Crim 1025; [2004] 2 Cr.App.R. 27.

give too much weight to the enactment under review and too little to the presumption of innocence and the obligation imposed on the court by s.3 of the Human Rights Act.[118] Elsewhere in his speech Lord Bingham referred to what he described as the important but uncontroversial principle reiterated in *Brown v Stott* that substantial respect should be paid by the courts to the considered decisions of democratic assemblies and governments.[119]

Beyond indicating that deference is a matter of degree, this divergence of view **11–025** leaves the issue rather unclear. However, we can refine Lord Hope's statement in *Kebilene* by distinguishing more sharply between legitimate aim and proportionality. In this context identifying a legitimate aim requires the courts to consider the policy goals of criminalisation being pursued by the relevant provisions. It would surely be an exceptional case in which it would be constitutionally proper for the courts to hold that the offence-creating provisions did not pursue a legitimate aim. Certainly the courts have so far had no trouble in identifying the social or economic objectives to be attained by the penal provisions they have examined in the context of reverse onuses and regarding them as legitimate.

However, the further question whether the imposition of a reverse onus is proportionate to the achievement of the policy goal of the offence is not a question of the substance of the policy but of the procedure to implement it. Here the courts are on firmer ground. They have a valid claim to be the guardians of principles of procedural justice, a claim founded partly on their expertise in procedural justice and partly on their constitutional role in upholding the rule of law, which includes key constitutional principles of due process such as the presumption of innocence.[120] If this is right, then judgments of proportionality about reverse onuses entail an adjustment of competing constitutional claims. A strong principle of deference would seem to be inappropriate in resolving these claims, certainly if there is no evidence that Parliament gave thought to the presumption of innocence when it enacted the reverse onus.[121] If the arguments about proportionality appear to be balanced then it is suggested that the issue should not be resolved according to a principle of deference but that the importance of art.6(2) should prevail. It is for the state to justify a derogation from the presumption of innocence, and justifying arguments should be compelling if they are to succeed.[122]

(B)   Classification of offences

In *Lambert,* Lord Clyde referred to the traditional distinction in criminal law **11–026** between acts that are "truly criminal" and acts that are not truly criminal but are regulated in the public interest. This was in the context of his dictum that legal burdens to prove possession of licences to do acts of the second type may be

---

[118] *Sheldrake v DPP* [2004] UKHL 43; [2005] 1 All E.R. 237 at [31].
[119] *Sheldrake v DPP* [2004] UKHL 43; [2005] 1 All E.R. 237 at [23].
[120] See, e.g. the judgment of Laws L.J. in *International Transport Roth GmbH v Secretary of State for the Home Department* [2003] Q.B. 728 at [86] and [87].
[121] It would be appropriate for the courts to look at the parliamentary debates in a case of doubt about this.
[122] *Johnstone* [2003] UKHL 28; [2003] 2 Cr.App.R. 493 at [48], [49] per Lord Nicholls.

compatible with art.6(2).[123] Similarly, in the Divisional Court in *Sheldrake v DPP*, Jack J. referred to the recognised distinction between truly criminal offences and those which are regulatory or quasi-criminal, and suggested that it is easier to justify an interference with the presumption of innocence the lower in the scale the offence is.[124]

However, the classification of offences into *mala in se* and *mala prohibita* is problematic as a guide to the justifiable proportionality of a reverse onus. This is for more than one reason. First, the distinction is not particularly robust. If it depends on the moral quality of the act then the classification of numerous offences is likely to be contestable. Many might regard certain "public welfare" offences, say offences against the environment, or serious breaches of health and safety legislation, as immoral. In *Davies v Health and Safety Executive*,[125] an employer was charged under health and safety legislation with failure to ensure that his employees were not exposed to health and safety risks.[126] The relevant employee had died, which gave a morally reprehensible colour to conduct otherwise punishable under regulatory legislation only with a fine. If the distinction depends on penalties, so that regulatory offences are characterised as generally punishable by fine, many offences of a regulatory hue now carry the possibility of a custodial sentence on conviction.[127] Moreover, some summary offences punishable only by a fine may be far from "mere regulatory criminality", but may be "of great social and emotional importance to a large number of people".[128] Secondly, it does not follow that a statutory defence to a regulatory offence will be any easier for the defendant to prove than an equivalent defence to a truly criminal offence. There is no necessary relationship between the degree of onerousness of a reverse onus and the type of crime involved. The difficulty of proving, say, a due diligence defence, may vary considerably according to the economic and social context of the conduct involved and not because of anything to do with its moral quality.

(C) Construction of criminal liability: elements of offences and defences

11–027   The idea that the presumption of innocence might require the prosecution to prove at least all the essential elements of offences is one that seems to have an intuitive and enduring appeal for many judges. In *Attorney-General for Hong Kong v Lee Kwong-kut*,[129] Lord Woolf for the Privy Council remarked that if the

---

[123] *Lambert* [2002] 2 A.C. 545 at [154].

[124] *Sheldrake v DPP* [2003] 2 Cr.App.R. 14. See also *Davies v Health and Safety Executive* [2002] EWCA Crim 2949 (health and safety at work); *Clarke* [2008] EWCA Crim 651 (providing immigration services when not qualified to do so).

[125] *Davies v Health and Safety Executive* [2002] EWCA Crim 2949.

[126] Health and Safety at Work Act 1974 ss.3(1) and 33(1).

[127] e.g. offences under ss.136 and 137 of the Licensing Act 2003. There is a due diligence defence in s.139. The nature of the burden on the defendant in relation to this defence is not specified, but it is likely that s.101 of the Magistrates' Courts Act 1980 will apply so that it will be a legal burden.

[128] A distinction made by the Divisional Court in *DPP v Wright* [2009] EWHC 105 (Admin), in relation to determining the burden of proof on whether certain hunting is "exempt" for the purposes of the controversial offence of hunting a wild mammal with a dog under s.1 of the Hunting Act 2004.

[129] *Attorney-General for Hong Kong v Lee Kwong-kut* [1993] A.C. 951.

prosecution retain responsibility for proving the essential ingredients of the offence, the less likely it is that an exception will be regarded as unacceptable. In *Lambert,* Lord Hope distinguished between essential elements of offences and exculpatory defences of the type referred to in *Edwards*,[130] and suggested that reversing the onus of proof of such defences might be more easily justifiable.[131] In *Sheldrake v DPP,* Lord Rodger, in the minority, argued that Parliament had prescribed in s.11(1) of the Terrorism Act 2000 the ingredients of the offence of belonging or professing to belong to a terrorist organisation. Parliament could have left it at that. Article 6 does not prohibit offences that require proof only of simple objective facts. Therefore, since there was no requirement to include the s.11(2) defence at all, there was no objection to reversing the onus for a defendant who wanted to take advantage of this favourable provision.[132]

However, other judges have been more sceptical of the value of a formal distinction between elements and defences. In *Lambert,* Lord Steyn noted that the difference between elements of the offence and defensive issues was sometimes only a matter of drafting technique.[133] He suggested that it was preferable to focus on the issue of substance. For him this issue was that of moral blameworthiness. Defences such as those discussed in *Edwards* (by implication not concerned with moral blameworthiness) should be distinguished from:

> "other cases where the defence is so closely linked with *mens rea* and moral blameworthiness that it would derogate from the presumption of innocence to transfer the legal burden to the defendant."[134]

He instanced the example of provocation, and could well have referred also to such general common law defences as self-defence, duress and necessity. All these defences incorporate moral evaluations of the defendant's conduct. They go to the issue of the defendant's culpability in a way that is analogous to requirements of mens rea.[135] It is now well-established that any burden on the defendant in relation to these common law defences is evidential only.[136] Once the issue is raised the prosecution must disprove the availability of the defence.

In *Attorney-General's Reference (No.4 of 2002),*[137] the Court of Appeal adopted an analogous approach, but used different terminology. The court held that art.6(2) requires the prosecution to prove the "true nature" or the "gravamen" of the offence. This principle appears to require the court to discover the rationale of the offence, including any elements of moral blameworthiness. However, the court clearly took the view that the application of this principle did not depend on a formal statutory separation of elements and defences. Some statutory defences

---

[130] *Edwards* [1975] Q.B. 27.
[131] *Lambert* [2002] 2 A.C. 545 at [74].
[132] *Sheldrake v DPP* [2004] UKHL 43 at [65]–[71]. See also *Williams* [2012] EWCA Crim 2162.
[133] *Lambert* [2002] 2 A.C. 545 at [35].
[134] *Lambert* [2002] 2 A.C. 545 at [35].
[135] See, e.g. the well-known debate whether in *Steane* [1947] K.B. 997 a defendant who broadcast for the enemy in wartime under threats to send his family to a concentration camp should be acquitted of assisting the enemy with intent on the ground of lack of specific intent or on the basis of duress. The premise of both doctrinal analyses is that he lacked moral blameworthiness.
[136] Insanity is the (anomalous) exception.
[137] *Attorney-General's Reference (No.4 of 2002)* [2003] EWCA Crim 762; [2003] 2 Cr.App.R. 22.

might not form part of the gravamen of the offence, whereas others might. *Lambert* would be an example of the latter type of case, where the issue of the defendant's guilty knowledge of his possession of a controlled drug was part of the gravamen of the offence, but it appeared in the statute as a formal defence that imposed a reverse onus.

11–028 At the same time it is important not to assume that a reverse onus on an essential element of the offence will necessarily be unjustifiable. Not having a licence to drive is an essential element of the offence of driving without a licence; an offence of "driving" without further elements would not make sense. Equally, the gravamen of the offence is surely the risk to others created by unqualified drivers. However, placing a burden on the defendant to prove possession of a licence to do regulated acts requiring a licence is commonplace,[138] and can be justified on pragmatic grounds.

(D)   Significance of maximum penalties

11–029 One of the functions of maximum penalties is to provide indicators of gradings of seriousness of offences.[139] If we accept the powerful argument that the weight of the presumption of innocence ought to increase in proportion to the gravity of the offence,[140] then we might expect some correlation between maximum penalties and decisions on compatibility. In *Lambert* Lord Steyn attached importance to the penalty of life imprisonment when reading down the reverse onus in that case. By contrast in *Sheldrake v DPP* the House of Lords upheld the reverse onus under s.5(2) of the Road Traffic Act 1988, where the maximum penalty for the offence of being in charge of a motor vehicle while over the limit for alcohol was six months. In *Attorney-General's Reference (No.4 of 2002),* the House refused to uphold the reverse onus under s.11(2) of the Terrorism Act 2000, where the maximum penalty for the offence under s.11(1) is ten years.

These results might suggest a principle that reverse onuses in offences with maximum penalties of substantial terms of imprisonment are unlikely to be justified. However, in *Johnstone* the House of Lords upheld the reverse onus under s.92(5) of the Trade Marks Act 1994, where the maximum penalty for the offence under s.92(1) is ten years.[141] In *Attorney-General's Reference (No.1 of 2004)*[142] the Court of Appeal struck down one reverse onus under the Insolvency Act 1986 but upheld another. The relevant maximum penalties on indictment for the two offences in question were two years and seven years respectively. In a conjoined appeal the Court of Appeal upheld a reverse onus under the Criminal

---

[138] See, e.g. *John v Humphreys* [1955] 1 W.L.R. 325; *Edwards* [1975] Q.B. 27.

[139] See generally A. Ashworth, *Sentencing and Criminal Justice,* 4th edn (Cambridge: Cambridge University Press, 2005), Ch 4.

[140] The argument was eloquently made by Sachs J. in *State v Coetzee* [1997] 2 L.R.C. 593 South African Constitutional Court, in the passage set out above in para.11–8.

[141] In *Makuwa* [2006] EWCA Crim 175; [2006] 2 Cr.App.R. 11, where the Court of Appeal upheld a reverse onus under s.31 of the Immigration and Asylum Act 1999, which provides a defence to a charge of using a false instrument with the intention of inducing somebody to accept it as genuine, contrary to s.3 of the Forgery and Counterfeiting Act 1981. The maximum penalty for an offence under s.3 is 10 years. See also *Williams* [2012] EWCA Crim 2162.

[142] *Attorney-General's Reference (No.1 of 2004)* [2004] EWCA Crim 1025; [2004] 2 Cr.App.R. 27.

Justice and Public Order Act 1994[143] in relation to the offence of witness intimidation, an offence punishable with a maximum of five years on indictment.

Divergences of view are also present in respect of reverse onuses in offences punishable only with pecuniary penalties. In the *Roth* case[144] the Court of Appeal divided on whether a reverse onus under s.34 of the Immigration and Asylum Act 1999 was disproportionate in relation to the offence of carrying clandestine entrants into the United Kingdom, an offence punishable with a fixed penalty of £2,000 per clandestine entrant. Jonathan Parker L.J. thought that it was, Simon Brown L.J. thought that it was not, and Laws L.J. held that art.6(2) was not engaged since in his view the relevant penalty scheme was civil and not criminal in nature.[145]

In the light of these cases it would seem that maximum penalties are a very uncertain guide as to whether a reverse onus will be held to be proportionate to the legitimate aim of the offence in question. The nature of the penalty—custodial or pecuniary—is certainly not conclusive either way. It ought to be the case that the more serious the offence the more compelling should be the justification for a reverse onus, but the application of such a principle has been patchy to say the least. **11–030**

(E) Ease of proof and peculiar knowledge

Ease of proof is by no means the same concept as peculiar knowledge. A defendant who has a licence to drive or sell intoxicating liquor can easily produce it if required. It is easier for him to do this than for the prosecution to prove the negative proposition that he did not have a licence. In such a case the prosecution would have to adduce evidence such as registers of licence-holders, or perhaps evidence that the defendant failed to produce a licence on demand. The former may entail trouble and expense, the latter may result in conflicts of testimony or disputes over whether non-possession is a reasonable inference from non-production. It should be noted, however, that the defendant does not have peculiar knowledge of his possession of a licence; that knowledge is available to the prosecution from evidence such as registers, but it is more burdensome and costly to locate it. On the other hand, the defendant does have peculiar knowledge of his state of mind at the time of a criminal act; he has privileged access to his intention, knowledge or belief. But does it follow from his peculiar knowledge that it is easier for him to prove absence of a criminal intention than for the prosecution to prove its presence? That seems to be contestable, particularly if the defendant is likely to cut a poor figure as a witness,[146] so that his testimony is **11–031**

---

[143] Criminal Justice and Public Order Act 1994 s.51(7).

[144] *International Transport Roth GmbH v Secretary of State for the Home Department* [2003] Q.B. 728.

[145] *International Transport Roth GmbH v Secretary of State for the Home Department* [2003] Q.B. 728. Laws L.J. implied (at [109]) that he would have taken a different view of the acceptability of s.34 if he had held that the scheme was criminal in nature.

[146] As Lord Bingham noted in *Sheldrake v DPP* [2004] UKHL 43; [2005] 1 All E.R. 237 at [51](2).

unlikely to be believed. In some cases the existence of intention may be an overwhelming inference from the circumstantial evidence of what the defendant did at the time.

Some judges have tended to regard peculiar knowledge and ease of proof as independent reasons in justifying a reverse onus. In *Kebilene,* Lord Hope suggested that in striking the balance required by the principle of proportionality, one of the questions to be asked was whether the burden on the defendant related to something that was within his own knowledge or to which he readily had access.[147] This suggestion was followed by Lord Nicholls in *Johnstone,* who similarly referred to the defendant's own knowledge or ready access as alternative relevant factors in a decision about compatibility of a reverse onus.[148] In *Lambert,* Lord Clyde referred to peculiar knowledge and ease of proof cumulatively as considerations that might have supported a reverse onus in that case.[149] Other judges have assumed a contingent relationship. In *Attorney-General's Reference (No.1 of 2004),* one of the Court of Appeal's list of points of guidance for trial judges stated that the easier it is for the accused to discharge the burden the more likely it is that the reverse burden is justified: "This will be the case where the facts are within the defendant's own knowledge".[150]

Peculiar knowledge has been a persistent factor in judicial thinking about reverse onuses despite the fact that it is over-inclusive. As Clarke L.J. put it in the Divisional Court in *Sheldrake v DPP*, "there are very many aspects of the criminal law in which the state of mind of the accused is of crucial importance but where the burden of proving it is on the prosecution".[151] It should also be remembered that in *Lambert* the factor of the defendant's peculiar means of knowledge of what was in the duffle bag he was carrying did not prevail over considerations of a maximum penalty of life imprisonment and the unfairness of convicting the defendant where the jury thought that his story was as likely to be true as not.

11–032   The significance of the defendant's peculiar knowledge of certain facts is not therefore that it supports the imposition of a legal burden on the defendant to prove those facts. Peculiar knowledge can at best support the imposition of an *evidential* burden to raise the issue of those facts, in circumstances where the prosecution would not otherwise know in what form a defence based on those facts might arise. It is for this reason that the defence bear the burden of raising the issue of common law defences such as self-defence or duress. It would not be reasonable to expect the prosecution to negative such justifications and excuses without being made aware of the facts relied on to support them, and in most of these cases it is only the defendant who knows those facts.

Ease or difficulty of proof also needs careful handling as a relevant factor. The point of a reverse onus is always to ease the task of the prosecution in establishing the defendant's liability. It does not of course follow that Parliament will intend to reverse the onus only where it would be difficult for the prosecution

---

[147] *Kebilene* [2000] 2 A.C. 326 at [386].
[148] *Johnstone* [2003] UKHL 28; [2003] 2 Cr.App.R. 493 at [50].
[149] *Lambert* [2002] 2 A.C. 545 at [153].
[150] *Attorney-General's Reference (No.1 of 2004)* [2004] EWCA Crim 1025; [2004] 2 Cr.App.R 27.
[151] *Sheldrake v DPP* [2003] 2 Cr.App.R. 14 at [61].

to prove guilt. It might be done as a matter of convenience or as a cost-saving measure, particularly for regulatory crimes the enforcement of which is in the hands of an agency with a limited budget. Moreover, even where proof of guilt would be difficult for the prosecution, it does not follow that disproof of guilt would be easy for the defendant. If a reverse onus is to be justified by reference to ease of proof the focus should be on the weight of the burden the reverse onus would impose on the defendant. However, in *Makuwa*,[152] the Court of Appeal upheld a reverse onus under s.31 of the Immigration and Asylum Act 1999 almost entirely on the basis of the difficulty of proof for the prosecution if they were held to bear the legal burden on the matters in question. These matters were that the defendant's life or freedom was threatened in the country from which she had come to the United Kingdom, that she presented herself to the authorities in the United Kingdom without delay, that she showed good cause for her illegal entry or presence, and that she made a claim for asylum as soon as was reasonably practicable after her arrival in the United Kingdom. If the defendant could prove all these matters she would have a defence to a charge under s.3 of the Forgery and Counterfeiting Act 1981 of using a false instrument (a passport) with the intention of inducing somebody to accept it as genuine. The court glossed over any difficulties of proof that the defendant might have on any of these matters, emphasising instead the policy need to maintain proper immigration controls by restricting the use of forged passports.

In contrast, in *DPP v Wright*,[153] the Divisional Court held that a burden on the defendant to prove that his hunting was "exempt", on a charge of hunting a wild mammal with a dog, would be "oppressive, disproportionate, unfair, and an unnecessary intrusion on the presumption of innocence". Schedule 1 of the Hunting Act 2004 contained a list of exempt forms of hunting: some of the matters would be within the defendant's knowledge, some would be easy for him to prove, but some would be neither. In these circumstances the Act should be read as imposing only an evidential burden on the defendant; once the prosecution knew which form of exemption was in issue it would not be unduly burdensome to require them to disprove it.

(F) Presumption of innocence

The Strasbourg jurisprudence has emphasised the *procedural* significance of the presumption of innocence. The presumption has been said to be the foundation of the right to fair trial under art.6. In *Salabiaku v France*,[154] the European Court of Human Rights stressed that the presumption prevented legislatures from stripping trial courts of their powers to assess the evidence of the defendant's guilt. Protecting the courts' freedom of assessment of guilt from presumptions of fact or law that assumed guilt was necessary to uphold the courts' duty of impartiality and the fundamental principle of the rule of law. This conception of the presumption of innocence has led to a strong focus in Strasbourg on how presumptions of fact or law are actually applied to the defendant in the case in

11–033

---

[152] *Makuwa* [2006] EWCA Crim 175; [2006] 2 Cr.App.R. 11.
[153] *DPP v Wright* [2009] EWHC 105 (Admin).
[154] *Salabiaku v France* (1988) 13 E.H.R.R. 379.

question. The concern has been more with adjudicative independence and the courts' freedom of evaluation rather than with substantive issues of fairness. The European Court of Human Rights has the capacity to conduct this exercise because it reviews the fairness of the trial as a whole after the event.

In *Sheldrake v DPP,* Lord Bingham summed up the effect of the Strasbourg conception of the presumption of innocence in these terms:

> "The overriding concern is that a trial should be fair, and the presumption of innocence is a fundamental right directed to that end. The Convention does not outlaw presumptions of fact or law but requires that these should be kept within reasonable limits and should not be arbitrary. It is open to states to define the constituent elements of a criminal offence, excluding the requirement of mens rea. But the substance and effect of any presumption adverse to a defendant must be examined, and must be reasonable. Relevant to any judgment on reasonableness or proportionality will be the opportunity given to the defendant to rebut the presumption, maintenance of the rights of the defence, flexibility in application of the presumption, retention by the court of a power to assess the evidence, the importance of what is at stake and the difficulty which a prosecutor may face in the absence of a presumption. Security concerns do not absolve member states from their duty to observe basic standards of fairness. The justifiability of any infringement of the presumption of innocence cannot be resolved by any rule of thumb, but on examination of all the facts and circumstances of the particular provision as applied in the particular case."[155]

11–034 Domestic courts that have to decide on the justifiability of reverse onuses will generally be doing so before the trial when rulings on the burden of proof have to be made. At this stage it may not be clear how presumptions of fact or law are likely to be applied at the trial. This point may help to account for why the English case law has tended to take a less procedural and more morally substantive view of the presumption of innocence. In *Lambert,*[156] Lord Steyn conceived of the presumption as ensuring that issues of the defendant's moral blameworthiness had to be proved by the prosecution. As mentioned above, this was why he rejected a strong distinction between definitional elements of offences and defences; as he put it, some defences are so closely linked with mens rea and moral blameworthiness that it would derogate from the presumption to transfer the legal burden to the defendant. This second conception of the presumption thus emphasises fairness in both process and outcome. As noted above, in *Lambert* one of Lord Steyn's reasons for rejecting a reverse onus under s.28 of the Misuse of Drugs Act 1971 was that it would oblige the court to convict the defendant where it thought his version of the facts was as likely to be true as not.[157] This was thought to be unfair and unacceptable for an offence punishable with life imprisonment. Lord Bingham took a similar approach in *Attorney-General's Reference (No.4 of 2002)* to the reverse onus under s.11(2) of the Terrorism Act 2000.

(G) Principles and proportionality

11–035 It seems reasonable to conclude in the light of this analysis that the debate about the justifiability of a reverse onus is a debate about proportionality. The aim of a

---

[155] *Sheldrake v DPP* [2004] UKHL 43; [2005] 1 All E.R. 237 at [21].
[156] *Lambert* [2002] 2 A.C. 545.
[157] *Lambert* [2002] 2 A.C. 545 at [38].

reverse onus will invariably be to make the task of the prosecution easier by allocating part of the burden of proof to the defendant. This allocation aims to promote the enforcement of the relevant criminal offence, which will, as far as the courts are concerned, invariably be enacted in pursuit of a legitimate aim. But not all reverse onuses are proportionate to the legitimate aim of the offence. It is inconceivable, for example, that Parliament could reverse the decision in *Woolmington* by placing on the defendant the legal burden of disproving the intention required for murder and expect this to be upheld as a proportionate measure to the aim of preventing intentional killings.

The question now is whether proportionality is determined by some broad, unstructured balancing of the various relevant factors discussed above. If it is, we should expect decisions on particular reverse onuses to be made on a case-by-case basis, with authorities on reverse onuses in different contexts being of limited value. However, if courts are free to pick and choose amongst the six factors discussed above, and to assign weight to different factors as they think fit, then almost inevitably the result will be uncertainty and inconsistency. It is strongly arguable that this is the position we have now reached. The case law resembles a forensic lottery and shows clearly the extent to which experienced judges may disagree about the judgments required on issues of compatibility of reverse onuses.

It seems therefore highly desirable to identify general principles that would afford trial judges more structured guidance and enable decisions about this fundamental issue to be made with a greater degree of consistency and coherence. Granted that there is no universally applicable rule to reverse onuses, it is nonetheless arguable that the cases can be accounted for by reference to certain broad principles, and these principles could serve as some guide to future decision-making. The principles involve both pragmatic and moral considerations.

The pragmatic consideration is the relative ease or difficulty of proof for prosecution and defence. It has been suggested earlier that some clearer thinking is needed about the difference between ease of proof and peculiar knowledge. Several of the judgments in the cases have expressed approval in one form or another of the principle set out in *Edwards* relating to the burden on defendants to prove qualifications to do certain acts regulated in the public interest. It seems unobjectionable to require a defendant to prove a formal qualification to do an act that is otherwise prohibited by regulatory legislation.[158] If the defendant has a licence it is not a hardship to ask him to produce it. If he does produce it that is the end of the case[159]; in the usual case it is not a contestable form of proof. But it should be emphasised that ease of production—based on the idea that a defendant has peculiar knowledge of the matter in question—is not the same as ease of proof. It is easy for a defendant to produce evidence of his state of mind. He has peculiar knowledge of what he intended or knew at the relevant time and

11–036

---

[158] This is particularly the case where there are several possible qualifications, and it would be difficult and costly for the prosecution to prove that the defendant had none of them. See, e.g. *Clarke* [2008] EWCA Crim 651.

[159] In reality of course if the defendant has a licence and has produced it at an earlier stage there will be no prosecution.

can simply testify to it. But his testimony may well be contestable; his state of mind is not so easily proved as his possession of a licence. Similarly a defendant may have peculiar knowledge of any inquiries he made by way of due diligence and has easy access to his records. But the evidence is still contestable in the sense that it may be argued to be insufficient to reach the required standard of due diligence. The defendant remains at risk in such a case of an adverse moral evaluation; a finding that he did not exercise due diligence is a finding of objective fault analogous to a finding of mens rea.

At this point we return to Lord Steyn's view in *Lambert* that this is a key factor. If the presumption of innocence has a morally substantive character, as Lord Steyn suggested, then it supports the principle that the prosecution should always have the burden of persuasion where liability requires judgments of moral blameworthiness. These judgments will be entailed by all requirements of mens rea (whether expressly imposed by the statute or presumed by the court) and all defences that incorporate moral evaluations as part of their elements. Judgments of moral blameworthiness may therefore cross the offence/defence boundary. This principle would be further underpinned by the theory that one function of a guilty verdict in a criminal trial is to make a morally authoritative statement of the defendant's guilt and fitness for punishment.[160] The authority of this official pronouncement derives principally from the public demonstration by state agencies of the defendant's commission of the offence. Accordingly if liability for the offence incorporates elements of adverse moral evaluation of the defendant's conduct the state's prosecuting agencies should justify to the court why it should make those adverse moral evaluations. Any burdens on the defendant in respect of these evaluations should be evidential only.

There is, however, an argument for recognising one principled exception to this foundational principle. Such an exception would account for a number of the cases in which the courts have upheld reverse onuses as justified. In *Johnstone,* Lord Nicholls stressed that "those who trade in brand products are aware of the need to be on guard against counterfeit goods. They are aware of the need to deal with reputable suppliers and keep records and of the risks they take if they do not".[161] The principle that underlies this statement could be expressed in the form that individuals who voluntarily participate in a regulated activity from which they intend to derive benefit accept the associated burden. This burden is the risk that they may have to account for any apparent wrongdoing in the course of that activity, even where the liability involves an adverse moral evaluation of their conduct. The moral principle involved is strengthened by the pragmatic argument that this is not an unreasonable burden to impose because in the normal course of events it will be easy for the defendant to produce the relevant records—often easier than for the prosecution to do so—and written records are generally a reliable form of proof. The main objection would be that some of the offences involved carry high maximum penalties, as in *Johnstone* itself. Accordingly the principle may be considered by some to be insufficient to outweigh the importance of maintaining the presumption of innocence in serious offences.

---

[160] See Ch.2.
[161] *Johnstone* [2003] UKHL 28; [2003] 2 Cr.App.R. 493 at [52].

As well as *Johnstone* other cases which might be accounted for on this basis are **11–037** *International Transport Roth GmbH v Secretary of State for the Home Department*[162] (burden on a carrier to prove no knowledge or reasonable suspicion of carrying clandestine entrants into the United Kingdom), *Attorney-General's Reference (No.1 of 2004)*[163] (burden on a landlord to prove belief or reasonable cause to believe that a residential occupier had ceased to reside in the let premises), and *Davies v Health and Safety Executive*[164] (burden on an employer in relation to health and safety in the workplace). In *Chargot Ltd,*[165] the House of Lords cited *Davies* in upholding the express legal burden on an employer under s.40 of the Health and Safety at Work 1974. Lord Hope commented that the case was analogous to the position of the trader in *Johnstone*, and summarised part of the reasoning of Tuckey L.J. in *Davies*:

> "Regard had to be had to the fact that the Act's purpose was both social and economic, to the fact that duty holders were persons who had chosen to engage in work or commercial activity and were in charge of it and that in choosing to operate in a regulated sphere they must be taken to have accepted the regulatory controls that went with it."[166]

At this stage therefore two types of case have been identified where reverse onuses may be justified as reasonable and proportionate to a legitimate aim. However, these are not the only types of case where issues of justification of reverse onuses may arise. Many reverse onuses may relate to matters that do not involve either formal qualifications or voluntary acceptance of risk. A great variety of issues may arise under this heading. They may include such questions as whether the defendant had "lawful authority" or "reasonable excuse" to do a certain act, or they may include issues of fact and circumstance that amount to a statutory defence to the offence. In *Sheldrake v DPP* the reverse onus related to the likelihood of the defendant driving his car while over the alcohol limit. In *Attorney-General's Reference (No.4 of 2002)* the reverse onus related to the time when the defendant joined a proscribed organisation and whether he had taken part in its activities when it was proscribed. A further principle is needed at this point, as Lord Bingham recognised in his speech in *Sheldrake v DPP*.

Lord Bingham's approach to both cases was founded on his rehabilitation of *Lambert* and focused on the issue of moral blameworthiness. In relation to *Sheldrake v DPP* he argued that the gravamen of the offence was the risk that the defendant might drive his car while over the alcohol limit. Being in charge of his car in these circumstances was the conduct Parliament intended to criminalise, and could be thought to be morally blameworthy. But the defendant might be able to show that he was not within the risk encompassed by the offence because he had taken steps to put it out of his power to drive and therefore was unlikely to do so. There would then be no justification for proceeding on the implicit judgment of blameworthiness arising from his conduct of being in charge while over the limit. Conversely, in *Attorney-General's Reference (No.4 of 2002)* Lord Bingham

---

[162] *Roth* [2003] 3 Q.B. 728.
[163] *Attorney-General's Reference (No.1 of 2004)* [2004] EWCA Crim 1025; [2004] 2 Cr.App.R. 27.
[164] *Davies v Health and Safety Executive* [2002] EWCA Crim 2949.
[165] *Chargot Ltd* [2008] UKHL 73; [2009] 2 All ER 645.
[166] *Chargot Ltd* [2008] UKHL 73; [2009] 2 All ER 645 at [29].

argued that the definition of the offence in s.11(1) of the Terrorism Act 2000 was sufficiently wide and uncertain as to include persons whose conduct could not reasonably be regarded as "blameworthy or such as should properly attract criminal sanctions". In these circumstances he thought that there would be a clear breach of the presumption of innocence, and a "real risk of unfair conviction" if such persons could only exonerate themselves by discharging a legal burden of proving the defence in s.11(2). This burden might be extremely difficult for the defendant to discharge.

11–038   This approach seeks to go beyond formal criteria of moral blameworthiness required by the definition of the offence (e.g. fault elements of intention or recklessness or negligence) or included in the elements of a statutory[167] or common law defence. It looks to the rationale of the offence in question and asks how far the prohibited conduct is "blameworthy or properly criminal". If the prohibition extends to conduct that is not blameworthy or properly criminal, the effect of a reverse onus provision may be to require the defendant to prove his innocence in morally substantive terms. If the provision does have this effect it will be prima facie objectionable as disproportionate. According to the analysis set out above it may then be saved only by a countervailing moral principle such as voluntary assumption of risk or the pragmatic principle of ease of proof of a formal qualification.

This type of case is apparently to be distinguished from a case where the prohibited conduct is morally blameworthy, but the defendant is given an opportunity by the reverse onus provision to show that his conduct fell outside the risk that led to the creation of the offence. Such a reverse onus may be justifiable, provided the rights of the defence are maintained and the burden is not unreasonable. To put the distinction another way, the principle adopted by Lord Bingham appears to ask how far the defendant has to negative a presumption of culpability. If the parameters of the offence define conduct that is presumptively blameworthy, a reverse onus provision that requires the defendant in effect to rebut the presumption by proving matters of exculpation may be justifiable. If an offence is widely defined so as to include conduct that is not presumptively blameworthy, a reverse onus provision that requires the defendant in effect to prove that he was not blameworthy infringes the presumption of innocence and is unlikely to be justifiable.

There are two advantages to this approach but it carries some significant problems. One advantage is its theoretical coherence. If prohibited conduct incorporates an element of moral blameworthiness, whether or not that element is expressed in the criteria of liability, or implicit in the prohibited conduct, it is right in principle that the prosecution should prove that moral condemnation of the defendant is justified. Most serious offences carrying substantial maximum penalties will carry this element of moral blameworthiness either expressly or impliedly. A second advantage is that this approach helps to account for cases such as *Matthews*.[168] This case concerned the offence under s.139 of the Criminal Justice Act 1988 of having a bladed article in a public place. This offence, like a

---

[167] e.g. s.28 of the Misuse of Drugs Act 1971.

[168] *Matthews* [2004] Q.B. 690. See also the earlier decision of the Divisional Court in *L v DPP* [2003] 1 Q.B. 137.

number of other similar offences, has an obvious endangerment rationale. By prohibiting the carrying of knives and other offensive weapons in public places these offences aim to prevent the risk that they will be used to cause harm to others. The voluntary carrying of such an article in public is presumptively blameworthy. The statute then allows the defendant an opportunity to negative the presumptive judgment of blameworthiness by showing that he had a good reason or lawful authority to carry the article.

However, turning to the problems with the principle, the first difficulty is that the **11–039** moral colour of many offences of the regulatory or public welfare type may be contestable. The examples were given earlier of offences against the environment or against health and safety legislation. It may well be a moot point whether such offences concern moral blameworthiness. Moreover, as noted earlier, some regulatory offences carry the possibility of imprisonment on conviction. It is not clear how far the penalties for the offence relate to the moral blameworthiness analysis, or whether they are intended to relate to it at all.

A second problem is that establishing the rationale of a given offence may not always be straightforward. There is likely to be much scope for argument and disagreement in many cases, as seen for example in *Attorney-General's Reference (No.4 of 2002)*, where the House of Lords split 3–2 on the justifiability of the reverse onus under s.11(2) of the Terrorism Act 2000. Lord Bingham and Lord Rodger, in the majority and minority respectively, took radically different views of the scope and rationale of the offence in s.11(1) of the Act. It is not difficult to envisage many similar disagreements, given the proliferation of reverse onuses.

Thirdly, Lord Bingham's approach may require courts to make some finely nuanced distinctions between offences of the same type. In *Attorney-General's Reference (No.1 of 2004)*,[169] the Court of Appeal dealt with a number of reverse onus provisions across a range of offences, including offences under the Insolvency Act 1986. In one case the court held that a legal burden to prove a lack of intention to defraud was justifiable[170]; in another it was held to be disproportionate and read down to an evidential burden.[171] On the face of it these different results are hard to account for. Intention to defraud is a significant indicator of moral blameworthiness. It would seem that its existence ought always to be proved by the prosecution, by analogy with *Lambert* and Lord Bingham's approval in *Sheldrake v DPP* of Lord Steyn's focus on moral blameworthiness in *Lambert*. However, the Court of Appeal's close analysis of the two offences concerned suggests that in the first case the court regarded the defendant's conduct as presumptively blameworthy, whereas in the second case it was not. In *Sheldrake v DPP* Lord Bingham approved the Court of Appeal's conclusions.

It is clear from this example that the principle will entail detailed analysis of the **11–040** scope of the offence as well as its rationale. Again there will be much room for

---

[169] *Attorney-General's Reference (No.1 of 2004)* [2004] EWCA Crim 1025; [2004] 2 Cr.App.R. 27.
[170] That is, the offence under s.353(1) of failing to inform the official receiver of a disposal of property.
[171] That is, the offence under s.357(1) of making a transfer of property within five years of becoming bankrupt.

disagreement.[172] This conclusion then leads to a fourth problem, which is how workable is a test based on presumptive moral blameworthiness? Will it not be possible in some cases, perhaps most, to think of situations where the width of the offence catches people who are not blameworthy? Take the offence in issue in *Sheldrake v DPP*. D drives to a party intending to drink only lemonade. His friends spike his lemonade with vodka, which D only realises when he is about to get into his car after the party. If he is then arrested for being in charge of the vehicle while over the limit, he can try to argue that, having realised that he was involuntarily drunk, he would have called a taxi to take him home. But should he carry the legal burden of proving that he was not likely to drive, given that he was not blameworthy in getting into the situation? In this example the driver's position approximates to that of an innocent joiner of an organisation that later becomes proscribed. It will be recalled that the reverse onus in the latter case was held to be unjustified.

A final problem is the inconsistency between this principle for statutory defences and the general common law defences. This principle allows for reverse onuses to be upheld where the statute provides an exculpatory defence to prohibited conduct that is presumptively morally blameworthy. This can cover defences to a wide range of crimes, including some very serious crimes. Common law defences also provide exculpation for prohibited conduct that is presumptively blameworthy; for example, duress excuses an act done with mens rea and extends to all crimes except murder and attempted murder. But the defendant does not bear the legal burden. Cases of duress, and other common law defences, remain subject to the presumption of innocence.

(H)   Reading down a reverse onus

11–041   If a court holds that a reverse onus is unjustified it is then faced with two possible courses of action. The first is to "read down" the legal burden to an evidential burden, using the interpretative power under s.3 of the Human Rights Act 1998 ("HRA"). The second is to declare that the provision reversing the onus is incompatible with art.6(2) under s.4 of the HRA. The first is clearly the alternative to be preferred. This is because s.3 provides that so far as it is possible to do so legislation must be read and given effect in a way that is compatible with Convention rights. After some initial hesitation[173] it has become clear that s.3 enables a court to disregard the ordinary (incompatible) meaning of a statutory

---

[172] Consider the fate of *Carass* [2002] 2 Cr.App.R. 77: the Court of Appeal held that a legal burden under s.206(4) of the Insolvency Act 1986 to prove lack of intention to defraud in relation to a charge under s.206(1) of concealment of a debt of a company in anticipation of a winding-up was not justified. *Carass* was followed, reluctantly, by the Court of Appeal in *Daniel* [2003] 1 Cr.App.R. 99 (in relation to an offence under s.354(1) of the Insolvency Act 1986 of concealing a debt due to the defendant bankrupt), then not followed by the Court of Appeal in *Attorney-General's Reference (No.1 of 2004)* [2004] EWCA Crim 1025; [2004] 2 Cr.App.R. 27, and finally effectively overruled by Lord Bingham in *Sheldrake v DPP*. In *R. (on the application of Griffin) v Richmond Magistrates' Court* [2008] EWHC (Admin); [2008] 3 All E.R. 274 the Divisional Court accepted that *Carass* was wrongly decided in upholding as proportionate the legal burden under s.208(4) of the Insolvency Act 1986 to prove no intention to defraud on a charge under s.208(1)(c) of failing to deliver up books and papers to the liquidator.

[173] See, e.g. Lord Hope in *R. v DPP Ex p. Kebilene* [2000] 2 A.C. 326.

provision in favour of a secondary and perhaps contrived meaning if the latter would facilitate a compatible reading. On this basis the House of Lords in *Lambert*[174] interpreted the words "to prove" in s.28(2) of the Misuse of Drugs Act 1971 to mean "to adduce sufficient evidence". As noted in Ch.2, the courts have reinforced the interpretative obligation imposed by s.3 by saying that declarations of incompatibility are the last resort.

This being so, are there any circumstances in which it will not be possible to read down a legal burden using s.3 of the HRA? Prior to *Attorney-General's Reference (No.4 of 2002)*[175] it might have been argued that this could not be done where it would be in direct contradiction of the clear intention of Parliament. If, for example, Parliament expressly sets out a list of defences in a particular statute and provides that the defendant bears only an evidential burden in respect of these defences, there seems to be a necessary implication that other defences in the statute not in the list are intended to impose a legal burden. Accordingly, reading down a defence in this group would seem to flout the intention of the legislature. Nevertheless, this is exactly what a majority of the House of Lords did in *Attorney-General's Reference (No.4 of 2002)*. The reverse onus in question was imposed by s.11(2) of the Terrorism Act 2000. Section 11(2) was not listed in s.118(2) of the Act as one of the provisions creating (only) an evidential burden. Lord Bingham and his colleagues were not deterred. In a remarkable passage Lord Bingham explained:

> "It was argued for the Attorney-General that section 11(2) could not be read down under section 3 of the 1998 Act so as to impose an evidential rather than a legal burden if (contrary to his submissions) the subsection were held to infringe, impermissibly, the presumption of innocence. He submitted that if the presumption of innocence were found to be infringed, a declaration of incompatibility should be made. I cannot accept this submission . . . In my opinion, reading down section 11(2) so as to impose an evidential instead of a legal burden falls well within the interpretative principles discussed above. The subsection should be treated as if section 118(2) applied to it. Such was not the intention of Parliament when enacting the 2000 Act, but it was the intention of Parliament when enacting section 3 of the 1998 Act. I would [rule] that section 11(2) should be read and given effect as imposing on the defendant an evidential burden only."[176]

To say that Parliament "intended" this result by virtue of s.3 is ingenious, but, with respect, unconvincing. The Terrorism Act was passed after the HRA, and Parliament must be taken to have had full knowledge of s.3. It made its intentions very plain in s.118(2) of the later Act; the only way to have made its intentions plainer would have been for the statute to provide expressly that under s.11(2) the legal burden was on the defendant to prove the relevant matters on the balance of probabilities. Nevertheless, in this case Parliament's clear expression of view is overridden and the relevant part of the statute rewritten. The logical implication of this approach is that all unjustified reverse onuses can now receive the same treatment. The argument from s.3 has become the ace of trumps. It will not matter what Parliament says in the statute creating the reverse onus; it can always be contradicted by the contrary intention that the courts derive from s.3 of the HRA.

---

[174] *Lambert* [2002] 2 A.C. 545.

[175] *Attorney-General's Reference (No.4 of 2002)* [2004] UKHL 43; [2005] 1 All E.R. 237.

[176] *Attorney-General's Reference (No.4 of 2002)* [2004] UKHL 43 at [53]. Lord Steyn and Lord Phillips of Worth Matravers agreed.

D. ALLOCATIONS OF BURDENS IN CIVIL CASES

11–042 We have seen already that the allocation of both legal and evidential burdens is a question of law. Once the burdens have been determined they do not shift during the course of a trial. In many types of civil proceeding, case law or statute has settled the burdens, and disputes about the allocation are likely to be rare.[177] It is difficult to state confidently that there are *any* principles of general application relating to this topic. It is broadly true that "he who asserts must prove", meaning that a party bears the burden of proof of every matter that is an essential part of the party's cause of action.[178] This principle was referred to by Bowen L.J. in *Abrath v North Eastern Rly Co*,[179] when rejecting an argument that the burden of proof should change when a negative assertion is an element of the cause of action. Accordingly, he held that in an action for the tort of malicious prosecution the burden is on the plaintiff to prove that the defendant brought a prosecution with "no reasonable or probable cause". However, the principle is less helpful than first appears because it begs the question of what is an "essential part of a cause of action". How is this to be determined? What criteria should the courts use when the burdens are unclear?

The first point is that there is no direct equivalent in civil cases of the *Woolmington* principle that the prosecution should prove all the elements that make up guilt.[180] Because the parties are theoretically equal, and considerations of stigma and punishment are not usually involved, there is no compelling reason why claimants should bear the burden of disproving any possible defences. So in libel actions, for example, once the claimant has proved the publication of a defamatory statement, the burden is on the defendant to prove defences such as justification or fair comment.

On the other hand, the law may be reluctant to presume fault on the part of a party to civil proceedings, and this may affect the courts' attitude to the proof and disproof of defences. In *Joseph Constantine Steamship Line Ltd v Imperial Smelting Corp Ltd,*[181] the charterers of a ship brought an action against the shipowners for damages for breach of contract in failing to load. The shipowners pleaded that the contract had been frustrated by an explosion on board the ship that had disabled it from making the chartered voyage. As a matter of law the defence of frustration is not available where the frustrating event is brought about by the negligence of the party relying upon the event. The question for the House of Lords was the burden of proof on the issue of negligence: did the owners have to prove that the explosion was not caused by their negligence, as an element of their defence, or did the charterers have to prove that it was, by way of rebutting the defence? The Lords held that the burden was on the charterers to prove that

---

[177] Non-standard form contracts may be an exception.

[178] "Generally, although there are exceptions, a plaintiff or applicant must establish the existence of all the preconditions and other facts entitling him to the order he seeks": per Lord Nicholls in *Re H (Minors)* [1996] A.C. 563 at 586 HL.

[179] *Abrath v North Eastern Rly Co* (1883) 11 Q.B.D. 440 CA.

[180] And art.6(2) of the ECHR applies only to a person "charged with a criminal offence".

[181] *Joseph Constantine v Imperial Smelting* [1942] A.C. 154 HL. See also the comment on the case by J. Stone in (1944) 60 L.Q.R. 262.

the explosion was the fault of the owners.[182] Considerable importance was attached to the factor of ease of proof. Viscount Simon L.C. pointed to the difficulty for the owners of proving the negative of lack of fault, particularly given the number of employees involved and the uncertain state of the evidence about the actual cause of the explosion. He offered further examples of the unfairness of placing the burden on the owners: where the ship disappeared during a storm on the high seas, and where the ship was sunk by enemy action with the loss of all hands. In such cases it would be impossible to prove that the crew had been operating the ship properly before the sinking occurred that frustrated the contract. Lord Wright referred to the presumption of innocence, saying that it was applicable in civil disputes as well as criminal matters. In his view a person was not to be held guilty of fault unless fault was established and found by the court. Fraud, for example, had to be alleged and proved. It could not be presumed, and the same was true of other wrongful acts.[183]

In addition to these considerations of principle, it is likely that arguments of policy will also play a major role in the allocation of burdens in civil cases. One policy might be minimising the risk of erroneous outcomes of trials. If Stone was right to say[184] that in the great majority of cases of frustration of contract there is no operative fault of the parties, but that it would be difficult or impossible to prove lack of fault, then a rule placing a burden of proof of fault on the claimant is clearly right. The number of claimants who fail to prove fault where it does exist and who are thereby denied justice, will inevitably be less than the number of defendants who fail to prove lack of fault where there is in fact none. A second policy might be to allocate burdens according to principles of loss distribution. In a consumer contract of bailment, for example, it would be appropriate for a bailee who fails to return the bailor's goods as agreed to have the burden of proving that the loss or theft of the goods occurred without his negligence or fundamental breach of contract. The commercial bailee is better able to bear the loss than the individual bailor; the latter of course has the additional difficulty of not knowing what has happened to the goods in the hands of the bailee.[185] **11–043**

E.   STANDARD OF PROOF IN CRIMINAL CASES

Two expressions exist to describe the standard of proof that the prosecution must meet in a criminal case. One is the classic formula of proof "beyond reasonable doubt". In *Miller v Minister of Pensions*[186] Denning J. described this as follows: **11–044**

---

[182] The Court of Appeal reached a similar conclusion in the earlier case of *The Glendarroch* [1894] P. 226: where a defendant relies, in an action on a bill of lading, on an exception clause for perils of the sea, the exception is not available if its operation was brought about by the negligence of the defendant or the unseaworthiness of the defendant's ship, but the burden of proving negligence or unseaworthiness is on the plaintiff.

[183] *Joseph Constantine v Imperial Smelting* [1942] A.C. 154 at 192.

[184] *Joseph Constantine v Imperial Smelting* [1942] A.C. 154; (1944) 60 L.Q.R. 262.

[185] See *Levison v Patent Steam Carpet Cleaning Co Ltd* [1978] 1 Q.B. 69 CA, distinguishing the shipping cases on bills of lading and frustration.

[186] *Miller v Minister of Pensions* [1947] 2 All E.R. 372 at 373 KBD.

> "the ... degree of cogency ... required in a criminal case before an accused person is found guilty ... is well settled. It need not reach certainty, but it must carry a high degree of probability. Proof beyond reasonable doubt does not mean proof beyond the shadow of a doubt. The law would fail to protect the community if it admitted fanciful possibilities to deflect the course of justice. If the evidence is so strong against a man as to leave only a remote possibility in his favour which can be dismissed with the sentence 'of course it is possible, but not in the least probable,' the case is proved, but nothing short of that will suffice."

The merit of this explanation is that it tries to confront what has always been the problem with the classic formula, namely that it appears to permit conviction where there is a doubt about the accused's guilt, and the question is whether the doubt is a "reasonable" one. Reasonableness is a question of values, and values might well vary amongst a group of lay factfinders. Denning J.'s explanation provides a helpful reminder of the practical function of the test in the administration of criminal justice, and emphasises that speculative doubts are insufficient to justify not convicting. Whether the explanation goes far enough to answer a juror determined to find out what might be a reasonable doubt is itself uncertain, and trial judges have attempted from time to time to give juries further explanations. Appeal courts have sometimes upheld particular examples of such explanations.[187] On other occasions the terms of particular explanations have been disapproved,[188] and some courts have suggested that judges should stop trying to define that which is almost impossible to define,[189] and keep the direction on the standard of proof short and clear.[190]

The other expression is whether the prosecution have satisfied the factfinder so that the factfinder is sure of the accused's guilt. This was introduced into the law in *Summers*,[191] in order to meet difficulties that were being felt about the concept of a reasonable doubt. The two expressions mean the same, and for many years courts regarded them as alternative formulations for directing juries as to the standard of proof they should apply. However, the modern preference is for judges to avoid using "beyond reasonable doubt" because of the problem of having to explain the concept of a reasonable doubt if a jury asks for clarification.[192] Accordingly, the 2010 revision of the Crown Court Bench Book simply advises judges to direct juries that they must be sure of the defendant's guilt before they can convict. This advice is generally followed. For the Court of

---

[187] As in *Walters v R.* [1969] 2 A.C. 26, where the Privy Council described the following direction by a trial judge as unexceptionable: "a reasonable doubt is that quality and kind of doubt which, when you are dealing with matters of importance in your own affairs, you allow to influence you one way or the other". See also *Ching* (1976) 63 Cr.App.R. 7, where the Court of Appeal said that there was nothing wrong in telling a jury that a reasonable doubt is the kind of doubt that "might influence you if you were to consider some business matter. A matter, for example, of a mortgage concerning your house, or something of that nature".

[188] As in *Stafford* [1968] 3 All E.R. 752, where the Court of Appeal disapproved of a direction to a jury to "remember that a reasonable doubt is one for which you could give reasons if you were asked". See also *Gray* (1973) 58 Cr.App.R. 177, where the Court of Appeal said that a judge's statement that a reasonable doubt was the "sort of doubt which might affect you in the conduct of your everyday affairs" set the standard too low.

[189] *Ching* (1976) 63 Cr.App.R. 7 CA.

[190] *Penny* (1992) 94 Cr.App.R. 345 at 350 CA.

[191] *Summers* [1952] 1 All E.R. 1059 CCA.

[192] *Majid* [2009] EWCA Crim 2563.

Appeal the crucial question is the effect of the summing-up considered as a whole. Provided that the judge makes clear that the burden of proof is on the prosecution and that the jury must not convict the defendant unless they are sure of his guilt, it does not matter whether any particular form of words is used.[193] The point about taking the summing-up as a whole is that judges may well make several references to the burden and standard of proof. A slightly ambiguous or incomplete expression at one stage may be cured by the language used in other parts of the summing-up. Where the case against the accused depends wholly or partly on inferences from circumstantial evidence, factfinders cannot logically convict unless they are sure that inferences of guilt are the only ones that can reasonably be drawn. If they think that there are possible innocent explanations for circumstantial evidence that are not "merely fanciful", it must follow that there is a reasonable doubt about guilt. There is no rule, however, that judges must direct juries in terms not to convict unless they are sure that the evidence bears no other explanation than guilt. It is sufficient to direct simply that the burden on the prosecution is to satisfy the jury beyond reasonable doubt,[194] or so that they are sure.

The very high standard of proof required in criminal cases minimises the risk of a wrongful conviction. It means that someone whom, on the evidence, the factfinder believes is "probably" guilty, or "likely" to be guilty will be acquitted, since these judgments of probability necessarily admit that the factfinder is not "sure". It is generally accepted that some at least of these acquittals will be of persons who are in fact guilty of the offences charged, and who would be convicted if the standard of proof were the lower civil standard of the balance of probabilities. Such acquittals are the price paid for the safeguard provided by the "beyond reasonable doubt" standard against wrongful conviction. It is impossible to know the frequency of wrongful acquittals, but given the high acquittal rates generally in the Crown Court,[195] it seems that it is almost certainly greater than the frequency of wrongful convictions.[196] This allocation of the risk of misdecision reflects Dworkin's claim that a wrongful conviction is a particularly grave species of moral harm, one that is significantly worse than a wrongful acquittal.[197]

11–045

---

[193] *Ferguson v R.* [1979] 1 W.L.R. 94 PC. The judge should not, however, risk confusing the jury by distinguishing between being "sure" of guilt and being 'certain' of guilt: *Majid* [2009] EWCA Crim 2563.

[194] *McGreevy v DPP* [1973] 1 W.L.R. 276 HL.

[195] M. Zander and P. Henderson, *Crown Court Study* (RCCJ Research Study No.19, London, 1993), para.6.1.2 suggested a figure of around 40% of defendants acquitted of all charges, with a further 3–4% of cases having hung juries who failed to agree a verdict.

[196] In the study referred to above, there was a very striking difference in reactions to jury verdicts, with many more respondents to the study, including the judges, being surprised by acquittals than by convictions: para.6.1.6. This does not of course prove that the acquittals were wrong, only that most other participants in the trial would have decided the case differently.

[197] R. M. Dworkin, "Principle, Policy, Procedure" in C. Tapper (ed), *Crime Proof and Punishment* (London, 1981), p.193.

F.   STANDARD OF PROOF IN CIVIL CASES

11–046   The normal standard of proof in civil cases, and also the standard of proof where the accused bears the burden of proof in a criminal case, is proof on the balance of probabilities. Another term for it is the preponderance of probabilities. In *Miller v Minister of Pensions*,[198] Denning J. contrasted the civil and criminal standards. After explaining the criminal standard in the terms set out above, he continued:

> "The . . . degree of cogency . . . required to discharge a burden in a civil case . . . is well settled. It must carry a reasonable degree of probability, but not so high as is required in a criminal case. If the evidence is such that the tribunal can say: 'We think it more probable than not' the burden is discharged, but, if the probabilities are equal, it is not."

Although this is the standard generally used in civil cases, there are several examples of civil proceedings where courts have held that certain matters must be proved to the criminal standard of proof. Contempt of court in civil proceedings must be proved beyond reasonable doubt,[199] a rule based largely on the fact that the liberty of the subject is involved in such proceedings.[200] In *Re A Solicitor*,[201] the Divisional Court held that, in proceedings before a solicitors' disciplinary tribunal, allegations of professional misconduct had to be proved to the criminal standard where what was alleged was tantamount to a criminal offence. In applications for anti-social behaviour orders, breach of which is a criminal offence with a substantial maximum penalty of five years imprisonment, the standard of proof required should be equivalent to the criminal standard.[202] The rationale for requiring the higher standard in these types of case is the seriousness of the consequences for the defendant of an adverse finding, as Lord Brown commented in *Re Doherty*.[203]

11–047   The House of Lords[204] and the Supreme Court[205] have recently been at pains to emphasise that there are only two standards of proof in English law. They have rejected any notion that there might be an intermediate standard or standards between the balance of probabilities and beyond reasonable doubt, or that there are degrees of probability within the concept of the balance of probabilities, so that the court might, for example, vary the degree of probability required

---

[198] *Miller v Minister of Pensions* [1947] 2 All E.R. 372 at 374 KBD.

[199] *Re Bramblevale Ltd* [1970] Ch. 128. See further *Witham v Holloway* (1995) 69 A.L.J.R. 847 High Court of Australia; C.J. Miller, "Proof of Civil Contempt" (1996) 112 L.Q.R. 539.

[200] cf. *DPP v Havering Magistrates' Court* [2001] 3 All E.R. 997 (not necessary for compliance with art.5 of the ECHR to prove breach of bail conditions to the criminal standard of proof).

[201] *Re A Solicitor* [1993] Q.B. 69 DC. See also *R. v Milk Marketing Board Ex p. Austin, The Times*, March 21, 1983.

[202] *R. (on the application of McCann) v Manchester Crown Court* [2002] UKHL 39; [2003] 1 A.C. 787. Similar rulings have been made for applications for sex offender orders (*R. v Chief Constable of Avon and Somerset Constabulary* [2001] 1 W.L.R. 340) and for football banning orders (*Gough v Chief Constable of the Derbyshire Constabulary* [2002] Q.B. 1213).

[203] *Re Doherty* [2008] UKHL 33.

[204] *Re Doherty* [2008] UKHL 33 at [25] per Lord Carswell; *Re B (Children)* [2008] UKHL 35; [2008] 4 All E.R. 1 at [13] per Lord Hoffmann.

[205] *Re S-B (Children)* [2009] UKSC 17; [2010] 1 All ER 705 at [11] per Lady Hale.

according to the seriousness of the allegation. Some earlier authorities[206] had suggested this approach to civil cases involving allegations of criminal conduct, or other conduct of similar gravity, but it is now clear that such an approach is thought to produce over-complication and confusion.

This is not to say that the gravity of the allegation is irrelevant to considering whether the standard of proof on the balance of probabilities has been met. The question is how it should be taken into account. An alternative view is that the matter is not one of the degree of probability required, but is a matter of the weight of the evidence needed to tip the balance of probabilities. In *Hornal v Neuberger Products Ltd* Morris L.J. explained the approach as follows:

> "Though no court and no jury would give less attention to issues lacking gravity than to those marked by it, the very elements of gravity become a part of the whole range of circumstances which have to be weighed in the scale when deciding as to the balance of probabilities."[207]

Similarly, in *Thomas Bates & Son v Wyndhams (Lingerie) Ltd*,[208] which concerned the rectification of a lease, Buckley L.J. commented that "in civil proceedings a fact must be proved with that degree of certainty which justice requires in the circumstances of the particular case. In every case the balance of probability must be discharged, but in some cases that balance may be tipped more easily than in others". In more recent cases the courts have not dissented from the claim that more cogent evidence may be needed to prove more serious allegations. But they have tended to base the claim on the inherent *likelihood* of the allegations being true rather than the seriousness of the *consequences* which might follow from proof of the allegations.[209]

This approach was developed in the context of allegations of sexual abuse in child care proceedings. In *Re H (Minors)*,[210] the House of Lords had to decide whether the standard of proof for such allegations is the ordinary civil standard, or whether suggestions in one or two earlier cases were correct that some higher degree of probability is required.[211] It was held that these suggestions were not accurate. The House of Lords confirmed that the standard is the normal balance of probability. Lord Nicholls of Birkenhead,[212] who gave the main speech for the majority, discussed at some length the argument that the seriousness of the   **11–048**

---

[206] For discussion of these cases see the 3rd edition of this book at pp.482–484.
[207] *Hornal v Neuberger Products Ltd* [1957] 1 Q.B. 247 at 266. For a searching discussion of the interpretation of the civil standard of proof, see A. Stein, "An Essay on Uncertainty and Fact-Finding in Civil Litigation, with Special Reference to Contract Cases" (1998) 48 U. of Toronto L.J. 299.
[208] *Thomas Bates v Wyndhams* [1981] 1 W.L.R. 505 at 514.
[209] Of course a grave consequence might be relevant to the likelihood of an event occurring: consider the example of the probability of a bank manager committing a minor theft from the bank given the risk of the loss of his job if discovered. See the comment by Mirfield in (2009) 125 LQR 31.
[210] *Re H (Minors)* [1996] A.C. 563 HL.
[211] See *Re G (A Minor) (Child Abuse: Standards of Proof)* [1987] 1 W.L.R. 1461; *Re W (Minors) (Sexual Abuse: Standard of Proof)* [1994] 1 F.L.R. 419. Other authorities supported the application of the ordinary civil standard: *H v H (Minors) (Child Abuse: Evidence)* [1990] Fam. 86; *Re M (A Minor) (Appeal) (No.2)* [1994] 1 F.L.R. 59.
[212] With whom Lord Goff and Lord Mustill agreed. Lord Browne-Wilkinson and Lord Lloyd dissented on the question whether s.31(2) of the Children Act 1989 imposed on a local authority applying for a care order a legal burden to prove facts on the balance of probabilities to support an inference that the occurrence of sexual harm to the child in question was a real possibility. The

allegation goes to the weight of the evidence required to establish the balance of probability. He suggested that the more serious the allegation the less likely it may be that the event occurred. Accordingly the stronger should be the evidence that the allegation is established on the balance of probability. As Lord Nicholls put it:

> "Fraud is usually less likely than negligence. Deliberate physical injury is usually less likely than accidental physical injury. A stepfather is usually less likely to have repeatedly raped and had non-consensual oral sex with his under age stepdaughter than on some occasion to have lost his temper and slapped her. Built into the preponderance of probability standard is a generous degree of flexibility in respect of the seriousness of the allegation.
>
> Although the result is much the same, this does not mean that where a serious allegation is in issue the standard of proof required is higher. It means only that the inherent probability or improbability of an event is itself a matter to be taken into account when weighing the probabilities and deciding whether, on balance, the event occurred. The more improbable the event, the stronger must be the evidence that it did occur before, on the balance of probability, its occurrence will be established . . .
>
> This approach also provides a means by which the balance of probability standard can accommodate one's instinctive feeling that even in civil proceedings a court should be more sure before finding serious allegations proved than when deciding less serious or trivial matters."[213]

Lord Nicholls provided no evidence to support his claim about the improbability of serious events. He offered it as an a priori truth. Empirically, the notion that serious events are less likely than non-serious ones seems debatable at best, and there is much scope in any event for disagreement about what counts as "serious". However, the House of Lords approved this approach on several occasions subsequently,[214] although Lady Hale emphasised in *Re S-B (Children)*,[215] that there is no necessary connection between seriousness and inherent probability. It seems clear that as so often in the law of evidence much depends on the specific circumstances of the case, the precise issue in question and the state of the other evidence in the case. If, for example, the issue in care proceedings is whether a child was sexually abused by her male relative, it may be appropriate for a court to require cogent evidence to overcome the claim that sexual abuse by fathers or stepfathers of children in their care is inherently unlikely. But where there is cogent medical evidence that a child has been sexually abused, and the issue is the identity of the perpetrator, there is now little weight in an argument that sexual abuse of a child by its father or stepfather is improbable.

Lord Nicholls' rejection in *Re H (Minors)* of a third standard of proof in some civil cases is not wholly persuasive. The existence of a third standard is well recognised in the United States in the form of the "clear and convincing" standard. Burger C.J. explained in *Addington v Texas*[216] that this standard is typically used in civil cases involving allegations of fraud and other

---

majority held that the authority had such a burden. The minority held that the authority merely had a burden of adducing evidence capable of giving rise to such an inference.

[213] *Re H (Minors)* [1996] A.C. 563 at 586–587.

[214] See *Secretary of State for the Home Department v Rehman* [2003] 1 A.C. 153; *Re Doherty* [2008] UKHL 33; *Re B (Children)* [2008] UKHL 35; [2008] 4 All E.R. 1.

[215] *Re S-B (Children)* [2009] UKSC 17; [2010] 1 All E.R. 705 at [12].

[216] *Addington v Texas* (1979) 441 U.S. 418 Supreme Court of the US.

"quasi-criminal wrongdoing", and to protect certain other particularly important individual interests in civil cases, such as the interest that a person has in not being deported or in not losing his status as a citizen by being denaturalised. In *Addington v Texas,* the Supreme Court held that this standard applies in civil proceedings against an individual for mandatory commitment to a mental hospital. It is clear therefore that it is used to mark the importance of the interests at stake: these cases involve the risk of serious harm to a person's character or reputation, or involve the interests of the state in a person's continuing status or liberty.

However, exactly how the "clear and convincing" standard differs from the criminal standard of proof beyond reasonable doubt is somewhat obscure. On one view evidence about past facts that is clear and that convinces the factfinder has satisfied the criminal standard; being convinced that an allegation of misconduct is true and being sure about it are the same thing. On the other hand, as the Supreme Court pointed out, an issue in civil proceedings may turn on expert interpretation of primary facts. In a civil commitment case a psychiatrist may give a clear and convincing diagnosis that a person is mentally ill and likely to be dangerous, but psychiatric diagnosis can be fallible, and it may often involve "subtleties and nuances" which render practical certainty unattainable. These factors might suggest that a reasonable doubt could co-exist with a clear and convincing diagnosis. The court was therefore right to say that the criminal standard is not appropriate for proof of facts that are essentially predictive in nature. Even where the practical difference between the standards is not so apparent, the "clear and convincing" standard may have an important communicative function. It may tell the factfinder that because of the interests at stake the risks of error in decision-making are not to be distributed more or less equally between the parties, which is the function performed by the normal civil standard of the balance of probabilities. At the same time it indicates that a certain risk of error is acceptable in view of the fact that the object of the proceedings is not the enforcement of the criminal law and the punishment of an offender. Thus a factfinder does not have to be satisfied that there is no more than a "fanciful" doubt that the factual decision is correct. These considerations suggest that the rejection in *Re H (Minors)* of a third standard of proof was perhaps over-hasty. It is not apparent that leaving the matter of serious allegations as one affecting the weight of the evidence needed to tip the balance of probability is significantly more certain and less confusing.

11–049

G.   BURDEN AND STANDARD OF PROOF OF FOUNDATION FACTS FOR ADMISSIBILITY OF EVIDENCE[217]

The admissibility of evidence sometimes depends on certain facts, the existence of which is a condition precedent for the admission of the evidence. These facts can be called for convenience foundation facts. An example comes from the law of confessions: a confession by the accused is not admissible in proof of his or

11–050

---

[217] See R. Pattenden, "The proof rules of pre-verdict judicial fact-finding in criminal trials by jury" (2009) 125 L.Q.R. 79.

her guilt unless the confession was not obtained by oppression or by anything said or done likely to render any confession by that person unreliable.[218] The existence of foundation facts may be disputed, in which case the court (the trial judge or the bench of magistrates) will almost certainly have to hear evidence about them in order to decide whether their existence has been proved. In jury trials the procedure for doing this is known as the voir dire, or trial within a trial. The jury are absent from court when a voir dire is held, so that the jury do not hear evidence which may be held to be inadmissible. The question that arises now is what is the burden and standard of proof of foundation facts for the admissibility of evidence?

The general rule is that the party adducing the evidence bears the burden of proving any foundation facts for the admission of that evidence. The rule is supported by common sense, by the principle "he who asserts must prove", and by judicial decisions and statutory rules relating to proof of particular foundation facts. Thus, s.76(2) of PACE stipulates that if the prosecution wish to adduce the accused's confession in evidence they must prove that it was not obtained in either of the prohibited ways. The standard of proof is expressed to be beyond reasonable doubt. This is a logical rule; it would be inconsistent to require the prosecution to prove guilt beyond reasonable doubt and then to admit evidence probative of guilt where there was or might be a reasonable doubt whether the facts rendering that evidence admissible had been proved. Similarly, at common law it was held in *Jenkins*[219] that where the prosecution sought to rely on a dying declaration of the victim in a murder case, the prosecution had to prove beyond reasonable doubt that when the victim made the declaration he or she had no hope of recovery (was under a "settled hopeless expectation of death"), an essential condition of the admissibility of such declarations as common law exceptions to the hearsay rule. In *Ewing*,[220] the Court of Appeal held that where the prosecution produce samples of the accused's handwriting for comparative purposes under s.8 of the Criminal Procedure Act 1865, the prosecution must prove beyond reasonable doubt that the samples are indeed those of the accused. If a question arises whether a witness is competent to give evidence it is for the party calling the witness, whether prosecution or defence, to satisfy the court on the balance of probabilities that the witness is competent.[221]

In these examples the judge and jury are deciding different questions, and there is no danger that the judge may be usurping the function of the jury. Thus the judge decides on the legitimacy of the methods used to obtain a confession, whereas the jury decide whether the confession was true.[222] The judge decides whether a handwriting sample is the writing of the accused, whereas the jury decide whether the sample matches the disputed writing with which it is being compared. Sometimes, however, judge and jury may have to decide the same question, which raises the risk that the judge's prior decision on admissibility will effectively usurp the jury's function. Suppose, for example, it is disputed whether

---

[218] PACE s.76(2).
[219] *Jenkins* (1869) L.R. 1 C.C.R. 187.
[220] *Ewing* [1983] Q.B. 1039 CA.
[221] Youth Justice and Criminal Evidence Act 1999 s.54(2).
[222] But note *Mushtaq* [2005] UKHL 25, which effectively allows the jury to second-guess the judge on the legitimacy question. The decision is discussed and criticised in Ch.6.

an alleged confession was made at all, or whether an incriminating tape-recording is authentic, in the sense that it is an original recording that has not been tampered with. The judge should not let such evidence go to the jury unless he or she is satisfied that there is proof of its authenticity; the jury should not act on such evidence unless sure that it is authentic. In *Robson*,[223] the Court of Appeal resolved the problem by holding that in deciding whether a recording was genuine a judge had only to be satisfied by evidence to the standard of the balance of probabilities. To apply the criminal standard would mean that the judge would be directly usurping the task of the jury to decide whether the recording was genuine beyond reasonable doubt. Cross and Tapper offer an alternative conceptualisation of the problem.[224] This argues that authenticity is not a foundation fact at all, but only a fact of which there should be prima facie evidence before the recording can go to the jury. In effect the judge would have to be satisfied that the prosecution had discharged an evidential burden on the issue, but would not himself have to decide the question whether the recording was authentic. There is an attractive simplicity to this approach, although it offers no principled way of distinguishing between foundation facts, which the judge must settle conclusively before the evidence is admitted, and facts of which prima facie evidence must be given. In a criminal case, of course, prima facie evidence would be evidence capable of proving the matter beyond reasonable doubt.

---

[223] *Robson* [1972] 1 W.L.R. 651 CA.
[224] Cross and Tapper, p.184.

CHAPTER 12

FORMS OF PROOF AND ALTERNATIVES TO PROOF

A. INTRODUCTION

Having considered the nature and extent of the obligation to prove facts, we now   **12–001**
turn to the ways in which this obligation can be met. The law of evidence
recognises three forms of proof: the testimony of witnesses, documentary
evidence and so-called real evidence. These three forms of evidence are known
collectively as "judicial evidence". It should be emphasised that, whatever the

form in which evidence is adduced, it is always subject to the general principles of relevance, admissibility and discretionary exclusion, which are discussed elsewhere in this book. The rule against hearsay, for example, may prevent a court receiving evidence of an out-of-court statement by X, irrespective of whether the evidence takes the form of W's testimony that he heard X make the statement, or of a letter from X containing the statement. Similarly, a court may exclude under s.78 of PACE evidence in the form not only of a taped confession by the defendant that he stabbed the victim, made following deliberate breaches by the police of PACE and the Codes of Practice, but also of the knife that the defendant revealed following the confession.[1] Broadly speaking, the rules discussed in this chapter deal with formal issues concerned with the process of adducing judicial evidence. These rules are distinct from the principles of relevance and admissibility, although they presuppose the existence of those principles and interact with them.

In relation to judicial evidence, section B provides a short introduction to the subject of witness testimony. This is a large topic that is covered in more detail in the following three chapters. Section C, on documentary evidence, deals with the formal requirements relating to proof of the contents and of the execution of documents. Section D discusses formalities relating to proof of real evidence.

This chapter also includes three sections dealing with certain doctrines that have the effect of reducing, or dispensing with, the need for proof of certain facts. These doctrines should be regarded as aids, or even as alternatives to proof, rather than forms of proof, but their function is similar in that they enable facts to be established for adjudicative purposes. This is why they are discussed in the same context as judicial evidence. Section E deals briefly with the rules permitting parties to make formal admissions of fact that are binding for the purposes of the litigation in question. Section F provides an introduction to presumptions. This term is used rather loosely in the law of evidence, but in this context a presumption properly refers to an inference of fact, the "presumed" fact, that may or must be drawn from proof of another fact, often called the "basic" fact. Presumptions vary in their strength; some may function as a means of proof in the sense that they may oblige the factfinder to draw a certain inference unless there is evidence to the contrary. Section G deals with the doctrine of judicial notice. This doctrine applies in respect of certain types of facts; it empowers a judge to dispense with the normal requirement for parties to adduce evidence of such facts. The judge will say that judicial notice is taken of them, which means that their existence is taken to be established for the purposes of the proceedings. An important aspect of this topic is the issue of when a court may act upon personal knowledge of facts in issue.

---

[1] cf. *Lam Chi-Ming v R.* [1991] 2 A.C. 212 PC.

B. TESTIMONY

Testimony is the evidence of a witness, normally given on oath.[2] The sworn **12–002** statements of the witness are offered to the court as evidence of the facts stated, in other words as statements that are true because the witness says they are. The term is often used to refer only to *oral* testimony in court, but in many types of civil proceeding a witness may give written testimony in the form of an affidavit. This is a formal written statement made on oath, for the purpose of being used as evidence in the proceedings. Affidavits are thus distinguished from statements in documents not made on oath, and from transcripts of statements made on oath in other proceedings. Affidavits normally constitute the only evidence in interlocutory proceedings, proceedings for judicial review, and certain other proceedings.[3] Statute occasionally makes provision for the use of affidavits in criminal proceedings.[4]

Historically, oral testimony was the foundation of the common law trial, and in criminal proceedings there is still a strong attachment to the principle of orality. In *Butera v DPP*,[5] the High Court of Australia set out a concise statement of the value of oral evidence. This passage sums up much of the traditional view supporting orality as the guiding principle for jury trial:

> "A witness who gives evidence orally demonstrates, for good or ill, more about his or her credibility than a witness whose evidence is given in documentary form. Oral evidence is public; written evidence may not be. Oral evidence gives to the trial the atmosphere which, though intangible, is often critical to the jury's estimate of the witnesses. By generally restricting the jury to consideration of testimonial evidence in its oral form, it is thought that the jury's discussion of the case in the jury room will be more open, the exchange of views among jurors will more easily occur than if the evidence were given in writing or the jurors were each armed with a written transcript of the evidence."

The orality principle requires that as far as possible witnesses to fact should appear in person at court to give oral evidence in chief on which they can then be cross-examined. The success of this technique as a method of accurate factfinding depends on the witnesses giving testimony that is credible and reliable. The common law developed a number of rules and techniques aimed at ensuring the credibility and reliability of testimony. There is first the general rule that a witness may give testimony only about matters of which the witness has personal knowledge. Secondly, testimony must be given on oath or affirmation, a requirement that signifies a liability to prosecution for perjury where a person knowingly makes a material statement that is false. Thirdly, a requirement for oral testimony enables the factfinder to observe the demeanour of the witness when giving evidence, and to take this into account in deciding the weight to be attached to the testimony. Fourthly, witnesses who give oral testimony can be cross-examined in person at the time, thereby enabling the cross-examiner to

---

[2] Children under 14 give evidence in criminal proceedings unsworn: Youth Justice and Criminal Evidence Act 1999 s.56(1) and (2). See further Ch.13.

[3] See further CPR r.32.15.

[4] See, e.g. Bankers' Books Evidence Act 1879 ss.4 and 5, as amended by Criminal Procedure and Investigations Act 1996 s.47 Sch.1 Pt II para.16.

[5] *Butera v DPP* (1987) 164 C.L.R. 180 at 189.

maximise the impact and efficiency of the questioning. Fifthly, collateral evidence of the witness's credibility can sometimes be adduced in the form of evidence of the witness's bias, bad character and disability.

12–003 The requirement of personal knowledge raises the question of hearsay statements as a form of proof. A hearsay statement is a statement made by a person other than while giving oral testimony in the proceedings, adduced as evidence of the facts stated. Hearsay statements are generally inadmissible, partly because of the personal knowledge rule. A witness who reports to the court a statement made out of court by a third party may have no personal knowledge of the matters asserted by the third party.[6] However, there are numerous exceptions to the rule against hearsay. When one of the exceptions applies, the "evidence" consists of the witness's testimony that X made a statement out of court and the terms of X's statement as reported by the witness. Hearsay statements are analytically different from direct testimony, but as regards formal requirements of proof nothing turns on their classification. Admissible hearsay in written form is, like all documentary evidence, subject to the principles relating to documentary evidence that are considered in the next section. The normal rules of testimony apply where a witness gives evidence of an admissible oral hearsay statement, whether by the witness himself or a third party. The weight of admissible oral hearsay partly depends, like the witness's non-hearsay testimony, on the credibility and reliability of the witness as a reporter of things done, said and heard out of court.

C. DOCUMENTARY EVIDENCE

12–004 Documents must generally be "proved" by a witness who can verify the nature and authenticity of the document. The same rule applies to items admitted as real evidence. In this sense all forms of judicial evidence are forms of testimony, but documents need separate consideration because of the particular rules that regulate how a witness may prove, first, the contents of a document, and, secondly, the due execution of the document.[7]

Documents can be relevant in more than one way. Most commonly a document has testimonial relevance by virtue of its contents. The statements it contains may themselves be in issue, such as the terms of a will or the publication of a libel, or they may be relevant because of the facts they record, such as the results of a medical examination or the questions and answers in a police interview. As a record of a fact, a document may have considerably more weight than oral testimony about the fact; it will generally have been made at the time, or at least much nearer the time, of the facts it records, and its terms are settled. It is not therefore so subject to testimonial infirmities such as defective memory and ambiguity of narration. The classic piece of common sense advice, "Get it in writing", reflects this point. More rarely a document may be relevant as a thing, in the sense that its physical condition is relevant to some issue to be decided in

---

[6] This does not apply where the out-of-court statement was made by the witness himself.

[7] A separate question about documentary evidence is the extent to which extrinsic evidence is admissible to explain, vary or contradict the terms of a document. This question is more appropriately dealt with as part of the substantive law of contracts, wills, etc and is not discussed further in this book.

the proceedings. A rare book, for example, may bear the fingerprint of the accused who is alleged to have stolen it. In such a case, when the book is adduced in evidence, it is not relied on "testimonially", and the rules relating to proof of the contents and execution of documents do not apply.

1. *Proof of the contents of documents*

(A) *Special statutory provision*

Documents of a public nature, such as various types of public record, are frequently subject to special statutory provision that sets out certain formalities for proof of them. This is particularly so where the kind of facts recorded can be expected to recur often in legal proceedings. There is little point in trying to compile a complete list of such documents, but a few examples can be given of different types of statutory provision. The fact of a person's birth or death can be proved by the production of a certified copy of an entry in the registers of births and deaths respectively.[8] A judgment of the Court of Appeal or the High Court can be proved in civil proceedings by the production of an office copy made in the central office or district registry in which the judgment is filed.[9] In criminal proceedings a previous conviction of a person can be proved by the production of a certificate of conviction and evidence that the person named in the certificate as having been convicted is the person whose conviction is to be proved.[10]

12–005

As regards private documents, the most important special statutory provisions are contained in the Bankers' Books Evidence Act 1879. Given the frequency with which evidence about bank accounts is needed in litigation, it would be highly inconvenient, if not downright impossible, for the original bankers' books to be produced on every occasion. Accordingly the 1879 Act recognises the practical necessity of providing for the admission of copies of entries in bankers' books. Under s.3 of the Act a copy of any entry in a banker's book is admissible in all legal proceedings as prima facie evidence of such entry and of all the transactions and accounts recorded by the entry. Sections 4 and 5 of the Act then set out a number of conditions to be satisfied before the copy is admitted: the book must be one of the ordinary books of the bank, the entry must have been made in the ordinary course of business, the book must be in the custody or control of the bank, and the copy must have been examined against the original entry and found to be correct. Proof of all these matters must be given by an officer of the bank, and may be given orally or by an affidavit. The definition of

---

[8] Births and Deaths Registration Act 1953 s.34. A certified copy is a copy accompanied by a certificate verifying its accuracy, issued by the appropriate official. Note that the entry is admissible as evidence of the fact (birth or death) stated by virtue of the common law exception to the hearsay rule for statements in public documents; this exception is preserved in the statutory scheme for the admissibility of hearsay by the Criminal Justice Act 2003 s.118(1). See Ch.17. Note also that the court must be satisfied that the person referred to in the entry is the person whose birth or death is in issue in the proceedings.

[9] Senior Courts Act 1981 s.132. Again, it may be necessary to adduce evidence to identify the parties named in the judgment with the person whose rights and liabilities are in issue in the proceedings.

[10] PACE s.73.

"bankers' books" in s.9(2) has been extended[11] to take account of technological developments in record-keeping; it does not matter whether the records are in written form or are kept on microfilm,[12] magnetic tape or any other form of mechanical or electronic data retrieval mechanism. However, the Act does not apply to all banking business, but only to books that are "ledgers, day books, cash books, account books, and other records used in the ordinary business of the bank".[13] It has been held that the Act does not extend to copies of letters written and sent by the bank to a customer,[14] or to bundles of cheques and paying-in slips.[15] Even on the assumption that these documents form part of the bank's records, the addition of another cheque to a bundle of used cheques, or of a copy letter to a file of correspondence, is not regarded by the courts as the making of an "entry" in the records. Similarly records made by the bank of conversations between its employees and customers are not "other records used in the ordinary business of the bank".[16]

Section 7 of the Act contains a provision regarding access to evidence relating to bank accounts. On its face the provision is extremely wide. Any party to a legal proceeding may apply for an order that he be at liberty to inspect and take copies of any entries in a banker's book for the purposes of the proceeding. The application for the order can be made ex parte without notice to the bank or any other party. The order itself must be served on the bank three clear days before it is due to be obeyed unless the court or judge directs otherwise. Section 7 has been held to extend to the making of an order to inspect the account of a third party, not a party to the proceedings, even if that person is not compellable as a witness.[17]

12–006 It is apparent therefore that this is a draconian power that, if not used with restraint, could sanction large-scale invasions of privacy and "fishing expeditions". In practice, however, its application has been significantly restricted. In civil cases, where an order is sought against another party to the litigation, the ordinary rules of discovery will be applied.[18] This means that the limits on what is normally discoverable in a civil action cannot be outflanked by the use of s.7. It means also that the other party can invoke the privilege against self-incrimination.[19] Where an application is made under s.7 against a third party, the court must be satisfied that the account of the third party is the account of the other party to the action, or is an account with which he is so connected that items in it would be evidence against him, and that the party asking for inspection can show very strong grounds for suspicion, almost amounting to certainty, that there

---

[11] By the Banking Act 1979, substituting an amended provision.

[12] The courts had already made this extension: *Barker v Wilson* [1980] 1 W.L.R. 884.

[13] For the definition of "bank", see s.9(1).

[14] *Dadson* (1983) 77 Cr.App.R. 91 CA. In such a case the defendant should be served with a notice to produce the original letter; if he fails to do so, a copy can be admitted as secondary evidence at common law.

[15] *Williams v Williams* [1988] Q.B. 161 CA.

[16] *Re Howglen Ltd* [2001] 1 All E.R. 376.

[17] *R. v Andover Justices Ex p. Rhodes* [1980] Crim. L.R. 644 DC (order for inspection of the account of the defendant's husband).

[18] *Re Bankers' Books Evidence Act 1879, R. v Bono* (1913) 29 T.L.R. 635.

[19] *Waterhouse v Barker* [1924] 2 K.B. 759.

are items in the account that would be material evidence against the other party.[20] In relation to criminal proceedings, the Divisional Court held in *Williams v Summerfield*,[21] that the privilege against self-incrimination could not be used to resist an application, otherwise s.7 would almost never be able to apply in criminal cases. The Divisional Court went on to say that since the order could be a serious interference with the liberty of the subject, it should only be made after the most careful thought and on the clearest grounds.[22] In particular, a court should consider whether the prosecution already have other evidence to support the charge; the application should be refused if it is no more than a fishing expedition in the hope of finding material on which to hang a charge.[23]

(B)   General statutory provision: criminal proceedings

In addition to special statutory provisions, there are in s.133 of the Criminal Justice Act 2003 general rules relating to proof in criminal proceedings of the contents of a document. The section provides as follows: **12–007**

> "Where a statement in a document is admissible as evidence in criminal proceedings, the statement may be proved by producing either—
> (a)   the document; or
> (b)   (whether or not that document exists) a copy of the document, or of the material part of it, authenticated in whatever way the court may approve."

For the purposes of this section, a "statement" is "any representation of fact or opinion made by a person by whatever means; and it includes a representation made in a sketch, photofit or other pictorial form",[24] and "document" is given the widest possible meaning of "anything in which information of any description is recorded".[25] It will thus include, in addition to any writing, a map, plan, sketch, photograph, tape recording (audio or video), film, microfilm, fax and computer disk. Websites on the internet are clearly included, so that, for example, evidence of postings on social networking sites will count as documentary evidence.[26] Less obvious media for recording information also fall within the definition of a document: a wall, tombstone, flag, vehicle, even an animal.[27] A "copy" of a

---

[20] *South Staffordshire Tramways Co v Ebbsmith* [1895] 2 Q.B. 669 CA (pre-trial application); *DB Deniz Nakliyati TAS v Yugopetrol* [1992] 1 All E.R. 205 CA (post-judgment application in aid of enforcement of a judgment debt; the Court of Appeal indicated that the application was premature and that the creditor should first use the remedies provided by RSC Ord.48).
[21] *Williams v Summerfield* [1972] 2 Q.B. 512.
[22] See also *Grossman* (1981) 73 Cr.App.R. 302 CA (an order should be made only in exceptional circumstances, and where the private interest in keeping a bank account confidential is outweighed by the public interest in assisting a prosecution).
[23] See, e.g. *R. v Nottingham City Justices Ex p. Lynn* [1984] Crim. L.R. 554 DC (order for inspection of a defendant's bank accounts over a 3-year period varied to cover only a period of 6 months before an alleged incident of drug smuggling).
[24] Criminal Justice Act 2003 s.115(2).
[25] Criminal Justice Act 2003 s.134(1).
[26] For discussion of issues associated with this type of evidence see M. O'Floinn and D. Ormerod, "Social Networking Material as Criminal Evidence" [2012] Crim. L.R. 486.
[27] Consider a brand on the animal as evidence of its ownership.

document is anything on to which information recorded in the document has been copied, by whatever means and whether directly or indirectly.[28]

The aim of s.133 (as of its predecessor, s.27 of the Criminal Justice Act 1988) is to replace the old common law rule that a party seeking to rely on the contents of a document had to adduce primary evidence of the contents in the form of the original document. In criminal proceedings a party may now adduce the original or a copy of the document, irrespective of whether the original still exists, provided that the document or copy is authenticated in an approved manner. The Act says nothing further about approved methods of authentication, so it is assumed that the court is intended to have a wide discretion. Clearly in the case of a copy it will be sufficient for a witness with personal knowledge to testify that the copy is a true copy of the original. Many original documents are now in electronic form, such as an email or a posting on a social networking site. The accuracy of this type of document might be established by evidence from the person who created the communication, or from "distinctive characteristics of the material or other circumstantial evidence."[29] It is unclear whether authentication of a document under s 133 has to be proved as a foundation fact,[30] or whether it is sufficient for prima facie evidence of authenticity to be adduced, or whether there must simply be *some* evidence from which authenticity could be inferred.[31]

It ought not to matter whether the contents of the document are relied on for a hearsay purpose, as evidence of the facts stated, or whether they are relied on to show that certain statements were made, such as the terms of a libel.[32] There would be no merit in interpreting the section narrowly to apply only to documentary hearsay,[33] and in *Foxley*,[34] the Court of Appeal assumed without argument that copies of credit notes, adduced as original evidence of payments alleged to be corrupt, were admissible under s.27 of the Criminal Justice Act 1988 (the predecessor of s.133 and couched in almost identical terms).

12–008   Section 133 is not, however, a comprehensive provision for proof of the contents of documents in criminal proceedings. Section 71 of PACE provides that in any proceedings the contents of a document, whether or not the document is still in existence, may be proved by the production of an enlargement of a microfilm copy of the document. Where, under either of these provisions, appropriate copies

---

[28] Criminal Justice Act 2003 s.134(1).

[29] For the latter possibility see M. O'Floinn and D. Ormerod, "Social Networking Material as Criminal Evidence" [2012] Crim. L.R. 486, 489, citing Federal Rules of Evidence r.901(b)(4). For a case of inadequate evidence of authentication see *Skinner* [2005] EWCA Crim 1439, and compare *Saward* [2005] EWCA Crim 3183 at [44].

[30] The authenticity of a tape recording was treated in *Robson* [1972] 1 W.L.R. 651 as a foundation fact to be proved by the prosecution on the balance of probabilities, but the decision is doubted by M. O'Floinn and D. Ormerod, "Social Networking Material as Criminal Evidence" [2012] Crim. L.R. 486, 492, and by Cross and Tapper, p.184.

[31] See R. Pattenden, "Authenticating 'things' in English law: principles for adducing tangible evidence in common law jury trials" (2008) 12 E. & P. 273.

[32] For discussion of the distinction between using out-of-court statements for a hearsay purpose and as "original" evidence, see Ch.16.

[33] There is nothing in s.133 itself to support such a distinction. The only argument for it is that s.133 appears in Ch.2 of Pt 11 of the Criminal Justice Act 2003, and Ch.2 has the sub-heading "Hearsay Evidence".

[34] *Foxley* [1995] 2 Cr.App.R. 523 CA.

of documents are not available, the common law rules relating to proof of documents must apply. These rules also apply where a question arises in any criminal proceedings of giving oral evidence of the contents of a document. Section 133 of the Criminal Justice Act 2003 deals only with proof by means of a copy of the document and does not refer to oral evidence.[35]

(C)   Common law rules

Given their largely residual role in modern law, the common law rules relating to proof of the contents of documents will not be discussed in detail. In summary the rules are as follows. The general rule is that only primary evidence, meaning the original, is admissible as evidence of the contents of a document.[36] The rule has a very long history, dating back to the days when all copying of documents had to be done by hand, and the scope for mistakes and forgeries was considerable. The rule was thus underpinned by the rationale that the original document was the best evidence obtainable and was not subject to the risks of inaccuracy associated with manual copying, or with a witness giving oral evidence of the contents of a document from memory. In modern times this rationale has been comprehensively undermined by developments in technology; first the invention of carbon paper for making simultaneous copies of typewritten documents and, in recent years, the arrival of the photocopier, fax machine and computer. There is now little, if any, justification in most cases for insistence on the original of the document. Even before the introduction of s.27 of the Criminal Justice Act 1988 (the predecessor to s.133 of the Criminal Justice Act 2003) the courts had begun to take a restrictive attitude to the operation of the primary evidence rule. It had been established for many years that a relationship, such as landlord and tenant, which is created by a document, could be proved by evidence other than the original lease.[37] The existence of a document, as opposed to its contents, could be proved by evidence other than the production of the document itself.[38] In *Kajala v Noble*,[39] it was held that the primary evidence rule applied only to written documents in the strict sense and did not apply to "documents" such as tapes and films. Accordingly the Divisional Court held that the prosecution had rightly been allowed to adduce a video recording of the original BBC news film showing the defendant taking part in a riot.[40]

12–009

There are certain exceptions to the common law rule requiring production of the original of a written document. These are all referable to a broad principle of practical necessity, whereby the court will accept secondary evidence if satisfied that the original is genuinely unavailable and the copy or other secondary evidence is authentic. Thus, if the original document has been destroyed or lost,

---

[35] See *Nazeer* [1998] Crim. L.R. 750 (decided under the equivalent provision in s.27 of the Criminal Justice Act 1988), and accompanying Commentary by Professor Birch.
[36] For confirmation and application of the rule, see *Augustien v Challis* (1847) 1 Ex. 279; *MacDonnell v Evans* (1852) 11 C.B. 930.
[37] *R. v Holy Trinity, Kingston-upon-Hull, Inhabitants* (1827) 7 B. & C. 611.
[38] See, e.g. *Elworthy* (1867) L.R. 1 C.C.R. 103.
[39] *Kajala v Noble* (1982) 75 Cr.App.R. 149 DC.
[40] It was BBC policy not to allow original film to leave the Corporation's premises. The Corporation could have been subpoenaed to produce it, but the court clearly felt that this was an unnecessary step.

the party seeking to rely on it may adduce secondary evidence of its contents. Older authorities required the party relying on secondary evidence to show that due search was made for the original; what amounted to due search depended on the circumstances of each case.[41] However, the general approach in modern law is to admit secondary evidence provided there is a reasonable explanation for non-production of the original, and then to make a judgment as to the weight of the evidence.[42] Similarly, if the original is in existence, but it is impossible,[43] or highly inconvenient,[44] to produce it, secondary evidence is admissible of its contents. Again, if the original is in the possession of a third party who lawfully refuses to produce it,[45] or against whom a witness summons cannot be issued,[46] secondary evidence of the contents of the document is admissible. Secondary evidence for the purposes of these exceptions may be a copy of the document, duly authenticated, or it may be oral evidence of the contents of the original document, provided that the witness has first-hand knowledge of the contents.[47]

(D) General statutory provision: civil proceedings

12–010   Section 8 of the Civil Evidence Act 1995 provides:

> "(1)   Where a statement contained in a document is admissible in evidence in civil proceedings, it may be proved—
> (a)   by the production of that document, or
> (b)   whether or not that document is still in existence, by the production of a copy of that document or the material part of it, authenticated in such manner as the court may approve.
> (2)   It is immaterial for this purpose how many removes there are between a copy and the original."

The civil proceedings to which the section applies are "civil proceedings, before any tribunal, in relation to which the strict rules of evidence apply, whether as a matter of law or by agreement of the parties".[48] In all material respects s.8 is identical to s.27 of the Criminal Justice Act 1988, the predecessor to s.133 of the Criminal Justice Act 2003 and worded in almost identical terms. "Document" and

---

[41] *Brewster v Sewell* (1820) 3 B. & Ald. 296. The general principle is that "it is not necessary to negative every possibility . . . it is enough to negative . . . every reasonable probability . . . of anything being kept back": *M'Gahey v Alston* (1836) 2 M. & W. 206 at 214 per Alderson B.

[42] See *Masquerade Music Ltd v Springsteen* [2001] EWCA Civ 563; *Post Office Counters Ltd v Mahida* [2003] EWCA Civ 1583.

[43] Impossibility may be physical, as in the case of an inscription on a wall, or legal, as in the case of a notice that is required by law to remain attached to the wall of a particular place such as a factory (*Owner v Bee Hive Spinning Co Ltd* [1914] 1 K.B. 105).

[44] As in the case of an inscription on a tombstone (*Mortimer v M'Callan* (1840) 6 M. & W. 58 at 58, 63, 72) or a flag or banner (*Hunt* (1820) 3 B. & Ald. 566).

[45] A third party within the jurisdiction of the court can normally be issued with a witness summons to produce the document at trial, but the third party may be able to claim privilege for the document, as in *Mills v Oddy* (1834) 6 C. & P. 728.

[46] Because the third party is outside the jurisdiction (*Kilgour v Owen* (1889) 88 LT. Jo. 7) or is entitled to diplomatic immunity (*Nowaz* [1976] 1 W.L.R. 830). Powers of the English courts to obtain evidence outside the jurisdiction are not dealt with in this book.

[47] See, e.g. *Sugden v Lord St Leonards* (1876) 1 P.D. 154 (daughter of testator giving oral evidence of the contents of her father's will).

[48] Civil Evidence Act 1995 s.11.

"copy" have the same extensive meanings.[49] It follows that s.8 of the Civil Evidence Act 1995 has the same effects in civil proceedings as s.133 of the Criminal Justice Act 2003 has in criminal proceedings, as regards the form in which the contents of a document are proved. The party relying on the document can therefore produce the original or any copy, duly authenticated in an approved manner. It should be noted that a wider range of documents is admissible in civil proceedings, since s.1 of the Civil Evidence Act 1995 abolished the hearsay rule in civil cases, whereas it continues to apply, subject to important exceptions, in criminal cases.[50] However, s.8 of the Civil Evidence Act 1995, like s.133 of the Criminal Justice Act 2003, refers only to original documents and copies of documents. It does not allow in terms for the admission of oral evidence of a statement in a document. It would seem therefore that the abolition of the hearsay rule effected by s.1 has not affected the rules about the form in which the contents of admissible documents can be proved. As regards oral evidence of the contents, the common law continues to apply. This is right as a matter of principle. A party relying on a document should be required to explain the absence of the document (or a copy of it) before being permitted to give oral evidence of the contents.

2. *Proof of the execution of documents*

The general principle is that a party relying on a document must not only prove, in proper form, the contents of the document, but must also prove that the document was duly executed. This normally requires proof that it was made and/or signed by the person who is alleged to be the author and/or signatory, and, where the document is not legally valid unless attested (witnessed), that that person's signature was duly witnessed as required by law. These formal requirements may sometimes be dispensed with. In civil proceedings a party is deemed to admit the authenticity of a document disclosed to him under Pt 31 of the Civil Procedure Rules unless he serves notice that he wishes the document to be proved at trial.[51] Parties can make formal admissions of due execution of documents in criminal proceedings.[52] In the case of public documents, statutes that provide for proof of the contents of such documents by copies generally dispense with the need to prove due execution of the original. A party relying on the document will only need to produce a copy in the appropriate form to have it received in evidence. Even if the need for proof of execution is not dispensed with, there is a rebuttable presumption at common law that official documents that appear on their face to have been properly executed have in fact been properly executed.[53] As regards private documents, the common law presumes due execution in the case of an "ancient document",[54] that is regular on its face

12–011

---

[49] Civil Evidence Act 1995 s.13.
[50] See further Ch.17.
[51] CPR r.32.19(1). See, e.g. *Rall v Hume* [2001] 3 All E.R. 248.
[52] Criminal Justice Act 1967 s.10.
[53] This is an application of the general presumption of regularity, often cited as the Latin maxim *praesumuntur rite esse acta*. See *Phipson on Evidence*, 16th edn (London: Sweet & Maxwell, 2005), para.6–29.
[54] Meaning not less than 20 years old: Evidence Act 1938 s.4. The period at common law was 30 years.

and that is produced from proper custody. Proper custody for this purpose is custody that is reasonable and natural in the circumstances; it does not have to be the best and most proper place of deposit.[55] Other presumptions applying to all documents are that a document is presumed to have been executed on the date that it bears,[56] and that any alterations to a document were made before its execution.[57]

(A) Proof of handwriting and signatures

12–012　Where it is necessary to prove that a document was written or signed by a particular person there are three ways of doing this. The easiest and most obvious way is by direct evidence from the person in question that he wrote or signed as the case may be, or by direct evidence from someone else who saw the person writing or signing the document. The second possibility is evidence from someone familiar with the handwriting of the person in question. A non-expert witness can give opinion evidence identifying a person's handwriting provided the witness has had adequate means of acquiring personal knowledge of it.[58] This is a question of degree: the witness must have had a sufficient opportunity to become familiar with the handwriting, but the capacity in which the witness did so is immaterial, and it is not necessary that the witness ever saw the person in question write.

The third possibility is by comparison, often assisted by a witness able to give an expert opinion. Section 8 of the Criminal Procedure Act 1865, which applies to both civil and criminal proceedings, provides:

> "Comparison of a disputed writing with any writing proved to the satisfaction of the judge to be genuine shall be permitted to be made by witnesses; and such writings, and the evidence of witnesses respecting the same, may be submitted to the court and jury as evidence of the genuineness or otherwise of the writing in dispute."

This provision requires the sample offered for the purpose of comparison to be proved to "the satisfaction of the judge" to be genuine. The standard of proof required follows the normal rules. It therefore differs according to whether the proceedings are civil, when the test of the balance of probabilities applies, or criminal, when proof of genuineness beyond reasonable doubt is required.[59]

12–013　The statute does not say that evidence of comparison by a witness is always necessary. It seems to envisage that, once the judge is satisfied as to the genuineness of the sample, the sample and the disputed writing may simply be compared by the factfinder. Even if a witness as to comparison is called, there is

---

[55] *Meath (Bishop) v Marquess of Winchester* (1836) 3 Bing. N.C. 183 (papers belonging to a deceased bishop by virtue of his office held to be in "proper custody" when found among his private papers in the possession of his family, even though they ought to have been in the possession of his successor as bishop).

[56] *Anderson v Weston* (1840) 6 Bing. N.C. 296.

[57] Unless the document is a will, in which case the presumption is that any alterations were made after execution, because they would not then invalidate the entire will. See *Doe d. Tatum v Catomore* (1851) 16 Q.B. 745.

[58] *Doe d. Mudd v Suckermore* (1837) 5 Ad. & El. 703.

[59] *Ewing* [1983] Q.B. 1039 CA.

[502]

no express requirement that the witness should be an expert. However, the opinion of a non-expert who has no previous familiarity with the handwriting in question seems to have little, if any, more weight than the opinion of the tribunal of fact itself. Moreover, there are obvious dangers in letting an uninstructed tribunal loose on this kind of comparison without help, and in criminal cases it has been held that a jury should not be invited to make a comparison of handwriting without the benefit of expert evidence.[60]

D.   REAL EVIDENCE

We have seen that a court can receive evidence in the form of the oral testimony of a witness or of a duly authenticated document. A third way in which evidence can be presented is in the form of real evidence. This is a term used to refer to physical objects produced for the court's inspection. When a factfinder acts on real evidence it acts on its own perceptions of the nature and qualities of the object in question, although this does not of course prevent a witness from testifying as to the significance of the object, for example in relation to the bloodstains on a weapon produced as an exhibit. "Real evidence" is not a term of art, and there is no authoritative definition of what it includes. Most writers would accept that it embraces material objects, the appearance of persons, the demeanour of witnesses, views of machinery, buildings and landscapes, and various types of mechanical record and output that do not involve the intervention of a human mind.

12–014

1.   *Material objects*

Where the nature or quality of a material object is a fact in issue, or an evidentiary fact, the object itself is relevant and admissible as an item of evidence. Thus an allegedly offensive weapon might well be produced in evidence to enable the factfinder to observe at first hand whether it is an article "adapted to cause injury".[61] In *Line v Taylor*,[62] which concerned an action against the defendant for keeping a vicious dog, the trial judge permitted the dog to be brought into court so that the jury could assess its temper for themselves, based on their own experience of dogs and their observation of this particular animal. In modern cases involving disputes about the ownership of animals, judges have permitted a parrot,[63] and cats,[64] to be in court so that their reactions to persons claiming to be their rightful owners could be observed. No particular formalities are necessary for the proof of material objects, although evidence identifying the object will be necessary from the witness producing it.[65] It appears that the primary evidence rule for documents does not apply. Secondary and oral

12–015

---

[60] *Harden* [1963] 1 Q.B. 8 CCA. See also *Tilley* [1961] 1 W.L.R. 1309 CCA.
[61] Prevention of Crime Act 1953 s.1(4).
[62] *Line v Taylor* (1862) 3 F. & F. 731.
[63] *The Times*, February 16, 1995.
[64] *The Times*, April 26, 1995.
[65] See generally R. Pattenden, "Authenticating 'things' in English law: principles for adducing tangible evidence in common law jury trials" (2008) 12 E. & P. 273.

evidence of the object is admissible,[66] although a party would be well advised to produce the thing itself if it is feasible to do so. A failure to produce any evidence of a material object may be the subject of an adverse inference where appropriate.[67]

2. *Appearance of persons*

12–016 A person's physical appearance may have probative value in many different ways. Characteristics such as height, build, colouring, the presence of facial hair or scars, etc. may all be important in identification cases; the pitch of a person's voice or the possession of a particular accent might also provide evidence of identity. Hale said that a physical deformity such as a rupture would almost inevitably lead to the conclusion that the man in question was not guilty of rape.[68] A physical resemblance between a child and its alleged father is some evidence of parentage, although it may have very little weight, depending on the circumstances.[69] A court may also permit injuries or wounds to be exhibited to establish their nature and extent, but there is considerable potential for prejudice in doing this, particularly in criminal cases, and such evidence might well be excluded for this reason if there is other, less emotive evidence of the injuries. A film taken out of court of the claimant in a personal injuries action is admissible to show the extent of a disability, or even that the claimant's symptoms are faked.[70]

3. *Demeanour of witnesses*

12–017 The common law has traditionally regarded the demeanour of a witness as relevant to the witness's credibility. The attitude of the witness, and the way the witness answers questions—whether he or she is clear or confused, helpful or evasive, confident or nervous, etc—have been thought to be useful guides to the weight that can be placed on the witness's evidence. This is shown by the frequent refusal of appeal courts to reverse decisions of fact at trial on the ground that the trial court had the opportunity to see and hear the witnesses in the case. Another indication of the importance attached to demeanour is found in the

---

[66] *Francis* (1874) L.R. 2 C.C.R. 128.

[67] *Francis* (1874) L.R. 2 C.C.R. 128.

[68] Sir M. Hale, *Pleas of the Crown*, Vol.1 p.635.

[69] *Slingsby v Att-Gen* (1916) 33 T.L.R. 120; *C v C and C* [1972] 1 W.L.R. 1335 (where photographic evidence of resemblance was admitted).

[70] This can of course also be demonstrated in court. A story, possibly apocryphal, is told of a case in which the plaintiff claimed that an accident had severely restricted the mobility of his right arm. Counsel for the defendant, in an appropriately sympathetic manner, asked the plaintiff to demonstrate how far he could now raise his arm. With much wincing the plaintiff gingerly raised his arm to the level of his shoulder. In the same sympathetic way counsel then asked the plaintiff to show how far he could raise his arm before the accident. With an expression of triumph the plaintiff promptly shot his arm straight up in the air.

rationales for the hearsay rule; a standard justification for excluding hearsay is that the factfinder has no opportunity for observing the demeanour of the person making the hearsay statement.[71]

When a court takes note of a witness's demeanour it is in effect observing for itself an evidentiary fact. The demeanour is an item of information from which inferences may be drawn about the probative value of the testimony, in the same way as inferences might be drawn from proof, for example, that the witness has previous convictions for perjury. Accordingly, demeanour is rightly treated as an item of real evidence analogous to the appearance of persons and the observable qualities of an object.

4.   *Views and reconstructions*

A view is an inspection by the court of an object or place outside the courtroom during the course of a trial. Objects inspected in this way include, for example, things that it is impossible or inconvenient to produce in court, such as vehicles and factory machines. Similarly, visits by the court to the scene of an accident or a crime,[72] or to land that is the subject of litigation, may take place during a trial. In *Tito v Waddell*,[73] Megarry J., together with the parties and counsel, visited an island in the Pacific Ocean alleged to have been rendered uninhabitable by phosphate mining.

12–018

Views frequently involve reconstructions. For example, witnesses may indicate where they were standing or what they were doing at the material time, or the operation of a machine may be demonstrated. In *Buckingham v Daily News Ltd*,[74] the plaintiff sued his employers in respect of injuries he suffered while cleaning a machine at his place of work. The court inspected the machine and watched a demonstration of its operation. The Court of Appeal held that the trial judge had been entitled to take into account the opinion he had formed when making the view. It was said that the situation was the same as if the machine had been brought into court and a demonstration had been made in the well of the court. Birkett L.J. expressed agreement with the statement by Denning L.J. in *Goold v Evans and Co*,[75] that a view was as much part of the evidence as an exhibit: "It is real evidence. The tribunal sees the real thing instead of having a drawing or a photograph of it".[76] Because the court is receiving evidence at a view it follows that the judge, the parties, their legal advisers and the jury, if there

---

[71] This, along with the other rationales for the hearsay rule, is discussed in Ch.16. For a sceptical discussion of the significance of demeanour see M. Stone, "Instant Lie Detection? Demeanour and Credibility in Criminal Trials" [1991] Crim. L.R. 821, who argues that there is no sound basis from physiology or psychology for assessing credibility from demeanour.

[72] As in *Sawoniuk* [2000] 2 Cr.App.R. 220, discussed and criticised by D. Ormerod, "A Prejudicial View?" [2000] Crim. L.R. 452.

[73] *Tito v Waddell* [1975] 1 W.L.R. 1303.

[74] *Buckingham v Daily News Ltd* [1956] 2 Q.B. 534 CA.

[75] *Goold v Evans and Co* [1951] 2 T.L.R. 1189.

[76] cf. the opinion of Hodson L.J. in the same case that a view was no more than a means of interpreting evidence given in court.

is one, should all be present.[77] Even if no demonstration is involved, and a judge simply wishes to see a public place in order better to understand the evidence given in court, the judge should not do this informally, but should give the parties notice of the proposed visit. The parties then have an opportunity to deal with points arising at the view and to indicate any features that may have changed since the events in question.[78]

Demonstrations and reconstructions may present problems of relevance and admissibility. In *Quinn and Bloom*,[79] discussed in Ch.3, the Court of Criminal Appeal upheld a trial judge's refusal to admit a filmed reconstruction of an allegedly obscene striptease performance, on the ground that its accuracy was impossible to assess. The evidence was therefore insufficiently relevant. This can be compared with *Thomas*,[80] where a police video of the route of a car chase was held to have been rightly admitted as relevant to the issue of the accused's reckless driving. Where the accused himself re-enacts a crime at the invitation of the police, the re-enactment is the visual equivalent of a verbal confession, and will accordingly be admissible under the exception to the hearsay rule for confessions,[81] provided that the conditions for the admissibility of a confession have been complied with.[82]

5. *Mechanical recordings and computer output*

12–019   Mechanical recordings, of a variety of types, are an increasingly common form of evidence in both civil and criminal litigation. Some examples have already been referred to, and there are many others. Still photographs, audiotapes, film, videotapes and computer printouts may all record events and information relevant to legal proceedings. Security cameras may record the actual commission of an offence, interviews in police stations are routinely tape-recorded, computers may make electronic records of the serial numbers of banknotes, purchases at shop tills, cash withdrawals from banks, and so on. Two issues arise regarding the use of such recordings in evidence. The first is their admissibility, and in particular the extent to which they are subject to the hearsay rule. The second, which arises on the assumption that particular recordings are admissible, is whether there are any formal requirements for admission that must be complied with.[83]

The general rules of admissibility apply equally to mechanical recordings as they do to any other items of evidence. If what is recorded is relevant to the issues in the case, then the recording is prima facie admissible. This approach has been

---

[77] See *Salusbury v Woodland* [1970] 1 Q.B. 324; *Hunter* [1985] 1 W.L.R. 613; *R. v Ely Justices Ex p. Burgess* [1992] Crim. L.R. 888.

[78] *Salusbury v Woodland* [1970] 1 Q.B. 324; *Parry v Boyle* (1986) 83 Cr.App.R. 310.

[79] *Quinn and Bloom* [1962] 2 Q.B. 245 CCA.

[80] *Thomas* [1986] Crim. L.R. 682 CA.

[81] *Li Shu-Ling v R.* [1989] A.C. 270 PC.

[82] *Lam Chi-Ming v R.* [1991] 2 A.C. 212 PC (the defendant's oral confession to murder by stabbing was inadmissible because it was obtained by oppression; a film made two days later in which the defendant demonstrated how he had thrown the knife into Hong Kong harbour was tainted by the earlier oppression and was also inadmissible).

[83] On the question of authentication of such evidence see the article by Pattenden, "Authenticating 'things' in English law" (2008) 12 E. & P. 273, 290–292.

made clear in a series of cases in which the courts have plainly been aware of the evidential advantages offered by developments in technology.[84] In the leading case of *Maqsud Ali*,[85] the police had covertly tape-recorded an incriminating conversation between two men suspected of murder. The Court of Criminal Appeal held that the trial judge had rightly admitted the tape-recording in evidence. Noting that the courts had admitted photographs in evidence for many years, Marshall J. said that there was no difference in principle between a photograph and a tape-recording. The former "reproduced by means of mechanical and chemical devices" things seen with the naked eye or with the aid of telescopes or binoculars. The latter was the product of a device for picking up, transmitting and recording conversations. This was a strong case, since the original recorded conversation was in Punjabi, and the trial judge had admitted a copy of the tape in the form of a transcript containing an English translation, the accuracy of which had to be verified by the translator. Subsequently, in *The Statue of Liberty*,[86] the court permitted the plaintiff in an action arising out of a collision between two ships to adduce evidence of a film showing radar echoes recorded automatically by a shore radar station. Sir Jocelyn Simon P. reasoned that if tape-recordings were admissible, as they had been held to be in *Maqsud Ali*,[87] then a photograph of radar reception, or any other type of photograph, was equally admissible. No distinction could be made between cases where recording machines were manually operated and cases where the recording mechanism was triggered automatically. Similarly, photographs taken by an automatic security camera of a robbery at a building society are admissible because they are relevant to the issues of whether an offence was committed and who committed it[88]; news film of a violent demonstration is admissible for the same reason.[89]

The hearsay rule will affect a mechanical recording only if the recording consists of or contains a statement by a *person* other than while giving oral testimony that is offered as evidence of the facts stated. In the case of a tape-recording of an incriminating conversation or interview, the statements on tape by the accused are clearly caught by the rule, although they will be admissible nonetheless by virtue of the exception for informal admissions by parties to litigation. In the case of photographs of the commission of crimes the visual images are not hearsay if the purpose of adducing them is to show the performance of the relevant acts and the identity of the actors. No statements by anyone are being relied on in such a case. These examples are straightforward. More complicated are cases involving material generated by computers. In deciding whether the admission of a computer printout contravenes the hearsay rule the court will have to determine the function that the computer was performing, and the source of the information on which it performed that function. If it was recording and then printing out material keyed into it by a

---

[84] *Maqsud Ali* [1966] 1 Q.B. 688 CCA (audiotapes); *The Statue of Liberty* [1968] 1 W.L.R. 739 (radar tracings); *Kajala v Noble* (1982) 75 Cr.App.R. 149 DC (news film); *Dodson and Williams* (1984) 79 Cr.App.R. 220 CA (security camera photographs); *Re G* [1987] 1 W.L.R. 1461 (video recordings).
[85] *Maqsud Ali* [1966] 1 Q.B. 688 CCA.
[86] *The Statue of Liberty* [1968] 1 W.L.R. 739.
[87] *Maqsud Ali* [1966] 1 Q.B. 688 CCA. See also *Senat and Sin* (1968) 52 Cr.App.R. 282 CA.
[88] *Dodson and Williams* (1984) 79 Cr.App.R. 220 CA.
[89] *Kajala v Noble* (1982) 75 Cr.App.R. 149 DC.

human operator, then the contents of the printout represent information that "has passed through a human mind", and the printout will be hearsay if it is sought to rely on the printout as containing true statements. On the other hand, if the computer was operating as no more than a mechanical calculator, then the printout it produces is an item of real evidence that is admitted as "original" evidence. Accordingly, the test record printout produced by an automatic breath-testing device is not hearsay, but is admissible as real evidence.[90] Similarly, in *Spiby*,[91] the Court of Appeal held that the hearsay rule did not extend to the printout from a device that automatically recorded the numbers to which telephone calls were made; nothing in the operation of the device depended on any "input of information provided by the human mind".[92] Even if a document produced by a computer constitutes hearsay because it contains such an input, it may still be admissible under the provisions for the admission of hearsay in the Criminal Justice Act 2003.[93] Note, however, that s.129 of these provisions has the effect that where a representation of fact is made by a machine, and the representation depends for its accuracy on information supplied by a person, the representation is not admissible as evidence of the fact unless it is proved that the information was accurate.

12–020   As regards the form in which evidence of recordings is admitted, mechanical recordings are "documents" for the purposes of s.133 of the Criminal Justice Act 2003 and s.8 of the Civil Evidence Act 1995. Duly authenticated copies are therefore admissible whether or not the original recording is still in existence.[94] In any event, at common law the best evidence rule was held not to apply to these forms of document,[95] so there is no general requirement to produce the original. If a suitable copy is not available, oral evidence of the contents of the recording may be admissible. In *Taylor v Chief Constable of Cheshire*,[96] police officers had watched a video recording of an incident of shoplifting. They identified the defendants, whom they knew, from the recording. When the videotape was accidentally erased before the trial the officers were permitted to give oral evidence of its contents. The Divisional Court held that their evidence was direct evidence of the commission of the offence in the same way as the evidence of a security officer who had directly observed the action of the alleged shoplifter. Questions about the quality of the recording, and about the reliability of the officers' recollection of it, were regarded therefore as affecting the weight of their

---

[90]   *Castle v Cross* [1985] 1 All E.R. 87 DC.

[91]   *Spiby* (1990) 91 Cr.App.R. 186 CA.

[92]   The phrase used by Lord Griffiths in *Shephard* [1993] A.C. 380 at 384. For other examples of computer-produced real evidence, see *Wood* (1982) 76 Cr.App.R. 110 CA (computer calculation of the composition of certain metals); *Shephard* [1993] A.C. 380 HL (till rolls produced by computerised checkouts using barcodes to identify goods sold). See also *R. v Governor of Brixton Prison Ex p. Levin* [1997] 3 W.L.R. 117 HL. In *Pettigrew* (1980) 71 Cr.App.R. 39 the Court of Appeal held that a computer record of the serial numbers of banknotes fed into the computer was hearsay (although admissible nonetheless under s.1(1)(a) of the Criminal Evidence Act 1965); it is generally agreed that this reasoning was wrong since no statement by any person formed part of the record.

[93]   See Ch.17.

[94]   On authentication of a copy where computer screen images were copied electronically to another computer, see *Skinner* [2005] EWCA Crim 1439; [2006] Crim. L.R. 56.

[95]   *Kajala v Noble* (1982) 75 Cr.App.R. 149.

[96]   *Taylor v Chief Constable of Cheshire* [1987] 1 All E.R. 225 DC.

evidence rather than its admissibility, although Ralph Gibson L.J. went on to say that "when the film or recording is not available, or is not produced, the court will, and in my view must, hesitate and consider very carefully indeed before finding themselves made sure of guilt on such evidence".[97] In *Attorney-General's Reference (No.2 of 2002)*,[98] the Court of Appeal approved the decision in *Taylor v Chief Constable of Cheshire*, but confirmed that the position is different where the witness is able to identify the defendant, not on the basis of recognition of a person known to the witness, but on the basis of a detailed analysis the witness has made comparing the photographic images from the scene with a reasonably contemporary photograph of the defendant. In such a case both the original images and the photograph used for the comparison must be available for the jury.

In civil proceedings r.33.6 of the Civil Procedure Rules requires a party to give notice of intention to adduce evidence (such as a plan, photograph or model) that is not contained in a witness statement, affidavit or expert's report, or is not to be given orally at trial, or is not hearsay evidence of which prior notice must be given under r.33.2. The object of the notice is to give the other parties an opportunity to inspect the evidence and to agree to its admission without further proof. If the notice is not given the evidence is not receivable at trial unless the court orders otherwise. It seems clear that this rule is not restricted to plans, photographs and models, but will include other forms of evidence not in writing such as films, tapes, and so on. Pre-trial disclosure of such evidence is the norm under the modern approach to civil litigation. In a personal injuries case, for example, a party will not be permitted to hold back evidence until trial for tactical reasons.[99]

Where evidence is in the form of a document produced by a computer there are no longer any formal requirements of proof that the computer was functioning properly when it produced the document in question. When the possibility of computer-produced evidence first emerged in the 1960s there was a good deal of concern about the reliability of such evidence. This led to some quite elaborate statutory regulation intended to provide guarantees of accuracy.[100] However, as the use of computers became more widespread, and many more people became familiar with their operation, so the fear of unreliability and of the production of inaccurate documents diminished. The statutory formalities were increasingly seen as both unnecessary and difficult to comply with, a view that eventually persuaded the Law Commission to propose the repeal of the relevant provisions without replacement.[101] These recommendations have now been carried into effect.[102]

---

[97] *Taylor v Chief Constable of Cheshire* [1987] 1 All E.R. 225 at 230.

[98] *Attorney-General's Reference (No.2 of 2002)* [2002] EWCA Crim 2373; [2003] Crim. L.R. 192.

[99] See *Khan v Armaguard Ltd* [1994] 3 All E.R. 545 CA, decided under the old RSC Ord.38 r.5.

[100] Civil Evidence Act 1968 s.5; PACE s.69.

[101] See Law Com. No.216, *The Hearsay Rule in Civil Proceedings* (1993), para.4.43; Law Com. No.245, *Evidence in Criminal Proceedings: Hearsay and Related Topics* (1997), para.13.23.

[102] The Civil Evidence Act 1968 s.5 was repealed by the Civil Evidence Act 1995. PACE s.69 was repealed by s.60 of the Youth Justice and Criminal Evidence Act 1999.

12–021   In the absence of formal statutory requirements it appears, as the Law Commission suggested,[103] that the courts will apply the presumption of proper functioning of machines.[104] This means that when a party adduces evidence of a computer-produced document, the party may rely on a presumption that the computer was operating properly at the material time. An evidential burden is then on the party objecting to the admission of the document to produce some evidence to show that it was not. In the event of the issue of proper functioning being successfully raised, the burden will be on the party relying on the document to prove by evidence that the computer was operating properly. In accordance with the usual rules in criminal proceedings,[105] if the prosecution have this burden they will have to prove the matter beyond reasonable doubt, whereas if the defence have the burden the standard of proof will be the balance of probabilities.

E. FORMAL ADMISSIONS

12–022   In both civil and criminal proceedings parties may make formal admissions of fact for the purposes of the proceedings. A formal admission is a form of proof in itself rather than an item of evidence from which inferences may be drawn.[106] Its function is to absolve the party who would otherwise have the burden of proof of the fact in question from the necessity to adduce any evidence of the fact. The existence of the fact is taken to be conclusively established. Because the fact is no longer in issue evidence as to its existence is not only not required it is not even admissible. Formal admissions bind the party who makes them. The party will not be permitted to contradict them, although they may be withdrawn with the leave of the court.

In civil proceedings formal admissions can be made under the Civil Procedure Rules at various stages of the proceedings.[107] The incentive to make admissions in civil litigation is the costs factor. A party who unreasonably puts an opponent to proof of a fact that is not seriously in dispute may well be ordered to pay the costs involved, even if the party refusing to admit the fact is ultimately successful in the litigation.

In criminal proceedings both the prosecution and the defence can make formal admissions under s.10 of the Criminal Justice Act 1967. A fact formally admitted by either party under the section "shall as against that party be conclusive

---

[103] Law Com. No.245 paras 13.13 and 13.14.

[104] *Castle v Cross* [1985] 1 All E.R. 87. This is an important presumption in practice and its application is not unproblematic; see, e.g. *Kelly Communications Ltd v DPP* [2002] EWHC Admin 2752; and the Commentary in [2003] Crim. L.R. 479 and 875.

[105] See Ch.11.

[106] Unlike an informal admission by a party, which is admissible in evidence as an exception to the hearsay rule; see Ch.17. An informal admission is not binding on its maker, who is entitled to try to explain it away if possible.

[107] See CPR rr.14.1(1) and (2) (notice in writing); 16.5(1)(c) (admission in the party's defence); 18.1 and 26.5(3) (in response to a written request, or court order, to give additional information); 32.18 (in response to a notice to admit facts).

evidence in those proceedings of the fact admitted".[108] A formal admission must be in writing if made pre-trial; if made at trial it can be made orally or in writing. An important safeguard for defendants is that any pre-trial formal admissions they make must be approved by their counsel or solicitor. The main rationale for admissions in criminal proceedings is efficiency. The Criminal Law Revision Committee, which proposed the provision in s.10,[109] argued that there was no need to insist on formal proof of facts that were not in dispute. If the common law rule was maintained, that a defendant could never waive the rules of evidence by consent in a criminal case,[110] a considerable waste of time and money could be incurred. In some cases considerations of justice and fairness may prompt the prosecution to make formal admissions. An example of a case in which the prosecution made important formal admissions is *Blastland*,[111] discussed in Ch.3.

F. PRESUMPTIONS

1. *Nature and classification of presumptions*

The term "presumption" is used in more than one way in the law of evidence. Sometimes the term is simply a method of stating specific rules about the allocation of the burden of proof. In this usage it indicates that a certain conclusion must be drawn or a certain state of affairs must be taken to exist at the beginning of the case, and this conclusion continues to be presumed until the contrary is proved. Thus one usage of the "presumption of innocence" refers to the rule that the legal burden of proving guilt rests on the prosecution in criminal proceedings; if the prosecution cannot discharge this burden to the required standard of proof the accused must be acquitted. Similarly, the "presumption of sanity" refers to the rule that a person accused of an offence is taken to be sane until he discharges the burden of proving that he was insane at the time of the offence. The language of presumption adds nothing to the substance of these rules about the allocation of the burden of proof, but the phrases "presumption of innocence" and "presumption of sanity" are convenient shorthand expressions.

12–023

Two further points should be made about the presumption of innocence. Sometimes this term is used in a wider sense to denote a major principle of political morality about the relationship between the state and the citizen. In this usage the presumption is a normative principle that can generate or support other rules of evidence, such as the privilege against self-incrimination.[112]

Secondly, it is essential to avoid the misconceptions that the presumption of innocence is an item of evidence in itself, or that it expresses any kind of proposition about the probability of the facts in issue. Suppose that a defendant is charged with robbery, and that eyewitnesses have identified him as the man who held up a post office at gunpoint. When the jury evaluate the evidence in the case

---

[108] Criminal Justice Act 1967 s.10(1). Note that the fact formally admitted must be one of which direct oral evidence could have been given.
[109] *Ninth Report on Evidence*, Cmnd.3145 (1966).
[110] See, e.g. *Attorney-General for New South Wales v Bertrand* (1867) L.R. 1 PC 520.
[111] *Blastland* [1986] A.C. 41 HL.
[112] See further Ch.5.

they do not include in the evidence as a separate item an assumption that the defendant is in fact innocent.[113] They take the evidence on its merits to see what conclusions about guilt or innocence can be drawn from it. Only *after* these conclusions have been drawn does the presumption of innocence—the burden of proof of guilt—become relevant in determining whether the defendant should be convicted on those conclusions.

12–024   Sometimes rules of substantive law are stated in presumptive form. It was a rule at one time that a boy under 14 was conclusively presumed to be incapable of committing the crime of rape.[114] That rule could equally well have been stated in terms that a boy under 14 could not be guilty of rape as a principal offender. The language of "presumption" added nothing to the rule.

The main and most helpful use of the term "presumption" is in connection with the drawing of inferences from proof of certain facts. A presumption is a conclusion that fact B may or must be presumed to exist once fact A has been proved; for purposes of discussion it is convenient to refer to fact A as the "basic fact" and fact B as the "presumed fact". Presumptions in this sense operate as a means of discharging burdens of proof. By stipulating the weight of certain inferences, presumptions may have the effect of dispensing with the need for further evidence of the presumed fact.

There are numerous presumptions that vary widely in their subject-matter, and it is beyond the scope of this book to describe and discuss them all in detail. Certain common characteristics are worth noting. The rationale of any particular presumption is generally based on one or more factors of logic, convenience and policy. For example, where the paternity of a child is in issue, the common law presumption of legitimacy states that on proof of the basic fact of the birth of the child to a married woman during lawful wedlock the child is presumed to be the legitimate offspring of the parties to the marriage until the contrary is proved.[115] This is supported by the logical argument, grounded in general experience, that children born during marriage are usually legitimate, and by the social policy that children should not lightly be found to be illegitimate. Another presumption at common law relates to proof of the death of a person. Where certain basic facts are proved—that there is no acceptable evidence that X was alive at some time during a continuous period of seven years, that there are persons likely to have heard of X if he were alive, that those persons have not heard of X during the period of seven years, and that all due enquiries have been made appropriate to the circumstances—then X will be presumed to have died.[116]

There is no particular logic in the figure of seven years' absence.[117] This presumption is based largely on convenience. It enables legal affairs, such as the

---

[113] For an instructive case where even the Supreme Court of the United States made this elementary error: see *Coffin v US* (1895) 156 U.S. 432.

[114] The rule was abolished by the Sexual Offences Act 1993 s.1.

[115] *Phipson*, 16th edn (2005), paras 6–22 and 6–23, where the authorities are collected.

[116] *Chard v Chard* [1956] P. 259.

[117] The absence of X for a period of less than 7 years may give rise to an inference of fact that X is dead. The point about 7 years' absence is that the law then gives what might otherwise be an inference of fact artificial weight by inflating the inference into a presumption of law. See further Law of

status of a marriage or the distribution of property, to be settled within a reasonable timescale; this is further supported by the need to minimise the continuing anxiety and insecurity likely to be caused to the person's family if it is not clear whether the person is alive or dead.

The common law traditionally classified presumptions into presumptions of fact **12–025** and presumptions of law, with a further subdivision of the latter into rebuttable and irrebuttable presumptions. A more useful classification is one that aims to explain more precisely the effect of presumptions on legal and evidential burdens in civil and criminal proceedings. This classification is as follows:

(a) *Provisional presumptions*—these correspond to the common law's category of presumptions of fact. They denote a conclusion that *may* be drawn from proof of the basic fact of the presumption, but the factfinder is under no obligation to draw the conclusion, even in the absence of any rebutting evidence. However, the factfinder is likely to draw the relevant conclusion and accept the presumed fact as true if its existence is not challenged by the party disputing the presumption. In this way the presumption imposes a "provisional" or "tactical" burden on the party against whom it is operating. That party will generally need to respond by adducing some evidence to rebut the presumed fact. An example of this type of presumption is the presumption of intention: once the basic fact is proved that a certain event was the natural and probable consequence of the defendant's act, the defendant may be presumed to have intended or foreseen that consequence, but s.8 of the Criminal Justice Act 1967 states expressly that a court or jury is not bound in law to draw this inference.

(b) *Evidential presumptions*—these are a subdivision of the common law's category of rebuttable presumptions of law. They denote a conclusion that *must* be drawn by the factfinder on proof of the basic fact of the presumption in the absence of any evidence to the contrary. An illustrative example is the presumption of testamentary capacity. Once the basic fact has been proved that the testator duly executed an apparently rational will, it will be presumed as a fact that the testator was sane when he executed it. This is a conclusion that the factfinder is obliged to draw unless the party disputing the will discharges an evidential burden of adducing sufficient evidence to raise the issue of whether the presumed fact is true. In accordance with the normal rules, this means that there must be enough evidence to the contrary to justify a finding in favour of the party bearing the evidential burden if the case stopped at that point. In civil cases this amounts to saying that the party disputing the will would have to show that the probabilities were equal that the testator was sane or insane when he made the will. If this evidential burden is discharged, then the legal burden resting on the party relying on the will to prove the testator's testamentary capacity will come back into play. Further evidence of the testator's

---

Property Act 1925 s.184(1) for the statutory presumption regarding the order in which deaths are presumed to occur where this is uncertain on the facts, but needs to be resolved for the purposes of settling title to property.

rationality at the time is likely to be necessary, and eventually the factfinder will have to decide the issue of capacity without the aid of presumptions.[118]

(c) *Persuasive presumptions*—these are a second subdivision of the common law's rebuttable presumptions of law. They denote a conclusion that *must* be drawn by the factfinder on proof of the basic fact of the presumption unless and until the conclusion is disproved by the party disputing it. These presumptions accordingly operate to place a legal, as opposed to an evidential, burden on the party challenging the presumed fact. If the factfinder is left in doubt at the conclusion of all the evidence this legal burden will be decisive. An example of a persuasive persumption is the presumption of legitimacy referred to above. At common law this was one of the strongest presumptions that required rebuttal to a very high standard of proof,[119] but s.26 of the Family Law Reform Act 1969 now provides:

> "Any presumption of law as to the legitimacy or illegitimacy of any person may in any civil proceedings be rebutted by evidence which shows that it is more probable than not that the person is illegitimate or legitimate as the case may be and it shall not be necessary to prove that fact beyond reasonable doubt in order to rebut the presumption."

(d) *Conclusive presumptions*—these can be mentioned briefly for the sake of convenience. They correspond to the common law's irrebuttable presumptions of law, and denote conclusions that must be drawn by the factfinder on proof of the basic fact of the presumption. Since no evidence is admissible to rebut them they function in the same way as rules of law that are not stated in the language of presumptions.

This classification is only a guide to the operation of different types of presumption. It is based on formal concepts, and it is necessary to make two important qualifications about its practical application. The first is that in its pure form it is applicable only to presumptions operating in civil proceedings. In criminal cases the *Woolmington*[120] rule states that the burden of proving guilt is always on the prosecution. The only exceptions where the onus is reversed are the common law defence of insanity, and express and implied statutory exceptions. It is generally agreed therefore that presumptions in criminal cases can never operate to place more than an evidential burden on the accused. If the defendant is charged with incest with his daughter, and claims that she is his wife's child by another man, he will not bear a legal burden of proof of that fact. If the presumption of legitimacy applies at all, it can only have the effect that the defendant will need to discharge only an evidential burden of adducing sufficient evidence to raise a reasonable doubt about legitimacy in order to displace the presumption. In *Dillon v R.*,[121] the Privy Council went further and held that the prosecution cannot rely on presumptions to prove facts central to an offence. That case concerned a charge against a police officer of negligently permitting the escape of two persons in lawful custody. The prosecution failed to adduce any evidence of the lawfulness of the custody, and the Privy Council held that the

---

[118] See *Sutton v Sadler* (1857) 3 C.B.N.S. 87.
[119] *Preston-Jones v Preston-Jones* [1951] A.C. 391 HL; cf. *Blyth v Blyth (No.2)* [1966] A.C. 643 HL.
[120] *Woolmington* [1935] A.C. 462 HL.
[121] *Dillon v R.* [1982] A.C. 484 PC.

prosecution could not rely on the presumption of regularity—*praesumuntur rite esse acta*—to make good the deficiency. If the presumption did not apply it followed that the defendant had to be acquitted since there was no evidence capable of proving beyond reasonable doubt that the custody was lawful. The mere fact that the persons in question were in custody was insufficient. In other cases, even if no presumptions of law can apply, proof of the basic facts of a presumption may be sufficient to support an inference of fact. In the hypothetical example of the legitimacy of the defendant's daughter, her legitimacy could be logically inferred as a fact from proof of her birth during her mother's marriage to the defendant, even if that conclusion could not be presumed.

This leads on to the second qualification. The strength of any conclusion of fact, whether inferred or presumed from a basic fact, varies considerably from case to case depending on the circumstances. The inference in some examples of provisional presumptions may be very strong and virtually impossible to displace. Suppose that D is filmed by a hidden security camera fixing a bomb under P's car shortly before P is due to drive off. The bomb explodes five minutes after P drives off, reducing the car to fragments and killing P. If the jury believe on the basis of expert evidence that the bomb was virtually guaranteed to kill the occupant of the car, the inference that D intended to kill P is overwhelming. On the other hand, the strength of the presumed fact in some examples of persuasive presumptions may in the circumstances be extremely weak and easily displaced. Consider the issue of the legitimacy of a child born to W while she was still married to H, but in circumstances where she had left him 12 months earlier to begin living with X in Australia. The legal presumption that H is the father is decisively rebutted by the evidence of W's cohabitation with X at the time of conception. **12–026**

The compatibility of presumptions with art.6(2) of the ECHR is dealt with in Ch.11.

2. *Particular presumptions and proof of frequently recurring facts*

Many common law presumptions are designed to help proof of facts that frequently recur in litigation, in circumstances where other evidence of those facts may be lacking, or difficult to obtain, or unduly time-consuming and expensive, or essentially a formality. For example, two of the best-known rebuttable presumptions of law, those relating to proof of marriage and of death,[122] were developed at a time before the introduction of statutory systems of registration, when parish records might be incomplete or missing or simply hard to get hold of. With the advent of statutory registration, and its accompanying provisions for proof of marriage and death by production of the relevant certificates, these presumptions are now very much less important in practice than they used to be. Hence further details of them are not discussed in this book. **12–027**

---

[122] A report by the House of Commons Justice Committee, *Presumption of Death* (2012) has recommended legislation to clarify the legal position in relation to a person who has been missing for several years.

Other important presumptions of fact relate to the proof of such common issues as a person's intention[123] and the continuance of a state of affairs.[124]

G. JUDICIAL NOTICE

12–028 Judicial notice is the name of a doctrine of the law of evidence that empowers a court (judge or bench of magistrates) to declare that it finds certain facts[125] to exist without the need for any evidence to be given as the existence of the facts. This finding is made on the basis that the fact is within the knowledge of the court itself. The doctrine of judicial notice thus enables a court to dispense with the normal requirement for proof of facts that are not formally admitted. Such dispensation clearly assists the party who would otherwise bear legal and evidential burdens with respect to proof of those facts. The doctrine has existed in the law for centuries.[126] Its rationale is debated[127]; most writers tend to highlight two main justifying arguments, one concerned with efficiency and the other with the desirability of consistency. Efficiency is undoubtedly a key element insofar as judicial notice saves the time and money that would otherwise be wasted on proof of matters that could not be the subject of serious dispute. Sometimes policy considerations suggest that consistency of approach to certain facts is desirable. Judicial notice helps to avoid inconsistency, particularly where it enables a judge to control a jury's factfinding by directing them that certain facts are established for the purposes of the case.

Before dealing with the common law doctrine in more detail, two important general points should be made. First, there are numerous instances where statute expressly stipulates for the taking of judicial notice. For example, judicial notice is to be taken of all Acts of Parliament passed after 1850,[128] of the European Community Treaties, the *Official Journal of the Communities* and decisions or opinions of the European Court of Justice,[129] and of the validity of signatures on many types of official documents.[130]

Secondly, this section discusses situations where courts are overtly taking judicial notice of certain facts. In any litigation there are countless occasions when courts draw, sometimes unconsciously, on a mass of factual knowledge and experience about the world and the ordinary course of human affairs. This is used

---

[123] See para.12–25 above.

[124] See, e.g. *Lumley* (1869) L.R. 1 C.C.R. 196 (continuance of life is a question of fact, not of legal presumption).

[125] Judicial notice is also taken of some matters of law; see below.

[126] See J. B. Thayer, *A Preliminary Treatise on Evidence at the Common Law* (1898, Boston), p.277, who cites cases going back to 1302.

[127] See generally E. M. Morgan, *Some Problems of Proof under the Anglo-American System of Litigation* (1956), p.36; G. D. Nokes, "The Limits of Judicial Notice" (1958) 74 L.Q.R. 59; P. B. Carter, "Judicial Notice: Related and Unrelated Matters" in E. Campbell and L. Waller (eds), *Well and Truly Tried* (Sydney, 1982), p.88.

[128] Interpretation Act 1978 ss.3, 22(1), and Sch.2 para.2. The common law permits judicial notice to be taken of public Acts passed before 1850; private Acts passed before this date must be pleaded and proved by evidence in the absence of an express provision for the taking of judicial notice of them.

[129] European Communities Act 1972 s.3(2).

[130] An example is the Evidence Act 1845 s.2, providing for judicial notice to be taken of the signatures of the judges of the superior courts on any judicial or official document.

as part of the essential process of understanding and evaluating the evidence given in the case.[131] Inferential reasoning presupposes its existence. Almost invariably, none of this knowledge and experience is ever proved by evidence. It is simply assumed that the factfinders have access to it.[132] No one suggests that it could or should be made the subject of proof; litigation would become impossible. As Thayer put it:

> "In conducting a process of judicial reasoning, as of other reasoning, not a step can be taken without assuming something which has not been proved; and the capacity to do this, with competent judgment and efficiency, is imputed to judges and juries as part of their necessary mental outfit."[133]

For the purposes of discussion this section distinguishes between three applications of the doctrine: to notorious facts, to facts judicially noticed after proper enquiry, and to facts of which the factfinder has personal knowledge.

1. *Notorious facts*

A judge may take judicial notice of facts that are matters of common knowledge and could not be the subject of serious dispute. Hence it would be pointless and wasteful to require evidence of them. Hypothetical possibilities for notorious facts are limitless: textbook writers frequently cite as illustrations the date of Christmas and the death of Queen Victoria as facts that would be judicially noticed. Reported cases contain many examples. The courts have taken judicial notice of the fact that by the laws of nature, a fortnight is too short a period for human gestation[134]; that cats are kept for domestic purposes[135]; that London streets carry a large volume of traffic, so that a boy employed to ride a bicycle through them runs a risk of injury[136]; that the reception of television is a common feature of domestic life enjoyed primarily for purposes of recreation[137]; and that one of the popular forms of entertainment on television is a series of reconstructed trials that have a striking degree of realism.[138] Occasionally "notorious" facts acquire a normative tinge, as in *Burns v Edman*,[139] where Crichton J. halved the conventional award of damages for loss of expectation of life to the wife of a deceased criminal after taking judicial notice of the fact that

12–029

---

[131] This is not properly to be regarded as judicial notice: *Burns v Lipman* (1974) 132 C.L.R. 157 High Court of Australia.

[132] Judges make this assumption every time they direct juries to use their common sense in evaluating the evidence in the case. They do not direct juries in mandatory terms as to what common sense consists of.

[133] Thayer, *A Preliminary Treatise on Evidence* (1898), pp.279–280. See also K. C. Davis, "Judicial Notice" (1955) 55 Col. L.R. 975.

[134] *Luffe* (1807) 8 East 193.

[135] And hence protected by the Malicious Damage Act 1861: *Nye v Niblett* [1918] 1 K.B. 23.

[136] *Dennis v AJ White and Co* [1916] 2 K.B. 6.

[137] *Bridlington Relay Ltd v Yorkshire Electricity Board* [1965] Ch. 436.

[138] *Yap Chuan Ching* (1976) 63 Cr.App.R. 7 CA. The fact judicially noticed in this case was a collateral fact relevant to the appropriateness of the judge's direction on the burden and standard of proof.

[139] *Burns v Edman* [1970] 2 Q.B. 541 QBD.

"the life of a criminal is an unhappy one". This qualitative judgment is of a rather different order from the easily demonstrable facts in the other examples.

What is a matter of common knowledge may of course change with time. In 1848 a court had no difficulty in assuming general knowledge of Aesop's fables.[140] That assumption could not be made today. It may not always be necessary that the fact is "notorious" amongst an entire population. Some facts may be common knowledge only to a certain group, such as the residents of a particular town[141] or the practitioners of a particular business. Judicial notice can still be taken of such facts if they are within the court's knowledge, and the court is satisfied that they could not be seriously disputed. However, the difference between what might be called "general local knowledge", and personal knowledge by the factfinder of facts in issue, may be a difficult question of degree. This point is discussed further below.[142]

2.   Facts judicially noticed after enquiry

12–030   This is a somewhat miscellaneous group of cases in which the courts declare certain facts to exist after consulting sources of authority. The facts in question are by definition not "notorious", but they are mostly facts which the reference to authoritative sources can render no longer subject to serious dispute. In some cases there may be a significant normative element involved; policy considerations may dictate that the facts in question should not be the subject of dispute and possible inconsistent decision. Three main types of case are commonly identified.

(A)   Political and diplomatic issues

12–031   A clear example of policy-driven uses of judicial notice occurs in relation to political and diplomatic issues. In *Duff Development Co v Government of Kelantan*,[143] a question arose whether an arbitration award could be enforced against the defendant. An inquiry was made of the relevant government minister whether Kelantan was an independent sovereign state. The Secretary of the State for the Colonies replied that it was, and the House of Lords held that the reply was decisive of the issue:

> "It has for some time been the practice of our courts, when such a question is raised, to take judicial notice of the sovereignty of a state, and for that purpose (in case of any uncertainty) to seek information from a Secretary of State; and when information is so obtained the court does not permit it to be questioned by the parties."[144]

---

[140] *Hoare v Silverlock* (1848) 12 Q.B. 624.
[141] e.g. the American case of *Varcoe v Lee* (1919) 181 P. 233 (judicial notice that Mission Street in San Francisco is in a business district).
[142] And see C. F. Parker, "Judicial Notice and Personal Knowledge" [1982] C.L.P. 77.
[143] *Duff Development Co v Government of Kelantan* [1924] A.C. 797 HL.
[144] *Duff Development Co v Government of Kelantan* [1924] A.C. 797 at 805 per Lord Cave.

The same approach is adopted to similar issues such as the extent of territorial waters,[145] the diplomatic status of individuals,[146] and whether a state of war continues to exist.[147] The policy aim in these cases is to ensure consistency between the courts and the executive as regards matters of the country's external relations; it would be undesirable for conflicting views to be taken on matters that might be extremely sensitive and have extensive political implications. The courts give the final word on these matters to the executive largely out of necessity. It would be impracticable in many cases to investigate the matters forensically, and wider political judgments are unsuitable for judicial decision.

(B) Historical, scientific and other issues of learning

Litigation frequently involves issues of the interpretation of language. If a judge decides that a word is used in a statute or legal instrument in its ordinary meaning, the judge may seek clarification of that meaning from a dictionary, usually the *Oxford English Dictionary*. This is treated as an authoritative source, and parties will not be allowed to dispute its accuracy, although they may of course argue that a word is not used in its dictionary meaning. Facts such as the meaning of words are sometimes called "legislative facts", to indicate that they are facts that the court must decide in making a ruling on a question of law such as the meaning of a legal instrument.   **12–032**

Other legislative facts include the legislative history of a statute,[148] and related legislation. In *DPP v Hynde*[149] the respondent was found to be in possession of a butterfly knife at Heathrow Airport. She was charged with an offence under the Aviation Security Act 1982[150] of having with her an article made or adapted for causing injury to a person. At her trial the stipendiary magistrate dismissed the charge on the ground that the prosecution had adduced no evidence to show that such a knife was made or adapted for causing injury, and had therefore failed to make out an essential element of the offence. Allowing the Crown's appeal, the Divisional Court held that the magistrate should have taken judicial notice of the fact that a butterfly knife is made or adapted for use for causing injury to a person. The court's reasoning was founded partly on the design of the knife, which operates with the same elements of speed and surprise as a flick-knife, and partly on the fact that Parliament had expressly included butterfly knives in the schedule of offensive weapons applicable to the separate offence under s.141 of the Criminal Justice Act 1988. Although the court refers to taking judicial notice of a "fact", the effect of the decision is to turn the "fact" into a matter of legal classification; henceforth butterfly knives will be treated, like flick-knives,[151] as

---

[145] *The Fagernes* [1927] P. 311.
[146] *Engelke v Musmann* [1928] A.C. 433.
[147] *R. v Bottrill Ex p. Kuechenmeister* [1947] K.B. 41.
[148] Which may be determined by reference to *Hansard*, in a case where the legislative history is a permissible aid to the interpretation of a statute under the ruling of the House of Lords, in *Pepper v Hart* [1993] A.C. 593.
[149] *DPP v Hynde* [1998] 1 All E.R. 649 DC.
[150] Aviation Security Act 1982 s.4.
[151] *Simpson* [1983] 1 W.L.R. 1494 CA.

articles "made or adapted for causing injury". The justification is consistency of decision. The Divisional Court commented in *DPP v Hynde* that:

> "justice would be affronted if... the same butterfly knife might be found to be an offensive weapon by one fact finding tribunal and not by another."[152]

12–033   Courts may sometimes need to investigate historical and scientific issues in order to resolve a question of law. In *Read v Bishop of Lincoln*,[153] the Privy Council held that where it was necessary to decide whether certain ecclesiastical practices were contrary to the law of the church, it was permissible to consult historical and theological works. The court thought that this was an application of a principle that historical works could be used to ascertain ancient facts of a public nature.[154] There is authority that judicial notice cannot be taken of facts of contemporary history, such as the date of a particular event in a modern war.[155] However, this seems an arbitrary limitation on the scope of the doctrine, and it is contradicted by *Monarch Steamship Co Ltd v Karlshamns Oljefabriker (A/B)*,[156] where several members of the House of Lords took judicial notice of the fact that as a matter of recent history there had been a general fear in 1939 of an outbreak of war.

12–034   In *McQuaker v Goddard*,[157] a judge had to decide whether a camel should be classed as a wild animal (*ferae naturae*) or a tame one (*mansuetae naturae*) for the purposes of an action against the manager of a zoo for injury caused to a visitor by a bite from a camel. The Court of Appeal upheld the judge's decision that camels were tame, a decision that the judge reached after consulting books about camels and hearing expert witnesses speak of the habits of camels. The Court of Appeal held that the judge was entitled to take judicial notice of the nature of camels, and for this purpose to inform himself by reference to appropriate sources. Clauson L.J. pointed out that this process was not the same as taking evidence in the normal way about facts in issue. The function of the witnesses was to help the judge in "forming his view as to what the ordinary course of nature in this regard in fact is, a matter of which he is supposed to have complete knowledge".[158] This tends to confirm that judicial notice is better regarded as a substitute for proof rather than as a form of proof.

(C)   Issues of custom and practice

12–035   A court may take judicial notice of the general customs of a particular profession or business, where these have been satisfactorily proved in other cases.[159] The aim is to prevent pointless repetition of evidence about the existence of the

---

[152]   *DPP v Hynde* [1998] 1 All E.R. 649 at 656.

[153]   *Read v Bishop of Lincoln* [1892] A.C. 644.

[154]   The judgment of Lord Halsbury L.C. in this case does not refer in terms to judicial notice, but it seems clear that this doctrine is being relied on.

[155]   *Commonwealth Shipping Representative v P and O Branch Service* [1923] A.C. 191.

[156]   *Monarch Steamship v Karlshamns* [1949] A.C. 196.

[157]   *McQuaker v Goddard* [1940] 1 K.B. 687 CA.

[158]   *McQuaker v Goddard* [1940] 1 K.B. 687 at 700.

[159]   This is an exception to a general rule that a court cannot hold that a fact is proved on the basis of evidence given in another case. See, e.g. *Roper v Taylor's Central Garages (Exeter) Ltd* (1951) 2 T.L.R. 284.

custom. Thus, for example, judicial notice has been taken of the custom of bankers' liens on the securities of their customers,[160] of customary terms in contracts of domestic service,[161] and of the practices of ordnance surveyors when compiling Ordnance Survey maps.[162]

3. *Personal knowledge*

It is clear from what has been said above that factfinders, whether judges, juries or magistrates, may make use of their general knowledge, either by taking judicial notice of notorious facts or as part of the common stock of knowledge and experience used in the understanding and assessment of evidence. The question now is whether factfinders can use any personal knowledge they have of facts in issue or of evidentiary facts. In principle the answer should be "No"; if facts are not so well-known as to be incapable of serious dispute they should be proved by evidence. However, matters are not that simple.

12–036

First, the question itself makes too sharp a division between general and personal knowledge. As mentioned earlier, what is "notorious" may be so only within a particular locality or a particular trade or profession. It seems that there is no objection to adjudicative factfinders taking account of matters of which they have knowledge and that are within the common knowledge of persons in the district. Thus in *Reynolds v Llanelly Associated Tinplate Co Ltd*,[163] the Court of Appeal held that a county court judge, acting as an arbitrator in a workmen's compensation case,[164] could take into account his knowledge of local wage rates, provided that this knowledge was generally known in the area. He could not rely on some particular knowledge of specialised matters that he had acquired personally. Similarly, there is authority that lay magistrates can make use of their knowledge of local conditions, where these are notorious locally,[165] and of common trade practices.[166] In *Chesson v Jordan*,[167] the Divisional Court upheld the use of local road knowledge by a judge in the Crown Court hearing an appeal against conviction from a magistrates' court.

Secondly, lay justices, at least, are allowed to take specialised knowledge into account in the evaluation of evidence given in cases before them. In *Wetherall v*

---

[160] *Brandao v Barnett* (1846) 12 Cl. & Fin. 787.

[161] *George v Davies* [1911] 2 K.B. 445 DC.

[162] *Davey v Harrow Corp* [1958] 1 Q.B. 60 CA.

[163] *Reynolds v Llanelly Associated Tinplate Co Ltd* [1948] 1 All E.R. 140.

[164] Allen regards *Reynolds v Llanelly Associated Tinplate Co Ltd*, and the line of authority on which it is based, as stating a rule peculiar to workmen's compensation cases: see C. Allen, "Judicial notice extended: *Mullen v Hackney London Borough Council*" (1998) 2 E. & P. 37 at 42.

[165] *Clift v Long* [1961] Crim. L.R. 121 (whether a car park was public or private); *Borthwick v Vickers* [1973] R.T.R. 390 (layout of public roads). See also *Bowman v DPP* [1990] Crim. L.R. 600, where the Divisional Court held that the justices could use their local knowledge to decide that a particular car park was a public place, but mysteriously added that the use of actual local knowledge by justices was not "judicial notice". It is hard to see why, since local knowledge was being used, like judicial notice of notorious facts, as a substitute for evidence on the point.

[166] *R. v Field Ex p. White* (1895) 64 L.J.M.C. 158 (composition of cocoa, as an article of commerce, with other ingredients).

[167] *Chesson v Jordan* [1981] Crim. L.R. 333 DC.

Harrison,[168] the issue was whether the defendant had a reasonable excuse for failing to give a specimen of blood in a drink-driving case.[169] The defendant had given evidence of "needle phobia", claiming that he had suffered a hysterical reaction when a doctor had tried to take a specimen. One of the justices was a doctor who passed on to his colleagues on the bench his professional opinion as to whether the defendant's reaction was genuine. The defendant was acquitted. On appeal by the prosecutor the Divisional Court stressed that while lay justices[170] could use specialised knowledge to evaluate evidence, they must not use that knowledge in contradiction of, or substitution for, the evidence actually given.

12–037 It ought to follow from these principles that magistrates should not make use of, as a form of *proof*, their specialised knowledge, or their local knowledge if the matter is not generally known in the locality. However, two cases contradict these conclusions. In *Ingram v Percival*,[171] the defendant was charged with an offence of illegal fishing in tidal waters. The prosecution led evidence to prove the illegal method of fishing, which was a fixed net designed to catch salmon and trout. No evidence was adduced to show that the waters in which the net was fixed were tidal. The justices stated that they knew that the waters were tidal at that point, and convicted the defendant. The Divisional Court upheld the conviction, saying that in this case the justices were fully entitled to make use of their local knowledge. This is very dubious because it does not appear that the matter was notorious in the locality. The justices had in effect acted as extra prosecution witnesses to supply the missing proof of an element of the offence. Since the "proof" was by way of judicial notice, no cross-examination or evidence in rebuttal was possible. If this case were to recur today it would probably involve a breach of art.6 of the ECHR. The defendant would effectively be denied the opportunity to examine the witnesses against him; the principle of "equality of arms" would be violated.

In *Mullen v Hackney LBC*,[172] the issue was whether a county court judge could take into consideration his knowledge of other breaches by the defendant council of undertakings given to the court in repairing cases when fixing the penalty for breach of the undertaking in question. The Court of Appeal held that the judge was entitled to take judicial notice, based on his special local knowledge of how the council had behaved in relation to undertakings in similar cases. This again seems objectionable.[173] The council's breaches of court undertakings were hardly notorious facts, even in the locality. They would not be facts forming part of local knowledge, like local knowledge of the nature of a particular car park. These facts could of course be ascertained after enquiry from court records, but there might still be dispute as to whether all such breaches of

---

[168] *Wetherall v Harrison* [1976] Q.B. 773 DC.
[169] See Road Traffic Act 1972 s.9(3).
[170] But not "trained judges", who are apparently expected to exclude such knowledge from their consideration of their evidence. But if a judge has to evaluate a conflict of specialised (expert) opinion, it seems inevitable that his judgment will be influenced by his own expertise, as Wills J. recognised in *R. v Field Ex p. White* (1895) 64 L.J.M.C. 158 at 160.
[171] *Ingram v Percival* [1969] 1 Q.B. 548 DC.
[172] *Mullen v Hackney LBC* [1997] 1 W.L.R. 1103 CA.
[173] Allen, "Judicial notice extended" (1998) 2 E. & P. 37.

all such undertakings should properly be taken into account. This was the point of the council's objection that no schedule of such breaches had been put in evidence. Therefore the defence was prevented from taking issue on them.

CHAPTER 13

WITNESSES

A. INTRODUCTION

This is the first of three chapters dealing with the testimony of witnesses. This   **13–001**
chapter covers the power to call witnesses, the rules of competence to testify, the
limits of compulsion to testify and the formal requirements for giving evidence
on oath. Before looking at the law in more detail, we should note as a preliminary
point the fundamental shift that took place in the focus of the law of evidence in
the nineteenth century. The repercussions of this shift are still being felt in
various ways in modern law.

The principle of orality is one of the traditional foundations of the contested
trial in common law systems of adjudication.[1] Given the importance attached to
oral testimony, it is perhaps not surprising that the early common law was greatly
concerned with the qualifications of persons to be witnesses. An extensive list
developed of categories of persons disqualified from giving evidence by reason
of presumed untrustworthiness. By the end of the eighteenth century the list
included non-Christians, convicted felons, the parties to cases, the spouses of
parties and any other persons with an interest in the outcome of a case, such as a
beneficiary in litigation concerning trust property. Any person falling into one of
these categories was an incompetent witness, in the sense that he could not
lawfully be called to give evidence.

---

[1] See Ch.1.

The common law rules of competency formed one of Bentham's main targets in his attacks on the law of evidence. As Bentham put it, in his inimitable style:

"in principle there is but one mode of searching out the truth . . . Be the dispute what it may,—see every thing that is to be seen; hear every body who is likely to know any thing about the matter: hear every body, but most attentively of all, and first of all, those who are likely to know most about it, the parties."[2]

13–002   The attacks by Bentham and others on the rules of competency were ultimately extremely successful. Throughout the nineteenth century a series of reforming statutes gradually dismantled the common law rules, culminating in the Criminal Evidence Act 1898, which made the accused in a criminal case a competent witness for the defence in all cases.

The focus on the competence of witnesses to give evidence was replaced by a concern with the relevance of their testimony. The general approach in modern law is to regard relevance of testimony, and not formal competence of the witness, as the fundamental requirement of admissibility. Thus the basic principle now is that any person can be a competent witness. A person is a competent witness if he or she may lawfully be called to give evidence. Competence normally implies compellability. A person is a compellable witness if he or she may lawfully be *obliged* to give evidence.

However, the historical process of using piecemeal legislative interventions to modify the old common law principles of competency has left its mark on the law of witnesses in a number of ways. The modern basic principles of competence and compellability are still modified in certain respects for certain types of witness. After dealing briefly with the power to call witnesses, we will consider in turn the position of an accused in a criminal case, a co-accused, the accused's spouse, child witnesses and persons suffering from mental disability. The chapter concludes with a short account of the formal requirements for witnesses to take the oath or make an affirmation.

B.   THE POWER TO CALL WITNESSES

13–003   The principle of party autonomy in adversarial proceedings means that, as a general rule, it is the parties to litigation who decide which witnesses are to be called and in what order. This is certainly the situation in civil cases, where a judge has no power to call a witness without the consent of the parties.[3] However, a civil court does have powers under the Civil Procedure Rules to limit the number of expert witnesses who may be called at the trial,[4] to make an order concerning the form in which evidence of particular facts may be given,[5] and, in

---

[2] J. Bentham, *Rationale of Judicial Evidence* (J. S. Mill (ed)) (London, 1827), Vol.5, p.743.

[3] *Re Enoch and Zaretsky, Bock & Co's Arbitration* [1910] 1 K.B. 327. This fundamental rule does not seem to be affected by the court's power to control evidence under CPR r.32.1, although the court may now have the power to direct the parties as to the order in which witnesses should be called.

[4] CPR rr.35.1 and 35.4.

[5] CPR r.32.1.

an action begun by writ, to order that the affidavit of a witness may be read at the trial if in the circumstances of the case the court thinks it reasonable so to order.[6]

In criminal cases the prosecution's autonomy in the calling of witnesses is limited to some extent by the imposition of a duty to act fairly. There is a discretion to decide which witnesses are to be called to prove the prosecution's case, but it must be exercised in accordance with the prosecutor's "overall duty of fairness, as a minister of justice".[7] The relevant principles for the exercise of this discretion were summarised by the Court of Appeal in *Brown and Brown*[8]:

"(1) The prosecution have a discretion in deciding which witnesses it will rely on for the purpose of establishing a prima facie case ... [at] ... committal proceedings ..., and will serve their statements accordingly. It must normally disclose any potentially material statement not served.[9]

(2) Counsel for the prosecution must have at court all witnesses whose statements have been served, whether as part of the depositions or as additional evidence, upon whom he intends to rely, unless any such witness is conditionally bound or the defence agree that he need not attend because, for example, his evidence can be admitted.

(3) Counsel for the prosecution enjoys a discretion whether to call or to tender a particular witness whom he has required to attend. Further, counsel may refuse even to tender a witness, notwithstanding that the witness's statement has been included in the depositions, if he decides that the witness is unworthy of belief.[10] Our adversarial system requires counsel for the prosecution to present a case against the defendant. He must always act in the interests of justice and to promote a fair trial, and his discretion must be exercised with these objects in mind. He should not refuse to call a witness merely because his evidence does not fit in exactly with the case he is seeking to prove. But he need not call a witness whose evidence is inconsistent with, or contrary to, the case he is prosecuting since such witnesses' evidence will be unworthy of belief if his case be correct.

(4) Counsel for the prosecution ought normally to call, or offer to call, all the witnesses who give direct evidence of the primary facts of the case unless the prosecutor regards the witness's evidence as unworthy of belief.

(5) It is for counsel for the prosecution to decide which witnesses give direct evidence of the primary facts of the case. He may reasonably take the view that what a particular witness has to say is, at best, marginal.

(6) Counsel for the prosecution is also the primary judge of whether or not a witness to the material events is unworthy of belief.

(7) Counsel for the prosecution, properly exercising his discretion, is not obliged to offer a witness upon whom the Crown does not rely merely in order to give the defence material with which to attack the credit of other witnesses on whom the Crown does rely. The law does not insist that the prosecution are obliged to call a witness for no purpose other than to assist the defence in its endeavours to destroy the Crown's case. Such a course would merely serve to confuse a jury. The Crown's obligation is to make such witnesses available to the defence so that the defence can call them if they choose to do so. The jury will then be clear that evidence is led by the party who wishes to rely upon it and can be tested by cross-examination by the other party, if that party wishes to challenge the evidence."

---

[6] CPR r.32.15.

[7] *Russell-Jones* [1995] 1 Cr.App.R. 538 at 544 per Kennedy L.J. See also the remarks of Lord Parker C.J. in the earlier case of *Oliva* [1965] 3 All E.R. 116 at 122.

[8] *Brown and Brown* [1997] 1 Cr.App.R. 112 at 113–114.

[9] For the prosecution's duty of disclosure of unused material see Ch.9.

[10] There is no principle of law or justice requiring the prosecution to regard the whole of a witness's evidence as reliable before calling him. Since the jury may accept the evidence of a witness in part only, the prosecution may properly exercise their discretion to call the witness if they consider that part of the evidence of that witness is reliable but would not rely on other parts: see *Cairns* [2002] EWCA Crim 2838; [2003] 1 Cr.App.R. 38.

In criminal cases a judge has a discretion to call a witness up to the time that the jury retire to consider their verdict. This is an exceptional procedure because the exercise of the discretion may look like an interference with the adversarial process; the judge must not appear to abandon his neutrality by "descending into the arena". However, if, for example, a matter arises that could not reasonably have been anticipated, the interests of justice may justify the judge calling a witness to deal with it.[11] The Court of Appeal will be very unwilling to interfere with the judge's exercise of discretion, particularly if the judge refused to exercise it to call a witness.[12]

13–004 There is no obligation on the defence to call any witnesses at all, let alone any particular person as a witness. This is subject to the point that in practice it may be necessary for the defendant to testify himself or to call an appropriate witness if the defendant is successfully to discharge some evidential burden that rests on him.[13] Where the defence fail to call a witness who might reasonably be expected to support the defence story, a question arises whether any evidential consequences can ensue from the failure. It has been held[14] that the judge has power to comment on the absence of a potential defence witness,[15] but the judge must exercise care in making comment, in the same way that care was required in making the kind of restricted comment permitted at common law on the accused's own failure to testify.[16] In particular the judge must take care to avoid the possibility of leaving the jury under the impression that the failure to call a witness is something of importance when there may be a valid reason for not calling him.[17] It might be appropriate to comment where the prosecution had no possible means of knowing that the witness had relevant evidence to give until the accused himself came to give evidence at trial. In *Weller*,[18] the Court of Appeal emphasised the need for circumspection and reserve in making comment. The court added that, as regards the terms of any comment it could not envisage any case where it would be appropriate to say that if there were any truth in the accused's story he would have been expected to call a particular witness.

For the same reason that a judge should not normally call a witness, a judge should not normally engage in the questioning of a witness. The danger arises of the judge appearing to abandon impartiality by helping one side or the other. There are limited exceptions to this principle, which are discussed in Ch.14.

---

[11] See *Tregear* [1967] 2 Q.B. 574; *Cleghorn* [1967] 2 Q.B. 584.

[12] *Roberts* (1985) 80 Cr.App.R. 89.

[13] e.g. if witness X is the defendant's doctor, and medical evidence is needed to raise the issue of automatism.

[14] *Gallagher* [1974] 3 All E.R. 118 CA.

[15] In *Khan* [2001] EWCA Crim 486; [2001] 4 Archbold News 3, the Court of Appeal said that the absence of any power to comment would be an encouragement to dishonest evidence, naming individuals in the knowledge that the jury will be directed not to speculate on why they have not been called.

[16] See section C below.

[17] *Gallagher* [1974] 3 All E.R. 118 CA. See also *Wilmot* (1989) 89 Cr.App.R. 341 CA.

[18] *Weller* [1994] Crim. L.R. 856.

C.   THE ACCUSED AS A WITNESS FOR THE DEFENCE

1.   *Competence and compellability*

Section 53(1) of the Youth Justice and Criminal Evidence Act 1999 sets out the general rule applicable to all witnesses: **13–005**

> "At every stage in criminal proceedings all persons are (whatever their age) competent to give evidence."

This rule of competency takes effect subject to subs.(3) of s.53, which provides a test of the minimum intellectual qualities required of any witness. This test is discussed in section F of this chapter dealing with children as witnesses. In the case of the accused s.53(1) also takes effect subject to subs.(4) of s.53:

> "A person charged in criminal proceedings is not competent to give evidence in the proceedings for the prosecution (whether he is the only person, or is one of two or more persons, charged in the proceedings)."

These provisions did not make any change of substance to the former law concerning the competency of the accused. At common law the accused was not a competent witness for the prosecution. This long-standing rule means that the prosecution cannot call an accused person to testify against himself or against any other person charged with him. If the prosecution wish to obtain D1's testimony against D2, they have to make use of one of the various procedures by which D1 ceases to be a co-accused with D2. These are discussed in the next section.

The common law rule of the accused's incompetency originally also applied to testimony for the defence. This part of the rule was reversed by s.1 of the Criminal Evidence Act 1898. As noted above, that Act represented the final stage of a legislative process that went on intermittently throughout the second half of the nineteenth century and consisted of the progressive dismantling of the disabilities the common law had attached to certain types of witness in both criminal and civil proceedings. Thus the ban on the parties to civil cases giving evidence finally disappeared in 1869,[19] but the corresponding rule relating to the accused in a criminal case took longer to dispose of.[20] Section 1 of the Criminal Evidence Act 1898 provided for the defendant to be a competent witness for the defence in all cases, but the Act stopped short of providing for compellability as well. As amended by the Youth Justice and Criminal Evidence Act 1999 s.1 provides: **13–006**

> "(1)   A person charged in criminal proceedings shall not be called as a witness in the proceedings except upon his own application."

---

[19]   Evidence Further Amendment Act 1869.

[20]   To ameliorate some of the harsh effects of this incompetency a practice developed of permitting the accused to make an unsworn statement from the dock. This did at least allow the accused to get his story before the jury, but such statements could not be made the subject of cross-examination and their precise evidential status remained obscure. The accused's power to make an unsworn statement was preserved by s.1(h) of the Criminal Evidence Act 1898 but eventually abolished by the Criminal Justice Act 1982 s.78 Sch.16.

The effect of this provision is to make the accused a competent witness in his own defence and also for the defence of a co-accused. The accused is not, however, compellable; he can be called as a witness only upon his own application.[21] This lack of any formal compulsion to testify in defence must in turn be qualified by the point that a decision by an accused not to give evidence has never been entirely risk-free. The right to silence in court was not an absolute right, as will shortly be seen, and there is now a statutory power to draw adverse inferences from a failure to testify.[22] This curtailment of what was already a limited right means that there is now an element of de facto compellability for all accused persons. A decision not to give evidence will require justification, if it is not to count against an accused.

2. *Failure to testify: the right to silence in court*

13–007 One of the reasons why the 1898 reform took so long was the strength of the opposition from some MPs concerned that it would put pressure on accused persons to give evidence. They feared that some defendants, unwillingly coerced into the witness box, would be susceptible to tricky cross-examination from prosecution counsel and would incriminate themselves falsely. It was to placate this opposition that the 1898 Act contained a provision that was intended to remove any element of pressure to testify. Proviso (b) (now repealed)[23] to s.1 stated that the failure of an accused person to give evidence could not be made the subject of any comment by the prosecution. The prosecution could not therefore invite the court to draw adverse inferences from the accused's non-appearance in the witness box.

The accused's immunity from comment turned out to be a restricted one. The Act did not deal with the position of the judge or a co-accused as regards adverse comment on an accused's decision not to testify. The Court of Appeal has held that a co-accused has an unfettered right to comment; the judge has no discretion to prevent comment by a co-accused or to control the extent of it.[24] All that the judge can do to lessen the damage caused by prejudicial comment from a co-accused is to remind the jury that the defendant does have a right to silence and is not obliged to testify. A good deal of case law developed concerning the scope of the judicial power to comment. The cases were not easy to reconcile since they reflected shifting attitudes on the part of the courts to the questions both of whether there were any limits on the power to comment and, if so, the precise nature of those limits.

---

[21] However the defendant's opportunity to give evidence in defence is usually only available once. In *Ikram* [2008] EWCA Crim 586 the Court of Appeal upheld a trial judge's refusal to allow a defendant to be recalled to testify a second time. "It is difficult to imagine circumstances—unless bizarre in the extreme—in which the defendant should be granted the privilege of giving evidence twice in order to advance contradictory defences at the same trial" (at [52]). It may be different where a recall is necessary to enable the defendant to clarify some feature of his evidence or to deal with new allegations by a co-accused.

[22] Criminal Justice and Public Order Act 1994 s.35.

[23] Criminal Justice and Public Order Act 1994 s.168(3) Sch.11.

[24] *Wickham* (1971) 55 Cr.App.R. 199 CA.

Initially the orthodox view was that set out by Lord Russell of Killowen C.J. in the Court for Crown Cases Reserved in *Rhodes*.[25] Reading the Criminal Evidence Act 1898 literally, he held that there was nothing in it to affect the right of the court to comment on the evidence in the case. He continued:

> "The nature and degree of such comment must rest entirely in the discretion of the judge who tries the case; and it is impossible to lay down any rule as to the cases in which he ought or ought not to comment on the failure of the prisoner to give evidence, or as to what those comments should be."[26]

This forthright statement was taken as indicating that judges had a free and unfettered discretion as to when and how they commented on an accused's failure to testify.[27] It was not until the decision of the Privy Council in *Waugh v R.*,[28] 50 years later, that it became clear that the discretion was not absolute. In that case the prosecution evidence on a murder charge had been weak, but in his summing-up the trial judge had commented nine times on the failure of the defendant to give evidence and had twice suggested that the jury could treat the failure to testify as evidence suggestive of guilt. The Privy Council held that these comments amounted to a wrongful exercise of discretion and quashed the conviction. The judge had a duty to be careful in commenting on a failure to give evidence, and his repeated comments and suggestions that silence was indicative of guilt was a serious departure from justice.

13–008

The decision was notable, partly because it confirmed that the discretion to comment was reviewable on appeal, and partly because it effectively recognised a derivative application of the privilege against self-incrimination.[29] Whatever inferences common sense might draw from a defendant's failure to testify, *Waugh* appeared to say that it was wrong in principle to make a direct inference of guilt from such a failure. This was accepted in subsequent discussions of the discretion to comment, which were directed to clarifying what other evidential significance, if any, could be attached to a failure to testify. In *Bathurst*,[30] Lord Parker C.J. set out, obiter, some influential[31] guidelines for trial judges on appropriate forms of comment:

> "the accepted form of comment is to inform the jury that, of course, the accused is not bound to give evidence, that he can sit back and see if the prosecution have proved their case, and that,

---

[25] *Rhodes* [1899] 1 Q.B. 77.

[26] *Rhodes* [1899] 1 Q.B. 77 at 83.

[27] See *Voisin* [1918] 1 K.B. 531 CCA, holding that the exercise of the discretion was not reviewable on appeal. cf. *Corrie and Watson* (1904) 20 T.L.R. 365; and *Bernard* (1908) 1 Cr.App.R. 218, distinguishing between weak cases, where no inference should be drawn from the defendants' failure to testify, and cases where the proven facts called strongly for an explanation from the defendant if one existed, so that an inference could be drawn from a failure to give evidence.

[28] *Waugh v R.* [1950] A.C. 203.

[29] See Ch.5 on primary and derivative applications of the privilege against self-incrimination, and the relationship between the privilege and the right to silence.

[30] *Bathurst* [1968] 2 Q.B. 99 CA.

[31] The guidelines formed the basis of the specimen direction issued by the Judicial Studies Board before the reform effected by the Criminal Justice and Public Order Act 1994. The text of the direction was set out in *Martinez-Tobon* (1994) 98 Cr.App.R. 375 at 380.

while the jury had been deprived of the opportunity of hearing his story tested in cross-examination, the one thing they must not do is to assume that he is guilty because he has not gone into the witness box."[32]

Implicit in these guidelines was the idea that failure to support the defence "story" from the witness box might weaken the defence. This idea was developed further in *Sparrow*[33] where Lawton L.J. indicated that in some cases a judge might make a stronger comment than envisaged by the *Bathurst* guidelines. The defendant and a co-accused Skingle were charged with murdering a police officer in the course of a joint car theft. There was clear evidence that Skingle had shot the officer with a gun that was in the car in which the defendant and Skingle had been travelling. The defendant's defence, which his counsel put to Skingle in cross-examination, was that the defendant had agreed that the gun was to be used only to frighten and that he had not contemplated shooting anyone. The defendant did not give evidence. The trial judge asked the jury whether it was not essential that the defendant should go into the witness box to tell this story and be cross-examined on it. The Court of Appeal held that this went too far since it suggested that the defence could not succeed unless the defendant gave evidence, which was not so.[34] However, Lawton L.J. said[35] that what was appropriate comment depended on the facts of the case. In some cases, of which this was one, the interests of justice might call for a stronger comment than normal. There was a very strong prima facie case against the defendant who was denying mens rea and seeking to throw all the blame on to his co-accused. The Court of Appeal clearly thought that the defendant's failure to establish this defence by his own evidence weakened the defence and thereby strengthened the prosecution case. In *Mutch*,[36] Lawton L.J. drew a distinction between cases of simple denial of the prosecution case, when strong comment would not be appropriate, and cases of "confession and avoidance", where the defendant is seeking to give an innocent explanation of prima facie incriminating prosecution evidence. If the explanation is one within the defendant's own knowledge, his failure to support it from the witness box yields an inference that he may be afraid that it will not stand up to cross-examination.[37]

13–009   A further issue, on which the cases were not in harmony, was whether a judge had a duty in all cases where the defendant did not testify to direct the jury that they could not infer guilt from the failure to give evidence. In *Harris*,[38] Lawton L.J. denied the existence of such a general duty, but later authorities took the view that it was necessary in all cases for the judge to deal with the issue in the kind of terms approved in the specimen direction.[39]

The state of the common law on the right to silence in court was thoroughly reviewed by the Court of Appeal just before the reforms made by the Criminal

---

[32] *Bathurst* [1968] 2 Q.B. 99 at 107–108.
[33] *Sparrow* [1973] 1 W.L.R. 488 CA.
[34] The court applied the proviso to uphold the conviction, despite the irregularity of the comment.
[35] *Sparrow* [1973] 1 W.L.R. 488 at 496.
[36] *Mutch* [1973] 1 All E.R. 178 CA.
[37] *Mutch* [1973] 1 All E.R. 178 at 181.
[38] *Harris* (1987) 84 Cr.App.R. 75 CA. See also *Squire* [1990] Crim. L.R. 341.
[39] *Taylor* [1993] Crim. L.R. 223 CA; *Fullerton* [1994] Crim. L.R. 63 CA.

Justice and Public Order Act 1994 were enacted. The judgment in *Martinez-Tobon*,[40] summarised the principles as follows:

> "(1) The judge should give the jury a direction along the lines of the Judicial Studies Board specimen direction based on *R. v Bathurst* [1968] 1 All E.R. 1175 at 1178; [1968] 2 Q.B. 99 at 107. (2) The essentials of that direction are that the defendant is under no obligation to testify and the jury should not assume he is guilty because he has not given evidence. (3) Provided those essentials are complied with, the judge may think it appropriate to make a stronger comment where the defence case involves alleged facts which (a) are at variance with prosecution evidence or additional to it and exculpatory, and (b) must, if true, be within the knowledge of the defendant. (4) The nature and strength of such comment must be a matter for the discretion of the judge and will depend upon the circumstances of the individual case. However, it must not be such as to contradict or nullify the essentials of the conventional direction."

3. *Failure to testify: reform of the right to silence*

Section 35 of the Criminal Justice and Public Order Act 1994 curtails the right to silence in court.[41] Like the reforms to the right to silence in the police station, this reform derived originally from a proposal by the Criminal Law Revision Committee[42] and had similarly been tried out in Northern Ireland for some years. Although most of the subsequent debate has centred on pre-trial silence, s.35 also is controversial and raises the same issue of compatibility with art.6 of the ECHR. It is dealt with separately from the earlier discussion of the right to silence out of court for two reasons. One is that in practice, s.35 functions as a measure of de facto compellability for the accused, so that it is appropriate to consider it in the context of the law relating to witnesses. The other is that the procedural context of trial is so different from that of interrogation in the police station that the theoretical arguments for curtailing the right to silence require different treatment. These arguments will be considered after the nature and scope of the reform have been discussed.

13–010

Section 35 allows for the drawing of adverse inferences where the accused fails to testify if certain conditions are satisfied.[43] The first of the statutory conditions is that the physical or mental condition of the accused must not be such as to make it undesirable for him to give evidence.[44] The defence bear the burden of adducing evidence of the accused's condition if they claim that the subsection applies.[45] It is not sufficient that the defendant suffers from *some* physical or mental condition. It must be a condition which makes it undesirable for him to give evidence, and this has been restrictively interpreted to mean that because of the accused's physical or mental state, if he gives evidence it will have

---

[40] *Martinez-Tobon* (1994) 98 Cr.App.R. 375 CA.

[41] See generally M. Redmayne, "English Warnings" (2008) 30 Cardozo L.R. 1047, esp.1071–1080.

[42] *Eleventh Report* paras 110–113.

[43] These conditions originally included a condition that the accused should not be a child (i.e. that the accused should be aged 14 or over), but the age limitation for inferences from failure to testify was repealed by the Crime and Disorder Act 1998 s.35.

[44] Criminal Justice and Public Order Act 1994 s.35(1)(b). For discussion see A. Owusu-Bempah, "Judging the Desirability of a Defendant's Evidence: An Unfortunate Approach to s. 35(1)(b) of the Criminal Justice and Public Order Act 1994" [2011] Crim. L.R. 690.

[45] *R. v A* [1997] Crim. L.R. 883 CA

a significantly adverse effect on him.[46] In *Friend*,[47] Otton L.J. suggested that it would only be in very rare cases that a judge would have to consider whether it is undesirable for an accused to give evidence on account of his mental condition. This is because an accused who has sufficient mental capacity to be fit to plead will normally be able to testify. An exception might be a physical condition which included a risk of an epileptic attack or a mental condition such as "latent schizophrenia, where the experience of giving evidence might trigger a florid state".[48] It will not be enough that the physical or mental condition may merely cause the defendant some difficulty in giving evidence.[49] Moreover, it appears that the judge may also take into account the importance of the defendant's evidence to the issues in the case when deciding whether it would be undesirable for him to testify.[50]

The other conditions to be satisfied for inferences to be possible under s.35 are:

- the court must be satisfied that the accused is aware of his choice whether to testify and of the consequences of failing to testify[51];
- the prosecution must have made out a prima facie case on the basis of their own evidence.[52]

13–011   When the conditions are satisfied, the inferences that may be drawn are such as "appear proper" from the failure of the accused to give evidence, and the court may draw them in determining whether the accused is guilty of the offence

---

[46] *Ensor* [2009] EWCA Crim 2519; [2010] 1 Cr.App.R. 18.

[47] *Friend* [1997] 2 Cr.App.R. 231.

[48] P. 242. In *Friend* the accused was aged 15, but had a mental age of 9. The Court of Appeal held that the trial judge had not erred in directing the jury that they could draw adverse inferences from the accused's failure to testify. Although there was expert evidence that he had difficulty in concentrating and expressing himself, he was not abnormally suggestible and was capable, as demonstrated in his police interviews, of giving a coherent account of his actions. Subsequently, however, in a further appeal in *Friend* [2004] EWCA Crim 2661, the Court of Appeal quashed the defendant's conviction for murder in the light of new evidence that he suffered from attention deficit hyperactivity disorder which would have affected his ability to participate effectively in the trial and might have caused him to be inconsistent and give conflicting evidence. The focus on the effect of the accused's condition on the *quality* of the evidence that he might have given contrasts with the rejection in other cases of difficulty in giving evidence as grounds for a finding of undesirability under s.35(1)(b).

[49] *R. (on the application of DPP) v Kavanagh* [2005] EWHC 820 (Admin), approved in *Ensor* [2009] EWCA Crim 2519; [2010] 1 Cr.App.R. 18.

[50] *Tabbakh* [2009] EWCA Crim 464, where the defendant's condition presented a risk of self-harm (albeit not severe) from the stress of giving evidence.

[51] Criminal Justice and Public Order Act 1994 s.35(2). The judge will normally do this by asking the accused's counsel. This requirement does not apply if, at the close of the prosecution evidence, the accused's lawyer informs the court that the accused will give evidence (s.35(1)). For the procedure in such a case see the Practice Note [2002] 1 W.L.R. 2870 and *Cowan* [1996] Q.B. 373 at 383 CA.

[52] This requirement is implicit in s.35 because if the prosecution have not made out a prima facie case by the close of their evidence, no question of the accused testifying in defence can arise. The logic of this position is reinforced by the contrast between s.34(2)(c) and (d) (adverse inferences may be drawn from failure to mention facts when questioned by a constable in determining whether there is a case to answer and in determining whether the accused is guilty of the offence charged) and s.35(3) (adverse inferences may be drawn from failure to testify [only] in determining whether the accused is guilty). The point was confirmed in *Cowan* [1996] Q.B. 373 CA.

charged.[53] Section 35 has been held to be of general application and not to be restricted to exceptional cases.[54] However, a judge retains a discretion as to the direction to be given to a jury on the proper inferences to be drawn from a failure to testify, and in an appropriate case a judge should direct the jury that it would not be proper to draw any adverse inference.

In *Cowan*,[55] the Court of Appeal highlighted essential elements of the direction that trial judges should now give in a case where the defendant does not testify[56]:

"(1)   The judge will have told the jury that the burden of proof remains upon the prosecution throughout and what the required standard is.

(2)   It is necessary for the judge to make clear to the jury that the defendant is entitled to remain silent. That is his right and his choice. The right of silence remains.[[57]]

(3)   An inference from failure to give evidence cannot on its own prove guilt. That is expressly stated in s.38(3) of the Act.

(4)   Therefore, the jury must be satisfied that the prosecution have established a case to answer before drawing any inferences from silence. Of course, the judge must have thought so or the question whether the defendant was to give evidence would not have arisen. But the jury may not believe the witnesses whose evidence the judge considered sufficient to raise a prima facie case. It must therefore be made clear to them that they must find there to be a case to answer on the prosecution evidence before drawing an adverse inference from the defendant's silence.

(5)   If, despite any evidence relied upon to explain his silence or in the absence of any such evidence, the jury conclude the silence can only sensibly be attributed to the defendant's having no answer or none that would stand up to cross-examination, they may draw an adverse inference."

A number of matters call for discussion and comment. Point (4) in this list is a way of making sense of s.38(3), as it applies to s.35. Section 38(3) aims to ensure that no one can be convicted of an offence on the basis of silence alone. In the event that the jury accept *none* of the prosecution evidence, despite the judge finding that it did amount to a prima facie case, the provision prevents the accused then being convicted purely on the basis that he did not give evidence. However, Lord Taylor's reference to the jury needing to find "a case to answer on the prosecution evidence" before drawing an adverse inference from the defendant's silence is not as clear as it might be. When a judge finds that there is a case to answer, this is a conclusion that the prosecution have adduced sufficient evidence on which a reasonable jury, if they accepted it, could find the case against the accused proved beyond reasonable doubt. But what is involved in a

---

[53] Criminal Justice and Public Order Act 1994 s.35(3).

[54] *Cowan* [1996] Q.B. 373 CA.

[55] *Cowan* [1996] Q.B. 373 at 381 CA.

[56] The Judicial Studies Board had published a specimen direction. In *Cowan* [1996] Q.B. 373 at 380–381 the Court of Appeal referred to it as generally a sound guide, although the court noted that it might be necessary to adapt or add to it in the circumstances of a particular case. In *Becouarn* [2005] UKHL 55; [2006] 1 Cr.App.R. 2 the House of Lords stated that the JSB direction was sufficiently fair to defendants and approved *Cowan*. As noted in Ch.5, the model direction in *Cowan* was approved and adapted by the Court of Appeal for directions as to the drawing of adverse inferences under s.34 of the Criminal Justice and Public Order Act 1994, where the defendant fails to mention facts in a police interview on which he later relies in his defence.

[57] See s.35(4), which maintains the primary application of the privilege against self-incrimination by providing that "the section does not render the accused compellable to give evidence on his own behalf, and he shall accordingly not be guilty of contempt of court by reason of a failure to do so".

jury finding that there is a case to answer? It cannot mean that the jury have to be satisfied that the prosecution have in fact proved the case beyond reasonable doubt before any adverse inferences from silence fall to be considered. If this were so, adverse inferences would be redundant and s.35 would be robbed of much of its intended effect. It would seem therefore that what is envisaged is a provisional conclusion by the jury that the prosecution evidence is sufficiently credible, reliable and probative to incriminate the accused as to the offence charged and therefore to call for an explanation from the accused.[58] At this stage in their reasoning the jury would not need to have reached any conclusion whether the prosecution had discharged the burden of proof.

This approach accommodates the statement in *Cowan* that an inference from failure to testify may be "a further evidential factor in support of the prosecution case".[59] This naturally suggests that the jury might regard the accused's absence from the witness box as a further piece of evidence that resolves any doubt they might feel about his guilt, and therefore as something that takes the prosecution case to the required standard of proof. A useful illustration of the reasoning involved appears in the judgment of the House of Lords in *Murray v DPP*,[60] a case concerned with the virtually identical provisions of the Northern Ireland legislation.[61] The defendant was charged with attempted murder and possession of a firearm with intent to endanger life. Cogent circumstantial evidence pointed to his involvement with the attack on the victim. The trial judge expressed surprise that the defendant did not give evidence, and drew a common sense inference that the defendant was guilty because he was not prepared to assert his innocence on oath. Dismissing the defendant's appeal against conviction, the House of Lords held that an adverse inference from failure to testify is not necessarily restricted to an inference about specific facts, but may extend to a general inference of guilt of the offence charged. The latter inference is founded on the argument that the defendant does not controvert the prosecution case by evidence on oath because he is unable to do so, and/ or that any defence he puts forward but does not support from the witness box is a sham. Lord Mustill explained this with great clarity:

> "if the defendant does not go on oath to say that the witnesses who have spoken to his actions are untruthful or unreliable, or that an inference which appears on its face to be plausible is in reality unsound for reasons within his knowledge, the factfinder may suspect that the defendant does not tell his story because he has no story to tell, or none that will stand up to scrutiny; and this suspicion may be sufficient to convert a provable prosecution case into one which is actually proved... So also if the defendant seeks to outflank the case for the prosecution by means of a 'positive' defence—as for example where he replies in relation to a charge of murder that although he did kill the deceased he acted under provocation. If he does not give evidence in support of this allegation there will in very many cases be a legitimate inference that the defence is untrue."[62]

---

[58] See *Murray v DPP* (1993) 97 Cr.App.R. 151 HL.

[59] *Cowan* [1996] Q.B. 373 at 379.

[60] *Murray v DPP* (1993) 97 Cr.App.R. 151.

[61] Criminal Evidence (NI) Order 1988 (SI 1988/1987) art.4. See, on the interpretation of this and other corresponding provisions of the Northern Ireland legislation, J. Jackson, "Inferences from Silence—From Common Law to Common Sense" (1993) 44 N.I.L.Q. 103; "Interpreting the Silence Provisions: The Northern Ireland Cases" [1995] Crim. L.R. 587.

[62] *Murray v DPP* (1993) 97 Cr.App.R. 151 at 155.

It seems, however, that the House of Lords in *Murray v DPP* took the view that **13–012** this inferential reasoning could not be employed unless the prosecution had made out a clear or strong prima facie case,[63] and the means of denial or explanation were within the defendant's own knowledge.[64] This restrictive approach to when adverse inferences are "proper" is highly reminiscent of the view taken at common law as to the cases in which judges could make strong comment on a failure to testify. However, it seems unlikely that the effect of s.35 is limited to permitting general inferences of guilt to be drawn in the exceptional circumstances where strong comment was allowed at common law on failure to testify. The limitations involved do not appear in the judgment of the Court of Appeal in *Cowan*, which cited the Northern Irish case of *McLernon*[65] for the propositions that the court has a complete discretion whether to draw any, and, if so, what, adverse inferences from failure to testify, and that it would be improper and unwise to set limits to the discretion. This approach fits better with the generality of the terms of s.35, but the dicta of the Law Lords in *Murray v DPP* are more likely to find favour with those who would wish to cut down the scope of the reform made by the section.

The cases where it would not be proper to draw adverse inferences thus remain to be clarified. Apart from the uncertainty whether anything turns on the strength of the prosecution case, there is an unresolved issue as to what counts as a legitimate excuse for failure to testify. In *Becouarn*,[66] the House of Lords approved the ruling of the Court of Appeal in *Cowan*[67] that the possibility that the defendant could be cross-examined on his previous criminal record was not a good reason to avoid adverse inferences from failing to testify.[68] Otherwise, as the Court of Appeal rightly said, a defendant with convictions would be in a more privileged position than one with a clean record. The former could attack prosecution witnesses and then avoid submitting himself to cross-examination with impunity. The latter could not. In *Napper*,[69] the defendant argued on appeal that he was justified in failing to testify because the failure by the police to interview him had deprived him of an opportunity of giving his side of the story while events were still fresh in his mind. By the time of the trial, he said, he could not be expected to remember details. The Court of Appeal held that the trial judge had correctly directed the jury on the possibility of drawing an adverse inference. This reluctance to cut down the scope of s.35 by reference to asserted excuses is an example of the interpretative principle of giving the reforms of the right to

---

[63] See the speech of Lord Slynn (*Murray v DPP* (1993) 97 Cr.App.R. 151 at 160), who stated that it would not be proper to draw adverse inferences of guilt from a failure to answer "parts of the prosecution case [that] had so little evidential value that they called for no answer".

[64] *Murray v DPP* (1993) 97 Cr.App.R. 151 at 160–161. See also *Birchall* [1999] Crim. L.R. 311 CA: the jury must be directed that they should not draw adverse inferences from the defendant's failure to testify until they have concluded that the prosecution have made out a sufficiently compelling case to answer as to call for an answer by the defendant.

[65] *McLernon* [1990] 10 N.I.J.B. 91.

[66] *Becouarn* [2005] UKHL 55; [2006] 1 Cr.App.R. 2.

[67] *Cowan* [1996] Q.B. 373.

[68] cf. R. Pattenden, "Inferences from Silence" [1995] Crim. L.R. 602, 607.

[69] *Napper* [1996] Crim. L.R. 591 CA.

silence their "proper effect".[70] The courts will require some evidential basis for directing a jury that adverse inferences would not be proper, or some exceptional factors in the case making that a fair course to take.[71] In *Hamidi and Cherazi*,[72] it was not an exceptional factor that a co-accused (D3) had absented himself from the trial. This meant that the statutory procedure for a s 35 direction could not be applied in respect of D3, but the Court of Appeal held this did not make it unfair to give the direction in respect of D1 and D2 who were present at the trial. The fact that the defendant may have been suffering from diminished responsibility is not without more an exceptional factor. In *Barry*,[73] where D was relying on evidence of alcohol dependency syndrome to support the defence, the Court of Appeal upheld a s 35 direction on the basis that D could have given relevant evidence on the central issue in the case, namely the degree of impairment of his responsibility for the killing in question.

It was noted in Ch.5 that the privilege against self-incrimination and the right to silence have been implied into art.6 of the ECHR as generally recognised international standards that lie at the heart of the notion of a fair procedure.[74] Accordingly, the issue arises, as it does with silence in the police station, of how far reform of the accused's right to remain silent at his trial is compatible with art.6. *Murray v United Kingdom*[75] is the leading case. The applicant had been found in a house where a suspected police informer had been held captive and interrogated on tape. The applicant had refused to answer police questions[76] and did not give evidence at his trial. In finding him guilty of aiding and abetting unlawful imprisonment, the trial judge stated that he had drawn adverse inferences[77] from the applicant's failure at any time to give an explanation for his presence in the house. By a majority of 14–5 the European Court of Human Rights found that there had been no violation of art.6 arising out of the drawing of adverse inferences from silence. In reaching this conclusion the court did not distinguish between silence in the police station and silence at trial. However, the court emphasised that it was concerned with the fairness of the applicant's trial,

---

[70] *Bowden* [1999] 2 Cr.App.R. 176. The courts have said on several occasions that the operation of s.35 is not to be reduced or marginalised: see *Becouarn* [2005] UKHL 55; [2006] 1 Cr.App.R. 2 at [23].

[71] *Cowan* [1996] Q.B. 373 at 380. In *Becouarn* [2005] UKHL 55; [2006] 1 Cr.App.R. 2 the House of Lords reinforced the point by holding that the jury need not be directed that there might have been reasons for the defendant not giving evidence other than his inability to give an explanation or answer the prosecution case. In the absence of evidence of what those reasons might be, the jury would be engaging in unfounded speculation. Counsel may not address the jury on the basis that he advised the defendant not to testify without disclosing the reason for the advice, for which he would need the defendant's consent to waive privilege: *Branchflower* [2009] EWCA Crim 1239 at [36].

[72] *Hamidi and Cherazi* [2010] EWCA Crim 66.

[73] *Barry* [2010] EWCA Crim 195.

[74] *Funke v France* (1993) 16 E.H.R.R. 297; *Saunders v United Kingdom* (1997) 23 E.H.R.R. 313; *Murray v United Kingdom* (1996) 22 E.H.R.R. 29.

[75] *Murray v United Kingdom* (1996) 22 E.H.R.R. 29. This is not the same case as *Murray v DPP* (1993) 97 Cr.App.R. 151 discussed above, which concerned a different defendant and a different incident.

[76] The police denied him access to a solicitor for 48 hours after arrest, pursuant to s.15(1) of the Northern Ireland (Emergency Provisions) Act 1987. It does not appear that the refusal to answer questions was causally related to the delay in receiving legal advice.

[77] Under arts 4 and 6 of the Criminal Evidence (NI) Order 1988 (SI 1988/1987).

and that it was not the court's role to examine generally whether the drawing of adverse inferences under the relevant Order was incompatible with art.6. On the facts the court held that, having regard to the weight of the prosecution evidence against the applicant, the drawing of an adverse inference from his refusal to explain his presence in the house was "a matter of common sense and cannot be regarded as unfair or unreasonable in the circumstances".[78]

This leaves open the question whether, on different facts, the drawing of adverse inferences from failure to testify might amount to a violation of the right to a fair trial. The answer is probably "No", as a general principle. We have seen already that the European Court of Human Rights has stated consistently that the privilege against self-incrimination and the right to silence are not absolute rights.[79] They may be qualified or restricted under certain conditions. It seems likely that the same four minimum conditions required for inferences under s.34 of the Criminal Justice and Public Order Act 1994 to satisfy art.6[80] apply, mutatis mutandis, to inferences under s.35. Thus in *Murray v United Kingdom* the majority of the court stated that, as long as silence did not constitute the sole or main evidence for conviction, the implied rights under art.6 did not prevent silence being taken into account as a matter of evidence in situations where the prosecution had established a prima facie case clearly calling for an explanation from the defendant. The majority admitted that the possibility of inferences from silence did involve a certain level of indirect compulsion. But since the applicant could not be directly compelled to testify, this consideration was not decisive. The majority then looked carefully at the safeguards designed to respect the rights of the defence and to ensure that the trial is fair. The following safeguards were specifically highlighted: the requirement under the Order of appropriate warnings to the accused as to the legal effect of silence; the need for the prosecution first to establish a prima facie case; only "proper" common sense inferences can be drawn from silence; the discretion of the trial judge to decide whether any inferences could or should be drawn; the requirement in Northern Ireland for trial judges sitting without juries to give reasons for decisions to draw inferences; the possibility of review by appellate courts of the exercise of discretion.

13–013

Of this list, only the duty to give reasons has no counterpart under the English legislation. However, although the judgment of the European Court noted the difference, it did not attach particular importance to it, and in *Cowan,*[81] Lord Taylor C.J. dismissed it with the comment that juries in criminal trials are required to draw inferences in numerous situations. Provided, he said, that judges give proper directions, he could see no reason why the reasoning in *Murray v United Kingdom* should not apply equally to jury trials. His point was effectively endorsed for inferences under s.34 by the European Court of Human Rights in *Condron v United Kingdom.*[82] It seems safe to assume that an analogous

---

[78] *Murray v United Kingdom* (1996) 22 E.H.R.R. 29 at 63.
[79] See Ch.5.
[80] See Ch.5 para.5–24.
[81] *Cowan* [1996] Q.B. 373.
[82] *Condron v United Kingdom* (2000) 31 E.H.R.R. 1, discussed in Ch.5 para.5–24.

requirement for a proper direction would be insisted on by Strasbourg in a jury trial involving possible inferences under s.35.

It should be remembered that any delay in giving the accused access to a lawyer in pre-trial investigations may be critical in any assessment of the fairness of the accused's trial. In *Murray v United Kingdom*,[83] the European Court of Human Rights held that the delay of 48 hours in the applicant's case amounted to a breach of art.6(1). The possibility of drawing adverse inferences under the scheme established by the Criminal Evidence (NI) Order 1998 was a major factor in this decision. Because the scheme attached such significant evidential consequences to the accused's attitude and behaviour in the initial stages of police investigation, decisions made at this time might irretrievably prejudice the rights of the defence in all subsequent stages of the proceedings. It was therefore of "paramount importance" for the accused to have access to a lawyer in the initial stages. To deny access, whether or not the denial was independently justified, was said to be incompatible with the rights of the accused under art.6.[84] Therefore, if there is an issue at trial of possible adverse inferences under s.34, a violation of art.6 at the earlier stage will not be cured by the accused waiving his right to silence in court and electing to testify on legal advice.

13–014   Chapter 5 discussed at length the theoretical justifications for the accused's privilege against self-incrimination. The claim was developed that most of the traditional justifying arguments for the privilege have significant weaknesses. In relation to pre-trial interrogation it was suggested that the most satisfying justifying account of the privilege is one that characterises the privilege as a functional necessity, intended as a safeguard against the abuse of power by state enforcement authorities in circumstances where silence in the police station is systemically unreliable as evidence of guilt. This account was located in the context of a general theory about the proper aims of the law of evidence being to promote the legitimacy of the verdict in its factual, moral and expressive dimensions. The approach to the privilege as a functional necessity in the police investigation accounted for both its primary application (no enforceable duty to answer questions) and its derivative application (no adverse inferences from a failure to answer questions).

The procedural context of the criminal trial is very different from that of a police interrogation. The accused knows the precise charges against him, has heard the evidence against him and has had an opportunity to challenge it, has the opportunity to present his own evidence in reply, and is participating in a public hearing before an impartial tribunal. In the context of a police investigation most of these conditions—which liberal theory suggests are central to notions of natural justice and a fair trial[85]—do not exist most of the time. This radical difference in the procedural context has important implications for the privilege against self-incrimination at trial. The argument for the privilege as a functional necessity against abuse of power is not applicable where the investigation of the charges takes place in conditions of natural justice. Moreover, the systemic factors that tend to make silence in the police station unreliable evidence of guilt

---

[83] *Murray v United Kingdom* (1996) 22 E.H.R.R. 29.
[84] *Murray v United Kingdom* (1996) 22 E.H.R.R. 29 at [67].
[85] See art.6 of the ECHR and the discussion in Ch.2.

are either not present in the trial context or not present to the same degree. A different justifying argument is needed for the right to silence in court, and on analysis the argument turns out to be limited and weak.

It was suggested in Ch.5 that the well-known claim that the privilege protects the accused from cruel choices (to commit perjury by lying, to commit contempt by refusing to testify, to incriminate by truthful answers) fails to convince because of its flimsy moral basis. It assumes the accused's guilt, then claims that it is unfair to place pressure on the guilty to admit their guilt. But, although the premises of this argument are unsatisfactory, its central focus is not. This focus is correctly directed at the political relationship between the state and the accused. The crucial question to be asked in the present context is whether it is improper for the state to place any pressure on the accused to respond to a prima facie prosecution case at a criminal trial and, if not, what the legitimate limits of that pressure should be. This is ultimately a political question and depends for its resolution on a view of political obligation between state and citizen. A strongly libertarian view would hold that citizens must be accorded complete freedom of choice whether to co-operate with state investigations by answering questions even if they are guilty,[86] and that no pressure of a direct or indirect form is permissible. This position accords maximum value to individual autonomy, but at some cost to community interests in the correct enforcement of the criminal law and the protection of victims.

A compromise view would argue that it is not in principle unfair to expect a citizen to respond to well-founded claims that he appears to have abused his autonomy by committing an offence. The argument would continue that, provided the claims are well-founded in the sense that a prima facie case has been made out in a formal proceeding conducted in accordance with the principles of natural justice, a citizen cannot reasonably complain if his failure to answer the case is taken as confirmation of its accuracy. In this way the use of adverse inferences as a form of indirect pressure on defendants could be justified. It might then be asked why such an argument should not justify doing away with the primary application of the privilege against self-incrimination. Why should it not become an offence or a contempt to refuse to testify? The answer to this begins with the point that such direct coercive pressure is unnecessary if the use of adverse inferences will serve the same purpose. One of the cardinal principles of liberal theory is, or should be, that the criminal law should be used with restraint and only when no other means of influencing behaviour is likely to be effective. If the use of the criminal law is not required in this context, then its deployment would represent an unacceptable use of state power, particularly against a citizen in a vulnerable position. Accordingly the primary application of the privilege can be maintained, but not the derivative application that would refuse to allow adverse inferences from a decision not to testify. The approach of the European Court of Human Rights in *Murray v United Kingdom*[87] seems to be consistent with this theoretical view.

---

[86] A libertarian would of course invoke the presumption of innocence at this point.
[87] *Murray v United Kingdom* (1996) 22 E.H.R.R. 29.

D.   THE ACCUSED AS A WITNESS FOR THE PROSECUTION

13–015   An accused person is not a competent witness for the prosecution,[88] hence one accused (D1) cannot be called to give evidence against a co-accused (D2).[89] A co-accused for this purpose is a person being tried jointly with the accused when the issue of D1's competency arises. If the prosecution wish to make use of D1's evidence against D2 they will have to adopt one of the four methods by which D1 will cease to be a co-accused with D2 within this definition.[90] The methods are:

(a)   the Attorney-General discontinues the proceedings against D1 by the entry of a formal plea known as a *nolle prosequi;*

(b)   the prosecution obtain an order for separate trials of D1, and D2;

(c)   at the trial of D1 and D2 the prosecution offer no evidence against D1 who is then formally acquitted of the charges against him;

(d)   at the trial[91] of D1 and D2, D1 pleads guilty to one or more of the charges against him (or, alternatively, to a lesser charge as part of a bargain with the prosecution).[92]

In the last case it is desirable in principle for D1 to be sentenced before he is called to give evidence for the prosecution against D2, otherwise there will inevitably be a suspicion that D1 has a continuing interest in trimming his evidence to suit the prosecution case. There is some authority supporting this as a general rule,[93] but the issue is ultimately a matter of discretion for the court.[94] The law seems to have developed on similar lines in the case where proceedings are still pending against D1 at the time that he is called as a witness against D2.[95]

Where an accused testifies in his own defence, it is possible that he may give evidence incriminating a co-accused. It is generally accepted that the accused's evidence on oath is evidence for all purposes in the case, therefore any testimony given by him that incriminates a co-accused may be taken into account by the factfinder when considering the case against the co-accused. This applies whether D1 gives the evidence in chief[96] or under cross-examination.[97]

---

[88] Youth Justice and Criminal Evidence Act 1999 s.53(4), restating the former law in *Rhodes* [1899] 1 Q.B. 77.

[89] Youth Justice and Criminal Evidence Act 1999 s.53(4). This was the position both before and after the Criminal Evidence Act 1898: *Payne* (1872) L.R. 1 C.C.R. 349; *Grant* (1944) 30 Cr.App.R. 99; *Sharrock* (1948) 32 Cr.App.R. 124.

[90] Following Youth Justice and Criminal Evidence Act 1999 s 53(5), which provides "In subsection (4) the reference to a person charged in criminal proceedings does not include a person who is not, or is no longer, liable to be convicted of any offence in the proceedings (whether as a result of pleading guilty or for any other reason)".

[91] Or committal: see *Palmer* (1994) 99 Cr.App.R. 83 CA.

[92] It is immaterial that D1 later gives evidence suggesting that his plea of guilty was equivocal if it was unequivocal at the time: *McEwan* [2011] EWCA Crim 1026.

[93] *Weekes* (1982) 74 Cr.App.R. 161 at 166 per Boreham J.

[94] *Palmer* (1994) 99 Cr.App.R. 83 CA.

[95] See *Pipe* (1966) 51 Cr.App.R. 17; and cf. *Turner* (1975) 61 Cr.App.R. 67.

[96] *Rudd* (1948) 32 Cr.App.R. 138 CCA.

[97] *Paul* [1920] 2 K.B. 183 CCA.

In any case where one accomplice has given evidence against another, whether as **13–016** a witness for the prosecution or in his own defence, an issue may arise about the approach to be adopted in evaluating his evidence. This issue is considered in Ch.15, which deals generally with the use of warnings and directions to use care in respect of potentially suspect testimony. The further issue concerning cross-examination of an accused who gives evidence against a co-accused, on the accused's bad character, is dealt with in Ch.19.

E. THE SPOUSE OF THE ACCUSED

Under s.53(1) of the Youth Justice and Criminal Evidence Act 1999 the spouse of **13–017** the accused is competent to give evidence for all parties in criminal proceedings. This provision replaced the earlier rule in s.80(1) of PACE to the same effect.

As noted above, subs.(1) of s.53 of the Youth Justice and Criminal Evidence Act 1999 is subject to subs.(4). Under this provision a person charged in criminal proceedings is not competent to give evidence for the prosecution, whether he is the only person charged or is one of two or more persons. Therefore a wife who is charged with her husband in the same proceedings will not be competent for the prosecution against her husband irrespective of whether they are charged jointly with an offence or with different offences.

The basic principles of compellability of spouses are set out in subs.(2) and (3) of s.80 of PACE, as amended by the 1999 Act. Under subs.(2) the spouse or civil partner of the accused is compellable on behalf of the accused in all cases. The Criminal Law Revision Committee ("CLRC"), the architect of s.80, was in no doubt that this was the desirable rule. The principle that an accused person should have access to all relevant evidence capable of proving innocence has great force in this context. As the Committee said, "a husband might feel a great grievance if he could not compel his possibly estranged wife to give evidence for him".[98] The only exception arises where both the spouses or civil partners are charged in the same proceedings. In this case one accused will not be able to compel his or her spouse or civil partner to give evidence unless the latter is no longer liable to be convicted of any offence in the proceedings (whether as a result of pleading guilty or for any other reason).[99]

Compellability for the prosecution or for a co-accused is more problematic. The CLRC discussed the matter in some detail, and although the Government accepted its decision to adopt a principle of limited compellability in selected types of offence it extended the relevant categories in the legislation. Arguments in favour of a general principle of compellability include the public interests in the prosecution of offenders and the protection of victims and potential victims, plus a possible need to give wives some measure of protection against pressures to withdraw co-operation with the prosecution. A wife may be less subject to intimidation if she can say that she has no choice whether to testify against her husband. The arguments against compellability include the unedifying spectacle of publicly requiring one spouse to inform against the other, the forced disclosure of confidences and the disruption to marital harmony, together with the ethical

---

[98] *Eleventh Report* para.153.
[99] PACE s.80(4) and (4A), as substituted by Youth Justice and Criminal Evidence Act 1999.

stance that, while it is right to make a wife competent, she alone is the best person to judge whether her interest in the preservation of marital stability is sufficient reason for her not to testify. A further point is that compellability is unlikely to stop intimidation altogether, and may even be counter-productive because it reduces a victim's degree of control over the criminal justice process. It might even contribute to a decision not to report marital violence in the first place. This was a concern expressed particularly by organisations dealing with rape victims in responding to the Law Commission's working paper on the subject of rape within marriage.[100]

13–018   The CLRC's solution to the dilemma presented by these conflicting considerations was based on two main criteria. One was the necessity of the wife's evidence for proving the charge against the accused, the other was the seriousness of the offence itself. The Committee proposed that the wife should be compellable in cases of violence to her by her husband and violence to children under 16 belonging to the same household as the accused. The seriousness of such assaults, plus the special position of the wife as a witness of offences in the family, was thought to justify overriding her possible reluctance to testify. The Committee noted also that the wife herself may sometimes be a party to the violence, even though she is not prosecuted for it. Presumably the thinking was that her fault in this respect weakened her case for non-disclosure of her husband's conduct. To these cases of physical abuse the CLRC added sexual offences against children under 16 belonging to the accused's household. In the event, however, the Government did not accept the limitation of offences against children to children of the family, and widened the category to include any child under 16. This extension has been said to downgrade the importance of the necessity criterion, since there is no reason to believe that a wife will have special knowledge of her husband's offences against children who are not part of her family. The point is a fair one, although it has to be said that trials of paedophile gangs in recent years have shown that married couples may not infrequently be involved in offences against both their own children and the children of others.

Turning to the terms of the law, subs.(2A) and (3) provide:

> "(2A)   In any proceedings the spouse or civil partner of a person charged in the proceedings shall, subject to subsection (4) below, be compellable—
>   (a)   to give evidence on behalf of any other person charged in the proceedings, but only in respect of any specified offence with which that other person is charged; or
>   (b)   to give evidence for the prosecution but only in respect of any specified offence with which any person is charged in the proceedings.
> (3)   In relation to the spouse or civil partner of a person charged in any proceedings, an offence is a specified offence for the purposes of subsection (2A) above if—
>   (a)   it involves an assault on, or injury or a threat of injury to, the spouse or civil partner or a person who was at the material time under the age of 16;[101]

---

[100]   Law Com. No.205, *Criminal Law: Rape within Marriage* (1992) para.4.21.

[101]   This paragraph is concerned with the nature of the offence and not the specific factual circumstances in which the offence was committed: *R. v BA* [2012] EWCA Crim 1529. According to the Court of Appeal in this case the offence does not have to have as one of its ingredients an assault on or injury or threat of injury to the spouse; it is sufficient if the offence "encompasses the real possibility" of such an assault etc, as for example, an offence of arson endangering life. But if the

> (b)   it is a sexual offence alleged to have been committed in respect of a person who
>   was at the material time under that age;
> (c)   it consists of attempting or conspiring to commit, or of aiding, abetting,
>   counselling, procuring or inciting the commission of, an offence falling within
>   paragraph (a) or (b) above."

Once again this provision will be subject to the limitation in subs.(4) for cases where a spouse or civil partner is charged with his or her spouse or civil partner in the same proceedings. To take an example of a case involving an alleged paedophile ring, H and W might be charged jointly with P with sexual assaults on persons under 16. Neither H nor W would be a competent witness for the prosecution. Both would be competent for P, but neither would be compellable. The age limit in paras (a) and (b) of subs.(3) may be problematic where the husband is charged with a series of offences against his daughter committed both when she was under and over the age of 16. Such a case was *RL*,[102] where the defendant's wife had made a statement to the police which had the effect of destroying his defence to a count charging him with raping his daughter when she was 19. The wife subsequently described her statement as "all lies" and was unwilling to testify for the prosecution. Had the count of rape stood alone she would clearly not have been compellable. The Court of Appeal described it as a "nice point" whether she would have been compellable on the basis that her evidence of what happened on that occasion was relevant to the counts alleging indecent assaults on the daughter when under 16. However, it was not necessary to decide the point since the court upheld the trial judge's decision to admit the wife's statement to the police in the interests of justice under s.114(1)(d) of the Criminal Justice Act 2003.[103] Section 80 of PACE was said not to present a bar to the admission of such hearsay evidence[104]; any unfairness could be dealt with as a matter of the judge's discretion under s.114, or under s.78 of PACE.

A divorced spouse or former civil partner is as competent and compellable to give evidence as if he or she had never been married to, or a civil partner of, the accused.[105] The spouse or civil partner may therefore testify to matters occurring before, during and after the marriage or partnership. The law takes the view that since the marriage or civil partnership has formally ended, any interest in preserving confidence and stability between the parties has lapsed, or is at least outweighed by the principle of allowing the parties unrestricted access to relevant evidence.

In *Pearce*,[106] the Court of Appeal resisted an attempt to extend the general rule of no compellability for spouses to cohabitees. It was held that the woman who had lived with the defendant for 19 years and borne three children by him had been rightly compelled to testify for the prosecution on a charge against him of

13–019

---

offence does not fulfil this requirement (for example, the charge is criminal damage) it is not sufficient that the evidence reveals that there was a threat of assault or injury.

[102] *RL* [2008] EWCA Crim 973; [2008] 2 Cr.App.R. 18.

[103] See Ch.17.

[104] The court held further that there was no requirement on the police when interviewing a spouse to inform her that she was not a compellable witness against her husband.

[105] This is the combined effect of s.53(1) of the Youth Justice and Criminal Evidence Act 1999 and PACE s.80(5), as amended.

[106] *Pearce* [2001] EWCA Crim 2834; [2002] 1 Cr.App.R. 39.

murdering his brother. The defendant argued that the court should read down the words "wife or husband" so as to ensure that his partner's right to respect for family life under art.8 of the ECHR would be protected. The Court of Appeal held that this was an area where the interests of the family had to be weighed against those of the community, and that art.8 did not require that a limited concession made to husbands and wives should be extended. Even if her rights under art.8(1) had been infringed the interference was justified under art.8(2) as necessary in a democratic society for the prevention of crime. The court commented that if the compellability concession to spouses were to be widened it was not easy to see where, logically, it should stop. However, the Civil Partnership Act 2004 recently extended the compellability rules for spouses to include civil partners.[107]

There is an unresolved issue concerning the compellability of a wife in a prosecution against her husband for raping her. The question was not considered by the CLRC in 1972, or by Parliament in 1984, presumably because of the husband's traditional immunity at common law in respect of marital rape. When the immunity was judicially abolished by the House of Lords in *R. v R*,[108] the issue arose of whether the wife is compellable for the prosecution under subs.(3)(a). At first sight the answer appears clearly to be "Yes", because if the wife does not consent to the intercourse the husband commits an assault by forcing this unwanted physical contact upon her, and subs.(3)(a) says that the wife is compellable if the offence charged involves an assault upon her. However, subs.(3)(b) refers to sexual offences committed in respect of persons under 16, and these include rape, since subs.(7) defines "sexual offence" to mean an offence under the Protection of Children Act 1978 or Pt 1 of the Sexual Offences Act 2003. Since rape of an adult is not therefore included in subs.(3)(b), this might imply an intention that a wife should not be compellable for the prosecution where her husband is charged with raping her. The question may well be academic in most cases, since the prosecution are unlikely to want to call a reluctant complainant of rape, but it is submitted that in principle the wife ought to be treated as compellable.

In terms of principle the current law represents a compromise between opposing views on compellability of spouses.[109] As we have seen, subs.(3) provides for a spouse to be compellable for the prosecution in cases of child physical or sexual abuse and intra-spousal violence. The CLRC justified these cases partly by the need to punish violence, and also sexual offences against children, and partly on the ground of necessity—a wife's evidence may be essential to prove offences committed within the family or, we might add, within a paedophile ring involving a number of adults. This leaves many other serious offences, including murder, where the prosecution will not be able to call a wife or husband who is unwilling to testify against her or his spouse. It is easy to see that a spouse's evidence might be critically important in these other serious cases, and arguments based on the protection of potential victims might also apply with

---

[107] Civil Partnership Act 2004 s.261(1) and Sch.27 para.97, amending the relevant provisions of s.80 of PACE.
[108] *R. v R* [1992] 1 A.C. 599.
[109] See the discussion in J. Brabyn, "A Criminal Defendant's Spouse as a Prosecution Witness" [2011] Crim. L.R. 613.

great force. Such considerations suggest that it might be preferable to abandon attempts at compromise and to adopt a general rule that a spouse should be a compellable witness in all cases. This would have the additional advantage of removing the anomaly that other family members, and also partners who are unmarried but who are cohabiting in stable relationships, are not subject to any restrictions on compellability.

F. CHILDREN

1. *Historical background to the modern law*

At common law the testimony of a witness had to be given on oath. In its original **13–020** form the oath was a solemn promise, sworn on the Bible, to tell the truth. Because the promise was made at the same time to God and to the court, the theory was that breach in the form of deliberate lying was punishable by both divine and secular sanctions. The offence of perjury has existed in the law since the early years of the seventeenth century. For these sanctions to be meaningful to the promisor the common law insisted quite logically that before a person could take an oath the person had to understand the nature and consequences of an oath.

This requirement presented problems in relation to children. Young children are likely to lack the required understanding and hence are likely to be excluded from testifying. However, the exclusion of children's evidence causes significant difficulties for the administration of criminal justice. Children may be the only witnesses to offences against themselves, particularly sexual offences. They may also be important witnesses to other offences, including offences against other children. If their evidence is not available serious offenders may go unpunished, and other potential victims may be unprotected against dangerous persons. Hence repeated efforts have been made to escape from the rigour of the common law test of competency.

The first strategy consisted of the creation of a category of inferior, unsworn, testimony. Section 38 of the Children and Young Persons Act 1933 permitted a child of tender years to give unsworn evidence in a criminal case if two conditions were satisfied, namely that the child understood the duty of speaking the truth and was possessed of sufficient intelligence to justify the reception of the evidence. This was an inferior type of evidence in the sense that it had to be corroborated as a matter of law. In contrast with sworn testimony, on which an accused could be convicted in law without more,[110] the Act originally stipulated in a proviso to s.38 that no one could be convicted on unsworn testimony unless it was corroborated by some other evidence that implicated the accused in a material particular.

A second move was undertaken by the courts. In *Hayes*,[111] the Court of Appeal **13–021** acknowledged the reality that religious education in the late 20th century might

---

[110] Although the judge had to give a warning in respect of the sworn evidence of a child that it would be dangerous to convict in the absence of corroboration, the judge could also say, somewhat inconsistently, that the jury could convict on the child's evidence if they were convinced that the child was telling the truth. See further Ch.15.

[111] *Hayes* (1977) 64 Cr.App.R. 194 CA.

not correspond with the assumptions of an earlier and more devout age. Two boys aged 11 and 13 were questioned by the trial judge on their knowledge of God and on the religious instruction they received at school. Both claimed to be ignorant of the existence of God and to have received no religious instruction. Both, however, claimed also to be aware of the importance of telling the truth, particularly when they were in court. Upholding the judge's decision to allow them to give sworn testimony the Court of Appeal took a policy decision to secularise the common law test. It was sufficient, said Bridge L.J.,[112] that the child in question should have a sufficient appreciation of the solemnity of the occasion, and should understand that the duty of speaking the truth in court involved a higher duty than in everyday life. If these conditions were satisfied, it was not necessary that the child should be aware of the religious significance of an oath.

This decision may well have had the effect of making it easier for pre-teenage children to give sworn evidence. At the same time it reduced almost to vanishing point the difference between the tests for sworn and unsworn testimony of children. This in turn called into question the necessity for a requirement of actual corroboration for unsworn testimony when the sworn testimony of a child required only a corroboration warning to the jury.

There were other criticisms of the state of the law relating to children's evidence. Although the 1933 Act did not specify a lower age limit for the giving of unsworn testimony, in *Wallwork*,[113] the Court of Criminal Appeal had indicated, in an influential dictum,[114] that children as young as five and six should not be called as witnesses at all. This seemed to have been responsible for a widespread view in the profession that the effective minimum age for a child witness was seven or even eight.[115] Critics argued powerfully that such a rule failed to protect younger children. In a climate of increasing awareness of the scale of physical and sexual abuse of children, arguments for enhancing possibilities of conviction by allowing more evidence from younger victims had much appeal. The reform lobby pointed also to the emergence of empirical studies suggesting that children's evidence was not as unreliable as was traditionally alleged. In particular the research argued that children were not significantly worse than adults on matters of eyewitness observation and recall. Scepticism was expressed whether the dangers of possible fantasy, suggestibility or malice on the part of children had not been overstated. The general tenor of the campaign for reform was for removal of all technical restrictions on child witnesses, and the adoption of a policy of listening to the evidence of any child capable of giving an intelligible story.[116]

---

[112] *Hayes* (1977) 64 Cr.App.R. 194 at 196.

[113] *Wallwork* (1958) 42 Cr.App.R. 153 CCA.

[114] Approved as recently as 1987 by Ognall J. in *Wright and Ormerod* (1990) 90 Cr.App.R. 91 CA, where he commented that quite exceptional circumstances were required to justify the reception of the evidence of a child of extremely tender years, a 6-year-old girl in that case.

[115] In *Hayes* (1977) 64 Cr.App.R. 194 defence counsel made a concession, apparently accepted by the Court of Appeal, that the effective dividing line between children old enough to take the oath and those too young to do so fell between the ages of 8 and 10.

[116] The nature of the campaign, and the arguments used, are well demonstrated in the articles by Professor J. R. Spencer, one of the leading protagonists. See his "Child Witnesses Video Technology and the Law of Evidence" [1987] Crim. L.R. 76; "Child Witnesses and Video Technology: Thoughts

The reform campaign of the 1980s was very successful. It generated a succession of legislative and judicial innovations relating both to the competency of children and to the ways in which children may give their evidence. The introduction of courtroom screens, video links and video recordings has done much to lessen the trauma of testifying in the courtroom, a matter that had greatly concerned Lord Goddard in *Wallwork*. These developments are discussed in more detail in Ch.15. In relation to competency the Court of Appeal took the opportunity in Z[117] to repudiate as outdated the dictum in *Wallwork* concerning the minimum age for child witnesses, holding that the matter was entirely within the judge's discretion.

13–022

2. *The modern law of competency: criminal cases*

The modern law of competency of child witnesses in criminal cases is found in the provisions of ss.53–57 of the Youth Justice and Criminal Evidence Act 1999 ("YJCEA"). As we have seen, s.53(1) makes all persons (whatever their age) competent to give evidence at every stage in criminal proceedings. This subsection takes effect subject to the test of competence in s.53(3):

13–023

> "A person is not competent to give evidence in criminal proceedings if it appears to the court that he is not a person who is able to—
> (a)   understand questions put to him as a witness, and
> (b)   give answers to them which can be understood."

It is for the party calling the child witness to satisfy the court on the balance of probabilities that the child is competent to give evidence in the proceedings.[118] In determining that question the court shall treat the witness as having the benefit of any special measures directions that the court has given, or proposes to give, in respect of the witness.[119] Any questioning of the witness considered necessary to determine his or her competence shall be conducted by the court in the presence of the parties.[120] The court may receive expert evidence on the question.[121] Any such proceedings to determine competence must be held in the absence of the jury.[122]

Only witnesses aged 14 or over may give sworn evidence. A witness may not be sworn unless he has a sufficient appreciation of the solemnity of the occasion and of the particular responsibility to tell the truth that is involved in taking an oath.[123] There is a statutory presumption that a witness has a sufficient appreciation of these matters if he is able to give intelligible testimony.[124] The

---

for the Home Office" (1987) 51 Jo. Crim. Law 44; "Reforming the Competency Requirement" [1988] N.L.J. 147. For an excellent survey of children as witnesses see J. McEwan, *Evidence and the Adversarial Process,* 2nd edn (Oxford, 1998), pp.135–157.

[117] *Z* [1990] 2 Q.B. 355 CA.

[118] YJCEA s.54(2); *MacPherson* [2005] EWCA Crim 3605; [2006] 1 Cr.App.R. 30.

[119] YJCEA s.54(3). Special measures directions are discussed in Ch.15.

[120] YJCEA s.54(6).

[121] YJCEA s.54(5).

[122] YJCEA s.54(4).

[123] YJCEA s.55(2). This reflects the common law on oath-taking as stated by the Court of Appeal in *Hayes* (1977) 64 Cr.App.R. 194.

[124] YJCEA s.55(3).

test of intelligibility is the same as the test in s.53(1) for competence.[125] The presumption of sufficient appreciation is an evidential one, so that if there is evidence adduced tending to show the contrary, the burden is on the party seeking to have the witness sworn to satisfy the court on the balance of probabilities that the witness does meet these statutory conditions for sworn evidence.[126]

13–024 A child under the age of 14 who is competent to testify may give unsworn evidence.[127] This includes evidence by way of deposition.[128] No appeal in criminal proceedings may succeed on the ground only that a witness who gave evidence unsworn should have been required to take the oath.[129] It is a summary offence, similar to perjury, for a person giving evidence unsworn wilfully to give false evidence.[130] The difference between this offence and the indictable offence of perjury for false evidence on oath appears to be the only practical distinction between unsworn and sworn testimony. The Act does not specify any difference in the weight to be attached to the different forms of testimony, and there is no requirement of corroboration for unsworn evidence.

There is no express presumption of competency under the YJCEA provisions, although it is arguably implicit in s.54(1) that a child will normally be assumed to be competent, unless there is reason to doubt this. Section 54(1) refers to the question being raised by a party or by the court itself; the question might be raised when the child begins to give evidence or beforehand. In practice the issue will often emerge where leave is sought to admit a video recording of an interview with the child as the child's evidence in chief under s.27 of the YJCEA.

The judge will determine the issue of the child's competency as a matter of the admissibility of evidence in any case where the issue is raised. Where the prosecution apply to put in evidence a pre-recorded interview with the child, the judge can normally form a view about the child's competence when viewing the recording. If, however, the judge is left in doubt, or if the child's evidence in chief is not to be given by a video recording and competence is in issue, the judge should investigate the issue as part of the trial. The judge can do this by asking general questions of the child in open court in the presence of the accused,[131] but must not do so in the presence of the jury.[132] The purpose of the questions will be to see whether the child can give evidence that is capable of being understood. This test has rightly been said to be a simple one well within the capacity of a judge or lay magistrate,[133] but nonetheless expert evidence may be received on the question of competence.[134] Expert evidence is most likely to be of assistance where a witness, whether a child or an adult, suffers from mental illness or disability.

---

[125] YJCEA s.55(8).
[126] YJCEA s.55(4).
[127] YJCEA s.56(1) and (2).
[128] YJCEA s.56(3).
[129] YJCEA s.56(5).
[130] YJCEA s.57.
[131] *Hampshire* [1995] 2 Cr.App.R. 319 CA; *DPP v M* [1997] 2 Cr.App.R. 70 DC.
[132] YJCEA s.54(4).
[133] *G v DPP* [1997] 2 Cr.App.R. 78 DC.
[134] YJCEA s.54(5).

In *Barker*,[135] the Court of Appeal emphasised that the test of competency requires a judgment by the trial judge that is witness-specific, and that the clear words of s.53 should not be glossed or reinterpreted:

"These statutory provisions are not limited to the evidence of children. They apply to individuals of unsound mind. They apply to the infirm. The question in each case is whether the individual witness, or, as in this case, the individual child, is competent to give evidence in the particular trial. The question is entirely witness or child specific. There are no presumptions or preconceptions. The witness need not understand the special importance that the truth should be told in court, and the witness need not understand every single question or give a readily understood answer to every question. Many competent adult witnesses would fail such a competency test. Dealing with it broadly and fairly, provided the witness can understand the questions put to him and can also provide understandable answers, he or she is competent. If the witness cannot understand the questions or his answers to questions which he understands cannot themselves be understood he is not. The questions come, of course, from both sides. If the child is called as a witness by the prosecution he or she must have the ability to understand the questions put to him by the defence as well as the prosecution and to provide answers to them which are understandable. The provisions of the statute are clear and unequivocal, and do not require reinterpretation."[136]

It is worth emphasising the difference in the tests for giving sworn and unsworn evidence. The test for sworn testimony follows the common law as set out in *Hayes*. The test for competence in s.53(3), and competence is all that is needed for unsworn evidence, directs the court to assess the child's intellectual capacities, notably the child's powers of speech and narration. What it does not do is make any reference to the child's moral sense. As *Barker* confirms, there is no formal requirement for unsworn testimony in a criminal case that the child should understand the duty of speaking the truth. In *MacPherson*,[137] the Court of Appeal expressly rejected an attempt by defence counsel to reintroduce a requirement for competency that the child should appreciate the difference between truth and falsehood. But it does not follow that the abandonment of a test whether the child can tell truth from lies means that all ability to distinguish truth and reality from fiction and fantasy is now irrelevant. Built into the notions of the ability to understand questions about the offence, and to answer them in a way that the jury can understand, seems to be an essential basic sense of the objectivity of experience. In other words, the court must surely be satisfied, if the issue is raised, that the "intelligibility" of the child's evidence incorporates an understanding of the concept of "what really happened" and of the ability to describe it. In *Malicki* the child complainant was four years and eight months old at the time of the alleged offence. When the trial came on after a delay of 14 months she could no longer distinguish between her memory of the event and her memory of her video interview which she had seen twice shortly before being cross-examined. In these circumstances the Court of Appeal considered that effective cross-examination was impossible and that the trial judge should have stopped the case. Her competency was subsequently described in *Barker* as "at least doubtful".[138]

---

[135] *Barker* [2010] EWCA Crim 4.
[136] *Barker* [2010] EWCA Crim 4 at [38].
[137] *MacPherson* [2005] EWCA Crim 3605; [2006] 1 Cr.App.R. 30.
[138] *Barker* [2010] EWCA Crim 4 at [50]. *Malicki* [2009] EWCA Crim 365 should be compared with *DPP v R.* [2007] EWHC 1842 (Admin), where the Divisional Court held that a loss of memory of the

13–025   *Malicki* is part of a line of authority[139] holding that the trial judge should keep the issue of competency under review and be prepared to reconsider it at the end of the child's evidence. According to the Court of Appeal in *Barker*, which described this as a judicially created extra-statutory jurisdiction:

> "The second test should be viewed as an element in the defendant's entitlement to a fair trial ... If the child witness has been unable to provide intelligible answers to questions in cross-examination (as in *Powell*) or a meaningful cross-examination was impossible (as in *Malicki*) the first competency decision will not have produced a fair trial, and in that event the evidence admitted on the basis of a competency decision which turned out to be wrong could reasonably be excluded under section 78 of the 1984 Act."[140]

At the same time the Court of Appeal has stressed that competence is not the same as credibility. If the judge is satisfied that the child is competent according to the statutory criteria it is for the jury to decide whether the child has given truthful and accurate evidence. Moreover, there is no implication that children are in general less credible than adults:

> "if competent, as defined by the statutory criteria, in the context of credibility in the forensic process, the child witness starts off on the basis of equality with every other witness."[141]

In *Barker,* the Court of Appeal upheld a conviction for rape of a child aged just under three at the time of the offence and four and a half at the time of trial. The court described her as a "compelling as well as a competent witness",[142] and confirmed that it is open to a properly directed jury to reach a safe conclusion on the evidence of a single competent witness whatever her age or disability. However, where a very young child complainant is concerned delay in bringing the case to trial is a significant concern, because of the risk that counsel will not be able to put the defence case fairly to the child. It is not a rule that delay necessarily results in unfairness, as the decision in *Barker* demonstrates, but in other cases judges have emphasised the desirability of fast-tracking trials involving such young witnesses.[143] In a case where there is evidence capable of supporting an allegation of fabrication or fantasy on the part of a child, a judge might well think it appropriate to direct the jury to approach the child's evidence with caution in view of the challenge and to look for any evidence tending to support the child's evidence. The precise terms and strength of the warning would be within the judge's discretion. Contamination of a child's evidence by suggestive pre-trial questioning from police officers or other adults is a potentially serious risk, as the Butler-Sloss report into the Cleveland child abuse

---

events in question, which occurs between the video interview and the trial and results in the defendant being unable to cross-examine effectively, is not the same as incompetence and goes to weight not admissibility.

[139]   *MacPherson* [2005] EWCA Crim 3605; [2006] 1 Cr.App.R. 30; *Powell* [2006] EWCA Crim 3; [2006] 1 Cr.App.R. 31; *R. v M* [2008] EWCA Crim 2751; *Malicki* [2009] EWCA Crim 365; *Barker* [2010] EWCA Crim 4.

[140]   *Barker* [2010] EWCA Crim 4 at [43].

[141]   *Barker* [2010] EWCA Crim 4 at [40].

[142]   *Barker* [2010] EWCA Crim 4 at [52].

[143]   *Powell* [2006] EWCA Crim 3; [2006] 1 Cr.App.R. 31; *Malicki* [2009] EWCA Crim 365.

controversy recognised.[144] A judge who took the view that the risk in a particular case was so great that no reliance could safely be placed on the child's evidence could exclude the evidence altogether under s.78 of PACE.

3. *The modern law of competency: civil cases*

The position of child witnesses in civil cases is slightly more complicated. The basic common law principle applies that the child may give evidence on oath if he or she understands the nature of an oath. Although authority is lacking, it would seem likely that the interpretation of this requirement expounded by the Court of Appeal in the criminal case of *Hayes* would be held to apply. However, the common law is supplemented, as the criminal law used to be before 1991, by a provision allowing for the child's evidence to be heard unsworn if the child does not understand the nature of an oath. The Children Act 1989 s.96 provides that the child's evidence may be heard if the child understands the duty to speak the truth and has sufficient understanding to justify the evidence being heard.[145]   **13–026**

It is unclear whether this second condition goes further than the requirement in the YJCEA that a child should understand questions being put to him and give answers that can be understood (intelligible answers). However, the first condition in s.96 of the Children Act is certainly stricter than the criminal law, because it retains the requirement, now dropped by the criminal law, that the child understands the duty of truth-telling. Whether this strictness is justifiable is debatable. Its effect may be to exclude the testimony of very young children in civil cases. Yet a civil court might well have to investigate the same issues, say, of alleged child sexual abuse, as a criminal court, in which case exclusion seems anomalous and undesirable. On the other hand the Children Act has effectively abolished the hearsay rule in those types of civil case where the evidence of children is most likely to be heard.[146] If evidence of younger children is to reach the court in the form of hearsay statements on any regular basis then the stricter conditions of admissibility may be justified as offering greater circumstantial guarantees of reliability.

G.   PERSONS UNDER MENTAL DISABILITY

The scheme established by ss.53–57 of the YJCEA applies to persons under disability as it does to all witnesses in criminal proceedings. This means that an adult witness under disability, who was formerly unable to testify if he or she lacked sufficient understanding to take the oath,[147] is now able to give evidence unsworn provided he or she passes the basic test of competence.[148] In this way vulnerable adults who have been the victims of physical or sexual abuse may be   **13–027**

---

[144] Cm.412 (1988). See further Ch.15.

[145] A child, for this purpose, is a person under the age of 18: s.105.

[146] That is, evidence in connection with the upbringing, maintenance or welfare of a child: see Children Act 1989 s.96(3) and the orders made thereunder.

[147] On the application of the common law principle of competency to mentally ill or handicapped witnesses see *Hill* (1851) 2 Den. 254; *Bellamy* (1986) 82 Cr.App.R. 222.

[148] YJCEA s.56(1) and (2).

able to help bring their abusers to justice. Their position is helped further by the possibility of special measures directions[149] that may include the examination of them through an approved intermediary.[150] In assessing a witness's competence the court may treat the witness as having the benefit of any special measures directions that it has given or proposes to give in relation to the witness.[151] The court may hear expert evidence on the issue of competency.[152] This should be taken in open court in the presence of the accused but not the jury.[153]

According to the Court of Appeal in *Sed*,[154] the test of competence in s.53(3) of the YJCEA does not necessarily require 100 per cent mutual comprehension of material exchanges giving rise to potential evidence. In this case an 81-year-old complainant of rape, who suffered from moderate to severe Alzheimer's disease, had given a video-recorded interview to the police. Her account and her responses to questions were somewhat patchy—sometimes her answers were hard to understand or bore little relation to the question asked—but "the abiding picture was of a woman who was nevertheless complaining repeatedly of a particular recent sexual assault".[155] Upholding the judge's decision to admit the recording,[156] the Court of Appeal said that, taking the potential witness's performance as a whole, if there is a common and comprehensible thread in his or her responses to the questions, however patchy, and on critical matters the witness can be seen and heard to be intelligible, then the test of competence is satisfied and it is for the jury to determine matters of reliability and general cogency. This purposive approach to the s.53 test is to be applauded. It gives effect to the policy we have already noted in connection with children of protecting vulnerable persons from exploitation and abuse by giving them a voice in court whenever possible.

In *Sed,* the Court of Appeal was much influenced by the earlier decision in *R. v D*,[157] where on rather similar facts the court had upheld the admission of a recorded interview by reference to the test in s.53, and had also referred to the "right" of the witness to have her complaint placed before a jury and have the jury assess whether they are sure the complaint is established. The source of this "right" was not stated, but it is clear from the more recent decision in *R. (on the application of B) v DPP*[158] that art.3 of the ECHR may be engaged in prosecutions involving vulnerable complainants. In that case a prosecution for causing grievous bodily harm with intent was discontinued because counsel had advised that he could not put forward the complainant as a reliable witness. A

---

[149] For further discussion see D. Birch, "A Better Deal for Vulnerable Witnesses?" [2000] Crim. L.R. 223.

[150] YJCEA s.29. For discussion see L. Ellison, "Cross-Examination and the Intermediary: Bridging the Language Divide?" [2002] Crim. L.R. 114.

[151] YJCEA s.54(3).

[152] YJCEA s.54(5).

[153] See *Deakin* [1994] 4 All E.R. 769 CA; and *Hampshire* [1995] 2 Cr.App.R. 319.

[154] *Sed* [2004] EWCA Crim 1294; [2005] 1 Cr.App.R. 4.

[155] *Sed* [2004] EWCA Crim 1294; [2005] 1 Cr.App.R. 4 at [42].

[156] As an exception to the hearsay rule under s.23 of the Criminal Justice Act 1988. Section 23, and the other provisions of the 1988 Act dealing with documentary hearsay, have been repealed by the Criminal Justice Act 2003 and replaced by the new scheme in Ch.2 of Pt 11 of that Act. See Ch.17.

[157] *R. v D* [2002] EWCA Crim 990; [2002] 2 Cr.App.R. 36.

[158] *R. (on the application of B) v DPP* [2009] EWHC 106 (Admin).

psychiatric report had stated that the complainant suffered from a condition which *might* affect his perception and recollection of events so as to make his evidence unreliable. In a forceful judgment the Divisional Court ruled that the discontinuance decision was irrational and unlawful. The complainant's account was factually credible, and the conclusion that he could not be put forward as a credible witness was either based on a misreading of the psychiatric report or on unfounded stereotyping of the complainant in vew of his history of mental illness. The decision was also said to be a violation of the complainant's rights under art.3 because it amounted to a failure by the state to fulfil its positive obligation to provide protection through the criminal justice system against serious assaults.

H.   OATHS AND AFFIRMATIONS

Centuries ago the common law required all witnesses to give evidence on oath, and a witness was not competent unless he was prepared to swear an oath on the Gospel. This strict rule was gradually relaxed over the years. While witnesses are still required to give sworn evidence, except when they give unsworn evidence under s.56 of the YJCEA, they can now take an oath or make an affirmation in accordance with the broader rules contained in the Oaths Act 1978.   **13–028**

Section 1 of the Oaths Act 1978 sets out the form in which oaths are to be administered to Christians or Jews. This form is to be followed unless the witness objects or the witness is physically incapable of taking the oath in the way prescribed. A witness who wishes to affirm instead of taking the oath may do so, and the affirmation has the same force and effect as an oath.[159] Where the witness is neither a Christian nor a Jew, the witness may make an affirmation or take an oath in the manner prescribed by another religion, provided that the court and the witness considers the oath to be binding on his conscience.[160] Where the ground has been properly laid for an expectation that a witness would normally take the oath on a holy book relevant to their religious belief, sensitive questioning may be permissible on why the witness chose to affirm instead.[161] By s.4(2) the validity of an oath duly administered and taken is not affected by the lack of any religious belief on the part of the witness.

---

[159] Oaths Act 1978 s.5. This means that the witness who gives false evidence on affirmation is liable for perjury in the same way as if he had lied on oath.
[160] Oaths Act 1978 s.4(1); *Kemble* [1990] 1 W.L.R. 1111.
[161] *Mehrban* [2001] EWCA Crim 2627; [2002] 1 Cr.App.R. 40.

CHAPTER 14

EXAMINATION OF WITNESSES

A. INTRODUCTION

This chapter deals with the questioning of witnesses at trial, a topic that raises **14–001** numerous issues about the scope and limits of examination in chief and cross-examination. A substantial body of law has developed in relation to these issues, but much of the law makes use of imprecise concepts and flexible rules that leave judges with a good deal of discretion as to their application. To gain a full understanding of how the law works in practice, it is a good idea to visit both a Crown Court and a magistrates' court to observe a number of trials.

There are other aspects of the law relating to witnesses that are dealt with elsewhere in this book. The power to call witnesses, the rules of competence to testify, the limits of compulsion to testify and the formal requirements for giving evidence on oath are all covered in Ch.13. Issues of whether a witness can claim a privilege or an immunity from answering questions or producing documents frequently arise first in pre-trial process concerned with disclosure and production of evidence. For this reason such issues are dealt with in various chapters in Pt II. In recent years there has been increasing concern over the way vulnerable witnesses are treated in legal proceedings, and Ch.15 devotes a special section to this topic. Chapter 15 also considers the issue of protection of the accused from witnesses whose evidence is suspect for one reason or another. Chapter 19, which deals with the admissibility of evidence of an accused's bad character under the Criminal Justice Act 2003, covers cross-examination of an accused on bad character when he testifies as a witness in his own defence. Lastly, the evidence of expert witnesses is discussed in Ch.20.

One topic not covered in this book is the technique of questioning witnesses. This topic belongs to the study of advocacy rather than the law of evidence; the process of questioning a witness effectively is a highly skilled forensic art. Specialist manuals of advocacy provide useful discussion of courtroom technique, as well as salutary warnings about pitfalls to be avoided. Again, much can be learnt from observing trials and seeing how counsel conduct examinations and cross-examinations in court. Ultimately, though, there is no substitute for practical experience, a process which for some advocates at least may be literally one of trial and error.

14–002   A further introductory point is that the rules for the examination of witnesses embody two fundamental principles that sometimes exert contradictory influences on the shape of the law. First, it should be remembered that the rules developed in the context of an adversarial system of procedure. Historically the law was designed to function in a system of adjudication where, broadly speaking, it is the parties who define the issues, find the evidence and present the evidence to an essentially passive adjudicative tribunal. Under this system witnesses are called by one side or the other because they are expected, in the normal course of events, to testify in support of the version of the facts put forward by the party calling them. This means that a witness's testimony in chief will be intended to be demonstrative. Counsel's aim will be to get the witness to give evidence in a way that shows the party's case to its best advantage. Cross-examination, on the other hand, will usually be aimed at destroying or reducing this advantageous effect, either directly by getting the witness to retract or modify the testimony, and/or indirectly by discrediting the witness generally. Because of their passive, umpireal, role judges should in principle not engage in questioning of witnesses at all; if they do intervene it should only be for the purpose of clarification.[1] It follows that witnesses will not generally be

---

[1] That is, to clarify matters that the judge does not understand or thinks the jury may not understand: *Sharp* [1993] 3 All E.R. 225 at 235 CA. In *R. v MM* [2011] EWCA Crim 1291 at [35] the Court of Appeal explained that it is permissible for a judge to pose questions to a witness (including a

questioned by anyone involved in the proceedings in a spirit of free impartial inquiry. Partisan, controlled questioning is the norm, and free report by the witness is the exception. This point helps to explain why some witnesses find the process of testifying at best bewildering, because they are unable to tell their story in their own way, or at worst traumatic, because of "robust" cross-examination that may have the effect of making them feel that they themselves are on trial.

Secondly, however, courts frequently maintain that they are engaged in a search for the truth regarding the facts in issue.[2] A commitment to rectitude of decision as the main aim of adjudication entails a commitment to discovering the "true facts" of the issue. Consequently the courts may set limits to the partisan presentation of the evidence, in the interests of promoting the truth-finding objective. A concern with the quality of evidence is a pervasive theme in the law relating to witnesses, as it is throughout the law of evidence. One of the most important manifestations of this concern is the rule that forbids the training or coaching of witnesses. The rule was emphatically affirmed by the Court of Appeal in the leading case of *Momodou and Limani*,[3] where an issue arose about a witness training programme arranged by a security company for a number of their employees involved in a major disturbance at an immigration detention centre managed by the company. A number of the detainees were charged with offences arising out of the disturbance. The training programme was severely criticised by both prosecution and defence at the trial as "wholly inappropriate and improper". The trial judge expressly associated himself with this agreed fact and directed the jury in robust terms that it was unlawful. Agreeing, Judge L.J. took the opportunity to restate the relevant principles:

> "There is a dramatic distinction between witness training or coaching, and witness familiarization. Training or coaching for witnesses in criminal proceedings (whether for prosecution or defence) is not permitted. This is the logical consequence of the well-known principle that discussions between witnesses should not take place, and that the statements and proofs of one witness should not be disclosed to any other witness ... The witness should give his or her own evidence, so far as practicable uninfluenced by what anyone else has said, whether in formal discussion or informal conversations. The rule reduces, indeed hopefully avoids, any possibility that one witness may tailor his evidence in the light of what anyone else has said, and equally avoids any unfounded perception that he may have done so. These risks are inherent in witness training. Even if the training takes place one-to-one with someone completely remote from the facts of the case itself, the witness may come, even unconsciously, to appreciate which aspects of his evidence are perhaps not quite consistent with what others are saying, or indeed not quite what is required of him. An honest witness may alter the

---

defendant) for the purpose of resolving ambiguity. "Ambiguity may arise, in our judgment, on occasions when the jury without assistance from the witness himself is likely to speculate when otherwise evidence may be given by way of explanation." Applying this principle, the court upheld a judge's questions to a defendant in a rape case whether he had done or said anything which might have caused V to make an admitted 999 call to the police, and whether there had been any reaction by V to indicate pain or discomfort during the sexual activity that D maintained was consensual, but which V said was not and which had caused her injury. The court agreed that in the absence of D's answers the jury might otherwise have speculated about the reasons for the call and whether V's injuries were consistent with D's account of the activity. The dividing line between asking clarificatory questions of this type and acting as prosecution counsel may be a fine one.
[2] For a recent reaffirmation of this principle see *R. v A (No.2)* [2001] UKHL 25; [2001] 2 Cr.App.R. 21 at [55] per Lord Hope.
[3] *Momodou and Limani* [2005] EWCA Crim 177; [2005] 2 Cr.App.R. 6.

emphasis of his evidence to accommodate what he thinks may be a different, more accurate, or simply better remembered perception of events. A dishonest witness will very rapidly calculate how his testimony may be 'improved'. These dangers are present in one-to-one witness training. Where, however, the witness is jointly trained with other witnesses to the same events, the dangers dramatically increase. Recollections change. Memories are contaminated. Witnesses may bring their respective accounts into what they believe to be better alignment with others. They may be encouraged to do so, consciously or unconsciously. They may collude deliberately. They may be inadvertently contaminated. Whether deliberately or inadvertently, the evidence may no longer be their own. Although none of this is inevitable, the risk that training or coaching may adversely affect the accuracy of the evidence of the individual witness is constant. So we repeat, witness training for criminal trials is prohibited.

This principle does not preclude pre-trial arrangements to familiarize the witness with the layout of the court, the likely sequence of events when the witness is giving evidence, and a balanced appraisal of the different responsibilities of the various participants. Indeed such arrangements, usually in the form of a pre-trial visit to the court, are generally to be welcomed. Witnesses should not be disadvantaged by ignorance of the process, nor, when they come to give evidence, taken by surprise at the way it works. None of this however involves discussions about proposed or intended evidence. Sensible preparation for the experience of giving evidence, which assists the witness to give of his or her best at the forthcoming trial, is permissible. Such experience can also be provided by out of court familiarization techniques. The process may improve the manner in which the witness gives evidence by, for example, reducing the nervous tension arising from inexperience of the process. Nevertheless the evidence remains the witness's own uncontaminated evidence... The critical feature of training of this kind is that it should not be arranged in the context of nor related to any forthcoming trial, and it can therefore have no impact whatever on it."[4]

Both principles, party autonomy and the truth-finding role of the court, are in turn subject to the disciplines of necessity and efficiency. Human beings are mortal, and the resources of the legal system are not infinite. Therefore limits have to be set to the scope of the inquiry and to the length and cost of the proceedings. The interaction of these principles and policies helps to explain much of the complex, and apparently arbitrary, nature of the law.

B. EXAMINATION IN CHIEF

14–003 The party who calls a witness is generally the first to question the witness, and this stage of questioning is known as the examination in chief. It is also sometimes called direct examination. The general principle is that a witness must give oral testimony in chief,[5] but there are important exceptions to this principle. First, in civil proceedings, a written statement by a witness, which has been served on the other parties in accordance with the directions of the court in the action, will normally be ordered to stand as the witness's evidence in chief.[6]

---

[4] *Momodou and Limani* [2005] EWCA Crim 177; [2005] 2 Cr.App.R. 6 at [61] and [62]. Judge L.J. went on to give broad guidance about the procedure to be followed where arrangements are made for witness familiarisation by outside agencies (and not, e.g. by the Witness Service). This includes consultation with the Crown Prosecution Service ("CPS") where prosecution witnesses are concerned, advice of counsel where defence witnesses are concerned, supervision of the training by a solicitor or barrister, and so on (see [63]–[65]).

[5] See CPR r.32.2.

[6] CPR r.32.5(2) provides that the witness statement of a witness called to give oral evidence shall stand as the evidence in chief of the witness concerned unless otherwise ordered. Where there is a conflict of evidence on the facts a judge might usefully exercise the discretion to require the witness to give oral testimony in chief: *Cole v Kivells, The Times*, May 2, 1997.

Secondly, in criminal proceedings, one of the special measures directions that may be given for vulnerable and intimidated witnesses is an order that a video-recorded interview with the witness is to be admitted as the evidence in chief of the witness. Such orders were first introduced for certain cases involving child witnesses; s.27 of the Youth Justice and Criminal Evidence Act 1999 subsequently extended their availability as part of the package of special measures directions for eligible categories of witness. The details of the package, and the eligible categories of witness, are considered in the next chapter. For present purposes it can be noted that, where a video recording is admitted as the witness's evidence in chief, the witness may not without the permission of the court give evidence in chief otherwise than by means of the recording as to any matter which, in the opinion of the court, is dealt with in the witness's recorded testimony.[7] The court should not make a direction for the admission of a video recording under s.27 if it would not be in the interests of justice for it to be admitted,[8] and in certain circumstances where a direction has been made the court may subsequently decline to admit the recording—for example where it appears that the witness will not be available for cross-examination.[9] The rationale of s.27 directions, in common with other special measures, is the policy of witness protection. Admitting video-recorded interviews as their evidence in chief helps to reduce the stress on vulnerable witnesses when testifying, and may improve the quality of the evidence they give. It is not a formal condition of the admissibility of a video recording under s.27 that the recording should have been made at a time when the events in question were fresh in the witness's memory, although this will usually be the case.

Thirdly, s.137 of the Criminal Justice Act 2003 provides a general power to admit a video recording as the evidence in chief of a witness in cases of serious offences. The section gives effect to a recommendation in the Auld Review[10] and has similar objectives to s.27 of the Youth Justice and Criminal Evidence Act 1999, namely the reduction of stress on witnesses and the promotion of the giving of best evidence via a recording made when the events were fresh in the witness's memory. The two sections partly duplicate each other as far as vulnerable witnesses to serious crimes are concerned, but s.27 remains the governing provision for special measures directions for eligible witnesses.[11] There would be no advantage in using s.137 for admitting video recordings of witnesses eligible for special measures because s.137 provides for greater conditions of admissibility than s.27.

Section 137 has not yet been brought into force, probably due to its resource implications for the police and the Crown Prosecution Service. It is unclear when, if ever, it will take effect. On the assumption that it may be brought into force at some stage, a brief summary is provided here. Under s.137 a court may direct that

---

[7] Youth Justice and Criminal Evidence Act 1999 s.27(5)(b), as substituted by Coroners and Justice Act 2009 s.103(2).

[8] Youth Justice and Criminal Evidence Act 1999 s.27(2). See further Ch.15.

[9] Youth Justice and Criminal Evidence Act 1999 s.27(4).

[10] *Review of the Criminal Courts of England and Wales* (2001), p.555.

[11] Criminal Justice Act 2003 s.138(5) provides that nothing in s.137 affects the admissibility of any video recording that would be admissible apart from that section.

a video recording should be admitted as evidence in chief of a witness where the following set of conditions is satisfied[12]:

(a)   a person is called as a witness in proceedings for an offence triable only on indictment, or for a prescribed offence triable either way;

(b)   the person claims to have witnessed the conduct constituting the offence or part of it, or events closely connected with it;

(c)   the person has previously given an account of what he witnessed (whether or not in response to questions) at a time when the events in question were fresh in his memory;

(d)   a video recording was made of the account;

(e)   the witness's memory of the events is likely to have been significantly better when he gave the recorded account than it will be when he gives oral evidence in the proceedings; and

(f)   it must be in the interests of justice for the recording to be admitted.[13]

14–004   Directions can be made in respect of both prosecution and defence witnesses, except that the defendant himself is excluded.[14] A defendant who wishes to give evidence in his defence will always have to give oral testimony.[15]

The effect of s.137(2) is that where a video recording is admitted under the section, the statements made by the witness in the recording are treated as having been made by him in his oral evidence in the proceedings, to the extent that he asserts that they are true. In such a case therefore the statements will not be hearsay evidence. Section 138 of the Criminal Justice Act 2003 sets out some consequential provisions for cases where video recordings are admitted under s.137. The direction may be that only part of a recording may be admitted; in this way recordings may be edited to avoid a risk of prejudice to the defendant, although the court must still make an estimate of whether the interests of justice nevertheless require the whole of the recorded interview to be shown.[16]

1.   *Relevance, credit and previous consistent statements*

14–005   The general rule is that a witness may be asked any question in examination in chief that is relevant to a fact in issue in the proceedings, and that is not inadmissible by virtue of an exclusory rule. Relevance is determined according to the normal principles, but there are important refinements to be

---

[12] Criminal Justice Act 2003 s.137(1) and (3)(b).

[13] Criminal Justice Act 2003 s.137(3)(b)(ii) provides that in determining the interests of justice the court should have regard in particular to the matters mentioned in subs.(4), namely the time interval between the events witnessed and the making of the recorded account, any other factors that might affect the reliability of the account, the quality of the recording, and any views of the witness as to whether his evidence should be given orally or by means of the recording.

[14] Criminal Justice Act 2003 s.137(3)(a).

[15] The defendant is excluded from any category of witness eligible for special measures (Youth Justice and Criminal Evidence Act 1999 ss.16(1) and 17(1)), with the exception of the use of live link (Youth Justice and Criminal Evidence 1999 s.33A) and intermediaries (Youth Justice and Criminal Evidence Act 1999 s.33BA). See Ch.15.

[16] Criminal Justice Act 2003 s.138(2) and (3).

noted in this context. A party calling a witness is taken to be putting forward the witness as a witness worthy of belief,[17] hence the examiner in chief is not generally permitted to adduce evidence relating solely to the witness's credibility. In *Turner*,[18] Lawton L.J. referred to:

> "what have long been thought to be the rules relating to the calling of evidence on the issue of credibility, i.e. that in general evidence can be called to impugn the credibility of witnesses but not led in chief to bolster it up."[19]

Although evidence supporting the witness's credibility might be thought to be relevant to the weight to be attached to the witness's evidence, it is not sufficiently relevant to be admitted. This is partly because it is superfluous (the witness is presumed to be capable of belief), and partly because of its incidental costs (the time and expense involved in hearing it, the side issues to which it might give rise, and the risk it creates of multiplying the issues and confusing the factfinder).

One form of evidence supporting a witness's credibility is evidence that a witness has made a previous statement that is consistent with the witness's testimony at trial. The consistency of a witness's story might be some indication of its truth; certainly inconsistency is often regarded as a sign that the witness may not be worthy of credit. Following the principle stated in the previous paragraph, a previous consistent statement of a witness is not generally admissible, but there are exceptions, discussed below. However, the reliability of evidence going to credit may be an additional problem. Even if an exception is applicable, a further doubt may arise where the previous statement was made using an allegedly "scientific" test that purports to demonstrate the statement's reliability. One case is where a person makes a statement when interviewed after being given a so-called "truth drug". In New Zealand, evidence of such statements made by an accused, which were consistent with the accused's testimony at trial, has been rejected, partly because of doubts about the reliability of statements made in these circumstances.[20] An English court would almost

---

[17] However, there is no principle of law or justice that requires the prosecution to regard the whole of a witness's evidence to be reliable before he can be called as a prosecution witness. A prosecutor is entitled to call a witness if he forms the view that part of the witness's evidence is capable of belief, even though he does not rely on another part: *Cairns* [2002] EWCA Crim 2838; [2003] 1 Cr.App.R. 38 at [36]. At common law, if the prosecution in a criminal case were aware that their witness was of bad character, they had a duty to inform the defence of the witness's previous convictions: *Collister and Warhurst* (1955) 39 Cr.App.R. 100 CCA; *Paraskeva* (1983) 76 Cr.App.R. 162 CA; *Brown (Winston)* [1998] A.C. 367 HL. Such convictions must now be disclosed as part of the duty of initial prosecution disclosure under s.3(1) of the Criminal Procedure and Investigations Act 1996. The prosecution will then be asking the court to accept the witness's evidence despite his admitted bad character.

[18] *Turner* [1975] Q.B. 834 at 842.

[19] For further examples of judicial disapproval of "oath-helping" see *Robinson* (1994) 98 Cr.App.R. 370 CA; and *R. v T (AB)* [2006] EWCA Crim 2006; [2007] 1 Cr.App.R.4, where the Court of Appeal allowed the defendant's appeal and ordered a retrial of sexual abuse charges in relation to his young niece after the trial judge permitted the prosecution to lead evidence that the girl's grandfather had admitted abusing her and that her step-grandfather had been convicted of doing so. According to the court, this evidence was not relevant to the issue of whether her uncle had abused her. Its only purpose was to bolster her credibility as a witness against him.

[20] *McKay* [1967] N.Z.L.R. 139 New Zealand Court of Appeal.

certainly take the same line. Similarly, it is generally assumed that in England evidence of statements made by a witness who has taken a polygraph (lie-detector) test would be excluded, in view of the unproven accuracy of the technique.[21] On the other hand, it appears that statements made by witnesses under hypnosis may be admitted, provided they have been obtained in accordance with the Home Office guidelines on the use of hypnosis.[22]

14–006   We now examine the rule about previous consistent statements in more detail. The starting-point is two general rules at common law. The hearsay rule generally prevents a witness's previous consistent statement being admitted as evidence of the facts stated. A second and independent rule prevents such a statement being admitted to show the witness's consistency. The rationale of exclusion in the latter case derives from the factors mentioned above as justifying the general ban on parties accrediting their own witnesses. In the case of previous consistent statements the ease with which such statements can be manufactured and their superfluity to the proceedings are the two reasons most commonly given.[23] This exclusionary rule is sometimes called the rule against narrative, meaning that a witness may not testify that he narrated the substance of the evidence to a third party out of court. Where the witness is one of the parties to the case, the rule is sometimes called the rule against self-serving statements, reflecting the point that a previous consistent statement clearly serves the interest of the person making it and is very easy to manufacture.

A standard illustration of the rule against previous consistent statements is *Roberts*.[24] The defendant was charged with the murder of his former girlfriend by shooting her. His defence was that the shooting was an accident. The trial judge refused to allow the defendant's father to testify that the defendant, shortly after his arrest, had told him that there had been an accident. Upholding the defendant's conviction for murder, Humphreys J., giving the judgment of the Court of Criminal Appeal, emphasised that the rule did not permit a party to make evidence for himself and roundly asserted that the reason for the rule was that evidence of a previous consistent statement had no evidential value. It was therefore irrelevant. This was almost certainly putting the point too strongly. In some cases previous consistent statements may well have very little or no weight. A flimsy defence does not get any better by being repeated numerous times. On the other hand, in certain circumstances a previous consistent statement might have considerable probative value in suggesting that the present testimony is

---

[21] Offender Management Act 2007 s.28 provides that participation in a polygraph test may be made a condition of the release of a sexual offender on licence, but s.30 goes on to provide that evidence obtained from such a test is inadmissible in any proceedings against the released person for an offence. Polygraph evidence has been rejected in Canada: *R. v Phillion* [1978] 1 S.C.R. 18; *R. v Beland* [1987] 2 S.C.R. 398. For a good review of the issues, see D. W. Elliott, "LieDetector Evidence: Lessons from the American Experience" in E. Campbell and L. Waller (eds), *Well and Truly Tried* (Sydney, 1982), p.100.

[22] See *Browning* [1995] Crim. L.R. 227 CA; cf. *R. v Trochym* [2007] 1 S.C.R. 239 Supreme Court of Canada, where the majority held that post-hypnotic testimony is presumptively inadmissible.

[23] See, e.g. *Law Commission, Evidence in Criminal Proceedings: Hearsay and Related Topics*, Law Com. No.245, (1997), paras 10.12, 10.15.

[24] *Roberts* [1942] 1 All E.R. 187 CCA.

true.[25] The common law effectively acknowledged this point by recognising a number of exceptions and qualifications to the rule in criminal cases. At this point the law becomes complex because of its interaction with the hearsay rule, which gives rise to questions about the purposes for which previous statements can be admitted. The common law exceptions to the rule against previous consistent statements were significantly affected by the Criminal Justice Act 2003, both as to the scope of some of the exceptions and as to the use that can be made of previous consistent statements when admitted.

(A) Exceptions to the rules against narrative and hearsay: previous statements of witnesses admissible as evidence of the facts stated as well as evidence of consistency

(1) Previous identifications

Chapter 7 explained that at common law a witness can give evidence that he made a previous identification of the accused.[26] This can be a formal[27] or an informal[28] identification, and the evidence is admissible whether or not the witness has identified the accused in court.[29] If the witness cannot remember who it was he identified on the previous occasion, or even whether he identified anyone, a person who observed the identification may give evidence of it.[30] There seems no doubt that, where the witness fails to identify the defendant in court, such previous identifications are evidence of the facts stated (i.e. that the identification is true),[31] and that this exception to the hearsay rule is well-established despite the somewhat unconvincing reasoning in the relevant authorities.[32] If the witness does identify the defendant in court, the previous identification would be evidence of the witness's consistency, as well as evidence

14–007

---

[25] Consider the civil case of *Corke v Corke and Cook* [1958] 1 All E.R. 224, decided under the old law of divorce. The wife denied the husband's claim that she had committed adultery with Cook, and gave evidence that, a few minutes after her husband had discovered her with Cook on the occasion in question and accused her of adultery, she had telephoned her doctor with a request for him to come and examine her to see if she had recently had intercourse. The majority of the Court of Appeal held that this evidence was irrelevant and inadmissible. According to Hodson L.J., her statement at the time that she was willing to be medically examined (the doctor did not in fact come) was of no probative value. This is very dubious: in the absence of a deliberate and risky bluff, her confidence in the truth of her claim and her willingness to put it to the test might well be a useful guide to whether her denial of adultery was likely to be true. Under the law as it is now in civil proceedings, a witness's previous statement is admissible, with the leave of the court, as evidence of the facts stated: Civil Evidence Act 1995 s.6(1), (2).

[26] *Christie* [1914] A.C. 545 HL.

[27] As in *Osbourne and Virtue* [1973] Q.B. 678 CA; and *McCay* (1990) 91 Cr.App.R. 84 CA.

[28] As in *Christie* [1914] A.C. 545 HL.

[29] In *Christie* [1914] A.C. 545 HL the witness had identified the accused in court; in *Osbourne and Virtue* [1973] Q.B. 678 the witnesses had not.

[30] See the cases referred to in fn.27.

[31] See, in particular, *McCay* (1990) 91 Cr.App.R. 84 CA; Law Commission Consultation Paper, *Evidence in Criminal Proceedings: Hearsay and Related Topics*, Law Com. No.138, (1995), paras 13.10–13.16.

[32] See further Ch.7.

of the facts stated. However, the common law exception extends only to previous identifications of people; it does not cover identifications of vehicles.[33]

This is one of the exceptions affected by the Criminal Justice Act 2003, as far as treating previous identifications as evidence of the facts stated is concerned. As discussed in Ch.7, the effect of s.120(4) and (5) of the 2003 Act is that a previous statement by a witness is admissible as evidence of any matter stated if the statement identifies or describes a person, object or place, [34] and while giving evidence the witness indicates that to the best of his belief he made the statement and that it is true. Accordingly, a previous identification by an eyewitness, who can confirm at trial making the statement of identification and confirm its truth, is now admissible as evidence of the facts stated. It is a statutory exception to the rule against hearsay. The previous identification will also be evidence of the witness's consistency by virtue of the common law.

Section 120(4) and (5) will not apply in cases such as *Osbourne and Virtue*[35] and *McCay*,[36] where the witness cannot remember making the earlier identification or cannot confirm its truth. However, s.118 of the Criminal Justice Act 2003 preserves as part of the statutory scheme for hearsay evidence certain common law categories of admissible hearsay. These include the rule of res gestae, whereby a statement is admissible as evidence of any matter stated if it accompanied an act that can be properly evaluated as evidence only if considered in conjunction with the statement.[37] This is the rule that provided the first reason for upholding the admission of the identification evidence in *McCay*. It seems therefore that previous identifications in this type of case will continue to be admissible as evidence of the facts stated, although the question of consistency of the witness clearly does not arise where the witness cannot identify the defendant in court.

(2) Res gestae

14–008 Evidence of acts and statements that form part of the res gestae is generally admissible at common law, notwithstanding the operation of any exclusionary rule. The justification for admission is that such evidence may have a high degree of relevance because of its contemporaneity with the facts in issue.[38] Depending on the use to which it is being put, it may be admitted as an exception to the hearsay rule or the rule against previous consistent statements. A useful authority in the context of previous consistent statements is the old case of *Fowkes*.[39] The accused was charged with the murder of B by shooting him. Lord Campbell C.J. is reported as having permitted B's son to testify that he was in a room with B just before B was shot and that he saw a man with a gun in his hand pass the window,

---

[33] *Jones v Metcalfe* [1967] 1 W.L.R. 1286; *McLean* (1967) 52 Cr.App.R. 80; *Kelsey* (1982) 74 Cr.App.R. 213.

[34] As explained in *Chinn* [2012] EWCA Crim 501; [2012] 2 Cr App R 4: see Ch 7.

[35] *Osbourne and Virtue* [1973] Q.B. 678.

[36] *McCay* (1990) 91 Cr.App.R. 84.

[37] Criminal Justice Act 2003 s.118(1)4(b)

[38] See the discussion of res gestae in Ch.17.

[39] *The Times*, March 8, 1856; J. F. Stephen, *A Digest of the Law of Evidence,* 12th edn (London: Macmillan, 1946), pp.7–8.

whereupon the son shouted "There's Butcher". "Butcher" was the accused's nickname. Stephen cited the case in the Digest as illustrative of the admission of a statement relevant to a fact in issue, here obviously the identity of the killer. This may suggest that he conceived of admission of the statement as a hearsay exception.[40] However, given that the son had also tentatively identified the accused at the trial, Stephen may have thought that the evidence of his previous statement was admissible both as to the issue of the son's consistency as an identifying witness and as evidence of the facts stated.[41] It would be very odd if it could be used for the latter purpose but not the former. The common law rules relating to the admission of statements as part of the res gestae are preserved by the Criminal Justice Act 2003.[42]

(3)   Statements rebutting suggestions of recent fabrication

This rule is not quite as straightforward as it first appears. The basic idea is simple enough. If a cross-examiner suggests to a witness that his testimony is a recent invention, at common law evidence may be given in rebuttal[43] that the witness made a statement at an earlier time consistent with the challenged testimony.[44] In this way the witness's credit can be repaired. However, the trial judge has to be careful in applying the rule. It is a necessary condition for its operation that the "account given by the witness in his testimony is attacked on the ground of recent invention or reconstruction or that a foundation for such an attack has been laid".[45] Accordingly it is not enough by itself that the cross-examiner proves that the witness has made a previous inconsistent statement,[46] or that the cross-examiner attacks the whole of the witness's testimony.[47] The cross-examiner has to go further, so that the cross-examination amounts to an allegation that the witness in effect fabricated the testimony after the events in question for the purposes of the trial.[48] Such allegations can carry

14–009

---

[40] The Law Commission cites *Fowkes* as an example of the res gestae exception to the hearsay rule for spontaneous statements made by way of reaction to a relevant act or event: Law Com No.245, para.8.115.

[41] cf. the old civil case of *Milne v Leisler* (1862) 7 H. & N. 786, where certain letters written by the plaintiff were admitted as confirmation of the plaintiff's testimony at trial regarding the facts in issue and not as direct proof of those facts. The letters would now be admissible for the latter purpose under the provisions of the Civil Evidence Act 1995.

[42] Criminal Justice Act 2003 s.118(1)4.

[43] By questions in re-examination of the witness, or by calling the person to whom the earlier statement was made. See, e.g. *Wilmot* (1989) 89 Cr.App.R. 341.

[44] *Oyesiku* (1971) 56 Cr.App.R. 240 CA, citing the influential judgment of Dixon C.J. in the High Court of Australia in *Nominal Defendant v Clements* (1961) 104 C.L.R. 104.

[45] *Nominal Defendant v Clements* (1961) 104 C.L.R. 476 at 479 per Dixon C.J.

[46] *Coll* (1889) 25 L.R. Ir. 522; *Beattie* (1989) 89 Cr.App.R. 302 CA; *P(GR)* [1998] Crim. L.R. 663 CA. cf. *Ali* [2003] EWCA Crim 3214; [2004] 1 Cr.App.R. 39, where the Court of Appeal stated that there is a "residual discretion", based on the interests of justice, to permit re-examination to show consistency. It appears that this might be exercisable, for example, where there is something in the nature of the inconsistency, or the use made of it by the cross-examiner, that might mislead the jury as to the existence of some fact or the terms of an earlier statement.

[47] *Fox v General Medical Council* [1960] 1 W.L.R. 1017.

[48] See, e.g. *Gregson* [2003] EWCA Crim 1099; [2003] 2 Cr.App.R. 34: allegation that the defendant invented his story, relating to his lack of intention to supply drugs in his possession, only after the

considerable risks; if made to a police officer, for example, they may result in the officer's notebook being put in evidence to rebut the allegation.[49]

At common law a previous statement admitted under this rule was admitted as an item of circumstantial evidence for the specific purpose of rebutting the allegation of recent invention and thereby bolstering the witness's credit. It was not admissible as evidence of the facts stated in the previous statement, and the judge had to give a direction to this effect in a jury trial. The Law Commission criticised this limitation as creating a distinction without a difference,[50] and recommended reform. Section 120(2) of the Criminal Justice Act 2003 accordingly provides that if a witness's previous statement is admitted to rebut a suggestion that his oral evidence has been fabricated, the statement is admissible of any matter stated of which oral evidence by the witness would be admissible. In this way the fact of the previous statement can be used as before to support the witness's testimony and rebut the suggestion of fabrication,[51] and in addition the terms of the statement can be relied on as being true.[52] The provision in s.120(2) does not refer to the suggestion being one of *recent* fabrication, unlike the statements in the common law cases referred to above. However, this should not be interpreted as some kind of relaxation of the common law rule. The subsection does not deal with admissibility; it is concerned only with the effect of the statement once it has been admitted in accordance with the common law requirements. As David Clarke J. noted in *Trewin*:

> "It seems to us that the subsection says nothing about whether such evidence may or may not be admitted. Accordingly the admissibility of evidence to rebut fabrication must be considered by reference to the principles which have governed the question in the past."[53]

The position in civil cases is that a previous statement of a witness is now formally admissible as evidence of the facts stated by virtue of the provisions of ss.2–6 of the Civil Evidence Act 1995. Under s.6(2) a party who calls a person as

---

police searched his home and found the drugs; Court of Appeal held that the judge should have permitted the defence to call witnesses to prove that before the search the defendant had spoken to them in terms consistent with his story. See also *R. v MH* [2012] EWCA Crim 2725: a defence case that a 3 year old child had been put up by his mother to make allegations of sexual offences on him by D amounted to a claim of recent fabrication, and enabled evidence of the child's earlier complaints to the mother to be admitted.

[49] *Benjamin* (1913) 8 Cr.App.R. 641 CCA. They might also constitute an attack on the witness's character and result in the admission of evidence of the accused's bad character under the provisions of the Criminal Justice Act 2003 s.101(1)(g), discussed in Ch.19.

[50] Law Com No.245, para.10.17.

[51] Assuming that the previous statement is substantially similar to the testimony, and that there is something different in the circumstances in which the previous statement was made which suggests that evidence of the previous statement may fairly assist the jury in ascertaining where the truth lies: *Athwal* [2009] EWCA Crim 789; [2009] 2 Cr.App.R. 14.

[52] It follows that where the previous statement consists of a complaint of an offence, it may qualify as a hearsay exception under both this provision and the provision for complaints in s.120(4) and (7) of the Criminal Justice Act 2003 (discussed below); see, e.g. *Kirk* [2008] EWCA Crim 434.

[53] *Trewin* [2008] EWCA Crim 484. It is submitted, with respect, that the contrary suggestion in *Athwal* [2009] EWCA Crim 789; [2009] 2 Cr.App.R. 14 at [61], that s.118 of the Criminal Justice Act 2003 has had the effect of abolishing the common law on rebutting recent fabrication, and that s.120(2) now governs admissibility of previous statements for this purpose, is wrong. See further Ch.17.

a witness may not adduce evidence of a previous statement by the person without leave of the court, *unless* the purpose is to rebut a suggestion that the person's evidence has been fabricated. It follows that in both civil and criminal proceedings previous statements admitted to rebut suggestions of recent fabrication of oral testimony are now evidence of the facts stated and of the witness's consistency (and therefore credibility).

(4)   Complaints by victims

A fourth exception to the rule against previous consistent statements concerns **14–010** complaints. At common law a complaint, for the purposes of the exception, was an allegation by a person that a sexual offence had been committed against him or her.[54] The common law exception can be summarised as follows. Evidence of a complaint was admissible if the complaint was made within a reasonable time of the alleged offence[55] and at the first reasonable opportunity,[56] and was not made in response to leading questions.[57] If these conditions were satisfied evidence could be given both of the fact of a complaint and of its terms.[58] The complainant should testify to the making of the complaint, but the terms of the complaint should be proved by the person to whom it was made.[59] The complaint was admissible as an item of circumstantial evidence for the purposes of showing the witness's consistency with his or her testimony at trial, and of negativing consent, by virtue of its inconsistency with consent, if consent was in issue.[60] It followed that if consent was not in issue, and the complainant did not testify, the complaint had to be excluded.[61] The complaint was not admissible as evidence of the facts stated,[62] and a jury had to be specifically instructed to this effect.[63]

The common law rule about complaints was undoubtedly one of the more technical rules of the law of evidence. The restrictions attached to it attracted much criticism,[64] which focused particularly on the limitation of the rule to

---

[54] According to Ridley J., giving the judgment of the Court for Crown Cases Reserved in *Osborne* [1905] 1 K.B. 551, the rule for complaints derived from the medieval rule that a victim of rape had to raise the "hue and cry" if her appeal of rape were to succeed. In the absence of such outcry her testimony alleging rape was presumed to be false (Hale, P.C., Vol.1, p.633). See also *Islam* [1999] 1 Cr.App.R. 22, where the Court of Appeal described the complaints rule as "a perverted survival of the ancient requirement of . . . hue and cry". The extension of the exception to complaints by males was made by the Court of Criminal Appeal in *Camelleri* [1922] 2 K.B. 122.

[55] *Valentine* [1996] 2 Cr.App.R. 213 CA; *Birks* [2002] EWCA Crim 3091; [2003] 2 Cr.App.R. 7.

[56] *Osborne* [1905] 1 K.B. 551 CCCR; *Cummings* [1948] 1 All E.R. 551 CCA; *Valentine* [1996] 2 Cr.App.R. 213 CA.

[57] See *Osborne* [1905] 1 K.B. 551 CCCR, where a distinction was drawn between questions of a "suggestive or leading" character, and what might be called natural questions of concern such as "What is the matter?" or "Why are you crying?".

[58] *Lillyman* [1896] 2 Q.B. 167 CCCR.

[59] per Lord Hoffmann, giving the opinion of the Privy Council in *White v R.* [1999] 1 Cr.App.R. 153 at 157.

[60] *White v R.* [1999] 1 Cr.App.R. 153; *Osborne* [1905] 1 K.B. 551 CCCR.

[61] This might happen where the victim was a young child and unable to testify: see, e.g. *Sparks v R.* [1964] A.C. 964 at 979 PC.

[62] *Lillyman* [1896] 2 Q.B. 167 CCCR.

[63] *Osborne* [1905] 1 K.B. 551 CCCR; *Islam* [1999] 1 Cr.App.R. 22 CA.

[64] For details see the second edition of this book at p.466, and Law Com. No.245 paras 10.53–10.61.

complaints only of sexual offences, and the limitation on the use that could be made of a complaint when admitted. The idea that a complaint might be considered as evidence that the complainant was now telling the truth in court, but might not be considered as evidence of the truth of the complaint itself, is subtle, to say the least. The Criminal Law Revision Committee described a judicial direction in these terms as "wholly unrealistic and difficult for a jury to appreciate".[65]

The Criminal Justice Act 2003 addressed these criticisms and recast the complaints rule, making some substantial changes. The relevant subsections of s.120 provide as follows:

> "(1) This section applies where a person (the witness) is called to give evidence in criminal proceedings.
>
> ...
>
> (4) A previous statement by the witness is admissible as evidence of any matter stated of which oral evidence by him would be admissible, if—
>   (a) any of the following three conditions is satisfied, and
>   (b) while giving evidence the witness indicates that to the best of his belief he made the statement, and that to the best of his belief it states the truth.[66]
>
> ...
>
> (7) The third condition is that—
>   (a) the witness claims to be a person against whom an offence has been committed,
>   (b) the offence is one to which the proceedings relate,
>   (c) the statement consists of a complaint made by the witness (whether to a person in authority or not) about conduct which would, if proved, constitute the offence, or part of the offence,
>   (d) [repealed by the Coroners and Justice Act 2009 s.112];
>   (e) the complaint was not made as the result of a threat or a promise, and
>   (f) before the statement is adduced the witness gives oral evidence in connection with its subject matter.
>
> (8) For the purposes of subsection (7) the fact that the complaint was elicited (for example, by a leading question) is irrelevant unless a threat or promise was involved."

14–011   Under these provisions, which give effect to the recommendations of the Law Commission, the admissibility of complaints is no longer limited to sexual offences, but applies to a complaint of any offence. The voluntariness condition has been relaxed with the dropping of the requirement that no leading questions should have been used to elicit the complaint. It is only threats and promises that now render the complaint inadmissible. When admitted, complaints are now admissible as evidence of any fact stated in the complaint, as well as being evidence of the complainant's consistency. Judges no longer have to give mystifying directions about the distinction between these uses of the complaint. These were all welcome reforms.

A further widening of the exception for complaints was made by s.112 of the Coroners and Justice Act 2009.[67] This dropped the former requirement in s.120(7)(d) of the 2003 Act that the complaint had to be made as soon as could

---

[65] *Eleventh Report* para.232.
[66] It follows that if the witness is not asked to confirm the making of the complaint and its truth, or is unable to do so, the complaint is inadmissible under s.120(4) and (7), as in *R. v MH* [2012] EWCA Crim 2725. However, this case also shows that, depending on the facts of the case, evidence of a prior complaint may be admissible to rebut a suggestion of recent fabrication of testimony, or in the interests of justice under s.114(1)(d) of the Criminal Justice Act 2003.
[67] In force from February 1, 2010.

reasonably be expected after the alleged conduct. There is now no temporal restriction on when complaints must be made. A period of delay between the alleged offence and the making of a complaint about it may affect the weight to be attached to the complaint, and the testimony with which it is consistent, but it no longer goes to the admissibility of the complaint. The abolition of the requirement is the culmination of a greater appreciation of the psychology of victims of offences, particularly sexual offences. It is now generally accepted that the old expectation that a rape victim, for example, would make a prompt complaint, is outdated. As Roch L.J. commented in *Valentine*[68]:

> "We now have greater understanding that those who are the victims of sexual offences, be they male or female, often need time before they can bring themselves to tell what has been done to them; that some victims will find it impossible to complain to anyone other than a parent or member of their family whereas others may feel it quite impossible to tell their parents or members of their family."[69]

Much depends on the context of the offence and the character of the victim as to when a complaint is likely to be made. Children who are the victims of sexual and/or physical abuse within the family may feel unable to complain until some considerable time later when they have reached adulthood and left the family unit. Even then it may take years before they can face telling what happened to them and accusing a parent, step-parent or other family member of very serious crimes.

As regards the operation of the modern complaints rule, as restated in s.120(7), a number of matters not expressly dealt with by the statutory provision require comment. It seems first, that the common law rule has been preserved that a complaint is admissible only where it relates to an offence charged on the indictment [70] The provision cannot be used therefore to admit hearsay evidence of complaints by victims of "similar fact" offences if these have not been charged. Secondly, the provision does not prevent the prosecution from adducing evidence of more than one complaint by the same victim,[71] where it is relevant to do so. It may well be appropriate, for example, for evidence of the terms of a child's complaint to be given by its mother and by a police officer or doctor to whom the complaint was repeated. Section 78 of PACE would be available to prevent any unfairness arising from the admission of multiple complaints. Thirdly, in relation to the consistency of the complaint with the witness's testimony, at common law it was not necessary that the terms of the complaint should disclose the ingredients of the offence charged, provided they disclosed evidence of relevant unlawful sexual conduct on the part of the defendant that could support the credibility of the complainant in testifying about the offence.[72] Sufficient consistency between the testimony and the complaint was required, rather than exact consistency. It is probable that this is still the case, given the policy of the legislation to enlarge rather than restrict the scope of the complaints

14–012

---

[68] *Valentine* [1996] 2 Cr.App.R. 213.
[69] *Valentine* [1996] 2 Cr.App.R. 213 at 224.
[70] See the dictum to this effect by David Clarke J. in *Trewin* [2008] EWCA Crim 484 at [17].
[71] See *R. v O* [2006] EWCA Crim 556; [2006] 2 Cr.App.R. 27; *Kirk* [2008] EWCA Crim 434.
[72] *R. v S* [2004] EWCA Crim 1320; [2004] 2 Cr.App.R. 39.

rule. Major inconsistencies between the complaint and the evidence would clearly call for a careful direction from the trial judge about the reasons for them and their potential significance for the jury's decision whether the complainant is telling the truth. Fourthly, the trial judge should ordinarily direct the jury that a complaint is not evidence independent of the complainant, and that this might affect the weight a jury could give to evidence of the complaint.[73]

(B)   Unclear exceptions: statements by the accused when arrested, when interviewed and when confronted with the discovery of incriminating articles

14–013   If the accused makes any statement before trial which is wholly or partly adverse to his case, under PACE the statement amounts to a confession.[74] It will be admissible against him as evidence of its truth provided the conditions for the admissibility of confessions are satisfied.[75] It does not matter for this purpose whether the accused made the statement on arrest, in a formal interview or an informal conversation, or as a result of the finding of incriminating articles or other evidence. Where the statement is "mixed", in the sense of containing both incriminating and exculpatory parts, then both parts are admissible as evidence of the facts they state. The jury will be directed to consider the statement as a whole in order to determine where the truth lies.[76] The rationale for this position is that it would be unfair and potentially misleading for only the incriminating part of the statement to be admitted; the prosecution should not be able to take admissions out of context. Once the whole statement is admitted, it would be a virtually impossible task for the judge to explain that whereas the incriminating parts may be treated as being true the excusing parts are not evidence of their truth but are something less. However, the judge may tell the jury that the exculpatory parts may deserve less weight because they are in the accused's interest, whereas incriminating statements, being against his interest, are more likely to be true. Mixed statements, as well as confessions, are preserved as exceptions to the hearsay rule by s.118(1)5 of the Criminal Justice Act 2003.

The issue then arises about the status of pre-trial statements by the accused that are wholly exculpatory. Are they admissible at all, and, if so, for what purpose? On principle they should be excluded by the hearsay rule as evidence of the facts they state, and by the general rule against previous consistent statements as evidence of consistency with the accused's testimony at trial. In *Storey*,[77] the police had entered the defendant's flat under a search warrant and found a quantity of cannabis. The defendant's immediate response was that it did not belong to her and that it had been brought to the flat against her will. The Court of

---

[73] *R. v A* [2011] EWCA Crim 1517, approving *R. v AA* [2007] EWCA Crim 1779. However, a failure to give a direction in these terms will not necessarily be fatal to the safety of a conviction: *R. v H* [2011] EWCA Crim 2344; [2012] 1 Cr.App.R. 30.
[74] PACE s.82(1).
[75] See Ch.6.
[76] See *Sharp* [1988] 1 All E.R. 65 HL, confirming the approach of the Court of Appeal in *Duncan* (1981) 73 Cr.App.R. 359.
[77] *Storey* (1968) 52 Cr.App.R. 334 CA.

Appeal held that evidence of this statement could be given at her trial. According to Widgery L.J. it was not evidence of the facts stated, but it was admissible:

"because of its vital relevance as showing the reaction of the accused when first taxed with the incriminating facts ... it is evidence of the reaction of the accused which forms part of the general picture to be considered by the jury at the trial."[78]

The point of this rather cloudy distinction[79] seems to be that the jury may take the statement into account in deciding the issue of guilt, but that if the statement is not evidence of its truth, the trial judge need not take account of it in deciding whether there is a case to answer[80] or include it in any summary of the evidence for the defence.

In the later case of *Pearce*,[81] the trial judge had excluded two voluntary statements by the defendant and part of an interview with the defendant on the ground that they were self-serving statements and not admissible. Allowing the appeal, the Court of Appeal adopted the approach taken in *Storey*, but took the opportunity to restate and generalise the applicable principles. Lord Widgery C.J. summarised the principles as follows:

"(1)   A statement which contains an admission is always admissible as a declaration against interest and is evidence of the facts admitted. With this exception a statement made by an accused person is never evidence of the facts in the statement.

(2)   (a) A statement that is not an admission is admissible to show the attitude of the accused at the time when he made it. This however is not to be limited to a statement made on the first encounter with the police. The reference in *Storey* to the reaction of the accused 'when first taxed' should not be read as circumscribing the limits of admissibility. The longer the time that has elapsed after the first encounter the less the weight which will be attached to the denial. The judge is able to direct the jury about the value of such statements. (b) A statement that is not in itself an admission is admissible if it is made in the same context as an admission, whether in the course of an interview, or in the form of a voluntary statement. It would be unfair to admit only the statements against interest while excluding part of the same interview or series of interviews. It is the duty of the prosecution to present the case fairly to the jury; to exclude answers which are favourable to the accused while admitting those unfavourable would be misleading. (c) The prosecution may wish to draw attention to inconsistent denials. A denial does not become an admission because it is inconsistent with another denial. There must be many cases however where convictions have resulted from such inconsistencies between two denials ...

In the light of the principles which we have ventured to state, there can be no reason for casting doubt on ... the practice of admitting statements by the accused even where their evidential value is small."[82]

It seems therefore that pre-trial exculpatory statements by the accused are generally admissible to show consistency with testimony and/or the accused's reaction at the time. Such evidence is not restricted to statements made on the first encounter with the police or to statements made when other incriminating

14–014

---

[78] *Storey* (1968) 52 Cr.App.R. 334 at 337–338.
[79] The statement showing the defendant's reaction may be useful evidence of consistency if the defendant testifies to the same effect at trial, but the statement is seemingly admissible under this principle even if the defendant does not testify at trial.
[80] *Storey* (1968) 52 Cr.App.R. 334 CA.
[81] *Pearce* (1979) 69 Cr.App.R. 365 CA.
[82] *Pearce* (1979) 69 Cr.App.R. 365 at 369–370.

evidence is discovered. It extends to statements made on other occasions including both formal interviews and informal exchanges with the police. Thus transcripts of taped interviews will show all the accused's reactions to the police questions, whether they consist of admissions, denials, "no comment" answers, or silence. At the same time it is not the case that all exculpatory statements will automatically be admitted. In *Pearce*, Lord Widgery C.J. added to the above principles:

> "(3)   Although in practice most statements are given in evidence even when they are largely self-serving, there may be a rare occasion when an accused produces a carefully prepared written statement to the police, with a view to it being made part of the prosecution evidence. The trial judge would plainly exclude such a statement as inadmissible."[83]

In *Tooke*,[84] the Court of Appeal upheld a trial judge who had excluded the defendant's voluntary written witness statement, made a short time after the defendant had made an oral statement giving his first reaction that the victim of an assault was in fact the aggressor. The court took the view that the written statement added nothing to the evidence of first reaction and was not therefore relevant. This decision now needs to be viewed in the light of s.34 of the Criminal Justice and Public Order Act 1994. Suppose the written statement was given to the police in the course of an interview, or when the defendant was charged with the offence, and mentioned a fact on which the defendant relied in his defence at trial. The statement is now admissible to show that the fact was mentioned at the time and thereby to prevent the possibility of the court drawing adverse inferences under s.34 where, say, the defendant has otherwise given a "No comment" interview.[85]

2.   *Leading questions*

14–015   In principle, any witness may be asked any question in chief that is relevant to the facts in issue, but there is an important restriction on the way in which questions can be asked. Leading questions are not permitted in examination in chief. A leading question may take one of two forms. Most commonly it is a question that suggests the desired answer, such as "Did you see D hit P?". This is leading the witness to give the answer "Yes", since this is clearly the answer counsel is expecting. A proper line of questioning would be to ask the witness where he was on the particular day, whether he saw anything happen, and then to ask the witness what he saw. Questions that simply invite the witness to assent to a proposition about the facts in issue will frequently be leading. The reasons why an examiner in chief should not use leading questions are: first, the witness can be expected to favour the party calling him and is likely therefore to agree with counsel who puts words in his mouth; secondly, allowing counsel to lead a

---

[83] *Pearce* (1979) 69 Cr.App.R. 365 at 370. For an example of a self serving statement ruled inadmissible on this ground, see *Newsome* (1980) 71 Cr.App.R. 325 CA, where the Court of Appeal expressed doubts about the width of the second proposition stated by Lord Widgery C.J. in *Pearce*.
[84] *Tooke* (1990) 90 Cr.App.R. 417 CA.
[85] See *Knight* [2003] EWCA Crim 1977; [2004] 1 Cr.App.R. 9; *Turner* [2004] 1 All E.R. 1025 CA.

witness increases the risk that only favourable testimony will emerge and that unfavourable testimony will be suppressed, thus impairing the truth-finding function of the proceedings; thirdly, a witness may be misled into agreeing to a question put in terms that do not completely express the true meaning of his evidence.[86]

An exception to the rule is made in the interests of efficiency for matters that are introductory (such as the witness's name, address and occupation) or are not contested by the other side (for example, that D did hit P, in a case where the issue is whether D was acting in self-defence). The latter example shows the difference between directing the witness's attention to the subject about which he or she is to be questioned, which is unobjectionable, and suggesting the answer to a matter in dispute, which is objectionable. Leading questions of this type may, however, be put in cross-examination and to a party's own witness where the judge has given leave for the witness to be treated as hostile. In addition, in practice a judge may give counsel a certain amount of latitude in dealing with witnesses whose memory or intelligence may be so defective that they cannot be brought to the point at issue without some degree of prompting. The fact that evidence is adduced by means of leading questions does not make it inadmissible, but it may affect its weight.[87]

The other form of leading question is one that assumes the existence of a disputed fact. A question such as "When did you stop beating your wife?" is plainly objectionable if it is in issue whether the witness does beat his wife. This is in effect a trick question, unfair to the witness, and is never permissible.

3. *Refreshing memory*

There may be a considerable delay between a trial and the events in question in the trial. It is a commonplace of experience that memory fades with time, and yet witnesses are frequently expected to give detailed oral evidence on oath about events that happened months or even years earlier. The problem of accurate recall of single past events may be worse for witnesses, such as police officers, who deal with a great many frequently recurring events in the course of their work. However, witnesses will often have made statements about these events well before the trial, at times when the memory of the events was sharper in the witnesses' minds. At the beginning of this chapter it was noted that in civil proceedings a pre-trial written statement may be ordered to be admitted as the witness's evidence in chief. In criminal proceedings if the witness's pre-trial statements are in the form of a video-recorded interview, which satisfies the requirements of s.137 of the Criminal Justice Act 2003, or s.27 of the Youth Justice and Criminal Evidence Act 1999, the court may direct that the recording should be admitted as the witness's evidence in chief. Where these provisions are not applicable a question may arise whether a witness may look at a previous written statement to refresh his memory while giving evidence or beforehand.

14–016

---

[86] See W. M. Best, *A Treatise on the Principles of Evidence* (London, 1849), pp.478–480; *Maves v Grand Trunk Pacific Rail Co* (1913) 14 D.L.R. 70.
[87] *Moor v Moor* [1954] 1 W.L.R. 927.

The law on this issue of refreshing memory, like the law on previous consistent statements, is a somewhat complex mix of common law and reforms enacted by the Criminal Justice Act 2003. The Act has supplemented the common law in some respects, superseded it in others, and left some parts untouched. Discussion begins with the broad distinction made at common law between refreshing memory in court while testifying, and out of court before testifying.

(A) Refreshing memory in court while testifying

14–017 At common law a witness may refresh his memory while testifying from a statement in a document, provided that the document was made contemporaneously with the events in question, and was made or verified by the witness. A standard illustration is a police officer giving evidence about events that he recorded in his notebook. The officer may refer to his notes while testifying once he has confirmed that he made the notes at about the time of the events recorded. Contemporaneity for this purpose is a flexible standard. It does not mean that the document must have been made simultaneously with the events or even at the first subsequent opportunity: "It is sufficient, for the purposes of the rule, if the writing was made or verified at a time when the facts were still fresh in the witness's memory".[88] Thus in *Simmonds*,[89] the Court of Appeal upheld a ruling that customs officers could read to the trial court their notes of lengthy interviews, which they had compiled at the first convenient opportunity after returning to their office after the interviews.[90] The document used to refresh memory can be made by someone other than the witness, but in such a case the witness must have verified the accuracy of the document at the time, either by reading it himself[91] or by having it read over to him.[92]

The common sense principle underlying the common law rule is that the quality of the witness's evidence is likely to be improved if the witness is allowed to use a statement made nearer the time as an aide-memoire. The same principle underlies s.139(1) of the Criminal Justice Act 2003, which sets out a different rule for refreshing memory. This has largely superseded the common law rule, although the Act has not abolished the old rule. Section 139(1) provides that a witness giving oral evidence in criminal proceedings about any matter may at any stage refresh his memory of it from a document made or verified by him at an earlier time if two conditions are satisfied. The first is that the witness states in his oral evidence that the document records his recollection of the matter at the earlier time, and the second is that his recollection of the matter is likely to have

---

[88] *Attorney General's Reference (No.3 of 1979)* (1979) 69 Cr.App.R. 411 at 414 CA per Lord Lane C.J. In that case the Court of Appeal held that it was acceptable for police officers to record later in their notebooks a fair copy of an interview made from notes jotted down at the time of the interview.
[89] *Simmonds* [1969] 1 Q.B. 685 CA.
[90] Note that there has never been a technical objection to police officers collaborating in the preparation of their notes of an interview (*Bass* [1953] 1 Q.B. 680 CCA), despite the persistent belief of many police officers and counsel to the contrary.
[91] See, e.g. *Dyer v Best* (1866) 4 H. & C. 189.
[92] As in *Kelsey* (1982) 74 Cr.App.R. 213 CA. In such a case the doctrine of refreshing memory functions as a disguised method of admitting hearsay evidence.

been significantly better at that time than it is at the time of his oral evidence.[93] The common law requirement that the statement should have been contemporaneous with the matters it deals with has been dropped.

It is important to note that under both the common law rule and s.139(1) the evidence is the witness's oral testimony, not the document used to refresh memory. Where use of the document does in fact revive a hazy or forgotten memory, there is no artificiality involved in maintaining this position. However, the common law doctrine of refreshing memory also extends to the case where the witness's memory of the event does not revive, but the witness is prepared to testify to it on the basis that the contemporaneous record is accurate. In the old case of *Maugham v Hubbard*,[94] the issue was whether the witness had been paid £20 by the plaintiff six years earlier. The witness was shown the plaintiff's cash book, which contained an entry recording the payment and an acknowledgment of it by the witness in the form of his initials. The witness testified that he had no memory of receiving the money, but said that in view of his initials in the book, he was in no doubt that he had received it. The Court of King's Bench held that although the entry in the cash book could not be used to prove the receipt directly, because it was unstamped, it could nevertheless be used by the witness to refresh his memory. The doctrine of refreshing memory operates as a benevolent fiction in this type of case; the court in effect is permitting the witness to give reliable hearsay evidence, on the basis that the witness is prepared to vouch for the accuracy of the contemporaneous record.[95] It is consistent with this function that the common law requires a document used to "refresh memory" in this type of case to be the original document.[96] In other cases the witness may *revive* memory from any contemporaneous document made or verified by him.

Section 120 of the Criminal Justice Act 2003 contains a useful provision to take account of this point about the hearsay use of documents where the witness's memory is not in fact refreshed by reference to the document. This eliminates some of the need to rely on the fiction just described. The effect of s.120(1), (4) and (6), is that where a witness in criminal proceedings does not, and cannot reasonably be expected to, remember a matter well enough to be able to give oral evidence of it, but has made a previous statement when the matters stated were fresh in his memory, and indicates while giving evidence that, to the best of his belief, he made the statement and it is true, the statement is admissible as evidence of any matter stated of which oral evidence by him would be admissible.[97] This applies only to statements *made* by the witness, not to

14–018

---

[93] See also s.139(2), dealing with refreshing memory from a transcript of an account previously given by the witness in a sound recording.

[94] *Maugham v Hubbard* (1828) 8 B. & C. 14. See also *Topham v McGregor* (1844) 1 Car. & Kir. 320.

[95] As the Law Commission has recognised: Law Com No.245 para.10.66.

[96] *Doe d. Church and Phillips v Perkins* (1790) 3 Term Rep. 749; *Harvey* (1869) 11 Cox C.C. 546.

[97] According to the Court of Appeal in *Chinn* [2012] EWCA Crim 501; [2012] 2 Cr.App.R. 4 this provision is not intended to apply only when the matters sought to be adduced are "routine"; a suggestion to the contrary in *Archbold*, 2012 edn para.11-39 was not followed.

statements *verified* by him.[98] When the statutory provision applies the witness's evidence will be the oral testimony plus the earlier hearsay statement.

There are exceptional circumstances at common law in which a document used to refresh a witness's memory may itself become an item of evidence. These circumstances were explained by Sir Jocelyn Simon P. in *Senat v Senat*.[99] His Lordship confirmed that where a witness uses a contemporaneous document to refresh memory in the witness box, cross-examining counsel may call for the document to inspect it.[100] Counsel can do this for the purpose of checking the document without being bound to put it in evidence. In addition, counsel can cross-examine the witness on the parts of the document used to refresh memory without the document becoming evidence, provided that the cross-examination is restricted to those parts.[101] If, however, the cross-examination extends to other parts of the document not used to refresh memory, counsel for the party calling the witness can insist on the document being made evidence in the case.[102] If this happens, the document will become an exhibit and will therefore be available for inspection by the jury. As Allen has noted, this has the potential disadvantage for the cross-examiner that the document will be a permanent reminder to the jury of the witness's testimony.[103]

If the document does become evidence, the common law rule is that the document is not evidence of the facts stated in it. The document may be used only to support the witness's credibility by demonstrating his consistency.[104] It thus functions in a similar way to a complaint in a sexual case as an exception to the rule against previous consistent statements. The common law has again been superseded by statute to some extent. In civil cases a document made evidence in the case will be admissible as evidence of the facts stated, notwithstanding that it is hearsay, under the provisions of the Civil Evidence Act 1995.[105] In criminal cases s.120(3) of the Criminal Justice Act 2003 provides that a statement made by the witness in a document used to refresh memory while giving evidence, on which he is cross-examined and which consequently is received in evidence in the proceedings, is admissible as evidence of any matter stated of which oral evidence by him would be admissible. It is therefore admissible hearsay evidence. Like the provisions in the Act relating to complaints, this provision gives effect to a recommendation of the Law Commission.[106] It should be noted, however, that the provision applies only to statements *made* by the witness in a

---

[98] cf. Criminal Justice Act 2003 s.139(1), dealing with the use of documents to refresh memory (which refers to a document "made or verified" by a person at an earlier time). Such a document can include a witness statement: *Mangena* [2009] EWCA Crim 2535.

[99] *Senat v Senat* [1965] P.172.

[100] The same rule applies where the witness refreshes memory outside court from notes that the witness does not use in court: *Owen v Edwards* (1983) 77 Cr.App.R. 191 DC.

[101] Note, however, that if it is suggested, expressly or by implication, that the documentary record used to refresh memory is a fabrication, "the record may be admissible to rebut this suggestion and, if the nature of the record assists as to this, to show whether or not it is genuine, that is to say whether or not it has the appearance of being a contemporaneous record which has not subsequently been altered": per Woolf L.J. in *Sekhon* (1986) 85 Cr.App.R. 19 at 22 CA.

[102] *Britton* [1987] 2 All E.R. 412 CA.

[103] C. Allen, *Practical Guide to Evidence,* 3rd edn (London: Routledge-Cavendish, 2004), p.99.

[104] *Virgo* (1978) 67 Cr.App.R. 323 CA; *Sekhon* (1986) 85 Cr.App.R. 19 CA.

[105] For discussion of these provisions, see Ch.17.

[106] Law Com No.245 para.10.82.

document; it does not extend to statements *verified* by the witness at the time. If the document in question becomes evidence in the case, statements verified, but not made, by the witness will be subject to the common law rule and evidence only of the witness's consistency. The merit of this difference is not immediately apparent.

(B)   Refreshing memory out of court

At common law witnesses may also refresh their memories from documents that **14–019** were not made contemporaneously in the sense explained above. An example of such a document would be a statement by the witness to a party's solicitor made some time after the events in question. It is natural that a witness who did not make a contemporaneous record might want to look at the witness statement before giving evidence about the matter, since the statement will almost certainly have been made at a time when the matter was fresher in the witness's mind than it is at the trial. It is also natural that the legal advisers of the party calling the witness might want to invite the witness to read the statement before testifying; the questions counsel will ask the witness will usually be framed on the basis of the witness statement. This practice received the blessing of the Court of Appeal in *Richardson*[107] where prosecution witnesses were told outside court that they might refresh their memories from the statements they had given to the police a few weeks after the offences in question were committed. The offences had been committed 18 months before the trial. Dismissing the defendant's appeal, Sachs L.J. approved some concise comments of the Supreme Court of Hong Kong[108]:

> "Testimony in the witness box becomes more of a test of memory than of truthfulness if witnesses are deprived of the opportunity of checking their recollection beforehand by reference to statements or notes made at a time closer to the events in question.
> Refusal of access to statements would tend to create difficulties for honest witnesses but be likely to do little to hamper dishonest witnesses."

The court added a note of warning to the effect that it would be wrong for several witnesses to be handed their statements in circumstances that enabled them to compare with each other what they had said. Subsequently the Court of Appeal made it clear that there is no rule that witnesses must be allowed to see their statements before giving evidence[109]; there may be cases where this would not be appropriate.[110] It is desirable for the prosecution to inform the defence where prosecution witnesses have been shown their statements, although an omission to do so will not by itself be a ground for quashing a conviction.[111] In any event the

---

[107] *Richardson* [1971] 2 Q.B. 484.
[108] In *Lau Pak Ngam v R.* [1966] Crim. L.R. 443.
[109] *Westwell* [1976] 2 All E.R. 812.
[110] Because, e.g. the witness has some improper purpose in mind. See also *Thomas* [1994] Crim. L.R. 745, where the Court of Appeal upheld a trial judge's ruling that it would be undesirable to show a child aged 8 her statement before the child testified. The Commentary in the *Criminal Law Review* suggests the reason may have been that the child would not appreciate that she had to testify about what she remembered of the day in question and not about what she had been shown in her statement. A similar point might well apply to some adult witnesses.
[111] *Westwell* [1976] 2 All E.R. 812 CA.

defence could elicit the fact in cross-examination, with a view to challenging the weight that could safely be attached to the witness's evidence.

It used to be the case that at common law non-contemporaneous documents could only be looked at out of court and could not be taken into the witness box for the purpose of refreshing memory.[112] In more recent years the courts modified this rule and to some extent blurred the boundary between the two forms of refreshing memory. In *Da Silva*,[113] a witness (W) in a robbery case was called to give evidence relating to an alleged confession made to him by the accused in a police cell. W had made a statement to the police one month after the relevant conversation, but had not looked at the statement before giving evidence. When W said that he could not remember what had happened a year earlier, the trial judge invited W to withdraw to read his statement. W did so and then returned to the witness box to complete his evidence. Approving this procedure and dismissing the defendant's appeal, the Court of Appeal said that a judge had a discretion to allow a witness to refresh his memory from a non-contemporaneous statement if certain conditions were satisfied:

(1) the witness cannot recall the details of events because of the lapse of time since they took place;

(2) the witness made a statement much nearer the time of the events and the contents of the statement represented his recollection at the time that he made it[114];

(3) the witness had not read the statement before entering the witness box;

(4) the witness wished to have an opportunity to read the statement before continuing to give evidence.

14–020 The court added that it did not matter whether the witness withdrew from the witness box to read the statement or read it in the box, provided that in either case the statement was removed from him when he came to give his evidence and he should not be permitted to refer to it again. The inroad made by this case into the traditional separation of the two types of refreshing memory was taken one stage further by the Divisional Court in *R. v South Ribble Magistrates Ex p. Cochrane*.[115] Here the witness (W) had read his witness statements before starting to give evidence at committal proceedings for conspiracy to pervert the course of justice. He then claimed not to remember details of conversations referred to in his statements, which had been made 12–18 months earlier. The stipendiary magistrate allowed W to look at the statements again before continuing with his evidence. Despite the failure to satisfy the third of the conditions set out in *Da Silva*, that the witness should not have read the statement before starting to give evidence, the Divisional Court approved this procedure and refused an application for judicial review of the committal. According to

---

[112] *Richardson* [1971] 2 Q.B. 484 at 489–490 CA per Sachs L.J.

[113] *Da Silva* [1990] 1 All E.R. 29 CA.

[114] Note the difference in wording from the test of a "contemporaneous" document that requires that the memory of the events be fresh in the witness's mind when he makes the statement in the document.

[115] *R. v South Ribble Magistrates Ex p. Cochrane* [1996] 2 Cr.App.R. 544.

Henry L.J., a judge has a "strong discretion"[116] to decide whether to permit a witness to refresh his memory from a non-contemporaneous document. He explained that the criteria in *Da Silva* represented sufficient rather than necessary conditions for the exercise of the discretion, and went on to say that, provided the judge complied with the requirements of fairness and justice, an appeal court would give the judge a generous margin of appreciation in applying the discretion.

In the light of this decision, there appears to be nothing to stop a judge allowing a witness to refer repeatedly to a non-contemporaneous document in the course of testifying. Cases are quite conceivable where this would be proper: a complex serious fraud where the witness statements are lengthy and detailed, or where the witness is a nervous, confused and flustered old lady.[117] If repeated reading is to be allowed, then the courts have substantially abolished the distinction between contemporaneous and non-contemporaneous documents in refreshing memory.[118] This is probably a good thing, since it is not clear that the distinction ever served a very useful purpose. It is worth recalling at this point that s.139 of the Criminal Justice Act 2003, which allows a witness to refresh his memory while giving evidence from a document made or verified by him at an earlier time, does not require the document to be contemporaneous with the matter in question. It is sufficient if the witness states in his oral evidence that the document records his recollection of the matter at the earlier time and his recollection is likely to have been significantly better at that time. With this, and the other provisions noted above, the Act has made valuable reforms to the doctrine of refreshing memory. However, it is submitted that the subject remains unnecessarily technical and complex; it would benefit from further simplification, and restatement in a modern statutory code of evidence.

4.   *Unfavourable and hostile witnesses*

A party who calls a witness to prove certain facts may find that the witness "fails to come up to proof", meaning that the witness does not testify in accordance with his or her witness statement. The witness may simply not prove the facts that he was expected to prove, or the witness may prove something different. Such a witness is "unfavourable". This is a technical term used to distinguish this type of witness from the witness who is "hostile" to the party calling him or her. Hostile witnesses are considered below. At common law a party calling a witness who turns out to be unfavourable is not permitted to attack the credibility of the witness. Having put the witness forward as a witness of truth, the party may not now invite the court to disbelieve the witness on the basis that no credit can be

14–021

---

[116] *R. v South Ribble Magistrates Ex p. Cochrane* [1996] 2 Cr.App.R. 544 at 552.

[117] *R. v South Ribble Magistrates Ex p. Cochrane* [1996] 2 Cr.App.R. 544, where these examples are given to illustrate the point that a pretrial reading of the statements may be inadequate for the purpose of refreshing memory.

[118] This move is endorsed by the Auld Review, which recommends (p.551) that the only condition for use of a written statement to refresh a witness's memory should be that there is good reason to believe that he would have been significantly better able to recall the events in question when he made or verified it than at the time of giving evidence.

given to the testimony.[119] In particular the party is not allowed to discredit the witness by adopting the technique of cross-examining the witness on a previous inconsistent statement. All that the party can do is to call another witness to contradict the unfavourable witness. In *Ewer v Ambrose*,[120] the defendant called a witness to prove the existence of a partnership, but the witness proved the opposite. It was held that the defendant could call other witnesses to prove the partnership. He could not:

> "give general evidence to show that the witness was not to be believed on his oath, but he may show by other evidence that he is mistaken as to the fact which he is called to prove."[121]

If the law were otherwise, a party's ability to prove his case might depend on the chance of the order in which he happened to call his witnesses.

The standard definition of a hostile witness was given by Stephen: a witness who is not desirous of telling the truth at the instance of the party calling him.[122] Hostility[123] is partly a question of the witness's demeanour, partly a question of the nature of the evidence the witness gives, and partly a question of the evidence that the witness does not or will not give. Thus hostility may be demonstrated by the witness's apparent animus against the party, but an animus is not a necessary condition. A prosecution witness who refuses to give evidence through fear of reprisals from the defendant or his associates may have no animus against the prosecution, but will nonetheless be unwilling to tell the truth when questioned by counsel for the prosecution.[124] Hostility may exist where a witness plainly contradicts a statement that he has previously given to the party calling him.[125] Again, however, inconsistent testimony is not a necessary condition. A witness who is sworn and then refuses to say anything further may also be treated as hostile.[126]

The significance of having the judge declare a witness "hostile" is that the party calling the witness then has leave to cross-examine the witness to some extent. At common law the party may ask a hostile witness leading questions, but

---

[119] Thus a party may not seek to discredit an unfavourable witness with evidence of the witness's bad character, or previous inconsistent statements, or any other technique that might be used in cross-examining the other side's witnesses as to their credit. For a sceptical view of the rationale of the rule prohibiting a party from impeaching the credit of the party's own witness see R. Munday, "Calling a Hostile Witness" [1989] Crim. L.R. 866, 868.

[120] *Ewer v Ambrose* (1825) 3 B. & C. 746.

[121] *Ewer v Ambrose* (1825) 3 B. & C. 746 at 750 per Holroyd J. See *Clarke* [2011] EWCA Crim 407 for an example of a case where the prosecution was entitled to ask the jury to prefer the evidence of one group of prosecution witnesses to that of two other prosecution witnesses whose testimony was unfavourable to the prosecution case. The Court of Appeal went on to confirm that where counsel had not obtained leave to treat the latter witnesses as hostile he could not attack their credibility by suggesting that they were lying.

[122] *Digest of the Law of Evidence*, 12th edn, art.147.

[123] It is essentially a matter of the trial judge's discretion whether to declare a witness hostile. See *Fraser and Warren* (1956) 40 Cr.App.R. 160; *Mann* (1972) 56 Cr.App.R. 750.

[124] See, e.g. *Honeyghon and Sayles* [1999] Crim. L.R. 221 CA, on the procedure prosecutors and courts should adopt where a witness appears likely to persist in a refusal to assist the court.

[125] As in *Bashir* [2011] EWCA Crim 2763 where a wife withdrew a complaint of domestic violence by her husband, claiming that her statement to the police was all lies, fabricated by interpreters at the instigation of the police.

[126] *Thompson* (1976) 64 Cr.App.R. 96 CA.

may not cross-examine the witness on the witness's convictions or previous misconduct or bad character generally. If the hostile witness's testimony is inconsistent with a previous statement by him, then under s.3 of the Criminal Procedure Act 1865 the party can cross-examine him or her on the previous inconsistent statement.[127] This section provides[128]:

> "A party producing a witness shall not be allowed to impeach his credit by general evidence of bad character, but he may, in case the witness shall, in the opinion of the judge, prove adverse, contradict him by other evidence, or, by leave of the judge, prove that he has made at other times a statement inconsistent with his present testimony; but before such last mentioned proof can be given the circumstances of the supposed statement, sufficient to designate the particular occasion, must be mentioned to the witness, and he must be asked whether or not he has made such statement."

The section is not well drafted, because it fails to distinguish between unfavourable and hostile witnesses, and it does not make clear the nature of the relationship between the common law power to contradict a party's own witness and the statutory power to ask about previous inconsistent statements. In *Greenough v Eccles*,[129] the court drew attention to the defects in the identically worded predecessor of s.3,[130] and engaged in some judicial rationalisation of the provision. It was held that the word "adverse" means "hostile", with the result that the section is to be interpreted as saying nothing about the power at common law to contradict an unfavourable witness by other testimony. What the section does on this view, therefore, is to enact that a hostile witness can not only be contradicted by other evidence (as he could be at common law) but, with leave, can also be asked about previous inconsistent statements. It is unclear whether the common law permitted this. In *Thompson*,[131] the defendant was charged with indecent assault on, and incest with, his daughter. The daughter had previously made a statement to the police implicating the defendant. When the prosecution called her as a witness at the trial, after being sworn she stood "mute of malice" and refused to say anything more. Given her defiant demeanour, the judge gave leave for her to be treated as hostile, whereupon counsel for the prosecution asked her about her statement to the police. She eventually admitted that the statement was true. On appeal the defendant's counsel argued that she should not have been treated as hostile. He put the simple but powerful point that s.3 of the 1865 Act did not apply, since the daughter had not given any testimony that was inconsistent with her previous statement. She had given no statement in evidence at all. Apparently conceding the logical force of this, the Court of Appeal held that the matter was covered by the common law.[132] Dismissing the defendant's

14–022

---

[127] This power provides the main reason for calling a witness known or suspected to be hostile. The party calling the witness will hope that the witness, when confronted with the earlier statement, will acknowledge its truth. For further discussion see R. Munday, "Calling a Hostile Witness" [1989] Crim. L.R. 866.

[128] Despite the name of the statute this provision applies to both criminal and civil proceedings: Criminal Procedure Act 1865 s.1.

[129] *Greenough v Eccles* (1859) 5 C.B.N.S. 786.

[130] Namely s.22 of the Common Law Procedure (Amendment) Act 1856, repealed and reenacted in s.3 of the 1865 Act.

[131] *Thompson* (1976) 64 Cr.App.R. 96 CA.

[132] See *Clarke v Saffery* (1824) Ry. & M. 126; *Bastin v Carew* (1824) Ry. & M. 127.

appeal, the court held that the common law empowered a trial judge to permit the cross-examination of a hostile witness to the extent of asking the witness leading questions. Such leading questions could apparently include asking the witness about the existence of the statement to the police and about whether the contents of the statement were true. The court in *Thompson* declined to express a view about the application of s.3, and inferentially the common law, in cases where the witness's testimony was inconsistent with a previous statement.

Where the witness, as in *Thompson*, admits the truth of the earlier statement, the witness in effect adopts the contents of the statement as part of the witness's testimony. Assuming that the factfinder decides that the witness is credible, the testimony can be accepted as evidence of the facts that the witness has testified to. Where the previous inconsistent statement is proved, but the witness does not admit its truth, then at common law the previous statement cannot be used as evidence of the facts stated. The factfinder cannot choose between the previous statement and the present testimony.[133] The previous statement can be used only for the purpose of casting doubt on the credibility of the witness. One view is that it has the effect of cancelling out the testimony at the trial, so that the factfinder should be directed to disregard the witness altogether. According to the Court of Criminal Appeal:

> "When a witness is shown to have made previous statements inconsistent with the evidence given by that witness at the trial the jury should not merely be directed that the evidence given at the trial should be regarded as unreliable; they should also be directed that the previous statements, whether sworn or unsworn, do not constitute evidence upon which they can act."[134]

If this proposition means that a previous statement always neutralises present testimony, so that the jury must be directed to disregard the testimony, then it is almost certainly inaccurate because it is overbroad. First, the witness may be able to give a satisfactory explanation of the inconsistency. The witness may be able to show, for example, that the previous statement resulted from improper pressure brought to bear on him, or that it resulted from a misunderstanding, or from an honest mistake based on the witness's faulty memory of a matter that the witness was later able to check from documentary sources. In such cases it would seem that the factfinder ought to be able to rely on the trial testimony,[135] taking into account that its weight might be somewhat affected by the inconsistency. Secondly, inconsistency may be a matter of degree and there may not be a complete contradiction between the previous statement and the testimony. Thirdly, depending on the circumstances of the case, an earlier retracted statement may carry less weight than the testimony being relied on.[136] The better

---

[133] See, for a clear statement of this view, *White* (1922) 17 Cr.App.R. 60 CCA.

[134] *Golder* [1960] 1 W.L.R. 1169 at 1172–1173 CCA per Lord Parker C.J. See also *Oliva* [1965] 1 W.L.R. 1028 CCA.

[135] See *Maw* [1994] Crim. L.R. 841 CA.

[136] cf. *Thomas* [1985] Crim. L.R. 445 CA, where the defendant was charged with the murder of his young baby. His sister, a defence witness, had made some incriminating admissions to the police, regarding her violent treatment of the child, which she retracted when called by the defence to testify. After being ruled to be hostile, she confirmed the substance of her police statements. The Court of

view therefore, which is supported by a number of authorities,[137] is that the proposition in *Golder* should not be treated as setting out an inflexible rule of law or practice whereby the testimony of an inconsistent witness is always to be disregarded.

In both civil and criminal proceedings the factfinder now has the option of preferring the previous inconsistent statement to the trial testimony, and treating the former as reliable evidence. In civil cases, by virtue of the combined operation of ss.1 and 6(3) and (5) of the Civil Evidence Act 1995, a witness's previous inconsistent statement that is adduced under s.3 of the Criminal Procedure Act 1865 is admissible as evidence of the facts stated notwithstanding its hearsay nature. In criminal cases s.119 of the Criminal Justice Act 2003 provides that where a person giving oral evidence admits making a previous inconsistent statement, or such a statement made by him is proved by virtue of s.3 of the Criminal Procedure Act 1865, the previous statement is admissible as evidence of any matter stated of which oral evidence by him would be admissible.[138] In all proceedings, therefore, a factfinder has three alternatives when confronted with an inconsistent witness: the first is to regard the witness as wholly unreliable; the second is to accept the whole or part of the trial testimony; and the third is to accept the whole or part of the previous statement.[139]

14–023

A further simplification of the law would be to abolish the distinction between unfavourable and hostile witnesses. It is not obvious that this distinction serves any useful purpose. It would be more consistent with the court's truth-finding function to allow all witnesses to be challenged where their testimony contradicts their previous statements, and not just those witnesses whom the judge thinks display a hostile demeanour. The Australian Evidence Act 1995 has taken this step by providing[140] that a party who called a witness may, with leave, question the witness about whether the witness has at any time made a prior inconsistent statement. The grant of leave is not made dependent on any finding of "hostility".

C. CROSS-EXAMINATION

Cross-examination has a number of aims. Two of them are, in Allen's concise phrase, "to complete and correct the story told by the witness during evidence in chief".[141] The cross-examiner may wish to get from the witness a part of the story that was missing from the evidence in chief and that is favourable to the cross-examiner's case. The cross-examiner may also wish to test and challenge

14–024

Appeal held that the jury should have been invited to consider whether her evidence cast doubt on the Crown case, and that the judge should have pointed out that she would have far fewer motives for admitting violence than denying it.

[137] See *Driscoll v R.* (1977) 137 C.L.R. 517 High Court of Australia; *Pestano* [1981] Crim. L.R. 397 CA; *Alves v DPP* [1992] 4 All E.R. 787 HL (see Lord Goff of Chieveley at 792).

[138] This welcome reform gives effect to a recommendation of the Law Commission: Law Com No.245 paras 10.91–10.101.

[139] However, if a previous inconsistent statement can still be admitted at common law, it cannot be evidence of the facts stated, because s.119 of the Criminal Justice Act applies only to statements admitted under ss.3, 4 and 5 of the Criminal Procedure Act 1865.

[140] Australian Evidence Act 1995 s.38.

[141] C. Allen, *Practical Guide to Evidence*, 3rd edn (2004), p.82.

the unfavourable testimony that the witness has given in chief, hoping to get the witness to modify or qualify it, or even to admit that it was a lie or a mistake. A further possibility is that the cross-examiner may wish to cast doubt on the witness's testimony generally, by putting questions intended to show that the witness is not worthy of belief on oath. Cross-examination as to credit (or credibility), as this is known, aims to attack unfavourable testimony indirectly, by persuading the factfinder that it is not safe to place reliance on anything the witness says in evidence.

The right to cross-examine is available to any party whose interests may be affected by the testimony of the witness. In criminal cases this means, for example, that one accused may cross-examine a co-accused, even if the latter has given no evidence in chief against the accused.[142] The point is that cross-examination might permit the extraction of some evidence favourable to the defence of the accused.

Cross-examination of witnesses is an essential feature of adversarial procedure, and it has attracted a good deal of supporting rhetoric in the past. Wigmore famously described it as "beyond any doubt the greatest legal engine ever invented for the discovery of truth".[143] In Viscount Sankey's view, it was "a powerful and valuable weapon for the purpose of testing the veracity of a witness and the accuracy and completeness of his story".[144] However, there is also a view that some of the claims made for its value have been exaggerated. Sceptics have doubted in particular whether it is effective in exposing the witness who is determined to commit perjury. Neither does it seem to have been conspicuously successful in demonstrating the unreliability of some eyewitness identification evidence. Part of the reason for this may be that cross-examination works best where the witness has a "story" to tell that can be probed for consistency and plausibility. Evidence of visual identification tends to lack the story context, and to stand more as an isolated item of evidence the weight of which may be partly dependent on the witness's confidence. An honest and strong-minded witness may not find it too difficult to repel a direct assault on his confidence made in cross-examination. The focus of this debate about the merits of cross-examination tends to be the rationale of the hearsay rule; the absence of an opportunity to cross-examine is often said to be one of the principal reasons for the rule. Further discussion is therefore postponed to Ch.16.

1. *General principles*

(A) *Relevance and admissibility*

14–025   Cross-examination differs from examination in chief in two major respects. The first relates to the manner of questioning. In cross-examination, leading questions of the first type are permissible.[145] Because the witness is not presumed to be

---

[142] *Hilton* [1972] 1 Q.B. 421 CA.
[143] *Evidence* (Chadbourn rev., 1974), Vol.V p.32.
[144] *Mechanical and General Inventions Co and Lehwess v Austin and Austin Motor Co* [1935] A.C. 346 at 359 HL.
[145] *Parkin v Moon* (1836) 7 C. & P. 408.

favourable to the cross-examiner's case, the cross-examiner can suggest facts to the witness, seek the witness's agreement to factual propositions and put words in the witness's mouth. This liberty does not, however, extend to leading questions of the second type, which assume the existence of disputed facts.

The second point of difference concerns the scope of the questioning. All questions to witnesses must, as ever, be relevant to an issue in the case. However, the cross-examiner is permitted to make the credibility of the witness an issue in the case, and this means that questions may be asked in cross-examination that relate solely to the credit of the witness:

> "When a witness has given evidence material to the issues in the case you can cross-examine him on matters not directly material to the case in order to ask the jury to infer from his answers that he is not worthy of belief, not a credible person, and therefore that they should not accept his answers on questions material to the case as true. This is cross-examination as to his credibility, commonly called cross-examination to credit."[146]

Cross-examination to credit is discussed in more detail below, but it should be noted at this stage that the liberty to cross-examine on credit does not entitle the cross-examiner to investigate any and every detail of the witness's life and character that might conceivably be relevant to the witness's credibility: "Since the purpose of cross-examination as to credit is to show that the witness ought not to be believed on oath, the matters about which he is questioned must relate to his likely standing after cross-examination with the tribunal".[147] There is a requirement therefore that the questions should have a sufficient degree of relevance to credit to justify an obligation on the witness to answer them. In *Hobbs v Tinling,* Sankey L.J. explained the considerations that the court ought to take into account in deciding whether a witness should be compelled to answer a question as to credit:

> "(1)   Such questions are proper if they are of such a nature that the truth of the imputation conveyed by them would seriously affect the opinion of the Court as to the credibility of the witness on the matter to which he testifies.
>
> (2)   Such questions are improper if the imputation which they convey relates to matters so remote in time, or of such a character, that the truth of the imputation would not affect, or would affect in a slight degree, the opinion of the Court as to the credibility of the witness on the matter to which he testifies.
>
> (3)   Such questions are improper if there is a great disproportion between the importance of the imputation made against the witness's character and the importance of his evidence."[148]

These common law principles apply to civil and criminal cases alike. Questions in cross-examination, whether relevant to issue or credit, must also comply with any applicable rules of admissibility. In criminal cases questions in cross-examination concerning the bad character of witnesses are now governed not by the common law, but by the provisions of Ch.1 of Pt 11 of the Criminal Justice

14–026

---

[146] *Hobbs v Tinling and Co Ltd* [1929] 2 K.B. 1 at 18–19 CA per Scrutton L.J.

[147] *Sweet-Escott* (1971) 55 Cr.App.R. 316 at 320 per Lawton J., holding that a witness's convictions, that were more than 20 years old, were not "material" to the proceedings in which the witness gave evidence, since in the circumstances of the case they could not have adversely affected his credit.

[148] *Hobbs v Tinling* [1929] 2 K.B. 1 at 51 CA. See also *Sweet-Escott* (1971) 55 Cr.App.R. 316 at 320 CA per Lawton J.

Act 2003.[149] The rules differ according to whether the witness is the defendant or a non-defendant. The scheme of the Act relating to evidence of the bad character of defendants, including cross-examination on their bad character, is considered in Chs 18 and 19. Cross-examination of non-defendants on their bad character is dealt with below.

In *Treacy*,[150] the trial judge allowed the prosecution to cross-examine the accused on a confession that the judge had ruled to be inadmissible for the prosecution in chief. The terms of the confession were inconsistent with the defendant's testimony. The Court of Criminal Appeal held that the cross-examination was improper because the confession was inadmissible evidence for the prosecution irrespective of the use they wished to make of it. Humphreys J. put the matter concisely:

"if [the statement] is not admissible, nothing more ought to be heard of it, and it is quite a mistake to think that a document can be made admissible in evidence which is otherwise inadmissible simply because it is put to a person in cross-examination."[151]

This is a categorical statement, but it needs qualifying in one important respect. A confession by one accused (D1) may be inadmissible evidence for the prosecution against D1, but it may be relevant to the defence of a co-accused (D2), and it may be so relevant whether or not D1's testimony at trial includes evidence against D2. In such a case D2 may be able to cross-examine D1 on the confession,[152] although the judge must then direct the jury that they may take the confession into account only in considering the evidence against D2 and may not use it as evidence against D1.

(B)   The obligation to challenge the evidence given in chief

14–027   Cross-examination should concern questions of fact. It is improper for counsel to put questions to a witness that are really invitations to an argument.[153] One of the reasons for this is efficiency; the appropriate time for counsel to argue about the interpretation of evidence is in counsel's closing speech after all the evidence has been heard. The other reason is fairness to the witness. The witness in the box is an amateur, and it is not an equal contest to pit him against a professional conductor of argument. A trial judge has the power where necessary to prevent the use of argumentative questions by exercising a discretion to control bullying or inappropriate cross-examination.

However, it is not always easy to discern the line between fact and argument, particularly where inferential facts are concerned. In addition the point is affected by a second general principle regarding cross-examination. If a party proposes to contradict evidence given in chief by a witness for the other side, the party must

---

[149] Criminal Justice Act 2003 s.99 abolished the common law rules governing the admissibility of evidence of bad character in criminal proceedings.
[150] *Treacy* [1944] 2 All E.R. 228 CCA.
[151] *Treacy* [1944] 2 All E.R. 228 at 236.
[152] *Rowson* [1986] Q.B. 174 CA; *Lui Mei Lin v R.* [1989] A.C. 288 PC; *Myers* [1998] A.C. 124 HL; and see Ch.6.
[153] *Baldwin* (1925) 18 Cr.App.R. 175 CCA.

normally challenge the evidence by putting the contradictory matter to the witness. This is sometimes called the rule in *Browne v Dunn*,[154] after the obscurely reported case in which the House of Lords stated the obligation. The obligation is founded on fairness to the witness; it is thought that the witness should be given the opportunity to rebut the challenge and explain any contradiction. A failure to make the challenge may result in the court inferring that the party accepts the witness's evidence and refusing to permit the party to invite the jury to reject the evidence. The rule is, however, a flexible one,[155] and is not always strictly applied, particularly in magistrates' courts.[156] The rule may also be significantly qualified in relation to the cross-examination of young children and other vulnerable witnesses, where trial judges have discretion to restrict both the scope and the style of questioning by defence advocates.[157]

2. Cross-examination as to credit

(A) Collateral issues and the finality rule

The credibility of a witness is not a fact in issue in the sense of a fact that must be proved in order to ground a civil claim or establish the elements of a criminal offence. It is indirectly relevant to the determination of those facts that give rise to legal consequences, but it is essentially a side or collateral issue. There is a general rule in the law of evidence that a witness's answers to collateral questions must be treated as final.[158] This is not to say that they must be accepted as true[159]; the point is that a cross-examiner may not go behind the answers and call evidence in rebuttal. The rationale of the rule is mainly the need to avoid indefinite multiplication of the issues in a case, and all the accompanying disadvantages of increasing the length and cost of the proceedings and risking distraction and confusion of the factfinder.[160] A further reason is the need to be fair to the witness who may have had no notice before coming into court that these issues were to be raised.[161]

14–028

The operation of the finality rule in relation to the credit of a witness is illustrated by *Edwards*.[162] The prosecution evidence against the defendant on a charge of robbery included testimony from police officers that the defendant had made oral admissions. The defendant had refused to sign the interview notes saying that the admissions were fabrications. A question arose on appeal as to

---

[154] *Browne v Dunn* (1893) 6 R. 67. See also *Fenlon* (1980) 71 Cr.App.R. 307 CA; *Lovelock* [1997] Crim. L.R. 821 CA.
[155] It may not, e.g. always be essential to put to the witness expressly that he is lying, provided that counsel makes clear that the evidence is not accepted. See *Lovelock* [1997] Crim. L.R. 821 CA: a "raised eyebrow" approach may be sufficient.
[156] See *O'Connell v Adams* [1973] Crim. L.R. 313.
[157] See, e.g. *R. v E* [2011] EWCA Crim 3028; [2012] Crim. L.R. 563; *Wills* [2011] EWCA Crim 1938; [2012] Crim. L.R. 565.
[158] *Harris v Tippett* (1811) 2 Camp. 637; *Att-Gen v Hitchcock* (1847) 1 Ex. Ch. 91.
[159] *Hobbs v Tinling and Co Ltd* [1929] 2 K.B. 1.
[160] *Att-Gen v Hitchcock* (1847) 1 Ex. Ch. 91.
[161] *Hobbs v Tinling and Co Ltd* [1929] 2 K.B. 1.
[162] *Edwards* [1991] 2 All E.R. 266 CA.

whether the defendant could cross-examine the officers concerned on evidence they had given in other trials, where the issue was again one of whether they had fabricated oral admissions. The defendants in those other cases had been acquitted, suggesting that the juries had disbelieved the police evidence. The Court of Appeal held that the cross-examination would have been permissible. Given that the same issue of fabrication was involved, questions about the evidence given by the officers in the other trials had a sufficient connection with the outcomes of those trials to be relevant to the officers' credibility as witnesses against the defendant. This line of cross-examination could seriously affect the credibility of their testimony, in the opinion of the court. At the same time the Court of Appeal reaffirmed the rule that evidence would not be admissible to rebut any replies by the officers that were unfavourable to the defence. The officers' credibility was a collateral issue, and their answers to questions relating to credit were final unless one of the exceptions applied. The exceptions are considered below.

This was a clear case where questions about evidence in other cases could only be relevant to credit.[163] Consequently the rule about the finality of answers to collateral issues was not difficult to apply. Sometimes, however, the distinction between the issue in the case and matters collateral to the issue may be very difficult to draw, because ultimately the distinction depends on the degree of relevance involved. According to Pollock C.B. in *Att-Gen v Hitchcock*,[164] the test of whether a matter is collateral is whether the party cross-examining the witness in question would be permitted to adduce evidence in chief of the matter because of its connection with the facts in issue. If not, the matter is collateral and the cross-examiner may not as a general rule call evidence to rebut the witness's answers. This test has a strong element of circularity,[165] but it also has the merit of focusing attention on the need for a matter to have a sufficient degree of relevance to justify further investigation. Thus, in *Att-General v Hitchcock* the question was whether a cross-examiner could go behind a witness's denial that he had said out of court to C that he had been offered a bribe to give certain testimony. It was held that the cross-examiner could not call C to prove that the witness made this statement to him. Given that it was not contended that the witness had in fact accepted a bribe, it was not sufficiently relevant to either the issue or to his credit whether or not he had *said* that he had been offered one. The cross-examiner could certainly never have led evidence in chief of any such statement.

14–029 Where the outcome of a case depends essentially on whether the factfinder believes the testimony of a complainant or the testimony of the accused, the dividing line between issue and credit becomes increasingly blurred. Sexual offences frequently give rise to what might be called a credibility contest. In *Funderburk*,[166] the defendant was charged with offences of unlawful sexual intercourse with a girl aged 13. The girl's testimony to the acts of intercourse with the defendant included a claim that the first act involved the loss of her virginity.

---

[163] For a further example, see *Irish* [1995] Crim. L.R. 145 CA.

[164] *Att-Gen v Hitchcock* (1847) 1 Ex. Ch. 91 at 99.

[165] As Henry J. acknowledged in *Funderburk* [1990] 2 All E.R. 482 at 491.

[166] *Funderburk* [1990] 2 All E.R. 482 CA.

The defendant's case was that he never had intercourse with the girl, and that the acts to which she testified were the product of fantasy or acts that she had experienced with other men. The trial judge refused to permit the defendant to cross-examine the girl on a previous statement she had made to X in which she told X that, before the first alleged incident with the defendant, she had had sex with two other men. If the girl had denied making this statement the defendant had wanted to call X to prove it. The Court of Appeal held that the cross-examination on the previous inconsistent statement should have been allowed. If the jury had known that the girl was not a virgin, as she had claimed in evidence, they might have reappraised her credibility. On the question of rebutting evidence, if the girl had denied the statement to X, the court said that "where the disputed issue is a sexual one between two persons in private the difference between questions going to credit and questions going to the issue is reduced to vanishing point".[167] Given the importance that the claim about loss of virginity had assumed, its refutation went to the issue in the case and was not merely a matter of the girl's credit. Therefore the defendant would have been able to prove the previous statement if the girl had denied it.

This is probably a defensible decision on the particular facts, but *Funderburk* seems to have been interpreted as authority for a wide principle that in sexual cases generally the court should not draw too fine a line between matters going to the issue and matters going to credit.[168] In *Nagrecha*,[169] the complainant alleged that the defendant, her employer, had indecently assaulted her on the first and only occasion that she went to work for him. The defendant denied the assault. When cross-examined, the complainant denied making allegations of sexual impropriety against other men. The Court of Appeal held that the trial judge had erred in refusing to let D call evidence of the making of other complaints by the complainant. According to Rose L.J.:

> "Such evidence went not merely to credit, but to the heart of the case, in that it bore on the crucial issue as to whether there had been any indecent assault. As to that matter, only the complainant and the appellant were able to give evidence. In our judgment, that being so, the learned judge ought to have permitted the evidence to be called because it might well have led the jury to take different view of the complainant's evidence."[170]

This looks like a green light to the defence to investigate any and all inconsistencies in a complainant's evidence, in a case where the essential issue is whether she or the accused is telling the truth. A passage in Cross and Tapper,[171] cited with apparent approval in *Nagrecha*,[172] comments that there are signs of a more liberal approach to rebuttal evidence, substituting a test of substantial relevance for the older distinction between facts in issue and collateral issues. A focus on substance rather than form is usually a good thing, and there is no doubt

---

[167] *Funderburk* [1990] 2 All E.R. 482 at 491 per Henry J.
[168] See *Gibson* [1993] Crim. L.R. 453 CA; *Nagrecha* [1997] 2 Cr.App.R. 401 CA.
[169] *Nagrecha* [1997] 2 Cr.App.R. 401 CA.
[170] *Nagrecha* [1997] 2 Cr.App.R. 401 at 410.
[171] See now Cross and Tapper, 10th edn, p.387.
[172] *Nagrecha* [1997] 2 Cr.App.R. 401 at 407. *Nagrecha* should be compared with *Neale* [1998] Crim. L.R. 737, where the Court of Appeal, on different facts, reasserted the orthodox rule.

that the traditional distinction in the law of evidence between issue and credit has been the subject of much well-merited criticism.

14–030 However, the danger of its abandonment in this context is that the test of "substantial relevance" will be set too low, with consequent unfairness to the complainant as well as unprofitable confusion of the issues. In *Nagrecha*, for example, C (the complainant) had been cross-examined about her relationship with a previous employer, L. She admitted complaining about his aggressive behaviour, but denied making any complaint against him of a sexual nature. The rebutting evidence consisted of a statement by L. After describing C as "very difficult" and suffering from "severe mood changes", L stated that she had made "allegations of a sexual nature against me". The vagueness of these various claims and counterclaims makes it hard to see how they could significantly affect the question of C's credibility in complaining about an assault by the defendant. They seem to require a good deal of further investigation before we can know what to make of them. As Birch has said, elucidating the meaning of these claims initiates "precisely the sort of debate which the rule of finality exists to prevent".[173] The cost of clarification is likely to be out of all proportion to any benefit to the factfinder in deciding where the truth lies about what happened on a completely different occasion. Moreover, there is unfairness to the witness in confronting her without warning with instances of such unrelated behaviour.[174] On the other hand, cross-examination as to whether a complainant has made false complaints of a very similar nature in similar situations does seem to be substantially relevant to her credibility. An accused who was prevented from asking about such complaints might well feel that he had not had a fair trial.

As well as this flexibility in its application, there are certain exceptions to the finality rule as far as cross-examination as to credit is concerned. These relate to previous inconsistent statements of the witness, the witness's bad character and previous convictions, bias of the witness, and disability of the witness affecting his or her reliability.

(B)   Previous inconsistent statements

14–031 Section 4 of the Criminal Procedure Act 1865 provides:

> "If a witness, upon cross-examination as to a former statement made by him relative to the subject-matter of the indictment or proceeding, and inconsistent with his present testimony, does not distinctly admit that he has made such statement, proof may be given that he did in fact make it; but before such proof can be given the circumstances of the supposed statement, sufficient to designate the particular occasion, must be mentioned to the witness, and he must be asked whether or not he has made such statement."

This section deals with when and how a witness's previous inconsistent statement can be proved if the witness does not admit making it. Whether a witness can be asked at all about a previous statement that is inconsistent with present testimony

---

[173] See commentary on *Nagrecha* in [1998] Crim. L.R. 65 at 66.
[174] It should be noted that questions and evidence about "sexual behaviour" of a complainant are subject to the regulatory regime in s.41 of the Youth Justice and Criminal Evidence Act 1999, discussed in Ch.15.

is determined by the common law, which says that it depends on the relevance of the question.[175] Questions going to previous inconsistent statements about facts in issue are by definition always relevant.[176] Questions going to previous inconsistent statements about collateral issues can be asked if they are sufficiently relevant according to the criteria discussed above.[177] Where a question is allowed to be asked about a previous inconsistent statement, and the witness does not admit making the statement,[178] s.4 allows the statement to be proved if it relates "to the subject-matter of the indictment or proceeding". This phrase is generally thought to signify the common law's distinction between facts in issue and collateral facts, so that a witness's denial of a previous inconsistent statement can be rebutted by proof of the statement only where the statement concerns the issue raised by the proceedings. This distinction is not always clear-cut and allows a trial judge a good deal of flexibility in its application. Where proof of the issue essentially comes down to whether the factfinder believes a complainant or a defendant, as in many cases of sexual offences, the distinction between issue and credit may be reduced to vanishing point.[179]

Assuming that a witness's previous inconsistent statement is proved under s.4 of the Criminal Procedure Act 1865, and assuming that the witness does not admit that the previous statement is true, the question then is the use that can be made of the statement. At common law the hearsay rule prevented use of the previous statement as evidence of the facts stated.[180] The previous statement went only to the credibility of the witness and might affect the weight to be given to the witness's testimony. However, reform of the hearsay rule in both civil and criminal cases has resulted in abolition of this limitation on the use of previous inconsistent statements. In civil cases the previous statement can be used as evidence of the facts stated by virtue of the Civil Evidence Act 1995.[181] In criminal cases s.119(1) of the Criminal Justice Act 2003 provides that where a witness admits making a previous inconsistent statement, or a previous inconsistent statement is proved against him by virtue of s.3, 4 or 5 of the Criminal Procedure Act 1865, the statement is admissible as evidence of any matter stated of which oral evidence by him would be admissible.

---

[175] See *Hart* (1957) 42 Cr.App.R. 47 CCA; *Funderburk* [1990] 2 All E.R. 482 CA.

[176] Note that a defendant may make an inconsistent previous statement by his authorised agent, namely his solicitor or counsel. This might happen, for example, where the lawyer indicates on the plea and case management form ("PCMH") what the issue at the trial will be, but the defendant subsequently raises a different and inconsistent issue. In *Newell* [2012] EWCA Crim 650 the Court of Appeal held that in the usual case the trial judge should exclude the statement on the PCMH form under s.78 of PACE provided that the defence has adhered to the letter and spirit of the Criminal Procedure Rules.

[177] See in particular *Hobbs v Tinling and Co Ltd* [1929] 2 K.B. 1; *Sweet-Escott* (1971) 55 Cr.App.R. 316.

[178] This phrase covers the witness who expressly denies the statement, the witness who claims not to remember making it, and the witness who refuses to answer.

[179] *Funderburk* [1990] 2 All E.R. 482 CA, and see the discussion in the text above. See also S. Seabrooke, "The Vanishing Trick–blurring the line between credit and issue" [1999] Crim. L.R. 387.

[180] *Golder* [1960] 1 W.L.R. 1169 CCA; *Askew* [1981] Crim. L.R. 398 CA.

[181] See Civil Evidence Act 1995 ss.1, 6(3) and (5).

14-032   In *Gibbons*,[182] the Court of Appeal commented that s.119 comes into play principally when a witness maintains that the contents of a prior statement which inculpates the defendant are not true. The change made by the section was to permit the jury to rely upon the prior statement, albeit that the witness in evidence declines to adopt it, or goes further and says that it is not true. In this way the section addresses the issue of a witness who is too frightened, perhaps as the result of intimidation, to admit that the statement is true. A different, and unusual, scenario occurred in *Coates*,[183] where a complainant of rape first gave an account of the rape which she subsequently disavowed in a different account in her evidence at the defendant's court-martial. The defence had no real choice but to cross-examine her on the previous statement in order to challenge the reliability of her testimony. Notwithstanding that the prosecution were not seeking to rely on the prior statement the defendant was convicted on the strength of it, a course of action which s.119 appears to allow. The Courts-Martial Appeal Court thought that as a matter of "discretion and overall fairness" s.78 of PACE should have been applied so as to prevent the use of the prior statement for this purpose. It is doubtful, to say the least, whether the wording of s.78 is apt for this purpose, since it is concerned with whether prosecution evidence should be "given", not with the *use* of evidence admitted at the instance of the defence. However, it may be that the decision can be accounted for as a "reading down" of s.78 under s.3 of the Human Rights Act 1998 where this is necessary to ensure a fair trial compatibly with art.6 of the ECHR. Where a previous inconsistent statement is *exculpatory* of the defendant, and the testimony of the witness is crucial to the prosecution, it will be sufficient for acquittal if the jury think that the previous statement *may be* true.[184]

Section 4 applies to both oral statements and statements in writing.[185] Section 5 of the Criminal Procedure Act 1865 sets out additional provisions concerning proof of previous inconsistent statements in writing:

> "A witness may be cross-examined as to previous statements made by him in writing or reduced into writing relative to the subject-matter of the indictment or proceeding, without such writing being shown to him; but if it is intended to contradict such witness by the writing, his attention must, before such contradictory proof can be given, be called to those parts of the writing which are to be used for the purpose of so contradicting him; provided always, that it shall be competent for the judge, at any time during the trial, to require the production of the writing for his inspection, and he may thereupon make such use of it for the purposes of the trial as he may think fit."

Section 5 did not affect the use that could be made of previous inconsistent statements at common law, despite the proviso that the judge can make such use of the statement for the purposes of the trial as he thinks fit. It was held that this did not enable him to direct the jury that they could choose between the previous

---

[182] *Gibbons* [2008] EWCA Crim 1574.
[183] *Coates* [2007] EWCA Crim 1471; [2008] 1 Cr.App.R. 3.
[184] See *Billingham* [2009] EWCA Crim 19; [2009] 2 Cr.App.R. 20, where the Court of Appeal suggested that the JSB direction on s.119 should be amended to clarify this point.
[185] *R. v Derby Magistrates' Court Ex p. B* [1996] 1 A.C. 487 HL.

statement and the witness's testimony.[186] However, as noted above, this limitation has now been removed. In both civil and criminal cases a previous statement admitted under s.5 of the 1865 Act is evidence of any matter stated of which the witness could have given direct oral evidence.

(C) Bad character and previous convictions

A cross-examiner might want to question a witness about discreditable aspects of the witness's character, with a view to persuading the factfinder that the witness should not be believed on oath. The cross-examiner might, for example, want to ask the witness whether he lied in the past to get a job, or was an alcoholic, or had a conviction for handling stolen goods. Any of these matters might found an argument that the witness should not be trusted. Before the Criminal Justice Act 2003 questions about discreditable matters were permitted if they fell within the principles set out in the leading authorities of *Hobbs v Tinling*[187] and *Sweet-Escott*,[188] discussed above. Because these matters were usually collateral the witness's answers had to be accepted as final under the general rule. However, the common law allowed the cross-examiner to adduce evidence to rebut a denial of the imputation made by the question to show bias on the part of the witness, or to demonstrate the witness's bad reputation for veracity. Section 6 of the Criminal Procedure Act 1865, which applied to civil as well as criminal proceedings, allowed for proof of the witness's previous convictions. The section used to be phrased in terms that permitted cross-examination on any previous conviction, although its width was restricted somewhat in both civil and criminal cases, as noted below.

14–033

Both the common law on cross-examination of witnesses as to their bad character, and the original wording of s.6 of the Criminal Procedure Act 1865, have been superseded. The Criminal Justice Act 2003 comprehensively recast the law on evidence of bad character and previous convictions. Chapter 1 of Pt 11 of the Act sets out a new scheme of admissibility for evidence of bad character in relation to both defendants and non-defendants in criminal proceedings. This book deals later with the bad character of defendants, since the relevant law is extensive and complex, and needs separate treatment in the context of a discussion of the relevance of character evidence to guilt. Accordingly, most of the discussion of the scheme in the Criminal Justice Act 2003 is in Ch.19. This section will focus on the new law relating to non-defendants, a category that includes all witnesses who are not defendants in the proceedings, as well as others such as victims and police officers not called as witnesses.

Broadly speaking the object of the Act's scheme is to "rebalance" criminal justice in this area. Evidence of the bad character of defendants is intended to be more freely admissible, whereas the admission of evidence of the bad character

---

[186] *Birch* (1924) 18 Cr.App.R. 26 CCA. The proviso does, however, enable the judge to edit the statement, so that in an appropriate case a jury should see only the part of the statement concerning the point on which the witness has been cross-examined: *Beattie* (1989) 89 Cr.App.R. 302 CA.

[187] *Hobbs v Tinling* [1929] 2 K.B. 1.

[188] *Sweet-Escott* (1971) 55 Cr.App.R. 316.

of non-defendants is intended to be more restrictively controlled. In *Somana-than*,[189] the Court of Appeal noted that there is a higher test for the introduction of a non-defendant's bad character under s.100 of the Act than the test for the introduction of a defendant's bad character under s.101. The provisions of the Act relating to non-defendants are largely based on the proposals of the Law Commission.[190] The Commission took the view that the common law gave inadequate protection to witnesses from irrelevant and unfair cross-examination on their character, and that there was a need for courts "to control gratuitous and offensive cross-examination of little or no purpose other than to intimidate or embarrass the witness or muddy the waters".[191] The Commission argued that tightening the law would reduce the power of evidence of bad character to distort the factfinding process and would encourage witnesses to give evidence. The legislation reflects these aims in three main ways: by specifying more precisely the circumstances in which evidence of a witness's bad character is admissible; by requiring the leave of the court for its admission; and by providing for a test of enhanced relevance to be satisfied.[192]

14–034 Section 99(1) abolished the common law rules governing the admissibility of evidence of bad character in criminal proceedings. This provision did not refer expressly to the putting of questions to witnesses in cross-examination on their bad character, but it seems clear that the common law rules relating to such questions were intended to be included in the abolition.[193] Several reasons support this view. Such questions are not "evidence" in themselves, but they are put with a view to eliciting from the witness evidence of bad character. It can therefore be said that the common law rules used to govern the admissibility of such evidence; if the question was not permitted by the rules the evidence could not be elicited. Secondly, if the witness denied the imputation, it was the common law that determined whether evidence of bad character could then be adduced under one of the exceptions to the finality rule for answers to collateral questions. Thirdly, the Criminal Justice Act 2003 repealed the provision in s.1(3) of the Criminal Evidence Act 1898 relating to cross-examination of the defendant on his bad character. It would make no sense for a new comprehensive statutory scheme to replace that part of the old law while leaving intact the common law on cross-examination of non-defendants on bad character.

It was argued after the passing of the Act that the abolition of the common law *rules* governing the admissibility of evidence of bad character did not extend to abolition of the *discretion* at common law to exclude evidence where its

---

[189] One of a number of appeals reported as *Weir* [2005] EWCA Crim 2866; [2006] 2 All E.R. 570 at [36].

[190] *Evidence of Bad Character in Criminal Proceedings*, Law Com. No.273 (2001), Pt IX.

[191] *Evidence of Bad Character in Criminal Proceedings* (2001), Pt IX para.9.35(3). In *Brewster and Cromwell* [2010] EWCA Crim 1194; [2010] 2 Cr.App.R. 20 at [21] the Court of Appeal agreed with the view of Professor J. R. Spencer, *Evidence of Bad Character,* 2nd edn (Oxford: Hart Publishing, 2009) that the purpose of s.100 was to remove from the criminal trial the right to introduce by cross-examination old or irrelevant or trivial behaviour in an attempt unfairly to diminish in the eyes of the tribunal of fact the standing of the witness, or to permit unsubstantiated attacks on credit.

[192] *Evidence of Bad Character in Criminal Proceedings* (2001), Pt IX paras 9.41 and 9.42.

[193] This was clearly the intention of the Law Commission in Pt IX of *Evidence of Bad Character in Criminal Proceedings* (2001).

prejudicial effect exceeds its probative value.[194] The position in relation to discretion to exclude evidence of the bad character of defendants is considered in chapter 19. As regards evidence of the bad character of non-defendants, it has been stated expressly that there is no residual discretion to refuse to admit the evidence if the admissibility conditions of s. 100 are satisfied,[195] although case management powers may be used to regulate the manner of presentation of the evidence to the jury and to restrict cross-examination to relevant matters.[196]

The concept of "bad character" is defined in s.98, which must be read together with s.112(1). According to s.98 references to evidence of a person's bad character are to evidence of, or of a disposition towards, misconduct on his part. Section 112(1) defines "misconduct" to mean the commission of an offence or other reprehensible behaviour. The interpretation of "reprehensible behaviour" is considered more fully in Ch.19; for present purposes it is sufficient to say that it is conduct that may not amount to the commission of an offence, but that carries with it some element of culpability or blameworthiness.[197] Section 98 excludes from its definition of bad character evidence that:

(a)   has to do with the alleged facts of the offence with which the defendant is charged; or
(b)   is evidence of misconduct in connection with the investigation or prosecution of that offence.

The operation of these exclusions is illustrated by the following examples. D is **14–035** charged with assaulting P. D wishes to cross-examine P to show that P hit him first and that D hit P in self-defence. This is evidence of misconduct by P (the commission of an assault by P on D), but it is evidence "to do with" the alleged facts of the offence with which D is charged. The questions are not therefore questions about "bad character" as defined in s.98; they are not therefore subject to the conditions of admissibility set out in s.100. They are relevant to D's defence and can be asked without the necessity to obtain the leave of the court. Alternatively, suppose that D denies hitting P, but a police officer testifies that D confessed to doing so when arrested. D wishes to cross-examine the officer to show that the officer has fabricated the alleged confession. This is evidence of misconduct by the officer (a probable offence of attempting to pervert the course of justice, and certainly reprehensible behaviour), but it is evidence of misconduct in connection with the investigation of the offence. Again, the questions are not about "bad character" as defined in s.98, and so again they are not subject to s.100. They are relevant and can be asked without leave. These results are in accordance with the recommendations of the Law Commission. Under their scheme questions and evidence about the "central set of facts" of the offence should be admissible without restriction, even if they disclose bad character in the sense of misconduct or other reprehensible behaviour. This is

[194] C. Tapper, "The Criminal Justice Act 2003: Evidence of Bad Character" [2004] Crim. L.R. 533, 540.
[195] *Braithwaite* [2010] EWCA Crim 1082; [2010] 2 Cr.App.R. 18.
[196] *Brewster and Cromwell* [2010] EWCA Crim 1194; [2010] 2 Cr.App.R. 20 at [24].
[197] See *Renda* [2005] EWCA Crim 2826; [2006] 2 All E.R. 553 at [24]. See also *Manister*, one of a number of appeals reported as *Weir* [2005] EWCA Crim 2866; [2006] 2 All E.R. 570 at [94] and [97].

coherent and sensible. Such questions and evidence will usually be more directly relevant to the issues in the case than to the witness's credibility in general.

Where questions and evidence relating to non-defendants are about "bad character", as defined in s.98, their admissibility is determined by the provisions of s.100 of the Criminal Justice Act 2003. Like s.99, s.100 does not refer in terms to questions in cross-examination, but only to the admissibility of evidence. Nevertheless, for the reasons given above, the intention is plainly to cover the putting of questions with a view to eliciting evidence of bad character. [198] Section 100(1) provides:

> " In criminal proceedings evidence of the bad character of a person other than the defendant is admissible if and only if—
>
> (a) it is important explanatory evidence,
> (b) it has substantial probative value in relation to a matter which—
> (i) is a matter in issue in the proceedings, and
> (ii) is of substantial importance in the context of the case as a whole, or
> (c) all parties to the proceedings agree to the evidence being admissible."

There are therefore three categories of case where cross-examination of non-defendants on their bad character can take place. Under s.100(4) leave of the court is required for the giving of such evidence under the first two categories in subs.(1)(a) and (b), but where all parties to the proceedings agree to the evidence being admissible leave is not required.

(1) Subsection (1)(a): important explanatory evidence

14–036   Subsection (2) of s.100 provides that evidence is important explanatory evidence if, without it, the court or jury would find it impossible or difficult properly to understand other evidence in the case, and its value for understanding the case as a whole is substantial. Such evidence is therefore "explanatory" in the sense of explaining other evidence in the case. The principle that evidence of the bad character of a non-defendant should have enhanced relevance to be admissible is given effect in the requirement that, as explanatory evidence, it should have "substantial" value for understanding the case as a whole. At this point we should recall the common law on "background" evidence. Chapter 1 explained that evidence is admissible at common law if it is part of a relevant background history to the offence charged, and without it the account of the offence put before the jury would be incomplete or incomprehensible. Section 100 replaces that principle in so far as it covers evidence of bad character. It extends the principle by stipulating that the other evidence need only be "difficult" to understand, but restricts it by the requirement that the evidence of bad character should have substantial value.

The Law Commission's example of a case covered by this provision is one of intra-familial abuse. It may not only be abusive behaviour by the defendant on other occasions that is valuable in explaining the case as a whole, but also

---

[198] In *Brewster and Cromwell* [2010] EWCA Crim 1194; [2010] 2 Cr.App.R. 20 the Court of Appeal noted with apparent assent the "common ground" between the appellants and the Crown that while s.100 is expressed in terms of the admissibility of evidence, it governs also cross-examination upon the bad character alleged.

abusive behaviour by other members of the family.[199] Evidence of the latter behaviour may be essential in helping the jury understand why, for example, the complainant did not complain to other family members about the abuse she was suffering from the defendant. In *Miller*,[200] the Court of Appeal agreed with a submission that if bad character evidence could expose a witness's motive for giving false evidence it could constitute important explanatory evidence. This illustrates the extension that the statutory test has made to the common law. The witness in question was a friend of the defendant who testified that drugs and money found at D's flat belonged to him and not to D. This evidence was certainly not 'incomprehensible' in the absence of any evidence about the witness's character. But the court seems to have assumed that the jury would find it difficult to understand why, as the prosecution claimed, the witness would falsely take responsibility for the drugs and money unless they knew that he was in fact guilty of two serious offences with which he had been charged and was facing a lengthy term of imprisonment.[201]

(2) Subsection (1)(b): evidence having substantial probative value in relation to a matter in issue

An issue in the proceedings obviously includes all the facts in issue in the case, and it can also include the credibility of a witness.[202] Accordingly, if the credibility of a witness is of substantial importance in the context of the case as a whole, and the evidence of the witness's bad character has substantial probative value in relation to his credibility, the evidence is admissible with leave. Subsection (3) directs the court, when it is assessing the probative value of evidence for the purposes of subs.(1)(b), to have regard to a number of specified factors (and to any others that it considers relevant). The specified factors include the nature and number of the events, or other things, to which the evidence relates; when those events or things are alleged to have happened or existed; the nature and extent of the similarities and dissimilarities where similarity between alleged instances of misconduct is relied on for the probative value of evidence of misconduct; and the extent to which evidence of misconduct tends to show that the same person was responsible for that misconduct and the misconduct charged, where identity is in issue.

14–037

The operation of this provision is illustrated by *Osbourne*.[203] D was charged with robbery of a publican (V). His defence was that V had fabricated the complaint to cover up his own misconduct as the licensee of the pub in question. The trial judge gave leave under s.100 for defence counsel to adduce evidence of V's mismanagement of the pub, resulting till shortages, and regular free after-hours drinking for staff and late customers. He refused leave for evidence of V's drug-taking during these sessions. The Court of Appeal agreed that the latter evidence lacked substantial probative value in relation to the issue of whether V

---

[199] Law Com. No.237 para.9.43.
[200] *Miller* [2010] EWCA Crim 1153; [2010] 2 Cr.App.R. 19.
[201] See also *McCluskey* [2010] EWCA Crim 1197.
[202] *Yaxley-Lennon*, one of a number of appeals reported as *Weir* [2005] EWCA Crim 2866 at [73].
[203] One of a number of appeals reported as *Renda* [2005] EWCA Crim 2826; [2006] 2 All E.R. 553.

had fabricated the complaint of robbery. The court also upheld the judge's decision to permit the cross-examination of a defence witness on his recent conviction for an offence of serious violence. This was thought to have substantial probative value on the issue of the witness's credibility in testifying in support of the defence that V had fabricated the complaint. On the other hand, in *Yaxley-Lennon*,[204] the Court of Appeal held that the trial judge had erred in permitting a defence witness to be cross-examined about a caution for possession of cocaine. This was thought to have little or no probative value on the issue of her credibility in testifying in support of her boyfriend's version of an incident with the victim of an alleged assault by the boyfriend in the street. There is no inconsistency of principle in these decisions. The difference in result is explicable by reference to the different factual matrix in the two cases, the nature of the previous misconduct of the witness, its relevance to the particular issue of credibility in the case, and the judgment of the degree of probative value, if any, that the evidence has.[205]

In *Brewster and Cromwell*,[206] the Court of Appeal suggested that it is helpful to distinguish between two forms of probative value of evidence bearing on credibility. Convictions might have a direct bearing on credibility because they might provide a reason for doubting the particular evidence given by the witness. So if the main issue in the case is whether it was D or V who was the aggressor in a fight, and V has testified that D hit him first, evidence that V has convictions for violence is plainly of substantial probative value. The evidence of V's propensity is directly relevant to whether he is telling the truth that he was the victim and not the aggressor.[207]

On the other hand, convictions may bear on credibility more indirectly by suggesting that the witness is not the kind of person whose word can be taken on trust. This is a more general claim than a claim that the witness has a specific relevant propensity, and potentially opens up a wide scope for admission of the witness's convictions. The test of admissibility under s.100 is therefore crucial. In *Brewster and Cromwell*,[208] the Court of Appeal rejected a narrow approach which would permit only convictions showing a propensity of the witness to be untruthful by making false statements or giving false evidence.[209] This was

---

[204] One of a number of appeals reported as *Weir* [2005] EWCA Crim 2866; [2006] 2 All E.R. 570.

[205] Mere allegations of the commission of offences, which have not been proved, are very unlikely to have substantial probative value: *Braithwaite* [2010] EWCA Crim 1082; [2010] 2 Cr.App.R. 18 (commenting on Crime Report Information System ("CRIS") reports in which no conviction, caution or penalty notice had ensued). See also *Miller* [2010] EWCA Crim 1153; [2010] 2 Cr.App.R. 19 (unproved charges of offences).

[206] *Brewster and Cromwell* [2010] EWCA Crim 1194; [2010] 2 Cr.App.R. 20.

[207] See, e.g. *Razaq and Razaq,* one of a number of appeals reported as *Renda* [2005] EWCA Crim 2826; [2006] 2 All E.R. 553. See also *R. v S (Andrew)* [2006] EWCA Crim 1303; [2006] 2 Cr.App.R. 31, where the Court of Appeal held that D should have been permitted to adduce evidence of V's convictions for theft, handling stolen goods and burglary since they showed that V, a prostitute, had a propensity to act dishonestly, and this supported his defence to a charge of indecent assault on V that she had demanded more money for sex than they had agreed and tried to snatch a gold chain from him.

[208] *Brewster and Cromwell* [2010] EWCA Crim 1194; [2010] 2 Cr.App.R. 20.

[209] See *Hanson* [2005] EWCA Crim 824;[2005] 2 Cr.App.R. 21, where the Court of Appeal adopted this test for the purposes of s. 101(1)(d) of the Criminal Justice Act 2003. See further Ch.19.

thought to be unduly restrictive of the right of a person to defend himself against a criminal charge.[210] Instead the court expressed the test in terms of whether:

> "the evidence of previous convictions, or bad behaviour, is sufficiently persuasive to be worthy of consideration by a fair-minded tribunal upon the issue of the witness's creditworthiness."

Applying this test, the court quashed convictions for kidnapping and theft where the trial judge had ruled that evidence of the alleged victim's (V) convictions for burglary, theft and manslaughter were not of substantial probative value and had refused leave for her to be cross-examined on them. The case involved radically different accounts of a meeting between V and the defendants; it was their case that V had fabricated her account and that her convictions as a whole went to give a more complete picture of her standing as a witness. The court agreed,[211] while also saying that the persuasive value of convictions on the issue of creditworthiness will depend principally on the nature, number and age of the convictions, and that not all convictions will necessarily qualify.[212] In *Braithwaite*,[213] Hughes L.J. commented that the probative value of the bad character evidence falls to be assessed in the context of the case as a whole, and that means that it may in some cases be appropriate to consider whether or not it adds significantly to other more probative evidence directed to the same issue.

We should now note the amended provision in s.6 of the Criminal Procedure Act 1865:

> "If, upon a witness being lawfully questioned as to whether he has been convicted of any felony or misdemeanour, he either denies or does not admit the fact, or refuses to answer, it shall be lawful for the cross-examining party to prove such conviction."

The question then is when a witness may "lawfully" be questioned about a previous conviction. Section 6 applies to both civil and criminal proceedings. As originally worded, s.6 permitted cross-examination as to any previous conviction, even if it was not one concerned with an offence against the administration of justice or dishonesty.[214] However, even before the Rehabilitation of Offenders Act 1974 a judge could take the view that a particular conviction was so stale and/or trivial that it was not sufficiently relevant to the question of credibility. The judge might therefore disallow cross-examination on it, or discourage counsel from pursuing the point.[215] Section 4(1) of the Rehabilitation of

---

[210] See the remarks of Hughes L.J. in *Stephenson* [2006] EWCA Crim 2325 at [27], and the cases on s.101(1)(e) of the Criminal Justice Act 2003, discussed in Ch.19.

[211] *Brewster and Cromwell* [2010] EWCA Crim 1194; [2010] 2 Cr.App.R. 20 at [24], where the court notes also that V's conviction for manslaughter was directly relevant to her credibility because the circumstances of the conviction showed a propensity to conduct resembling that alleged by the defendants.

[212] As in *Ul-Haq* [2010] EWCA Crim 1683, where a witness's convictions, principally for dishonesty, were said to be of considerable antiquity and to concern events which had no similarity to the present case.

[213] *Braithwaite* [2010] EWCA Crim 1082; [2010] 2 Cr.App.R. 18.

[214] See *Clifford v Clifford* [1961] 1 W.L.R. 1274.

[215] *Sweet-Escott* (1971) 55 Cr.App.R. 316 CA; *Thomas v Commissioner of Police* [1997] 1 All E.R. 747 CA.

Offenders Act 1974 provides that evidence of "spent"[216] convictions is inadmissible in civil legal proceedings. This is subject to s.7(3), which permits such evidence to be given if the interests of justice require it to be admitted. The Court of Appeal considered s.7(3) in *Thomas v Commissioner of Police*,[217] holding that it requires the judge to weigh the degree of relevance of the spent conviction to the issues, including the issue of the witness's credibility, against the amount of prejudice that it might cause the factfinder to have against the witness. An unfair degree of prejudice might result in an unfair trial for the party calling the witness. These are not the only considerations relating to the "interests of justice", but they are ones the judge should take into account in every case, because:

> "some prejudice is inevitable [i.e. from proof of the fact of a previous conviction] except in cases of total and obvious irrelevance where... the evidence should be excluded in any event."[218]

A judge also has the general exclusionary discretion under r.32 of the Civil Procedure Rules as a means of regulating the scope of cross-examination.

Section 4 of the Rehabilitation of Offenders Act 1974 does not apply to criminal proceedings, so that spent convictions remain technically admissible. However, questions to witnesses about any previous convictions are now of course subject to the conditions of admissibility in s.100 of the Criminal Justice Act 2003. If the convictions are spent it is unlikely that they will satisfy the requirement of enhanced relevance embodied in the statutory conditions. Moreover, a Practice Direction issued before the 2003 Act requires a cross-examiner to obtain the leave of the court before questioning a witness in a criminal case about a spent conviction.[219] It would seem that in exercising discretion to disallow the questions, the court should as far as possible regard the interests of the accused as paramount.[220]

14–038 Finally, in relation to this exception to the finality rule, police officers could be cross-examined at common law on findings of guilt against them on disciplinary charges.[221] If such findings were denied evidence was admissible in rebuttal to prove them. In *Guney,* Judge L.J., giving the judgment of the Court of Appeal, said: "If and when discreditable behaviour has resulted in findings of professional misconduct we see no justification for limiting the principle to police officers".[222] In criminal proceedings the admissibility of such evidence is now determined by s.100 of the Criminal Justice Act 2003. Such findings of guilt are likely to have substantial probative value on the issue of the officers' credibility, certainly where the findings relate to evidential matters. It seems likely therefore that the application of s.100 will produce similar results to the common law principle.

---

[216] The Act contains detailed provisions on when a conviction may become "spent", which are not considered in this book.

[217] *Thomas v Commissioner of Police* [1997] 1 All E.R. 747.

[218] *Thomas v Commissioner of Police* [1997] 1 All E.R. 747 at 765.

[219] Practice Note [1975] 2 All E.R. 1072.

[220] *Nye* (1982) 75 Cr.App.R. 247 CA; *O'Shea* [1993] Crim. L.R. 951 CA.

[221] *Edwards* [1991] 2 All E.R. 266 CA.

[222] *Guney* [1998] 2 Cr.App.R. 242 at 259–260.

However, it should be noted that the common law principle was restricted to cases where allegations of professional misconduct had been proved. Judge L.J. went on in *Guney* to say that cross-examination of police officers on the basis of unresolved criminal charges or complaints to the Police Complaints Authority was not permitted; mere allegations did not provide a secure foundation for cross-examination. The same reasoning would apply a fortiori if the complaint had been heard and dismissed or if the witness had been acquitted of the criminal charge.

(D)   Bias

At common law a cross-examiner may ask questions designed to show that the witness is biased in favour of the party calling the witness, since the existence of bias may seriously affect the weight that can safely be given to the witness's testimony. In many cases, of course, an admitted relationship between the witness and the party (spouse, parent, brother, etc) will itself suggest the possibility of bias, and there is no need for any special rule about cross-examination designed to bring this out. In other cases a witness's denial of a relationship, or of other facts indicating bias, need not be taken as final. The cross-examiner may call evidence in rebuttal to show, for example, that a witness for the plaintiff was the plaintiff's mistress,[223] or that witnesses had been coached in their evidence.[224]

14–039

In criminal proceedings, where evidence showing bias is not evidence of the witness's bad character within the meaning of s.98 of the Criminal Justice Act 2003, the common law rule continues to apply. This rule will cover a good many cases, since it may be quite possible to show a witness's bias or partiality towards a party in ways that do not amount to showing misconduct or other reprehensible behaviour by the witness. Proof that a witness has been instructed on how to give their evidence is an example. Where the evidence of bias is evidence of bad character, the common law rule is abolished by s.99 of the 2003 Act, and the admissibility of the evidence is governed by s.100 of the Act. As noted above, the credibility of a witness can be an issue in the proceedings. Under s.100(1)(b) evidence of the bad character of a witness can be admitted if it has substantial probative value to a matter in issue and is of substantial importance in the context of the case as a whole. Since bias is likely to affect the credibility of the witness substantially, it seems that evidence of bad character that demonstrates that the witness is biased is likely to pass the statutory test. It is submitted therefore that the results in the cases applying the common law rule are likely to be the same under the rule in s.100. If so, the development of the common law is worth consideration as a guide to the operation of the statutory rule.

It seems that the bias exception at common law to the finality rule extended to proof of any impropriety on the part of the witness in relation to evidence in the case given by the witness himself or by other witnesses, if this could seriously

---

[223] *Thomas v David* (1836) 7 C. & P. 350.
[224] *Phillips* (1936) 26 Cr.App.R. 17 CCA. This was a case of incest where the alleged child victims denied in court that they had been schooled by their mother. The court held that the denials could be rebutted by proof of their earlier admissions to third parties that they had been coached.

reflect on the witness's credibility. In *Mendy*,[225] the defendant was charged with assault. During her trial the defendant's husband was seen talking to a man who had been sitting in the public gallery taking notes when a police officer was giving evidence about the assault. The inference was that this discussion was aimed at priming the husband for evidence he would give showing that he, and not his wife, had committed the assault. The husband denied the incident with the man, and a question arose whether evidence could be adduced to rebut the denial. The Court of Appeal held that the prosecution could call witnesses to the incident; the jury were entitled to be apprised of the fact that the husband was prepared to cheat[226] in order to deceive the jury and help his wife. An element of bias might have been presumed in any event from their relationship, but the rebutting evidence here clearly showed the full extent of the husband's partiality.

14–040 The bias exception has also been suggested as the best explanation of the problematic case of *Busby*.[227] Police witnesses for the prosecution gave evidence of oral admissions by the defendant to burglary. In cross-examination it was suggested to the officers that they had fabricated the admissions, and also that they had threatened a potential witness for the defendant to prevent him testifying. The trial judge refused to let the defence question the witness who had been threatened so as to obtain from him evidence rebutting the officers' denials of threats. The Court of Appeal quashed the defendant's conviction, holding that the rebuttal evidence went to an issue in the case because it showed that the officers concerned were prepared to go to improper lengths to secure D's conviction. The case is problematic in the sense that, if it cannot be explained as an example of the bias rule, it looks on its face to be inconsistent with the old authority of *Harris v Tippett*.[228] This is generally taken to have established the principle that other discreditable acts of the witness are collateral issues and are therefore subject to the finality rule.

However, there remains a possibility that *Busby* did create a new broad exception to the finality rule for evidence that tends to show that the police were prepared to go to improper lengths to secure a conviction.[229] The point arose in two sets of cases concerned with alleged repeated malpractice by police officers, one set involving officers of the former West Midlands Serious Crimes Squad, the

---

[225] *Mendy* (1976) 64 Cr.App.R. 4 CA.

[226] By getting round the rule that prospective witnesses must stay out of court until their time comes to give evidence; a rule which is necessary to prevent trimming of evidence.

[227] *Busby* (1982) 74 Cr.App.R. 79 CA. The case was explained on this basis by the Court of Appeal in *Edwards* [1991] 2 All E.R. 266.

[228] *Harris v Tippett* (1811) 2 Camp. 637. See further R. Pattenden, "Evidence of Previous Malpractice by Police Witnesses and *R. v Edwards*" [1992] Crim. L.R. 549.

[229] The possibility was first suggested in these terms by Henry J., giving the judgment of the Court of Appeal in *Funderburk* [1990] 2 All E.R. 482 at 486. See also the earlier case of *Marsh* (1986) 83 Cr.App.R. 165 CA where Mustill L.J. referred to the excluded evidence in *Busby* as "material to the quality of the testimony adduced in relation to the central issue; on the one side to the alleged admissions and on the other to the reliability of the officers who had sought to establish them". This might be taken as meaning that evidence of other police misconduct is admissible in rebuttal of police denials, where the main issue is the respective credibility of the police officers and the accused in relation to an alleged confession or, say, possession of articles that the accused maintains were planted on him.

other set involving officers of the Stoke Newington Drugs Squad. In *Edwards*,[230] one of the West Midlands cases, the Court of Appeal rejected the wider view of *Busby*, and impliedly restricted the exceptions to the finality rule to the well-established ones such as bias. Thus, as noted above, the court said that evidence would not be admissible to rebut a police officer's answers in cross-examination as to credit on evidence given by the officer in other cases. The Court of Appeal took a similar line in *Clancy*,[231] another of the West Midlands cases, emphasising that courts should not permit the defence to call evidence tending to show a systematic course of conduct by police officers belonging to a particular unit to circumvent the constraints imposed by PACE and the Codes of Practice. This is understandable as far as *other* officers are concerned. There is a clear danger then of guilt by association, which is unfair in principle to the officer who is being cross-examined on the misconduct of the others.[232] However, if the officers concerned are those whose credibility is in issue vis-à-vis the accused, evidence of their similar misconduct in other cases—if it can be proved—does seem sufficiently relevant to justify admission.[233] In *Maxine Edwards*,[234] one of the Stoke Newington cases, the Court of Appeal quashed the defendant's conviction for possession of crack cocaine with intent to supply, on the ground that one of the two officers who gave evidence against the defendant had been involved in other cases that had resulted in acquittals after allegations that police evidence had been fabricated, or in which prosecutions had been dropped, or in which the Crown had not contested appeals. According to Beldam L.J.:

> "Once the suspicion of perjury starts to infect the evidence and permeate cases in which the witnesses have been involved, and which are closely similar, the evidence on which such convictions are based becomes as questionable as it was in the cases in which the appeals have already been allowed.
>
> It is impossible to be confident that had the jury which convicted this appellant known the facts and circumstances in the other cases in which Constable Carroll had been involved, that they would have been bound to convict this appellant. In our view, that is the appropriate test."[235]

Unfortunately this statement of what many would say is a desirable principle is weakened by the fact that no cases are referred to in the judgment. In fact none of the relevant authorities appears even to have been cited to the Court of Appeal. Given that the principle, as stated, envisages the defence leading evidence of other cases in which the relevant officer was involved, it is inconsistent with

---

[230] *Edwards* [1991] 2 All E.R. 266.

[231] *Clancy* [1997] Crim. L.R. 290.

[232] *Guney* [1998] 2 Cr.App.R. 242 at 260 CA. It would be very doubtful in any event whether such evidence would be sufficiently relevant to justify its admission, given the time involved in investigating other cases and the remoteness of those cases from the issues in the instant trial.

[233] If the prosecution can use sufficiently relevant "similar fact" evidence to incriminate the accused as to the offence charged, it is hard to see why the defence should not use sufficiently relevant evidence of similar misconduct by prosecution witnesses to discredit their testimony implicating the accused. Or is this another example of relevance being construed more strictly against the accused than the prosecution? cf. *Blastland* [1986] A.C. 41 HL.

[234] *Maxine Edwards* [1996] 2 Cr.App.R. 345 CA.

[235] *Maxine Edwards* [1996] 2 Cr.App.R. 345 at 350.

Edwards, and it may be that the decision is simply per incuriam. In *Guney*,[236] the Court of Appeal noted the possible conflict of authority, and went on to say that the court regarded itself as bound by *Edwards*, explaining *Maxine Edwards* as a case effectively decided on the Court of Appeal's doubts about the safety of a particular conviction based on the evidence of a particular witness. On this basis *Maxine Edwards* would not be an authority for any proposition of law regarding cross-examination as to credit.

14–041 However, it seems that in practice *Maxine Edwards* is being followed. Dein has argued[237] that in later cases involving unresolved allegations of malpractice against police witnesses courts have expressly relied on the dicta of Beldam L.J. concerning the "suspicion of perjury" about the police evidence. Dein suggests that attempts to restrict the decision in *Maxine Edwards* to its particular facts have failed. The Court of Appeal has preferred a wider view to the effect that "the court ought seriously to consider quashing any conviction where a potentially tainted police officer(s) had made a significant contribution to the prosecution case".[238] In *Hutchings*,[239] the Court of Appeal accepted that, where the evidence of police officers from a particular squad is challenged, then , depending on the precise circumstances of the case, it may be relevant to their credibility to allow cross-examination on their awareness of admitted corrupt practices by other members of the squad.

(E)   Disability of the witness

14–042 A witness's credibility may be significantly affected by some disability from which the witness suffers. A physical disability, such as myopia, could obviously affect the weight of eyewitness identification evidence if the witness swears he made a careful observation of the accused at some distance without the aid of glasses. There is no doubt that evidence is admissible to rebut a witness's denial of some disability where that would colour the factfinder's view of his evidence. In *Toohey v Metropolitan Police Commissioner*,[240] the defendants were charged with assault with intent to rob. The victim of the assault was a young man whom the defendants said was drunk and whom they were trying to assist home when he became hysterical and accused them of attacking him. A doctor examined the victim shortly afterwards. A dispute arose at a retrial as to whether the doctor could testify that the victim was unusually prone to hysteria and that his hysteria would be exacerbated by alcohol. The House of Lords was in no doubt that such medical evidence was admissible, and Lord Pearce stated the rule as follows:

> "Medical evidence is admissible to show that a witness suffers from some disease or defect or abnormality of mind that affects the reliability of his evidence. Such evidence is not confined to a general opinion of the unreliability of the witness, but may give all the matters necessary

---

[236] *Guney* [1998] 2 Cr.App.R. 242 at 262 CA.

[237] J. Dein, "Police Misconduct Revisited" [2000] Crim. L.R. 801.

[238] Dein, "Police Misconduct Revisited" [2000] Crim. L.R. 801 at 811; cf. *Malik* [2000] Crim. L.R. 197.

[239] *Hutchings* [2011] EWCA Crim 2535.

[240] *Toohey v Metropolitan Police Commissioner* [1965] A.C. 595 HL.

to show not only the foundation of and the reasons for the diagnosis but also the extent to which the credibility of the witness is affected."[241]

The sense of this is clear, given that the witness is testifying about a matter that is outside the knowledge and experience of the factfinder. On the other hand, where the issue is simply whether a witness, not suffering from a disability, is telling the truth in court, expert opinion on that issue will not be permitted. This general proposition was stated by the Court of Appeal in *Mackenney*,[242] and is supported by statements in other cases against the admissibility of evidence of "oath-helping".[243] However, its scope clearly depends on how widely or narrowly the concept of a disability is interpreted. In recent years the courts have been taking a more expansive view of the cases in which expert psychiatric or psychological evidence on issues of credibility may be admissible. Thus in *Pinfold and Mackenney*,[244] the Court of Appeal, on a reference from the Criminal Cases Review Commission, revisited its earlier decision in *Mackenney* that the evidence of a psychologist about a key prosecution witness at the defendant's trial for murder was inadmissible. The psychologist had not examined the witness but had observed him giving evidence and had formed the view that the witness had a psychopathic personality. This meant that although he was capable of giving reliable evidence he might choose not to do so, and that his demeanour when testifying might not exhibit the normal signs of fabrication so as to enable the jury to detect when he was lying. The court held that the psychologist's opinion would now be admissible. The fact that he had not examined the witness would affect the weight of his opinion, not its admissibility.[245]

D. RE-EXAMINATION

The party calling a witness has a right to re-examine the witness after he or she has been cross-examined. However, the re-examination may not be used to rehearse again the evidence given in chief or to introduce new matters. Its purpose is to allow the party to deal with matters arising out of the cross-examination—for example, to get the witness to clarify or qualify the meaning of the answers given in cross-examination. New matters can be introduced at this stage only with the leave of the judge. In the leading case of *Prince v Samo*,[246] Lord Denman C.J. held that a witness who had given evidence in cross-examination about certain statements made by the plaintiff in other proceedings could be re-examined about the plaintiff's testimony only as far as it was connected with those statements; the witness could not be asked about other unconnected parts of the plaintiff's earlier evidence.

14–043

---

[241] *Toohey v Metropolitan Police Commissioner* [1965] A.C. 595 at 609.

[242] *Mackenney* (1981) 76 Cr.App.R. 271 CA.

[243] e.g. *Robinson* [1994] 3 All E.R. 346 CA. cf. *R. v E* [2011] EWCA Crim 1690.

[244] *Pinfold and Mackenney* [2003] EWCA Crim 3643; [2004] 2 Cr.App.R. 5.

[245] The Court of Appeal heard fresh evidence from a psychiatrist. He also had not examined the witness in question, but his opinion concurred with the psychologist who had attended the original trial. In the light of this the court quashed the conviction as unsafe. See further Ch.20.

[246] *Prince v Samo* (1838) 7 Ad. & El. 627.

In general the rules that apply to examination-in-chief apply also to re-examination. Thus a witness cannot be asked leading questions, or about his previous consistent statements, unless one of the exceptional cases applies. It may be, however, that the cross-examination itself has brought one of the exceptions into play, as where the cross-examination has suggested that the witness's testimony was a recent fabrication. In such a case, the witness's previous consistent statement can be proved on re-examination to rebut the suggestion.[247] In the hands of a skilful and well-prepared advocate, re-examination can do much to lessen the impact of a damaging cross-examination.

---

[247] See *Ali* [2003] EWCA Crim 3214; [2004] 1 Cr.App.R. 39.

CHAPTER 15

VULNERABLE AND SUSPECT WITNESSES

A. INTRODUCTION

15–001 This chapter deals with two different, but related, problems concerning witnesses. The first is the problem of how the law of evidence should respond to the vulnerable witness. It is widely accepted that certain witnesses are "vulnerable" in the sense that their experiences as victims of offences, or their particular personality characteristics, or their susceptibility to intimidation, may mean that they are liable to suffer more than the normal amount of stress associated with being a witness, and are unlikely to be able to give best evidence without the help of certain protective measures. The Youth Justice and Criminal Evidence Act 1999 ("YJCEA") overhauled this area of the law and considerably increased the scope of protection. The Act helps a greater range of witnesses, with a greater range of measures, and to a greater extent, than under the previous law.

The main problem for the law of evidence centres on the questioning of this type of witness.[1] Cross-examination in particular may prove intrusive and distressing. The most notorious example of this problem is the questioning by the defence of complainants of sex offences on their previous sexual history. This has been a source of acute controversy for many years, with virulent criticism directed at the perceived failure of the law to protect complainants adequately. The questioning of children who (may) have been the subject of abuse is another aspect of the topic that has aroused great professional and public concern. These issues present a pressing question of how far the general principles for examination of witnesses, discussed in the previous chapter, should be modified to take account of a witness's particular susceptibilities. There are powerful arguments for special techniques of protection. The proper enforcement of the criminal law partly depends on these types of witness. Their evidence may be crucial for the conviction of dangerous and violent offenders, and for ensuring the future safety of the witnesses themselves and other potential victims. Moreover, irrespective of the importance of their evidence, witnesses have rights under the ECHR to life (art.2), to freedom from torture and inhuman or degrading treatment (art. 3), to liberty (art.5) and to privacy (art.8). Certain forms of cross-examination could engage the right to privacy, and the intimidation of witnesses could engage any or all of these rights. In *Doorson v Netherlands*,[2] the European Court of Human Rights stated that these interests implied that criminal proceedings should be organised in such a way that the interests were not unjustifiably imperilled. "Against this background, principles of fair trial also require that in appropriate cases the interests of the defence are balanced against those of witnesses or victims called upon to testify."[3]

This statement highlights the inevitable conflicts that arise when special techniques of witness protection are adopted. Many of these measures have implications for the way an accused person conducts his defence, and raise the question how far restrictions on the nature and conduct of defences are compatible with the right to a fair trial under art.6. It is notable that only a year

---

[1] Other issues about the treatment of vulnerable witnesses, such as keeping them informed of the progress of the case and providing decent waiting facilities at court, are outside the scope of this book.

[2] *Doorson v Netherlands* (1996) 22 E.H.R.R. 330.

[3] *Doorson v Netherlands* (1996) 22 E.H.R.R. 330 at 70.

after the *Doorson* judgment the European Court of Human Rights stated that if prosecution witnesses were granted anonymity to protect their rights:

"the defence will be faced with difficulties which criminal proceedings should not normally involve. Accordingly ... art.6 ... requires that the handicaps under which the defence labours be sufficiently counterbalanced by the procedures followed by the judicial authorities."[4]

Subsequently the Human Rights Act 1998 has resulted in the English courts having to grapple with these problems of balancing rights of victims and defendants under the Convention.[5]

The second problem covered in this chapter is how the law of evidence should respond to the suspect witness. Unlike "vulnerable witness", a term used in the YJCEA,[6] "suspect witness" is not a term of art. It is used here to refer to a witness whose evidence is alleged to be perjured, or unreliable, for one or more of a variety of reasons. Historically the common law included in its categories of suspect witnesses children, and complainants of sexual offences, regarding their evidence as potentially unreliable for reasons at least partly associated with their vulnerability. The law has changed significantly in recent years for both types of witness, but the general question remains of how to evaluate the evidence of a witness perceived as suspect for whatever reason. As we have seen, debate still continues about confession evidence and eyewitness identification evidence, and more will be said about these subjects later.

15–002

The issue of suspect evidence, and safeguards against it, has taken on renewed currency with the development in recent years of the theory of "recovered memory". According to this theory, certain adults, who may be suffering from psychiatric symptoms such as depression or low self-esteem, can be encouraged by therapists and counsellors to "recover" long-repressed memories of the childhood sexual abuse that is thought to account for the patients' current problems.[7] If a prosecution ensues against the alleged abuser, typically a parent who vehemently denies the charge, a critical issue arises about what safeguards, if any, are required to prevent incorrect evaluation of the witness's testimony and a potential miscarriage of justice. Various techniques of protection are available for dealing with suspect evidence. A decision whether to use any of these inevitably raises again the question of adjusting the competing interests of witnesses and defendants. Ultimately, however, it has to be remembered that it is the accused who has most to lose from the criminal process, and in situations of real doubt about the appropriate rules, the interests of avoiding wrongful convictions should be the primary concern.

---

[4] *Van Mechelen v Netherlands* (1997) 25 E.H.R.R. 647 at 54.
[5] Most notably in *R. v A (No.2)* [2001] UKHL 25; [2001] 2 Cr.App.R. 21 HL, see below.
[6] It appears in the heading to Ch.1 of Pt II.
[7] There is an extensive literature about this theory, which has polarised professional psychiatric opinion, particularly in the US. For measured reviews of the literature and the evidence see S. Brandon, J. Boakes, D. Glaser and R. Green, "Recovered memories of childhood sexual abuse" (1998) 172 *British Journal of Psychiatry* 296; P. Lewis, *Delayed Prosecution for Childhood Sexual Abuse* (Oxford: Oxford University Press, 2006), pp.10–17; C. R. Brewin, "Recovered Memory and False Memory" in A. Heaton-Armstrong (eds), *Witness Testimony—Psychological Investigative and Evidential Perspectives* (2006), p.89.

B.   VULNERABLE WITNESSES[8]

15–003   The YJCEA contains a large number of protective measures for vulnerable witnesses. We can group these under three headings. First, there are "special measures directions" that relate to how and when witnesses eligible for the assistance provided by these measures give their evidence. The scheme in ss.16–33, which establish these measures, is very detailed and extremely complex. Secondly, ss.34–40 impose restrictions on defendants cross-examining certain witnesses in person. These provisions include a power for the court to appoint a representative to conduct cross-examination on behalf of the accused where the accused is unrepresented and subject to a prohibition on cross-examining in person. Thirdly, s.41 (together with ancillary provisions in ss.42 and 43) deals with the vexed subject of sexual history evidence. It restricts very considerably the circumstances in which evidence and questions about a complainant's sexual behaviour on occasions other than the event in question will be admissible. It is convenient to discuss these measures in reverse order since the rules governing sexual history evidence are connected to the general principles governing cross-examination considered in Ch.14. They represent a specialised and modified application of those principles.

1.   *Complainants of sexual offences: the use of sexual history evidence*

(A)   Some general comments

15–004   We have seen in the previous chapter that witnesses can be asked in cross-examination about their conduct on other occasions where this is sufficiently relevant to their credibility in giving evidence on oath. In the case of complainants of rape there are acute difficulties as to how far this power should extend to cross-examination about a complainant's previous sexual history. When, if ever, is it relevant to ask about the complainant's sexual experience with men other than the accused, or about her[9] previous relationship, if any, with the accused? If she denies any such relationships, when, if ever, can the defendant adduce evidence to rebut her denials?

Before looking at the complex and controversial law on the point, it is worth making a number of introductory comments. Sex offences (rape, sexual assault, etc) raise more acute conflicts of credibility than any other type of crime. This is because, by their nature, these offences tend to take place in the absence of other witnesses. In some cases, of course, there may be scientific evidence, such as a DNA profile from traces of semen or blood, that can be used to establish the identity of a rapist, if that is in issue. In other cases, however, particularly where consent or the actual existence of a sexual assault is in issue, there may be little or

---

[8] See generally L. Ellison, *The Adversarial Process and the Vulnerable Witness* (Oxford: Oxford University Press, 2001).

[9] The offence of rape has extended to rape of males since 1994 (Criminal Justice and Public Order Act 1994 s.142). Since the great majority of cases concern female complainants, the female pronoun alone is used to avoid tedious repetition of "her or his", etc.

no independent evidence to confirm the testimony of the complainant. In such cases a jury may be faced with a straight choice as to who is telling the truth—it may literally be a case of the complainant's word against the defendant's.[10] Historically, however, this choice did not present itself as a decision on which of two witnesses was more credible. Before 1898 the jury could not hear from the defendant directly. He was incompetent to testify in his own defence.[11] The only way in which he could dispute the complainant's evidence as to what had happened between them was by cross-examining her on the details of the alleged offence and by challenging her credibility. This necessarily tended to switch the focus of the trial on to the complainant. Even after 1898 there was no compulsion on the defendant to testify in his own defence, and many accused may have felt, or been advised, that their best chance of acquittal lay in attacking the complainant's evidence and character,[12] rather than responding to the evidence in person. The standard of proof is an important factor in this calculation; an accused need only create a reasonable doubt about the credibility of the complainant, where the complainant's testimony is the only substantial evidence against him, in order to ask a conscientious jury to acquit him.

Much critical writing on the law of rape concerns this focus on the complainant, and more will be said about this later. However, it is worth emphasising at this stage that any evaluation of the law must take account of the distinctive procedural context of rape trials and the stark conflicts of credibility that they often entail.[13] This point bears particularly on two matters that have attracted a good deal of adverse comment. Research by Adler[14] and others[15] suggests that in practice much importance is attached by police, prosecutors and courts to the concept of the "ideal rape". McColgan[16] cites Adler's description of the concept:

> "[A] rape where the victim is sexually inexperienced and has a 'respectable' lifestyle, whose assailant is a stranger and whose company she had not willingly found herself in. She will have fought back, been physically hurt and, afterwards, promptly reported the offence."[17]

McColgan summarises the research findings by concluding that the further the complainant's experience strays from this "ideal" model, the less likely the police are to record a complaint as a "rape" and the less likely a jury is to convict the accused of rape.[18] One explanation for this, put forward by McColgan,[19] is that

15–005

---

[10] A typical example is *Hamadi* [2007] EWCA Crim 3048.

[11] See Ch.13.

[12] This is still a standard defence strategy: J. Temkin, "Prosecuting and Defending Rape: Perspectives From The Bar" (2000) 27 *Journal of Law and Society* 219, 231–236.

[13] These conflicts have not disappeared with the redefinition of rape in s.1 of the Sexual Offences Act 2003. They will continue as long as non-consensual sex remains the essence of the offence and sex continues to be an essentially private matter. Conflicts of credibility are inevitable.

[14] Z. Adler, *Rape on Trial* (London, 1987).

[15] G. Chambers and A. Millar, *Prosecuting Sexual Assault* (1983); L. Smith, *Concerns About Rape* (1989); C. Lloyd and R. Walmsley, *Changes in Rape Offences and Sentencing* (1989).

[16] A. McColgan, "Common Law and the Relevance of Sexual History Evidence" (1996) 16 O.J.L.S. 275, 278.

[17] Z. Adler, *Rape on Trial* (London, 1987), p.119.

[18] A. McColgan, "Common Law and the Relevance of Sexual History Evidence" (1996) 16 O.J.L.S. 275, 278–279, 287.

the "ideal rape" reflects a popular stereotype of the offence, based on a representation of sex as an activity in which a sexually aggressive male dominates an essentially passive woman.[20] A woman who is sexually active outside marriage fails to conform to the behaviour expected by the stereotype; she may as a result find that her complaint of non-consensual sex is more likely to be interpreted by police and juries as "sex" or "rough sex", rather than rape, particularly if she has known the accused socially beforehand. Whether or not this theory is accurate, a more prosaic explanation can also be offered. The "ideal rape" stereotype is significant because it modifies the credibility conflict. It provides two externally verifiable items of evidence, namely physical injury and prompt complaint, that are inconsistent with any representation of the complainant as someone who has invented an allegation of sexual assault, or who has redefined to herself a consensual sexual experience as rape. Accordingly, such evidence, additional to the complainant's testimony, may enable a jury to decide more confidently that the complainant is telling the truth. This is quite apart from any conclusions the jury might be tempted to draw from the facts that the complainant was a virgin and the accused a stranger.

Secondly, critics have attacked the "myth" that women lie about rape. To quote McColgan again[21]:

"There is no evidence that women lie about sexual assault any more than people generally lie about other offences. Nevertheless, mistrust about such allegations pervades the handling of rape complaints throughout the criminal justice system. Chambers and Millar's Scottish study, conducted in 1980–1, found '(a)n underlying assumption . . . held by many criminal justice agents . . . that women, in particular, those who are promiscuous, are prone to untruthfulness and are unreliable witnesses'."

The Law Commission found no empirical evidence to back up such claims,[22] and there seems little doubt that anecdotally based fears of unreliability have been greatly exaggerated.[23] At the same time it is important not to overstate the case the other way. False complaints of rape and other sexual misconduct do occasionally occur.[24] When they do occur they may be difficult to repel, precisely

---

[19] A. McColgan, "Common Law and the Relevance of Sexual History Evidence" (1996) 16 O.J.L.S. 275, 302–307.

[20] See N. Naffine, "Possession: Erotic Love in the Law of Rape" (1994) 57 M.L.R. 10.

[21] A. McColgan, "Common Law and the Relevance of Sexual History Evidence" (1996) 16 O.J.L.S. 275, 276 (footnotes omitted).

[22] *Corroboration of Evidence in Criminal Trials*, Law Com. No.115 (1990), para.4.31.

[23] The classic example of a sweeping unsupported generalisation about complainant unreliability is the remark of Salmon L.J. in *Henry and Manning* (1968) 53 Cr.App.R. 150 at 153 CA: "Human experience has shown that . . . girls and women [in these courts] do sometimes tell an entirely false story which is very easy to fabricate, but extremely difficult to refute. Such stories are fabricated for all sorts of reasons, which I need not now enumerate, and sometimes for no reason at all".

[24] A few examples can be given. Sandra Harris falsely identified a complete stranger as a man who had raped her, in order to hide from her lesbian lover that she had had consensual sex with a male friend in an attempt to have a child. She was convicted of perverting the course of justice: *The Times*, August 6, 1991. A married vicar accused by a woman parishioner of committing adultery with her in his car was acquitted by a consistory court after evidence was presented that the complainant suffered delusions resulting from a psychiatric disorder: *The Times*, January 24, 1997. Samantha Heywood admitted 7 charges of perverting the course of justice by making false allegations of rape and abuse against 6 men and her mother. She was placed on probation with a condition of psychiatric treatment:

because of the lack of independent evidence contradicting the complainant. A great deal is at stake for the accused: rape is a very serious offence carrying severe penalties, a conviction for it is highly stigmatic, and it may result in the loss of a man's livelihood and status, the break-up of his marriage and denial of access to his children. It is essential that a man who has been falsely accused should be able to expose the falsity of the accusation, and it may well be that the only way of doing this in the absence of other evidence is by attacking the credibility of the complainant.

A final introductory point is that the traditional common law distinction between cross-examination as to the issue and cross-examination on collateral matters such as a witness's credibility is extremely problematic in the context of sexual offences. Where the complainant's testimony provides the only substantial evidence against the accused, her credibility effectively becomes the issue.[25] The point in dispute may be whether a sexual act took place at all, or whether it took place without her consent, but in either case if the jury find that the complainant is not, or might not be, telling the truth on oath, the charge is not proved and the accused must be acquitted. It is not surprising therefore to find contradictions and confusions in the cases as courts struggle with a distinction that is artificial at best, and in this context may be more or less unworkable.

15–006

(B)   The common law

The rule at common law was that questions about the complainant's sexual history were admissible if they were directly relevant to a fact in issue, such as consent or identity, or if they went to the issue of the complainant's credibility in bringing a complaint of rape. An example of the former would be where the accused, who denied alleged intercourse with the complainant at a party, sought to cross-examine her on whether she had had sex with another man at the party, with a view to showing that semen found on the complainant came from the other man. In relation to credibility, the common law regarded previous sexual experience as relevant on the basis that it tended to show promiscuity. In an age of different sexual mores, promiscuity was associated with a general willingness to consent to sex and a tendency to lie about it. Hale argued that women of good character made a prompt complaint if they were raped; an absence of prompt complaint gave rise to a presumption that the complainant's testimony as to rape was "false or feigned".[26] Additionally a danger of sexual fantasy on the part of a "loose" woman was sometimes invoked. Wigmore, for example, feared that an "unchaste ... mentality finds incidental but direct expression in the narration of

15–007

The Times, January 20, 1999. Nadine Milroy-Sloan was sentenced to 3 years' imprisonment for perverting the course of justice after falsely accusing former MP Neil Hamilton and his wife Christine of rape: *The Times*, June 14, 2003. Mother and daughter Louise and Ada Brazil received custodial sentences for attempting to pervert the course of justice by falsely accusing the daughter's former boyfriend of rape: *The Times*, April 28, 2006.

[25] As Henry J. put it in *Funderburk* [1990] 2 All E.R. 482 at 491: "where the disputed issue is a sexual one between two persons in private the difference between questions going to credit and questions going to the issue is reduced to vanishing point". On the possible use of expert witness testimony in sexual assault cases see Ellison in (2005) 9 E. & P. 239.

[26] Sir M. Hale, *Pleas of the Crown* (London: 1736), Vol.1 p.633.

imaginary sex incidents of which the narrator is the heroine or the victim".[27] Accordingly, cross-examination was permitted at common law on a complainant's previous sexual history.[28] A defendant who succeeded in getting a complainant to admit to promiscuity could appeal to the assumed probative value of this fact in weakening her testimony. He could also invite the jury to consider the moral status of a complainant who had been revealed as a loose woman. If he had no previous convictions himself he could invite a direct comparison between his own good character and the flawed character of the complainant. A jury unsure of whom to believe might well give the benefit of the doubt to the accused in such a case.

However, a complainant's sexual acts on other occasions are plainly collateral issues. Answers to questions about them normally had to be treated as final under the general rule discussed in Ch.14. This was so even if the defence could adduce convincing evidence in rebuttal to show that a denial of other sexual experience was false. The rebuttal evidence would be inadmissible unless an exception to the finality rule applied. The common law recognised a number of exceptions in the case of sexual history evidence. These exceptions constituted an acknowledgment by the courts that the line between credit and issue becomes hopelessly blurred in certain cases. First, the defence could adduce evidence of the complainant's other acts of intercourse with the defendant himself[29] if she denied them. The rationale was that if the complainant had previously had consensual sex with the accused, the probability of further intercourse also being with consent was increased. Secondly, it appears that evidence was admissible of other sexual incidents forming part of the surrounding circumstances of the offence, by what amounts to a generous application of the res gestae principle relating to relevant evidence of context.[30] The argument for relevance in this type of case seems to be based on an idea of showing the complainant to have been in a continuing state of heightened sexual awareness or arousal at the time, thus increasing the probability of her consent. Thirdly, and most far-reaching, was the rule that evidence was admissible that the complainant was a prostitute.[31] Prostitution for this purpose was not restricted to the sale of sex for money. The rule extended to evidence showing the complainant to be a woman of "notorious immoral character and reputation".[32] In *Krausz*,[33] Stephenson L.J. summarised the development of the common law by suggesting that the authorities supported the crude proposition that "Evidence which proves that a woman is in the habit of submitting her body to different men without discrimination, whether for pay or not, would seem to be admissible". If this is right, the dividing line between promiscuity and prostitution becomes impossible to define. Assuming that evidence of prostitution

---

[27] Wigmore, Vol. IIIA (Chadbourn rev. 1970), para.924a.

[28] *Holmes* (1871) L.R. 1 C.C.R. 334.

[29] *Riley* (1887) 18 Q.B.D. 481.

[30] This conclusion seems necessarily to follow from the decision of the Court of Appeal in *Viola* [1982] 1 W.L.R. 1138, discussed below. Evidence of "contemporaneous" sexual incidents involving the complainant and men other than the accused was held to be relevant to the issue of consent "according to the ordinary common law rules of evidence": at 1141.

[31] *Barker* (1829) 3 C. & P. 589.

[32] *Krausz* (1973) 57 Cr.App.R. 466 at 474 CA per Stephenson L.J. interpreting the earlier decision of the Court of Criminal Appeal in *Greenberg* (1923) 17 Cr.App.R. 107.

[33] *Krausz* (1973) 57 Cr.App.R. 466 at 474 CA.

was admissible on the issue of consent, as it seems to have been, the conclusion is inescapable that the distinction between credit and issue had effectively been collapsed altogether.

(C) "Rape shield" legislation: YJCEA s.41[34]

Criticism of the common law was widespread and strong. One line of attack pointed to the unfortunate consequences of the cross-examination rules: many felt that the rules resulted in the complainant being on trial, rather than the defendant, and there was a broad consensus that the prospect of a robust and intrusive cross-examination was a significant contributing factor to the reluctance of many women to report rape or to press charges in contested cases.[35] A second criticism challenged what have been called the twin myths: "that unchaste women were more likely to consent to intercourse and in any event were less worthy of belief".[36] Critics flatly denied the claims that because a woman had consented to sex with A or B or C, she was therefore more likely to have consented to sex with D and in any event was less trustworthy in testifying on sexual matters. In *R. v A (No.2)*,[37] the House of Lords signalled judicial acceptance of the criticism. Lord Steyn described such claims as "outmoded beliefs" and as "generalised, stereotyped and unfounded prejudices which ought to have no place in our legal system".[38]

15–008

The force of the criticism has persuaded the legislatures in all common law jurisdictions to enact "rape shield" statutes. The content of these varies,[39] but they all aim to protect complainants to a greater or lesser extent from questions and evidence about their previous sexual experience. The first such legislation in England and Wales was s.2 of the Sexual Offences (Amendment) Act 1976.[40] This prohibited evidence and questions in cross-examination about any sexual experience of a complainant with a person other than the defendant, except with the leave of the judge. The judge was permitted to give leave only if he was satisfied that it would be unfair to the defendant to refuse to allow the evidence to be adduced or the question to be asked. Although well-intentioned, this provision came to be regarded widely as unsatisfactory, and, as applied in practice, little

---

[34] N. Kibble, "The Sexual History Provisions: Charting a course between inflexible legislative rules and wholly untrammelled judicial discretion?" [2000] Crim. L.R. 274; G. Young, "The Sexual History Provisions in the Youth Justice and Criminal Evidence Act 1999—A Violation of the Right to a Fair Trial" (2001) 41 Med.Sci.Law 217.

[35] See generally J. Temkin, *Rape and the Legal Process*, 2nd edn (Oxford, 2002), pp.8–11, 17–19, 197. See also J. Harris and S. Grace, *A Question of Evidence? Investigating and Prosecuting Rape in the 1990s* (Home Office, 1999).

[36] *Seaboyer* (1991) 83 D.L.R. (4th) 193 at 258, 278 per McLachlin J. cited with approval by Lord Steyn in *R. v A (No.2)* [2001] UKHL 25; [2001] 2 Cr.App.R. 21 at [27].

[37] *R. v A (No.2)* [2001] UKHL 25; [2001] 2 Cr.App.R. 21 at [27].

[38] For a more sceptical approach to the (political) "correctness" embodied in s.41 see D. Birch, "A Better Deal for Vulnerable Witnesses?" [2000] Crim. L.R. 223, 247–249.

[39] See the concise but valuable summary by Lord Hope of Craighead in *R. v A (No.2)* [2001] UKHL 25; [2001] 2 Cr.App.R. 21 at [100]–[102] and the literature there cited.

[40] Enacted following the recommendations of the Heilbron Committee's *Report of the Advisory Group on the Law of Rape*, Cmnd. 6352 (1976). For a discussion of s.2 and its associated jurisprudence see the first edition of this book at pp.473–480.

better than the common law. Following proposals in the report *Speaking Up For Justice*,[41] s.2 of the Sexual Offences (Amendment) Act 1976 was repealed, and replaced by s.41 of the YJCEA.

15–009 Section 41 is structurally similar to the earlier "rape shield", in the sense that it imposes a general ban on evidence and questions concerning the other sexual behaviour of the complainant, and then provides that the shield may be lifted in certain cases. However, the shield is larger, and the exceptions much more restrictively defined, than under the previous law. Section 41(1) contains the general ban:

> " If at a trial a person is charged with a sexual offence, then, except with the leave of the court—
>
> (a)   no evidence may be adduced, and
> (b)   no question may be asked in cross-examination, by or on behalf of any accused at the trial, about any sexual behaviour of the complainant."

"Sexual offence" is widely defined under s.62(1) of the YJCEA to mean any offence under Pt 1 of the Sexual Offences Act 2003. A "complainant" means a person against or in relation to whom any offence was or is alleged to have been committed.[42]

15–010 As well as extending the range of offences to which the general ban applies, the YJCEA extends the ban to sexual behaviour of the complainant with the accused.[43] Under s.42(1)(c) "sexual behaviour" means "any sexual behaviour or other sexual experience, whether or not involving any accused or other person". This extension of the general ban, which makes no distinction at all between the accused and third parties, presented a problem of compatibility with art.6 of the ECHR, as will appear below. "Sexual behaviour" does not include "anything alleged to have taken place as part of the event which is the subject matter of the charge against the accused". Thus the general ban does not extend to evidence and questions about the facts that make up the event giving rise to the proceedings against the accused. The accused can cross-examine the complainant, for example, on whether she made sexual overtures to him on the occasion of a date when he is alleged to have raped her, or on whether she was encouraging other men to have sex with her at a party, where it is the defendant's case that the complainant willingly took part with him and others in a session of group sex.

Section 41(1) indicates that the court may give leave for the accused to adduce evidence or ask questions about the complainant's sexual behaviour, but leave can only be given if the conditions in s.41(2) are satisfied. These are that the case falls within one of the exceptional categories of case in subs.(3) or (5) of s.41, *and* "that a refusal of leave might have the result of rendering unsafe a conclusion

---

[41] Report of the Interdepartmental Working Group on the Treatment of Vulnerable or Intimidated Witnesses in the Criminal Justice System (London, 1998).

[42] YJCEA s.63(1).

[43] It is worth noting that the main aim of s.41, as revealed in *Speaking Up For Justice* (London, 1998), was to tighten the law on sexual history evidence regarding the complainant's relationships with third parties. Although some extension of the ban to sexual behaviour with the accused had been proposed in some of the literature, the travaux preparatoires of the YJCEA never made a reasoned case for it.

of the jury or (as the case may be) the court on any relevant issue in the case". Thus in all exceptional cases the court granting leave must be satisfied that not permitting the accused to adduce the evidence or ask the question might result in an unsafe conclusion on any relevant issue.[44] It should be noted that s.41 does not provide for any residual discretion in the court to grant leave in the interests of justice, or of fairness to the accused.

The exceptional categories of case under subss.(3) and (5) can be classified under four headings. The categories of admissibility are not mutually exclusive. Evidence of the complainant's sexual behaviour may be admissible under more than one heading.[45] It is convenient to deal first with the type of case set out in subs.(5). This is the case where the prosecution adduce evidence about any sexual behaviour of the complainant,[46] and the evidence to be adduced or the question to be asked by or on behalf of the accused relates to the prosecution evidence and goes no further than is necessary to rebut or explain it. Two examples of the operation of the provision can be given. *R. v F*,[47] was a child sexual abuse case in which the defendant was charged with specimen counts of rape and gross indecency with his stepdaughter (P), when she was aged between seven and 16. D denied all the alleged incidents. The issue concerned evidence of the admitted sexual relationship they had had for a number of years when P was an adult. It was D's case that the relationship was uncoerced and consensual on P's part, and that she had a motive of revenge for bringing a false complaint against him after he terminated the relationship. According to P the relationship was a continuation of the childhood abuse, and she was too scared of D to refuse him. The trial judge ruled that under s.41(3)(a) (see below) evidence of the relationship should be disclosed to the jury as relevant to D's case that the alleged acts of sexual abuse never occurred. Following this ruling the prosecution solicited P's account of the relationship during her evidence in chief. The Court of Appeal held that under s.41(5) D had been entitled to rebut that account, but had been wrongly prevented by a further ruling of the trial judge from calling certain evidence that P had participated willingly in the relationship. This evidence consisted of videos and photographs that showed P stripping for D, engaging in sexual behaviour, and appearing to be happy and enjoying herself. In the view of the court the dispute about the nature of the adult relationship was vital to the jury's decision whether there had been an earlier abusive relationship, and the excluded evidence showing P's demeanour was of potential value to the resolution of that dispute. In the second case, also called *R. v F*,[48] the complainant testified as to a rape by the defendant which had resulted in her becoming pregnant. The Court of Appeal held that the trial judge had wrongly refused to permit cross-examination of the

---

[44] For cases where the Court of Appeal applied s.41(2)(b) and held that a refusal of leave did not tend to make the jury's conclusion of guilt unsafe see *Mokrecovas* [2001] EWCA Crim 1644; [2002] 1 Cr.App.R. 20; *Bahador* [2005] EWCA Crim 396.

[45] As in *R. v F* [2005] EWCA Crim 493; [2005] 2 Cr.App.R. 13 (s.41(3)(a) and (5)).

[46] The wording of the provision naturally refers to evidence adduced in chief by the prosecution, but could extend to evidence volunteered by the complainant in cross-examination: see *Hamadi* [2007] EWCA Crim 3048, where the Court of Appeal distinguished the latter possibility from evidence deliberately elicited from the complainant by defence counsel.

[47] *R. v F* [2005] EWCA Crim 493; [2005] 2 Cr.App.R. 13.

[48] *R. v F* [2008] EWCA Crim 2859.

complainant on medical notes revealing that she had told her doctor at the time that she was pregnant as the result of a "condom accident" involving her boyfriend. It seems clear that in both these cases it would have been unfair to deprive the defendant of the potential support that could have been provided for his rebuttal by the objective evidence that the trial judges excluded.

15–011   The second category of exception is in s.41(3)(a). This permits the court to give leave where the evidence or question relates to a relevant issue[49] in the case that is not an issue of consent. The phrase "issue of consent" means "any issue whether the complainant in fact consented to the conduct constituting the offence with which the accused is charged (and accordingly does not include any issue as to the belief of the accused that the complainant so consented".[50] Thus a "defence"[51] that the accused honestly and reasonably, but mistakenly, believed that the complainant was consenting, is included in this category and is not subject to the more restrictive rules that apply where the issue is one of actual consent. Other relevant issues that are not issues of consent are whether the alleged act, e.g. of penetration or sexual assault, occurred at all, and whether the act, assuming that it occurred, was committed by the accused or by some other person. In these types of case evidence and questions about the complainant's sexual behaviour may be relevant because of the specific inferences they may permit that point to the accused's innocence. Thus, as Lord Hope noted in *R. v A (No.2)*,[52] the evidence and questions may show that the complainant was biased against the accused or had a motive to fabricate the evidence, or that there is an alternative explanation for the physical conditions that the prosecution claim establish that penetration took place, or, especially in the case of young complainants, that the detail of their account must have come from some other sexual activity before or after the event that provides an explanation for their knowledge of that activity. If the accused is to have a fair trial it is essential that he should be able to show, for example, that bruising of the complainant, which the prosecution rely on to show that the accused sexually assaulted her, was caused during an act of penetration by a third party before the event in question.

The third and fourth exceptions to the general ban apply where the relevant issue is an issue of consent, and the evidence or question relates to that issue. Under s.41(3)(b) the court may give leave where the "sexual behaviour of the complainant to which the evidence or question relates is alleged to have taken place at or about the same time as the event which is the subject matter of the charge against the accused". This exception seems to be founded on the common law principle of relevance via contemporaneity with the facts in issue, but its scope is uncertain. Two problems arise. First, what are the temporal limits of the condition that the sexual behaviour took place "at or about the same time" as the event in question? Does this mean within minutes, hours, days or even weeks of

---

[49] i.e. any issue falling to be proved by the prosecution or defence in the trial of the accused: s.42(1)(a).

[50] YJCEA s.42(1)(b).

[51] The "defence" is a denial of the mens rea that the prosecution must prove by virtue of s.1(1)(c) of the Sexual Offences Act 2003, namely that the accused did not reasonably believe that the complainant consented.

[52] *R. v A (No.2)* [2001] UKHL 25; [2001] 2 Cr.App.R. 21.

the event? And does the context of the event in question, for example a party, make any difference? The YJCEA itself gives no further guidance.

In *R. v A (No.2)*,[53] which is discussed in more detail below, the accused wanted to cross-examine the complainant on the sexual relationship he claimed they had been having before the alleged rape. He said that the relationship had continued for a three-week period prior to the rape, and that the last act of intercourse had taken place approximately one week beforehand. All five members of the House of Lords held that this fell outside the scope of s.41(3)(b).[54] None of the Lords was prepared to assign a specific temporal limit to the phrase "at or about the same time". There was general agreement that the test was a flexible one that had to be determined in the light of the circumstances of each particular case. But their Lordships' differing dicta present trial judges with confusing guidance. Lord Slynn thought that the words should be given a narrow meaning that would restrict evidence and questions to sexual behaviour of the complainant that was "really contemporaneous" with the event in issue.[55] Lord Steyn said that an example covered by s.41(3)(b) would be where the accused alleged that the complainant invited him to have sex with her earlier in the evening, but in his opinion the temporal restriction would not extend to days, weeks or months.[56] Lord Hope referred to the Home Office's explanatory notes to the Act, which state that the phrase "at or about the same time" is expected to be interpreted no more widely than 24 hours before or after the offence.[57] This limit was expressly included in the Bill as introduced in Parliament, but it was dropped after criticism that it was arbitrary. Lord Clyde noted that incidents within s.41(3)(b) must be outwith anything that takes place as part of the event that forms the subject matter of the charge, since such things are excluded from the definition of "sexual behaviour" in s.42(1)(c). He thought that it would be difficult to extend the concept of the time of the event to a period of several days.[58] Lord Hutton was clear that an act one week before the offence was outside the scope of the provision,[59] but did not express a view on what that scope was.

The second problem is the degree of relevance necessary for leave to be given, assuming that the other sexual behaviour of the complainant comes within the temporal limit of s.41(3)(b), whatever that limit may be. Where the other sexual behaviour was with third parties it seems clear that some kind of link with the offence alleged against the accused will be necessary. In the absence of a link making the complainant's consent more likely the evidence or question will not be relevant.[60] In *R. v A (No.2)*, the trial judge had given the accused leave to ask the complainant about an incident of sexual intercourse with a third party (the

---

[53] *R. v A (No.2)* [2001] UKHL 25; [2001] 2 Cr.App.R. 21.
[54] See *R. v A (No.2)* [2001] UKHL 25; [2001] 2 Cr.App.R. 21 per Lord Slynn at [12]; Lord Steyn at [40]; Lord Hope at [82]; Lord Clyde at [132]; Lord Hutton at [156].
[55] *R. v A (No.2)* [2001] UKHL 25; [2001] 2 Cr.App.R. 21.
[56] *R. v A (No.2)* [2001] UKHL 25; [2001] 2 Cr.App.R. 21 at [40].
[57] *R. v A (No.2)* [2001] UKHL 25; [2001] 2 Cr.App.R. 21 at [82].
[58] *R. v A (No.2)* [2001] UKHL 25; [2001] 2 Cr.App.R. 21 at [132].
[59] *R. v A (No.2)* [2001] UKHL 25; [2001] 2 Cr.App.R. 21 at [156].
[60] For a case involving a dubious link, see *Mukadi* [2004] Crim L.R. 373, and the critical commentary by Professor Birch.

accused's flatmate) some hours before the alleged rape. This would certainly have been within the temporal limit envisaged by Lord Hope, and probably within the limits envisaged by Lord Steyn and Lord Clyde. However, the Court of Appeal thought that the evidence was not relevant and reversed the trial judge on this point.[61] The point was not in issue in the House of Lords, but it seems likely that the Lords would have agreed with the Court of Appeal in view of their comments about the "twin myths", mentioned above. Where the other sexual behaviour was with the accused himself it may well be possible to draw an inference about the complainant's favourable mindset towards the accused. Granted that a woman has the right to say "No" at any time, common sense suggests that a reversal of the complainant's attitude to sex with the accused within a matter of hours would call for an explanation.

15–012   Section 41(3)(c) permits leave to be given where the evidence or question relates to an issue of consent, and the sexual behaviour of the complainant is so similar to any of her sexual behaviour that took place as part of the event in question, or that took place at or about the same time, that the similarity cannot be explained as a coincidence. On its face this allows the accused to introduce "similar fact" evidence of the complainant's sexual behaviour, as originally recommended by the Heilbron Committee.[62] During the debates on the Bill in the House of Lords Baroness Mallalieu gave the celebrated example of a complainant who claims that the accused raped her after climbing up on to her balcony and into her bedroom; the accused should be able to support his defence of her consent to intercourse by showing that on several other occasions the complainant had invited a man to re-enact the balcony scene from *Romeo and Juliet* prior to having sex with him.[63] This unlikely story hardly provides a compelling case for the provision. This exception seems vulnerable to the criticism that women give consent to sex with a particular partner and not to a particular occasion, so that situational similarities are essentially irrelevant. However, in *R. v T*,[64] the Court of Appeal assumed that a sufficient degree of circumstantial similarity was enough for admissibility, and did not probe the argument for its relevance. The defendant, who was charged with raping P inside a climbing frame in a children's play area in a park, was refused leave to cross-examine P on whether they had not had consensual sex in the climbing frame, adopting the same respective positions, on an occasion three or four weeks earlier. The Court of Appeal held that s.41(3)(c)(i) applied, and quashed the conviction.[65] Moreover, Durston[66] has argued that sexual history evidence that shows some situational similarity with the incident involving the accused is acceptable where the use of the evidence is

---

[61] *R. v A (No.2)* [2001] EWCA Crim 4. The Court of Appeal reached the same conclusion in *Mokrecovas* [2002] 1 Cr.App.R. 20, in relation to a claim that the complainant had sex with the accused's brother on the night in question. In view of these decisions we can be reasonably confident that if the facts of *Viola* [1982] 1 W.L.R. 1138 recurred the result would now be different.

[62] *Report of the Advisory Group on the Law of Rape*, Cmnd.6352 (1976), para.137.

[63] HL Committee Stage, *Hansard* February 1, 1999 col.45.

[64] *R. v T* [2004] EWCA Crim 1220; [2004] 2 Cr.App.R. 32.

[65] The trial judge had wrongly incorporated a temporal limitation to the "similarity" exception. *R. v T* can be compared on the facts with *Hamadi* [2007[EWCA Crim 3048, where the circumstantial similarities were not sufficient to be inexplicable as coincidence.

[66] Durston (1998) 62 Jo. Crim. Law 91.

to challenge some background generalisation the jury might employ. Such evidence might be, for example, that the complainant has previously had sex with a much older man ("teenage girls don't usually agree to sex with men of 50"), or sex with a group of men, or sex in a public place, and so on. Finally, the House of Lords has given s.41(3)(c) an unexpected interpretation in order to safeguard the accused's right to a fair trial, a matter to be discussed shortly.

This analysis of the scope and purposes of s.41 needs to take account of two **15–013** further limits on what is permitted by way of evidence and questions relating to a complainant's sexual behaviour. For the purposes of all the exceptional cases in subss.(3) and (5) the evidence or question must relate to a specific instance or instances of alleged sexual behaviour on the part of the complainant.[67] In *White*,[68] the Court of Appeal held that this provision prevented the defence from asking the complainant whether she was working as a prostitute at the time of the alleged rape. According to Laws L.J., "there must be something about the circumstances of a specific episode of alleged sexual conduct by a complainant which has potential probative force".[69] It follows that evidence of the complainant's reputation for sexual behaviour, or of a witness's opinion of the complainant's sexual behaviour, remains subject to the general ban and is not admissible.

Secondly, for the purposes of subs.(3) no evidence or question shall be regarded as relating to a relevant issue in the case if it appears to the court to be reasonable to assume that the purpose (or main purpose) for which it would be adduced or asked is to establish or elicit material for impugning the credibility of the complainant as a witness.[70] This attempt to prevent the use of sexual history evidence to attack the credibility of the complainant presents courts with some difficult decisions, bearing in mind the problem of distinguishing issue and credit in sexual cases. In *R. v A (No.2)*, Lord Clyde commented that "a very sharp knife may be required to separate what may be admitted from what may not".[71] Both he and Lord Hope thought that evidence would be admissible under s.41(3)(a) about a sexual experience of a young complainant (a boy aged 15), which had occurred two years after the abuse that was the subject of the charge but that could provide an alternative explanation for his evidence.[72] The purpose of adducing this evidence is to show that the boy's evidence of abuse by the accused should not be believed, which seems to amount to impugning his credibility. So, despite the view of their Lordships, it ought to be ruled out by s.41(4). However, applying s.41(4) in this way would cut away most of the ground covered by the exceptions in subs.(3) and leave them with a very restricted area of operation. Moreover, where the complainant's credibility is effectively the issue, it would seem to deny the accused a fair trial if he cannot prove a motive or an explanation for false testimony by the complainant.

---

[67] YJCEA s.41(6).
[68] *White* [2004] EWCA Crim 946.
[69] *White* [2004] EWCA Crim 946 at [16].
[70] YJCEA s.41(4).
[71] *R. v A (No.2)* [2001] UKHL 25; [2001] 2 Cr.App.R. 21 at [138].
[72] *R. v A (No.2)* [2001] UKHL 25; [2001] 2 Cr.App.R. 21 at [79], [129]; citing *Love v HM Advocate* 1999 S.C.C.R. 783.

In *Martin*,[73] the Court of Appeal sought to limit the restrictive tendency of s.41(4) by distinguishing between different purposes of a cross-examination. D's defence to charges of indecent assault and assault occasioning actual bodily harm was that the complainant had fabricated the incident in question because she was angry with him for rejecting her sexual advances to him two days earlier. The trial judge refused leave for D to cross-examine the complainant, in relation to that occasion, on whether she had pestered him for sex and performed an act of oral sex on him before he rejected her suggestion of further intimacy. The Court of Appeal held that the judge had erred. The cross-examination was relevant to the issue of whether the complainant had a motive for fabricating the charges against D; it was one purpose, but not "the purpose" or "the main purpose" to impugn the credibility of the complainant.[74] On its face this distinction is unconvincing, since the whole point of the cross-examination about the complainant's sexual behaviour on the earlier occasion is to ask the jury to disbelieve her testimony about the events that form the subject of the charge. However, the court seems to have had in mind that, if necessary, s.41(4) might be interpreted as a prohibition on direct attacks on the credibility of a complainant, rather than questions or evidence going to the issue of her credibility on the facts of the case.[75] From this perspective the "purpose" distinction makes more sense, and is defensible as a pragmatic device to ensure that the accused has a fair opportunity to present his defence.

15–014 Another way of attacking the credibility of a complainant is to suggest that she has made previous false complaints, or has failed to complain when a complaint might be expected if an allegation were true. If such facts could be proved they would ground an argument that she has a tendency to lie about sexual attacks on her. In the leading case of *BT, MH*,[76] the Court of Appeal held that questions about, respectively, a failure to complain when other sexual allegations were being investigated, and previous lies about sexual matters, were not questions about any "sexual behaviour" of the complainant and therefore fell outside s.41 altogether. However, the court also made it clear that if D is to take the cross-examination outside the scope of s.41 he must first seek a ruling from the trial judge that the section does not apply, and he will need to have an evidential foundation for the allegations of falsity.[77] There is some inconsistency in the authorities as to what constitutes a sufficient evidential foundation. One view is that it is enough for D to point to some evidence on which a jury could be satisfied that the previous allegation was false.[78] Other cases seem to require stronger proof by referring to a more solid foundation than inconsistencies between the complainant's statement and other witness statements and comments in a police report, such as an admission by the complainant that the earlier

---

[73] *Martin* [2004] EWCA Crim 916; [2004] 2 Cr.App.R. 22.

[74] *Martin* [2004] EWCA Crim 916; [2004] 2 Cr.App.R. 22 at [37]. On the facts it was held that, despite the wrong ruling, the conviction was safe.

[75] *Martin* [2004] EWCA Crim 916; [2004] 2 Cr.App.R. 22 at [38].

[76] *BT, MH* [2001] EWCA Crim 1877; [2002] 1 Cr.App.R. 22; followed in *R. v C and B* [2003] EWCA Crim 29; *R. v E* [2004] EWCA Crim 1313; *R. v TW* [2004] EWCA Crim 3103; *Abdelrahman* [2005] EWCA Crim 1367.

[77] *BT, MH* [2002] 1 Cr.App.R. 22 at [41].

[78] *Murray* [2009] EWCA Crim 618; *Davarifar* [2009] EWCA Crim 2294.

allegation was false.[79] It does, however, seem to be clear that it is not enough to show that the police[80] or the CPS[81] decided not to prosecute the earlier allegation. Where no evidential foundation for falsity exists, the questions about previous complaints will be treated as questions about previous sexual behaviour and therefore subject to s.41. In such a case they are likely to be ruled out by s.41(4), on the ground that their purpose or main purpose is to impugn the credibility of the complainant.[82]

Questions about false complaints that are held to fall outside s.41 will almost certainly need to satisfy s.100 of the Criminal Justice Act 2003. They will usually amount to evidence of the bad character of the complainant, by suggesting that she has committed an offence or been guilty of reprehensible behaviour by making false accusations on other occasions. The credibility of the complainant will be an issue in the proceedings, and so the admissibility of the questions will depend on whether they have substantial probative value in relation to her credibility, and whether her credibility is of substantial importance in the context of the case as a whole. If she can be shown to have lied about sexual matters in the past, trial judges are likely to rule that the conditions of s.100 have been satisfied. It is conceivable that cases could arise in which D wishes to cross-examine the complainant on other sexual behaviour about which she told lies. In such a case both s.100 of the Criminal Justice Act 2003 and s.41 of the YJCEA would be engaged. It seems that the provisions are cumulative, and D would have to satisfy the conditions of both for the questions to be admissible.

(D)   Section 41 and the ECHR article 6

Section 41 restricts the right of the accused to examine a complainant witness against him. A question arises therefore of its compatibility with art.6 of the ECHR. It will be recalled that art.6(3)(d) confers on everyone charged with a criminal offence the right to examine or have examined witnesses against him. The issue of compatibility was very fully considered by the House of Lords in the leading case of *R. v A (No.2)*.[83] The defendant (D) was charged with rape. The complainant (P) alleged that D raped her on a towpath in the early hours of the morning when she and D were walking from a flat (which D shared with a friend, with whom P had been having a relationship) to a hospital where the friend had been taken after collapsing the night before. D said that the intercourse was consensual, alternatively that he had believed that she had consented. He claimed that he and P had been having a sexual relationship for three weeks beforehand. At a preparatory hearing D sought leave under s.41 to adduce evidence of this relationship. The trial judge ruled that such evidence was prohibited by s.41. He did, however, give leave under s.41(3)(b) for D to ask P about an incident of sexual intercourse between P and the friend the previous evening. On appeal under s.35 of the Criminal Procedure and Investigations Act 1996 the Court of

15–015

---

[79] *R. v RD* [2009] EWCA Crim 2137; *R. v MC* [2012] EWCA Crim 213.
[80] *R. v RD* [2009] EWCA Crim 2137.
[81] *Davarifar* [2009] EWCA Crim 2294.
[82] As in *Abdelrahman* [2005] EWCA Crim 1367.
[83] *R. v A (No.2)* [2001] UKHL 25; [2001] 2 Cr.App.R. 21.

Appeal, as noted above, reversed the judge's ruling on the latter point. On the first point the court allowed D's appeal, holding that the evidence and questions about the alleged previous sexual relationship between P and D was admissible under s.41(3)(a) in relation to the issue of D's *belief* in consent. However, the Court of Appeal stated that the evidence and questions would be inadmissible on the issue of actual consent. This result caused the Court of Appeal some concern and led the court to certify the following question for the House of Lords[84]:

> "May a sexual relationship between a defendant and complainant be relevant to the issue of consent so as to render its exclusion under section 41 of the Youth Justice and Criminal Evidence Act 1999 a contravention of the defendant's right to a fair trial?"

The response of the House to this question was a qualified "Yes". The ratio of the case appears in the speech of Lord Steyn, in a passage[85] with which all the other Lords agreed[86]:

> "under section 41(3)(c) of the 1999 Act, construed where necessary by applying the interpretative obligation under section 3 of the Human Rights Act 1998, and due regard always being paid to the importance of seeking to protect the complainant from indignity and from humiliating questions, the test of admissibility is whether the evidence (and questioning in relation to it) is nevertheless so relevant to the issue of consent that to exclude it would endanger the fairness of the trial under Article 6 of the Convention. If this test is satisfied the evidence should not be excluded."

The House then held that the application of this test to the facts of the case was a matter for the trial judge to rule on at the resumed trial.

15–016   Counsel for the accused had indicated that he would invite the House to construe s.41 according to its interpretative duty under s.3 of the Human Rights Act 1998 ("HRA"), alternatively that he would seek a declaration of incompatibility under s.4 of the HRA. The speeches demonstrate that while the Lords are willing to use s.3 to give creative interpretation to potentially incompatible legislation they are extremely reluctant to make a s.4 declaration. Lord Steyn said that a declaration of incompatibility "is a measure of last resort. It must be avoided unless it is plainly impossible to do so".[87] Lord Hutton said that it is clearly desirable that a court should seek to avoid having to make a declaration of incompatibility unless the clear and express wording of the provision makes this impossible.[88] None of the Lords thought that s.41 imposed a clear limitation on Convention rights in express terms.

To what extent, then, is the use of the interpretative obligation in s.3 of the Human Rights Act necessary? The reasoning of the Lords begins once again from the proposition that the specific rights in art.6 are not absolute. According to the familiar methodology they may be restricted in pursuance of a legitimate aim,

---

[84] The curious form of the appeal to the House of Lords is explained in the speech of Lord Hutton at [165]–[173] in *R. v A (No.2)* [2001] UKHL 25; [2001] 2 Cr.App.R. 21.

[85] *R. v A (No.2)* [2001] UKHL 25; [2001] 2 Cr.App.R. 21 at [46].

[86] See *R. v A (No.2)* [2001] UKHL 25; [2001] 2 Cr.App.R. 21 per Lord Slynn at [15]; Lord Hope at [110]; Lord Clyde at [140]; Lord Hutton at [163].

[87] *R. v A (No.2)* [2001] UKHL 25; [2001] 2 Cr.App.R. 21 at [44].

[88] *R. v A (No.2)* [2001] UKHL 25; [2001] 2 Cr.App.R. 21 at [162].

provided that the restriction is proportionate to the aim.[89] In deciding whether the restrictions are in pursuance of a legitimate aim the courts pay a degree of deference to the democratic judgment of the legislature as to where the balance is to be struck between the rights of the individual and the needs of society.[90] Parliament's judgment that complainants must be protected from unnecessary humiliation and distress when giving evidence was considered to pursue a legitimate aim, bearing in mind the prevalence of sexual offences that are unreported because of the reluctance of complainants to submit to the process of giving evidence at trial.[91] The unnecessary humiliation and distress arises from the use of evidence and questions founded on the "twin myths" mentioned above. On this basis Lord Steyn expressed the view that s.41:

> "deals fairly and sensibly with questioning and evidence about the complainant's sexual experience *with other men*. Such matters are almost always irrelevant to the issue whether the complainant consented to sexual intercourse on the occasion alleged in the indictment or to her credibility. To that extent the scope of the reform of the law by the 1999 Act was justified."[92]

However, the extension of this protection without distinction to evidence and questions about the complainant's sexual experience with the accused himself was considered to raise a critical issue of proportionality. All the Lords thought that such experience could in some cases be sufficiently relevant to the issue of consent to require its admission in the interests of fairness.[93] But the ordinary meaning of the restrictive language in s.41(3)(b) and (c) would not always permit the admission of the evidence of such experience. The sexual behaviour of the complainant with the accused might not have been at or about the same time as the event in question, nor might it have been so similar as not to be a coincidence. Thus the application of the ordinary meaning of these provisions might result in the exclusion of evidence relevant to the accused's defence and hence in a violation of his right to a fair trial. In this way the Lords arrived at the need to invoke the interpretative obligation under s.3 of the Human Rights Act 1998. This, in the words of Lord Steyn:

> "requires the court to subordinate the niceties of the language of s.41(3)(c), and in particular, the touchstone of coincidence, to broader considerations of relevance judged by logical and common sense criteria of time and circumstances."[94]

Lord Steyn proceeded to justify this solution to the problem of disproportionality with the comment:

---

[89] See in particular *R. v A (No.2)* [2001] UKHL 25; [2001] 2 Cr.App.R. 21 per Lord Hope at [91].

[90] *R. v A (No.2)* [2001] UKHL 25; [2001] 2 Cr.App.R. 21 per Lord Hope at [58], citing *R. v DPP Ex p. Kebilene* [2000] 2 A.C. 326; *Brown v Stott* [2001] 2 All E.R. 97.

[91] *R. v A (No.2)* [2001] UKHL 25; [2001] 2 Cr.App.R. 21 per Lord Hope at [92].

[92] *R. v A (No.2)* [2001] UKHL 25; [2001] 2 Cr.App.R. 21 at [30] (emphasis supplied).

[93] *R. v A (No.2)* [2001] UKHL 25; [2001] 2 Cr.App.R. 21 per Lord Slynn at [10]; Lord Steyn at [31]; Lord Clyde at [136]; Lord Hutton at [161]. Lord Hope was less explicit, but the point is implied in his speech at [105].

[94] *R. v A (No.2)* [2001] UKHL 25; [2001] 2 Cr.App.R. 21 at [45].

> "after all, it is realistic to proceed on the basis that the legislature would not, if alerted to the problem, have wished to deny the right to an accused to put forward a full and complete defence by advancing truly probative material."[95]

15–017 At this point doubts about the legitimacy of the solution begin to emerge. Lord Hope was surely right to say that the highly structured scheme of s.41 contradicts any idea that it is possible to read in a new provision that entitles the court to give leave whenever it thinks this is necessary to ensure a fair trial.[96] Yet this is the effect of the decision in *R. v A (No.2)*. The decision supplies the residual inclusionary discretion that is so conspicuously lacking in the text of s.41. The peg on which the decision hangs, namely the reading down of s.41(3)(c), is inadequate for the purpose. It is hard to see how the actual words of this provision can be read in any secondary meaning to achieve the result the Lords wish to produce. It may be very important for the accused to show the existence of a previous affectionate relationship between him and the complainant if he pleads her consent to sex. But this simply does not fit the concept of her previous behaviour being so similar as not to be a coincidence.[97] That concept suggests an inquiry into the circumstantial detail and peculiarity of the behaviour, not its emotional content.

However, whilst the Lords may have in substance partly rewritten s.41, the practical impact of the decision may not be great. First, there was no encouragement in *R. v A (No.2)* for counsel seeking to bypass the restrictions on evidence and questions about the sexual behaviour of the complainant with third parties. The Lords clearly regarded these as proportionate to the legitimate aim of protecting complainants. Secondly, where the existence of a previous sexual relationship between the defendant and the complainant is not disputed, the prosecution may make a formal admission to that effect.[98] Thirdly, the relevance of the complainant's sexual behaviour with the accused remains a matter of degree. It is not the case that any evidence of a previous sexual relationship between the complainant and the accused will suffice. Dicta of Lord Hope, Lord Clyde and Lord Hutton suggested that more will be needed than evidence of just a previous act of intercourse.[99] The evidence and questions will need to show something like a background of an affectionate relationship, which would go to demonstrate the complainant's attitude towards sex with the accused—her "specific mindset" towards the accused, as Galvin puts it.[100] Another possibility, according to Lord Clyde, is some detail of similarity of conduct by the complainant that is not so unremarkable as to be reasonably explained as a

---

[95] *R. v A (No.2)* [2001] UKHL 25; [2001] 2 Cr.App.R. 21 at [45].

[96] *R. v A (No.2)* [2001] UKHL 25; [2001] 2 Cr.App.R. 21 at [109].

[97] A conclusion frankly admitted by Lord Steyn at [43] in *R. v A (No.2)* [2001] UKHL 25; [2001] 2 Cr.App.R. 21.

[98] As in *R. v MM* [2011] EWCA Crim 1291, where the CA upheld a trial judge who had refused leave for D to cross-examine V on two specific instances of their previous sexual activity, on the ground that they were insufficiently similar to the events constituting the alleged rape for the purposes of s. 41(3)(c).

[99] *R. v A (No.2)* [2001] UKHL 25; [2001] 2 Cr.App.R. 21at [85], [135] and [152] respectively. See also Lord Steyn at [45].

[100] Harriet Galvin, "Shielding Rape Victims in the State and Federal Courts: A Proposal for the Second Decade" (1986) 70 Minn. L.R. 763, 903; cited in *R. v A (No.2)* [2001] UKHL 25; [2001] 2 Cr.App.R. 21 per Lord Hutton at [151].

coincidence.[101] This gets closer to the kind of case envisaged in s.41(3)(c), although Lord Clyde was at pains to say that the similarity does not have to be in some rare or bizarre conduct. For him at least, the *Romeo and Juliet* scenario did not seem to provide the benchmark.[102]

(E)   Further reform?

Sexual history evidence continues to generate vigorous debate.[103] There has been much discussion of whether s.41 adopted the right strategy in dealing with this controversial subject. One issue is whether it went too far in eliminating any inclusionary discretion for trial judges and in making no distinction between the complainant's previous sexual behaviour with the accused and with third parties. A second issue is whether the categories of admissibility are too narrowly or, alternatively, too widely drawn.

    As noted above, there are problems, for example, with the formulation of all three categories of admissibility provided for in s.41(3). A third issue is how well, or badly, the provision is working in practice. The case law on s.41 suggests that the senior judiciary have been well aware of the policy objectives of the legislation, and that they have conscientiously tried to give effect to the aims of protecting complainants while continuing to ensure fair trials for defendants. Their interpretation of some of the provisions, particularly subss.(3)(c) and (4), has enabled a pragmatic relaxation of restrictive measures that were arguably too inflexible. How far a fair balance is being achieved by trial judges in all cases remains uncertain. The empirical research to date has come up with mixed messages,[104] although there does now seem to be broad agreement that better judicial training has resulted in fewer complainants being subjected to the lengthy and humiliating questioning that used to be a feature of many rape trials.

15–018

2.   *Cross-examination by the accused in person*

One consequence of a defendant's right to defend himself in person is that the defendant is able personally to question the witnesses against him. In the case of rape complainants this right was sometimes grossly abused. In 1997, Ralston Edwards spent six days at his trial for rape cross-examining in person his victim, Julia Mason. He was wearing the same clothes as he wore during the 16 hours

15–019

---

[101] *R. v A (No.2)* [2001] UKHL 25; [2001] 2 Cr.App.R. 21 at [135].

[102] cf. *R. v A (No.2)* [2001] UKHL 25; [2001] 2 Cr.App.R. 21 per Lord Hope at [83]–[88], who takes the view that the test in s.41(3)(c) appears to impose a test of a unique or striking similarity that will not be easy to satisfy.

[103] See M. Redmayne, "Myths, Relationships and Coincidences: the New Problems of Sexual History" (2003) 7 E. & P. 75; and the lively debate between Professors Birch and Temkin in: D. Birch, "Rethinking Sexual History Evidence: Proposals for Fairer Trials" [2002] Crim. L.R. 531; J. Temkin, "Sexual History Evidence–Beware the Backlash" [2003] Crim. L.R. 217; and D. Birch, "Untangling Sexual History Evidence: a Rejoinder to Professor Temkin" [2003] Crim. L.R. 370.

[104] N. Kibble, "Judicial Perspectives on the Operation of s.41 and the Relevance and Admissibility of Prior Sexual History Evidence: Four Scenarios" [2005] Crim. L.R. 190; L. Kelly, J. Temkin and S. Griffiths, *Section 41: an evaluation of new legislation limiting sexual history evidence in rape trials* (Home Office Online Report 20/06, 2006).

that he had attacked her at her home. She claimed subsequently that he was "reliving the rape moment by moment".[105] In *Brown (Milton)*,[106] the defendant sacked his defence lawyers early in his trial for rape and subsequently subjected the two complainants to "repetitious and irrelevant questions designed to intimidate and humiliate them". On the hearing of the defendant's appeal in this case the Court of Appeal took the opportunity to remind trial judges of their duty to do all that they can, consistently with the accused's right to a fair trial, to minimise the trauma suffered by other parties to the proceedings. Lord Bingham C.J. said that the judge should intervene to protect the complainant where the accused engaged in humiliating, intimidating or abusive questioning. The judge should be prepared to instruct the accused as to the course of the questioning, and of the need to move on after the accused had put a point to the complainant. If the accused proved unable or unwilling to comply with the judge's instructions the judge should if necessary take over the questioning himself. In addition, he should not hesitate to order the use of a screen to shield the complainant where the accused sought by his dress, bearing, manner or questions to dominate, intimidate or humiliate the complainant. Lord Bingham C.J. added that the Court of Appeal would support trial judges who had to exercise careful judgment in such difficult cases, and would be extremely slow to disturb any conviction where the judge had made decisions about the conduct of the proceedings with due regard to the interests of all parties involved.

This was a welcome, albeit somewhat late reminder that the courts are not impotent in the face of abuse. It has now been overtaken by the YJCEA. Section 34 prohibits a defendant charged with a sexual offence[107] from cross-examining in person a witness who is a complainant in connection with that offence or any other offence with which the defendant is charged in the proceedings. Section 35[108] imposes a similar prohibition on the cross-examination of a child complainant, and other child witnesses,[109] of an offence to which the section applies. The protection for children is wider than the protection for adult complainants under s.34, since the offences to which s.35 applies[110] extend beyond sexual offences to include kidnapping, false imprisonment, child abduction, wilful neglect, and any offence involving assault on or injury or a threat of injury to any person. Section 36 additionally empowers a court to prohibit the accused from cross-examining in person a witness not falling within ss.34 or 35. An application for an order can be made by the prosecutor, or the court may raise the issue of its own motion. The ground for making the order is that the quality of the witness's evidence is likely to be diminished if the cross-examination is conducted by the accused in person and likely to be improved if an order is made. The test also requires the court to balance the

---

[105] See *The Times*, May 7, 1998.
[106] *Brown (Milton)* [1998] 2 Cr.App.R. 364.
[107] As defined in s.62(1); see above.
[108] Section 35 replaced and extended the earlier ban on cross-examination of children by the defendant in person, contained in s.34A of the Criminal Justice Act 1988.
[109] A "child" complainant or witness in relation to a sexual offence is a person under 18: YJCEA s.35(4)(a), as amended by Coroners and Justice Act 2009 s.105. Oddly, a "child" in relation to the other offences to which the section applies is a person under 14: s.35(4)(b).
[110] YJCEA s.35(3).

quality of the witness's evidence against the interests of justice.[111] In making its judgment regarding the quality of the witness's evidence the court must take into account a list of criteria,[112] including any views of the witness, the nature of the questions likely to be asked, the conduct of the accused, and so on. An order under s.36 might be appropriate, for example, where an adult witness is in fear of the accused.

Where an accused is not represented, and is subject to a prohibition on conducting a cross-examination in person, an issue arises as to how his case is to be properly presented. Article 6(3)(d) of the ECHR guarantees an accused the right to examine or have examined the witnesses against him. Section 38 of the YJCEA deals with the issue by giving the court power to appoint a legal representative to conduct any necessary cross-examination on behalf of the accused. Any such representative is centrally funded,[113] and is not responsible to the accused.[114] Section 39 of the YJCEA requires an appropriate judicial warning to a jury in a trial on indictment to counter any risk of prejudicial inferences from the accused being prohibited from cross-examining in person, or of prejudice from the fact that the cross-examination was carried out by a court-appointed representative not acting as the accused's own legal representative. These measures seem sufficient to ensure compliance with art.6.[115] They "counterbalance" the protection given to vulnerable witnesses against cross-examination by the accused in person, and respect the rights of the defence.[116]

3. *Special measures directions*

The YJCEA introduced powers in ss.16–33 for trial judges to make "special measures directions" ("SMDs") to protect vulnerable and intimidated witnesses. All the provisions of the scheme are in force with the exception of s.28, which provides for video-recorded cross-examination. At the time of writing it is unclear when, if ever, this provision will be brought into force.[117] The Act divides witnesses into two categories for the purposes of eligibility for assistance.[118] The first category consists of children under 18, and adult witnesses suffering from a physical or mental disorder or disability likely to diminish the quality of their

15–020

---

[111] YJCEA s.36(2).

[112] YJCEA s.36(3).

[113] YJCEA s.40.

[114] YJCEA s.38(5).

[115] See *Croissant v Germany* (1993) 16 E.H.R.R. 135.

[116] *Van Mechelen v Netherlands* (1997) 25 E.H.R.R. 647 at 54.

[117] For discussion see D. Cooper, "Pigot Unfulfilled: Video-recorded Cross-examination under s.28 of the Youth Justice and Criminal Evidence Act 1999" [2005] Crim. L.R. 456.

[118] As suggested in *Speaking Up For Justice*, (London, 1998). On the difficulties of identifying eligible witnesses see M. Burton, R. Evans and A. Sanders, "Implementing Special Measures for Vulnerable and Intimidated Witnesses: The Problem of Identification" [2006] Crim. L.R. 229. The report by D. Cooper and P. Roberts, *Special Measures for Vulnerable and Intimidated Witnesses: An Analysis of Crown Prosecution Service Monitoring Data* (CPS, 2005) shows that some 6,000 witnesses were identified as vulnerable or intimidated in a first-phase 12-month period of operation for special measures; almost three-quarters of those were child witnesses, 15% were vulnerable adults and the remaining 11% intimidated. The success rate for applications for special measures was remarkably high at 98%.

evidence.[119] The second category consists of witnesses suffering from fear or distress in connection with testifying that is likely to diminish the quality of their evidence.[120] The second category thus covers vulnerable adult witnesses who do not come within s.16, including witnesses who are in fear as a result of intimidation.[121] A complainant of a sex offence who is a witness in proceedings relating to that offence is automatically included in the second category unless the witness informs the court of her or his wish not to be so eligible.[122] Similarly a witness in proceedings relating to a "relevant offence" (meaning offences against the person involving guns or knives, as set out in Sch.1A) is automatically eligible for assistance by SMDs unless the witness opts out.[123] The difference between the two categories is that witnesses in the first category will be eligible for a wider range of assistance, namely any of the measures in ss.23–30, whereas witnesses in the second category are eligible for assistance from measures in ss.23–28.[124] The position of the accused, who is excluded from the categories of eligible witnesses under ss.16 and 17, will be dealt with separately after we have examined the provisions of the Act for eligible non-defendant witnesses.

15–021   Section 19 provides the authority to a court to make an SMD. Where a court determines that a witness is eligible for assistance,[125] the court must then determine whether any of the special measures available would, either singly or in combination, be likely to improve the quality of the witness's evidence. If so, the court must then decide which measures would be likely to maximise so far as practicable the quality of the evidence, and make an SMD applying such measure(s) to evidence given by the witness.[126] It should be noted that the court has no discretion to refuse to make an SMD once it has determined that special measures would be likely to improve the quality of the witness's evidence. The scope for "discretion" lies in the initial decisions on whether any special measures, and if so which, would be likely to have this effect. In making these decisions the court must consider all the circumstances of the case, including the witness's own views and the extent to which the measure(s) might inhibit effective testing of the evidence by a party to the proceedings.[127] Once made, an SMD is binding until the relevant proceedings are determined or abandoned.[128] The court may discharge or vary an SMD in the interests of justice of its own motion, or on application by a party, but in the latter case only where there has

---

[119] YJCEA s.16. Witnesses in this category are eligible for a wider range of assistance than witnesses in the second category; see below.

[120] YJCEA s.17.

[121] For a useful discussion of witness intimidation, in the context of non-forensic witness protection schemes, see N. R. Fyfe and H. McKay, "Desperately Seeking Safety: Witnesses' Experiences of Intimidation, Protection and Relocation" (2000) 40 B.J. Crim. 675.

[122] YJCEA s.17(4).

[123] YJCEA s.17(5), added by Coroners and Justice Act 2009 s.99(2).

[124] YJCEA s.18(1).

[125] By virtue of YJCEA s.16 or 17.

[126] YJCEA s.19(2).

[127] YJCEA s.19(3).

[128] YJCEA s.20(1).

been a material change of circumstances since the direction was given or varied previously.[129] A number of other provisions of a procedural nature, relating to the making of an SMD, are set out in s.20.

Child witnesses. Where the eligible witness is a child, the court's decision-making duties under s.19(2) are subject to the special provisions set out in s.21. The original version of s.21 was fearsomely complex, but it has been somewhat simplified by the amendments made by s.100 of the Coroners and Justice Act 2009,[130] and the account here is written on the assumption that those amendments are in force. Essentially the section creates an elaborate structure of decision-making based on the concept of the "primary rule". Even in its amended version s.21 presents a challenge, which is not made any easier by some convoluted drafting.[131]

15–022

The "primary rule" requires the court to give a SMD directing that the child's evidence in chief should be given by way of video-recorded interview (under s.27), and that cross-examination and re-examination should be by way of live link (under s.24). There is no requirement for a finding by the court that the video recording is likely to improve the quality of the child's evidence,[132] although it is reasonable to expect that an interview much nearer the time of the event will produce better evidence from the child. However, the primary rule does not apply where the court is satisfied[133] that compliance would *not* be likely to maximise the quality of the child's evidence.[134] In this case the court must then consider optional SMDs under s.19(2). The court also has power to disapply the primary rule where the child wishes to give oral evidence in chief and/or to testify in the court room rather than using live link.[135] Some older teenagers, for example, might want to take advantage of this possibility. The court must be satisfied that this would not diminish the quality of the child's evidence, having regard to the witness's age and maturity, the witness's ability to understand the consequences of giving evidence in a different way, the relationship (if any) between the witness and the accused, the witness's social and cultural background and ethnic origins, and the nature and alleged circumstances of the offence.[136] If the court does disapply the primary rule under this power it must then direct the use of a

---

[129] YJCEA s.20(2) and (3).

[130] Following a Review Group Consultation Paper, *Improving the Criminal Trial Process for Young Witnesses* (2007), discussed by L. C. H. Hoyano, "The Child Witness Review: Much Ado About Too Little" [2007] Crim. L.R. 849.

[131] See, e.g. YJCEA s.21(4)(ba), which contains four negative propositions. Any court struggling with SMDs, and with s.21 in particular, will get considerable help from L. C. H. Hoyano, "Special Measures Directions Take Two: Entrenching Unequal Access to Justice?" [2010] Crim. L.R. 345), to which I am indebted. Earlier discussions of SMDs include L. C. H. Hoyano, "Variations on a Theme By Pigot: Special Measures Directions for Child Witnesses" [2000] Crim. L.R. 250; J. McEwan, "In defence of vulnerable witnesses: the Youth Justice and Criminal Evidence Act 1999" (2000) 4 E. & P. 1.

[132] The primary rule displaces the court's duty under s.19(2) in relation to child witnesses, so that it is presumed that these measures will have the likely effect of improving the quality of the child's evidence: see s.21(2) and (3), read together.

[133] Presumably on the balance of probabilities.

[134] YJCEA s.21(4)(c).

[135] YJCEA s.21(4)(ba).

[136] YJCEA s.21(4C).

screen for the witness's oral evidence (under s.23), unless the witness does not want it and the court is satisfied that its absence would not diminish the quality of the witness's evidence.[137] The primary rule is subject to the special measures being "available"[138] in relation to the witness, and to a court deciding that a video recording should not be admitted under s.27 in the interests of justice.[139] This might happen, for example, where the court considers that the recording is of poor quality or where the child's answers were given in response to unacceptable leading questions.[140] If the video interview is ruled out, or the special measures are not "available", then the SMD must provide for the child's evidence to be given (at trial) by live link (under s.24).[141] After applying the primary rule the court must then consider under s.19(2) whether any other special measures are likely to improve the quality of the evidence and should therefore be directed.

15–023 *Complainants of sexual offences.* As noted above, adult complainants of sexual offences are eligible for SMDs under s.17 of the YJCEA by virtue of being deemed to be in fear or distress about testifying. This is subject to their wish to decline assistance.[142] Section 22A[143] of the YJCEA further provides that where the trial takes place in the Crown Court, then on an application by a party to the proceedings, a video recorded interview of the complainant is to be (automatically) admissible under s.27, unless the court thinks that it would not be in the interests of justice to admit the recording, or the court is satisfied that compliance would not be likely to maximise the quality of the witness's evidence so far as practicable. In the magistrates' court the position is different in that the prosecution must satisfy the court under s.19(2) that admission of the video recording would be likely to maximise the quality of the witness's evidence. The necessity for the difference is not apparent.[144]

15–024 *Defendants.* Under the original scheme of the YJCEA the accused was and still is expressly excluded from the categories of witness eligible for SMDs under ss.16 and 17.[145] This disqualification raised issues of compatibility with art.6 of the ECHR.[146] First, in relation to child defendants, it was arguable that it infringed the right to participate effectively in the trial.[147] The quality of the child's evidence in his defence might be improved, for example, by being given via a video link[148] or through an intermediary.[149] The non-availability of these

---

[137] YJCEA s.21(4B)(a). The court can also dispense with the use of a screen if satisfied that it would not maximise the quality of the witness's evidence: s.21(4B)(b).

[138] Within the meaning of s.18(2); see s.21(4)(a). On the effect of s.18(2) see *R. v R(SA)* [2008] EWCA Crim 678.

[139] YJCEA s.21(4)(b).

[140] McEwan, "In defence of vulnerable witnesses" (2000) 4 E. & P. 1, 8.

[141] YJCEA s.21(3)(b).

[142] YJCEA s.17(4).

[143] Inserted by Coroners and Justice Act 2009 s.101.

[144] See further L. C. H. Hoyano, "Special Measures Directions Take Two: Entrenching Unequal Access to Justice?" [2010] Crim. L.R. 345.

[145] YJCEA ss.16(1), 17(1), 18(1), 19(1)(a).

[146] D. Birch, "A Better Deal for Vulnerable Witnesses?" [2000] Crim. L.R. 223, 242–243.

[147] *T and V v United Kingdom* (1999) 30 E.H.R.R. 121; Laura C. H. Hoyano, "Striking a Balance between the Rights of Defendants and Vulnerable Witnesses: Will Special Measures Directions Contravene Guarantees of a Fair Trial?" [2001] Crim. L.R. 948, 968).

[148] YJCEA s.24.

measures might in some cases result in a denial to the child of an opportunity to give the best evidence that he or she could. Secondly, if a defendant, whether a child or an adult under disability, cannot have the benefit of such measures but prosecution witnesses can, an issue arises of whether the principle of equality of arms is being properly respected. The European Court of Human Rights takes the view that the principle applies to the presentation of each party's own evidence, so that one party must not be at a substantial disadvantage compared with his opponent.[150]

This position has now been modified in a number of respects. First, s.33A[151] of the YJCEA allows for the use of a live link for the evidence of certain accused persons. The defendants eligible for a live link direction are children under 18 and adults suffering from a mental disorder. In all cases the court must be satisfied that it is in the interests of justice for the accused to give evidence through a live link.[152] If the defendant is under 18 the court must be satisfied that his ability to participate effectively in the proceedings as a witness giving oral evidence in court is compromised by his level of intellectual ability or social functioning, and that use of a live link would enable him to participate more effectively in the proceedings as a witness (whether by improving the quality of his evidence or otherwise).[153] As regards an adult defendant the court can direct use of a live link only if satisfied that the defendant suffers from a mental disorder (within the meaning of the Mental Health Act 1983) or otherwise has a significant impairment of intelligence and social function, that for that reason he is unable to participate effectively in the proceedings as a witness giving oral evidence in court, and that use of a live link would enable him to participate more effectively in the proceedings as a witness (whether by improving the quality of his evidence or otherwise).[154] The court must state its reasons for giving or refusing a live link direction. The meaning of "live link" is set out in s.33B.

Secondly, s.33BA[155] of the YJCEA allows for the use of intermediaries for the examination of certain accused persons. The categories of defendant eligible for this form of assistance are the same as those eligible for the use of a live link, and the conditions for making the direction are the same, except that in the case of intermediaries the court must be satisfied that the direction is necessary to ensure that the accused receives a fair trial. It is quite unclear what the difference is, if any, between this condition and "the interests of justice" condition for the use of a live link for the same categories of defendant.

Thirdly, some of the special measures provided for by the Act, such as the use of screens and the removal of wigs and gowns, were available at common law. The Act places these measures on a statutory footing for the witnesses eligible for them, but the Act does not abolish any inherent powers of the court at common law to control its own procedure. Indeed s.19(6) expressly preserves any power of a court to make an order in the exercise of its inherent jurisdiction in relation to

---

[149] YJCEA s.29.
[150] *Dombo Beheer NV v The Netherlands* (1994) 18 E.H.R.R. 213 at 33; and see Ch.2.
[151] Inserted by Police and Justice Act 2006 s.47.
[152] YJCEA s.33A(2)(b).
[153] YJCEA s.33A(4).
[154] YJCEA s.33A(5).
[155] Inserted by Coroners and Justice Act 2009 s.104, but not yet in force.

a witness who is not an eligible witness. It appears therefore that such common law powers can be used to assist *defendants* who are not eligible for a live link or intermediaries, where the measure in question is likely to improve the quality of their evidence and/or enable them to participate more effectively in the trial.

However, there is some doubt about the extent of the common law powers. It is clearly established that there is a common law power to direct the use of an intermediary for a defendant with communication difficulties.[156] But in *Ukpabio*,[157] the Court of Appeal approved the earlier decision of the Divisional Court in *R. (on the application of S) v Waltham Forest Youth Court*,[158] that there is no power at common law to direct the use of a live link facility for a defendant to give evidence. According to the Court of Appeal in *Ukpabio*, the YJCEA provides a complete statutory scheme for the giving of evidence by video link, being based on the premise that in the absence of the statutory provisions evidence should be given orally by a witness in court "subject to such protective measures short of video link which the court considers to be appropriate to provide such protection as is necessary to ensure that the witness is able to give evidence properly and fully and in particular without fear".[159]

This suggests that the common law power might extend to all the special measures in the YJCEA, except those which change elements of the basic principle that a witness should give oral evidence in the court room. On this basis the common law of assistance to witnesses would not extend to the use of video link, or the admission of video recorded evidence in chief or cross-examination. In *R. (on the application of D) v Camberwell Green Youth Court*,[160] Baroness Hale cited the view of the Court of Appeal in *R. v SH*[161] that the court has wide and flexible inherent powers to ensure that the accused receives a fair trial, and this includes a fair opportunity of giving the best evidence he can. She noted that in that case, where the defendant had learning and communication difficulties, the court could allow him the equivalent of an interpreter to assist with communication. In addition, a detailed written statement could be read to the jury so that they knew what he wanted to say, and he might even be asked leading questions based upon that document, all in an attempt to enable him to give a proper and coherent account.

Baroness Hale's further dictum to the effect that the common law might permit the use of live link for defendants to give evidence in some cases, such as where a younger child defendant is too scared to give evidence in the presence of her co-accused,[162] was not applied in *Ukpabio*.[163] But the matter remains open at the

---

[156] *R. (on the application of C) v Sevenoaks Youth Court* [2009] EWHC 3088 (Admin); *Cox* [2012] EWCA Crim 549; [2012] 2 Cr.App.R. 6. In *Cox*, the Court of Appeal held that where attempts to identify an available intermediary have failed the proceedings do not necessarily have to be stayed. If the defendant is fit to plead it is a decision for the trial judge whether a fair trial can still be held.

[157] *Ukpabio* [2007] EWCA Crim 2108; [2008] 1 Cr.App.R. 6.

[158] *R. (on the application of S) v Waltham Forest Youth Court* [2004] EWHC 715 (Admin); [2004] 2 Cr.App.R. 21.

[159] *Ukpabio* [2007] EWCA Crim 2108 at [14].

[160] *R. (on the application of D) v Camberwell Green Youth Court* [2005] UKHL 4; [2005] 2 Cr.App.R. 1.

[161] *R. v SH* [2003] EWCA Crim 1208.

[162] *R. (on the application of D) v Camberwell Green Youth Court* [2005] UKHL 4; [2005] 2 Cr.App.R. 1 at [63].

level of the Supreme Court, particularly given the disparity of treatment of both child and vulnerable adult defendants compared with child and vulnerable adult witnesses. The conditions of eligibility for special measures are stricter for both categories of defendants.[164] There remains a concern whether the YJCEA scheme is compatible in this respect with art.6; the principle of "equality of arms" would seem clearly to be engaged.[165] If s.41 of the YJCEA can be read down to ensure a fair trial for the defendant, then is the same true for ss.33A and 33BA?

We can now turn to consider the range of special measures available to assist eligible witnesses under the YJCEA scheme.

(A) Use of screens

Under s.23 of the YJCEA an SMD may provide for any eligible witness, while giving testimony or being sworn in court, to be prevented from seeing the accused by means of a screen or other arrangement. The screen must not prevent the witness from seeing, and being seen by, the judge, justices, jury, the legal representatives acting in the proceedings, and any interpreter or other person appointed to assist the witness. The use of screens for child witnesses is likely to be rare in future, as a result of the provisions of s.21, but they may become more common for vulnerable adult witnesses. Their use is unlikely to raise a problem of compatibility with art.6 of the ECHR. As Hoyano has noted,[166] the European Commission of Human Rights approved the use of screens in Northern Ireland to shield intimidated witnesses from the accused, the public and the media.[167]

15–025

It was clear before the YJCEA that a judge has inherent power at common law to vary the physical arrangement of the court. This includes a power to allow witnesses to give their evidence from behind a screen. For example, in *X, Y, Z*,[168] the Court of Appeal approved the use of a screen for child witnesses where the test of "the balance of fairness" is satisfied. This requires the judge to take account not only of the interests of the accused but also the interests of the prosecution and the witnesses. It appears that the power to direct the use of a screen is available in all courts and all types of proceedings.[169] As noted above, this common law power will continue to be available to assist non-eligible witnesses.[170] It is suggested that the use of a screen may be justified where the

---

[163] Although the Court of Appeal did say that the common law could permit the defendant on his own application to *participate* in the trial (other than by giving evidence) via a live link.

[164] See further L. C. H. Hoyano, "Special Measures Directions Take Two: Entrenching Unequal Access to Justice?" [2010] Crim. L.R. 345.

[165] The criticism by the European Court of Human Rights in *SC v United Kingdom* [2004] ECHR 263 of the trial arrangements for a learning-disabled boy of 11 rather confirm the view that the Strasbourg court will rigorously scrutinise a disparity in the assistance available to witnesses and defendants.

[166] Laura C. H. Hoyano, "Striking a Balance between the Rights of Defendants and Vulnerable Witnesses: Will Special Measures Directions Contravene Guarantees of a Fair Trial?" [2001] Crim. L.R. 948, 964.

[167] *X v United Kingdom* (1992) 15 E.H.R.R. CD 113.

[168] *X, Y, Z* (1990) 91 Cr.App.R. 36.

[169] The use of the power in magistrates' courts was officially encouraged by Home Office Circular 61/1990.

[170] Screens can be used to protect witnesses whose identity must be kept secret, such as certain members of the armed forces, the security services and so on.

necessity of trying to ensure that the witness will be able to give evidence outweighs any possible prejudice to the accused by the erection of the screen. The judge should counter any possible prejudice by telling the jury that the screen is there solely to help the witness give evidence, and that they should not allow it to affect their view of the accused.

(B) Live link

15–026 Under s.24 of the YJCEA an SMD may provide for any eligible witness to give evidence by means of a live link.[171] This is a live television link or other arrangement.[172] The witness, while absent from the courtroom, must be able to see and hear a person there and to be seen and heard by the judge, justices, jury, legal representatives, and any interpreter or other person appointed to assist the witness.[173] The direction may now provide for a specified person to accompany the witness while the witness is giving evidence via live link and the court must have regard to the wishes of the witness in determining who the person is to be.[174] This is welcome; the "support person" may increase the quality of the witness's evidence by decreasing anxiety.[175]

The possibility of giving evidence via a live television link was first introduced in 1988 for child witnesses.[176] The procedure has been widely used in cases of physical and sexual abuse of children. It is unclear whether it has had any effect on the conviction rate for such offences, but early research suggested that it may have helped to reduce the stress on some child witnesses.[177] Other research suggested that some prosecutors still preferred the child to be in the courtroom because this was thought to maximise the impact of the child's testimony on the jury.[178] The provisions of s.21 of the YJCEA, discussed above, imply that bringing a child witness back into the courtroom to give evidence will be an exceptional measure.

In *R. v Redbridge Youth Court Ex p. DPP*,[179] Latham L.J. said that in making orders under s.32 of the Criminal Justice Act 1988 (the predecessor to s.24 of the YJCEA) "the court will bear in mind that the paradigm or norm in our courts is that a witness should give evidence in court in the presence of the defendant".[180] It followed that some good reason had to be shown, in accordance with the

---

[171] YJCEA s.24(1).

[172] There is no power in an English court to receive evidence by telephone. The common law principle applies that witnesses must appear in person to give their evidence, except where there are hearsay exceptions and where evidence by video link is permitted: *Diane* [2009] EWCA Crim 1494; [2010] 2 Cr.App.R. 1.

[173] YJCEA s.24(8).

[174] YJCEA s.24(1A) and (1B), inserted by Coroners and Justice Act 2009 s.102(1).

[175] McEwan, "In defence of vulnerable witnesses" (2000) 4 E. & P. 1, 6.

[176] Criminal Justice Act 1988 s.32(1)(b).

[177] G. Davies and E. Noon, *An Evaluation of the Live Link for Child Witnesses* (London, Home Office, 1991).

[178] G. Davis, L. Hoyano, C. Keenan, L. Maitland and R. Morgan, *An Assessment of the Admissibility and Sufficiency of Evidence in Child Abuse Prosecutions* (the "Bristol study") (London, Home Office, 1999), pp.58–60.

[179] *R. v Redbridge Youth Court Ex p. DPP* [2001] 4 All E.R. 411 DC.

[180] *R. v Redbridge Youth Court Ex p. DPP* [2001] 4 All E.R. 411 at 421.

legislative purpose of enabling the child witness to give as full an account as possible of the events in question, for an order to be made under s.32. This approach has been changed for child witnesses by the primary rule contained in s.21(3) of the YJCEA. As discussed above, this *requires* an SMD to provide for a child's evidence to be given by video-recorded interview or live link.[181] However, no such presumptive rule applies for other eligible witnesses. For these witnesses the court must determine whether the use of a live link would be likely to improve the quality of their evidence.[182] To make such a judgment the court is likely to require evidence of how the experience of testifying may affect the witness.[183] In the *Redbridge* case, Latham L.J. envisaged material, such as a statement from the child, that established that "the witness could be upset, intimidated or traumatised by appearing in court as a result of which there was a real risk that the quality of the child's evidence would be affected or that no evidence would be forthcoming". Where the choice for a vulnerable or intimidated adult witness is between testimony in the courtroom and via a live link, material of this kind may be necessary to tip the balance in favour of the live link. Exceptionally, the circumstances of the case, for example a severe disability of the witness and a severe attack on him or her, might justify the relevant inference in the absence of such material.[184]

(C)   Evidence given in private

Under s.25 an SMD may provide for the exclusion from the court, during the witness's evidence, of any person except the accused, the legal representatives acting in the proceedings, and any interpreter or other person appointed to assist the witness.[185] In addition one representative of the media is permitted to remain when the court is cleared pursuant to a direction under this section.[186] This power of exclusion is limited to proceedings related to sexual offences, or where the court has reasonable grounds for believing that someone other than the accused has tried or will try to intimidate the witness.[187]

15–027

The power is an exception to the fundamental principle of public justice, a principle embodied in art.6(1) of the ECHR.[188] However, art.6(1) states in terms

---

[181] Confirmed by the House of Lords in *R. (on the application of D) v Camberwell Green Youth Court* [2005] UKHL 4; [2005] 2 Cr.App.R. 1 at [45]: "It is clear that, by enacting the primary rule and limiting the circumstances in which it may be disapplied, Parliament did not mean to allow defendants to challenge the use of a video recording or live link simply because it is a departure from the normal procedure in criminal trials. There is no question, as there was for live link applications under the old law, of the court striking a balance between the 'right of the defendant to have a hearing in accordance with the norm' and 'the interests not only of the child witness but also of justice, to ensure that the witness will be able to give evidence . . . unaffected by the stress of appearing in court itself'."

[182] YJCEA s.19(2).

[183] Rules of court may provide for expert evidence to be given in connection with the making of an SMD: YJCEA s.20(6)(c).

[184] cf. *R. (on the application of T) v Redbridge Youth Court* [2002] EWHC 414.

[185] YJCEA s.25(1)(2).

[186] YJCEA s.25(3).

[187] YJCEA s.25(4).

[188] The importance of the principle was emphasised in *Riepan v Austria* [2001] Crim. L.R. 230 (trial held in a prison in which the applicant was detained—violation of art.6(1) because the trial was insufficiently publicised to ensure effective public and media access).

that the press and public may be excluded from all or part of the trial where the interests of juveniles require it, or where the protection of the private life of the parties so requires. The latter is apt to cover adult complainants of sexual offences.[189]

(D)   Removal of wigs and gowns

15–028   Under s.26 an SMD may provide for the court to dispense with the wearing of wigs and gowns during the witness's evidence. Almost certainly the court has inherent power to do this, but the YJCEA removes any doubt about the existence of the power. Counsel would presumably have a duty to comply with the terms of a direction providing for removal of wigs and gowns.[190] A direction under this section can be made to assist any eligible witness. There appears to be no problem of compatibility with art.6 in respect of such directions.

(E)   Video-recorded evidence in chief

15–029   Section 27 of the YJCEA provides for the admission in evidence of video recordings of interviews with eligible witnesses. Such a provision had existed in the law since 1992 for child witnesses in certain types of case,[191] but s.27 extended it to all eligible witnesses (as defined by the YJCEA) and to all criminal proceedings. When a direction is made under s.27 it allows a video recording of an interview of the witness to be admitted as the witness's evidence in chief. The recording is regarded as the equivalent of direct oral testimony, so that statements by the witness in the interview are admitted as evidence of any fact stated of which the witness could have given direct oral evidence.[192] The witness must be called by the party adducing the recording in evidence, but may not without the permission of the court be questioned in chief as to any matter that, in the court's opinion, is dealt with in the recorded testimony.[193] After the recording has been shown the witness may be cross-examined; the cross-examination may, and often will, be via a live television link. The court may decline to admit the whole or part of a video-recorded interview if it would not be in the interests of justice to admit it.[194] This power allows for an interview to be edited if it contains, for example, inadmissible material about the accused's bad character. However, the court must consider in such a case whether any prejudice to the accused that might result from that part being admitted is outweighed by the desirability of showing the whole, or substantially the whole, of the recorded interview.[195]

---

[189] See Laura C. H. Hoyano, "Striking a Balance between the Rights of Defendants and Vulnerable Witnesses: Will Special Measures Directions Contravene Guarantees of a Fair Trial?" [2001] Crim. L.R. 948, 967, citing *Hols v Netherlands* (25206/94), ruled inadmissible October 19, 1995, European Commission of Human Rights, approving closure of the court for adult complainants of incest.

[190] cf. McEwan, "In defence of vulnerable witnesses" (2000) 4 E. & P. 1, 12.

[191] The governing provision was s.32A of the Criminal Justice Act 1988, inserted by s.54 of the Criminal Justice Act 1991.

[192] YJCEA s.31(2).

[193] YJCEA s.27(5)(b).

[194] YJCEA s.27(2).

[195] YJCEA s.27(3).

An important factor in the decision whether to refuse to admit a video recording will be the way in which the interview was conducted. It is critical that the interviewer should not ask leading questions and give the child cues as to the answers the interviewer expects, or worse, requires. Concern has been expressed in the past about the use of overzealous interviewing techniques, often involving the use of anatomically correct dolls, in the creation of evidence for forensic use. There is a government memorandum of good practice on the interviewing of child witnesses,[196] and the court will take account of the extent to which the guidelines in the memorandum were followed.[197] The memorandum does not, however, have the force of a Code of Practice. Departures from the guidelines will not necessarily be a ground for quashing a conviction.[198] The prime consideration is the reliability of the videoed evidence. This will normally be assessed by reference to the interview itself, the conditions under which it was held, the age of the child, and the nature and extent of any breach of the interviewing code. Other evidence in the case may help to show that breaches of the code have not had the effect of undermining the credibility or accuracy of the video interview, but such other evidence is not a necessary condition for admitting the video where breaches of the code have occurred.[199]

Where a transcript of the interview is available, the jury may be given copies of it for the purpose of enabling them better to follow the interview. This is a sensible practice as an aid to understanding, particularly in the case of a long interview or where the witness speaks with a strong accent. However, the jury must be told that it is the oral evidence of the child that counts, and the judge should warn them against attaching undue weight to the transcript.[200] Because of the danger that they might give it undue weight, the judge should not normally permit the jury to take the transcript with them when they retire, unless the defence consents.[201] A separate issue is whether a judge should ever permit the video recording to be played a second time after the conclusion of the rest of the evidence. It is easy to see that a jury might want to be reminded of the way in which the child witness spoke, or of the precise terms of the child's evidence, but there is an obvious potential for unfairness in that the jury may be influenced by hearing prosecution evidence repeated when they have heard the defence evidence only once. For this reason the Court of Appeal has said that replaying of the recording is generally to be discouraged, and that the judge should permit it

---

[196] *Achieving Best Evidence in Criminal Proceedings: Guidance for Vulnerable or Intimidated Witnesses, Including Children* ("The Memorandum") (2002); available on the CPS website *http://www.cps.gov.uk* [Accessed January 2013]. This is a non-statutory code that replaced an earlier memorandum from 1992 that, amongst other things, incorporated recommendations made in the Butler-Sloss Report, Cm.412, (1988). The Bristol study (London, 1999, Ch.VII) recommended revision of the earlier Memorandum in response to findings that some of the guidance, or its interpretation, hampered the collection of evidence that might have helped the prosecution case.

[197] *G v DPP* [1997] 2 Cr.App.R. 78 DC.

[198] *Dunphy* (1994) 98 Cr.App.R. 393 CA.

[199] *R. v K* [2006] EWCA Crim 472; [2006] 2 Cr.App.R. 10, explaining some comments of the Divisional Court in *G v DPP* [1997] 2 Cr.App.R.78.

[200] *Springer* [1996] Crim. L.R. 903 CA.

[201] *Welstead* [1996] 1 Cr.App.R. 59 CA. In *Popescu* [2010] EWCA Crim 1230 the Court of Appeal made a stronger pronouncement that a jury should be permitted to retire with a transcript only in exceptional circumstances, such as when the defence positively wants the jury to have the transcript and the judge is satisfied that there are very good reasons why they should have it.

only in exceptional cases.[202] It is not clear what counts as an exceptional case—one may be where the jury specifically requests a replay so that they can study the child's demeanour.[203] Where a replay does take place a number of conditions must be satisfied: it should be in court with judge, counsel and defendant present; the judge should warn the jury about giving the recording undue weight on the basis that they were hearing it a second time after all the other evidence; and the judge should remind the jury from his own notes about the cross-examination and re-examination of the child.[204]

15–030   In *R. (on the application of D) v Camberwell Green Youth Court*,[205] the House of Lords held that the previous version of the primary rule in s.21 of the YJCEA, requiring the admission under s.27 of a video-recorded interview with a child "in need of special protection", in preference to live testimony in the courtroom, did not violate art.6 of the ECHR. In principle, as we have seen, art.6 requires all evidence to be produced in the presence of the accused at a public hearing with a view to adversarial argument.[206] The protection of vulnerable witnesses is a legitimate aim that may justify modification of this principle,[207] provided that any restrictions are proportionate to the aim, and that any handicaps to the defence are sufficiently counterbalanced by the procedures followed by the judicial authorities.[208] Thus the interest in enabling a vulnerable witness to give better evidence, in the form of a contemporaneous account in circumstances conducive to a full account, supports the use of video-recorded interviews.[209] It is clear that the right of the defendant to examine witnesses against him is respected if he has the opportunity to question the witness either when the witness makes the statement or at a later stage in the proceedings.[210] Accordingly the availability of the witness for cross-examination at the trial satisfies art.6 despite the gap in time between the interview and the trial. In the light of these considerations, taken together with the decision and the reasoning in the *Camberwell Green Youth Court* case (above), it would seem that the admission of a video-recorded interview with any eligible witness will not raise problems of compatibility with art.6.

---

[202] *R. v M* [1996] 2 Cr.App.R. 56 CA.

[203] cf. *Rawlings and Broadbent* [1995] 1 W.L.R. 178 CA. See also *Mullen* [2004] 2 Cr.App.R. 18, where the Court of Appeal held that the judge's discretion to allow a replaying of video evidence in exceptional circumstances extended to the evidence of a supporting child witness, provided the balancing direction is given.

[204] *Rawlings and Broadbent* [1995] 1 W.L.R. 178 CA; *R. v M* [1996] 2 Cr.App.R. 56 CA; *R. v W* [2011] EWCA Crim 1142.

[205] *R. (on the application of D) v Camberwell Green Youth Court* [2005] UKHL 4; [2005] 2 Cr.App.R. 1.

[206] *Kostovski v Netherlands* (1989) 12 E.H.R.R. 434.

[207] *Doorson v Netherlands* (1996) 22 E.H.R.R. 330. See also *R. v A (No.2)* [2001] 2 Cr.App.R. 351.

[208] *Van Mechelen v Netherlands* (1997) 25 E.H.R.R. 647.

[209] *R. v Redbridge Youth Court Ex p. DPP* [2001] 4 All E.R. 411 at 420.

[210] *Unterpertinger v Austria* (1991) 13 E.H.R.R. 175; *Kostovski v Netherlands* (1989) 12 E.H.R.R. 434.

(F)   Video-recorded cross-examination

Under s.28 an SMD that provides for a video-recorded interview to be admitted **15–031** as the witness's evidence in chief may also provide for any cross-examination and re-examination of the witness to be video recorded, and for the recording to be admitted as the witness's evidence under cross-examination and on re-examination.[211] The recording must be made in the presence of such persons as rules of court or the direction may provide and in the absence of the accused.[212] The judge or magistrates, and the legal representatives acting in the proceedings, must be able to see and hear the examination of the witness and to communicate with the persons in whose presence the recording is being made. The accused must be able to see and hear the examination and to communicate with his legal representatives.[213] Once the recording has been made further cross-examination is not possible without a further SMD.[214] The court may only give such a further direction if the party seeking it (which will usually be the defence) can show that they have become aware since the recording was made of a matter that they could not have ascertained by reasonable diligence before the time of the recording.[215]

Section 28 thus implements for all eligible witnesses the "full Pigot" scheme originally recommended for child witnesses.[216] Since the cross-examination is under the control of the judicial authorities, and the rights of the defence are respected by ensuring the defendant's effective participation through his ability to communicate with his legal representatives who are conducting the examination, the procedure appears to be compliant with art.6.[217] The right to a fair trial under the ECHR does not imply a right to physical confrontation[218] between witness and defendant, nor does it require the presence of the witness at the trial, provided the defendant has had an opportunity to challenge the witness's evidence.[219]

---

[211] YJCEA s.28(1).

[212] YJCEA s.28(2).

[213] YJCEA s.28(2).

[214] YJCEA s.28(5).

[215] YJCEA s.28(6).

[216] See further McEwan, "In defence of vulnerable witnesses" (2000) 4 E. & P. 1, 9–10; D. Cooper, "Pigot Unfulfilled: Video-recorded Cross-examination under s.28 of the Youth Justice and Criminal Evidence Act 1999" [2005] Crim. L.R. 456 contains a useful review of the Pigot scheme for video-recorded cross-examination and a discussion of the reasons why s.28 is unlikely to be brought into force. These derive from concerns about both the practicality and the fairness of requiring all cross-examination to be conducted in pre-trial proceedings.

[217] Laura C. H. Hoyano, "Striking a Balance between the Rights of Defendants and Vulnerable Witnesses: Will Special Measures Directions Contravene Guarantees of a Fair Trial?" [2001] Crim. L.R. 948, 959.

[218] *R. (on the application of D) v Camberwell Green Youth Court* [2005] UKHL 4; [2005] 2 Cr.App.R. 1. The Strasbourg Court occasionally refers loosely to a lack of "confrontation" as a ground for finding a violation of art.6: see, e.g. *Saidi v France* (1994) 17 E.H.R.R. 251 at 44. See further Ch.16.

[219] See Ch.17 for the position where the witness is not available for cross-examination but their hearsay evidence is admitted in chief via a video recording or written statement.

(G)   Examination of witness through intermediary

15–032   Section 29 introduced a new power into English law. The use of interpreters for witnesses unable to speak English is familiar, but under s.29 an SMD may provide for the use of a different kind of intermediary. This measure is available for witnesses eligible for assistance under s.16, namely children and witnesses with physical or mental disabilities or disorders, and for the categories of defendants specified in s.33BA, discussed above. The direction may provide for the examination of such a witness through an approved interpreter or other person whose function is to explain to the witness the questions being put and to explain to the questioner the witness's answers.[220] Before acting the intermediary must make a declaration, in such form as may be prescribed by rules of court, that he will faithfully perform his function as intermediary.[221] An intermediary may be used in connection with a video-recorded interview under s.27, provided he made the statutory declaration before the interview and was approved by the court before the direction was given.[222] The judge or justices, and the legal representatives acting in the proceedings, must be able to see and hear the examination of the witness and to communicate with the intermediary. Except in the case of a video-recorded examination the jury, if there is one, must be able to see and hear the examination of the witness.[223]

This is a praiseworthy innovation designed to enable very young witnesses, or witnesses with significant learning disability, to give evidence.[224] The practical problems associated with its implementation, relating to the identity, training and accreditation of an intermediary, appear to have been overcome; according to Hoyano, England and Wales are leading the common law world in developing the infrastructure for intermediaries to give effective and impartial assistance to vulnerable witnesses.[225] It is not thought likely that the use of intermediaries will present any problems regarding compliance with art.6. In continental jurisdictions defence questions sometimes have to be put through the investigating judge, a procedure that the European Commission of Human Rights upheld in *Baegen v Netherlands*.[226] In *Cameron*,[227] the Court of Appeal rejected a claim that it was an abuse of process for a trial judge to take over the questioning of a rape

---

[220] YJCEA s.29(1)(2). The explanatory function serves to distinguish a s.29 intermediary from a person, akin to an interpreter, who merely translates the witness's unintelligible replies, as in *Duffy* [1999] Q.B. 919.

[221] YJCEA s.29(5).

[222] YJCEA s.29(6).

[223] YJCEA s.29(3).

[224] In assessing the competence of a witness to give evidence the court shall treat the witness as having the benefit of any SMD that the court has given or proposes to give in relation to the witness: YJCEA s.54(3). Such direction could include the use of an intermediary for a witness eligible under s.16 for assistance. For general discussion see L. Ellison, "Cross-examination and the Intermediary: Bridging the Language Divide?" [2002] Crim. L.R. 114.

[225] L. C. H. Hoyano, "Special Measures Directions Take Two: Entrenching Unequal Access to Justice?" [2010] Crim. L.R. 345. See also J. Plotnikoff and R. Woolfson, "Making the Most of the Intermediary Special Measure at Trial" [2008] Crim. L.R. 91.

[226] *Baegen v Netherlands* (16696/90) (1995) A. 327-B.

[227] *Cameron* [2001] Crim. L.R. 587. The age of the witness was a material fact in this case; the result might have been different had the recalcitrant witness been an adult.

complainant aged 14, on issues identified by defence counsel, when she refused to answer any further questions from counsel.

(H)   Aids to communication

Under s.30 an SMD may provide for a witness, eligible for assistance under s.16, to have such a device while giving evidence as the court considers appropriate with a view to enabling questions or answers to be communicated to or by the witness, despite any disability or disorder of the witness. A specially modified computer, to provide a witness with an artificial voice, where the witness has lost the power of speech, would be an example. It is most unlikely that the use of such devices will present any art.6 problems.

15–033

4.   Anonymity for witnesses[228]

Witness intimidation is a serious problem, particularly in gang-related crime, which often involves the use of firearms.[229] Special measures may not be sufficient to reassure witnesses who are terrified of giving evidence at a trial, either as a result of specific threats by the defendant or his associates or because they fear reprisals generally if they are known to have violated a culture of no co-operation with the authorities. Fearful witnesses are usually witnesses for the prosecution, but the problem is not restricted to them. It is possible that a witness for a co-accused might also be subject to intimidation and wish to give evidence anonymously. A further problem concerns police officers or other law enforcement agents working under cover. Like civilian witnesses they may fear that revealing their identity will expose them to the risk of reprisals. In addition their superiors may wish not to imperil their use for future operations. If their cover were to be blown the authorities might well lose valuable investigators in whom they had invested considerable resources. In this way the public interest in effective criminal justice could be seriously harmed.

15–034

For fearful witnesses there are two possible courses of action available to the prosecution. The first is not to call the witnesses at the trial, but to adduce evidence of their statements to the police, using the hearsay provisions of the Criminal Justice Act 2003. The use of these provisions, and the compatibility of this strategy with art.6 of the ECHR, is considered in Ch.17. This is in any event only a partial answer to the problem, since the witnesses' identities will become known. The alternative is to call the witnesses and to seek an order from the trial judge that their identity should not be revealed. The witnesses would then give

---

[228] See generally J. Doak and R. Huxley-Binns, "Anonymous Witnesses in England and Wales: Charting a Course from Strasbourg" (2009) 73 J. Crim. Law 508; I. Dennis, "Witness Anonymity in the Criminal Process" in J. Chalmers, F. Leverick and L. Farmer (eds), *Essays in Criminal Law in Honour of Sir Gerald Gordon* (Edinburgh UP, 2010), Ch.14; D. Ormerod, A. Choo and R. Easter, "Coroners and Justice Act 2009: The 'Witness Anonymity' and 'Investigation Anonymity' Provisions" [2010] Crim. L.R. 368.

[229] See the remarks of Sir Igor Judge P. in *Davis, Ellis* [2006] EWCA Crim 1155; [2006] 2 Cr.App.R. 32 at [8]–[10].

their evidence anonymously. Until the decision of the House of Lords in *Davis*,[230] it was assumed that there was an inherent power in the courts at common law to grant anonymity to witnesses in appropriate cases, and a growing practice of doing so had developed.[231] However, in *Davis* the House of Lords put an abrupt stop to the practice, holding that anonymity was contrary to the long-established right of a defendant at common law to confront witnesses against him.[232] It was held that where the testimony of an anonymous witness constituted the sole or decisive evidence for conviction its use amounted to an unlawful constraint at common law on the conduct of the defence and also constituted a violation of the right to a fair trial under art.6 of the ECHR. Following this decision it was unclear when, if ever, anonymity could lawfully be granted. Consequently Parliament hastily passed temporary legislation to restore legality to orders for witness anonymity[233]; that legislation was subsequently replaced by virtually identical provisions in the Coroners and Justice Act 2009.

15–035 The purpose of the Coroners and Justice Act 2009 is to provide statutory authority for the making of orders to secure the anonymity of witnesses in criminal proceedings. To that end s.86(1) empowers a court to make an order that requires such specified measures to be taken in relation to a witness as the court considers appropriate to ensure that the identity of the witness is not disclosed. These measures include, but are not restricted to, withholding the witness's name and other identifying details, the use of a pseudonym, a ban on questions that might lead to the identification of the witness, screening of the witness, and the use of voice modulation technology. Screening must still enable the witness to be seen by judge and jury, and voice modulation must still allow the witness's natural voice to be heard by judge and jury.

Section 88 of the Act provides for three conditions to be satisfied before a witness anonymity order can be made.[234] Condition A is that the order must be necessary to protect the safety of the witness or another person or to prevent serious damage to property, or to prevent "real harm to the public interest" (s.88(3)).[235] Condition B is that, having regard to all the circumstances, the effect of the proposed order would be consistent with the defendant receiving a fair trial (s.88(4)). Condition C is that the importance of the witness's testimony must be

---

[230] *Davis* [2008] UKHL 36; [2008] 3 All E.R. 461. For a critique of the decision see I. Dennis, "Witness Anonymity in the Criminal Process" in J. Chalmers, F. Leverick and L. Farmer (eds), *Essays in Criminal Law in Honour of Sir Gerald Gordon* (Edinburgh UP, 2010).

[231] The practice was reviewed by the Court of Appeal in *Davis, Ellis* [2006] EWCA Crim 1155; [2006] 2 Cr.App.R. 32.

[232] On the meaning and importance of this right see Ch.16.

[233] Criminal Evidence (Witness Anonymity) Act 2008, replaced with effect from January 1, 2010 by Ch.2 of Pt 3 of the Coroners and Justice Act 2009. Section 1(2) of the 2008 Act abolished the common law rules relating to the power of a court to make an order for the anonymity of a witness in criminal proceedings. The legislation should be read together with the guidelines issued by the Attorney-General, *The Prosecutor's Role in Applications for Witness Anonymity Orders* (2008), and by the Director of Public Prosecutions, *Guidance on Witness Anonymity* (2008). See also the *Practice Direction* [2010] 2 Cr.App.R. 6, and Pt 29 of the Criminal Procedure Rules 2012 (SI 2012/1726).

[234] The judge need not give in open court the reasons for making the order: *Chisholm* [2010] EWCA Crim 258.

[235] The concept of harm to the public interest will cover the danger that revealing the identity of police undercover officers will jeopardise their utility for future operations as well as their safety.

such that in the interests of justice the witness ought to testify and the witness would not testify if the proposed order were not made, or there would be real harm to the public interest if the witness were to testify without the proposed order being made (s.88(5)). In deciding on the first of these conditions the court must have regard to any reasonable fear on the part of the witness that if the witness were identified the witness or another person would suffer death or injury or there would be serious damage to property (s.88(6)). In *Chisholm*,[236] the Court of Appeal held that it would be enough to satisfy Condition A that the witness had a real and reasonable fear for their own safety; if such a fear existed the court would not then have to decide objectively that the witness's safety would in fact be jeopardised without the anonymity order. However, the witness's fear does have to be a reasonable fear for their safety if their identity is revealed. Where the defendant is already aware of the witness's identity, an order for anonymity cannot be necessary.[237]

The court is further directed by s.89 to have regard to a number of "relevant considerations" in deciding whether the three conditions are met. These considerations are expressed to be:

(a)   the general right of a defendant in criminal proceedings to know the identity of a witness in the proceedings;

(b)   the extent to which the credibility of the witness concerned would be a relevant factor when the weight of his or her evidence comes to be assessed;

(c)   whether evidence given by the witness might be the sole or decisive evidence implicating the defendant;

(d)   whether the witness's evidence could be properly tested (whether on grounds of credibility or otherwise) without his or her identity being disclosed;

(e)   whether there is any reason to believe that the witness has a tendency to be dishonest, or has any motive to be dishonest in the circumstances of the case, having regard to any previous convictions of the witness, and to any relationship between the witness and the defendant or any associates of the defendant;

(f)   whether it would be reasonably practicable to protect the witness's identity by any means other than by making a witness anonymity order.

These considerations go primarily to the fair trial condition since they mostly concern the importance of the witness's evidence, its likely reliability, and the defendant's ability to challenge it. It seems to follow from the considerations that the Act would not change the result in a case such as *Davis*. Where as in that case the evidence of the identification witnesses to a fatal shooting is potentially decisive, and the defendant would be hampered significantly by anonymity orders in conducting a defence that the witnesses in question had been put up to give false testimony against him, he would not receive a fair trial and the

---

[236] *Chisholm* [2010] EWCA Crim 258.
[237] *Willett* [2011] EWCA Crim 2710.

anonymity orders could not therefore be validly made.[238] The same applies where a witness may have a motive for falsely incriminating the defendant.[239] Given the importance attached by the European Court of Human Rights to the "sole or decisive evidence" principle,[240] it is highly unlikely[241] that the court would not find a violation of art.6 if anonymity is granted where the essence of the defence is a frontal attack on the credibility of the identifying prosecution witnesses. Such a defence is virtually impossible to conduct if the identities of the witnesses are withheld.

15–036 Certain principles concerning the operation of the statutory power are beginning to emerge from the case-law. The leading authority is *Mayers*,[242] the first case under the 2008 Act to reach the Court of Appeal. First, the operation of the power is not to be restricted to cases where the evidence is of largely formal significance.[243] There is nothing in the wording of the Act to support such an approach, and in *Mayers* Lord Judge C.J. suggested to the contrary that an anonymity order should not be made unless the oral testimony is potentially important.[244] Secondly, in *Powar and Powar* the Court of Appeal rejected a submission that witness anonymity orders should be confined to cases of specific types of crime, such as terrorism or gangland killings.[245] Thirdly, however, in *Mayers* Lord Judge C.J. described a witness anonymity order as a new statutory special measure, and, having referred to the ancient principle that the defendant is entitled to know the identity of the witnesses who incriminate him, said that it should be regarded as "the special measure of last practicable resort".[246] The

---

[238] The *Guidance on Witness Anonymity*, issued to the CPS by the Director of Public Prosecutions, comments that where it is clear that the credibility of a witness may be in issue, and the witness's evidence remains the sole or decisive evidence, it is unlikely that the defendant will be able effectively to cross-examine an anonymised witness.

[239] As in *Donovan* [2012] EWCA Crim 2749, a case of robbery and violent disorder where two identifying eyewitnesses claimed to know the defendants well, but material in their statements raised questions as to their objectivity and impartiality. The Court of Appeal quashed the convictions because the anonymity orders had prevented the defendants from cross-examining the witnesses on their motives.

[240] *Al-Khawaja and Tahery v United Kingdom* (2012) 54 E.H.R.R. 23. See further Ch.17, where the Strasbourg principle, and its reception in England, is discussed.

[241] Even if the evidence of an anonymous witness were "decisive", that would not mean that the making of the order would be unlawful: *Chisholm* [2010] EWCA Crim 258, citing the judgment of the Supreme Court in *Horncastle* [2009] UKSC 14; [2010] 2 All E.R. 359.

[242] *Mayers* [2008] EWCA Crim 2989; [2009] 1 W.L.R. 1915.

[243] As in *Murphy and Maguire* [1990] N.I. 306, a case concerning an anonymity order at common law for television journalists identifying certain TV footage of an incident involving the murder of two army corporals in Belfast. The evidence of the journalists did not itself implicate the defendants and the credibility of the journalists was not in issue. In *Davis* [2008] UKHL 36, the House of Lords approved the decision upholding the order, although Lord Brown thought it came close to the limits to which the court should go in permitting invasion of the right to confrontation.

[244] *Mayers* [2008] EWCA Crim 2989; [2009] 1 W.L.R. 1915 at [26]. See also [13], where Lord Judge C.J. envisages that anonymous witnesses may give *crucial* incriminating evidence.

[245] *Powar and Powar* [2009] EWCA Crim 594; [2009] 2 Cr.App.R. 8 at [63].

[246] *Mayers* [2008] EWCA Crim 2989; [2009] 1 W.L.R. 1915 at [4], [8]. However, the figures cited in the article by Ormerod, Choo and Easter, "Coroners and Justice Act 2009" [2010] Crim. L.R. 368, for successful applications for anonymity orders in the first 6 months of the 2008 Act (129 orders granted out of 135 applications) do not suggest that the orders will rarely be used. It is worth noting that two thirds of the successful applications involved police witnesses.

special measures he had in mind were those under the YJCEA, discussed above. These should be considered first as a a means of protecting the fearful witness, before an anonymity order is considered. As regards other measures the court in *Mayers* dismissed a submission that witness relocation would normally provide a practicable alternative to an anonymity order. Quite apart from the obvious resource problem, there is the objection that relocation is disruptive and unfair to the witnesses and their families who are cut off from their roots and compelled to start new lives.[247] Moreover relocation may not be effective in concealing witnesses' identities where the community from which they are removed is small and close-knit, so that their sudden departure is apparent.

In *Mayers,* Lord Judge C.J. suggested that the "most helpful" approach in deciding whether to grant an anonymity order would be to address conditions C and A first.[248] There is an obvious common sense to this suggestion, in that if the order is not *necessary* for the purposes of either condition then it should not be granted, and its effect on the fairness of the defendant's trial does not need to be considered. The danger with this approach is that the fair trial condition comes to be seen simply as a possible constraint on the grant of an order that appears to be necessary in the interests of justice. In this way the defendant's rights of confrontation and challenge of the witnesses against him may be downgraded to a kind of secondary status; the necessity for the order becomes the primary consideration and will generate a presumption in favour of the order. This danger is heightened by the fact that the "relevant considerations" in s. 89 are stated as a list; neither the defendant's right to know the identity of the witness nor the right to properly test the evidence of the witness is assigned any priority or special weight. These rights thus appear to be negotiable as part of a context-specific balancing exercise which takes account of a large number of factors. This is undesirable in principle; rights thought to be essential elements of a fair trial should not be treated as freely tradeable. Their importance suggests they should attract some form of presumptive priority. However, this is not to say that either of the rights should be overriding. Nor should we claim that the "sole or decisive evidence" principle, which is another of the relevant considerations, should be given any overriding importance. Rather, as will be argued in Ch.17, the fair trial condition should be regarded as mandating a proportionality inquiry. The court should ask whether an anonymity order is justified as a proportionate restriction on the defendant's right under art.6 to examine witnesses against him. To structure the question in this way would assign primary value to the defendant's right; consequently good justifying reasons for limiting it would have to be found. The necessity for the order would be one good reason, but it would be one element in the overall calculation of proportionality. It is suggested that this approach puts the emphasis in the right place and would be preferable.

15–037

Four final matters should be noted. First, under s.90, where a witness gives evidence anonymously in a jury trial, the judge must give the jury an appropriate warning to ensure that the anonymity of the witness does not prejudice the defendant. Secondly, the DPP's *Guidance on Witness Anonymity* makes clear that

---

[247] *Mayers* [2008] EWCA Crim 2989; [2009] 1 W.L.R. 1915 at [9].
[248] *Mayers* [2008] EWCA Crim 2989; [2009] 1 W.L.R. 1915 at [26], [29]. This approach was followed by the Court of Appeal in *Powar and Powar* [2009] EWCA Crim 594; [2009] 2 Cr.App.R. 8.

the prosecution has an "absolute duty" to provide the defence with as much information as possible—commensurate with a grant of anonymity—to enable the defendant effectively to cross-examine the anonymous witness. In *Mayers,* Lord Judge C.J. emphasised that the prosecution must be proactive in its duty of disclosure, "focusing closely on the credibility of the anonymous witness and the interests of justice".[249] Thirdly, the Act makes no formal provision for the appointment of special counsel to protect the defendant's interests where an application for an anonymity order is made at an ex parte hearing. The Government resisted attempts to add such a provision to both the 2008 and the 2009 Acts.[250] However, as the Attorney-General's *Guidelines for Prosecutors* make clear, it is always open to the court to request the Attorney-General to appoint special counsel in the exceptional circumstances set out by Lord Bingham in the House of Lords in *R. v H and C*.[251] This might be appropriate, for example, where considerations of public interest immunity might prevent full disclosure of matters going to the witness's credibility. Fourthly, it has been said that there is no power under the legislation for anonymity orders, or under the Criminal Justice Act 2003, to admit anonymous hearsay evidence.[252] This is debatable; it will be argued in Ch. 17 that certain hearsay exceptions in the 2003 Act may have the effect of permitting some anonymous hearsay statements to be admissible.

C. SUSPECT WITNESSES

15–038   A party to legal proceedings might challenge the testimony of a witness against him on any number of grounds, but ultimately these all boil down to one or other of two basic questions[253]: Is the witness lying?; and Is the witness mistaken? Any witness can be said to be "suspect" whose evidence about the facts in issue, or about relevant evidentiary facts, is challenged on the basis that there is a plausible reason for regarding his evidence as lying or mistaken. The reason may be some attribute personal to the witness, such as a particular motive for lying or some perceptual disorder. Alternatively the reason may be some risk that evidence of that type is thought to have generally, such as the risk that eyewitness identifications may be unreliable.

Where a witness is suspect in this sense there is a clear risk of error in the evaluation of the witness's evidence. The factfinder may be deceived by a lie or misled by a mistake. This may in turn lead to decisions that are factually inaccurate and hence illegitimate. In criminal cases wrongful convictions may result. The question for the law of evidence is what measures, if any, should be

---

[249] *Mayers* [2008] EWCA Crim 2989; [2009] 1 W.L.R. 1915 [12]. So, e.g.in *Nazir* [2009] EWCA Crim 213 the prosecution disclosed that the anonymous witness was an illegal immigrant as a matter relevant to her credibility.

[250] See Ormerod, Choo and Easter, "Coroners and Justice Act 2009" [2010] Crim. L.R. 368.

[251] *R. v H and C* [2004] 2 A.C. 134.

[252] *Mayers* [2008] EWCA Crim 2989; [2009] 1 W.L.R. 1915 at[113]; *Horncastle* [2009] UKSC 14; [2010] 2 All E.R. 359 at Annexe 4 [13]; *Ford* [2010] EWCA Crim 2250.

[253] This is leaving aside questions of what inferences are to be drawn from a witness's evidence and the strength of any such inferences. These may depend on the view that is taken of the witness's credibility and reliability, but can arise even where a witness is accepted as honest and accurate.

taken against the risk of error from accepting the evidence of suspect witnesses.[254] There are numerous possibilities. These vary in generality from evidential rules of universal application in all adjudicative proceedings, to rules relating to particular types of witness or particular types of evidence, to rules designed to respond to the circumstances of individual cases. The choice of measure is itself influenced by a range of factors: historical tradition,[255] institutional structure,[256] legal and social culture,[257] the nature and degree of the perceived risk of error, and extraneous policy considerations. We will look briefly at the various possible strategies before considering special cases in the modern law.

1.   *Rules of competence*

One technique for dealing with suspect witnesses is to provide that certain classes of person are not competent to give evidence at all. It might be argued that if factfinders are not exposed to evidence from dubious sources there is much less likelihood of them making errors in evaluation. At one time English law adopted this technique quite extensively. Rules of competence disqualified several types of important potential witnesses, including the parties to the proceedings.[258] The main problems with this technique are that it is over-inclusive, unfair and counter-productive. It is over-inclusive in the sense that it presumes that the witness is suspect from the fact that the witness has a particular formal status, and incompetence is founded on that status. It is unable to take account of variations between cases, or of factors pointing to the reliability of individual witnesses within the excluded class. It is unfair in the sense that it deprives interested persons from participation in the process of decision-making and may leave them with a sense of grievance. It is counter-productive in the sense that it deprives the factfinder of important evidence from those who may know most about the matter under inquiry. It may thus reduce rather than promote the chances of the factfinder arriving at the correct decision on the facts. The violation of the process value of participation in the decision-making may detract from the legitimacy of the decision.

These arguments, as developed at length by Bentham and others, led to the abandonment of the disqualifying rules of competence in the 19th century. The

15–039

---

[254] For theoretical discussion of the problem of allocating the risk of error in adjudicative factfinding see A. Stein, "The Refoundation of Evidence Law" (1996) IX *Canadian Journal of Law & Jurisprudence* 279, and the argument developed further in his *Foundations of Evidence Law* (2005).

[255] There is a broad historical divergence between common law and continental systems on the requirements of proof in legal proceedings. In the early modern period continental procedure was dominated by the quantitative system of formal proofs ("full" and "fractional" proofs) derived from Roman law. See further J. Stone (rev. W.A.N. Wells), *Evidence: Its History and Policies* (1991), pp.13–14. In this period the common law adopted a more eclectic approach founded on a general principle of examining the quality of the evidence, tempered by class-based exceptions for the incompetency of certain witnesses and a few cases where a plurality of evidence was required.

[256] Particularly the division of function between judge and jury in English law, whereby the evaluation of evidence is regarded as the province of the jury.

[257] e.g. the development of feminism has had important effects on a number of evidential rules relating to complainants in cases of sexual offences.

[258] For a brief summary of these rules see Ch.13.

modern approach is to allow any witness with relevant evidence to give to be heard unless the witness is actually unintelligible.[259]

2. *Exclusionary rules and/or exclusionary discretion*

15–040   Two alternatives to rules of competence for certain witnesses are exclusionary rules and/or exclusionary discretion for certain types of evidence. An exclusionary rule might be considered appropriate for evidence that is thought to present systemic risks of unreliability such that it would be unsafe to give factfinders a free hand in its evaluation. It is arguable that the rule against hearsay is founded on this basis,[260] and it has been suggested that prohibiting adverse inferences from the accused's silence in police interviews would be at least partly justified on the same basis.[261] A number of factors militate against the widespread use of exclusionary rules. First, like rules of competency, they deprive factfinders of relevant evidence that *may* be of considerable probative value. Thus, while they may eliminate errors against the party invoking the rule, they necessarily create the possibility of error against the party who would have adduced the excluded evidence. Secondly, developing this point, exclusionary rules tend to produce complexity and technicality in the law. This is because of the need to make exceptions to the rules where the evidence has circumstantial guarantees of reliability and it is the best available evidence. The numerous exceptions to the hearsay rule provide a good example. Thirdly, exclusionary rules reveal a mistrust of the ability of factfinders to do their jobs properly. This lack of confidence in tribunals of fact is most noticeable in common law jurisdictions that use lay factfinders in the form of juries and magistrates. It is in these jurisdictions that we tend to find the greatest concentration of exclusionary rules. In proceedings where factfinding is assigned to professional judges there tends to be less enthusiasm for rules that exclude whole categories of evidence.[262] The case for exclusionary rules is also weakened where perceptions of the abilities of lay factfinders change due to better education or training. However, changing perceptions of factfinding abilities will not affect rules whose rationale is based largely on the need to safeguard the moral authority of verdicts, such as the rule excluding confessions obtained by oppression.

In English law there has been an increasing tendency in recent years to rely on exclusionary discretion as a means of dealing with concerns about the reliability of evidence in individual cases. Discretion can be used equally to respond to evidence that may carry significant risks of impairing the moral authority of the verdict. While the use of discretion can avoid some of the complexity and technicality associated with exclusionary rules, in the view of some it replaces

---

[259] The rule of competence for all witnesses in criminal proceedings laid down by s.53 of the YJCEA, discussed in Ch.13.
[260] See the discussion of the rationale of the hearsay rule in Ch.16.
[261] See Ch.5.
[262] The attrition of the rules of evidence in civil cases in England is a striking example of this tendency.

those problems with others of inconsistency and uncertainty in its exercise.[263] Its exercise may, as in the case of exclusionary rules, display a mistrust of the competence of the factfinder to evaluate the suspect evidence.

3. *A general requirement of corroboration for all evidence*

Corroboration simply means evidence that supports or confirms other evidence.[264] The concept does, however, have strong and weak versions. The strong version of corroboration denotes supporting evidence that is independent of the witness to be corroborated and that itself tends to implicate the accused in the commission of the offence charged.[265] The weak version denotes any supporting evidence that tends to confirm that the witness requiring corroboration is telling the truth. An example of the difference is a complaint made by a rape victim shortly after the commission of the rape. The fact of the complaint tends to confirm that the witness is telling the truth when she testifies that she did not consent to intercourse, but it is not corroboration in the strong sense because it is not independent of the complainant.

15–041

English law has never adopted a general requirement of corroboration in either sense of the term. The general principle has been that the evidence of one credible and reliable witness is sufficient to support a finding of fact, even a finding of guilt of a criminal offence beyond reasonable doubt. The obligation on a witness to take the oath is intended to provide some guarantee of credibility, while the forensic tests of demeanour and cross-examination provide means of estimating the degree to which it is safe to act on the witness's evidence. This approach is underpinned by the general epistemological assumption that factfinders have a sufficient degree of cognitive competence and consensus to evaluate evidence correctly. On this theory the risk of error is in general distributed by the burden and standard of proof. As discussed in Ch.11, the higher standard of proof required in criminal proceedings represents a weighting of the seriousness of wrongful conviction as compared to wrongful acquittal. It follows that for English law measures to deal with suspect witnesses have always had an exceptional quality. They have been thought to require particular justification showing why it is necessary to depart from the general principles of evaluation of witness evidence. Scots law, by contrast, has adopted a general principle that corroboration of evidence is required for adjudicative findings of fact.[266] The weak version of corroboration is employed for this purpose because it is facts, not witnesses as such, that have to be corroborated. Therefore it is not a necessary condition of confirming evidence that it should be independent of the witness who provides the main source of evidence, as long as it tends to confirm the evidence that the witness has given.

---

[263] This is something that particularly concerned the Law Commission in its consideration of whether to replace the hearsay rule and its exceptions with a general discretion either to include or exclude hearsay. See the discussion of hearsay in Chs 16 and 17.

[264] *DPP v Hester* [1973] A.C. 296 at 325 HL per Lord Morris.

[265] *Baskerville* [1916] 2 K.B. 658 CCA.

[266] M. Ross and J. Chalmers, *Walker and Walker: The Law of Evidence in Scotland,* 3rd edn (2009) paras 5.1-5.2. See further P. Duff, "The Requirement for Corroboration in Scottish Criminal Cases: One Argument Against Retention" [2012] Crim. L.R. 513.

4. *Corroboration requirements for certain types of evidence*

15–042   A fifth technique is to impose corroboration requirements on an exceptional basis for particular types of evidence. The requirement might take the form of a condition precedent to conviction, so that no one could be convicted of a particular offence on the evidence of one witness alone, or of any offence on a particular type of evidence such as an uncorroborated confession. Alternatively the requirement might take the form of a mandatory judicial warning to the jury that it would be dangerous to convict on certain evidence without corroboration (in the strong sense), coupled with an explanation of what evidence could or could not be corroborative on the facts of the case. The second form would have much the same effect in practice as the first, with the difference that the jury would have the option of convicting if, having heard the warning, they were convinced that it was safe to act on the evidence in question despite an absence of corroboration.

Both forms of this technique have been used in English law in the past, but almost all such requirements have suffered the same fate as the old rules of competency and for very similar reasons. There are now very few cases where corroboration is a legal requirement, and none where a judge is required to give a corroboration warning. The proposed introduction of new corroboration requirements for certain types of case has been rejected on several occasions in recent years. The most recent was the response of the Royal Commission on Criminal Justice[267] to calls for a corroboration requirement for disputed confessions.[268] The majority of the Commission accepted the case for an additional safeguard against conviction on a false confession, but was not persuaded that more was required than a strong warning of the need for care before convicting on the basis of the confession alone. There remains a good case for the introduction of such a warning requirement, but to date no legislation has implemented this recommendation and the courts have shown no inclination to give effect to it.

5. *Caution warnings*

15–043   The sixth technique is essentially a less formal and less technical version of the fifth. It requires the judge to warn the jury to proceed with caution in view of the reasons why the evidence may be suspect. If the reasons are generally applicable to evidence of that type, as in the case of eyewitness identifications, the judge should explain the reasons for caution. If the defence have offered particular reasons in the case the judge should remind the jury of those as part of the judicial duty to present the defence fairly to the jury. The judge may, and sometimes must, advise the jury to look for supporting evidence before acting on the suspect evidence. The terms and strength of the direction are otherwise within

---

[267] RCCJ Report Ch.4 para.4.77.
[268] For discussion of this possible safeguard against wrongful conviction on confession evidence see A. Choo, "Confessions and Corroboration: a Comparative Perspective" [1991] Crim. L.R. 867; R. Pattenden, "Should Confessions be Corroborated?" (1991) 107 L.Q.R. 317; P. Mirfield, *Silence, Confessions and Improperly Obtained Evidence* (1997), pp.345–352.

the judge's discretion, and the Court of Appeal will be reluctant to interfere. The main differences from the old strict corroboration warnings are as follows. First, the judge is not obliged to tell the jury that it would be dangerous to convict on the suspect evidence without corroboration. Secondly, the judge is not required to itemise the evidence that could or could not be corroborative. Supporting evidence is a looser notion than corroboration in the strong sense. In principle any evidence that tends to confirm the truth of the suspect evidence will do, although the judge is obliged to explain the conditions under which adverse inferences can be drawn against the accused from certain items of circumstantial evidence.

The use of caution warnings has become the preferred technique of both the courts and Parliament in recent years. This is in line with the more general move in the law of evidence away from strict rules of evidence, with limited categories of exception, to more flexible principles that give substantially greater discretion to trial judges both as to the evidence they admit and to how they direct juries on its evaluation. In the light of this general summary we can now turn to examine the modern law dealing with suspect witnesses.

6. *Statutory requirements*

There is a very small number of statutory provisions that effectively require corroboration as a matter of law as a condition of conviction for certain offences. These provisions are set out below. This list used to be longer, but there are now only three provisions that require consideration. **15–044**

(A) *Perjury*

Section 13 of the Perjury Act 1911 provides: **15–045**

> "A person shall not be liable to be convicted of any offence against this Act, or of any offence declared by any other Act to be perjury or subornation of perjury, or to be punishable as perjury or subornation of perjury, solely upon the evidence of one witness as to the falsity of any statement alleged to be false."

The section does not use the word "corroboration", but it has been held to impose a legal requirement of corroboration.[269] There must be evidence to go to the jury of more than one witness as to the falsity of the perjured statement. Such evidence may be that of another witness or witnesses, or it may be some other supporting evidence amounting to corroboration, such as a confession. A business documentary record could provide the necessary corroboration of a witness as to the falsity of the perjured statement, but it must be independent of the witness and not prepared by him.[270]

In *Hamid and Hamid*,[271] Lawton L.J. said that the justification for this requirement is that in many cases the person proving the falsity of the statement is connected with the accused and may have a motive for giving untrue testimony

---

[269] *Hamid and Hamid* (1979) 69 Cr.App.R. 324 CA; *Carroll* (1994) 99 Cr.App.R. 381 CA.
[270] *Cooper* [2010[EWCA Crim 979.
[271] *Hamid and Hamid* (1979) 69 Cr.App.R. 324 CA.

against the accused. This argument envisages therefore the possible use as a Crown witness of an accomplice of the accused or at least of a person with something to gain by falsely incriminating the accused. Such a justifying argument is no longer tenable in the light of *Beck*,[272] and of the abolition of the common law rule concerning the mandatory direction regarding corroboration of accomplices (see below). An alternative justification is suggested by Cross and Tapper that the requirement encourages witnesses to testify because it inhibits possible prosecutions for perjury:

> "nothing must be allowed to discourage witnesses from testifying, and the fact that a conviction for perjury might be secured on the oath of one witness could have this effect."[273]

This is unconvincing. Witnesses may be reluctant to give evidence for many reasons, of which intimidation and the fear of reprisals are almost certainly the most common. One doubts whether one witness in a thousand is even aware of the corroboration requirement, and the number of potential witnesses who would regard it as a determining factor in their decision to testify must be minute. The truth is that this corroboration requirement no longer has a plausible justification and could be scrapped without loss.

(B) Speeding

15–046   Section 89(1) of the Road Traffic Regulation Act 1984 creates the offence of speeding, which consists of driving a motor vehicle on a road at a speed exceeding a prescribed limit. Subsection (2) provides:

> "A person prosecuted for such an offence shall not be liable to be convicted solely on the evidence of one witness to the effect that, in the opinion of the witness, the person prosecuted was driving the vehicle at a speed exceeding a specified limit."

This provision has not been held in terms to require corroboration, but the effect of the decisions concerning the subsection is that the opinion of the witness (invariably a police officer) must be supported by other evidence that will amount to corroboration. Such supporting evidence may take a variety of forms: a second opinion from another witness concerning the vehicle's speed at the same time and place[274]; a confirmation of the opinion by the speedometer reading of a police car following the accused[275]; or a foundation for the opinion by real evidence such as skid marks or damage sustained in a collision. In the last of these, a different type of opinion is involved. It is not an opinion based on a direct observation of the vehicle at the time of the offence, but is an expert's opinion based on a post-accident reconstruction.[276]

The provision has an obvious justification in the likely unreliability of one person's estimate of the speed of a moving object such as a car. In practice the

---

[272] *Beck* [1982] 1 W.L.R. 461 CA.
[273] Cross and Tapper, p.280.
[274] See *Brighty v Pearson* [1938] 4 All E.R. 127 DC.
[275] *Nicholas v Penny* [1950] 2 K.B. 466 DC.
[276] See *Crossland v DPP* [1988] 3 All E.R. 712 DC.

great majority of cases of speeding are proved by reliable evidence from mechanical devices such as radar guns and automatic cameras.

(C)   Attempts to commit either of the above

Under s.2(2)(g) of the Criminal Attempts Act 1981, all "provisions whereby a person may not be convicted . . . on the uncorroborated evidence of one witness (including any provision requiring the evidence of not less than two credible witnesses)" apply also to attempts to commit the offences in question.

15–047

7.   Abolition of common law requirements

The common law developed "rules of practice" whereby trial judges were required to warn juries that it was dangerous to convict on the evidence of certain types of witness without corroboration. These types of witness were accomplices of the accused testifying for the prosecution, complainants of sexual offences, and children giving sworn evidence. The law relating to these mandatory corroboration warnings was complex, technical and much criticised.[277] Parliament abolished the warning requirement for children in s.34(2) of the Criminal Justice Act 1988, and for accomplices and complainants in s.32(1) of the Criminal Justice and Public Order Act 1994. This provides:

15–048

> "Any requirement whereby at a trial on indictment it is obligatory for the court to give the jury a warning about convicting the accused on the uncorroborated evidence of a person merely because that person is—
> (a)   an alleged accomplice of the accused, or
> (b)   where the offence charged is a sexual offence, the person in respect of whom it is alleged to have been committed, is hereby abrogated."[278]

The section thus abolished the duty to give a warning based on the witness's formal status as an accomplice of the accused or as a complainant of a sexual offence. The Act gave no further guidance on when, if ever, it would be appropriate for a trial judge to give a corroboration warning as a matter of discretion, or on how challenges to the credibility of accomplices and complainants should be dealt with in future.[279]

The Court of Appeal considered these issues, soon after the section came into force, in *Makanjuola*.[280] Lord Taylor C.J. reviewed the policy of the Act and held that its aim was to remove the special status the common law attached to these witnesses as presumptively unreliable. Such witnesses were to be treated in future

---

[277] See Law Com. No.202, *Corroboration of Evidence in Criminal Trials* (1991); RCCJ Report, Ch.8, para.35; I. Dennis, "Corroboration Requirements Reconsidered" [1984] Crim. L.R. 316; D. J. Birch, "Corroboration in Criminal Trials: a Review of the Law Commission's Working Paper" [1990] Crim. L.R. 667. cf. J. D. Jackson, "Credibility, Morality and the Corroboration Warning" [1988] C.L.J. 428.
[278] Criminal Justice and Public Order Act 1994 s.32(3) abrogates the analogous requirement for summary trials.
[279] For exploration of these issues, before *Makanjuola* [1995] 3 All E.R. 730, see P. Mirfield, "'Corroboration' After the 1994 Act" [1995] Crim. L.R. 448; D. Birch, "Corroboration: Goodbye To All That?" [1995] Crim. L.R. 524.
[280] *Makanjuola* [1995] 3 All E.R. 730.

like any other witnesses in criminal trials. Accordingly, to carry on giving discretionary warnings generally and in the same terms as were previously obligatory, as counsel had optimistically argued for, would, in Lord Taylor's view, be contrary to the policy and purpose of the Act. He summarised the court's conclusions in the form of a number of propositions:

> "(1) Section 32(1) abrogated the requirement to give a corroboration direction in respect of an alleged accomplice or a complainant of a sexual offence, simply because a witness falls into one of those categories. (2) It is a matter for the judge's discretion what, if any warning, he considers appropriate in respect of such a witness as indeed in respect of any other witness in whatever type of case. Whether he chooses to give a warning and in what terms will depend on the circumstances of the case, the issues raised and the content and quality of the witness's evidence. (3) In some cases, it may be appropriate for the judge to warn the jury to exercise caution before acting upon the unsupported evidence of a witness. This will not be so simply because the witness is a complainant of a sexual offence nor will it necessarily be so because the witness is alleged to be an accomplice. There will need to be an evidential basis for suggesting that the evidence of the witness may be unreliable. An evidential basis does not include mere suggestion by cross-examining counsel. (4) If any question arises as to whether the judge should give a special warning in respect of a witness, it is desirable that the question be resolved by discussion with counsel in the absence of the jury before final speeches. (5) Where the judge does decide to give some warning in respect of a witness, it will be appropriate to do so as part of the judge's review of the evidence and his comments as to how the jury should evaluate it rather than as a set-piece legal direction. (6) Where some warning is required, it will be for the judge to decide the strength and terms of the warning. It does not have to be invested with the whole florid regime of the old corroboration rules. (7) ... Attempts to re-impose the straitjacket of the old corroboration rules are strongly to be deprecated. (8) Finally, this court will be disinclined to interfere with a trial judge's exercise of his discretion save in a case where that exercise is unreasonable in the *Wednesbury* sense."[281]

15–049   These principles are in line with the expectations of the Law Commission about the approach to be adopted under the Act to accomplices and complainants. The fundamental principle is that the trial judge has an overriding duty to ensure a fair trial for the accused, with a corresponding obligation to put the defence case fairly and adequately to the jury.[282] So, for example, where the defence claims that there are grounds for thinking that an accomplice has a motive for falsely incriminating the accused, or exaggerating the accused's part in the offence, the jury might be directed to proceed with caution and to consider this allegation carefully when assessing the accomplice's evidence. A failure to give such a warning could be grounds for appeal. On the other hand the strength and terms of the warning would be within the judge's discretion. The test should be the overall spirit and effect of the directions, not whether particular words or formulae were used.

This is not to say, as Lord Taylor C.J. acknowledged in *Makanjuola*, that a caution warning should automatically be given in every case involving an accomplice witness. The Law Commission suggested that the question of giving such a warning would arise:

> "where the accomplice may himself be in danger of conviction, and probably also in any other case where he is identified as having any 'interest' in giving false evidence."[283]

---

[281] *Makanjuola* [1995] 3 All E.R. 730 at 1351–1352.
[282] Law Com No.202 paras 3.12–3.14.
[283] Law Com No.202, para.3.17. "Supergrass" evidence may well come within this principle.

However, in other cases, as the Criminal Law Revision Committee noted,[284] there may be no real possibility that the accomplice is acting out of spite against the accused or trying to minimise his own part in the offence. Where the circumstances suggest that the accomplice's evidence is likely to be reliable there will be no obligation to give any kind of warning.

Similar points can be made about complainants. A specific defence that a complainant is lying or fantasising about a sexual assault must be put squarely before the jury. As with any direct challenge to the credibility of a witness, a trial judge might well think it appropriate to advise the jury to look carefully at the other evidence in the case in deciding on the weight to be given to the impugned testimony. The judge should not, however, go further and indulge in broad generalisations about false complaints or suggest that it would be desirable to have confirmatory evidence before convicting in this type of case. This is so even if such comments are intended to be helpful. It is precisely this kind of speculation about the dangers of complainant testimony that made the common law rule so offensive to women[285] and formed a substantial part of the case for its abolition. In the course of its deliberations the Law Commission even considered whether the legislation should positively seek to prohibit warnings in these terms. Its conclusion was that it would be unnecessary and impracticable to do so, and that it would be preferable to trust judges to make the comments that fairness and the interests of justice required.[286] It remains to be seen whether the Commission's confidence that judicial "dislike of and embarrassment at the use of the standard direction in sexual cases"[287] will prevent the reappearance of this aspect of the direction in future.

A group of cases raises the problem of long delay between the occurrence of an alleged sexual offence and the complaint by the victim. Typically the victim complains that a father, stepfather or other male relative or friend sexually abused her as a child, sometimes over many years. The delay in making a complaint may be explained on a variety of grounds: lack of confidence, anxiety that she would not be believed, fear of upsetting the mother, a wish not to be responsible for the break-up of the family, and so on. Sometimes a victim may say that she had forgotten about the abuse, until counselling in adult life for psychiatric problems caused her to "recover" the memory. When these cases come to trial they may cause great difficulties for both complainants and defendants. It may be hard to recall details of incidents many years previously, and witnesses who could have provided important evidence for one side or the other may have died or become untraceable.

15–050

One of the earlier cases of extreme delay is *Jenkins*.[288] The defendant was convicted in 1997 of a number of offences against S and J (two sisters) between 1963 and 1967. At the time of the offences S and J were between two and six years old. Neither complained until 1995; S explained that she remembered the

---

[284] *Eleventh Report* para.183.
[285] See generally J. Temkin, *Rape and the Legal Process*, 2nd edn (Oxford: Oxford University Press, 2002), pp.255 onwards.
[286] Law Com. No.202 paras 4.1–4.7. For contrary arguments see K. Mack, "Continuing Barriers to Women's Credibility: A Feminist Perspective on the Proof Process" (1993) 4 Crim. Law Forum 327.
[287] Law Com. No.202 para.4.5.
[288] *Jenkins* [1998] Crim. L.R. 411 CA.

incidents only after counselling in 1995. Allowing the defendant's appeal, the Court of Appeal held that the trial judge should have exercised his discretion to stay the proceedings as an abuse of process. The exceptional delay of 30 years had prejudiced the defendant in putting his defence; this, together with evidence suggesting that S's memory had mysteriously "improved" after her first visit to the police and that J's evidence was contaminated, made the convictions unsafe.[289] A number of later cases demonstrate that the Court of Appeal is anxious that the nature and extent of any prejudice to the defendant in cases of extreme delay should be carefully examined.[290] Where important evidence that could have supported the defendant's case and provided material for specific rather than speculative cross-examination of the complainants no longer exists (as where witnesses have died or documentary records have been destroyed or gone missing,) the court may well conclude that a fair trial was impossible.[291] At the same time it has been said that staying the proceedings altogether is the ultimate safeguard against suspect evidence, and is an exceptional measure.[292] Proceedings should generally go ahead even where the delay is unjustifiable, and it will rarely be appropriate to order a stay in the absence of "fault" on the part of a complainant or the prosecution.[293] In cases of substantial delay where the case is left to the jury it will be desirable for the judge to give the jury a direction as to possible difficulties the defence face as the result of the delay. The direction is not mandatory in all cases,[294] but it will invariably be required where some significant difficulty or aspect of prejudice is raised by the defence or otherwise becomes apparent to the judge at trial.[295]

Such a direction is not a corroboration warning as such. It is rather a matter of bringing specifically to the jury's attention the significance of delay in terms of its effect on the ability of the parties to adduce evidence relating to the alleged offences and on the nature of the credibility conflict that inevitably arises in this type of case.

15–051   It is submitted, however, that one situation does call for at least a corroboration warning in respect of the evidence of a complainant. This situation concerns instances of "recovered memory", where a complainant purports after receiving psychotherapy or counselling to recall incidents of sexual abuse in childhood many years earlier.[296] There appears to be a significant risk that evidence of this

---

[289] The court also quashed the defendant's convictions for other offences committed against another pair of sisters between 1981 and 1985, on the ground that they were tainted by the admission as "similar fact" evidence of the offences against S and J.

[290] See *R. v B* [2003] EWCA Crim 319; [2003] 2 Cr.App.R. 13; *Joynson* [2008] EWCA Crim 3049; *R. v F* [2011] EWCA Crim 726.

[291] See, e.g. *R. v F* [2011] EWCA Crim 726.

[292] *Smolinski* [2004] EWCA Crim 1270; [2004] 2 Cr.App.R. 40; *MacKreth* [2009] EWCA Crim 1849. The application for a stay should normally not be made until all the evidence has been heard.

[293] *Attorney-General's Reference (No.1 of 1990)* [1992] 1 Q.B. 643 CA.

[294] See, e.g. *Henry* [1998] 2 Cr.App.R. 161 CA.

[295] See *Dutton* [1994] Crim. L.R. 910 CA (delay of 14–20 years before complaint; potential defence witnesses had died); *Birchall, The Times*, March 23, 1995 (delay of 16–20 years before trial; witnesses to whom complaint was allegedly made were dead or untraceable); *John* [1996] 1 Cr.App.R. 88 CA (delay of 17–23 years; important family witnesses had died).

[296] It is *not* suggested that all cases of delay by victims of child sexual abuse in making complaint are cases of "recovered" memory, or that a corroboration warning should be required in all cases of delay.

type may be false,[297] but the complainants concerned may honestly and strongly believe it to be true. Cases of recovered but false memory may therefore be difficult to detect by the usual forensic tests. The risk of falsity is highlighted in the debate about the underlying theory concerning the repression and recovery of memories of such abuse; the theory is supported by many clinicians, but has been strongly attacked as fundamentally flawed. Critics claim that there is a high risk that such "memories", in which complainants may sincerely believe, are false, having been implanted by therapists and counsellors. One authoritative review, by a working party of the Royal College of Psychiatrists, of this highly controversial topic concluded[298]:

> "Evidence does not support the view that memory enhancement techniques actually enhance memory. There is evidence to support the view that these are powerful and dangerous methods of persuasion. Many of the memories 'recovered' using these measures refer to events in the early months or years of life which fall within the period of infantile amnesia and must be regarded as implausible for that reason. There is sufficient evidence of distortion and/or elaboration of memories to assert that entirely new and false memories can be created, not only experimentally but also in clinical practice . . .
>
> The common experience of remembering is for a memory to return suddenly and completely. 'Recovered memories' differ from other forms of forgotten and remembered events in being built-up over time. Close examination reveals that they resemble narrative rather than memory, with more being added at each attempt at recall, often becoming increasingly elaborate and bizarre . . .
>
> There is no reliable means of distinguishing a true memory from an illusory one other than by external confirmation."

8. *Use of caution warnings*

The approach taken by the Court of Appeal in *Makanjuola* to challenges to the credibility and reliability of accomplices and complainants is part of a pattern. For some 20 years the courts have resisted attempts to persuade them to create new corroboration requirements for prosecution witnesses whose evidence may be suspect for one reason or another. These attempts were made in several

15–052

For further discussion of these cases see P. Lewis and A. Mullis, "Delayed Criminal Prosecutions for Childhood Sexual Abuse: Ensuring a Fair Trial" (1999) 115 L.Q.R. 265; M. Redmayne, "A Corroboration Approach to Recovered Memories of Sexual Abuse: A Note of Caution" (2000) 116 L.Q.R. 147. The further debate between Lewis and Mullis and Redmayne, at (2001) 5 E. & P. 111 and 121, is more about the nature of corroboration than the issues of recovered memory.

[297] In *Clark* [2006] EWCA Crim 231, the Court of Appeal quashed convictions for sexual offences where the trial judge wrongly excluded evidence from a defence expert witness that cast doubt on the reliability of the evidence of one of the complainants, who had first complained some 20 years after the alleged offences. The complaint emerged while the complainant was undergoing hypnotherapy as part of her counselling programme.

[298] Brandon, "Recovered memories of childhood sexual abuse" (1998) 172 *British Journal of Psychiatry* 296. See also the sustained and trenchant critique by R. Ofshe and E. Watters, *Making Monsters: False Memories, Psychotherapy and Sexual Hysteria* (London: Andre Deutsch Ltd, 1995); J. D. Read, "The Recovered Memory Debate: Three Steps Forward, Two Steps Back?" (1999) 7 *Expert Evidence* 1; S. Ring, "Due process and the admission of expert evidence on recovered memory in historic child sexual abuse cases: lessons from America" (2012) 16 E. & P. 66. P. Lewis, *Delayed Prosecution for Childhood Sexual Abuse* (2006), Ch.10 reviews four options for dealing with the problem of suspect memories of childhood sexual abuse and recommends a warning, founded on an analogy with the *Turnbull* warning in cases of disputed eyewitness identification evidence (see below), which would be in similar terms, although not quite as stringent, as the one suggested here.

different contexts. In each case the courts' preferred response has been for a requirement of a judicial direction to be couched in terms of the special need for caution in considering the suspect evidence, but to be given without all the trappings of a full corroboration warning. In particular such warnings to use caution do not require a statement that it would be dangerous to convict in the absence of supporting evidence. Nor do they require judges to become enmeshed in the technicalities of what evidence may or may not amount to corroboration, although there is a certain amount of case law on the question of when the accused's lies may be used as support for disputed prosecution evidence. Failure to give a caution warning when one should have been given will generally be grounds for appeal. However, it is more difficult to challenge the terms in which the warning is given since the strength of the advice to proceed with caution will vary according to the facts of the case.[299]

(A) Eyewitness identification evidence

15–053   The modern trend began with *Turnbull*.[300] The Court of Appeal, in what was effectively judicial legislation, set out detailed guidelines for trial judges in cases of disputed eyewitness identification evidence. The guidelines include directions to juries to proceed with caution before convicting in reliance on the correctness of the identification. Where the quality of the identifying evidence is poor it should not be left to the jury unless there is some evidence capable of supporting its correctness, and the jury must be sure that the effect of such evidence is to support the correctness of the identification. The support may be corroboration in the technical sense but does not have to be. The *Turnbull* guidelines are discussed in detail in Ch.7. The important point for present purposes is the attitude of the Court of Appeal to the appropriate safeguards against wrongful conviction on disputed prosecution evidence. The challenge in identification cases is usually to the reliability of the evidence rather than to the witness's credibility, and there is a high degree of consensus that the potential unreliability of eyewitness identifications presents the biggest single danger of wrongful convictions. Nevertheless the Court of Appeal was not persuaded that a new corroboration requirement was the appropriate response to this danger. The court preferred the less technical and more flexible requirement of a caution warning. Whether this was the best solution to the particular problem of identification evidence is debatable, but there is no doubt that *Turnbull* was highly influential in the thinking of the Court of Appeal when later cases raised similar issues about strategies for dealing with suspect evidence.[301]

---

[299] *Beck* [1982] 1 All E.R. 807 at 813 CA per Ackner L.J.
[300] *Turnbull* [1977] Q.B. 224 CA.
[301] See, e.g. *Nembhard v R.* [1982] 1 All E.R. 183 PC (dying declaration by the victim of a homicide identifying the defendant as the assailant—caution warning sufficient to deal with the risk of error in identification).

(B)   Witnesses with purposes of their own to serve

In *Beck*,[302] the defendant was charged with conspiracy to defraud a finance   **15–054**
company. Prosecution witnesses included directors of the finance company who
testified that they had no knowledge of the allegedly fraudulent transactions
carried out by the defendant in collusion with the managing director of a
subsidiary of the finance company. The defendant, whose case was that the
directors did have such knowledge, claimed that they were lying due to a desire
to cover up a false insurance claim for the subsidiary's losses. It was not
suggested that the directors were the defendant's accomplices in the fraud. The
issue was a pure question of their credibility in claiming lack of knowledge of the
relevant trading methods. The Court of Appeal held that in dealing with this
challenge the judge had correctly directed the jury to proceed with caution.
Rejecting earlier dicta suggesting the need for a corroboration warning in such
cases,[303] Ackner L.J. said that this would be a "totally unjustifiable addition" to
the burden on the trial judge. The court clearly took the view that the complexity
and technicality of corroboration warnings outweighed any benefits they might
offer. The decision indicated that a caution warning was adequate to protect the
accused from the risk of perjured evidence, in the same way that the Turnbull
caution warning was thought to be adequate to protect the accused from wrongful
conviction on unreliable identification evidence.

The Court of Appeal has also held, consistently with *Beck*, that a caution
warning is appropriate as far as co-accused are concerned. A co-accused who
gives evidence in his own defence incriminating the accused may well be
challenged by the accused on the basis that the co-accused has a motive to
exculpate himself by exaggerating or inventing the accused's part in the offence.
A line of authority indicates that the judge should generally direct the jury to
approach the co-accused's evidence with caution because the co-accused may
have an interest to serve.[304] In *Cheema*,[305] the Court of Appeal reviewed all the
earlier authorities and expressly rejected the argument that they should be
interpreted so as to require the full corroboration warning then applicable to
accomplices to be given. In *Jones and Jenkins*,[306] the Court of Appeal followed
the approach in *Cheema* to the evidence of a co-accused, and confirmed that it
should apply where two or more accused are running "cut-throat" defences.
Accordingly, where one defendant has given evidence adverse to another, the
judge should warn the jury in a neutral way to examine the evidence of each with
care because each has or may have an interest of his own to serve. There may be
a particular need for such a warning where one accused has refused to answer
questions in interview and has therefore been able if he wished to tailor his
evidence to the facts given in evidence.

---

[302] *Beck* [1982] 1 All E.R. 807 CA.
[303] See *Prater* [1960] 2 Q.B. 464 at 466 per Edmund Davies J.; *DPP v Kilbourne* [1973] A.C. 729 at
740 per Lord Hailsham L.C.
[304] *Bagley* [1980] Crim. L.R. 572 CA; *Loveridge* (1982) 76 Cr.App.R. 125 CA; *Knowlden* (1983) 77
Cr.App.R. 94 CA; *Cheema* [1994] 1 All E.R. 639 CA.
[305] *Cheema* [1994] 1 All E.R. 639 CA.
[306] *Jones and Jenkins* [2003] EWCA Crim 1966; [2004] 1 Cr.App.R. 5.

A problem that has caused much concern for many years is the "cell confession". The typical scenario is a prisoner giving evidence of a confession made to him by the defendant when the defendant was on remand sharing a cell with the prisoner. Such a confession may be a major part of the prosecution case. But it is easy to invent, and prisoners might have several incentives to lie in terms of receiving more favourable treatment from the authorities for assistance given. In *Benedetto v R.*,[307] the Privy Council took a strong view of the need for safeguards. It was held that in view of the inherent unreliability of such evidence, and its potential for causing a miscarriage of justice, the judge should always advise the jury to be cautious before accepting the evidence, drawing their attention to the indications that may justify the inference that the prisoner's evidence is tainted. However, in *Stone*,[308] the Court of Appeal clearly thought that this went too far and sought to explain the judgment in *Benedetto*. It said that in the standard case of the "two line cell confession" the judge should generally give the warning, pointing out that such confessions are easy to concoct, and that prisoners may have many motives to lie. If they have signficant criminal records or a history of lying this should also be pointed out. But not every case would require a warning. If the confession, for example, contains detail that it would have been difficult for the prisoner to invent, it would not make sense to warn about the ease of concoction. If a motive to lie has not been put to the witness in cross-examination it should not be obligatory to issue a warning about potential motives. The case has therefore, consistently with *Makanjuola*, rejected a general rule that there is a distinct category of cases involving cell confessions where a caution warning is always required. As in all these cases where witnesses may have an interest of their own to serve, a duty to give a warning should arise out of the facts of the case and the issues raised about the credibility of the witness rather than the existence of a formal classification of evidence.

(C)   Mental patients of bad character

15–055   In *Spencer*,[309] the suspect evidence was the testimony of mental patients in Rampton special hospital who had been sent or transferred there following conviction for serious offences. A series of trials took place in which a number of such patients testified to ill-treatment by the defendant and other nurses at the hospital. This testimony was very largely unsupported. The trial judge directed the jury in each case to approach the patients' evidence with the greatest caution and to examine it with the greatest care. He reminded the jury of the dangers involved: the patients' mental illness at the time, their convictions for serious offences, the medical evidence that they suffered from delusions and had a tendency to lie or exaggerate, and the risk that they might have conspired together to bring false accusations. The House of Lords upheld these directions and dismissed the defendants' appeals. The Lords held that where individual prosecution witnesses fulfilled analogous criteria to those that were presumed in

---

[307] *Benedetto v R.* [2003] UKPC 27; [2003] 2 Cr.App.R. 25.
[308] *Stone* [2005] EWCA Crim 105; [2005] Crim.L.R. 569.
[309] *Spencer* [1987] A.C. 128 HL.

the "accepted categories of suspect witnesses"[310] an adequate warning had to be given. The Lords stopped short of saying that this should be the traditional corroboration warning required for accomplices and complainants. Lord Ackner insisted that no magic formula of wording was required; in particular it was not necessary to say that it would be dangerous to convict on such evidence provided it was made clear that there were dangers in doing so.[311] He added that if potential corroborative material existed the extent to which the judge referred to that material depended on the facts of the case. Lord Hailsham agreed that each direction should be tailor-made to suit the requirements of the individual case.[312]

This was a strong case, since the risks involved included both possible perjury and possible delusions on the part of the suspect witnesses. Challenges were being made to their reliability as well as to their credibility. Again the court took the view that the correct response was a caution warning geared to the facts of the case, the strength of the warning being dependent on the strength of the risks present.

(D) Confessions by mentally handicapped persons[313]

Section 77 of PACE requires a judge in a trial on indictment to warn the jury of the special need for caution before convicting in reliance on the accused's confession where three conditions apply. These are that the case against the accused depends wholly or substantially on the confession, that the accused is mentally handicapped and that the confession was not made in the presence of an independent person. The warning should explain that the need for caution arises because of the existence of these circumstances relating to the confession. An "independent person" is expressed not to include a police officer or a person employed for or engaged on police purposes; in many cases the "appropriate adult", who is required by Code C to be present when a mentally handicapped suspect is interviewed, will be the independent person. The two terms are not, however, synonymous. The suspect's solicitor, for example, may assume the role of an independent person,[314] but may not act as an appropriate adult.[315] A person is mentally handicapped for the purposes of s.77 if he "is in a state of arrested or incomplete development of mind which includes significant impairment of intelligence and social functioning".[316]

Section 77 is an odd and rather marginal provision. It is odd because it applies only in respect of confessions made by one group of vulnerable suspects. It does not apply where confessions are made by persons suffering from mental illness, or by juveniles. Yet these types of vulnerable suspect are bracketed with mentally handicapped suspects for the purposes of the "appropriate adult" provisions of Code C, and in many cases their confessions might be thought to present similar

15–056

---

[310] i.e. those categories of witness in respect of whom a mandatory corroboration warning had to be given at the time.
[311] *Spencer* [1987] A.C. 128 at 142.
[312] *Spencer* [1987] A.C. 128 at 135.
[313] See P. Mirfield, *Silence, Confessions and Improperly Obtained Evidence* (1997), pp.296–299.
[314] *Lewis (Martin)* [1996] Crim. L.R. 260 CA.
[315] Code C, Note for Guidance 1F.
[316] PACE s.77(3).

risks of unreliability. In practice a judge might well decide that a similar caution warning was therefore justified if no independent person was present when the suspect made the confession, but it is hard to see why s.77 does not make it obligatory. The section is marginal in the sense that it may apply in only a few cases of confessions by mentally handicapped persons.[317] This is because trial judges may well exclude confessions by the mentally handicapped under ss.76(2) and 78 of PACE, on the basis of their likely unreliability or the unfairness of their use in the circumstances.[318] Alternatively, a judge may withdraw the case from the jury altogether under the rule in *Galbraith*[319] as interpreted in *Mackenzie*.[320] The use of these alternative strategies for dealing with confessions by the mentally handicapped may leave relatively little room for the operation of s.77. In *Moss*,[321] it was suggested that such confessions might go to the jury where the suspect had been interviewed in the absence of an appropriate adult in a case of urgency,[322] or where a confession was made in a single interview during a short period of custody. These are not the only possibilities. In *Bailey*,[323] three interviews took place at which no independent person was present, and there was a time gap between the second and third interviews. The Court of Appeal rejected an argument that the trial judge was wrong not to exclude the confession, but the court went on to allow the appeal because the judge had failed to give the warning he ought to have given under s.77.

---

[317] *Blackstones's Criminal Practice,* 2011 edn, para.F.17.23. "Mentally handicapped" is a question of degree, and some significantly disadvantaged defendants may be held not to come within the description; see, e.g. *Foster* [2003] EWCA Crim 178.

[318] See, e.g. *Moss* (1990) 91 Cr.App.R. 371 CA; *Weekes* (1993) 97 Cr.App.R. 222 CA.

[319] *Galbraith* [1981] 2 All E.R. 1060 CA.

[320] *Mackenzie* (1993) 96 Cr.App.R. 98 CA. See also *Wood* [1994] Crim. L.R. 222 CA.

[321] *Moss* (1990) 91 Cr.App.R. 371 at 377 CA.

[322] Code C para.11.1 and Annex E para.1.

[323] *Bailey* [1995] 2 Cr.App.R. 262 CA.

PART IV

USING EVIDENCE: THE SCOPE AND LIMITS OF EXCLUSIONARY RULES

CHAPTER 16

HEARSAY AT COMMON LAW AND IN CIVIL PROCEEDINGS

A.   INTRODUCTION

The rule against hearsay evidence was one of the main exclusionary rules   **16–001**
developed by the common law. According to Wigmore the rule was recognised by
the end of the 17th century,[1] and it has remained one of the cornerstones of
Anglo-American laws of evidence to the present day. In English law the common
law of hearsay has now been replaced by statutory regulation in both civil and
criminal cases, but the regulatory schemes cannot be fully understood without
some appreciation of the common law background. The common law rule had a
deserved reputation for being technical and difficult. It puzzled generations of
students, and sometimes provoked striking judicial confusion[2] or disagreement.[3]

---

[1] Wigmore Vol.V (Chadbourn rev. 1974), pp.12 onwards. See also on the history of the rule R. W.
Baker, *The Hearsay Rule* (London: Pitman, 1950), Ch.2; E. M. Morgan, *Some Problems of Proof
Under the AngloAmerican System of Litigation* (New York: Columbia University Press, 1956), pp.106
onwards; S. Landsman, "The Rise of the Contentious Spirit: Adversary Procedure in Eighteenth
Century England" (1990) 75 Cornell L.R. 497, 564–572 showing the gradual entrenchment of the rule
in trial courts during the 18th century.
[2] As in *Pettigrew* (1980) 71 Cr.App.R. 39 where a computer printout recording the serial numbers of
banknotes fed into the computer was wrongly treated by the Court of Appeal as hearsay evidence. See
J.C. Smith, *Criminal Evidence* (London: Sweet & Maxwell, 1995), p.68. For discussion of the
admissibility of statements produced by computer, see Ch.12.

However, it is worth emphasising at the outset that the underlying ideas of a rule against hearsay are reasonably clear and are not difficult to relate to general concerns of the law of evidence. This is not to say that the rationale of such a rule should be uncritically accepted. On the contrary, the justification for a systemic exclusionary rule has been keenly debated,[4] particularly in some situations at the margins of hearsay where the limits of the rule at common law were notably obscure.

This chapter begins with an explanation of the underlying ideas of the common law rule against hearsay and relates them to fundamental principles of the law of evidence. The chapter then considers in a little more detail the formulation, rationale and application of the common law rule. The purpose of this discussion is to provide a context for the far-reaching statutory reforms of recent years and to enable their significance to be properly understood. This chapter concludes with a short account of the legislative reform of the hearsay rule in civil cases, which has resulted in the complete abolition of the rule.[5] The next chapter deals with the comprehensive recasting of the hearsay rule in criminal cases effected by the Criminal Justice Act 2003. This scheme has retained the structure of an exclusionary rule ameliorated by a considerable number of exceptions, but the statutory rule is in narrower terms than the common law, and the exceptions are wider. We are still some way from complete abolition of the rule in criminal cases, but the new scheme represents a radical move in the direction of admitting much more hearsay evidence where it has potential probative value and the interests of justice require admission.

The starting-point for analysis of a rule against hearsay is the proposition that the rule is a rule about the admissibility and use of evidence. The rule presupposes that the evidence in question is relevant to the issues in the case. Relevance is assessed in accordance with the criteria set out in Ch.3. If the evidence is irrelevant it is inadmissible for that reason. Strictly speaking there is then no need to ask whether it is hearsay, but, given that relevance is a question of degree, courts have sometimes considered the application of the hearsay rule on the assumption that the evidence does have some relevance. Assuming, therefore, that the evidence is relevant, the common law rule against hearsay was designed to prevent a party using evidence of an out-of-court statement for the purpose of proving that a fact stated in the statement was true. A simple example to illustrate the rule is a statement made out of court by X, a shopper, to W, a store detective, that "D picked up a book and ran off without paying". If D is charged with theft of the book this statement is relevant, but the hearsay rule will prevent the prosecution calling W to testify that he heard X say this, since the purpose of doing so is to ask the court to accept that the facts stated in X's statement are true,

---

[3] As in *Kearley* [1992] 2 A.C. 228 at 237 where Lord Griffiths, dissenting, opined that the law as applied by the majority of the House of Lords in the case would be regarded by a layman as asinine.
[4] There is an extensive secondary literature on the scope and rationale of the hearsay rule. For a full discussion and bibliography, see A. Choo, *Hearsay and Confrontation in Criminal Trials* (Oxford: Oxford University Press, 1996).
[5] Civil Evidence Act 1995, giving effect to recommendations of the Law Commission in Law Com. No.216, Cm.2321 (London, 1993).

namely that D did take the book without paying. The rule thus obliges the prosecution to call X as a witness to give direct evidence that she saw D take the book.

It is worth recalling at this stage that relevant evidence is presumptively admissible, on the basis that admitting as much relevant evidence as possible will help to maximise the factual accuracy of the decision. The more reliable and probative the evidence appears to be, the more a court may want to admit it. This may result in pressure to avoid or even ignore the operation of an exclusionary rule where it would be inconvenient to apply the rule. These pressures led in the past to the creation of numerous exceptions to the hearsay rule at common law and, in more modern times, to the use of artificial devices to avoid the operation of the rule. However, not all courts were willing to circumvent the rule in these ways. The consequence was a tension in the cases between what Birch[6] aptly described as "hearsay logic", when the rule was applied, and "hearsay fiddles", when its operation was in some way avoided. The theme is a recurring one throughout the discussion of hearsay.

16–002

An outline of the basic theory of the hearsay rule runs as follows.[7] As we have seen, the common law trial was originally founded on a principle of orality that requires witnesses to give oral testimony based on their personal knowledge of the matters in issue. For this method of factfinding to produce correct decisions the witnesses have to be credible and their evidence has to be subject to satisfactory testing by the court. The requirements of personal knowledge and forensic testing mean that the court can estimate how much reliance to place on the witness before it, given the four possible testimonial infirmities to which all witnesses are subject: defective observation, defective memory, ambiguity of narration and insincerity. The forensic tools available in the common law trial for assessing the credibility of witnesses are the oath, the demeanour of the witness, cross-examination of the witness and external evidence relevant to credibility, such as a witness's previous convictions. If the court is asked to place reliance on other persons not then before the court, it is not in a position to use most of its forensic tools to test the credibility of those other persons. It is therefore generally less safe and satisfactory to make factual judgments based on material supplied by them. One important function of the rule against hearsay is to obviate this problem by refusing to permit the parties to ask the court to place reliance on persons not before the court whose possible testimonial infirmities cannot be tested by the usual procedures. The rule was never absolute, however, and the common law recognised a number of exceptions where certain circumstantial guarantees of trustworthiness of the statement were thought to exist.

A further function of the rule, which has been increasingly emphasised in modern debates,[8] is to give effect to rights of parties to confront and challenge witnesses against them. These rights derive from the interests that parties have,

---

[6] D. J. Birch, "Hearsay-Logic and Hearsay-Fiddles: *Blastland* Revisited" in P.F. Smith (ed) *Criminal Law Essays in, Honour of JC Smith* (London: Butterworths, 1987), p.24.

[7] E. M. Morgan, "Hearsay Dangers and the Application of the Hearsay Concept" (1948) 62 Harv. L.R. 177.

[8] M. R. Kadish and M. Davis, "Defending the Hearsay Rule" (1989) 8 *Law and Philosophy* 333; E. A. Scallen, "Constitutional Dimensions of Hearsay Reform: Toward a Three-Dimensional

first, in the instrumental benefits of challenge as a means of testing the probative value of the evidence and, secondly, in the importance of confrontation and challenge as a "process value", enhancing the parties' participation in the process of decision-making and thereby reinforcing the legitimacy of the adjudication.[9]

B. STATEMENT AND RATIONALE OF THE HEARSAY RULE AT COMMON LAW

1. *Statement of the rule*

16–003 The definition of the hearsay rule at common law was "assertion-based", meaning that it was founded on the concept of a "statement" or "assertion"[10] made by a person. The definition regulated the use in evidence of any statement or assertion not made by a person while testifying in the current proceedings. It treated as subject to the hearsay rule any such statement or assertion when it was offered to prove the truth of the matter stated or asserted.

Before dealing in more detail with the formulation of this definition and the application of the rule it embodied, it is useful to note that other approaches to defining hearsay are possible.[11] The most important of these is an approach that focuses on the credibility of the declarant whose out-of-court statement is being reported to the court.[12] Park suggests that a "declarant-oriented definition is one that defines an act or utterance as hearsay if it is offered for an inference about a belief of the declarant".[13] This approach can also be called "dangers analysis" since it treats the inability to test an absent declarant on possible hearsay dangers as prima facie justification for exclusion of the statement. In most cases the two types of definition will produce the same result, but the declarant-based type is potentially wider in its ambit since it is capable of embracing some so-called "implied assertions" that may fall outside a literal assertion-based definition.[14] Apart from the drawback of its width, the declarant-based approach is valuable in

---

Confrontation Clause" (1992) 76 Minn. L.R. 623; E. Swift, "Smoke and Mirrors: The Failure of the Supreme Court's Accuracy Rationale in *White v Illinois* Requires a New Look at Confrontation" (1993) 22 Capital Univ. L.R. 145.

[9] Nesson offers a further consequentialist argument that the hearsay rule promotes the social acceptability of verdicts by insulating them from attack by declarants who subsequently retract hearsay statements: C. R. Nesson, "The Evidence or the Event: On Judicial Proof and the Acceptability of Verdicts" (1985) 98 Harv. L.R. 1357, 1372–1375. For discussion of this view see R. C. Park, "The Hearsay Rule and the Stability of Verdicts: A Response to Professor Nesson" (1986) 70 Minn. L.R. 1057.

[10] These terms are interchangeable as far as express oral or written statements are concerned. "Assertion" is more commonly used when an issue arises of whether evidence of a person's *conduct* amounts to or involves hearsay.

[11] C. Callen, "Wallace Stevens, Blackbirds and the Hearsay Rule" (1995) 16 Mississippi Coll. L.R. 1; R. C. Park, "The Definition of Hearsay: To Each Its Own" (1995) 16 Mississippi Coll. L.R. 125.

[12] See L. H. Tribe, "Triangulating Hearsay" (1974) 87 Harv. L.R. 957; M. H. Graham, "Stickperson Hearsay: A Simplified Approach to Understanding the Rule against Hearsay" [1982] Univ. of Illinois L.R. 887.

[13] Park, "The Definition of Hearsay" (1995) 16 Mississippi Coll. L.R. 125.

[14] The best example is an out-of-court statement offered as a lie. This is not hearsay on an assertion-based definition, since the statement is not offered as evidence of the truth of the facts stated. On the other hand it may be hearsay on a declarant-based definition if the court is being asked

tying the rule more closely to its rationale and in helping to account for exceptions to the hearsay rule. However, the "assertion-based" definition has the advantage that it accounts more easily for the exclusion of out-of-court statements both of third parties and of the testifying witness. At common law a witness's previous statements could not generally be admitted as evidence of the facts stated despite the fact that the witness was present in court and available for cross-examination on them.[15]

The generally accepted definition of the hearsay rule at common law was the one formulated by Cross. This achieved very wide acceptance, including judicial approval at the highest level:

> "an assertion other than one made by a person while giving oral evidence in the proceedings is inadmissible as evidence of any fact [or opinion] asserted."[16]

This may be compared with the definition of "hearsay" given in the Civil Evidence Act 1995. Section 1(1) of the Act provides that in civil proceedings evidence shall not be excluded on the ground that it is hearsay. Section 1(2)(a) states that in the Act " 'hearsay' means a statement made otherwise than by a person while giving oral evidence in the proceedings which is tendered as evidence of the matters stated".

16–004

Cross's proposition stipulated that a person's out-of-court statement could not be used "testimonially"[17] to prove the truth of some fact narrated by the statement. A court could not, in other words, be asked to accept that something was true because X (who made the statement being reported to the court) said it was. It made no difference for the purposes of the rule whether the statement in question was made on oath. Testimony in other judicial proceedings, or other statement on oath, was still hearsay when reported to another court as evidence of the facts testified or sworn to.[18] The rule applied to all parties to litigation. There was no question of more lenient application to the defence in criminal cases.[19] As indicated above, the rule applied equally to statements out of court by third parties and to a witness's own out-of-court statements. At common law a witness's previous statement was inadmissible as evidence of the facts asserted in

---

to treat the lie as an implied statement by the declarant of his belief in his guilt. Hearsay dangers of faulty perception, faulty memory or ambiguity on the part of the speaker may be present.

[15] Nor could such statements be admitted as relevant to the witness's credibility (by showing consistency) by virtue of the general rule against narrative: see Ch.14.

[16] See the Law Commission's Consultation Paper, *Evidence in Criminal Proceedings: Hearsay and Related Topics* (1995) ("Law Com. CP 138"), para.2.3; citing the 7th edn of *Cross on Evidence* (1990), p.509. An earlier version (that did not contain the words in parentheses) was approved by Lord Havers in *Sharp* [1988] 1 W.L.R. 7 at 11, with whom the other members of the House of Lords concurred, and by Lord Ackner in *Kearley* [1992] 2 A.C. 228 at 254. See also the virtually identical statement of the hearsay rule by Lord Oliver in the same case at 259. Later editions of *Cross and Tapper on Evidence* have replaced "assertion" with "statement".

[17] *Ratten v R.* [1972] A.C. 378 at 387 PC per Lord Wilberforce.

[18] *R. v Eriswell (Inhabitants)* (1790) 3 Term Rep. 707; *Haines v Guthrie* (1884) 13 Q.B.D. 818.

[19] *Turner* (1975) 61 Cr.App.R. 67 at 88 CA, where Milmo J. stated emphatically that "The idea, which may be gaining prevalence in some quarters, that in a criminal trial the defence is entitled to adduce hearsay evidence to establish facts, which if proved would be relevant and would assist the defence, is wholly erroneous".

the previous statement. This remained true even if, exceptionally, the previous statement was admissible to show consistency with the present testimony.[20]

The concluding words of the definition made clear that it was the purpose for which the assertion was offered in evidence that was crucial. The question that should always be asked in relation to possible hearsay evidence is: What is the purpose of adducing this evidence? What is the party adducing it trying to prove by it? According to the common law rule the hearsay rule applied only if the purpose was to prove the truth of some fact stated in the assertion. If the assertion was offered in evidence for some other purpose, for example to show that a statement was made, as opposed to showing that it was true, the hearsay rule did not apply and the evidence of the assertion was admissible. The classic expression of this fundamental distinction was in the judgment of the Privy Council in *Subramaniam v Public Prosecutor*[21]:

> "Evidence of a statement made to a witness by a person who is not himself called as a witness may or may not be hearsay. It is hearsay and inadmissible when the object of the evidence is to establish the truth of what is contained in the statement. It is not hearsay and is admissible when it is proposed to establish by the evidence, not the truth of the statement, but the fact that it was made."

16–005   A straightforward example of an assertion adduced in evidence for a non-hearsay purpose is proof of a libel. The claimant calls a witness to produce a letter from the defendant to the witness in which the defendant wrote that the claimant was a thief. Clearly the claimant's purpose in adducing this letter in evidence is not to prove that he is a thief (the truth of the fact asserted by the defendant) but to prove that the defendant made this statement. A statement in these terms is defamatory, so proof that the statement was made establishes the claimant's cause of action. If the defendant's defence is that the statement was true (a plea of justification), the burden will be on him to prove it.

This section concludes with some instructive examples of hearsay evidence taken from leading criminal cases. In *Gibson*,[22] the defendant was charged with maliciously wounding P. P testified that after he had been hit by a stone, a woman at the scene pointed to the door of the defendant's house and said, "The man who threw the stone went in there". The Court for Crown Cases Reserved quashed the defendant's conviction because the evidence of the woman's statement was inadmissible. In terms of the preceding analysis the court was being asked to assume that it was true that the stone-thrower had gone into the defendant's house, yielding an inference that the person was the defendant himself, because the woman said he had. The court was not, however, in a position to assess the woman's reliability as a reporter of events. A sceptic might point out that her statement was unambiguous and might query whether there was any real reason to think that she might be lying. On the other hand, even though her assertion was almost contemporaneous with the event, her observation might have been mistaken. At all events the decision was a logical application of the rule, even though only one of the hearsay dangers was possibly present.

---

[20] This rule has now been changed in both civil and criminal proceedings.

[21] *Subramaniam v Public Prosecutor* [1956] 1 W.L.R. 965 at 969.

[22] *Gibson* (1887) 18 Q.B.D. 537.

The second case is *Sparks v R*.[23] The defendant, a white man, was convicted of indecent assault on a three-year-old girl. The girl did not give evidence at the trial. The trial judge refused to allow the defence to call the girl's mother to testify that the child had said to her, about an hour-and-a-half after the event, that a coloured boy had done it. The Privy Council upheld this decision as a correct application of the hearsay rule, although the conviction was quashed on other grounds. Again the logic is faultless; the purpose of producing the child's statement was as evidence of the facts stated, that is, to show that it was true that a coloured boy had done it because the little girl said that he had. The case is notable because it provides a striking example of the point made earlier that the hearsay rule at common law applied equally to defence hearsay. The court was not prepared to disapply the rule, or create an exception, in deference to an argument that it was necessary to do so in order to prevent a possible miscarriage of justice. The court reached its conclusion despite the fact that the girl's statement was not ambiguous; she was unlikely to have mistaken the colour of her attacker or to have misremembered it so soon after the incident, and she was probably too young to lie about the matter. This was a clear case of the rule being applied in the absence of any significant hearsay danger. Other authorities followed the logic of this case by holding that an out-of-court confession by a third party, that he committed the offence with which the defendant was charged, was also a mere hearsay statement and inadmissible for the defence under the rule.[24]

Gibson and *Sparks* were both concerned with oral statements. The hearsay rule applied equally to assertions by physical gesture[25] and to statements in writing. In *Myers v DPP*,[26] the defendant was charged with conspiracy to receive stolen goods and conspiracy to defraud. The prosecution case was that the defendant acquired stolen cars, which he disguised to conform with wrecked cars he had previously bought. He then sold the stolen vehicles as renovated wrecks. As part of their evidence identifying the cars sold by the defendant as stolen, the prosecution called as a witness the employee who was in charge of the records kept by the manufacturers of the stolen cars. The records in question were microfilms containing photographs of cards filled in by production line workers; the cards showed details of the numbers stamped on the cylinder blocks of the cars on the production line. This evidence went to show that the cylinder block numbers of the stolen cars and the cars sold by the defendant were identical. On the defendant's appeal against conviction the House of Lords held that the evidence of the manufacturers' records was inadmissible hearsay.[27] The purpose of producing the records was to show that certain cars carried certain numbers on them when they left the production line. But the only way in which these numbers could be established was by relying on the cards filled in by the workers

16–006

---

[23] *Sparks v R.* [1964] A.C. 964 PC.
[24] *Turner* (1975) 61 Cr.App.R. 67 CA; *Blastland* [1986] A.C. 41 HL.
[25] The standard illustration of an intentional assertion by conduct is *Chandrasekera v R.* [1937] A.C. 220 where the victim, whose throat had been cut, nodded her head when asked whether it was the defendant who had done it. The Privy Council held that this was a hearsay statement, although admissible under an exception contained in the Ceylon Evidence Ordinance 1895.
[26] *Myers v DPP* [1965] A.C. 1001 HL.
[27] The convictions were nonetheless upheld by application of the proviso.

at the time. These cards were, in the words of Lord Reid, "assertions by the unidentifiable men who made them that they had entered numbers which they had seen on the cars".[28] In effect the trial court was asked to rely on the accuracy of observation and recording of workers who could not now be identified and tested on their reliability.

The case is an excellent example of both the logic and the technicality of the hearsay rule at common law. The facts fell neatly outside a number of existing exceptions to the rule,[29] and the Lords were invited to create a new exception in view of the point that the reliability of the records was not seriously in doubt. Again the hearsay dangers were slight if not non-existent. The numbers were clearly stated; the workers had no reason to falsify the numbers; defects in memory were unlikely since the records were contemporaneous; the only possible doubt could be over the accuracy of their observation, and this was speculative. Yet the majority of the Lords refused to invent a new exception for this kind of business record. Instead they argued that the hearsay rule had reached the limit of its development at common law and claimed that any future exceptions should be created by Parliament.[30] This self-denying ordinance, unusual in procedural law,[31] attracted criticism for its inflexibility,[32] particularly when applied to the facts of the case. The actual decision was almost immediately reversed by the Criminal Evidence Act 1965, which provided for the admissibility of trade and business records in criminal cases.[33]

The technicality of the law established by *Myers v DPP* was underlined by the decision of the Court of Appeal in *McLean*.[34] G, the victim of a robbery, observed the registration number of the robbers' getaway car. Not more than three minutes later he dictated a number to C, who wrote down HKB138D on a card. A car bearing this registration number had been hired before the robbery by the defendant using a different name. G did not see what C wrote down and did not check its accuracy. By the time of the defendant's trial G had forgotten the number he had observed. The trial judge allowed C to testify that he, C, had written down the number that G had told him was the number of the robbers' car. Quashing the defendant's conviction "with the utmost reluctance", Edmund Davies L.J. held that C's evidence contravened the hearsay rule. This is logically

---

[28] *Myers v DPP* [1965] A.C. 1001 at 1022.

[29] See the dissenting speech of Lord Pearce: *Myers v DPP* [1965] A.C. 1001 at 1034 onwards.

[30] *Myers v DPP* [1965] A.C. 1001 at 1022 per Lord Reid, 1028–1029 per Lord Morris of Borth-y-Gest, 1034 per Lord Hodson.

[31] Compare the initiative shown by the civil courts in inventing in the 1970s the forms of interlocutory relief then known as *Mareva* injunctions and *Anton Piller* orders. The argument that the courts should wash their hands of further hearsay reform and leave it to the legislature has a superficial plausibility, but overlooks the point that the courts are better equipped, by virtue of their practical experience, than Parliament to refashion adjectival rules that have become ossified and inconvenient. Constitutional objections to judges making *substantive* criminal law do not apply.

[32] J. A. Andrews, "The Shackles of Rigidity and Formalism" (1964) 27 M.L.R. 606. In *Ares v Venner* (1970) 14 D.L.R. (3d) 4 the Supreme Court of Canada refused to follow the decision in *Myers* and held that hospital records having circumstantial guarantees of reliability were admissible at common law.

[33] That legislation was replaced by s.68 of PACE, which was itself replaced by ss.23–26 of the Criminal Justice Act 1988. Those provisions were in turn replaced by the scheme in the Criminal Justice Act 2003, discussed in Ch.17.

[34] *McLean* (1967) 52 Cr.App.R. 80.

correct in that G's statement to C of the registration number was clearly being adduced as evidence that the car did bear that number. However, if G had written down the number himself or checked the accuracy of C's note at the time, he would have been able at trial to refresh his memory from the writing and give direct evidence of the number.[35] It is very doubtful whether this difference in the form in which the evidence of the number reached the court justified the different outcome of the case.

2. *Rationale*[36]

The leading judicial account of the reasons for the hearsay rule is in the opinion of Lord Normand in *Teper v R.*[37]:

    16–007

> "[Hearsay] is not the best evidence and it is not delivered on oath. The truthfulness and accuracy of the person whose words are spoken to by another witness cannot be tested by cross-examination and the light which his demeanour would throw on his testimony is lost."

This is not a complete account of the possible justifying arguments for the rule[38] but it is a convenient starting-point for discussion. The object of the discussion is to consider the cogency of the arguments, either individually or collectively, as support for a general exclusionary rule, albeit a rule that can be ameliorated by certain categories of exceptions. The question is whether hearsay evidence is so systemically objectionable as to require a general rule of inadmissibility or whether the problems it presents can be dealt with by some less drastic measure. There are several alternative strategies for regulating hearsay evidence, including leaving the whole matter as an issue of weight for the factfinder, perhaps with appropriate directions and warnings for lay tribunals of fact. As we shall see, different reform strategies have been adopted for civil and criminal proceedings.

(A) Hearsay is not the best evidence[39]

In most cases hearsay is only indirect secondary evidence of facts in issue.[40] Its very nature suggests that, in theory at least, better primary evidence might be available. The shoplifting hypothetical example given above illustrates the point:

    16–008

---

[35] A possibility suggested in *Jones v Metcalfe* [1967] 3 All E.R. 205 DC; and applied in *Kelsey* (1982) 74 Cr.App.R. 213 CA.

[36] A summary of the main arguments appears in Pt VI of Law Com. CP 138. See further A. Choo, *Hearsay and Confrontation in Criminal Trials* (1996), Ch.2, and for a good judicial discussion see *R. v Khelawon* [2006] 2 S.C.R. 787.

[37] *Teper v R.* [1952] A.C. 480 at 486 PC. Lord Normand's statement was cited by Lord Bridge of Harwich in *Blastland* [1986] A.C. 41 at 54; and by Lord Oliver of Aylmerton in *Kearley* [1992] 2 A.C. 228 at 259.

[38] See further R. C. Park, "A Subject Matter Approach to Hearsay Reform" (1987) 86 Mich. L.R. 51.

[39] See generally D. A. Nance, "The Best Evidence Principle" (1988) 73 Iowa L.R. 227, esp. 282–283; M. L. Seigel, "Rationalizing Hearsay: A Proposal for a Best Evidence Hearsay Rule" (1992) 72 Boston U.L.R. 893.

[40] Some facts in issue, such as a person's state of mind, cannot be observed. Thus direct evidence cannot be given of them, but when hearsay evidence is admitted of a person's statements about his state of mind at the time, the courts sometimes talk loosely of such evidence as direct. What they mean is that no better, or more direct, evidence is available.

the best evidence is the testimony of the eyewitness who saw the offence committed; to adduce evidence of her hearsay report of the offence is to use indirect and inferior evidence. It does not, for example, allow the accuracy of her identification to be tested, and it requires the factfinder to draw two inferences rather than one (that is, as to the reliability of the reporter of the hearsay statement as well as to the reliability of the maker of the statement). As a general principle it seems axiomatic that a court should have access to the best available sources of evidence. If therefore there is a choice between seeing and hearing a person in the witness box and having that person's statement reported to the court, the law should generally require direct evidence from the witness.

However, the move from this counsel of prudence to the proposition that hearsay evidence is excluded simply because it is not the best evidence is too crude. There are at least three cogent objections to an argument in this form as a justification for the common law form of the hearsay rule. In some cases a choice is not available, as where the maker of a hearsay statement has died before trial. In these circumstances the hearsay statement is the best evidence in the sense that there is nothing better to be obtained from that person. It can then be argued that, if the evidence is relevant, it is preferable in such a case to admit the hearsay for what it is worth than to have no evidence. Secondly, it is not true that direct testimony is always superior to hearsay. As the Law Commission pointed out,[41] the manufacturers' records in *Myers v DPP*[42] were likely to be much more reliable than the workers' memories in the witness box of the numbers they had observed three years earlier, even assuming that the workers could be traced and that they could remember the numbers at all.[43] Thirdly, the exceptions to the hearsay rule, of which there are many at common law and under the statutory scheme in criminal cases, sometimes admit hearsay when direct evidence is available,[44] but do not always admit hearsay even when it is the best available.[45] There is no necessary correlation.

A more sophisticated form of this rationale might say that hearsay is normally excluded because it is not the best evidence *reasonably available*. The purpose of the rule excluding hearsay would thus be to encourage parties to adduce direct evidence if possible, not least because direct evidence in the form of witness testimony can be tested by cross-examination. It would then follow that if direct testimony is not reasonably available, indirect evidence in the form of hearsay may become the best substitute. This adequately meets the first objection to the cruder form of the rationale, but does not dispose of the other objections. Even when hearsay is the best evidence reasonably available it is not always admitted. Sometimes it is admitted when direct evidence is available, and in some cases indirect evidence in the form of a written report of an event would be better than direct testimony from a witness who has forgotten all the details of the event.

---

[41] Law Com. CP 138 para.6.4.

[42] *Myers v DPP* [1965] A.C. 1001.

[43] They would be able to refresh their memories from the cards they had completed at the time, thus illustrating how the device of refreshing memory may function as a disguised way of admitting reliable hearsay.

[44] e.g. "excited utterances" by spectators at events in issue may be admitted under the res gestae doctrine even if the maker of the statement is available as a witness.

[45] e.g. an oral confession to the offence in question by a third party who has since died.

This rationale seems unsatisfying, therefore, because it places too much emphasis on the form of the evidence, and the chance of a particular form, oral testimony, being available. The notion of the best evidence reasonably available is not strong enough to carry the full weight of the rule, although it does go a long way towards explaining many of the exceptions to the rule.

(B)　Hearsay is not given on oath

The oath sworn by a witness is one of the traditional guarantees at common law of the witness's sincerity. Historically the significance of the oath was founded on the belief that perjury, involving the deliberate breach of a promise made to God to tell the truth, would be punished by divine sanction in the next world. The oath also served as a reminder to the witness that secular punishment for perjury was available in the present world. Since hearsay statements were made out of court neither of these threats against false statement could apply. An alternative claim for the value of the oath is that it serves to remind witnesses of the importance and solemnity of giving evidence in court. The reminder may provide an incentive to witnesses to take greater care in memory recall and in the narration of their evidence. No such incentive applies to a person making an out-of-court statement. **16–009**

Such arguments are not persuasive. The main argument addresses only one of the testimonial infirmities, namely the risk that the person relied on will make a false statement deliberately or recklessly. The oath is no safeguard against mistakes in the original observation, and one may be sceptical whether it makes any significant difference to the risk of defective memory. Equally the oath probably does little to prevent testimony from being ambiguous or unclear in the same way that a hearsay statement might be. A second objection is that the hearsay rule applies to all out-of-court statements, including statements made on oath in previous legal proceedings or otherwise.[46] The justification fails to account for this application of the rule. Thirdly, as well as being under-inclusive, the argument carries little conviction today. Most people have simply ceased to believe in the possibility of divine sanctions for lying,[47] and the risk of prosecution for perjury is rightly thought to be very slight. In 1972 the CLRC commented, "The oath has not prevented an enormous amount of perjury in the courts".[48] The Law Commission concluded that "there is no clear evidence which indicates that an oath or affirmation in itself promotes truthful testimony".[49] Collectively these points suggest that the absence of an oath has no serious claim to be a justifying explanation of the hearsay rule.

---

[46] See above.
[47] *Hayes* [1977] 1 W.L.R. 234 at 237 per Bridge L.J.
[48] *Eleventh Report* para.280(vi).
[49] Law Com. CP 138 para.6.35.

(C) *Absence of cross-examination and the difficulty of assessing the weight of hearsay*

16–010   Lord Normand's third point in *Teper* was that the truthfulness and accuracy of the person whose words are spoken to by another witness cannot be tested by cross-examination. This is often considered to be the most important rationale of the rule. Its advocates point to the instrumental benefits of cross-examination as a means of testing and exposing testimonial infirmities; the claim is that it will reveal insincerity, mistakes and ambiguity in testimony. If these matters cannot be tested it will be more difficult for any factfinder to know what weight to attach to the evidence.[50] It is sometimes argued that juries in particular find it very difficult to assess the weight of hearsay, with the result that there is a substantial risk that they will overestimate its probative value.[51] The absence of cross-examination equals, therefore, the absence of an essential guide to the weight of evidence. If these claims for the benefits of cross-examination are justified, they offer a powerful reason for maintaining the general prohibition on hearsay. In principle the absence of an opportunity for cross-examination when a hearsay statement is given in evidence would provide a systemically valid reason for exclusion. This would still be true even if the hearsay statement was made in previous proceedings and was subject to cross-examination. Clearly, the objection to its later use as a hearsay statement has much less force, but the later evidential context may differ in important ways. If so, a later cross-examiner might want to put additional or different questions.

However, the argument for the importance of cross-examination is open to attack. Despite Wigmore's rhetoric,[52] the effectiveness of cross-examination as a forensic tool for the discovery of truth can be questioned. First, in relation to insincerity, Morgan argued that although exposure of lying is the most dramatic function of cross-examination it is in fact rarely demonstrated.[53] His view is echoed by Allen, who regards the main value of cross-examination as being its effectiveness in "eliminating or limiting the danger of inaccuracy caused by faults in perception and memory rather than in discovering deceit".[54] Even so, the earlier discussion of the weaknesses of identification evidence has shown that while honest witnesses may well be mistaken, cross-examination may not only fail to detect error but in fact increase the confidence of certain witnesses in their accuracy.

---

[50] Lord Phillips in *Horncastle* [2009] UKSC 14; [2010] 1 Cr.App.R. 17 at [21].

[51] A point emphasised by Lord Bridge in *Blastland* [1986] A.C. 41 at 54; repeated by Lord Ackner in *Kearley* [1992] 2 A.C. 228 at 258. These dicta suggest that the supposed fallibility of juries in dealing with hearsay provides an independent rationale for the rule, although this fails to account for the application of the common law rule in all courts, irrespective of whether the tribunal of fact consisted of lay persons or judges.

[52] "[Cross-examination is] ... beyond any doubt the greatest legal engine ever invented for the discovery of truth. However difficult it may be for the layman, the scientist, or the foreign jurist to appreciate this its wonderful power, there has probably never been a moment's doubt upon this point in the mind of a lawyer of experience.": Wigmore, Vol.5 (Chadbourn rev. 1974), para.1367.

[53] E. M. Morgan, "Hearsay Dangers and the Application of the Hearsay Concept" (1948) 62 Harv. L.R. 177, 186.

[54] J. Allen, "The Working and Rationale of the Hearsay Rule and the Implications of Modern Psychological Knowledge" [1991] C.L.P. 217, 230.

Secondly, as the Law Commission pointed out,[55] the techniques of cross-examination are not designed in any event to promote objective truth-finding. This takes us back to the conflict at the heart of the adversarial process. Examination in chief is generally highly structured, with the aim of ensuring that a witness gives evidence in a way that supports the case of the party calling the witness. Free report, qualifications and explanations by the witness are likely to be discouraged. One necessary objective of cross-examination is to correct and complete the witness's narrative by bringing out any such qualifications and explanations that are to the cross-examiner's advantage. But matters do not stop there. Because witnesses are thought of in adversarial terms, as supporters of one "side" or the other, most cross-examiners regard it as their job to weaken or destroy the opposing evidence by showing that the witness who gives the evidence is not to be relied upon.[56] A cross-examiner may frequently try to do this by discrediting the witness. The cross-examiner may use leading or suggestive questions to unsettle and confuse the witness. Another technique is to insist on testimony from the witness about matters of minute detail, sometimes of dubious relevance, with a view to revealing apparent inconsistencies and gaps in the witness's knowledge. Intrusive and aggressive questioning may be used to attack the witness's composure and confidence. If these tactics succeed, so that witnesses become nervous, hesitant or incoherent, it is not necessarily the case that the process of questioning has succeeded in giving a court or jury helpful guidance for assessing the evidence given by the witness. The truth may well be obscured, or lost altogether in the drama of the contest.

By contrast, cross-examination is not likely to make much impression in many cases involving documentary evidence. Questioning the production line workers in *Myers v DPP*[57] would only have detracted from the value of the records in the improbable event of the workers admitting to inventing the numbers or to regularly making mistakes. The nature of such records, and the circumstances in which they are made, suggest they are likely to be reliable. This is an example of the more general point that there may be other features of hearsay statements that provide useful guidance to their reliability irrespective of whether their makers are questioned. These features include how far the statement is consistent with the evidence of other witnesses, how far it is consistent with any admitted facts, and how far it is inherently plausible as part of the "story" of the party relying on it. **16–011**

The objections to the value of cross-examination should not be overstated. They are far from a complete refutation of this particular rationale for a generalised hearsay rule. There will be many cases where the probative value of hearsay evidence, especially in the form of oral assertions, is highly problematic in the absence of cross-examination. It may be that lay factfinders, juries and lay magistrates, do have particular difficulty evaluating hearsay, although this claim

---

[55] Law Com. CP 138 paras 6.45 onwards. See also J. McEwan, *Evidence and the Adversarial Process*, 2nd edn (1998), pp.14–16.

[56] See Ch.14. For further discussion, see M. Stone, *Proof of Fact in Criminal Trials* (1984), Ch.15.

[57] *Myers v DPP* [1965] A.C. 1001.

has been questioned by some American empirical research.[58] Nevertheless, the objections offer an important corrective to an uncritical acceptance of the frequent rhetorical claims for the value of cross-examination.

(D)   Demeanour of the witness

16–012   The Law Commission noted that opinions differ about the value of a witness's demeanour as a guide to reliability.[59] Some judges and commentators regard it as a great advantage for a factfinder to be able to observe first-hand the way in which a witness gives evidence. The assumption they make is that a person's body language, manner of delivery, confidence, ability to deal with questions and so on may all provide important clues to whether the person can be relied on as truthful. Others believe that it is very difficult to discern from such aspects of demeanour whether a witness is telling the truth. Physical signs that some people think of as symptoms of lying may in fact be reactions to stress, and it should be remembered that the process of testifying is in itself a stressful experience for many witnesses. The Commission cites Spencer and Flin, who concluded after a review of the relevant psychological literature:

> "The most that can be said for the value of the demeanour of a witness as an indicator of the truth is that it is one factor, which must be weighed up together with everything else. It would be quite wrong to promote it to the level where we use it to accept or reject the oral testimony of a witness in the face of other weighty matters all of which point the other way."[60]

If we accept that behavioural research does not bear out the assumptions about the value of demeanour, and to some extent contradicts them,[61] it follows that this argument provides a very shaky foundation for the hearsay rule. Furthermore, the argument is under-inclusive insofar as it fails to account for the full width of the rule. The rule currently extends to hearsay in documentary form, where the demeanour of the witness producing the document may be comparatively unimportant, and even to pre-recorded interviews on film or video with absent witnesses, where demeanour can be observed. The argument is probably best regarded, therefore, as an aspect of the objection to hearsay based on the lack of opportunity to cross-examine when the evidence is given.

(E)   Risk of manufactured evidence

16–013   Lord Normand did not include the risk of manufacture in his list of reasons against hearsay, but others have insisted on its importance. For example, in

---

[58] P. Miene, R. C. Park and E. Borgida, "Jury Decision Making and the Evaluation of Hearsay Evidence" (1992) 76 Minn. L.R. 683; M. B. Kovera, R. C. Park and S. D. Penrod, "Jurors' Perceptions of Eyewitness and Hearsay Evidence" (1992) 76 Minn. L.R. 703.
[59] Law Com. CP 138 paras 6.20–6.30.
[60] J. R. Spencer and R. Flin, *The Evidence of Children*, 2nd edn (London: Blackstone, 1993), p.280.
[61] e.g. Allen, "The Working and Rationale of the Hearsay Rule" [1991] C.L.P. 217, 225, cites psychological studies on eyewitness evidence as seeming "to indicate that frequently the confidence of a witness, by proving not to be any consistent indicator of accuracy, may mislead the trier of fact who subscribes to the intuitive connection between the two".

Kearley,[62] Lord Ackner referred to the danger of concoction of hearsay evidence as one reason for excluding police evidence of alleged incriminating telephone calls when the callers did not testify. The CLRC, on the other hand, was greatly exercised by the possibility of hearsay manufactured by the defence,[63] and its attitude was supported by the Bar Council in its response to the *Eleventh Report*.[64] Subscribers to this fear of defence hearsay sometimes reinforce their anxiety by pointing out that the defence need only raise a reasonable doubt in order to secure an acquittal. This may lead to an argument that the law should not make it too easy for the defence to raise doubts by adducing evidence of dubious or speculative worth.

Of course the risk of manufacture may also exist in direct testimony. The testifying witness can be cross-examined as to his sincerity whether he is giving direct evidence or evidence of a hearsay assertion, but in the latter case it is not also possible to cross-examine the maker of the alleged assertion. It is undeniable that this increases the danger presented by hearsay, and the risk increases further with multiple hearsay involving several repetitions by one person to another. Whether this is enough to justify a categorical rule of inadmissibility of hearsay evidence is doubtful. The degree of danger is very variable, and the argument based on risk of manufacture is weak where much documentary hearsay is concerned, particularly if the evidence in question was recorded on film or video. This is not to say that the risk is negligible even in these cases. It is rather to argue that the issue is better regarded as an issue about the weight of the evidence, and that factfinders should be left to determine weight in the normal way, perhaps with an appropriate judicial warning in the case of a jury. The Law Commission's conclusion was that the risk is a good justification only for excluding multiple hearsay (i.e. other than first-hand hearsay) and the hearsay evidence of unidentified witnesses. As far as police evidence of out-of-court statements by witnesses is concerned, it has been suggested that codes of practice should be drawn up to govern the recording of such statements, the codes being backed by the exclusionary discretion under s.78 of PACE.[65] This would be valuable in reducing the risk of police fabrication of hearsay statements.

(F) Risk of error in transmission

This argument complements the previous one. Just as a witness may concoct a hearsay assertion, or unwittingly repeat a concocted assertion, so may a witness misreport an assertion by another. People may mishear, misunderstand or misinterpret things said to them[66]; moreover, the phenomenon of a person hearing what the person wants or expects to hear is a commonplace of experience.[67] Again, the risk of error increases with the number of repetitions.

16–014

---

[62] *Kearley* [1992] 2 A.C. 228 at 258.
[63] *Eleventh Report* para.229.
[64] Cited in Law Com. CP 138 p.76 fn.11.
[65] See J. D. Jackson in (1995) 16 Mississippi Coll. L.R. 104.
[66] R. Lempert and S. Saltzburg, *A Modern Approach to Evidence*, 2nd edn (West Publishing, 1983), p.353.
[67] R. C. Park, "A Subject Matter Approach to Hearsay Reform" (1987) 86 Mich. L.R. 51.

This is probably an undervalued argument. It adds a further element to the traditional hearsay dangers discussed earlier. We should note, also, that even where an oral assertion has been heard correctly it may be reported to a court in the form of a paraphrase that changes the emphasis or the meaning itself. These risks are greatest when only oral assertions are involved, but they may still apply when the hearsay statement takes the form of a written report of something that the writer of the report has read or heard from another source. Multiple hearsay is then involved. However, a film or tape of a person making an oral hearsay assertion is outwith the risk, because there is no doubt about the words used. To that extent the argument is under-inclusive.

The Law Commission's provisional view was that this risk should be treated in the same way as the risk of manufacture, namely as going to the weight of the evidence. The risk of error in transmission was thought to be a good justification only for excluding multiple hearsay. If the argument is considered in isolation this view makes practical sense, although it draws a somewhat arbitrary line between first-hand and multiple hearsay. However, it is stronger when coupled with the argument based on absence of cross-examination because we then identify at least two sources of potential error as a reason for exclusion; mistakes by the maker of the assertion and mistakes by the transmitting witness.

(G)   Right to confront one's accusers[68]

16–015   The justifying arguments for the hearsay rule that we have considered so far are all concerned with the probative value of hearsay evidence. They offer reasons why the evidence may be unreliable and/or its weight may be difficult to assess. In theoretical terms these issues go to the accuracy component of factfinding, and the location of the debate is the allocation we make between matters affecting admissibility and matters affecting weight. A recurring theme of this book is that rules of admissibility designed to promote rectitude of decision are only justified if the evidence in question presents systemic risks of unreliability such that it is unsafe to give factfinders a free hand in evaluating it. If the case for a general exclusionary rule is not established, we then consider the role of judicial discretion in excluding particular items of evidence if they present significant risks of unreliability in the circumstances of the individual case. Further alternatives involve the use of corroboration requirements and/or judicial instructions and guidance to lay tribunals on the determination of the weight of the evidence. It is not clear at this stage that the justifying arguments have positively demonstrated the need for a general prohibition on hearsay evidence, certainly not a rule as widely formulated as the one set out above.

We turn therefore to consider a different kind of argument. This argument is founded on the principle that a defendant has a *right* to confront the witnesses against him. Advocates of a right to confrontation[69] argue that it can protect two

---

[68] See I. Dennis, "The Right to Confront Witnesses: Meanings, Myths and Human Rights" [2010] Crim. L.R. 255; W. E. O'Brian, "The right of confrontation: US and European perspectives" (2005) 121 L.Q.R. 481.

[69] See fn 8 above.

kinds of interests. The first is the interest of a party in accurate fact-determination. This argument focuses attention on the instrumental benefits of confrontation, maintaining that it is crucial in helping to determine the probative value of evidence and claiming that parties who submit or who are forced to submit their disputes to official adjudication should be entitled to use techniques calculated to maximise rectitude of decision. The second approach argues that a right of confrontation demonstrates official concern and respect for human personality.[70] Irrespective of its instrumental benefits for accuracy of decision the confrontation right delivers opportunities to parties to maximise their participation in the process of decision-making and in this way it promotes legitimacy of decision in the eyes of the parties and the public generally. In order to evaluate the claims of these arguments as a justification for a general rule against hearsay we need to be clear about what we understand by "confrontation".

However, it is clear on analysis that judges and scholars understand different things by the term "confrontation". The term is a convenient and evocative descriptor, but its users appear to have no common conception of its meaning.[71] In the light of these disagreements it is suggested that it is more accurate to understand "confrontation" not as a single unified right, but rather as a bundle of rights. These rights are closely linked, but have different meanings because they emphasise different aspects of the testimonial process in a criminal trial. Analysis suggests four such meanings. First, there is the right to public trial, meaning that witnesses should give their evidence openly in court in public rather than having it taken in private and then reported to the court. Secondly, there is the right to a face-to-face confrontation: the right to have an accusing witness physically present in the court so that the adverse testimony can be given to the defendant's face and not behind his back. Thirdly, there is the right to cross-examine a witness against the defendant, sometimes called a right of challenge. Of course physical confrontation is itself a kind of challenge, and a right to physical confrontation would normally imply a right of challenge by questioning.[72] The converse, however, is not true; challenge does not necessarily imply physical confrontation. A defendant might, for example, be able to challenge evidence by means of questions from his counsel to a witness not physically present, or, in some legal systems, by questions put by a judge or investigating magistrate at a preliminary hearing in the absence of the defendant. It is obvious that the admission of hearsay evidence may limit all three of these forms of a right to confrontation. The maker of a hearsay statement may have made it in private, may not be in court when evidence of the statement is given, and may never be be available for cross-examination. The fourth form of a right to confrontation is the defendant's right to know the identity of a witness against him. This is the form of the right to confrontation which is at the heart of the debate about witness anonymity.[73] Anonymity, like the admission of hearsay, may impact on the other

---

[70] T. Massaro, "The Dignity Value of Face-to-Face Confrontations" (1988) 40 Fla. L.R. 863; E. Scallen, "Constitutional Dimensions of Hearsay Reform: Toward a Three Dimensional Confrontation Clause" (1992) 76 Minn. L.R. 623.

[71] Dennis, "The Right to Confront Witnesses" [2010] Crim. L.R. 255, 256.

[72] Friedman claims that a confrontation right signifies an "absolute right" of cross-examination: (1995) 16 Mississippi Coll. L.R. 87, 88.

[73] See Ch.15.

three forms of confrontation. It may limit cross-examination as to credibility, and measures of screening and voice modulation cut back the principle of public trial and may largely deny face-to-face confrontation.

16–016   It is important to distinguish between these meanings of the right to confrontation, because the strength of the different rights varies, and not all of them are recognised in all jurisdictions. For example, one of the best-known expressions of a right to confrontation is in the Sixth Amendment to the United States Constitution. The US Supreme Court has held on a number of occasions that this constitutional right to confront one's accuser guarantees a face-to-face meeting.[74] However, there is no right of physical confrontation in English law. As noted in the previous chapter, witnesses may be screened from the accused in court, or in some cases they may give their evidence away from the courtroom via a video link.[75] Very exceptionally, a disruptive accused may be removed from the court and the trial will proceed in his absence.[76] Even granted that these procedures are exceptional, the non-recognition of a strong right of physical confrontation of witnesses[77] makes it difficult to account for the hearsay rule on this basis. In addition, as the Law Commission has pointed out, there is no evidence supporting the claim that physical confrontation increases witness veracity.[78] If anything, the stress involved is likely to inhibit a witness's coherence and confidence, as the use of screens for vulnerable witnesses clearly suggests. Thirdly, if the maker of a hearsay assertion were available to be confronted in court at some stage, there would be little reason to apply the rule if its basis is a right to confrontation. Yet the general rule applies irrespective of whether the maker of the assertion is available as a witness. For these reasons a right to physical confrontation cannot convincingly justify the hearsay rule in English law.

What about the right to challenge the accuser by cross-examination? Like physical confrontation, this is an essential element of the constitutional right to confrontation in the US.[79] There is no doubt that this form of the right is also recognised in English law. The right to question witnesses is regarded as one of the elements of natural justice in adjudicative decision-making.[80] The right of challenge by cross-examination also finds expression in art.6(3)(d) of the ECHR. This provides that:

---

[74] e.g. *Coy v Iowa* (1988) 487 U.S. 1012 at 1016.

[75] See Ch.15.

[76] A defendant has a right to attend his trial, and in a trial on indictment, an obligation to do so. But the court retains a discretion to direct that in exceptional circumstances a trial should take place, or continue, in the defendant's absence: *Jones* [2002] UKHL 5; [2003] A.C. 1 HL. Disruption of the proceedings is one such circumstance; see e.g. *Lee Kun* [1916] 1 K.B. 337.

[77] The ECHR does not guarantee a right to a face-to-face confrontation, as Baroness Hale noted in *R. v Camberwell Green Youth Court* [2005] UKHL 4; [2005] 2 Cr.App.R. 1 at [49].

[78] Law Com. CP 138 para.6.88.

[79] See *Crawford v Washington* (2004) 124 S.Ct. 1354, where the Supreme Court held that the Sixth Amendment bars the admission of "testimonial" statements by unavailable witnesses whom the defendant has had no opportunity to cross-examine. For discussion see the articles by Friedman and Ho in (2004) 8 E. & P. at 1 and 147 respectively.

[80] *R. v Edmonton Justices Ex p. Brooks* [1960] 2 All E.R. 475 DC; *Blaise v Blaise* [1969] 2 All E.R. 1032 CA; *R. v Birmingham City Juvenile Court Ex p. Birmingham City Council* [1988] 1 All E.R. 683 CA.

"Everyone charged with a criminal offence has the following minimum rights... (d) to examine or have examined witnesses against him..."

Accordingly this requirement is one of the factors that determines whether there has been a fair trial within the meaning of art.6(1). As regards its significance for the hearsay rule, it seems clear that a general ban on the admission of hearsay evidence for the prosecution is consistent with the requirement, since the maker of a hearsay statement will often not be available for examination at trial. The rule also applies to the defence, and in *Blastland v United Kingdom*[81] the European Commission of Human Rights was faced with a challenge to the hearsay rule in the form of a claim that its exclusion of defence hearsay vitiated the accused's right to a fair trial. The Commission rejected the claim, ruling that the purposes of the hearsay rule were legitimate and that the rule did not in principle entail a breach of art.6(1). This was a strong case because the defence had argued that the evidence in question was necessary in order to avoid wrongful conviction, but the Commission in effect refused to allow defendants to have the benefit of the rule in terms of prohibiting prosecution hearsay without the burden of the restrictions it might impose on defence evidence. This ruling follows from the principle that one of the purposes of art.6(3)(d) is to secure equality of arms between prosecution and accused.[82]

To say that the hearsay rule does not breach the Convention is not of course to say that the English rule is a necessary condition of a fair trial. A series of cases in Strasbourg has examined the extent to which various presentations of prosecution "hearsay" have resulted in the accused failing to receive a fair trial. The "hearsay" is usually in the form of statements from witnesses given before trial, to police or investigating judges. "Witness" in art.6(3)(d) has an autonomous meaning that includes a person who makes a pre-trial statement subsequently adduced in evidence at the trial, but who does not appear as a witness at the trial to give oral evidence.[83] Certain conclusions emerge from the cases that are significant for both the scope and the rationale of the rule in England.

    The first, and crucial, point is that the rights of the defence under art.6(3)(d) must be respected but they are not absolute.[84] Like the other express and implied rights in art.6 they may be subject to some qualification. The general principle is that "all the evidence must... be produced in the presence of the accused with a view to adversarial argument".[85] However, this does not prevent the prosecution relying on pre-trial statements in certain circumstances. Thus, according to Strasbourg, the prosecution can use a hearsay statement by a witness without violating art.6 if the defence had an opportunity to question the witness in pre-trial proceedings.[86] Even if the defence did not have this opportunity the use

16–017

---

[81] *Blastland v United Kingdom* (1988) 10 E.H.R.R. 528.

[82] *X v FRG* (1151/61); *Ochensberger v Austria* (1995) 18 E.H.R.R. C.D. 170 at 171.

[83] *Kostovski v Netherlands* (1990) 12 E.H.R.R. 434.

[84] See Emmerson, Ashworth and Macdonald, para.15–122.

[85] *Barbera, Messegue and Jabardo v Spain* (1989) 11 E.H.R.R. 360 at [78].

[86] *Kostovski v The Netherlands* (1990) 12 E.H.R.R. 434; *SN v Sweden* (2004) 39 E.H.R.R. 13, where defence counsel waived the right to attend an interview with the child complainant of sexual abuse, but questions drafted by him were put to the child by the police. See also *Isgro v Italy* (1991) Series A No.194 (the defendant was allowed to question a key witness at a pre-trial confrontation before the

of the statement may not render the trial unfair if the witness is identified (so that the defence were able to question his or her credibility), and there is other evidence to support the conviction.[87] Where however a hearsay statement was the sole or decisive evidence for conviction, and there was no (or only a restricted) opportunity for questioning of the witness by the defence, the European Court of Human Rights has stated on several occasions that there would be a violation of art. 6.[88] This limitation, that untested hearsay evidence may not constitute the sole or decisive evidence for conviction, would suggest that the right to confrontation by examination of witnesses provides a foundation for the general rule against hearsay. It implies that the exceptions to the hearsay rule can only go so far. But the limitation is highly controversial. It was firmly rejected by the UK Supreme Court in *Horncastle*.[89] Subsequently in *Al-Khawaja and Tahery v United Kingdom*,[90] the Grand Chamber of the European Court of Human Rights modified its stance by holding that the limitation should not be applied as an inflexible rule, but it remains as an important consideration in decisions whether the defendant's trial complies with the requirements of art.6. Since the "sole or decisive evidence" principle also affects the use of witness anonymity orders, as noted in the previous chapter, its status is of major practical importance for criminal justice in England. In order to appreciate fully its significance, we need to consider the system of exceptions to the hearsay rule established by the Criminal Justice Act 2003. The next chapter deals with these and then returns to discuss the Strasbourg limitation on the use of hearsay and anonymous evidence in more detail.

16–018   This survey of the justifying arguments for the hearsay rule shows that the case for its retention is not compelling. There are objections to all the systemic arguments relating to the probative value of hearsay. Even considered collectively rather than individually, they do not produce a strong case in favour of a broad strict rule of exclusion. The argument for a right of confrontation suffers from a lack of clarity of meaning. The form of the right consisting of physical confrontation of a witness is not recognised in either English law or the jurisprudence of the ECHR. The form of the right consisting of challenge to the witness by examination is recognised, but it is not clear that it adds much to the systemic arguments for the rule, *unless* the "sole or decisive evidence" principle turns out to be a necessary condition of a fair trial. The further, non-consequentialist, argument that a right of confrontation acknowledges the defendant's entitlement to respect for his dignity and autonomy and maximises his opportunity for participation in the process of adjudication, represents a mainly American constitutional view of confrontation that is not replicated in the

---

investigating judge, but without the benefit of advice from his lawyer, who had been excluded from the confrontation. The court held that no violation of art.6(3)(d) had occurred. This is doubtful, in view of the importance of the right to legal representation, particularly in relation to the questioning of witnesses).

[87] *Asch v Austria* (1993) 15 E.H.R.R. 597; *Ferrantelli and Santangelo v Italy* (1997) 23 E.H.R.R. 288.

[88] See the cases cited in Ch.17 fn 269.

[89] *Horncastle* [2009] UKSC 14; [2009] 2 W.L.R. 47.

[90] *Al-Khawaja and Tahery v United Kingdom* (2012) 54 E.H.R.R. 23.

English approach to the right.[91] In one sense, the weakness of the justification for the hearsay rule has always been recognised in the form of the numerous exceptions at common law and under statute. In due course this chapter will show that this acknowledgment has reached its logical conclusion in civil cases with the abolition of the rule. Hearsay is now generally admissible in civil cases subject to certain procedural requirements. This is not so in criminal cases, but the narrowing of the exclusionary rule and the extension of the exceptions made by the Criminal Justice Act 2003 are further indications of the fragility of the rationale for the rule.

C. Application of the Common Law Rule: Hearsay and Original Evidence

Section A of this chapter explained that it is essential to analyse the purpose for which a party is adducing evidence of an out-of-court statement. At common law it was only where the purpose was to ask the factfinder to accept that the statement was evidence of the facts stated (in other words, that the statement was proof of its own truth) that the hearsay rule applied. If the party's purpose was to show only that the statement was made, the evidence of the statement fell outside the hearsay rule and would be admissible provided, of course, that it was relevant to an issue in the case to prove that the statement was made. Evidence admitted to prove that an out-of-court statement was made is often called original evidence, as a way of distinguishing it from hearsay evidence offered to prove that an out-of-court statement was true.

16–019

The distinction between original and hearsay evidence is very clear in the example of evidence of the speaking or writing of a defamatory statement. This is because the making of a defamatory statement by the defendant is a fact in issue itself; its making gives rise to the claimant's cause of action. The last thing the claimant wants to do is to prove that the statement was true. There are other situations where the speaking or writing of certain words may, as a matter of substantive law, give rise to legal rights and obligations. Proof that such statements were made is sometimes called proof of "operative words", meaning words whose utterance has legal consequences by virtue of rules of law. An example is a statement by D to P "I will sell you my car for £1,000". According to the law of contract this is a valid contractual offer if a reasonable man would interpret D's words as signifying an intention to be bound on acceptance. Irrespective of D's "real" intentions, a binding contract will exist if P accepts the offer. Therefore, when witness W testifies that he heard D speak these words he is giving original evidence of a fact in issue, namely whether D made a statement amounting to an offer. The evidence is not being offered for a hearsay purpose because it is not necessary for P to prove that D's statement was true in the sense that D had a subjective intention to make an offer. It is sufficient for P to show that D uttered words that, on the objective test prescribed by the law of contract, would reasonably be understood to signify an intention to be bound. Similarly,

---

[91] See *Grant v R.* [2006] UKPC 2; [2007] 1 A.C. 1, where the Privy Council summarily dismissed an argument for the adoption of the American view of confrontation in the interpretation of the Jamaican constitutional right to examine witnesses.

words that accompany a handing-over of money are admissible as original evidence to explain the nature of the transaction.[92]

The making of an out-of-court statement may be relevant to a fact in issue irrespective of the truth of the statement. If so, evidence of it will be admissible as original evidence and will not contravene the hearsay rule. Clear examples occur in relation to defences in criminal law founded on the defendant's reaction to things said by others. Evidence that a deceased person, whom the defendant is charged with murdering, said to the defendant "You are a child abuser" is admissible, not for the purpose of showing that the defendant is a child abuser, but for the purpose of showing that the victim made a highly provocative accusation that might have caused the defendant to lose his self-control. In *Subramaniam v Public Prosecutor*,[93] the defendant was charged with unlawful possession of ammunition. His defence was that he had been acting under duress from terrorists and he tendered evidence of threatening statements made to him by the terrorists capable of amounting to duress. The Privy Council held that the trial judge had wrongly excluded evidence of the terrorists' statements as hearsay. After stating the general principle set out above the Privy Council went on to say that the relevant issue was the defendant's conduct and his accompanying state of mind, in particular whether he believed that threats had been made against him. Irrespective of whether the threatening statements were true (in the sense that the terrorists sincerely intended to carry out the threats) the defendant could nonetheless have believed them to be true, thus satisfying one of the conditions of the defence of duress. Accordingly it was relevant to show simply that the threats were made. Putting the point another way, the court was not being asked to rely upon the terrorists as speakers of truth. The person whose credibility was in issue was the defendant when he claimed to have a certain state of mind as a result of what he had been told. The defendant was of course a witness and available for cross-examination.

16–020   Accurate analysis of the substantive law will help to decide the relevance of an out-of-court statement. For example, relevance may well alter according to how the elements of a crime are defined. If the substantive law is that it is enough to prove that a statement in certain terms was made, evidence of the making of it will be direct evidence and not hearsay.[94] The use of a statement as original evidence, on the basis that its making is relevant to a fact in issue, will also depend on the state of the other evidence. Depending on what it is sought to prove in the context of the case as a whole, a statement may or may not be used

---

[92] *Hayslep v Gymer* (1834) 1 Ad. & El. 162.

[93] *Subramaniam v Public Prosecutor* [1956] 1 W.L.R. 965. The principle stated in this case was applied in *R. v T* [2007] EWCA Crim 1250, where in a murder case a letter written to the defendant by a co-accused, telling him that his knife (the murder weapon) had been found, was held admissible as original evidence. In the circumstances of the case the letter was relevant to show the close association between the defendant and the co-accused, and it was also relevant to show the defendant's state of mind when he made a written statement to the police saying that he had lent his knife to a third person named in the letter.

[94] See, e.g. *Woodhouse v Hall* (1980) 72 Cr.App.R. 39 (statements amounting to offers of sexual sevices not hearsay where the substantive law of acting in the management of a brothel required only that the offers were made; but see the comment on this case by R. Pattenden, "Conceptual versus Pragmatic Approaches to Hearsay" (1993) 56 M.L.R. 138, 143).

for a hearsay purpose. This can lead to sophisticated analysis of items of evidence that any lay person would assume to be important for the decision in the case. *Ratten v R.*[95] provides a dramatic example. The defendant was charged with the murder of his wife by shooting her at their home. His defence was that the gun had gone off accidentally while he was cleaning it. The other evidence established that the shooting occurred between 1.12pm and 1.20pm when the defendant telephoned for an ambulance. The defendant denied that any telephone call had been made from the house during the previous eight minutes. The prosecution called evidence from a telephonist at the local exchange who testified that at about 1.15pm she received a call from the defendant's house. When she answered she heard a female voice, hysterical and sobbing, say "Get me the police please". The speaker then rang off. The defendant appealed against his conviction for murder on the ground that the telephonist's evidence should have been excluded as inadmissible hearsay. Dismissing the appeal the Privy Council held that the evidence did not amount to hearsay, but that if there was a hearsay element involved, it was still admissible under the exception relating to res gestae.

The latter point is discussed in Ch.17; for the moment we are concerned with whether the evidence was hearsay at all. If we begin with its relevance, the fact that a call was made, and was made by the defendant's wife, who was the only woman in the house, contradicted the defendant's story in an important respect about what happened during the crucial eight minutes and suggested that he was lying. The evidence of these facts was plainly not hearsay, since the telephonist was able to give direct evidence that a female person made a call at that time. No out-of-court assertion is relied on to prove this fact. This point does not, however, account for the admission of the evidence relating to the tone of the woman's voice or the words she used. The Privy Council suggested that the relevance of this was possibly to show that the wife was in a state of emotion or fear at some existing or impending emergency; this would tend to rebut the defence of accident, which implied a state of normality in the house prior to the gun going off. On this view, evidence as to the hysterical and sobbing tone of the woman's voice is not hearsay because no assertion is being relied on to establish the woman's state of emotion. There would be a reasonable inference, in the light of the other evidence, that the emotion was produced by the defendant's actions at the time. But to strengthen the inference that the defendant's actions were threatening, we need the actual words spoken by the caller. Lord Wilberforce lumped these in with the rest of the evidence about the call on the basis that "they were relevant and necessary evidence in order to explain and complete the fact of the call being made. A telephone call is a composite act, made up of manual operations together with the utterance of words".[96] The whole of the telephonist's evidence was, on this view, evidence of relevant facts; in particular, the woman's request for the police was not being used "testimonially" to establish any fact.

This is not to say that the wife's statement was not capable of being used as an implied assertion that the defendant was attacking her. Lord Wilberforce argued rather that this was not how the case was presented to the jury. His analysis

---

[95] *Ratten v R.* [1972] A.C. 378.
[96] *Ratten v R.* [1972] A.C. 378 at 388.

proceeds on the basis that the words spoken as an integral part of the call were sufficiently relevant in the light of the evidence in the case as a whole without the need to rely on any such implied assertion. This is surely right, given the defendant's story that no call was made and that the shooting was accidental; had he not said this the prosecution might well have needed to rely on an implied assertion by the wife that the defendant was attacking her. In such a case the relevance of the call would be unclear unless it were being offered as equivalent to an express statement by the wife to the effect: "Help! My husband is threatening to shoot me".

16–021 A final aspect of the distinction between original and hearsay evidence is concerned with the admissibility of articles bearing marks of identification. We have already seen how in *Myers v DPP*[97] the cards containing records of engine numbers filled in by unidentified employees were treated as hearsay evidence of the "identity" of the cars containing those engines. It follows that if goods bear a label saying "Made in Hong Kong" or "Produce of Morocco", the label is hearsay evidence that the goods were in fact made in Hong Kong or produced in Morocco.[98] The label is being used "testimonially" to establish a fact, and the court is asked to rely on the unidentified writer of the label as having made an accurate record. This is again a logical application of the hearsay rule to an express assertion, although it has to be said that in many cases it is a formal one. In many cases the hearsay dangers will not be present and cross-examination would be unproductive. The exceptions are cases where there is reason to think that the producers of goods had a motive to misrepresent their origin.[99] This is pre-eminently a question of weight on the facts of the case and should be left accordingly to the factfinder. One major recent codification of evidence law has made express provision for this kind of identifying mark to be admissible.[100]

16–022 Occasionally a court may be able to avoid the hearsay rule by a process of reasoning that treats a mark of identification as a relevant fact and not as an assertion. This depends entirely on the issue in the case and the state of the other evidence. An illustration is provided by the much-debated case of *Rice*.[101] This was a conspiracy case in which an issue arose as to whether Rice had been a passenger on a certain flight to Manchester. An airline representative was allowed to give evidence that a ticket found in the file of tickets used on that flight bore the name of Rice. The Court of Criminal Appeal held that this was not hearsay evidence. Winn L.J. explained:

> "the ticket and the fact of the presence of that ticket in the file or other place where tickets used by passengers would in the ordinary course be found, were facts which were in logic relevant to the issue whether or not there flew on those flights two men [one] of whom was a Mr Rice ... The relevance of that ticket in logic and its legal admissibility as a piece of real evidence both stem from the same root, viz., the balance of probability recognised by common

---

[97] *Myers v DPP* [1965] A.C. 1001.
[98] *Patel v Comptroller of Customs* [1966] A.C. 356; *Comptroller of Customs v Western Electric Ltd* [1966] A.C. 367.
[99] See the example given by J. C. Smith, *Criminal Evidence* (1995), p.62 fn.6.
[100] Evidence Act 1995 (Commonwealth of Australia) s.70.
[101] *Rice* [1963] 1 Q.B. 857.

sense and common knowledge that an air ticket which has been used on a flight and which has a name upon it has more likely than not been used by a man of that name."[102]

Winn L.J. went on to say that he doubted whether the ticket could have been used for the purpose of proving that the booking had been made by Rice. This would require reliance on an implied assertion by the booking clerk that he or she was issuing the ticket to a man named Rice, and would infringe the hearsay rule. The decision has been strongly criticised,[103] and some commentators take the view that it is inconsistent with *Myers v DPP* and may have been impliedly overruled by that case.[104] However, it is submitted that the case was rightly decided for the reason given in the judgment. The other evidence showed that the ticket had been used on the flight in question. We can then ask: "Who had used it?" The most likely answer was someone whose name corresponded to the name on the ticket. The background generalisation that underpins this conclusion is that things bearing marks of identification that are found in certain places are likely to have been in the physical control of a person with that identity who took them there. This reasoning does not require the court to rely on anything expressly or impliedly asserted in the thing itself. Suppose, to change the facts, that after the flight a cleaner of the plane had found under a seat a diary bearing an inscription "This diary belongs to J. Rice". If the ownership of the diary is in issue the inscription is clearly hearsay evidence that J. Rice is the owner.[105] If, on the other hand, the issue is how the diary came to be in that place, the probable inference is that it was left there by someone of that name. The same would be true if instead of an inscription the diary bore a photograph of a person. Can there be any doubt that the finding of the diary would be admissible evidence to show that the person whose photograph it was had probably been on the aircraft? In summary, the point is that the criticisms of *Rice* confuse the use of a document for a hearsay purpose with the use of the document as a thing for the purpose of identifying a particular person at a particular place and time. This conclusion gains support from the decision of the Court of Appeal in *Lydon (Sean)*.[106] The defendant was charged with robbery. The prosecution adduced evidence that two pieces of paper were found in the immediate vicinity of a gun allegedly used in the robbery. Written on the pieces of paper were the words "Sean rules" and "Sean rules 85" respectively. The Court of Appeal held that the evidence was admissible to found inferences that the paper had previously been in the possession of someone either named Sean or associated with someone named Sean, and that Sean had therefore been in the area where the papers were found. Clearly the pieces of paper were not being used as documentary evidence that Sean ruled anything.[107]

---

[102] *Rice* [1963] 1 Q.B. 857 at 871.

[103] R. Cross, "The Periphery of Hearsay" (1969) 7 Melbourne Univ. L.R. 1; A. Rein, "The Scope of Hearsay" (1994) 110 L.Q.R. 431.

[104] J. A. Andrews and M. Hirst, *Criminal Evidence*, 3rd edn (London: Jordans Ltd, 1997), para.17–029; A. Choo, *Hearsay and Confrontation in Criminal Trials* (1996), p.45.

[105] cf. *US v Snow* (1975) 517 F.2d. 441 (name on a briefcase tag held not to be hearsay evidence that the person named was the owner of the briefcase); criticised by Graham, "Stickperson Hearsay" [1982] Univ. of Illinois L.R. 887, 912–913.

[106] *Lydon (Sean)* (1987) 85 Cr.App.R. 221.

[107] A. Choo, *Hearsay and Confrontation in Criminal Trials* (1996), p.46. Curiously, Woolf L.J. was doubtful whether *Rice* was still good law but, on the argument presented here, the 2 decisions were in

D. APPLICATION OF THE COMMON LAW RULE: IMPLIED ASSERTIONS

16–023   To summarise the discussion so far, the hearsay rule at common law applied to express assertions (other than those of a testifying witness) when these were adduced to prove the truth of the facts asserted. Express assertions can be made orally, in writing, or by conduct, as where a person nods in response to a question or points to someone present when asked to name her attacker.[108] Statements adduced as facts were outside the scope of the rule, provided of course it was relevant to prove that the statement was made, as opposed to proving that the statement was true.

We turn now to consider the application of the common law rule to implied assertions.[109] This was one of the most difficult and controversial aspects of the rule, and it generated some problematic case law and a substantial secondary literature. Fortunately it is not now necessary to consider the problem in the detail that used to be required. As we shall see in Ch.17, the reforms made by the Criminal Justice Act 2003 for criminal cases include a redefinition of the rule against hearsay in terms that take most implied assertions outside the scope of the rule. In civil cases the statutory formulation of the rule is in the same terms as the common law, but even if implied assertions remain subject to the rule, hearsay evidence is now generally admissible in civil proceedings.

The problem concerns evidence of a statement and/or conduct by a person that was not intended by that person to assert the fact the evidence is tendered to prove but that was nonetheless founded on a belief in the existence of that fact. The argument for the application of the hearsay rule is that the court is being asked to treat the statement and/or conduct as equivalent to an express assertion of the fact to be proved. A well-known example of the problem is the hypothetical put by Parke B. in *Wright v Doe d. Tatham*[110] of the conduct of a deceased ship's captain carefully examining a ship before embarking on it with his family. If evidence of this conduct is tendered as relevant to an issue of whether the ship was seaworthy when it set sail, the court is being asked to conclude that the ship was seaworthy on the basis that the captain was an expert and would not have embarked unless he thought it was seaworthy. His conduct is thus being used as evidence that the captain held this opinion; it is being offered as an implied equivalent of an express statement by him at the time that the ship was seaworthy. Put in this way it appears logical to apply the rule. The court is asked to rely on the expertise of the captain and his credibility is in issue. An inquirer would want

---

harmony. For a further example of the same reasoning see *McIntosh* [1992] Crim. L.R. 651. Contrast *Horne* [1992] Crim. L.R. 304 where the Court of Appeal held inadmissible against the defendant evidence of the finding of two pieces of paper referring to the defendant and containing calculations that possibly related to the cost of importing drugs. The papers were found in the flat of a co-accused and may have been treated as an implied admission by the co-accused incriminating the defendant.

[108]   *Chandrasekera v R.* [1937] A.C. 220.

[109]   There is an extensive literature on this topic. See, e.g. J. F. Falknor, "The 'Hear-Say' Rule as a 'See-Do' Rule: Evidence of Conduct" (1961) 33 Rocky Mount. L.R. 133; T. Finman, "Implied Assertions as Hearsay: Some Criticisms of the Uniform Rules of Evidence" (1962) 14 Stan. L.R. 682; M. Weinberg, "Implied Assertions and the Scope of the Hearsay Rule" (1973) 9 Melbourne U.L.R. 268; R. C. Park, " 'I Didn't Tell Them Anything About You': Implied Assertions as Hearsay under the Federal Rules of Evidence" (1990) 74 Minn. L.R. 783.

[110]   *Wright v Doe d. Tatham* (1837) 7 Ad. & E. 313 at 388.

to know, for example, how thorough his inspection was, whether he had any reservations about the ship's seaworthiness, whether he had any choice about travelling on the ship, and so on. Without the benefit of cross-examination it is difficult to know how much weight to give to this evidence.[111] On the other hand, at least one of the traditional hearsay dangers is not likely to be present in most of these cases. Insincerity will rarely be an issue; it would be a very elaborate kind of lie that sought to deceive observers by a statement and/or conduct that was not intended to assert facts. As Cross put it, in relation to another standard example, "People do not say 'Hello X', in order to deceive passers-by into thinking that X is present".[112] Any small risk of insincerity could safely be left as a matter of weight for the factfinder.

Three leading authorities support the view that at common law the hearsay rule **16–024** extended to assertions implied in statements. The first case is *Wright v Doe d. Tatham*,[113] a civil action in which the issue was whether a deceased testator, Marsden, had sufficient mental capacity to make a valid will. The party relying on the will tendered evidence of letters written to Marsden by third parties, long since dead, that were couched in terms suggesting that the writers believed they were dealing with a sane person. The letters seem to have been offered as a riposte to evidence of Marsden's incompetency, which included evidence of how he was treated as a child by his servants and of how boys in the street had shouted that he was crazy. A majority of the judges in the court of Exchequer Chamber held that the letters were inadmissible. The clearest judgment, and the one generally cited, was given by Parke B. He explained that the relevance of the letters was to show the opinion of the third parties as to Marsden's sanity as revealed in the language they used to address him. But, he said, a statement by the writers of their opinion would be inadmissible if not made on oath and therefore the evidence of the implied statements of opinion should also be rejected. As Choo puts it, the reasoning is that "the letters contained an implied assertion that Marsden was a rational person, and because an express assertion to that effect would have been subject to the hearsay rule, so too should be an implied assertion".[114] There was sense to this conclusion, in that most of the same objections applied equally to the letters and to express hearsay statements of opinion: in neither case could the court find out the basis of the opinion, how well the third parties knew Marsden, how far they were being conventionally polite, and so on.[115] The surprising feature of the case is that the evidence of incompetency was apparently admitted without challenge despite being open to exactly the same hearsay objections.

---

[111] Note, however, that Parke B. was apparently prepared to concede that a court sitting without a jury might "be more safely trusted with the consideration of such evidence": *Wright v Doe d. Tatham* (1837) 7 Ad. & E. 313 at 389.

[112] *Cross on Evidence*, 5th edn (1979), p.470.

[113] *Wright v Doe d. Tatham* (1837) 7 Ad. & E. 313.

[114] Choo, *Hearsay and Confrontation in Criminal Trials* (1996), p.75.

[115] The probative value of the letters was rendered even more doubtful by their age. They were written many years before the date of the will, and there was no means of knowing whether the writers held the same opinion of the testator's sanity at the later date. Morgan commented that the letters were of slight value ("Hearsay Dangers and the Application of the Hearsay Concept" (1948) 62 Harv. L.R. 177, 208). They could have been excluded on the ground of insufficient relevance.

The issue concerned an assertion implied in *statements* by the writers that were not intended to make the assertion. The writers were not, as it were, consciously reporting on Marsden's sanity to a third party. Nevertheless, *Wright v Doe d. Tatham* treated the hearsay rule as applying to such implied assertions, and the same proposition underpins the judgment of the Privy Council in *Teper v R*.[116] The defendant was charged with arson of the shop belonging to his wife where he carried on business. He set up an alibi; the only evidence to contradict it was the testimony of a police officer who stated that at some distance from the shop and about 25 minutes after the fire had started he heard an unidentified woman in the crowd of spectators shout "Your place burning and you going away from the fire". The woman appeared to be shouting to a man in a car whom the officer said resembled the defendant. Quashing the defendant's conviction the Privy Council held that the evidence of the woman's shout was inadmissible hearsay[117] and was too remote from the event to come within the exception for statements forming part of the res gestae. Putting the res gestae point on one side for the moment, the relevance of the evidence was clearly the woman's claim, necessarily implied in her exclamation, that she had recognised the defendant at the scene. This claim was tendered as evidence that the recognition was accurate. The court was thus being asked to rely on the powers of observation of an unidentified woman at night in an excited crowd who had caught a glimpse of a man who might have been the accused. This was almost the weakest form of identification evidence that it was possible to have and the defendant was in no position to challenge the woman's credibility by cross-examination or otherwise. There was therefore a sound case for excluding the evidence, although if the case occurred today the same result could be achieved by use of the exclusionary discretion under s.78 of PACE.

16–025 The third case is the decision of the House of Lords in *Kearley*.[118] The police arrested the defendant at his home after a search revealed a quantity of drugs hidden on the premises. The police had suspected the defendant of being a dealer in drugs, but the quantity found was insufficient to raise a prima facie inference that he was in possession with intent to supply—the offence with which he was charged. Accordingly the police remained on the premises for several hours. During that time they answered ten telephone calls in which the callers asked for "Chippie" (the defendant's nickname) and asked for drugs. In addition seven visitors came to the house asking for "Chippie" and indicating they wanted to buy drugs. At trial the prosecution did not call as witnesses any of the telephone callers or visitors but, over defence objections, called the police officers concerned to give evidence of the conversations they had had with the callers and visitors. The purpose of doing so was to prove that the latter were calling at the premises as customers or potential customers for drugs who believed that the

---

[116] *Teper v R*. [1952] A.C. 480.

[117] Similarly in *Walton v R*. (1989) 166 C.L.R. 283 the High Court of Australia held that a telephone greeting, "Hello Daddy", was an implied assertion of identity, subject to the hearsay rule.

[118] *Kearley* [1992] 2 A.C. 228. For comment and criticism see M. Hirst, "Conduct, Relevance and the Hearsay Rule" (1993) 13 L.S. 54; R. Pattenden, "Conceptual Versus Pragmatic Approaches to Hearsay" (1993) 56 M.L.R. 138; J. R. Spencer, "Hearsay, Relevance and Implied Assertions" [1993] C.L.J. 40.

defendant would supply them; from this the jury could be asked to infer that the drugs in the defendant's possession were intended for sale and not for his own use.

This issue provoked a sharp division of opinion in the House of Lords. A bare majority of three–two held that the police evidence of the telephone calls and visits was inadmissible. Two reasons were given for this conclusion. The first was that the evidence was not relevant. Lord Ackner argued that the evidence of the calls went to prove the state of mind of the callers but, he said, the state of mind of a person calling with a request for drugs was not a fact in issue at the trial, nor was the fact that the person wanted drugs and thought that the defendant would be willing to supply drugs probative of the defendant's intention to supply them.[119] There is a sense in which this point about the circumstantial significance of the calls is plainly correct. The mere fact that X believes the defendant to be a drug dealer, child abuser, murderer or any other species of criminal does not, without more,[120] make it probable that the defendant is any of those things. Lords Griffiths and Browne-Wilkinson, the dissenting judges, accepted this point[121] but argued that the fact of the calls was relevant for a different reason. Their argument was that the large number of calls yielded a reasonable inference that the defendant had established a market for drugs that he was willing to supply and was attracting customers.[122] The probative value thus depended on the number of callers making the same request. To put it colloquially, 17 people could not be wrong. One or two might have been mistaken, or might even have conspired to frame the defendant as a dealer,[123] but it defied belief that all the callers had made the same error or were all party to the same conspiracy. On this argument the prosecution did not need to rely on any hearsay element in the evidence. It was enough to prove that a large number of calls were made at the defendant's house by persons asking for drugs. The minority relied for support on certain Commonwealth cases holding that evidence of telephone calls to particular premises by persons seeking to place bets is admissible evidence that the premises are being used for illegal gambling.[124]

The majority did not accept this view, maintaining that the existence of a body of customers did not make it more likely that a given individual intended to

---

[119] *Kearley* [1992] 2 A.C. 228 at 253–254. See to similar effect Lord Bridge of Harwich at 243; Lord Oliver of Aylmerton at 263–264.

[120] It may be different where we are confident that X has grounds for the belief. In everyday life, as Stephen Guest has pointed out to me, we frequently rely on the beliefs of others to establish facts about the world: the sight of people in the street beginning to put up umbrellas will indicate to me that they believe it is starting to rain, and I will assume this belief is correct on the basis that they have felt the first drops.

[121] *Kearley* [1992] 2 A.C. 228 at 238 per Lord Griffiths, by implication, 279 per Lord Browne-Wilkinson, expressly.

[122] *Kearley* [1992] 2 A.C. 228 at 238 per Lord Griffiths, 279 per Lord Browne-Wilkinson.

[123] Accordingly the minority suggested that evidence of just one such call, although relevant, should be excluded on the ground that its probative value would be exceeded by its prejudicial effect.

[124] *Davidson v Quirke* [1923] N.Z.L.R. 552; *McGregor v Stokes* [1952] V.L.R. 347; *Marshall v Watt* [1953] Tas. S.R. 1; *Police v Machirus* [1977] 1 N.Z.L.R. 288; cf. *US v Zenni* (1980) 492 F. Supp. 464, decided under the definition of hearsay in the Federal Rules of Evidence restricting the rule to intentional assertions.

satisfy their requirements.[125] The majority maintained that there was an alternative argument for the relevance of the calls, namely that each caller was impliedly asserting not his or her belief that the defendant was a drug dealer, but the *fact* that the defendant was a drug dealer. Two of the callers asked for the "usual", thereby impliedly asserting that the defendant had supplied them with drugs in the past and would therefore be willing to do so again. The majority held that the use of the evidence for this purpose would be excluded by the hearsay rule because:

> "evidence of words spoken by a person not called as a witness which are said to assert a relevant fact by necessary implication are inadmissible as hearsay just as evidence of an express statement made by the speaker asserting the same fact would be."[126]

Wright v Doe d. Tatham was cited as authority for applying the rule to such assertions.

If the prosecution had wanted to use the evidence for implied assertions that Kearley had in fact supplied each of the callers with drugs in the past, then its admissibility looks problematic. The rule against the admission of evidence of an accused's past misconduct could provide one reason for excluding implied assertions about the defendant's past offences of drug-dealing.[127] Even if this hurdle can be overcome, it is not clear that there is a necessary implication in the requests that the defendant had previously supplied drugs to each person making a request.[128] The beliefs of some of the callers might have been the result of what the callers had been told by others or of seeing others obtain drugs from the defendant. The majority sidestepped the problems by using the hearsay rule to prevent proof of any such further implied assertions; this was their second line of argument, after the claim that the evidence of the callers' simple assertions of belief was irrelevant. However, the exclusion of this highly probative evidence of the numerous calls[129] was a technical and counter-intuitive application of the hearsay rule.

---

[125] To justify this view Lord Oliver posed an analogy of a charity collector: "Can one, for instance, legitimately infer an intention to make a gift to charity from evidence of calls made by collectors seeking donations?" ([1992] 2 A.C. 228 at 271). This is unpersuasive because, as Spencer points out, "buyers of drugs, unlike charity collectors, do not usually go systematically down the street, knocking at every door" ("Hearsay, Relevance and Implied Assertions" [1993] C.L.J. 40 at 41). The fact that several intending purchasers of drugs call at one particular house tends to suggest that the occupier may be willing to supply them: "people are more likely to try to buy a product from someone who makes a habit of selling it than from someone who does not" (Spencer).

[126] *Kearley* [1992] 2 A.C. 228 at 245 per Lord Bridge of Harwich.

[127] Although Lord Ackner seems to have had no doubt that the callers would have been able to give evidence in chief of their previous transactions with the defendant: *Kearley* [1992] 2 A.C. 228 at 255.

[128] Only two of the callers requested their "usual" supply; others simply inquired about the availability of drugs.

[129] Lord Bridge agreed with the minority that the calls were powerful evidence of guilt (*Kearley* [1992] 2 A.C. 228 at 247) and Lord Oliver conceded that they would be so regarded by the layman (262). One respected American writer has commented: "The only mistake the poor jury could have made would have been to underestimate not overestimate its probative value": R. Allen, "Rules, Logic and Judgment" (1995) 16 Mississippi Coll. L.R. 65.

These authorities clearly supported the application of the hearsay rule to   **16–026**
assertions implied in statements,[130] but there was much less certainty about
assertions implied in *conduct*. In *Wright v Doe d. Tatham*,[131] Parke B. assumed
that the rule would also apply in these cases. He gave a number of hypothetical
examples of what he called "mere instances of hearsay evidence, mere statements
not on oath but implied in or vouched by the actual conduct of persons",
suggesting that such evidence would be excluded by the rule in the same way as
the letters in the case. One of his examples was the hypothetical instance
discussed above of the conduct of a deceased ship's captain inspecting a vessel
whose seaworthiness is in issue. We have already seen that some, but not all,
objections to hearsay apply in this type of case.

    These examples were not discussed by the Lords in *Kearley*, but the approval
by the majority of the reasoning of Parke B. in relation to the letters to
Marsden[132] suggests they would accept the logic of applying the reasoning to
assertions implied in conduct. The conclusion that the hearsay rule does apply to
assertions implied in conduct gains some support from dicta in the Australian
case of *Holloway v McFeeters*.[133] In relation to an issue whether a hit-and-run
driver had negligently caused a collision, two members of the High Court of
Australia stated that the driver's conduct in fleeing the scene of the accident was
not admissible as an implied admission by the driver that he was conscious of
being at fault.[134] This necessarily assumed that the hearsay rule did apply to the
conduct in question.

    If the hearsay rule did extend so far it was extraordinarily wide.[135] Evidence of
conduct is frequently admitted as the basis for inferences, including inferences
about the actor's state of mind. If the process of inference were treated as
potentially involving reliance on an implied assertion by the actor about his or her
state of mind courts would have to decide in every case whether an implied
assertion was being relied on and, if so, whether an exception to the hearsay rule
applied. The possibilities for confusion and technicality would be endless.

Given that hearsay dangers are often significantly reduced in cases of implied   **16–027**
assertions, there is no compelling systemic reason for applying the hearsay rule to
them. This is not to say that particular statements or instances of conduct may not
present unusual difficulties of evaluation, because, for example, of real doubts
about the actor's perceptions or ambiguities of behaviour. However, a judge has

---

[130] cf. *Mawaz Khan v R.* [1967] 1 A.C. 454, where the Privy Council held that the hearsay rule did not
apply to statements adduced as lies, although it is arguable that if the jury are being asked to infer that
the lie results from a consciousness of guilt on the part of the speaker, they are in effect being asked to
rely on an implied assertion by him of his belief in his guilt. However, a conclusion that the rule did
apply in such a case would be counter-intuitive; it would turn on its head the traditional formulation of
the rule as excluding a statement adduced as evidence of the matters stated in it.

[131] *Wright v Doe d. Tatham* (1837) 7 Ad. & E. 313 at 388.

[132] *Kearley* [1992] 2 A.C. 228 at 244–245 per Lord Bridge, 256 per Lord Ackner, 265–266 per Lord
Oliver.

[133] *Holloway v McFeeters* (1956) 94 C.L.R. 470.

[134] The driver was not a party to the litigation, nor was the (nominal) defendant being sued on his
behalf, therefore the hearsay exception for informal admissions by parties was inapplicable. See
further Weinberg, "Implied Assertions and the Scope of the Hearsay Rule" (1973) 9 Melbourne
U.L.R. 268, 277–279.

[135] See S. Guest, "The Scope of the Hearsay Rule" (1985) 101 L.Q.R. 385, 400.

adequate powers to exclude the evidence if necessary on the grounds of insufficient relevance or by virtue of the fairness discretion. It is noteworthy that major restatements of hearsay doctrine in modern times generally begin with the proposition that the basic rule of exclusion should apply only to intentional assertions.[136] In its Consultation Paper the Law Commission commented[137] that it found persuasive the argument by Cross:

> "concentration upon the presence of an intention to assert provides the most defensible watershed between hearsay and non-hearsay both as a matter of logical coherence and of practical common-sense."[138]

The Commission's final recommendation for the redefinition of hearsay pursued a modified version of this idea[139]; Ch.17 will discuss how this recommendation was taken forward in the recasting by the Criminal Justice Act 2003 of the hearsay rule in criminal cases. First, however, the modern law of hearsay in civil cases will be considered.

E. STATUTORY REFORM—CIVIL CASES

16–028 Reform of the hearsay rule in civil cases began earlier and has gone much further than in criminal cases. The reform process started in civil proceedings with the Evidence Act 1938, which made hearsay statements in documents admissible under certain conditions. The Civil Evidence Act 1968 extended admissibility to first-hand oral hearsay statements, enlarged the provision for documentary hearsay, made new provision for statements produced by computer, and instituted an elaborate notice procedure for parties wishing to adduce hearsay evidence at trial. The third and final stage of the development came when the Civil Evidence Act 1995 abolished the hearsay rule altogether in civil proceedings, leaving the issue of reliance upon hearsay statements as essentially a question of weight rather than admissibility.

Before looking in more detail at the Civil Evidence Act 1995 it is useful to consider briefly the context of civil litigation in England and the essentially practical considerations that drove the reform process. There is no doubt that both the institutional context, and the culture, of civil litigation changed radically in the second half of the twentieth century. Three main reasons for this change should be highlighted. The first is the decline of the jury in civil proceedings. Juries are now used in only a handful of civil trials annually.[140] Factfinding and the evaluation of evidence in the High Court and the county court is now undertaken almost entirely by professional judges. Lay participation in civil

---

[136] Leading examples are the Federal Rules of Evidence (US) r.801(a) and the Evidence Act 1995 (Cth of Australia and NSW) s.59.

[137] Law Com. CP 138 para.7.67.

[138] *Cross on Evidence*, 7th edn (1990), p.517. For discussion of some difficulties associated with a test of a person's intention to assert, see D. Ormerod, "Reform of Implied Assertions" (1996) 60 Jo.Crim.L. 201.

[139] Law Commission, *Evidence in Criminal Proceedings: Hearsay and Related Topics*, Law Com. No.245 (1997), para.7.40. The Law Commission's scheme of reform is considered further in Ch.17.

[140] For discussion of the use of the jury in civil litigation see *Smith Bailey and Gunn on the Modern English Legal System*, 4th edn (London: Sweet & Maxwell, 2002), pp.1035–1039.

litigation is effectively restricted to magistrates, whose civil jurisdiction is in any event much less important than their criminal jurisdiction. As a result, that part of the rationale for the hearsay rule that argues that the rule is necessary because of the difficulty that lay factfinders have in evaluating the weight of hearsay evidence has largely disappeared.

Secondly, in a great deal of civil litigation the evidence is primarily and increasingly in documentary form, often in documents generated by computer. There are of course some exceptions, but in general oral hearsay statements of witnesses do not have the degree of importance they have in criminal trials. Insofar as the hearsay rule protects against mishearing and misreporting of hearsay statements it is not applicable to documents. Moreover cross-examination of witnesses is less important where the evidence is substantially documentary.

Thirdly, the culture of civil litigation has changed in recent years. It has become less overtly adversarial, more responsive to the needs of its "consumers" and has been significantly affected by the drive to managerial efficiency. When the Law Commission reported on civil hearsay in 1993[141] it noted that civil litigation is now conducted in a more open climate. There is greater emphasis on identifying and refining the issues in advance of trial, with the result that parties are less able to take tactical evidential points at trial.[142] This is complemented by an approach that aims to ensure that, as far as possible, all relevant evidence is adduced,[143] and that intelligent witnesses and litigants are not frustrated by rules of evidence from giving testimony of matters they regard as relevant and cogent.[144] The Woolf reforms, and the Civil Procedure Rules that came into effect in 1999, have consolidated and extended these developments. **16–029**

The Law Commission's report concluded that the time had come to abandon the hearsay rule in civil proceedings altogether. Consultation had revealed that the scheme established by the Civil Evidence Act 1968 was outmoded, unwanted and frequently ignored in practice. The Commission's policy, now embodied in the Civil Evidence Act 1995, was based on two fundamental guiding principles:

"(1)   The law should be simplified to the greatest degree consistent with the proper functioning of a law of evidence.

(2)   As a general rule all evidence should be admissible unless there is good reason for it to be treated as inadmissible."[145]

The scheme of the Civil Evidence Act 1995 is, in summary, as follows. Section 1 provides that in civil proceedings[146] evidence shall not be excluded on the ground that it is hearsay. This wording makes clear that it is only the hearsay rule that is **16–030**

---

[141] Law Com. No.216, *The Hearsay Rule in Civil Proceedings* (1993). See also the Law Commission's earlier consultation paper with the same title: Law Com. CP No.117 (London, 1991).

[142] Law Com. No.216 para.1.5.

[143] Law Com. No.216 para.1.5 citing Balcombe L.J. in *Ventouris v Mountain (No.2)* [1992] 1 W.L.R. 887 at 899: "The modern tendency in civil proceedings is to admit all relevant evidence, and the judge should be trusted to give only proper weight to evidence which is not the best evidence".

[144] Law Com. No.216,para.1.6.

[145] Law Com. No.216 para.4.1.

[146] Defined as "civil proceedings, before any tribunal, in relation to which the strict rules of evidence apply, whether as a matter of law or by agreement of the parties": s.11. This means that the Act applies to all civil proceedings in the ordinary courts, and to those tribunals and arbitrations that apply the

abolished. The section leaves open the possibility of exclusion of evidence on other grounds, such as legal privilege.[147] "Hearsay" is defined in terms virtually identical to the definition at common law,[148] and includes any degree of hearsay.[149] Section 5 establishes the important precondition of competence as a witness in relation to the admissibility of a hearsay statement. This requirement applies to the maker of any hearsay statement, including the maker of a statement recording another hearsay statement. Section 5(1) states:

> "Hearsay evidence shall not be admitted in civil proceedings if or to the extent that it is shown to consist of, or to be proved by means of, a statement made by a person who at the time he made the statement was not competent as a witness.
>
> For this purpose 'not competent as a witness' means suffering from such mental or physical infirmity, or lack of understanding, as would render a person incompetent as a witness in civil proceedings; but a child shall be treated as competent as a witness if he satisfies the requirements of section 96(2)(a) and (b) of the Children Act 1989 (conditions for reception of unsworn evidence of child)."

Accordingly a party who wishes to rely on an oral hearsay statement by X must show, if necessary, that X would have been a competent witness at the time he made the statement. If X's statement is being proved by Y's written record of what X said, and Y is not a witness in the civil proceedings, it must be shown that Y would have been a competent witness at the time he made the record.

The Act contains a number of provisions designed to prevent unfair use of hearsay evidence and to help courts in evaluating its weight. First, a party proposing to adduce hearsay evidence must give such advance notice as is "reasonable and practicable in the circumstances for the purpose of enabling the other party or parties to deal with any matters arising from its being hearsay".[150] A failure to give notice where it is reasonable and practicable to do so does not affect the admissibility of the hearsay evidence.[151] However, the court may take the failure into account in exercising control over the proceedings, for example by granting an adjournment to allow a party time to respond to the evidence, or when dealing with costs. The court may also treat the failure to give notice as a matter affecting the weight to be given to the evidence.[152] If the maker of the statement is called as a witness the leave of the court is required before a previous

---

strict rules of evidence, but it does not apply to the wardship jurisdiction of the High Court, the Court of Protection or the Coroners' Court, none of which apply the strict rules of evidence.

[147] Civil Evidence Act 1995 s.14(1) states the point expressly.

[148] Civil Evidence Act 1995 s.1(2)(a): "hearsay" means a statement made otherwise than by a person while giving oral evidence in the proceedings that is tendered as evidence of the matters stated. According to s.13, a "statement" is any representation of fact or opinion however made. It is unclear whether implied assertions amount to "representations" and hence fall within the Act's definition of hearsay. Logically they should where a party relies on a fact or belief expressly or impliedly "narrated" by the statement. Moreover, Parliament cannot have intended the absurd result of a contrary conclusion, which would entail holding that the Act had abolished the hearsay rule for express assertions but retained the common law exclusionary rule for implied assertions.

[149] Civil Evidence Act 1995 s.1(2)(b).

[150] Civil Evidence Act 1995 s.2(1). Under s.2(2) rules of court can disapply the notice requirement in specified classes of proceedings and can prescribe how the notice requirement is to be complied with where it does apply. See CPR rr.33.2 and 33.3.

[151] Civil Evidence Act 1995 s.2(4).

[152] Civil Evidence Act 1995 s.2(4).

(hearsay) statement by that person can be given.[153] This is designed to prevent unnecessary repetition of evidence; consequently the condition of leave does not apply where the previous statement has independent probative value because it tends to rebut a suggestion of recent fabrication.

The party against whom a hearsay statement is given may, with the leave of the court, call the maker of the statement as a witness and cross-examine him on the statement.[154] Where the maker is not called as a witness evidence is still admissible to attack his credibility as if he had been called.[155] This will include evidence of any previous convictions of the maker, of bias on his part, and of any inconsistent statement whether made before or after the hearsay statement.[156]

16–031

Section 4(1) of the Act directs the court, when evaluating the weight (if any) of hearsay evidence, to have regard to any circumstances from which inferences can reasonably be drawn as to the reliability or otherwise of the evidence. It follows that if the court is sufficiently doubtful about the reliability of the hearsay it could give it no weight at all. Under s. 4(2) such circumstances may include:

"(a)   whether it would have been reasonable and practicable for the party by whom the evidence was adduced to have produced the maker of the original statement[[157]] as a witness;

(b)   whether the original statement was made contemporaneously with the occurrence or existence of the matters stated;

(c)   whether the evidence involves multiple hearsay;

(d)   whether any person involved had any motive to conceal or misrepresent matters;

(e)   whether the original statement was an edited account, or was made in collaboration with another or for a particular purpose;

(f)   whether the circumstances in which the evidence is adduced as hearsay are such as to suggest an attempt to prevent proper evaluation of its weight."[158]

Most of these considerations are self-explanatory, and should be readily apparent to an astute tribunal. Keane and McKeown note[159] that there is some obscurity in the reference in para.(d) to "any person involved". Bearing in mind the scheme of the Act, their suggestion is surely right that this extends beyond the maker of the original statement to include any witness of the statement who heard and/or recorded it and also any intermediary who supplied it to an ultimate "receiver". If any of these classes of person had a motive to conceal or misrepresent this could affect the reliability of the hearsay evidence. It remains to note that in an appropriate case a court may make a finding solely on the strength of hearsay

---

[153] Civil Evidence Act 1995 s.6(2).

[154] Civil Evidence Act 1995 s.3.

[155] Civil Evidence Act 1995 s.5(2).

[156] Civil Evidence Act 1995 s.5(2)(b). Under this provision an inconsistent statement is admissible for the purpose of showing that the maker of the hearsay statement contradicted himself; by implication it would not be admissible as evidence of the facts stated. The position is otherwise for a previous inconsistent statement of a witness admitted under s.3, 4 or 5 of the Criminal Procedure Act 1865. The Civil Evidence Act 1995 s.6(5) makes clear that such a statement is capable of being used as evidence of the facts stated under s.1.

[157] "Original statement" is defined in s.13. In the case of a statement of fact it means the underlying statement by a person having personal knowledge of the fact.

[158] Civil Evidence Act 1995 s.4(2).

[159] A. Keane and P. McKeown, *The Modern Law of Evidence*, 9th edn (Oxford: Oxford University Press, 2012), p.338.

evidence; "there is no rule of law which prohibits a court from giving weight to hearsay evidence merely because it is uncorroborated and cannot be tested or contradicted by the other party".[160]

16–032 Finally, on its face the Civil Evidence Act 1995 made significant changes to the regime established by the Civil Evidence Act 1968. How far it has been successful in practice in dealing with the problems that arose under the old regime is unclear. Not long after its passing Peysner expressed scepticism, pointing out[161] that the simplified notice procedure still requires parties intending to rely on hearsay evidence to identify hearsay before trial and to advise opposing parties of its existence. If these requirements were unworkable before the new Act it is hard to see that much has changed to make them workable now. It seems quite possible therefore that parties will continue in some cases to ignore or overlook the statutory procedure. Failure to comply with the procedure does not now affect the admissibility of the evidence, but the judge may impose a sanction for non-compliance in the form of discounting the weight to be attached to the evidence. Since judges used to examine the weight of hearsay admitted under the 1968 Act carefully in any event,[162] results under the new regime may not be very different. There is much to be said for Peysner's proposal that English law should drop notice requirements altogether and allow hearsay to be admissible without more as it is in Scotland.[163]

---

[160] *Welsh v Stokes* [2008] 1 W.L.R. 1224 at [23] per Dyson L.J.
[161] J. Peysner, "Hearsay is Dead! Long Live Hearsay!" (1998) 2 E. & P. 232.
[162] See, e.g. *Morris v Stratford-on-Avon RDC* [1973] 1 W.L.R. 1059 CA.
[163] Peysner, "Hearsay is Dead! Long Live Hearsay!" (1998) 2 E. & P. 232, 244–246, noting the Civil Evidence (Scotland) Act 1988.

CHAPTER 17

THE MODERN LAW OF HEARSAY IN CRIMINAL CASES

A. INTRODUCTION

17–001   The Criminal Justice Act 2003 recast the law of hearsay in criminal cases. Chapter 2 of Pt 11 of the Act created what is in effect a new mini-code of rules regulating the admissibility of hearsay evidence. The new code replaced the common law, and in this sense the Act marked a fresh start. However, although the rules of the common law were abolished, the Act retained the common law structure of an exclusionary rule plus exceptions (that include certain common law exceptions expressly preserved by the Act). Accordingly, the discussion in Ch.16 of the rationale for a general exclusionary rule, and of the distinction between hearsay and original evidence, remains relevant to a critical appreciation of the new law.

The new law is largely based on the recommendations of the Law Commission, which reported on hearsay in criminal cases in 1997.[1] In dealing with hearsay in criminal cases the Commission adopted the same guiding principles for reform that inspired its earlier report on hearsay in civil proceedings.[2] However, the principles led the Commission to a rather different conclusion. First, and most fundamentally, it recommended that the hearsay rule should live on for criminal cases. Despite the weaknesses of its various rationales the hearsay rule has proved surprisingly resistant to outright abolition in criminal proceedings.[3] In its report the Commission firmly rejected the reform option that would have taken criminal cases down the same path it had previously recommended for civil cases.[4]

The Commission was concerned that outright abolition of the rule would produce unacceptable problems. Although it would result in the admission of all cogent hearsay, and all hearsay tending to exculpate the accused, it might also result in the admission of poor quality multiple hearsay that lay factfinders would find very difficult to assess.[5] If the defence had no opportunity to cross-examine the maker of a hearsay statement adduced by the prosecution, there might be a breach of art.6(3)(d) of the ECHR, particularly if the witness was available but not called.[6] The Commission referred also to the danger that large quantities of superfluous hearsay evidence might be adduced by defendants in the hope of confusing factfinders so that they could not be sure of guilt. If trial judges attempted to deal with this on the basis of excluding evidence that was not sufficiently relevant, the hearsay rule might resurface under a different name.[7]

---

[1] Law Com. No.245, *Evidence in Criminal Proceedings: Hearsay and Related Topics,* Cm.3670 (1997) ("Law Com. 245").

[2] See Ch.16.

[3] J. D. Jackson, "Hearsay: the sacred cow that won't be slaughtered?" (1998) 2 E. & P. 166.

[4] Law Com. 245 para.6.16.

[5] Law Com. 245 para.6.11.

[6] Law Com. 245 para.6.10.

[7] Law Com. 245 para.6.13.

Finally, the legal profession was strongly opposed to free admissibility of hearsay.[8] The response to the Commission's Consultation Paper on the subject had been so anxious about the implications of abolition of the hearsay rule for the justice and efficiency of criminal trials that this was not a politically feasible option.

In the event therefore the Law Commission opted to stick with its provisional proposal in the Consultation Paper. This made the least structural change to the common law short of doing nothing at all, but the change was in the direction of more complexity rather than less. The Commission's preferred option[9] accepted the need for a general exclusionary rule. It accepted the need to qualify the rule with class-based exceptions, which would continue to be subject to the general exclusionary discretion under s.78 of PACE or at common law. It then added to the categories of admissibility what the Commission called a "very limited" discretion to admit otherwise inadmissible hearsay in the interests of justice. This was intended to be a "safety-valve" provision to ensure fairness in individual cases. In the event it took 13 sections of the Criminal Justice Act 2003 to give effect to the Commission's hearsay proposals, and the statutory provisions are further augmented by the preserved common law exceptions to the exclusionary rule. Whatever else these reforms have done to the law of evidence, on balance they have certainly not made it simpler.[10]

    This is not to say that they have not improved the previous law in terms of principle and policy. Almost anything would have been better than the mess that existed before. The common law exclusionary rule was complex and unclear in its scope. Its operation was mediated by a large number of class-based exceptions, but if the objective was to ensure the admission of credible and reliable hearsay evidence where hearsay was the best available evidence, the technique had two flaws. One was that the formal conditions of the exceptions were intended to provide circumstantial guarantees of sincerity and reliability, but they did not take account of variations in the weight of the evidence in individual cases. Consequently they might permit the admission of some hearsay of very doubtful probative value. The other flaw was that the category technique left gaps through which some hearsay of considerable probative value might fall, and thus remain inadmissible. The classic example is the manufacturers' records in *Myers v DPP*,[11] which fell neatly outside several of the common law exceptions. In addition to these defects, the previous law was capable of producing results that were contrary to common sense, as in *Kearley*,[12] or that might contribute to a potential miscarriage of justice.[13]

Giving effect to the Commission's recommendations improved the law in the following ways. First, the new statutory definition of the exclusionary rule took nearly all "implied assertions" outside the scope of the rule, and reversed the part

17–002

17–003

---

[8] Law Com. 245 para.6.15.
[9] Law Com. 245 paras 6.48–6.53.
[10] See the comments of Lord Cooke of Thorndon in the course of the parliamentary debates on the Criminal Justice Bill: *Hansard*, HL, Vol.652, col.1110.
[11] *Myers v DPP* [1965] A.C. 1001.
[12] *Kearley* [1992] 2 A.C. 228 HL.
[13] As in *Sparks v R.* [1964] A.C. 964 PC.

of the decision in *Kearley* that held the evidence of callers to the defendant's home asking for drugs to be inadmissible hearsay. Secondly, the admissibility of statements of witnesses not available to testify was extended to cover first-hand oral statements as well as statements in documents, provided that the maker of the statement is identifiable. Thirdly, the exception for business records is more satisfactory than its predecessor,[14] which suffered from significant drafting defects. Fourthly, the "safety-valve" discretion softens the rigidity of the class-based exceptions and helps to ensure that no hearsay of significant probative value is likely to be excluded. It is right in principle that this inclusionary discretion should be available in respect of both prosecution and defence evidence,[15] although the impact of art.6(3)(d) of the ECHR needs to be borne in mind when considering the admission of any hearsay evidence for the prosecution. Finally, the provisions relating to a witness's previous statements abolished some artificial and mystifying distinctions between use of such statements as evidence of the facts stated and use of them as relevant (only) to the witness's credibility.[16] These were all desirable changes and, as a matter of practical politics, they represented the most that could be achieved in the current climate of professional opinion.[17] They are unlikely to be the end of the reform story. As Jackson has commented, "many more Commission reports and legislative changes may be needed to chip away incrementally at the foundations of the hearsay rule before the rule is finally abolished".[18]

B. THE SCHEME OF THE ACT AND THE EXCLUSIONARY RULE

1. *Structure of the scheme*

17–004 The scheme in Ch.2 of Pt 11 of the Criminal Justice Act 2003[19] has been in force since April 4, 2005. It applies to all trials and retrials beginning on or after that date. Section 114 is headed "Admissibility of hearsay evidence". Subsection (1) provides as follows:

> "In criminal proceedings a statement not made in oral evidence in the proceedings is admissible as evidence of any matter stated if, but only if—
> (a)   any provision of this Chapter or any other statutory provision makes it admissible,
> (b)   any rule of law preserved by s.118 makes it admissible,
> (c)   all parties to the proceedings agree to it being admissible, or
> (d)   the court is satisfied that it is in the interests of justice for it to be admissible."

At first sight this provision appears to reverse the common law approach to hearsay because it refers to hearsay being "admissible" if certain -conditions are satisfied, whereas the common law rule was a rule of "inadmissibility" of hearsay

---

[14] Criminal Justice Act 1988 s.24.
[15] Law Com. 245 para.8.149.
[16] Law Com. 245 Pt X, and see Ch.14 above.
[17] The Government appeared to accept the Law Commission's view of how far practitioners and judges would be willing to be re-educated as regards the admission of hearsay.
[18] Jackson, "Hearsay" (1998) 2 E. & P. 166, 189.
[19] For discussion see D. Birch, "Criminal Justice Act 2003 (4) Hearsay: Same Old Story, Same Old Song?" [2004] Crim. L.R. 556.

evidence. However, the inclusion of the words "if but only if" in s.114(1) makes it clear that the admission of hearsay is exceptional; if the statement in question does not fit into one of the specified categories of admissibility the necessary implication is that it is inadmissible. In substance, therefore, the Act retains a general rule of exclusion in criminal proceedings[20] for statements not made in oral evidence[21] in the proceedings when these are tendered as evidence of the matters stated.

Section 114(1) should be read together with s.118(2), which provides that "With the exception of the rules preserved by this section, the common law rules governing the admissibility of hearsay evidence in criminal proceedings are abolished". The combined effect of these provisions is threefold. First, hearsay statements remain subject to a general exclusionary rule as evidence of the matters stated, but the rule is now statutory and not common law. Secondly, to be admissible a hearsay statement must now be brought within one of the four paragraphs of s.114(1): these allow a hearsay statement to be admitted if it comes within a statutory exception in Ch.2 of Pt 11 of the Criminal Justice Act 2003, or any other statutory provision, if it comes within one of the common law exceptions preserved by s.118(1), if all parties agree to it being admitted, or if the court is satisfied that it should be admitted in the interests of justice. Thirdly, where a statement would have been defined as hearsay at common law, but it is not covered by the definitions of "statement" and "matter stated" in s.115 of the Act, it falls outside the statutory scheme. Since the common law rules have been abolished, the admissibility of such a statement is no longer governed by the law relating to hearsay.[22] It is now simply a question of the relevance of the statement, with the possibility of exclusionary discretion arising if it is prosecution evidence.

2. The scope of the exclusionary rule

(A) Generally

The rule stated in s.114(1) clearly derives from the general common law rule set out in Ch.16. It refers, as did the common law rule, to statements not made while giving oral evidence in the proceedings, and thus covers both statements by third parties on other occasions and previous statements by testifying witnesses. Like the common law, the statutory rule makes no distinction between statements on oath and statements made informally; both types are subject to the rule. Furthermore, the statutory rule is concerned, like the common law, with the purpose for which the statement is adduced. The rule in s.114(1) only bites when the statement is adduced as "evidence of any matter stated". The rule does not

17–005

---

[20] This term means criminal proceedings in relation to which the strict rules of evidence apply: Criminal Justice Act 2003 s.134(1).

[21] "Oral evidence" includes evidence that, by reason of any disability, disorder or other impairment, a person called as a witness gives in writing or by signs or by way of any device: Criminal Justice Act 2003 s.134(1).

[22] *Singh* [2006] EWCA Crim 660; [2006] 2 Cr.App.R. 12; *Twist* [2011] EWCA Crim 1143; [2011] 2 Cr.App.R. 17.

apply therefore when evidence of the statement is adduced to show the fact that it was made and not to establish its truth. In this way the statutory rule reproduces the distinction at common law between hearsay and "original" evidence. This distinction was discussed in Ch.16; the details will not be repeated here save to recall that sometimes the making of a statement may be a fact in issue itself, and sometimes it may be relevant to a fact in issue. Both types of case will require accurate analysis of the relevance of the statement. The cases and examples considered in the discussion in Ch.16 will provide valuable guidance for the operation of the statutory rule.

However, the scope of the statutory rule is not precisely the same as the scope of the common law rule. This becomes clear when we turn to the definitions of "statement" and "matter stated" in s.115. Section 115 provides:

> "(1)   In this Chapter references to a statement or to a matter stated are to be read as follows.
> (2)   A statement is any representation of fact or opinion made by a person by whatever means; and it includes a representation made in a sketch, photofit or other pictorial form.
> (3)   A matter stated is one to which this Chapter applies if (and only if) the purpose, or one of the purposes, of the person making the statement appears to the court to have been—
>   (a)   to cause another person to believe the matter, or
>   (b)   to cause another person to act or a machine to operate on the basis that the matter is as stated."

The definition of a "statement" is in wide terms. It includes, as well as any representation of fact, a representation of opinion. The admissibility of statements of opinion generally is discussed in Ch.20; the point of including a reference to them in s.115 is to make clear that where statements of opinion are made otherwise than by a witness while giving oral evidence in the proceedings they are subject to the hearsay rule, as well as the rules governing opinion evidence.[23] The reference to a statement made "by whatever means" indicates that the statutory rule will extend, like the common law rule, to oral statements, written statements and statements by conduct, as when a person nods in answer to a question, or points to a person or place.[24] The final part of subs.(2) extends the definition of "statement" to include a representation made in a sketch, photofit or other pictorial form. This reverses decisions under the common law holding that photofit pictures of suspects compiled from eyewitness descriptions are a species of real evidence sui generis[25]; analogous to a photograph. It was argued in Ch.7 that this reasoning was flawed in that a picture compiled from a witness's description, unlike a photograph, necessarily incorporates the witness's statement as to the person's appearance. The point holds true no matter whether the picture is compiled by a police artist, or by the witness herself, or by anyone else. If the picture is adduced in evidence as an accurate representation of the appearance of the person the witness observed, the court is being asked to rely on the witness's out of court verbal or pictorial assertion as a true representation of the person's

---

[23] Criminal Justice Act 2003 s.114(3) states that "nothing in this Chapter affects the exclusion of evidence of a statement on grounds other than the fact that it is a statement not made in oral evidence in the proceedings". This preserves the operation of all other exclusionary rules of evidence.

[24] See, e.g. *Chandrasekera v R.* [1937] A.C. 220 PC.

[25] *Cook* [1987] 1 All E.R. 1049 CA; *Constantinou* (1990) 91 Cr.App.R. 74 CA.

appearance. The photofit does not speak for itself in the way that a photograph does. It is the product of a human mind (the witness) making an intentional communication as to a fact (the appearance of the person observed). The Act correctly treats such a statement as hearsay.

In this respect the statutory rule has a wider reach than the common law rule, but in another respect it is narrower. This follows from the definition of a "matter stated" as one that depends on the purpose of the maker of the statement. Under subs.(3)(a) of s.115 it is only where the maker had a purpose to cause another person to believe that the matter stated in the statement is true that the evidence of the statement will be covered by the rule in s.114. The objectives of this provision are discussed below. Under subs.(3)(b) it is only where the maker had a purpose to cause another person to act on the basis that the matter stated in the statement is true, or to cause a machine to act on that basis, that the evidence of the statement will be covered by the rule in s.114. The first of these alternatives is to cover cases where a person does not necessarily intend someone else to believe the statement, but does intend them to do something on the basis that the statement is true; the example given by the Law Commission was an expenses claim submitted to an accounts clerk.[26] In the Commission's view this should be subject to the hearsay rule because of the risk that the claim might be fabricated. The second alternative is to cater for cases where the processing of claims and similar statements is carried out by computer.[27]

17–006

(B) Implied assertions

The aim of introducing consideration of the maker's purpose into the definition of a "matter stated" is to take implied assertions outside the scope of the statutory rule against hearsay. As discussed in Ch.16, an implied assertion is a statement and/or conduct by a person that was not *intended* by that person to assert the fact that the evidence is adduced to prove, but that was nevertheless founded on a belief by the person in the existence of the fact. The common law treated implied assertions as subject to the hearsay rule on the basis that the court was being asked to accept the statement and/or conduct as equivalent to an express assertion of the fact to be proved. Thus, notoriously, a majority of the House of Lords held as part of their decision in the leading case of *Kearley*[28] that evidence of 17 telephone and personal calls, to the house of a person charged with possession of drugs with intent to supply, in which the callers asked for the defendant and enquired about the availability of drugs, was inadmissible hearsay because the calls contained implied assertions by the callers that the defendant was a drug dealer. If the callers had said in terms to the police officers who took the calls that the defendant was a drug dealer that would plainly be hearsay evidence when testified to by the officers. The majority took the view that it should make no difference when the court was being asked to infer that he was a dealer from the fact of calls linking him to the sale of drugs. The court was still being asked to rely on the callers as reliable reporters of the defendant's behaviour. The decision

17–007

---

[26] Law Com. 245 para.7.34.
[27] Law Com. 245 para.7.35.
[28] *Kearley* [1992] 2 A.C. 228.

attracted much criticism as a formal application of the hearsay rule that was contrary to common sense and deprived the court of highly probative evidence of the defendant's guilt.[29]

The Law Commission agreed with the critics. It recommended that *Kearley*, and other cases applying the hearsay rule to implied assertions, should be reversed. Arguing that the main danger the rule sought to guard against was the risk of fabrication by the maker of a hearsay statement, the Commission suggested that the risk of insincerity was very much less when the maker of the statement was not intending to communicate a fact or opinion to another. It would only be where the maker was not intending another person to believe the truth of a statement that it could "safely be inferred that he or she was not deliberately seeking to mislead".[30] The Commission employed the notion of the maker's "purpose" in making the statement, rather than their "intention", because the concept of intention was said to be wider and to include consequences known to be inevitable side-effects of the consequences desired.[31] It was the desired consequence that should be the focus of inquiry; the hearsay rule should operate only where the maker of a statement was seeking to cause another to believe that the statement, or an implication in the statement, is true. The terms of s.115(3) follow this recommendation.

Has the provision achieved its objective? It is submitted that it probably has, although there may be room for argument in certain cases. Let us consider first the leading cases on implied assertions at common law. In *Teper v R.*,[32] the evidence in question was that of a police officer who heard an unidentified woman shout to a person in a car "Your place burning and you going away from the fire". The person resembled the defendant, who was charged with arson of the premises in question. The officer's testimony was the only evidence to contradict the defendant's alibi. As suggested in Ch.16, the relevance of the woman's shout was her claim, implied in her exclamation, that she had recognised the defendant at the scene. Was it her purpose, or one of her purposes, to cause him to believe the "matter stated"? It seems clear that she was not trying to cause him to believe what she stated expressly, namely that his place was on fire and that he was leaving. Presumably she believed that he knew this already. One of her purposes was undoubtedly to cause him to believe that she was surprised at his conduct, but her surprise as such is not relevant and her exclamation is not being relied on to prove it. What is relevant is her purported recognition of him. Was she seeking to cause him to believe that she had recognised him? This question can be plausibly answered both ways. She was communicating to him indirectly that she had recognised him, but she was not, as it were, deliberately reporting that fact to him or to anyone else. In the circumstances there seems to be no risk of her fabricating recognition of the defendant. On the Law Commission's rationale of the hearsay rule, there seems to be no case for applying it in this case. The

---

[29] See para.16–025 above, and the articles and notes there cited.
[30] Law Com. 245 para.7.25.
[31] Law Com. 245 para.7.36.
[32] *Teper v R.* [1952] A.C. 480.

considerable risk that her purported recognition was mistaken could be dealt with by the exclusionary discretion and the *Turnbull*[33] guidelines for identification evidence of poor quality.

Kearley is more straightforward. The callers' purpose appears plainly to have been to contact the defendant and obtain drugs from him. Assuming the callers thought they were talking to a friend of the defendant, rather than a police officer, their purpose cannot plausibly be said to have been to cause the friend to believe that the defendant was a drug dealer. The terms of the calls would suggest that the callers assumed that the friend already knew this. The case does not therefore fall within subs.(3)(a) of s.115. Could it be said that the callers had a purpose of causing the receiver of the calls to act on the basis that the defendant was a drug dealer, so as to bring the case within subs.(3)(b)? This would be a strained interpretation; the callers were presumably only asking the receiver to act as a messenger to the defendant. It was not necessary for this purpose that the receiver of the calls should do so on the basis that he accepted that the defendant was a dealer. The case seems therefore to fall outside s.115(3) and therefore outside the rule in s.114.[34]

17–008

As regards *Wright v Doe d. Tatham*,[35] it seems highly unlikely that the writers of the letters to the deceased testator Marsden had a purpose of causing Marsden to believe that he was sane, which was said to be the assertion implied in the letters. Since the letters were written to him personally, it cannot be said that the writers had a purpose of causing anyone else to believe in his sanity. Section 115(3) has clearly reversed the decision that the letters were subject to the rule against hearsay. It can safely be assumed also that the examples given by Parke B. of hearsay assertions implied in conduct will equally fall outside s.115(3). Evidence of the inspection, by his hypothetical deceased ship's captain, of a ship whose seaworthiness was in issue will now be admissible simply as an item of circumstantial evidence. It was not the captain's purpose, in making the inspection and then embarking on the vessel, to cause anyone to believe that the ship was seaworthy. It would be different if he had written a report setting out his opinion of the ship's seaworthiness.

In the first case to reach the Court of Appeal on s.115 the court was in no doubt that implied assertions were no longer subject to the hearsay rule. In *Singh*,[36] D was charged with conspiracy to kidnap. In order to prove his participation in the conspiracy the prosecution adduced evidence of entries in the memories of the mobile telephones of his co-accused; these entries contained the numbers of telephones allegedly used by D extensively at the time of the

---

[33] *Turnbull* [1977] Q.B. 224.

[34] Birch and Hirst, "Interpreting the new concept of hearsay" (2010) 69 C.L.J. 72 make the point that the Act does not address the first part of the majority decision in *Kearley*, namely that evidence of the callers' *beliefs* that D was a drug dealer was irrelevant. This is true, but the cases, discussed below, on text messages to the defendant asking about drugs suggest that in practice prosecutors are now seeking to adduce evidence of such communications as relevant items of circumstantial evidence, on the basis that they are the kind of messages that a drug dealer would receive (see, e.g. *Bains* [2010] EWCA Crim 873). The same argument would apply to evidence of personal and telephone calls about drugs (see, e.g. *R. v K(M)* [2007] EWCA Crim 3150).

[35] *Wright v Doe d. Tatham* (1837) 7 Ad. & E. 313.

[36] *Singh* [2006] EWCA Crim 660; [2006] 2 Cr.App.R. 12.

kidnapping. D argued on appeal against conviction that the entries amounted to unintentional implied assertions that were outwith s.115(3), but subject to the common law rule of exclusion of such assertions as inadmissible hearsay. The Court of Appeal held that the common law rule had been abolished by s.118(2), and that s.114 had created a new rule against hearsay that did not extend to implied assertions. In the court's view the telephone entries were not a matter stated within s.115. They were implied assertions that were admissible because they were relevant and no longer hearsay.[37]

17–009   The short judgment did not analyse the nature of the implied assertions or the terms of s.115(3). It is submitted, with respect, that the court's conclusion was correct that the entries were not subject to the rule against hearsay set out in s.114, but the reasoning to this conclusion requires some explanation. Most of the entries consisted simply of the numbers of the telephones in question. On the assumption that the entries had been inserted into the memories by the co-accused who owned the telephones containing the memories, the entries amounted to implied assertions by them that the numbers were correct. But it was not their purpose to cause anyone else to believe that fact. One of the co-accused's telephones also contained the name "Alex" and a telephone number. This seems to be an express assertion that someone called Alex had that number, but again it was not the purpose of the person who made the entry to cause anyone else to believe that fact. The point would be the same if the police had discovered an address book owned by a co-accused containing a written statement of D's name, address and telephone number. Under the common law this would have been an express hearsay statement if adduced to show that the defendant did have that address and number, but it falls outside s.115(3) if it is written only for the writer's use. It follows from this example that a private diary, not intended to be read by anyone else, that records information, will not amount to hearsay if adduced as evidence of the truth of the matters recorded.[38] Section 115(3) has therefore not only taken most implied assertions outside the scope of the statutory rule against hearsay, but also some express assertions.

This is not to say that the application of s.115(3) is always straightforward. As *Kearley* illustrates, tricky problems can arise with communications to a defendant (or sometimes a third party) which involve greetings or requests or questions. In drugs cases such communications often take the form of text messages on the defendant's mobile phone commenting on drugs supplied by the defendant or inquiring about the availability of drugs.. In a series of cases the Court of Appeal appeared to take inconsistent views on whether evidence of such communications was hearsay and, if so, whether it could be admitted under the Act.[39] These cases

---

[37] The court held, somewhat inconsistently, that they were also admissible under the co-conspirator exception to the hearsay rule (s.118(1)(7) and possibly under s.114(1)(d)).

[38] *R. v N(K)* [2006] EWCA Crim 3309; *Knight* [2007] EWCA Crim 3027. For critical discussion see Birch and Hirst, "Interpreting the new concept of hearsay" (2010) 69 C.L.J. 72, 93–94.

[39] See *Leonard* [2009] EWCA Crim 1251 (text messages to D referring to the quality and quantity of drugs, impliedly supplied by him, hearsay and inadmissible on the issue of D's intent to supply drugs in his possession); *Bains* [2010] EWCA Crim 873 (text messages from street drug dealers to D hearsay and admissible on the issue whether D was concerned in the supply of drugs); *Chrysostomou* [2010] EWCA Crim 1403 (text messages to D asking about the availability of drugs not hearsay and admissible on the issue whether D dealt in drugs as evidence of bad character). See also *R. v K(M)*

were reviewed in an authoritative judgment by Hughes L.J. in the Court of Appeal in the leading case of *Twist*.[40] According to Hughes L.J. a court should approach the question whether such a communication is hearsay in three stages:

(i)   identify what relevant fact (matter) it is sought to prove;

(ii) ask whether there is a statement of *that matter* in the communication. If no, then no question of hearsay arises (whatever other matters may be contained in the communication);

(iii) if yes, ask whether it was one of the purposes (not necessarily the only or dominant purpose) of the maker of the communication that the recipient, or any other person, should believe *that matter* or act upon it as true? If yes, it is hearsay. If no, it is not.

This approach begins by focusing on the purpose for which the communication is sought to be adduced in evidence. The question is what fact or matter the party adducing the evidence is trying to prove by it. It is important to distinguish the purpose of the party in adducing the evidence from the purpose of the person who sent the message or made the call because the two can easily be confused. This seems to have happened in *Leonard*[41] where the prosecution wanted to adduce two text messages on the mobile phone of the defendant, who was charged with possession of drugs with intent to supply. One message complimented D on the quality of drugs, the other was a complaint about the quantity of drugs; in both it was necessarily implied that the defendant had supplied the drugs. The Court of Appeal held that the messages were inadmissible hearsay evidence. This is surely wrong.[42] The prosecution did not need to rely on the "matters stated" in the messages, in the sense of the senders' happiness or unhappiness with the drugs supplied, which it was their purpose to communicate to the defendant. That was irrelevant. The relevance of the messages was the implicit claims that the defendant had supplied drugs, but it was not the senders' purpose to cause the defendant to believe that. Like the callers in *Kearley* they assumed that the recipient of the messages knew this already.

In terms of the approach suggested in *Twist* the correct analysis of *Leonard* seems to be as follows. (1) The fact or matter to be proved is D's intention to supply drugs. This can be inferred from evidence that he is a dealer. (2) That he is a dealer is not a matter expressly stated in the messages. It is a matter necessarily

---

[2007] EWCA Crim 3150 (telephone call to D inquiring about the availability and price of a drug not hearsay and admissible on the issue whether D was guilty of offences of drug trafficking).

[40] *Twist* [2011] EWCA Crim 1143; [2011] 2 Cr.App.R. 17. In *Mateza* [2011] EWCA Crim 2587 Thomas L.J. commended the analysis in *Twist* and advised future courts that it would be "entirely unnecessary" to look at earlier cases because the judgment in *Twist* "set out all of the relevant considerations and the correct approach" ([23]). cf. the commentary on *Twist* in [2011] Crim. L.R. 796 by D. Ormerod.

[41] *Leonard* [2009] EWCA Crim 1251.

[42] In *Twist* [2011] EWCA Crim 1143; [2011] 2 Cr.App.R. 17 at [24], Hughes L.J. defended the decision in *Leonard* [2009] EWCA Crim 1251 on the basis that the prosecution were in fact relying on the truth of the claims about the quality and quantity of the drugs as part of their argument that D was a dealer. That is debatable, but if it was so, such reliance was unnecessary and self-defeating.

implied in the messages.[43] (3) But it is not the purpose of the senders of the messages to cause D to believe that matter. The messages are sent on the basis of a common knowledge or understanding that D deals in drugs. Therefore the messages are not within the Act's concept of hearsay. Similar conclusions were reached in the four separate appeals heard together in *Twist*. In two of them, *Twist* and *Boothman,* the messages were requests to the defendant to supply drugs or comments on past supplies. The court held that the messages were not hearsay since even if they contained implied assertions that the defendant was dealing drugs, the senders did not have a purpose of causing him to believe that he was. In the third case, *Tomlinson and Kelly,* a case of robbery, the message to T, one of the defendants, was a request for a gun to be delivered to the sender. This was held not to be hearsay. The relevant fact to be proved was that T was in possession of a gun. That was implicit in the message, if not expressly stated. But it was not the sender's purpose to cause T to believe that. That was simply their common understanding underlying the communication. The fourth case, *L,* concerned messages sent by the defendant to a girl he was charged with raping, which the prosecution argued amounted to confessions of rape. The court held that the messages were not hearsay. They were adduced to prove that the sexual intercourse between D and the girl was rape and not consensual as D claimed. The messages amounted to statements of the fact of rape, but D did not have a purpose when he sent the messages of causing the girl to believe that she had been raped.[44]

One of the authorities explained and approved in *Twist* was *Elliott*.[45] D was charged with firearms and drug offences after both were found at his home. An issue arose of whether the prosecution could adduce bad character evidence that D was a member of a violent local gang involved in gun and drug crime. The evidence included letters written to D while he was in prison which included approving references to the gang and signed in the form of the gang's emblem. It was agreed that these letters had been rightly held not to be hearsay. The authors did not have a purpose of causing D to believe any representation that the letters might contain. They were rather expressing the shared support of D and the authors for the gang; "common membership of the gang was simply the shared basis of the communications".[46]

(C) Negative hearsay

17–010 In some cases it may be relevant to prove that a particular express statement has not been made. Can the absence of an entry in a record of events be adduced as evidence that a relevant event has not occurred? At common law the Court of Appeal chose to regard the absence of an entry in a record as not raising a hearsay

---

[43] In *Twist* [2011] EWCA Crim 1143; [2011] 2 Cr.App.R. 17 at [19] the Court of Appeal strongly recommended avoidance of the "difficult concept" of the implied assertion when applying its suggested approach to the application of the Act.

[44] Of course, if they were hearsay they would still be admissible as confessions by virtue of ss.114(1)(b) and 118.

[45] *Elliott* [2010] EWCA Crim 2378. See also *Mullings* [2010] EWCA Crim 2820; [2011] 2 Cr.App.R. 2 at [20].

[46] *Twist* [2011] EWCA Crim 1143; [2011] 2 Cr.App.R. 17 at [26].

problem. In *Patel*,[47] to prove that X was an illegal immigrant, the prosecution called an immigration officer to testify that X's name did not appear in the relevant Home Office records of persons entitled to a certificate of registration in the United Kingdom. The Court of Appeal held, applying *Myers v DPP*, that the officer's testimony was hearsay, but this seems to have been on the basis that he was not responsible for the compilation of the records and had therefore necessarily to rely on the assertions of others that the records were accurate. The Court went on to say that an official who was in charge of the compilation and custody of the records would have been able to give evidence that the system of compilation was such that if X's name was not present he must be an illegal immigrant. The Court of Appeal subsequently applied this dictum in *Shone*[48] where persons in charge of stock records were held to have been rightly allowed to testify that certain items of stock were not recorded as having been used or sold. If the items were missing from stock, as was the case, it followed that they must have been stolen. In these two cases, therefore, the Court of Appeal regarded evidence of the absence of an entry in a properly authenticated record not as hearsay but as original evidence in the form of direct evidence of a relevant fact. The probative value of the evidence clearly derived from the factual presumption that the employees who supplied the information generally did their jobs efficiently. Therefore if a particular fact was not recorded, it could reasonably be inferred that it did not exist. The decisions can be defended on the basis that hearsay dangers are not generally significant in these cases. The employees will usually be making contemporaneous records of transactions in which they have been personally engaged, so the possibilities of mistaken perception or memory are unlikely. The absence of an entry in a record does not present a problem of ambiguity, and the possibility that the employees have deliberately falsified their returns is entirely speculative in the absence of any evidence that they may be concealing their own or another's dishonesty. There is a chance that cross-examination of every single employee who supplies information to the compiler of a record might throw up something untoward about that employee's returns, but most of the time an employee can be expected simply to swear to the accuracy of his or her returns.

The position is unchanged under the Act. In *DPP v Leigh*,[49] L, the registered keeper of a vehicle, was charged with failing to give information identifying the driver who had been caught speeding in it on two separate occasions.[50] W testified that he had checked the relevant records and had found no reply from L on either occasion. The Divisional Court followed *Patel* and *Shone* in holding that no issue of hearsay arose. The court treated the absence of a record where one would normally be expected if it existed as a fact, and not as involving any 'statement' by anyone. As the court put it:

---

[47] *Patel* [1981] 3 All E.R. 94.
[48] *Shone* (1982) 76 Cr.App.R. 72.
[49] *DPP v Leigh* [2010] EWHC 345 (Admin).
[50] Road Traffic Act 1988 s.172(3).

> "it is artificial to suggest that anyone by failing to put anything in the record concerning a particular individual is thereby seeking to assert that no reply has been given by that person. That is not the purpose behind their inaction in not recording a response that has not been made."

This analysis will hold good as long as the witness who testifies as to the absence of the entry in the record is able to give first-hand evidence about the method of compilation of the record. If the witness has to rely on what he has been told by others about the record then his evidence will be hearsay. However, it may nonetheless still be admissible under the business records exception in s.117, or under the "interests of justice" exception in s.114(1)(d) (see below).

C. STATUTORY EXCEPTIONS: SECTION 116—WITNESS UNAVAILABILITY

1. *Terms and scope of the exception*

17–011   Section 116 provides for the admissibility of hearsay evidence where the maker of a hearsay statement is unavailable as a witness. The section replaced and extended s.23 of the Criminal Justice Act 1988, which had permitted the admission of hearsay statements in documents under certain conditions. Section 116 extended the previous law in two important ways. First, it widened admissibility so as to include all forms of hearsay statements: oral, written and by conduct. Secondly, in all but one type of case, where the conditions of admissibility are satisfied, admissibility is now automatic. It does not require the leave of the court, even where the hearsay is in the form of a witness statement.[51] The only situation where leave is required to admit a hearsay statement under s.116 is where the witness (whom the section describes as the "relevant person") is unavailable through fear. The conditions of admissibility provided by s.116 are that the maker of the hearsay statement can be identified, that he or she would have been able to give oral evidence of the matter stated in the statement, and that he or she is unavailable for one of a number of specified reasons.[52] The section provides as follows:

> "(1)   In criminal proceedings a statement not made in oral evidence in the proceedings is admissible as evidence of any matter stated if—
> (a)   oral evidence given in the proceedings by the person who made the statement would be admissible as evidence of that matter,

---

[51] Under the scheme in ss.23–26 of the Criminal Justice Act 1988 leave of the court was required for the admission of hearsay in witness statements in all cases, and the court was directed by s.26 not to give leave unless it was of the opinion that the statement ought to be admitted in the interests of justice.

[52] According to Hughes L.J. in *Adams* [2007] EWCA Crim 3025 at [15] it is not relevant for a trial judge to consider the factors listed in s.114(2) of the 2003 Act in an application to admit evidence under s.116. Those factors are relevant to an application to admit hearsay in the interests of justice under s.114(1)(d). However, it is submitted that where the judge is asked to exclude a statement, otherwise admissible under s.116, under the "fairness" discretion in s.78 of PACE the s.114(2) factors are likely to be material considerations. As the Court of Appeal commented in *Cole, Keet* [2007] EWCA Crim 1924; [2008] 1 Cr.App.R. 5 at [7], the test under s.78 "is unlikely to produce a different result from that of the 'interests of justice' in s. 114(1)(d)".

[718]

(b)   the person who made the statement (the relevant person) is identified to the court's satisfaction, and

(c)   any of the five conditions mentioned in subsection (2) is satisfied.

(2)   The conditions are—

(a)   that the relevant person is dead;

(b)   that the relevant person is unfit to be a witness because of his bodily or mental condition;

(c)   that the relevant person is outside the United Kingdom and it is not reasonably practicable to secure his attendance;

(d)   that the relevant person cannot be found although such steps as it is reasonably practicable to take to find him have been taken;

(e)   that through fear the relevant person does not give (or does not continue to give) oral evidence in the proceedings, either at all or in connection with the subject matter of the statement, and the court gives leave for the statement to be given in evidence.

(3)   For the purposes of subsection (2)(e) 'fear' is to be widely construed and (for example) includes fear of the death or injury of another person or of financial loss.

(4)   Leave may be given under subsection (2)(e) only if the court considers that the statement ought to be admitted in the interests of justice, having regard—

(a)   to the statement's contents,

(b)   to any risk that its admission or exclusion will result in unfairness to any party to the proceedings (and in particular to how difficult it will be to challenge the statement if the relevant person does not give oral evidence),

(c)   in appropriate cases, to the fact that a direction under section 19 of the Youth Justice and Criminal Evidence Act 1999 (c.23) (special measures for the giving of evidence by fearful witnesses etc.) could be made in relation to the relevant person, and

(d)   to any other relevant circumstances.

(5)   A condition set out in any paragraph of subsection (2) which is in fact satisfied is to be treated as not satisfied if it is shown that the circumstances described in that paragraph are caused—

(a)   by the person in support of whose case it is sought to give the statement in evidence, or

(b)   by a person acting on his behalf, in order to prevent the relevant person giving oral evidence in the proceedings (whether at all or in connection with the subject matter of the statement)."

Section 116 should be read in conjunction with s.121, which deals with multiple hearsay. The effect of s.121 is that generally only first-hand hearsay will be admissible under s.116. This is because s.121 does not permit one hearsay statement to be proved by another hearsay statement, except where either statement is admissible under one of a number of specified provisions in the Act that do not include s.116. To illustrate the point, suppose that A, an eyewitness of a hit-and-run accident, tells her friend B the registration number of the car involved and B writes down the number in a statement to the police. A does not verify the number. A then disappears without trace and B is too ill to testify at D's trial. B's written statement of the number will not be admissible under s.116. It is a hearsay statement that records another hearsay statement. The prosecution would have to try to bring it within s.117 (see below) or ask the judge to exercise the inclusionary discretion conferred by s.121(1)(c) to admit B's written statement in the interests of justice. It would be different if A had verified the number because it would then be her statement in the document, and that statement could be proved under s.116 by production by the police of the document. Similarly, if B were not ill, she would be able to testify under s.116 as to A's hearsay statement of the number.

Potentially s.116 has a very wide field of application. In relation to hearsay statements in writing it will cover, in addition to witness statements to the police, all correspondence, memoranda, reports, files, emails, entries in books of accounts, and so on.[53] Statements in audio tapes, video tapes, films and computer files will all be included. Oral statements not recorded in any permanent form are also included. In this way evidence of confessions to crimes by third parties will be admissible, whether made orally or in writing, subject to the requirements that the maker of the confession must be identified, and unavailable as a witness for one of the specified reasons. It is worth noting in this connection that where the reason for non-availability is other than fear on the part of the relevant person, for example he is abroad and it is not reasonably practicable to secure his attendance, and the evidence of his confession is adduced by the defence, the trial judge may have no discretion to exclude it. Section 78 of PACE applies only to prosecution evidence, and there is no discretion at common law to exclude defence evidence. Section 126(1) of the Criminal Justice Act 2003 (discussed below) provides a general exclusionary discretion where the court is satisfied that the case for excluding a hearsay statement, taking account of the danger that to admit it would result in undue waste of time, substantially outweighs the case for admitting it, taking account of the value of the evidence. Given the potential importance of a third-party confession in preventing a possible miscarriage of justice, this discretion is unlikely to be exercised against the defendant unless the evidence of the confession is so tenuous or suspect that no reliance could safely be placed upon it.

Whichever reason for the witness's non-availability is relied on, the existence of that reason must be proved as a fact,[54] unless it is formally admitted.[55] Proof of the reason in question should be by admissible evidence,[56] but such evidence can itself be hearsay that is admissible under one of the preserved common law exceptions[57] or under s.116.[58]

---

[53] Provided in all cases that the maker of the statement can be identified and that he "made" the statement by writing it himself, signing it, or otherwise verifying his acceptance of it as his statement: *McGillivray* (1993) 97 Cr.App.R. 232 CA (a case under s.23 of the Criminal Justice Act 1988).

[54] *Wood and Fitzsimmons* [1998] Crim. L.R. 213 CA.

[55] See *Bermudez v Chief Constable of Avon and Somerset* [1988] Crim. L.R. 452.

[56] *Neill v North Antrim Magistrates' Court* [1992] 4 All E.R. 846 HL.

[57] Thus a police officer can state that the witness told the officer of being in fear, by virtue of the common law exception relating to declarations of contemporaneous states of mind. See *Neill v North Antrim Magistrates' Court* [1992] 4 All E.R. 846 at 854 per Lord Mustill. See also *Fairfax* [1995] Crim. L.R. 949 CA.

[58] *Castillo* [1996] 1 Cr.App.R. 438 CA (evidence of the inability of the maker of the statement, who was a travel agent in Venezuela, to attend the trial was provided by a statement from a customs liaison officer based in Venezuela, the latter statement itself being admitted under s.23 of the Criminal Justice Act 1988). In *R. v Belmarsh Magistrates' Court Ex p. Gilligan* [1998] 1 Cr.App.R. 14 the Divisional Court held that a witness's fear could not be proved by the production of a written statement by him in which he stated that he was afraid to give evidence; oral evidence as to fear would be necessary, for example from a police officer. This is quite plainly wrong. Evidence of a person's statement that he is in fear is admissible at common law under the rule relating to declarations as to contemporaneous states of mind (see *Blastland* [1986] A.C. 41). It can make no possible difference whether that statement is an oral one reported to the court by a police officer, or whether it is in writing in a statement made to the police. If the court was asserting that oral evidence was always necessary to establish the conditions of unavailability of the witness under s.23 of the Criminal Justice Act 1988,

2. Reasons for unavailability of the witness (the "relevant person")

Turning to the specified reasons for unavailability of the relevant person, the first **17–012** is that the person is dead. This is straightforward. Several of the reported cases illustrate the reception of witness statements by deceased victims of the alleged offences[59] or other misconduct[60] of the defendant. In *Musone*,[61] for example, the Court of Appeal upheld the admission of a statement by the victim of a stabbing in a prison cell identifying the defendant as his attacker. Describing it as a "dying declaration"[62] the court held it admissible under s.116 and said the trial judge had been right not to exclude it under s.78 of PACE despite doubts about the reliability of the prisoner who gave evidence of the statement. The main issue arising here, as with other situations where hearsay is admitted, is whether its use violates the defendant's right to a fair trial under art.6 where the evidence is the sole or decisive evidence for conviction. Since this is a general issue it will be dealt with after all the hearsay exceptions have been considered.

The second reason for unavailability is where the person is unfit to be a witness because of his bodily or mental condition. Clearly someone unable to attend court because of physical illness or frailty is "unfit" to be a witness; equally, a person may be physically fit but mentally unfit, as where he suffers from a mental condition, such as Alzheimer's disease, that results in him being unable to remember the events in issue. In *Keet*,[63] for example, the Court of Appeal upheld the admission of a witness statement by the elderly victim of an attempted fraud by the defendant. The trial did not take place until four years later as a result of the defendant absconding, by which time the victim was mentally unfit to give evidence. Her statement was the sole evidence against the defendant.

In relation to a relevant person who is abroad, the cases decided under the virtually identically worded paragraph in s.23(2) of the Criminal Justice Act 1988 are likely to be helpful. The Court of Appeal held that a trial judge must consider a number of matters in deciding whether it was not "reasonably practicable" to secure the attendance of the person in question.[64] First, the judge must consider the importance of the evidence and the extent to which the absence of the witness would prejudice the defence. It seems that more may be required in the way of insuperable difficulty for a key witness than for a peripheral one. Secondly, the judge must consider the expense and inconvenience of securing the witness's attendance. It might not be reasonable, for example, to require the prosecution to incur considerable expense in flying a witness from South America to give

---

the decision was per incuriam because it was inconsistent with *Castillo*, which was not cited. Written statements as to fear were accepted in *Rutherford* [1998] Crim. L.R. 490; and *Denton* [2001] Crim.L.R. 225.

[59] *Musone* [2007] EWCA Crim 1237; [2007] 2 Cr.App.R. 29; *Cole* [2007] EWCA Crim 1924; [2008] 1 Cr.App.R. 5.

[60] *R. v Z* [2009] EWCA Crim 20.

[61] *Musone* [2007] EWCA Crim 1237; [2007] 2 Cr.App.R. 29.

[62] A well-known exception to the hearsay rule at common law, abolished by s.118(2) of the Criminal Justice Act 2003.

[63] *Keet* [2007] EWCA Crim 1924; [2008] 1 Cr.App.R. 5 (reported with *Cole* [2007] EWCA Crim 1924 above). See also *R. v D* [2002] EWCA Crim 990; [2002] 2 Cr.App.R. 36, a case under ss.23 and 26 of the Criminal Justice Act 1988.

[64] *Castillo* [1996] 1 Cr.App.R. 438.

evidence on an essentially formal matter that could not be seriously challenged in cross-examination.[65] Thirdly, the judge must consider the reasons why it is not convenient or reasonably practicable for the witness to attend. An illustration of the interaction of these factors is *Gokal*,[66] where an important witness in a major fraud case was in Pakistan and refused to come to England to give evidence. The Court of Appeal held that it was not reasonably practicable for the prosecution to do more to secure his attendance than offer to pay the witness's expenses and to compensate him for any financial loss. Postponing the trial, which might be appropriate where a key witness was unable to attend because he had to take an examination or undergo an operation, was not an option in view of the witness's refusal to attend at all. In *Gyima*,[67] the parents of a 14-year-old eyewitness resident in the United States refused to let him return to England for the trial. The Crown Prosecution Service had made repeated phone calls over a number of weeks to the parents in an effort to persuade them to change their minds but to no avail. The Court of Appeal was satisfied that the boy's witness statement had been rightly admitted.

The "reasonably practicable" standard also applies where the relevant person cannot be found, and the question is whether the party seeking to rely on the witness's hearsay statement has made sufficient efforts to trace her. It seems likely that in deciding whether the party has taken such steps as it is reasonably practicable to take the courts will apply some of the same considerations as those applied where the witness is abroad. The expense and delay involved in trying to find the witness will be relevant factors, and it will be reasonable to expect more to be done in respect of a key witness. The ease, and the likely efficacy, of the steps that it is open to the party to take must obviously be taken into account. In *Adams*,[68] a key witness was missing on the day of the trial and could not then be contacted. The Court of Appeal held that the judge should not have admitted his witness statement under s.116(2)(d) because reasonably practicable steps had not been taken to find him beforehand.[69] The trial date had been fixed months earlier, but no contact was made with the witness until the last working day before the trial when a voicemail message was left on his mobile phone. The court said this was not good enough; a visit to his address and/or place of work, or at least telephone contact with either, would have been reasonably practicable. Similarly, in *Kamuhuza*,[70] the Court of Appeal described the efforts to locate a police officer who had left the force as "desultory", and pointed out that it should have been easy to find his address since as a former public servant he would have been in receipt of a pension.

17–013   The most likely reason in practice for a witness being unavailable is that the witness is in fear. Where the witness is a potential witness for the prosecution the

---

[65] *Castillo* [1996] 1 Cr.App.R. 438.

[66] *Gokal* [1997] 2 Cr.App.R. 266 CA.

[67] *Gyima* [2007] EWCA Crim 429.

[68] *Adams* [2007] EWCA Crim 3025.

[69] However, the court went on to say that the statement was admissible under s.114(1)(d) in the interests of justice because it went to prove the defendant's possession of drugs, an issue which was not in dispute on the facts of the case.

[70] *Kamuhuza* [2008] EWCA Crim 3060. However, the court went on to say that the officer's report was admissible under s.117 as a business document: see below.

most common cause of fear of giving evidence will be threats or intimidation from the accused or his associates. However, subs.(2)(e) does not require the fear to derive from such a cause. It refers simply to the witness not giving evidence "through fear", and is therefore capable of applying where the witness is not intimidated but is fearful of the process of giving evidence in itself. According to subs.(3) "fear" is to be widely construed, and includes, for example, fear of the death or injury of another person or of financial loss. This will cover such forms of intimidation as threats directed at a witness's family or friends, or threats to stop payments to the witness such as child support. It is not necessary that the witness should be absent from the trial for subs.(2)(e) to apply. The provision expressly covers also the cases where the witness starts to give evidence, but through fear does not continue, or where the witness testifies about other matters, but does not give evidence about the subject-matter of the hearsay statement.[71]

The reference in subs.(3) to giving "fear" a wide construction should encourage courts to reject arguments for imposing an objective test of fear. In *Acton Justices Ex p. McMullen*,[72] the Divisional Court rejected an implied limitation under s.23 of the Criminal Justice Act 1988 that the fear should be based on reasonable grounds. Watkins L.J. said:

> "it will be sufficient that the court on the evidence is sure that the witness is in fear as a consequence of the commission of the material offence or of something said or done subsequently in relation to that offence and the possibility of the witness testifying to it."[73]

On one view, this fell short of full acceptance of the literal interpretation of "fear" if it was saying that the court must make some inquiry into the cause of the fear and must be satisfied that the fear is linked to the offence or the consequences of testifying about it. However, in *Martin*,[74] the Court of Appeal saw no reason to qualify the wide statutory wording. The fact of fear was said to be sufficient; it was not necessary to inquire into the precise basis for it. The court pointed out that a witness might be genuinely fearful, having mistaken something said or done as a threat when it was not. A judge would still be faced with a potential witness who was not prepared to give evidence. Parliament's policy was to combat the possibility of witness intimidation by rendering the written statements of frightened witnesses admissible, subject to the protection for the accused provided by the requirement for leave of the court to admit the hearsay statement. In *Davies*,[75] a case under the 2003 Act, the Court of Appeal held that there was no obligation on a trial judge to test the witness's fear by means of video link or tape recording. As the court put it, "courts are ill-advised to seek to test the basis of fear by calling witnesses before them, since that may create the very situation which s. 116 is designed to avoid".[76] At the same time it is clear that judges should require good evidence of the fear and the basis for it. The court in *Davies* continued:

---

[71] Resolving the problem which arose under s.23 of the Criminal Justice Act 1988 in *Ashford Magistrates' Court Ex p. Hilden* [1993] Q.B. 555.

[72] *Acton Justices Ex p. McMullen* (1991) 92 Cr.App.R. 98.

[73] *Acton Justices Ex p. McMullen* (1991) 92 Cr.App.R. 98 at 105–106.

[74] *Martin* [1996] Crim. L.R. 589 CA.

[75] *Davies* [2006] EWCA Crim 2643; [2007] 2 All E.R. 1070.

[76] *Davies* [2006] EWCA Crim 2643; [2007] 2 All E.R. 1070 at [14].

"Of course, judges must be astute not to skew a fair trial by a too-ready acceptance of assertions of fear since it is all too easy for witnesses to avoid the inconvenience and anxiety of a trial by saying they do not want to come."[77]

3. The requirement of leave for admission of a hearsay statement by a witness in fear

17–014   Under subs.(2)(e) leave of the court is required for the admission of a hearsay statement by a relevant person in fear. This is intended as a safeguard against the possibility that a witness might conveniently become fearful after making a witness statement, so as to avoid giving oral testimony and being cross-examined on it. Subsection (4) provides that leave may be given to admit the hearsay statement only if the court considers that the statement ought to be admitted in the interests of justice. The subsection goes on to list a number of factors to be taken into account in this decision. In summary these are the contents of the statement, the fairness of admission or exclusion, including the difficulty of challenge to the statement in the absence of the witness, the protection that could be afforded to the relevant person by any special measures available for fearful witnesses, and any other relevant circumstances.

These factors are in very similar terms, apart from the reference to special measures, to the factors specified in s.26 of the Criminal Justice Act 1988 which imposed a similar requirement of leave for any statement admissible under ss.23 or 24 that was prepared for the purposes of pending or contemplated criminal proceedings or of a criminal investigation. Like s.116, s.26 presumed that such witness statements should not be admitted, unless the interests of justice required inclusion. The operation of that section was not restricted to the case of a witness in fear, but applied whatever the reason for unavailability of the witness. Given the similarity of the leave requirement under s.116, and the similarity of the factors to be taken into account, the courts are likely to find that principles developed under the 1988 Act provide valuable guidance in decisions whether to grant leave, despite the difference in the extent of the requirement. However, these principles must also take account of art.6 of the ECHR, in particular the status of the "sole or decisive evidence" limitation which is discussed later.

The Court of Appeal said that the application of s.26 required the judge to balance three principal considerations bearing on the interests of justice[78]: the quality of the evidence, the importance of the evidence, and the degree of unfairness to the accused in being unable to test the evidence by cross-examination of the witness and to have the witness's demeanour observed by the factfinder. The character of the witness concerned was not an overriding factor.[79] The Court of Appeal regarded the decision of the judge as to where the balance lay in a particular case as an exercise of judicial discretion. Therefore the court would interfere with the decision only if persuaded that the judge erred in principle, by, for example omitting to take account of a relevant factor. Otherwise if the decision was one that the judge could reasonably come to having

---

[77] *Davies* [2006] EWCA Crim 2643; [2007] 2 All E.R. 1070 at [15].
[78] See *Cole* (1990) 90 Cr.App.R. 478; *French and Gowhar* (1993) 97 Cr.App.R. 421.
[79] *Lockley and Corah* [1995] 2 Cr.App.R. 554 CA.

considered the relevant factors, it would be upheld. Thus much depended on the circumstances of the individual case, and it is not easy to identify any consistent pattern to the application of the "interests of justice" test. One group of authorities tended to suggest that where the evidence was important to the prosecution case, and was prima facie of good quality, it was likely to be admitted. Certainly this was so if the court thought that the defendant could controvert it by giving evidence himself or calling other defence witnesses. In several cases the Court of Appeal upheld the admission on these grounds of witness statements of eyewitnesses to the commission of offences.[80] Any residual unfairness arising from the lack of opportunity to cross-examine could be compensated for by appropriate judicial warnings, and explanations of any weaknesses in the hearsay evidence.[81]

Where the evidence is important, but its quality is dubious, cross-examination is potentially crucial. In such cases the interests of justice are likely to point to the hearsay statements being kept out. Thus in *Lockley and Corah*,[82] the statement concerned an uncorroborated confession to murder allegedly made by one defendant to a person with whom she was sharing a prison cell while on remand. There was evidence of the witness's dishonesty and bad character. Recognising that evidence of uncorroborated cell confessions was to be treated with caution, the Court of Appeal held[83] that in this case it was important that the jury should be able to see the witness and observe her demeanour under cross-examination. Clearly there was a significant problem of credibility in that case.[84]

    Identification evidence may present equally significant problems of reliability. In *Setz-Dempsey*,[85] the witness's identification of the defendant as present when a stolen aircraft engine was taken to the place where it was subsequently found was the only evidence against the defendant. The witness was mentally unfit to give

17–015

---

[80] See, e.g. *Cole* (1990) 90 Cr.App.R. 478 (assault: statement of deceased eyewitness would give the jury a "fuller picture"); *Dragic* [1996] 2 Cr.App.R. 232 (burglary: identification evidence by victim was good quality evidence of recognition, and was rightly admitted despite being the only evidence against the defendant); *Martin* [1996] Crim. L.R. 589 (arson: statement of fearful eyewitness admitted; not unfair since defence was a conspiracy between witness and others falsely to accuse the defendant, and this defence could be put to the others who did give evidence). A more difficult case was *James* [1996] 2 Cr.App.R. 38 (murder: the eyewitness was the co-accused's girlfriend who disappeared before trial; she had made inconsistent statements; the Court of Appeal thought that there was considerable strength in defence counsel's argument that the admission of her statement incriminating the defendant was unfairly prejudicial given the inability to cross-examine, but held that it had not been shown that the trial judge erred in the exercise of his discretion).

[81] *Cole* (1990) 90 Cr.App.R. 478 CA. In *Gokal* [1997] 2 Cr.App.R. 266 the Court of Appeal held that the fact that a witness was an accomplice of the accused, or was otherwise a suspect witness, was not by itself a reason for refusing to admit the witness's statement, since the issue of the witness's credibility could be appropriately dealt with by a warning to the jury.

[82] *Lockley and Corah* [1995] 2 Cr.App.R. 554.

[83] The Court of Appeal exercised the statutory discretion afresh since the trial judge had purported to admit a transcript of the witness's evidence at an earlier trial under a power at common law, and had not been referred to s.26.

[84] See also *R. v W* [1997] Crim. L.R. 678, where the Court of Appeal upheld a judge's refusal to admit a written statement by the defendant's wife, made 5 weeks into the trial and after most of the prosecution evidence had been given. Much depended on the credit of the wife, but the Crown would have no opportunity to cross-examine her and observe her demeanour.

[85] *Setz-Dempsey* (1994) 98 Cr.App.R. 23 CA.

evidence at the defendant's trial. Allowing the defendant's appeal against conviction the Court of Appeal held that the trial judge should not have admitted the written statement. He had failed to take into account the effect of the medical evidence about the witness's state of mind on the quality of the identification evidence, and the unfairness to the defendant in being unable to probe the witness's testimony. The inability to cross-examine was said in this case to be of "the utmost significance". Similarly, in *French and Gowhar*,[86] a robbery victim's identification of the accused was central to the prosecution case, but was alleged to be mistaken. The victim was a foreign student whose attendance it was not reasonably practicable to secure. Allowing the appeal, the Court of Appeal said that the trial judge had seriously underestimated the importance of the evidence to the case, and that he would not have admitted it in view of the challenge to it had he realised its importance. The Court of Appeal also took into account the fact that the prosecution had brought the situation on themselves by refusing to agree to a severance of charges at an earlier trial when the witness was present. This undoubtedly compounded the unfairness to the accused in being unable to cross-examine the witness at the second trial, which he could not attend.

Where the witness is proving a formal matter, such as the inability of another witness to attend, and cross-examination could not seriously challenge the substance of the witness's statement, the interests of justice and fairness are unlikely to require exclusion.[87] On the other hand, exclusion might be appropriate for a statement by a witness abroad and unwilling to attend the trial in England, if the prosecution could obtain oral evidence from the witness on commission[88] and the defendant would have an opportunity to cross-examine.[89]

D. STATUTORY EXCEPTIONS: SECTION 117—BUSINESS DOCUMENTS

17–016 Section 117 deals with business documents. The section provides:

"(1)   In criminal proceedings a statement contained in a document is admissible as evidence of any matter stated if—

(a)   oral evidence given in the proceedings would be admissible as evidence of that matter,

(b)   the requirements of subsection (2) are satisfied, and

(c)   the requirements of subsection (5) are satisfied, in a case where subsection (4) requires them to be.

(2)   The requirements of this subsection are satisfied if—

(a)   the document or the part containing the statement was created or received by a person in the course of a trade, business, profession or other occupation, or as the holder of a paid or unpaid office,

(b)   the person who supplied the information contained in the statement (the relevant person) had or may reasonably be supposed to have had personal knowledge of the matters dealt with, and

(c)   each person (if any) through whom the information was supplied from the relevant person to the person mentioned in paragraph (a) received the

---

[86] *French and Gowhar* (1993) 97 Cr.App.R. 421 CA. See also *Radak* [1999] 1 Cr.App.R. 187 CA.

[87] See *Castillo* [1996] 1 Cr.App.R. 438 CA.

[88] See the Crime (International Co-Operation) Act 2003 ss.7–9.

[89] *Radak* [1999] 1 Cr.App.R. 187 CA. See also the earlier decision in *Gokal* [1997] 2 Cr.App.R. 266 CA.

information in the course of a trade, business, profession or other occupation, or as the holder of a paid or unpaid office.

(3)   The persons mentioned in paragraphs (a) and (b) of subsection (2) may be the same person.

(4)   The additional requirements of subsection (5) must be satisfied if the statement—

    (a)   was prepared for the purpose of pending or contemplated criminal proceedings, or for a criminal investigation, but

    (b)   was not obtained pursuant to a request under section 7 of the Crime (International Co-operation) Act 2003 (c.32) or an order under paragraph 6 of Schedule 13 to the Criminal Justice Act 1988 (c.33) (which relate to overseas evidence).

(5)   The requirements of this subsection are satisfied if—

    (a)   any of the five conditions mentioned in section 116(2) is satisfied (absence of relevant person etc), or

    (b)   the relevant person cannot reasonably be expected to have any recollection of the matters dealt with in the statement (having regard to the length of time since he supplied the information and all other circumstances).

(6)   A statement is not admissible under this section if the court makes a direction to that effect under subsection (7).

(7)   The court may make a direction under this subsection if satisfied that the statement's reliability as evidence for the purpose for which it is tendered is doubtful in view of—

    (a)   its contents,

    (b)   the source of the information contained in it,

    (c)   the way in which or the circumstances in which the information was supplied or received, or

    (d)   the way in which or the circumstances in which the document concerned was created or received."

Section 117 replaced the earlier provision in s.24 of the Criminal Justice Act 1988, which was itself traceable through s.68 of PACE to the Criminal Evidence Act 1965. The 1965 Act was passed to reverse the effect of the decision of the House of Lords in *Myers v DPP*,[90] which excluded manufacturers' records of car engine numbers as inadmissible hearsay. The issue for trade and business records has essentially been one of the circumstantial guarantees of reliability that should be required, first, to compensate for the lack of opportunity to cross-examine on the information in the record and, secondly, to obviate the need for elaborate formal proof of documents of evidential value. The law has evolved to the point where s.117 requires only that the document containing the hearsay statement was created or received in the course of a trade, business, etc. of which the supplier of the information in the statement had personal knowledge, and that any intermediaries received the information in the course of a trade, business, etc.

Section 117 has a wide area of application. Its predecessor, s.24 of the Criminal Justice Act 1988, which was in broadly similar terms, was held to cover, for example, a bank's reports on lost and stolen credit cards,[91] a computer printout of stock records,[92] a manufacturer's records of contractual payments,[93]

---

[90] *Myers v DPP* [1965] A.C. 1001.

[91] *Bedi and Bedi* (1992) 95 Cr.App.R. 21 CA.

[92] *Burr v DPP* [1996] Crim. L.R. 324 QBD. In this case, and in *Motor Depot Ltd v Kingston upon Hull City Council* [2012] EWHC 3257 (Admin) the courts refused to admit under the business records exceptions *oral* evidence of what documents would have said.

[93] *Foxley* [1995] 2 Cr.App.R. 523 CA. However, as Professor J.C. Smith pointed out, since the documents in question were copies of the actual payments themselves they were original evidence (an example of "operative words") and not hearsay at all. See [1995] Crim. L.R. 637.

and a transcript of evidence.[94] A letter written or received in the course of business is clearly covered by s.117.[95] Other examples under s. 117 include a report by a scenes of crime police officer relating to a fingerprint he had found,[96] and a Notice signed by a prison governor and the defendant recording the defendant's release from prison on licence and stating the conditions of the licence.[97]

17–017 The existence of the statutory conditions can be inferred from the documents themselves and the evidence of how they have come to be produced before the court. It is not always necessary to have oral evidence from the supplier of the information, or the creator or keeper of the document. This point, confirmed in *Foxley*,[98] derives from the policy of letting the documents as far as possible speak for themselves. So in *O'Connor*[99] the Court of Appeal stated that a judge is entitled to look at the documents and to admit them under s. 117 if on the face of them the conditions of subs. (2) are satisfied. The documents in question were mobile phone records supplied to English police by police in Belgium. The records were in a form familiar to English courts. According to the Court of Appeal it was not a fatal objection to admissibility that the records were not accompanied by a written statement explaining their provenance. This case also provides an example of how anonymous hearsay can be admitted under s. 117. The person who made the statement constituting the record was not identified, but s. 117(2), unlike s. 116, does not require the maker of the statement to be identified. The court thought that the person must have been either an employee of the Belgian phone company or a police officer; in either case he would have been acting in the course of a trade or business and could reasonably be supposed to have had personal knowledge of the matters dealt with.

Unlike s.116, s.117 is not restricted to first-hand hearsay. Section 117(1) provides only that oral evidence of the matter stated would have to have been admissible; it does not stipulate that the *maker of the statement* should have been able to give such evidence. Accordingly subs.(2)(c) indicates that the information in the statement contained in the document may reach the maker of the statement indirectly through one or more intermediaries. For example, A, an employee, orally informs B, his supervisor, that he has witnessed an accident at their place of employment; B then makes an oral report to C, a manager, who writes down the details of the accident. The written report would be admissible in criminal

---

[94] *Lockley and Corah* [1995] 2 Cr.App.R. 554 CA. Note that a transcript would also be admissible under s.116 as well as s.117 if made by the shorthand writer who heard the evidence being given, and the witness is unavailable. There is considerable overlap between these sections as regards first-hand hearsay.

[95] See, e.g. the letter in issue in *Foxley* [1995] 2 Cr.App.R. 523 CA, written to the defendant by a third party, which implied that the defendant had made incriminating statements in an earlier letter to the third party. It is debatable whether the letter would amount to hearsay evidence at all applying s.115(3) of the 2003 Act, but it would clearly fall within s.117 in any event.

[96] *Kamuhuza* [2008] EWCA Crim 3060.

[97] *West Midlands Probation Board v French* [2008] EWHC 2631 (Admin). The decision is criticised by Birch and Hirst, "Interpreting the new concept of hearsay" (2010) 69 C.L.J. 72, 87–88, on the ground that the Notice was not a hearsay document at all since the purpose of adducing it was to prove the defendant's awareness of the conditions of the licence by virtue of his signature on the Notice.

[98] *Foxley* [1995] 2 Cr.App.R. 523 CA.

[99] *O'Connor* [2010] EWCA Crim 2287.

proceedings arising out of the accident. C created the document in the course of a trade or business; the information contained in it was supplied by A who had personal knowledge, and the information was passed to C by B who had received it from A in the course of his occupation. In this example it would be immaterial whether A, B or C was available as a witness.

Matters become more complex where a written statement was prepared for the purposes of a criminal investigation or of pending or contemplated criminal proceedings. Such a statement is admissible under s.117 only if "the relevant person" is not available as a witness for one of the reasons listed in s.116(2) or because he cannot reasonably be expected to remember the matter in question.[100] The relevant person for this purpose is the person who supplied the information contained in the statement. It is that person who is the material witness, and it is that person's veracity and reliability that would be in issue in deciding whether the statement should be excluded in the court's discretion under subs.(7). An example of a case where a statement by a relevant unavailable witness was held admissible under s.117 is *Kamuhuza*.[101] The statement was a report by a scenes of crime police officer recording the finding of a fingerprint on the window of a flat that the defendant was alleged to have burgled. The officer had left the police force in the five years that had elapsed between the offence and the trial, and could not be traced. The defence resisted the admission of the report, arguing that they needed to question the officer on whether the window opened to the left or the right, and whether other fingerprints had been found in the flat. The Court of Appeal held that the report was rightly admitted under s.117. The conditions in subs.(2) were satisfied, and subs.(5)(b) was satisfied because an officer who attended a great many crime scenes could not reasonably be expected to remember the matters in the statement; presumably certainly not in the kind of detail the defence wished to raise.

Unlike s.116, s.117 provides (in subs.(6)) for a power of discretionary exclusion **17–018** of statements that would otherwise be admissible under the section. According to subs.(7) the discretion may be exercised where the statement's reliability is doubtful. The doubt may be in view of the contents of the statement (as where it is internally contradictory), or the source of the information contained in it (as where it comes from a person of doubtful veracity), or the way in which the information was supplied or received (as where it is in the form of an anonymous letter), or the way in which or the circumstances in which the document was created or received (as where a report is ambiguous or incomplete). This discretion is more restricted than its predecessor, s.25 of the Criminal Justice Act 1988, that applied to both ss.23 and 24 of the 1988 Act and referred to exclusion in the interests of justice. This extended beyond consideration of the reliability of the statement to include its importance, relevance to the issues in the case, and any risk that its admission or exclusion would result in unfairness to the accused. However, s.78 of PACE continues to be available in respect of both ss.116 and 117 of the 2003 Act, and will allow the court to exclude otherwise admissible

---

[100] Criminal Justice Act 2003 s.117(4)(iii).
[101] *Kamuhuza* [2008] EWCA Crim 3060.

prosecution hearsay where required to safeguard the fairness of the proceedings. Defence hearsay statements, on the other hand, will only be excludable under s.117(6).

17–019 Finally, it is worth noting in relation to ss.116 and 117 that the courts have generally been unwilling to find any significant unfairness to an accused in the indirect restrictions placed by statutory hearsay exceptions on the exercise of the privilege against self-incrimination. In *Gokal*,[102] the Court of Appeal held expressly that it was not an abrogation of the privilege to say that a defendant could controvert a hearsay statement by giving evidence himself. It simply made the privilege more difficult to exercise. In this respect, as the court rightly pointed out, the situation is no different from any case where the prosecution adduce incriminating evidence that calls for an answer from the defendant if there is one.

E. STATUTORY EXCEPTIONS: SECTIONS 119 AND 120—PREVIOUS STATEMENTS OF WITNESSES

17–020 Section 119(1) of the Criminal Justice Act 2003 provides that where a person giving oral evidence admits making a previous inconsistent statement, or a previous inconsistent statement is proved against him by virtue of ss.3, 4 or 5 of the Criminal Procedure Act 1865, the statement is admissible as evidence of any matter stated of which oral evidence by him would be admissible. This provision changes the rule at common law, whereby a previous inconsistent statement of a witness was admissible only in relation to the witness's credibility and could not be used as evidence of the facts stated. Section 119(1) is discussed in more detail in Ch.14.

Subsection (2) of s.119 enacts a corresponding provision for the case where a hearsay statement is admitted that was made by a person who does not give oral evidence in the proceedings, and it is proved under s.124(2)(c) that that person made an inconsistent statement (at whatever time). The inconsistent statement is admissible under s.124(2)(c) for the purpose of showing that the maker of the hearsay statement contradicted himself, and by virtue of s.119(2) it may then be used as evidence of the matters stated.

Section 120 of the Criminal Justice Act 2003 contains a number of important provisions relating to other previous statements by witnesses. The section is largely an adjunct to the common law on the admissibility and use of previous consistent statements by witnesses. The common law, and the effect of the various provisions of s.120, is discussed in Ch.14. In summary, s.120(2) provides that a witness's previous statement admitted to rebut a suggestion that his oral evidence has been fabricated is admissible as evidence of any matter stated of which oral evidence by him would be admissible. Section 120(3) makes a similar provision for hearsay use of a statement in a document used to refresh memory where the document becomes evidence in the case as a result of cross-examination of the witness on it. Section 120(4) allows for the admission of previous statements by a witness, as evidence of any matter stated of which oral evidence by the witness would be admissible, in three types of case, provided in

---

[102] *Gokal* [1997] 2 Cr.App.R. 266 CA.

each case that the witness confirms in evidence that he made the statement and that he believes it to be true. The first case is previous identifications of a person, object or place (subs.(5)). The second case is where the previous statement was made when the matters stated were fresh in the witness's memory, but he does not now remember them and cannot reasonably be expected to remember them well enough to give oral evidence of them (subs.(6)). The third case is complaints by victims of offences. These are dealt with in subss.(7) and (8), which relax and extend the restrictive common law rules about complaints. The admissibility of a complaint is no longer confined to complaints of sexual offences but extends to complaints of any offence, and the requirement that a complaint should not have been made in response to a leading question is dropped in favour of a condition only that it should not have been made in response to a threat or a promise. The common law rule that the complaint was not evidence of the facts it stated, but was evidence of the consistency of the witness's story, has at last been changed, so that judges no longer have to explain to juries this baffling distinction without a difference.

F.   THE PRESERVED COMMON LAW EXCEPTIONS: SECTION 118

Section 118(1) of the Criminal Justice Act 2003 states: "The following rules of law are preserved". There then follows a list of eight paragraphs itemising the common law exceptions to the hearsay rule that are preserved by this provision. Any common law exception not in this list is abolished by s.118(2), along with all other common law rules governing the admissibility of hearsay evidence in criminal proceedings. Each of the eight paragraphs describes the rule in question, but does not codify it. It is therefore necessary to refer to the common law authorities to determine the scope and limits of each of the preserved rules.   **17–021**

1.   *Public information, etc*

Paragraph 1 of s.118(1) preserves: **17–022**

> "Any rule of law under which in criminal proceedings—
> (a)   published works dealing with matters of a public nature (such as histories, scientific works, dictionaries and maps) are admissible as evidence of facts of a public nature stated in them,
> (b)   public documents (such as public registers, and returns made under public authority with respect to matters of public interest) are admissible as evidence of facts stated in them,
> (c)   records (such as the records of certain courts, treaties, Crown grants, pardons and commissions) are admissible as evidence of facts stated in them, or
> (d)   evidence relating to a person's age or date or place of birth may be given by a person without personal knowledge of the matter."

Sub-paragraphs (a), (b) and (c) are in virtually identical terms to the three paragraphs of s.7(2) of the Civil Evidence Act 1995, which preserved these common law rules for civil proceedings. Their preservation for criminal proceedings was a recommendation of the Law Commission.[103] It is not necessary to say a great deal about these rules. The first rule permits published works of reference dealing with matters of a public nature, where the courts regard the work in question as authoritative, to be used as evidence of the facts stated in the works.[104] Such works are treated in effect as a specialised kind of expert evidence in documentary form, the reliability of which is presumed from the qualifications, study and expertise of their authors.

The second and third rules permit public documents and records to be used as evidence of the facts stated in them. There are a great many such documents and records; the examples given in sub-paras (b) and (c) are by no means exhaustive. The leading case of *Sturla v Freccia*[105] indicated that in general three conditions must be satisfied for this exception to the hearsay rule to operate: the document must concern a public matter; the document must have been made by a public officer acting under a duty to inquire into and record the matter in question; the document must have been intended to be retained for public reference and inspection. The second of these conditions suggests that there is a considerable overlap between this common law exception and the statutory business records exception in s.117 (discussed above), which deals, inter alia, with documents created by a person as the holder of an office.[106] The same presumption of reliability of the record, based on the conscientious performance of his duty by the creator of the document, underpins both exceptions. It should also be noted that the admissibility of many public documents, or of copies thereof, is regulated by separate statutory provision: examples include certified copies of entries in registers of births and deaths,[107] certificates of conviction,[108] and so on. There may not therefore be many cases in practice where it is necessary to rely on the common law exception for public documents.

17–023 The fourth rule may also not have a great deal of application in practice. A person's age or date or place of birth might well be the subject of a formal admission if it cannot be seriously disputed. If any of these matters is in issue, then, as just indicated, proof of a person's date and place of birth, and hence of their age, will normally be made by production of a certified copy of an entry in the register. It would be necessary to have evidence identifying the person in question with the person named in the certified copy if such identity is in issue. It is at this point that the rule stated in sub-para.(d) might be useful because it

---

[103] Law Com. 245 para.8.132.

[104] e.g. see *Read v Bishop of Lincoln* [1892] A.C. 644 PC.

[105] *Sturla v Freccia* (1880) 5 App.Cas. 623, HL.

[106] An illustration of the overlap is *West Midlands Probation Board v French* [2008] EWHC 2631 (Admin), where the Divisional Court held that a Notice signed by a prison governor and the defendant recording the defendant's release on licence from prison and stating the conditions of the licence was admissible under both s.117 and s.118(1)(b).

[107] Births and Deaths Registration Act 1953 s.34.

[108] PACE s.73.

allows someone without personal knowledge of the person's age to give evidence of the matter, such as the person himself[109] or a relative who was present at the birth.[110]

2. *Reputation as to character*

Paragraph 2 of s.118(1) preserves: 17–024

> "Any rule of law under which in criminal proceedings evidence of a person's reputation is admissible for the purpose of proving his good or bad character." It adds a note: "The rule is preserved only so far as it allows the court to treat such evidence as proving the matter concerned."

This provision is the counterpart for criminal proceedings of s.7(3)(a) of the Civil Evidence Act 1995, which preserved for civil cases the common law rule that evidence of a person's reputation is admissible to prove his character, whether good or bad, provided such character is a proper object of proof. The continuation of the rule in criminal cases was again a recommendation of the Law Commission.[111] The subject of character evidence is discussed in detail in Chs 18 and 19. That discussion will include reference to the common law rule providing for proof of character by evidence of reputation, although it is worth noting at this stage that "reputation" is unlikely to be the most informative or reliable evidence of character in most cases.

3. *Reputation or family tradition*

Paragraph 3 of s.118(1) preserves: 17–025

> "Any rule of law under which in criminal proceedings evidence of reputation or family tradition is admissible for the purpose of proving or disproving—
> (a)   pedigree or the existence of a marriage,
> (b)   the existence of any public or general right, or
> (c)   the identity of any person or thing.
>   Note
>   The rule is preserved only so far as it allows the court to treat such evidence as proving or disproving the matter concerned."

This provision is the counterpart for criminal proceedings of s.7(3)(b) of the Civil Evidence Act 1995, which preserved for civil cases two rules of the common law relating to declarations by deceased persons about matters of pedigree or public or general rights. Like the other common law rules preserved in the first two paragraphs of s.118(1), these rules were preserved on the recommendation of the Law Commission.[112] Other common law exceptions to the hearsay rule related to

---

[109] Someone giving evidence of their own age is necessarily relying on hearsay statements by their parents, or others present at their birth, but it would be pedantic in the extreme, and highly inconvenient, to apply hearsay logic at this point.

[110] *Weaver* (1873) L.R. 2 C.C.R. 85.

[111] Law Com. 245 para.8.132.

[112] Law Com. 245 para.8.132.

various types of declaration by deceased persons included declarations against interest, declarations in the course of duty, and dying declarations by victims of homicide. None of these exceptions has been preserved, the thinking being that all worthwhile hearsay that would have been covered by them can now be brought within the statutory exceptions in the 2003 Act or other preserved common law exceptions.

(A)   Declarations as to pedigree

17–026   Pedigree refers to relationships by blood or marriage between persons. Issues of pedigree include, for example, dates of birth, legitimacy of children, existence of marriages, the fact of death, identity of next of kin, and so on. Such issues may arise in many different contexts, including criminal proceedings.[113] The common law rule[114] is that an oral or written statement by a deceased person concerning a matter of pedigree is admissible as evidence of the truth of the facts stated, provided that the declarant was a blood relation or spouse of a blood relation of the person whose pedigree is in issue and that the declaration was made before the dispute arose. A question of pedigree must be directly in issue; the declaration may not be used for a collateral purpose, such as proof of a person's age in an action for breach of contract where the defence is one of infancy.[115]

The rationale of this exception is largely based on necessity. Given that the facts relevant to the issue of pedigree may have occurred many years before the trial, declarations by deceased members of the family may be not only the best, but also the only evidence available to determine the issue. Reliability may fairly be presumed since family members are the persons generally best placed to know the truth about such issues, and the requirement that the declaration should have been made before the dispute arose helps to dispel the possibility that the statement's probative value is rendered doubtful by an interest of the declarant. However, it should be noted that this exception does not require personal knowledge on the part of the declarant. These declarations may be founded on family tradition or reputation passed on through the generations,[116] hence they permit the use of multiple hearsay.

This last point could present a problem for any scheme of reform that aims to avoid unfairness by requiring particulars of hearsay statements to be given to the other parties to the case and provides for various factors to be taken into account in assessing the weight of hearsay statements, such as whether a person with personal knowledge made an original statement contemporaneously with the facts stated. Such provisions for notice and weighing of evidence are simply unworkable as far as evidence of reputation and family tradition based on multiple hearsay is concerned. The Civil Evidence Act 1995 met the difficulty in the following way. The Act provides in s.7(3) that the common law rules whereby

---

[113]   e.g. where the defendant is charged with incest, and he denies that the other party was a person within the prohibited degrees of relationship.

[114]   The leading cases establishing the scope and limits of the rule are *Goodright d. Stevens v Moss* (1777) 2 Cowp. 591; *Berkeley Peerage Case* (1811) 4 Camp. 401; *Shrewsbury Peerage Case* (1858) 7 H.L. Cas. 1; *Butler v Mountgarret* (1859) 7 H.L. Cas. 633.

[115]   See *Haines v Guthrie* (1884) 13 Q.B.D. 818 CA.

[116]   *Davies v Lowndes* (1843) 6 Man. & G. 471.

evidence of reputation or family tradition is admissible to prove or disprove pedigree or the existence of a marriage shall continue to have effect insofar as they authorise the court to treat such evidence as proving or disproving that matter. Where any such rule applies, reputation or family tradition is to be treated for the purposes of the Act as a fact and not as a statement or multiplicity of statements about the matter in question. This has the effect of deeming the declarations of deceased persons as to pedigree not to be hearsay evidence at all for the purposes of the provisions of the Act relating to notice and weighing of such evidence.

(B) Declarations as to public or general rights

At common law an oral or written statement by a deceased person concerning the reputed existence[117] of a public or general right is admissible as evidence of the existence of that right, provided that the declaration was made before a dispute had arisen[118] and, in the case of a general right, that the declarant had competent knowledge of the right.[119] A public right is one that affects the whole population, such as the existence of a public footpath over certain land.[120] A general right affects particular classes of people, such as the right of the inhabitants of a parish to use common land for certain purposes.[121]

17–027

The rationale of this exception is similar to the rationale for declarations as to pedigree. Other, or better, evidence of the existence of such rights may not be available, particularly where the right in question is of ancient origin. Local people may be presumed to know about local matters affecting the community, in the same way as family members usually know about matters affecting the family. It should be noted, however, that this is another exception that may allow in effect for the admission of multiple hearsay. This may have led Lord Ellenborough C.J. to comment in *Weeks v Sparke*[122] that reputation is in general weak evidence, and the judge should impress on the jury how little weight it ought to have.

By its nature this hearsay exception has little application in criminal proceedings. It was preserved for civil cases by s.7(3) of the Civil Evidence Act 1995, on the same terms and for the same reasons as declarations as to pedigree.

(C) Reputation as to identity

At common law evidence of reputation was admissible to prove the identity of a person or thing. Common sense and necessity provide the rationale. People generally do not have first-hand knowledge of the names of other people; they rely on what they are told are the names or what they heard the others are called.

17–028

---

[117] See *Mercer v Denne* [1905] 2 Ch. 538 CA (the exception does not extend to statements of particular facts relevant to the existence or non-existence of the right in issue; it only covers statements directly about matters of reputation).

[118] *Berkeley Peerage Case* (1811) 4 Camp. 401 HL.

[119] *Crease v Barrett* (1835) 1 Cr. M. & R. 919.

[120] See, e.g. *Radcliffe v Marsden UDC* (1908) 72 J.P. 475.

[121] See, e.g. *Weeks v Sparke* (1813) 1 M. & S. 679.

[122] *Weeks v Sparke* (1813) 1 M. & S. 679.

A modern application of the exception is seen in *Phillips*,[123] where a witness (W) to an assault in a barrack room recognised D as the assailant, but at the time of the attack knew him only by a nickname. It was held to be no objection to W's evidence of identification that he learnt D's name subsequently when they attended a course together and heard what D was called.

4. Res gestae

17–029   Paragraph 4 of s.118(1) preserves:

> "Any rule of law under which in criminal proceedings a statement is admissible as evidence of any matter stated if—
>
> (a)   the statement was made by a person so emotionally overpowered by an event that the possibility of concoction or distortion can be disregarded,
>
> (b)   the statement accompanied an act which can be properly evaluated as evidence only if considered in conjunction with the statement, or
>
> (c)   the statement relates to a physical sensation or a mental state (such as intention or emotion)."

Res gestae is a long-established concept in the law of evidence. But the term has given judges, and writers on evidence, a good deal of trouble because its precise doctrinal significance at common law has remained persistently unclear. Roughly translated the term means "the transaction", or in a looser sense "the story", but these are only descriptive labels and tell us nothing about rules of evidence concerning matters that form part of the transaction or the story. It appears that the term has been used in two main ways in relation to the admissibility of evidence, but in neither context is the term actually necessary since the principles concerned can be equally well described without reference to it. Little would be lost if the term were dropped from the law of evidence altogether.

One usage relates to the admissibility of evidentiary *facts*. A fact that is relevant to the case by virtue of its close association with the facts in issue is sometimes said to form part of the transaction with which the case is concerned, and hence to be admissible as part of the res gestae.[124] In Ch.1 proof of such facts was referred to as evidence of context. This denotes the idea that decisions about the existence, meaning and significance of the facts in issue may be facilitated by evidence of the context (time, place and other circumstances) in which they are alleged to have occurred. Such contextual facts may be admissible, because of their degree of relevance, notwithstanding that they might otherwise fall foul of one of the exclusionary rules of evidence. An example is *Ellis*[125] where the defendant, a shop assistant, was charged with stealing six marked shillings from the till. There was evidence that the marked coins had been placed in the till with other money at the beginning of the day, and that a watch had then been kept on the till. The defendant was observed taking money from the till on several occasions during the day. On arrest he was found to be in possession of the marked coins plus a further sum of money that matched the amount by which the

---

[123]   *Phillips* [2010] EWCA Crim 378.
[124]   Cross and Tapper, pp.34–35.
[125]   *Ellis* (1826) 6 B. & C. 145.

till was short. Proof that the defendant had taken other money, as well as the money he was actually charged with stealing, would normally have been prohibited by the common law rule against the admission of "similar fact" evidence. This rule stated that evidence of the defendant's similar misconduct on other occasions was inadmissible because of its prejudicial tendency. However, in this case the evidence of the other takings was held to be admissible because it helped to explain the history of the till from the time the marked coins were placed in it up to the time when they were found on the defendant. As Bayley J. put it:

> "Generally speaking, it is not competent to a prosecutor to prove a man guilty of one felony, by proving him guilty of another unconnected felony; but where several felonies are connected together, and form part of one entire transaction, then the one is evidence to show the character of the other."[126]

The other usage of res gestaeres gestae relates to the admission of certain **17–030** *statements* of fact or opinion. These statements are the subject of para.4 of s.118(1).[127] As we have seen, the making of a statement may be a fact in issue itself, as in the case of a defamatory statement, or it may be relevant as an evidentiary fact in the same way as contemporaneous conduct, as where a person tells a lie or runs away when caught doing a criminal act. In these situations the statement or the conduct is not adduced as evidence of any facts stated, and there is therefore no hearsay problem.[128] The group of exceptions set out in para.4 concerns the use of contemporaneous statements as evidence of the facts stated. When a statement is admitted for this purpose under one of these exceptions it is commonly said to be admitted as part of the res gestae. Paragraph 4 follows the generally accepted classification of such statements propounded by Cross and Tapper.[129] It is worth noting, however, that the classification is an attempt to impose order on a sprawling mass of cases. These cases are united only by the facts that the statements concerned throw some light on the existence, meaning and significance of the facts in issue by virtue of their association in time and place with the facts in issue, and that the maker of the statement is generally unavailable to give evidence. There is therefore a degree of overlap with s.116. Most first-hand oral hearsay statements admissible by virtue of para.4 will also be admissible under s.116 where the maker of the statement can be identified[130] but is not available as a witness for one of the reasons stated in s.116(2).[131]

---

[126] *Ellis* (1826) 6 B. & C. 145 at 147–148.

[127] Preserved, like the other common law exceptions in s.118(1), on the recommendation of the Law Commission: Law Com. 245 paras 8.121–8.129.

[128] But see the earlier discussion of whether these instances amount to implied assertions by the actor of his consciousness of guilt, and whether the hearsay rule applies to such assertions. Whatever the position at common law, it is submitted that under the definition of "a matter stated" in s.115(3) in the 2003 Act it does not.

[129] Cross and Tapper, pp.569–577. For an earlier, more elaborate analysis see the classic articles by R. N. Gooderson, "*Res Gesta* in Criminal Cases" [1956] C.L.J. 199 and [1957] C.L.J. 55.

[130] If the maker cannot be identified then s.116 cannot be used, and evidence of the statement can only be admitted as res gestae. The possibility of exclusion for unfairness under s.78 of PACE should be borne in mind where evidence of the statement is tendered by the prosecution.

[131] Where the witness is absent through fear, leave will not be required to admit the hearsay statement as res gestae, as it would be under s.116; again, s.78 of PACE may need to be considered.

The lack of judicial discipline in the reasoning of these cases is reflected in the impurity of the classification. Its categories overlap to some extent, and some cases do not necessarily fit neatly into one category or another. A warning is also needed against undue conceptualism in the application of the categories. In recent years the courts have shown a welcome tendency to focus less on formal conditions of admissibility and more on the relevance and reliability of the statements in question. With these caveats in mind, we can now turn to consider these applications of the res gestae principle.

(A)   Spontaneous statements about events in issue: the "excited utterance rule"

17–031   Paragraph 4(a) of s.118(1) preserves the common law rule of res gestae, which is often described as the doctrine relating to spontaneous statements about events in issue, or, in American terminology, as the "excited utterance" rule. The doctrine established by the leading modern[132] cases of *Ratten v R.*[133] and *Andrews*[134] is that a statement by a person about an event in issue, made in such circumstances of spontaneity or involvement in the event that the possibility of concoction or error can be disregarded, is admissible as evidence of the facts stated. The idea that to be admissible the statement should be an instinctive reaction to the drama of the event is captured in the American term "excited utterance"[135]; where the speaker has had time for detached reflection on the event so as to be able to construct or distort his account of it, the statement should be excluded.[136] The rationale of this hearsay exception is that such statements may have great probative value in establishing or understanding the events in question, and that the emotional involvement of the speaker in the event provides a guarantee of sincerity.

The scope and limits of this doctrine have been worked out in some detail in the cases, and it is the most developed of the res gestae exceptions to the hearsay rule. Historically there was some tendency to give it a narrow operation by confining it to statements that were contemporaneous in the sense of actually being part of the event in issue. In the notorious case of *Bedingfield*,[137] the defendant was charged with the murder of a woman. Cockburn C.J., the trial judge, refused to admit a statement by the deceased, who had emerged from a room in which she had been with the defendant, walked 30 yards, and met two witnesses to whom she had said, pointing to her throat, which was cut: "See what Harry [Bedingfield] has done to me". Cockburn C.J. held that this was not admissible as part of the res gestae[138] since it was "something stated by her after

---

[132] The historical origins of the doctrine are commonly traced to *Thompson v Trevanion* (1693) Skin. 402.

[133] *Ratten v R.* [1972] A.C. 378 PC.

[134] *Andrews* [1987] A.C. 281 HL.

[135] Federal Rules of Evidence r.803(2).

[136] See Lord Wilberforce in *Ratten v R.* [1972] A.C. 378 at 389.

[137] *Bedingfield* (1879) 14 Cox C.C. 341.

[138] The statement was not admissible as a dying declaration, since there was no evidence that the woman had a settled hopeless expectation of death at the time she made it; and because it was not

it was all over, whatever it was, and after the act was completed".[139] He contrasted this with a cry such as "Don't Harry!", uttered while the act was being done.[140] This approach[141] was a classic illustration of legal formalism, concentrating on a conceptual issue of when a "transaction" or an "act" began and ended, in preference to considering the substantive question of whether the statement was likely to be reliable in the circumstances. In restating the modern form of the doctrine in *Ratten v R.* Lord Wilberforce commented that the statement in *Bedingfield* was clearly one that carried "the mark of spontaneity and intense involvement",[142] and in *Andrews* Lord Ackner stated that *Bedingfield* would be decided differently today.[143] The case has been effectively overruled.

The facts of *Ratten v R.* were given in the previous chapter where the issue was discussed of whether evidence of a telephone call, made by a sobbing hysterical woman who said "Get me the police please", was adduced for an implied assertion that she was being attacked by her husband, the defendant. Such an assertion would have been subject to the hearsay rule at common law. It will be recalled that the Privy Council held that no such assertion was being relied on, but Lord Wilberforce went on to consider the admissibility of the evidence on the alternative basis that it was being used for a hearsay purpose. He held that it would still be admissible as part of the res gestae. Although it could not be shown that the call was made at the precise time of the shooting of the defendant's wife, it was closely associated in time and place with that event, and the tone of the woman's voice and her request for the police showed that her statement was being forced from her by the "overwhelming pressure of contemporary events".[144] This was sufficient to "exclude the possibility of concoction or distortion to the advantage of the maker [of the hearsay statement] or the disadvantage of the accused".[145] By adopting this test Lord Wilberforce was deliberately abandoning the concept of a statement forming "part of the transaction", with its difficulty and uncertainty of application, in favour of a principle linked directly to the rationale for admission.

Lord Wilberforce's formulation of the principle did not refer to excluding the possibility of error in addition to the risk of concoction or distortion.[146] This was an important omission in view of the likelihood that the statement might purport

17–032

---

made in the defendant's presence there was no possibility of finding an informal admission by the defendant's silence or conduct of the truth of the statement.

[139] *Bedingfield* (1879) 14 Cox C.C. 341 at 342–343.
[140] *Bedingfield* (1879) 14 Cox C.C. 341 at 342–343.
[141] *Bedingfield* can be compared with Foster (1834) 6 C. & P. 325, a manslaughter case where a statement by a person made just after he had been run over was admitted as evidence of the cause of the collision.
[142] *Ratten v R.* [1972] A.C. 378 at 390.
[143] *Andrews* [1987] A.C. 281 at 300.
[144] *Ratten v R.* [1972] A.C. 378 at 391. *Ratten* may be compared with *Newport* [1998] Crim. L.R. 581, where a call by an "agitated and frightened" deceased wife to her friend 20 minutes before her husband stabbed her was held by the Court of Appeal not to be a spontaneous and unconsidered reaction to an immediately impending emergency. Sed quaere.
[145] *Ratten v R.* [1972] A.C. 378 at 391.
[146] In *Lawson* [1998] Crim. L.R. 883 the Court of Appeal referred also to risks of "fabrication" and "dishonest motive" on the part of the maker of the statement. It is unclear what these references add to Lord Wilberforce's use of "concoction" and "distortion".

to identify an assailant or other wrongdoer, with the risk that the identification could be mistaken. In *Nye and Loan*,[147] the Court of Appeal remedied the omission by adding a "gloss" to the principle, requiring the judge to exclude the risk of error as well as the risk of fabrication. In that case a motorist, L, was assaulted by a person travelling in another car involved in a collision with L's vehicle. While L was sitting in his car recovering from the effects of the blow received, the police arrived on the scene. L then made a statement identifying the second defendant (Loan), a passenger in the other car, as his attacker. Upholding the admission of L's statement, the Court of Appeal held that L had had no opportunity for concoction and there was no chance of error, given the very short time involved before L made the statement and given that his mind was still dominated at the time by the event. Paragraph 4(a) refers only to the possibility of "concoction or distortion" and does not mention the possibility of error arising from the person being emotionally overpowered by the event. It remains to be seen what significance, if any, the courts will attach to this omission. It is submitted that they should not regard the wording of the provision as an attempt to enlarge the scope of the doctrine and should, if necessary, interpret "distortion" widely to include mistake, particularly where identity is in issue.

In *Andrews*,[148] Lord Ackner stressed the idea of a person's mind being so dominated by an event that the statement can be regarded as an instinctive reaction, produced by the speaker without the opportunity for reasoned reflection. His judgment went on to draw out the implications of this idea, and in so doing provided a useful elucidation of the test of spontaneity or involvement in the event. Contemporaneity of the statement with the event is seen as a matter of degree; the statement should be made in conditions of approximate but not exact contemporaneity. Secondly, provided that the "trigger mechanism" for the statement is still operative, it may not be a bar to admissibility that the statement was made in response to a question. It is not a necessary condition that the statement should have been spontaneous in the sense of being unprompted by any inquiry. In *Andrews* the victim had been fatally stabbed by one of two men who attacked him when he opened the door of his flat in response to their knock. The victim, bleeding heavily, sought help from the flat below. When the police arrived, some minutes after the attack, they asked the victim how he had come by his injuries. He said that one of the attackers was someone called "Donald", which was the defendant's first name. The officer taking notes apparently misheard the name because he wrote down that the victim had said "Donavon", but it seems to have been accepted that this was a mistake probably due to the victim's Scottish accent and the fact that he had been drinking very heavily. There was some evidence that the victim might have had a malicious motive to incriminate the defendant, since he believed that the defendant and the other man, O'Neill, had attacked and damaged his house on an earlier occasion. The House of Lords upheld the trial judge's admission of the victim's identification of the

---

[147] *Nye and Loan* (1977) 66 Cr.App.R. 252 CA. See also *Turnbull* (1984) 80 Cr.App.R. 104 CA.
[148] *Andrews* [1987] A.C. 281.

defendant as res gestae, saying that the victim's thoughts were so dominated by the severity of the attack that the possibility of fabrication could be ignored.[149]

In *Gilfoyle*,[150] there was a hint that the courts might be prepared to rely on the *Andrews* rationale to justify extending the exception to statements about evidentiary facts as opposed to restricting it to statements about facts in issue. The defendant was convicted of the murder of his wife. She had been found hanging from a beam in the garage of their home. It was thought at first that she had killed herself because the defendant had produced a suicide note in her handwriting. However, a number of the dead woman's colleagues at work came forward to say that a few weeks earlier she had told them that she was worried because on the previous evening the defendant had asked her to write suicide notes. He had said to her that this was in connection with a suicide course he was doing at work. He had told her what to say and had then taken her into the garage to show her how to put up a rope. Further investigation led to the defendant being charged with his wife's murder. At trial the defendant maintained the defence that his wife had committed suicide. The trial judge excluded the evidence of the witnesses as to the wife's statements about the notes, on the ground that the evidence was inadmissible hearsay. On appeal the Court of Appeal held that the court had power on an application to receive fresh evidence[151] to reconsider decisions at trial on the admissibility of evidence. It was then held that evidence of the wife's statements was admissible to prove that she was not in a suicidal frame of mind when she wrote the notes and that she wrote them in the belief that she was assisting the defendant in a course at work. The ground of admissibility here is the res gestae exception, discussed below, relating to declarations by a person about their state of mind. This is a well-established principle, but it would not permit use of the declaration to prove other facts, such as the fact that the defendant had asked his wife to write the notes and had told her what to write. The Court of Appeal said that it was not necessary to decide the admissibility of the statements for this purpose, but in an earlier passage the court cited *Ratten* and *Andrews* and commented that:

> "In this case the statements themselves suggested that the events which prompted them were still dominating [the wife's] mind. The statements were made the morning after the letters had been written as soon after as would ordinarily have been expected. The possibility of invention or unreliability could be discounted and there was little room for inaccuracy in the reporting of the statements."[152]

This dictum seems to suggest that the wife's statements could be admitted to prove that the defendant asked her to write the notes and told her what to write. Suicide was of course a fact in issue, and the notes were a key item of circumstantial evidence pointing towards suicide. However, the statements were about the *notes*, rather than the "transaction" of the wife's death. The Court of

17–033

---

[149] See also *Turnbull* (1984) 80 Cr.App.R. 104 CA (a similar case where a stabbed victim identified his assailant by various names, including the defendant's nickname of "Tommo": statement admitted); *Cartnall* [1995] Crim. L.R. 944 CA (victim with very severe injuries named his attacker an hour after the attack in answer to questions: statement admitted).

[150] *Gilfoyle* [1996] 1 Cr.App.R. 302 CA.

[151] Under the Criminal Appeal Act 1968 s.23.

[152] *Gilfoyle* [1996] 1 Cr.App.R. 302 at 323 per Beldam L.J.

Appeal was surely right to say that in the circumstances the risk of concoction or error was remote, but if this dictum is correct, it moves the law a long way from the concept of a spontaneous statement forced from the speaker by the overwhelming pressure of contemporary events (that is, the events in issue). Such an extension would swallow up Cross's second category of res gestae statements—statements accompanying and explaining relevant acts—while also removing the limitation that such statements are not admissible to prove the existence of facts mentioned by the maker of the statement when giving the reasons for the act.[153] A general test of circumstantial guarantees of trustworthiness would in fact make most of the formal categories of admissible hearsay redundant. It remains to be seen whether the dictum in *Gilfoyle* will provide a basis for extension of the doctrine of spontaneous statements; possible support for an extension might be that para.4(a) refers to a person being emotionally overpowered by "an event" and does not, for example, limit this to an event that is the subject-matter of the charge against the accused.[154]

Although nearly all of the leading cases have concerned statements by deceased victims, it is not a necessary condition of this doctrine that the maker of the statement should be dead at the time when it is sought to use his hearsay statement. The doctrine can apply equally when the maker of the statement is unavailable for other reasons or fails to attend the trial,[155] and even when he is called as a witness.[156] However, the doctrine should not be used as a device to avoid calling the maker of the statement as a witness when he is available.[157] In *Tobi v Nicholas*,[158] the Divisional Court fired a warning shot at prosecutors by refusing to apply the doctrine in a case where it was sought to use a statement by the driver of a coach identifying the defendant as the other driver involved in a collision between their vehicles. The coach driver was not called as a witness at the defendant's trial on a charge of failing to stop after an accident. The court was not persuaded that the collision was such a dramatic incident that it would necessarily have so dominated the mind of the coach driver when he made his statement 20 minutes afterwards that the possibility of concoction could be excluded.

(B) Statements accompanying and explaining relevant acts

17–034 Paragraph 4(b) of s.118(1) preserves the common law rule of res gestae that where the doing of a certain act is a fact in issue, or is relevant to the issue as an item of circumstantial evidence, a statement by the actor that accompanies and

---

[153] See further below.

[154] cf. Youth Justice and Criminal Evidence Act 1999 s.41(3)(b).

[155] As in *Edwards and Osakwe v DPP* [1992] Crim. L.R. 576 DC.

[156] As in *Nye and Loan* (1977) 66 Cr.App.R. 252.

[157] *Andrews* [1987] A.C. 281 at 302 per Lord Ackner. This dictum does not mean that this res gestae exception is to be disapplied if better or the best evidence is available: *Attorney-Generals Reference (No.1 of 2003)* [2003] EWCA Crim 1286; [2003] 2 Cr.App.R. 29. In that case, the prosecution had wanted to adduce a spontaneous res gestae statement of the victim, who later retracted her statement and who the prosecution believed would be hostile if called as a witness. The Court of Appeal held that her statement would be admissible, but was liable to exclusion under s.78 of PACE because of the lack of opportunity to cross-examine.

[158] *Tobi v Nicholas* [1987] Crim. L.R. 774.

explains the act is admissible as evidence of what is stated.[159] The act must be relevant in the absence of the statement; the justification for admitting the statement is that it may be necessary to resolve a doubt about the precise significance of the act by showing its nature or the intention with which it was done. Paragraph 4(b) expresses this in terms that the statement should accompany an act that can be properly evaluated as evidence only if considered in conjunction with the statement. So, for example, if the issue is whether a transfer of money from the claimant to the defendant was a gift or a loan, and the act of delivery of the money is proved, evidence can be given by a witness that he heard the claimant say on handing over the money, "I'm giving you this for your birthday". The claimant's statement can be used to prove that the money was a gift. It should be noted, however, that the statement cannot be used to prove any other facts mentioned in connection with the nature or purpose of the act. In *Skinner & Co v Shew & Co*,[160] the plaintiffs sued the defendants for interference with contract by threatening a third party with legal proceedings so as to cause him to repudiate a contract with the plaintiffs. The Court of Appeal held that the plaintiffs had been rightly permitted to adduce in evidence a letter from the third party in which the latter broke off the contract and explained that he was doing so as a result of the defendants' threats. However, the existence of the threats themselves was required to be proved by other evidence.

The three conditions of this exception to the hearsay rule are that the statement must be made by the actor, the statement must relate to the act done, and the statement must be roughly contemporaneous with the act. The first condition is illustrated by *Howe v Malkin*[161] where the court rejected a statement about the boundary of property because the statement was about work being done on the land by builders, not by the maker of the statement himself. The second condition is illustrated by *Bliss*,[162] where the court rejected a statement by the deceased owner of property when planting a tree that he was doing so on the boundary of his land with a road. The reason given for rejection was that the statement had no connection with the act done, although a simpler reason would have been that in any event evidence of the act of planting the tree was irrelevant to the issue in the case of whether the road was public or private. Contemporaneity of act and statement is a question of degree. Where the act is a continuing one, a statement explaining the act appears to be admissible if made at any time during the continuance of the act.[163]

This type of res gestae exception applies equally to facts constituting circumstantial evidence, including evidence of identification. In *McCay*,[164] an eyewitness had picked out a man at a parade, but by the time of the trial the witness was unable to remember the number of the man in the parade that the

---

[159] The leading old cases are *Rawson v Haigh* (1824) 2 Bing. 99; *Bliss* (1837) 7 Ad. & El. 550; *Howe v Malkin* (1878) 40 L.T. 196. For modern recognition of the rule see *McCay* [1991] 1 All E.R. 232 CA; *Kearley* [1992] 2 A.C. 228 at 246 per Lord Bridge of Harwich.

[160] *Skinner & Co v Shew & Co* [1894] 2 Ch. 581 CA.

[161] *Howe v Malkin* (1878) 40 L.T. 196.

[162] *Bliss* (1837) 7 Ad. & El. 550.

[163] See *Rawson v Haigh* (1824) 2 Bing. 99 (letters written by a bankrupt during his absence abroad admissible to prove that his intention in leaving the country was to hinder his creditors).

[164] *McCay* [1991] 1 All E.R. 232 CA.

witness had viewed from behind a two-way mirror. A police officer present during the parade was permitted to testify that the witness had said "It is number eight". According to the Court of Appeal this statement accompanied and explained a relevant act of identification that consisted of the physical act of viewing the suspect and the intellectual act of recognising him. The reasoning is dubious because the statement did not explain an otherwise equivocal act; there was no such act independent of the statement—it was a case of the statement being a verbal "act" in itself. As an expedient to justify the admission of a reliable piece of hearsay this contrived argument is understandable, but the case is an example of the ways in which courts have sometimes "fiddled" the hearsay rule and its exceptions to achieve what they regard as acceptable results.

(C)   Statements relating to physical sensations or mental states

17–035   Paragraph 4(c) of s.118(1) preserves two rules of the common law of res gestae relating to the admissibility of a person's contemporaneous statements about his physical sensations or mental states. We will deal first with statements about mental states since the law relating to these is more complex.

(1)   The general rule for statements relating to mental states

17–036   Where a person's state of mind or emotion is in issue, or is relevant to an issue,[165] evidence of a contemporaneous statement by that person about his or her state of mind or emotion is admissible to show its existence. Questions of intention,[166] knowledge,[167] belief,[168] opinion[169] and emotion[170] can all be proved in this way. It seems clear that such statements are logically hearsay on either an assertion-based or a declarant-based definition of hearsay, although this is sometimes denied. The rationale of the exception is a combination of best evidence and necessity principles. No better evidence of a person's past state of mind is available than the person's own statements at the time, and such statements may be the only evidence if there is no relevant conduct from which inferences could be drawn. The contemporaneity of the statement is a pointer to

---

[165] For cases where the states of mind of third parties were controversially held not to be relevant to the issue of the defendant's liability for an offence, see *Blastland* [1986] A.C. 41 (knowledge of a murder before the news of the murder became public—discussed in Ch.3) and *Kearley* [1992] 2 A.C. 228 (belief that the defendant was a drug dealer—discussed in Ch.16).

[166] *Sugden v Lord St Leonards* (1876) 1 P.D. 154 at 251 per Mellish L.J.

[167] See *Thomas v Connell* (1838) M. & W. 267 (statement by bankrupt admissible to prove knowledge of his insolvency at the time of making a payment of money).

[168] *Du Bost v Beresford* (1810) 2 Camp. 511; *Jozwiak v Sadek* [1954] 1 All E.R. 3 (declarations admissible to show belief of maker that certain defamatory statements referred to particular individuals).

[169] *Tooke* (1794) 25 St. Tr. 344.

[170] *Vincent Frost and Edwards* (1840) 9 C. & P. 275 (statements by bystanders at a public meeting admissible to prove that they were frightened by the meeting); *Neill v North Antrim Magistrates' Court* [1992] 4 All E.R. 846 HL (statement by witness admissible to prove fear of giving evidence). See also *Gilfoyle* [1996] 1 Cr.App.R. 302 CA (statements by writer of suicide notes as to reasons for writing the notes admissible to prove that she was not in a suicidal frame of mind).

its credibility, although the factfinder may clearly have to consider whether the person making the statement had any motive to misrepresent his state of mind at the time.

This rationale does not extend to proof of facts that exist independently of the maker's state of mind. Hence such statements are not admissible to prove any facts stated other than the relevant state of mind or emotion. The standard illustration is *Thomas v Connell*,[171] where a statement admitted to prove a bankrupt's knowledge of his insolvency when making a payment to the defendant could not be used to prove the insolvency itself. However, if the dictum in *Gilfoyle* is correct, this limitation may be bypassed in future in some cases. According to that dictum the whole of a statement about relevant facts may be admissible as evidence of what is stated if the statement is made under such conditions of involvement in or domination by the fact in question as to negative the possibility of concoction or mistake.

As with all the res gestae exceptions, the requirement of contemporaneity is one of degree. The risk of manufacture of a self-serving statement clearly increases with any time gap between the state of mind in question and the statement about its existence. If it is relevant whether X knew a particular fact on January 1, an isolated statement by him on February 1, that he did know the fact on January 1, is unlikely to be admissible under this rule.[172]

(2) Declarations of intention[173]

We have seen above that when a relevant act is accompanied by an explanatory statement the statement is admissible to show the intention with which the act was done. The question now is the use, if any, that can be made of an isolated declaration of intention, when by definition the statement is not accompanied by a relevant act.

It is clear that such a declaration is admissible as circumstantial evidence of the prior[174] or subsequent[175] existence of the intention. Suppose the issue is whether D deliberately attacked P on March 1. D's statement on February 1 that he intended to attack P in the future is admissible to show that he had such an intention on February 1. This fact is a relevant item of circumstantial evidence because a reasonable inference can be drawn, based on the factual presumption of continuance, that the intention continued for a month. If it continued to the time of the assault this would tend to prove mens rea and to negative any question of self-defence. A similar argument can work in reverse for statements made after relevant acts have occurred. In *Re Fletcher* Cozens-Hardy M.R. commented, "It is common practice, particularly in criminal cases, to prove intention at a particular time by words and acts at a subsequent date".[176]

17–037

---

[171] *Thomas v Connell* (1838) 4 M. & W. 267.

[172] If the person is a party to the case the statement will be admissible as an informal admission, assuming that it is adverse to the person's case.

[173] See R. Munday, "Legislation that would 'preserve' the common law: the case of the declaration of intention" (2008) 124 L.Q.R. 46.

[174] *Re Fletcher* [1917] 1 Ch. 339.

[175] *Robson v Kemp* (1802) 4 Esp. 233.

[176] *Re Fletcher* [1917] 1 Ch. 339 at 342.

It is less clear whether a declaration of intention to do an act in the future can be used to prove the performance of the act in the absence of any other evidence that the act was done. At first sight it is surprising how little authority there is on this question, given its apparent importance. However, it should be remembered that the issue is most likely to arise in connection with alleged acts by the parties to the case, in particular the accused in a criminal case. In these cases the declaration of intention to do the act will amount to an informal admission and will be admissible on that basis. Evidence of a threat by the defendant to kill the deceased is admissible to help prove both mens rea and actus reus of murder.[177] The problem for the common law has concerned declarations by third parties, usually deceased by the time of trial, that are not admissible under any other exception. The English authorities on the point are not consistent, but the majority of the cases support the view that such a declaration is not admissible to prove performance of the act.

17–038   In *Thomson*,[178] the defendant was convicted of using an instrument to procure a miscarriage on a woman who had since died from an unrelated cause. His defence was that she had operated on herself. The Court of Criminal Appeal held that the trial judge had rightly excluded evidence that the woman had said before the miscarriage that she intended to operate on herself and that after it had happened she said that she had operated on herself. The latter statement was clearly hearsay if adduced as evidence of the fact stated; it was the equivalent of a third-party confession. It was logical therefore for the court also to reject the former statement. The law would be absurd if it permitted a statement of intention to prove the performance of an act, but rejected better (because more incriminating) evidence that the maker of the statement had done the act.[179] *Thomson* is consistent with the earlier first instance decision of Lord Cockburn C.J. in *Wainwright*[180] where he held inadmissible a statement by a deceased victim of murder when leaving her house that she was going to visit the defendant. The rejection was apparently on the basis of insufficient probative value: "it was only a statement of intention which might or might not have been carried out". *Wainwright* is frequently contrasted with *Buckley*,[181] where Lush J. admitted a statement by a deceased police officer to his superior that he intended to go in search of the defendant, who was charged with the officer's murder, after dark that evening. The hearsay point is not addressed in the report of the case, but it may be that Lush J. thought that since the officer's statement was made in the

---

[177] See *Ball* [1911] A.C. 47 at 68; *Williams* (1987) 84 Cr.App.R. 298.
[178] *Thomson* [1912] 3 K.B. 19 CCA.
[179] cf. *Moghal* (1977) 65 Cr.App.R. 56, where the Court of Appeal thought that a person's declaration of intention to kill the deceased was admissible to support the defence of the defendant (who was alleged to have been an accessory to the murder) that the killing had been perpetrated solely by that person. The court also held that the declarant's subsequent confession to murder was inadmissible hearsay. It is very doubtful whether this case can be taken as authority for any proposition of law. *Thomson* was not cited; the dictum regarding the admissibility of the pre-act declaration was subsequently doubted by Lord Bridge in *Blastland* [1986] A.C. 41 at 60, and in any event the prosecution had conceded that the declarant was the principal party in the murder.
[180] *Wainwright* (1875) 13 Cox C.C. 171.
[181] *Buckley* (1873) 13 Cox C.C. 293.

course of duty, his intention was likely to have been carried out. In this way the cases might be reconcilable on their facts, although the point of distinction is thin.

The issue in these cases will now need to be considered in relation not only to the preserved common law of res gestae, but also to the statutory exceptions to the hearsay rule in the Criminal Justice Act 2003. Section 116 will permit the admission of first-hand oral statements by an identified person who is not available as a witness at the trial for one of the specified reasons. Leave of the court will not be required where the reason for unavailability is the person's death. Accordingly, it appears that all the statements in question in the cases discussed in the previous paragraph would be automatically admissible under s.116. However, where the statements are tendered as evidence for the prosecution, as in *Wainwright* and *Buckley*, they will be subject to the exclusionary discretion under s.78 of PACE. Where they are tendered for the defence, as in *Thomson*, s.78 is not applicable. The only possibility for exclusion then is s.126 of the 2003 Act. This refers to exclusion on the ground that admitting the statement would result in undue waste of time, taking account of the value of the evidence. It seems most unlikely that admitting the statements of the deceased in *Thomson* could be regarded as time-wasting. A further possibility under the 2003 Act for these statements is s.114(1)(d), the provision that allows for the admission of hearsay statements in the interests of justice. This provision is discussed below.

In Australia the High Court has held, in a case where a husband was charged with the murder of his wife, that the wife's statement that she intended to meet her husband in the town centre was admissible as original evidence of her intention.[182] In the view of the court the jury could draw appropriate inferences about the likelihood of her having acted upon her intention, although the statement could not be used as direct evidence that she did meet him. The latter point is clearly right since the conclusion that there was a meeting depends on two inferences, namely that the wife tried to carry out her intention to meet, and also that the husband did likewise. On the facts, there was independent evidence to justify the second inference as well as the first, since the husband had told another witness of his arrangement to meet his wife in the town centre on the night in question. The conclusion that declarations of intention are original rather than hearsay evidence follows classic American authority,[183] but it contradicts the logic of the hearsay rule and is unlikely to be followed in England.

(3)   Statements relating to physical sensations

This is the counterpart of the previous rule. A statement by a person about the   **17–039**
state of his health or bodily sensations at the time is admissible as part of the res gestae to prove the existence of that state of health or those sensations. If, for example, it is relevant to show that X suffered food poisoning at a certain time, a statement by him at the time that he felt nauseous can be proved. In the old case

---

[182] *Walton v R.* (1989) 84 A.L.R. 59.
[183] *Mutual Life Insurance Co v Hillmon* (1892) 145 U.S. 284. For further discussion of the problem raised by this and the other cases, see A. Choo, *Hearsay and Confrontation in Criminal Trials* (1996), pp.129–137.

of *Aveson v Lord Kinnaird*[184] the issue was whether the plaintiff's wife was in good health at the time the plaintiff took out an insurance policy on her life. The Court of King's Bench held that the evidence of a friend had been rightly admitted that when the friend had visited the plaintiff's wife about that time, she was in bed looking ill and made a number of statements about why she was in bed and how she had been ill for about ten days. Lord Ellenborough C.J. noted that the wife had been questioned by the friend about her bodily infirmity, and continued:

> "She said it was of some duration, several days... What were the complaints, what the symptoms, what the conduct of the parties themselves at the time, are always received in evidence upon such inquiries, and must be resorted to from the very nature of the thing."[185]

The rationale for admitting this type of statement is again a combination of best evidence and necessity principles, as Lord Ellenborough recognised. His statement also suggests that the requirement of contemporaneity in this rule is not strict. The evidence in this case seems to have been received to establish not only the state of the wife's health at the time of making the statement, but also the state of health going back over the previous ten days. This is both inevitable and desirable. States of health and bodily sensations are very often not transient events (unlike emotions), but extend over a period of time. It would be absurd to say that a person could testify that he heard X say that she was suffering from a pain in the head at the time she spoke, but not that she had been suffering from the same pain for a week. Given the rationale of the rule it would seem logical to admit evidence of a statement by X that she had been ill a week earlier even if she was no longer ill at the time of making this statement. However, the authorities are not clear that the rule always permits a narrative of past symptoms.[186] It seems likely that a degree of contemporaneity will be required, although the modern approach of asking whether the speaker had any motive to misrepresent or distort the facts, or might have made a mistake, could allow very considerable relaxation of this requirement.

It is generally said that declarations as to health are admissible to prove the existence of bodily symptoms, but are not admissible to prove their cause.[187] The reason for this limitation may be a combination of the rule against opinion evidence, where the hearsay statement relates to an issue the court has to decide or on which expert evidence is required, and the danger of prejudice to the accused in a criminal case through the admission of statements whose probative value cannot be tested.[188]

---

[184] *Aveson v Lord Kinnaird* (1805) 6 East 188.

[185] *Aveson v Lord Kinnaird* (1805) 6 East 188 at 194–195.

[186] Compare *Gloster* (1888) 16 Cox C.C. 471 with *Black* (1922) 16 Cr.App.R. 118 (Salter J., in argument); and see further R. N. Gooderson, "*Res Gesta* in Criminal Cases" [1956] C.L.J. 199, 211–215, suggesting that in poisoning cases, statements by victims were often admitted that they had felt unwell at earlier times, when the issue was whether poison had been administered to them at those times.

[187] *Gilbey v GWR Co* (1910) 102 L.T. 202 is the leading case.

[188] Again, however, poisoning cases may be an exception to the prohibition on statements about causes of physical sensations: see Gooderson, "*Res Gesta* in Criminal Cases" [1956] C.L.J. 199.

5. *Confessions etc*

Paragraph 5 preserves "Any rule of law relating to the admissibility of confessions or mixed statements in criminal proceedings".   **17–040**

The general principle at common law is that an informal admission by a party to litigation is admissible against the party as evidence of the truth of what is admitted. This common law principle applied equally to civil and criminal cases, but in relation to civil cases it has now been superseded by the Civil Evidence Act 1995. The principle is still applicable in criminal cases and is preserved by para.5. An admission by the accused in a criminal case will invariably amount to a confession for the purposes of PACE, since it is adverse to the accused. This means that if the prosecution wish to adduce it they will have to satisfy the conditions of admissibility in s.76 of PACE. As discussed in Ch.6, an admission/confession is a statement that is adverse to its maker at the time it is made.[189] An admission only has probative value if the maker has personal knowledge of the matter admitted.[190]

Admissions are usually express but they can be implied by a party's silence or in their conduct. The application of the principle to express admissions in a context other than police questioning is illustrated by such cases as *Simons*,[191] where the defendant was overheard making an incriminating remark to his wife on leaving the magistrates' court after his committal for trial on a charge of arson. Alderson B., the trial judge, allowed a witness to prove the making of this statement: "What a person is overheard saying to his wife, or even saying to himself, is evidence". Similarly, in *Rumping v DPP*[192] the House of Lords held admissible a letter written by the defendant to his wife that the police had intercepted and that contained what amounted to an admission of murder.[193] Implied admissions may result from the operation of the principle confirmed in *Christie*[194]: a failure by the defendant to deny an accusation made in his presence may amount to an implied admission by him of the truth of the accusation, if in the circumstances it would be reasonable to expect a denial if the accusation were untrue. The operation of this principle was discussed in detail in Ch.5 in connection with the accused's right to silence at common law. An example of its

---

[189] *Hasan* [2005] 2 Cr.App.R. 22 HL. Is a person's statement "I am X" an admission where X is a defendant and the statement was made in circumstances subsequently alleged to be incriminating? See *Ward, Andrews and Broadley* [2001] Crim. L.R. 316 (and Commentary by DJB).

[190] *Comptroller of Customs v Western Electric Co* [1966] A.C. 367 PC. Hence an admission as to the place of manufacture of certain goods that is based on markings on the goods themselves has no more value than those markings, and is inadmissible hearsay at common law. cf. *Bird v Adams* [1972] Crim. L.R. 174 DC (admission by drug dealer as to the nature of the drugs found in his possession admissible as founded on personal experience). On the question of admissions that goods found in the defendant's possession are in fact stolen (as opposed to admissions of the defendant's belief that they are), see *Hulbert* (1979) 69 Cr.App.R. 243 CA; *Korniak* (1983) 76 Cr.App.R. 145 CA.

[191] *Simons* (1834) 6 C. & P. 540 at 541.

[192] *Rumping v DPP* [1962] 3 All E.R. 256.

[193] The letter was not protected by the privilege that attached at that time to marital communications, because the privilege was only one against compulsory disclosure. It did not avail where third parties had learnt of the contents of the communication. This head of privilege was abolished for civil cases by Civil Evidence Act 1968 s.16(3) and for criminal cases by PACE s.80(9).

[194] *Christie* [1914] A.C. 545 HL.

operation in a context other than police interrogation is *Parkes*,[195] where the defendant was confronted by the mother of a murder victim who accused him of stabbing her daughter. The defendant made no reply to the accusation, then tried to stab the mother when she said she would detain him until the police arrived. Dismissing his appeal, the Privy Council cited *Christie* and held that since the parties were speaking on equal terms it was reasonable to expect the defendant to deny the mother's charge if it were untrue. Hence the trial judge had been right to allow the jury to consider the defendant's reaction as part of the evidence pointing to his guilt.

17–041   Under s.82(1) of PACE, "any statement wholly or partly adverse to the person who made it" amounts to a confession for the purposes of Pt VIII of PACE. This means that the definition extends to mixed statements, that is statements that are partly incriminating and partly exculpatory. If the prosecution wish to rely on the incriminating parts of the confession they will have to satisfy the conditions of admissibility of confessions under s.76(2), and put in the whole of the confession. They are not permitted to take the incriminating parts out of context. The direction that the judge should give the jury about a mixed statement is discussed in Ch.6.

Two rationales have been suggested for the admissions rule.[196] One is that informal admissions are one of the best forms of evidence and are likely to be reliable, based on the crude psychological assumption that no one would make a statement against their interest unless it were true. Although in many cases this may be so, in Ch.6 we noted persuasive evidence against this view as a general truth. False confessions, whether of the voluntary type or coerced by the pressure of police interrogation, are a significant risk, particularly with vulnerable defendants who are highly suggestible or who suffer from mental handicap, mental illness or personality disorder. The use of the exclusionary discretion under s.78 of PACE or at common law to control the admission of such unreliable confessions should be borne in mind at this point. The other rationale is founded on the logic of the adversarial process.[197] This argues that parties cannot reasonably object to the use in evidence against them of their own (voluntary) statements. This is because a party can hardly complain about the absence of an opportunity to cross-examine himself at the time he made the statement, and the party always has the opportunity to explain the statement by giving evidence at trial. This argument has the merit of convincingly distinguishing the situation of third-party admissions, which were not admissible at common law, although they may now be admitted under ss.116 or 114(1)(d) of the 2003 Act if the conditions of those sections are satisfied. The argument does not necessarily invoke the presumed reliability of admissions, although it may do so. It maintains that in the circumstances the question of reliability can properly be left to the factfinder, subject to the judge's overriding discretion to exclude admissions to which no probative value could safely be attached.

---

[195] *Parkes* [1976] 1 W.L.R. 1251 PC; cf. *Watson* [1997] Crim. L.R. 680 CA.

[196] For discussion see I. R. Scott, "Controlling the Reception in Evidence of Unreliable Admissions" [1981] Crim. L.R. 285; J. C. Smith, "Exculpatory Statements and Confessions" [1995] Crim. L.R. 280.

[197] See Smith, "Exculpatory Statements" [1995] Crim L.R. 280.

6. *Admissions by agents, etc*

Paragraph 6 of s.118(1) preserves: **17–042**

"Any rule of law under which in criminal proceedings—
 (a)   an admission made by an agent of a defendant is admissible against the defendant as
        evidence of any matter stated, or
 (b)   a statement made by a person to whom a defendant refers a person for information is
        admissible against the defendant as evidence of any matter stated."

The common law recognised the possibility of "vicarious" admissions. A party might sometimes have admitted against him an admission made by another person. This could only happen where the other was in "privity" with the party in question. Privity was a concept the limits of which were never fully clarified. It included predecessors in title,[198] and persons having an identity of interest in the property or obligation in question,[199] such as partners[200] or trustees. It also extended to agents who had the authority of the party to act for the party and/or to speak about the matter in question to others.[201] The limits of the agency principle were particularly uncertain. It was never clearly settled how far it extended to employees who made statements amounting to admissions of negligence in cases where their employers would be liable contractually,[202] or vicariously in tort.[203] The problem is now largely a matter of legal history following the abolition of the hearsay rule in civil cases. A statement by a party's agent or employee is now admissible in civil proceedings, despite its hearsay nature, provided of course that it is relevant to the facts in issue and that the maker of the statement would have been a competent witness when he made the statement.[204]

In criminal cases the possibility of a vicarious admission is exceptional due to the essentially personal nature of criminal liability. Co-defendants, for example, are not generally regarded as being in privity with each other, hence a confession by D1 that incriminates D2 is not generally admissible against D2. This rule is discussed in Ch.6, along with the exceptions to it. The principal cases of vicarious admissions in criminal proceedings are those arising in cases of conspiracy and joint enterprise, which are preserved separately by para.7 below, and admissions by the defendant's lawyers that they are authorised to make on his behalf. The lawyers are regarded as agents of the defendant in the conduct of proceedings against the defendant, and hence an admission by his counsel or solicitor is

---

[198] *Woolway v Rowe* (1834) 1 Ad. & El. 114; *Falcon v Famous Players Film Co Ltd* [1926] 2 K.B. 474.
[199] e.g. *Jaggers v Binnings* (1815) 1 Stark. 64.
[200] The common law rule that an admission by one partner about partnership matters made in the ordinary course of business is evidence against the firm is now contained in the Partnership Act 1890 s.15.
[201] *Williams v Innes* (1808) 1 Camp. 364 (executors bound by statements of third party to whom they had referred the plaintiff for information concerning the estate); *Kirkstall Brewery Co v Furness Rly Co* (1874) L.R. 9 Q.B. 468 (statement by the defendants' stationmaster to a police officer suggesting that the plaintiff's lost parcel had been stolen by another employee of the defendants admissible against the defendants).
[202] Compare the *Kirkstall Brewery* case with *Great Western Rly Co v Willis* (1865) 18 C.B.N.S. 748.
[203] See *Burr v Ware RDC* [1939] 2 All E.R. 688 CA.
[204] Civil Evidence Act 1995 ss.1, 5.

admissible against the defendant as evidence of any matter stated. This rule received an important application in *R. (on the application of Firth) v Epping Magistrates' Court*,[205] where a statement by D's counsel on a case progression form that D's defence to a charge of assault would be self-defence was held admissible as an admission that she had been involved in an altercation with the victim and thereby provided necessary evidence of identification for committal proceedings when the CPS decided to increase the charge to assault occasioning actual bodily harm.[206]

7. *Common enterprise*[207]

17–043   Paragraph 7 of s.118(1) preserves:

> "Any rule of law under which in criminal proceedings a statement made by a party to a common enterprise is admissible against another party to the enterprise as evidence of any matter stated."

A further important principle exists at common law for cases of conspiracy and joint enterprise. The principle is that acts done and statements made by a party to a conspiracy or joint enterprise are admissible against other parties to the conspiracy or enterprise as evidence of its scope and purposes,[208] but they are not admissible to show the participation of the other parties, which must be proved by independent evidence.[209] The latter rule is to ensure that an alleged conspirator is not at risk of conviction on narrative hearsay evidence alone.[210] The underlying theory of admissibility is debatable.[211] The most convincing approach is implied agency: each conspirator, or party to a joint enterprise, is deemed by the law to have implied authority from the others to act or speak in furtherance of the common purpose.[212] To be admissible against other conspirators the act or

---

[205] *R. (on the application of Firth) v Epping Magistrates' Court* [2011] EWHC 388 (Admin); [2011] 4 All E.R. 326.

[206] See the critical discussion of this case by Edwards in [2011] Crim. L.R. 547, and see also *Newell* [2012] EWCA Crim 650; [2012] 2 Cr.App.R. 10 (statements in plea and case management forms should generally be excluded under s.78 of PACE), and the discussion in Ch.9.

[207] K. Spencer, "The Common Enterprise Exception to the Hearsay Rule" (2007) 11 E. & P. 106.

[208] *Blake and Tye* (1844) 6 Q.B. 126 (conspiracy to evade customs duty); *Devonport, Pirano and White* [1996] 1 Cr.App.R. 221 CA (conspiracy to defraud); *Jones* [1997] 2 Cr.App.R. 119 CA (conspiracy and joint enterprise to evade prohibition on importation of cannabis). It seems that this exception to the hearsay rule applies only where the accused are *charged* with conspiracy and/or the joint commission of offences. It does not apply where they are charged with separate substantive offences: *Gray* [1995] 2 Cr.App.R. 100 CA; as explained in *Murray, Morgan and Sheridan* [1997] 2 Cr.App.R. 136 CA.

[209] Hence at common law a confession to the police by D1 as to D2's participation in the conspiracy is not admissible against D2. D2's participation in a conspiracy or joint enterprise may often be inferred from surveillance records and/or logs of mobile phone conversation with the co-accused, as in *Onyeabor* [2009] EWCA Crim 534.

[210] *King and Provan* [2012] EWCA Crim 805, confirming the limitation and clarifying that it is for the judge to decide the sufficiency of evidence for the purposes of this exception to the hearsay rule.

[211] See the discussion by Spencer, "The Common Enterprise Exception to the Hearsay Rule" (2007) 11 E. & P. 106.

[212] *Gray* [1995] 2 Cr.App.R. 100 at 129 CA; citing the judgment of Dixon C.J. in the High Court of Australia in *Tripodi v R.* (1961) 104 C.L.R. 1. For an alternative view that the admissibility of

statement in question must be in *furtherance or advancement* of the conspiracy. This suggests that the common purpose must be continuing at the time of the act or statement; a statement made after it has been completed recording what has been done is not within the scope of this principle.

The operation of the principle is illustrated by *Devonport, Pirano, and White*.[213] Five defendants were convicted of conspiracy to defraud a bank of £310,000. There was circumstantial evidence to link all the defendants with a scheme whereby the money was transferred from two bank accounts in London to other accounts, including one in Munich, from which the money was then never traced. A further item of evidence was a document found in the home of the girlfriend of one of the defendants. The document was written by her at his dictation, and showed the division of the money obtained from the conspiracy among the five defendants. The trial judge admitted the document in evidence against all the defendants, despite the fact that there was no evidence that the other four conspirators had had anything to do with its preparation. Upholding the convictions of the appellants, the Court of Appeal held that the document was admissible against the others as a declaration by the conspirator who dictated it. It was in furtherance of the conspiracy in the sense that, prima facie, it was "an indication of the intended or prospective distribution of the proceeds of the conspiracy when it had been fulfilled".[214]

8. *Expert evidence*

Paragraph 8 of s.118(1) preserves "Any rule of law under which in criminal proceedings an expert witness may draw on the body of expertise relevant to his field".   **17–044**

When an expert witness gives an opinion, drawing on material (other than findings of primary fact) produced by other persons in the relevant field of expertise, the expert is expressly or impliedly asserting that the statements contained in the material are true. Thus the expert is giving evidence that is logically hearsay, but the common law acknowledged the existence of a dispensation from the hearsay rule[215]—otherwise, expert evidence would become an impossibility. Paragraph 8 preserves this essential exception to the rule.

G. STATUTORY EXCEPTIONS: SECTION 114(1)(D)— INTERESTS OF JUSTICE

The Criminal Justice Act 2003 contains two further provisions that permit a court to admit hearsay statements in the interests of justice. The first of these is s.114(1)(d). This refers simply to the court being satisfied that it is in the interests   **17–045**

---

declarations of co-conspirators is a species of res gestae see J. A. Andrews and M. Hirst, *Criminal Evidence*, 4th edn (Bristol: Jordan's Ltd, 2001), para.20.26.
[213] *Devonport, Pirano and White* [1996] 1 Cr.App.R. 221 CA.
[214] *Devonport, Pirano and White* [1996] 1 Cr.App.R. 221 at 227 per Judge J.; distinguishing *Tye (Blake and Tye* (1844) 6 Q.B. 126) where a document made after the conspiracy had been completed was held to have been wrongly admitted under this principle.
[215] See *Abadom* [1983] 1 All E.R. 364 CA, and the discussion in Ch.20 at paras 20–023 and 20–024.

of justice for a hearsay statement to be admissible. In deciding this question the court must have regard to the factors set out in subs.(2) and to any others it considers relevant. The subsection provides:

> "In deciding whether a statement not made in oral evidence should be admitted under subs.(1)(d) the court must have regard to the following factors (and to any others it considers relevant)—
> (a) how much probative value the statement has (assuming it to be true) in relation to a matter in issue in the proceedings, or how valuable it is for the understanding of other evidence in the case;
> (b) what other evidence has been, or can be, given on the matter or evidence mentioned in paragraph (a);
> (c) how important the matter or evidence mentioned in paragraph (a) is in the context of the case as a whole;
> (d) the circumstances in which the statement was made;
> (e) how reliable the maker of the statement appears to be;
> (f) how reliable the evidence of the making of the statement appears to be;
> (g) whether oral evidence of the matter stated can be given and, if not, why it cannot;
> (h) the amount of difficulty involved in challenging the statement;
> (i) the extent to which that difficulty would be likely to prejudice the party facing it."

In *Taylor*,[216] the Court of Appeal held that s.114(2) does not require a trial judge to inquire into each of the nine factors listed and reach a conclusion on each of them. As the court pointed out, the contrary interpretation would result in some cases in the judge having to hear evidence about the factors. A proper investigation would lengthen the trial considerably. Rejecting this construction, Rose L.J. stated that the provision requires the judge to give consideration to the listed factors, and to any others the judge considers relevant, and to assess their significance and weight, both individually and in relation to each other. The only conclusion he is required to reach is whether, having regard to the various factors, the evidence should be admitted. This is a decision requiring an exercise of judgment.[217] However, in terms of the appealability of the decision, the Court of Appeal regards it as a matter of discretion,[218] which means that it will be difficult to challenge it effectively if the judge has given consideration to all the relevant factors, [219] and the decision is within the range of reasonable decisions that the judge could have reached.

Section 114(1)(d) is based on a recommendation of the Law Commission. The Commission proposed what it described as a "very limited" discretion to admit hearsay that would otherwise be inadmissible, if that was necessary to ensure that justice was done.[220] It saw the discretion as a "safety valve" that would introduce a measure of flexibility into a scheme of reform that might otherwise be too rigid. It intended the discretion to be available for both prosecution and defence, although its main examples were of hearsay statements favourable to the defence. These examples included the statement by the child victim in *Sparks v R*.[221] as to

---

[216] *Taylor* [2006] EWCA Crim 260; [2006] 2 Cr.App.R. 14.
[217] *Ibrahim* [2010] EWCA Crim 1176.
[218] *Taylor* [2006] EWCA Crim 260; [2006] 2 Cr.App.R. 14 at [39]; *Sadiq* [2009] EWCA Crim 712.
[219] For an instructive case where the judge did not attend to a number of factors see *Bucknor* [2010] EWCA Crim 1152.
[220] Law Com. 245 paras 8.133 onwards.
[221] *Sparks v R*. [1964] A.C. 964. This case is discussed in Ch.16.

the colour of her assailant, and an out-of-court confession by a third party to the crime with which the defendant is charged.[222] It was envisaged that it would be possible to admit multiple hearsay using this discretion.

Structurally, however, subs.(1)(d) is one of four alternative ways of admitting hearsay under the scheme established by s.114. Giving the words of subs.(1) their ordinary meaning, para.(d) is free-standing, available to both prosecution and defence,[223] and not expressed to be subject to any of the other methods. Nor is there anything in the Act to suggest that the discretion should be confined to exceptional cases, or to suggest that it should be used only where necessary to avoid a miscarriage of justice.[224] A literal approach to construction, therefore, would give the 'interests of justice' exception a potentially broad area of application. On the other hand, a purposive approach based on the Law Commission's report would produce a much narrower application. An important contextual consideration is the danger that an extensive application of s. 114(1)(d) could bypass the limits placed on other category-based hearsay exceptions. A comprehensive fact-specific discretion to admit hearsay evidence in the interests of justice would have the potential to make an exception like s.116 unnecessary; the conditions of unavailability of the witness would simply become factors to be considered in applying the wider standard of the interests of justice.[225]

17–046

Since its introduction the provision in s. 114(1(d) has generated an extensive jurisprudence. The cases do not show a consistent approach to the operation of the provision. Initially the courts were not minded to read restrictions into it, and certainly not to reserve it mainly for the kinds of cases envisaged by the Law Commission, where it is necessary to admit hearsay for the defence. Several of the earlier cases concerned hearsay evidence adduced by the prosecution. Thus in *Taylor*,[226] two prosecution witnesses to a serious assault were permitted to testify that they had been told the name of the defendant, whom they had seen participating in the assault. The Court of Appeal saw no reason to interfere with the judge's decision to admit the hearsay statements under s.114(1)(d). There appears to have been nothing unusual or exceptional about this case. The fact that the testimony of one of the witnesses involved double hearsay was thought to make no difference. The court did comment that there was considerable other evidence against the accused; that was regarded as confirming the reliability of the hearsay, but there is no suggestion in the judgment that such confirmation is a necessary condition of admitting the hearsay evidence under this provision.

---

[222] Such a confession was inadmissible at common law: *Cooper* [1969] 1 Q.B. 267; *Turner* (1975) 61 Cr.App.R. 67; *Blastland* [1986] A.C. 41.

[223] As the Court of Appeal commented in *R. v Y* [2008] EWCA Crim 10; [2008] 2 All E.R. 484: "The provisions of s. 114(1) are quite clearly general in application. They govern when hearsay is admissible, irrespective of who seeks to have it admitted ..." (at [53]).

[224] Note, however, that in *Horncastle* [2009] UKSC 14; [2010] 2 All E.R. 359 at [31] Lord Phillips, in summarising the statutory code relating to hearsay evidence, said that s.114(1)(d) "provides for a limited residual power to admit hearsay if the interests of justice require it".

[225] This point should not be pushed too far, since hearsay may be admissible under a category-based exception as of *right* (as it is under s.116 except where the witness is in fear), which is better for the party seeking to adduce the evidence than reliance on a general *discretion* to admit hearsay.

[226] *Taylor* [2006] EWCA Crim 260; [2006] 2 Cr.App.R. 14.

In *Xhabri*,[227] D was charged with false imprisonment, rape, threats to kill and control of prostitution for gain. The complainant testified that D had raped her and forced her to work as a prostitute by threats of physical violence. The trial judge admitted evidence from her mother, father, a friend and a police officer of communications she had made, directly or indirectly, indicating that she had been kidnapped and was being held against her will and threatened. Dismissing D's appeal, the Court of Appeal held that this evidence of the complainant's statements had been rightly admitted as evidence of the facts she had stated. This was for more than one reason. First, the court thought that the evidence of the statements to the mother, father and friend was admissible as evidence of complaints under s.120(4) and (7). Secondly, even if s.120 was not satisfied, the evidence of the statements was admissible in the interests of justice under s.114(1)(d). Thirdly, the evidence of the police officer involved double hearsay, because he reported what two witnesses told him what the complainant had said to them. Its admissibility was therefore governed by s.121. The court held that in view of the very high probative value of the officer's evidence it was rightly admitted in the interests of justice under s.121(1)(c). As in *Taylor*, there is no suggestion in *Xhabri* that this was in any way an exceptional case. The Court of Appeal approached the "interests of justice" hearsay exceptions in ss.114 and 121 on the basis that they could be applied to the facts of the case in the same way as the other statutory exceptions.[228]

17–047 Before turning to the cases adopting a more cautious approach to s. 114(1)(d), we should note that early cases recognised an important consequence of admitting hearsay under the provision. The evidence becomes evidence in the case generally.[229] When this point is coupled with the abolition of the common law rules of hearsay it follows that the old rule, that an out-of-court statement by one defendant incriminating a co-accused is never admissible against the latter, has gone. In *McLean*, D1 sought to adduce evidence of a hearsay statement by D2 which indicated that D3 had committed the murder with which all three were charged. Since D2's statement was not a confession it fell outside s.76A of PACE.[230] Relying on the common law rule, the trial judge ruled D2's statement inadmissible under s.114(1)(d). The Court of Appeal held that the ruling was wrong, quashed all three convictions and ordered a retrial. According to the court, if it was in the interests of justice to admit the statement—as to which the court expressed no view since it would depend on a proper consideration of the factors listed in subs.(2)—then the jury would be entitled to consider it as evidence in the

---

[227] *Xhabri* [2006] 1 All E.R. 776 CA.
[228] Other cases upholding the admission of prosecution hearsay under s.114(1)(d) include *Musone* [2007] EWCA Crim 1237; [2007] 2 Cr.App.R. 29 (eyewitness statement about the immediate aftermath of a stabbing); *Lynch* [2007] EWCA Crim 3035; [2008] 1 Cr.App.R. 24 (eyewitness's statement at an identification parade); *Sak v Crown Prosecution Service* [2007] EWHC 2886 (Admin) (doctor's report on defendant's physical condition); *R. v RL* [2008] EWCA Crim 973; [2008] 2 Cr.App.R. 18 (wife's statement to police undermining husband's defence); *Sadiq* [2009] EWCA Crim 712 (victim's account of the attack on him). See also the unusual case of *Turner* [2012] EWCA Crim 1786 (witness too embarrassed to testify publicly as to the details of sexual offences committed against her permitted to have her witness statement read to her in court so that she could adopt it).
[229] *McLean* [2007] EWCA Crim 219; [2008] 1 Cr.App.R. 11.
[230] Discussed in Ch.6.

case generally, "to determine its weight, and to make up its mind whether it can or cannot rely upon it".[231] Subsequently, in *R. v Y*,[232] the Court of Appeal applied similar reasoning in favour of the prosecution and reversed a judge's preliminary ruling that refused the prosecution leave to adduce evidence of a confession by X to murder which implicated the defendant. X had already pleaded guilty to the murder. The court held that the judge had wrongly accepted the argument that the common law restriction on the use of a confession had been preserved as part of the preservation by s.118(1) para.5 of the common law rule that a confession is admissible against its maker. The argument was wrong because s.118(1) preserved common law rules of admissibility, not inadmissibility. The latter had been replaced by the scheme of admissibility set out in s.114(1). Accordingly:

> "It follows that neither the fact that the hearsay in question is an accusation against the defendant, rather than an admission against interest by the maker, nor the fact that it is the Crown which seeks to adduce it, can rule out the application of s. 114(1)(d) as a matter of law."

However, the court went on to emphasise that this did not mean that police interviews of one defendant could routinely be admitted against co-defendants using s.114(1)(d). Since the provision was capable of applying to any out of court statement it was *capable* of applying to a hearsay statement contained in a police interview. But the interests of justice test still has to be satisfied, and that requires attention to the factors listed in sub.(2). The court in *R. v Y* thought that the identity of the applicant (that is, the defendant) is plainly relevant to the interests of justice test; that test may not necessarily produce the same result on an application by the prosecution as it might on an application by the defendant. In particular, attention should be given to any difficulty the defendant would face in challenging the hearsay statement, and also to the question whether oral evidence could be given in place of reliance on the hearsay statement. It was suggested that, depending on the circumstances of each case, justice might be better served by putting the witness before the jury, if that is possible, so that they can see him, with the possibility of applying to cross-examine him upon the previous statement.[233]

This last suggestion is an application of a "best evidence" principle. It is founded **17–048** on the assumption that it is generally preferable to call the witness to give oral testimony rather than to rely upon her hearsay statement. In several cases this has proved to be an important strand of thinking in a more cautious approach to the application of s.114(1)(d). In *R. v Z*,[234] the Court of Appeal held that a trial judge had wrongly admitted a hearsay statement under the provision where the witness was well and able to testify, although reluctant to do so. The statement related to a sexual attack on the witness by the defendant and was being adduced by the prosecution as bad character evidence. As the court said, it was important

---

[231] *McLean* [2007] EWCA Crim 219; [2008] 1 Cr.App.R. 11 at[1.20].

[232] *R. v Y* [2008] EWCA Crim 10; [2008] 2 All E.R. 484 at [54].

[233] That is, as a hostile witness. A previous statement adduced in cross-examination of a hostile witness can now be evidence of the facts stated under s.119. The same point would apply in a case of a witness called by the defence: *Khan* [2009] EWCA Crim 86.

[234] *R. v Z* [2009] EWCA Crim 20.

evidence, potentially prejudicial, and difficult for the defendant to deal with other than by a simple denial. The judge had failed to take proper account of the s.114(2) factors, particularly para.(g) which relates to the inability of the witness to give oral evidence. Similarly there are cases where prosecution hearsay from important eyewitnesses has been excluded where the witnesses were available to testify,[235] and the principle has been applied to defence hearsay as well. In *Finch*,[236] for example, D1 sought to adduce a confession to the police by D2 which exonerated D1 of complicity in offences of possession of a prohibited firearm and of ammunition. D2 pleaded guilty. He was available to give evidence for D1 but reluctant to do so. The Court of Appeal upheld the trial judge's decision that the interests of justice did not call for his police interview to be admitted, commenting that D2's reluctance to support his statement on oath undermined its reliability.[237]

17–049 A further argument supporting the decisions in these cases is the danger, noted above, of rendering s.116 redundant by an expansive use of s.114(1)(d). A related danger is the use of s.114(1)(d) to supplement s.116 by admitting hearsay statements where the witnesses are "unavailable" for reasons other than those listed in s.116. This was a concern for the Court of Appeal in *R. v Z* where the court commented that s.114(1)(d) should be "cautiously applied, since otherwise the conditions laid down by Parliament in s.116 would be circumvented".[238] This advice has been influential in several subsequent cases. In *R. v C*,[239] the Court of Appeal held that a trial judge had wrongly admitted hearsay evidence of a complaint of child sexual abuse. It had not been established that the girl in question was unable or unwilling to testify; the judge had apparently accepted the view of the girl's adoptive mother that it would be undesirable for her to give evidence of the abuse. The court cited the advice in *Z* and continued:

> "To repeat ... a cautious approach is necessary when consideration is being given to the admission of hearsay evidence when a witness of primary fact is alive and well and, on the face of it, able to give oral evidence to the court. In our judgment this approach must be followed strictly when, as here, the witness of primary fact is an alleged victim of serious crimes."[240]

---

[235] See, e.g. *McEwan v DPP* [2007] EWHC 740 (Admin); *Williams (Dion Mark)* [2007] EWCA Crim 211.

[236] *Finch* [2007] EWCA Crim 36; [2007] 1 Cr.App.R. 33.

[237] For other examples of defence hearsay being refused admission under s.114(1)(d), where the witness was available and there were doubts about the reliability of the hearsay statements, see *Khan* [2009] EWCA Crim 86; *Marsh* [2008] EWCA Crim 1816.

[238] *R. v Z* [2009] EWCA Crim 20 at [20]. See also *O'Hare* [2006] EWCA Crim 2512 at [30], where Scott Baker L.J. said that s.114(1)(d) should not be applied so as to render s.116 "nugatory".

[239] *R. v C* [2010] EWCA Crim 72; [2010] Crim. L.R. 858.

[240] *R. v C* [2010] EWCA Crim 72; [2010] Crim. L.R. 858 at [40]. See also *M v R.* [2011] EWCA Crim 2341 (evidence of a 999 call and a witness statement by the victim of domestic violence should not have been admitted under s.114(1)(d) where this evidence was virtually the whole of the prosecution case. The complainant had sought to withdraw her complaint and had moved house, but the judge found that the prosecution had failed to take reasonable steps to locate her and that no attempt had been made to persuade her to change her mind about giving evidence).

In *R. v EED*,[241] a witness to a complaint by the victim of sexual abuse was unwilling to testify at D's trial because she had been warned late of the date of the trial and would be on a family holiday. The Court of Appeal held that the trial judge should not have admitted her witness statement under s. 114(1)(d). According to the court:

> "[Z] is important because it reinforces the court's view that it should not countenance the use of s. 114(1)(d) to circumvent the requirements of other gateways to admissibility *higher up the s.114 hierarchy*. (Emphasis supplied) It is not permissible to nod through hearsay evidence merely because it is convenient to the party seeking its admission and the evidence is of value upon an important issue in the trial."[242]

However, this restrictive approach to reluctant witnesses is not applied as a blanket rule. Where the hearsay evidence is of subsidiary and not major importance, and it is clear that there is no point in trying to call the witness to give oral evidence, the court may be more accommodating to the use of s. 114(1)(d). In *Burton*,[243] the Court of Appeal upheld the admission of a statement to a police officer by a 14 year old girl about her relationship with D. He was charged with sexual activity with a child; she had flatly refused to make a witness statement or to testify. The court described this as an exceptional case, pointing to the girl's age, the desirability of the jury knowing of her immediate reaction to the discovery of letters written to her by D, and the prosecution's intention to use her statement not as sole or primary evidence but to confirm the accuracy of statements D had made in interview. There are examples of other cases, before *Z*, where hearsay was admitted under s.114(1)(d) where the witness was available,[244] and other cases where hearsay was admitted where the witness was unavailable for reasons not covered by s.116.[245] None of these cases has been overruled. It seems clear therefore that a "best evidence" approach, although now dominant, has not hardened into a general rule of application of s. 114(1)(d). The discretion remains one to be exercised in all the circumstances of the case, having regard to the factors listed in s.114(2) and any others the court considers relevant.

The factors set out in s.114(2) are not stated in any order of priority, nor have the courts attempted to assign priorities amongst them.[246] However, the discussion above demonstrates the importance attached to the question whether oral evidence of the matter stated can be given and, if not, why not (para. (2)(g)). Another factor likely to be particularly important is the amount of difficulty   **17–050**

---

[241] *R. v EED* [2010] EWCA Crim 1213; [2010] Crim. L.R. 862.

[242] *R. v EED* [2010] EWCA Crim 1213; [2010] Crim. L.R. 862 at [17]. For other cases adopting the approach in *Z* see *Ibrahim* [2010] EWCA Crim 1176; *Freeman* [2010] EWCA Crim 1997.

[243] *Burton* [2011] EWCA Crim 1990.

[244] *Musone* [2007] EWCA Crim 1237; [2007] 2 Cr.App.R. 29; *Meade* [2007] EWCA Crim 1116.

[245] *Sak v Crown Prosecution Service* [2007] EWHC 2886 (Admin); *R. v RL* [2008] EWCA Crim 973; [2008] 2 Cr.App.R. 18. See also *Seton* [2010] EWCA Crim 450, a post *Z* case, where evidence was admitted of a phone call by a serving prisoner (P) denying responsibility for a murder which D alleged that P, and not D, had committed. P had refused point blank to give a statement to the police or to testify at D's trial. The Court of Appeal upheld the judge's decision.

[246] An instructive example of a case where the Court of Appeal concisely summarised its view of the application of all the s.114(2) factors to a hearsay statement by the defendant's wife, who was not a compellable witness for the prosecution, is *R. v RL* [2008] EWCA Crim 973; [2008] 2 Cr.App.R. 18.

involved in challenging the hearsay evidence (para. (2)(h). In *Lynch*,[247] for example, an eyewitness had identified the defendant at a parade as being present when the victim was attacked by a group of youths following an altercation between the victim and the defendant. The officer conducting the parade had then asked her what she had seen the defendant do. She replied that she had seen the defendant swear at the victim when he had been knocked to the ground by another member of the group. At the trial of the defendant for violent disorder the prosecution successfully applied for evidence of the witness's statement at the parade to be admitted after she had given evidence of her identification and been cross-examined about the incident. The Court of Appeal held that it was in the interests of justice for her statement to be admitted and dismissed the defendant's appeal:

> "... it seems to this court that this is the sort of out-of-court statement which s. 114(1)(d) was intended to cover. The statement made at the identification process was made very much closer in time to the date of the incident than was her evidence at trial, over a year before the trial even began. As has been said many times in this court, a trial is not, or should not be, primarily a test of memory or recollection, and when one has a reliable record of a statement made by a witness at a time much closer to the event and officially recorded, it will often be in the interests of justice for it to go before the jury."[248]

In this case the witness was not only available but had testified, and the trial judge had made it clear that she could be recalled for further cross-examination if the defence wished. There was therefore no difficulty for the defendant in challenging her statement. *Lynch* can be compared with *R, v Z*, mentioned above, where the evidence was equally important, but the witness, although available, was unwilling to testify, and the defendant would have had great difficulty in challenging her evidence if he could not cross-examine her. In *R. v Y*,[249] the Court of Appeal commented that although s.114(1)(d) is available to the Crown as it is to a defendant, it does not necessarily follow that the interests of justice would point in the same direction upon an application by the Crown as they might upon an application by a defendant.[250] In this connection one factor not mentioned in s.114(2), but which the judge must keep in mind when considering the admission of prosecution hearsay under any of the provisions in the Act, is its compatibility with the defendant's fair trial rights under art.6 of the ECHR. We will return to this topic in the final section of this chapter.

H.   STATUTORY EXCEPTIONS: SECTION 121—MULTIPLE HEARSAY

17–051   Section 121 deals with multiple hearsay. It provides:

> "(1)   A hearsay statement is not admissible to prove the fact that an earlier hearsay statement was made unless—

---

[247] *Lynch* [2007] EWCA Crim 3035; [2008] 1 Cr.App.R. 24.
[248] *Lynch* [2007] EWCA Crim 3035; [2008] 1 Cr.App.R. 24 at [32].
[249] *R. v Y* [2008] EWCA Crim 10; [2008] 2 All E.R. 484.
[250] Where a defendant seeks to adduce a hearsay statement which would be highly prejudicial to a co-defendant the judge will have to balance the interests of the two defendants in deciding whether to admit the statement in the interests of justice: *Atkinson* [2011] EWCA Crim 1746.

(a)   either of the statements is admissible under section 117, 119 or 120,
(b)   all parties to the proceedings agree, or
(c)   the court is satisfied that the value of the evidence in question, taking into account how reliable the statements appear to be, is so high that the interests of justice require the later statement to be admissible for that purpose.

(2)   In this section 'hearsay statement' means a statement, not made in oral evidence that is relied on as evidence of a matter stated in it."

The effect of s.121(1)(a) is that one hearsay statement cannot be proved by another hearsay statement, except where either statement is admissible under one of a number of specified provisions in the Act. These are ss.117 (business documents), 119 (previous inconsistent statements of witnesses) and 120 (certain previous consistent statements of witnesses). It follows that in general only first-hand hearsay will be admissible under ss.116 (hearsay statements where the witness is unavailable) and 118 (the preserved common law hearsay exceptions). This restrictive approach follows the recommendation of the Law Commission, which was concerned about the increased risk of fabrication, or error in transmission, with each increased link in the chain of hearsay, plus the increased complexity of the directions which the judge would have to give the jury about assessing the reliability of multiple hearsay.[251] These objections do not apply with the same force to *documentary* hearsay which fulfils the reliability conditions of s.117, nor to cases involving previous consistent or inconsistent statements, where the maker of the statement is available for cross-examination.

Moreover, the court is given a discretion by s.121(1)(c) in effect to override this limitation in the interests of justice, where the evidence (that is, the multiple hearsay statements) has a high degree of reliability and probative value. An example of the use of the inclusionary discretion under s.121(1)(c) is seen in *Xhabri*, the facts of which are set out above.[252] However, it should be noted that, although the standard of the "interests of justice" is used again in this provision, the test for admissibility under s.121(1)(c) is more onerous than the general test in s.114(1)(d).[253] In *Scorah,* the Court of Appeal held that a judge was wrong to admit evidence of a hearsay statement to the police by the defendant's mother, which if true destroyed the defendant's alibi on a charge of wounding with intent to cause grievous bodily harm. The statement recounted something which the mother had been told by a source that could not be identified. Thus although the evidence was important, its reliability was uncertain given its unknown provenance, and the defendant would have had difficulty in challenging it. By contrast, in *Thakrar,*[254] the Court of Appeal upheld the admission under s. 121(1)(c) of the evidence of a Northern Cypriot police officer of statements he

---

[251] Law Com No. 245 paras 8.15–8.22.
[252] For a further example see *Maher v DPP* [2006] EWHC 1271 (Admin), where a police log recording the registration number of a car involved in a collision in a car park was allowed to be proved under s.121(1)(c) on a charge of careless driving. The number was passed to the police by the girlfriend of the owner of the parked car after an eyewitness of the collision had put a note of the number on the parked car's windscreen. By the time of trial the note had been lost, but the Divisional Court held that the log had been rightly admitted in view of the likely reliability of the original identification of the number and the fact that the defendant had admitted driving her car in the car park at the material time.
[253] *Scorah* [2008] EWCA Crim 1786 at [32].
[254] *Thakrar* [2010] EWCA Crim 1505.

had taken in Cyprus from three associates of D, in which they had reported conversations with D in which he had admitted and indeed boasted of carrying out the killings with which he was charged. None of the associates had been willing to come to England to give evidence. In the court's view, the statements had high probative value, they appeared to be reliable in view of the amount of detail about the murders that they contained, and it was difficult to see any motive for the associates to invent D's confessions or for the police officer to concoct the statements.

I. OTHER PROVISIONS

17–052 Sections 122–134 of the Criminal Justice Act 2003 contain a number of provisions of an ancillary nature relating to the admission or exclusion of hearsay evidence under the Act. They form a somewhat miscellaneous group, and this book does not aim to deal with all of them in detail. Section 124 contains an important safeguard for a party against whom a hearsay statement is admitted, where the maker of the statement does not give oral evidence in connection with the subject-matter of the statement. Under s.124(2) evidence may be adduced relating to the credibility of the maker of the statement. In summary this includes any statement inconsistent with the hearsay statement,[255] any evidence that could have been given as relevant to the maker's credibility if the maker had testified (that is, under an exception to the rule of finality for answers to questions on collateral matters such as credibility),[256] and, with leave of the court, evidence of any (other) matter going to credibility which could have been put in cross-examination if the maker had testified, but where the rule of finality would have applied to exclude evidence in rebuttal.[257]

Section 125 provides a further safeguard in cases of jury trial. The judge is given power to stop the case where the case against the defendant is based wholly or partly on hearsay evidence, and the evidence is so unconvincing that, considering its importance to the case, a conviction would be unsafe. This is an exception to the rule in *Galbraith*,[258] discussed in Ch.4, whereby issues of the reliability and weight of evidence are generally regarded as matters for the jury to determine and not the judge. This power, and the power under s.124 to adduce evidence going to the credibility of the maker of a hearsay statement, constitute important factors in the determination of whether the admission of hearsay evidence against a defendant violates the right to a fair trial.

Section 126 confers a discretion on the court to exclude hearsay where "the court is satisfied that the case for excluding the statement, taking account of the danger that to admit it would result in undue waste of time, substantially outweighs the case for admitting it, taking account of the value of the evidence". The provision is largely a case management power, since it appears to be targeting hearsay of little probative value which is probably superfluous in the

---

[255] Criminal Justice Act 2003 s.124(2)(c).
[256] Criminal Justice Act 2003 s.124(2)(a), and see Ch.14.
[257] Criminal Justice Act 2003 s.124(2)(b).
[258] *Galbraith* [1981] 1 W.L.R. 1039.

circumstances of the case. This discretion is conferred without prejudice to the discretion under s.78 of PACE to exclude unfair evidence or any discretion at common law to exclude evidence.[259]

J. THE IMPACT OF ARTICLE 6 OF THE ECHR

Under art.6(3)(d) of the ECHR one of the rights of a person charged with a criminal offence is the right to examine or have examined the witnesses against him. It is a question of fundamental importance how far the provisions of the Criminal Justice Act 2003 which allow for the admission of hearsay evidence under certain conditions are compatible with this right, given that the defendant may have no opportunity to cross-examine the maker of the hearsay statement. As we have seen in Ch.15, a similar question of compatibility arises where a witness gives evidence anonymously; the defendant's cross-examination of the witness may be significantly hampered by ignorance of the identity of the witness. These questions have generated an acute controversy which led recently to a major clash between the Supreme Court and the European Court of Human Rights. The controversy now seems to have been settled in favour of the view that the admission of hearsay statements or anonymous testimony does not necessarily result in a violation of art.6, even where the evidence is potentially decisive of the case. However, it is also clear that the need to ensure a fair trial for the defendant imposes substantial obligations on courts in relation to both these types of evidence. The case for admitting hearsay or anonymous evidence must be searchingly examined, as must the extent to which the rights of the defence can be safeguarded, and judges must ensure that they give appropriate directions to the jury where evidence of either type is admitted. This section will discuss the nature of the controversy before turning to its resolution and the recent guidance from the Court of Appeal[260] to trial judges on the compatibility issue. The discussion will focus mainly on hearsay evidence although reference will be made to the position of anonymous evidence in relation to art.6. The statutory regime for the admission of anonymous testimony is covered in Ch.15.

17–053

The starting point of the discussion is the reminder that Strasbourg jurisprudence has consistently acknowledged that the rights of the defence under art.6(3)(d) are not absolute.[261] Accordingly, the absence of an opportunity to cross-examine the maker of a hearsay statement, or to conduct a full cross-examination of an anonymous witness, is not automatically a violation of art.6. This point enabled the Court of Appeal in *Xhabri*[262] to make short work of a defence argument that insofar as s.114 permitted the court to adduce evidence of a hearsay statement by a witness not available for cross-examination it was incompatible with art.6(3)(d) of the ECHR. Given that art.6(3)(d) does not give a defendant an absolute right to examine every witness against him, the touchstone is whether fairness of the trial requires this. In that case the requirement of fairness was satisfied by the point that almost all the hearsay evidence derived

---

[259] See Criminal Justice Act 2003 s.126(2).
[260] *Ibrahim* [2012] EWCA Crim 837; [2012] 2 Cr.App.R. 32; *Riat* [2012] EWCA Crim 1509.
[261] See Ch.16 para.16–017, and *Grant v R.* [2006] UKPC 2.
[262] *Xhabri* [2005] EWCA Crim 3135; [2006] 1 All E.R. 776.

directly or indirectly from the complainant, and she was available for cross-examination at the trial. In other cases, where the maker of the hearsay statement is absent from the trial the requirements of fairness may become more demanding.

17–054 Just how demanding was demonstrated by the judgment of the Fourth Section of the European Court of Human Rights in *Al-Khawaja and Tahery v United Kingdom.*[263] In these two conjoined cases the European Court of Human Rights found in respect of both applicants a violation of art.6(1) read in conjunction with art.6(3)(d). In *Al-Khawaja,* the applicant (A) had been convicted of indecent assault largely on the evidence of a deceased witness whom he had had no opportunity to cross-examine. There was no suggestion that the complainant's death (she committed suicide) was connected with the alleged assault. The Court of Appeal had upheld the trial judge's admission of her witness statement under ss.23 and 26 of the Criminal Justice Act 1988. The witness was a patient of A, a doctor, and her statement was the main evidence against him of an assault committed during a consultation. The Court of Appeal had held that there had been no violation of art.6.[264] According to the court, there was a strong public interest in the admission of a witness statement by the sole witness to a crime who had since died.[265] That could not be allowed to override A's right to a fair trial, but the right of examination of witnesses was only one specific aspect of a fair trial. If that opportunity was not available, the question was still whether the proceedings as a whole were fair. The court considered that in the circumstances of the case they were, although the judge should have given the jury a stronger direction about the disadvantage to A resulting from the absence of the deceased witness. In *Tahery,* the applicant (T) had been convicted of wounding with intent to do grievous bodily harm and attempting to pervert the course of justice. The main evidence against him was the written statement to the police by an eyewitness of the stabbing of the victim; the witness was too fearful to attend the trial to give evidence before the jury. Again T had had no opportunity to cross-examine the eyewitness. The trial judge had admitted the witness statement under s. 116(2)(e) of the Criminal Justice Act 2003. T's appeal was dismissed.[266]

In reaching its conclusion that art. 6 had been violated in both cases the European Court of Human Rights emphasised that the provisions of art. 6(3) are aspects of the right to a fair trial guaranteed by art.6(1). They state minimum rights which constitute express guarantees, and they cannot be read, as the Court of Appeal had maintained in *Sellick,*[267] as simply illustrations of matters to be taken into account when determining whether a fair trial has been held. Having restated the well-established principle that evidence must normally be produced in the presence of the accused in a public hearing with a view to adversarial argument, the European Court of Human Rights went on to say that if a witness

---

[263] *Al-Khawaja and Tahery v United Kingdom* (2009) 49 E.H.R.R. 1. For further discussion, especially of the unclear rationale of the rule adopted in the case, see Dennis, "The Right to Confront Witnesses: Meanings, Myths and Human Rights" [2010] Crim. L.R. 255.

[264] *Al-Khawaja* [2005] EWCA Crim 2697; [2006] 1 Cr.App.R. 9.

[265] The witness was also the alleged victim of the offence, and the court may have thought that what the deceased victim said about the offence ought to be heard as a matter of justice to her.

[266] *Tahery* [2006] EWCA Crim 529.

[267] *Sellick* [2005] EWCA Crim 651; [2005] 2 Cr.App.R. 15.

statement is read to the court the rights of the defence mean that in principle the accused must be given a proper and adequate opportunity to challenge and question a witness against him, either when the witness made the statement or at a later stage. Other Strasbourg cases had made it clear that when this right under art. 6(3)(d) is restricted the requirement of a fair trial means that the handicaps to the defence must be sufficiently counter-balanced by the procedures followed by the judicial authorities.[268] However, the court then invoked the principle stated in a line of cases in Strasbourg,[269] that where a conviction is based solely or to a decisive degree on depositions from a person whom the accused has had no opportunity to examine or have examined, whether during the investigation or at the trial, the rights of the defence are restricted to an extent incompatible with art.6. A second line of authority had stated that the same principle applied to evidence from an anonymous witness.[270] In relation to the admission of hearsay statements the court doubted whether in the *absence of special circumstances* any counter-balancing measures would be sufficient to justify the introduction in evidence of an untested statement which was the sole or decisive basis for conviction. The reference to special circumstances was a reference to the situation in *Sellick,* where the defendants were convicted of murder following the admission of statements by witnesses who were in fear of testifying at the trial, or who had disappeared, as a result of the conduct of the defendants or their associates. The court in *Al-Khawaja and Tahery v United Kingdom* appeared to accept that a defendant who procures the absence of a key witness by intimidation cannot legitimately complain of a violation of the right to a fair trial by reason of his inability to examine the witness. However, that exception to the 'sole or decisive' principle was not applicable to the case of either applicant. None of the counter-balancing measures relied on by the UK Government in the two cases were thought to be adequate to meet the prejudice and disadvantage caused to the applicants by the admission of the written statements by the key witnesses against them. This decision caused major concern in England. Its espousal of what appeared to be a blanket rule, subject to a single limited exception, would have had far-reaching implications for the use of hearsay and anonymous evidence in all criminal trials.

A few months later came the riposte from the English courts. In *Horncastle,* a five-member Court of Appeal firmly rejected the "sole or decisive" limitation on the use of hearsay evidence.[271] That judgment was subsequently approved and reinforced by the judgment of a seven-member Supreme Court.[272] This case involved two conjoined appeals. Horncastle and Blackmore had been convicted

17–055

---

[268] *Doorson v Netherlands* (1996) 22 E.H.R.R. 330; *Van Mechelen v Netherlands* (1997) 25 E.H.R.R. 647.

[269] *Doorson v Netherlands* (1996) 22 E.H.R.R. 330; *AM v Italy* [1999] ECHR 141; *PS v Germany* (2003) 36 E.H.R.R. 61; *Luca v Italy* (2003) 36 E.H.R.R. 807.

[270] *Van Mechelen v Netherlands* (1997) 25 E.H.R.R. 647; *Visser v Netherlands* BAILII: [2002] ECHR 108; *Birutis v Lithuania* BAILII: [2002] ECHR 349; *Krasniki v Czech Republic* BAILII: [2006] ECHR 176.

[271] *Horncastle* [2009] EWCA Crim 964.

[272] *Horncastle* [2009] UKSC 14; [2010] 1 Cr.App.R. 17. Lord Phillips stated expressly that the Supreme Court's judgment should be read as complementary to that of the Court of Appeal and not as a substitute for it.

of causing grievous bodily harm with intent. The victim, who died before trial from unrelated causes, had made a witness statement which was read at the trial. Marquis and Graham had been convicted of kidnapping a young woman who was too frightened to give evidence. Her statement was read at the trial. Both statements were admitted pursuant to the provisions of s.116 of the Criminal Justice Act 2003. All the defendants argued that the admission of the statements violated their rights to a fair trial, relying on the "sole or decisive evidence" principle which had been affirmed in *Al-Khawaja and Tahery v United Kingdom*.

The Supreme Court's judgment began by rejecting the argument that the court was bound to follow the Strasbourg decision. Lord Phillips stated:

> "The requirement to 'take into account' the Strasbourg jurisprudence will normally result in this Court applying principles that are clearly established by the Strasbourg Court. There will, however, be rare occasions where this court has concerns as to whether a decision of the Strasbourg Court sufficiently appreciates or accommodates particular aspects of our domestic process. In such circumstances it is open to this court to decline to follow the Strasbourg decision, giving reasons for adopting this course. This is likely to give the Strasbourg Court the opportunity to reconsider the particular aspect of the decision that is in issue, so that there takes place what may prove to be a valuable dialogue between this court and the Strasbourg Court. This is such a case."[273]

He continued with a detailed analysis of the English law relating to both hearsay evidence and anonymous witnesses, suggesting that there was no difference in principle between them as far as the "sole or decisive" rule was concerned.[274] In both situations the critical question is whether the demands of a fair trial require such a rule, having regard to the cogency of the evidence in question and the safeguards provided by the legislation which permits such evidence to be given. In relation to hearsay evidence Lord Phillips argued that the "crafted code" in the Criminal Justice Act 2003 ensures that apparently reliable hearsay is admitted only when it is fair that it should be, and that there is no need for the "sole or decisive" rule to guarantee fairness.

17–056   He went on to offer a number of criticisms of the rule. First, he suggested that the rule is impracticable because it lacks clarity and is therefore difficult to apply. If the rule is a rule of *admissibility*, how is a trial judge, or an appeal court, to know when evidence is 'sole or decisive'? The answer may be obvious in some instances, as where a statement by a deceased victim constitutes virtually all the prosecution case. But there will be many other cases where hearsay is mixed with some direct evidence and/or some circumstantial evidence. All the evidence will be capable of being probative to some degree, otherwise it would not be admissible at all. But it may be very difficult to say how much each type of evidence contributes to the overall case against the defendant. As Lord Phillips said, "If 'decisive' means capable of making the difference between a finding of guilt and innocence, then all hearsay evidence will have to be excluded".[275]

---

[273] *Horncastle* [2009] UKSC 14; [2010] 1 Cr.App.R. 17 at [11].

[274] This was the main point on which the Supreme Court disagreed with the Court of Appeal, which had suggested that different considerations applied to anonymous witnesses: *Horncastle* [2009] EWCA Crim 964 at [48]–[51]. In treating the two types of evidence as raising the same issue of principle the Supreme Court and the European Court of Human Rights are in agreement.

[275] *Horncastle* [2009] UKSC 14 at [90].

Secondly, if the rule is a rule about the *use* of hearsay evidence, it would follow that a jury would have to be directed that they could have regard to a witness statement as supporting evidence but not as decisive evidence. Again this would be impracticable: "[such a direction] would involve them in mental gymnastics that few would be equipped to perform".[276]

Thirdly, Lord Phillips argued, as the Court of Appeal had done, that the rule confuses the importance of the evidence with its reliability. There is no necessary relationship. Hearsay evidence may be critically important, as it was in these cases, but if it is demonstrably reliable, or we have satisfactory procedures for estimating its reliability, why should it be unfair to the defendant to act upon it? He suggested that the rule produces the paradox that the court can have regard to the hearsay evidence if it gives peripheral support to the prosecution case, but not where it is decisive. "The more cogent the evidence the less it can be relied upon."[277]

Lord Phillips concluded his judgment on the general issue by saying:

"... it would not be right for this court to hold that the sole or decisive test should have been applied rather than the provisions of the 2003 Act, interpreted in accordance with their natural meaning. I believe that those provisions strike the right balance between the imperative that a trial must be fair and the interests of victims in particular and society in general that a criminal should not be immune from conviction where a witness, who has given critical evidence in a statement that can be shown to be reliable, dies or cannot be called to give evidence for some other reason. In so concluding I have taken careful account of the Strasbourg jurisprudence. I hope that in due course the Strasbourg court may also take account of the reasons that have led me not to apply the sole or decisive test in this case."[278]

Horncastle settled the law as far as the English courts are concerned. The **17–057** Supreme Court had made it clear that the "sole or decisive" test was not to be overriding in respect of either hearsay evidence or witness anonymity. At best it was to be a factor in the calculation of what the interests of justice and fairness required when the admission of either type of evidence was being considered. There was, however, considerable uncertainty as to how Strasbourg would respond to the challenge made to the rule. *Al-Khawaja and Tahery v United Kingdom* was a judgment of the Fourth Section of the Court of Human Rights. At the request of the UK Government the case was referred to the Grand Chamber for further consideration. It took 18 months for the Grand Chamber to reach its decision, which was finally handed down in December 2011. In this section we will refer to this judgment as *Al-Khawaja and Tahery v United Kingdom (GC)*.[279]

This is a landmark judgment. The Grand Chamber backed away from outright confrontation with the Supreme Court. It accepted both the need for the dialogue between the courts which Lord Phillips had called for in *Horncastle,* and the need to re-examine the provisions in English law for the admission of hearsay evidence, particularly the safeguards for the interests of the defence. It held that the "sole or decisive" principle should not be applied as an inflexible rule. Where hearsay evidence is the sole or decisive evidence against a defendant, its

---

[276] *Horncastle* [2009] UKSC 14 at [90].
[277] *Horncastle* [2009] UKSC 14 at [91].
[278] *Horncastle* [2009] UKSC 14 at [108].
[279] *Al-Khawaja and Tahery v United Kingdom (GC)* (2012) 54 E.H.R.R. 23.

admission in evidence should not automatically result in a violation of art.6. The same would appear to apply to the evidence of an anonymous witness. In the Grand Chamber's view, to apply the "sole or decisive" rule inflexibly, ignoring the specificities of the particular legal system concerned and in particular its rules of evidence,

> "would transform the rule into a blunt and indiscriminate instrument that runs counter to the traditional way in which the Court approaches the issue of the overall fairness of the proceedings, namely to weigh in the balance the competing interests of the defence, the victim, and witnesses, and the public interest in the effective administration of justice."[280]

However, the Grand Chamber's judgment is not a complete vindication of *Horncastle*. The court rejected most of Lord Phillips' criticisms of the "sole or decisive" rule.[281] In particular it argued that the rule is not imprecise and difficult to apply. It suggested that 'decisive' means more than "probative"; the word "should be narrowly understood as indicating evidence of such significance or importance as is likely to be determinative of the outcome of the case".[282] It then explained that how far hearsay evidence is treated as decisive may depend on the extent to which it is supported by other corroborative evidence. The court noted that while a trial judge might find it difficult in some cases to determine in advance whether evidence would be decisive, once the prosecution had concluded its case the significance and weight of the untested evidence could be assessed against the background of the other evidence against the accused. The court reinforced its retort by noting that in *Davis*[283] the House of Lords had appeared to foresee no difficulty in applying the "sole or decisive" rule in the context of anonymous witnesses. Moreover, the expression had been incorporated into the Coroners and Justice Act 2009 as a factor to be considered in the making of a witness anonymity order.[284]

The Grand Chamber went on to say that where a conviction is based solely or decisively on the evidence of absent witnesses, the court must subject the proceedings "to the most searching scrutiny". This means firstly, that the court must be satisfied that there is a good reason for the non-attendance of the witness, and that in the case of a witness excused from testifying on grounds of fear, that all available alternatives, such as witness anonymity and other special measures, would be inappropriate or impracticable. Secondly, because of the dangers presented by this kind of evidence, its admission requires sufficient counter-balancing factors, including the existence of "strong procedural safeguards".

> "The question in each case is whether there are sufficient counter-balancing factors in place, including measures that permit a fair and proper assessment of the reliability of that evidence to take place."[285]

---

[280] *Al-Khawaja and Tahery v United Kingdom (GC)* (2012) 54 E.H.R.R. 23 at [146].
[281] *Al-Khawaja and Tahery v United Kingdom (GC)* (2012) 54 E.H.R.R. 23 at [130]–[142].
[282] *Al-Khawaja and Tahery v United Kingdom (GC)* (2012) 54 E.H.R.R. 23 at [131].
[283] *Davis* [2008] UKHL 36; [2008] 1 A.C. 1128.
[284] *Al-Khawaja and Tahery v United Kingdom (GC)* (2012) 54 E.H.R.R. 23 at [137].
[285] *Al-Khawaja and Tahery v United Kingdom (GC)* (2012) 54 E.H.R.R. 23 at [147].

The court then reviewed the counter-balancing measures available in English law. It noted the requirement for leave for the admission of the statement of a fearful witness, the duty on the judge to consider special measures for such a witness, the provision in s.124 of the 2003 Act for the admission of evidence going to the credibility of the maker of a hearsay statement, the power of the judge under s.125 of the 2003 Act to stop a case based wholly or partly on hearsay evidence where the evidence is so unconvincing that a conviction would be unsafe, and the discretion under s. 78 of PACE to exclude evidence where necessary to protect the fairness of the proceedings. In the court's judgment these measures collectively "are, in principle, strong safeguards designed to ensure fairness".[286]

The court then examined how the safeguards were applied in the two cases before it. In A's case it agreed that the statement of the deceased witness was decisive,[287] and that the interests of justice were in favour of admitting it. The reliability of the statement was supported by the fact that the deceased had made prompt complaint to two friends who gave evidence at the trial of what the deceased had said, and more importantly by the strong similarities between her account of the assault and a separate assault testified to by another of A's patients. The court commented:

> "In a case of indecent assault by a doctor on his patient, which took place during a private consultation, where only he and the victim were present, it would be difficult to conceive of stronger corroborative evidence …"[288]

Given this support, and the judge's direction that the deceased's statement should carry less weight in view of A's inability to cross-examine her, the court considered that the jury was able to conduct a fair and proper assessment of its reliability. Viewing the proceedings as a whole, the court held that there were sufficient counter balancing factors to conclude that the admission of the hearsay statement did not result in a breach of art.6. On the other hand, in T's case the Grand Chamber did find a violation of art.6. This was because the witness's uncorroborated eyewitness statement "was, if not the sole, at least the decisive evidence against the applicant for that reason. It was obviously evidence of great weight and without it the chances of a conviction would have significantly receded." In the absence of any strong corroborative evidence the jury were unable to conduct a fair and proper assessment of the reliability of the statement. The factors of T's ability to give evidence rebutting the statement and the judge's clear caution warning to the jury about the danger of relying on untested evidence were thought to be insufficient to counter-balance the handicap to the defence of being unable to cross-examine the witness.

Where does this judgment leave English law? It is clear that the statutory regimes **17–058** for the admission of hearsay and anonymous evidence can continue to be applied even where the evidence in question is the sole or decisive evidence for conviction. It is not the case that such evidence can only be used in a supporting role for other more probative evidence of guilt. However, it is also clear that the

---

[286] *Al-Khawaja and Tahery v United Kingdom (GC)* (2012) 54 E.H.R.R. 23 at [151].

[287] Accepting the view of the trial judge who had observed "no statement, no count one".

[288] *Al-Khawaja and Tahery v United Kingdom (GC)* (2012) 54 E.H.R.R. 23 at [156].

Strasbourg rule has not been completely abandoned. It has only been relaxed. Where hearsay or anonymous evidence is the sole or decisive evidence against the accused the court must pay particular attention to the necessity to safeguard the interests of the defence so as to comply with the requirement for a fair trial. Recently, in *Ibrahim*[289] and in *Riat*[290] the Court of Appeal has reviewed the admission and treatment of hearsay evidence in the light of *Horncastle* and *Al-Khawaja and Tahery v United Kingdom (GC)*. It is to these cases and the guidance they offer to trial judges that we now turn.

In *Ibrahim*, the Court of Appeal examined the judgments of the Supreme Court and the Grand Chamber and concluded that any difference between them was more one of form than substance. In *Horncastle* the Supreme Court had declined to apply the "sole or decisive" test to the cases before it, whereas in *Al-Khawaja and Tahery v United Kingdom (GC)* the Grand Chamber had confirmed that the test remained part of the Strasbourg jurisprudence. In so far as there is an inconsistency the Court of Appeal is bound to follow *Horncastle*.[291] However, the Supreme Court had referred to the position where a hearsay statement is "critical evidence" which, as the Court of Appeal rightly said, may not be very different from the concept of "sole or decisive". The court might have added that Lord Phillips' rejection of the Strasbourg test was premised on it being a blanket rule. In its modified form his attitude might have been different, especially since the expression is used in the Coroners and Justice Act 2009 as a factor relevant to the grant of a witness anonymity order. At all events the Court of Appeal thought that the approach of the Supreme Court and the Grand Chamber to the admission of untested hearsay statements was substantially the same. In *Riat,* the Cout of Appeal reiterated that the importance of the hearsay evidence to the case is a vital consideration when deciding upon its admissibility and treatment, but emphasised that there is no over-arching rule, either in the Strasbourg jurisprudence or English law, that a piece of hearsay evidence which is "sole or decisive" is for that reason automatically inadmissible.

The court went on in *Riat* to suggest that the statutory framework for hearsay evidence can usefully be considered in a number of successive steps:

(i)   Is there a specific statutory justification (or "gateway") permitting the admission of hearsay evidence (s. 116-118 of the 2003 Act)?

(ii)   What material is there which can help to test or assess the hearsay (s.124)?

(iii)   Is there a specific "interests of justice" test at the admissibility stage?

(iv)   If there is no other justification or gateway, should the evidence nevertheless be considered for admission on the grounds that admission is, despite the difficulties, in the interests of justice (s.114(1)(d))?

(v)   Even if prima facie admissible, ought the evidence to be ruled inadmissible (s.78 PACE and/or s.126 of the 2003 Act)?

(vi)   If the evidence is admitted, then should the case subsequently be stopped under s.125?

---

[289] *Ibrahim* [2012] EWCA Crim 837; [2012] 2 Cr.App.R. 32.
[290] *Riat* [2012] EWCA Crim 1509.
[291] *Ibrahim* [2012] EWCA Crim 837; [2012] 2 Cr.App.R. 32 at [87], citing *R. (on the application of RJM) v Secretary of State for Work and Pensions* [2008] UKHL 63; [2009] 1 A.C. 311.

The court might have added a step (vii) to the effect that if the evidence is admitted, and the case is not stopped, what direction should the judge in a jury trial give about the evidence? In *Ibrahim*, the Court of Appeal emphasised that a jury should be reminded that a hearsay statement will not (usually) have been verified on oath and will certainly not have been tested by cross-examination:

> "The judge should identify and point out the specific risks of relying on that evidence and should invite the jury to scrutinise it with particular care. The jury's attention should be drawn to the context in which the statement was made and to all the other evidence in relation to it. If there are discrepancies between the hearsay statement and the evidence of other witnesses the jury's attention should be specifically drawn to them."[292]

In *Riat*, the Court of Appeal, having set out the six steps mentioned above, offered further comment on their application. In relation to (i) the court stressed that the necessity for resorting to second-hand evidence must be demonstrated. In particular, where a witness is in fear of testifying, all possible steps should be taken to enable the witness to give evidence. "This may be impossible, but very frequently it is perfectly practicable; a degree of (properly supported) fortitude can legitimately be expected in the fight against crime."[293] In *Wilson*, one of the cases heard with *Riat*, the Court of Appeal held that the trial judge's finding that the witnesses to an assault were in fear was not soundly based and their hearsay statements should not have been admitted. The court observed that if the witnesses had been compelled to come to court they might well have been persuaded to give evidence. If any had refused it would not inevitably have been wrong to treat him or her as hostile. The point of so doing would of course be to enable the prosecution to confront the witness with her or his previous statement.[294]

17–059

In relation to step (ii) the Court of Appeal suggested that if a specific gateway is passed the court should always then consider the linked questions of the apparent reliability of the evidence and the practicability of the jury testing and assessing its reliability. As the court said, s.124 of the 2003 Act is critical at this point. The more important the evidence, the greater the need for full enquiries to have been made as to the witness's credibility and for full disclosure of relevant material to have been made. Steps (iii), (iv) and (v) are logically distinct in terms of the framework of admission or exclusion of hearsay. In practice the decisions they require will raise much the same considerations in relation to satisfying fair trial requirements. This is acknowledged in *Riat* where the Court of Appeal suggested that the factors listed in s.114(2) are "useful *aides memoire*" for any judge considering the admissibility of hearsay evidence, whether under s. 114(1)(d) or under s. 78 of PACE.

To this list one should add the nature and extent of any supporting evidence for the reliability of the hearsay. As noted above, the Grand Chamber attached considerable importance to the presence or absence of corroboration in determining the fairness of admitting potentially decisive hearsay statements. So

---

[292] *Ibrahim* [2012] EWCA Crim 837; [2012] 2 Cr.App.R. 32 at [112]..
[293] *Riat* [2012] EWCA Crim 1509 at [16].
[294] See the discussion of hostile witnesses in Ch.14.

too did the Court of Appeal in some of the cases reported as *Riat*. In *Riat*[295] itself the Court of Appeal upheld the admission of video-recorded interviews with the deceased child victim (V) of alleged sexual offences. The reliability of the interviews was thought to be assured by evidence of V's frequent spontaneous statements about her sexual relationship with D, a detailed account of the relationship which V gave to a nurse she had consulted about possible pregnancy, and evidence from one of V's friends that she had seen V and D go into a bedroom in D's flat, heard sounds of sexual activity, and then been threatened by D at knifepoint if she did not swear to secrecy. Assuming the friend was telling the truth it would be hard to think of stronger corroboration. In *Doran,* the court upheld the admission of the witness statement of a deceased victim of robbery and theft. His account of how he had been coerced into paying a vastly inflated sum for work done by D at his house was supported by a note in D's handwriting for the amount of the supposed debt, D's initial lie to the police that he had never visited the house, and his record of exactly this kind of extortion from householders. By contrast, in *Wilson,* mentioned above, a further reason for not admitting the witness statement of one of the eyewitnesses to the assault (which took place late at night outside a pub) was that it stood alone as a bare allegation against the defendant. It could not be sufficiently tested and assessed, and was clearly not demonstrably reliable.

In relation to step (vi) the Court of Appeal explained in *Riat* that the power under s.125 of the 2003 Act to stop a case where hearsay evidence is unconvincing requires the judge to assess the reliability of the evidence. "That means looking at its strengths and weaknesses, at the tools available to the jury for testing it, and at its importance to the case as a whole."[296] This is a different task from the one required by *Galbraith,*[297] when the judge is ruling on whether the prosecution have made out a case to answer. Then the judge has only to decide whether there is sufficient evidence on which a properly directed jury could convict. The judge's own view of the reliability of the evidence is immaterial. Under s.125 the judge must reach a conclusion on how convincing or otherwise he or she finds the hearsay evidence.

K.   ANONYMOUS HEARSAY

17–060   The final question to consider in this chapter is whether anonymous hearsay is ever admissible. Can evidence of a hearsay statement be admitted where the identity of the maker of the statement is unknown or concealed? There is powerful authority that this is never permissible. In *Mayers,* Lord Judge C.J., giving the judgment of the Court of Appeal, upheld a ruling by a trial judge that he had no power to admit the hearsay statement of an anonymous witness.

---

[295] See also *Clare,* where evidence of the complaint of a child aged 3 to her mother about a sexual assault was "powerfully supported" by 3 separate items of other evidence.
[296] *Riat* [2012] EWCA Crim 1509 at [28].
[297] *Galbraith* [1981] 1 W.L.R. 1039.

"... we are being invited to rewrite the 2008 Act by extending anonymous witness orders to permit anonymous hearsay evidence to be read to the jury. We cannot do so. Neither the common law, nor the 2003 Act, nor the 2008 Act, permits it."[298]

In *Horncastle,* Lord Judge C.J. reaffirmed this proposition in his Annexe to the judgment of the Supreme Court.[299] The Court of Appeal has subsequently applied the proposition in two cases. In *Fox*[300] a passer-by who witnessed a street robbery made a 999 call reporting the incident. He gave his name and address but insisted on remaining anonymous and refused to give evidence at the trial. The trial judge had admitted evidence of the call under s.114(1)(d) of the 2003 Act, but the Court of Appeal held that he was wrong to do so. There was no power to admit anonymous hearsay. In *Ford,*[301] police attending the scene of a shooting were handed a piece of paper and a note by an unknown woman. The paper contained a car registration number, and the note said that the woman had "heard gun shots and saw them getting into this car but I don't want to get involved". The Court of Appeal characterised this as anonymous hearsay evidence and held that it was inadmissible.

The proposition stated in *Mayers* and relied on in *Fox* and *Ford* deserves some critical scrutiny.[302] It is true that the statutory provision in the Coroners and Justice Act 2009 for witness anonymity orders is silent on the question whether an order can permit the statement of an anonymous *and* absent witness to be admitted. Since the whole scheme of the legislation is premised on the identity of the witness being known, but concealed when the witness testifies, the argument is compelling that the legislation was not intended to permit an available witness to make an anonymous hearsay statement. It would then seem to be right that s.114(1)(d) of the 2003 Act should not be used to bypass this restriction, in the same way that it should not be used to circumvent the limits of the provision for unavailable witnesses in s.116.

However, suppose that the identity of the maker of a hearsay statement is not known, so that the issue of calling the maker to give evidence simply does not arise. *Ford* indicates that this makes no difference, but it is submitted that it may do. This is because, unlike s.116, some of the other hearsay exceptions in the 2003 Act do not require the maker of the statement to be identified before the statement can be admitted. The most obvious one is s.117. The business records exception refers in s.117(2)(b) to:

"the person who supplied the information contained in the statement ... [who] had *or may reasonably be supposed to have had* personal knowledge of the matters dealt with." (emphasis added)

This seems to envisage that the supplier of the information in a business record may be unknown, but in the circumstances her or his knowledge is likely to have been reliably reported. An obvious example would be the unidentified production

---

[298] *Mayers* [2008] EWCA Crim 2989; [2009] 1 W.L.R. 1915 at [113].
[299] *Horncastle* [2009] UKSC 14; [2010] 1 Cr.App.R. 17 Annexe 4 at [13].
[300] *Fox* [2010] EWCA Crim 1280.
[301] *Ford* [2010] EWCA Crim 2250; [2011] Crim. L.R. 475.
[302] See the Commentary by Professor Ormerod in [2011] Crim. L.R. 477.

line workers in the notorious case of *Myers v DPP*.[303] It has been assumed for nearly half a century that the decision that the cards which they filled in recording engine numbers were inadmissible was reversed by legislation in 1965. It is surely inconceivable that this is no longer true under the successor legislation in the 2003 Act. On the facts of *Ford,* it is strongly arguable that the paper and note were admissible under s. 117, since all the statutory conditions of admissibility were satisfied. Some of the preserved common law exceptions in s.118 may also permit hearsay where the maker of the statement is not identified. Evidence of reputation is a clear example, and it may be that the res gestae exception for spontaneous statements may also allow the admission of a hearsay statement by an unknown person. It is suggested therefore that the proposition in *Mayers* is stated too widely and will need to be qualified on a suitable occasion.

---

[303] *Myers v DPP* [1965] A.C. 1001. See also *O'Connor* [2010] EWCA Civ 2287, and para.17–017 above.

CHAPTER 18

CHARACTER AND CREDIBILITY: AN OVERVIEW

A. INTRODUCTION

Evidence of character is a large subject in the law of evidence. An important part **18–001** of it deals with the character of witnesses, particularly the extent to which evidence of a witness's bad character can be adduced at trial. This topic was dealt with in Ch.14 on the examination of witnesses, which discussed the tightening of the law made by s.100 of the Criminal Justice Act 2003. The major part of the subject has been reserved for this part of the book because character evidence has in the past been closely associated with the exclusionary rules of the common law and the Criminal Evidence Act 1898 relating to evidence of the accused's bad character and misconduct on other occasions.[1] These rules were replaced by the new comprehensive statutory scheme, established by Ch.1 of Pt 11 of the Criminal Justice Act 2003,[2] which regulates the admission of evidence of bad character in criminal proceedings generally. The new scheme utilises some of the structure and concepts of the previous law, but relaxes its strictness, so as to make more evidence of the accused's bad character admissible for the prosecution. This scheme is discussed in detail in Ch.19.

This chapter presents an overview of the issues relating to character and credibility in the law of evidence. One aim is to provide some theoretical and contextual discussion to inform the analysis of the new scheme for bad character evidence in criminal cases. A second aim is to discuss the common law of evidence relating to character and credibility. The common law still governs character evidence of the parties in civil proceedings, and evidence in criminal proceedings of the accused's good character. It no longer applies to evidence of bad character in criminal proceedings. But an outline of the old law and the reasons for reform will help in understanding the new scheme set out in the next chapter.

The discussion begins with an introduction to the nature and scale of the problems that evidence of bad character can present. "Character" in this context simply means a person's tendency to behave in a particular way. "Disposition" and "propensity" are alternative terms with the same meaning, which are frequently found both in the primary sources of law and in the secondary literature on the subject.[3] Thus a person might be described as having a violent disposition if he has several convictions for assault, or as having an honest character if she has a reputation for integrity. These examples indicate that a person's character can be shown in different ways. Bad character might be revealed by previous convictions, the commission of other criminal acts, other discreditable conduct, possession of incriminating or discreditable materials (e.g. paedophile literature), criminal associations,[4] and reputation. Similarly, good character might be shown by the absence of convictions, by virtuous conduct on other occasions, by the good opinions of others and by reputation.

18–002 In criminal cases character evidence is generally thought to have probative value on the issue of guilt or innocence. A revealing study was carried out for the Home Office into the effect on mock juries of knowing that the defendant has a previous conviction.[5] The strongest finding was that participants who were told of a defendant's recent similar conviction rated him as significantly more likely to have committed the crime charged than when they were told that he had a

---

[1] The Law Commission reviewed this topic in a Consultation Paper, *Evidence in Criminal Proceedings: Previous Misconduct of a Defendant* ("Law Com. CP 141") (1996) and the subsequent report, *Evidence of Bad Character in Criminal Proceedings*, Cm.5257 ("Law Com. 273") (2001).

[2] In Pt 11 Ch.1.

[3] The Criminal Justice Act 2003 uses all 3 terms in Pt 11.

[4] "You may know a person by the company he keeps." We shall see later that the definition of "bad character" in the Criminal Justice Act 2003 is not apt to cover all the forms of evidence that might reveal bad character.

[5] Law Com. CP 141 Appendix D ("The Oxford Study"). See further S. Lloyd-Bostock, "The Effects on Juries on Hearing About the Defendant's Previous Criminal Record: A Simulation Study" [2000] Crim. L.R. 734.

dissimilar conviction or no convictions.[6] At the same time evidence of bad character is potentially prejudicial to the accused and is capable of seriously distorting the factfinding process. A further finding of the study was that a previous conviction for indecent assault on a child tended to produce a markedly adverse evaluation of the defendant. Amongst other things such a defendant was likely to be viewed as being least trustworthy, most deserving of punishment and most likely to lie to the court.[7]

These findings neatly encapsulate the conflict at the heart of the debate about bad character evidence. The conflict is between the probative value for the offence charged of evidence that tends to show the accused's bad character and the tendency of that evidence to prejudice the factfinder against the accused. The common law attempted to resolve the conflict by establishing a general rule that the prosecution could not adduce evidence in chief for the purpose of proving the accused's bad character unless that evidence had a sufficient degree of relevance to the issues in the case to make it just to admit it, notwithstanding its prejudicial effect.[8] Insofar as the rule generally excluded such evidence at trial it was peculiar to common law systems. It has no counterpart in continental criminal procedure where the accused's criminal record generally forms part of the dossier of the case and is available to the court of trial.[9] While the Criminal Justice Act 2003 has enlarged the admissibility of evidence of bad character, it has still left English law some way from the continental position.

The exclusionary rule of the common law was often referred to as the rule about "similar fact evidence". This was a misleading term since the rule extended to evidence that did not necessarily have any similarity to the facts of the offence charged, but that tended to show the accused's character in a bad light.[10] Despite this drawback the term was too well established to be ignored, and it is still occasionally used in this chapter as a convenient shorthand reference. Like the common law rule against hearsay evidence, the common law rule against similar fact evidence had a deserved reputation for difficulty. Three major attempts were made by the higher courts to state the essential elements of the rule, but it gave much trouble in practice[11] and a massive reported case law dealt with its refinements. An equally extensive body of case law interpreting the provisions of the Criminal Evidence Act 1898 dealt with cross-examination of the accused on

---

[6] Law Com. CP 141 para.D.21.

[7] Law Com. CP 141 para.D.26. Lloyd-Bostock's comparable research on the effect on magistrates of knowing of a defendant's criminal record showed that, as with mock jurors, previous convictions generally affected magistrates' impressions and verdicts unfavourably. However, an interesting difference between magistrates and mock jurors was that magistrates were most influenced by information that the defendant had a previous conviction for intentionally causing grievous bodily harm, whereas the defendant's previous conviction for indecent assault on a child had most effect on the mock jurors: see Law Com. 273 Appendix A.

[8] *DPP v P* [1991] 2 A.C. 447 HL.

[9] Law Com. CP 141 paras B.104–B.118; M. R. Damaska, "Propensity Evidence in Continental Legal Systems" (1994) 70 Chicago-Kent L.R. 55.

[10] As in *Thompson v R.* [1918] A.C. 221 HL; and, less controversially, *Lewis* (1982) 76 Cr.App.R. 33 CA. See further the discussion by the High Court of Australia in *Pfennig v R.* (1995) 127 A.L.R. 99.

[11] Lord Hailsham once referred to the subject as a "pitted battlefield": *DPP v Boardman* [1975] A.C. 421 at 445. The common law rules were analysed in detail in Ch.18 of the 2nd edn of this book.

his previous convictions and bad character. This body of law was regarded as equal in complexity to the common law similar fact rule and probably more unsatisfactory in terms of principle.[12]

18–003   The broad objectives of both the common law similar fact rule and the scheme of the Criminal Evidence Act 1898 were protective. They aimed to protect the accused from the prejudice that revelation of his bad character might cause. However, the exclusionary rules were not absolute. The Criminal Evidence Act 1898 provided for a number of exceptions where the accused could lose the shield provided by the Act against cross-examination on his record. The majority of these exceptions depended on how the accused conducted his defence. Even in the exceptional cases where the shield was lost the courts retained a discretion to exclude cross-examination on bad character evidence where its prejudicial effect outweighed any probative value it had. Likewise, the similar fact rule generally excluded evidence of previous convictions and bad character as part of the prosecution case, but such evidence could exceptionally be admitted where its probative value exceeded its prejudicial tendency. This principle of weighing probative value and prejudicial effect is a familiar one in the law of evidence. However, its application in this context was complicated by the facts that proof and prejudice are more complex concepts than they first appear, and the similar fact rule was beset by continuing uncertainty over whether the admissibility decision was one of law or discretion, or both.

The scheme established by the Criminal Justice Act 2003 does not in terms require courts to weigh probative value against prejudicial effect. However, as we shall see, the availability of discretion to exclude admissible bad character evidence, based on its adverse effect on the fairness of the proceedings, is likely to require courts to continue to address this issue in substance.[13] Accordingly, the next section of this chapter will discuss further the concepts of proof and prejudice. The chapter will then deal briefly with character evidence in civil cases, and with good character in criminal cases, before turning to the reasons for the reforms carried out in the new statutory scheme for evidence of bad character in criminal cases. Chapter 19 will then deal with the new scheme in detail.

B.   PROOF AND PREJUDICE

1.   *The relevance of evidence of good character*

18–004   A fruitful way of analysing the probative value of evidence of bad character is to begin with its converse, and to ask why evidence of good character may be thought to have probative value. Evidence of the accused's good character may have relevance to the issue of guilt in the following way. It may yield an inference that the accused is unlikely to have committed the offence charged because he is a law-abiding citizen, as demonstrated by the lack of a criminal record. The accused may seek to argue that he is "not the kind of person who does this kind of thing". Accordingly, any incriminating evidence may be explained on

---

[12]   See Ch.19 of the 2nd edn of this book.
[13]   See, e.g. *Edwards* [2006] 1 Cr.App.R. 31 at [16].

the basis that it is a lie, a mistake, or has an innocent explanation. In support of this argument for relevance, Zuckerman points to common beliefs that human behaviour is not entirely arbitrary and unpredictable, but may be dictated by the mental make-up of the actor. In this way, he suggests, "Character has both predictive force and probabilistic significance concerning a person's past acts or omissions".[14] The common law has long acted on this assumption, allowing the accused to adduce evidence of good character in support of a not guilty plea from an early stage.[15]

Evidence of good character may also be relevant to the issue of the accused's credibility if he gives evidence in his defence at trial or evidence is given of his exculpatory statements to the police. He may seek to argue that his statements and testimony should be accepted as true because his record shows that he is trustworthy, that he is not the kind of person who tells lies on serious matters. As will be seen later, the law accepts that good character may have relevance to both guilt and credibility, and the judge will generally have to give an appropriate direction to the jury on this point.

These arguments for relevance are directed to the factual issue of criminal liability, the issue of whether the defendant did in fact commit the offence charged. As Zuckerman rightly points out,[16] good character may also have a bearing on the moral choice facing the factfinder. According to the theory of legitimacy presented in this book the factfinder must decide not only whether the defendant in fact committed the offence charged but also whether, if so, the defendant deserves to be convicted. A verdict of guilty is a public assignment of moral blame, and the factfinder should be satisfied that it is merited. Drawing attention to the accused's good character draws the factfinder's attention to the significance of this judgment of blameworthiness. The stigma attached to conviction is likely to destroy the person's moral standing in the community. The more serious the offence, the greater is the likelihood of this happening. In the long term the loss of moral standing may have more severe effects than the actual punishment imposed by the court. This consideration might influence the factfinder's process of decision in favour of the accused in two ways. In some cases it might lead to a literal interpretation, or even a revision, of the standard of proof: the factfinder might be unwilling to convict unless the factual commission of the offence were proved beyond any conceivable doubt, whether reasonable or otherwise. Alternatively it might lead in exceptional and rare cases to a frank exercise of jury equity, whereby the jury refused to convict a person of such moral worth despite concluding that the person did commit the offence. The general verdict of not guilty conceals the use of this device, as it does in other cases of jury equity such as where the jury disapproves of the criminal law in question or the bringing of the particular prosecution.

---

[14] A. A. S. Zuckerman, "Similar Fact Evidence—The Unobservable Rule" (1987) 103 L.Q.R. 187, 190.

[15] The leading authority on this aspect of the common law before 1898 is *Stannard* (1837) 7 C. & P. 673.

[16] A. A. S. Zuckerman, "Similar Fact Evidence—The Unobservable Rule" (1987) 103 L.Q.R. 187, 198.

2. The relevance of evidence of bad character

18–005   Understanding the relevance of good character is helpful in understanding the relevance of evidence of bad character and the conflicts it may involve. First, such evidence tends to rebut any arguments made by the defence founded on good character. The law has always taken the view that the accused should not be allowed to mislead the court by false assertions of a good character that he does not have. This is so whether the good character is asserted to be relevant to guilt or to credibility, or both. The accused might raise the issue by giving evidence himself of his good character, or by calling character witnesses, or by cross-examining prosecution witnesses about it. As we shall see in the next chapter, one of the "gateways" through which evidence of the defendant's bad character may be admitted under the Criminal Justice Act 2003 is where it is "evidence to correct a false impression given by the defendant".[17]

    Whether or not the accused lays claim to a good character, the question can still arise whether the prosecution may take the initiative in adducing evidence of bad character. Parity of reasoning suggests that, just as good character may make guilt less likely, so bad character may make guilt more likely. As noted above, the probability of guilt may be increased in the eyes of factfinders by knowledge that the person in question is shown to have a propensity for lawbreaking,[18] more so if there is evidence of past lawbreaking in the form of similar offences to the one charged. In this way the law has a symmetry that requires it to admit the possibility that bad character could be logically relevant to guilt, and to the credibility of the defendant in giving evidence or making statements to the police. Although judges have sometimes denied this possibility, there are explicit acknowledgments of it in the cases.[19] As with good character, the argument for the logical relevance of evidence of bad character is founded on generalisations about human behaviour that are the product of observation and experience of the repetitive and patterned nature of much human action. As Redmayne has noted, modern psychological research tends to see behaviour as determined by a combination of personality characteristics and situational factors.[20] The acknowledgment by social science that individuals may act in accordance with established character traits provides useful theoretical backing for the claim that past criminal behaviour has probabilistic value for legal factfinding. However, this is not to say that the particular psychological assumptions that underpinned the common law relating to evidence of bad character, and the provisions of the Criminal Evidence Act 1898 relating to cross-examination of the accused on his bad character, were necessarily sound. It is strongly arguable that they were not, as we shall see in the next section.

---

[17] Criminal Justice Act 2003 s.101(1)(f).

[18] Interestingly the Oxford study showed that a defendant with a *dissimilar* conviction was rated by the participants as significantly less likely to have committed the offence charged: Law Com. CP 141 para.D.22. However, a conviction for indecent assault was apparently an exception, and it may be that a study using a greater range of other offences would confirm that the effect of introducing convictions for dissimilar offences is variable.

[19] *Clarke* [1995] 2 Cr.App.R. 425 at 433; *Randall* [2004] UKHL 69; [2004] 1 W.L.R. 36 at [22]; Law Com. CP 141, Pt VI.

[20] M. Redmayne, "The Relevance of Bad Character" [2002] C.L.J. 684.

Nevertheless the application of these generalisations about behaviour in the context of criminality gains further support from the statistics on recidivism. Some years ago Tapper pointed out that:

> "less than 1 in 138 of the population is likely to commit a serious crime in a given year, while 1 in 2 of those found guilty in the year of committing such crimes will have a record of having committed such a crime."[21]

Similarly, Redmayne suggests that a study of comparative propensity—meaning how much more likely a person with a conviction for a particular crime is to commit that type of crime, compared with someone without a previous conviction for that crime—produces figures that at face value imply that recent same-crime previous convictions have considerable probative value.[22]

These arguments are strong, but they should not be overstated. The claim is only **18–006** that evidence of bad character and other misconduct is generally capable of having logical relevance, and hence probative value, to the issue of guilt. Whether particular evidence does have relevance in the circumstances of a particular case, and, if so, how much probative value it has, depends on three key variables. These are:

- the cogency of the evidence of bad character and other misconduct;
- the precise issue or issues in the case;
- the state of the other evidence in the case.[23]

Cogency refers to the strength of the evidence that the accused does have the bad character claimed. As the Law Commission have said, if the evidence of the other misconduct is untrue then it has no probative value at all and can only be prejudicial.[24] Particular problems can arise in this connection with the risk of collusion between witnesses to "similar fact" offences and with weak circumstantial evidence of the accused's commission of other offences. Assuming, however, that the evidence showing bad character is true, its degree of relevance inevitably depends on the issue to which it is directed. For example, the common law similar fact rule drew a distinction between the use of bad character evidence to prove the mens rea of an offence, where the accused admitted doing the prohibited act but denied having the requisite intent, and its use to prove the actus reus of the offence, where the accused denied doing the prohibited act at all.

---

[21] C. Tapper, "Proof and Prejudice" in E. Campbell and L. Waller (eds), *Well and Truly Tried* (Melbourne:1982), pp.177, 199. See also Law Com. CP 141 para.7.7 fn.10.

[22] Redmayne "The Relevance of Bad Character" [2002] C.L.J. 684, 691–698, esp. 695. Later in this article Redmayne casts doubt on how far such figures should determine evidence policy, but his caution does not detract from the key point that some propensity evidence may be more probative and less prejudicial than is sometimes asserted.

[23] For the importance of these variables under the old law see L. H. Hoffmann, "Similar Facts After Boardman" (1975) 91 L.Q.R. 193; Tapper, "Proof and Prejudice" (1982), pp.199–203; *Clarke* [1995] 2 Cr.App.R. 425, 433–435. It is submitted that they continue to play important roles under the Criminal Justice Act 2003 scheme, not least when the exercise of exclusionary discretion is being considered.

[24] Law Com. CP 141 para.6.3.

Evidence that suggested that a particular admitted act was not accidental, or was done with an indecent motive, might not be sufficient to prove the commission of another act that the accused denied.[25]

Importantly, the state of the other evidence may critically affect the amount of "work" the similar fact evidence has to do. Speaking broadly, the more the similar fact evidence has to prove, the greater the degree of relevance it will need to have. A good example is *Ball*,[26] where evidence that a brother and sister had committed incest before that conduct was criminalised in 1908[27] was admitted to prove that they had committed incest after the statute took effect. The evidence of what the House of Lords called their "guilty passion" for each other was highly probative, given that the other evidence showed that they had continued to share a bed in the house they occupied after 1908. This fact was unusual for adult siblings, and suspicious in the absence of an explanation. However, as Hoffmann convincingly argued,[28] the result of the case should have been different if the other evidence had showed that two bedrooms were in use. In that case the evidence of the defendants' previous incestuous association would be inadequate to bear the whole weight of proving that a particular sexual relationship continued after it had been prohibited.

3. *The prejudicial effect of evidence of bad character and other misconduct*

18–007   Tapper defined prejudice as:

> "the tendency of evidence of discreditable extrinsic conduct or disposition to persuade the jury to convict the accused for reasons other than the logical force which constitutes the justification for admitting such evidence."[29]

This emphasises that prejudice means more than an inference that is simply unfavourable to the accused,[30] and more than an adverse inference that is logically warranted by the evidence.[31] Prejudice in this sense is unfair to the accused because it carries the risk that he will be convicted when he is in fact innocent, or when the evidence is insufficient to prove the charge against him beyond reasonable doubt.

The Law Commission has helpfully distinguished between two forms of prejudice, namely "reasoning prejudice" and "moral prejudice":

---

[25] See, e.g. *Lewis* (1982) 76 Cr.App.R. 33.
[26] *Ball* [1911] A.C. 47 HL.
[27] Punishment of Incest Act 1908.
[28] Hoffmann, "Similar Facts after Boardman" (1975) 91 L.Q.R. 193, 202.
[29] Tapper, "Proof and Prejudice" (1982), p.204.
[30] Any evidence of guilt is in a broad sense prejudicial to the accused because it worsens his position, but this usage is unhelpful and best avoided.
[31] A. A. S. Zuckerman, "Similar Fact Evidence—The Unobservable Rule" (1987) 103 L.Q.R. 187, 194.

"We take 'prejudicial effect' to mean that a verdict is reached, not as a valid conclusion from a logical line of reasoning, but either by giving too much weight to the evidence of bad character ('reasoning prejudice') or by convicting otherwise than on the evidence ('moral prejudice')."[32]

Reasoning prejudice may occur in a variety of ways. The factfinder may, for example, overestimate the probative value of evidence that the defendant has committed similar offences in the past. This may be the result of statistical naivety, as where the factfinder believes that the evidence singles out the accused as the offender whereas it may only place him in a group of persons more likely than other persons to have committed the offence. In a burglary case, evidence that the defendant habitually burgles by breaking a kitchen window to gain entry does not without more identify him as the burglar who did so on this occasion. There may be many other burglars in the local population who use this method of entry. The Law Commission suggests that ignorance of police methods might result in an inaccurate estimate of the probability of an innocent person being arrested and charged.[33] The police may well, indeed often will, begin an inquiry by investigating the "usual suspects", who are of course those persons known to have a propensity to commit the type of crime in question. If the record is then used by the factfinder as a basis for conviction the accused may have been doubly prejudiced.

Other forms of reasoning prejudice are possible. The factfinder may be influenced by the defendant's record into rejection of innocent explanations without adequate consideration. A further possibility is that the factfinder may be tempted to weaken the standard of proof required, and to be satisfied with a probability of guilt less than beyond a reasonable doubt.[34] If the defendant is charged with several offences, and the factfinder is not sure of guilt on any one of them considered in isolation, there may be a temptation to think that there is "no smoke without fire". This might lead the factfinder to assume that the defendant's apparent propensity to commit offences, as revealed by the evidence on each offence, is sufficient to justify conviction on one of the offences; that conviction might then be used to resolve the uncertainty about guilt of the other charges.[35]

18–008

There is a certain amount of empirical evidence to back up these fears. The Oxford study and the earlier jury research carried out by the LSE both found that mock jurors were more likely to convict a defendant if they knew that he had a recent previous conviction for a similar offence.[36] In the revealing case of *Bills*[37] a jury that had returned a verdict of unlawful wounding sought to change the verdict to the more serious offence of wounding with intent to do grievous bodily harm after it heard for the first time at the sentencing stage of the accused's record for violence.

Moral prejudice arises from the nature of the evidence of bad character rather than from any probative inferences to be drawn from it. If the bad character

---

[32] Law Com. CP 141 para.7.2. See also Law Com. 273 para.5.18.
[33] Law Com. CP 141 para.7.8.
[34] A. A. S. Zuckerman, "Similar Fact Evidence—The Unobservable Rule" (1987) 103 L.Q.R. 187, 195.
[35] Law Com. CP 141 para.7.9.
[36] Law Com. CP 141 para.7.7.
[37] *Bills, The Times*, March 1, 1995.

evidence shows that the accused is a morally repugnant person, a lay factfinder may be sufficiently influenced by the revulsion felt to the point where there is a willingness to convict irrespective of the probative force of the evidence relating to the charge. The factfinder might justify this on the basis that if the defendant has not committed the offence charged, he has probably committed others, or that his record shows him to be a dangerous and unpleasant person from whom society deserves to be protected and who merits conviction in any event. Indecent assault on a child is a clear example. The Oxford study found that if a defendant had a previous conviction for such an offence mock jurors were more likely to convict him and more likely to believe that he would commit other offences in the future.[38] If such prejudice does occur, a guilty verdict cannot be legitimate. It lacks moral authority because it is founded on a violation of one of the fundamental principles of criminal justice—namely that a person may fairly be blamed and punished only for what he has done (proved to the requisite standard) and not for what he is.[39]

18–009 Spencer has put forward the argument that because bad character evidence is typically weak, it presents a danger where the other evidence of the defendant's guilt is slender. In his view it should not be a substitute for "hard evidence" that implicates the defendant more directly, and should not therefore be admitted where the other evidence is thin:

> "On the other hand, . . . there is no unfairness involved in admitting this sort of evidence where the other evidence is strong, and in particular where it may clinch the case."[40]

Certainly, if the other evidence against the defendant is thin, the dangers presented by reasoning and moral prejudice are greatly increased because there is more scope for them to fill the "gap" between a weak prosecution case and proof beyond reasonable doubt. However, it would be going too far to insist that bad character evidence can *never* be used where the other evidence is weak. As Spencer himself notes, the degree of relevance of bad character evidence may vary considerably. This is particularly so where it is "similar fact" evidence. If, for example, the similar fact offences involving the defendant show a very unusual modus operandi, something in the nature of a criminal signature, then this is strong evidence of his identity as the offender if the offence charged was committed in the same very unusual way.[41] It is arguable that it should be admitted even if the other evidence against the defendant is not much more than evidence of his opportunity to commit the offence. Because it tends to place the defendant in a class of his own as the offender its probative value is difficult to overestimate.

Finally, it is important to locate this issue about evidence of bad character in its practical context. The Crown Court study for the Royal Commission on Criminal Justice[42] showed that in contested cases the defendant had previous

---

[38] Law Com. CP 141 para.7.11.

[39] A. A. S. Zuckerman, "Similar Fact Evidence—The Unobservable Rule" (1987) 103 L.Q.R. 187, 195–196; Law Com. CP 141 para.7.10; Law Com. 273 para.5.13.

[40] J. R. Spencer, *Evidence of Bad Character* (2006), paras 1.58 onwards.

[41] The celebrated case of *Straffen* [1952] 2 Q.B. 911 CCA is an example.

[42] M. Zander and P. Henderson, RCCJ Research Study No.19 (London, 1993).

convictions in 77 per cent of cases.[43] In more than half the cases the convictions were for similar offences.[44] The trial judges in the study rated the seriousness of the convictions as follows: 10 per cent were "very serious"; 53 per cent were "fairly serious"; and 37 per cent were "not very serious".[45] Given the potential for knowledge of convictions to prejudice the factfinder there is plainly a large-scale problem for the law to resolve.

The Crown Court study showed that the defendant's convictions emerged during the trial in approximately 20 per cent of cases.[46] In considerably more than half the cases where the convictions emerged they were introduced by the defence rather than by the prosecution.[47] It seems that there was no single explanation for this. In some cases the defence strategy was to introduce stale or minor convictions as part of a reasonably positive claim to good character. In other cases the strategy was to defuse in advance a potentially damaging cross-examination where the defendant was making imputations against prosecution witnesses or giving evidence against a co-accused.[48] In a third group of cases convictions emerged inadvertently, blurted out by the defendant or by someone else. In cases where the prosecution introduced the defendant's convictions almost half the cases concerned the "tit for tat" rule, i.e. where the defendant lost the shield against cross-examination on his character by making imputations against prosecution witnesses.

The study also asked about the extent to which the defence was inhibited by the "tit for tat" rule.[49] The response was that the defence was inhibited by the rule in 28 per cent of cases, and not inhibited in 72 per cent of cases (either because there was no need to attack the prosecution evidence or otherwise). The significant number of cases where the defence did feel inhibited should be borne in mind when we consider how the Criminal Justice Act 2003 has reproduced the substance of this rule.

18–010

C.   CHARACTER AND CREDIBILITY: THE PSYCHOLOGY OF THE LAW RELATING TO BAD CHARACTER EVIDENCE

Certain psychological assumptions underpinned the common law rules governing evidence of the accused's bad character and the statutory provisions regulating cross-examination of the accused on his bad character. These assumptions were fundamental, but they were far from being generally accepted as uncontroversial. Prior to the Criminal Justice Act 2003 they had been increasingly questioned by

18–011

---

[43] M. Zander and P. Henderson, RCCJ Research Study No.19 (London, 1993), para.4.6.1.

[44] M. Zander and P. Henderson, RCCJ Research Study No.19 (London, 1993), para.4.6.5.

[45] M. Zander and P. Henderson, RCCJ Research Study No.19 (London, 1993), para.4.6.4. No guidance was given to the judges on the meaning of these terms.

[46] M. Zander and P. Henderson, RCCJ Research Study No.19 (London, 1993), para.4.6.6.

[47] M. Zander and P. Henderson, RCCJ Research Study No.19 (London, 1993). Interestingly, the judges differed from the defence barristers in their perceptions of how frequently the defence introduced the convictions (81% of cases compared to 60% of cases).

[48] These were 2 of the cases in which the accused lost the shield against cross-examination on his record.

[49] M. Zander and P. Henderson, RCCJ Research Study No.19 (London, 1993), para.4.6.8.

sceptical commentators,[50] and in its Consultation Paper the Law Commission had subjected them to detailed scrutiny.[51] It is useful to state these assumptions in summary form to establish the relationships between them. The first was that a person's character is unitary and indivisible, so that there is a link between behaviour in different contexts. Accordingly it might be relevant to adduce evidence or cross-examine an accused about an offence of a different type from the offence charged. The second derived logically from the first and claimed that a connection exists between criminal behaviour and truthfulness on oath; in other words, an accused's bad disposition is relevant to his credibility as a witness. The third was that juries would understand and apply a judicial direction to use evidence of the accused's bad character only for certain purposes, such as relevance to the accused's credibility, and not to his guilt of the offence charged. The old law has gone, but these assumptions remain relevant to understanding the scheme for bad character evidence introduced by the Criminal Justice Act 2003.

1. *The divisibility of character*

18–012 The common law took the straightforward view that a person's character is indivisible. Thus, if a defendant claimed to have a good character and referred to one particular type of good behaviour, the prosecution could refute the claim by cross-examining him on misconduct in another respect.[52] As the Law Commission suggested, this view seemed to be founded on the theory that a person's character consists of certain personality traits that remain consistent across different situations. Accordingly, a person who could be described as "dishonest" on the basis of certain examples of dishonest behaviour (say, convictions for theft) might reliably be expected to act dishonestly in different situations. In this way evidence of bad behaviour in one context rebutted claims of good behaviour in another context.

Modern psychology, however, has rejected both the simplicity and the universality of this approach. The preferred view now is that even if character traits do exist they are at best unreliable predictors of behaviour. Rather, behaviour is conceived to be "a function of both disposition and situation, and their mutual interaction".[53] Some people may behave more consistently across a variety of situations than others, so that factors in situations that result in behavioural changes in one person may not affect another. Even then prediction of the behaviour of a given individual based on how he has behaved in the past is fraught with uncertainty. The Australian Law Reform Commission has said that valid predictions are unlikely unless the individual is placed in similar situations,[54] and its view is echoed by the New Zealand Law Commission, which

---

[50] See R. J. C. Munday, "Reflections on the Criminal Evidence Act 1898" [1985] C.L.J. 62; S. M. Davies, "Evidence of Character to Prove Conduct: A Reassessment of Relevancy" (1991) 27 Crim. Law Bull. 504. See also, more generally, Zuckerman, *Principles*, Ch.13.

[51] Law Com. CP 141.

[52] *Winfield* (1939) 27 Cr.App.R. 139 at 141 per Humphreys J.; *Stirland v DPP* [1944] A.C. 315 at 326 per Viscount Simon L.C.

[53] Davies, "Evidence of Character" (1991) 27 Crim. Law Bull. 504, 518.

[54] ALRC Report No.26 (1985), Vol.1 para.394.

summarised the findings of the psychological research by saying "true predictive value is dependent upon a number of instances of conduct and a degree of similarity between the situations".[55]

This does not go quite so far as to destroy the claim that character is indivisible. It does not repudiate outright the notion that valid inferences may be drawn from evidence of misconduct in one context about a person's misconduct in a different context. However, it highlights the lack of confidence with which such inferences can be made and reinforces the need for a principle that directs trial judges to examine the probative value of the other misconduct very carefully.

A further feature of the psychological research also requires emphasis. The Law Commission pointed to a consistent finding about the way in which people interpret the behaviour of others. This is the so-called "halo" effect, meaning that people have a tendency:

    18–013

> "to form a complete, integrated impression of another person's personality, even where only limited information about that person is available to them. Thus the person is presumed to have attributes that fit with what is known, but that he or she may or may not have."[56]

In this way certain character traits might be ascribed to individuals based on expectations of how individuals of that type (the typecasting being made on the partial information available) might be expected to behave. Such a psychological process would be consistent with the story-telling model of factfinding discussed in Ch.4. Factfinders who construct stories to account for the evidence in a case must create the characters that drive the stories, and we have already seen how factfinders may supply "missing" parts of the evidence on the basis of their own knowledge and experience. We must expect therefore that factfinders will tend to round out the characters in their narratives with assumptions about the goals and actions of those characters. If those assumptions include ideas about the indivisibility of character and the predictive value of certain character traits, the scope for prejudice arising from evidence of other misconduct is obvious.

2. The relationship between other misconduct and untruthfulness on oath

It follows from the above that the relationship between other misconduct and the accused's credibility as a witness is likely to be at best contingent and uncertain. There is little psychological support for the proposition that possession of a criminal record is indicative of a propensity to lie on oath, irrespective of the type of crime involved. On the other hand, if there is evidence that the accused has lied on oath in similar situations previously and has done this more than once, a much more confident prediction might be made about the likelihood of a further repetition of this conduct. Between these two extremes are two other types of case that have given rise to much discussion, and at one time a striking divergence of view in the Court of Appeal.[57] These cases concern first,

    18–014

---

[55] See Law Com. CP 141 para.6.16.
[56] Law Com. CP 141 para.6.19.
[57] *Watts* (1983) 77 Cr.App.R. 126 CA;

convictions for offences of dishonesty and, secondly, convictions for offences similar to the offence for which the accused is currently on trial.

Taking convictions for dishonesty first, these have sometimes been regarded as particularly relevant to issues of credibility.[58] This is on the basis that such convictions demonstrate a lack of probity on the part of the accused and/or a willingness to use deception to achieve his ends. These character traits are assumed to have predictive value on the question whether the accused is likely to lie on oath. Munday disputed this assumption, claiming that "the link between 'commercial' and 'testimonial' dishonesty is weak, if not pure juridical fiction".[59] The Law Commission was much more equivocal, saying simply that convictions for dishonesty may be relevant in some circumstances.[60] This bland statement contrasted curiously with the finding of the research study on mock juries set out in the Consultation Paper:

> "In the Oxford study it was found that, if mock jurors were told that the defendant had a previous conviction for a dishonesty offence, they were not significantly more likely to say that they disbelieved his evidence, or that he was untrustworthy, or that he was more likely than other men of his age and background to lie on oath to a court of law."[61]

Perhaps there was a feeling that the finding was counter-intuitive, although in fact it cohered with the view that behaviour in different situations may not be consistent.

18–015   Previous convictions for similar offences have a greater degree of relevance to the accused's credibility as a witness, but it is important to understand the nature of the argument involved. Suppose that the defendant is charged with indecent assault on a woman. In his evidence he denies the charge and explains police evidence of a confession by him as a fabrication. Suppose further that in consequence the law permits the prosecution to put to him his previous convictions for indecent assault on children. A factfinder might well reason that the convictions show that the defendant is the type of man who would commit an assault on a woman and therefore that he cannot be believed when he denies such an offence. Note that this reasoning necessarily entails an inference as to the defendant's propensity to commit a type of offence; the factfinder then draws a conclusion from that propensity about the defendant's truthfulness on oath in denying the commission of another offence showing the same propensity. Propensity reasoning is invited in all cases where the defendant's past convictions are adduced on the issue of his credibility. The more similar the past offences the more convincing the reasoning, precisely because of the argument discussed above about consistency of behaviour across different situations. Yet it is also this type of case that presented the greatest danger that the factfinder would reason directly from proof of propensity to a conclusion that the defendant was guilty of the offence charged because he was the type of person who committed this type

---

[58] See *Watts* (1983) 77 Cr.App.R. 126 CA.
[59] Munday, "Reflections on the Criminal Evidence Act 1898" [1985] C.L.J. 62, 71.
[60] Law Com. CP 141 para.6.63.
[61] Law Com. CP 141, para.6.34. See further S. Lloyd-Bostock, "The Effects on Juries of Hearing About the Defendant's Previous Criminal Record: A Simulation Study" [2000] Crim. L.R. 734; "The Effects on Magistrates of Knowing of a Defendant's Criminal Record" in Law Com. 273 Appendix A.

of offence. This seemed to be borne out by the Law Commission's research, which showed that a recent conviction for an offence similar to that charged significantly increased the rate of conviction.[62]

3. *Judicial directions on the use of previous convictions and the distinction between issues of guilt and credibility*

The distinction between the guilt and the credibility of the defendant has been much criticised,[63] and much of the criticism is justified. However, the relationship between guilt and credibility is more complex than the critics sometimes allow. The issues of whether the defendant is guilty of the offence charged and whether the defendant's testimony is credible are conceptually different questions. Moreover there is no necessary direct connection between these issues. For example, suppose that D1 and D2, charged with robbery, both give evidence of an alibi and assert that they are persons whose word can be trusted. The prosecution then cross-examine D1 on his previous inconsistent statement to the police about his whereabouts at the time of the offence and D2 on his previous convictions for perjury. The effect of the cross-examinations may be to persuade the factfinder that in neither case can the alibi be believed, but it would be a fallacy to conclude without more that either D1 or D2 was guilty of the offence in question. Before the factfinder could make the connection between a false alibi and guilt the factfinder would need to rule out other motives for lying; the false alibi might, for example, have resulted from the desire of the defendants to conceal other discreditable but non-criminal behaviour.[64] In this type of case the relationship between the defendant's guilt and his credibility as a witness is therefore contingent and indirect. Further facts need to be found before an adverse conclusion as to guilt can follow from an adverse conclusion as to credibility. In these circumstances, and given that perjury and robbery are dissimilar crimes, a direction that D2's convictions for perjury are relevant to the question of his credibility as a witness, but should be ignored in considering his guilt of robbery, makes logical sense.

The connection between guilt and credibility may, however, be much more direct. For example, the defendant's defence may be of the "confession and avoidance type", such as self-defence or duress. If the factfinder rejects the exculpatory part of the defendant's testimony as incredible, perhaps on the basis of the defendant's repeated use of these defences when accused of offences of violence, the defendant will thereby stand to be convicted on the confessional part of the testimony. Another type of direct connection occurs where there is a straight conflict of testimony between a complainant and a defendant on whether the defendant did a particular act, such as a sexual assault, when they were alone together. A rejection of the defendant's denial of the act as incredible leads

18–016

---

[62] Law Com. CP 141, para.6.61. This seems to be true for magistrates as well as juries: see the studies cited by Lloyd-Bostock, "The Effects on Juries" [2000] Crim. L.R. 734.

[63] See, for a valuable critique, R. Munday, "The Paradox of Cross-Examination to Credit–Simply too Close for Comfort" [1994] C.L.J. 303.

[64] For further discussion of the process of inferential reasoning see Ch.4; and for the use of the accused's lies as supporting evidence of guilt, see Ch.3.

directly to the conclusion that he is guilty on the evidence of the complainant. In these cases a direction that distinguishes between use of a criminal record as going to credibility but not to guilt will be hard to understand. To a lay factfinder these questions will look like two sides of the same coin. It will be even more mystifying for the factfinder where the record is for similar offences to the one charged.

D. THE COMMON LAW: EVIDENCE OF CHARACTER IN CIVIL CASES

18–017   Questions of evidence of character can arise in civil cases. As well as issues about the character of witnesses that may be relevant to their credibility,[65] issues can arise about the admissibility of similar fact evidence against the parties to the proceedings. The general rule applies that all evidence must have logical relevance to the facts in issue, and this requirement may enable the court to dispose of some claims for the admission of evidence on the ground of irrelevance or marginal relevance to the issues.[66] In other cases the nature of the cause of action may actually require evidence of patterns of behaviour,[67] or suggest the need for evidence of multiple instances of conduct to prove negligent practice[68] or other violation of right.[69] However, outside such cases there remains a question of the degree of relevance of similar fact evidence necessary for its admission, and whether the law should adopt the same strictness towards such evidence that it does in criminal cases.

At first sight the arguments for exclusion of similar fact evidence in civil cases seem much weaker than in criminal cases. There is rarely a jury, so the dangers of reasoning and moral prejudice are that much less, and the consequences arising from the use of unfairly prejudicial evidence in terms of stigma and punishment are absent or much reduced. While accepting these points as generally true it is important to remember that civil cases are not a homogeneous group. Some are civil in form but in substance are analogous in many respects to criminal proceedings. Disciplinary proceedings concerned with charges of serious professional misconduct are a good example. Here the consequences attached to a finding of guilt, in terms of adverse publicity, loss of reputation and loss of livelihood, may be equally as serious as those attached to a conviction. In *Lanford v General Medical Council*,[70] the Privy Council accepted without question a submission that in disciplinary proceedings before the General Medical Council the relevant legal principles were those applicable to a criminal trial. Hence the criminal law rules applied to the admission of similar fact evidence; this meant that the testimony of two female complainants was admissible for the purpose of

---

[65] See Ch.14.
[66] See, e.g. *British Coal Corp v Dennis Rye Ltd (No.2)* [1988] 1 W.L.R. 1113 (plaintiff's evidence of fraudulent overcharging by the defendant for similar services provided on other occasions rejected). Evidence of good character of the parties to civil cases is usually rejected as irrelevant: see, e.g. *Attorney-General v Radloff* (1854) 10 Exch. 84.
[67] As in discrimination cases: see *West Midlands Passenger Executive v Singh* [1988] 2 All E.R. 873.
[68] *Hales v Kerr* [1908] 2 K.B. 601 (three customers of the same barber contracting ringworm).
[69] See, e.g. *Brown v Eastern and Midlands Rly Co* (1889) 22 Q.B.D. 391.
[70] *Lanford v General Medical Council* [1990] 1 A.C. 13 PC.

mutual corroboration if, but only if, their evidence showed striking similarities.[71] The strictness of this test will presumably be relaxed in future in line with the less demanding degree of relevance now required in criminal proceedings.[72]

Where factors that make the case analogous to a criminal trial are not present, the test for the admissibility of similar fact evidence in criminal cases does not apply. The principles for civil cases were authoritatively reviewed by the House of Lords in the leading case of *O'Brien v Chief Constable of South Wales Police*.[73] The claimant brought an action against the defendant alleging misfeasance in public office and malicious prosecution. He claimed that two officers of the defendant's police force had acted with deliberate and flagrant impropriety to "frame" him for a murder for which he had been convicted and served 11 years in prison before the conviction was quashed by the Court of Appeal. To support his claim he wished to adduce evidence that the officers had acted with similar impropriety on other occasions. Upholding the admissibility of the evidence, the House of Lords held that there was no warrant for introducing into civil proceedings a test of enhanced relevance or substantial probative value applicable in criminal cases.[74] Nor was it the case, as the defendant had argued, that similar fact evidence was only admissible in a civil suit if it was likely to be reasonably conclusive of a primary issue in the proceedings. To adopt either of these tests would build into civil procedure an inflexibility that would be inappropriate and undesirable. According to Lord Phillips, the test is simply whether the similar fact evidence is relevant to the issues in the action; it will be admissible if it is potentially probative of an issue.

Although the House rejected a general standard of enhanced relevance, it also emphasised that the test of admissibility is flexible, and will take account of the "costs" of admitting similar fact evidence. This seems to have been regarded as a separate exercise from the initial judgment of the logical relevance of the similar fact evidence. After setting out the test of relevance Lord Phillips went on to refer to "policy" considerations that the case management judge should bear in mind. Under the Civil Procedure Rules a civil court now has a discretionary power, under r.32.1(2), to exclude evidence that would otherwise be admissible. The court must exercise the power, as it must exercise any power under the Rules, in order to further the overriding objective of dealing with cases justly. This objective includes ensuring that the parties are on an equal footing, saving expense, and ensuring that the case is dealt with expeditiously and fairly. In relation to fairness, Lord Phillips said that similar fact evidence will not necessarily carry a risk of causing unfair prejudice to the party against whom it is admitted. But if it does carry such a risk, the judge should consider whether that is disproportionate to its relevance, particularly in a jury trial. The risk would need to be justified by the "probative cogency" of the similar fact evidence. Other factors that will need to be considered include the danger of creating side or

18–018

---

[71] Applying *DPP v Boardman* [1975] A.C. 421 HL.

[72] The *Boardman* standard was relaxed at common law by the House of Lords in *DPP v P* [1991] 2 A.C. 447, and was relaxed still further by Criminal Justice Act 2003 s.101(1)(d), as discussed in Ch.19.

[73] *O'Brien v Chief Constable of South Wales Police* [2005] UKHL 26; [2005] 2 All E.R. 931.

[74] This was a requirement of the *common law* in criminal cases. It is not a requirement for the admission of bad character evidence under s.101(1)(d) of the Criminal Justice Act 2003.

collateral issues that might unbalance the trial and distract the factfinder, the burden on the party against whom the evidence is directed in terms of time, cost and resources, and the difficulties for witnesses to the similar fact events, particularly if they occurred some time ago.

In reaching the decision in *O'Brien v Chief Constable of South Wales Police* the House of Lords approved the earlier decision of the Court of Appeal in *Mood Music Publishing Co Ltd v De Wolfe Ltd*.[75] This case concerned an action for breach of copyright in which the defence was that no copying had taken place and that any resemblance between the defendants' published song and the plaintiffs' song was coincidental. The Court of Appeal held that the plaintiffs had been rightly permitted to call evidence of other works published by the defendants bearing a marked similarity to works in which other people owned the copyright. One of these instances was an example set up by agents of the plaintiffs specifically to trap the defendants. Lord Denning M.R. commented that the civil courts had taken a similar line to the criminal cases on similar fact evidence but had not been so cautious about admitting such evidence. He went on:

> "In civil cases the courts will admit evidence of similar facts if it is logically probative, that is, if it is logically relevant in determining the matter which is in issue: provided that it is not oppressive or unfair to the other side; and also that the other side has fair notice of it and is able to deal with it."[76]

It is noticeable that this statement makes no reference to prejudice. The statement lists oppression, unfairness and surprise as grounds for exclusion. Lord Denning M.R. apparently regarded these as factors forming elements of the judge's decision on admissibility as a matter of law. He did not refer to any discretion in civil cases to exclude otherwise admissible evidence, and it seems clear that no such discretion existed at common law.[77] Now that the Civil Procedure Rules have introduced such a discretion, it seems from *O'Brien v Chief Constable of South Wales Police* that the courts will treat these factors as material to the exercise of the discretion, and not as part of the decision on the relevance of the evidence. The terms "oppression" and "unfairness" were not further defined in *Mood Music Publishing Co Ltd v De Wolfe Ltd*. In applying the test stated the Court of Appeal thought that it was clear that the evidence had probative value: similarity might be due to coincidence in one case, but it was unlikely to be so in four cases. In the language of some of the old criminal law cases this was evidence of "system" adduced to prove deliberate wrongdoing. It is implicit in the Court of Appeal's decision that it was not oppressive or unfair to admit the evidence, notwithstanding that one example of the similar misconduct had been procured by the entrapment of the defendants by an agent provocateur of the

---

[75] *Music Mood Publishing Co Ltd v De Wolfe Ltd* [1976] Ch.119 CA.

[76] *Music Mood Publishing Co Ltd v De Wolfe Ltd* [1976] Ch.119 at 127. In *Thorpe v Chief Constable of the Greater Manchester Police* [1989] 2 All E.R. 827 Dillon L.J. expressed the view that Lord Denning's statement did not apply to a civil *jury* trial, where the rule in criminal cases stated in *Boardman v DPP* [1975] A.C. 421 should be applied. This dictum was not disapproved in *O'Brien v Chief Constable of South Wales Police*, but it cannot stand with the principles stated by the House of Lords.

[77] See Ch.3, and, for further discussion, see R. Pattenden, "The Discretionary Exclusion of Relevant Evidence in English Civil Proceedings" (1997) 1 E. & P. 361.

plaintiffs. In *Berger v Raymond & Son Ltd*,[78] Warner J. excluded some of the plaintiff's evidence of other alleged forgeries of documents by the defendant as "oppressive", because it was adduced at very short notice, had doubtful probative value and would place a heavy burden on the defendant to investigate it.

E. THE COMMON LAW: GOOD CHARACTER OF THE ACCUSED IN CRIMINAL CASES

Section B of this chapter discussed the relevance of evidence of good character.   **18–019**
The common law has recognised for many years that in criminal proceedings good character is relevant to the issue of the accused's guilt, and that it is also relevant to the issue of the accused's credibility if he gives evidence, or if evidence is adduced of his pre-trial statements or answers to questions. The issue of how evidence of good character may be rebutted is dealt with in Ch.19. As we shall see, s.101(1)(f) of the Criminal Justice Act 2003 provides for the admission of evidence of bad character to correct a false impression given by the defendant. In this section we are concerned with the use of good character evidence and the directions that judges must give about it.

A surprising amount of case law has developed around this question. The subject has become a technical one, with some refinements and distinctions that are dubious, if not downright disreputable.[79] The starting-point for discussion is the leading case of *Vye*.[80] In that case the Court of Appeal was faced with a series of decisions that had given rise to much uncertainty and some inconsistency on how far a trial judge had a duty to give a direction on good character and on the form that good character directions should take.[81] The court attempted to resolve the problems by laying down a set of guidelines for trial judges. Lord Taylor C.J. summarised the guidelines as follows:

(1) "A direction as to the relevance of his good character to a defendant's credibility is to be given where he has testified or made pre-trial answers or statements." This is often called the first limb of a *Vye* direction. The direction must be given even where the defendant, on his own admission, has told lies to the police in interview.[82]

(2) "A direction as to the relevance of his good character to the likelihood of his having committed the offence charged is to be given, whether or not he has testified, or made pre-trial answers or statements." This is the second limb of a *Vye* direction.

(3) "Where defendant A of good character is jointly tried with defendant B of bad character, (1) and (2) still apply."

---

[78] *Berger v Raymond & Son Ltd* [1984] 1 W.L.R. 625.
[79] See R. Munday, "What Constitutes a Good Character?" [1997] Crim. L.R. 247 for an effective critique.
[80] *Vye* [1993] 1 W.L.R. 471 CA.
[81] Starting with *Berrada* (1990) 91 Cr.App.R. 131 CA.
[82] *Kabariti* (1991) 92 Cr.App.R. 362 CA, a decision that some may feel is generous, to say the least.

18–020   When Lord Taylor C.J. set out para.(3) he had in mind a case where B is in fact of bad character, but adduces no evidence either way about his character. Lord Taylor said that in such a case the judge has a discretion whether to make any comment at all about B's character. Depending on the circumstances it might be best to say nothing at all, while in other cases it might be appropriate to warn the jury about the danger of speculating about B's character in the absence of any evidence. Where there is positive evidence before the jury of B's bad character, say in the form of evidence of B's previous convictions, the use to which that evidence can be put will depend on the "gateway" through which it was admitted[83] and its relevance in the case.

A *Vye* direction does not require any particular form of words, but the judge should make clear to the jury that good character is a factor that they should take into account when considering either purpose to which evidence of good character is relevant. In this sense the jury do not have an option whether to take it into account[84] in deciding either whether they believe the defendant's evidence[85] or in deciding whether he is guilty of the offence.[86] The relevance of good character should be explained, namely that it may make it more likely that the defendant is telling the truth in his evidence and admissible out-of-court statements, and less likely that he is guilty of the offence charged.

"Good" character is not the same as a wholly unblemished record. The courts have given this concept a somewhat generous interpretation. First, as noted above, the right to a *Vye* direction is not necessarily forfeited by admitted lies to the police. Secondly, the defendant does not necessarily lose the right by admitting that he was guilty of other offences[87] and/or discreditable conduct in relation to the events that are the subject of the charge.[88] Thirdly, even where the defendant has previous convictions, if those convictions are old or trivial,[89] it is open to the trial judge to disregard them for the purposes of the character direction. However, these indulgent tendencies have been checked in two respects. The House of Lords has made it clear that the mere absence of convictions does not give an absolute right to a *Vye* direction. In *Aziz*[90] the House of Lords confirmed, obiter, that the judge has a residual discretion not to give the good character direction at all if the defendant's claim to a good character is spurious and it would be "an insult to common sense" to give the direction. This would be the case, for example, where the defendant has no previous convictions but is shown beyond reasonable doubt to have been guilty of serious criminal

---

[83] Under s.101 of the Criminal Justice Act 2003: see Ch.19.
[84] As the Court of Appeal confirmed in *R. v CM* [2009] EWCA Crim 158.
[85] *Gray* [2004] 2 Cr.App.R. 30 CA.
[86] *Boyson* [1991] Crim. L.R. 274 CA; *Miah* [1997] 2 Cr.App.R. 12 CA.
[87] *Richens* [1993] 4 All E.R. 877 CA.
[88] *Durbin* [1995] 2 Cr.App.R. 84 CA. This is another generous decision. The defendant was charged with illegally importing a very large amount of cannabis. He admitted to lying to two prosecution witnesses in connection with the whereabouts of his co-accused, to lying about his movements when interviewed about his alleged involvement in the drug-smuggling, and to his involvement in smuggling other goods during the relevant journey in Europe. He also had two spent convictions for offences of dishonesty. Can such a person really be said to have a "good" character?
[89] *R. v H* [1994] Crim. L.R. 205 CA.
[90] *Aziz* [1996] 1 A.C. 41 HL.

behaviour similar to the offence charged.[91] Secondly, in cases where the blemish is not so serious, other authorities emphasise that the appropriate course may be to give the *Vye* direction and then to qualify it by reference to the other proved or possible misconduct that has emerged during the trial.[92]

These principles have been discussed by the Court of Appeal on a number of occasions. The leading case is *Gray*,[93] where Rix L.J. set out the framework of the law:

"(1) The primary rule is that a person of previous good character must be given a full direction covering both credibility and propensity. Where there are no further acts to complicate the position, such a direction is mandatory and should be unqualified (*Vye, Aziz*);

(2) If a defendant has a previous conviction which, either because of its age or nature, may entitle him to be treated as of effective good character, the trial judge has a discretion so to treat him, and if he does so the defendant is entitled to a *Vye* direction; but

(3) Where the previous conviction can only be regarded as irrelevant or of no significance in relation to the offence charged, that discretion ought to be exercised in favour of treating the defendant as of good character (*H, Durbin* and, to the extent that it cited *H* with apparent approval, *Aziz*). In such a case the defendant is again entitled to a *Vye* direction. It would seem to be consistent with principle (4) below that, where there is room for uncertainty as to how a defendant of effective good character should be treated, a judge would be entitled to give an appropriately modified direction.

(4) Where a defendant of previous good character, whether absolute or we would suggest effective, has been shown at trial, whether by admission or otherwise, to be guilty of criminal conduct,[94] the prima facie rule of practice is to deal with this by qualifying a *Vye* direction rather than by withholding it (*Vye, Durbin, Aziz*); but

(5) In such a case, there remains a narrowly circumscribed residual discretion to withhold a good character direction in whole, or presumably in part, where it would make no sense or would be meaningless or absurd or an insult to commonsense, to do otherwise (*Zoppola-Barraza* and dicta in *Durbin* and *Aziz*) ..."

The application of the principles is illustrated by a number of recent cases. In *R. v PD*,[95] D was charged with offences of anal rape on his wife. He had no previous convictions but admitted having been violent towards his wife from time to time. The trial judge indicated that he would give a modified good character direction on the propensity limb,[96] but did not in the event do so. Quashing D's convictions, the Court of Appeal cited principle (4) from *Gray* and commented that character directions are particularly important where a verdict will turn on whether a complainant or a defendant is believed. In *King and Provan*,[97] King

---

[91] *Aziz* [1996] 1 A.C. 41 at 62. *Durbin* [1995] 2 Cr.App.R. 84 CA was not cited to the House of Lords in *Aziz*, but the effect of both cases, in the light of their citation of *Zoppola-Barraza* [1994] Crim. L.R. 833 CA, is to support a distinction between the defendant's admitted misconduct on the occasion giving rise to the charge (which does not lose the right to a good character direction) and misconduct on other occasions (which may do). The merit of this distinction is not immediately apparent.

[92] *Aziz* [1996] 1 A.C. 41; *Hickmet* [1996] Crim.L.R. 588 CA.

[93] *Gray* [2004] EWCA Crim 1074; [2004] 2 Cr.App.R. 30, followed in *R. v PD* [2012] EWCA Crim 19; (2012) 1 Cr.App.R. 33, and *GAI v R.* [2012] EWCA Crim 2033.

[94] A penalty notice for disorder does not count: *Hamer* [2010] EWCA Crim 2053. It is not a conviction or a caution, and does not involve an admission of guilt.

[95] *R. v PD* [2012] EWCA Crim 19.

[96] The reason for not including the credibility limb in the proposed direction was that D had described himself in interview as "non-violent", and he had also admitted acts of dishonesty relating to his financial affairs.

[97] *King and Provan* [2012] EWCA Crim 805.

was charged with conspiracy to supply drugs and possession of firearms. He had no convictions for drugs or firearms offences, but had two convictions for other minor offences and he admitted recent dealing in stolen goods. The judge gave the propensity limb of the good character direction, but declined to give the credibility limb. Upholding the direction, the Court of Appeal held that, following *Aziz,* the judge was entitled to modify the direction in the light of D's admitted dishonesty. In *GAI v R*,[98] D was charged with offences of rape of a child under 13. He had a conviction for burglary 28 years earlier and a police caution three years earlier in relation to a domestic incident of common assault on his wife. On a retrial the judge refused to give a good character direction on the ground that the facts of the incident giving rise to the caution were relevant to both his guilt and credibility in relation to the offences charged. Allowing the appeal, the Court of Appeal disagreed and held that D should have been treated as a man of "effective" good character, so that the judge should have given a modified *Vye* direction. The importance of such a direction could not be dismissed since the case turned on an evaluation of the evidence of the complainant and D respectively. It seems clear therefore that the courts will continue to scrutinise the necessity for good character directions, and their terms, with some care. This will be especially so in cases turning on credibility contests between the victim and the defendant, of which of course sexual offences provide the paradigm example.

An interesting problem can arise more often now that evidence of the bad character of a defendant is more freely admissible under the Criminal Justice Act 2003. It is possible for someone to have no previous convictions, and thus be entitled on the face of it to a good character direction, and at the same time to have bad character evidence, other than convictions, admitted against him, which might require a direction as to its relevance to both propensity and credibility. Clearly the judge cannot be expected to give contradictory directions. In *Doncaster*,[99] the Court of Appeal addressed the issue by proposing that the bad character direction might be modified so as to allow the jury to choose which type of character evidence weighed with them more:

> "We consider that in the post-2003 Act world, where bad character directions as to propensity have more frequently become necessary, even in the absence of previous convictions, it may be possible similarly to tailor a modified bad character direction, along the following lines. Thus when a judge is directing the jury about the relevance of bad character to propensity or propensities, he could remind them that the defendant has no previous convictions and say that, in the ordinary case, where there was no evidence of bad character, a defendant of no previous convictions would have been entitled to a direction that the jury should consider that that counted in his favour on the questions of both propensity and credibility; as it was, it was for the jury to consider which counted with them more—the absence of previous convictions or the evidence of bad character; and if the former then they should take that into account in favour of the defendant, and if the latter, then they would be entitled to take that into account against him."[100]

---

[98] *GAI v R.* [2012] EWCA Crim 2033.
[99] *Doncaster* [2008] EWCA Crim 5.
[100] *Doncaster* [2008] EWCA Crim 5 at [43].

F. BAD CHARACTER OF THE ACCUSED IN CRIMINAL CASES: THE BACKGROUND TO THE CRIMINAL JUSTICE ACT 2003

1. *The common law similar fact rule*

The law that the Criminal Justice Act 2003 replaced was extensive and complex.   **18–021**
It is not necessary to analyse it in detail, but a summary of its structure and main
principles is useful in understanding the scheme of the Act and the extent to
which it set the law on bad character evidence on a new path. We will deal first
with the common law similar fact rule, which regulated the admissibility for the
prosecution of evidence of the accused's bad character and other misconduct as
evidence of his guilt of the offence charged.

The starting-point of the law was that evidence that tended to show that the
accused was of bad character and/or was guilty of misconduct on other occasions
was prima facie inadmissible. This was not because such evidence was thought to
be logically irrelevant; rather it was assumed to be unfairly prejudicial to the
accused. In one of the leading cases, *DPP v Boardman*,[101] Lord Wilberforce
commented that the admission of "similar fact evidence" (using the term in its
broad and misleading sense) was exceptional. In previous editions of this book it
was suggested that this rule of prima facie exclusion applied whenever a
factfinder was asked to use reasoning that required or invited a finding that the
accused had a bad character and/or had committed other misconduct. This was
because in all such cases the risks arose of both reasoning prejudice and moral
prejudice. The essential question therefore was whether the prosecution were
asserting that the evidence showed that the accused had committed other offences
or other discreditable conduct, or that the accused had a propensity to commit
offences or discreditable acts. Proof of those facts might be the basis of an
argument that because the defendant had a general, or a particular, criminal
disposition he was therefore more likely to have committed the offence
charged.[102] Alternatively, proof of those facts might be an integral part of a
different type of argument not depending on criminal disposition, such as the
unlikelihood of coincidence as the explanation for a mass of similar incriminating
circumstantial evidence, or a plurality of witnesses all testifying to similar acts by
the accused, where the function of the similar fact evidence was to provide
mutual corroboration of the witnesses.[103]

In some cases both types of argument were involved. In *West*,[104] four
witnesses testified that Rosemary West had taken part with her husband Fred in
sadistic sexual acts on them in the cellar of the Wests' house. The prosecution

---

[101] *DPP v Boardman* [1975] A.C. 421.

[102] It was sometimes claimed that such an argument from disposition was a "forbidden chain of
reasoning" (per Lord Hailsham in *DPP v Boardman* [1975] A.C. 421, referring to a famous statement
of principle by Lord Herschell in *Makin v Att-Gen for New South Wales* [1894] A.C. 57). But it was
clear that a complete ban on arguments from disposition was neither workable nor desirable, as Lord
Cross conceded in *Boardman*. A number of cases decided under the similar fact rule were explicable
only on the basis that evidence showing the accused's propensity had a high degree of relevance on
the facts of the case and was rightly admitted.

[103] As in *DPP v Boardman* [1975] A.C. 421; and *DPP v P* [1991] 2 A.C. 447.

[104] *West* [1996] 2 Cr.App.R. 374 CA.

adduced this evidence in support of the allegation that the accused had participated in the murder by Fred West (which he had admitted before committing suicide) of a number of other girls whose bodies had been found buried on the premises. The argument for the relevance of this evidence takes the following form. The testimony of each witness was used first to establish that the others were telling the truth by negativing the coincidence that each had independently come up with strikingly similar false stories. From this conclusion it could be inferred that Rosemary West had a disposition to engage in concert with her husband in the sexual and sadistic abuse of young girls in the cellar of their house for their joint pleasure. The other evidence of the killings carried out by Fred West showed that they were part of or were followed by the same type of sexual and sadistic abuse. Given Rosemary West's propensity, it would be an extraordinary coincidence if all these killings had occurred without her participation.

18–022 In contrast, the rule of prima facie exclusion of similar fact evidence did *not* apply where prosecution evidence revealed as an incidental side-effect that the accused might have committed other offences or might be of bad character, but proof of these facts was not part of the purpose of adducing the evidence. An example would be where the prosecution wanted to prove that the defendant knew a particular fact at the time of the offence, and adduced evidence that he had been told the fact at an earlier time when he was in prison. His presence in prison shows that he may have committed other offences, but this is not the purpose of admitting the evidence. The point is whether and when he knew the fact, and the reference to his presence in prison simply identifies the occasion. The occasion might equally have been when he was in hospital.[105] In such cases no *reasoning* prejudice would arise because no reasoning involving bad character and/or other misconduct was entailed. The test of admissibility in such cases was therefore the normal test of relevance. The risk of *moral* prejudice from incidental revelation of the accused's record was left appropriately to the general exclusionary discretion. This discretion is discussed further below.

18–023 The prima facie rule of exclusion for similar fact evidence was subject to a broad proviso that the evidence was admissible if it had a sufficient degree of relevance to the issues in the case. The test for admissibility was authoritatively stated by the House of Lords in *DPP v P*[106] and was confirmed by the Lords in *R. v H*.[107] The test was whether the evidence had a sufficient degree of relevance to make it just to admit the evidence notwithstanding its prejudicial effect. The prejudice in question was reasoning prejudice, as Lord Cross made clear in *Boardman* when he said that the risk of the jury overestimating the probative value of similar fact evidence was the reason for the rule against it.[108] This meant that when the judge was deciding on the admissibility of similar fact evidence he proceeded on an assumption[109] that there was always a risk that the probative value of the

---

[105] cf. *Miller* [1952] 2 All E.R. 667 CCA.
[106] *DPP v P* [1991] 2 A.C. 447.
[107] *R. v H* [1995] 2 A.C. 596.
[108] *Boardman* [1975] A.C. 421 at 456.
[109] This important point was well made by A. Palmer, "The Scope of the Similar Fact Rule" (1994) 16 Adel. L.R. 161.

evidence would be overestimated by the factfinder. The question for decision at that stage was whether the evidence had a high enough degree of relevance to make the risk of an overestimate negligible in the circumstances. The circumstances for this purpose were those that always apply when questions of sufficient relevance arise, namely the issue to which the similar fact evidence is directed and the state of the other evidence in the case. Part of the explanation for the extensive and complex case law on the similar fact rule is the need that the appellate courts felt to give guidance to trial judges and the legal profession on how the test of a sufficiently high degree of relevance should be applied in the infinite variety of cases that could arise.

On this analysis the role of the exclusionary discretion was to deal with the problem of moral prejudice.[110] But the test here needs careful formulation. It was not simply whether the risk of moral prejudice outweighed the probative value of the similar fact evidence. Viewed out of context, these are incommensurable factors that could not be meaningfully "balanced" in the way that the risk of reasoning prejudice could be set against judgments of degree of relevance. The necessary context for dealing with the risk of moral prejudice is the fairness of the trial as a whole, and the concern should be with the effect of such a risk on the moral authority of the trial verdict. This is why the test should be the one set out in s.78 of PACE, which applies to all evidence on which the prosecution proposes to rely.[111] It is whether in all the circumstances the admission of the similar fact evidence would carry such a significant risk of moral prejudice—of the jury convicting the accused for reasons unconnected with the probative value of the evidence—that the fairness of the trial would be substantially affected. This risk could of course be present even where the evidence had a high degree of relevance. An example is *Mackie*.[112] The defendant was charged with the manslaughter of a three-year-old boy. The boy had fallen downstairs, apparently while trying to escape from the defendant, from whom he feared excessive punishment. In order to show that the boy's fear of the defendant was reasonable the prosecution adduced evidence of previous assaults by the defendant on the boy. The judge directed the jury that this evidence was relevant only to the boy's state of mind immediately before he ran away from the defendant; the jury should not use it as evidence of the defendant's violent disposition towards the boy. It appears that the judge thought that the evidence was not subject to the similar fact rule, and he declined to exclude it in the exercise of his discretion. The Court of Appeal thought that the prejudicial effect of the evidence far outweighed its probative value,[113] apparently on the basis that the jury might well conclude that the defendant was a persistent child-batterer who was "*morally* responsible for the boy's death"[114] (emphasis added).

The respective roles of law and discretion in this analysis of similar fact evidence can thus be seen to be underpinned by the theory of legitimacy. It has

---

[110] T. R. S. Allan, "Some favourite fallacies about similar facts" (1988) 8 L.S. 35, 37–38.

[111] The potential application of s.78 to similar fact evidence was acknowledged in *R. v H* [1995] 2 A.C. 596 by Lord Mackay L.C. (at 612) and by Lord Nicholls (at 627); and by the Court of Appeal in *Johnson* [1995] 2 Cr.App.R. 41.

[112] *Mackie* (1973) 57 Cr.App.R. 453 CA.

[113] Although the court declined to interfere with the judge's decision.

[114] *Mackie* (1973) 57 Cr.App.R. 453 at 464.

been suggested in earlier chapters of this book that exclusionary rules of law may be appropriate for evidence that carries systemic risks of impairing the factual accuracy of verdicts. If a particular type of evidence presents difficulties for the factfinders who have to determine its probative value, because of the kind of evidence it is, then this may give prima facie reason for excluding all evidence of that type. The rule against hearsay may be explained on this ground, as discussed in Ch.16. An alternative technique for dealing with evidence of doubtful probative value is judicial education and instruction of the factfinder. This is the technique adopted for eyewitness identification evidence. Prosecution evidence tendered to prove bad character and/or other misconduct of the accused always has a risk that the factfinder may be the victim of reasoning prejudice which produces an overestimate of probative value. On this approach the law took a coherent view that the evidence should prima facie be excluded unless the prosecution could satisfy the judge that its probative value was such that the risk of an overestimate was negligible. This is how the familiar calculation of probative value and prejudicial effect should be understood. If the evidence had a sufficient degree of probative value to pass this test it should have been admitted on the usual justification that the admission of relevant evidence would promote the factual accuracy of decision-making.

18–024   However, this would be subject to the right of the accused to object that the admission of the evidence might, despite its probative value, so adversely affect the fairness of the proceedings that it ought not to be admitted. In the case of similar fact evidence exclusion would be justified on this ground if there were a significant risk that the factfinder would be morally prejudiced to the extent of convicting the accused irrespective of the probative value of the evidence. Normatively such an event would be exceptional and rare; it would envisage the factfinder ignoring or being distracted from the fundamental duty to determine the defendant's guilt of the offence charged on the evidence that he committed the offence charged. The greater the probative value of the similar fact evidence, the less the chance of this happening. This is why the defendant should have borne the burden of raising the issue of moral prejudice as a ground for exclusion of the evidence under s.78 of PACE.[115] Because any such risk depended on all the circumstances of the particular case it was appropriate for the trial judge, who had the "feel" of the whole case, to make the decision as an exercise of "discretion". This was discretion in a weak sense. If the judge concluded that the risk of moral prejudice was such as to compromise the fairness of the trial substantially, then the judge should have excluded the evidence as a matter of duty. The "discretion" consisted in the large scope for evaluation of the risk in the circumstances of the individual case.

No doubt in practice many trial judges felt unable or unwilling to distinguish consciously between the two types of prejudice. They probably preferred to make one global judgment that attempted to balance probative value against prejudice in whatever form. In such cases the rule of admissibility merged with the exclusionary discretion. The judge in effect applied the rule and exercised the discretion simultaneously. This helps to explain the confusion in some appellate

---

[115] On the location of the burden of persuasion under s.78, see Ch.3 para.3–041.

cases over the nature of the decision. Some cases referred to the judge's decision on admissibility as an exercise of discretion, whereas others talked of the application of a rule of law. The better view is that it was both. The Court of Appeal could choose to characterise it as one or the other depending on how willing the court was to interfere with the decision. No great harm was done by the elision of these stages of decision-making, but it is important not to lose sight of the fact that they were logically and theoretically distinct. It is also essential to remember that the exclusionary discretion was available in cases where the similar fact rule did not apply, but prosecution evidence incidentally disclosed that the defendant was of bad character and/or had been guilty of other misconduct.[116]

2. Cross-examination of the accused: The Criminal Evidence Act 1898 section 1(3)

The other part of the law that dealt with evidence of the accused's bad character and other misconduct was s.1(3)—previously 1(f)—of the Criminal Evidence Act 1898. This regulated cross-examination of the accused who elected to give evidence in his defence. Cross-examination of the accused is a topic that presents problems for the law of evidence. In one sense the accused is simply another witness in the trial when giving evidence about the facts in issue, and one might expect the normal rules governing the questioning of witnesses in court to apply.[117] On the other hand, the defendant is unlike any other witness in that he is still the accused and remains the object of the forensic enquiry. Accordingly, protective principles, such as the principle that generally prevents the prosecution adducing evidence of the accused's bad character, might still have a role to play. The result is that the law cannot escape having to make some accommodation between the principles of proof and the principles of protection against prejudice.

18–025

Section 1 of the Criminal Evidence Act 1898 made the accused for the first time a competent witness for the defence in all cases. Parliament acknowledged the special position of the accused by enacting a number of provisoes to s. 1. The first was the one noted in Ch. 13: the accused could be called as a witness in the proceedings against him only on his own application, so he was not compellable. The second—in subs. (2) of the 1898 Act and still in force—removes the privilege against self-incrimination for questions in cross-examination as to the offence charged. If the accused elects to testify in his defence he cannot refuse to answer questions in cross-examination on the ground that they might incriminate him. Otherwise he would be able to deny guilt and assert all manner of facts in defence without fear of having to respond to incriminating questions from the prosecution. This would place the accused in a very favourable position.

---

[116] A good example is evidence that the defendant was identified from police photographs. The similar fact rule did not apply because it was not part of the prosecution's purpose to prove that the defendant had been in trouble with the police; the probative value of the evidence would be the same if the witness had picked the defendant out from an exhibition of photographs at the National Portrait Gallery. Nevertheless, there is a possibility of moral prejudice that may make the evidence appropriate for discretionary exclusion.

[117] See Ch.14.

The third proviso related to cross-examination as to credit. This could involve questions as to bad character, including previous convictions for similar offences. The risk then would be that the factfinder might treat the previous convictions as relevant not to credibility but to guilt, reasoning via the accused's propensity to commit offences to an increased probability of guilt on this occasion. In this way the common law rule against evidence of bad character and other misconduct would simply be bypassed in any case where the accused elected to testify. Prejudicial evidence might come in via cross-examination, which the prosecution would not have been permitted to adduce in their evidence in chief. This problem might have been met by the grant of an immunity to the accused from cross-examination to credit, but then the accused would be in the privileged position of being able to make all kinds of allegations in the witness box without fear of having his own lack of credibility exposed.

18–026   Parliament's response to this issue took the form of an elaborate legislative compromise:

> "(3)   A person charged and called as a witness in pursuance of this Act shall not be asked, and if asked shall not be required to answer, any question tending to show that he has committed or been convicted of or been charged with any offence other than that wherewith he is then charged, or is of bad character, unless—
>
> (i)   the proof that he has committed or been convicted of such other offence is admissible evidence to show that he is guilty of the offence wherewith he is then charged; or
>
> (ii)   he has personally or by his advocate asked questions of the witnesses for the prosecution with a view to establish his own good character, or has given evidence of his good character, or the nature or conduct of the defence is such as to involve imputations on the character of the prosecutor or the witnesses for the prosecution [or the deceased victim of the alleged crime];[118] or
>
> (iii)   he has given evidence against any other person charged [in the same proceedings]."[119]

18–027   In summary this provision gave the accused a shield against certain types of potentially prejudicial questions. The accused could not be asked questions that showed previous convictions, the commission of other offences, previous charges or bad character. The shield could be lost in any of the four sets of circumstances specified in sub-provisoes (i), (ii) and (iii). The first of these operated independently of the way the accused conducted the defence and linked cross-examination of the accused on other misconduct to the rules on the admission of such evidence in chief. Sub-provisoes (ii) and (iii) indicated that the accused could lose the shield by the way in which he ran the defence. The first way was by adducing evidence of his good character, the second was by attacking the character of prosecution witnesses and the third was by giving evidence against a co-accused. In each of these three situations the protection of the shield was lost and the accused could be cross-examined on the matters otherwise prohibited. It is important to note that this consequence did not follow automatically. In the first place questions in cross-examination were still subject to the overriding requirement of relevance; the provisions of s.1(3) took effect

---

[118] Words in square brackets added by the Criminal Justice and Public Order Act 1994 s.31.
[119] Words in square brackets substituted for the original words "with the same offence" by the Criminal Evidence Act 1979 s.1.

subject to the other rules of the law of evidence. Secondly, the trial judge retained a discretion to control cross-examination by the prosecution. Even where the accused had lost the shield the judge could still refuse leave to the prosecution to ask any question the prejudicial effect of which exceeded its probative value. However, no such discretion existed to control cross-examination by a co-accused; in this respect there was an important difference between the operation of s.1(3)(ii) and s.1(3)(iii).

3. Reform of the law: the Law Commission proposals

Following a reference by the Home Secretary in 1994 the Law Commission examined the subject of evidence of previous misconduct and bad character in criminal proceedings. The Commission produced an extensive Consultation Paper in 1996,[120] and a subsequent Report in 2001.[121] The report made important recommendations for the reform of the law. It dealt generally with evidence of bad character, which the Commission defined as evidence that tends to show that a person has committed an offence, or has behaved, or is disposed to behave, in a way that might be viewed with disapproval by a reasonable person.[122] Following the Consultation Paper, which focused on evidence of the bad character and previous misconduct of a *defendant*, the Commission extended its inquiry to evidence of the bad character of witnesses as well as defendants.

18–028

The report set out in summary form what the Commission regarded as the principal defects of the previous law. First, the rules on the admissibility of similar fact evidence were said to be unclear and difficult to apply.[123] The confusion extended to the problem of distinguishing inadmissible similar fact evidence from admissible "background" evidence, which might well include prejudicial elements. Secondly, witnesses were thought to be inadequately protected from irrelevant and unfair cross-examination on their character.[124] Thirdly, the rules on cross-examination of the accused were criticised on several grounds. Treating the accused's character as indivisible was unjustifiable and could work unfairly.[125] There was a lack of clarity about the circumstances in which an accused made a claim to good character that would lose the shield against introduction of his record.[126] The loss of the shield through the making of imputations against prosecution witnesses could be harsh on defendants who had to make the imputations as part of their defence. It might inhibit the proper presentation of the defence.[127] There was an over-reliance on judicial discretion to compensate for the defects of the statutory rules under s.1(3)(ii) of the Criminal Evidence Act 1898.[128] By contrast there was no discretion at all to

---

[120] Law Com. CP 141.
[121] Law Com. 273.
[122] Law Com. 273 para.8.19 and preceding discussion.
[123] Law Com. 273 paras 4.2–4.12.
[124] Law Com. 273 paras 4.54–4.56.
[125] Law Com. 273 para.4.27.
[126] Law Com. 273 paras 4.30–4.31.
[127] Law Com. 273 paras 4.33–4.42.
[128] Law Com. 273 paras 4.44–4.46.

soften the rigour and occasional unfairness of the rule that the accused lost the shield by giving evidence against a co-accused.[129]

The Law Commission proposed to deal with this raft of problems by recasting the law as a whole, in a new statute that would follow a new approach. The report included a draft Bill of 21 clauses and two schedules to give effect to the recommended scheme. The scheme was a conscientious and thoughtful attempt to synthesise the law, to improve its coherence and to treat witnesses and defendants more fairly.[130] It is fair to say, however, that although the Commission's revision of the law was radical in form, it was not particularly radical in substance.[131] The Commission accepted that the fundamental problem would continue to be how to reconcile the competition presented by evidence of bad character between its probative value and its prejudicial effect. It accepted a continuing structure of the law into an exclusionary rule for such evidence, ameliorated by category-based exceptions. It rejected any idea of routine disclosure of a defendant's criminal record.

18–029   The structure of the Law Commission's scheme[132] was as follows. A basic rule was proposed that leave of the court would be required for the -admission of any evidence of a person's bad character. The rule would apply equally to defendants and to any person not a defendant, such as a prosecution witness or a police officer. Leave would not be required in three situations: where all parties agreed to the evidence being admissible, where the defendant adduced evidence of his own bad character, and where the evidence was evidence of what the Commission called "the central set of facts".[133] Under this exception evidence would be admissible that concerned the alleged facts of the offence with which the defendant was charged, or that was evidence of misconduct in connection with the investigation or prosecution of that offence. Examples[134] would be prosecution evidence that the defendant committed the burglary charged, or committed an assault in the course of the burglary (this is all evidence that "has to do with" the alleged facts of the offence), or that the defendant tried to intimidate a prosecution witness (this is evidence of misconduct in connection with the investigation or prosecution of the offence). Similarly, defence evidence that a police officer planted evidence on, or fabricated a confession by, the defendant would be admissible without leave.

Leave would generally be required for all evidence of bad character, whether of defendants, witnesses or other persons, relating to behaviour on occasions that

---

[129] Law Com. 273 paras 4.71–4.75.

[130] For discussion see J. McEwan, "Previous Misconduct at the Crossroads: Which 'Way Ahead'?" [2002] Crim. L.R. 180.

[131] See Spencer, *Evidence of Bad Character* (2006), paras 1.6 onwards.

[132] See Pt VII of Law Com. 273. The Commission founded its scheme on "five fundamental considerations" (para.7.2). Common to all five was the key concept of relevance. This provided the means for settling the competing principles: "The fact-finders in any criminal trial must have all relevant material placed before them so as to enable them to perform their function ... [but] ... to adduce evidence of a person's bad character in a public forum is, prima facie, such an invasion of their privacy and so prejudicial to them that it should not be adduced where any relevance it may have to the issues the fact-finders have to decide is of no real significance or is only marginal" (para.7.2(2)(3)).

[133] Law Com. 273 para.7.4.

[134] See the Explanatory Notes to cl.2 of the draft Bill: Law Com. 273 at p.211.

were not part of the central set of facts. There would no longer be any automatic right in any party to cross-examine any witness, including the defendant, on his or her bad character. Moreover, the power of the court to give leave would not be a general inclusionary discretion. It would be a tightly regulated power, in the form of a number of specific categories of exceptional case in which leave could be given provided the statutory conditions were satisfied. However, since the Government did not accept important parts of the Law Commission's scheme we will not set out the scheme in detail. It suffices to say that the Commission's carefully worked out set of safeguards proposed as protective measures against the risk of prejudice received a mixed reception, positive in the case of victims and witnesses, largely negative in the case of defendants.

4. Reform of the law: Government policy

The Law Commission's scheme of reform was the product of an extensive **18–030** consultation exercise. It was a full and carefully worked out set of proposals grounded in clear statements of principle. However, the scheme was not designed to produce many more cases where evidence of the defendant's bad character would be admitted. There was certainly a policy agenda to improve the position of *witnesses* in relation to attacks on their character, but this was not accompanied by any aim of decreasing the protection available to defendants. The Commission stated at the beginning of the Report that it was unclear whether its scheme would result in any wider admissibility of evidence of the accused's bad character.[135] The Commission was more concerned with the quality of decision-making about bad character evidence than with the quantity of such evidence admitted against defendants in criminal trials. As it stated:

> "we have not started from a position that the admittance of more or less bad character evidence should be the outcome of our recommendations. We have sought, rather, to construct a consistent and balanced process under which the conflicting interests of the various parties may best be advanced and protected, and the fairness of criminal trials generally enhanced."[136]

This stance received only a partial endorsement from the Government, which was very much in favour of greater protection for victims and witnesses from attacks on their character. Improving the position of victims and witnesses has been a consistent policy in much reform of the law of evidence in recent years; notable steps in this direction had been taken only a year or two earlier in the Youth Justice and Criminal Evidence Act 1999. The Government therefore adopted the Commission's proposals in relation to this aspect of bad character evidence. Section 100 of the Criminal Justice Act 2003 enacted them largely unchanged. This section was discussed in Ch.14.

However, the proposals in relation to the bad character of defendants were thought to be too conservative. Lord Justice Auld, in his *Review of the Criminal Courts of England and Wales*,[137] had expressed a view, shortly before the publication of the Law Commission Report, that there was much to be said for a

---

[135] Law Com. 273 para.1.10.
[136] Law Com. 273 para.1.11.
[137] The Stationery Office, London, 2001.

more radical view than had so far found favour with the Commission. He would prefer to place more trust in factfinders and to introduce "some reality in this complex corner of the law".[138] This view was more in line with the Government's general wish to "rebalance" the criminal justice system so as to be more favourable to victims and witnesses and less favourable to defendants. Consequently, in the important White Paper, *Justice For All*,[139] the Government stated that it would:

> "overhaul the rules of evidence to ensure the widest possible range of relevant material is available for a judgment. This includes making information available to judges and juries on previous convictions and misconduct where it is relevant and put in context."[140]

18–031   The provisions of the Criminal Justice Bill were accordingly "informed" by the Law Commission's report, but the Commission's recommendations relating to evidence of the bad character of defendants were adopted only in part. Most of the safeguards proposed as protective measures against the risk of prejudice when bad character evidence was to be tendered by the prosecution, such as the obligation to obtain leave, and a requirement for the evidence to have enhanced relevance, were dropped. This was politically controversial and generated much opposition, particularly in the House of Lords. Consequently the provisions in the Bill dealing with evidence of bad character had a difficult passage through Parliament, with the outcome being in doubt until the last minute. However, in the event the Government's modifications of the Law Commission scheme survived largely intact. The new statutory scheme is therefore a patchwork. In relation to some topics it represents the cautious and balanced approach of the Law Commission; in relation to others it gives effect to the policy of "rebalancing" the criminal justice system by being overtly less favourable to defendants. As a whole the scheme lacks coherence and has some gaps in it. As we shall see, this resulted in the courts taking the scheme in hand and issuing a series of guideline judgments in its first year of operation with the aim of trying to ensure that the scheme is applied in accordance with the intentions of Parliament, while taking proper account of the interests of defendants in having a fair trial. Those judgments have been followed by a mass of further case law as the courts and the legal profession have explored the ramifications of the scheme.

---

[138] The Stationery Office (2001), p.567 para.120.
[139] Cm. 5563 (London, 2002).
[140] Cm. 5563 (London, 2002), p.68.

A.   INTRODUCTION

19–001   Chapter 1 of Pt 11 of the Criminal Justice Act 2003 ("the 2003 Act") is a landmark in the development of the law of evidence. It presupposed the potential relevance of evidence of bad character in criminal proceedings and enacted a new statutory scheme to govern its admissibility. The new scheme entailed the abolition of almost two centuries' worth of common law learning about similar fact evidence. The scheme also dispensed with a further extensive body of learning by repealing s.1(3) of the Criminal Evidence Act 1898, which had governed cross-examination of the accused on previous convictions and bad character ever since the accused first became a competent witness for the defence in all cases. The new scheme required extensive training for all judges and magistrates trying criminal cases. The radical nature of the scheme led to the Court of Appeal producing no less than seven guideline judgments in its first year of operation, covering a total of 26 conjoined appeals. Predictably, the case law has continued to grow rapidly.

The previous chapter explained the history of the reform and the government policy embodied in the new scheme. It is clear from the case law that the new scheme has led to greater admissibility of evidence of the bad character of defendants,[1] in line with the Government's intentions. It is unclear whether overall conviction rates have increased as a result. This is not an easy matter to determine, since other important changes to the law of criminal procedure and evidence came into force a few months after the bad character provisions, including the new regime under Ch.2 of Pt 11 of the 2003 Act for hearsay evidence.

Section B of this chapter sets out the structure and scope of the new scheme. In summary the scheme begins by defining the concept of "bad character" (s.98). It then abolishes all the common law rules governing the admissibility of evidence of bad character in criminal proceedings (s.99); this includes the rules governing bad character evidence in relation to non-defendants as well as defendants. In

---

[1]   As noted by Lord Phillips C.J. in *Campbell* [2007] EWCA Crim 1472; [2007] 2 Cr.App.R. 28 at [1].

place of the previous law the scheme provides rules for the admissibility of bad character evidence under certain conditions, but the evidence is admissible only if those conditions are satisfied. Section 100 deals with the admissibility of evidence of bad character of non-defendants; this is discussed in Ch.14 on the examination of witnesses. Section 101 deals with the admissibility of the bad character of defendants. It sets out seven "gateways" through which such evidence may be admitted against defendants. Each of the last five gateways has an accompanying explanatory and interpretative provision; these are set out in ss.102–106 of the 2003 Act.

Section C of this chapter discusses the general principles of interpretation of the new scheme that have emerged from the prolific case law. Section D then examines each of the s.101 gateways in detail. Section E concludes the chapter by dealing with some problems concerning the cogency of evidence of bad character, and the powers of the court where the evidence may be "contaminated".[2] **19–002**

B.   STRUCTURE AND SCOPE OF THE ACT

1.   *The meaning of "bad character"*

Consideration of the scope of Ch.1 of Pt 11 of the 2003 Act begins with the definition of "bad character". Section 98 provides: **19–003**

> "References in this Chapter to evidence of a person's 'bad character' are to evidence of, or a disposition towards, misconduct on his part, other than evidence which—
> (a)   has to do with the alleged facts of the offence with which the defendant is charged, or
> (b)   is evidence of misconduct in connection with the investigation or prosecution of that offence."

This provision must be read together with the definition of "misconduct" in the interpretation provisions of s.112(1): " 'misconduct' means the commission of an offence or other reprehensible behaviour".

(A)   *What is included in section 98*

Evidence of the commission of an offence, other than the one with which the defendant is charged, is a central case of evidence of bad character. The evidence may take the form of proof of *conviction* for a previous offence,[3] or it may be evidence showing that the defendant has committed other offences charged in the current proceedings,[4] or it may be evidence indicating that the defendant has **19–004**

---

[2] Criminal Justice Act 2003 s.107.

[3] On proof of a conviction for an offence, the accused is to be taken to have committed the offence unless the contrary is proved: PACE s.74(3).

[4] A common situation is where the defendant is charged with a number of offences against different victims. If each victim testifies to the commission of an offence against him or her, the question of the cross-admissibility of the evidence of each victim on the charges against the other victims is likely to arise. The Act applies: s.112(2), and see the discussion of gateway (d) below.

committed previous offences, irrespective of whether he has been tried for them.[5] It makes no difference for this purpose that the defendant has been tried and *acquitted* of the other offences. The fact of the acquittal does not prevent the prosecution or a co-accused tendering evidence of what the defendant did on the previous occasions as relevant to prove that he committed the offence for which he is now on trial, by, for example, showing a strikingly similar method of operation to prove his identity.[6] If the evidence shows the commission of a previous offence by the defendant it will be evidence of misconduct and therefore of the bad character of the defendant within s.98. Its admissibility will then depend on whether it can pass through one of the gateways in s.101.

Secondly, s.98 extends to evidence showing a "disposition towards" the commission of offences. This would include evidence of the defendant's preparation for offences, where the conduct involved did not amount to an attempt, or evidence of statements showing the defendant's inclination to commit certain types of offence, such as his admission of sexual interest in children, or evidence of the defendant's possession of materials indicating such an inclination.[7]

Thirdly, s.98 extends to evidence of "other reprehensible behaviour". This term is not defined in the Act. It extends the concept of "misconduct", and therefore "bad character" beyond the commission of other offences, but how far the extension goes and what it includes is left unclear. The term was inserted into the Criminal Justice Bill at a late stage in place of the Law Commission's formulation of behaviour "that, in the opinion of the court, might be viewed with disapproval by a reasonable person". The change was made because the latter expression had been criticised as too wide and vague.[8] Whether "reprehensible" is narrower and more precise is debatable. In an entertaining article Munday argued that the term is somewhat archaic, has uninformative dictionary meanings, and when used elsewhere in legal contexts tends to denote a conclusion rather than set out a norm.[9]

An early judicial pronouncement on the interpretation of the term was the statement by Sir Igor Judge P. in *Renda*[10] that "as a matter of ordinary language, the word 'reprehensible' carries with it some element of culpability or blameworthiness". This is indeed a standard dictionary explanation of the term,

---

[5] The classic example is "similar fact" evidence, suggesting that the defendant has committed a number of offences, even though he has not been charged with all of them, as in *Smith* (1915) 11 Cr.App.R. 229 CCA (the "Brides in the Bath" case). In *Tirnaveanu* [2007] EWCA Crim 1239; [2007] 2 Cr.App.R. 23 the Court of Appeal confirmed that evidence of allegations of misconduct untested by judicial findings is evidence of bad character. Note though that evidence of a *charge* of an offence is not, without more, evidence of misconduct and will therefore fall outside s.98: *Hussain* [2008] EWCA Crim 1117.

[6] See *R. v Z* [2000] 2 A.C. 483 HL. The same principle applies where the defendant was charged with the other offences but the prosecution was stayed as an abuse of process: *David Smith*, reported with *Edwards and Rowlands* [2005] EWCA Crim 3244; [2006] 2 Cr.App.R. 4; or the CPS decided not to prosecute for the earlier offences: *Nguyen* [2008] EWCA Crim 585; [2008] 2 Cr.App.R. 9.

[7] See further Law Com. 273 para.8.18; Spencer, *Evidence of Bad Character* (2006), paras 2.16 and 2.17.

[8] R. Munday, "What Constitutes 'Other Reprehensible Behaviour' under the Bad Character Provisions of the Criminal Justice Act 2003?" [2005] Crim. L.R. 24, 30–31.

[9] Munday, "What Constitutes 'Other Reprehensible Behaviour'" [2005] Crim L.R. 24.

[10] *Renda* [2005] EWCA Crim 2826; [2006] 2 All E.R. 553 at [24].

and its invocation is consistent with the idea that the term is used in its ordinary meaning and is not intended to have a technical definition. If this is so, then its limits will remain uncertain. Four cases, two on either side of the line, illustrate how the concept is being applied in practice. In *Renda,* the Court of Appeal held that it was evidence of "reprehensible behaviour" to show that a defendant, who was charged with attempted robbery and who asserted his good character, had been charged on a previous occasion with assault occasioning actual bodily harm, and that, although found unfit to plead, he was also found by the jury to have committed the physical act of assault. The commission of this act was thought to be reprehensible, although there was no finding by the jury that the defendant was culpable in committing it. In *Saleem*,[11] a defendant charged with taking part in a knife attack by photographing the attack on his mobile phone was found to have violent images on his computer, along with some violent rap lyrics which he had rewritten to refer to his birthday and to a violent attack planned for that day. The offence charged had taken place on the defendant's birthday. The Court of Appeal held that the images and lyrics "were at least evidence of reprehensible behaviour" and therefore evidence of bad character. The court then held them admissible under s.101(1)(d) as relevant to the important issue of whether the defendant's presence at the scene was innocent, as he claimed.

On the other hand, in *Manister*, discussed below, "unattractive" behaviour in the form of a sexually suggestive statement to an under-age girl, which reasonable people might well view with disapproval, was held not to be "reprehensible". In *Osbourne*,[12] the defendant was charged with murder. The prosecution adduced evidence from a former girlfriend that if the defendant did not take the medication he had been prescribed for schizophrenia he was liable to become aggressive and shout, but she said he did not become violent. The Court of Appeal held that this was not evidence of "reprehensible behaviour". In the court's view, while shouting at a partner over the care of a young child "was not of course to be commended", in the context of a charge of murdering a close friend it did not cross the threshold contemplated by the words of the statute. No clear principles emerge from these examples. The moral judgment which determines whether behaviour is "reprehensible" appears to be fact-specific; *Osbourne* may imply that the judgment can take account of the issue in the case to which the evidence is relevant.

The Divisional Court has stated that a district judge was right to hold that the Act does not extend the scope of evidence of bad character at common law.[13] If this is right, and the statutory definition encapsulates the meaning of bad character at common law, then evidence of "reprehensible behaviour" will include any evidence of discreditable conduct, whether it shows the commission of offences or a disposition to commit offences. Examples under the old law of evidence of bad character, which would therefore be subject to the Act's restrictions on admissibility, would include evidence of the possession of discreditable

19–005

---

[11] *Saleem* [2007] EWCA Crim 1923.
[12] *Osbourne* [2007] EWCA Crim 481.
[13] *Gleadall v Huddersfield Magistrates' Court* [2005] EWHC 2283.

materials, such as paedophile literature,[14] association with known criminals,[15] and discreditable conduct in relation to an earlier civil action.[16]

(B)   What is not included in section 98

19–006   Only where evidence is evidence of "bad character" is its admissibility determined by the provisions of the Act. It is important to note that although the Act abolished the common law rules governing the admissibility of evidence of bad character (see below) it did not abolish the common law relating to relevance and probative value. It assumes the continued existence and application of these concepts, subject to the clarification contained in s.109.[17] The scheme of the Act is to require the evidence of bad character to have relevance and probative value in the normal way, and then *in addition* it will have to satisfy the conditions of admissibility in ss.100 (non-defendants) or 101 (defendants). Evidence of bad character may therefore be inadmissible either if it is not relevant to the case or if it fails to meet the statutory conditions. It follows that if the evidence is not evidence of bad character, as defined in s.98, its admissibility will be determined simply by the usual common law principles of relevance, plus exclusionary discretion if it is prosecution evidence.

In *Manister*,[18] the defendant was charged with indecent assault on a girl aged 13. His defence was that they were just friends and that nothing of a sexual nature had taken place between them. On appeal against conviction he challenged the decision of the trial judge to admit evidence under s.101(1)(d) of his previous sexual relationship, when aged 34, with a girl aged 16, and evidence of a statement he made to the complainant's 15-year-old sister indicating that he was sexually attracted to her. In relation to the former the Court of Appeal held that the relationship was a lawful one, and there were no features that showed "reprehensible behaviour" by D; there was no evidence, for example, that D had groomed the girl before she was 16, or that her parents disapproved and communicated their disapproval to D, or that the girl was intellectually, emotionally or physically immature for her age. Therefore since the evidence of the relationship was not evidence of bad character, the trial judge's analysis of its admissibility was wrong. He should not have admitted it under the provisions of the Act. However, the court had no doubt that the evidence was admissible at common law. It was said to be relevant to the issue of whether D had a sexual interest in the complainant because it showed a sexual interest in early or mid-teenage girls, and tended to cast doubt on his claim of a purely friendly relationship with the complainant. The evidence of the statement to the sister was said to show "unattractive" behaviour by D, but his conduct could not safely be said to be reprehensible. Once again, however, the court thought the evidence of the statement would be admissible at common law, for the same reasons as

---

[14] *Lewis* (1983) 76 Cr.App.R. 33 CA. Possession of such material might also show a disposition to commit offences against children, as suggested above.

[15] *Davis and Murphy* (1972) 56 Cr.App.R. 249 CA.

[16] *Carter* (1997) 161 J.P. 207.

[17] The continued application of these common law concepts is assumed at several points in Pt 1 of Ch.11: see, e.g. ss.100(1)(b) and (3), 101(1)(d) and (e), 104(1), 105(1)(b), 109.

[18] Reported with *Weir* [2005] EWCA Crim 2866; [2006] 2 All E.R. 570 at 591.

applied to the evidence of the relationship. It is interesting to note that the relevance of both items of evidence rested on an argument from D's disposition, but the disposition was thought not to be within the scope of s.98 because it was not "reprehensible". By contrast, in *Osbourne*,[19] the evidence of the defendant's behaviour when not taking his medication was held simply to be irrelevant to the issue of whether the defendant had murdered his friend by stabbing him during an argument.

Manister concerned prosecution evidence. Other cases show that defence evidence that does not come within the definition of evidence of bad character in s.98 is similarly outside the scheme of the Act. It does not have to pass through any of the gateways in s.101 where it is evidence against the defendant. Nor does it have to satisfy the conditions in s.100 if it is evidence against a non-defendant. In both types of case its admissibility is a matter for the common law. If it is irrelevant on the normal principles of relevance it will be inadmissible for that reason. In *Edwards and Rowlands*,[20] the defendants were charged with conspiracy to supply a class A drug. At trial they ran cut-throat defences, each blaming the other. The Court of Appeal held that the trial judge had been wrong to permit D1 to cross-examine D2 on his possession of a pistol. The pistol was an antique firearm, for the purposes of the Firearms Act 1968, which it was lawful for D2 to possess. The evidence was not evidence of bad character, and therefore no question of its admissibility arose under s.101. The court clearly thought that it was irrelevant to D2's liability for the offence charged, as was evidence of his possession of an ammunition cartridge, also found in his home. Possession of the cartridge was an offence, and therefore evidence of possession would be evidence of D2's misconduct within s.98, but it had been found when D2's home was searched after his arrest. On this basis the Court of Appeal held that the evidence had "to do with the alleged facts of the offence" within s.98(a), which took it back outside the scope of s.98. The court did not refer to the common law on relevance, instead stating simply, but rightly, that the evidence was irrelevant to the jury's verdict on the offence charged.[21]

Section 98 contains two express exceptions for evidence that would otherwise come within its scope. The first (s.98(a)) is "evidence which has to do with the alleged facts of the offence with which the defendant is charged". This excludes from s.98 evidence of what the common law called the res gestae, and the Law Commission described as "the central set of facts". In other words, evidence will not be evidence of "bad character" where it goes directly to prove that the **19–007**

---

[19] *Osbourne* [2007] EWCA Crim 481.
[20] *Edwards and Rowlands* [2005] EWCA Crim 3244; [2006] 2 Cr.App.R. 4.
[21] See also *Hong Qiang He,* reported with *Weir* [2005] EWCA Crim 2866; [2006] 2 All E.R. 570 at 596: one defendant sought to adduce evidence that his co-defendants had on a previous occasion been the victims of a knife attack and refused to provide statements to the police, and that on another occasion they had been arrested on suspicion of a serious assault but released without charge. CA held that this was not evidence of bad character, and therefore the Act did not apply. It was not admissible at common law because the evidence was irrelevant on charges of wounding with intent to cause grievous bodily harm since it did not show the co-defendants had a propensity for violence. cf. *Cambridge* [2011] EWCA Crim 2009, where prosecution evidence was admissible at common law that D had previously been the victim of a shooting; this was relevant because it provided a possible motive for him to be in possession of a firearm and ammunition and tended to rebut his defence to those charges of "innocent association".

defendant committed the offence charged. Nor will it be evidence of "bad character" where it is evidence showing that the defendant committed other offences[22] or behaved reprehensibly in connection with the offence charged, whether at the same time and place or in some other way. In these cases the evidence will not have to pass through any of the gateways in s.101. It will be admissible at common law provided it is relevant to the facts in issue, either directly or because it is part of the contemporaneous factual context that enables the other evidence to be better understood and evaluated.[23] Such evidence may not, of course, always be relevant. In *Edwards and Rowlands*, noted above, evidence of D's unlawful possession of ammunition found during a search of D's house following his arrest for a drug offence was held to be evidence "to do with the alleged facts of the offence" charged. It was therefore excluded from the scope of s.98, but in the view of the Court of Appeal it was irrelevant to the defendant's liability for the drug offence.

The authorities are not unanimous on how far there is a requirement that the evidence of other misconduct should be contemporaneous with the facts of the offence charged in order to come within s. 98(a). In *Tirnaveanu*,[24] the Court of Appeal said that there should be "some nexus in time" between the evidence of other misconduct and the offence charged. This test was satisfied in *Machado*[25] where D had wished to cross-examine the victim of an alleged robbery on whether the victim had taken drugs on the night of the robbery and had offered to supply drugs to the defendant; this was apparently to support the defence that the victim had fallen over and had not been assaulted. The trial judge had ruled that the evidence was of bad character of the victim and not admissible under s.100 of the 2003 Act. The Court of Appeal held that this was wrong. The evidence related:

> "to the very circumstances in which this offence had occurred. All the matters were in effect contemporaneous to and closely associated with the alleged facts of the offence. It seems to us, looking at the facts of this case and applying the simple English of the provision, that these matters were to do with the alleged facts of the offence. They were, therefore, not evidence of bad character."

In *McNeill*,[26] D was charged with threatening to kill a neighbour whom she suspected of stealing a bottle of brandy from her flat. There was evidence that two days after the incident she had repeated the threat to an official at a Housing Office when she was seeking alternative accommodation. The Court of Appeal held that this was evidence within the exception in s.98(a) and was not therefore evidence of bad character. Citing *Machado*, the court suggested that the words "has to do with":

---

[22] e.g. that D committed an assault occasioning actual bodily harm in the course of a rape, or that he was carrying an offensive weapon in a public place before inflicting grievous bodily harm on the victim.

[23] For an old but still instructive example see *Ellis* (1826) 6 B. & C. 145.

[24] *Tirnaveanu* [2007] EWCA Crim 1239; [2007] 2 Cr.App.R. 23. See also *Saleem* [2007] EWCA Crim 1923, discussed above, where the evidence of the violent images and rap lyrics in the defendant's possession was said to have "insufficient connection in time with the facts of the offence" to come within s.98(a).

[25] *Machado* [2006] EWCA Crim 837.

[26] *McNeill* [2007] EWCA Crim 2927.

> "either clearly encompass evidence relating to the alleged facts of an offence which would have been admissible under the common law outside the context of bad character or propensity, even before the Act, or alternatively as embracing anything directly relevant to the offence charged, provided at any rate they were reasonably contemporaneous with and closely associated with its alleged facts."

In *Mullings*,[27] a question arose about letters written to D while he was in prison. The letters expressed hatred for a gang (the Doddington gang) to which the writer's gang (the Gooch gang) was opposed. D was charged with joint possession of a firearm with intent to endanger life, arising out of a melee between the two gangs. D admitted being present at the scene but denied knowledge of any firearms being carried by the people he was with. In the course of analysing the admissibility of the letters, the Court of Appeal considered, obiter, that if they were tendered to prove D's membership of the Gooch gang they would be evidence of misconduct.[28] Would they nevertheless fall back outside s.98 on the basis that they were to do with the alleged facts of the offence? The court thought not, adopting a distinction between evidence relevant to an offence (which the letters would be) and evidence having to do with the alleged facts of the offence (which the letters would not be). The latter was said to require "a close link in time" between the offence charged and the other misconduct.

These cases should be compared with *Sule*,[29] where D was charged with shooting V in an execution-style killing. The Court of Appeal upheld the trial judge's admission of evidence of previous incidents of shooting involving D as a victim and as an alleged avenger, as evidence of a motive for D to kill X, for whom V might have been mistaken. The judge had admitted the evidence at common law, on the ground that it was evidence to do with the facts of the offence charged. Agreeing, the Court of Appeal distinguished *McNeill* and *Tirnaveanu,* and said that a nexus in time was not always required to bring the evidence within s. 98(a).

> "The words of the statute are straightforward, and clearly apply to evidence of incidents alleged to have created the motive for the index offence. Indeed, where the evidence is reasonably relied upon for motive, it would be irrational to introduce a temporal requirement."

Whether this approach to s. 98(a) states a special application for evidence of motive, or whether there are other applications not requiring a nexus in time, or whether *Sule* is followed at all, remains to be seen, Ultimately it may not matter a great deal as far as prosecution evidence of misconduct is concerned, because if it is not within the exception in s.98(a) its admissibility is covered by the scheme of the Act. If the evidence is relevant to an important matter in issue between the prosecution and the defence it can then be admitted via s.101(1)(d), which is supplemented by an exclusionary discretion. If it is within the exception its

---

[27] *Mullings* [2010] EWCA Crim 2820; [2011] 2 Cr.App.R. 21.
[28] The actual decision in the case upheld the trial judge's decision to admit the letters, not as showing bad character via gang membership, but simply as evidence relevant to D's knowledge that his associates might be carrying arms if they went on to Doddington territory.
[29] *Sule* [2012] EWCA Crim 1130.

admissibility is determined by the common law of relevance, supplemented by an exclusionary discretion in virtually identical terms.

19–008 The second exclusion (s.98(b)) is of evidence of "misconduct in connection with the investigation or prosecution of the offence". In relation to non-defendants, we noted in Ch.14 that this exclusion would cover evidence from a defendant that a police officer had fabricated a confession by the defendant, and similar evidence of other police misconduct in connection with the investigation of the offence. Since such evidence is not within the scope of s.98, the leave of the judge that would otherwise be required under s.100 to admit it, is not necessary. However, it should be noted that a defendant who adduces evidence of this type against a police officer will be held to have made an attack on the character of the officer for the purposes of s.101(1)(g).[30] The gateway will then be open for the prosecution to adduce evidence of the defendant's own bad character. In *Apabhai*,[31] the Court of Appeal held that s.98(b) is not restricted to evidence of misconduct by the police or prosecuting authorities. It can apply to evidence adduced by one defendant of misconduct by a co-defendant, such as evidence that the latter tried to blackmail the former in connection with the prosecution. In such a case, if the judge regards the evidence as relevant at common law to the issues between the defendants, there is no discretion to exclude it.

2. *Effect of the Act on the previous law*

19–009 Section 99 provides:

> "(1)   The common law rules governing the admissibility of evidence of bad character in criminal proceedings are abolished.
>
> (2)   Subsection (1) is subject to section 118(1) in so far as it preserves the rule under which in criminal proceedings a person's reputation is admissible for the purpose of proving his bad character."

In addition, s.332 of and Sch.37 Pt 5 to the 2003 Act repeal s.1(3) of the Criminal Evidence Act 1898. The combined effect of the abolition of the common law rules on bad character evidence and this repeal is therefore to abrogate the whole of the previous law relating to admissibility of evidence of the defendant's bad character, as defined in s.98. The scheme of the Act is to replace both the common law on the use of similar fact evidence by the prosecution in chief and the provisions of the Criminal Evidence Act 1898 regulating cross-examination of the defendant on his previous convictions and bad character. In their place the Act sets up a unified scheme of admissibility for evidence of the defendant's bad character; this scheme does not distinguish between the stages in the trial when such evidence is adduced.

Tapper has argued that the abolition of the common law rules governing the admissibility of evidence of bad character does not extend to abolition of the *discretion* at common law to exclude evidence where its prejudicial effect

---

[30] Criminal Justice Act 2003 s.106(2).
[31] *Apabhai* [2011] EWCA Crim 917.

exceeds its probative value.[32] The argument is attractive, although it might be said in response that in relation to bad character evidence at common law the discretion had become absorbed into the formulation of the similar fact rule, and was no longer distinguishable from it.[33] In *Somanathan*,[34] the Court of Appeal commented in relation to the 2003 Act that "the pre-existing one-stage test which balanced probative value against prejudicial effect is obsolete".[35] The possible survival of the common law discretion may not matter a great deal as far as evidence of the bad character of defendants is concerned, because the Court of Appeal has said that the fairness discretion under s.78 of PACE remains available where the prosecution seek to adduce the evidence.[36]

3. *Admissibility of evidence of the defendant's bad character: the seven "gateways"*

Section 101 of the Criminal Justice Act 2003 provides as follows: 19–010

"(1)   In criminal proceedings evidence of the defendant's bad character is admissible if, but only if—

(a)   all parties to the proceedings agree to the evidence being admissible,

(b)   the evidence is adduced by the defendant himself or is given in answer to a question asked by him in cross-examination and intended to elicit it,

(c)   it is important explanatory evidence,

(d)   it is relevant to an important matter in issue between the defendant and the prosecution,

(e)   it has substantial probative value in relation to an important matter in issue between the defendant and a co-defendant,

(f)   it is evidence to correct a false impression given by the defendant, or

(g)   the defendant has made an attack on another person's character.

(2)   Sections 102 to 106 contain provision supplementing subs.(1).

(3)   The court must not admit evidence under subs.(1)(d) or (g) if, on an application by the defendant to exclude it, it appears to the court that the admission of the evidence would have such an adverse effect on the fairness of the proceedings that the court ought not to admit it.

(4)   On an application to exclude evidence under subs.(3) the court must have regard, in particular, to the length of time between the matters to which that evidence relates and the matters which form the subject of the offence charged."

C.   GENERAL PRINCIPLES OF INTERPRETATION OF THE NEW SCHEME

The new scheme for evidence of bad character has generated a substantial case   19–011
law as prosecution and defence lawyers have sought to test its scope and limits. In the scheme's first year of operation the Court of Appeal adopted the technique of hearing a number of appeals at the same time and giving a single judgment covering the several cases. These were effectively a set of guideline judgments, in

---

[32] C. Tapper, "The Criminal Justice Act 2003: Evidence of Bad Character" [2004] Crim. L.R. 533, 540.

[33] See *DPP v P* [1991] 2 A.C. 447 HL

[34] Reported with *Weir* [2005] EWCA Crim 2866; [2006] 2 All E.R. 570.

[35] *Weir* [2005] EWCA Crim 2866; [2006] 2 All E.R. 570 at [36].

[36] See section C below. For comment about the common law discretion in relation to the admission of evidence of bad character of non-defendants under s.100 of the Criminal Justice Act 2003 see Ch.14.

the sense that the Court of Appeal used them to establish a number of general principles regarding the interpretation and application of the scheme. These principles were clearly aimed at guiding trial judges in their decision-making about the admissibility of bad character evidence.[37] However, the Court of Appeal was also careful to say that the guidance, for example on the contents of a summing-up, is not intended as a blueprint, departure from which will result in the quashing of a conviction.[38] It is useful to set out these principles in this section before turning to consider the gateways to admissibility in more detail.

First, the aim of the legislation is to assist in the evidence-based conviction of the guilty, while not putting those who are not guilty at risk of conviction by prejudice. Therefore, according to the Court of Appeal in *Hanson*,[39] the first of the "guideline" cases, applications to admit bad character evidence should not be made routinely. They should be based on the particular circumstances of each case. This is a key point. The routine disclosure of the defendant's criminal record had been trailed in the Auld Review as a possible reform, but the Court of Appeal was quick to discourage prosecutors from thinking that the scheme of the Act could be used in this way. *Hanson* reinforced the message that bad character evidence should be used with restraint by emphasising that previous convictions of the defendant should not be used to bolster a weak prosecution case, or to prejudice the minds of a jury against the defendant.[40]

Secondly, where past events (that is, those that form the subject-matter of evidence of bad character) are disputed, the judge should be careful not to let the trial be diverted to examination of matters not charged.[41] In *David Smith*,[42] the Court of Appeal repeated the warning given by Rose L.J. in *Bovell*[43] about the undesirability of having "satellite litigation" introduced into the trial. Juries, the court said, should not be required to explore satellite issues one stage removed from the charges they are trying unless this is really necessary.[44] Such issues may arise particularly where the evidence of bad character is in the form of allegations of misconduct that have not been tried and are denied, or where a previous conviction was founded on a plea of guilty, and the defendant disputes the factual basis of the plea.

19–012   Thirdly, where bad character evidence is adduced, it is essential for trial judges to give juries clear warnings, explanation and guidance as to its use. According to Rose L.J. in *Edwards*[45]:

---

[37] See *Hanson* [2005] EWCA Crim 824; [2005] 2 Cr.App.R. 21 at [3]–[18]; *Bovell* [2005] EWCA Crim 1091; [2005] 2 Cr.App.R. 27 at [2], [22]; *Edwards* [2005] EWCA Crim 1813; [2006] 1 Cr.App.R. 3 at [3], [77]; *Highton* [2005] EWCA Crim 1985; [2006] 1 Cr.App.R. 7 at [11]–[14]; *Renda* [2005] EWCA Crim 2826; [2006] 2 All E.R. 553 at [3]; *Weir* [2005] EWCA Crim 2866; [2006] 2 All E.R. 570 at [7], [38]; *Edwards and Rowlands* [2005] EWCA Crim 3244; [2006] 2 Cr.App.R. 4 at [1], [82].

[38] *Edwards* [2005] EWCA Crim 1813; [2006] 1 Cr.App.R. 3 at [3].

[39] *Hanson* [2005] EWCA Crim 824; [2005] 2 Cr.App.R. 21.

[40] *Hanson* [2005] EWCA Crim 824; [2005] 2 Cr.App.R. 21 at [18].

[41] *Hanson* [2005] EWCA Crim 824; [2005] 2 Cr.App.R. 21 at [12].

[42] See *Edwards and Rowlands* [2005] EWCA Crim 3244; [2006] 2 Cr.App.R. 4.

[43] *Bovell* [2005] EWCA Crim 1091; [2005] 2 Cr.App.R. 27 at [22].

[44] *Edwards and Rowlands* [2005] EWCA Crim 3244; [2006] 2 Cr.App.R. 4 at [86]. For a striking affirmation of this principle in a difficult rape case see *O'Dowd* [2009] EWCA Crim 905.

[45] *Edwards* [2005] EWCA Crim 1813; [2006] 1 Cr.App.R. 3.

"What the summing-up must contain is a clear warning to the jury against placing undue reliance on previous convictions, which cannot, by themselves, prove guilt. It should be explained why the jury has heard the evidence and the ways in which it is relevant to and may help their decision, bearing in mind that relevance will depend primarily, though not exclusively, on the gateway in s.101 (1) of the Criminal Justice Act 2003 through which the evidence has been admitted. For example, some evidence admitted through gateway (g), because of an attack on another person's character, may be relevant or irrelevant to propensity, so as to require a direction on this aspect."

Picking up the last point in this quotation, the jury should be told that even if they find that the defendant has a propensity to commit offences or to be untruthful, that propensity is only one relevant factor, and the jury must assess its significance in the light of all the other evidence in the case.[46] However, provided the judge has given suitably clear warnings, explanation and guidance, the terms in which he or she did so can differ. There is no rigid formula to be adhered to.[47]

Fourthly, the application of the scheme in the Act is primarily a matter for trial judges. The Court of Appeal has said that it will interfere with the decisions of trial judges only in limited circumstances. This will be so whether the decision or ruling of the judge that is questioned on appeal was either a judgment in the specific factual context of the individual case or the exercise of a judicial discretion. In either case the principles applicable to review of discretion will be adopted.[48] In *Renda*, Sir Igor Judge P. explained that this is because the trial judge's "feel" for the case is usually the critical ingredient of the decision at first instance which the Court of Appeal lacks, and that context is vital. On this approach it is appropriate to interfere with the decision only where the trial judge went wrong in principle.

Fifthly, the effect of s.101(3) is that the court must not admit evidence of bad **19–013** character via gateways (d) or (g) of s.101(1) if the court thinks that its admission would have such an adverse effect on the fairness of the proceedings that the court ought not to admit it. The wording of this provision is plainly derived from s.78 of PACE. In fact the wording is so close to s.78 as to imply that Parliament intended the possibility of exclusion on the ground of fairness to be restricted to the two gateways specified. If so, it follows that no exclusionary discretion would be available in respect of evidence of bad character admissible via any of the other gateways. However, in *Highton*, Lord Woolf L.C.J. suggested that s.78 of PACE provides an additional protection to a defendant.[49] While emphasising that the Court of Appeal had not heard full argument and was therefore not expressing a concluded view, he advised judges that it would be a sensible precaution, when making rulings as to the use of evidence of bad character, to apply s.78 and exclude evidence where appropriate to do so, pending a definitive ruling to the contrary. He reinforced the point by noting that s.78 enables the court to comply with its obligations under art.6 of the ECHR, and therefore that its application to the scheme in the 2003 Act would avoid any risk of non-compliance. Since s.78 allows for exclusion only of prosecution evidence it cannot apply in respect of

---

[46] *Hanson* [2005] EWCA Crim 824; [2005] 2 Cr.App.R. 21 at [18].
[47] *Edwards* [2005] EWCA Crim 1813; [2006] 1 Cr.App.R. 3 at [3].
[48] See the remarks of Sir Igor Judge P. in *Renda* [2005] EWCA Crim 2826; [2006] 2 All E.R 553 at [3].
[49] *Highton* [2005] EWCA Crim 1985; [2006] 1 Cr.App.R. 7 at [13].

gateway (e), where the evidence of bad character is adduced by a co-accused. But this dictum can certainly make a difference as regards gateways (c) and (f), for which there would otherwise be no exclusionary discretion. The question does not arise as regards gateway (a), where the parties agree to admit the evidence, or (b), where the defendant adduces it.

Sixthly, the gateways deal only with the admissibility, not with the *use* of evidence of bad character. In *Highton,* the Court of Appeal held that evidence admitted through gateway (g), because the defendant had made an attack on another person's character, could, depending on the particular facts, be relevant not only to the defendant's credibility but also his propensity to commit offences of the kind with which he was charged. This marked a change from the previous law. The court in *Highton* was not prepared to recreate the distinction under the 2003 Act, whereby evidence admitted under the 'tit for tat' principle could only be used as relevant to the accused's credibility in making the attack on the other peron's character. Instead the court preferred to argue that the scheme of the Act suggested that wherever bad character evidence is admitted, it can be admitted for any purpose for which it is relevant in the case. Any unfairness, the court said, could be dealt with by the exclusionary discretions in ss.101(3) and 103(3), or s.78 of PACE. *Highton* has been criticised,[50] but was followed by the Court of Appeal in *Enright and Gray.*[51] In this case Enright, who was charged with offences of possession of drugs (ecstasy, amphetamine and cannabis) with intent to supply, led evidence himself under s.101(b) of his previous convictions for a variety of offences, only one of which related to drugs. One reason for taking this course was to minimise the potentially prejudicial effect of evidence that when the police raided his flat and arrested him he was handcuffed. The trial judge directed the jury that previous convictions could be relevant both when deciding whether a defendant's evidence was truthful and when deciding whether he had committed the offences charged. The Court of Appeal rejected the argument that convictions admitted under s.101(b) could be used only for the purpose for which the defendant had adduced them. Evidence of bad character, applying *Highton,* could be used, once admitted, for any purpose for which it is relevant.[52]

In addition, the Criminal Procedure Rules 2012 provide for the giving of notice of applications to admit evidence of bad character. One important function of the notice is to require the prosecution to decide whether they propose to rely simply upon the fact of conviction or also upon the circumstances of it.[53] Identifying the relevant circumstances will be necessary, for example, where the prosecution rely on factual similarities between the previous offence and the offence the defendant is now charged with. The Court of Appeal has stressed more than once the importance of compliance with the rules so as to ensure that

---

[50] See R. Munday, "The Purposes of Gateway (g): Yet Another Problematic of the Criminal Justice Act 2003" [2006] Crim. L.R. 300.

[51] Reported with *Edwards and Rowlands* [2005] EWCA Crim 3244; [2006] 2 Cr.App.R. 4 at [87].

[52] *Edwards and Rowlands* [2005] EWCA Crim 3244; [2006] 2 Cr.App.R. 4 at [100]. The Court of Appeal went on to say that, on the facts of the case, the trial judge should have made it clearer that the convictions did not assist the Crown on either truthfulness or propensity. Nevertheless the conviction was held to be safe in view of the strong evidence against the defendant of drugs and drug paraphernalia all over his flat.

[53] *Hanson* [2005] EWCA Crim 824; [2005] 2 Cr.App.R. 21 at [17].

all parties have the appropriate information in relation to convictions and other evidence of bad character, in good time.[54] The interests of fairness require that the defendant should have an opportunity adequately to prepare his defence against arguments founded on his bad character. For example, as the court pointed out in *Bovell*, the basis of plea in relation to an earlier conviction may be relevant where it demonstrates differences from the way in which the prosecution initially put the case.[55] Accordingly, a mere reference to the statement of a complainant in an earlier case may not provide the later court with the material needed to make a decision as to the admissibility of the earlier conviction. However, it seems that in practice failure to comply with the notice provisions will probably not affect the decision as to the admissibility of the evidence, provided the defendant has not been prejudiced by the failure. Moreover, even if there is an element of prejudice arising from a lack of notice, the admission of the evidence may not be sufficient to render a conviction unsafe.[56]

Finally, the Explanatory Notes on the 2003 Act prepared by the Home Office are a permissible aid to construction of the Act,[57] and the Court of Appeal has already used them for this purpose.[58]

19–014

D. THE GATEWAYS IN DETAIL

1. *Gateway (a): evidence adduced by agreement of all parties*

Evidence of the bad character of the defendant is admissible through gateway (a) if all parties agree, that is, prosecution, defendant and any co-defendants. This provision gives effect to a recommendation of the Law Commission.[59] Leave of the court is not required. An example of its operation is seen in *Hussain*.[60] Two defendants charged jointly with attempted robbery agreed that their respective convictions for offences of dishonesty were bound to be admitted since each was blaming the other. The prosecution accepted the agreement.

19–015

---

[54] *Bovell* [2005] EWCA Crim 1091; [2005] 2 Cr.App.R. 27 at [2]; *Fysh* (reported with *Edwards*) [2005] EWCA Crim 1813; [2006] 1 Cr.App.R. 3 at [32].

[55] For an example of the importance of establishing the basis of plea in a case of late notice see *Atkinson* [2006] EWCA Crim 1424.

[56] See, e.g. *Fysh* (reported with *Edwards*) [2005] EWCA Crim 1813; [2006] 1 Cr.App.R. 3 where the other evidence against the defendant was strong and the judge restricted the number of previous convictions admitted.

[57] See Spencer, *Evidence of Bad Character* (2006), paras 1.65 and 1.66, taking issue with the argument to the contrary by Munday, "Bad Character Rules and Riddles: 'Explanatory Notes' and True Meanings of s.103(1) of the Criminal Justice Act 2003" [2005] Crim. L.R. 337.

[58] *Weir* [2005] EWCA Crim 2866; [2006] 2 All E.R. 570 at [35] and [36].

[59] Law Com. 273 para.8.29.

[60] *Hussain* [2008] EWCA Crim 1117.

2. *Gateway (b): evidence adduced by the defendant himself*

19–016   Section 101(b) preserves the possibility of admitting bad character evidence where the evidence is adduced by the defendant himself or is given in answer to a question asked by him in cross-examination and intended to elicit it. An example of the latter situation is where a defendant asks questions of a police officer in cross-examination designed to bring out the defendant's previous convictions. The provision gives effect to a recommendation of the Law Commission.[61] Leave of the court is not required.

A defendant might have a number of reasons for making what, on the face of it, is a surprising choice to reveal his discreditable past. The example given by the Law Commission was where the defendant had an alibi for the crime charged because he was in prison for another offence at the time. Other reasons might have a more tactical quality. If the convictions are few in number, and old and stale, the defendant might try to portray himself to the jury as a person of reformed, and therefore good, character. In addition, he might wish to prevent possible speculation by the jury that if he says nothing about his character it must be a bad one. Alternatively, where his defence will involve an attack on the character of another person, such as a police officer or a witness for the prosecution, he will render himself liable to have his bad character admitted through gateway (g). In this situation he might well wish to defuse a potentially damaging cross-examination by the prosecution by bringing out his bad character himself, when he can portray himself as being open with the court. Another tactical move was seen in *Enright and Gray*, discussed above, where the defendant adduced evidence of his previous convictions to counter possible prejudice arising from police evidence that when his flat was searched and he was arrested he was handcuffed.

However, the Court of Appeal made clear in *Enright and Gray* that if the defendant adopts such a tactic he cannot restrict the use of the convictions to the tactical purpose for which he adduced them. Once admitted through gateway (b) they can be used for whatever purpose they are relevant. If therefore they demonstrate a propensity on the part of the defendant to commit the kind of offence with which he is charged, or to be untruthful, they can be used for those purposes.

3. *Gateway (c): important explanatory evidence*

19–017   Evidence of the bad character of the defendant is admissible via gateway (c) of s.101(1) if it is "important explanatory evidence". Section 102 defines this concept in the following terms:

> "For the purposes of s.101(1)(c) evidence is important explanatory evidence if—
> (a)   without it, the court or jury would find it impossible or difficult properly to understand other evidence in the case, and
> (b)   its value for understanding the case as a whole is substantial."

---

[61] Law Com. 273 para.8.30.

This gateway, as defined in s.102, represents a modified version of a recommendation of the Law Commission.[62] The Government rejected a proposed further condition that the court would have to be satisfied that either the evidence was not prejudicial to the defendant, or that its value for understanding the case as a whole was such that the interests of justice required its admission despite the risk of prejudice. Accordingly, when the court decides on the admissibility of evidence via this gateway, there is no formal requirement that the court should balance the explanatory value of the evidence against any prejudicial effect it might have. However, if s.78 of PACE can apply in respect of this gateway[63] then in an appropriate case the court may engage in precisely this balancing exercise in deciding on the fairness of admitting the evidence. Nevertheless, given that gateway (c) cannot open unless the value of the explanatory evidence for understanding the case as a whole is substantial, and it must be impossible or difficult properly to understand the other evidence without it, the evidence will need to have a good deal of explanatory value to be admissible at all. Accordingly, if the evidence shows bad character, say in the form of previous convictions or other misconduct of the defendant, the bad character evidence will have to be seriously prejudicial for the exercise of exclusionary discretion to be a real issue.[64]

The Law Commission intended gateway (c) to give statutory effect to the common law principle allowing for "background" evidence to be admissible. This principle was discussed in Ch.1 where it was suggested that evidence may be relevant to the proceedings because it enables other evidence about the facts in issue to be better understood and evaluated. Evidence of contemporaneous context, or evidence of background or history, are central examples of such relevance. However, the more context, or the more background or history, that is introduced into the proceedings the greater the "costs", in terms of expense, delay and risks of multiplying the issues and distracting the factfinder. The risk of prejudice where the evidence shows bad character is a further cost of admission. The common law adopted therefore what was in effect a test of enhanced relevance for the admission of background evidence. In the unreported but influential case of *Pettman*[65] the Court of Appeal referred to:

> "evidence of part of a continual background of history relevant to the offence charged .. and without the totality of which the account placed before the jury would be *incomplete or incomprehensible*." (emphasis added)

The formulation in s.102 is not in precisely the same terms, but the principle of enhanced relevance for the explanatory purpose is maintained.

Gateway (c) has received some consideration in the cases arising under the Act. In *Chohan*,[66] a witness claimed to recognise the defendant as a man she saw in the street, running away from the scene of a robbery. The Court of Appeal upheld

19–018

---

[62] Law Com. 273, Pt X.
[63] See *Highton* [2005] EWCA Crim 1985; [2006] 1 Cr.App.R. 7, and the discussion in the text above.
[64] For a case where the exclusionary discretion was considered for background evidence but not used see *Sawoniuk* [2000] 2 Cr.App.R. 220 CA.
[65] *Pettman* Unreported May 2, 1985.
[66] Reported with *Edwards* [2005] EWCA Crim 1813; [2006] 1 Cr.App.R. 3.

the trial judge's decision to admit, through gateway (c), a statement from the witness explaining that she had been able to recognise the defendant because she had regularly bought heroin from him. The judge had concluded that it would be difficult for the jury to understand—which in this context must include evaluate—her evidence of recognition without knowing the basis of the recognition. This decision seems to be plainly right. The *Turnbull* guidelines on identification evidence require the jury to consider the circumstances in which the witness came to make the identification.[67] The jury's task is much more difficult, and verges on the impossible, if they are kept in ignorance of how the witness is acquainted with the defendant. Moreover, the fact that the acquaintance is through the defendant's drug-dealing is beside the point. No reliance need be placed on this misconduct, which helps to reduce the risk of prejudice. Her statement would have the same value if she had said that she bought groceries from him, or that he was a neighbour she saw several times a week. Accordingly, the evidence satisfied the conditions for admission through gateway (c) and there was no case for excluding it in the interests of fairness.

On the other hand, it has been confirmed that if the other evidence is clear and can be understood without more, gateway (c) will not be available. It will not be enough that the evidence of the defendant's bad character might make it easier to evaluate the other evidence, in the sense of making it more likely that the jury will disbelieve the defendant's story. In *Beverley*,[68] D was charged with conspiracy to import cocaine. Newly imported cocaine was found in the possession of a passenger in D's car, and the issue was whether D was a knowing participant in the conspiracy. The trial judge permitted the prosecution to adduce evidence under gateways (c) and (d) of two previous convictions of the defendant, one for possession of cannabis with intent to supply and one for simple possession of cannabis. The Court of Appeal had no hesitation in ruling that gateway (c) was unavailable. The court was unable to see how the jury would have been disabled or disadvantaged in understanding any of the evidence connecting D with the crime charged: "The evidence was perfectly clear. It required no footnote or lexicon".[69] Even if his convictions showed that D was no stranger to the use and supply of controlled drugs, as the prosecution argued, that did not make the evidence of what was found in his car any more comprehensible.[70] In *Saint*,[71] D was charged with rape and false imprisonment of a woman abducted from a car park late at night. The Court of Appeal held that the

---

[67] See Ch.7.

[68] *Beverley* [2006] EWCA Crim 1287.

[69] *Beverley* [2006] EWCA Crim 1287 at [7].

[70] *Davis* [2008] EWCA Crim 1156 is similar: where the defence to a murder charge was provocation by an unfaithful wife, prosecution evidence from the defendant's former girlfriend of his jealous and controlling behaviour in their relationship 20 years earlier should not have been admitted via gateway (c). As the Court of Appeal said, the evidence did not explain anything, or make anything comprehensible that was impossible or difficult to understand; its purpose was rather to contradict the defendant's story of gross provocation. This can be compared with the tax fraud case of *Doncaster* [2008] EWCA Crim 5, where evidence of the defendant's non-disclosures and lies in two previous Revenue inquiries into his tax affairs was admissible via gateway (c) because the evidence of the first two inquiries helped substantially in understanding the third inquiry out of which the charges arose, and which had referred to the first two.

[71] *Saint* [2010] EWCA Crim 1924.

trial judge had been wrong to admit via gateway (c) evidence of D's interest in "dogging", his use of a night vision aid and habit of wearing camouflage clothing and a blackened face to patrol the car park at night. It was not "important explanatory evidence", since the evidence to which it was relevant, namely the hearing by the woman and a companion of footsteps in the car park, was not impossible or difficult to understand. The message of such cases is that the prosecution should not try to smuggle through gateway (c) evidence of propensity, when the other evidence is comprehensible without it. Gateway (d) is the appropriate provision to consider in these cases.

4. Gateway (d): evidence relevant to an important matter in issue between the defendant and the prosecution

Evidence of the defendant's bad character is admissible via gateway (d) if it is relevant to an important matter in issue between the prosecution and the defendant. Section 103 explains: **19–019**

> "(1) For the purposes of section 101(1)(d) the matters in issue between the defendant and the prosecution include—
>   (a) the question whether the defendant has a propensity to commit offences of the kind with which he is charged, e.g. except where his having such a propensity makes it no more likely that he is guilty of the offence;
>   (b) the question whether the defendant has a propensity to be untruthful, except where it is not suggested that the defendant's case is untruthful in any respect.
> (2) Where subsection (1)(a) applies, a defendant's propensity to commit offences of the kind with which he is charged may (without prejudice to any other way of doing so) be established by evidence that he has been convicted of—
>   (a) an offence of the same description as the one with which he is charged, or
>   (b) an offence of the same category as the one with which he is charged.
> (3) Subsection (2) does not apply in the case of a particular defendant if the court is satisfied, by reason of the length of time since the conviction or for any other reason, that it would be unjust for it to apply in his case.
> (4) For the purposes of subsection (2)—
>   (a) two offences are of the same description as each other if the statement of the offence in a written charge or indictment would, in each case, be in the same terms;
>   (b) two offences are of the same category as each other if they belong to the same category of offences prescribed for the purposes of this section by an order made by the Secretary of State.
> (5) A category prescribed by an order under subsection (4)(b) must consist of offences of the same type.
> (6) Only prosecution evidence is admissible under section 101(1)(d)."

Gateway (d) is the most important of the gateways. It is the one that replaced the common law rule against similar fact evidence and other evidence showing the accused's bad character. It deals with the conditions under which the prosecution can lead such evidence against the accused, irrespective of how the accused conducts his defence. For the purposes of gateway (d) it is immaterial whether the accused puts his character in issue or attacks the character of another person. If he does do either of those things then gateways (f) or (g) may also open. It is possible for evidence of bad character to be admitted through more than one gateway.

19–020 Gateway (d) embodies the greatest departure made by the 2003 Act from the Law Commission's recommendations. The Government rejected the conservative approach[72] which would have imposed requirements for leave, substantial probative value, and admission of the evidence in the interests of justice despite the risk of prejudice. It is enough if the evidence is (simply) relevant to an important matter in issue between prosecution and defence. There is no doubt that it was the intention of Parliament to relax the strictness of the common law by dropping any requirement for enhanced relevance for similar fact evidence. This approach is consistent with the Government's declared policy of "rebalancing" the criminal justice system, as is seen by a comparison of s.101(1)(d) with s.100 of the Act. Section 100 aims to restrict the amount of bad character evidence adduced against non-defendants, but s.101(1)(d) is worded so as to enlarge the admissibility of bad character evidence against defendants.

In *Somanathan*,[73] the Court of Appeal confirmed that there is no requirement for gateway (d) of "enhanced relevance" or "enhanced probative value", and that the test under the previous law that balanced probative value against prejudicial effect is obsolete. The court reinforced its point by saying that the terms of s.100 "clearly impose a higher test in respect of the introduction of a non-defendant's bad character than the test for the introduction of a defendant's bad character".[74] It even went so far as to state that the 2003 Act completely reverses the pre-existing general rule: "Evidence of bad character is now admissible if it satisfies certain criteria (see s.101(1), and the approach is no longer one of inadmissibility subject to exceptions".[75] This is something of an exaggeration because s.101(1) begins by providing that evidence of the defendant's bad character is admissible *if, but only if* . . . (emphasis added), which implies that in all other cases it will be inadmissible. The structure therefore continues to be a general rule of exclusion of such evidence subject to a number of defined exceptions, but the exception in gateway (d) has been deliberately widened from the previous law.

The basic test for gateway (d) is whether the evidence is relevant to an important matter in issue between the defendant and the prosecution. An "important matter" means a matter of substantial importance in the context of the case as a whole (s.112(1)). This will clearly include any specific factual issue having a bearing on the defendant's liability for the offence, such as whether the defendant was mistakenly identified as the offender,[76] or whether an admitted use

---

[72] For a summary of the legislative history see Spencer, *Evidence of Bad Character* (Hart Publishing, Oxford, 2006), paras 4.18 and 4.19.

[73] Reported with *Weir* [2005] EWCA Crim 2866; [2006] 2 All E.R. 570.

[74] *Weir* [2005] EWCA Crim 2866; [2006] 2 All E.R. 570 at [36]. In reaching this conclusion the Court of Appeal considered and rejected a dictum by Lord Phillips in the civil case of *O'Brien v Chief Constable of South Wales Police* [2005] UKHL 26; [2005] 2 All E.R. 931 at [33], that the Criminal Justice Act 2003 preserves the requirement that similar fact evidence should have an enhanced probative value to be admissible. The dictum had been cited and applied by a differently constituted Court of Appeal in *Duggan* (reported with *Edwards* [2005] EWCA Crim 1813; [2006] 1 Cr.App.R.3 at [54]. It is submitted, with respect, that the view in *Somanathan* [2005] EWCA Crim 2866; [2006] 2 All E.R. 570 is clearly correct.

[75] *Weir* [2005] EWCA Crim 2866; [2006] 2 All E.R. 570 at [35].

[76] e.g. *Crawford* [2008] EWCA Crim 1863; [2009] 1 Cr.App.R. 11.

of force by him was not done in self-defence.[77] As under the previous law, evidence of similar facts or other offences involving the defendant will be admissible if it is relevant to such a specific issue.

The argument for relevance in relation to gateway (d) may or may not involve an argument from the defendant's propensity.[78] Three types of case can be considered which do not require reasoning from a proved propensity.[79] First, evidence of previous convictions may be relevant to a specific issue irrespective of its tendency to prove that the defendant has a bad character. In *Isichei*,[80] D was charged with offences of assault occasioning actual bodily harm and robbery, arising out of an incident in which two men accosted two female students in the street late at night, said they wanted "coke" (cocaine), then took the girls to a bank cash dispenser where they assaulted them and required them to withdraw money. One of the girls identified D as a man they had seen earlier in the evening when he had helped to secure entry for them to a club. To rebut D's defence of mistaken identity the prosecution adduced evidence of D's conviction some six years earlier for having been concerned in the importation of cocaine. Dismissing D's appeal, the Court of Appeal agreed with the trial judge that the conviction was not admitted to show any propensity of D to commit robbery and/or assault (to which it was not relevant). Rather it was relevant to support the identification because it showed that D was connected to cocaine in the sense of having an interest in the drug. Although the court did not use the term, the argument was one based on the unlikelihood of coincidence. The victim's identification of D was one of good quality in the circumstances; if the jury were satisfied that she was accurate in saying that the attacker referred to cocaine, it would be an odd coincidence if she had wrongly identified someone who happened to have an interest in cocaine.

19–021

A second type of case which does not involve an argument from propensity is where the defendant is charged with a number of offences against different victims, and the question is whether the evidence of each victim is admissible in relation to the charges in respect of the other victims. The relevance of such evidence usually lies in the similarities of the victims' accounts: in the absence of collusion or contamination of their stories it would be an unlikely coincidence if they had all come up with the same false story. So in *Freeman*,[81] the Court of Appeal upheld the trial judge's ruling that the evidence of two young girls was cross-admissible on the two counts of sexual offences committed by the defendant against them. Because of the similar nature of the allegations the evidence of each girl tended to support the truth of the evidence of the other. In substance the case is one of mutual corroboration of the victims.[82] The same analysis applies where the 'similar fact' evidence is of an uncharged offence. The evidence of the victim of that offence can be admissible to support the evidence

---

[77] e.g. *Duggan*, reported with *Edwards* [2005] EWCA Crim 1813; [2006] 1 Cr.App.R. 3.

[78] The arguments for the relevance of evidence of bad character are discussed in Ch.18. For an instructive case involving arguments based on disposition, *and* on the unlikelihood of coincidence, see *West* [1996] 2 Cr.App.R. 374.

[79] cf. M. Redmayne, "Recognising Propensity" [2011] Crim. L.R. 177.

[80] *Isichei* [2006] EWCA Crim 1815. See also *Eastlake* [2007] EWCA Crim 603.

[81] *Freeman* [2008] EWCA Crim 1863; [2009] 1 Cr.App.R. 11.

[82] See also *Chopra* [2006] EWCA Crim 2133; [2007] 1 Cr.App.R. 16.

of the victims of the offences that have been charged.[83] However, it is not the case that the evidence of the victims of a series of alleged offences by the defendant will always be cross-admissible. In *R. v SW*,[84] D was charged with offences of rape of a child, plus a number of other lesser sexual offences against his female child relatives. The Court of Appeal held that the trial judge should not have treated the evidence of all the complainants as cross-admissible. He should have distinguished between the evidence of the victims of the different groups of offences according to their seriousness.

The third type of case, also involving the issue of cross-admissibility,[85] is illustrated by *Wallace*.[86] The defendant was charged with four counts of robbery. The robberies had a number of features in common, and there was circumstantial evidence linking the defendant to all four. The trial judge allowed the evidence on each count to be cross-admissible on the others, but in relation to each count did not treat the evidence tending to show the defendant's participation in the other robberies as evidence of "bad character". It was simply regarded as relevant circumstantial evidence. Hence no application was made by the prosecution to admit it under s.101(1)(d). Dismissing the appeal, the Court of Appeal held that the evidence did come within s.98 because it was evidence of the defendant's commission of an offence, although it was not tendered to prove bad character in the sense of propensity. This, with respect, is clearly right; the argument for cross-admissibility is again based on the unlikelihood that there is an innocent explanation for the incriminating evidence that the defendant had participated in all four robberies. But since the evidence would inevitably have been admitted via gateway (d) if an application had been made, no injustice had been done to the defendant. Again, a similar analysis can be applied to evidence of other uncharged incidents which the prosecution say help to prove the identity of the defendant as the perpetrator of the offences that have been charged. In *Suleman*,[87] D was charged with offences of arson and public nuisance by making hoax calls to the emergency services. The prosecution case was that D had engaged in a long campaign targeting the business run by members of his family. The Court of Appeal held that the trial judge had rightly admitted evidence of a series of earlier uncharged fires at the business which D had had the opportunity to set; these went "to establish the pattern and progression of offending upon which the prosecution relied to prove the identity of the fire raiser". No argument from a proved propensity is involved in such a case.

---

[83] As in *Nicholson* [2012] EWCA Crim 1568; [2012] 2 Cr.App.R. 31. In the course of the judgment the court repeated the point made in *Suleman* [2012] EWCA Crim 1569; [2012] 2 Cr.App.R. 30 that "cross-admissibility" is a term applicable only to the issue of whether evidence on one *count* in the indictment is admissible to support the evidence on another *count*. It should not be applied to similar fact evidence of uncharged offences or other misconduct.

[84] *R. v SW* [2011] EWCA Crim 2463.

[85] On the problems associated with cross-admissibility generally, see R. Fortson and D. Ormerod, "Bad Character Evidence and Cross-admissibility" [2009] Crim. L.R. 313.

[86] *Wallace* [2007] EWCA Crim 1760; [2007] 2 Cr.App.R. 30. See also *McAllister* [2008] EWCA Crim 1544; [2009] 1 Cr.App.R. 10.

[87] *Suleman* [2012] EWCA Crim 1569; [2012] 2 Cr.App.R. 30.

(A)   Evidence of bad character to prove D's propensity to commit the kind of offence charged

Section 103(1)(a) provides that for the purposes of gateway (d) the matters in issue between the defendant and the prosecution include the question whether the defendant has a propensity to commit offences of the kind with which he is charged, except where his having such a propensity makes it no more likely that he is guilty of the offence. This provision clearly enables, and is intended to enable, the prosecution to adduce evidence of the defendant's record as the basis of an argument that his proved disposition to commit offences of the kind charged makes it more likely that he is guilty. What Lord Hailsham once described[88] as "the forbidden chain of reasoning" at common law is therefore no longer forbidden. Indeed it is now positively encouraged. The provision does not say that the matters in issue "may" include the defendant's propensity, which would be permissive; it simply says that the matters in issue do include propensity. The conclusion must be therefore that the defendant's propensity is deemed to be in issue in all cases unless the exception applies. It is something that it is always capable of being relevant for the jury to take into account in deciding on the defendant's guilt[89] unless on the facts of the case it can make no difference to his likely guilt. According to the Explanatory Notes to the Act[90] this exception is to cater for cases where there is no dispute as to what the defendant did, and the issue is whether the undisputed facts constitute the offence. An example would be an issue of causation in a homicide case, where the defendant claims that a grossly negligent medical intervention broke the causal link between his assault and the death of the victim.

19–022

Given that the test of admissibility for gateway (d) is (simple) relevance, and that "enhanced relevance" or "substantial probative value" is not required, the kind of detailed factual similarities between the previous offences and the one charged that might have been looked for at common law are not necessary.[91] This was confirmed by early cases under the 2003 Act. In *Gilmore*,[92] D was charged with theft of goods stolen from a shed after they were found in his possession. His defence was that he believed that the bag containing the goods had been thrown out as rubbish. The Court of Appeal held that his three convictions for theft by shoplifting had been rightly admitted to show his recent persistent propensity to steal. It is doubtful that these convictions would have been admissible at common law since they did not demonstrate "similar facts" to the offence charged. In *Duggan*,[93] D was charged with wounding with intent to cause grievous bodily harm arising out of an altercation with the victim in a pub. The central issue was self-defence in the context of who was the aggressor. The Court of Appeal held that the trial judge had rightly admitted evidence of D's previous convictions for assault and public order offences; they showed D's propensity to violence, which was relevant to the issue of self-defence. It does not appear from

---

[88] In *DPP v Boardman* [1975] A.C. 421.
[89] See further the analysis by Spencer, *Evidence of Bad Character* (2006), paras 4.24 onwards.
[90] Explanatory Notes to the Act para.371.
[91] *Hanson* [2005] EWCA Crim 824; [2005] 2 Cr.App.R. 21.
[92] Reported with *Hanson* [2005] EWCA Crim 824; [2005] 2 Cr.App.R. 21.
[93] Reported with *Edwards* [2005] EWCA Crim 1813; [2006] 1 Cr.App.R. 3.

the report that any evidence of the facts of the convictions was given, as opposed to the bare fact of conviction for these offences. However, it remains important to identify the precise issue in the case to which the alleged propensity is relevant. In *Bullen*,[94] the defendant was charged with murder. He pleaded to manslaughter on the basis of hitting the victim with a bottle during a drunken fight but denied having the specific intent to kill or cause serious injury. The Court of Appeal held that the trial judge was wrong to admit evidence of the defendant's previous convictions for violence. They were all for offences of basic intent and none had resulted in serious injury. They were therefore not relevant to the issue whether the defendant had the specific intent for murder. *Duggan* was distinguished as a case concerned with the different issue of self-defence, to which a propensity to violence was relevant.[95]

Propensity to commit offences of the kind charged can be shown not only by previous convictions but also by evidence of the defendant's misconduct on other occasions for which he has not been convicted. In *Weir*,[96] evidence that the defendant had been cautioned on a previous occasion for making an indecent photograph of a child was held to be admissible evidence of propensity on a charge of sexual assault on a girl under 13.[97] In *David Smith*,[98] D was charged with a number of sexual offences against three children. The counts relating to offences against two of the children were stayed as an abuse of process, and the trial proceeded on the counts relating to the third. The trial judge admitted the evidence of the first two children relating to the alleged offences against them to prove D's propensity to commit the offences for which he was being tried. Upholding the convictions the Court of Appeal held that there were no grounds for interfering with the judge's decision. The court rejected the argument that an allegation which is untested by a judicial or quasi-judicial finding cannot be evidence of a defendant's bad character for the purposes of s.101. The fact that the counts had been stayed against the witnesses in question was immaterial.[99] It was for the jury to decide whether the allegations were true.

19–023 Section 103(2) provides that a defendant's propensity to commit offences of the kind charged can be proved by evidence that he has been convicted of either an

---

[94] *Bullen* [2008] EWCA Crim 4; [2008] 2 Cr.App.R. 25.

[95] See also *Brima* [2006] EWCA Crim 408; [2007] 1 Cr.App.R. 24, where previous convictions for assault occasioning actual bodily harm and robbery were admissible to show the defendant had a propensity to commit offences of violence by using knives to inflict or threaten injury, which was relevant to rebut his defence of mistaken identity to a charge of murder by stabbing.

[96] *Weir* [2005] EWCA Crim 2866; [2006] 2 All E.R. 570.

[97] However, where a caution has been given after an admission made without legal advice there may be a good argument for excluding it on the basis of unfairness, given variations in police practice in administering cautions: see *Olu* [2010] EWCA Crim 2975. A caution can be contrasted with a penalty notice for disorder, which is not a conviction and does not involve any admission of guilt. However, evidence that a penalty notice was issued to D would seem to be evidence of reprehensible behaviour and therefore evidence of bad character, contrary to the view of the Court of Appeal in *Hamer* [2010] EWCA Crim 2053.

[98] Reported with *Edwards and Rowlands* [2005] EWCA Crim 3244; [2006] 2 Cr.App.R. 4. See also *Nguyen* [2008] EWCA Crim 585; [2008] 2 Cr.App.R. 9, where the CPS had decided not to prosecute for the earlier offence.

[99] Similarly, it is no answer that the defendant has been acquitted of the other charges if the evidence of the complainants relating to those charges is relevant to the offence for which the defendant is on trial: *R. v Z* [2000] 2 A.C. 483 HL.

offence of the same *description* as the one charged, or an offence of the same *category* as the one charged. The subsection states explicitly that this is without prejudice to any other way of proving propensity, and the cases cited in the previous paragraph offer examples of other ways. In *Johnson*,[100] where the defendants were charged with a large-scale conspiracy to burgle, the trial judge ruled that the convictions of four of the defendants for offences of burglary and attempted theft were not evidence of propensity under s.103(2) since they were not offences of the same description or category as conspiracy. But they were relevant and admissible on the important issue of whether the defendants "would participate in a conspiracy to burgle". The Court of Appeal held that this was synonymous with the concept of propensity, but since the subsection expressly allowed for propensity to be proved by other means the convictions were rightly admitted.

Two offences are of the same description as each other if the statement of the offence in a written charge or indictment would in each case be in the same terms (s.103(4)(a)). Two offences are of the same category as each other if they belong to the same category of offences prescribed for the purposes of s.103 by an order made by the Secretary of State (s.103(4)(b)). Such a category must consist of offences of the same type (s.103(5)). So far two categories of offences have been prescribed by order under these provisions.[101] The first consists of theft and related offences, such as burglary, robbery, taking vehicles without consent, handling stolen goods, going equipped for stealing and making off without payment. The second consists of sexual offences against minors and includes a total of 36 offences, mostly under the Sexual Offences Act 2003.

Thus a defendant charged with theft may have his previous convictions for theft proved against him, as offences of the same description, and his convictions for burglary and handling may also be proved, as offences of the same category. It will not matter, as *Gilmore* demonstrates, that the underlying facts of the offences for which the defendant was convicted are different from the facts of the offence charged. However, the mere fact of those convictions will not necessarily open gateway (d). According to the Court of Appeal in *Hanson*,[102] where propensity to commit the offence charged is relied on there are three questions to be considered:

(1) Does the history of conviction(s) establish a propensity to commit offences of the kind charged?
(2) Does that propensity make it more likely that the defendant committed the offence charged?
(3) Is it unjust to rely on the conviction(s) of the same description or category; and, in any event, will the proceedings be unfair if they admitted?

The court went on to offer further clarification of the application of s.103(2):

"In referring to offences of the same description or category, s.103(2) is not exhaustive of the types of conviction which might be relied upon to show evidence of propensity to commit

---

[100] *Johnson* [2009] EWCA Crim 649; [2009] 2 Cr.App.R. 7.
[101] Criminal Justice Act 2003 (Categories of Offences) Order 2004 (SI 2004/3346).
[102] *Hanson* [2005] EWCA Crim 824; [2005] 2 Cr.App.R. 21.

offences of the kind charged. Nor, however, is it necessarily sufficient, in order to show such propensity, that a conviction should be of the same description or category as that charged.

There is no minimum number of events necessary to demonstrate such a propensity. The fewer the number of convictions the weaker is likely to be the evidence of propensity. A single previous conviction for an offence of the same description or category will often not show propensity. But it may do so where, for example, it shows a tendency to unusual behaviour or where its circumstances demonstrate probative force in relation to the offence charged... Circumstances demonstrating probative force are not confined to those sharing striking similarity."[103]

This has proved to be an important statement of principle. On a number of occasions the Court of Appeal has upheld the admission of evidence of just one previous conviction to show propensity. In *Jackson*,[104] D was charged with the murder of an elderly man by strangulation. Evidence was admitted of D's conviction for a murder 20 years earlier when he had strangled a much younger victim in different circumstances. The Court of Appeal said that the evidence was rightly admitted, not on a "strikingly similar fact" or "signature" basis, but to show the propensity of D to carry out a serious attack by strangulation. It seems that the fact of the other killing, by the same method, was sufficient to give the evidence probative force in relation to the murder charged. Similarly, in *Miller*[105] D was charged with rape of a child under 13. At the time of the rape D was aged 25. Evidence was admitted of a conviction for an earlier rape when he was 16. The victim had been 15, and the offence took place in the very different circumstances of a gang rape. Nevertheless the Court of Appeal took the view that the conviction showed D's propensity to have sex with non-consenting young girls by means involving an abuse of power. It may well be therefore that where a single conviction is for the same type of serious crime, relatively little will be needed in the way of similarity for it to have probative force in relation to the crime charged.[106]

(B)   Evidence of bad character to prove D's propensity to be untruthful

19–024   Section 103(1)(b) provides that the matters in issue between the defendant and the prosecution include the question whether the defendant has a propensity to be untruthful, except where it is not suggested that the defendant's case is untruthful in any respect. This provision thus stipulates for the defendant's credibility to be in issue in the same way as s.103(1)(a) stipulates for his disposition to commit the kind of offence charged to be in issue. It might seem as a matter of first impression that the defendant's truthfulness will generally be in issue where he gives evidence in his defence denying the charge, or evidence is adduced of his exculpatory statements out of court, say on arrest or in a police interview. However, in *Campbell* the Court of Appeal was extremely sceptical of the distinction between bad character evidence going to guilt of the offence charged

---

[103] *Hanson* [2005] EWCA Crim 824; [2005] 2 Cr.App.R. 21 at [8], [9].

[104] *Jackson* [2011] EWCA Crim 1870.

[105] *Miller* [2010] EWCA Crim 1578.

[106] See also *Nguyen* [2008] EWCA Crim 585; [2008] 2 Cr.App.R. 9 for an example of a case where one previous incident of uncharged misconduct was held admissible to prove a propensity to violence, on the basis that the facts of the previous incident were substantially similar to the offence charged.

and bad character evidence going to the defendant's credibility. Describing the distinction as contrary to common sense and wholly unrealistic, Lord Phillips C.J. said:

> "If the jury learn that a defendant has shown a propensity to commit criminal acts they may well at one and the same time conclude that it is more likely that he is guilty and that he is less likely to be telling the truth when he says that he is not."[107]

This comment was made in the context of a case where the defendant was charged with false imprisonment and assault occasioning actual bodily harm. The prosecution case was that he had kept his girlfriend prisoner in her flat and had assaulted her when she escaped to the flat of a friend nearby. The defence was a complete denial. Having admitted via gateway (d) the defendant's previous convictions for violence against former girlfriends involving similar conduct, the judge directed the jury that they could take the convictions into account in deciding whether the defendant's evidence denying the offences charged was truthful. Dismissing the appeal, the court described this direction as unhelpful because it did not sufficiently relate the convictions to the facts of the case, but held that the convictions were safe. After the passage cited above, Lord Phillips C.J. continued:

> "The question of whether a defendant has a propensity for being untruthful will not normally be capable of being described as an *important* matter in issue between the defendant and the prosecution. A propensity for untruthfulness will not, of itself, go very far to establishing the committal of a criminal offence. To suggest that a propensity for untruthfulness makes it more likely that a defendant has lied to the jury is not likely to help them. If they apply common sense they will conclude that a defendant who has committed a criminal offence may well be prepared to lie about it, even if he has not shown a propensity for lying whereas a defendant who has not committed the offence charged will be likely to tell the truth, even if he has shown a propensity for telling lies. In short, whether or not a defendant is telling the truth to the jury is likely to depend simply on whether or not he has committed the offence charged. The jury should focus on the latter question rather than on whether or not he has a propensity for telling lies.
>
> For these reasons, the only circumstances in which there is likely to be an *important* issue as to whether a defendant has a propensity to tell lies is where telling lies is an element of the offence charged. Even then, the propensity to tell lies is only likely to be significant if the lying is in the context of committing criminal offences, in which case the evidence is likely to be admissible under s.103(1)(a)."[108]

Lord Phillips' view of when credibility of the defendant will be in issue for the purposes of gateway (d) stands in some contrast, as we shall see, to the significance of the defendant's credibility in relation to gateways (e) and (g).[109] It is also somewhat at odds with the view of the Court of Appeal in *Hanson*,[110] where the court had taken a restrictive line on propensity for untruthfulness in gateway (d), but one that was less narrow than *Campbell*. In *Hanson,* the court rejected the view of the law before the Act that character is indivisible, so that in principle all convictions could be relevant to credibility. In particular the court

---

rejected the idea that commercial dishonesty is, without more, relevant to the question of testimonial dishonesty. The Court of Appeal stated:

> "As to propensity to untruthfulness, this, as it seems to us, is not the same as propensity to dishonesty. It is to be assumed, bearing in mind the frequency with which the words honest and dishonest appear in the criminal law, that Parliament deliberately chose the word 'untruthful' to convey a different meaning, reflecting a defendant's account of his behaviour, or lies told when committing an offence. Previous convictions, whether for offences of dishonesty or otherwise, are therefore only likely to be capable of showing a propensity to be untruthful where, in the present case, truthfulness is an issue and, in the earlier case, either there was a plea of not guilty and the defendant gave an account, on arrest, in interview, or in evidence, which the jury must have disbelieved, or the way in which the offence was committed shows a propensity for untruthfulness, for example, by the making of false representations."[111]

The logic of Lord Phillips C.J. in *Campbell* renders the "propensity to be untruthful" side of gateway (d) very largely redundant. *Hanson* makes it narrow, but allows passage for bad character evidence involving deception not limited to cases where the offences charged also involve deception. In relation to gateway (d), Mirfield's analysis a few years ago suggested that most of the later cases followed or were at least consistent with *Hanson*.[112] This position is further illustrated by *Ellis*,[113] where the issue was whether D had a reasonable excuse for possessing an offensive weapon in a public place. He had at first lied to the police and then came up with a second story. The admissibility of his convictions five years earlier for obtaining services by deception, and using a false instrument, in relation to fraudulent time sheets he had submitted, was unchallenged. However, as we shall see, neither the *Campbell* nor the *Hanson* approach has prevailed in relation to gateways (e) or (g).

(C)   Discretionary exclusion of evidence of bad character via gateway (d)

19–025   Section 101(3) provides that the court must not admit evidence under subs.(1)(d) if, on an application by the defendant to exclude it, it appears to the court that the admission of the evidence would have such an adverse effect on the fairness of the proceedings that the court ought not to admit it. This principle of fairness is clearly derived from s.78 of PACE, which was applicable under the previous law to similar fact evidence adduced by the prosecution.[114] In addition, s.103(3) provides in effect that a court should not admit a conviction by virtue of s.103(2) for an offence of the same description or category as the offence charged, in order to show the defendant's propensity to commit the kind of offence charged, if the

---

[111] *Hanson* [2005] EWCA Crim 824; [2005] 2 Cr.App.R. 21 at [13].

[112] Mirfield, "Character and Credibility" [2009] Crim. L.R. 135, 139–141. At least one case, *Belogun* [2008] EWCA Crim 2006, appeared to be inconsistent with *Campbell* [2007] EWCA Crim 1472; [2007] 2 Cr.App.R. 28.

[113] *Ellis* [2010] EWCA Crim 163.

[114] See *R. v H* [1995] 2 A.C. 596 at 612 per Lord Mackay L.C. and 627 per Lord Nicholls; *Johnson* [1995] 2 Cr.App.R. 41 CA. For a case under the new law, where the Court of Appeal thought that evidence of D's bad character (not involving convictions) should have been excluded from gateway (d) as more prejudicial than probative, see *Saint* [2010] EWCA Crim 1924.

court is satisfied, by reason of the length of time since the conviction or for any other reason, that it would be unjust to admit it.

Section 101(3) applies generally to all cases of bad character evidence admissible via gateway (d), whereas s.103(3) applies only to convictions admissible under s.103(2). The two provisions refer to fairness and justice respectively, but it is not clear that s.103(3) adds anything to s.101(3) in cases where they both apply.[115] The factor of lapse of time could be considered as part of the issue of fairness in any event. In *Hanson,* the Court of Appeal commented on the relationship between these two provisions, and on the factors relevant to their application:

> "In a conviction case, the decisions required of the trial judge under s.101(3) and 103(3), though not identical, are closely related ... When considering what is just under s.103(3), and the fairness of the proceedings under s.101(3), the judge may, among other factors, take into consideration the degree of similarity between the previous conviction and the offence charged, albeit they are both within the same description or prescribed category. For example, theft and assault occasioning actual bodily harm may each embrace a wide spectrum of conduct. This does not however mean that what used to be referred to as striking similarity must be shown before convictions become admissible. The judge may also take into consideration the respective gravity of the past and present offences. He or she must always consider the strength of the prosecution case. If there is no or very little other evidence against a defendant, it is unlikely to be just to admit his previous convictions, whatever they are.
>
> In principle, if there is a substantial gap between the dates of commission of and conviction for the earlier offences, we would regard the date of commission as generally being of more significance than the date of conviction when assessing admissibility. Old convictions, with no special feature shared with the offence charged, are likely seriously to affect the fairness of proceedings adversely, unless, despite their age, it can properly be said that they show a continuing propensity."[116]

5. Gateway (e): substantial probative value in relation to an important matter in issue between the defendant and a co-defendant

Evidence of the bad character of a defendant is admissible via gateway (e) of s.101(1) if it has substantial probative value in relation to an important matter in issue between the defendant and a co-defendant. Section 104 supplements this by providing:

19–026

> "(1) Evidence which is relevant to the question whether the defendant has a propensity to be untruthful is admissible on that basis under section 101(1)(e) only if the nature or conduct of his defence is such as to undermine the co-defendant's defence.
> (2) Only evidence—
> (a) which is to be (or has been) adduced by the co-defendant, or
> (b) which a witness is to be invited to give (or has given) in cross-examination by the co-defendant, is admissible under section 101(1)(e)."

Section 104(2) makes clear that only the co-accused can adduce evidence via gateway (e), whether in chief or by cross-examination. This gateway is not

---

[115] Subject to the point that the defendant has to make an application for evidence to be excluded under s.101(3), whereas the court can apply s.103(3) of its own motion.
[116] *Hanson* [2005] EWCA Crim 824; [2005] 2 Cr.App.R. 21 at [10], [11].

available to the prosecution.[117] If the prosecution wish to adduce evidence of the accused's bad character they will have to use one of gateways (c), (d), (f) or (g). Gateways (f) and (g) will only be available respectively where the accused conducts his defence in such a way as to give an impression of his good character or to attack the character of another person. If the defendant does neither of these things the prosecution will be restricted to gateways (c) and (d). Gateway (e) will be available to a co-accused only where the evidence of the accused's bad character is of substantial probative value in relation to an important matter in issue between them. An "important matter" means a matter of substantial importance in the context of the case as a whole.[118]

Evidence that satisfies the test for gateway (e) will be admissible for the co-accused as of right. The section gives the judge no discretion to exclude it, even if he regards it as having great potential for prejudice compared with its probative value. The statutory exclusionary discretion in s.101(3) is not available for gateway (e), and s.78 of PACE is available only for evidence on which the prosecution propose to rely. Assuming that the discretion at common law to exclude evidence where its prejudicial effect exceeds its probative value has survived the abolition of the common law *rules* governing the admissibility of evidence of bad character,[119] it did not extend to the exclusion of defence evidence in any event.[120] However, in *Musone*[121] the Court of Appeal held that the rules of court made under s.111 of the Act conferred power on a court to exclude evidence that would be admissible via gateway (e) where there had been a breach of a prescribed requirement.[122] So if a defendant's failure to give notice of intention to adduce evidence of the bad character of a co-accused was not due to oversight, but because of a deliberate intention to ambush the co-accused and make it difficult for him to deal with the evidence, the judge was entitled to exclude that evidence. In this way the co-accused's right to a fair trial could be protected.

19–027   Section 104(1) necessarily implies that evidence of bad character can be adduced via gateway (e) where it is relevant to the accused's credibility. The credibility of the accused will be an important matter in issue between the accused and a co-accused where the accused's evidence or admissible statements tend to undermine the co-accused's defence; an example would be where the accused's testimony, if believed, would destroy the co-accused's alibi. But the accused's credibility is not the only possible matter in issue between him and the co-accused. The matter in issue may be which of them committed an offence with which they are jointly charged. Each may run a classic "cut-throat" defence and explicitly blame the other. Alternatively their denials of liability may in the circumstances of the case necessarily imply that the other was responsible. In such a case the co-accused may wish to bring out the bad character of the accused

---

[117] It is a separate question whether the prosecution can *use* evidence adduced by a co-accused via gateway (e). See the discussion in the text below.

[118] Criminal Justice Act 2003 s.112(1).

[119] See the discussion in section B above.

[120] *Lobban v R.* [1995] 2 All E.R. 602 PC; *Randall* [2003] UKHL 69; [2004] 1 Cr.App.R. 26.

[121] *Musone* [2007] EWCA Crim 1237; [2007] 2 Cr.App.R. 29.

[122] See also *Jarvis* [2008] EWCA Crim 488 at [34] and *Phillips* [2011] EWCA Crim 2935; [2012] 1 Cr.App.R. 25 at [54]–[55] to the same effect.

to support an argument that the accused is more likely by virtue of his disposition to have committed the offence than the co-accused. In this way the bad character evidence would go directly to the respective guilt and innocence of the accused and co-accused.

The wording of s.101(1)(e) allows for both types of use of evidence of bad character, provided the evidence has substantial probative value in relation to the matter in issue between the co-defendants. The Act largely follows the recommendations of the Law Commission in relation to co-defendants.[123] The Commission proposed the criteria of "substantial" probative value and "important" matter in issue to give effect to a requirement for "enhanced relevance" for the admission of bad character evidence via gateway (e). This requirement was intended to go some way to compensate for the lack of a discretion to exclude very prejudicial evidence of bad character via this gateway. In *Phillips,* the Court of Appeal emphasised the significance of this function of the test in s. 101(1)(e):

> "It is important, in our view, that the threshold for admissibility is not understated. The purpose of the requirement is to ensure as far as possible that the probative strength of the evidence removes the risk of *unfair* prejudice."[124] (emphasis original)

The court went on to say that the ability of one accused to lead evidence of the bad character of a co-accused under s.101(1)(e) meant that the potential for satellite litigation was increased. This added to the need to maintain the rigour of the test of *substantial* probative value on an issue of *substantial* importance between the defendants. Accordingly the court thought that the Law Commission's reference to "substantial probative value" meaning "more than trivial probative value"[125] could be misleading. It seems that a greater degree of probative value is required than is implied by this description. This is reinforced by the further point made in *Phillips* that the trial judge should not consider the item of bad character evidence in isolation. He should take into account the other evidence going to the issue in question between the defendants, and in effect ask whether the disputed evidence will add substantially to what is already available.

We can now look in more detail at the use of bad character evidence via gateway (e), first as relevant to the co-accused's defence, and, secondly as relevant to the accused's credibility. The discussion will include some reference to leading cases decided under the old law, since although the old rules of admissibility have been abolished, these cases provide useful illustrations of how the principles of gateway (e) may be applied.

(A) Evidence of the bad character of the accused (D1) adduced by a co-accused (D2) as relevant to D2's defence

As noted above, it may be an important matter in issue between co-accused as to which of them committed the criminal act charged, or which of them did admitted acts with the requisite mens rea. Using gateway (e) D2 may lead, or elicit by cross-examination of prosecution witnesses, evidence showing D1's criminal

19–028

---

[123] Law Com. 273 Pt XIV.
[124] *Phillips* [2011] EWCA Crim 2935; [2012] 1 Cr.App.R. 25 at [40].
[125] Law Com. 273 para.14.43.

propensity or other misconduct if such evidence is relevant to D2's defence and has substantial probative value on the fact in issue between them. An illustration of a case of the use of bad character evidence for this purpose, which does not depend on an argument from propensity, is the common law decision in *Miller*.[126] Three accused were charged with conspiracy to evade customs duties. The defence of one, D2, was that he was not involved and that the offences were committed by one of the others, D1, who had masqueraded as him. Devlin J., the trial judge, permitted D2 to cross-examine a prosecution witness on whether the offences had stopped when D1 was in prison and re-started only when D1 was released. This evidence was relevant to support D2's defence that the offences were committed by D1 without D2's participation. In this case the revelation that D1 had been in prison was incidental. The relevance of the evidence would have been exactly the same if it had shown that D1 was in hospital at the material time. It is submitted that this case would be decided the same way under gateway (e) of the 2003 Act.

19–029   Where the respective characters of D1 and D2 become an important issue in the case D2 may wish to support his defence by relying on an argument from D1's propensity. The leading case at common law was the decision of the House of Lords in *Randall*.[127] Randall (D2) was charged jointly with Glean (D1) with murder. The prosecution case was that they jointly or independently attacked and killed the victim. Each gave evidence blaming the other, with the result that the bad character of both became admissible and each was cross-examined by the other on his previous convictions. D2 had relatively minor convictions for driving offences and disorderly behaviour, but it was suggested that he had used violence towards his former girlfriend. D1 had a worse record, which included convictions for robbery and burglary involving the use of weapons to threaten violence. The trial judge directed the jury that the evidence of bad character was relevant only to the defendants' credibility and that D1's convictions were irrelevant to the likelihood of him having attacked the victim. The jury convicted D2 of manslaughter and acquitted D1. The Court of Appeal held that the judge had misdirected the jury; the court allowed D2's appeal and ordered a retrial. The House of Lords dismissed the prosecution's appeal. Lord Steyn, with whom all the other Lords agreed, held that where in a joint trial a propensity to violence of an accused is relevant to the facts in issue, a co-accused is entitled to disprove his own guilt by tendering evidence of the accused's propensity to show that his version of the facts is more probable than that of the accused. Propensity was relevant in this case because each accused blamed the other. It was not necessary that character was expressly put in issue. Lord Steyn put the argument for the relevance of propensity to guilt, as well as credibility, in this type of case very clearly:

> "Postulate a joint trial involving two accused arising from an assault committed in a pub. Assume it to be clear that one of the two men committed the assault. The one man has a long list of previous convictions involving assaults in pubs. It shows him to be prone to fighting when he had consumed alcohol. The other man has an unblemished record. Relying on experience and common sense one may rhetorically ask why the propensity to violence of one

---

[126] *Miller* [1952] 2 All E.R. 667.
[127] *Randall* [2003] UKHL 69; [2004] 1 Cr.App.R. 26.

man should not be deployed by the other man as part of his defence that he did not commit the assault. Surely such evidence is capable, depending on the jury's assessment of all the evidence, of making it more probable that the man with the violent disposition when he had consumed alcohol committed the assault. To rule that the jury may use the convictions in regard to his credibility but that convictions revealing his propensity to violence must otherwise be ignored is to ask the jury to put to one side their common sense and experience. It would be curious if the law compelled such an unrealistic result."[128]

The position appears to be the same under the 2003 Act. In *Hussain*,[129] two defendants were charged jointly with attempted robbery at D1's workplace. The defence of both included claims that the other was a drug supplier who had persuaded the hapless addicted purchaser of drugs to attempt the robbery. The trial judge permitted D2 to adduce evidence from the manageress of the workplace that she had seen D1 engaged in drug transactions, on the basis that this evidence had substantial probative value upon an important issue arising between them. In the course of its judgment on a separate issue the Court of Appeal commented that the judge "was plainly right about that and there is no complaint about that part of his ruling".[130] In *Phillips*,[131] the defendants were charged with conspiracy to cheat the public revenue arising out of a complex construction industry fraud. Both accepted that a fraud must have taken place while they were working together, but both denied responsibility, thereby impliedly blaming each other. The trial judge allowed D2 to admit evidence of D1's previous conviction some years earlier for conspiracy to defraud, but refused to allow D2 to lead evidence of D1's involvement in a similar construction industry fraud before the period covered by the indictment in the case. The Court of Appeal held that this evidence should have been admitted since it had substantial probative value on the important issue whether D2, as he claimed, had been recruited to perpetrate an existing fraud set up by D1. D1's propensity to commit such frauds was clearly relevant to that defence. The court confirmed that once a judge is satisfied that the conditions of gateway (e) are met, the judge has no discretion to exclude the evidence to prevent satellite litigation or unfairness to D1.

It follows therefore that in considering the prosecution case against D2 the jury can take into account D1's disposition where that is relevant to D2's claim that it was not him but D1 who committed the offence. It is relevant because it may ground an inference that D1 is more likely than D2 to have committed the offence. This leads naturally to a further question. What is the position with regard to the *prosecution's* case against D1? Can the jury take D1's disposition into account in deciding whether he is guilty? In *Randall* Lord Steyn added:

"For the avoidance of doubt I would further add that in my view where evidence of propensity of a co-accused is relevant to a fact in issue between the Crown and the other accused it is not necessary for a trial judge to direct the jury to ignore that evidence in considering the case against the co-accused. Justice does not require that such a direction be given. Moreover, such a direction would needlessly perplex juries."[132]

---

[128] *Randall* [2003] UKHL 69; [2004] 1 Cr.App.R. 26 at [22].
[129] *Hussain* [2008] EWCA Crim 1117.
[130] *Hussain* [2008] EWCA Crim 1117 at [8].
[131] *Phillips* [2011] EWCA Crim 2935; [2012] 1 Cr.App.R. 25.
[132] *Randall* [2003] UKHL; [2004] 1 Cr.App.R. at [35].

19–030   This view has powerful support from logic and common sense. If D1's propensity is relevant to D2's guilt because it tends to decrease the probability of D2 having committed the crime, it is a necessary step in the reasoning that it tends to increase the probability that D1 committed the offence, given the premise that it must have been one or both of them. A jury would surely be baffled if directed to discard this logic when considering D1's guilt. Their bafflement would be even greater when told that they could take D1's propensity into account in considering his credibility in claiming that it was not him but D2 who did it. However, a problem then arises of whether the prosecution are getting an unfair "windfall". If the prosecution would not have been able to adduce evidence of D1's propensity in their evidence in chief against him because it did not satisfy the test for the admission of evidence via gateway (d), should they be permitted to rely on it when it is adduced by D2?

This problem produced inconsistent decisions in two Court of Appeal cases at common law. In *Price*,[133] the Court of Appeal followed Lord Steyn's dictum in *Randall*, saying that once the evidence of D1's previous violence and reputation for violence was in, the jury might use that evidence as they saw fit. In that case D1's propensity to aggression, and his reputation for aggression, was relevant not only to whether it was D2 who had killed the victim, but also to whether, if it was D1, D2 had been a party to the attack or whether, as he claimed, he had been too scared of D1 to intervene. In *Mertens*,[134] a differently constituted Court of Appeal held that Lord Steyn's dictum in *Randall* was concerned with evidence of disposition that was relevant as similar fact evidence; it could not therefore be relied on by the prosecution unless adduced by the prosecution as similar fact evidence. The textual support for this reading of Lord Steyn's dictum is very thin, and its accuracy was doubted subsequently by the Court of Appeal in *Robinson*.[135] In *Robinson* the Court of Appeal upheld a direction that all the evidence could be taken into account when considering the case of each defendant, including the evidence of D1's bad character. However, the court's endorsement of the principle stated by Lord Steyn in his dictum in *Randall* was less than wholehearted; it was suggested that where the evidence of bad character is not admissible for the prosecution, "it is to be hoped that the prosecution do not seek in closing the case to the jury to rely on it".[136]

The position under the 2003 Act is unclear. In *McLean*,[137] McLean (D1) was jointly charged with D2 with wounding V with intent to cause grievous bodily harm. D1 and D2 gave entirely separate versions of the event. The trial judge described these as not cut-throat defences in the classic sense, perhaps because both defendants alleged that the other must have carried out the attack with a third person. Nevertheless the judge held that there was an important matter in issue between them. He then held that D1's convictions for violence had substantial probative value in relation to that issue and allowed D2 to adduce

---

[133] *Price* [2005] Crim. L.R. 304.

[134] *Mertens* [2005] Crim. L.R. 301. See also *Murrell* [2005] EWCA Crim 382; [2005] Crim. L.R. 869, another cut-throat defence case, where the Court of Appeal upheld a judge's direction not to take an accused's conviction into account when considering the prosecution case against him.

[135] *Robinson* [2005] EWCA Crim 3233; [2006] 1 Cr.App.R. 32.

[136] *Robinson* [2005] EWCA Crim 3233; [2006] 1 Cr.App.R. 32 at [83].

[137] Reported with *Edwards and Rowlands* [2005] EWCA Crim 3244; [2006] 2 Cr.App.R. 4 at [34].

evidence of them. The jury convicted D1 and acquitted D2. D1's main ground of appeal was that the convictions should not have been admitted via gateway (e) because on the previous day the judge had refused an application by the prosecution to admit them via gateway (d). Dismissing the appeal the Court of Appeal was plainly doubtful whether the judge had been right to refuse the prosecution's application, but went on to say that different considerations applied to the two gateways and that the judge had applied the test for gateway (e) correctly. The court concluded by saying that once gateway (e) was open the evidence "was in". It is not clear whether this means that it could be used by the prosecution as part of their case against D1, despite the judge's earlier ruling. However, the decision in *Highton*,[138] not referred to in *McLean*, is authority for the proposition that evidence admitted via any of the gateways can be used for whatever purpose it is relevant. D1's convictions in *McLean*, like those of D1 in *Price*, were relevant to the issue of his guilt where his case was that he did not commit the offence and D2 did.

It is apparent that cases involving multiple defendants may give rise to difficult problems of fairness where they are running "cut-throat" defences.[139] An order for separate trials remains an option for dealing with cases where very prejudicial evidence of disposition is likely to be relevant. However, according to Lord Steyn in *Randall*[140] it is established practice that those who are charged with an offence allegedly committed in a joint criminal enterprise should generally be tried in a joint trial. In such a case a judge will be unlikely to consider that the interests of justice require separate trials, given the resulting costs, the hardship caused to victims and witnesses by having to attend successive trials, and the desirability of having the issues of responsibility arising out of the incident determined in a single hearing.

19–031

(B) Evidence adduced by a co-accused (D2) to prove the propensity of the accused (D1) to be untruthful

Under the Criminal Evidence Act 1898 s.1(3)(iii) the accused lost the statutory shield against cross-examination on his bad character if he gave evidence against any other person charged in the same proceedings. "Giving evidence against" was interpreted to mean giving evidence that either supported the prosecution case against the co-accused in a material particular or undermined the defence of the co-accused.[141] If D1 lost the shield in this way D2 could cross-examine D1 on his bad character for the purpose of attacking his credibility in testifying against D2. Although this provision has been repealed by the Act, most of its effect is preserved by ss.101(1)(e) and 104. D2 can adduce evidence of D1's bad character to show D1's propensity to be untruthful where D1's credibility is an important

19–032

---

[138] *Highton* [2005] EWCA Crim 1985; [2006] 1 Cr.App.R. 7.
[139] Where they are not, and the evidence of D1's disposition is not otherwise relevant to D2's defence, the evidence is irrelevant and inadmissible: *R. v B(C)* [2004] EWCA Crim 1254; [2004] 2 Cr.App.R. 34.
[140] *Randall* [2003] UKHL 69; [2004] 1 Cr.App.R. 26 at [16].
[141] *Murdoch v Taylor* [1965] A.C. 574.

matter in issue between them, the evidence has substantial probative value on the issue of credibility, and the nature or conduct of D1's defence is such as to undermine D2's defence.

However, the scope for D2 to adduce evidence of D1's bad character as relevant to D1's credibility may be narrower than under the 1898 Act in two ways. The first is that the evidence must be relevant to the question whether D1 has a "propensity to be untruthful". Under the 1898 Act, where D1 lost the shield, D2 could cross-examine on *any* conviction of D1, even if it had no apparent connection with not telling the truth. But, as discussed above, in *Hanson* the Court of Appeal stated in relation to gateway (d) that a propensity to be untruthful is not the same as a propensity to dishonesty. According to the court, previous convictions, whether for offences of dishonesty or otherwise, are likely to be capable of showing a propensity to be untruthful only if, in the earlier case, either there was a plea of not guilty and D1 gave an account that the jury must have disbelieved, or the way in which the offence was committed showed a propensity for untruthfulness, for example by the making of false representations. As we have seen, *Campbell* took an even more restrictive view of the propensity to be untruthful in gateway (d).[142]

It is doubtful whether either of these restrictive approaches applies to gateway (e). Munday argued that the analysis in *Hanson* did apply[143]; Spencer disagreed.[144] The cases appear to support Spencer's view, although not all of them have considered the issue fully.[145] In *Lawson*,[146] the Court of Appeal distinguished *Hanson*, holding that the trial judge had rightly found that D1's conviction for assault, put to him by D2, who was jointly charged with D1 with manslaughter, was relevant to D1's credibility in giving evidence of incriminating remarks by D2:

> "A defendant who is defending himself against the evidence of a person whose history of criminal behaviour or other misconduct is such as to be capable of showing him to be unscrupulous or otherwise unreliable should be enabled to present that history before the jury for its evaluation of the evidence of the witness. Such suggested unreliability may be capable of being shown by conduct which does not involve an element of untruthfulness; it may be capable of being shown by widely differing conduct, ranging from large-scale drug—or people- trafficking via housebreaking to criminal violence. Whether in a particular case it is capable of having substantial probative value in relation to the witness's reliability is for the trial judge to determine on all the facts of the case."[147]

The court added that the Act addresses different occasions on which bad character evidence may be admissible and provides a different framework of rules for each situation. In *Rosato,* two accused charged with arson each blamed the other for starting the fire. The judge ruled that D2 could adduce evidence via gateway (e)

---

[142] *Campbell* [2007] EWCA Crim 1472; [2007] 2 Cr.App.R. 28. See para.19–24 above.
[143] R. Munday, "Cut-Throat Defences and the 'Propensity to be Untruthful' under s.104 of the Criminal Justice Act 2003" [2005] Crim. L.R. 624.
[144] Spencer, *Evidence of Bad Character* (2006), para.4.70.
[145] See Mirfield, "Character and Credibility" [2009] Crim. L.R. 135, 141–143.
[146] *Lawson* [2006] EWCA Crim 2572; [2007] 1 Cr.App.R. 11.
[147] *Lawson* [2006] EWCA Crim 2572; [2007] 1 Cr.App.R. 11 at [34].

of D1's convictions for offences of dishonesty, including burglary and theft. Upholding the ruling, the Court of Appeal cited *Lawson*, making no reference to either *Hanson* or *Campbell*, and said:

> "When looking at the matter as between co-defendants, the court is not narrowly constrained to consider simply whether the defendant has a past history of offences which in themselves involve lies or deceit . . . the approach adopted by the court in *Lawson* is based on the recognition that there may be other forms of misconduct which could reasonably cause a fair-minded jury to suppose that somebody guilty of that misconduct would not scruple to tell a lie if necessary for his own protection."[148]

It seems in the light of these cases that neither of the restrictive approaches that have been suggested to apply to gateway (d) is applicable to gateway (e). At the same time none of the cases decided under the 2003 Act has suggested that *any* confession of an accused can be admitted by a co-accused when gateway (e) is available.

The second way in which the scope given to the co-accused by the 2003 Act may be narrower than the corresponding provision in the 1898 Act is that the co-accused can adduce evidence of the accused's bad character as relevant to the accused's credibility only where the nature or conduct of the accused's defence is such as to undermine the co-accused's defence. Unlike the position under the 1898 Act, it will not be sufficient that the accused's evidence supports the prosecution case against the co-accused if it does not undermine the latter's defence. In many cases, of course, the accused's evidence against the co-accused will do both. Nevertheless, it is possible to imagine cases where D1's evidence incriminates D2 as to one or more of the elements of the offence charged, for example by showing that D2 hit the victim or appropriated property belonging to another, but does not touch on D2's defence of lack of mens rea or duress. In such a case gateway (e) will not open.

19–033

The concept of undermining the co-accused's defence received much consideration in the case law under the 1898 Act. Since the 2003 Act employs the same concept in the same context the principles established by the old case law could provide valuable guidance for the operation of gateway (e). The House of Lords considered most of the issues in the leading case of *Murdoch v Taylor*[149]; and their conclusions were subsequently restated and expanded by the Court of Appeal in *Varley*.[150]

The first of those principles is that it is not necessary that the accused should have any hostile intent towards the co-accused. In *Murdoch v Taylor,* the defence had argued that s.1(3)(iii) of the 1898 Act should be interpreted to apply only to evidence given by D1 against D2 with hostile intent, on the basis that the provision was concerned to protect a co-accused where he was the subject of intentional attack by the accused. The response of the House of Lords was that it is the effect of the evidence on the jury that is important, and that is an objective test. D1's state of mind when he gave the evidence against D2 was immaterial.

---

[148] *Rosato* [2008] EWCA Crim 1243 at [21]. The court went on to give the example of a defendant with a history of armed robbery.

[149] *Murdoch v Taylor* [1965] A.C. 574.

[150] *Varley* [1982] 2 All E.R. 519 at 522.

However, this objective test is not always an easy one to apply. The idea of undermining the defence of the co-accused is troublesome because it is capable of very sweeping operation. It could be argued that any inconsistency with or contradiction of the co-accused's evidence tends to undermine his defence. On the other hand total congruence of the stories of the accused and the co-accused would probably be regarded with deep suspicion by any jury. The courts were aware of this difficulty and certain principles stated in *Varley* represented an attempt to produce some further practical guidance on the application of the test:

> "(4)   If consideration has to be given to the undermining of the other's defence care must be taken to see that the evidence clearly undermines the defence. Inconvenience to or inconsistency with the other's defence is not of itself sufficient. (5) Mere denial of participation in a joint venture is not of itself sufficient to rank as evidence against the co-defendant. For the proviso to apply, such denial must lead to the conclusion that if the witness did not participate then it must[151] have been the other who did. (6) Where the one defendant asserts or in due course would assert one view of the joint venture which is directly contradicted by the other such contradiction may be evidence against the co-defendant."[152]

19–034   The principle set out at the beginning of this quotation confirms the point already made that trivial inconsistencies should be ignored. It is not the case that any inconsistency or contradiction should be regarded as an undermining of the defence. This is why the remaining principles draw attention to the nature of the inconsistency rather than the fact of its existence. However, these principles set up certain distinctions that are somewhat obscure and that need to be explored by reference to some of the relevant cases.

The fifth principle stated in *Varley* distinguished between a "mere" denial of participation in a joint venture and a denial that tended to identify by inference the co-accused as the perpetrator of the offence in question. *Davis*[153] provides an illustration of the latter point. The defendant (D1) and O (D2) were charged with theft of valuable articles from a house that they had visited for the ostensible purpose of buying antiques. The articles included a gold cross on a chain and a tureen. D2 testified that after they had left the house D1 produced the cross and chain from his pocket, whereupon D1 cross-examined D2 on D2's previous convictions. In his evidence in chief D1 denied the allegation of theft but was careful not to say anything positive against D2. After cross-examination on a previous statement in which he had incriminated D2, D1 was finally driven to say "I am not suggesting [D2] took the cross and chain. As I never, and it is missing, he must have done but I am not saying he did". The Court of Appeal upheld the cross-examination of the defendant by D2's counsel on D1's previous convictions. This was a case where D1's denial of participation in theft necessarily implicated D2 because the prosecution evidence pointed very strongly to theft by one or both of them. If D1 was genuinely not involved, the conclusion was inevitable that D2 must have stolen the articles.

---

[151] "Must" was later held to be too strong. In *Crawford* [1998] 1 Cr.App.R. 338 the Court of Appeal agreed with the trial judge who thought that "may" would be more appropriate.
[152] *Varley* [1982] 2 All E.R. 519 at 522.
[153] *Davis* [1975] 1 All E.R. 233.

Even where the accused's evidence does not compel this implication it is sufficient if the defendant denies participation in a joint venture, where the denial has the effect of significantly damaging D2's defence that he also was not involved.[154]

It would seem therefore that a mere denial of complicity in the offence that did not have this effect did not lose the shield under the 1898 Act.[155] However, there is still the sixth principle to consider, which related to a view of the joint venture that directly contradicted the view asserted by the co-accused. Presumably this was not intended to cover a case where the accused directly contradicted the co-accused by denying participation in the joint venture altogether. Were it otherwise, the fifth and sixth principles would be inconsistent. Similarly the contradiction must be something other than inconvenience to or inconsistency with the other's defence, which the fourth principle stated to be insufficient. If these situations were outside the scope of the sixth principle it is not easy to identify the cases to which it might apply. The puzzle can only be resolved by bringing out a latent ambiguity in the meaning of "joint venture". This could refer, narrowly, to the actual act(s) charged, and this seems to be its meaning in the fifth principle. For example, Davis' denial of participation in a joint venture of stealing the specified articles was not evidence against his co-accused unless the denial led to the inference that the co-accused must have taken them. The alternative is that "joint venture" referred more broadly to the surrounding circumstances of the offence, or to the transaction out of which the offence was alleged to have arisen.

This alternative interpretation helps to explain *Hatton*.[156] Hatton (D1) was **19–035** charged jointly with D2 and D3 with theft of scrap metal. The prosecution case was that the three of them had gone together to the site in question and taken the metal dishonestly in accordance with a pre-arranged plan. D2 had given evidence in defence denying any plan to take metal from the site. D1 then testified that all three of them had been sent by D2's stepbrother to collect the metal, which the stepbrother had bought and paid for. The Court of Appeal held that he had given evidence against D2. His evidence supported the prosecution allegation of a plan to take metal from the site and undermined D2's defence that he only met up casually with D1 and D3 at the site. In terms of the sixth principle, D1's view of the joint venture, i.e. the circumstances of the reason for going to the site and the persons who went there together, directly contradicted D2's account.

It seems therefore that the fifth and sixth principles from *Varley* can be distinguished by giving different meanings to the concept of a "joint venture", although the significance of doing so is only apparent when the facts of cases such as *Davis* and *Hatton* are investigated.

The distinction between the fourth and sixth principles seems to be a matter of degree. The direct contradiction in *Hatton* involved more than a mere inconsistency with D2's defence. If D1's view of the joint venture was believed D2's defence was destroyed. Although D1 asserted a lack of dishonesty for all three defendants, the Court of Appeal thought that on balance his evidence made

---

[154] *Crawford* [1998] 1 Cr.App.R. 338 CA.
[155] e.g. see *Kirkpatrick* [1998] Crim. L.R. 63 CA.
[156] *Hatton* (1976) 64 Cr.App.R. 88.

the conviction of D2 more likely. An example of a case covered by the fourth principle, which would not involve a "direct contradiction of a view of the joint venture", would be where the co-accused asserted an alibi for the offence that the accused failed to support but did not knock down. This should not be regarded as undermining the co-accused's defence.

A final comment is that the principles set out in *Varley* did not provide a complete guide to the application of s.1(3)(iii) of the 1898 Act. The accused might contradict the defence put up by the co-accused but, according to the cases, might do it in such a way as to improve the co-accused's prospects of acquittal. If the effect of the accused's evidence was to make the conviction of the co-accused less likely then the accused did not lose the shield. In *Bruce*,[157] B (the accused) was charged with M (the co-accused) and other youths with robbery from a man in a railway carriage. The prosecution case was that the youths, acting in pursuance of an agreement to rob, had intimidated the man into handing over money. M testified that there had been an agreement to rob, but that he had taken no part in carrying out the plan. B gave evidence that there had been no plan to rob anyone. The Court of Appeal held that he had not given evidence against M, and that the cross-examination by M on B's previous convictions was improper. The overall effect of B's evidence was to weaken the prosecution case that there had been a robbery. Although M's defence had been partly undermined, B had provided him with a different and possibly better defence and this made his acquittal more likely. In *Hatton, Bruce* was distinguished on the facts, but no doubt was cast on the gloss that *Bruce* put on the concept of undermining the defence of the co-accused.

19–036   As far as the scope of the right to adduce evidence of the bad character of D1 via gateway (e) is concerned, it seems that this will extend to the facts of previous offences if such facts are relevant to the issues to be decided in the present case. Thus in *Reid*,[158] a case under the 1898 Act, the Court of Appeal held that the defendant was properly questioned about his defence to a previous charge of robbery because there was a live issue on the current charge of robbery whether his defence amounted to an attempt falsely to incriminate others. In both cases the defendant said that the robbery in question was committed by others either shortly before he arrived on the scene or just after he had left the scene.

6.   Gateway (f): evidence to correct a false impression given by the defendant

19–037   Evidence of the bad character of a defendant is admissible via gateway (f) of s.101(1) if it is evidence to correct a false impression given by the defendant. Section 105 supplements this by providing:

> "(1)   For the purposes of section 101(1)(f)—
>
> (a)   the defendant gives a false impression if he is responsible for the making of an express or implied assertion which is apt to give the court or jury a false or misleading impression about the defendant;

---

[157] *Bruce* [1975] 3 All E.R. 277.
[158] *Reid* [1989] Crim. L.R. 719.

       (b)   evidence to correct such an impression is evidence which has probative value in correcting it.

(2)   A defendant is treated as being responsible for the making of an assertion if—

       (a)   the assertion is made by the defendant in the proceedings (whether or not in evidence given by him),

       (b)   the assertion was made by the defendant—

             (i)   on being questioned under caution, before charge, about the offence with which he is charged, or

             (ii)   on being charged with the offence or officially informed that he might be prosecuted for it,

           and evidence of the assertion is given in the proceedings.

       (c)   the assertion is made by a witness called by the defendant,

       (d)   the assertion is made by any witness in cross-examination in response to a question asked by the defendant that is intended to elicit it, or is likely to do so, or

       (e)   the assertion was made by any person out of court, and the defendant adduces evidence of it in the proceedings.

(3)   A defendant who would otherwise be treated as responsible for the making of an assertion shall not be so treated if, or to the extent that, he withdraws it or dissociates himself from it.

(4)   Where it appears to the court that a defendant, by means of his conduct (other than the giving of evidence) in the proceedings, is seeking to give the court or jury an impression about himself that is false or misleading, the court may if it appears just to do so treat the defendant as being responsible for the making of an assertion which is apt to give that impression.

(5)   In subsection (4) "conduct includes appearance or dress.

(6)   Evidence is admissible under section 101(1)(f) only if it goes no further than is necessary to correct that impression.

(7)   Only prosecution evidence is admissible under section 101(1)(f)."

(A) Evidence of good character and its rebuttal: the previous law

In Ch.18 "character" was described as the tendency of a person to behave in a particular way. We noted that such tendency, good or bad, can be proved in various ways: by the existence or absence of convictions for other offences, by evidence of other virtuous or discreditable acts, by a person's reputation in the community and by the individual opinions of others. Before 1898 a defendant who wanted to raise the issue of his good character could do so only by calling a "character" witness or by cross-examining prosecution witnesses. Since he was incompetent to testify himself he could not raise the issue by direct assertion from the witness box. In the old leading case of *Rowton*[159] a majority of the Court for Crown Cases Reserved held that a witness called to testify as to the defendant's character should testify only as to his knowledge of the defendant's reputation and not as to his personal opinion of the defendant's disposition. By implication this would exclude the witness giving evidence of particular examples of the defendant's good conduct on other occasions. This decision was never formally overruled. However, it was criticised by Stephen even before 1898[160] and seems to have been generally ignored in practice virtually ever since the case was decided.[161] When the Criminal Evidence Act 1898 made the accused a competent witness in his own defence, s.1(3)(ii)—formerly s.1(f)(ii)—envisaged that the

19–038

---

[159] *Rowton* (1865) Le. & Ca. 520 CCCR.
[160] J. F. Stephen, *History of Criminal Law* (1882), Vol.1 p.450.
[161] For a rare example of its continuing application see *Redgrave* (1981) 74 Cr.App.R. 10 CA.

accused could raise the issue of his good character in his own evidence. This made the *Rowton* rule more or less unworkable, since a person can hardly give reliable evidence of his own reputation, at least not without blatantly contravening the hearsay rule. Subsequently "character" in the 1898 Act was said to mean both reputation and disposition[162]; this confirmed the view that the defendant could testify to his absence of convictions and good behaviour, and if he did raise the issue of his good character in this way his bad disposition could be proved by questions in cross-examination on previous convictions and the commission of other offences.

Accordingly, from 1898 a defendant was able to raise the issue of his good character by his own evidence, or through the evidence of a defence witness, or by cross-examination of a prosecution witness. His counsel might, for example, elicit from a police officer that the defendant had no criminal convictions. The question of how a claim to good character made through a defence witness or through cross-examination of a prosecution witness could be rebutted was governed by the common law. According to Evans L.J. in *Durbin*[163]:

> "Character, bad or good, is not simply a matter of the presence or absence of previous convictions, nor is it the same as reputation, though the one may be evidence of the other."

Accordingly the defendant's claim to good character could be rebutted by adducing evidence of his previous convictions,[164] or other discreditable conduct,[165] as well as by evidence of reputation. At common law the defendant's character was regarded as indivisible, so there was no requirement that rebuttal evidence should be restricted to a particular character trait that the defendant had raised. According to Humphreys J. in *Winfield*[166]: "there is no such thing known to our procedure as putting half your character in issue and leaving out the other half". If the defendant raised the issue of his good character, he was treated as putting the whole of his past record in issue.[167]

(B)   Evidence to correct a false impression: the new law

19–039   Section 101(1)(f) of the 2003 Act, together with its explanatory s.105, is the replacement for both the common law and s.1(3)(ii) of the 1898 Act on rebuttal of claims by the defendant to good character by proof of his bad character. Sections 101(1)(f) and 105 talk in terms of "evidence to correct a false impression", rather than in the language of evidence rebutting a claim to good character, but the principle is the same. Evidence of a person's reputation is still admissible under

---

[162] *Stirland v DPP* [1944] A.C. 315 at 324–325 per Viscount Simon L.C.
[163] *Durbin* [1995] 2 Cr.App.R. 84 CA.
[164] *Redd* [1923] 1 K.B. 104 CCA; *Waldman* (1934) 24 Cr.App.R. 204; *Winfield* (1939) 27 Cr.App.R. 139 CCA (which also established the rule that the accused's character is indivisible); *R. v B, R. v A* [1979] 1 W.L.R. 1185 CA.
[165] *Hodgkiss* (1836) 7 C. & P. 298; *Rogan and Elliott* (1846) 1 Cox CC 291; *Bracewell* (1978) 68 Cr.App.R. 44 CA.
[166] *Winfield* (1939) 27 Cr.App.R. 139 CCA.
[167] *Stirland v DPP* [1944] A.C. 315 at 326–327 per Viscount Simon L.C.

the 2003 Act for the purpose of proving his good or bad character,[168] but the effect of s.99(1) is to abolish any lingering vestige of the *Rowton* rule that evidence of reputation is the only permitted means of proof of character. The provisions of the 2003 Act relating to gateway (f) are based mainly on the recommendations of the Law Commission,[169] although the Commission's proposed additional safeguards against unfair prejudice were dropped.

(1)   The creation of a false impression

There was no authoritative test under the previous law for determining when the defendant put his good character in issue. An appeal to other conduct of a virtuous nature would generally suffice to lose the shield under the 1898 Act, as where the defendant testified to his regular attendance at mass,[170] or to his regular employment,[171] or to past occasions when he returned lost property to its owner.[172] Adducing evidence of the defendant's lack of previous convictions would also count as an assertion of the defendant's good character.[173] On the other hand, where the defendant confined his evidence to the circumstances of the offence charged with a view to providing an innocent explanation, the exception would not apply. In *Ellis*,[174] an early case on the 1898 Act, Bray J. commented:

19–040

> "In our opinion, if we were to give the slightest colour to the idea that a general examination as to the surrounding circumstances was such evidence of good character as to entitle the prosecution to prove or to cross-examine as to other offences or convictions, we should deprive the prisoner of the protection which the statute has given him. [Section 1(3)(ii)] ... was not intended to apply ... to mere assertions of innocence or repudiation of guilt on the part of the prisoner, nor to reasons given by him for such assertion or repudiation."

Similarly, it appears that the 2003 Act contains no general test for the application of this gateway. The Court of Appeal has accepted that, as under the 1898 Act, "a simple denial of the offence or offences alleged, cannot, for the purposes of s.101(1)(f), be treated as a false impression given by the appellant".[175] According

---

[168] See ss.99(2) and 118(1) of the Criminal Justice Act 2003, preserving the common law rule that reputation is admissible evidence of character.

[169] Law Com. 273 Pt XIII.

[170] *Ferguson* (1909) 2 Cr.App.R. 250.

[171] *Baker* (1912) 7 Cr.App.R. 252 (evidence from the defendant that for four years he had been earning an honest living was evidence of good character); *Coulman* (1927) 20 Cr.App.R. 106 ("If you ask a man whether he is a married man with a family, in regular work, and has a wife and three children, you are setting up his character": per Swift J.).

[172] *Samuel* (1956) 40 Cr.App.R. 8. The defendant was charged with larceny, and the purpose of the questions was clearly to establish a disposition to deal honestly with other people's property.

[173] As the cases dealing with the direction to be given about such evidence implicitly accept; see Ch.18. cf. *Lee (Paul)* [1976] 1 W.L.R. 71 (questions in cross-examination of a prosecution witness about the criminal records of other persons did not imply an assertion of good character by the defendant).

[174] *Ellis* [1910] 2 K.B. 746 at 763. The defendant was charged with obtaining cheques for the price of goods sold to P by false pretences as to the cost price of the goods. The defendant's evidence as to his course of dealing with P and to other similar transactions was held not to amount to evidence of good character.

[175] *Somanathan*, reported with *Weir* [2005] EWCA Crim 2866; [2006] 2 All E.R. 570 at [43]; followed in *Chable* [2009] EWCA Crim 496.

to the Court of Appeal in *Renda*,[176] "for the purposes of s.101(1)(f) of the 2003 Act the question whether the defendant has given a 'false impression' about himself, and whether there is evidence which may properly serve to correct such a false impression within s.105(1)(a) and (b) is fact-specific". In *Renda*, D, who was charged with attempted robbery, testified that he had served as a soldier in the armed forces and had sustained a serious head injury while so employed, and also that at the date of his arrest he was in regular employment as a security guard. The court was in no doubt that he was plainly seeking to convey that he was a man of positive good character. It made no difference to the opening of gateway (f) that he subsequently admitted in cross-examination that the head injury had occurred in a car accident while he was on holiday, and that his duties as a security guard involved no more than checking passes. These concessions that he had not told the truth in his evidence in chief were held not to amount to a withdrawal or disassociation from the original assertion for the purposes of s.105(3). There was a significant difference between a defendant obliged by the process of cross-examination to make such concessions, and a defendant "who makes a specific and positive decision to correct a false impression for which he is responsible, or to disassociate himself with [sic] false impressions conveyed by the assertions of others".[177]

According to s.105(1)(a) a defendant can open gateway (f) by making an express or implied assertion that is apt to give the court or jury a false or misleading impression about the defendant. Express assertions for this purpose would include, for example, explicit false or misleading claims by the defendant that he is an honest man, is non-violent, has no sexual interest in children,[178] and so on. In *Chable*,[179] the defendant was charged with blackmail on the basis that he had demanded money from the victim backed up by threats with a knife. In his police interview and in his evidence he put himself forward as an honest plumber who "did not do" knives. The trial judge admitted evidence via gateway (f) that when the defendant was arrested two days later a similar knife was found under his pillow. Dismissing the appeal, the Court of Appeal said that this was not evidence of the commission of an offence or of reprehensible behaviour, but it was evidence of a *disposition* towards reprehensible behaviour, namely to put knives to illegitimate use when necessary. The court clearly thought that a jury might be properly sceptical of the defendant's explanation that he had hidden the knife under his pillow to prevent his nephew, who had an unhealthy interest in knives, from taking it. Implied assertions would cover, for example, false or misleading claims about the defendant's conduct and circumstances so as to imply that he has a virtuous character (that he is a person of integrity, is law-abiding, etc.). The claims in *Renda* would fall into this category.

Under s.105(4) a court may treat a defendant as giving a false or misleading impression about himself by his conduct in the proceedings (other than by giving evidence). For this purpose conduct includes appearance or dress.[180] So a defendant who tries falsely to pass himself off as a soldier by wearing military

---

[176] *Renda* [2005] EWCA Crim 2826; [2006] 2 All E.R. 553 at [19].
[177] *Renda* [2005] EWCA Crim 2826; [2006] 2 All E.R. 553 at [21].
[178] As in *Dixon* [2012] EWCA Crim 2163.
[179] *Chable* [2009] EWCA Crim 496.
[180] Criminal Justice Act 2003 s.105(5).

uniform in court is likely to open gateway (f) to evidence of his bad character. But the court should only treat the defendant as having made a false or misleading impression by conduct where it "appears just to do so". This will probably not be the case where a normally scruffy defendant has a shave and puts on a collar and tie for his appearance in court. He is certainly trying to give a favourable impression of himself, and in a sense the impression is false or misleading, but it would be harsh to hold that this rather minimal effort to impress amounted to putting good character in issue.

An express or implied assertion about the defendant can be made in more than one context and by persons other than the defendant himself. Section 105(2) sets out the various possibilities. Paragraph (a) states the most usual case, namely where the defendant himself makes the assertion in the proceedings "(whether or not in evidence given by him)".[181] The defendant may also make the assertion in a police interview or when charged with the offence (para.(b)). As under the previous law the defendant can adduce evidence of his good character by means of an assertion made by a defence witness (para.(c)), or by means of an assertion made by a witness in cross-examination in response to a question intended or likely to elicit the assertion (para.(d)). Finally, the assertion may be made by any person out of court, and the defendant adduces evidence of it in the proceedings (para.(e)). If a witness volunteers an assertion that is apt to give a false or misleading impression of the defendant, without being asked, the defendant can avoid opening gateway (f) by disassociating himself from the assertion.[182]

19–041

(2)   The correction of a false impression

Section 105(6) provides that evidence of bad character is admissible via gateway (f) only if it goes no further than is necessary to correct the false impression. It follows that if the defendant has made only a limited claim to good character, the prosecution's evidence in rebuttal will be restricted to that limited claim. If the defendant claims to be an honest man the prosecution will not be able to adduce evidence of his convictions for sexual offences through gateway (f). In *Somanathan* the Court of Appeal accepted that this is a statutory reversal of the common law rule that character is indivisible.[183] As we saw in Ch.18, the Law Commission had recommended the abolition of this rule on grounds of unfairness and in the light of psychological research rejecting the theory that character has a unitary quality across different contexts.[184] Of course, if the defendant makes a comprehensive claim to good character, asserting that he is a law-abiding citizen in all respects, he can hardly complain if the law permits the prosecution to rebut this claim by proof of any previous conviction.[185]

19–042

---

[181] The parenthesis caters for the case where the defendant's lawyer makes the assertion on his behalf in presenting the case: Explanatory Notes to s.105 para.309.

[182] Criminal Justice Act 2003 s.105(3).

[183] *Somanathan* [2005] EWCA Crim 2866; [2006] 2 All E.R. 570 at [43].

[184] Law Com. CP 141 para.11.42; Law Com. 273 paras 13.22–13.28.

[185] Subject to the possibility that the conviction may be for an offence committed many years previously or for a very trivial offence. Such a case is probably best dealt with by allowing the accused still to have the benefit of the judge's direction on the relevance of good character, modified as appropriate in the circumstances.

In *Somanathan* the defendant was a priest at a Hindu temple who was convicted of twice raping a woman worshipper at the temple. His defence included claims that he had always behaved properly towards female members of his congregation and that there had been no trouble when he was a priest at another temple in Tooting. To rebut these claims the prosecution called two other women to give evidence of the defendant's sexually suggestive approaches to them, and the chairman of the trustees of the temple in Tooting to give an account of how the defendant had been dismissed from his employment there because he had lied to the chairman and because his behaviour towards women had caused concern. On appeal the defendant argued that, as regards what had happened at Tooting, the prosecution should have been restricted to a statement from the chairman that a decision had been taken not to renew the defendant's contract because of complaints received. Rejecting this argument, the Court of Appeal held that once the gateway had been opened the prosecution were entitled to adduce "a full account of what, according to their witness, brought the Tooting contract to an end".[186]

19–043 The purpose of adducing evidence of bad character to correct a false impression is an issue that requires some discussion. There are three possibilities. The first is use of the evidence to attack the defendant's credibility. If the false impression has been given by the defendant himself, whether in his evidence or in a statement out of court, it is clear that, whatever other purposes may be involved, evidence about the accused's bad character may be adduced to discredit the accused. Such evidence is relevant to the general credibility of the accused. Under the previous law the jury were not required to limit their consideration of the evidence of bad character to the issue of how far the defendant could be believed, in claiming to have a good character.[187] They could give the evidence of bad character such weight as they thought fit in assessing the accused's testimony on any matter in the case. This appears also to be the case under the 2003 Act.

The second possibility is that the evidence of bad character may be used to rebut the defendant's argument from good disposition. If, in other words, the defendant is seeking to argue that his good character means that he is less likely to be guilty of the offence, the prosecution can try to displace any such inference by negativing the initial premise of good character. It is submitted that it would be absurd if the evidence could not be used for this purpose. The defendant would otherwise be permitted to reason from a factual assertion that the factfinder knows to have been challenged if not falsified altogether. In *Maxwell v DPP*,[188] a case under the 1898 Act, Lord Sankey clearly recognised the point:

> "if the prisoner by himself or his witness seeks to give evidence of his own good character, for the purpose of showing that it is unlikely that he committed the offence charged, he raises by way of defence an issue as to his good character so that he may fairly be cross-examined on that issue just as any witness called by him as to his good character may be cross-examined to show the contrary."

---

[186] *Somanathan* [2005] EWCA Crim 2866; [2006] 2 All E.R. 570 at [43].
[187] *Richardson and Longman* [1969] 1 Q.B. 299.
[188] *Maxwell v DPP* [1935] A.C. 309 at 319.

There is a narrow distinction to be made between this situation and the third **19–044**
possibility, which is that the prosecution may go further and use the defendant's
bad character as probative of guilt. Under the previous law, with its strong
distinction between credibility and guilt, this should not have been permitted. The
prosecution would have had to bring the evidence of bad character within the
rules of admissibility for their evidence in chief, and would therefore have to
show that its positive probative value exceeded its prejudicial effect. Under the
2003 Act the position is different. The Court of Appeal has made it clear that once
the evidence of bad character has been admitted, it may be used for any purpose
for which it is relevant, irrespective of the gateway through which it was
admitted.[189] If, therefore, the evidence of bad character shows a propensity on the
part of the defendant to commit the offence charged, or is relevant to his guilt in
some other way, it seems that the prosecution may use it in proof of guilt,
notwithstanding that it was admitted in order to correct a false impression of the
defendant's character.[190] In such a case, the prosecution will usually have sought
to adduce the evidence via gateway (d) in any event,[191] so the issue of its use for
this purpose when admitted via gateway (f) will be academic. However, if the
evidence is tendered only via gateway (f) the importance of judicial discretion
should be remembered. The statutory exclusionary discretion under s.101(3) does
not apply in respect of evidence of bad character admissible via gateway (f), but
s.78 of PACE does.[192] The common law discretion to exclude evidence where its
prejudicial effect outweighs its probative value may also be available. The judge
might use s.78 or the common law discretion to regulate the extent of the
admission of such evidence. The judge might, for example, permit the
prosecution to question the accused about some previous convictions but not
others. The judge's duty is as always to secure a fair trial for the accused, and this
might require the judge to exclude evidence of bad character where the
prejudicial effect of the matters revealed by the questions would outweigh any
probative value they have. Under the previous law the application of the common
law discretion to the case where the defendant asserted good character was
undoubted.[193]

---

[189] *Highton* [2005] EWCA Crim 1985; [2006] 1 Cr.App.R. 7; *Campbell* [2007] EWCA Crim 1472;
[2007] 2 Cr.App.R. 28.

[190] In *Chable* [2009] EWCA Crim 496, discussed above, the Court of Appeal noted that it was a very
small step from admitting the evidence of the knife found under the defendant's pillow, to correct a
false impression that the defendant had nothing to do with knives, to considering the defendant's
propensity to misuse knives.

[191] But not always: in *Dixon* [2012] EWCA Crim 2163 D's 2 convictions for indecent assault on
under-age girls were admitted via gateway (f) to correct the false impression he had given that he had
no sexual interest in children. But in view of the age of the convictions (they were more than 30 years
old) the prosecution did not rely on them as evidence of his propensity to commit sexual assault on
children.

[192] *Somanathan*, reported with *Weir* [2005] EWCA Crim 2866; [2006] 2 All E.R. 570 at [44];
following the judgment of Lord Woolf C.J. in *Highton* [2005] EWCA Crim 1985; [2006] 1 Cr.App.R.
7 at [13].

[193] *Thompson* [1966] 1 All E.R. 505; *Marsh* [1994] Crim. L.R. 52.

7. Gateway (g): the defendant has made an attack on another person's character

19–045   Evidence of the bad character of a defendant is admissible under gateway (g) of s.101(1) if the defendant has made an attack on another person's character. Section 106 supplements this by providing:

> "(1)   For the purposes of section 101(1)(g) a defendant makes an attack on another person's character if—
>   (a)   he adduces evidence attacking the other person's character,
>   (b)   he (or any legal representative appointed under section 38(4) of the Youth Justice and Criminal Evidence Act 1999 (c.23) to cross-examine a witness in his interests) asks questions in cross-examination that are intended to elicit such evidence, or are likely to do so, or
>   (c)   evidence is given of an imputation about the other person made by the defendant—
>   (i)   on being questioned under caution, before charge, about the offence with which he is charged, or
>   (ii)   on being charged with the offence or officially informed that he might be prosecuted for it.
> (2)   In subsection (1) 'evidence attacking the other person's character' means evidence to the effect that the other person—
>   (a)   has committed an offence (whether a different offence from the one with which the defendant is charged or the same one), or
>   (b)   has behaved, or is disposed to behave, in a reprehensible way; and 'imputation about the other person' means an assertion to that effect.
> (3)   Only prosecution evidence is admissible under section 101(1)(g)."

19–046   Gateway (g) is founded on the same principle as the previous law contained in the second "limb" of s.1(3)(ii) of the Criminal Evidence Act 1898. Section 1(3)(ii) provided that the accused lost the shield against cross-examination on his previous convictions and bad character if the nature or conduct of his defence was such as to involve imputations on the character of the prosecutor or the witnesses for the prosecution or the deceased victim of the alleged crime. The underlying principle was that the defendant should not be able to make attacks on the character of prosecution witnesses and others with impunity; if he chose to conduct his defence by making such attacks it was fair that the prosecution should be entitled to put his character before the jury. In *Selvey v DPP*,[194] Lord Pearce referred to this as the "tit for tat" argument, and continued:

> "If the accused is seeking to cast discredit on the prosecution, then the prosecution should be allowed to do likewise. If the accused is seeking to persuade the jury that the prosecutor behaved like a knave, then the jury should know the character of the man who makes these accusations, so that it may judge fairly between them instead of being in the dark as to one of them."

There is a primitive appeal to this retaliatory principle. It offers some practical justice to witnesses and victims who are subject to scurrilous and humiliating attacks from the defence, and helps to ensure that some at least of these attacks are not undertaken lightly. But the principle has always been flawed in the sense that it proceeds by placing witnesses and defendants on a false footing of

---

[194] *Selvey v DPP* [1970] A.C. 304 at 353.

equality. In formal terms, and for most practical purposes, the defendant has more to lose simply because he is the person on trial. Witnesses are not subject to an increased risk of conviction and punishment through revelations of their bad character. Concerns over the fairness of the principle led the Law Commission to propose elaborate safeguards for the replacement provision for the old law. However, the Government dropped all of them and enacted the simple provisions of s.106. This is an area of the law on bad character evidence where the policy of victim and witness protection has taken clear precedence in the legislation over concerns of fairness to defendants.

(A) Interpretation of gateway (g) and section 106: when is an attack made?

Section 106(1)(a) refers to a defendant making an attack on another person's **19–047** character if he adduces evidence attacking the other person's character. This wording will certainly cover evidence given by a witness called by the defendant, and it is presumably intended to cover evidence given by the defendant himself, although it is curious that this is not spelt out expressly (compare s.105(2)(a), dealing with the defendant asserting his good character). Secondly, an attack can be made in cross-examination of a witness by means of questions intended or likely to elicit such evidence. Thirdly, evidence may be given (this will usually be adduced by the prosecution) of an imputation made by the defendant in an out-of-court statement when interviewed or charged. In *Ball*,[195] the defendant had said in his police interview that P, who had complained that he had raped her, was very promiscuous: "She's a bag really, you know what I mean, a slag". The prosecution led evidence of this statement to show the defendant's attitude towards the complainant that they said was relevant to the question of his mens rea for rape. The Court of Appeal upheld the decision of the trial judge that this statement was evidence of an attack on the complainant's character, and agreed that he had properly permitted the prosecution to cross-examine the defendant on his previous convictions and breaches of court orders.

(B) Interpretation of gateway (g) and section 106: who can be attacked?

Both s.101(1)(g) and s.106 refer to an attack on the character of "another person". **19–048** This is very wide. It will include witnesses, victims, police officers, co-accused[196]; in short anyone, irrespective of their connection with the offence or its investigation or prosecution. Does "another person" include a deceased person? Section 1(3)(ii) of the 1898 Act expressly included "deceased victims of the alleged crime" in the list of targets, attacks on whom would result in the loss of the shield. This reference has not been retained in the 2003 Act, but it would be strange if they were not now included, particularly given the policy adopted for

---

[195] Reported with *Renda* [2005] EWCA Crim 2826; [2006] 2 All E.R. 553.
[196] See *Dowds*, reported with *Bovell* [2005] EWCA Crim 1091; [2005] 2 Cr.App.R. 27, where D, charged jointly with burglary, testified that his co-accused had committed another burglary the day before.

gateway (g) of victim and witness protection. In *Hanson*,[197] the Court of Appeal commented that gateway (g) could be relied on by the prosecution "where the defendant has made an attack on the character of another person who will often, though not always, be the victim of the alleged crime, whether alive or dead". In *Wainwright*,[198] a case under the 1898 Act, the defendant, who was serving a prison sentence for attempted murder, was charged with the murder of a fellow prisoner. The defendant claimed to have acted in self-defence and adduced evidence of the victim's bad reputation for violence. The Court of Appeal held that the trial judge had correctly allowed the prosecution to cross-examine the defendant on his own criminal record. He had attacked the character of the deceased victim, and it made no difference in the court's view that the prosecution had not disputed the victim's bad character. Imputations could still be made even where the faults alleged by the defendant about the victim were agreed. It is submitted that the position is the same under the 2003 Act.

(C)   Interpretation of gateway (g) and section 106: what is an attack on character?

19–049   According to s.106(2) evidence attacking another person's character means evidence that the other person has committed an offence or has behaved, or is disposed to behave, in a reprehensible way. An "imputation" is an assertion to that effect. In *Hanson,* the Court of Appeal's guidance on the scheme of the 2003 Act included the statement:

> "As to section 101(1)(g), pre 2003 Act authorities will continue to apply when assessing whether an attack has been made on another person's character, to the extent that they are compatible with section 106."[199]

This simple statement has important implications that the court did not explore. Under s.1(3)(ii) of the 1898 Act attacks on the general reputation of a witness for honesty and truthfulness,[200] and specific allegations against a witness of misconduct on a particular occasion,[201] were equally held to be imputations on character. This will not change under the 2003 Act. However, the courts were conscious of competing pressures in applying the 1898 Act. They did not wish to permit defendants to make serious, and possibly unfounded, allegations with impunity, but equally they were conscious of the danger of over-expansive application of this part of s.1(3)(ii). It is arguable that in many cases in which the defendant denies guilt in the witness box, and rejects or explains away incriminating evidence, he is impliedly asserting lies or other flaws on the part of prosecution witnesses. A wide application of the provision carried the danger that the defendant would not be able to develop any kind of defence without losing

---

[197] *Hanson* [2005] EWCA Crim 824; [2005] 2 Cr.App.R. 21 at [5].

[198] *Wainwright* [1998] Crim. L.R. 665 CA.

[199] *Hanson* [2005] EWCA Crim 824; [2005] 2 Cr.App.R. 21 at [14]. The Court of Appeal affirmed the point in *Lamaletie* [2008] EWCA Crim 314.

[200] *Rappolt* (1911) 6 Cr.App.R. 156.

[201] e.g. an allegation that a police officer had fabricated or extorted a confession by the defendant. See below.

the shield against cross-examination on record. Hence the courts developed a number of devices to limit the operation of the provision in practice, although these were not always applied consistently. It remains to be seen how far this statement in *Hanson* will result in the continued application of these devices.

Some examples from the previous law of allegations by the accused that were held to be imputations on character include the following: that the complainant of an offence of buggery was a male prostitute[202]; that a prosecution witness had committed the offence in question[203]; that the police had fabricated,[204] or extorted,[205] the accused's confession. All such allegations will continue to be attacks on character under the 2003 Act. By contrast in *Bishop*,[206] the defendant alleged by way of defence to a charge of burglary that he had been having homosexual relations with P in the room in P's house in which the defendant's fingerprints had been found. In 1974 that was regarded as an allegation of a fault or vice against P. Decades later, and in the light of the law allowing for same-sex civil partnerships, it is inconceivable that an allegation that a person is homosexual will be held to be an allegation of "reprehensible" behaviour. It will be different, as Spencer has pointed out, if the defendant alleges that the other committed a sexual offence against him.[207]

It was an established rule under the previous law that in rape cases the defendant could allege consent by the complainant to intercourse without losing the shield. In earlier times an allegation of consent might have suggested immorality on the part of the complainant, but there was clear authority that it was not an imputation on character under s.1(3)(ii).[208] It is likely to be different if, as in *Ball*,[209] the defendant goes further and suggests that the complainant has a disposition to promiscuity.   **19–050**

A further limitation on the concept of an attack on character was the so-called rule in *Rouse*.[210] In that case the defendant testified in his defence that the chief witness for the prosecution was a liar and that his evidence was a lie. The Court for Crown Cases Reserved held that this was not an imputation because "it was a plea of not guilty put in forcible language such as would not be unnatural in a person in [the defendant's] rank of life".[211] In *Selvey v DPP*, Viscount Dilhorne, summarising propositions he took to be established by the cases, said:

> "If what is said amounts in reality to no more than a denial of the charge, expressed, it may be, in emphatic language, it should not be regarded as coming within the section."[212]

If this limitation still holds good, it is a principle that is easier to state than to apply. The line between a denial and an imputation can be so fine as to be

---

[202] *Selvey v DPP* [1970] A.C. 304.
[203] *Hudson* [1912] 2 K.B. 464 CCA.
[204] *Clark* [1955] 2 Q.B. 469.
[205] *Cook* [1959] 2 Q.B. 340.
[206] *Bishop* [1975] Q.B. 274.
[207] Spencer, *Evidence of Bad Character* (Hart Publishing, Oxford, 2006), para.4.95.
[208] *Turner* [1944] K.B. 463 CCA; *Selvey v DPP* [1970] A.C. 304 HL.
[209] Reported with *Renda* [2005] EWCA Crim 2826; [2006] 2 All E.R. 553.
[210] *Rouse* [1904] 1 K.B. 184.
[211] *Rouse* [1904] 1 K.B. 184 at 186.
[212] *Selvey v DPP* [1970] A.C. 304 at 339.

indistinguishable. When is a claim that prosecution evidence is a lie only an emphatic denial of the charge and when is it an allegation of perjury on the part of the witness in question and perhaps of other offences as well? In *Somanathan*,[213] the defendant said in his defence statement that the complainant, who had alleged that he had raped her, "is not a witness of truth and has some ulterior motive in making and indeed pursuing this complaint". It was accepted by the defence that this opened gateway (g).

19–051 A further question is whether it makes any difference if the defendant does not make the allegation of fabrication explicit but it is nonetheless implied in his denial of the incriminating evidence. This question arose in an acute form under the previous law in relation to the evidence of police officers testifying as to confessions made by defendants. It was clear that express allegations that the police had manufactured[214] or improperly procured[215] a confession amounted to imputations on the character of the officers concerned. This was so despite the fact that on one view all that the defendant was doing was denying part of the evidence against him and giving a reason why it should not be accepted. There does not seem to be much difference in kind between these cases and the situation where the defendant claims that a non-police witness has lied on oath about the occurrence of an actual event some time previously. Nevertheless, the principle of the police cases was confirmed and extended. In *Britzman*,[216] two police officers testified that the defendant had made incriminating statements in the course of a long interview with them, and one officer also testified that he had overheard the defendant shouting something incriminating to a co-accused whilst in a police cell. In his evidence, the defendant denied the existence of the interview and said that he had not had a shouting-match with his co-accused in the cells. He was careful not to make any overt allegations of impropriety against the officers in question, but the Court of Appeal held that to deny the conversations necessarily implied that the officers had given false testimony deliberately in order to secure the defendant's conviction. Accordingly the trial judge had been entitled to exercise his discretion to allow cross-examination on the defendant's previous convictions. The implication of fabrication seems to have been regarded as necessary because on the facts the court thought that there was no question of the defendant saying that the officers had made a mistake, or misunderstood, or were confused about what had been said, for example, in a short interview.

In *Britzman*, Lawton L.J. regarded the distinction between a denial and an imputation as a matter affecting the exercise of discretion rather than a rule about the scope of s.1(3)(ii). He indicated that defences that suggest deliberate fabrication of evidence by prosecution witnesses must involve imputations on the character of the witnesses, with the result that judges may exercise discretion to

---

[213] Reported with *Weir* [2005] EWCA Crim 2866; [2006] 2 All E.R. 570.
[214] *Clark* [1955] 2 Q.B. 469 CCA; *Tanner* (1977) 66 Cr.App.R. 56 CA; cf. *Nelson* (1978) 68 Cr.App.R. 12 CA.
[215] *Cook* [1959] 2 Q.B. 340 CCA.
[216] *Britzman* [1983] 1 All E.R. 369. In this case the Court of Appeal preferred its earlier decision in *Tanner* (1977) 66 Cr.App.R. 56 to that in *Nelson* (1978) 68 Cr.App.R. 12. *Britzman* was followed in *Owen* (1986) 83 Cr.App.R. 100 CA.

allow cross-examination of the defendant on his previous convictions. However, he went on to suggest a number of guidelines for the exercise of discretion in favour of defendants:

> "First, it should be used if there is nothing more than a denial, however emphatic or offensively made, of an act or even a short series of acts amounting to one incident or in what was said to have been a short interview. Examples are provided by the kind of evidence given in pickpocket cases and where the defendant is alleged to have said 'Who grassed on me this time?' The position would be different however if there were a denial of evidence of a long period of detailed observation extending over hours . . . [or] denials of long conversations.
>
> Second, cross-examination should only be allowed if the judge is sure that there is no possibility of mistake, misunderstanding or confusion and that the jury will inevitably have to decide whether the prosecution witnesses have fabricated evidence. Defendants sometimes make wild allegations when giving evidence. Allowance should be made for the strain of being in the witness box and the exaggerated use of language which sometimes results from such strain or lack of education or mental instability. Particular care should be used when a defendant is led into making allegations during cross-examination . . . Finally, there is no need for the prosecution to rely upon section 1[3](ii) if the evidence against a defendant is overwhelming."[217]

These guidelines may prove helpful in appropriate cases under the 2003 Act. What about imputations that are necessary for the proper development of the defence? It seems that, as under the old law,[218] there is no principle that an exclusionary discretion should be exercised in D's favour in a case of necessary imputation. In *Lamaletie*,[219] the defendant was charged with inflicting grievous bodily harm on a minicab driver with whom he had had a dispute over the fare. His defence was that the driver had attacked him and his girlfriend and that he had acted in self-defence. The trial judge permitted the prosecution to adduce via gateway (g) the defendant's six previous convictions for offences of violence. Dismissing the defendant's appeal the Court of Appeal held that it was not a rule of law under either the 1898 Act or the 2003 Act that an imputation which was necessary for the defence, such as the claim that the victim struck the first blow, precludes the admission of the defendant's previous convictions. Equally, the court showed no inclination to suggest that there was any general principle that exclusionary discretion should be used to exclude the convictions in such a case.

19–052

(D) Interpretation of gateway (g) and section 106: the scope and purpose of the evidence of the defendant's bad character

One point of difference from the previous law is that evidence of the defendant's bad character can be adduced via gateway (g) even if the defendant does not give evidence and therefore cannot be cross-examined. Under the previous law, if the defendant attacked the character of the prosecution witnesses, but did not put his own character in issue and did not give evidence, the prosecution were not permitted to retaliate with evidence of the defendant's own bad character.[220] This

19–053

---

[217] *Britzman* [1983] 1 All E.R. 369 at 373–374.
[218] See *Selvey v DPP* [1970] AC 304.
[219] *Lamaletie* [2008] EWCA Crim 314.
[220] *Butterwasser* [1948] 1 K.B. 4 CCA.

rule was strongly criticised[221] and has now gone. The prosecution can adduce evidence of the defendant's bad character, once gateway (g) is open, irrespective of whether he gives evidence.

If gateway (g) has opened, as a result of the defendant making an attack on another person's character, the trial judge may, as under the previous law, restrict the evidence of the defendant's bad character that the prosecution may adduce. In *Fysh*,[222] for example, where the defendant alleged that the prosecution witnesses had conspired to accuse him falsely of assault, the trial judge had indicated that he would not permit evidence of the defendant's criminal record to go back beyond 1986. In the event the prosecution applied to adduce only a few of the defendant's convictions; these were convictions since 1999 for assault, theft and benefit fraud. It seems clear that the primary purpose of admitting the defendant's convictions via gateway (g) is to enable the jury to evaluate the defendant's credibility. For this purpose the prosecution are not restricted to convictions that bear directly on the defendant's propensity to be truthful. In *Fysh* the Court of Appeal appeared to accept that its earlier statement in *Hanson*, that offences of dishonesty did not necessarily equate to a propensity to be untruthful in relation to gateway (d), did not apply in relation to gateway (g). Later cases confirm that the courts are not minded to apply the restrictive approach of *Hanson*, and a fortiori, of *Campbell*, to gateway (g). Thus in *Nelson*,[223] the Court of Appeal upheld the trial judge's ruling permitting the prosecution to adduce evidence of the defendant's convictions for drug offences after he had attacked the character of the chief prosecution witness. The case involved a charge of affray, which the defendant alleged was a story fabricated by the witness in a conspiracy with the defendant's neighbour, whom the defendant accused of drug-taking. The court said that the credibility of the defendant and the witness were central to the case, and that the judge had correctly directed the jury that the convictions were relevant to the credibility of the allegations the defendant was making about the witness and the neighbour. In *Lamaletie*,[224] noted above, the defendant's previous convictions for violence were admitted as relevant to his credibility in putting forward the claim of self-defence to an unlawful attack by the minicab driver. In *Clarke*,[225] D claimed that allegations of sexual offences against two children were fabrications and the result of collusion between the girls in question. The Court of Appeal upheld the trial judge's admission via gateway (g) of D's extensive criminal record. None of the convictions demonstrated D's propensity to be untruthful in the *Hanson* sense, but that case was expressly said not to apply to gateway (g). In the court's view the position under gateway (g) is the same as it was under the 1898 Act, namely that in principle all of D's previous convictions are admissible to show the character of the person making an attack on the character of another person.

---

[221] RCCJ Report Ch.8 para.34. Note that if the defendant wants now to cross-examine prosecution witnesses on their previous convictions, as he did in *Butterwasser*, he will need the leave of the judge under s.100 of the Criminal Justice Act 2003, and the convictions will have to have substantial probative value on the issue of their credibility.

[222] Reported with *Edwards* [2005] EWCA Crim 1813; [2006] 1 Cr.App.R. 3.

[223] *Nelson* [2006] EWCA Crim 3412.

[224] *Lamaletie* [2008] EWCA Crim 314.

[225] *Clarke* [2011] EWCA Crim 939.

It seems therefore that if the defendant attacks the character of another person he **19–054** lays himself open to having the whole of his bad character put in, subject to the possible exercise of the statutory exclusionary discretion under s.101(3). In *Edwards*, the Court of Appeal expressed the view that recent convictions for violence, of a defendant charged with common assault and having a bladed article in a public place, might well, if admitted via gateway (g), have had a significantly prejudicial effect against the defendant: "an impact which far outweighed the probative value of those offences".[226] The court approved the decision of the trial judge to admit instead the defendant's convictions for robbery and dwelling-house burglary as relevant to his credibility. If this view implies that recent convictions for similar offences should be admitted only via gateway (d) it must be read subject to the decision of the Court of Appeal in *Highton*,[227] discussed earlier in this chapter. In that case the court held that the s.101 gateways control only the admissibility of the evidence and not its use. Once evidence of the defendant's bad character has been admitted via a particular gateway it can be used for any purpose for which it is relevant. It follows that if convictions for similar offences are admitted against the defendant via gateway (g), and they are relevant to prove his disposition to commit the kind of offence charged, then they can be used for that purpose. The court commented in *Lamaletie*[228] that the defendant's previous convictions for violence could probably have been used to prove his propensity to violence; it seems that in that case the prosecution did not pursue the possibility because they lacked full details of the convictions in question.

The last point raises the question whether, if convictions for similar offences can **19–055** be adduced via gateway (g), to what extent can or should the prosecution investigate the facts and circumstances of the previous offences, as opposed to simply bringing out the bare fact of conviction? Where evidence is restricted to dissimilar offences, it would not normally be relevant to go beyond the fact of the accused's convictions, for example for theft or fraud. In *Clarke* the Court of Appeal suggested a restrictive approach:

> "The authorities demonstrate that under paragraph (g) all convictions are potentially relevant to assist the jury to assess the character of the accused, and it is not necessary, or at least not generally so, for detailed facts about the nature and circumstances of those convictions to be put before the jury. That is only likely to be required where it is necessary to demonstrate a propensity for untruthfulness in paragraph (g) cases."

This may be another indication that if the prosecution want to use previous convictions as the basis for an argument that D has a propensity to commit the kind of offence charged, then they should use gateway (d). It may also reflect the Court of Appeal's continuing concern that trial judges should avoid multiplying the issues in criminal trials and engaging juries in satellite litigation. It remains to be seen whether this approach in *Clarke* will be followed, and if it is, how a

---

[226] *Edwards* [2005] EWCA Crim 1813; [2006] 1 Cr.App.R. 3 at [16]. See also *Williams* [2011] EWCA Crim 2198.
[227] *Highton* [2005] EWCA Crim 1985; [2006] 1 Cr.App.R. 7.
[228] *Lamaletie* [2008] EWCA Crim 314.

"propensity for untruthfulness" might be interpreted in this context. It may well be, for example, that the courts will follow the principle stated under the old law that:

> "similarities of defences which have been rejected by juries on previous occasions, for example false alibis or the defence that the incriminating substance has been planted and whether or not the accused pleaded guilty or was disbelieved having given evidence on oath, may be a legitimate matter for questions. These matters do not show a disposition to commit the offence in question, but they are clearly relevant to credibility."[229]

E.   COGENCY AND CONTAMINATION

1.   *Cogency of evidence of bad character*

19–056   Section 109(1) of the 2003 Act provides that a reference to the relevance or probative value of evidence of bad character is a reference to its relevance or probative value on the assumption that the evidence is true. This is of course the usual practice where issues of relevance of evidence are concerned; the judge asks whether the evidence is capable of having a sufficient degree of relevance to justify admission, on the assumption that the evidence is true. The issue of the actual credibility of the evidence is then left to the factfinder to determine. However, in assessing the relevance or probative value of such an item of evidence the court need not assume its truth if it appears that no court or jury could reasonably find it to be true.[230] Clearly, if the evidence is so obviously false there can be no question of admitting it however relevant it might seem to be.

The truth of the evidence said to be evidence of bad character is one aspect of its cogency. A further problem concerned with cogency arises where the accused's connection with the evidence is not admitted[231] and there is no prima facie proof of it.[232] The problem arose at common law of how cogent the evidence of "similar facts" had to be before any question could arise of drawing inferences from the similar facts. In *Harris v DPP*,[233] the defendant, a police officer, was charged with eight counts of office-breaking and larceny from premises in a market that he patrolled. The evidence on the first seven counts was that the breakings and thefts were effected by the same means of access and that they occurred at times when the defendant was on duty in the market and when most of the gates to the market were closed to the general public. Apart from this evidence of opportunity there was no other evidence to link the defendant with

---

[229] *McLeod* [1994] 3 All E.R. 254 at 267.

[230] Criminal Justice Act 2003 s.109(2).

[231] The accused did admit to other misconduct in *Straffen* [1952] 2 Q.B. 911 CCA; and in *Pfennig v R.* (1995) 127 A.L.R. 99 High Ct of Australia, where the defendant pleaded guilty at a trial. Similarly the defendant may admit a particular propensity, such as homosexuality: *King* [1967] 2 Q.B. 338 CA.

[232] This term is used to refer to evidence that, if accepted, proves beyond reasonable doubt the existence of the facts said to constitute similar facts and the accused's connection with them. Such evidence could take many forms. Examples include things found on the accused's person (*Thompson v R.* [1918] A.C. 221 HL) or at his premises (*Lewis* (1982) 76 Cr.App.R. 33 CA); the direct testimony of a victim (*DPP v P* [1991] 2 A.C. 447 HL) or an eyewitness (*Mustafa* (1976) 65 Cr.App.R. 26 CA) and so on.

[233] *Harris v DPP* [1952] A.C. 694 HL.

any of these seven offences. The evidence on the eighth count was much more incriminating. The defendant was seen outside the premises just after an alarm bell in the premises had sounded; a quantity of marked money missing from the till was found in a bin a short distance away; the defendant did not immediately join other police officers who entered the market after the alarm sounded and whom he knew, but disappeared for a time just long enough for him to have secreted money in the bin before he returned. The jury convicted the defendant on the eighth count but acquitted him on the first seven counts. The House of Lords quashed his conviction because the judge failed to direct the jury to exclude the evidence relating to the first seven counts when they were considering the eighth. The majority held that this evidence was not admissible as similar fact evidence. According to Viscount Simon:

> "It is, of course, clear that evidence of 'similar facts' cannot in any case be admissible to support an accusation against the accused unless they are connected in some relevant way with the accused and with his participation in the crime . . . It is the fact that he was involved in the other occurrences which may negative the inference of accident or establish his *mens rea* . . . [or] prove his identity . . .
> . . . the accused denied that he was the thief and the fact that someone perpetrated the earlier thefts when the accused may have been somewhere in the market does not provide material confirmation of his identity as the thief on the last occasion."[234]

It was not clear at common law whether the evidence of the defendant's connection with the similar facts had to reach any particular standard of proof in order for it to be admissible.[235] The point was complicated by the fact that admissibility as similar fact evidence also depended on the strength of the inferences that could be drawn from it. This assessment was made by the judge on the assumption that the similar fact evidence was true, and the judge was not required to decide as a preliminary fact that the evidence was true. This was the task of the jury, and remains so under the 2003 Act. But there is nonetheless a question of the minimum level of cogency required before the evidence can be left to the jury at all. It is submitted that the answer in principle is that there should be prima facie evidence of the defendant's connection with the similar facts, that is, evidence capable of proving the connection beyond reasonable doubt.[236] This is the general standard that prosecution evidence of guilt must meet. There seems no good reason for accepting a lesser standard for evidence which, ex hypothesi, is prejudicial to the accused.

However, there is a further complication. Must the factfinder be satisfied that the **19–057** accused's link with the alleged similar misconduct is established by evidence independent of the evidence on the offence to which the similar fact evidence is said to be relevant (the "sequential" approach), or can the whole of the evidence be pooled to enable the factfinder to conclude that the same person was responsible for both the offence charged and the similar misconduct (the

---

[234] *Harris v DPP* [1952] A.C. 694 at 708, 711.
[235] See generally R. Mahoney, "Similar Fact Evidence and the Standard of Proof" [1993] Crim. L.R. 185.
[236] cf. *Mansfield* (1977) 65 Cr.App.R. 276, where the Court of Appeal distinguished *Harris v DPP* on the ground that there was "ample" evidence to connect the accused with the starting of other fires relied on as similar fact evidence in a case of arson.

"cumulative" approach)? This question arose in a number of cases at common law involving similar fact evidence of identity, and caused considerable difficulty.[237] Under the 2003 Act "cumulative" reasoning appears to be the preferred approach, certainly in relation to a case involving a number of charges where there is cross-admissible circumstantial evidence to support each charge.[238] The jury will be directed to consider the totality of the evidence in relation to each of the charges and will not necessarily have to reach a decision of guilt on charge A before proceeding to consider charge B and so on. In *Freeman*,[239] which was concerned with cross-admissible direct evidence from the victims of the alleged offences, Latham L.J. for the Court of Appeal said:

> "In some of the judgments since *Hanson*, the impression may have been given that the jury, in its decision-making process in cross-admissibility cases should first determine whether it is satisfied on the evidence in relation to one of the counts of the defendant's guilt before it can move on to using the evidence in relation to that count in dealing with any other count in the indictment. A good example is the judgment of this court in *R. v S* [2008] EWCA Crim 544. We consider that this is too restrictive an approach. Whilst the jury must be reminded that it has to reach a verdict on each count separately, it is entitled, in determining guilt in respect of any count, to have regard to the evidence in regard to any other count, or any other bad character evidence if that evidence is admissible and relevant in the way we have described. It may be that in some cases the jury will find it easier to decide the guilt of a defendant on the evidence relating to that count alone. That does not mean that it cannot, in other cases, use the evidence in relation to the other count or counts to help it decide on the defendant's guilt in respect of the count that it is considering. To do otherwise would fail to give proper effect to the decision on admissibility."[240]

2. *Contamination of evidence of bad character*

19–058   A further problem of cogency of evidence of bad character may arise if there is a suspicion that the evidence of witnesses to multiple alleged offences by the defendant is contaminated. This might be the result of deliberate collusion between the witnesses to fabricate complaints, or it could arise where one complainant's knowledge of what another complainant is saying causes the former consciously or even unconsciously to trim her evidence to eliminate any differences. The leading case at common law was *R. v H*.[241] The accused was charged with sexual offences against two girls living with him in the same house. The first (W1) was his adopted daughter aged nine against whom he was alleged to have committed offences over a period of two years. The second (W2) was his stepdaughter aged 14. Neither girl made a complaint until more than three years after the alleged offences. H denied all the relevant incidents. It was accepted on both sides that there was a risk of collusion between W1 and W2 to make false allegations against H. The issue for the House of Lords was whether the trial judge was correct in directing the jury that they could use the similarities in the

---

[237] For discussion see the 3rd edn of this book at pp.842–844.
[238] See, e.g. *Wallace* [2007] EWCA Crim 1760; [2007] 2 Cr.App.R. 30; *McAllister* [2008] EWCA Crim 1544; [2009] 1 Cr.App.R. 10.
[239] *Freeman* [2008] EWCA Crim 1863; [2009] 1 Cr.App.R. 15.
[240] *Freeman* [2008] EWCA Crim 1863; [2009] 1 Cr.App.R. 15 at [20]. See further Fortson and Ormerod, "Bad Character Evidence and Cross-admissibility" [2004] Crim L.R. 313.
[241] *R. v H*. [1995] 2 A.C. 596 HL.

stories of W1 and W2 as mutually corroborative, provided they were satisfied that the girls had not conspired to tell a false story. The judge had thus left the credibility of the similar fact evidence to the factfinder as a question of weight. The defence argued[242] that it was a condition of the admissibility of similar fact evidence as a matter of law that there should be no real risk of collusion between the witnesses concerned.[243] Therefore, the defence said, the judge should decide before admitting the evidence whether such a real risk of collusion existed, if necessary by holding a voir dire. If he concluded that it did, he should exclude the evidence. The House of Lords rejected the defence argument, overruled the Court of Appeal cases supporting it and dismissed H's appeal.

According to the House of Lords the admissibility of similar fact evidence should be approached on the assumption that the evidence was true. Then the trial judge, following the approach laid down in *DPP v P*,[244] should decide whether the probative force of the similar fact evidence made it fair to admit it, notwithstanding its prejudicial effect. The possibility of collusion was not generally relevant at this stage. The Lords went on to hold that the issue of collusion or contamination should generally be left to the jury as a question of fact. If the jury had a reasonable doubt whether the evidence was free from collusion or contamination they could not use it as corroboration or for any purpose adverse to the defence. This followed the normal division of function whereby issues of credibility of evidence are generally left to the factfinder as questions of weight. The Lords qualified their ruling only to the extent of saying that if in the course of the trial it became apparent that no reasonable jury could accept the evidence as free from collusion then the judge should direct the jury that they could not rely on the evidence for any purpose adverse to the defence.

The Law Commission took the view that this approach did not provide sufficient safeguards for defendants against the risk of contaminated evidence. The Commission proposed that the judge should have power to stop the case if he or she is satisfied at any time after the close of the case for the prosecution that the evidence is contaminated, and that the contamination is such that, considering the importance of the evidence to the case against the defendant, his conviction of the offence would be unsafe. Section 107(1) of the 2003 Act gives effect to this proposal. In such a case the judge must either direct the jury to acquit the defendant of the offence, or discharge the jury if the judge considers there ought to be a retrial. Under s.107(5) a person's evidence is contaminated where:

"(a) as a result of an agreement or understanding between the person and one or more others, or

(b) as a result of the person being aware of anything alleged by one or more others whose

evidence may, or has been, given in the proceedings,the evidence is false or misleading in any respect, or is different from what it would otherwise have been."

---

[242] Relying on *Ananthanarayanan* [1994] 2 All E.R. 847 CA; *Ryder* [1994] 2 All E.R. 859 CA; *R. v W* [1994] 2 All E.R. 872 CA.

[243] The defence argued that this condition extended beyond deliberate conspiracy to fabricate evidence to include contamination of evidence by innocent "infection" where witnesses discussed their evidence informally, although the latter possibility was not in issue on the facts of the case.

[244] *DPP v P* [1991] 2 A.C. 447.

19–059   The judge's power under s.107 is limited. According to the Court of Appeal in *Renda*,[245] "Section 107 deals with a particular situation where the evidence of 'bad character' has been admitted and *proves* to be false or misleading in the circumstances described in s.107(5)" (emphasis supplied).[246] If the judge merely suspects that the evidence may be contaminated the question whether it is should be left to the jury in the normal way. In *R. v N(H)*,[247] the Court of Appeal confirmed that there is an obligation on the judge, where the evidence of complainants is cross-admissible, usually to direct the jury that they must exclude collusion or innocent contamination as an explanation for the similarity of the complaints before they can assess the force of the argument that they are unlikely to be the product of coincidence. Where, as in that case, the prosecution are not relying on the complaints as cross-admissible, the need for a warning about the risk of contamination will depend on the circumstances of the case and how the evidence has developed at the trial.

---

[245] *Renda* [2005] EWCA Crim 2826; [2006] 2 All E.R. 553 at [27].
[246] In *Card* [2006] EWCA Crim 1079; [2006] 2 Cr.App.R. 28 the Court of Appeal confirmed that the duty under s.107 does not arise unless the judge is satisfied that there has been important contamination of the evidence. If the judge is so satisfied then the trial must be stopped.
[247] *R. v N(H)* [2011] EWCA Crim 730.

OPINION AND EXPERT EVIDENCE

A.   INTRODUCTION

The general rule at common law is that witnesses may only give evidence of facts   **20–001**
of which they have personal knowledge. In other words, witnesses may testify
only as to what they themselves did, said, heard or witnessed. This cardinal rule
provides the foundation not only for the hearsay rule, but also for a further
common law rule that prohibits witnesses from expressing their opinions about
what happened or may have happened.[1] In general, witnesses may not draw
inferences from the facts, or speculate as to the causes of the facts, or make value
judgments about them.[2] Thus in a case of theft, a witness can testify that he saw
the defendant do something with the property in question, but may not testify that
he thought the defendant's behaviour was dishonest. In a personal injuries action,

---

[1] *Robb* (1991) 93 Cr.App.R. 161 CA.
[2] J. A. Andrews and M. Hirst, *Criminal Evidence*, 4th edn (2001), para.21–01.

a witness can describe the manner of the defendant's driving, but the common law rule prevents the witness saying that in his view the defendant's negligence was the cause of the accident.

The rule against evidence of opinion is based on three main rationales. The first is that, generally speaking, witnesses' opinions are unnecessary and superfluous. The court is as well-equipped as the witness to draw inferences from the facts to which the witness testifies and to reach conclusions about the application of the law to the facts. The reception of opinion evidence from witnesses would thus produce delay and expense that could be avoided. The second rationale argues that the reception of opinions might raise collateral issues that would distract or confuse the factfinder. These include such issues as the qualifications of the witness to give an opinion, the basis for the opinion, how far it is consistent with other opinions, and so on. The third rationale is related to the first. It is the function of the factfinder in adjudicative proceedings to draw inferences from the facts and to reach decisions about the application of the law to the facts. The danger of admitting evidence of opinion is that the witness may usurp this function; the danger is thought to be particularly apparent in jury trials in criminal cases where the witness is a person to whose opinion the jury may give great weight.

20–002   For these reasons the common law has erected a general ban on evidence of opinion. However, the ban is subject to two types of exception where evidence of a witness's opinion is either inevitable or desirable. It is inevitable where it is not reasonably practicable for the witness to separate the observed facts from the inferences that the witness draws from the facts. In such cases the courts take the view that it is better to have the evidence in the form of an opinion than not to have it at all. Opinion evidence is desirable where it consists of inferences to be drawn in relation to some matter involving special skill or knowledge that is outside the normal experience and competence of the tribunal of fact. In such cases a court needs expert help in order for the court to discharge its duty of fair and accurate factfinding.

These exceptions thus allow for the admission in certain cases of non-expert opinion evidence and expert evidence respectively. The next two sections of this chapter deal with these exceptions in more detail. A further issue is the use, if any, that can be made of judicial findings in other legal proceedings. A question may arise whether, for example, a party can adduce evidence that the defendant, or a third party, has been convicted of an offence, in circumstances where the conviction is relevant to an issue in the current proceedings. In one sense the conviction, or other judicial finding, represents no more than the concluded opinion of another court on another occasion. As such it does not fit comfortably within either of the two exceptions to the general rule against opinion evidence, and yet it is clearly a peculiarly authoritative kind of opinion. This gives it considerable probative value, but its admission or exclusion raises issues both of policy and principle. These issues are considered in the final section of the chapter.

B.   NON-EXPERT OPINION

The general rule at common law is that a witness may not give an opinion on any **20–003** matter that does not call for the special skill or knowledge of an expert if the facts on which the opinion is based can be stated without reference to the opinion in a manner equally conducive to the ascertainment of the truth.[3] If, on the other hand, it is not reasonably practicable to expect the witness to separate observed facts from the inferences the witness draws from the facts, then the witness is allowed to give the evidence in the form of an opinion. Indeed, it has been recognised for at least a century that there is a basic sense in which all evidence of "fact" is evidence of "opinion".[4] Whenever a witness engages in the process of observing an event, storing the event in memory, retrieving it subsequently and narrating it to a court, the witness cannot help using inference, explanation and classification to make sense of what has been observed. These are the fundamental elements of the social construction of all knowledge. For example, a witness is allowed to say that he saw a white car drive across a road junction through a red traffic light. Nothing would be gained, and much confusion would be caused, if we tried to restrict the witness to saying that he saw a white irregularly shaped object change its position in relation to a long thin object with a red glow at the top. For his testimony to have any meaning it is necessary for the witness to organise his visual perceptions by reference to the relevant concepts of a car, a road, driving and a traffic light, and to the significance of their conjunction when the light is red. This kind of interpretation and classification of observed phenomena is, in a weak sense, all opinion evidence.

The cases now to be considered represent a development of this idea. Questions may arise in litigation about certain features or characteristics of the things observed by the witness. The witness is allowed to describe such features or characteristics in the form of an opinion, if it is not reasonably practicable to expect the witness to describe them in a way that separates facts from inferences. Common examples are the age of a person,[5] the identity of a person or thing,[6] the handwriting of someone known to the witness,[7] the speed of a vehicle,[8] the condition or value of an object,[9] and so on. In *Davies*,[10] the examples were taken a stage further where a non-medical witness was allowed to testify that he thought the defendant had been drinking. This is a case where the inference can

---

[3] Cross and Tapper, p.529; citing *Sherrard v Jacob* [1965] N.I. 151 at 157–158 per Lord MacDermott.
[4] J. B. Thayer, *A Preliminary Treatise on Evidence at the Common Law* (Boston, 1898), p.524; Wigmore, Vol.VII (Chadbourn rev. 1978), para.1919.
[5] *Cox* [1898] 1 Q.B. 179.
[6] *Fryer v Gathercole* (1849) 4 Ex. 262. For judicial concern about the reliability of lay evidence of *voice* recognition, see *Flynn* [2008] EWCA Crim 970; [2008] 2 Cr.App.R. 20. Where lay evidence of opinion, offered by the prosecution, is thought to be more prejudicial than probative, as it was in *Flynn*, the judge should exclude it under the discretion available under s.78 of PACE or at common law.
[7] *Doe d. Mudd v Suckermore* (1837) 5 Ad. & El. 703; *O'Brien* (1911) 7 Cr.App.R. 29.
[8] See Road Traffic Regulation Act 1984 s.89(2), providing that no one can be convicted of speeding solely on the basis of one person's opinion as to the speed of the vehicle.
[9] *Beckett* (1913) 8 Cr.App.R. 204.
[10] *Davies* [1962] 3 All E.R. 97 CMAC. See also *Tagg* [2001] EWCA Crim 1230; [2002] 1 Cr.App.R. 22 (opinion of witnesses admissible that D was "drunk" on an aircraft).

be distinguished from the underlying facts, meaning physical signs such as the defendant's unsteady gait, slurred speech and glazed eyes. The Courts Martial Appeal Court thought that it was acceptable for the witness to state his impression that the defendant had been drinking, provided that he then stated the facts on which the impression was based. In most of these situations it is inevitable that the witness will give evidence in the form of an opinion. Realistically there is no other way in which this kind of relevant evidence can be given, although the basis for the opinion can of course be probed in cross-examination with a view to challenging the weight of the evidence.

In criminal cases the common law continues to apply, although in practice it seems that the general ban on non-expert opinion is applied flexibly in a common sense way. In civil cases, on the other hand, the general rule against non-expert opinion was substantially abolished by the Civil Evidence Act 1972 s.3(2). This recognises the frequent difficulty of distinguishing fact and opinion when a witness is testifying about matters personally observed by him, and provides:

> "It is hereby declared that where a person is called as a witness in any civil proceedings, a statement of opinion by him on any relevant matter on which he is not qualified to give expert evidence, if made as a way of conveying relevant facts personally perceived by him, is admissible as evidence of what he perceived."

20–004 An example of the kind of evidence that would be covered by this provision is the statement in issue in *Rasool v West Midlands Passenger Transport Executive*.[11] An eyewitness of an accident in which a bus collided with a pedestrian made a written statement that:

> "The bus driver was in no way to blame for the accident. The pedestrian walked straight out into the road without looking in either direction. He had made no attempt to use the pedestrian crossing."

The case concerned the admissibility of this as a hearsay statement, since the witness had become untraceable. The point whether the statement was inadmissible opinion evidence was not argued, but it seems clear that the witness's conclusions about the fault of the parties represented her way of explaining what she had seen. As such, the statement would be admissible under s.3(2).[12] It follows that a non-expert's opinion, which is *not* given as a way of conveying relevant facts personally perceived by him, is still inadmissible by virtue of the general rule. If the same witness had gone on, for example, to express a view about the adequacy of the brakes on the bus, or the driver's qualifications, that opinion would have been inadmissible even if those matters had been in issue.

A further rule should be mentioned at this point. At common law no witness, whether expert or non-expert, was permitted to give an opinion on the ultimate issue in the case. This meant the issue that the court had to decide in order to dispose of the case, such as whether the defendant had defamed the claimant or had murdered the victim. The ultimate issue rule is discussed further in connection with expert evidence in criminal cases. In civil cases it has been

---

[11] *Rasool v West Midlands Passenger Transport Executive* [1974] 3 All E.R. 638 QBD.
[12] See J. A. Andrews and M. Hirst, *Criminal Evidence* (2001), para.21–03.

abolished altogether for expert witnesses[13]; for non-experts it is abolished only for the purposes of cases covered by the Civil Evidence Act 1972 s.3(2).

C.   EXPERT EVIDENCE[14]

The exception to the opinion rule for expert evidence on matters involving special skill or knowledge has existed for at least two centuries.[15] Although well-established, the exception is far from being unproblematic. Current law and practice is widely thought to be unsatisfactory in relation both to the criteria for the admission of expert evidence and its evaluation by the court. In an important recent report[16] the Law Commission identified several causes for concern. It noted a history of unreliable expert evidence contributing to wrongful convictions of major crimes.[17] It argued that the common law has adopted a laissez-faire approach to the admission of expert evidence which pays inadequate attention to whether the evidence is sufficiently reliable to be considered by a jury.[18] It queried whether the reliability of dubious expert evidence is adequately tested in cross-examination, suggesting that advocates who do not feel confident or equipped to challenge the underlying science may prefer to focus on the expert's credibility.[19] It referred to the danger of a lay jury, which may not be equipped by education or experience properly to evaluate technical or complex scientific evidence, simply deferring to the opinion of the specialist or concentrating on such matters as the witness's qualifications or demeanour.[20] These concerns led the Commission to recommend significant reforms, including the enactment of a new statutory test of admissibility requiring expert opinion evidence to have "sufficient reliability" to be admitted. This proposal is considered further below.

20–005

In addition to the Law Commission's report, we may note increasing judicial concern in several areas of medical and forensic science about the need to promote better practice in the giving of expert evidence. These cases restate and clarify the application of several central principles. In *Reed and Reed*,[21] the Court of Appeal gave a lengthy judgment reviewing DNA profiling technology and reminding counsel and witnesses about the boundaries of expert evidence in this area. The court emphasised in particular that an expert witness must not go

---

[13] Civil Evidence Act 1972 s.3(1) and (3).

[14] See generally M. Redmayne, *Expert Evidence and Criminal Justice* (Oxford: Oxford Uinversity Press, 2001); E. Beecher-Monas, *Evaluating Scientific Evidence* (Cambridge: Cambridge University Press, 2007); D. Dwyer, *The Judicial Assessment of Expert Evidence* (Oxford: Oxford University Press, 2008); Law Commission, *Expert Evidence in Criminal Proceedings in England and Wales* (Law Com No.325, TSO, London, 2011) ("Law Com 325").

[15] *Folkes v Chadd* (1782) 3 Doug K.B. 157 is the early leading case.

[16] Law Com 325. See also the report of a committee of the National Research Council of the US National Academy of Sciences, *Strengthening the Forensic Sciences in the US: A Path Forward* (The National Academies Press, 2009) which criticises the state of several areas of forensic science and the role of the courts in regulating evidence in these areas.

[17] Citing *Dallagher* [2002] EWCA Crim 1903; [2003] 1 Cr.App.R. 12; *Clark* [2003] EWCA Crim 1020; [2003] 2 F.C.R. 447; *Cannings* [2004] EWCA Crim 1; [2004] 2 Cr.App.R. 7.

[18] Law Com 325 para.1.8.

[19] Law Com 325 para.1.21.

[20] Law Com 325 para.1.15.

[21] *Reed and Reed* [2009] EWCA Crim 2698; [2010] 1 Cr.App.R. 23.

beyond the limit of her expertise,[22] so that the witness in the case could not testify as to her opinion that the defendants were handling the knives in question when the knives broke (Ds' DNA was found on the handles of two broken knives at the scene of the murder they were charged with committing). There was no underlying scientific basis for this opinion. In *Henderson*,[23] the Court of Appeal reviewed in another lengthy judgment the medical evidence in a number of "shaken baby" cases. The court gave guidance for the conduct of future cases, emphasising the importance of the medical expert being in current clinical practice when making his report, and of the need for the basis of the opinion to be fully explained. It stressed that a conviction in a case depending on contested medical evidence should be founded on a logically justifiable basis, and that juries should not decide between experts on the basis of impression. In *R. v T*,[24] the Court of Appeal quashed a conviction for murder as unsafe where an expert on footwear marks (shoeprint comparisons) had relied in forming his opinion on data that the court found to be incomplete and imprecise. In a forceful judgment the court said that an expert giving footwear mark evidence should not make use of likelihood ratios[25] in the absence of a sufficiently reliable statistical database, but should restrict himself to verbal expressions that a particular shoe belonging to the defendant 'could' have made the mark found at the crime scene.[26] In *R. v Smith (Peter)*,[27] the Court of Appeal reviewed a number of issues arising in connection with fingerprint evidence. It found that the practices of fingerprint examiners were unsatisfactory in several respects, including a failure to keep notes of their examinations and the reasons for their conclusions. The court issued a call for urgent review and reform by the appropriate bodies.

Despite the Court of Appeal's various concerns about expert evidence, it has not attempted in any of these cases to lay down a new test of admissibility. For the most part the judgments have reiterated the test set out by the Supreme Court of South Australia in the influential case of *R. v Bonython*, as adopted by the Court of Appeal in *Luttrell*.[28] This requires the judge to consider three matters in relation to expert opinion evidence. The first two, as expressed in *Bonython,* are:

(a) whether the subject matter of the opinion is such that a person without instruction or experience in the area of knowledge or human experience would be able to form a sound judgment on the matter without the assistance of witnesses possessing special knowledge or experience in the area;

---

[22] Citing *Atkins and Atkins* [2009] EWCA Crim 1876; [2010] 1 Cr.App.R. 8 (a case on expert evidence of "facial mapping").

[23] *Henderson* [2010] EWCA Crim 1269; [2011] 2 Cr.App.R. 24.

[24] *R. v T* [2010] EWCA Crim 2439; [2011] 1 Cr.App.R. 9.

[25] See Ch.4 for an explanation of this term in the context of a discussion of the use of Bayes' Theorem in criminal cases.

[26] It seems that the Court of Appeal thought that the same principle should apply in other areas of forensic science, although those areas were not in issue in the case. For discussion and criticism see M. Redmayne, "Forensic Science Evidence in Question" [2011] Crim. L.R. 347; G. S. Morrison, "The likelihood-ratio framework and forensic evidence in court: a response to *R v T*" (2012) 16 E. & P. 1.

[27] *R. v Smith (Peter)* [2011] EWCA Crim 1296; [2011] 2 Cr.App.R. 16.

[28] *Luttrell* [2004] EWCA Crim 1344; [2004] 2 Cr.App.R. 31 approving *Bonython* [1984] 38 S.A.S.R. 45.

(b)   whether the subject matter of the opinion forms part of a body of
knowledge or experience which is sufficiently organised or recognised to
be accepted as a reliable body of knowledge or experience, a special
acquaintance with which by the witness would render his opinion of
assistance to the court.

If the first two conditions are satisfied the third matter is whether the witness
is suitably qualified to express the expert opinion in question. Before dealing with
each of these matters in more detail we should note also the Court of Appeal's
references to a view expressed in Cross and Tapper:

> "The better, and now more widely accepted, view is that so long as the field is sufficiently
> well-established to pass the ordinary tests of relevance and reliability, then no enhanced test of
> admissibility should be applied, but the weight of the evidence should be established by the
> same adversarial forensic techniques applicable elsewhere."[29]

1.   Matters which the court considers call for the special skill or knowledge of an expert: the helpfulness test

It is a decision for the trial judge in each case whether the issue on which a party **20–006**
proposes to adduce expert evidence is one that requires such a degree of skill and
knowledge as to be outside the experience of the tribunal. Medical and scientific
questions are obvious examples, but there are a great many other matters on
which expert evidence can be given, and the list is growing.[30] Forensic science
does not stand still and the courts are conscious of how advances in technology
can improve detection and prosecution of crime. In *Clarke*,[31] a case concerned
with facial mapping by video superimposition, Steyn L.J. commented in relation
to developments in real evidence that:

> "if that real evidence is not sufficiently intelligible to the jury without expert evidence, it has
> always been accepted that it is possible to place before the jury the opinion of an expert in
> order to assist them in their interpretation of the real evidence... There are no closed
> categories where such evidence may be placed before a jury. It would be entirely wrong to
> deny to the law of evidence the advantages to be gained from new techniques and new
> advances in science."

The question of the requisite degree of reliability of expert evidence is considered
below. For the moment we should stress the significance of the helpfulness test.
An influential statement of the principle that the admissibility of expert opinion is
founded on necessity was given by Lawton L.J. in *Turner*:

---

[29] This passage is now at p.545 of the 12th edn. It was approved in earlier editions in *Dallagher*
[2002] EWCA Crim 1903; [2003] 1 Cr.App.R. 12 at [29]; *Luttrell* [2004] EWCA Crim 1344; [2004] 2
Cr.App.R. 31 at [37]; *Reed and Reed* [2009] EWCA Crim 2698; [2010] 1 Cr.App.R. 23 at [111].
[30] In recent years it has been held to include, e.g. identification by facial mapping (*Stockwell* (1993)
97 Cr.App.R. 260 CA); identification by earprints (*Dallagher* [2002] EWCA Crim 1903; [2003] 1
Cr.App.R. 12; lip-reading evidence (*Luttrell* [2004] EWCA Crim 1344; [2004] 2 Cr.App.R. 31, and
"walking gait" analysis (*Otway* [2011] EWCA Crim 3) .
[31] *Clarke* [1995] 2 Cr.App.R. 425 at 429–430 CA.

"An expert's opinion is admissible to furnish the court with scientific information which is likely to be outside the experience and knowledge of a judge or jury. If on the proven facts a judge or jury can form their own conclusions without help, then the opinion of an expert is unnecessary."[32]

Immediately after this passage Lawton L.J. went on to explain that where expert opinion is not necessary, since the matter is within the factfinder's own competence, the expert's evidence is excluded not just because it is superfluous but also because it may unduly dominate the factfinder's evaluation of the evidence in the case and thus tend to usurp the factfinder's function. Speaking of jury trials, he said:

"In such a case if it is given dressed up in scientific jargon it may make judgment more difficult. The fact that an expert witness has impressive scientific qualifications does not by that fact alone make his opinion on matters of human nature and behaviour within the limits of normality any more helpful than that of the jurors themselves; but there is a danger that they may think it does."

20–007 The context of these remarks was the admissibility of psychiatric and/or psychological evidence on behalf of the defence in a criminal case. This question has arisen in numerous cases over a period of years, and offers an instructive case-study of the use and limits of expert evidence.

First, in relation to issues of mens rea, the courts will not admit expert evidence unless it is alleged that the defendant was suffering from an abnormal mental state at the time of his act. In *Chard*,[33] the defendant was charged with murder. He sought to adduce psychiatric evidence relating to his intention at the material time, but the trial judge excluded the evidence on the basis that there was no question of D having had an abnormal mental state; neither insanity nor diminished responsibility was in issue. The Court of Appeal dismissed the defendant's appeal against conviction, saying that jurors did not need expert help in deciding on the intentions of a man with a normal mind. This was something they were well able to judge for themselves by their ordinary experience.[34]

The strict line the courts have taken on expert evidence relating to issues of mens rea is reinforced by other cases. It appears to make no difference that the accused is intellectually impaired or psychologically vulnerable. In *Masih*,[35] the Court of Appeal held expert evidence to be inadmissible in relation to an issue of whether the accused, who was charged with rape, had realised that the victim was not consenting. The accused had an IQ of 72 and was thus a borderline mental defective. Had his IQ been four points lower, he would have been classed as mentally defective and expert evidence would have been admissible. Similarly, in *Henry*,[36] the Court of Appeal held that the defendant, who had been convicted of

---

[32] *Turner* [1975] Q.B. 834 at 841 CA. The case is closely analysed by M. Redmayne, *Expert Evidence and Criminal Justice* (Oxford: Oxford Uinversity Press, 2001), pp.140–149.

[33] *Chard* (1971) 56 Cr.App.R. 268 CA.

[34] cf. *Toner* (1991) 93 Cr.App.R. 382 CA (expert evidence admissible concerning the effect of mild hypoglycaemia on a man's ability to form an intent; this was not something within the jury's ordinary experience).

[35] *Masih* [1986] Crim. L.R. 395.

[36] *Henry* [2005] EWCA Crim 1681; [2006] 1 Cr.App.R. 6. See also *Weightman* (1990) 92 Cr.App.R. 291 CA.

soliciting to murder and conspiracy to murder, could not adduce fresh evidence from a psychologist that he had an IQ of 75 and a mental age of about 12, and was an impulsive individual who tried to please others and who was easily imposed upon. The defendant had argued that the evidence went to the issue of his intention that murder should occur, but the court said that since the evidence did not show him to be either mentally ill or mentally defective it was not admissible. The IQ threshold invoked in these cases would seem to be a somewhat arbitrary figure.

Secondly, however, the mens rea cases can be compared with *Lowery v R.*,[37] which concerned not an abnormal mental state, but an accused's propensity to aggression compared with his co-accused. This was held to be relevant to establish his identity as the perpetrator of a murder. Lowery and his co-accused, King, were charged with the murder of a girl. The circumstances were such that the murder must have been committed by one of them, or both acting in concert. At the trial each sought to blame the other. Lowery gave evidence in his defence that he was a person of good character. The trial judge subsequently permitted King to adduce evidence from a clinical psychologist who had examined both accused that King was immature, emotionally shallow and likely to be dominated by a more aggressive man. He also testified that Lowery had a strong aggressive drive with weak controls. Dismissing Lowery's appeal against conviction the Privy Council held that the psychologist's evidence was rightly admitted. The ratio decidendi of this case is unclear. In *Turner*, Lawton L.J. described it as decided on its special facts,[38] and it is clear that there are two grounds for interpreting the decision narrowly. One is that Lowery had put his good character in issue as relevant to his credibility in maintaining his innocence. The psychologist's evidence was admissible for King in rebuttal of the claim of good character. The other ground is that the question of which of the two men had the more aggressive personality, a question that was relevant to the probability of their guilt, was not a question that the jury could resolve from their own experience. They needed the expert help provided by the psychologist. Neither of these grounds offers any basis for saying that *Lowery* is authority for the wider admission of expert evidence.[39] However, Lord Morris said at one point that:

20–008

> "we see no reason of policy or fairness which justifies or requires the exclusion of evidence relevant to prove the innocence of an accused person ... it would be unjust to prevent either [defendant] from calling any evidence of probative value which could point to the probability that the perpetrator was the one rather than the other."[40]

Abstracted from the factual context of the case, these statements might justify much greater admissibility of expert evidence in criminal trials. A difficulty with this reading is that it seems to state a special rule only for defence evidence. In

---

[37] *Lowery v R.* [1974] A.C. 85 PC.

[38] *Turner* [1975] Q.B. 834 at 842.

[39] In *Randall* [2003] UKHL 69; [2004] 1 Cr.App.R. 26 the House of Lords treated *Lowery* [1974] A.C. 85 as authority for the proposition that evidence of the propensity of the accused to violence is relevant and admissible on the issue of which of two co-accused is more likely to have used violence on the victim. However, Lord Steyn expressly refrained from commenting on the admissibility of expert evidence on the issue (at [30]).

[40] *Lowery* [1974] A.C. 85 at 102 and 101 respectively.

Turner, the Court of Appeal was quick to scotch any idea that the rules about expert evidence might be more generously applied to the defence:

> "We adjudge *Lowery v R.* to have been decided on its special facts. We do not consider that it is an authority for the proposition that in all cases psychologists and psychiatrists can be called to prove the probability of the accused's veracity. If any such rule was applied to our courts, trial by psychiatrists would be likely to take the place of trial by jury and magistrates. We do not find that prospect attractive and the law does not at present provide for it."[41]

Thirdly, turning to defences, it is clear that expert evidence is not only admissible, but is normally required to establish defences of insanity and diminished responsibility. By definition these defences concern abnormal mental states outside the experience of the jury. With other defences the position is more complex. *Turner* concerned the common law defence of provocation to murder. The defendant had battered his girlfriend to death with a hammer. He claimed that he had been provoked by her statements to him that she had been unfaithful to him and was pregnant by another man. The defendant wished to strengthen this defence with psychiatric evidence to the effect that the depth of the defendant's relationship with his girlfriend had been such that he could well have behaved as he did in an explosive outburst of rage, and that his anger and subsequent grief were consistent with the defendant's personality structure. Upholding the trial judge's refusal to admit this evidence, the Court of Appeal held that the defendant was not mentally ill, and that the jury did not need a psychiatrist to tell them how ordinary people were likely to react to the situation in which the defendant found himself.

20–009   Fourthly, the cases on expert evidence relating to credibility[42] show some movement towards a more relaxed approach. For example, the courts now regularly admit psychiatric or psychological evidence when considering the admissibility of an accused's out-of-court confession.[43] The accused's mental state during the relevant interview is one of "the circumstances existing at the time", which s.76(2)(b) of PACE requires to be taken into account in deciding on the reliability of any confession that the accused might have made in consequence of anything said or done. If the accused's mental state at the time is likely to have been outside the experience of the jury, then expert evidence will be admissible even if the mental state did not amount to mental illness or personality disorder. In *Blackburn,*[44] the Court of Appeal held that the phenomenon of a "coerced compliant confession",[45] made by a person rendered vulnerable by fatigue and age or other factors, fell outside the experience of a jury. It was therefore a topic on which expert evidence was admissible.

---

[41] *Turner* [1975] Q.B. 834 at 842.

[42] See generally T. Ward, "Usurping the Role of the Jury? Expert Evidence and Witness Credibility in English Criminal Trials" (2009) 13 E. & P. 83.

[43] *Raghip, The Times,* December 9, 1991. cf. *Weightman* (1991) 92 Cr.App.R. 291 CA, where the central issue was the truth of the defendant's confession to murdering her child. The Court of Appeal upheld the trial judge's refusal to admit psychiatric evidence relating to the defendant's abnormal personality.

[44] *Blackburn* [2005] EWCA Crim 1349; [2005] 2 Cr.App.R. 30.

[45] See Ch.6.

In *Mackenney*,[46] the defence sought to adduce the evidence of a psychologist, who had been observing a key prosecution witness at the defendant's trial for murder, that the witness had a psychopathic personality. This meant that although he was capable of giving reliable evidence, he might choose not to do so. In 1981 the Court of Appeal agreed that this was inadmissible. It was held that the question whether a witness was actually telling the truth was a question for the jury, on which they did not need expert help. The court said that expert evidence would be admissible on an issue of credibility only where the *capacity* of the witness to give any credible evidence was in issue. Twenty-three years later, in *Pinfold and Mackenney*,[47] the Court of Appeal revisited its earlier decision following a reference from the Criminal Cases Review Commission. The court acknowledged that the approach to the admission of expert evidence on issues of credibility had developed and was now more generous. Such evidence is now admissible if it demonstrates that a person is suffering from some form of abnormality, not necessarily fitting into any recognised category of illness or disorder, that is relevant to the reliability of their evidence. The absence of an examination of the person by the expert, which would usually be required, is a matter that goes to the weight of the expert's opinion and not its admissibility. However, some form of medical abnormality is necessary. It should be "a very significant deviation from the norm" and:

> "there should be a history pre-dating the making of the admissions or the giving of evidence which is not based solely on a history given by the subject, which points to or explains the abnormality."[48]

Such decisions are open to the charge that they attach too much significance to a conceptual distinction between "normal" and "abnormal" mental states, and overestimate the ability of lay factfinders to use common sense and general experience in assessing the behaviour of persons with complex psychological states.[49] The present law, founded on *Turner*, is arguably too concerned with a "turf war"—preventing psychiatrists and psychologists from playing a more extensive role in criminal trials—at the expense of giving factfinders possibly valuable professional help on difficult issues.[50] Outside the area of "abnormality" there is still considerable reluctance to relax the *Turner* principle. For example, in

20–010

---

[46] *Mackenney* (1981) 76 Cr.App.R. 271 CA.

[47] *Pinfold and Mackenney* [2003] EWCA Crim 3643; [2004] 2 Cr.App.R. 5.

[48] *Pinfold and Mackenney* [2003] EWCA Crim 3643; [2004] 2 Cr.App.R. 5 at [14]; citing Roch L.J. in the unreported case of *O'Brien* January 25, 2000.

[49] For further discussion see R. Pattenden, "Conflicting Approaches to Psychiatric Evidence" [1986] Crim. L.R. 92; R. D. Mackay and A. Colman, "Excluding Expert Evidence: A Tale of Ordinary Folk and Common Experience" [1991] Crim. L.R. 800.

[50] A dictum of Farquharson L.J. in *Strudwick and Merry* (1994) 99 Cr.App.R. 326 at 332 suggests that the law is in a state of development, and that there may be mental conditions, not amounting to mental illness, about which a jury might require expert assistance in order to understand and evaluate their effect on the issues in the case. In *Gilfoyle (No.2)* [2001] 2 Cr.App.R. 57 at 66–67 the Court of Appeal accepted the correctness of this dictum but refused to apply it so as to permit the admission of evidence of a "psychological autopsy" of a deceased wife allegedly murdered by her husband. cf. the cautionary remarks of Lord Hobhouse in *Pendleton* [2001] UKHL 66; [2002] 1 All E.R. 524 at [45].

R. v H (JR) (Childhood Amnesia)[51] the Court of Appeal held that expert evidence about childhood amnesia would be admissible only in exceptional circumstances, such as where the complainant of sexual abuse provides a description of events occurring very early in her childhood that contains an unrealistic amount of detail. Otherwise, said the court, the ability of a witness to remember events will be well within the ordinary experience of jurors.

There is a further consideration that should be mentioned at this point. One reason for the courts' reluctance to concede too much ground to the "mental experts" may be a lingering scepticism about the scientific credentials of some of the expertise on offer. This is not something peculiar to psychiatric and psychological evidence. The problem of what has been called "bad" or "junk" science[52]—the evidence of alleged experts based on unproved and deeply controversial scientific theories—is one that cuts across the whole subject of expert evidence,[53] although some of the fiercest debate has concerned theories of human behaviour. The furore over "recovered memory syndrome", discussed in Ch.15, is a recent example. Accordingly, we now turn to the second of the two matters set out in *Bonython,* which is the vexed question of the reliability of an expert opinion and how the validity of its scientific or other basis should be determined.

2. *Reliability of expert evidence*[54]

20–011 The assessment of expert evidence is generally left to the factfinder as a question of weight. Factfinders are not bound to accept a party's expert evidence, even if it is unequivocal and uncontradicted by expert witnesses on the other side, if there is other evidence that tends to conflict with it.[55] Equally, a judge has no obligation to accept the opinion of an expert jointly instructed by the parties; even if he cannot identify a flaw in it he may reject it in favour of contradictory evidence from other witnesses he finds to be credible and reliable.[56]

---

[51] *R. v H (JR) (Childhood Amnesia)* [2005] EWCA Crim 1828; [2006] 1 Cr.App.R. 10; followed in *Snell, Wilson* [2006] EWCA Crim 1404.

[52] S. J. Odgers and J. T. Richardson, "Keeping Bad Science Out of the Courtroom–Changes in American and Australian Expert Evidence Law" (1995) 18 U.N.S.W. L.J. 108; D. Bernstein, "Junk Science in the United States and the Commonwealth" (1996) 21 Yale J. Int'l Law 123.

[53] There is a rich literature on the objectivity of scientific knowledge, and on the ways in which scientific knowledge is represented and validated in litigation. It is beyond the scope of this book to explore the debate in detail; good starting-points are G. Edmond, "Judicial Representations of Scientific Evidence" (2000) 63 M.L.R. 216; Redmayne, *Expert Evidence and Criminal Justice* (2001), Chs 2 and 7.

[54] See Law Com 325, discussed by G. Edmond and A. Roberts, "The Law Commission's Report on Expert Evidence in Criminal Proceedings" [2011] Crim. L.R. 844. See also the earlier Law Commission Consultation Paper, *Expert Evidence in Criminal Trials* (CP No.190, London, 2009), reviewed by A. Roberts, "Rejecting General Acceptance, Confounding the Gate-keeper: the Law Commission and Expert Evidence" [2009] Crim. L.R. 551. For further discussion see G. Edmond, "Is reliability sufficient? The Law Commission and expert evidence in international and interdisciplinary perspective (Part 1)" (2012) 16 E. & P. 30 and "Advice for the courts? *Sufficiently reliable* assistance with forensic science and medicine (Part 2)" (2012) 16 E. & P. 263.

[55] *Sanders* (1991) 93 Cr.App.R. 245 CA (diminished responsibility).

[56] *Armstrong v First York Ltd* [2005] EWCA Civ 277; [2005] 1 W.L.R. 2751.

Furthermore, there is authority that an expert's opinion is admissible and may be left to the factfinder to consider even if it is a minority view in the profession. In *Robb*,[57] an issue arose concerning expert evidence of voice identification.[58] The question was whether the voice heard on recordings of telephone calls made by kidnappers demanding ransom money was the same voice heard on a video found in the defendant's home. It was not disputed that the video recorded the defendant's voice. The prosecution called a phonetics expert with extensive experience in the analysis of voice production. He testified, relying on auditory techniques alone,[59] that in his opinion the voice on the ransom tapes was the same as the voice on the video. His evidence was strongly challenged by the defence on the basis that auditory techniques were unreliable unless supplemented and verified by acoustic analysis based on physical measurement of resonance and frequency. The witness accepted that this view represented the great weight of informed opinion, including the world leaders in the field, but he maintained that voice identification was not an exact science and that his experience and training led him to believe that his conclusions based on auditory techniques were reliable. The Court of Appeal said that it did not find it an "entirely easy" question whether the expert's evidence was admissible. The court was concerned that no defendant should be asked to meet "evidence of opinion given by a quack, a charlatan, or an enthusiastic amateur". On the facts the witness was held not to fall anywhere near these categories, since he was well qualified by academic training and practical experience to express a judgment on voice identification. This judgment was said to "have a value significantly greater than that of the ordinary untutored layman, as the judgment of a handwriting expert is superior to that of the man in the street".[60] The fact that his reliance on the auditory technique alone was a minority view in his profession clearly worried the court, but the court seems to have been reassured by the witness's reasoned explanation for his preferred technique and by the failure of the defence to call evidence to contradict his opinion or to point out dissimilarities in the voices that he had overlooked or ignored.

Robb was not followed by the Court of Appeal for Northern Ireland in *O'Doherty*.[61] The court found that time had moved on since 1991, acoustic analysis was easier to carry out, and was now a method of voice identification deployed by almost all experts in the field. Accordingly, "in the present state of scientific knowledge no prosecution should be brought in Northern Ireland in which one of the planks is voice identification given by an expert which is solely confined to auditory analysis. There should also be expert evidence of acoustic analysis". However, in *Flynn*[62] the Court of Appeal confirmed the continuing validity of expert auditory analysis for English law by saying that "it is neither

---

[57] *Robb* (1991) 93 Cr.App.R. 161 at 166.
[58] On the problems associated with such evidence see generally D. Ormerod, "Sounds Familiar?—Voice Identification Evidence" [2001] Crim. L.R. 595.
[59] These involved careful and repeated listening to both the disputed tapes and the control tape, paying close attention to features of voice quality and pitch, and to the pronunciation of vowels and consonants, to see if there were any significant discrepancies between the tapes.
[60] *Robb* (1991) 93 Cr.App.R. 161 at 166.
[61] *O'Doherty* [2003] 1 Cr.App.R. 5.
[62] *Flynn* [2008] EWCA Crim 970; [2008] 2 Cr.App.R. 20.

possible nor desirable" to go as far as the court in *O'Doherty*. The latter decision is a useful reminder of the elementary but vital point that of course scientific knowledge and understanding does not stand still. Developments in expert techniques for analysing and interpreting evidence may mean that earlier judgments about the reliability of particular techniques have to be reassessed, although controversy may well remain, as these cases demonstrate. Given this point, the question then is whether English law has, or should have, any specific threshold requirements designed to ensure the reliability of expert evidence.

Where the expert does not set out the scientific criteria for testing the validity of his opinion, it has been said that the bare opinion will have little weight, since it cannot be tested by cross-examination or independently appraised.[63] More recent authorities suggest or imply that in such cases the evidence should be excluded as inadmissible.[64] More difficult is the case where the scientific criteria are set out, but are challenged by the defence as invalid, and therefore not constituting a reliable foundation for an expert opinion. In the United States the response to this problem was for many years the "general acceptance" test set out in *Frye v United States*[65]:

> "Just when a scientific principle or discovery crosses the line between the experimental and demonstrable stages is difficult to define. Somewhere in this twilight zone the evidential force of the principle must be recognised, and while the courts will go a long way in admitting expert testimony deduced from a well-recognised scientific principle or discovery, the thing from which the deduction is made must be sufficiently established to have gained general acceptance in the particular field to which it belongs."

20–012   This cautious principle has received a varying reception in England. In *Gilfoyle (No.2)*,[66] the Court of Appeal cited *Frye* for the proposition that evidence based on a developing new brand of science or medicine is not admissible until accepted by the scientific community as being able to provide accurate and reliable opinion. On this basis the court held inadmissible the conclusions of an expert in psychological profiling who had carried out a "psychological autopsy" on the accused's deceased wife. The court expressed considerable scepticism about the reliability of such evidence, referring to "unstructured and speculative conclusions",[67] and pointing out that the expert's views as to the likelihood of the wife having committed suicide were based on one-sided information from the defendant and his family. It concluded by saying that "the present academic status of psychological autopsies is not, in our judgment, such as to permit them to be admitted as a basis for expert opinion before a jury".[68]

---

[63] *Davie v Edinburgh Magistrates* (1953) S.C. 34.

[64] In *Gilfoyle (No.2)* [2001] 2 Cr.App.R. 57 at [67] the Court of Appeal appeared to say that an expert's failure to provide the court with the necessary scientific criteria for testing the accuracy of the expert's conclusions would render the evidence inadmissible. See also *R. v Smith (Peter)* [2011] EWCA Crim 1296; [2011] 2 Cr.App.R. 16.

[65] *Frye v United States* (1923) 293 F. 1013.

[66] *Gilfoyle (No.2)* [2001] 2 Cr.App.R. 57. The case is reported as *Gilfoyle*, but I have added the reference to No.2, so as to distinguish it from the first appeal by Gilfoyle against his conviction for murder of his wife, also reported as *Gilfoyle* at [1996] 3 All E.R. 883.

[67] *Gilfoyle (No.2)* [2001] 2 Cr.App.R. 57 at 67.

[68] *Gilfoyle (No.2)* [2001] 2 Cr.App.R. 57 at 68. For further discussion of this topic see D. Ormerod, "Psychological Autopsies: Legal implications and Admissibility" (2001) 5 E. & P. 1.

On the other hand, *Frye* was not applied in *Robb*, where the Court of Appeal upheld the admission of an expert opinion that was avowedly founded on a technique supported by only a minority in the relevant field of expertise. The court seems to have taken the view that, despite the lack of general acceptance of the technique involved, the opinion itself had probative value because of the formal qualifications and the practical experience of the witness. The importance of experience may be a ground on which *Robb* and *Gilfoyle (No.2)* can be distinguished on the facts. In the latter case the expert had never previously carried out the task he set himself, whereas the phonetics expert in *Robb* had been consulted in numerous previous cases involving voice identification. At the level of principle the cases are more difficult to reconcile. In *Gilfoyle (No.2)* the expert identified no criteria for testing the validity of his conclusions, and there was no substantial body of academic writing approving his methodology. In *Robb* the expert explained his methods, but he had published no material that would allow his methods to be tested or his results checked. He admitted that the great weight of informed opinion in the field was against his method. In *Dallagher*,[69] the Court of Appeal noted that at the time when *Gilfoyle (No.2)* was decided the *Frye* test was no longer in use in the United States. The court agreed with the view expressed in Cross and Tapper, set out above, that the question is one of whether the field is sufficiently well-established to passs the "ordinary tests of relevance and reliability", and that no enhanced test of admissibility should be applied. However, it is not entirely clear what is meant by the 'ordinary test of reliability'. If this refers simply to the principle that evidence should be excluded where its reliability is so uncertain that no weight could safely be given to it[70] then the test sets a very low threshold.

One advantage of such an approach to reliability is that it avoids the inhibiting effect on expert evidence of a rigid adherence to the *Frye* test. A common criticism of that test was that it could deny the courts the benefits of new developments in science while the process of general acceptance took place.[71] The approach also avoids the more extensive obligations placed on trial judges by the replacement for the *Frye* test in the United States, but whether this is desirable is more debatable. In *Daubert v Merrell Dow Pharmaceuticals Inc,*[72] the Supreme Court held that the *Frye* test had not survived the adoption of the Federal Rules of Evidence. Rule 702 of the Federal Rules originally provided:

20–013

> "If scientific, technical or other specialised knowledge will assist the trier of fact to understand the evidence or to determine a fact in issue, a witness qualified as an expert by knowledge, skill, experience, training, or education, may testify thereto in the form of an opinion or otherwise."

The Supreme Court noted that this rule makes no reference to a test of general acceptance of scientific validity, and took the view that the *Frye* test was inconsistent with the liberalising spirit of the Federal Rules generally. At the same

---

[69] *Dallagher* [2002] EWCA Crim 1903; [2003] 1 Cr.App.R. 12.
[70] As, e.g. in the case of certain confessions by persons suffering from mental illness: see Ch.6.
[71] There are also definitional issues about the "field" in question, and what constitutes "general acceptance".
[72] *Daubert v Merrell Dow Pharmaceuticals Inc* (1993) 509 U.S. 579.

time the court stipulated that trial judges should ensure that scientific evidence is both relevant and reliable before they admit it. This involves a preliminary enquiry into the expert's reasoning and methodology to see whether it can properly be applied to the facts in issue. A key question in this enquiry is whether the theory or technique on which the opinion is based can be and has been tested. Other indicators of reliability include publication and peer review of the science employed by the expert, the known or potential rate of error, and the existence and maintenance of standards controlling the operation of the particular scientific technique. The degree of acceptance within the relevant scientific community may also be taken into account.

By making trial judges the gatekeepers of scientific validity, while at the same time abandoning the *Frye* test, *Daubert* aimed to do two things. One was to expand the admissibility of helpful expert evidence, the other was to ensure that "junk" science did not survive the judge's scrutiny of its validity. However, the *Daubert* strategy requires judges to become amateur scientists, a task for which many may not be equipped and may require expensive judicial training programmes. A further problem is that criteria aimed at ensuring that only reliable "science" enters the courtroom may not be appropriate for non-scientific specialised knowledge based on study and experience.[73] From the perspective of English law the factors mentioned by the Supreme Court as material to the assessment of scientific validity offer useful guidance on whether expert evidence is likely to have probative value, but under the law as it is at present they are not conditions that always have to be satisfied in a given case.

20–014 The law may of course change, and the Law Commission's recent report on expert evidence[74] suggests that reform is desirable in view of the lack of clarity and consistency in the approach of the English courts to the reliability issue. The Commission's preference is to adopt a *Daubert*-style gatekeeping role for trial judges, rather than the more conservative *Frye* standard of general acceptance, with the associated concern that such a standard represents undue judical deference to the state of scientific opinion in the relevant field. As Edmond and Roberts have said, the Commission's emphasis on the need for more rigorous scrutiny of the reliability of expert opinion evidence is to be commended.[75] However, whether its recommendations will find their way into legislation remains to be seen. There are several issues to be resolved. First, as the report recognises, the new admissibility tests would entail a significant training programme for judges and lawyers, and restrictions on public spending may mean that the associated costs will not be regarded as justifiable. Secondly, the proposed reliability test is detailed and complex; it requires some 50 pages of explanation in the report. It seems very likely to lengthen trials and increase their costs, and it is virtually guaranteed to generate a flood of appeals. Thirdly, a key

---

[73] This point was taken by the US Supreme Court in *Kumho Tire Co v Carmichael* (1999) 526 U.S. 317, where the court acknowledged that not all the *Daubert* criteria are necessarily applicable to all forms of expert evidence. It should be noted that there is a very extensive American literature discussing *Daubert* and its successors, the details of which are beyond the scope of this book. See further the references above.

[74] Law Com 325.

[75] G. Edmond and A. Roberts, "The Law Commission's Report on Expert Evidence in Criminal Proceedings" [2011] Crim. L.R. 844.

element of the test is that the evidence will only be sufficiently reliable to be admitted if the strength of the opinion is warranted having regard to the grounds on which it is based. It appears from the Commission's report (although not the draft Bill) that the application of this requirement is intended to take account of the importance of the evidence in the case.[76] So, when considered in relation to the other evidence in the case, the more central the expert evidence is to the prosecution case, the stronger will have to be the reliability of the basis for the opinion. This seems very problematic. It suggests that "sufficient reliability" might be an infinitely flexible standard, which would lead to great uncertainty in the management of cases. It implies that in some cases trial judges might have to hear the whole of the evidence before being able to decide on the importance of the expert evidence. Fourthly, there is a fundamental question whether the enterprise of entrusting the courts with a gatekeeping role for all expert evidence is misconceived. Judges may be as equipped as anyone to decide whether non-scientific and ad hoc expert evidence is sufficiently reliable to be admitted. But there must be serious doubts whether judges in all criminal courts will be willing or able to acquire the degree of knowledge and understanding of scientific method that will be necessary to apply the Law Commission's test.[77]

What happens when experts disagree? This is not uncommon. Much expert evidence is about the existence of specialised primary facts; just as much, if not more, is about the significance of those facts and the inferences to be drawn from them. Consequently there is considerable scope for disagreement, particularly in the evaluation of evidence. As new fields of scientific inquiry develop, or established fields undergo rapid change, disagreements can be expected, and they may go to the heart of the case.   **20–015**

The orthodox view is that conflicts of view from expert witnesses are for the factfinder to evaluate and resolve,[78] as in the case of conflicts of evidence from any other witnesses. Factfinders will normally do this taking account of all the other available evidence in the case, and may accept or reject the evidence of experts on either side. The trial judge must, however, ensure that a conviction is one that a reasonable jury, properly directed, could reach on a logically justifiable basis. The Court of Appeal restated these principles in *Kai-Whitewind*,[79] where expert medical witnesses disagreed about the conclusions to be drawn from the post-mortem on the defendant's baby, who she was charged with murdering, and about the cause of death. The defence had argued on appeal that whenever there was a genuine conflict of opinion between reputable experts about the cause of an

---

[76] See in particular Law Com 325 para.3.92, discussing a hypothetical based on the medical evidence in *Harris* [2005] EWCA Crim 1980; [2006] 1 Cr.App.R. 5.

[77] See further G. Edmond and A. Roberts, "The Law Commission's Report on Expert Evidence in Criminal Proceedings" [2011] Crim. L.R. 844, and J. Hartshorne and J. Miola, "Expert evidence: difficulties and solutions in prosecutions for infant harm" (2010) 30 L.S. 279.

[78] A recent example is *Hookway* [2011] EWCA Crim 1989, where prosecution and defence experts agreed that DNA profiles suggested that both defendants had been in a car used in a robbery, but disagreed whether the findings were suitable for statistical interpretation, so that a match probability could be given. The Court of Appeal held that the difference could be attributed to different interpretational approaches between different forensic providers. This was a matter of weight for the jury to determine, and did not affect the admissibility of the evidence of the prosecution expert, who had given a match probability.

[79] *Kai-Whitewind* [2005] EWCA Crim 1092; [2005] 2 Cr.App.R. 31 at [89].

infant's death a prosecution for murder should not proceed. The basis for this submission was the court's earlier judgment in *Cannings*.[80] In that case three of the defendant's four children had died suddenly in infancy. The defendant was convicted of the murder of two of them after expert witnesses for the prosecution supported the argument that the history of three sudden unexplained infant deaths in the same family, an extremely rare occurrence, gave rise to a compelling inference that they had been deliberately harmed. The Court of Appeal had quashed the convictions after hearing fresh evidence from medical experts on sudden infant death syndrome ("SIDS") that, in the present state of medical research, where such deaths were unexplained natural causes could not be excluded as a reasonable possibility. In its judgment the court had stated that "if the outcome of the trial depends exclusively or almost exclusively on a serious disagreement between distinguished and reputable experts, it will often be unwise, and therefore unsafe, to proceed".[81] In *Kai-Whitewind,* Judge L.J., who had given the judgment in *Cannings*, explained that this statement referred only to cases that, in the light of contemporary medical knowledge, depended solely on inference based on coincidence, or the unlikelihood of two or more unexplained infant deaths in the same family. This was not the situation in *Kai-Whitewind* where there was only one infant death, other evidence pointing to the defendant's guilt and no need for reliance on an argument based on coincidence. It is not clear that this distinguishing of *Cannings* is successful,[82] especially in view of the evidence of the medical experts for the defence that the cause of the child's death in *Kai-Whitewind* remained unascertained. The orthodox view was asserted again in *Harris*,[83] where the Court of Appeal added that it saw no need for special rules for medical experts as far as the admissibility of expert evidence is concerned.

In *Henderson*,[84] where the principles set out in *Kai-Whitewind* were approved and applied, the Court of Appeal stressed the importance of Pt 33 of the Criminal Procedure Rules in ensuring the overriding objective of doing justice in cases involving expert evidence. The rules enable trial judges to manage the case by requiring the parties to marshal the evidence before the trial, particularly by clarifying the basis for the expert opinions and the nature and extent of any disagreements between the experts.[85]

---

[80] *Cannings* [2004] EWCA Crim 1; [2004] 2 Cr.App.R. 7. For critical comment see [2005] Crim. L.R. 126.

[81] *Cannings* [2004] EWCA Crim 1; [2004] 2 Cr.App.R. 7 at [178].

[82] See the Commentary on *Kai-Whitewind* by Walker in [2006] Crim. L.R. 348.

[83] *Harris* [2005] EWCA Crim 1980; [2006] 1 Cr.App.R. 5.

[84] *Henderson* [2010] EWCA Crim 1269; [2010] 2 Cr.App.R. 24.

[85] *Henderson* [2010] EWCA Crim 1269; [2010] 2 Cr.App.R. 24 at [209]–[210]. For further discussion of the problems with expert evidence in these medical cases see the article by J. Hartshorne and J. Miola, "Expert evidence: difficulties and solutions in prosecutions for infant harm" (2010) 30 L.S. 279.

3. Who is an expert?

It is a question for the trial judge in each case whether the proposed witness is an **20–016** expert on the matter that requires special skill, knowledge or expertise.[86] It is not always essential that the witness has appropriate professional qualifications or experience. For example, in the old case of *Silverlock*[87] a solicitor who had made a special study of handwriting in his spare time was permitted to testify as an expert on an issue of handwriting. Of course many branches of science have become so technical and specialised that the scope for amateurs to appear as expert witnesses is distinctly limited. The same is true of many other disciplines requiring special skill and knowledge. In the majority of cases professional qualifications or experience will be necessary for the witness to be regarded as an expert. But they are not always essential. In *Robb*,[88] Bingham L.J. set out a leading statement of principle:

> "The old-established, academically-based sciences such as medicine, geology or metallurgy, and the established professions such as architecture, quantity surveying or engineering, present no problem. The field will be regarded as one in which expertise may exist and any properly qualified member will be accepted without question as expert.
>
> Expert evidence is not, however, limited to these core areas. Expert evidence of fingerprints, handwriting and accident reconstruction is regularly given. Opinions may be given of the market value of land, ships, pictures or rights. Expert opinions may be given of the quality of commodities, or on the literary, artistic, scientific or other merit of works alleged to be obscene... Some of these fields are far removed from anything which could be called a formal scientific discipline. Yet while receiving this evidence the courts would not accept the evidence of an astrologer, a soothsayer, a witch-doctor or an amateur psychologist...
>
> The test which the English common law has developed is characteristically pragmatic. [Bingham L.J. then cited a passage from the judgment of Lord Russell of Killowen C.J. in *Silverlock* and continued:]... Thus the essential questions are whether study and experience will give a witness's opinion an authority which the opinion of one not so qualified will lack, and (if so) whether the witness in question is [skilled and has an adequate knowledge]... If these conditions are met the evidence of the witness is in law admissible, although the weight to be attached to his opinion must of course be assessed by the tribunal of fact."[89]

In this passage Bingham L.J. usefully drew attention to the broad distinction between truly scientific expertise, where academic and/or professional qualifications will invariably be required, and specialised non-scientific knowledge, which may be gained simply by appropriate study and experience. Such specialised knowledge may be the subject of expert witness testimony as much as scientific evidence, provided it passes the *Turner* helpfulness test.[90] Witnesses with such knowledge are sometimes known as "ad hoc experts". The criteria stated in the last paragraph of the quotation were applied by the Court of Appeal in

---

[86] The judge has a discretion to direct a voir dire to decide this issue, but it should be exercised sparingly so as to avoid satellite litigation: *R. v G* [2004] EWCA Crim 1240; [2004] 2 Cr.App.R. 38.

[87] *Silverlock* [1894] 2 Q.B. 766.

[88] *Robb* (1991) 93 Cr.App.R. 161 CA.

[89] *Robb* (1991) 93 Cr.App.R. 161 at 164–165.

[90] A good example of the admission of such specialised non-scientific knowledge is *Hodges* [2003] EWCA Crim 290; [2003] 2 Cr.App.R. 15, where a police officer who had 16 years' experience as a drugs officer was rightly permitted to give expert evidence on the usual method of supplying heroin, the street value of heroin, and whether the amount found on the defendant was more than would have been for personal use alone. cf. *Barnes* [2005] EWCA Crim 1158.

Dallagher,[91] where evidence of earprint comparisons by two prosecution experts was held to have been rightly admitted. One of the experts was a police officer with no formal qualifications, but he had become interested in the subject, had read widely and had built up an extensive portfolio of photographs and prints for purposes of comparison, specialising in the subject for more than a decade.

The burden of proving that the proposed witness is an expert lies on the party seeking to adduce the expert evidence. Even if the opposing party does not object to the witness giving opinion evidence as an expert, the judge has a duty to intervene if the witness is not qualified to do this.[92] However, where the competence of a person to give expert evidence is challenged, the court should be careful not to confuse competency with matters which go to the *weight* of the opinion. In *R. (on the application of Doughty) v Ely Magistrates' Court*,[93] the Divisional Court held that magistrates had wrongly refused to permit the applicant to give expert evidence about the reliability of a police speed detection device. The applicant was a retired police officer with extensive traffic department experience and a qualification in the use of the device. The facts that he had retired from the police force a few years earlier and had less expertise than the expert called for the prosecution did not disqualify him from giving an expert opinion, although that opinion might be less persuasive than one from a person with greater expertise and more recent experience of the device. The importance of current practical experience is a recurring theme in the case law. In the medical context the Court of Appeal emphasised in *Henderson* the importance of an expert witness in a "shaken baby" case being in current clinical practice.[94] This was clearly thought to be a matter going to the weight of the expert's opinion. Similarly, in *Weller*,[95] a case involving an issue of how the DNA of a victim of sexual assault had been transferred on to D's fingernails, the Court of Appeal implied that the opinion of a "scholar" who had studied relevant published papers but had no practical experience of DNA profiling was less weighty than that of an experienced practitioner in the field.

Finally in this section it should be stressed again that the expert witness must not give an opinion on a matter outside the limits of her or his expertise. At this point the general rule against opinion evidence applies. The Court of Appeal reiterated the limitation in *Reed and Reed*,[96] and again in *Cleobury*,[97] where the defence expert in a rape case involving DNA evidence had expressed views about the adequacy of the judge's summing-up to the jury about the evidence. The court stated explicitly that his report should not have included these comments; he should have restricted himself to the scientific issues arising.

---

[91] *Dallagher* [2002] EWCA Crim 1903; [2003] 1 Cr.App.R. 12. See further on the admissibility of earprint evidence, *Kempster (No.2)* [2008] EWCA Crim 975; [2008] 2 Cr.App.R. 19.

[92] *Inch* (1990) 91 Cr.App.R. 51 CMAC (judge-advocate should have ruled that a medical orderly was not qualified to express an opinion as to the cause of a wound, despite the failure of defence counsel to object to the orderly's evidence). See also *R. v G* [2004] 2 Cr.App.R. 38.

[93] *R. (on the application of Doughty) v Ely Magistrates' Court* [2008] EWHC 522 (Admin).

[94] *Henderson* [2010] EWCA Crim 1269; [2010] 2 Cr.App.R. 24 at [208].

[95] *Weller* [2010] EWCA Crim 1085.

[96] See para.20–005 above.

[97] *Cleobury* [2012] EWCA Crim 17.

4. The role of an expert witness[98]

The role of an expert witness was described by Cresswell J. in *National Justice Cia Naviera SA v Prudential Assurance Co Ltd, The Ikarian Reefer*.[99] This guidance has been said to be very relevant to criminal proceedings; it should be kept well in mind by both prosecution and defence[100]:

20–017

> "1. Expert evidence presented to the court should be, and should be seen to be, the independent product of the expert uninfluenced as to form or content by the exigencies of the litigation... 2. An expert witness should provide independent assistance to the Court by way of objective unbiased opinion in relation to matters within his expertise ... An expert witness in the High Court should never assume the role of an advocate. 3. An expert witness should state the facts or assumption upon which his opinion is based. He should not omit to consider material facts which could detract from his... concluded opinion... 4. An expert witness should make it clear when a particular question or issue falls outside his expertise... 5. If an expert's opinion is not properly researched because he considers that insufficient data is available then this must be stated with an indication that the opinion is no more than a provisional one. 6. If, after exchange of reports, an expert witness changes his view on a material matter having read the other side's expert's report or for any other reason, such change of view should be communicated (through legal representatives) to the other side without delay and when appropriate to the Court."

This passage was cited by Otton L.J. in *Stanton v Callaghan*[101] to demonstrate the unique role and responsibilities of the expert witness. Otton L.J. stressed that the expert witness owes a duty to the court as well as a duty to the client who has retained his services. The expert's duty to the court is "to assist the court in resolving the issues and coming to a just conclusion". This is said to be an overriding duty; it takes priority over any duty to the client.[102] A similar statement was made in the context of criminal proceedings by Gage L.J. in *R. v B (T)*,[103] where the court added a list of further factors to be included in an expert's report in addition to those mentioned by Cresswell J. in *The Ikarian Reefer*. These include the expert's qualifications and experience, the instructions received, information about the expert's methods in compiling the report, any range of opinion in the report and the reasons for it, details of relevant literature, and a statement that the expert has complied with the duty to provide independent assistance to the court by way of objective unbiased opinion.

This emphasis on the expert's duty to the court should be set in a wider context. There have undoubtedly been occasions when expert witnesses have identified with a particular cause, resulting in their failure to disclose experimental data adverse to "their" side. The most notorious examples were in

---

[98] M. Redmayne, *Expert Evidence and Criminal Justice* (Oxford, OUP, 2001), Ch.7.
[99] *The Ikarian Reefer* [1993] 2 Lloyd's Rep. 68 at 81–82.
[100] *Harris* [2005] EWCA Crim 1980; [2006] 1 Cr.App.R. 5 at [273], where the court also commended the guidance offered by Wall J. in *In Re AB (Child Abuse: Expert Witnesses)* [1995] 1 F.L.R. 181, in relation to expert evidence involving children.
[101] *Stanton v Callaghan* [1998] 4 All E.R. 961 at 990 CA. For an incisive critique of Cresswell J.'s principles, written from the standpoint of the civil practitioner, see A. Speaight, "Seven Essentials" (1996) 146 N.L.J. 1100.
[102] See, to the same effect, the Woolf Report, *Access to Justice* (London, 1996), Ch.13 pp.139, 143; CPR r.35.3.
[103] *R. v B(T)* [2006] EWCA Crim 417; [2006] 2 Cr.App.R. 3 at [176].

Maguire[104] and *Ward*.[105] In *Maguire,* a Home Office forensic scientist failed to disclose to the prosecution material that might have been significant for the defence case. In *Ward,* the Court of Appeal criticised three senior forensic scientists at RARDE[106] for becoming partisan and regarding it as their task to help the police. This had resulted in suppression of data that might have assisted the defence. The witnesses had "knowingly placed a false and distorted scientific picture before the jury". In both cases the Court of Appeal quashed the convictions as unsafe and unsatisfactory. It was emphasised that at common law a forensic scientist had a duty to disclose all his experimental data to the prosecution, and that in turn the prosecution had a duty to disclose to the defence any material that might undermine the prosecution case or assist the defence.[107]

20–018   Despite these clear statements of principle, it is worth recalling that it is still the parties who select the expert witnesses. They are inevitably selected on the basis of a reasonable expectation that they will support the case of the party calling them. This does not of course mean that they do not believe the evidence they give. Quite apart from issues of professional ethics, no litigant is likely to want to call an expert to testify to something in which he does not believe. However, as Redmayne has noted,[108] the adversarial system of litigation means that the experts selected by the parties are clearly not a random selection from the relevant scientific community, and may not necessarily be representative of that community.

We can therefore ask the question whether the court should appoint its own expert(s), particularly in cases where there is a significant disagreement between the parties' experts. There is power to do this in civil proceedings,[109] and the power is occasionally exercised.[110] The Royal Commission rejected a suggestion that court experts should be appointed in criminal cases, either instead of or in addition to the experts appearing for the prosecution and defence. The Commission's main objection was that a court expert's opinion would impliedly carry more weight than the opinion of a party's expert, but "there would be no guarantee that he or she was any nearer to the truth of the matter than the expert witnesses for the parties".[111] This is a controversial issue,[112] and some commentators have pointed to the example of continental jurisdictions, where the

---

[104] *Maguire* [1992] Q.B. 936 CA.

[105] *Ward* (1993) 96 Cr.App.R. 1 CA.

[106] Royal Armaments Research and Development Establishment.

[107] For the position on disclosure under Pt 1 of the Criminal Procedure and Investigations Act 1996, see Ch.9. Another serious example of non-disclosure by an expert witness occurred in *Clark* [2003] EWCA Crim 1020, where the Court of Appeal accepted that the witness (a Home Office pathologist) had not acted in bad faith but was severely critical of his failure to reveal certain results of his post-mortem examination of the body of one of the defendant's children.

[108] M. Redmayne, "Expert Evidence and Scientific Disagreement" (1997) 30 U.C. Davis L.R. 1027 at 1067.

[109] Under CPR r.35.7, where two or more parties wish to submit expert evidence on a particular issue, the court may direct that the evidence on that issue is to be given by one expert only ("a single joint expert").

[110] e.g. *Abbey National Mortgages Plc v Key Surveyors Nationwide Ltd* [1996] 3 All E.R. 184 CA.

[111] RCCJ Report Ch.9 para.74.

[112] See P. Alldridge, "Forensic Science and Expert Evidence" (1994) 21 Jo. Law and Society 136; P. Roberts, "Forensic Science Evidence after Runciman" [1994] Crim. L.R. 780.

use of court experts is common.[113] This practice, which is well illustrated by the system in France,[114] makes sense where an investigation is under the supervision of a judicial official from the beginning. It may not be easily transplantable to an adversarial culture. Nonetheless, the Law Commission has recently recommended that the Crown Court should have power to appoint its own expert to help it determine whether expert evidence which a party proposes to adduce is sufficiently reliable to be admitted.[115] This is not the same as the court appointing its own expert to provide evidence to it, but it may turn out to be a move in that direction.

5. *The ultimate issue rule*

The common law rule that a witness may not express an opinion on the ultimate issue that the court has to decide has already been referred to in connection with evidence of non-expert opinion. The rule applied equally to expert witnesses,[116] and to both civil and criminal cases. The rationale of the rule was generally agreed to be the danger of the witness usurping the function of the factfinder, particularly in jury trials.[117] This was never very convincing since the factfinder was always free to reject the opinion, and in any event it was never clear why the risk of usurpation became so great with ultimate issues as to preclude any evidence of opinion about them.

20–019

Moreover, if the rule is strictly applied, it can be inconvenient because it may prevent the expert witness giving the factfinder the maximum benefit of his expertise. It may well be that the factfinder can be properly helped only if the expert does explain his findings *and* explains his view of their significance for the issue that the court has to decide. The combination of these points—the weakness of the justification for the rule and its inconvenience in practice—has resulted in its virtual disappearance in modern law. In civil cases it has been abolished by statute. The Civil Evidence Act 1972 provides in s.3:

> "(1)   Subject to any rules of court made in pursuance ... of this Act, where a person is called as a witness in any civil proceedings, his opinion on any relevant matter on which he is qualified to give expert evidence shall be admissible in evidence.
>
>   . . .
>
> (3)   In this section 'relevant matter' includes an issue in the proceedings in question."

The Criminal Law Revision Committee recommended the enactment of a similar provision for criminal proceedings,[118] but this recommendation was never formally implemented. Instead the courts moved towards abandonment of the

---

[113] J. R. Spencer, "Court Experts and Expert Witnesses: Have We a Lesson to Learn from the French?" [1992] C.L.P. 213; P. Alldridge, "Scientific expertise and comparative criminal procedure" (1999) 3 E. & P. 141.

[114] See Spencer, "Court Experts and Expert Witnesses" [1992] C.L.P. 213; see also B. McKillop, *Anatomy of a French Murder Case* (Sydney, 1998) for a detailed and illuminating study of a murder case in France in which court experts were used.

[115] Law Com 325 Pt 6.

[116] See, e.g. *North Cheshire and Manchester Brewery Co v Manchester Brewery Co* [1899] A.C. 83.

[117] See, e.g. the comments of Lawton L.J. in *Turner* [1975] Q.B. 834 at 841.

[118] *Eleventh Report* para.268.

rule in criminal cases. To some extent the rule has always been applied inconsistently in the case of expert witnesses. In *Holmes*,[119] the Court of Criminal Appeal approved a cross-examination in which a psychiatric expert for the defence was asked whether the defendant's conduct showed that he knew the nature of his act and that it was wrong; these are of course the issues that the jury must decide in assessing the defence of insanity under the M'Naghten Rules. In *Davies*,[120] it was said in a drink-driving case that, while any witness could testify as to his opinion that the defendant had been drinking, an expert witness (and only an expert witness) could go further and say whether in his opinion the defendant was unfit to drive through drink. In *DPP v A & BC Chewing Gum Ltd*,[121] Lord Parker C.J. commented that he could not help feeling that "with the advance of science more and more inroads have been made into the old common law principles". He gave the example of expert witnesses called on the issue of diminished responsibility, and then said, "although technically the final question 'Do you think he was suffering from diminished responsibility?' is strictly inadmissible, it is allowed time and again without objection".

20–020　In this last case the defendant company was prosecuted under the Obscene Publications Act 1959 on the basis that "battle cards" sold with packets of bubble gum would tend to deprave and corrupt the children to whom the gum was sold. The prosecution sought to adduce expert evidence from child psychiatrists on the likely effect of the cards on children of various ages, but the magistrates ruled it inadmissible. Upholding the prosecutor's appeal, the Divisional Court held that the evidence was admissible. Since the court was dealing with the effect on children of the violent scenes depicted on the cards, the court needed all the help it could get in assessing the effects of the cards on different children. In reaching this conclusion Lord Parker C.J. was careful to say that it would be wrong for the expert witnesses to be asked the direct question whether any particular cards would tend to deprave and corrupt, since that was the issue that the justices ultimately had to determine. This nod in the direction of the ultimate issue rule was put in doubt both by the dicta noted above and by Lord Parker's further comment that a question from the defence as to whether a particular card could not corrupt would be allowed whatever the "strict position" might be.

Subsequent decisions have taken the view that expert evidence is not generally admissible on the issue of whether articles are obscene.[122] The question whether they have a tendency to "deprave and corrupt" is said to be a matter that factfinders can decide without the help of experts. Moreover expert evidence will not be admissible on the effects of allegedly obscene articles on the minds of likely recipients if that is a matter that the factfinder is capable of assessing without help. This is not to say that *DPP v A & BC Chewing Gum Ltd* is wrongly decided. It should be regarded as an exceptional case on the facts, where the

---

[119] *Holmes* [1953] 2 All E.R. 324 CCA.

[120] *Davies* [1962] 3 All E.R. 97.

[121] *DPP v A & BC Chewing Gum Ltd* [1968] 1 Q.B. 159 at 164 DC.

[122] *Anderson* [1972] 1 Q.B. 304; *Stamford* [1972] 2 Q.B. 391; *DPP v Jordan* [1977] A.C. 699. Note, however, s.4(2) of the Obscene Publications Act 1959, providing expressly for the admission of expert evidence on the question whether publication of an otherwise obscene article is justified as being for the public good, on the ground that it is in the interests of science, art, literature, learning or other objects of general concern.

factfinder's knowledge and experience needed supplementation in order for the factfinder to judge the effect of material on children.

A similar analysis accounts for the decision in *Skirving*,[123] where the Court of Appeal upheld a trial judge's admission of expert scientific evidence regarding the characteristics of cocaine and the effects on the human body of smoking it. The defendant was charged with publishing an obscene pamphlet that advocated the smoking of cocaine. The court founded its decision on a perception that ordinary juries might not be aware of the characteristics of cocaine and of its effects on the human mind and body when smoked.

Lord Parker C.J.'s scepticism about the force of the ultimate issue rule was taken further by the Court of Appeal in *Stockwell*.[124] The defendant was charged with robbery. He denied the charge, and the issue was whether he was the man who carried out the robbery, whose image had been captured on a poor quality security video. The trial judge permitted the prosecution to call an expert in "facial mapping", to say that, on the basis of the measurements he had carried out on the security photograph and the comparison he had made with the features of the defendant, there was strong support for the view that the defendant and the robber were the same man. Dismissing the defendant's appeal, Lord Taylor C.J. said that the rule was more a matter of form than substance. He held that it was acceptable for an expert witness to give his opinion on an ultimate issue, such as identification, provided the judge directed the jury that they were not bound to accept the opinion. Normally a jury would be able to reach a conclusion on identification without help if they have a clear photograph and there is no suggestion that the defendant has changed his appearance. Neither of these conditions applied in *Stockwell*, which was why the expert was able to provide the jury with information and assistance that they would otherwise lack for making an identification. Once the expert is permitted to testify he can hardly avoid expressing an opinion on the basic issue of identity that the jury will have to decide.[125]

Stockwell suggests that the courts will no longer apply the ultimate issue rule as an arbitrary limit on the scope of expert evidence. If it would be a necessary help to the factfinder to have an expert opinion on the ultimate issue, and the witness is qualified to give an expert opinion, then it seems that the witness may now give the opinion,[126] subject to the judicial direction that the jury are not obliged to accept it. The courts have made it clear, however, that they will continue to monitor carefully the limits of a witness's expertise. They will not permit the witness to "overstep the line which separates his province from that of the jury". This phrase comes from the important judgment of Phillips L.J. in *Doheny*.[127] This judgment explains the technique of DNA profiling, the significance of a DNA match and the "Prosecutor's Fallacy" concerning the

20–021

---

[123] *Skirving* [1985] Q.B. 819 CA.

[124] *Stockwell* (1993) 97 Cr.App.R. 20.

[125] See also *Clarke* [1995] 2 Cr.App.R. 425 CA; *Atkins* [2009] EWCA Crim 1876.

[126] As in the cases discussed above involving sudden infant deaths, for example. See also *Hodges* [2003] EWCA Crim 290; [2003] 2 Cr.App.R. 15 (police officer permitted to give expert opinion that drugs found on the defendant were not for personal use only).

[127] *Doheny* [1997] 1 Cr.App.R. 369 CA. See also *Reed and Reed* [2009] EWCA Crim 2698; [2010] 1 Cr.App.R. 23.

conclusions to be drawn from a match. Phillips L.J. went on to say that the scientist who carried out the DNA profiling[128]:

> "will properly explain to the jury the nature of the match ('the matching DNA characteristics') between the DNA in the crime stain and the DNA in the blood sample taken from the defendant. He will properly, on the basis of empirical statistical data, give the jury the random occurrence ratio–the frequency with which the matching DNA characteristics are likely to be found in the population at large. Provided that he has the necessary data, and the statistical expertise, it may be appropriate for him then to say how many people with the matching characteristics are likely to be found in the United Kingdom–or perhaps in a more limited relevant sub-group, such as, for instance, the caucasian, sexually active males in the Manchester area.
>
> This will often be the limit of the evidence which he can properly and usefully give. It will then be for the jury to decide, having regard to all the relevant evidence, whether they are sure that it was the defendant who left the crime stain, or whether it is possible that it was left by someone else with the same matching DNA characteristics.
>
> The scientist should not be asked his opinion on the likelihood that it was the defendant who left the crime stain, nor when giving evidence should he use terminology which may lead the jury to believe that he is expressing such an opinion.
>
> It has been suggested that it may be appropriate for the statistician to expound to the jury a statistical approach to evaluating the likelihood that the defendant left the crime stain, using a formula which gives a numerical probability weighting to other pieces of evidence which bear on that question. This approach uses what is known as the Bayes Theorem. In the case of *Adams (Denis)* [1996] 2 Cr.App.R. 467 this Court deprecated this exercise."

Thus the expert witness should *not* express a view on the probability of the defendant's guilt given the DNA match. That probability is a function of all the evidence in the case, which it is for the jury to evaluate. As Andrews and Hirst rightly say, much of the other evidence in the case may not be within the provenance of experts at all.[129] For example, the scientific evidence might show that there are probably only four or five white males in the United Kingdom from whom a semen stain on a rape victim could have come. If the defendant is one of them, but he has an alibi and does not fit the victim's description of her attacker, the jury will have to consider carefully the possibility that the stain was left by one of the other small group of men who have the same DNA characteristics.

6. *Hearsay and the foundation of expert opinion*[130]

20–022 An expert is a person who, as we have seen, is qualified by training and experience to give an informed opinion on a matter outside the normal competence of the factfinder. In principle all the facts on which an expert's opinion is based should be proved by admissible evidence. This would normally be thought to be essential if opposing parties are to have a fair opportunity to challenge and test the expert's evidence. Two kinds of problems can arise about facts forming the foundation of an expert opinion that raise issues about the

---

[128] *Doheny* [1997] 1 Cr.App.R. 369 at 374–375. The "Prosecutor's Fallacy" is discussed further in Ch.4.

[129] Andrews and Hirst, *Criminal Evidence* (2001), para.21–19.

[130] See generally R. Pattenden, "Expert Opinion Based on Hearsay" [1982] Crim. L.R. 85.

possible operation of the hearsay rule. These problems can be categorised according to Allen's useful distinction between "primary facts" and "expert's facts".[131]

(A) Primary facts

"Primary facts" for this purpose are the facts peculiar to the case; the facts that have to be investigated in order to decide the case. Sometimes the expert can prove these primary facts from personal knowledge; an example is a pathologist who carries out a post-mortem on a victim and who then testifies as to his opinion regarding the cause of death, based on his own findings. Where the expert does not have personal knowledge of the primary facts, a question arises whether he can nonetheless give evidence of his opinion in reliance on what he has been told of the primary facts by another person, for example a member of his research staff.

20–023

There is an obvious hearsay problem in this situation. The common law rule was that the primary facts should be proved by admissible evidence.[132] The expert could not therefore give hearsay evidence of primary facts found by another. The person with personal knowledge of the primary facts had to be called to prove them, in the absence of formal admissions of the facts by the opposing party. The expert could then be asked for his opinion on the assumed primary facts.[133] This position was not affected by the Criminal Justice Act 1988 s.30(1). This provides for the admission in criminal proceedings of an expert's report[134] whether or not the person making it attends to give oral evidence. If it is proposed that the person making the report shall not give oral evidence the report is admissible only with the leave of the court. When admitted under this section, an expert report shall be evidence of any fact or opinion of which the person making it could have given oral evidence.[135] It follows therefore that the section does not enable hearsay evidence of primary facts to be given via a written report.

However, in criminal proceedings the hearsay problem is now dealt with by s.127 of the Criminal Justice Act 2003. This provision gives effect to a recommendation of the Law Commission[136] to allow an expert to give an opinion based on the investigation of primary facts by an assistant, where the information supplied by the assistant related to matters of which the assistant had, or might reasonably be supposed to have had, personal knowledge. This permission for the expert to rely on a statement by another as to the primary facts is subject to the court's power to disapply the provision in the interest of justice (s.127(4)). This would result in the assistant having to be called to give oral evidence, but in deciding whether to make an order under subs.(4) the court must consider the expense of calling as a witness the person who prepared the statement, whether relevant evidence could be given by that person that could not be given by the

---

[131] C. Allen, *Practical Guide to Evidence*, 3rd edn (Cavendish Publishing, London, 2004), p.279.

[132] *Abadom* [1983] 1 All E.R. 364 CA; *Jackson* [1996] 2 Cr.App.R. 420 CA.

[133] As in *Mason* (1911) 7 Cr.App.R. 67 CCA.

[134] An "expert report" means a written report by a person dealing wholly or mainly with matters on which he is (or would if living be) qualified to give expert evidence: s.30(5).

[135] Criminal Justice Act 1988 s.30(4).

[136] See Law Com. No.245 (London, 1997), paras 9.23–9.29.

expert, and whether that person can reasonably be expected to remember the matters stated well enough to give oral evidence of them.[137]

In civil cases the hearsay issue has been eliminated by the Civil Evidence Act 1995. Under s.1 evidence shall not be excluded in civil proceedings on the ground that it is hearsay.[138] It is therefore open to an expert witness to testify as to primary facts established by others and as to his opinion based on those facts.

(B)   Expert's facts

20–024   "Expert's facts" are facts derived from other factual situations. These facts may be experimental data, or the fruits of scholarly research and analysis, or reports of similar instances to the one under investigation. Expert's facts may be available from a variety of sources—textbooks, journals, databases, and so on—or the expert may learn of them in an informal way. Irrespective of whether the expert is able to testify as to the primary facts, it is inevitable that part of the foundation of his opinion will include expert's facts. These will represent elements of his own previous experience and the learning that he has acquired through his training and his study of the work of others. The pathologist, for example, relies in forming his judgment on his medical training, his experience of other post-mortems, information he has acquired from colleagues in the field, and so on. The expert may well have no personal knowledge of the information used in the compilation of this source material. He generally relies on the good faith and accuracy of the authors concerned. Does this mean that when he gives his own expert opinion, drawing on these various sources, that he is giving a disguised form of hearsay evidence?

Logically the answer is "Yes". The expert is expressly or impliedly asserting that these out-of-court statements are true. However, to apply the hearsay rule to its full logical extent would cause immense inconvenience in this context. Strictly applied, the rule would make much expert evidence almost impossible to adduce. No expert could be expected to exclude from his consideration all his background knowledge derived from the work of others. This would tend to defeat the point of having expert evidence at all. Equally, it is inconceivable that the authors of all sources of information relied on by experts could be called in every case to verify their data and analysis. Consequently it is a necessity for there to be some exception to, or a dispensation from, the hearsay rule for information constituting expert's facts.

In civil cases the issue has been resolved by the Civil Evidence Act 1995. As noted above, under the Act the fact that an expert's opinion contains hearsay does not affect its admissibility.

20–025   In criminal cases s.118(1) para.8 of the Criminal Justice Act 2003 preserves as a common law category of admissible hearsay "Any rule of law under which in criminal proceedings an expert witness may draw on the body of expertise relevant to his field". The leading authority for the existence of this common law exception to the hearsay rule is the decision of the Court of Appeal in *Abadom*.[139]

---

[137] Criminal Justice Act 2003 s.127(5).
[138] For further discussion of the Civil Evidence Act 1995, see Ch.16.
[139] *Abadom* [1983] 1 All E.R. 364.

The defendant was alleged to be the leader of a gang who had carried out a robbery after breaking a window of the premises in question. Fragments of broken glass had been found embedded in a pair of shoes removed from the defendant's house after his arrest. One expert witness for the prosecution (W1) testified that he carried out a chemical analysis of the fragments found in the shoes, and found them to be similar in composition to particles of glass taken from the broken window. A second expert (W2) testified that the refractive index of the glass in the shoes was the same as the refractive index of a control sample from the window, and that this index was found in only 4 per cent of all glass samples analysed in forensic science laboratories. The source of this figure was statistics collated by the Home Office Central Research Establishment. W2 then expressed the view that, in the light of the analysis made by W1, the evidence as to the rarity of this particular refractive index was "very strong" evidence that the glass from the shoes originated from the glass in the window. Dismissing the defendant's appeal against conviction for robbery, the Court of Appeal rejected the argument that W2's evidence as to the frequency of the refractive index of the glass, based on the Home Office statistics, constituted inadmissible hearsay.[140] It was held that once the primary facts on which an expert opinion is based had been proved by admissible evidence,[141] the expert was entitled to draw on the work of others as part of the process of arriving at his conclusion. In this respect the evidence of experts was said not to be subject to the hearsay rule in the same way as the evidence of witnesses of fact.[142] Experts were not only entitled, but were expected, to take account of the material produced by others in the field of expertise. It was not an objection that they had not contributed to the bank of information of which they made use. Equally, it was immaterial whether the information used by the expert had been published: "part of [an expert's] experience and expertise may well lie in their knowledge of unpublished material and in their evaluation of it". The only rule applicable, according to the Court of Appeal, is that where experts have drawn on the work of others they should refer to this material in their evidence so that the cogency and probative value of their conclusions can be tested and evaluated by reference to it.

The decision in *Abadom* confirmed a broad exception to the hearsay rule for "expert's facts", but it should not be forgotten that the court has a discretion to exclude prosecution evidence at common law or under s.78 of PACE. It would rarely be appropriate to exclude evidence of an expert opinion founded on published sources of a general nature, but where a prosecution expert relied on, for example unpublished information about a specific incident allegedly similar to the one under investigation, a court might well want to look carefully at the probative value of the expert's opinion compared with its potential for causing prejudice to the accused.

---

[140] The statistical tables would now be admissible under s.117 of the Criminal Justice Act 2003.

[141] In so far as W2's opinion was based on facts found by W1 (the chemical composition of the glass) W1 had rightly been called to prove his analysis.

[142] Citing *English Exporters (London) Ltd v Eldonwall Ltd* [1973] Ch. 415.

D. JUDGMENTS AND VERDICTS IN OTHER PROCEEDINGS

20–026   This section deals with the issue of how far the judgments and verdicts of courts in other legal proceedings are admissible in evidence to prove the facts on which they are based. Suppose, for example, that D is convicted of rape of V. If D subsequently sues E for libel for writing that D is a rapist, a question arises whether E can adduce evidence of D's conviction in support of his plea of justification. If C is subsequently prosecuted for rape of V on the basis that C was D's accomplice in a joint enterprise of rape, can the prosecution use D's conviction in evidence against C? If D had been acquitted of raping V, similar questions could arise as to whether D and C respectively could rely upon the acquittal in the subsequent proceedings to support their denials of rape.

This issue should be distinguished from two other questions. First, all judgments and verdicts are conclusive as to the state of affairs that they create. If, for example, an issue arises as to whether a defendant has the status of a convicted rapist, a certificate in proper form[143] of the defendant's conviction for rape is conclusive as to the fact of conviction for that offence. Secondly, the parties to legal proceedings may be estopped from denying the facts on which a judgment was based if the same question arises in later proceedings between the same parties. The subject of estoppel is not dealt with in this book because it is more concerned with procedure and rules of public policy about finality in litigation than with rules of evidence.

1.   *The rule in Hollington v F Hewthorn & Co Ltd*

20–027   The issue in this leading case[144] at common law was whether a conviction of a car driver for careless driving was admissible as evidence of his negligence in a civil action brought by the plaintiff against the driver and his employer. The Court of Appeal held that it was not, partly on the ground that the conviction merely represented the opinion of the criminal court, acting on evidence not known to the civil court, that the driver was guilty of the offence charged. As such, said Goddard L.J., the evidence of the conviction was irrelevant and inadmissible in the civil proceedings. The decision was strongly criticised,[145] and few would now regard it as anything other than a particularly offensive example of legal formalism. The issue in the two sets of proceedings was identical, and the criminal court had to be satisfied to the higher standard of proof beyond reasonable doubt. Even if the conviction represented only an opinion, it was absurd to suggest that the opinion was irrelevant. Nevertheless, the decision is generally taken to have established a rule at common law that previous judgments and verdicts are inadmissible as evidence of the facts on which they were based,

---

[143] See PACE s.73.

[144] *Hollington v F Hewthorn & Co Ltd* [1943] K.B. 587 CA.

[145] Not least by the Law Reform Committee, Fifteenth Report (London, 1967), para.3. In *McIlkenny v Chief Constable of West Midlands* [1980] Q.B. 283 at 319, Lord Denning M.R. described *Hollington v F Hewthorn & Co Ltd* as wrongly decided and per incuriam, but this robust view was linked to Lord Denning's radical theory of the doctrine of issue estoppel. When the House of Lords heard the appeal in *McIlkenny* they did not find it necessary to decide the point.

at least as far as proceedings involving different parties are concerned.[146] Thus in *Spinks*,[147] where the defendant was charged with impeding the prosecution of a person, F, whom the defendant knew to be guilty of having committed an arrestable offence, the Court of Appeal held that the prosecution could not use F's conviction for wounding with intent to cause grievous bodily harm as evidence that he had committed that offence.

The rule has been substantially curtailed by statute in both civil and criminal cases. The position in civil cases is discussed below. As regards criminal cases, s.74 of PACE, discussed in the next section, effected a major limitation of the rule in relation to *convictions* by courts in the United Kingdom. Next, since evidence of a conviction is evidence of bad character under ss.98 and 112 of the Criminal Justice Act 2003, and s.99 of that Act has abolished the common law rules governing the admissibility of evidence of bad character in criminal proceedings, it follows that the rule has now gone completely as far as the admissibility of convictions is concerned, whether the conviction is by a UK or a foreign[148] court. Where does this leave evidence of previous *acquittals*? In *Kordasinski,* the Court of Appeal expressed the view that the rule in *Hollington v Hewthorn* "was abolished for criminal cases, in so far as it may ever have applied or have survived, by section 99(1) of the 2003 Act".[149] This view was stated without qualification, but acquittals were not in issue in the case, and the court may not have had them in mind. Where the defence seek to rely on an acquittal it is arguable that this is not evidence of bad character and therefore unaffected by s.99(1). If so, the rule in *Hollington v Hewthorn* may still apply, so that the fact of acquittal is inadmissible as evidence that the person acquitted was innocent of the offence in question.[150]

2.   *Criminal cases: PACE section 74*

PACE s.74, as amended by the Criminal Justice Act 2003,[151] provides: 20–028

"(1)   In any proceedings the fact that a person other than the accused has been convicted of an offence by or before any court in the United Kingdom ... shall be admissible in evidence for the purpose of proving that that person committed that offence, where evidence of his having done so is admissible, whether or not any other evidence of his having committed that offence is given.

(2)   In any proceedings in which by virtue of this section a person other than the accused is proved to have been convicted of an offence ... he shall be taken to have committed that offence unless the contrary is proved.

[146] Andrews and Hirst, *Criminal Evidence* (2001), para.22–21.
[147] *Spinks* (1982) 74 Cr.App.R. 246 CA. See also *Hassan* [1970] 1 Q.B. 423.
[148] *Kordasinski* [2006] EWCA Crim 2984 (foreign convictions for rape admissible under s.101(1)(d) of the Criminal Justice Act 2003).
[149] *Kordasinski* [2006] EWCA Crim 2984 at [72].
[150] *Hui Chi-Ming v R.* [1992] 1 A.C. 34 PC. However, prior to the 2003 Act it was thought that a previous acquittal may in some circumstances be so relevant to the issues that the jury has to determine that fairness requires its admission. See *Joseph Robert H* (1990) 90 Cr.App.R. 440; considering *Doosti* (1986) 82 Cr.App.R. 181; *Hay* (1983) 77 Cr.App.R. 70; *Cooke* (1987) 84 Cr.App.R. 286; and see also *Edwards* [1991] 2 All E.R. 266 CA.
[151] Criminal Justice Act 2003 s.331, Sch.36 para.85.

(3)   In any proceedings where evidence is admissible of the fact that the accused has committed an offence, if the accused is proved to have been convicted of the offence—
(a)   by or before any court in the United Kingdom ...
he shall be taken to have committed that offence unless the contrary is proved."

Section 74 gave effect to a recommendation of the Criminal Law Revision Committee.[152] The recommendation was that, where an element of the offence charged against the accused consists in the commission of an offence by a third party, then the prosecution should be able to rely on the conviction of the third party as evidence of the commission of the offence and should not have to prove the commission of the offence all over again. The Committee gave the example of handling stolen goods. It is an element of this offence that the goods the defendant is alleged to have handled were "stolen" goods. If X has already been convicted of theft of the goods, X's conviction should be admissible to prove that the goods were stolen when the defendant handled them. The Committee said that it would be "quite wrong, as well as being inconvenient" to require the prosecution to prove X's guilt of theft again at the defendant's trial for handling. Another example is the situation that occurred in *Spinks*,[153] where, as noted above, the prosecution were unable to rely on the conviction of a person whose prosecution the defendant was charged with impeding. There is an obvious justification for the recommendation in terms of efficiency; time and costs are saved by relieving the prosecution of the burden of establishing what they have already established in other proceedings. An argument that it would be wrong in principle to require such proof is more debatable, as will appear below.

(A)   Admissibility of the conviction of a person other than the accused

20–029   The amended version of s.74(1) refers to the fact of the conviction being admissible to prove the commission of an offence by a person other than the accused, where evidence that that person did commit the offence is admissible. No tests or criteria of admissibility are specified in the section. It seems to follow therefore that the normal rules of admissibility are intended to apply. The most important of these is relevance. The original version of s.74 referred expressly to the fact of conviction being admissible where it was "relevant to any issue in the proceedings" that the person in question had committed the offence. Since relevance to an issue in the proceedings is a condition of the admissibility of any evidence, it is submitted that the change of wording has made no change of substance to the admissibility of a conviction under s.74. The case law on the interpretation of the original version will continue to apply.

On this basis s.74(1) clearly applies to the Criminal Law Revision Committee's specific examples where the guilt of the accused depends in part on another person having committed an offence. The conviction of the other is relevant to an issue in the proceedings against the accused if it establishes an

---

[152] *Eleventh Report* para.218. For a helpful discussion of the provision see R. Munday, "Proof of Guilt by Association under section 74 of the Police and Criminal Evidence Act 1984" [1990] Crim. L.R. 236.
[153] *Spinks* (1982) 74 Cr.App.R. 246 CA.

element of the offence charged against the accused. In *Pigram*,[154] a conviction of one of two defendants charged with handling stolen goods, based upon his plea of guilty, was held to be admissible at the trial of the co-defendant to prove that the goods in question were stolen.

The application of the section is not, however, restricted to issues of the existence of elements of the offence. The authorities have held that it extends to evidentiary issues, such as the significance of potentially incriminating circumstantial evidence.[155] In *Castle*,[156] it was held to include a collateral issue relating to the credibility of a witness. A victim of robbery had identified two suspects at an identification parade, one of whom subsequently pleaded guilty to robbery. The conviction was held to be admissible under s.74, at the trial of the other suspect, because it tended to confirm the reliability of the victim's identifications.[157]

Relevance is determined on the normal principles discussed in Ch.3. One decision worth noting in this context, because it is demonstrably absurd, is *Potamitis*.[158] The defendant was charged with obtaining money from a number of elderly victims by a "bizarre and audacious" deception. His defence was that he was merely an innocent agent collecting money on behalf of his cousin. The trial judge permitted the prosecution to prove that the defendant's cousin, G, had been convicted of identical frauds the previous year, and that the defendant had visited G in prison before the defendant's involvement in the incidents that led to the charges against him. The Court of Appeal quashed the defendant's conviction, saying that the evidence of G's conviction was irrelevant. This decision is truly astonishing. The conviction, coupled with the fact of the defendant's visit to G in prison, gave rise to an overwhelming inference that the defendant knew perfectly well that the statements made to the victims of the frauds were false. It seems quite plain that the evidence tended to destroy his defence; it reduced its probability effectively to zero. The Court of Appeal's reasoning that the "boundary of relevance at a criminal trial is fixed by the dates and circumstances alleged in the indictment" is mystifying. It seems to represent an elementary confusion between the particulars necessary to identify the offence charged and the evidence admissible to prove the offences. Such evidence has never been restricted to facts falling within dates specified in an indictment. If any such rule existed, it would mean that virtually all the cases where "similar fact" evidence

20–030

---

[154] *Pigram* [1995] Crim. L.R. 808.

[155] See, e.g. *Warner and Jones* (1992) 96 Cr.App.R. 324 CA, where the defendants were charged with conspiracy to supply heroin, and the issue arose about the significance of there being a number of visitors to the house of one of the defendants. The fact that many of the callers had convictions for possession or supply of heroin was held to be relevant to the prosecution case because it had a bearing on the purpose of their visits. cf. *Kearley* [1992] 2 A.C. 228 HL, discussed in Ch.16.

[156] *Castle* [1989] Crim. L.R. 567.

[157] See also *Golder* [1987] 3 All E.R. 231 CA, where the convictions and guilty pleas of two co-accused in respect of two robberies were admitted as relevant to the issue of whether the defendant's alleged confession to one of the robberies was fabricated. The confession included details about the part played by the co-accused in the other robbery; proof that the other robbery occurred tended to confirm the evidence of the making of the confession.

[158] *Potamitis* [1994] Crim. L.R. 434 CA.

was admitted at common law were wrongly decided. *Potamitis* is a wholly aberrant decision and must be regarded as wrong.[159]

The Court of Appeal has also said, rightly, that trial judges should be astute to see that evidence is not admitted under s.74 that is irrelevant, inadmissible or prejudicial, on the basis that it enables the jury "to see the whole picture".[160] A conviction, whether of an alleged accomplice of the accused or of anyone else, should be admissible under s.74 only if it is relevant to an issue in the proceedings against the accused. If it is not relevant to an issue, as opposed say, to explaining to the jury why other persons are not being tried at the same time as the accused, then it should not be admitted.[161]

It may occasionally be relevant for the accused himself to use s.74. Take a variation on the facts of *Blastland*.[162] A defendant is charged with buggery and murder of a boy. The prosecution evidence shows that the act of buggery was carried out in a peculiar way. The defendant's defence is that these offences were carried out, not by him, but by a third party, Mark. If Mark has a previous conviction for buggery of a boy in the same peculiar way, there seems to be nothing to prevent the defendant from adducing evidence of the conviction under s.74(1) to support his defence. The judge would have no discretion to exclude it under s.78 of PACE because that applies only to evidence proposed to be given by the prosecution.[163]

20–031   Relevance is not of course the only condition of admissibility. Evidence of a conviction is capable of being evidence of "misconduct" for the purposes of the law on evidence of bad character.[164] It is necessary therefore to consider the rules of admissibility for evidence of bad character under Ch.1 of Pt 11 of the Criminal Justice Act 2003. These will not be a problem if the evidence of the other person's commission of the offence "has to do with the alleged facts of the offence with which the defendant is charged" (s.98(a)). The evidence will then fall outside the scheme of the Act. This will be so in many cases, such as where the evidence is relevant to establish an element of the offence charged against the defendant or the evidence is of a co-accused's plea of guilty to the conspiracy or joint offence charged against the defendant.[165] It is not clear that it will always be so: convictions of non-defendants for separate offences, such as those in issue in *Warner and Jones*,[166] might be held not "to do with the alleged facts" of the offence charged. If this is right, the convictions will be evidence of bad character

---

[159] It can be usefully contrasted with *Buckingham* (1994) 99 Cr.App.R. 303, where the Court of Appeal stated that anything that enables a jury better to understand the factual background against which the issue arises in the present case is properly to be described as relevant to that issue within the terms of s.74.

[160] *Boyson* [1991] Crim. L.R. 274.

[161] See, e.g. *Girma* [2009] EWCA Crim 912 (co-accused's plea of guilty to assisting an offender irrelevant where the issue was not whether acts capable of amounting to assistance were done, but the accused's state of mind in relation to those acts).

[162] *Blastland* [1986] A.C. 41 HL. The case is discussed in Ch.3.

[163] cf. *Hendrick* [1992] Crim. L.R. 427.

[164] Criminal Justice Act 2003 ss.98, 112(1).

[165] In *Smith* [2007] EWCA Crim 2105 the Court of Appeal confirmed that the admission of a co-accused's guilty plea to a joint offence with the accused is not evidence of bad character for the purposes of the Act and therefore does not need to pass the test of enhanced relevance under s.100.

[166] *Warner and Jones* (1992) 96 Cr.App.R. 324 CA.

for the purposes of the Act and will then have to satisfy the conditions of s.100. To be admissible under s.100 they will need to have enhanced relevance, in the sense of substantial probative value in relation to a matter that is in issue in the proceedings and is of substantial importance in the context of the case as a whole.[167] In future in appropriate cases courts may find that this requirement of enhanced relevance is not met, in circumstances where previously they might have excluded the evidence under s.78 of PACE, to which we now turn.

(B) Discretionary exclusion of the conviction under PACE section 78

It was not long after PACE came into force before enterprising prosecutors   **20–032**
realised that s.74 might apply in cases where a conspiracy or a joint enterprise is charged. If, for example D1 is charged with conspiracy to defraud with D2, and D2 is convicted at a separate trial of conspiracy to defraud with D1, D2's conviction is relevant to the issue of D1's guilt of conspiracy. Yet there is great potential for unfairness if D2's conviction is admitted at D1's trial. If the conviction was based on D2's plea of guilty, then using the conviction against D1 is equivalent to using a hearsay statement by D2 against D1, in a situation where D1 cannot cross-examine D2 on the statement and had no opportunity to do so at D2's trial. If the conviction was the outcome of a contested trial, the prosecution evidence is effectively being used again in the form of D2's conviction in a situation where D1 cannot cross-examine on it. Moreover, the effect of s.74(2) is to reverse the burden of proof. On proof of the conviction, D2 is taken to have committed the offence unless D1 proves the contrary.[168]

In *O'Connor*,[169] D1 was charged with conspiracy with D2 to obtain property by deception. D2 pleaded guilty to the conspiracy, and his conviction was subsequently admitted in evidence at D1's trial. The Court of Appeal held that it should not have been admitted. Since there were only two parties to the conspiracy the effect of proving the conviction of one of them for conspiracy with the other was to cast the burden on the other of proving his innocence. Moreover he had to do this without having the opportunity of cross-examining D2 in front of the jury. Proof of the conviction was therefore so unfairly prejudicial to D1 that it ought to have been excluded under s.78. The decision can now be reinforced by reference to the Human Rights Act 1998. There can be little doubt that in these circumstances D1 cannot receive a fair trial under art.6 of the ECHR: the presumption of innocence is violated, and D1 has no opportunity to examine the person who is effectively a witness against him.

This was a case where the conviction bore directly on the issue of D1's guilt. In *Kempster*,[170] the Court of Appeal suggested that s.74 should not be used in any case where the prosecution were seeking to adduce a conviction that expressly or by necessary inference imported the complicity of the accused. A conviction will have this effect where it proves all the elements of the offence charged, as in the

---

[167] For further discussion of the scheme of the Act and s.100 see Chs 14 and 19.
[168] The defendant is entitled to have this issue considered by the jury: *Dixon (Sarah Louise)* [2001] Crim. L.R. 126 CA.
[169] *O'Connor* (1987) 85 Cr.App.R. 304 CA.
[170] *Kempster* [1989] 1 W.L.R. 1125 CA.

case of a conspiracy with only two named parties, or where the accused is charged with the commission of an offence jointly with one other person who then pleads guilty to the joint offence.[171] By contrast, if the conviction tends to prove the existence of a conspiracy or a joint enterprise, but does not necessarily show that the accused was a party to it, its admission is not so prejudicial to the accused since the prosecution will still have to adduce other evidence to prove his participation. In *Robertson*,[172] the defendant was alleged to have conspired with two named men and with other persons unknown to commit burglary. The Court of Appeal held that the trial judge had rightly admitted evidence of the convictions of the two named accomplices for burglary. The difference from *O'Connor* is that these convictions, and the guilty pleas on which they were based, did not on their face incriminate the accused. They tended to suggest a conspiracy to burgle, but other evidence was needed to prove the defendant's membership of the conspiracy.[173]

In *Smith,* the Court of Appeal rejected a suggestion that the principles established by such cases as *O'Connor* and *Kempster* had been rendered outdated by the reforms of the Criminal Justice Act 2003, liberalising the admission of hearsay and bad character evidence:

> "It remains extremely relevant what the issue is in the case before the trial court. It remains of considerable importance to examine whether the case is one in which the admission of the plea of guilty of a now absent co-defendant would have an unfair effect upon the instant trial by closing off much, or in some cases all, of the issues which the jury is trying."[174]

In that case a prostitute (D2) and her boyfriend (D1) were charged jointly with robbery and possession of a firearm in relation to an incident in which money had been taken from one of her clients. D1 admitted theft but denied the offences charged. The Court of Appeal held that the trial judge should have excluded under s.78 evidence of D2's pleas of guilty to the offences. In the court's view, in a case such as this, where the real issue was whether the offence charged was committed at all the admission of the co-accused's guilty pleas was likely to have a weighty effect on the jury. It would effectively close off the issues which the jury had to try. This was unfair because the defendant would have no opportunity to cross-examine the co-accused, and the basis of her guilty pleas could not be explored.

20–033 A further problem, arising where several defendants are charged with separate offences committed during the course of a continuing incident, is that the admission against the other defendants of the conviction of one of them may be of dubious relevance and hence more prejudicial than probative. In *Mahmood and Manzur,*[175] D1 and D2 were charged, together with a co-accused L, with rape of a drunken girl whom they had picked up in their car. D1 and D2 admitted that

---

[171] See also *Mattison* [1990] Crim. L.R. 117 CA (D1 charged with gross indecency with D2 who pleaded guilty to a charge in a separate count of gross indecency with D1; Court of Appeal held that D2's conviction should have been excluded).

[172] *Robertson* (1987) 85 Cr.App.R. 304 CA.

[173] See also *Lunnon* (1989) 88 Cr.App.R. 71 CA, where the application of this principle was more debatable.

[174] *Smith* [2007] EWCA Crim 2105 at [17].

[175] *Mahmood and Manzur* [1997] 1 Cr.App.R. 414 CA.

they had each had intercourse with her, but claimed that she consented or that they believed she had consented. The trial judge allowed the Crown to adduce evidence of L's plea of guilty to rape as relevant to the issue of consent. The Court of Appeal allowed the defendants' appeals. In analysing this case the Court of Appeal approved the four propositions set out in *Boyson*[176]:

(1)　the conviction must be clearly relevant to an issue in the case;
(2)　s.74 should be used sparingly;
(3)　the judge should consider s.78 and whether the probative value of the conviction outweighs the prejudicial value;
(4)　the judge must direct the jury clearly as to the issues to which the conviction is not relevant, and also why the evidence is before them and to what issue it is directed.

　　The Court of Appeal held that it was not possible to identify any issue to which L's plea was relevant. The basis of L's guilty plea was not known. L might have pleaded guilty to rape on several possible bases; not all of them would be relevant to the issues that D1 and D2 were raising. However, there was a danger that the jury might assume that L's plea meant that he knew the girl was incapable from drink from giving any consent to intercourse (which was the Crown's case), and that this was knowledge shared by the defendants. This would be highly prejudicial to the defendants in that the jury would be encouraged to ignore full consideration of all the issues and "to ˙short circuit the decision making process".[177] Thus the judge should have excluded the evidence of L's conviction as either irrelevant, or more prejudicial than probative. Similarly, in *Downer*,[178] where the defendant was charged on an amended indictment with aggravated burglary under s.10(1)(a) of the Theft Act 1968, the Court of Appeal held that the guilty pleas of his co-accused to aggravated burglary under s.10(1)(b) should not have been admitted. If they had any probative value on the issue of the separate form of the offence with which the defendant was charged, which the court doubted, that was outweighed by the prejudicial effect on the minds of the jury who could easily conclude that all the defendants must have had the weapons or been aware of them when they entered the building in question.
　　Finally in this section, a brief word about s.74(3) is in order. This provides that where evidence is admissible of the fact that the *accused* has committed an offence, if he is proved to have been convicted of the offence he is then taken to have committed the offence unless the contrary is proved. In *Clift*,[179] D was charged with murder of V where V died some years after D violently attacked him. D had previously been convicted under s.18 of the Offences Against the Person Act 1861 of causing V grievous bodily harm with intent to cause grievous bodily harm. The Court of Appeal held that it was not unfair to admit evidence of this conviction. It was clearly relevant to show commission by D of some of the

---

[176] *Boyson* [1991] Crim. L.R. 274 CA.
[177] *Mahmood and Manzur* [1997] 1 Cr.App.R. 414 at 419.
[178] *Downer* [2009] EWCA Crim 1361.
[179] *Clift* [2012] EWCA Crim 2750.

elements of murder.[180] The effect of admitting the conviction was to reverse the burden of proof on the issue of intent: it was D's case that he had not intended to cause grievous bodily harm to V. There is no discussion in the judgment of the compatibility of this reverse onus with art.6(2) of the ECHR.[181]

3. Civil cases: Civil Evidence Act 1968 sections 11–13

20–034   Under s.11 of the Civil Evidence Act 1968 a conviction of a person for an offence may be proved in any civil proceedings, where the conviction is relevant to any issue in the proceedings. It is immaterial whether the conviction was founded on a plea of guilty or otherwise, and it is also immaterial whether the person convicted is a party to the civil proceedings. This section reverses the actual decision in *Hollington v F Hewthorn & Co Ltd*. It is now common in claims for damages for personal injuries caused by negligent driving for the claimant to allege and prove the conviction of the defendant for a driving offence arising out of the incident in question. The conviction usually provides prima facie evidence of negligence. The effect of proving the conviction is that the person convicted is taken to have committed the offence unless he proves the contrary. Where the conviction is of the defendant for dangerous or careless driving the burden of proof will thus be effectively reversed; the defendant will have to prove that he was not negligent.

A question then arises about the probative value of the conviction. Is its effect spent in reversing the burden of proof? Or can it function in addition as a weighty piece of evidence supporting the correctness of the conviction? This question received conflicting answers from two members of the Court of Appeal in *Stupple v Royal Insurance Co Ltd*.[182] Buckley L.J. said that no weight was to be given to the mere fact of conviction. In his view proof of conviction proved nothing relevant to the plaintiff's claim; it simply gave rise to the statutory presumption under subs.(2) whereby the burden of proof shifted to the defendant. This view was founded chiefly on the difficulty of assessing the weight of the conviction. Buckley L.J. thought that the weight could not be determined by such matters as the status of the court that convicted the defendant, or whether the verdict was unanimous or by a majority. On the other hand, Lord Denning M.R. was emphatic that the conviction "does not merely shift the burden of proof. It is a weighty piece of evidence of itself".[183] He gave the example of a conviction for careless driving founded on the evidence of a witness who dies before the civil trial takes place. The conviction, he said, would speak as clearly as the witness would have done had he lived. It would thus tell in the scale in the civil action, and would enable the plaintiff to answer a claim by the defendant that defence evidence negativing lack of care was not contradicted. As Lord Denning M.R. put

---

[180] It was therefore evidence to do with the facts of the offence charged, and not therefore subject to the rules on the admissibility of evidence of bad character: see Ch.19.

[181] See Ch.11 for discussion of compatibility of reverse onuses with the presumption of innocence.

[182] *Stupple v Royal Insurance Co Ltd* [1971] 1 Q.B. 50.

[183] *Stupple v Royal Insurance Co Ltd* [1971] 1 Q.B. 50 at 72.

it, the plaintiff could say to the defendant: "But your evidence is contradicted. It is contradicted by the very fact of your conviction".[184]

It may well be, as Lord Denning M.R. recognised, that the weight to be attached to a conviction might depend on the circumstances. A conviction returned by a jury after a contested trial might be entitled to much greater weight than a conviction on a plea of guilty. A guilty plea might be made for a number of reasons, including cases where the defendant pleaded guilty in error, or to save time and costs in a case of a minor offence, or to avoid the revelation of some other wrongdoing or embarrassing information. A defendant might find it easier to discharge the burden of disproof by explaining away a guilty plea than by trying to persuade a civil court that the verdict of a criminal jury, reached after a consideration of all the evidence, was wrong.[185]

---

[184] *Stupple v Royal Insurance Co Ltd* [1971] 1 Q.B. 50.
[185] In *Taylor v Taylor* [1970] 1 W.L.R. 1148 at 1152 CA, Davies L.J. commented, in support of Lord Denning's view, that it was "obvious that, when a man has been convicted by 12 of his fellow countrymen and countrywomen at a criminal trial, the verdict of the jury is a matter which is entitled to very great weight when the convicted person is seeking, in the words of the statute, to prove the contrary".

INDEX

This index has been prepared using Sweet and Maxwell's Legal Taxonomy. Main index entries conform to keywords provided by the Legal Taxonomy except where references to specific documents or non-standard terms (denoted by quotation marks) have been included. These keywords provide a means of identifying similar concepts in other Sweet and Maxwell publications and online services to which keywords from the Legal Taxonomy have been applied. Readers may find some minor differences between terms used in the text and those which appear in the index. Suggestions to *sweetandmaxwell.taxonomy@thomson.com*.

All references are to paragraph number

Abuse of power
privilege against self-incrimination,
5–050—5–052
Abuse of process
entrapment, 8–027—8–028
exclusionary discretion, 8–032—8–035
generally, 8–021—8–022
Accomplices
see also **Co-defendants**
corroboration, 15–049
witnesses, 13–015—13–016
Acquittals
previous acquittals
admissibility, 20–027
bad character, 19–004
Acts of Parliament
judicial notice, 12–028
Adjudication
avoidance of errors, 2–007
competing interests, 2–008—2–009
constraints on freedom of proof, 2–005—2–009
costs, 2–005
delay, 2–005
individual rights
generally, 2–010—2–011
right against wrongful conviction,
2–012—2–014
introduction, 2–001—2–002
legitimacy of decision-making
civil proceedings, 2–027—2–028
competing interests, 2–026
criminal proceedings, 2–023—2–025, 2–029
generally, 2–022
procedural fairness, 2–006

rationalist model
constraints on freedom of proof,
2–005—2–009
generally, 2–003—2–004
utilitarianism, 2–003, 2–009
rectitude of decision-making, 2–003 –2–004
utilitarianism, 2–003, 2–009
Admissibility
see also **Exclusionary discretion; Relevance**
facts relating to admissibility, 1–013
overview, 1–003, 1–014
Admissions
see also **Confessions**
formal admissions, 12–022
hearsay evidence
agents and employees, 17–042
informal admissions, 17–040—17–041
Adversarial proceedings
fact-finding, 4–014
generally, 1–015
Adverse inferences
see also **Right to silence**
defective defence disclosure, 9–018
failure to account, 5–022—5–023
failure to mention facts
common law, 5–038—5–039
conditions for adverse inferences, 5–025
exclusionary discretion, 5–037
facts relied on, 5–026—5–028
failure to mention, 5–029
generally, 5–022—5–023
legal advice to remain silent, 5–030—5–034
non-police investigations, 5–037
prima facie case, 5–035
proper inferences, 5–036
reasons for silence, 5–030